Fifth Edition # The Legal, Ethical and International Environment of Business

Herbert M. Bohlman

Associate Professor
Arizona State University
Judge Pro Tempore, Maricopa County Superior Court

Mary Jane Dundas

Associate Professor
Arizona State University

WEST
™
THOMSON LEARNING

Australia · Canada · Mexico · Singapore · Spain · United Kingdom · United States

The Legal, Ethical and International Environment of Business, Fifth Edition
by Herbert M. Bohlman and Mary Jane Dundas

Vice President/Publisher: Jack W. Calhoun
Senior Acquisitions Editor: Rob Dewey
Developmental Editor: Denise Simon
Marketing Manager: Nicole C. Moore
Media Technology Editor: Vicky True
Media Development Editor: Peggy Buskey
Media Production Editor: John Barans
Production Editor: Amy S. Gabriel, Kara ZumBahlen
Manufacturing Coordinator: Sandee Milewski
Internal Design: Carolyn Deacy Design/Carolyn Deacy, San Francisco
Cover Design: Jen2Design/Jennifer Lambert, Cincinnati
Cover Images: ©Randy Duchaine/The Stock Market; ©PhotoDisc, Inc.
Production House: Trejo Production
Printer: R.R. Donnelley & Sons Company, Willard Manufacturing Division

Printed in the United States of America
 2 3 4 5 04 03 02

For more information contact West Legal Studies in Business, 5191 Natorp Boulevard, Mason,
Ohio, 45040 or find us on the Internet at http://www.westbuslaw.com

For permission to use material from this text or product, contact us by
• **telephone: 1-800-730-2214**
• **fax: 1-800-730-2215**
• **web: http://www.thomsonrights.com**

Library of Congress Cataloging-in-Publication Data
Bohlman, Herbert M.
The legal, ethical, and international environment of business / Herbert M. Bohlman, Mary Jane Dundas.—
5th ed.
p. cm
ISBN 0-324-06183-8
1. Industrial laws and legislation—United Statees.   2. Trade regulation—United States.   3. Commercial
law—United States.   4. Business ethics—United States.   5. Business law-United States.   I. Dundas, Mary
Jane.   II. Title.
KF1600.B64 2001
346.7307—dc21

                                                                                          2001026215

Dedication

M. J. D. dedicates this book to the memory of her parents, R. J and Marie A. Dundas, and her sisters, Jean and Marilyn, and their families.

H. M. B. dedicates this book to his wife, Mimi, and his children, Bill, Patti, Mike, and Laura, and their families.

Brief Contents

Unit III Business Formation

Unit IV Business and Government Regulation

Appendices

Contents

Unit I   Introduction to Law

Unit II   Business and Private Law

Unit III   Business Formation

Unit IV   Business and Government Regulation

Appendices

Preface

During the last three decades, the legal scene in the United States has changed tremendously. The future of the law will be even more dynamic. As a result, businesses must influence and adapt to the dramatically changing legal environment. *The Legal, Ethical, and International Environment of Business,* Fifth Edition, was written with two goals in mind—to present to the student the breadth of the legal environment of business and to provide a legal, ethical, regulatory, international, and technological foundation that can be used in his or her business or government career. Where appropriate, comments are made about the political and social aspects of the legal environment.

To accomplish these goals, we have presented materials that cover both private and public legal aspects of business. Unit I provides students with an introduction to law, ethics, and the World Wide Web (WWW). This unit includes chapters on ethics, the judicial system, and alternatives to the judicial system called dispute resolution procedures. The chapters on constitutional law, administrative agencies, and criminal law introduce students to the regulatory issues. Unit II covers business and private law. Topics include torts; contracts; sales law; negotiable instruments; international business law; rights of consumers, debtors, and creditors; consumer protection; and property and computer law. Unit III examines the formation of business entities and agency and employment law. Unit IV sets out the various aspects of government regulation, which includes securities, antitrust, and labor and employment law; equal opportunity; and environmental law.

The fifth edition includes technological, ethical, and international sections in every chapter. Students are provided an opportunity to study the historical development of the U.S. legal system along with a general discussion of how constitutional issues affect businesses. The text integrates the American Assembly of Collegiate Schools of Business (AACSB) curriculum standards to cover ethical, global, political, social, legal, regulatory, environmental, and technological issues.

New to the Fifth Edition

Technological issues are in the forefront of business issues today. New to the fifth edition is the *CyberLaw* feature. Each chapter includes a legal discussion on how cyberspace has impacted, changed, or added new legal issues to a particular legal topic. *CyberLaw* acquaints students with current legal issues concerning technology. For example, businesses are adopting technology to drive down costs of purchasing. One method used is electronic business-to-business auctions. These auctions are compared with business-to-consumer auctions. Businesses use the web to sell items through electronic catalogs. Web businesses currently are exempt from sales taxes. Because sales taxes are not imposed on these transactions, how have state tax revenues been impacted? How are the state governments responding? These issues are explored to illustrate the ripple effect of decisions involving technology.

The *Using the World Wide Web* feature has been expanded. This edition has built a large web database with each chapter has its own summary of web addresses. The web addresses on the inside back cover have been updated and make it easy for students to find commonly used web addresses, such as www.whitehouse.gov. Because faculty and students have access to the web, each chapter has two *Web Activities*. Additionally, the last problem in the *Questions and Case Problems* section includes an additional web activity.

New to this edition is a reference in each chapter to a fictitious business called Artiste Login Products, Inc. This fictitious business is used to emphasize the overall view of each chapter.

Each chapter has a court case decided in 2000. These latest cases keep the students interested in the current law. Business-oriented issues, such as the blowouts of the Firestone/Bridgestone tires used primarily on Ford vehicles, are the focus of the *Legal Highlight* features. The new Third Restatements of Torts position on product liability is likewise presented in the text of the chapter on product liability.

The chapter on criminal law includes a discussion of the recent U.S. Supreme Court decision to uphold the 1960s case of *Miranda v. Arizona*. In the chapter of secured transactions, the new Uniform Commercial Code, Article 9, is fully discussed. The new Article 9 modifies prior law as to where to file a financing statement and broadens the different types of collateral.

This fifth edition has integrated technology issues, landmark cases with 2000 cases, and business and government web sites. Each chapter has questions that are designed such that the students should use the web to find answers, just as they will be doing in their business lives.

Total Learning/ Teaching Package

This text constitutes what we believe to be a total learning/teaching package. It contains numerous pedagogical aids and high-interest additions.

Case Selection and Presentation

Each chapter has several cases to illustrate the application of the law to specific business problems. We have tried to create a balance between classic cases that are well recognized and recent cases that have changed the

law significantly. Each case starts with the citation that includes the court, the date, the federal or state reporter (if available), the West reporter, and, when possible, a web citation.

The *Background and Facts* section focuses on the setting in which the case arose and identifies the plaintiffs and defendants. Text from an actual court case is then presented in an abbreviated form. Although the case is in an abbreviated form, enough judicial material is included to allow the professor to facilitate a discussion with the students to explore the reasoning and impact of the case. Finally, the *Decision and Remedy* section clearly states who prevailed in the case and why. When appropriate, we include a *Comment* section that presents additional material not available from the case itself or that indicates future trends. Each case ends with a *Critical Thinking* problem that helps the students reach a deeper level of understanding of the law and public policy.

Chapter Features

Each chapter includes one or more of the following special sections. These segments are designed to be instructive as well as interesting.

Quotations

Each chapter opens with a brief quotation that is appropriate to the chapter material. The source of the quote is included.

Ethical Considerations

The emphasis on ethics in academic studies is reflected in the standards set by the AACSB. These standards require that ethics be integrated into the study of business, and this text likewise integrates ethics into each chapter. Chapter 2, *Ethics and Corporate Social Responsibility*, covers ethical theories and provides a basis for class discussion of the ethical problems set out at the beginning of each chapter. A model is provided in Chapter 2 and reprinted on the inside front cover to assist students in resolving ethical issues.

Fictitious Business

Contained in each chapter is a fictitious business called Artiste Login Products, Inc. This business is featured in the *Introduction*. In some chapters, it is integrated, such as in Chapter 3 where Artiste Login Products, Inc., is involved in a lawsuit. In other chapters, the business is used in the *Web Activities* or the Internet problem at the end of the *Questions and Case Problems* section.

In the scenario, Artiste Login Products, Inc., has a web presence, sells both unique, handmade items, and a variety of other common goods, such as dinnerware. The instructor can build problems, current issues, and critical thinking around this business.

CyberLaw

The new feature entitled *CyberLaw* includes a discussion on a specific legal topic involving the web. New problems are discussed, such as the authentication of electronic signatures, along with new twists on old problems, such as privacy in the electronic age.

Exhibits

Most chapters have at least one exhibit to illustrate important aspects of the law. Some exhibits are charts, such as the one setting out the federal court system; others focus on classifications or summaries; and others illustrate forms used in the legal or business world, such as a sample credit sale contract.

Legal Highlights

All chapters have a feature entitled *Legal Highlight*. This feature is used to present stories and to provide practical advice, such as how to check on a Social Security account or examples of how the law was applied in an unusual situation.

International Considerations

The economic future of the United States is dependent on international trade. People involved with international business need a working knowledge of how international trade functions and the legal problems that may arise. The AACSB also is concerned with integrating global issues into the academic studies of business. Each chapter has an *International Consideration* that discusses international aspects of the chapter's subject matter. Chapter 13, *International Business Law*, covers various aspects of doing business in the global environment.

Legally Speaking

Toward the end of each chapter is material entitled *Legally Speaking*. In each such discussion we have attempted to present a factual situation that a businessperson could confront in his or her career. These situations concern problems that are collateral to the rest of the material contained within the chapter. They provide students with practical advice on how to apply the law.

Using the World Wide Web

Each chapter has a variety of references to web sites. This fifth edition integrates into the textual material references to web sites relating to cases, statutes, regulations, and organizations. Professors and students can use these references to find more information on the issues discussed in the chapter. *Using the World Wide Web* starts with a short discussion, followed by a summary of all the web sites in the chapter. This summary makes finding web sites easier. *Using the World Wide Web* ends with two *Web Activities*. At the end of each chapter is a research problem involving the use of the web.

Key Terms

Each chapter includes a list of *Key Terms*. The terms are first identified in the chapter by boldfaced type at which point a definition is provided. A key term used immediately prior to the definition is identified by the use of italics.

Questions and Case Problems

At the end of each chapter, there are ten *Questions and Case Problems*. The problems are a mix of hypothetical questions and actual case problems. The case problems are summaries of appellate court cases for which full citations are given. The last question involves a problem to be researched on the web.

Complete answers to all of the *Ethical Considerations* and the *Questions and Case Problems* are found in a separate manual entitled *Answers to Ethical Considerations, Critical Thinking, Web Activities, Questions and Case Problems*.

Appendices

This book can serve as a reference because of the appendices included. They are as follows:

A   The Constitution of the United States of America

B   The Uniform Commercial Code (Excerpts)

C   The Sherman Act (Excerpts)

D   The Clayton Act (Excerpts)

E   The Federal Trade Commission Act (Excerpts)

F   National Labor Relations Act (Excerpts)

G   The Federal Civil Rights Laws (Excerpts)

H   The Uniform Partnership Act (Excerpts)

I   International Top-Level Domains (ITLDs)

J   Critical Thinking

K   Selected World Wide Web Government Addresses

L   Spanish Equivalents for Important Legal Terms in English

Supplements

Study Guide

The *Study Guide* (0-324-06185-4) was written by Thomas Brierton of the University of the Pacific. Each chapter reinforces what the text has presented. The Study Guide consists of descriptions of general principles discussed in each chapter, chapter summaries in sentence outline form, and true-false, fill-in-the-blank, and multiple-choice questions to test students' comprehension.

Instructor's Manual

The *Instructor's Manual* (0-324-06184-6) was written by Dinah Payne of the University of New Orleans and Michael Hogg of Tulane University. Each chapter includes a chapter overview, chapter outline, case comments, discussion questions, ethical and international considerations comments, and instructional suggestions.

Test Bank

The *Test Bank* (0-324-06186-2) was written by Dinah Payne of the University of New Orleans and Michael Hogg of Tulane University. Each chapter of the *Test Bank* has approximately twenty-five true-false questions and seventy-five multiple-choice questions; many chapters have more items.

The *Test Bank* is available on *ExamView*™, a computerized testing software containing all of the questions in the printed test bank. This program is an easy-to-use test creation software package compatible with Microsoft Windows. Instructors can add or edit questions, instructions, and answers, and select questions by previewing them on the screen, selecting them randomly, or selecting them by number. Instructors can also create and administer quizzes online, whether over the Internet, a local-area network, or a wide-area network. Instructors should contact their West sales representative to inquire about acquiring *ExamView*™.

Answers to Ethical Considerations, Critical Thinking, Web Activities, Questions and Case Problems

The *Answer Manual* (0-324-06284-2) provides model answers to the *Ethical Considerations* that begin each chapter. This portion is followed by solutions to the *Questions and Case Problems* found in the end of each chapter.

Transparency Acetates

The supplements package contains a set of approximately thirty transparency acetates (0-324-06286-9).

PowerPoint Presentation Slides

Developed by Michael Hogg, more than 200 PowerPoint slides (0-324-06285-0) are available to supplement course content, adding structure and visual dimension to lectures.

Product Support Web Site

A rich web site at http://bohlman.westbuslaw.com complements the text providing many extras including learning and teaching resources, case updates, a product tour, and a guest book.

Acknowledgments

Many people are involved in the production of a textbook. The initial impetus for *The Legal, Ethical, and International Environment of Business,* Fifth Edition, came from Rob Dewey, our editor, who has been a strong supporter of this project. A heartfelt thanks to Denise Simon, our developmental editor, who coordinated all the reviews, provided expert analysis, and made suggestions that make for a stronger textbook. A hearty thanks to Amy S. Gabriel, our production editor, who kept the project moving in a timely manner.

We acknowledge the important contribution of Professor Arthur Gross Schaefer from Loyola Marymount University in Los Angeles. His credentials as an attorney, certified public accountant, and rabbi, along with his work in the development of ethical audits for profit and nonprofit organizations, make him a unique individual with a very broad background. His work as an ethicist with practicing attorneys and judges, moreover, has provided him with a critical ou look on dealing effectively with real-life situations. He has used these perspectives to create the ethics decision model, the ethics cases within each chapter, and model answers found in the *Answers to Ethical Considerations, Critical Thinking, Web Activities, Questions and Case Problems*. This material is an integral part of our book and greatly improved the book's overall presentation.

A number of reviewers were kind enough to give us their ideas and comments on various drafts of the manuscript. They are listed below for the five editions.

Reviewers for the Fifth Edition

Thomas M. Apke, California State University, Fullerton
Thomas D. Brierton, University of the Pacific
Marc. A. Hall, Auburn University
Glen Jones, Henderson State University
Frank Julian, Murray State University
Peter B. Macky, Susquehanna University
S. Andrew Ostapski, Valdosta State University
Dinah Payne, University of New Orleans
Daniel R. Vaughen, University of Central Florida
William B. Woodward, Jr., University of Alabama, Huntsville
Raymond A. Zimmerman, The University of Texas at El Paso

Reviewers for the Fourth Edition

Patricia Billow, University of Akron
Frank Cavaliere, Lamar University
Howard Ellis, Millersville University

George Generas, University of Hartford
Cliff Koen, University of New Orleans
A. Robert Lamb, The University of the Incarnate Word
Alan Schlact, Kennesaw State University
Mark E. Smith, University of Louisville

Reviewers for the Third Edition

Gamewell D. Gantt III, Idaho State University
Arthur Gross Schaefer, Loyola Marymount University
A. Robert Lamb, Sr., Incarnate Word College
Michael Litka, University of Akron
Michael G. Walsh, Villanova University
Kay Wilburn, The University of Alabama at Birmingham
Raymond A. Zimmerman, The University of Texas at El Paso

Reviewers for the Second Edition

Thomas M. Apke, California State University, Fullerton
Thomas D. Brierton, University of the Pacific
Frank J. Cavallere, Lamar University
Michael Litka, University of Akron
Paul Lyons, Frostburg State University
Charles W. McGuire, DeVry Institute
Dinah Payne, University of New Orleans
Jeffrey R. Pittman, Arkansas State University
Martha Sartoris, North Hennepin Community College
Darryl L. Webb, University of Alabama
Kay Wilburn, The University of Alabama at Birmingham

Reviewers for the First Edition

David L. Baumer, North Carolina State University
Katherine Beebe, Salt Lake Community College
Thomas H. Brucker, University of Washington
Mark A. Buchanan, St. Cloud State University
Daylin J. Butler, Kansas State University
Lawrence S. Clark, Louisiana State University in Shreveport
Gamewell D. Gantt III, Idaho State University
John Geary, Appalachian State University
Amy Zoe Gershenfeld, University of Kentucky
Martin F. Grace, Georgia State University
Gerard Halpern, University of Arkansas

Marsha E. Hass, College of Charleston
James P. Hill, Central Michigan University
E. C. Hipp, Clemson University
David D. Jaeger, University of Cincinnati
Marianne M. Jennings, Arizona State University
Jack E. Karns, University of North Dakota
Nancy P. Klintworth, University of Central Florida
Paul Lansing, University of Iowa
Andrew Laviano, University of Rhode Island
F. Raymond Lewis, Northeastern Illinois University
Nancy R. Mansfield, Georgia State University
S. Scott Massin, Emory University
John E. McDonald, Jr., University of North Carolina
    at Charlotte
Sheel P. Pawar, Idaho State University
Jordan B. Ray, University of Florida
Nim Razook, University of Oklahoma
Daniel L. Reynolds, Middle Tennessee State
    University
Rene Sacasas, University of Miami Florida
Scott Sibray, California State University, Chino
Lou Ann Simpson, Drake University
S. Jay Sklar, Temple University
Lucy L. Spalding, Illinois State University
Larry Strate, University of Nevada at Las Vegas

Donald J. Swanz, St. Bonaventure University
Irvin Tankersley, Memphis State University
Bernard F. Thiemann, Bellarmine College
Daphney Thomas, James Mason University
Wayne R. Wells, St. Cloud State University

We thank our colleagues who encouraged us, supported us, and spent hours reviewing our rough drafts: Professors Luis Aranda, Eileen Aranda, Marianne Moody Jennings, Ethan Lock, Peter Reiss, and the late Claude Olney, all of Arizona State University; and Professor Marc Ruzicka, University of Tennessee, Knoxville. They were extremely helpful with our initial drafts and with giving us their creative ideas and thoughts. They also gave us the motivation to keep going on all five editions.

As careful as we have attempted to be, there are, no doubt, errors in this text for which we take full responsibility. We welcome comments from all users of the text, for it is by incorporating such comments that we can make this text even better in future editions.

Herbert M. Bohlman
Mary Jane Dundas

Unit I   Introduction to Law

Chapter 1 Basics of the Law

Outline

The educated citizen has an obligation to uphold the law. This is the obligation of every citizen in a free and peaceful society—but the educated citizen has a special responsibility by the virtue of his greater understanding. For, whether he has ever studied history or current events, ethics or civics, the rules of a profession or the tools of a trade, he knows that only a respect for the law makes it possible for free men to dwell together in peace and progress.

He knows that law is the adhesive force of the cement of society, creating order out of chaos and coherence in place of anarchy. He knows that for one man to defy a law or court order he does not like is to invite others to defy those which they do not like, leading to a breakdown of all justice and all order.

He knows, too, that every fellow man is entitled to be regarded with decency and treated with dignity. Any educated citizen who seeks to subvert the law, to suppress freedom, or to subject other human beings to acts that are less than human, degrades his inheritance, ignores his learning, and betrays his obligations.

Certain other societies may respect the rule of force—we respect the rule of law.

Speech at Vanderbilt University, Nashville, Tennessee, May 13, 1963, as quoted in the *New York Times*, May 19, 1963, p. 62
John Fitzgerald Kennedy, 1917–1963
Thirty-fifth president of the United States of America, 1961–1963

http://www.cs.umb.edu/jfklibrary/index.htm

Ethical Consideration

Ethical Attitudes

Ethics are the principles used to differentiate right from wrong and govern a person's conduct. Ethical principles establish standards that provide the foundation for our legal system. In turn, the legal system attempts to set minimum ethical standards. Ethical standards are not the same as legal standards; ethical standards encompass more. To behave in an ethical manner requires more than simply meeting minimum legal standards.

Companies recognize that to ensure long-term profits they must strive to conduct their business with integrity and in an ethical manner, not only by setting corporate policies, but also by implementing those policies in their day-to-day operations. Corporate policies set the standards for ethical conduct toward all the business's stakeholders, including customers, employees, unions, government, competitors, suppliers, and the public. One step businesses can take to ensure ethical conduct is to adopt a formal code of ethics.

By having and enforcing a code of ethics, businesses can gain a reputation for integrity and honesty, thereby attracting investors, employees, and customers. They want to be welcomed into a community. For example, by developing and applying ethical standards, Levi Strauss & Co. has earned a positive worldwide reputation for its commitment to nonexploitative work practices in developing countries.

Business and society encourage ethical thinking. Chapter 2 discusses several theories of ethical conduct and provides a model for decision making. Subsequent chapters will begin with a short ethical dilemma to which you can apply the decision model.

Introduction

Entrepreneurs abound in the United States and around the world. Whether you decide to start your own business, work for a start-up company, or accept a position with an established firm, the law pervades the business world.

You are a well-known artist who has created an online business called Artiste Login Products, Inc., located on the World Wide Web (WWW). Customers can order from a large variety of items that can be personalized. Additionally, you can create a piece of art based on the customer's request. If you are unable to create the piece, you contract with other artists who will work with you. From the creation of your business, you are aware that you have very little knowledge of the legal issues that surround a business.

A variety of legal, regulatory, ethical, and international topics are covered within this text that should aid you in making business decisions whether your business is conducted online or in a bricks-and-mortar building. The unit you are now reading, *Introduction to Law,* covers seven chapters, each of which has importance to your business. Chapter 1 reviews the foundations of the law. Ethical approaches to business problems are set out in Chapter 2. An overview of the legal system is provided in Chapter 3.

Chapter 4 sets out several dispute resolution methods that are available as alternatives to long and costly legal actions. The impact of the U.S. Constitution on the business world is examined in Chapter 5.

Chapter 6 covers administrative agencies since all businesses have some contact with administrative agencies, such as the Internal Revenue Service. Chapter 7 covers crimes. A business can be the victim of a crime or, unfortunately, businesses can commit criminal acts. All of the remaining chapters within this text likewise have a direct application to the business environment.

Each chapter begins with an ethical problem that businesses face. At the end of the ethical problem is a question for you to decide. A decision-making model is provided in Chapter 2 and is reprinted on the inside front cover.

Court cases are placed throughout each of the chapters. Each case follows a particular legal issue and provides you with actual dilemmas that a business faced in court. Following each case is a critical thinking section, with questions to help you integrate legal, ethical, regulatory, international, and business issues. The supplementary material on critical thinking is set out in Appendix J. This material provides you with guidance to analyze and improve your decision-making skills. Additionally, World Wide Web citations to a host of legal and business sources are placed throughout each of the chapters.

This chapter discusses the background of the legal system and provides information on the sources of American law, the classifications within the law, and schools of legal philosophy. You will study the distinctions between the courts of law and the courts of equity. You will learn that cases, statutes, and administrative agencies each have different citation systems. The chapter ends with an explanation of and guidelines for briefing a case.

Definition of Law

Law is one of the most basic of all social institutions. Oliver Wendell Holmes, Jr., in a speech to the Suffolk Bar Association in 1885 observed "This abstract called the Law, wherein, as in a magic mirror, we see reflected not only our own lives, but the lives of all men that have been!"[1]

Kermit Hall, a legal historian, expands on Holmes's explanation with this observation:

> *Law is, after all, a human institution; its history is a tale of human choices. Its abstract rules deal with the most central of human issues: the preservation of life, the protection of property, the exercise of individual liberty, the fashioning of creative knowledge, and the allocating of scarce resources. All encounters in the law, therefore, have been personal, human encounters. Its history is that of individuals caught up in the efforts of the state to allocate blame, to deter criminal behavior, to punish wrongdoing, and encourage socially valuable activity.*[2]

Society could not exist if people did as they pleased without regard for the rights of others. You can read newspapers, watch television news, or use the Internet to observe how countries without a system of law fall into chaos and brutal civil wars. In order for society to function, its members must observe the rule of law, recognize their obligations toward each other, and abide by those obligations.

Law, in the plural sense, is how the whole society is governed. The law that governs our society arises from four basic sources: federal and state constitutions; **treaties**, that is, agreements signed by the federal government with other nations; laws passed by a legislative body, such as Congress or state legislatures; and court cases.

Law in the singular sense means a law that must be obeyed and followed by society's members. The member who disobeys a law is subject to a sanction or legal consequences. If a person breaks a contract without a valid reason, she can be sued and the party harmed can recover money damages. If a person robs a bank, he can be prosecuted by the government and sentenced to prison.

Sources of American Law

American law has evolved continuously since the first landings of English settlers at Jamestown, Virginia, in 1607, and at Plymouth Rock, Massachusetts, in 1620. The colonies naturally relied heavily on the English legal system.

During the new nation's early decades, however, Americans enriched their emerging legal system with French and German influences. These borrowed ideas and philosophies helped to shape our current legal system.

Constitutions

The constitution is the highest source to which a court will look when deciding a case. The two levels of constitutions are the U.S. Constitution and individual state constitutions. The U.S. Constitution has two functions: to establish the government and to protect people from overreaching government powers. A state constitution creates the state government and provides rights and protections to its residents.

The U.S. Constitution is the supreme law of the land.[3] The supreme law mandate is set out in the following provision:

> *This constitution, and the Laws of the United States which shall be made in Pursuance thereof; and all Treaties made, or which shall be made, under the*

---

[1] Oliver Wendell Holmes, Jr., *The Speeches of Oliver Wendell Holmes* (1891), p. 17.

[2] Kermit L. Hall, *The Magic Mirror: Law in American History* (Oxford, UK: Oxford University Press, 1989), p. 4.

[3] Article VI, Section 2, U.S. Constitution.

Authority of the United States, shall be the supreme Law of the Land; and the Judges in every State shall be bound thereby, any Thing in the Constitution or Laws of any State to the Contrary notwithstanding.

Any law in conflict with the federal Constitution, regardless of its source, cannot be enforced. Similarly, a state constitution, although supreme within that state's borders, must conform to the U.S. Constitution.

Statutes, Ordinances, and Administrative Regulations

A **statute** is a law passed by a legislative body, that is, Congress or a state legislature, and generally is signed into law by the president or a governor. An **ordinance** is a law enacted by a city or county legislative body.

Congress can only pass legislation that falls within the delegated powers granted to it under the U.S. Constitution.[4] State statutes and local ordinances must comply with the U.S. Constitution and the applicable state constitution. Cases before the courts often involve statutes. The courts must interpret the legislative intent of a law and apply that interpretation to the facts in the case.

Administrative agencies usually are created by Congress, or at the state level by state legislatures, to implement and administer statutes. Agencies regulate different aspects of society, such as education, public health, and taxation. To carry out their business, these agencies adopt **administrative regulations** that are published and have the force of law, absent successful challenge in the courts.

Case Law

Written court decisions constitute the **common law**, also known as **case law**. The origins of common law lie in England's ancient, unwritten law. Disputes were settled according to local custom. In 1066, the Normans, led by William the Conqueror, conquered England. He and his successors began the long process of unifying the country.

One of the means used for unification was the king's court. This court established a common or uniform set of customs for the whole country. A person was given the right to appeal a local decision to the king. Over time, so many appeals were made that the king established a separate court system to hear these appeals.

The rules set out in the cases heard by the king's court formed the beginnings of common law. As the number of courts and cases increased, each year's important decisions were recorded in yearbooks. Judges settling current disputes similar to ones that had been previously decided used the yearbooks as the basis for their decisions. If a case was unique, judges created new law by virtue of making a decision, but still based those decisions on the general principles suggested by earlier cases. The body of judge-made common law developed under this system is still used today in both England and the United States.

In many legal areas, statutory law has replaced common law. For example, landlord–tenant law originally was created by common law. Today, much of the landlord–tenant law is statutory. In a particular case, the court looks first for a statute, ordinance, or administrative regulation on which to base its decision. If it finds none, the court looks to case law.

When a case before the court involves an issue for which no legislation exists, the court refers to the common law to make a decision. Provided that a common law decision does not conflict with a constitutional provision or with a statute, common law carries the same authority as statutory law. Even when statutes have been substituted for common law, courts often rely on common law to interpret the legislation based on the supposition that the drafters of the statute had intended to codify a previous common law rule.

Most states have adopted common law by legislative decree. For example, the California Civil Code, Section 22.2, states that the "common law of England, so far as it is not repugnant to or inconsistent with the Constitution of the United States, or the Constitution or laws of this State, is the rule of decision in all the courts of this State."

Louisiana, formerly a French colony, is unique in that it adopted the *civil law system* that Napoleon[5] originated in continental Europe. The **civil law system** is based strictly upon statutory provisions.

Stare Decisis

A cornerstone of the American judicial system is the practice of deciding new cases with reference to decisions made in prior similar cases. Known as the doc-

[4] Amendment X, U.S. Constitution.

[5] Napoleon Bonaparte (1769–1821) was emperor of France from 1804 to 1815. France colonized Louisiana.

LEGAL HIGHLIGHT

Common Law Writs

The common law originally developed through the issuance of writs. Historically, a *writ* was a command; thus, only the English king or his emissaries could issue writs. The king issued substantive writs.

Substantive writs created rights. In past centuries, if you were injured in a horse-and-carriage accident caused by someone else, you could bring an action to recover damages from the wrongdoer under a writ called "trespass on the case."

Substantive writs no longer exist; they evolved over the centuries into many of our modern legal rights. People can file a lawsuit and not depend on writs issued by the king. The writ of trespass on the case evolved into

the modern negligence laws. Today, if you are injured in an automobile accident caused by someone else, you would bring a lawsuit based on negligence.

As centuries passed, the court system developed. Eventually, the king allowed the courts to issue substantive writs. Unlike the king, the courts, however, needed a way to enforce those writs. Over time, the courts began issuing procedural writs that were used to enforce rights created by the substantive writs.

Many of the procedural writs have survived the centuries and are still issued today by federal and many state courts. The following are examples of modern procedural writs used today to enforce your rights.

Common-Law Procedural Writs

Writ	Meaning	Purpose
Habeas corpus	You have the body.	*Habeas corpus* requires that the person held or detained be brought before the court. Used in criminal law and child custody cases.
Mandamus	We command.	*Mandamus* is used to require a specifically named public official to do her or his job. For example, *mandamus* may be sought to require the fire chief to activate a fire hydrant.
Quo warranto	By what authority?	*Quo warranto* may be sought to revoke a corporation's charter when the corporation is involved in illegal conduct.
Replevin	Redeliver.	*Replevin* directs the sheriff to seize personal property.
Certiorari	Review or inquiry.	*Certiorari* is a discretionary writ used by appellate courts to review a lower court's decision. If granted, the case will be reviewed. The writ of *certiorari* routinely is used by the U.S. Supreme Court.

trine of *stare decisis* (let the decision stand), the judge uses **precedent**, that is, the decision of a previous similar case, to decide the outcome of the current case. The process of *stare decisis* acknowledges the experience and wisdom of the past and at the same time creates the common law.

Functions of *Stare Decisis*. *Stare decisis* has several functions: efficiency, uniformity, stability, and predictability. *Stare decisis* allows the courts to be more efficient. A judge reads previous court decisions that set

out the reasons for a particular legal decision. If other judges have confronted similar issues, have reasoned through those problems, and have issued opinions, these previous court decisions can guide current decisions. The judge can adopt the reasoning used in previous cases to the current case.

Stare decisis also results in a more just and uniform decision-making system. Decisions based on precedent can neutralize the personal prejudices of individual judges. Judges are required to use precedent as the basis for their decisions. In spite of the use of precedent, however, some variations in law will occur because of the diverse applications of precedents in accordance with local law. Thus, reasonable judges can differ in their interpretation and application of the law.

Finally, use of precedent makes the law more stable and predictable. If case decisions for a particular subject are well established, people tend to abide by and accept the law as it is applied by the courts. For example, today no one would expect a lawsuit to segregate schools on the basis of race to succeed. A law that is stable encourages people to use the judicial system and to accept the results.

Flexibility of *Stare Decisis.*

Stare decisis provides stability, yet allows the law to be flexible. Kermit Hall described the history of U.S. law as "one of systematic change, of law and society reacting to and reinforcing one another."[6] When the precedent is no longer applicable, the courts can depart from it. For example, changes in technology, business practices, or social attitudes necessitate changes in the law.

Although judges are reluctant to overrule a precedent, they have the power to do so. Without that power, legal thinking and reasoning would be frozen in time. A judge's decision to deviate from precedent depends on the subject of the case, the number and prestige of prior decisions, the degree of social change affecting the case, and the identity of the deciding court. The United States Supreme Court, as the highest authority in the land, is freer than a lower court to change the direction of the law. The cases of *Plessy v. Ferguson* and *Brown v. Board of Education*, which are discussed later, illustrate how the Court influences the direction of the law.

Case of First Impression.

Occasionally, judges must make a decision on a case of first impression, that is, where no law exists on the topic, such as in evolving areas of electronic commerce (e-commerce) or the Internet. In these situations, a court uses one or more of the following guidelines in making its decision.

First, if the court can find a precedent that is relatively similar to the case under review, the court draws an analogy from the prior cases to the current case to make its decision. For example, the court can make the following analogy. States have passed laws governing the license and use of motorized vehicles, which historically are gas powered. The court will decide whether this law covers electrical vehicles or solar-powered vehicles, such as golf carts and scooters. The court could draw an analogy and apply the law to the electrical and solar-powered vehicles or the court could decide that the law does not apply.

Second, the court can consider social expectations to develop a policy. For example, the courts are currently debating the rights of ownership and privacy of electronic mail (e-mail). Does an e-mail user or recipient have the right to expect privacy? Does an e-mail message belong to the sender-creator, the employer, or the network owner? By studying e-mail users' expectations, the courts can establish legal rules for this newly emerging form of communication.

Third, the court can balance interests of the parties in the lawsuit. In making its decision, the court might consider employer versus employee interests, government versus individual interests, and state versus federal government interests. By weighing these interests, the court attempts to make a just decision.

Stare Decisis, Two Cases.

Cases that overturn precedent often receive much publicity. For example, the famous case of *Brown v. Board of Education* (1954), in essence, overruled *Plessy v. Ferguson* (1896) and marked the end of official racial segregation. The magnitude of the publicity that surrounds the reversal of major cases might lead the layperson to believe that case law frequently is overturned. Actually, most cases uphold the common law. The overturning of *Plessy v. Ferguson* by *Brown v. Board of Education* illustrates the Supreme Court's logic in reversing its position of sixty years earlier. A portion of the *Plessy v. Ferguson* case follows.

[6] Kermit L. Hall, *The Magic Mirror: Law in American History* (Oxford, UK: Oxford University Press, 1989), p. 336.

Case 1.1

Plessy v. Ferguson

Supreme Court of the
United States, 1896
163 U.S. 537, 16 S. Ct. 1138,
41 L. Ed. 256
http://www.findlaw.com/
http://supct.law.cornell.edu
/supct/
(See *Using the World Wide Web*
at the end of this chapter.)

LANDMARK CASE

BACKGROUND AND FACTS Plessy, the petitioner, a resident of Louisiana, was of mixed blood, seven-eighths Caucasian and one-eighth African. He purchased a first-class ticket on the East Louisiana Railway to travel from New Orleans to Covington, Louisiana. He sat in a vacant seat in a coach where only white passengers were accommodated.

The conductor requested that Plessy take a seat in another coach for persons who were not white. The only reason Plessy was asked to move was that he was deemed under Louisiana law not to be a white person. Upon his refusal to move, he was forcibly ejected from the coach, arrested, and jailed. He was charged with violation of the 1890 Louisiana criminal statute providing for separate railroad coaches for whites and blacks.

Plessy brought a petition against the criminal court judge to prevent the judge from enforcing the statute. Plessy argued that the statute violated his federal constitutional rights.

Justice BROWN delivered the opinion of the Court.

. . . .

So far, then, as a conflict with the fourteenth amendment is concerned, the case reduces itself to the question whether the statute of Louisiana is a reasonable regulation, and with respect to this there must necessarily be a large discretion on the part of the legislature. In determining the question of reasonableness, it is at liberty to act with reference to the established usages, customs, and traditions of the people, and with a view to the promotion of their comfort, and the preservation of the public peace and good order. Gauged by this standard, we cannot say that a law which authorizes or even requires the separation of the two races in public conveyances is unreasonable, or more obnoxious to the fourteenth amendment than the acts of congress requiring separate schools for colored children in the District of Columbia, the constitutionality of which does not seem to have been questioned, or the corresponding acts of state legislatures.

Justice HARLAN dissenting.

. . . .

The white race deems itself to be the dominant race in this country. And so it is, in prestige, in achievements, in education, in wealth, and in power. So, I doubt not, it will continue to be for all time, if it remains true to its great heritage, and holds fast to the principles of constitutional liberty. But in view of the constitution, in the eye of the law, there is in this country no superior, dominant, ruling class of citizens. There is no caste here. Our constitution is color-blind, and neither knows nor tolerates classes among citizens. In respect of civil rights, all citizens are equal before the law. The humblest is the peer of the most powerful. The law regards man as man, and takes no account of his surroundings or of his color when his civil rights as guaranteed by the supreme law of the land are involved. It is therefore to be regretted that this high tribunal, the final expositor of the fundamental law of the land, has reached the conclusion that it is competent for a state to regulate the enjoyment by citizens of their civil rights solely upon the basis of race.

In my opinion, the judgment this day rendered will, in time, prove to be quite as pernicious as the decision made by this tribunal in the *Dred Scott* Case.

DECISION AND REMEDY In 1896, the United States Supreme Court upheld the individual states' rights to require separate but equal facilities based solely on race. That decision legitimized an era of racial segregation in which the facilities were always separate, but never equal.

The *Dred Scott* case, to which the Court referred, was decided in 1857. Dred Scott was a black slave whose owner took him to a state that prohibited slavery. Later he was returned to a slave state. He brought a lawsuit in St. Louis, Missouri, to obtain his freedom based on previous decisions that residence in free territory conferred freedom. The United States Supreme Court found that no black, free or slave, could claim U.S. citizenship. Shortly after the Court's decision, Dred Scott was sold to a new owner who granted him his freedom two months later.

The ruling aroused angry resentment in the North and led the nation a step closer to the Civil War (1861–1865). It also influenced the introduction and passage of the Fourteenth Amendment to the U.S. Constitution in 1868. This amendment extended citizenship to former slaves and granted former male slaves full civil rights. As a side note, women, black or white, did not have full civil rights until the ratification in 1920 of the Nineteenth Amendment granting women the right to vote. People of the Chinese race (including those living in Hawaii) were not able to immigrate into the United States and could not apply for citizenship after Congress passed the Chinese Exclusion Act of 1882. The ban on both immigration and right to apply for citizenship was finally lifted in 1943 when Congress passed the Chinese Exclusion Repeal Act.

CRITICAL THINKING: REASONING Compare and contrast Justice Brown's opinion with Justice Harlan's opinion.

The next case, *Brown v. Board of Education*, illustrates the flexibility of the common law in adapting to changing social mores. During the fifty-eight years from *Plessy* in 1896 to *Brown* in 1954, two world wars had been fought, African Americans in large numbers had moved from the rural South to northern industrialized urban centers, and women had been granted the right to vote by the Nineteenth Amendment to the U.S. Constitution.

Fundamental structures and attitudes in our society had changed. Normally the law lags behind such societal changes. When these changes are momentous, however, the law adapts to accommodate them, as shown by the following case.

Case 1.2

Brown v. Board of Education

Supreme Court of the
United States, 1954
347 U.S. 483, 74 S. Ct. 686, 98
L. Ed. 873
http://www.findlaw.com/
http://supct.law.cornell.edu
/supct/

LANDMARK CASE

BACKGROUND AND FACTS Five cases originating one each from Kansas, South Carolina, Virginia, Delaware, and the District of Columbia were joined because of the common legal issues involved. The lead case was from Kansas. The plaintiff, Linda Brown, was an African-American five-year-old child living in Topeka. Her father brought this action on her behalf in the U.S. District Court to prohibit enforcement of a Kansas statute that permitted cities with a population of more than 15,000 to maintain separate school facilities for African-American students.

The Topeka Board of Education had elected to establish segregated elementary schools. Linda was assigned to an elementary school based on her race and not to the school which was closest. During the lawsuit, the three-judge federal district court found that segregation in public education had a detrimental effect on African-American children. The court denied a remedy, however, on the grounds that the African-American and white schools substantially were equal with respect to buildings, transportation, curricula, and the educational qualifications of their teachers. Brown appealed.

Chief Justice WARREN delivered the opinion of the Court.

. . . .

. . . It is true that public school education at the time of the [Fourteenth] Amendment had advanced further in the North, but the effect of the Amendment on Northern States was generally ignored in the congressional debates. Even in the North, the conditions of public education did not approximate those existing today. The curriculum was usually rudimentary; ungraded schools were common in rural areas; the school term was but three months a year in many states; and compulsory school attendance was virtually unknown. As a consequence, it is not surprising that there should be so little in the history of the Fourteenth Amendment relating to its intended effect on public education.

. . . .

Here, . . . there are findings below that the Negro and white schools involved have been equalized, or are being equalized, with respect to buildings, curricula, qualifications and salaries of teachers, and other "tangible" factors. Our decision, therefore, cannot turn on merely a comparison of these tangible factors in the Negro and white schools involved in each of the cases. We must look instead to the effect of segregation itself on public education.

In approaching this problem, we cannot turn the clock back to 1868 when the Amendment was adopted, or even to 1896 when *Plessy v. Ferguson* was written. We must consider public education in the light of its full development and its present place in American life throughout the Nation. Only in this way can it be determined if segregation in public schools deprives these plaintiffs of the equal protection of the laws.

Today, education is perhaps the most important function of state and local governments. Compulsory school attendance laws and the great expenditures for education both demonstrate our recognition of the importance of education to our democratic society. It is required in the performance of our most basic public responsibilities, even service in the armed forces. It is the very foundation of good citizenship. Today it is a principal instrument in awakening the child to cultural values, in preparing him for later professional training, and in helping him to adjust normally to his environment. In these days, it is doubtful that any child may reasonably be expected to succeed in life if he is denied the opportunity of an education. Such an opportunity, where the state has undertaken to provide it, is a right which must be made available to all on equal terms.

We come then to the question presented: Does segregation of children in public schools solely on the basis of race, even though the physical facilities and other "tangible" factors may be equal, deprive the children of the minority group of equal educational opportunities? We believe that it does.

. . . .

We conclude that in the field of public education the doctrine of "separate but equal" has no place. Separate educational facilities are inherently unequal.

Therefore, we hold that the plaintiffs and others similarly situated for whom the actions have been brought are, by reason of the segregation complained of, deprived of the equal protection of the laws guaranteed by the Fourteenth Amendment.

DECISION AND REMEDY The United States Supreme Court held that separate but equal public school facilities were inherently unconstitutional when the segregation was based on race. This decision laid the foundation for the desegregation of all public facilities. Ten years later the Civil Rights Act of 1964, which attempted to end all overt discrimination, was passed. Thus, *Plessy v. Ferguson* is no longer valid law.

COMMENT The *Brown* decision was pivotal for the nation. The Court understood the impact that its decision would have on the country; thus, the justices came together in a 9-to-0 vote.[a] The decision itself is only three and a half pages long. The Supreme Court rarely reads a decision in open court prior to releasing the material to the public. But to acknowledge the prestige of the decision, Chief Justice Warren read it in open court; that is, he read the opinion out loud in the courtroom packed with the parties to the case, visitors, and the press. One of the associate justices was Justice John Marshall Harlan,[b] the grandson of Justice John Marshall Harlan[c] who wrote the dissent in *Plessy v. Ferguson.*

The short opinion was reproduced in magazines and newspapers across the country. With no satellites to help speed transmission of this decision, the Voice of America, a radio broadcasting company, translated the *Brown* decision into thirty-four languages and, by the end of an hour, was broadcasting it around the world.

The *Brown* case did not include remedy, however. Instead, the Court set the case for a hearing. In 1955, in the case known as *Brown II,* the Court ordered the remedy to desegregate with "all deliberate speed." Unfortunately, desegregation did not mean automatic racial integration.

During the period between *Plessy* and *Brown,* neither Congress nor the state legislatures took steps toward overturning the concept of separate but equal because of political considerations. The courts were the impetus for change by declaring segregation illegal.

Thurgood Marshall[d] (1908–1993) represented the plaintiffs from the five cases. During his years of litigation, he won twenty-nine of the thirty-two cases he argued before the Court. In 1967, Justice Marshall was appointed to the Supreme Court by President Lyndon Johnson[e] (1908–1973). He served on the Court from 1967 to 1991.

CRITICAL THINKING: POLITICAL CONSIDERATION Why was it necessary for the federal government to become involved in school desegregation at the state level?

[a] *University of Detroit Law Journal* 18 (1954): 64.
[b] John Marshall Harlan (1899–1971) served as associate justice on the U.S. Supreme Court from 1955 to 1971.
[c] John Marshall Harlan (1833–1911) served as associate justice on the U.S. Supreme Court from 1877 to 1911.
[d] More information about Justice Thurgood Marshall is available at <http://www.thurgoodmarshall.com/>.
[e] The Lyndon Baines Johnson Library is part of a system of presidential libraries administered by the National Archives and Records Administration. The library can be accessed at <http://www.lbjlib.utexas.edu/>.

Brown v. Board of Education was first argued in 1952, but the Court decided that it needed more information and so reset the case for argument in 1953. Before the second hearing, Chief Justice Fred Vinson died, and President Dwight Eisenhower[7] (1890–1969) appointed Earl Warren[8] (1891–1974) as chief justice of the United States (1953–1969). Recognizing the importance of the case, the newly appointed chief justice decided that he needed to hear the oral arguments. The case was then argued a second time before the Court.

At first glance, the cases of *Plessy v. Ferguson* and *Brown v. Board of Education* may seem out of place in a textbook concerned with the legal environment of business. Both cases, however, had important impacts on the business world. *Plessy v. Ferguson* promoted an era of segregation. In response, businesses provided separate facilities for whites and nonwhites, including separate entrances, restrooms, and drinking fountains. Tremendous costs were incurred in building and maintaining separate facilities. Citizens of this country were discriminated against in the job market, in housing, and in transportation based on their skin color. Segregation also was applied to other ethnic and religious groups, such as Native Americans, Asians, Hispanics, Irish, Jews, and Catholics. Victims of discrimination varied according to the region and the era.

Brown v. Board of Education began the nation's long journey toward desegregation, a journey that continues today. Congress has passed a series of civil rights acts over the years. Businesses have spent and are still spending billions of dollars in attempts to comply with federal statutes and administrative regulations on equal opportunity and affirmative action, such as recruiting and training programs for minorities and women. Businesses are spending additional sums to defend against charges of violating an employee's constitutional and statutory rights. The financial losses resulting from wasted and unused talent are incalculable.

---

[7] The Dwight D. Eisenhower Library is part of a system of presidential libraries administered by the National Archives and Records Administration. The library can be accessed at <http://history.cc.ukans.edu/heritage/abilene/ikectr.ht ml>.

[8] A brief biography of Chief Justice Earl Warren can be found at <http://provost.ucsd.edu/warren/welcome/facts/earl.html>.

Classifications of Law

The law is very broad. As a result, the law is divided into a number of classifications, according to its various functions and jurisdictions, with some overlap. These classifications are somewhat arbitrary, but a study of the various classifications provides a sense of the depth and breadth of our legal system.

Substantive Law versus Procedural Law

Substantive law defines, describes, regulates, and creates legal rights and obligations. Take the following example. Restaurants are subject to health standards because they sell food and drinks to the public. A restaurant may be fined or even closed if found to be in violation of the health standards. Another example of substantive law is the rule that a person who, through his own fault, injures another must pay damages. Substantive law sets out our legal rights and liabilities.

Procedural law establishes methods of enforcing the rights created by substantive law. For example, procedural law regulates the procedures to initiate a lawsuit, to select the court in which the lawsuit should be filed, to select a jury, to enforce court decisions, and to determine which legal papers need to be filed. Procedural law sets out processes to enforce our legal rights.

Public Law versus Private Law

Public law addresses the relationship between the people and the government. An example is *constitutional law.* **Private law** governs the legal relationships among individuals, such as contracts. Both public and private law are subdivisions of substantive law.

Constitutional law is classified as public law because it involves questions regarding the federal, state, or local government's power to act. The U.S. Constitution empowers the federal government to perform certain acts. Often the issue is whether the government, that is, the legislative or the executive branch, has exceeded its delegated powers under the Constitution.

Constitutional law also limits the exercise of governmental power, preventing improper governmental action from endangering a person's life, liberty, or property. The Fourth and Fifth Amendments to the U.S. Constitution protect individuals from unreasonable searches and coerced confessions.

LEGAL HIGHLIGHT

Law Terms Are Easy to Learn!

At first glance, new legal terms seem like a foreign language. Legal terms are easy to decipher, however, if you know the code. The few legal terms that are in Latin are easy to learn. Whenever a Latin term is used in this text, an explanation follows.

Numerous legal terms end in one of two suffixes: "-or" or "-ee." See the following chart.

Examples of "or" and "ee"

"-or"	"-ee"
Promisor	Promisee
Offeror	Offeree
Grantor	Grantee
Trustor	Trustee
Mortgagor	Mortgagee

A word ending in "-or" is making or creating the word that precedes the "or." The promisor is the party making a promise; the offeror makes an offer; the grantor creates a grant, such as a conveyance of a title to real property; the trustor creates a trust; and the mortgagor creates a mortgage.

A word ending in "-ee" is receiving what precedes it. The promisee receives the promise, the offeree receives the offer, the grantee receives the grant, the trustee is the person who receives the assets for the trust, and the mortgagee receives the benefits of the mortgage. In a mortgage, the debtor, or mortgagor, is the one who creates the mortgage, thus the mortgagee is the creditor.

Administrative law consists of governmental agencies that issue regulations that regulate businesses and consumers. An example of administrative law is a proposal by the Occupational Safety and Health Administration (OSHA) requiring that restaurant noise be reduced. The restaurant industry could object on the grounds that the proposed regulation would raise costs excessively in comparison with any benefits that may result.

Other areas of the law, such as contract litigation, fall within the private law category. Businesspeople, who sue suppliers for breaking a contract, or pedestrians, who sue motorists for running into them, use private law. If a state government contracts to have a classroom building erected at the state university, this contract falls under public law, because the government is involved. Public law is involved if a gardener employed by the state university, while driving a university truck, hits a pedestrian. Thus, the same conduct may fall under public or private law depending upon whether the government or a private entity is involved.

Civil Law versus Criminal Law

Civil law encompasses the legal rights and duties that exist among persons or between citizens and their governments. Contract law, corporate law, and partnership law, for example, are part of the civil law. Civil law is concerned with a person's legally recognized rights and duties in relationship with others.

Criminal law involves a violation or wrong committed by a person. Although the criminal act may involve only one victim, it is also an offense against society. Criminal acts are prohibited by the government to protect the public. Criminal law falls under public law jurisdiction, whereas civil law is sometimes public and sometimes private. All law not classified as criminal is civil.

Criminal acts are defined by statutes enacted by local, state, or federal government. In a criminal case, the government seeks at trial to have the accused person found guilty and to have the court impose a penalty, such as a fine, a term of imprisonment, or even the death penalty. In civil law, the person seeks damages or other remedies, such as the return of a unique diamond. A criminal act often violates a civil right as well. For example, drunk driving is a criminal act. If an accident occurs, the government can prosecute the accused for driving under the influence of alcohol. If the accused injures someone in the accident, the victim also can sue in civil court for damages.

Courts of Law and Courts of Equity

Early in American legal history, the legal system followed the English model of courts and was divided into two systems, *courts of law* and *courts of equity*. A **court of law** grants a damage award, while a **court of equity** grants a **remedy**, a legal means to enforce personal rights or to correct a wrong. In most states, courts of law and courts of equity have merged, but vestiges of the distinctions between the two still exist.

Historically, the early English courts of law became so strict and complicated that justice was not served. In those days, the facts were presumed to be true. Thus, the outcome of the case depended on using the correct procedure. If the lawyer used the wrong procedural writ, the person would lose the case. The only appeal was to the king. The effect still lingers in the consciousness of society. We all have heard, for example, that "you must cross every t and dot every i" when dealing with legal matters, even though today that is not literally true.

By the thirteenth century, the courts of law were basically restricted to granting money damages and possession of property, such as a trial to determine the title to real estate, as a remedy. Depending on the degree of harm, a victim might not be compensated by these limited legal remedies. The only means of redress was to petition the king for justice for equitable relief. These petitions became so numerous that the king sent them to the lord **chancellor**, the king's principal minister, for resolution. By the fourteenth century, the petitions were sent directly to the chancellor.

By the middle of the fourteenth century, the chancery court became a separate court system. The chancellor had the ability to grant new and unique remedies that fit the facts of the particular case. Eventually, a body of rules and remedies was estab-lished for this new court. Chancery courts gradually became called courts of equity. The following sections clarify the distinctions that exist today between courts of law and courts of equity.

Distinctions

Several differences exist between courts of law and courts of equity. The major distinctions include the use of a jury, time limitations, and legal decisions.

First, a jury is allowed in a court of law, whereas in an equity court the judge makes the decision. Historically, juries were never used in courts of equity. Today, however, an advisory jury sometimes is allowed when equitable relief is sought, but its decision is not binding. For example, an injunction is decided by a judge, not a jury.

Second, the two courts differ in the time limitations for filing a lawsuit. In a court of law, the victim, after the harm has occurred, has a maximum time limitation to file a lawsuit or he forfeits the right to do so. The time limitations are set in the various **statutes of limitations** and are measured, usually, in years. For example, if a contract has been broken, the person who has been harmed may sue at any time during a four-year period. If the person sues one day after the four years have passed, the case will not be heard by a court. The statute of limitations is designed to prevent undue delay in bringing the suit to court so that the evidence on both sides is fresh and the witnesses still are available.

Similarly, courts of equity are bound by the **doctrine of laches**. Individuals who fail to act promptly to protect their rights will lose the right to the equity court's assistance. (See *Legal Highlight: Equitable Maxims*.) In other words, a person must sue within a reasonable time. For example, if a business seeks an injunction to prevent a labor union from carrying out its threat to strike within a week, management must file its request within a reasonable time period, usually within a few days. Because of the nature of the cases heard, a reasonable time may range from a few days to several decades; thus, setting specific time limitations is impossible.

Third, a court of law's **judgment** (legal decision) awards money damages. A court of equity, on the other hand, issues a *decree* or *order*. A **decree** determines the parties' rights in the case before the court. For example, a divorce decree dissolves the marital bonds between a husband and wife. An **order**, which is usually part of a decree, also determines the parties' temporary or permanent rights, such as child support.

Courts of law award monetary damages, whereas courts of equity grant other types of relief. The following are some differences between *remedies at law* and *equitable remedies.*

Courts of Law: Remedies at Law.

Today, most people who sue in court want monetary damages, that is, they want money to replace their loss. For example, a customer orders a bronze statue from you using the business WWW site. You and the customer work out all the details. You mold and cast the bronze statue and have it delivered to the customer's home as agreed. The customer does not pay for the statue. You would sue in a court of law for money damages, that is, the contract price on which you both agreed. If you prevail in court, the court will issue a judgment for money damages, also called a **remedy at law** or **legal remedy**.

Courts of Equity: Equitable Remedies.

Equity courts are grounded in justice and fair dealing. These courts grant **equitable remedies** that provide solutions other than the money damage remedies available in a court of law. Occasionally, people seeking equity may be granted money even though money was not the primary relief that they originally sought. In an equitable case, money is granted when the plaintiff asserts that the money is rightfully hers or his. In a case at law, money is awarded to compensate for specific damages caused by the wrongdoer.

Equitable remedies try to correct a situation by granting the harmed party relief. Generally, the courts will not consider applying equitable principles and granting equitable relief unless there is no adequate legal remedy available. The most common equitable remedies are *specific performance, injunction, rescission, reformation,* and *accounting.* Detailed explanations of each follow.

Specific Performance. A plaintiff may ask a court to issue a decree of **specific performance**, which orders a defendant to perform the acts that she promised to do in a contract. The subject matter of the contract must be unique for a court to order specific performance.

For example, in most states, land and one-of-a-kind personal property, like the Hope diamond,[9] are considered to be unique. A court of law can only order payment of money for damages, but, in many cases, this payment is not a satisfactory remedy. For example, the Hope diamond is for sale. The owner enters into a contract to sell the unique diamond.

The owner now regrets having sold the diamond and does not want to go through with the sale. The Hope diamond's buyer wants the gem, not monetary damages. A court of equity, then, can order the diamond's seller to turn the diamond over to the buyer. Failure to obey this order would result in a contempt of court charge.

In the case of your contract to sell the bronze statue, although you created the statue, you failed to deliver the statue. Assume the customer has paid in full. The customer could sue for specific performance. The statue is unique and the customer wants the statue, not money damages. If you failed to obey the court's order for specific performance, you could be held in contempt of court.

A court cannot order specific performance of personal services, however, because that would be considered involuntary servitude. Besides, such an order would be unenforceable in a practical sense. For example, you receive an order for a marble fountain. A dispute arises. If you had not already created the marble fountain, a court could not issue a specific performance order that in effect ordered you to construct the marble fountain, since it is a unique item. Another example is a professional softball player who refuses to play for her team. The softball club sues for specific performance. A court cannot order a softball player to play, because no one could enforce the order to make her play.

Injunction. A plaintiff might request an **injunction** to prevent a certain activity from happening or to stop an activity from continuing. For example, although a

---

[9] The Hope diamond now is owned by the U.S. government. The Hope diamond can be seen as part of the National Gem Collection at the Janet Annenberg Hooker Hall of Geology, Gems and Minerals, which is part of the Smithsonian's National Museum of Natural History in Washington, D.C. For a history of the previous owners of the Hope diamond and for more information, see <http://www.smithsonianmag.com/smithsonian/issuesall/issues97/sep97/gems.html>.

court cannot order the softball player to play, it could stop the softball player from playing for another team by issuing an injunction. The softball club would seek an injunction, in this case, an order refraining her from doing a particular act, in this case, playing for another team. A **temporary restraining order** (TRO) is a temporary injunction that orders a person to refrain from an activity for the time period between the filing of the lawsuit and the conclusion of the trial. A TRO might be issued to preserve evidence or to protect the plaintiff's rights. In this case, the softball club would first seek a TRO, which will be converted into a permanent injunction if the club prevails in court.

Rescission. Sometimes a person signs and performs a contract, but the basis of the contract was misrepresented by the other party. Upon discovery of the misrepresentation, the injured party wants to return to the position that he had before signing the contract. A court of equity can remedy the situation equitably by ordering a **rescission**. A rescission cancels the agreement and reinstates both parties to the status quo. For rescission to be granted, the injured party must show that he relied on misrepresentations when signing the contract. If the equity court grants rescission, the plaintiff is entitled to have any property or money returned to him. All rights and duties created by the agreement are rescinded.

For example, you sign a sales agreement not knowing that the supplier is misrepresenting the quality of the raw bronze metal you need to make a statue. If you discover the fraud before money or goods have changed hands, you can request the court for equitable relief to have the agreement rescinded, that is, to have the contract declared null and void. If, however, you paid the supplier before the fraud was discovered, you again can seek a recission of the contract and request the court to order the supplier to repay your money.

Reformation. Occasionally, a written contract does not correctly reflect the original oral agreement. The court of equity may order a **reformation** or change of the written contract to reflect the true intent of the parties. Reformation action results from either fraud or mistake in a contract situation.

For example, you go to an insurance agent to purchase disability insurance. Because you recently started an online business, you have very limited finances and can afford maximum monthly payments of $50. You need disability income coverage that will pay $400 a month to cover the loan payments on your truck. The insurance agent prepares the application for coverage of $400 a month. After you leave the office, the agent realizes that the $50 monthly premium will purchase coverage of only $200 a month. He strikes out the $400 and inserts $200. The insurance company does not realize that a change has been made and issues a policy for coverage of $200 per month. After six months, you become disabled and make a claim for income of $400 a month. The insurance company informs you that the maximum amount is $200 a month. You file a lawsuit seeking reformation of the contract. In this type of situation, the court may reform the contract to the original amount of $400 based on the fraud committed by the agent.

Accounting. When parties have a close relationship that involves money or other property, then have a disagreement, one or both may request a court of equity for an **accounting**. For example, one business partner accuses the other of misappropriating some of the business assets. The accuser may file a lawsuit in a court of equity and request a full accounting of the missing assets. Normally, the court appoints a certified public accountant to conduct a full accounting. The court could order the wrongdoer to pay for the value of the missing assets to the innocent party.

Merged Court Systems. A person filing a lawsuit during the period between the fourteenth century and the middle of the twentieth century had to decide whether to file in a court of law or in a court of equity as previously discussed. Many states today have merged the two court systems. Thus, a person may request both legal and equitable remedies in the same lawsuit.

In states that have merged the two systems, trial court judges have the authority to grant both forms of relief. Judges still decide questions of equity that have broad remedies. As noted previously, a jury rarely decides cases involving equitable relief. When a plaintiff requests only damages, a judge alone or a jury may hear the case. The merging of the courts of law and equity has not diminished the importance of distinguishing between these two systems.

LEGAL HIGHLIGHT

Equitable Maxims

How do judges make a decision when one party asks for an equitable remedy and the opposing party disagrees? For example, Racing Farms contracts with Jed to purchase from him a race horse named Speedster. One week after the contract was signed, Jed races Speedster one more time. Speedster wins the race and now Jed has seller's remorse and wants to keep Speedster because of the horse's potential for winning.

Racing Farms can sue for specific performance. Racing Farms requests the judge to order Jed to turn over the horse. Jed opposes the remedy. The judge is faced with making a decision as to whether to grant the request for specific performance.

From medieval times, judges have developed six principles, called *equitable maxims,* to guide their decision making. These equitable maxims are based on common sense and fairness.

1. Whoever seeks equity must do equity. Plaintiffs who seek an equitable remedy want to be treated fairly, but, to obtain justice, they, in turn, must have treated others fairly.

2. Where there is equal equity, the law must prevail. When both the plaintiff and the defendant have meritorious positions, the court must apply the law instead of searching for an equitable remedy.

3. Equity regards substance rather than form. The equity court is more interested in justice and fairness than in legal technicalities.

4. One seeking the aid of an equity court must come to the court with clean hands. The plaintiff must have acted honestly and fairly to seek aid from the court.

5. Equity will not suffer a right to exist without a remedy. When the plaintiff has a right to relief and no adequate remedy at law exists, the equity court is charged with identifying and awarding an equitable remedy.

6. Equity aids the vigilant, not those who rest on their rights. Individuals who find that they have been wronged must act within a reasonable time period to protect their rights. This maxim is the basis for the doctrine of laches, discussed earlier in this chapter.

The maxims do not have legal authority because they have not been codified. They do have precedential value, however, because they have been relied on for hundreds of years and are cited in numerous cases. These commonsense principles are often used by judges when deciding cases in equity. In this case, the judge should grant the request for specific performance and order Jed to turn the horse over to Racing Farms. Jed may have seller's remorse, but he does not have any legal reason not to turn over the horse.

Locating the Law

Trial courts hear factual issues and make decisions on cases that are brought before them. The side that loses has the right to appeal that decision to a higher court, called an **appellate court.** The following material examines the publication of trial court and appellate court decisions.

Publishing Court Decisions

Court decisions are published in chronological order and typically reflect only the decisions of appellate courts. A few states, including California and New York, publish their trial court decisions. The published decisions of the federal district courts, the trial courts for the federal government, are available in law libraries and on computer databases.

Of the thousands of trial court decisions made each year, less than 1 percent finish the appeal process, and only a few of those decisions are published. Published decisions made by state and federal courts of appeal are available in law libraries and in computer databases. The published appellate court cases are those that concern important legal issues.

The cases in this book have been taken from reported appellate court decisions. The following section addresses the system for locating reported cases.

Reporter System for Case Decisions

Many state governments publish their state appellate court decisions. State cases also appear in regional units of the *National Reporter System,* published privately by West Group (West)[10] (see Exhibit 1–1). If the state government does not publish its own material, it may designate West as the official publisher of the state's legal materials. West is the unofficial publisher of all the reported decisions by the federal trial and appellate courts.

United States Supreme Court decisions have three citations. First, the official reports are printed by the U.S. Government Printing Office in the *United States Reports* (U.S.). The second and third citations are to the two unofficial reporters, the *Supreme Court Reporter* (S. Ct.), published by West Group, and the *Lawyers' Edition* of the United States Supreme Court Reports (L. Ed.), published by Matthew Bender & Company, Inc.

Case Citations. Appellate court decisions normally have two citations: the official citation and the unofficial citation. The official citation is provided by the U.S. Government Printing Office and the unofficial citation is the one from the *National Reporter System*. The case is cited (referred to) by the case name, the volume number, name of the state report (if any), and page number; followed by the volume number, abbreviation of the *National Reporter,* and page number. The year in which the decision was filed appears at the end. (See Exhibit 1–2.)

For example, consider the following citation to a case decided by the Maryland Court of Appeals: *Harris v. State*, 344 Md. 497, 687 A.2d 970 (1997). The names of the parties, Harris and the State, appear first. The opinion appears in volume 344 of the official *Maryland Reports*, published by the state of Maryland, beginning on page 497, as well as in volume 687 of the *Atlantic Reporter*, Second Series, published by West Group, beginning on page 970. The appellate court decision was filed in 1997. In the title of a case, such as *Harris v. State*, the *v.* or *vs.* stands for *versus*, which means "against."

The appellate court often places the name of the party appealing the decision first. In this case, Harris appealed the trial court's decision. In some states, however, the appellate courts retain the order of names from the trial court. Thus, from the case name it is impossible to distinguish the **plaintiff**, the person filing the lawsuit and seeking relief from a harm, from the **defendant**, the person being sued and accused of causing harm. The facts of each case must be read carefully to identify each party's role; otherwise, the appellate court's discussion will be difficult to understand.

Uniform System of Citation. The American Bar Association (ABA)[11] has recommended a new uniform system of citation. This new system will standardize references to cases that are made available in print and electronic forms to the public. As of this writing, several states and one federal court have adopted the uniform system and its adoption is pending in other states.

Individual case references under the new system include (in order) the case name, the year of the decision, the court issuing the decision, and the decision's sequential number. Cases are numbered to correspond with the sequence in which the court decides them. To cite part of a case, a paragraph number, instead of a page number, follows the sequential number.

Since this system is new, a fictitious example follows: *Cotton v. Grady*, 2001 AZ 30, ¶58; 502 P.2d 1482. The name of the case is *Cotton v. Grady*. The case was decided in 2001. The court name, AZ, stands for Arizona Supreme Court. The number 30 indicates that this case was the thirtieth sent to publication. Finally, the symbol ¶58 indicates the specific paragraph. The second citation, 502 P.2d 1482, indicates that the case can be located in volume 502, on page 1482 in the Pacific second series of the *National Reporter System*.

Statute Publications

Statutes are passed by a legislative body as a bill that consists of various parts. These parts are individually assigned by topic to different areas of the statutory scheme. For publication purposes, statutes are organized by subject matter and published topically, in contrast to cases that are organized and published chronologically.

Statutory Citations. As a result of the fact that statutes are organized differently from cases, statutory citations differ from those of cases. In a statutory citation, the first number is the title number, and the second

---

[10] West Group is found at <http://www.westpub.com/>. West has published legal materials for more than 120 years.

[11] The American Bar Association's web site is at <http://www.abanet.org>.

Exhibit 1–1 National Reporter System—Regional and Federal

Regional Reporters	Coverage Beginning	Coverage
Atlantic Reporter (A. or A.2d)	1885	Connecticut, Delaware, Maine, Maryland, New Hampshire, New Jersey, Pennsylvania, Rhode Island, Vermont, and District of Columbia.
North Eastern Reporter (N.E. or N.E.2d)	1885	Illinois, Indiana, Massachusetts, New York, and Ohio.
North Western Reporter (N.W. or N.W.2d)	1879	Iowa, Michigan, Minnesota, Nebraska, North Dakota, South Dakota, and Wisconsin.
Pacific Reporter (P. or P.2d)*	1883	Alaska, Arizona, California, Colorado, Hawaii, Idaho, Kansas, Montana, Nevada, New Mexico, Oklahoma, Oregon, Utah, Washington, and Wyoming.
South Eastern Reporter (S.E. or S.E.2d)	1887	Georgia, North Carolina, South Carolina, Virginia, and West Virginia.
South Western Reporter (S.W. or S.W.2d)	1886	Arkansas, Kentucky, Missouri, Tennessee, and Texas.
Southern Reporter (So. or So.2d)	1887	Alabama, Florida, Louisiana, and Mississippi.
Federal Reporters		
Federal Reporter (F., F.2d or F.3d)	1880	U.S. Circuit Court from 1880 to 1912; Commerce Court of the United States from 1911 to 1913; U.S. district courts from 1880 to 1932; U.S. Court of Claims (now called U.S. Court of Federal Claims) from 1929 to 1932 and since 1960; U.S. Court of Appeals since 1891; U.S. Court of Customs and Patent Appeals since 1929; and U.S. Emergency Court of Appeals since 1943.
Federal Supplement (F.Supp.)	1932	U.S. Court of Claims from 1932 to 1960; U.S. district courts since 1932; and U.S. Customs Court since 1956.
Federal Rules Decisions (F.R.D.)	1939	U.S. district courts involving the Federal Rules of Civil Procedure since 1939 and Federal Rules of Criminal Procedure since 1946.
Supreme Court Reporter (S.Ct.)	1882	United States Supreme Court since the October term of 1882.
Bankruptcy Reporter (B.R.)	1980	Bankruptcy decisions of U.S. bankruptcy courts, U.S. district courts, U.S. Courts of Appeals, and United States Supreme Court.
Military Justice Reporter (M.J.)	1978	U.S. Court of Appeals for the Armed Forces and Army, Navy-Marine Corps, Air Force, and Coast Guard Courts of Criminal Appeals.

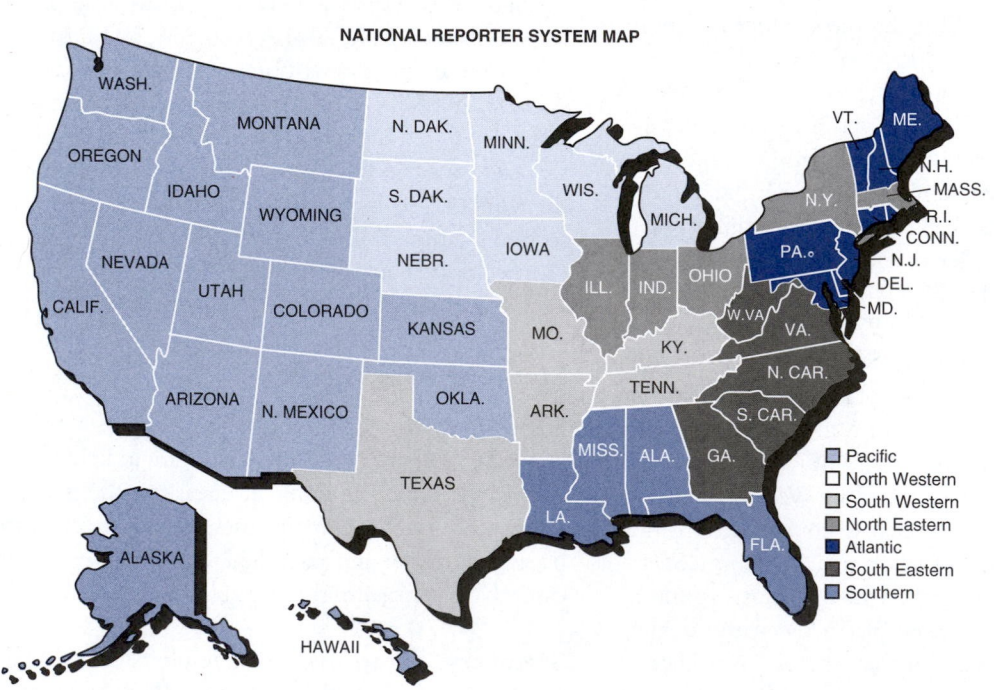

NATIONAL REPORTER SYSTEM MAP

Exhibit 1–2 **Case Citation Examples**

A. State Appellate Court Case

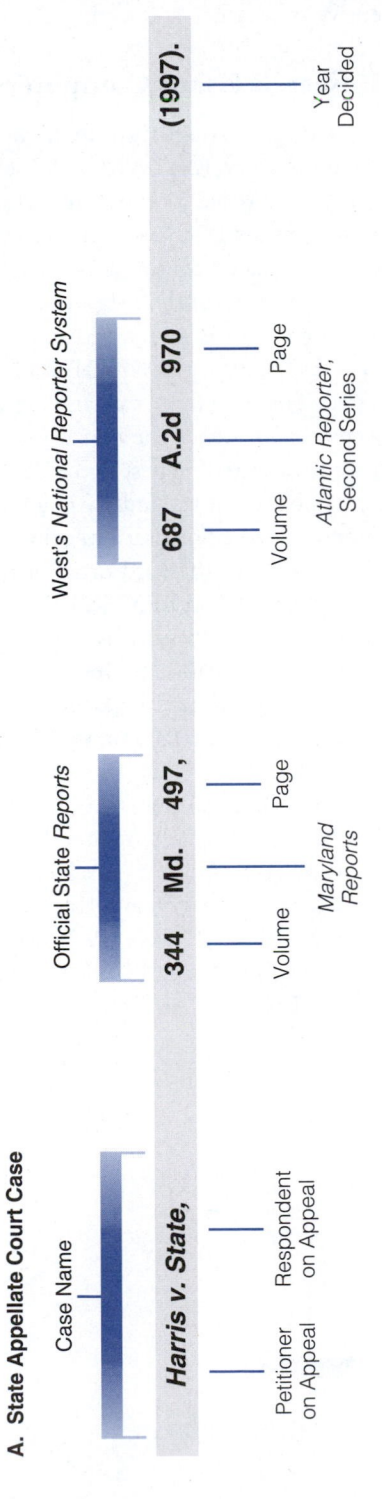

Harris v. State, 344 Md. 497, 687 A.2d 970 (1997).

Case Name | Official State *Reports* | West's *National Reporter System* | Year Decided

Petitioner on Appeal — Respondent on Appeal

Volume — Page (*Maryland Reports*)

Volume — A.2d — Page (*Atlantic Reporter, Second Series*)

Note: There is no way to tell who was the original plaintiff or defendant at the trial level. The order of the names at the appellate level is based on who brings the petition for appeal; this is usually the party who lost at the lower level. A few states, however, follow the rule that the plaintiff's name always appears first on the citation.

Note: Not all states have official reports, as Maryland does. Some states rely on West's *National Reporter System* as their official reports.

B. United States Supreme Court Case

Brown v. Board of Education, 347 U.S. 483, 74 S.Ct. 686, 98 L.Ed. 873 (1954).

Case Name | Official Reporter | West Reporter | Matthew Bender & Company, Inc. | Year Decided

Petitioner on Appeal — Respondent on Appeal

Volume — Page (*United States Reporter*)

Volume — S.Ct. — Page (*Supreme Court Reporter*)

Volume — L.Ed. — Page (*Lawyer's Edition*)

number indicates the section within the title in which the statute can be located. (See Exhibit 1–3.)

Federal statutes can be found in the *United States Code* (U.S.C., published by the U.S. Government Printing Office). The expanded version is the *United States Code Annotated* (U.S.C.A.) published by West Group, which provides short summaries of all the cases decided under that statute.

For example, a particular statute, coded as 18 U.S.C.A. § 2113, is published under Title 18, with all the other federal criminal statutes. Title 18 consists of many volumes. The number 18 is the title number, not the volume number. The symbol § stands for section, which is followed by the number. In this example, the title of section 2113 is *Bank Robbery and Incidental Crimes.*

Administrative Agency Regulations

An **administrative agency** is created by the legislative or, occasionally, the executive branch of the government. Each agency adopts regulations to facilitate the carrying out of its statutory duties. A regulation has the force of law unless a court overturns it. Federal agencies include the Federal Trade Commission, the Environmental Protection Agency, and the Internal Revenue Service. State and local agencies include the department of motor vehicles, public utility commissions, and pardon and parole boards.

The federal government publishes its administrative agencies' regulations in the *Code of Federal Regulations* (C.F.R.), a series of softbound books. Regulations issued by state governments are published either in softbound editions or in loose-leaf manuals.

Both federal and state regulations change frequently, which explains why they are published in a format that is inexpensive to produce and easy to change.

Legal Research Using Computers

The two most widely used private, high-speed data-delivery systems are WESTLAW by West Group and LEXIS-NEXIS by Reed Elsevier Properties, Inc. Both are computer-assisted legal research services that allow researchers to interact with the delivery system.

User interaction with the data-delivery system can be initiated anywhere in the world from a computer running a WESTLAW or LEXIS-NEXIS software access program. These systems can also be accessed by using a web browser. Once the user is logged onto the system, he sends a search request to the data bank. If the appropriate information is found, it appears on the user's computer screen. The user can print the information or download it to the hard drive or to a diskette.

For a fee, WESTLAW, LEXIS-NEXIS, and similar computerized data-search systems can access virtually any case, statute, or regulation in the United States with minimum time and effort. Today, the latest case outcomes are available within days on the computer, far in advance of printed copies that are sent to law libraries and subscribers. This legal information is also available on CD-ROM and is updated frequently.

A congressional mandate requires all governmental agencies to make information available on the Internet through the World Wide Web (WWW). Many state governments are also posting legal information on the Internet. (See Exhibit 1–4.) The legal information

Exhibit 1–3   Statute Citation Example

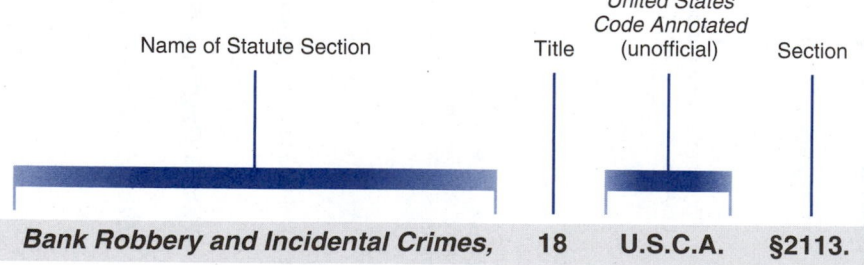

Note: Several other ways to cite statutes also are used, such as those found in *Statutes at Large, Public Law,* and in the official volumes of the *United States Code.*

available on the WWW is usually confined to relatively new information. Currently only high-profile historic cases are available. Additionally, unlike the private computer services described previously, the information on the WWW is still poorly organized, often difficult to locate, and may be unreliable because of errors or lack of updating.

This text provides reference addresses to WWW sites when appropriate. The user should be aware, however, that these sites often change or are removed without notice.

Schools of Legal Philosophy

Jurisprudence means the philosophy of law and describes the foundations and workings of our dynamic legal system. Jurisprudence explains the philosophical basis for the law, the reasons for the law, and the process by which the law can be changed. A number of schools of legal philosophy exist. In the following sections, we review five current schools of thought: the *natural law school,* the *analytical school,* the *historical school,* the *legal realists school,* and the *economic school.* Each school explains some areas of the law, but each has its limitations. There is no unified philosophy of the law that can be applied to all areas of the law.

Natural Law School

The **natural law school** holds that an ideal state of being exists that derives naturally from either human nature or a divine source. Natural law is discovered through reason and the knowledge of good and evil. Ethical values are the source of the law's authority.

Documents such as the Magna Carta, the Declaration of Independence, the U.S. Constitution (see Appendix A for the complete text), and the U.N. Declaration of Human Rights have the natural law as their philosophical basis. Natural law ideals are expressed in phrases such as this one from the Declaration of Independence: "We hold these truths to be self-evident, that all Men are created equal, that they are endowed by their Creator with certain unalienable Rights. . . ."

The civil rights movement of the late 1950s and early 1960s protested the existence of racial segregation. This movement used the natural law philosophy as its foundation. African Americans were arrested for sitting at lunch counters or at the front of buses, areas exclusively reserved for white patrons. The legal defense for these acts was based on the premise that segregation is inherently wrong. The defense asserted that a higher law provided meaning to the words found in the U.S. Constitution, such as equal protection in the Fourteenth Amendment, that sanctioned the defendants' acts of defiance. Although those defendants were convicted of criminal acts, the Congress eventually made the segregation laws illegal.

Analytical School

A proponent of the **analytical school** examines the structure and subject matter of legal codes and cases, analyzing them logically to extract the underlying principles. By analyzing cases and rules, the analytical school develops general principles. These principles form the basis for legal reasoning. Logic shapes the analytical school's approach to the law.

The American Law Institute (ALI) represents this philosophy in its ***Restatements***. The ALI has reviewed thousands of cases decided in the last 200 years to determine the law in specific areas. Based on this extensive review, the ALI has written *Restatements* for various sections of the law, including agency, contract, tort, and trust law.

In effect, the *Restatements* are volumes of sequentially organized compilations of cases on particular topics. The purpose of the *Restatements* is to set out the history, development and logic of particular laws. Judges often use the *Restatements* to support their case opinions. If a *Restatement* section is adopted by a state's supreme court, it becomes the law of that state.

Historical School

The **historical school** concentrates on the legal system's origin and history to determine the principles of contemporary law. Legal principles that have withstood the passage of time are best suited for shaping present laws. Statements are descriptive in nature, such as the following.

In 1540, the English Parliament passed the Statute of Wills. The statute permitted a person to sign a will; thus, the person was able to control to whom his real property was to be distributed after death. Prior to this statute, all real property belonged to the king and the king controlled how property was to be distributed after a person's death.

Centuries later, with the exception of Louisiana, all the other states in the United States have adopted some

Exhibit 1–4   Legal Research on the World Wide Web

The Internet is a data-delivery mechanism that consists of connected networks composed of several elements. The two most popular are electronic mail (e-mail) and the World Wide Web (WWW). The WWW is popular because it supports text, graphics, video, and audio capabilities and has interactive capabilities.

In the 1960s, the U.S. government began the development and construction of a system of computer networks, but its use was restricted to government, academic, and military users. After the end of the Cold War in 1989, the Internet was opened to the public. Since then, Internet use has grown exponentially. Millions of computers provide services linking the world's nations into a seamless web of computer connections, using telephone and cable lines, fiber optics, and satellite feeds.

The Internet can be accessed in a number of ways. You can subscribe to Internet service providers (ISPs), such as America Online, AT&T WorldNet Service,

MindSpring, and Microsoft Internet Network. Each service provides chat rooms, encyclopedias, financial and banking services, and access to the Internet for e-mail functions outside the service providers' clientele and for access to the WWW. These providers arrange information in an organized manner and allow their members access to the Internet. Keep in mind, however, that although these online services provide access to the Internet, they are not considered to be the Internet.

You can also subscribe to an ISP that provides Internet access and related services, such as home pages and e-mail, but generally no other services. Other common sources of Internet access and e-mail are places of employment, academic institutions, public libraries, and shopping malls.

Each computer that serves the WWW can be located through its Internet address. The address is based on the Domain Name System (DNS). Seven top-level domains exist in the United States. Country domains

The Original Magnificent Seven Generic Top-Level Domains (gTDLs)

Abbreviation	Explanation
World Wide Web gTLDs	
.com	Commercial organizations. Businesses use this domain. If the growth pattern continues, this category may be subdivided. Sites: 22,373,097
.edu	Educational and academic organizations. In the past, this domain was used for all U.S. educational institutions. Now, the .edu is restricted to four-year colleges and universities. Elementary and secondary schools and two-year colleges are registered in the country domain, such as <.us>, and use either K–12 (kindergarten through twelfth grade) or community college names. Sites: 3,092
.int	Organizations established by international treaties or having international databases.
.net	Network providers, that is, NIC (network information center) and NOC (network operations center) computers. Sites: 4,242,957
.org	Organizations not included in other domains, such as research and not-for-profit organizations. Sites: 2,671,526
United States Only gTLDs	
.gov	Originally intended for all government agencies. Now reserved for the U.S. government. State and local agencies are registered in the U.S. domain, such as for Arizona: <http://www.state.az.us>. Sites: 730
.mil	Military organizations within the U.S. Department of Defense.

Exhibit 1–4 (continued)

are identified by two-letter abbreviations. Each state in the United States is listed under the U.S. country domain of <.us>. Appendix I lists the two-letter country domain and those for each of the fifty states. The following table describes the top-level domains in the United States along with the number of sites carrying that domain. The numbers are rounded off because the numbers continually increase on any given day. The source for the numbers is <http://www.domainstats .com/internic.cfm>.

In this textbook, angle brackets (< >) set off the actual address. *Do not type in the letters URL: or < >.* An example of a WWW address follows:

URL: <http://www.law.cornell.edu>

Reading the example backwards, you can tell that the computer is located at an educational site, Cornell University, which contains law-related topics. Although this address is easy to read and figure out, most addresses are not so easily readable because the letters and symbols used in the address do not have any readily apparent meaning. All addresses, however, are converted to numbers through a domain name server. If you know these numbers, you can enter them and they will take you directly to the site.

Another example follows:

URL: <http://www.lawsoc.org.uk/>

The <org> in the address might lead you to think that the site is for a not-for-profit organization in the United States. A closer look shows <uk> follows <org>, indicating that this site is located in the United Kingdom. In fact, it is the site for the Law Society, an English not-for-profit organization. You will find English, not American, law at this web site.

Seven additional new generic top-level domains (gTLDs) have been adopted. Currently, a lawsuit is pending over the concerns of trademark and dispute mechanisms, and whether a .health domain should be adopted. The new ones are shown in the next table.

Millions of persons, businesses, and governments have their site names registered on the WWW. But sites, just like people, move or cease to exist. The WWW addresses provided in this textbook as references are current as of the print date.

New Magnificent Seven gTLDs

Abbreviation	Explanation
.aero	For the aviation industry.
.biz	For businesses and is an alternative to <.com>.
.coop	For business cooperatives.
.info	For those providing general information services.
.museum	For museums.
.name	For individual or personal nomenclature; a personal *nom de plume* identifier.
.pro	For professionals.

The popular Internet browsers, such as Netscape Navigator and Microsoft Internet Explorer, each has its own search engines. Search engines allow the user to locate information posted on the Internet. Some popular search engines are: Ask Jeeves, Excite, Infoseek, Lycos, Savvysearch, Webcrawler, Google, and Yahoo!.

HELPFUL HINTS. Have you ever typed in a top-domain address, but the site fails to respond? One reason might be that the server is busy, similar to a telephone busy signal. If it remains busy after repeated tries, one solution is to enter a forward slash (/) following the top domain (i.e., .com, .edu, .gov), so it reads <http://thomas.gov/>. That may do the trick. If the top-domain address has characters typed after a slash (/), try deleting everything to the right of the slash. For example, at one time <http://www.lawsoc.org.uk /lawsc02a.html> was a valid address, but today it no longer works. If you delete all the characters following the forward slash after the top domain, <http://www .lawsoc.org.uk/> the address works.

Sometimes you may not have seen in the address a small symbol that often follows the first slash after the top domain. Three symbols, the tilde (~), the underscore (_), and the hyphen (-), are used often and can be difficult to see. The tilde often follows the top domain and first forward slash (/).

version of this English law governing probate. **Probate** is the legal process of settling a person's estate by collecting property owned by the deceased (also called the decedent), paying his debts, and transferring ownership of the decedent's property to his heirs.

If a valid will exists, the probate court follows the instructions for distribution of the estate's property as lawfully expressed in his will. If no valid will exists, a state statute (commonly called statutes of descent and distribution or laws of intestacy) sets out the order of those entitled to inherit starting with the spouse, followed by children, grandchildren, and so on. The statute lists only people who are related by marriage or by blood.

For example, in many states if you are married to someone for one hour and die before you execute a will, your spouse inherits your full estate. In contrast, let's assume you lived happily with your lover as if you were husband and wife for fifty years, then you died without a will in a state that does not recognize common law marriage, that is, living together as husband and wife, though not officially married. Your lover inherits nothing because you were not legally married. If no relative listed in the statute survives you, your property goes to the state. These rules, based on historical precedent, have worked well for centuries, so they remain intact.

Legal Realists School

The **school of legal realism** acknowledges that law is shaped by social forces and is an instrument of social control. The legal realists school of philosophy relies on the pragmatic and empirical sides of law, that is, life experience.

For example, in 1919, the Constitution's Eighteenth Amendment was adopted, prohibiting the manufacture and sale of alcohol. People in large numbers, however, continued to manufacture and sell intoxicating beverages, albeit illegally. Police and judges basically ignored the law, although occasionally police staged raids, generally for publicity purposes, during which they smashed moonshine equipment and arrested notorious criminals. Prohibition proved to be a dismal failure. In 1933, the Twenty-First Amendment repealed the Eighteenth Amendment, ending Prohibition.

Legal realists see law as a means to a social end; thus, they try to predict and influence lawmaking. In the legal realist school, the same set of facts does not always result in the same conclusion. For the legal realist, the legitimacy of law and of legal institutions is measured by the degree to which they meet the needs of society.

Economic School

The **economic school** philosophy holds that people evaluate the law in accordance with economic principles. The theory assumes that everyone in the legal system is rational and will act to maximize personal welfare. For example, Jo has been injured in an automobile accident. She has a choice of filing a lawsuit or settling her claim. Chances are high that she will settle the claim because a settlement is faster and less costly than a trial. According to the economic school, efficiency is the key by which people analyze and evaluate the law.

The economic school of philosophy plays an important role in business decision making. For example, a manufacturer knows that one customer out of every 500,000 will be injured using its product. The manufacturer estimates the settlement cost for such an injury to be $300,000. The company considers this cost in pricing its product, reserving an appropriate amount for future claims.

The natural law, analytical, historical, legal realists, and economic schools provide different points of view for approaching legal decision making. The following sections describe various classifications of the law.

Analyzing Case Law

Reported court cases constitute the common law. A judge's written opinion reflects the reasoning process used to reach a decision about a case. Often, an opinion describes the important facts in the case and the judge's application of the law to those facts, including references to precedents.

The cases in this book were edited to make them easier for you to read. Each case is separated into the following sections: *Background and Facts*; the court's opinion; *Decision and Remedy; Comment,* when it is appropriate; and *Critical Thinking* questions. In the section that is the **court's opinion**, the focus is on that part which illustrates a point; thus, much of the case is omitted. Three ellipses (. . .) mean that part of a sentence or paragraph has been deleted; four ellipses (. . . .) mean that one or more paragraphs were deleted. To ease the reading of the cases, references to other cases or statutes usually are omitted.

How to Brief a Case

To brief a case, read the case carefully. Once you believe you understand the material, you can follow this checklist for an appellate court case brief.

1. *Case Name and Citation* State the case name, the level of court that decided the case, the decisions by prior courts, if given, and the year in which the case was decided.

2. *Facts* Summarize the facts. In this book, some of the facts appear in the Background and Facts section, while others appear more appropriately in the case description. This section can be fairly lengthy.

3. *Issue* Set out the issue of the case in the form of a question that can be answered yes or no. The issue is the question that the court answers to determine which party will prevail. The court often starts the issue with the words "whether or not" or "the issue is." This section is short.

4. *Holding* State the court's decision. This section is short.

5. *Reasoning* Summarize the court's reasoning that led to the holding. This section describes the court's application of the rule of law to the facts. The rule of law is a principle of general application that guides a judge in making a decision. This section is usually the longest part of a brief.

An appellate court has two alternatives when it reviews a case. If the court **affirms** a case, it is upholding (agreeing with) the lower court's decision. If the court **reverses** the case, it is disagreeing with the lower court's decision. An appellate court may choose to affirm part of a case and reverse the rest. Regardless of the appellate court's decision, the case is **remanded** (sent back) to the lower court to carry out the appellate court's instructions. The trial court is the one that normally carries out the decision of the appellate court.

CyberLaw

The Internet

The World Wide Web (WWW) was created at CERN, the European Laboratory for Particle Physics, located outside Geneva, Switzerland.[12] A team led by Tim Berners-Lee developed the three open-standard cores of the WWW. The first standard is the text formatting system, Hypertext Markup Language (HTML). The text is typed in with HTML tags to indicate to the computer where to place paragraphs, bold, italics, colors, and a number of other items to make the text readable on the computer screen. The second standard is the communications standard Hypertext Transfer Protocol (HTTP). HTTP creates a link that allows the user to move the mouse to point to a word or picture (often denoted by a different color or an underscore or by the cursor changing to another symbol, such as a hand) and then click on it to connect to another web server.

The third standard is the addressing scheme used to locate web sites, uniform resource locators (URLs). URLs start with http followed by a colon and two forward slashes, which are generally followed by www. For instance, the web server for the White House is <http://www.whitehouse.gov>. Today, many addresses do not require the www, or a number follows, such as www3. For example, the Legislative Reference Service of the U.S. Congress is found at <http://thomas.loc.gov>. To indicate a secured connection, the letter s will appear, such as wwws. Between www and the top domain, which concludes the URL address, is the computer address.

Two standards developed earlier completed the resources needed for the WWW. Users of the Internet can send and receive information by using File Transfer Protocol (FTP) which allows files to be transferred from one computer to another. The Transmission Control Protocol/Internet Protocol (TCP/IP) provides each computer hooked to the Internet with its own unique numbered address.

The WWW was released for universal use in 1991 with a rudimentary **browser**, which is a program that provides a graphical user interface with the web. A browser interfaces with **servers**, which are special software programs running on mainframe computers or personal computers (PCs). When connected to the Internet, the computers can serve information, including text, graphics, audio, and video, to the browser.

Not much happened with the WWW until Marc Andreessen, a graduate student at the University of Illinois, who worked for the National Center for

---

[12] CERN's web site is located at <www.cern.ch/Public>.

Supercomputing Applications (NCSA) located on the campus, created a browser called Mosaic. Mosaic was the first point-and-click graphical user interface to integrate graphics and multimedia features that could operate on a variety of computing platforms, such as Amiga, Macintosh, OS/2, Windows, or UNIX. In January 1993 when Mosaic was released, only fifty web servers were in existence. Mosaic was downloadable for free and millions of people took advantage. Mosaic was the Big Bang that exploded the WWW. Twenty-four months after Mosaic's release, more than 100,000 web servers were in existence.

Mosaic, however, faded as two new commercial browsers became available, both of which owe a debt to Mosaic. Andreessen went on to create Netscape, which eventually was purchased by America Online. Several years after the release of Netscape, Microsoft released its Internet browser, Internet Explorer. These browsers provided easy access to text, images, audio, streaming video, and conferencing-type video, all of which make the WWW interactive. Today any computing device with a database can be easily linked to anyone with a communications device, such as a telephone, wireless personal assistance device, cable television network, or satellite hookup.

In 1991, the Commercial Internet eXchange Association (CIX) was formed by commercial Internet providers.[13] It established cooperative agreements to let users communicate with each other. Organizations can access and use computers located virtually anywhere in the world. Originally, after the Internet was opened for public use, commercial activities were prohibited. Eventually, businesses were allowed to post web pages for informational purposes only, because it still was forbidden to use the Internet for commercial purposes. This prohibition soon was abandoned. With the creation of the multimedia browsers and secured lines for making purchases, commercial use of the Internet has driven its growth exponentially. The amount of business conducted on the web in 1993 was zero. By 2003, business-to-consumer e-commerce is projected to reach $146 billion and business-to-business e-commerce is predicted to be $1.3 trillion.

To purchase items online, a secure server is necessary. Once the purchaser is log on to a secure server, the address should read "https" or "wwws". Additionally, somewhere on the screen, usually in the lower lefthand corner, a lock or other symbol should show that it is locked or secured. Once those two items are visible, the purchaser can purchase the item in relative safety.

During the past decade, this technology has created new legal and social dilemmas. Are electronic contracts valid? What is a digital signature? Who owns e-mail? If the business owns the e-mail, does it have a right to monitor it? Concerns abound over the loss of privacy because of the information collected and stored in large databases without the knowledge of the consumer.

The WWW allows businesses another avenue to market and sell products and services. Called e-commerce (electronic commerce), brick-and-mortar businesses found another outlet to reach consumers, while new businesses pioneered an exclusive electronic presence on the web. New questions arose. Can the state and federal government tax the income of these electronic businesses? What about applying sales taxes to the web business transactions? If the e-merchant cannot send ordered items for a period of time, is the e-merchant obliged to notify the customer? How does the customer return the item if dissatisfied?

Other issues abound. Is the e-business able to sell shares of its company to investors over the web? Can a web site distribute copyrighted material without permission and without paying royalties? Which government has jurisdiction over crimes committed using the web? How can a person or company defend against untruths posted on the web? How do people vote in elections on the web?

No government or business owns the Internet. Yet, the Internet-related standards are global. The global Internet is powerful and is changing the dynamics of how business is conducted, how capital is raised, and how companies must be flexible to survive. The legal system is being challenged in the age of instantaneous and mass communications. For example, information on court cases, bills pending before a legislative body, and statutes, which were formerly available only in a few places, now are available on the WWW. The questions previously posed cover only a few of the legal issues that must be considered by the legislatures and courts in the future. These questions will be covered in the remaining chapters.

---

[13] The web page for the Commercial Internet eXchange Association is <http://www.cix.org/>.

International Consideration

Treaties, Conventions, and Agreements

The financial success of the United States depends on international trade. Every sovereign state (nation) has its own body of law (such as U.S. law, Japanese law, German law, Egyptian law, or Mexican law). **International law** does not exist as a unified set of codes. Instead, the trade and other political relationships among nations are established through treaties, *conventions,* and *agreements*.

Treaties are agreements made among nations. A nation that signs a treaty or a convention is referred to as a *signatory*. Treaties cover a wide scope of topics, ranging from regulation of migratory bird flight patterns to the destruction of nuclear weapons.

Treaties can create international organizations. Examples include the 1945 Charter of the United Nations, a treaty among many nations that created the United Nations. The 1957 Treaty of Rome created the European Economic Community (EEC).[14] Later amendments to the Treaty of Rome led to the European Union.

In the United States, the president signs treaties with his or her foreign counterparts. The U.S. Constitution requires treaties to be ratified by two-thirds of the Senate to become law.

A **convention** is a law adopted by an international organization that was created by a treaty, such as the United Nations' Convention on Climate Change. For a convention to be binding on a member nation, the treaty must grant the power for the organization to pass binding conventions. Each sovereign state has the power to adopt or disapprove conventions. If a nation adopts a convention, the treaty usually has provisions for a nation to later withdraw that permission. No nation has ever given up complete sovereignty to an international organization, nor can any international organization dictate a nation's adherence to the organization's code without that nation's permission.

An **agreement** is defined rather loosely as an agreement that can obligate a country, but that usually is less formal or less significant than a treaty or convention. Like treaties and conventions, agreements are made between or among heads of state. An example of an agreement is the North American Free Trade Agreement (NAFTA) which required approval from the U.S. Senate and House of Representatives.

A businessperson needs a working knowledge of the laws of the United States, the laws of the countries in which her business is conducted, and the international laws that govern the relationship among the countries. Businesspeople need to obtain independent legal advice from a professional who knows not only the laws of the other country, but also the laws contained within the treaties and lower level agreements, such as protocols.

The General Assembly of the United Nations declared the period from 1990 to 1999 the U.N. Decade of International Law. During the decade, nations were encouraged to develop and codify various proposals for international law that deal with subjects ranging from the protection, security, and safety of diplomatic personnel and premises to the newly emerging commercial transactions based on computer assistance.

---

[14] The European Economic Community (EEC) existed until 1992. The Treaty on European Union (commonly known as the Maastricht Treaty) was adopted in 1991 and amended the Treaty of Rome. The EEC evolved into the European Community (EC), which evolved into the European Union (EU). Although legal differences exist between the EC and the EU, the terms are used interchangeably.

LEGALLY SPEAKING

A Manager's Role in Preventive Law

According to an adage, "A business is not successful until it has been sued." This statement is based on the experience of many successful businesses. When a business has assets and is a functioning operation, it needs to be concerned with the prospect of litigation.

You are a manager in a new small business that has not employed attorneys, known as in-house legal counsel. You believe that the best approach is to conduct your business affairs with the idea of staying out of the courtroom. You understand that it is very easy for people to institute a legal action against a prosperous company. Litigation is expensive and time consuming even when the business prevails in the lawsuit. The key, you believe, is to practice preventive law.

To achieve this goal, as the manager, you need to retain a law firm that operates with the same philosophy. One good preventive law strategy is to have understandable contracts, training, and documentation.

Checklist for Preventive Law

✔ *Contracts in Plain English* Contracts with your employees, suppliers, and customers that are written in plain English will clarify your business obligations and support your working relations. For a contract to be effective, your employees, who will be working under the contract, must thoroughly review and understand it. As you plan the contents of the contract, consider including a clause that requires alternates to litigation in resolving disputes, such as the alternatives discussed in Chapter 4.

✔ *Training for Employees* Employees who deal with legal issues should be well versed in the legal aspects of their jobs. For example, human resources personnel should be trained in the pertinent statutes and cases pertaining to employment law. Other managers also should receive at least minimum training in personnel law, such as the laws involving sexual and racial harassment.

✔ *Effective Documentation* Documentation procedures and requirements should be well thought out. The length of document retention should be standardized based on legal requirements, if dictated, or on common sense. Document handling procedures should allow for swift and efficient filing and retrieval. If a governmental agency or a lawyer inquires about a particular action or procedure, the business must have access to the appropriate documentation. For example, documenting product design and test procedures may prevent or help to defend litigation concerning civil allegations if the product malfunctions.

Chapter Summary

As the English language evolved, the word *law* developed two definitions. First, law is a system that gives order to society by establishing rules of moral conduct that attempt to ensure justice. Second, law refers to specific principles represented by a rule or rules.

The court examines various sources of the law when making a decision. If applicable, the state or federal constitution, statutes, and regulations are examined. In addition, the courts review the case law also known as the common law.

Common law uses *stare decisis*. This doctrine of law makes the common law stable yet flexible with the passage of time.

The law also can be classified in several ways: substantive law or procedural law, public law or private law, and civil law or criminal law. The remedies that a court can apply can be divided into remedies at law and equitable remedies. Courts of law issue judgments for monetary damages, use juries, and apply the statute of limitations. Courts of equity issue decrees or orders for remedies other than monetary damages, normally do not have a jury, and apply the doctrine of laches.

The schools of legal philosophy are the natural law school, the analytical school, the historical school, the legal realists school, and the economic school. A number of methods can be used to locate the law. Law is covered by the Constitution, statutes, and cases. Also covered in this chapter is a method that can be used to analyze a case.

Using the World Wide Web

Two useful WWW sites referenced frequently throughout the book are the FindLaw web site and the legal site located at Cornell Law School.

The FindLaw web site is extensive with more than 15,000 publications available. The user can access cases, statutes, current news, and some administrative regulations. The Cornell site also contains a wide-ranging amount of legal material. Statutes, cases, international material and current news are available.

All federal government agencies and many officials, state governments, county and city governments, and other local governments, such as school boards, have web sites. Using e-mail, citizens can easily transmit their thoughts to most of their elected and appointed officials.

The federal government actively uses the WWW. To make information accessible to people, Congress has mandated that federal information be available on the Internet. Additionally, federal funding has been pumped into academic institutions, schools, libraries, and state and local governments to enable them to place materials on the WWW. A list of some useful sites is given here.

Finding the Law on the Web

White House
    http://www.whitehouse.gov
U.S. Senate
    http://www.senate.gov
U.S. House of Representatives
    http://www.house.gov
Alternative site for the U.S. Congress
    http://lcweb.loc.gov/global/legislative
    /congress.html#legbranch
Another alternative site for the U.S. Congress
    http://www.access.gpo.gov/congress/index.htm
Federal courts
    http://www.fjc.gov
Library of Congress
    http://lcweb.loc.gov

Legislative Reference Service of the U.S. Congress.
    The Thomas site is named after President Thomas
    Jefferson who donated his books to start the Library
    of Congress.
    http://thomas.loc.gov
Legal Information Institute located at
    Cornell University
    http://www.law.cornell.edu/rules/fre
    /overview.html
The FindLaw site is run by law librarians
    http://www.findlaw.com
U.S. Government Printing Office
    http://www.access.gpo.gov/index.html
World Wide Web Virtual Library
    http://www.law.indiana.edu/law/v-lib
    /lawindex.html
C-Span (Cable Satellite Public Affairs Network) is
    privately owned and operated by the consortium
    of cable networks.
    http://www.c-span.org
The Great American Web Site gives you access to every
    branch of government along with a brief review of
    each site.
    http://www.uncle-sam.com
The University of Houston Law Library has a good site
    on legal research and information for those thinking
    about law school.
    http://www.lawlib.uh.edu/guides
A nonprofit organization sponsors this site.
    http://www.criticalthinking.org

Chapter Web Sites

Dwight D. Eisenhower Library
    http://history.cc.ukans.edu/heritage/abilene
    /ikectr.ht ml
Biography of Chief Justice Earl Warren.
    http://provost.ucsd.edu/warren/welcome/facts
    /earl.html

Hope diamond
http://www.smithsonianmag.com/smithsonian
/issuesa ll/issues97/sep97/gems.html
Justice Thurgood Marshall
http://www.thurgoodmarshall.com/
Lyndon Baines Johnson Library
http://www.lbjlib.utexas.edu/
West Group
http://www.westpub.com/
American Bar Association
Listing of House representatives
http://www.abanet.org
http://www.house.gov/writerep/
Listing of state senators
http://www.senate.gov/senator/membmail.html

Web Activities

1–1 Reading the newspaper, you see that a bill in which you are interested has been introduced into the House of Representatives and the Senate. Go to the web site of each house of Congress and find a bill that is pending. Read the text and then track the bill. Determine whether the bill has been assigned to a committee, whether hearings have been held, whether the bill has been passed by both houses of Congress, and whether it has been assigned to a conference committee to rework the language. Has the language of the bill been agreed to? Has the Congress sent the bill to the president for his or her signature? Print out a bill from either site along with its legislative history. An easy way to check legislation is the Library of Congress web site at <http://thomas.loc.gov>.

1–2 You are listening to the radio. The newscaster summarizes a presidential speech. You are interested in reading the speech. Go to the White House web site at <http://www.whitehouse.gov> and find a speech given by the president. Print out the speech and analyze it using critical thinking tools from Appendix J. Describe what other information is available at the White House web site.

Key Terms

accounting	convention	jurisprudence	remedy
administrative agency	court of equity	law	remedy at law
administrative law	court of law	legal realists school	rescission
administrative regulation	court's opinion	legal remedy	*Restatements*
affirm	criminal law	natural law school	reverse
agreement	decree	order	server
analytical school	defendant	ordinance	specific performance
appellate court	doctrine of laches	plaintiff	*stare decisis*
browser	economic school	precedent	statute
case law	equitable remedy	private law	statute of limitations
chancellor	ethics	probate	substantive law
civil law	historical school	procedural law	temporary restraining
civil law system	injunction	public law	order (TRO)
common law	international law	reformation	treaty
constitutional law	judgment	remand	

Questions and Case Problems

1–1 Law Compare and contrast the definitions of the word *law*. Why are there two different definitions for one word?

1–2 Common Law Discuss the differences between common law and statutory law.

1–3 Philosophies of Law Identify and distinguish among the reasoning processes used to explain the law.

1–4 Philosophies of Law Describe the philosophical schools of law and classify each according to the appropriate reasoning process.

1–5 Citation Identify and describe the parts of the following citation: *Miranda v. Arizona,* 384 U.S. 436, 86 S. Ct. 1602, 16 L. Ed. 2d 694 (1966).

1–6 *Stare Decisis* Define *stare decisis* and describe its functions and flexibility.

1–7 Classification Discuss the differences between private law and public law.

1–8 Law and Equity Discuss the differences between courts of law and courts of equity.

1–9 Law or Equity Fully discuss whether each of the following breach of contract situations warrants specific performance or money damages as a remedy.

 a. Connie signs a contract to sell her house and lot to Juan. A few days later she finds another buyer who is willing to pay a higher price. Connie now refuses to sell to Juan. What remedies are available to Juan?

 b. Broken Hearts, a country music group, contracts to appear for a week at a Branson, Missouri, hotel showroom. Two days before the scheduled engagement, the group informs the management that it refuses to appear. What remedies are available to the Branson Hotel?

 c. Bill signs a contract to purchase a rare stamp from Al, who is breaking up his stamp collection. Before the stamp is turned over to Bill, Al decides to keep the stamp collection and refuses to deliver the stamp to Bill. What remedies are available to Bill?

1–10 Internet Go to <http://www.house.gov/writerep/> and find your representative to the House of Representatives. Go to <http://www.senate.gov/senator/membmail.html> and find your state's two senators. Find their e-mail addresses. What biographical information is posted at the site? What information is available that benefits the congressperson's constituency?

I would prefer to fail with honor than win by cheating.

> Sophocles, ca. 496–406 B.C.
> Sophocles was one of classical Athens' great writers of tragedy.

No man is justified in doing evil on the grounds of expedience.

> President Theodore Roosevelt, 1858–1919
> Twenty-sixth president of the United States of America, 1901–1909
> Nobel Peace Prize, 1906

Outline

Introduction

Anyone who owns a business, such as your online business, Artiste Login Products, Inc., is involved daily in making business decisions based on ethical standards. Most businesses have adopted a corporate code of ethics that is often displayed on their business web page. But to whom are ethical duties owed?

Businesses owe duties to groups that often have conflicting interests in the business's decisions. Your business needs to consider the interests of these various groups: the owners of the business, the shareholders; the employees of your business; the company's supply chain, which consists of suppliers and customers; the government that regulates your business; and the community or public at large where your business is located.

For example, your business funds academic scholarships for its employees' children. The business does not see any direct results from these scholarships, yet the long-term benefit to the business of funding these scholarships may be the goodwill it engenders among its employees.

The conflicting interests in this example arise with the shareholders. Your company has a responsibility to its shareholders and employees to make decisions that will help the business make a profit. A company's bottom-line goal, after all, is to minimize costs and to maximize profits. The monies spent on the academic scholarship program could have been paid in the form of dividends to the shareholders or increased wages to employees. In the case of the scholarship program, the business's decision makers not only fulfill their business's responsibility to benefit the public, but the gesture also benefits society by contributing to a well-educated population. Having satisfied employees also enhances the business's potential profit making. Fulfillment of these responsibilities constitutes ethical and socially responsible behavior.

Ethical businesspeople recognize the responsibility owed to the public and to themselves to maintain principles. The basis on which a business analyzes its goals, particularly its goal to make profits, influences its decisions and impacts its ethical standards. Emphasis on short-term profits sometimes creates the temptation to act unethically—although, certainly, a business's short-term success does not necessarily indicate that the business has been unethical. Still, when a business considers profits over the long term, rather than on a quarterly or annual basis, ethical considerations and social responsibility are enhanced.

Many businesses have adopted a code of ethics. Your online business, Artiste Login Products, Inc., should adopt a code of ethics, distribute the code among its employees, and post the code on the business web site. Additionally, your company may want to hire an ethics review consultant to conduct an ethics audit. This audit can reveal which parts of the code are followed and which are not. The consultant can recommend a plan of action.

In this chapter, you will review several ethical theories. You will examine the relationship between ethics and the law. You will see how various groups are affected by business decisions. You will be provided with an ethical decision-making model and see its application to a sample problem. The chapter concludes with a discussion of ethics in the legal profession.

Theories of Ethical Conduct

Ethics are systematic statements of right and wrong behavior based on a philosophical system. The term *ethics* is from the Greek word *ethos*; the word *moral* comes from the Latin word *moralis.* Morals reflects values about right and wrong.

Ethics, in their simplest form, set a standard for determining right and wrong by making reflective choices and by directing choice of action toward good. Constant clarification of those standards enables people to resolve value issues and to stimulate higher visions of what is good. For example, a common business practice in the mid-1800s was to drive competitors out of business by selling goods below cost and then to raise the price exorbitantly once the competitors were eliminated. By the late 1800s and the early 1900s, this practice was not only regarded as unethical, but also became illegal after Congress passed various laws.

Ethical decisions should neither depend on the technical aspects of an action (Can the action be taken?) nor on an action's legality (Is this action within the limitations of the law?). The ethical question is this: Should the action be taken based on social good?

Although ethics provide moral guidelines, individuals must apply these guidelines in making decisions. Ethics that apply to business (called business ethics) are not a separate theory of ethics, but rather an application of ethics. Although all people have ethical responsibilities, higher standards are imposed on professionals who serve as social models, such as physicians, attorneys, and accountants.

The Western foundation of ethics is based on the writings of the ancient Greek philosophers, such as Socrates,[1] Plato,[2] and Aristotle,[3] and writings from the various philosophical schools, such as the Cynics,[4] the Epicureans,[5] and the Stoics.[6] Over the centuries, a number of different philosophical frameworks have been developed that establish the standards of **ethical conduct**. The following subsections briefly describe only two major frameworks: ethical standards based on universal duties and ethical standards based on consequences.

Ethical Standards Based on Universal Duties

Deontology is the philosophical practice of defining and adhering to an absolute set of standards by which ethical behavior can be measured. Deontology tries to define universal duties that serve as moral guides to de-

cision making, such as those discussed by Immanuel Kant[7] and John Rawls.[8] When a moral dilemma arises, a person can apply these universal standards to determine whether a particular course of action is good.

In deontology, a person fulfills absolute moral duties regardless of whether good comes from the actions. A person decides on his actions in a situation by asking if a particular action is morally right or wrong. Importance is placed on the act of carrying out a duty and not on what the consequences of the act are.

A person who embraces deontology expects others to follow these universal duties without exception. For example, a person who believes that killing another is wrong must oppose capital punishment, war, and killing in self-defense. A person who follows the Ten Commandments without exception applies the concept of deontology.

In deontology, the moral duty embodies the concept of good. The outcome of following that moral duty—whether good or bad—is inconsequential. Deontology does not help a person resolve conflicts between universal standards.

For example, the universal standard (moral duty) to keep promises is good. You promise not to tell anyone where your friend lives. Under deontology that promise is morally binding; therefore, you keep the promise whether or not good results. Another universal standard, however, is to tell the truth. If the police ask you to tell them where your friend is because his life is in danger, do you tell the police? Compliance with the universal duty of truth-telling would compromise the universal duty of promise-keeping. Importance is placed on keeping the promise, not on the consequences. By keeping the promise, you say "no comment" to the police, thus keeping your promise to

[1] Socrates (ca. 469–399 B.C.), an ancient Greek, believed that wrong actions arose from ignorance. He believed that the way to discover universal rules was to use inductive reasoning. Through the questioning process, people would progress from general to more specific knowledge and eventually discover universal rules that applied to all examples. The Socratic method is named after him.
[2] Plato (ca. 428–354 B.C.), also an ancient Greek, was a student and friend of Socrates. Plato believed that all people desire happiness. Because people try to act in ways that produce happiness, actions contrary to this objective are mistakes caused by ignorance. According to Plato, if people know that moral virtue will lead to happiness, they will act virtuously.
[3] Aristotle (ca. 384–322 B.C.), an ancient Greek philosopher, was Plato's student. Aristotle regarded ethics as the study of practical knowledge. He believed that people's goal was to attain happiness, and they achieved it when they fulfilled a function. Thus, they had to discover what function made them happy. Moral virtue fell between extremes. For example, generosity fell between stinginess and wastefulness, and courage fell between the extremes of cowardice and foolhardiness.
[4] Founded by Antisthenes (ca. 444–366 B.C.) in ancient Greece, the Cynics claimed that people achieved happiness by leading a life of self-control and being free from material desires and pleasures. Antisthenes reasoned that individuals could not control these appetites for long.
[5] Founded by Epicurus (ca. 341–270 B.C.) in ancient Greece, the Epicureans equated happiness with seeking moderate pleasure and avoiding pain. Pleasure was gained through prudence, moderation, courage, justice, and friendships.
[6] Stoicism was founded by Zeno (ca. 336–261 B.C.), who was from Citium, a city located on Cyprus. The Stoics thought it was foolish to try to shape circumstances to human desires. A divine intelligence guides and governs circumstances and directs all things ultimately toward goodness.

[7] Kant (1724–1804) who was from Konigsberg, Prussia, based his philosophy in reason. He believed that a universal set of ethical principles existed that could serve as action-guiding rules. Through the reasoning process, this absolute and finite set of rules could be determined. His rules were duty based. For example, he believed that truth-telling was a universal rule. If lying were to become the universal rule—everyone lied—life would be impossible because no one could trust anyone. If truth-telling were the universal rule, everyone's moral duty would be to tell the truth. Kant's logic did not consider the consequences of the absolutism of universal rules.
[8] Rawls (1921–) was a professor of philosophy at Harvard University. He submits that because society is not heterogeneous, people hold opposing and sometimes irreconcilable views. Thus, democracy requires tolerance, which will lead to the principle of extensive individual liberty.

your friend and telling the truth, but the consequence is that your friend is killed. If you break your promise, thus breaking your moral duty, and tell the police of your friend's whereabouts, the consequence is that your friend will live.

As you can see from the example, one major problem with deontology is its lack of guidance for prioritizing duties, for example, between truth-telling and promise-keeping. Another major problem is the disregard for the consequences of keeping a moral duty. Following a universal rule usually is good, such as in keeping a promise. But sometimes consequences can be detrimental and harm can result from blindly obeying a moral duty.

Another school of philosophers developed the concept of utilitarianism. This school looks at the consequences of ethical standards.

Ethical Standards Based on Consequences

Utilitarianism is an approach to establishing ethical standards based on the consequences of an action. Philosophers, such as Jeremy Bentham[9] and John Stuart Mill,[10] believed that decisions should be made on the basis of their utility or usefulness. Utilitarianism defines good as "the greatest happiness for the greatest number." It judges ideas, institutions, and actions on the basis of their utility or benefit. Any source of happiness has utility, because individuals care about increasing their pleasure and decreasing their pain. Rather than supporting selfishness in the quest for personal happiness, however, utilitarianism encourages people to seek their own happiness in the happiness of others.

Often "the greatest happiness for the greatest number" is misinterpreted to mean that if the majority wants something, then the act that produces it is ethical. Instead, the moral act is judged by the good or bad

produced by its consequences in terms of social benefit or utility.

For example, the exclusionary rule in criminal cases prohibits a police search without permission or without a search warrant. Any evidence found in an unauthorized search is not allowed into evidence against an accused person. The reason for the exclusionary rule is to protect people from police abuse and to uphold the U.S. Constitution's Fourth Amendment right against unreasonable searches.

Polls taken of the American people, however, show that the majority disapproves of the exclusionary rule. The reasoning is that the rule sometimes prevents the courts from taking action against people who have committed crimes. Evidence that could potentially demonstrate their guilt is not allowed into evidence in the trial, thus the jury is not able to consider this information when rendering a verdict. The majority, therefore, would ban the exclusionary rule. But in spite of the majority's motivation for wanting the ban, the exclusionary rule benefits society, because the number of people exonerated from a crime under the rule is small compared with the number of people who might suffer from police abuse if the rule were abolished. The ethical person using utilitarianism to determine right from wrong must not ask, "What is my greatest satisfaction or happiness?" but instead, "What is the greatest benefit (happiness, utility) for the greatest number?"

The problem with utilitarian theory is that prediction of the success, failure, or utility of certain behaviors is impossible. In some situations, the temptation is to use profits or the accumulation of wealth as a tangible measure of success. Another problem with utilitarian theory is that individual well-being can be sacrificed for social benefit. One individual might suffer more as a result of behavior that brings society greater happiness. For example, the payment of substandard wages to illegal migrant farm workers lowers the cost of food available to society.

Ethical Behavior and Legal Behavior

Despite the differences in the approaches to developing ethical standards, all of us would readily agree that certain conduct is or is not ethical. In almost all cases, what is illegal is generally considered to be unethical.

[9] Bentham (1748–1832), a British philosopher, attempted to determine ethical judgments by observations and empirical study. He believed that an action's consequences in terms of its effect on others rather than an action's intended outcome mattered the most. He developed a method to measure happiness.

[10] Mill (1806–1873), a British philosopher, worked for the East India Company and eventually, like his father, became a director. He also served in the British Parliament. Mill believed that the quality of pleasure that an action produced was a crucial factor in determining the actions that one should take. He also believed that some actions were more valuable than others.

The converse is generally considered to be true in our society—that is, what is legal is considered to be ethical. Sometimes, however, conduct that is legal is considered unethical.

Many managers confuse legality and ethics, thinking that if an act is legal (or, at least, not forbidden), it is also ethical. Although legality and ethics often coincide, they are not one and the same.

The law is developed through ratification of constitutions, through court cases, through statutes passed by legislative bodies, and administrative rule making. Development of the law is basically a reactive process whether it is court cases or statutes. For example, laws forbidding computer crimes were not written before the first crime of that sort was committed. These laws were written only after computer crimes became rampant. Responding to a public outcry by victims of computer crimes, Congress and state legislatures passed statutes making this activity a crime. During the period when there were no specific laws forbidding theft by computer, were those thefts ethical? Of course not.

At times, no law exists when there is a need for one. Even when a law exists, it may not always be obeyed or even enforced. The law, thus, cannot cure ethical problems resulting from business behavior. For this reason, businesspeople must prioritize their inclusion of ethical guidelines and legal information in their decision-making process. They must examine which groups will be affected by their business, ethical, and legal decisions and must determine a balance when a conflict of interest arises among the groups.

Stakeholders

When dealing with ethical issues, a business must consider the good of at least five groups of people. These groups are called **stakeholders**, because they form a network affected by (with a stake in) the decisions made by the business. A business making a decision must determine which stakeholders will be affected and the impact the decision will have on them.

Stakeholders include (1) the shareholders, (2) the employees, (3) the supply chain which includes customers and suppliers, (4) the government, and (5) the community or public at large. Emphasizing one of these groups in making decisions sometimes has the ultimate effect of benefitting or harming other groups. Thus, business managers must balance the interests of all stakeholders in order to make ethical decisions.

Top management is responsible for embracing ethical standards. These standards are useless, however, until top management makes it clear to all employees that the standards must be upheld. Once the employees know and use these ethical standards, their conduct will affect all other stakeholders involved with the business.

Shareholders

One of the prime objectives of our capitalist society is for a business, over the long run, to maximize its profits. Businesses need profits to survive and to increase their viability.[11]

The owners and the primary investors in a business are the shareholders. As an owner and investor, the shareholder expects a monetary return from the business's activities. This return basically comes from the business's profits. Therefore, decisions made by management to increase employee wages and benefits, to lower prices or to improve product quality and safety for the consumer, or to contribute to community improvements lowers, at least for the short term, the shareholders' return.

Shareholders expect that their interests will be fully protected by management. When shareholders believe management has acted improperly, they have the right to file a lawsuit to correct any such mismanagement. Management, however, is given wide latitude in setting aside shareholder demands, including the board of directors' right to refuse to declare dividends.

Numerous reasons exist for a board's decision to refuse to declare dividends. Obviously, if those reasons are to improve the welfare of the business's employees and lower the cost to customers, an ethical conflict arises between management's behavior toward employees and customers versus its behavior toward the shareholders.

The following case, decided in 1919, illustrates the court's dilemma in resolving a conflict between a business's ethical behavior toward shareholders versus its ethical behavior toward employees and customers.

---

[11] Milton Friedman, "The Social Responsibility of Business Is to Increase Its Profits," *New York Times Magazine,* September 13, 1970.

Case 2.1

Dodge v. Ford Motor Co.

Supreme Court of Michigan, 1919

204 Mich. 459, 170 N.W. 668

BACKGROUND AND FACTS Ford Motor Company was formed in 1903. Henry Ford, the president and majority shareholder, attempted to run the corporation as if it were a one-person operation. The business expanded rapidly and, in addition to regular quarterly dividends, often paid special dividends. Sales and profits were as follows:

- 1910—18,664 cars; $4,521,509 profit
- 1911—34,466 cars; $6,275,031 profit
- 1912—68,544 cars; $13,057,312 profit; $14,475,095 surplus
- 1913—168,304 cars; $25,046,767 profit; $28,124,173 surplus
- 1914—248,307 cars; $30,338,454 profit; $48,827,032 surplus
- 1915—264,351 cars; $24,641,423 profit; $59,135,770 surplus.

By 1919, accumulated earnings totaled $111,960,907. Originally, the Ford car sold for more than $900. From time to time, the price was reduced. In 1916, it sold for $440. For the year beginning August 1, 1916, the price was reduced, again, to $360. In the interests of setting aside money for future investment and expansion, Ford Motor Company paid no special dividends after October 1915. The plaintiffs were minority stockholders, who owned one-tenth of the shares of the corporation. They petitioned the court to compel the directors to declare a dividend.

Chief Justice OSTRANDER

. . . .

. . . [I]t is charged that notwithstanding the earnings for the fiscal year ending July 31, 1916, the Ford Motor Company has not since that date declared any special dividends:

> "And the said Henry Ford, president of the company, has declared it to be the settled policy of the company not to pay in the future any special dividends, but to put back into the business for the future all of the earnings of the company, other than the regular dividend of five percent (5%) monthly upon the authorized capital stock of the company–two million dollars ($2,000,000)."

This declaration of the future policy, it is charged in the [complaint,] was published in the public press in the city of Detroit and throughout the United States in substantially the following language:

> "'My ambition,' declared Mr. Ford, 'is to employ still more men; to spread the benefits of this industrial system to the greatest possible number, to help them build up their lives and their homes. To do this, we are putting the greatest share of our profits back into the business.'"

It is charged further that the said Henry Ford stated to plaintiffs personally, in substance, that as all the stockholders had received back in dividends more than they had invested they were not entitled to receive anything additional to the regular dividend of 5 percent a month, and that it was not his policy to have larger dividends declared in the future, and that the profits and earnings of the company would be put back into the business for the purpose of extending its operations and increasing the number of its employe[e]s, and that, inasmuch as the profits were to be represented by investment in plants and capital investment, the stockholders would have no right to complain. . . .

. . . .

"It is a well-recognized principle of law that the directors of a corporation, and they alone, have the power to declare a dividend of the earnings of the corporation, and to determine its amount. Courts of equity will not interfere in the management of the directors unless it is clearly made to appear that they are guilty of fraud or misappropriation of the corporate funds, or refuse to declare a dividend when the corporation has a surplus of net profits which it can, without detriment to its business, divide among its stockholders, and when a refusal to do so would amount to such an abuse of discretion as would constitute a fraud, or breach of that good faith which they are bound to exercise towards the stockholders."

. . . .

There is committed to the discretion of directors, a discretion to be exercised in good faith, the infinite details of business, including the wages which shall be paid to employees, the number of hours they shall work, the conditions under which labor shall be carried on, and the price for which products shall be offered to the public.

. . . [I]t is not within the lawful powers of a board of directors to shape and conduct the affairs of a corporation for the merely incidental benefit of shareholders and for the primary purpose of benefiting others, and no one will contend that, if the avowed purpose of the defendant directors was to sacrifice the interests of shareholders, it would not be the duty of the courts to interfere.

. . . .

Defendants say, and it is true, that a considerable cash balance must be at all times carried by such a concern. But, as has been stated, there was a large daily, weekly, monthly, receipt of cash. The output was practically continuous and was continuously, and within a few days, turned into cash. Moreover, the contemplated expenditures were not to be immediately made. The large sum appropriated for the smelter plant was payable over a considerable period of time: *So that, without going further, it would appear that, accepting and approving the plan of the directors, it was their duty to distribute on or near the 1st of August, 1916, a very large sum of money to stockholders* (emphasis added).

In reaching this conclusion, we do not ignore, but recognize, the validity of the proposition that plaintiffs have from the beginning profited by, if they have not lately, officially, participated in, the general policy of expansion pursued by this corporation. We do not lose sight of the fact that it had been, upon an occasion, agreeable to the plaintiffs to increase the capital stock to $100,000,000 by a stock dividend of $98,000,000. These things go only to answer other contentions now made by plaintiffs, and do not and cannot operate to stop them to demand proper dividends upon the stock they own. It is obvious that an annual dividend of 60 percent upon $2,000,000 or $1,200,000 is the equivalent of a very small dividend upon $100,000,000, or more.

DECISION AND REMEDY The defendant, Ford Motor Company, was ordered by the court to declare a dividend.

COMMENT The two Dodge brothers received enough money from their share of the dividends and the sale of their stock to Henry Ford to establish their own automobile company, which produced Dodge automobiles. This company became part of the Chrysler Corporation (in 1998 it became DaimlerChrysler) in 1928.

Henry Ford was, at times, a farsighted business leader. He had a real concern for his employees. In 1914, when most of his competitors were requiring twelve-hour workdays, he instituted the eight-hour workday. When his competitors were paying $1 a day for unskilled labor and $2.50 for skilled workers, Henry Ford increased his minimum wage to $5 a day. This type of management resulted in more dedicated and efficient workers at Ford Motor Company.

As a result of the court decision, Ford purchased back all the outstanding stock and took the company private. The corporation went public again in 1956 after his death.

CRITICAL THINKING: MANAGEMENT CONSIDERATION What was Mr. Ford's management philosophy? Although this case was decided in 1919, does the same problem still face businesses today?

Shareholders have a financial stake in how well a business performs financially. According to *Business Week* in 1980, a chief executive officer (CEO) earned 42 times the pay earned by a factory worker. In 1990, a CEO's average salary was 85 times higher. By 1998, it was 419 times higher than the average wage.

Among major firms, CEO compensation averaged $30.5 million. This package included salary, short- and long-term bonuses, value of restricted stock, gains from exercising stock options, and the past year's rise in value of unexercised options.

A business is allowed a tax deduction of no more that $1 million per year for executive pay under a law passed by Congress. To deduct additional compensation on the business tax return, the tax statutes require the business to demonstrate that the CEO's pay is linked to performance. The Internal Revenue Service[12] must preapprove the performance guidelines that the business has adopted before any deduction is allowed. Although Congress intended to limit executive compensation, the result has been to make $1 million a base salary for executives.

Of all of the benefits a business can offer, the stock option is usually the most lucrative. As the stock market rose dramatically during the 1990s, stock options became an increasingly popular form of executive compensation. Stock options today make up two-thirds of the typical executive's pay. The best feature is that stock options are not counted against business earnings on its tax return. Thus, stock options are used to attract, reward, and retain business talent.

Currently, Securities and Exchange Commission[13] rules allow anyone who owns $1,000 or 1 percent of a company's stock to submit the executives' compensation package to the shareholders for a vote. The vote is not binding but will put pressure on the board to review the package. Institutional shareholders, such as insurance companies and pension funds, also can demand reform or elect boards that will tie salaries to performance.

Employees

Employees are essential to run a business. Some businesses have only one employee while others have tens of thousands of employees. Today, federal or state employment and civil rights statutes apply to businesses that have a minimum number of employees.

A business must comply with the laws with respect to the employee's statutory civil rights protections during the hiring, promotion, and termination processes. The business must follow safety laws in order to protect the employee while at the workplace. Employment statutes concerning wages and overtime must be met. If retirement, investment, or health insurance benefits are offered, the business must conform with federal law.

Employers have at a minimum an ethical duty to treat employees in a reasonable manner when hiring, training, compensating, and dismissing them. To do otherwise, especially if there is a legal duty, is costly because it invites lawsuits. Employment lawsuits have

[12] The home page for the Internal Revenue Service is <http://www.irs.gov/>.

[13] The home page for the Securities and Exchange Commission is <http://www.sec.gov>. For examples of executives' compensation, see <http://www.sec.gov/edaux/ec.htm>.

LEGAL HIGHLIGHT

Dynamic Duo, Milton and Chainsaw Al

Milton is Milton Friedman, recipient of the Nobel Prize for economics and professor emeritus at the University of Chicago. He advocates profit maximization. He has written "[T]here is one and only one social responsibility of business-to use its resources and engage in activities designed to increase its profits so long as it stays within the rules of the game, which is to say, engages in open and free competition, without deception or fraud."[a] He has a disciple in Albert J. Dunlap.

"Chainsaw Al" and "Rambo in Pinstripes" were nicknames for Dunlap, awarded to him over the years in response to his aggressive business activities. Businesses brought in Dunlap to reverse pending financial disasters. One of his trademarks was to announce a mass firing. Those employees who still held their jobs no longer needed to worry about further cuts because Dunlap restructured a business only once.

Dunlap started his turnaround artistry with Lily-Tulip Company (1983–1986), a manufacturer of disposable cups. He cut the headquarters staff by 50 percent and the salaried staff by 20 percent. From Lily-Tulip he moved to Crown-Zellerbach (1986–1989), where he cut staff by 22 percent and reduced the number of distribution centers from twenty-two to four.

He spent nearly a year at Australian National Industries (1989), where he reduced the workforce by 47 percent and staff headquarters from 200 to 23. Leaving there, he went to Consolidated Press Holdings (1991–1993), where he sold off 300 of the 413 companies that made up the large conglomerate.

Next up was Scott Paper Co. (1994–1995), where Dunlap laid off 11,200 employees, nearly 31 percent of the workforce, including 71 percent of the headquarters staff. He sold the palatial headquarters for $39 million and moved the corporate headquarters from Philadelphia, Pennsylvania, to Boca Raton, Florida. The move saved $6 million in maintenance and climate-control costs. Scott's $2.5-billion debt was nearly eliminated within two years. The value, measured by the outstanding shares, grew from $2.5 billion in 1993 to $9 billion by 1995. Scott was then sold to Kimberly-Clark and Dunlap personally made $100 million.

At Sunbeam-Oster (1996–1998), he laid off 6,000 of the 12,000 employees. He released layers of executives then sold the airplanes, automobiles, and condominiums, and cut or eliminated other benefits. The stock value increased from $12 to $39 within nine months. After Sunbeam acquired Coleman Co., Signature Brands USA, Inc., and First Alert, Inc. for $2.5 billion in 1997, Dunlap announced an additional 6,400 job cuts. The common stock, however, plunged 65 percent in just three months when Dunlap could not meet the earnings forecasts. Eventually he was terminated in June 1998 amid open cheers from Sunbeam-Oster employees. The board of directors issued a statement at the time of his dismissal that stated in part that it had lost confidence in his leadership.

Putting the shareholders first, wherever he went, Dunlap's first act was to end all philanthropical contributions by the business. He believes that individuals may choose to donate their assets, but that a business should not give away assets. For Dunlap, only one stakeholder exists: the shareholder.

[a] Milton Friedman, *Capitalism and Freedom* (Chicago: University of Chicago Press, 1962), p. 133.

become more frequent in recent years. To minimize losing a lawsuit, employers develop and maintain records on their employees. The extent and detail of these records create a conflict between the employer's potential legal liability and the employee's right of privacy. The trust between employer and employee can easily become strained. Thus, the employer has an ethical conflict: developing detailed records, sometimes

through spying, to protect the business from legal liability versus retaining the employee's privacy and trust.

Businesses may have an employee sign a separate arbitration agreement or, more frequently, place an arbitration clause in the employer's policy handbook. This clause prevents the employee from filing a lawsuit if an employment disagreement arises. Often the employee is not aware or is vaguely aware of the arbitration clause. More likely than not, the employee does not realize that with an arbitration clause she has waived her rights to file a lawsuit, to a jury trial, and to appeal the judgment, if she loses the lawsuit.

Businesses must balance the interests of their employees with those of its shareholders. When a business provides higher than competitive wages, better than reasonable working conditions, and other benefits, the cost per unit of production will be higher. When the price of the product is higher, compromising its competitive edge in the marketplace, the shareholders may receive a lower dividend in the short term.

An ethical equilibrium must be struck among the competing shareholders. Should the employee's wages, working conditions, and benefits be increased? Should the amount of the shareholder's dividends be increased? Or should the amount spent on improving the quality and safety of a product for the customer be increased? These choices present various conflicts that management must resolve. The more employees receive, presumably the less shareholders will receive. But higher wages may mean higher productivity, which, in turn, will reduce total costs and increase revenue, thus, benefiting the shareholders and customers.

Businesses have both legal and ethical mandates to provide a safe working environment for their employees. To ensure that employers provide safe working conditions for their employees, government regulation of the workplace has increased dramatically. These regulations are a reaction by Congress to employer abuses and inadequate employer action to protect workers.

Companies are required by law to use their own resources to eliminate health risks from airborne and waterborne by-products that are produced during the manufacturing process. Noise pollution laws apply to the work site as well. If the company manufactures or handles hazardous materials, additional laws come into play. Other businesses, such as the transportation industry, must provide their employees with rest breaks while on the job. For example, on a commercial airliner, the air crew must take turns resting during a sixteen-hour overseas flight.

Some critics argue that Congress has placed too much emphasis on safety and that regulation in the workplace upsets the balance between economic and ethical concerns. For many employers, the safer the workplace, the higher the cost related to labor in the production process. That higher cost is paid for by stockholders in the form of lower dividends, by employees in the form of lower wages, or by consumers in the form of higher prices. Once again, a conflict exists among the responsibilities of a business toward these groups of people.

The Supply Chain: Suppliers and Customers

The supply chain is defined as the management of all resources necessary to move a product from initial concept through its life cycle, that is, from the raw material stage to the product stage to the reuse, recycling, or final disposal stage. The supply chain encompasses both products and services. All businesses depend on both their suppliers and their customers.

Supplier and customer issues center around quality, safety, pricing, availability, fraudulent business practices, confidentiality, and advertising. The issue of service or product quality places pressure on middle managers, who are often the ones facing ethical dilemmas. Middle managers must be concerned with the needs and reactions of upper management, the needs of lower level employees, and the needs of the marketing, accounting, and operations departments. The profitability of the middle manager's department often is affected directly by customer satisfaction. Is it the middle manager's ethical responsibility, then, to disclose quality problems to customers or the government, even if the situation is clearly under someone else's control and that person is content to ignore the problem? Is it the business's ethical responsibility to ensure that ethical problems are discussed openly and guidance provided for managers?

Just as safety is important for employees, customer safety is an issue with which suppliers must be concerned. If the products or services are not safe, lawsuits may be filed and Congress may set up a regulatory scheme. For example, food product safety is regulated by the Food and Drug Administration; air passenger service safety is under the Federal Aviation Administration.

Common consumer products may not be regulated by a specific agency, but instead a consumer harmed by a defective product may be able to sue. For example, if you are badly injured by sitting in a chair that looks sturdy, but collapses when you sit on it, you may sue the manufacturer for inadequate design or improper assembly. Unless that manufacturer is the only one that produces chairs, you, as a consumer, may never purchase another product from the manufacturer again. It is in the best interests of a business to satisfy, rather than injure or defraud, the consumer.

Pricing issues affect not only consumers but also competitors of the business. If consumers believe they are being overcharged, they will seek out stores that sell the product at a lower price. A business can lower its prices on a product or service not for the benefit of its customers, but to drive its competitors out of business. If competitors complain to the government, a lawsuit may be filed against the business. A drop in pricing may have an anticompetitive effect and is discussed in more detail in Chapter 21.

The availability of the product or service may or may not be under the control of the business, because the business could, in turn, be dependent on its suppliers. When a manufacturer receives an order for a product and it does not have the raw materials on hand, it must order the materials from its suppliers. For example, an order comes in for three jumbo passenger aircraft. The manufacturer must order thousands of parts from hundreds of suppliers. If the product is common and usually on the shelf, such as lead pencils, availability usually is not an issue.

Businesses, however, may withhold a product or service hoping to increase the price. For example, foreign oil producers may drop the amount of oil pumped each month until the price of oil per barrel increases substantially. The customer, such as trucking firms, airlines, and individuals, must pay the increase or do without. This type of predatory business practice invites government regulation.

The consumer may be an individual buying for his personal needs, or a large business, such as Ford Motor Company, purchasing in large volume from its suppliers. Both types of consumers are concerned with being the victim of fraudulent or overreaching business practices.

Consumer protection laws guard individuals against abusive business practices. Over the decades fraudulent business practices by health spas, dancing studios, and used car dealerships have led to government regulation. The federal and state governments have adopted laws pertaining to specific businesses, from state laws regulating dancing studios to federal regulations governing used car dealerships.

Large business consumers are concerned with being the victim of fraud also. Aircraft manufacturers require nuts and bolts that meet specified strength requirements and are so marked. In the past, the manufacturers were supplied with look-alike bolts that were falsely marked. As a result of using these poorly manufactured nuts and bolts, airplanes crashed. What ethical duties did the supplier have when the supplier was not the manufacturer but the one who purchased the nuts and bolts from an overseas distributor?

Today, supply chains are being forged among large purchasers and many suppliers. For example, Ford Motor Company has 300 primary suppliers that, in turn, have their own suppliers of products and services. In the future, Ford will not compete as an individual company selling cars, but its whole supply chain will compete with other automobile sellers' supply chains. The supply chain that can supply its customer with the lowest price, the highest quality, and speedy availability will prevail over slower, more expensive supply chains.

Companies that have developed a supply chain relationship with their suppliers have an additional ethical concern about privacy. As these supply chain relationships develop, a partnership is formed among the company and its suppliers. The supplier is required to divulge information that in the past was confidential in nature, such as its pricing strategy. As more proprietary information is shared by the supplier with its purchaser, what ethical duties are imposed on the customer to keep this information confidential and not to use this information as a weapon against the supplier in order to force it to sell at lower prices?

Advertising must be truthful and must not deceive by omitting important information. As a result of fraudulent advertisements in the past, advertising is regulated by the Federal Trade Commission and is discussed in more detail in Chapter 14. All fifty states today have consumer protection laws and also regulate advertisements.

The following case represents a situation in which a corporation considered its short-term profits to be more important than its ethical responsibility for truthful advertising. In reviewing the case, consider whether these marketing practices best served this corporation's long-term interests.

Case 2.2

Oliveira v. Amoco Oil Company

Appellate Court of Illinois,
Fourth District, 2000
311 Ill.App.3d 886, 726
N.E.2d 51
http://caselaw.findlaw.com
/scripts/getcase.pl?court=
IL&vol=app\2000\4980199
&invol=3

BACKGROUND AND FACTS Plaintiff, Oliveira, appealed the dismissal of his complaint based on the Illinois Consumer Fraud and Deceptive Business Practices Act (Act) against the defendant, Amoco Oil Company (Amoco). Oliveira is an Illinois consumer who filed his complaint alleging that Amoco's advertisements for its premium gasolines were false and he and others purchased those premium brands because of the ads. He asserted that Amoco had violated the Illinois statute.

The complaint alleged Amoco began a multistate advertising campaign on November 6, 1991, which falsely represented:

> *(A) Amoco Ultimate gasoline is superior to all other brands of premium gasoline with respect to engine performance or environmental benefits because it is refined more than all other such brands;*
>
> *(B) The clear color of Amoco Ultimate gasoline demonstrates the superior engine performance and environmental benefits Amoco Ultimate provides compared to other premium brands of gasolines that are not clear in color;*
>
> *(C) A single tankful of Amoco Silver or Ultimate gasoline will make dirty or clogged fuel injectors clean;*
>
> *(D) Amoco Silver or Ultimate gasoline provides superior fuel injector cleaning compared to other brands of gasoline; and*
>
> *(E) Automobiles driven more than 15,000 miles with regular gasoline generally suffer from lost engine power or acceleration which will be restored by the higher octane of Amoco Silver gasoline.*

The complaint alleges Amoco knew these statements were untrue. The result of its deceptive advertising campaign was to increase demand for its premium gasoline thereby commanding an inflated and otherwise unsustainable price for the premium gasolines that all consumers paid whether or not they had relied on or seen the ads. Thus, Oliveira argued that all consumers who purchased defendant's premium gasolines during the advertising period were damaged by Amoco's misrepresentations. The trial court granted Amoco's motion to dismiss because it did not think that the marketing theory pleaded by Oliveira, that is, Amoco's misleading advertising, caused inflated prices for its gasoline. Therefore, there was no fraud by Amoco. Oliveira appealed.

Justice KNECHT

. . . .

Section 2 of the Act delineates an unlawful practice as follows:

> "Unfair methods of competition and unfair or deceptive acts or practices, including but not limited to the use or employment of any deception, fraud, false pretense, false promise, misrepresentation or the concealment, suppression or omission of any material fact, with intent that others rely upon the concealment, suppression or omission of such material fact, . . . in the conduct of any trade or commerce are hereby declared unlawful whether any person has in fact been misled, deceived or damaged thereby."

An action for damages under the Act may be brought pursuant to section 10a(a). "Any person who suffers actual damage as a result of a violation of this Act committed by any other person may bring an action against such person." The definition of "person" under the Act includes a corporation, company, or other business entity. Thus, defendant is included as a person who could commit a violation of the Act.

The Act has been construed liberally to give effect to the legislative goals behind its enactment. The Act's policy is to give broader protection than common law fraud by prohibiting any "deception, fraud, false pretense, false promise, misrepresentation or the concealment, suppression or omission of any material fact, with intent that others rely upon the concealment . . . in the conduct of any trade or commerce." The standard of proof for a violation of the Act is lenient as it does not require "any person has in fact been misled, deceived or damaged thereby."

A cause of action under section 2 of the Act has three elements: (1) a deceptive act or practice by the defendant, (2) the defendant's intent that plaintiff rely on the deception, and (3) the deception occurred during a course of conduct involving trade or commerce. Although the defendant's intent that its deception be relied on is an element of the offense, the Supreme Court of Illinois has stated no actual reliance is required to state a cause of action under the Act.

. . . .

Duran v. Leslie Oldsmobile, Inc. holds reliance is required for a private cause of action as opposed to those brought under the Act by the Attorney General. In support of its ruling, however, the *Duran* court relied on language in section 10a of the Act that deals with proximate causation: "Any person who suffers damage as a result of a violation of this Act . . . may bring an action . . . ."

While reliance is not required under the Act, a plaintiff must demonstrate the defendant's consumer fraud proximately caused his injuries. The required allegation of proximate causation has been termed minimal, however, as that determination is best left to the trier of fact. Defendant contends Illinois law under the Act requires a plaintiff to allege two components of causation: (1) "direct" or "proximate" causation and (2) "but for" or "transactional" causation. These two types of causation apparently originated in federal securities fraud cases.

. . . .

Since "but for" causation is not necessary because actual reliance is not necessary, the question under plaintiff's theory becomes whether defendant made misleading statements in its advertising that led to an increase in demand and inflated prices that were paid by all. Defendant argues, even if the advertising was misleading, it did not proximately cause any damage to plaintiff.

Defendant contends it provided affidavits to counter those supplied by plaintiff and which provide evidence the overall demand for its premium gasolines went down, as did prices during the relevant period; therefore, its advertising did not proximately cause any damages to plaintiff. . . . [T]he question is not whether demand for the premium gasolines went down but whether demand and prices were artificially high for the relevant time period due to misleading advertising. In other words, without the advertising, would the demand and prices of defendant's premium gasolines have been even lower during the relevant time period?

. . . .

DECISION AND REMEDY The court found Oliveira's complaint adequately stated a cause of action for consumer fraud under the Act. The complaint adequately pled a deceptive act or practice by defendant. Specifically, Oliveira alleged Amoco represented in its advertising that its premium gasolines had special features which would produce increased performance in automobiles and had environmental benefits, but that this information was false.

CRITICAL THINKING: LEGAL CONSIDERATION Do you think this type of advertising should be considered fraud or is it just trade puffing? Trade puffing refers to the use of words or phrases that do not promise anything or are not truly intended to be believed as in advertising for cosmetics.

With the global economy, suppliers must also consider their ethical responsibility to consumers in other countries. The Environmental Protection Agency prohibited the sale of insecticides containing DDT[14] in the United States because it might have long-term carcinogenic effects. Is it then ethical for the manufacturer sell the product in countries where its sale is still legal? This example demonstrates an ethical conflict between short-term profits for shareholders and long-term concern for the well-being of its customers. When such a conflict arises, ethical businesses consider the long-term effects of their products on customers rather than only considering the short-range profit picture.

Government

When businesses fail to act in an ethical manner, the government adopts statutes and regulations governing a particular business behavior. Once passed, a statute is assigned to a government agency to regulate and monitor as it applies to specific types of business behavior. As a result, the government incurs increased costs to administer these statutes. Increased costs translate into increased taxes paid by individuals and businesses to the government. Businesses now must comply with these new regulations or risk civil, and possibly criminal, charges.

The government's ability to tax and to adopt statutes influences business behavior. For example, when airline passengers had their flights delayed, baggage lost, and were generally treated poorly by airline personnel, Congress proposed a statute that would provide passengers with rights. The airline industry responded by voluntarily adopting rules governing their behavior in an effort to prevent Congress from passing any statutes. Congress, in response, delayed consideration of the airline passenger bill.

If a business disagrees with a law, it attempts to influence the legislature to modify or repeal the statute. (A business also has the option of suing, thus allowing a

court to decide the fate of a particular law.) Businesses have an interest in making certain that statutes reflect their views. Often one statutory scheme will generate lobbying, both for and against its adoption. For example, the automobile industry lobbied Congress against adopting seat belts and air bags because adoption would increase manufacturing costs, whereas the insurance industry lobbied Congress to adopt these measures because they would lower insurance costs by preventing or reducing injuries to passengers.

When Congress considers transportation bills, the trucking firms, the air carriers, and the railroad companies all provide information on the advantages and disadvantages of the proposed legislation. Congress provides tax support to the trucking industry by subsidizing the interstate highway system and provides tax support to air carriers by providing funds for the purchase of aircraft and for airport building, maintenance, and operations. Congress, however, decided not to support the railroad industry to the same extent and is requiring Amtrak eventually to become self-sufficient and support itself without any tax revenue from the federal government. Congress is lobbied by various special interest groups because legislation that supports one industry may be detrimental to another.

The U.S. government is one of the largest customers in the world. Unfortunately, the federal government discovered its suppliers were engaging in fraud and overcharging it. Congress reacted to this discovery by passing the **False Claims Act**[15] in 1986. The act authorizes the government to sue any party filing a fraudulent payment claim for products or services. The government receives information from a number of sources. One valuable source is the person known as a **whistleblower** who in-

---

[14] DDT stands for d(ichloro)d(iphenyl)t(richloroethane), a human-made toxic compound found in insecticides.

[15] 31 U.S.C.A. §§3729-3732. See also <http://www.law.cornell.edu/uscode/31/ch37.html>. The first formal False Claims Act was passed in 1863 as result of fraudulent suppliers selling faulty war supplies during the Civil War. The act was amended in 1943 which severely restricted the application of the original act. The 1986 amendments provide new life to the act by establishing the burden of proof as preponderance of the evidence, allowing the informant to seek damages, and protecting the informant from retaliation by the employer.

forms public officials or the news media of the company's unsafe, illegal, or unethical activities.

Assume the U.S. government pursues a lawsuit. If the evidence used to build the case comes from a whistleblower, that person may be awarded from 15 to 25 percent of any damages or fines awarded to the government. If the United States does not proceed with the litigation, but the informer continues with it and prevails, he is entitled to 25 to 30 percent of the awarded damages. Naturally, the law forbids a person who helped to plan and execute the fraud to collect under the federal False Claims Act.

Many whistleblowers are employees who must decide whether to become a whistleblower. The employee who keeps quiet compromises her own ethical standards and may be required by the employer to participate in the unsafe or illegal actions. Choosing the alternative, however, may lead to undesirable results. Whistleblowers usually are fired for some unrelated offense. Frequently, the whistleblower will not find another job in that industry.

The federal government offers statutory protection for whistleblowers. These laws authorize whistleblowers to sue their employer if they are discharged or suffer discrimination as the result of informing the federal government of the employer's illegal activities.[16] These statutes allow the court to award double the amount of back pay, attorneys' fees, and costs to an informer. If the employee is fired, the court can order that the employee be reinstated with the same seniority. To encourage employees to speak out, forty-five states have followed the lead of the federal government and have also enacted statutes that protect whistleblowers employed by the state government. Some state laws extend whistleblower protection to employees working in private industry.

In 1987, only thirty-three cases were filed under the act. By 1998, the number of cases had climbed to 417. Although the plaintiff has prevailed in only 11 percent of the cases, those who do prevail receive large awards because of the amounts involved. For example, in two different Medicare fraud cases, the plaintiffs received awards of $20 million and $9 million. The U.S. government was awarded a record $325 million in a third Medicare fraud case as the result of a whistleblower. Altogether, the total amount recovered since 1987 is $2,140,555,000 with a total of 2,420 cases filed.

Today, businesses that service or sell to the federal government must avoid fraudulent activities. Ethically, this standard has always held true. As a result of being overcharged and defrauded by businesses, the federal government has made fraud explicitly illegal and rewards the whistleblower.

Although the following case is not a business case, the concept is the same. A whistleblower was fired for insisting on maintaining testing standards and as a result she, in turn, filed this lawsuit.

---

[16] Whistleblower information is provided by the Department of Labor's Whistleblower Collection found at <http://www.oalj.dol.gov /libwhist.htm>.

Case 2.3

Rodriguez v. Laredo Independent School District

U.S. District Court, S.D. Tex., 2000

82 F. Supp. 2d 679

BACKGROUND AND FACTS Imelda Rodriguez (Rodriguez) was formerly the assistant superintendent for curriculum and program accountability for the Laredo Independent School District (LISD). She sued the Laredo Independent School District and Superintendent Paul Cruz (Cruz).

Rodriguez alleged that she was disciplined and demoted for her advocacy of strict compliance with testing procedures and her consistent reporting of testing irregularities, actions that conflicted with Cruz's goal of raising standardized scores. Rodriguez alleged that she was contacted by an administrator at the United Independent School District (UISD), an agency involved in the administration of statewide tests. The administrator notified her that a UISD investigation had revealed that a LISD teacher had improperly obtained an advance copy of a portion of a Texas Assessment of Academic Skills (TAAS) examination and had used it to prepare her students in violation of testing procedures.

Rodriguez previously had discovered that, while administering tests, teachers were engaging in a technique known as pacing. *Pacing* is a system by which the teacher conducting the testing instructs students, contrary to the mandated testing procedures, to work only on one or a small group of questions. The students work on the questions and do not proceed until told to do so by the teacher. This procedure provides improper and unlawful assistance. Rodriguez found that pacing was widely used throughout the school district during 1997. She advised principals that pacing would be discontinued for any further tests administered in 1998. The test scores for 1998 declined significantly.

In 1998, Cruz was appointed the superintendent for the school district. In August 1998 Rodriguez met with him to outline the results of her investigations including the previous use of pacing, the declining test scores, and her insistence on proper test procedures. She also discussed with him the advantages of norm-referenced tests in predicting college aptitude and recommended that the district adopt these tests.

At a subsequent meeting with LISD principals, Cruz indicated, contrary to Rodriguez's recommendations, that he would not require the norm referenced tests to be administered. Cruz also publicly predicted that, under his leadership, test performance would improve significantly. Rodriguez alleged that this announcement, in conjunction with his efforts to discourage norm referenced testing, indicated Cruz's primary emphasis on improving test scores at all costs, and his willingness to ignore compliance issues.

In September 1998, citing financial concerns, Cruz denied Rodriguez permission to attend a meeting that was typically attended by administrators at her level. Cruz subsequently issued a memorandum removing Rodriguez from her position as assistant superintendent and appointing her to a previously nonexistent administrative position, with responsibility for textbooks and janitorial service. Rodriguez was assigned to this new position even though that assignment conflicted with school board policy of approving new positions prior to their formal establishment.

Rodriguez filed a grievance that Cruz denied. Rodriguez appealed to the school board. Prior to her hearing, Cruz gave Rodriguez an unfavorable job evaluation. Rodriguez was granted a ten-minute period to make her presentation to the Board. Following private deliberations, the board took no action.

Rodriguez filed this suit alleging a violation of the Texas whistleblower law. Defendants filed a motion to dismiss Rodriguez's claim, asserting failure to state a claim on which relief can be granted. This decision arises from the motion to dismiss.

District Judge ELLISON

. . . .

LISD has also moved to dismiss Rodriguez's claim under the Texas Whistleblower Law. Rodriguez alleges that she suffered retaliation for reporting acts that she in good faith believed violated Texas law.

The Texas Government Code provides, in pertinent part, that:

> a) A state or local governmental entity may not . . . take . . . adverse personnel action against, a public employee who in good faith reports a violation of law by employing governmental entity or another public employee to an appropriate law enforcement agency. . . .

> b) In this section, a report is made to an appropriate law enforcement authority if the authority is part of a state or local government entity or of the federal government that the employee believes in good faith is authorized to:

> 1) regulate under or enforce the law alleged to be violated in the report. . . .

Thus, there is a two-pronged test to determine whether a violation of [the code] has occurred. As applied in this case, it is first, whether Rodriguez made a good faith report of cheating and second, whether she believed in good faith that

LISD had regulatory power with respect to violations of the TEA (Texas Education Agency) rules. Whether or not Rodriguez held a good faith belief that the rules were in fact being violated is a quintessential issue of fact. The same is true of her good faith belief that LISD had regulatory power with respect to such infractions.

Construing the facts in a manner that is favorable to Rodriguez, she has alleged enough in the pleadings to survive dismissal at this early stage. Her complaint includes reasonably detailed descriptions of the incidents that led her to believe that cheating was occurring and similarly detailed descriptions of the conversations supporting her belief that she was reporting these to the right authorities, namely, Cruz and the members of the School Board. It may be that later information indicates that these beliefs were not held in good faith. For the Court now to dismiss on these grounds, however, would be premature.

. . . .

DECISION AND REMEDY The court allowed the case to go to trial because of a possible violation of the Texas whistleblower law.

CRITICAL THINKING: LEGAL CONSIDERATION Rodriguez was an employee of the school district and her immediate supervisor was Cruz. Obviously, she knew that both the school district and her supervisor wanted higher test scores. Why do you think she opposed the actions taken to improve student scores?

The Community

When a business operates in a community, its treatment of employees is known in that community. Do people want to work for this company? Communities demand that local companies abide by legal and regulatory statutes. A community is unlikely to tolerate a company's pollution of the air, water, or land.

Most major corporations engage in philanthropic activities. They routinely donate to hospitals, the arts, and universities by giving money, employee time, and access to special assets, such as a supercomputer. Most major corporations screen charitable requests and determine organizations deserving of charitable contributions. IBM is a leader in contributing to education, social services, civil affairs, and the arts.

The following subsections describe two situations in which businesses have faced ethical, political, and legal problems in their relationships with a community.

Exxon Valdez. In 1989, Valdez, Alaska, became an instantly recognizable name and place after the tanker *Exxon Valdez* (owned by Exxon Corporation[17]) spilled

more than 11 million gallons of crude oil (out of the 53 million aboard ship) into Prince William Sound. The spill remains the worst environmental disaster in U.S. history.[18] The lawsuits continued more than a decade later, as did the effects on the people whose livelihood depended on the ocean. The spill still receives television and print media coverage.

The long-term environmental effects still are unknown.[19] In the short term, however, the spill spoiled the natural beauty of 1,200 miles of Alaskan shoreline and killed or maimed more than 100,000 migratory birds and unknown numbers of fish, including prized pink salmon. It halted the thriving fishing industry,

[17] In 1999, Exxon Corporation and Mobil Corporation merged to form ExxonMobil Corporation. Headquartered in Irving, Texas, ExxonMobil is in the petroleum and petrochemicals business. Its web page is <http://www.exxonmobil.com/index_flash.html>.

[18] In 1989, three other large oil spills occurred, in which 850,000 gallons of oil were spilled in Houston Ship Channel near Galveston Bay in Texas, the Delaware River, and off the coast of Rhode Island. Although the Exxon Valdez caused the largest single oil spill in U.S. waters, according to the National Academy of Sciences, Washington, D.C., the world's waters are polluted annually with 540 million gallons of oil, the equivalent of 50 Exxon Valdez accidents every year.
[19] The oil moved along the coastline of Alaska, contaminating portions of the shoreline of Prince William Sound, the Kenai Peninsula, lower Cook Inlet, the Kodiak Archipelago, and the Alaska Peninsula. Other areas the oil reached include a national forest, four national wildlife refuges, three national parks, five state parks, four state critical habitat areas, and a state game sanctuary. Oil eventually reached shorelines nearly 600 miles southwest of Bligh Reef, where the spill occurred.

forcing thousands of people out of work, even as late as 1998. How did such a cataclysmic event occur?

A harbor pilot guided the huge oil tanker through the Valdez Narrows (seven miles from Valdez) and for another seven miles before departing and turning the ship over to the captain of the ship, Joseph J. Hazelwood. The captain set a course to avoid icebergs and notified the Coast Guard[20] of his action. It was alleged that he ordered an accelerated speed, placed the ship on automatic pilot, left in charge the third mate (who allegedly was not qualified for this type of duty), and departed the bridge. In due course, the ship strayed from the outbound shipping lane, went through the separation lane, crossed through the inbound shipping lane,[21] and traveled several more miles before hitting Bligh Reef.[22]

The National Transportation Safety Board determined the probable causes of the grounding of the *Exxon Valdez* to be the failure of the third mate to properly maneuver the vessel because of fatigue and excessive workload; the failure of Captain Hazelwood to provide a proper navigation watch because he was impaired from drinking alcohol; the failure of Exxon to provide a fit ship captain since Exxon knew that Hazelwood had a drinking problem; the failure of Exxon to provide a rested and sufficient crew for the *Exxon Valdez*; the failure of the Coast Guard to provide an effective vessel traffic service because of inadequate equipment and manning levels, inadequate personnel training, and deficient management oversight; and the failure of the Coast Guard to provide effective pilotage services.

Are there others who should share the blame besides Captain Hazelwood? To cut expenses, Exxon[23] had reduced the number of employees on its tankers. Did this decision jeopardize the ship's safety? Further, Exxon was criticized for failing to have a double-hulled ship. Should Exxon have had this type of ship when very few of these types of ships had ever been built? Three-fourths of the oil tankers docking at Valdez had single hulls, because in 1975 the federal government refused to require tankers to have double hulls.[24]

Should Alyeska Pipeline Service Company share the blame[25] because it failed in its specific promises to the Department of the Interior[26] and to Congress to have trained personnel and equipment ready to meet such accidents? What were the failures of the Coast Guard, which tracked the ship on radar only as far as the Valdez Narrows? The Coast Guard had not informed the oil companies that ships were no longer tracked beyond the narrows. Nor were harbor pilots required to accompany these tankers out to the open sea. The Coast Guard also failed to install additional radar equipment at a site (at a cost of $100,000) further out at sea, a recommendation made in 1981. Its old, larger radar had been replaced with one half the size. Finally, the Coast Guard had no method of independent observation of the ice packs.[27]

Did the state of Alaska also fail by not having trained personnel and equipment ready for this type of disaster? The state earned an annual average of $1.5 billion from this venture,[28] yet it failed to fund any staff positions for oil-spill contingency planning and funded only 10 percent of what the state Department of Environmental

[20] The Coast Guard home page is at <http://www.dot.gov/dotinfo/uscg/>.
[21] Think of the sea lanes as a divided highway and Bligh Reef as the ditch alongside the road. Traveling down one side of the highway, the driver veers over the divider, crosses over all the opposing lanes, and ends up in the ditch. While highway accidents are measured in feet, problems at sea are measured in the equivalent of miles. Because of the length and weight of a fully loaded oil tanker, it may take up to five miles to stop the ship.
[22] The Exxon Valdez suffered $25 million in damages and the cost of the lost cargo was estimated at $3.4 million. After undergoing extensive repairs, the Exxon Valdez was renamed the Sea River Mediterranean and placed in service in the Mediterranean Sea. The 1990 Oil Pollution Act, written in the aftermath of the 11-million-gallon spill in Prince William Sound, contained a clause written by Senator Ted Stevens (R–Alaska) that barred the vessel from returning to Alaska. A lawsuit was filed by Exxon's shipping subsidiaries seeking to return the renamed tanker to service in the Alaska oil trade. This lawsuit is still pending.

[23] In 1968, a majority of the world's shipowners formed the International Tanker Owners Pollution Federation Limited (ITOPF). This nonprofit organization provides technical advice, expertise, assistance, and information on effective response to ship-source pollution. The ITOPF is found at <http://www.itopf.com/>.
[24] The Oil Pollution Act of 1990 requires double hulls on all new tankers. All single-hulled tankers are to be phased out by 2010. To date no double-hulled ships have been ordered or built.
[25] Alyeska Pipeline consisted of seven oil companies that owned the following percentages: British Petroleum, 50.01 percent; ARGO, 20 percent; Exxon, 20 percent; and Mobil, Amerada Hess, Unocal, and Phillips Petroleum shared the remaining 10 percent.
[26] The Department of Interior site is <http://www.doi.gov>.
[27] The Oil Pollution Act of 1990 provided the Coast Guard the statutory authority and funding needed to improve the policing of tanker activity. The act makes specific references to Bligh Reef.
[28] From 1969 to 1987, Alaska earned more than $29 billion in oil income. Alaska set aside part of this fund, about $400 million a year, to pay people a dividend for being residents.

Conservation had requested for oil regulation and monitoring.[29]

More than 185 major lawsuits were filed in state and federal courts as a result of the *Exxon Valdez* disaster. More than 75 law firms represented the 10,000 fishers, Alaska natives, and property owners who sued. Among the defendants were Exxon Corporation, Exxon Shipping Company, and Alyeska Pipeline Service Company, as well as each of its members.

In 1991, Exxon, the state of Alaska, and the U.S. government entered into a civil consent decree. Exxon must make ten annual payments totaling $900 million for injuries to natural resources and services, and for the restoration and replacement of natural resources. The first payment was made in December 1991; the last payment is due in September 2001. The money is to be used to "restore, rehabilitate, replace or enhance the natural resources and services" affected by the spill.

Altogether, by 1997, Exxon had paid about $3.5 billion in cleanup costs, government fines, and damage claims related to the spill. But even then, Exxon's troubles were not over. In 1994, a jury found Exxon liable and awarded approximately $19.6 million in compensatory damages, $38 million in prejudgment interest on the compensatory damages, and $5 billion in punitive damages.[30] The judge approved a plan that allocated 78 percent of the punitive award to oiled fisheries, 2 percent to unoiled fisheries, 2 percent to municipalities, and 16 percent to Alaska natives, processors, private businesses, and others. Exxon appealed the judgment, which is still pending.[31]

Whatever the business and governmental management decisions that led to the spill, it has cost Exxon financially and its reputation suffered. Although Exxon took the brunt of the blame, others also shoulder ethical responsibility.[32]

Bhopal. Bhopal, a town in India, was unknown in the United States until 1984, when forty tons of toxic gases were released from a Union Carbide[33] pesticide factory, killing approximately 1,800 people and injuring 200,000 others. That disaster stands as the worst industrial accident in history.

The plant was located in a heavily populated urban area; slums surrounded the plant. The actual occurrences on the night of the accident are unclear. What is known is that safety information was never distributed to the surrounding public, and the alarm that sounded that night was the same alarm that signaled practice drills, which occurred about thirty times a week. The plant did not meet U.S. standards for safety operations and had not been inspected in more than two years.

In 1986, the government of India, on behalf of the families harmed, filed a lawsuit against Union Carbide for $3.3 billion. In 1989, the case was settled. Union Carbide paid $470 million to the Indian government on behalf of the families. Yet through 1991, less than $5 million had been distributed.

Was this disaster a result of a poorly constructed physical plant or of poorly trained indigenous personnel working in a highly sophisticated factory? Did the company fail to heed warnings by experts that a serious accident could occur? Union Carbide asserts that the event was caused by sabotage. Was it caused instead by a combination of poor management decisions and negligent acts? Unless fully investigated or litigated in open court, the ethical and legal questions will remain unanswered.

Strategy for Ethical Decision Making

When confronted with a problem, a person can take any number of actions. Some actions may be useful, whereas others may create more problems. Philosophers have developed various ethical decision-making models to help a person to resolve a dilemma. Some models are more complex than others.

The following is a decision-making model you can use to resolve the ethical problems found at the

[29] The Oil Pollution Act of 1990 created the Oil-Spill Recovery Institute to study and evaluate oil spills and cleanup measures.
[30] Exxon had nearly 170 insurers. The insurers agreed to pay $780 million of Exxon's liability.
[31] Exxon's statement of the appeal is found at <http://www.exxonmobil.com/>; search for Exxon Valdez.
[32] Exxon's statement on the Valdez ten-year anniversary is at <http://www.exxonmobil.com/>; search for Exxon Valdez.

[33] Union Carbide's web page is <http://www.unioncarbide.com/>. Its only statement on the Bhopal incident is found in the Brief Chronology page where it is stated that the gas leak was an act of sabotage. Union Carbide and the Dow Chemical Company are in the process of merging. The Dow Chemical Company's web page is <http://www.dow.com/homepage/>.

LEGAL HIGHLIGHT

The Whistleblowers and Big Tobacco

In 1994, leaders of the seven largest U.S. tobacco companies testified under oath before Congress that they did not believe nicotine to be addictive or dangerous and that their companies did not manipulate nicotine levels. That moment would be a turning point in history.

Merrell Williams was a paralegal for a Louisville, Kentucky, law firm from 1989 to 1992. His job was to code internal records and research findings from Brown & Williamson Tobacco Corporation (B&W) that might damage the company's legal position if they were discovered and disclosed in court proceedings. Williams believed that the point of his work was to cover up detrimental information. Williams managed to copy 4,000 of B&W's documents and turn them over to opponents of the tobacco industry.

These documents provided the public's first look at the internal workings of a tobacco company. They were analyzed, and the findings were published first in the *Journal of the American Medical Association,* then in a 1996 book, *The Cigarette Papers,* by Stanton A. Glantz. Publication of these papers occurred at the right time to be useful to the attorney general of Mississippi, Michael Moore, who along with others was gathering information to sue tobacco companies to recover Medicaid costs for treating smoking-related illnesses. He filed the case in 1994, and eventually many other states joined in the lawsuit. Williams was sued by his former law firm, claiming theft, fraud, conversion, breach of fiduciary duties, and breach of contract.

Dr. Jeffrey Wigand was the highest ranking executive to blow the whistle on the tobacco industry. Between 1989 and 1993, he was employed with B&W as vice president for research and development at an estimated salary of $400,000. In 1993, Dr. Wigand was fired. Both before and after his firing, he signed four confidential agreements with B&W not to disclose information that he had discovered while employed by the company. He received a six-figure-per-year severance package, but this compensation ended after he offered to testify against his former employer for the federal government and for the Mississippi attorney general. Appearing on the CBS program *60 Minutes,* he alleged that B&W opposed work on a safer cigarette and used chemicals in its tobacco blends to enhance the effect of nicotine. He claimed that B&W executives knew that nicotine was addictive.

Although the program was taped, CBS did not broadcast it because the network feared being sued, because of the confidentiality agreements Dr. Wigand had signed. CBS's failure to broadcast the story became news itself. The program finally aired some seven months later in February 1996. In the meantime, B&W sued Dr. Wigand for breaching the confidentiality agreements. CBS agreed to pay for his defense.

Later in 1996, Dr. Wigand was caught between two conflicting court orders. In Kentucky, where B&W had filed the lawsuit against him, a court ordered him to cooperate with the company before he provided any testimony contrary to B&W's interests. In a separate case, a federal judge ruled that B&W could not interview Wigand until a federal grand jury had completed its tobacco industry probe investigating whether the tobacco leaders who testified before Congress had committed perjury.

Finally, in 1997, an historic $360-billion settlement between the attorneys general from forty states and the tobacco industry almost collapsed when B&W refused to agree to a clause that protected Dr. Wigand. The attorneys general negotiating the settlement agreed that they would walk away if Dr. Wigand, Merrell Williams, and other whistleblowers were not protected. As Attorney General Grant Woods from Arizona stated, "We won't leave any wounded behind." Finally, two and one half hours later, B&W agreed to drop the legal actions against Dr. Wigand and Merrell Williams by agreeing to the one sentence: "Furthermore, the Act would provide 'whistleblowers' in the tobacco industry with the maximum protection available under current federal statutes." Shortly thereafter, on June 20, 1997, the historic agreement was announced. It was finalized in writing on November 23, 1998.

But this agreement has not stopped all litigation. The Canadian government has filed an action against R. J. Reynolds in a New York federal court seeking a billion dollars in compensation. The U.S. Department of Justice also filed an action against all of the large tobacco companies. That lawsuit is still pending.

For more information, see the Tobacco BBS (Bulletin Board System), a free resource center focusing on tobacco and smoking issues at <http://www.tobacco.org/>. The Northeastern University School of Law in Boston, Massachusetts, operates Tobacco Control Resource Center, Inc., and the Tobacco Products Liability Project at <http://www.tobacco.neu.edu/>. The Digital Library of the University of California, San Francisco, maintains the Tobacco Control Archives at <http://galen.library.ucsf.edu/tobacco/>.

beginning each chapter. This model consists of the following six steps:

1. *Facts* Gather all the necessary facts, including whether any state or federal statutes or whether any administrative regulations apply. Once you have examined the facts, you will be able to define the problem.

2. *Stakeholders* List all the stakeholders that may be affected by the decision.

3. *Values* List all personal and work-related values involved in the particular case. These values may include one or more of the following:
   a. Personal values:
      Religious values or idea of good.
      Honesty, such as truth-telling, candidness, or openness.
      Integrity, such as acting on convictions, courageous acts, advocacy, or leadership by example.
   b. Institutional values:
      Responsible citizenship, such as respect for law or social consciousness.
      Pursuit of excellence, such as quality of work.
      Accountability, such as responsibility or independence.
   c. Interpersonal values:
      Promise-keeping, such as fulfilling the spirit of commitments.
      Loyalty, such as fidelity or confidentiality.
      Fairness, such as justice, equal treatment, diversity, or independence.
      Caring for others, such as compassion or kindness.
      Respect for others, such as human dignity or uniqueness.

4. *Alternative Actions* List all the possible alternative actions from which you could choose.

5. *Prioritization* Choose and prioritize by answering the following questions:

   a. Which stakeholder do you believe is the most important in this situation?
   b. Which value do you believe is the most important in this situation?
   c. Which of the choices do you believe will cause the greatest good or the least harm?

6. *Potential Action* Make a decision as to which stakeholder should prevail and determine a strategy (course of action) to carry out your decision.

A SAMPLE CASE

Using the Model for Ethical Decision Making

A secretary who has worked for your business for fifteen years is involved in a car accident in which she permanently loses the use of her right hand. Thus, she can no longer effectively type, file, or perform many of the other functions that she previously had performed and that are included in her job description. Your business has a very tight budget and does not have sufficient funds to pay for an additional secretary without reallocating budget items. The injured secretary has been very loyal to your business, and you have been very satisfied with her work and dedication. She wants to stay at her job. Moreover, she does not believe that she could find other employment at this time. Should your business fire her, lay her off with compensation, or find a way to retain her? The following steps apply the model to this case.

1. **Facts** These items need to be reviewed: the secretary, the job description, the statutes, the administrative regulations, the budget, disability insurance, and the impact on other employees. The Americans with Disabilities Act and its regulations may apply. Review with the injured secretary the specific duties that she can and cannot do

under her current job description. Determine if
the budget can be modified by allocating funds
from another category to the secretarial category
in case you decide to retain the worker.
Determine if there is any disability insurance
upon which the secretary may rely. Determine
the impact on other employees if the job duties
are shared with other employees.

In your interview with the secretary, you
must find out if any rehabilitation or treatment
programs would allow her to regain the use of
her right hand. Find out if a technological device
would allow her to type using a computer and to
perform other tasks with one hand. Ascertain her
current financial position and her wishes. Learn
how the remaining secretarial staff feels about
performing the additional duties once performed
by the injured secretary.

After reviewing the above, based on the
medical facts, you determine that the secretary
cannot physically perform many of the essential
duties of her job description. There is no way to
accommodate her. If you terminate her, the
Americans with Disabilities Act would not be
violated because she cannot perform the essential
functions of her job and your business cannot
reasonably accommodate her. The budget is very
tight but would allow a shift of funds among
some categories. The problem is whether to retain
the secretary, even though she cannot perform
many of the required duties. You may resolve this
problem by using the rest of the decision-making
model.

2. **Stakeholders** The stakeholders that may be
affected by the decision are:
a. Your business
b. The injured secretary
c. The secretarial staff
d. The management staff
e. The general community

3. **Values** The personal and work-related values
involved in the particular case are:
a. *Loyalty* As the secretary has given her loyalty
to your corporation, so the business should
demonstrate its loyalty to her.
b. *Fairness* The rest of the secretarial staff will
have to perform many of the secretary's
former duties.

c. *Respect* Although she now has a disability,
the secretary is still a very talented individual
who has contributed a great deal to your
corporation.
d. *Integrity* Your business should be in the forefront of making room for long-term loyal
employees who have disabilities.
e. *Accountability* The managerial staff is responsible for using business funds wisely and for
providing essential services within the financial
resources of the business.

4. **Alternative Actions** The possible alternative
actions from which you could choose are:
a. Do not retain the injured secretary because of
the budget.
b. Do not retain the injured secretary because of
the budget, but offer her an attractive severance
package.
c. Retain the secretary even though the budget
does not accommodate the salary of an additional secretary. Restructure the duties so that
the remaining secretarial staff will assume
many of her previous duties.
d. Retain the secretary by changing the budget-
ary priorities to accommodate the salary of an
additional secretary.

5. **Prioritization** Choose and prioritize by
answering the following questions.
a. Which stakeholder do you believe is the
most important in this situation? The injured
secretary.
b. Which value do you believe to be the most
important in this situation? Integrity that includes leadership by example.
c. Which of the choices do you believe will
cause the greatest good or the least harm?
Finding a means to increase or restructure the
budget to be able to retain the injured secretary and to hire additional secretarial help.

6. **Potential Action** Retaining the secretary by
increasing or restructuring the budget is the most
desirable action. Consider working with rehabilitation specialists from an insurance company, a
health care provider, or the state's workers' compensation office. This action will create an
affirmative atmosphere among the employees,
who will see your business as treating a fellow
employee with respect when she was confronted

with the potentially devastating combination of paralysis and unemployment. This action also will provide stability in the workplace.

The above solution represents one analysis of an ethical problem. Another decision with different results could be reached if, for example, the budget were not able to accommodate the retention of the secretary. No perfect answer exists.

Legal Ethics

Legal ethics involve the moral and professional duties that lawyers owe other lawyers, their clients, the courts, and the public. Although the legal profession is the butt of many jokes concerning ethical issues, most lawyers are ethical. Lawyers face legal and ethical issues every day.

The unanswered ethical issue of whether a lawyer should defend a criminal defendant that the lawyer knows to be guilty is just one example. The public often does not understand that a lawyer cannot pre-judge legal guilt. The prosecutor's job is to prove the defendant guilty "beyond a reasonable doubt" in a courtroom. The accused has a right to be presumed not guilty, has a constitutional right to assistance of counsel, and has a right to trial by jury under the Sixth Amendment. The lawyer's role is to ensure that the government respects a person's constitutional rights.

Courts increasingly are becoming irritated by frivolous lawsuits. It is true that a few lawyers, just to earn a fee, will take cases knowing that they cannot win on the merits (facts) while leading the clients to believe otherwise. The state's highest court has the authority to suspend or disbar attorneys who engage in this conduct. Further, courts today will force the lawyer to bear all the expenses of such frivolous suits.

The following U.S. Supreme Court case involves the issue of whether an attorney or his firm should be liable for instituting a groundless action. Federal court rules and many states permit the recovery of expenses when an attorney or a client brings a worthless claim. This recovery is commonly called a Rule 11 sanction. The following case looks at whether an attorney or his firm should pay the Rule 11 sanction.

Case 2.4

Pavelic & LeFlore v. Marvel Entertainment Group

Supreme Court of the United States, 1989
493 U.S. 120, 110 S. Ct. 456, 107 L. Ed. 2d 438
http://caselaw.findlaw.com /scripts/getcase.pl?navby= CASE&court=US&vol=493 &page=120

BACKGROUND AND FACTS Northern J. Calloway sued Marvel Entertainment Group for willful copyright infringement of his motion picture script. The original complaint-signed and filed by Calloway's attorney, Ray L. LeFlore, alleged that Calloway had developed an idea for a motion picture and had written a script. Further, the complaint alleged that Marvel had begun to develop Calloway's work without his permission.

Marvel filed a motion to dismiss, pointing to a series of documents annexed to the complaint that gave the production company the right to develop the work commercially. The district court dismissed the complaint (with leave to refile the complaint with the court), not on the ground that the documents authorized the alleged infringement, but on the ground that Calloway's complaint had failed to specify the registration number of his copyright and the dates on which the alleged acts of infringement had occurred.

Several weeks later an amended complaint, again signed by LeFlore, was filed. At the trial the jury found in favor of Marvel on all the claims. After the original case was completed, Marvel brought a Rule 11 motion and sought sanctions in the amount of $100,000 against both the law firm and Ray L. LeFlore. The Supreme Court took jurisdiction to decide whether a Rule 11 sanction should apply to the law firm or only to the individual lawyer.

Justice SCALIA delivered the opinion of the Court.

. . . .

But in any event it is not at all clear that respondents' strained interpretation would better achieve the purposes of the Rule. It would, to be sure, better guarantee reimbursement of the innocent party for expenses caused by the Rule 11 violation, since the partnership will normally have more funds than the individual signing attorney. The purpose of the provision in question, however, is not reimbursement but "sanction" and the purpose of Rule 11 as a whole is to bring home to the individual signer his personal, nondelegable responsibility. It is at least arguable that these purposes are better served by a provision which makes clear that, just as the court expects the signer personally—and not some nameless person within his law firm—to validate the truth and legal reasonableness of the papers filed, so also it will visit upon him personally—and not his law firm—its retribution for failing in that responsibility. The message thereby conveyed to the attorney, that this is not a "team effort" but in the last analysis yours alone, is precisely the point of Rule 11. Moreover, psychological effect aside, there will be greater economic deterrence upon the signing attorney, who will know for certain that the district court will impose its sanction entirely upon him, and not divert part of it to a partnership of which he may not (if he is only an associate) be a member, or which (if he is a member) may not choose to seek recompense from him. To be sure, the partnership's knowledge that it was subject to sanction might induce it to increase "internal monitoring," but one can reasonably believe that more will be achieved by directly increasing the incentive of the individual signer to take care. Such a belief is at least not so unthinkable as to compel the conclusion that the Rule does not mean what it most naturally seems to say.

DECISION AND REMEDY The United States Supreme Court found that an attorney, not her or his firm, is liable individually when a groundless action is instituted.

CRITICAL THINKING: ETHICAL CONSIDERATION If Microsoft Corporation is successfully sued, the chief executive officer, would not have to pay the judgment out of his personal funds. The Microsoft Corporation would be liable for the judgment. Should a law firm be treated the same as a corporation? Why should a lawyer be personally liable instead of the law firm?

Lawyers charge fees for their professional services. One common fee arrangement is the contingency fee, which is based generally on a percentage, typically between 20 and 40 percent, of an award granted by a court. This fee arrangement is used in cases such as automobile accidents.

Lawyers and clients can agree to an hourly fee arrangement. When a lawyer charges by the hour, law firms divide the hour into segments. At $200 to $300 per hour, this can add up. Some firms use fifteen-minute segments. Thus, if you consult with your lawyer for ten minutes, you are charged for fifteen.

Lawyers may charge a flat fee. For example, an attorney may charge a flat fee for a simple will.

The American Bar Association drafted a code of ethics for attorneys that is in effect in almost every state. Attorneys must follow the code's standards of professional ethics to be allowed to practice law. Ethics boards, usually an arm of the state's highest court, investigate complaints of alleged attorney misconduct and recommend to the appropriate authorities any corrective action.

LEGAL HIGHLIGHT

Caught Between a Rock and a Hard Place!

Although Richard Morris was licensed to practice law in Arizona and California, his practice was located in San Diego, California. There he had served as a deputy district attorney, as president of the local bar association, and as director of the local chamber of commerce.

One of Morris's clients was James G. Bryan, who owned the United States Tax Planning Service. In April 1982, Bryan sought legal advice from Morris concerning a tax plan. After conducting legal research, Morris advised Bryan that the Internal Revenue Service (IRS) would most likely disallow any deduction taken. Bryan was dissatisfied with Morris's advice and terminated their attorney–client relationship in May 1982.

Five years later, in 1987, a federal grand jury in Texas handed down a forty-page indictment involving twenty-two defendants. Morris was named as an alleged conspirator to defraud the United States by impeding the IRS. The majority of the acts occurred after Bryan had terminated his attorney–client relationship with Morris. The indictment attributed no overt acts of fraud to Morris.

After contacting several defense attorneys, Morris learned that his defense would cost from $60,000 to $100,000 and that the trial would take up to six weeks. Morris could not afford the potential attorney fees, hotel costs, and transportation costs and thought it would be too costly to abandon his practice in California and move to Dallas for the duration of the trial. As a result, Morris and the U.S. government agreed on a plea bargain. Morris pleaded guilty to the

charge that he knew Bryan and others had committed a felony. He was placed on probation for two years. The probation ended eight months early at the request of his probation officer.

Morris then faced having his license to practice law in Arizona suspended because of his guilty plea. The Arizona Bar found that Morris had been caught "between a rock and a hard spot" in choosing whether to reveal communications from his client or to face criminal prosecution. Because Morris had been convicted of a federal felony, however, the bar required some disciplinary action. The Bar suspended his license for six months and ordered him to pay the state bar of Arizona $594.50 for its expenses.[a]

Several mitigating factors persuaded the bar to impose the six months' suspension. Morris had been a member of the Arizona Bar for more than twenty years, had not had any prior disciplinary matters, and he had several letters of recommendation. Furthermore, Morris did not act for a dishonest or selfish motive or desire for pecuniary gain. He had fully cooperated with the IRS investigation and was cooperative throughout the disciplinary proceedings.

The lesson to be learned is that the federal government is cracking down on professionals, such as attorneys and accountants, who have anything to do with clients who cheat the government.

[a] *Matter of Morris*, 793 P.2d 544, 164 Ariz. 391 (Ariz. 1990).

CyberLaw

Internet Ethics

The Association of Ethical Internet Professionals[®34] promotes ethical standards. Its members recognize a moral and ethical obligation to the public, to other members, and to the association itself.

[34] The Association of Ethical Internet Professionals has a web page at <http://www.aeip.com/start.html>.

The members have adopted an ethical code that emphasizes the following:

1. To treat web site visitors with honesty and respect.

2. To not violate the confidential and private information obtained from web site visitors.

3. To properly exercise the authority and privileges provided them by their customers.

4. To protect customers' interests and provide them information needed to make informed decisions.

5. To protect information as private and confidential by providing secure servers for transmission of credit card, social security, and other personal information.

6. To not participate in, link to, or promote so-called "adult" material, exploitation of women, children, racial and ethnic division, or violence or hate groups.

7. To not use any client resources for personal advantage unless prior permission is given, not to take personal advantage of inexperienced customers, and to avoid conflicts of interest.

8. To not misrepresent or withhold facts about business policies, warranties, or quality of service or product.

New potential shoppers on the WWW are skeptical, for good reason, because of the number of scams and ripoffs. Web shoppers need help in discovering and recognizing web sites where they can shop in safety. Several web businesses provide seals of approval for members who agree to act in an ethical manner, such as the InterNET Bureau of Business Ethics[35] and the Better Business Bureau.[36] Others concerned about ethics and the Internet are Computer Professionals for Social Responsibility,[37] Internet Legal Services,[38] a legal site that combines legal ethics and the web, and Better Ethics Online.[39]

---

[35] The InterNET Bureau of Business Ethics is found at <http://www.inetbureau.com/default.htm>.

[36] The Better Business Bureau is at <http://www.bbb.org/>.

[37] The Computer Professionals for Social Responsibility is found at <http://www.cpsr.org/>.

[38] Internet Legal Services is at <http://www.legalethics.com/ethics.law>.

[39] Better Ethics Online is at <http://www.isp.cc/better-ethics-online/index.html>.

International Consideration

Codes and Guidelines that Emphasize Ethical Conduct

The United Nations has drafted a code of conduct to regulate the relations among transnational corporations, multinational corporations, host countries, and home countries. These relationships involve a dynamic combination of economic, political, historical, sociological, and cultural issues. While developing countries seek protection from the predatory business practices of multinational or transnational corporations, the corporations, in turn, seek protection from arbitrary government seizures in developing nations.

The Organization for Economic Cooperation and Development (OECD)[40] was created in 1961 as an intergovernmental institution for Western nations. Its purpose is to achieve the highest sustainable economic growth and employment, to maintain financial stability, and to contribute to the expansion of world trade. The OECD has adopted the Guidelines for Multinational Enterprises,[41] that used as a model by the United Nations. A multinational enterprise is to operate within the general policy objectives of the OECD members and to refrain from interfering with the host country's political activities. Businesses must consider the needs of the developing nation as an important factor when making decisions about investment opportunities that arise.

The transfer of technology from developed nations to developing nations is one example of an ethical issue facing the international community. In the past, large investments that transferred advanced technology to areas where people were impoverished have often failed to assist the host country because the local people did not benefit from the technology. A steel manufacturing plant in Egypt might give jobs to a few thousand people, for example, but the employees would not earn enough to stimulate the country's economy.

Would it not be better to encourage business opportunities that would improve conditions for the general population? Devices such as low-cost water pumps, windmills, solar heaters, and steam-driven turbines would benefit far more people in most developing countries than would factories involving advanced technology.

[40] The web site for the OECD is <http://www.oecd.org/>.

[41] Search for the guidelines at <http://www.oecd.org/search>.

LEGALLY SPEAKING

When Should You Blow the Whistle?

You are employed by a company that processes large amounts of hazardous material. Normally, the company is very careful to dispose of it in accordance with government guidelines.

On several occasions, however, you have observed your immediate superior and other managers getting rid of hazardous material by flushing it down the sewer or by dumping it on the ground in remote areas. These practices are not only illegal, but will result in pollution that may last for hundreds of years.

You are concerned about the environment and about possible civil or criminal liability if you do not inform the appropriate governmental officials. You still need your job, however, to pay the bills. Do you blow the whistle? If you do, the following checklist may provide you with some protection.

✔ Contact an attorney who will contact the appropriate law enforcement authorities on your behalf.

✔ Document illegal activity with a camera if possible. You would need a very small camera, so that the individuals involved do not know you are taking their picture.

✔ Document paperwork by making copies if possible.

✔ Attempt to convince other employees to go with you to the law enforcement officials.

✔ Be prepared for the worst, that is, the loss of your job. You may never find a job in that industry again.

✔ Prepare your family for the loss of your job and the difficulty in finding a new one. Your family should be your best supporters.

Chapter Summary

Ethics is the study of human behavior as it relates to right and wrong conduct. Ethics also is a system of moral standards that serve as guidelines for right behavior.

Two broad philosophies in ethical decision making were discussed. Ethics based on universal duties is deontology. A deontologist applies universal duties without exception to a situation. Ethics based on consequences is utilitarianism, which advocates that people should seek their own happiness in the happiness of others. An act is ethical if it benefits society.

Top management is responsible for embracing and disseminating ethical standards. Any business, when making decisions, must take into consideration various stakeholders, such as the shareholders, employees, its supply chain consisting of customers and suppliers, government, and community.

The legal profession also is responsible for incorporating ethical standards into the practice of law. Legal ethics incorporates the moral and professional duties that lawyers owe to each other, their clients, the courts, and the public. The courts and bar associations increasingly monitor the behavior of lawyers.

When making a business decision, a person should use an ethical decision-making model. One model consists of six steps: facts, stakeholders, values, alternative actions, prioritization, and potential action. Use of these steps helps a person to reach a decision based on ethical thinking rather than by making a rash decision.

 # Using the World Wide Web

A variety of academic and government sites include discussions about ethics on their web pages. Here is a list of a few sites.

Finding the Law on the Web

The American Legal Ethics Library at Cornell University Law School includes legal codes of ethics, court opinions, and other material.
http://www.law.cornell.edu/ethics

The Business Roundtable is an association of CEOs committed to improving public policy.
http://www.brtable.org

The Business for Social Responsibility compiles comprehensive reports on a variety of ethical topics.
http://www.bsr.org

The Center for Applied Ethics provides information on codes of ethics, articles, and links to ethical issues.
http://www.ethics.ubc.ca

Ethics Updates lists extensive links to a wide variety of other web resources.
http://ethics.acusd.edu/index.html

Institute for Business and Professional Ethics, DePaul University, Chicago, Illinois.
http://www.depaul.edu/ethics/

The International Business Ethics Institute's web page increases public awareness of global business ethics issues.
http://www.business-ethics.org

The Legal Ethics web site has links to other web resources and has a section on web ethics.
http://www.legalethics.com

The Novartis Foundation for Sustainable Development's site contains a collection of articles on corporate/business ethics.
http://foundation.novartis.com

Emerging business leaders have a web site at Net Impact.
http://www.net-impact.org/mission.htm

Sites for legal ethics for various government levels.
http://www.legalethics.com/govt.htm

U.S. statutes concerning ethics.
http://www.usoge.gov/

Whistleblower Collection on the U.S. Department of Labor's web site.
http://www.oalj.dol.gov/libwhist.htm

The AFL-CIO has a web site devoted to executive pay.
http://www.aflcio.org/paywatch

The Corporate Governance site provides news, links and a small library.
http://corpgov.net/

Chapter Web Sites

The Better Business Bureau maintains information on advertising and marketplace ethical issues.
http://www.bbb.org

Internal Revenue Service
http://www.irs.gov

Securities Exchange Commission
   http://www.sec.gov
Executives' compensation
   http://www.sec.gov/edaux/ec.htm
False Claims Act
   http://www.law.cornell.edu/uscode/31/ch37.html
Department of Labor's Whistleblower Collection
   http://www.oalj.dol.gov/libwhist.htm
Tobacco BBS (Bulletin Board System)
   http://www.tobacco.org/
Northeastern University, School of Law, Tobacco
   Control Resource Center, Inc. and Tobacco
   Products Liability Project
   http://www.tobacco.neu.edu
Digital Library, University of California, San Francisco,
   Tobacco Control Archives
   http://galen.library.ucsf.edu/tobacco
ExxonMobile Corporation
   http://www.exxonmobil.com/
Union Carbide
   http://www.unioncarbide.com/
The Dow Chemical Company
   http://www.dow.com/homepage/
Coast Guard
   http://www.dot.gov/dotinfo/uscg
International Tanker Owners Pollution Federation
   Limited (ITOPF)
   http://www.itopf.com
Department of Interior
   http://www.doi.gov
Pavelic & LeFlore v. Marvel Entertainment Group
   http://caselaw.findlaw.com/scripts/getcase
   .pl?navby=CASE&court=US&vol=493&page=120

Organization for Economic Cooperation and
   Development (OECD)
   http://www.oecd.org
Guidelines for Multinational Enterprises
   http://www.oecd.org/search
Net Impact
   http://www.net-impact.org/mission.htm
Association of Ethical Internet Professionals
   http://www.aeip.com/start.html
InterNET Bureau of Business Ethics
   http://www.inetbureau.com/default.htm
Computer Professionals for Social Responsibility
   http://www.cpsr.org/
Internet Legal Services
   http://www.legalethics.com/ethics.law
Better Ethics Online
   http://www.isp.cc/better-ethics-online/index.html
Corporate Governance
   http://corpgov.net

Web Activities

2–1 You are active in student activities and have an interest in business ethics. One resource is Net Impact, a site for emerging business leaders. Why does Net Impact exist? What is the mission of Net Impact? Go to <http://www.net-impact.org/mission.htm>.

2–2 News concerning businesses and ethics is fast moving. Go to the Corporate Governance site at <http://corpgov.net/> and prepare a review of two corporations that are in the news for ethics violations. Determine which steps the businesses should have taken to avoid the current situation.

Key Terms

deontology	legal ethics	utilitarianism	whistleblower
False Claims Act	stakeholder		

Questions and Case Problems

2–1 Ethics and Morals Define and distinguish among ethics, morals, and law.

2–2 Ethics To what extent should businesses be concerned with social or ethical goals in comparison with short-term, profit-making goals?

2–3 Ethics To what extent does marketplace competition increase or reduce the need for standards of business ethics?

2–4 Stakeholders Should ethics be solely a concern of top management or should it be a shared concern of all stakeholders?

2–5 Stakeholders Discuss the ethical issues that surface in the following situation. The retailer orders in large volume from a carpet manufacturer and is viewed as a major purchaser. One major expense is transportation of the heavy rolls of carpet. The retailer normally accepts nine out of ten carpet shipments. However, in approximately every tenth shipment, the retailer finds a minor flaw in several rolls of the carpet, such as a slight change in the color dye lot. The carpet could be—and is—sold in the ordinary course of business at full price. The retailer informs the manufacturer that it refuses to accept the shipment and is returning the shipment. The manufacturer is confronted with shouldering shipment costs both ways. The retailer then offers to accept the shipment at a 50 percent discount. The manufacturer agrees in order to keep a good customer and to avoid the transportation expense. The retailer does this with all its suppliers. What ethical issues do these facts present?

2–6 Stakeholders Various retail stores lobby the state legislature to pass a statute that allows retailers to sue in civil court for $500 whenever a person is convicted of shoplifting. The statute is passed. The theory underlying this statute is that a business incurs expenses, such as providing witnesses who are employees, whenever a shoplifter is prosecuted. The goods usually are recovered when the shoplifter is arrested. If a person is convicted of shoplifting but the goods are not recovered, she or he may be ordered by the court to pay restitution for the value of those goods. Once the person is convicted, the retailer can then sue for $500 in civil court. If the shoplifter is unable to pay the $500 but is employed, her or his salary can be garnished until the $500 has been paid. Consider that sometimes shoplifters steal food for themselves or their families. Is it ethical for the retailer, in addition to recovering the goods or their value, to recover an additional $500 in civil court without proof of real expenses? Should the retailer sue every shoplifter for the amount stolen?

2–7 Stakeholders The Roths purchased a 1988 Volkswagen Fox GL from Wheeler Motor Company (Wheeler) on October 2, 1989. The vehicle was the last 1988 model in stock. The Roths purchased the car for $8,000, reduced from the $9,813 sticker price. Although the Roths were the first owners of the vehicle, the car had been test driven 590 miles. The key ring submitted into evidence indicated that the car was "new," as did the sales contract. Within the first two weeks after purchase, the steel belt on the right front tire burst through the tread. A crack was found in the right front fender, the right headlight became loose, the right front suspension made a noise, and the right speaker blew out. Wheeler repaired each problem. These problems persisted throughout the twenty-three months during which the Roths drove the car. Matters came to a head when the Roths took the car to a car wash. Paint came off, revealing a primer that was not a Volkswagen primer. The Roths brought action against Wheeler requesting damages including punitive damages to punish them. The jury awarded $10,000 punitive damages and Wheeler appealed. What was the result and why? [*Wheeler Motor Co., Inc. v. Roth*, 867 S.W.2d 446 (1993)]

2–8 Whistleblower In January 1992, Terry Dysert began working as a one-year contract engineer at Florida Power Corporation's (FPC) Crystal River nuclear power plant. He raised safety and quality concerns about electrical relays that were to be used by FPC at the plant. In July, only six months later, FPC terminated him. Since the nuclear power industry falls under federal regulations, Dysert filed a complaint with the U.S. Department of Labor claiming that he was fired in retaliation for raising safety and quality concerns. Dysert alleged that his firing was a violation of the whistleblower protection provisions of the Energy Reorganization Act, 42 U.S.C. §5851. Under this statute, the Secretary of Labor could find that the employer unlawfully discriminated only if the complainant (Dysert) could demonstrate that his protected activity was a contributing factor in the unfavorable personnel action alleged in the complaint. Dysert lost his case after a two-day hearing in front of a hearing officer for the Department of Labor. He appealed. Did Dysert prevail in his appeal? [*Dysert v. Secretary of Labor*, 105 F.3d 607 (11th Cir. 1997)]

2–9 Stakeholders Audrey E. Vokes, fifty-one years old, was a widow who wanted to become an accomplished dancer. On several occasions, an instructor and other salespeople for Arthur Murray, Inc., told her that she had great dance potential and could reach her goal. In reality, she had difficulty hearing the beat of the music. With continued assurance of her progress, she contracted for more than $31,000 in dance lessons. At one time, she had more than 1,200 unused hours of credit when she was induced to buy an additional 175 hours of instruction at a cost of $4,472.75 to obtain a free trip to Mexico. Eventually, Vokes became disillusioned with her progress and sued Arthur Murray, Inc., for misrepresentation. The trial court dismissed her case because she had failed to state facts that would allow a court to grant her relief. Vokes appealed. Is she entitled to have her day in court? [*Vokes v. Arthur Murray, Inc.*, 212 So.2d 906 (Fla. 1968)]

2–10 Internet Go to the home page of a *Fortune 500* company that has published its code of ethics on the World Wide Web. What ethical concerns does it cover? Is it a detailed document or general in its terms?

Chapter 3

The Judicial System and Litigation

Litigation is a contest authorized by law in a court of justice for the purpose of enforcing a right.

> *Summerour v. Fortson,* 174 Ga. 862, 164 S.E. 809 (1932)

Outline

Ethical Consideration

To Play or Not to Play Hardball

You are the president of ABC Insurance Company, which insures elevator manufacturers and elevator maintenance companies. One of the company's clients is in the business of installing and maintaining elevators across the country. Most elevators have two braking systems, mechanical and electrical. If the primary brake fails, the secondary braking system becomes operative.

As a routine matter, you receive copies of all complaints filed against your insureds. You receive a copy of a complaint filed by a woman seeking unspecified damages for injuries suffered when an elevator fell in an uncontrolled manner from the fourth floor to the second floor, then abruptly stopped. This fall is similar to jumping from the roof of a two-story building. It is obvious that the plaintiff suffered serious injuries. Your insured had the elevators installed when the building was remodeled and hired a company to maintain the elevators in the building where the incident took place.

You call in the chief legal counsel for the insurance company, who has reviewed the complaint. He informs you that engineers hired by his office to investigate the claim have filed a report stating that the elevator was improperly maintained and, as a result of that negligence, the elevator fell. He also tells you that the law office handling the lawsuit for the injured woman is quite small and inexperienced. He suggests assigning a group of attorneys to the case. These attorneys will generate so much legal paperwork that the plaintiff and her attorneys will be overwhelmed. They will be forced to give up or to take a small settlement. If this approach does not work, your counsel will be able to intentionally postpone the trial for several years. This tactic will wear the plaintiff out financially, if not emotionally. It also will deter anyone else from trying to bring a legal action against your client.

Since you believe that the elevator caused the alleged injuries, what course of action should you follow? Use the ethical model presented in Chapter 2 and on the inside front cover to develop your answer.

Introduction

Your online business, Artiste Login Products, Inc., could be involved in a number of different types of lawsuits. The more you understand the legal system, the easier it is to understand the process. Why should a businessperson such as yourself understand the judicial system and the case litigation procedures?

First, everyone needs a basic working knowledge of the court system, at both the state and federal levels. This knowledge leads to a better understanding not only of how the system operates, but also of any flaws that need correction. Second, basic knowledge of trial procedure is necessary to understand trials covered by the media.

Third, as taxpayers, businesspeople have an interest in whether the legal system works as efficiently as possible without sacrificing the protections it should provide. Finally, businesspeople should understand what they will confront when litigation occurs. In our society, most businesspeople will be involved in litigation at some point in their careers.

This chapter looks at both the state and federal court systems. You will follow a sample case through a state trial court. The first question a court determines is whether it has **jurisdiction**, that is, the power to decide a particular case.

Jurisdiction

Juris means "law." *Diction* means to "speak." Thus, "the power to speak the law" is the literal meaning of jurisdiction. Before any court can hear a case legally, it must have jurisdiction. Having jurisdiction means that a court has the power to decide a case. When a court exercises jurisdiction, it does so based on its having power both over the person against whom the suit is brought and over the property or subject matter of the case. Without jurisdiction, a court has no power to act. Any judgment it enters without jurisdiction is null and void.

Proper jurisdiction ensures that a judgment obtained in one state is enforceable in all other states where the defendant may be located or may own property. The **full faith and credit clause** of the U.S. Constitution (Article IV, Section 1) mandates the enforcement of valid judgments made in other states.

Jurisdiction over the Person

To consider a case, a court must have power over the person against whom a suit is brought. A state court's power is limited to the territorial boundaries of the state in which the court is located, whereas a federal court has personal jurisdiction throughout the United States. Jurisdiction over the person is known as *in personam* **jurisdiction** or **personal jurisdiction**.

A court, whether city, county, state, or federal, has personal jurisdiction in the following situations. First, a court has personal jurisdiction over any resident of the judicial district even if he or she is temporarily out of the area on a business trip. Second, a court's jurisdiction also applies to any business within the judicial district, even if the business has its main plant or office elsewhere.

Third, a court has personal jurisdiction over anyone served with a summons in the judicial district, unless that person's presence was obtained by fraudulent means. An example of fraudulent means is seen in this example: A husband and wife plan to divorce. The wife moves to another state. She writes her husband to join her because she wants a reconciliation. He flies to the state where she lives. When he gets off the plane, he is served the divorce papers. Because his presence was obtained by fraudulent means, the court does not have personal jurisdiction over him. The court could grant a divorce because the court has jurisdiction over the marriage and the wife since she lives in that state. The court could not order him to pay spousal support or order property in his name to be divided because the court lacks personal jurisdiction over the husband.

Fourth, the court can exercise jurisdiction over a nonresident person or business by using the **long-arm statute**. This statute allows a court to obtain jurisdiction over a defendant who lives outside the state. If a person or business commits an act or acts within the state, which gives rise to minimum contacts within the state, the court has jurisdiction because the *traditional notions of fair play and substantial justice are not offended* (violated).

The phrase "traditional notions of fair play and substantial justice" is implied in the **due process clause** guaranteed in both the Fifth and Fourteenth Amendments. The phrase means that the person or business has had some contacts, although minimal, within the state. The court has jurisdiction over the person or business if it serves the person or business with the appropriate court papers that provide actual notice of the proceeding and an opportunity to be heard.

When a person is provided with both notice and the opportunity to be heard, the traditional notions of fair play and substantial justice, implicit in the due process clause, are satisfied. As the United States Supreme Court stated, "the defendant's conduct and connection with the forum [place of litigation] State are such that he should reasonably anticipate being hauled into court there." A person cannot bring a legal action in one state, however, if the defendant has never had contact with that state. Two examples follow.

Example 1. A business located out of state sends 100,000 mailers to residents all of whom are located within another state. The business receives more than 5,000 responses to purchase a watch. One customer is dissatisfied and sues the business. The business, after being served the appropriate court papers (usually a summons and complaint), can request that the lawsuit be dismissed because the court does not have jurisdiction over the business. The court finds that the business has committed an act within the state by mailing 100,000 mailers and that these mailers are the minimum contacts within the state. The court can decide it has jurisdiction over the business and the traditional notions of fair play and substantial justice are not offended because the court papers provide the business with the actual notice of the proceeding and an opportunity to be heard.

Example 2. A business's Internet server is located out of state. The business sends 100,000 mailers electronically (e-mails) to residents all of whom are located within another state. Where does a dissatisfied customer sue? Can she sue in the state court if she is dissatisfied with the watch? Does this example have any facts that are really different from the example using the postal system? What if, however, the business, its server, and the watches are all located outside the United States? What if the e-mail was accidentally sent into a state? Do these changes in facts alter whether the court has jurisdiction?

An inescapable fact of modern commercial life is that a substantial amount of business is transacted using the mail, telephone, and the Internet across state, national, and international boundaries; thus, the need for a physical presence no longer exists when business is conducted. The long-arm statutes will become more important in the future.

In all cases in which a court exercises personal jurisdiction, the defendants must be served with actual notice that they are being sued (usually by service of a summons and complaint). If the defendants are from out of state, the summons and complaint may be served either by a person or by certified mail containing the summons and complaint, for which the defendant must sign. Some states, however, are moving away from this rigid system. Today, many states allow the out-of-state defendant to be sent the paperwork by regular mail. This procedure allows the defendant to sign an acceptance of service, thus saving money on fees.

In the following case, the federal district court is confronted with the question of whether the court had subject matter jurisdiction and personal jurisdiction over the defendant. The court discusses the concept of due process of the law when determining the court's jurisdiction.

Case 3.1

Bilger v. Pereira

United States District Court,
Eastern District, Louisiana,
2000
2000 WL 108870

BACKGROUND AND FACTS Plaintiff Bilger claimed that she and defendant Pereira were visiting New Orleans, Louisiana, in an attempt to reconcile their relationship. One evening, while they were exiting the Mona Lisa Restaurant in the Vieux Carre, they began to argue. Plaintiff claimed that when she bent down to retrieve a souvenir that had fallen, defendant threw an unopened bottle of wine to the sidewalk, which shattered and injured plaintiff's wrist and forearm. Bilger went to a hospital and underwent surgery. Afterwards she was given drugs for her pain. In the meantime, Pereira obtained a marriage license. He took Bilger while she was in a drugged state and against her will to the House of Broel, in Metairie, where he "wrongfully" married her.

When Bilger recovered and was able to travel, Pereira took her to Sacramento, California, where he effected a "wrongful arrest" upon her by keeping her drugged and by denying her access to money. Bilger claimed that, during the "arrest," Pereira ridiculed, verbally assaulted, and threatened her. She finally escaped from Pereira when a friend wired her money. Pereira continued to threaten and harass her by repeatedly calling her and sending her e-mails and regular mail, and by hiring a private investigator to track her in Tennessee, where she had resided since March 1999. Bilger claimed that since she extricated herself from the situation, she had repeatedly requested that Pereira return plaintiff's property, which he refused to do.

On November 5, 1999, Bilger instituted legal action in Louisiana against Pereira alleging among other things negligent and intentional acts in violation of Louisiana, California, and Tennessee tort law. She sought compensatory and punitive damages, return of her personal property, injunctive relief, and costs.

Pereira moved to dismiss this case on the grounds that the federal court lacked subject matter jurisdiction, because both plaintiff and defendant were residents of California, and because the court lacked personal jurisdiction over defendant.

Judge VANCE

. . . .

A. Subject Matter Jurisdiction. This Court has federal question jurisdiction over this matter under . . . diversity jurisdiction. Defendant alleges that there is incomplete diversity because both plaintiff and defendant are residents of California, even though plaintiff states in her verified complaint that she is a resident of Tennessee. Defendant claims that although plaintiff has resided in Tennessee since March of 1999, she has failed to meet the six-month residency requirement of Tennessee law, because she traveled to California for a period of twelve days. Defendant has failed to cite any law or evidence to support this allegation, and his argument is meritless. In order for this Court to exercise diversity jurisdiction in this case, plaintiff must be "domiciled" in Tennessee. . . . The Fifth Circuit has stated that "residence in fact and the intention of making the place of residence one's home are essential elements of domicile." Although a plaintiff's statements of intent are entitled to little weight when they conflict with facts, there is no conflict in this case. Plaintiff states in her verified complaint that she resides in Tennessee, and defendant must come forward with more than his bald allegation that plaintiff is not a legal resident (in motion to dismiss for lack of subject matter jurisdiction, court accepts as true all allegations on the face of complaint). The parties agree that plaintiff resides in Tennessee, and there is simply no evidence that she did not intend to remain there when she filed this suit. Thus, this Court has diversity jurisdiction over the case. . . .

B. Personal Jurisdiction. When, as here, a nonresident defendant moves to dismiss for lack of personal jurisdiction, the plaintiff shoulders the burden of establishing jurisdiction over that defendant. Because this Court will rule on the issue without a full evidentiary hearing, the plaintiff need only make a prima facie (show a fact that will presumed to be true unless disproved by contrary evidence) showing of jurisdiction. . . . In determining whether plaintiff has made a prima facie showing of jurisdiction, the Court must accept as true all uncontroverted allegations in plaintiff's complaint, and resolve any factual disputes in her favor.

A court has personal jurisdiction over a nonresident defendant if (1) the forum state's long-arm statute confers personal jurisdiction over that defendant; and (2) the forum state's exercise of such jurisdiction complies with the due process clause of the Fourteenth Amendment. Under the Louisiana long-arm statute, jurisdiction is proper if the cause of action arises out of "injury or damage by an offense or quasi offense committed through an act or omission in this state." In addition, Louisiana's long-arm statute extends jurisdiction to the full limits of due process; thus, the Court must determine whether the exercise of jurisdiction satisfies the due process clause.

1. Due Process. The exercise of personal jurisdiction over a nonresident defendant satisfies due process when (1) the defendant has purposefully availed himself of the benefits and protections of the forum state by establishing "minimum contacts" with that state; and (2) exercising personal jurisdiction over the defendant does not offend "traditional notions of fair play and substantial justice."

(a) Minimum Contacts. The minimum contacts prong of the due process inquiry is satisfied if a court may exercise specific jurisdiction over the defendant. To determine whether specific jurisdiction exists, courts must examine whether the defendant purposefully availed himself of the privileges of conducting activity in the forum state, and whether the cause of action arises out of or relates to those activities. The defendant's connection with the forum state must be such that he "should reasonably anticipate being haled [sic] into court" there. A single act by the defendant directed at the forum state can be enough to confer *in personum* jurisdiction over him, if the cause of action arises out of that act.

In order to determine whether defendant purposefully availed himself of the privilege of conducting activities within this forum, the Court must consider factors such as the quality, nature and extent of defendant's activities in this forum, and the relationship between the cause of action and the contacts.

Here, plaintiff's claims against defendant arise, in part, out of defendant's activities in Louisiana. Plaintiff alleges in her verified complaint that defendant hurled an unopened wine bottle at the sidewalk upon which she was crouched, injuring her wrist and arm, and that following her surgery to deal with these injuries, he married her against her will while she was in a drugged state. Through these allegedly tortious acts, defendant certainly availed himself of the privileges of this state and should have reasonably anticipated being sued here. Thus, plaintiff has satisfied the minimum contacts prong of the due process analysis.

(b) Fair Play and Substantial Justice. In order to determine whether the exercise of personal jurisdiction over a nonresident defendant comports with traditional notions of fair play and substantial justice, this Court must consider the following factors: (1) the burden on the defendant; (2) the forum state's interests; (3) the plaintiff's interest in convenient and effective relief; (4) the judicial system's interest in efficient resolution of controversies; and (5) the state's shared interest in furthering fundamental social policies. Once minimum contacts are satisfied, the defendant must present a compelling case that conducting the litigation in this Court would impose severe hardship on him such that he would be at a considerable disadvantage in comparison to the plaintiff. In this case, defendant has failed to do so.

Pereira claims that he has very little money and will soon be unemployed and that the travel and lodging expenses of witnesses residing outside Louisiana would unduly burden him. By contrast, plaintiff states in her verified complaint that defendant has considerable resources. As stated above, this Court must resolve all factual disputes in plaintiff's favor. In any event, some of the witnesses involved in the case reside in Louisiana and, possibly, Tennessee, so that defendant would have to deal with the expense of deposing out-of-state witnesses even if the case were in California. Thus, this Court does not find that conducting the litigation in Louisiana overly burdens defendant. As to the second factor, the forum state clearly has an interest in trying the dispute that partially arose out of tortious activity within the state. Further, the plaintiff has submitted to jurisdiction in this state, and has an interest in convenient and effective resolution of this dispute. A substantial part of her claims against Pereira occurred in Louisiana, and many of the sources of proof are in this state, including her treating physician and other health care professionals who saw her when she received medical care at Tulane Medical Center, her medical records, the officer who married the parties and the marriage records. These factors also satisfy the judicial interest in convenient and effective relief in resolving this dispute in Louisiana. Finally, the state has a shared interest in discouraging violent and abusive acts toward other persons, and, in particular, women. Thus, the second prong of the due process analysis is satisfied, and the exercise of personal jurisdiction over defendant in Louisiana comports with traditional notions of fair play and substantial justice.

Because this Court finds that it has subject matter jurisdiction over this case, and that it may exercise specific jurisdiction over defendant, defendant's motion to dismiss must be denied.

DECISION AND REMEDY   Federal courts do not have jurisdiction over the marriage, only state courts have that jurisdiction. Although this federal court could not grant a divorce, it could consider the civil torts of fraud and assault once it found it had jurisdiction over the defendant.

CRITICAL THINKING: PUBLIC POLICY   What are the elements of jurisdiction?

Jurisdiction over Property

In *Shaffer v. Heitner,*[1] the United States Supreme Court distinguished between *in personam* and **in rem jurisdiction** or **quasi in rem jurisdiction**. When a court's jurisdiction is based on its authority over the defendant's person, the action and judgment are called *in personam* jurisdiction. With this kind of jurisdiction, a court can impose a personal obligation on the defendant in favor of the plaintiff.

If jurisdiction is based on the court's power over property located within its territory, the action is called *in rem* or *quasi in rem* jurisdiction. The effect of a judgment in such a case is limited to the property that supports the jurisdiction. No personal liability can be imposed on the property owner, because she does not fall under the court's jurisdiction.

A judgment *in rem* affects the interests of all persons in the designated property. A judgment *quasi in rem* affects the interests of particular persons in the property. For example, before a person purchases property that the government sells for unpaid taxes, the purchaser wants to be certain that no one else has an interest in the property. She can determine the property's previous owners through public records, which contain addresses that were valid at the time the entries were made. These addresses, however, may be out of date when the records are searched years later.

These previous owners are specific persons whose current whereabouts may be unknown. They might be deceased and their heirs may have a claim to the property. The new owner would file a suit to clear title to the property. The court has *quasi in rem* jurisdiction over the specified persons, the prior owners. As to the unknown heirs, the court has *in rem* jurisdiction. In either case, when the person's whereabouts are unknown, the jurisdiction is obtained by publishing appropriate notices in a newspaper of general circulation in the county where the property is located.

Subject Matter Jurisdiction

Subject matter jurisdiction imposes a limitation on the types of cases that a court can hear. The limitation is set by the constitution or statute creating the court.

[1] 433 U.S. 186, 97 S. Ct. 2569, 53 L. Ed. 2d 683 (1977).

A court's subject matter jurisdiction can be limited not only by the subject of the lawsuit, but also by the monetary amount in controversy, by the type of criminal case, or by whether the proceeding is a trial or an appeal. Probate courts (which handle only matters relating to wills and estates) and small-claims courts (which handle cases involving small amounts of money) are examples of courts with limited subject matter jurisdiction.

Venue

Jurisdiction is concerned with determining a court's authority over a specific subject matter or individual. **Venue** is concerned with the particular geographic area within a judicial district where a suit should be brought. The concept of venue reflects the policy of convenience. A trial court should be in the geographic neighborhood where the incident leading to the suit occurred or where the parties involved in the suit reside. Pretrial publicity or other factors may require a change of venue, that is, moving the trial to another community. A change of venue is used frequently in criminal cases if the defendant's right to a fair and impartial jury appears to be impaired within the current trial location.

CyberLaw

Cyber Jurisdiction

The Internet creates problems for the courts concerning jurisdiction over the parties. A business that has a web site reaches the entire world twenty-four hours a day. What happens if dissatisfied customers residing in China, Italy, or Russia decide to institute legal action in their respective countries? Does a business operating out of New York have to defend itself in a courtroom in another country that operates under a different legal system and is located thousands of miles away? A foreign country may have jurisdiction to hear the case. But is it reasonable to expect to be sued in another state's court located hundreds or thousands of miles away from the business or in a foreign country if the business does not have a physical location or operations there? The following case discusses this issue.

Case 3.2

Online Partners.Com Inc. v. Atlanticnet Media Corporation

United States District Court,
N.D. California, 2000
2000 WL 101242

BACKGROUND AND FACTS Plaintiff, Online Partners.Com Inc., filed this action claiming trademark infringement, unfair competition, dilution, and constructive trust under the Trademark Act of 1946. The defendant, Atlanticnet Media Corporation, was validly served with the summons and complaint but the defendant did not respond to the complaint and summons and, in accordance with the federal rules, a default judgment was entered against defendant.

The basis of the plaintiff's complaint was that the defendant used a web address exactly like the plaintiff's except it was in lowercase letters. The plaintiff's address appeared in all capital letters. Because the complaint requested an injunction be issued against the defendant, the court conducted a hearing. The court discussed its jurisdiction when the Internet was involved.

ILLSTON, J.

. . . .

Jurisdiction and Venue. California construes its long-arm statute to allow personal jurisdiction over a nonresident litigant to the maximum extent allowed by the federal constitution.

. . . .

Plaintiff has shown that defendant's Internet Web site is active, as opposed to passive, and actively solicits membership in a subscription service whereby members fill out a form, and provide a payment, by a credit card, to plaintiff or its designated agent or subscription service. Plaintiff has shown at least one member in this District who subscribed to the subscription service being offered by or through defendant under the domain name. . . .

This Court has personal jurisdiction over defendant because: a) defendant engaged in conduct that was intended to and did result in harmful effects to plaintiff, and plaintiff's . . . trademark in the United States, including California; and b) defendant has solicited business and made sales and has at least one subscriber in California, and defendant may be a cybersquatter, having registered the trademark of plaintiff in this district. . . .

. . . .

Internet jurisdiction cases have looked at the active nature of a defendant's Web site to find jurisdiction. For example, Internet cases have found purposeful availment by examining the "level of interactivity and commercial nature of the exchange of information that occurs on the website." *Zippo Mfg. Co. v. Zippo Dot Com, Inc.* (nonresident defendant's interactive Web site actively engaged in business with many forum residents constitutes purposeful availment). *Cybersell, Inc. v. Cybersell, Inc.* (following the rationale of *Zippo,* court held nonresident defendant's passive noninteractive Web site not constituting purposeful availment); *Inset Systems, Inc. v. Instruction Set, Inc.* (finding personal jurisdiction where nonresident defendant's Web site solicits business in the forum state); *Maritz, Inc. v. Cybergold, Inc.* (personal jurisdiction supported where nonresident defendant's interactive Web site was used by forum residents and generated business leads). *Panavision Int'l, L.P. v. Toeppen.* (Where a defendant operates a Web site that advertises and solicits business for defendant, provides an e-mail address for state residents to contact defendant, and provides a product order form, courts have found personal jurisdiction to exist in the forum state.)

. . . Similarly, here, where defendant operates a Web site that advertises defendant's services, and that offers and provides a subscription service accessible to, and joined by, California residents, personal jurisdiction is proper over defendant in California.

Here, defendant's Web site is not only an active subscription service, but plaintiff has shown that defendant's Web site would have, by its content, been directed at least in part to the population of this District, and plaintiff has provided evidence of membership by a resident of this District. This, together with defendant's having admitted the well-pleaded allegations of plaintiff's complaint, provides a basis for jurisdiction here.

Accordingly, this Court has subject matter jurisdiction over this action, and has supplemental jurisdiction under 28 U.S.C. § 1367(a) over plaintiff's claims under California law.

. . . .

DECISION AND REMEDY The court distinguished between interactive and noninteractive (passive) web sites. It was found that this web site was interactive because of the similarity between the names and that business was solicited by the site.

CRITICAL THINKING: PUBLIC POLICY Assuming there is personal service on a defendant, should there be limits placed on bringing an action in any state or country where a dispute occurs when a business sells on the Internet?

Res Judicata

Once a case has been fully litigated, neither party may institute another action based on the same facts or circumstances. This rule is known as the doctrine of **res judicata**. A final judgment on the merits by a court of competent jurisdiction is conclusive as to the rights of the parties. A settlement of a dispute within the court system, such as judicial arbitration, is treated as a final judgment or decree. Although not technically correct, some courts use the term *res adjudicata* to mean the same thing.

Court Systems in the United States

Today, in the United States, at least fifty-two separate court systems function. Each of the fifty states, the District of Columbia, and the federal government have their own fully developed and independent court systems.

The federal court system is authorized by Article III, Section 1, of the U.S. Constitution. The federal courts are not superior to the state courts; they are simply an independent system. The United States Supreme Court is the final controlling voice over all the court systems when questions arise concerning the U.S. Constitution, federal statutes and regulations, or treaties.

A Typical State Court System

Most court systems, including the federal system, are based on a three-tiered model. On the lowest tier is the trial court, which determines both questions of facts and questions of law. A jury (if no jury, the judge) determines the questions of facts and is called the trier of fact. In most jurisdictions, only the judge determines questions of law.

It is possible for both parties to appeal a judgment. The losing party in the trial court has the legal right to appeal the case to an appellate court. The prevailing party may also appeal, if all requested relief were not granted. These courts review the decisions of the lower courts generally on points of law, but if the fact finding were clearly in error, the court's judgment could be challenged and the case could be remanded (sent back to the court that originally heard the case) for further findings of fact. The losing party to a decision by an appellate court may appeal to the state supreme court located on the top tier. If a federal issue is involved in the decision of the state supreme court, that decision may be reviewed in the United States Supreme Court.

Exhibit 3–1 depicts the levels of a typical state court system. It has three main tiers: (1) the trial court of either general or limited jurisdiction, (2) the appellate court, and (3) the supreme court. The flow of appeal cases from the lower courts to the higher courts varies from state to state.[2]

General and Limited Jurisdiction Trial Courts.

Trial courts that have **general jurisdiction** can hear cases on a variety of subject matters. Other trial courts have **limited jurisdiction** and can hear only cases on a specific subject matter. For example, a probate court, family court, criminal court, municipal court, or small-claims court cannot hear cases that go beyond its stated jurisdiction. A criminal court can hear only criminal cases. The judge has no authority to make decisions in a divorce case, which must be heard by a family court. Trial courts have **original jurisdiction**, that is, cases first come before a trial court to be resolved.

Each state's constitution and statutes determine how a court system will work in that particular state. Trial courts are called by many names, such as county, district, superior, or circuit courts. For example, in Ohio the trial

court is called the court of common pleas, whereas in New York the trial court is called the supreme court.

Appellate Courts.

In some states, trial courts of general jurisdiction also have limited jurisdiction to hear appeals from the lower judiciary, such as small-claims courts or traffic courts. Generally, the term *appellate court* refers to the higher reviewing courts and not to trial courts.

Appellate courts also are called **courts of appeal** or courts of review. Every state has at least one appellate court. Many states have multiple intermediate reviewing courts and one supreme court. Often the intermediate reviewing court is called the court of appeals, and the highest court of the state is called the supreme court. New York and Maryland, however, call their highest courts, the court of appeals.

The appellate court has **appellate jurisdiction**; that is, the court hears appeals only on issues of law and does not retry the facts of the cases that it reviews. The justices examine the written record of the case on appeal to determine if the trial court committed an error of law. The appellate courts look at questions of law and procedure, not questions of fact. The only time an appellate court disagrees with a trial court's findings of fact is when the finding is clearly erroneous, such as when it is contrary to the evidence presented at trial or when no evidence supports the finding. Otherwise, all questions of fact remain within the trial court's jurisdiction.

---

[2] You can find information about specific state courts by going to <http://www.ncsc.dni.us/>. Another excellent site for information about all state courts is <http://www.courts.net/>.

Exhibit 3–1 Hypothetical State Court System

LEGAL HIGHLIGHT

Using a Small-Claims Court

Disputes often occur over small sums of money. For example, your former roommate owes you for last month's rent or for a telephone bill. To hire the services of a lawyer is expensive and not practical for such a small sum. States have small-claims courts that handle such claims in an expeditious manner.

You can sue your former roommate by filing a complaint in small-claims court. Normally the service of the summons and complaint is completed by sending them to the defendant using certified mail. The mailing of the documents eliminates the expense of paying a person to personally serve the summons and complaint on your roommate.

Your roommate, as the defendant, must file a writ-ten answer to your complaint with the court. If your roommate fails to respond to your lawsuit, you can obtain a default judgment.

If your roommate files an answer, the case proceeds to trial before a judge. In some small-claims courts, a jury is not allowed, nor are lawyers allowed to represent either party. Usually the hearing is very informal, with each party presenting her side of the case. The judge decides the case based on the facts as determined by the judge. Most decisions by small-claims courts cannot be appealed to a higher court. Small-claims courts provide a quick and inexpensive way to resolve minor disputes involving money damages.

In all questions of state law, the decisions of each state's highest court are final. When issues of the federal Constitution, treaties, or laws are involved, the decision by the state's highest court is subject to review by the United States Supreme Court.

The Federal Court System

The federal court system is similar in many ways to most state court systems. Also three tiered, it consists of (1) trial courts, (2) intermediate courts of appeal, and (3) the Supreme Court. The federal government also has special courts. Exhibit 3–2 shows the organization of the federal court system in some detail.

Article III of the U.S. Constitution establishes the one Supreme Court. Congress is empowered to create any other inferior courts that it deems necessary. Inferior courts include the U.S. courts of appeal; the district courts; and the other courts of limited, or specialized, jurisdiction.

District Courts. At the federal level, the trial court of general jurisdiction is the district court. Every state has at least one federal district court within its borders. Congress has divided the states and territories into ninety-four federal judicial districts. The number of ju-dicial districts varies over time primarily because of population changes and corresponding caseloads.

Most federal cases originate in the U.S. district courts. Whenever two or more district courts are within a single state, each court is limited to its geographic boundaries. The state of Florida, for example, has courts for northern, middle, and southern districts. Thus, a case that arises in the southern Florida district cannot be tried by a court in the northern district, unless a motion for a change of venue has been granted. A **motion** is an application made to the judge by a party to the lawsuit seeking relief for a wrong committed or asserting a procedural right. If the motion is granted, the judge issues an order to grant the relief sought. If the motion is denied, the relief is not granted.

U.S. district courts have original jurisdiction in federal matters; that is, federal cases start in the district courts. Other trial courts with original, limited jurisdiction include the U.S. Tax Court, the U.S. Bankruptcy Court, and the U.S. Claims Court, the court that hears claims against the United States on federal contracts. Certain administrative agencies and departments with quasi-judicial power also have original jurisdiction. These agencies and departments are listed in Exhibit 3–2.

Exhibit 3–2   Organization of the Federal Court System

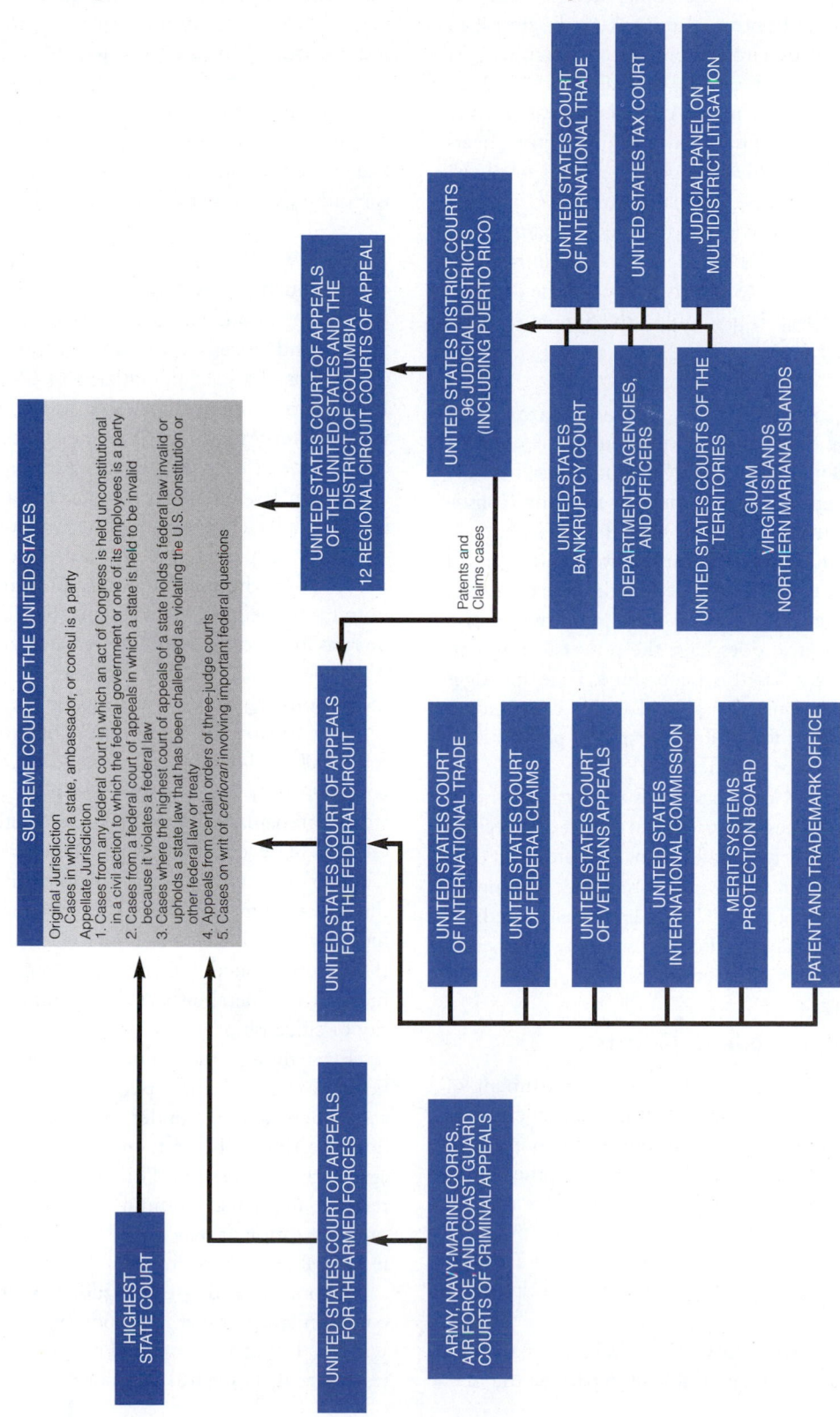

SUPREME COURT OF THE UNITED STATES

Original Jurisdiction
Cases in which a state, ambassador, or consul is a party
Appellate Jurisdiction
1. Cases from any federal court in which an act of Congress is held unconstitutional in a civil action to which the federal government or one of its employees is a party
2. Cases from a federal court of appeals in which a state is held to be invalid because it violates a federal law
3. Cases where the highest court of appeals of a state holds a federal law invalid or upholds a state law that has been challenged as violating the U.S. Constitution or other federal law or treaty
4. Appeals from certain orders of three-judge courts
5. Cases on writ of *certiorari* involving important federal questions

UNITED STATES COURT OF APPEALS OF THE UNITED STATES AND THE DISTRICT OF COLUMBIA
12 REGIONAL CIRCUIT COURTS OF APPEAL

UNITED STATES DISTRICT COURTS
96 JUDICIAL DISTRICTS
(INCLUDING PUERTO RICO)

UNITED STATES COURT OF INTERNATIONAL TRADE

UNITED STATES TAX COURT

JUDICIAL PANEL ON MULTIDISTRICT LITIGATION

UNITED STATES BANKRUPTCY COURT

DEPARTMENTS, AGENCIES, AND OFFICERS

UNITED STATES COURTS OF THE TERRITORIES
GUAM
VIRGIN ISLANDS
NORTHERN MARIANA ISLANDS

Patents and Claims cases

UNITED STATES COURT OF APPEALS FOR THE FEDERAL CIRCUIT

UNITED STATES COURT OF INTERNATIONAL TRADE

UNITED STATES COURT OF FEDERAL CLAIMS

UNITED STATES COURT OF VETERANS APPEALS

UNITED STATES INTERNATIONAL COMMISSION

MERIT SYSTEMS PROTECTION BOARD

PATENT AND TRADEMARK OFFICE

HIGHEST STATE COURT

UNITED STATES COURT OF APPEALS FOR THE ARMED FORCES

ARMY, NAVY-MARINE CORPS... AIR FORCE, AND COAST GUARD COURTS OF CRIMINAL APPEALS

Courts of Appeal. Congress has established twelve judicial circuits (regions), including the D.C. Circuit. The courts located within a judicial circuit are called courts of appeal or circuit courts. Each circuit court hears only appeals from the district courts located within its respective circuit. A thirteenth circuit, the Federal Circuit, which has a national jurisdiction, hears only cases in which the U.S. government is involved. Exhibit 3–3 shows these judicial circuits.

Appeals from decisions made by federal administrative agencies, such as the Federal Trade Commission, also are heard by the U.S. courts of appeal. The decision of a court of appeals is final unless the Supreme Court accepts the case.

Supreme Court of the United States. The highest level of the federal court system is the Supreme Court of the United States. The Supreme Court has nine justices. Although this number is not set by the Constitution, it has remained constant since the Civil War.

All federal judges are appointed by the president of the United States and confirmed by the Senate. Under Article III, they "hold their Offices during Good Behavior." Congress does have the power to impeach judges, but rarely has this been done. Federal judges (with few exceptions, such as bankruptcy court judges who are appointed for a fifteen-year time period) hold virtually lifetime appointments.

The Supreme Court has original, or trial, jurisdiction in rare instances as set forth in Article III, Section 2. Most of the time, it operates as an appellate court. The Supreme Court can review any case decided by any of the federal courts of appeal. It also has appellate authority over cases decided in the state supreme courts that involve the federal Constitution, treaties, or laws.

Jurisdiction of Federal Courts

Because the federal government is a government of limited powers, the jurisdiction of the federal courts is limited. Although the Constitution sets the outer limits of federal judicial power, Congress sets other limits on federal jurisdiction. The courts themselves also can establish rules that limit their jurisdiction over the types of cases that have certain characteristics. The following subsections examine these characteristics.

Federal Question Lawsuits. Whenever a plaintiff's cause of action is based, at least in part, on the U.S. Constitution, a treaty, or a federal law, a federal question arises. A case with a legal question that involves the federal Constitution, treaty or statute is called a **federal question case**. The federal courts have jurisdiction over such cases. Some lawsuits involving a federal question must originate in a federal court. For example, all bankruptcy cases must be brought in federal court. No minimum dollar amount in controversy is required when a case involves a federal question.

Diversity of Citizenship Lawsuits. **Diversity of citizenship cases** involve controversies between (1) citizens of different states, (2) a foreign country as plaintiff and citizens of the same or different states, and (3) citizens of a state and citizens of a foreign country. In diversity of citizenship cases, however, the amount in controversy must be $75,000 or more before a federal court can have jurisdiction. Although diversity of citizenship lawsuits need not involve a federal question, the federal courts cannot hear matters that are exclusively a state matter, such as a divorce.

Consider the following example. Smith is driving from his home state, New York, to Florida. In Georgia, he runs into a car owned by Able, a citizen of Georgia. Able's new Mercedes is demolished and, as a result of the personal injuries she sustained in the accident, Able is unable to work for six months. The property damage is $85,000, and her loss of income for the six months is $35,000; thus, this case involves more than $75,000 worth of damages. Able can sue Smith either in a Georgia state court or in the federal district court. Georgia has *in personam* jurisdiction over Smith through its long-arm statute. By driving on Georgia's highways, Smith has consented to Georgia jurisdiction. If Smith were sued in Georgia, he can have the suit removed to a federal district court on the basis of diversity of citizenship.

Even though most automobile accident cases are litigated in state courts, two reasons exist to take any case to federal court under the diversity of citizenship doctrine. First, the state courts may be prejudiced against the nonresident. This factor may be particularly relevant in smaller communities. Second, depending on the location, it may be faster to have the case heard in federal district court.

At one time, the federal judiciary created its own common law. At times, this body of law would conflict with the law that was applied by a state court. The end result was that you had two court systems in the same

Exhibit 3–3   ## Geographical Boundaries of U.S. Courts of Appeal and U.S. District Courts

Number and composition of circuits set forth by 28 U.S.C. §41.

state that were at times applying different law. This result caused litigants to look for a court that had law upholding their position so they could file their action in that particular, favorable court. This practice continued until the following landmark case declared that a federal court must apply the state's law when confronted with a factual situation not involving a federal question based on the federal constitution, statutes, and regulations.

Case 3.3

Erie R. Co. v. Tompkins

Supreme Court of the
United States, 1938
304 U.S. 64, 58 S. Ct. 817,
82 L. Ed. 1188
http://caselaw.findlaw.com/
http://www2.law.cornell
.edu/

LANDMARK CASE

BACKGROUND AND FACTS On a dark night Tompkins, a citizen of Pennsylvania, while walking along the railroad's right of way (located in Pennsylvania) was injured by a passing freight train owned by the Erie Railroad Company. He claimed that the accident occurred through negligence of the railroad. He brought an action in the federal court for Southern New York, which had jurisdiction because the company was a corporation formed in New York. Erie Railroad denied liability. The case went to trial where it was heard by a jury.

The question was which law would apply in this case, state or federal law? If the law of Pennsylvania applied, Tompkins would be denied recovery because he was a trespasser. Under federal law, Tompkins could recover because the federal law looked to the railroad's willful and wanton actions in injuring Tompkins and not to whether Tompkins was a trespasser. The federal trial court applied federal law. The court found for Tompkins and awarded him $30,000. This judgment was upheld by the Circuit Court of Appeals. The railroad appealed and the U.S. Supreme Court accepted jurisdiction.

Justice BRANDEIS delivered the opinion of the Court.

. . . .

First. *Swift v. Tyson,* held that federal courts exercising jurisdiction on the ground of diversity of citizenship need not, in matters of general jurisprudence, apply the unwritten law of the state as declared by its highest court; that they are free to exercise an independent judgment as to what the common law of the state is—or should be.

. . . .

Second. Experience in applying the doctrine of *Swift v. Tyson,* had revealed its defects, political and social; and the benefits expected to flow from the rule did not accrue. Persistence of state courts in their own opinions on questions of common law prevented uniformity; and the impossibility of discovering a satisfactory line of demarcation between the province of general law and that of local law developed a new well of uncertainties.

. . . .

The injustice and confusion incident to the doctrine of *Swift v. Tyson* have been repeatedly urged as reasons for abolishing or limiting diversity of citizenship jurisdiction. Other legislative relief has been proposed. If only a question of statutory construction were involved, we should not be prepared to abandon a doctrine so widely applied throughout nearly a century. But the unconstitutionality of the course pursued has now been made clear, and compels us to do so.

. . . .

Third. Except in matters governed by the Federal Constitution or by acts of Congress, the law to be applied in any case is the law of the state. And whether the law of the state shall be declared by its Legislature in a statute or by its highest court in a decision is not a matter of federal concern. There is no federal general common law. Congress has no power to declare substantive rules of common law applicable in a state whether they be local in their nature or 'general,' be they commercial law or a part of the law of torts. And no clause in the Constitution purports to confer such a power upon the federal courts. . . . .

DECISION AND REMEDY The railroad contended that under the common law of Pennsylvania, the only duty owed to the plaintiff was to refrain from willful or wanton injury. In support of their respective contentions, the parties cited decisions of the Pennsylvania Supreme Court. The case was returned to the trial court to determine what the law of Pennsylvania was at the time of the accident.

CRITICAL THINKING: ETHICS Should there be just one body of law for the entire United States?

Concurrent versus Exclusive Jurisdiction

Concurrent jurisdiction exists when both federal and state courts have the power to hear a case (such as in diversity of citizenship cases). When the subject matter of a case can be tried only in federal or only in state courts, there is **exclusive jurisdiction**. Federal courts have exclusive jurisdiction in cases involving federal crimes, bankruptcy, patents, copyrights, and lawsuits against the United States. States have exclusive jurisdiction in other types of legal matters, such as divorce, probate, and adoption cases.

Writ of *Certiorari*

The United States Supreme Court has appellate jurisdiction over cases involving a federal question, including the Constitution, "with such Exceptions, and under such Regulations as the Congress shall make" (Article III, Section 2, of the U.S. Constitution). Thousands of cases are filed with the Supreme Court each year, but it accepts and decides an average of only sixty to eighty cases annually.

Civil cases reach the Supreme Court when a party requests the Court to issue a **writ of *certiorari***. If the Court issues the writ, the case will be reviewed, but issuance of the writ is entirely at the Court's discretion. No set circumstance requires the court to issue a writ of *certiorari*.

When a writ of *certiorari* is issued, the Supreme Court orders a lower court to send the record of the case to it for review. The Court is more inclined to issue a writ in the following situations:

- When a state supreme court decides a substantial federal question that has not been decided by the Supreme Court.
- When two federal courts of appeal disagree.
- When a federal court of appeals decides an important federal question not yet addressed by the Supreme Court or has departed from the accepted and usual course of judicial proceedings.
- When a federal court of appeals holds a state statute invalid because it violates federal law.
- When a federal court holds an act of Congress unconstitutional and the federal government or one of its employees is a party.

The Supreme Court denies most petitions for writs of *certiorari*. A denial is not a decision on the merits of a case, nor does it indicate agreement with the lower court's opinion. Denial of the writ has no value as precedent. The Court will not issue a writ unless at least four justices approve it. Typically, only petitions for cases that may raise important constitutional questions are granted writs of *certiorari*.

Judicial Procedures: Following a Case through the Courts

American courts use the **adversary system** of justice where the judge acts as the decision maker between the opposing sides, the plaintiff and the defendant, at trial. Ideally, the judge plays an unbiased and mostly

LEGAL HIGHLIGHT

The Virtual Courtroom

The judiciary is often viewed as stodgy and lagging behind new technology by using procedures that date back to previous centuries. The motto seems to be "We have always done it that way, why change it?"

But change is coming to the judicial system. Transformations can be seen on television when a high profile case is being tried. Started in 1991, Court TV[a] broadcasts interesting court cases over cable and satellite. Court TV is owned by Liberty Programming Corporation, National Broadcasting Corporation, and AOL Time Warner, Inc. The programming is determined by "how important and interesting the issues in the case are; the newsworthiness of the case and the people involved; the quality and educational value of the trial; and the expected length of the trial."[b]

Standing contrary to the trend of television cameras in the courtroom are the U.S. Supreme Court and most federal courts. One strong exception exists at the federal level. The U.S. Court of Appeals for the Armed Forces[c] has invited cameras into its courtroom. Oral arguments before this court can be seen on C-SPAN.

The U.S. Supreme Court for the first time allowed audio tapes of oral argument to be released immediately because of the great national interest in the Election 2000 cases of *Bush v. Palm Beach County Canvassing Board*[d] and *Bush v. Gore*.[e] The normal procedure is to release the tapes after several months to the National Archives and Record Administration.

Today, in a trial courtroom a court reporter transcribes everything that is said in real time so the transcription can be viewed on a screen for the jury and the public to read. A monitor may be available for each member of the jury. In some states, all proceedings are video recorded, which removes the requirement of having a court reporter.

One problem that occurs during a trial involves written documents. A witness will be called to the stand. He will be handed a document and the attorney will have the witness testify about the document. The jury, however, does not know what the document contains until it is admitted into evidence by the judge. After the document is admitted into evidence, it is then circulated among the members of the jury. This passing of the document from one member to another is normally done while another witness is testifying. The document being passed from one to another causes the members of the jury either to not listen to the testimony or to ignore the document.

Today, many courtrooms have an electronic podium that includes a camera that sends a photocopy of the document to a computer and in turn back to the monitor directly in front of each juror. When this system is available, the jury member may see the document while testimony is given about it.

Another innovation is in the soliciting of evidence from a witness at a crime lab or another place instead of listening to the expert on the witness stand. A camera is taken into a crime lab where jurors can see how a DNA analysis or a blood alcohol test is conducted. This form of videoconferencing alleviates the need for the expert to appear in court, which really means sitting in the hall outside the courtroom or in a separate witness room. A witness may sit outside and not be called to the witness chair for many hours, if not days. Now the witness can continue working, but remains available for testifying. Instead of requiring a person to come to court (and often waste long periods of time), the courtroom is now going to the witness.

One advantage of videotaping is that attorneys to obtain a copy of the trial videotape to review before the next day. In the past it was possible to obtain a copy of the transcript by the next day, but this was very expensive. It meant that a court reporter would have to work additional hours to get it prepared for use the next day. This inconvenience is no longer necessary.

Money and time are also saved when people accused of crimes are arraigned in jail. In the past, those in jail had to be transported to and from the courthouse. This travel was not only costly, but the danger of escape was always present. Today, a room in the jail building can be set up for videoconferencing; the accused remains in jail while the judge is located in the courthouse miles away.

Innovation, new technologies, and imagination are bringing the stodgy courtrooms to life. The virtual courtroom is ready for the twenty-first century.

[a] Court TV can be found through cable and satellite listings. The web page is <http://courttv.com>.

[b] See <http://courttv.com/about>.

[c] The web site for the U.S. Court of Appeals for the Armed Forces is <http://www.armfor.uscourts.gov/>.

[d] *Bush v. Palm Beach County Canvassing Board*, 531 U.S. ___, 121 S. Ct. 471, 148 L. Ed.2d 366 (2000).

[e] *Bush v. Gore*, 531 U.S. 98, 121 S. Ct. 525, 148 L. Ed.2d 388 (2000).

passive role. Each party's lawyer functions as the client's advocate, presenting the client's version of the facts in an attempt to convince the judge, the jury, or both that the client's version is true.

Judges need not be entirely passive. They are responsible for the appropriate application of the law and do not have to accept the attorneys' legal reasoning. Instead, they can base a ruling on their own study of the law. Additionally, if a defendant chooses to act as his own counsel, the judge will often play more of an advocate role, intervening during the trial to assist the defendant and to preserve the record of the proceedings.

Procedure

Procedure involves the way that disputes are handled in the courts. Procedural law establishes the rules and standards for resolving disputes. The rules are complex and vary from court to court. The federal court system has rules of procedure that may differ from those of the various state court systems. In addition, rules of procedure differ between criminal and civil cases.

A SAMPLE CASE

Artiste Login Products, Inc. v. Acme Copiers, Inc.

Our sample case involves a dispute between Artiste Login Products, Inc. (Artiste) and Acme Copiers, Inc. (Copiers). Paul L. Lakin, has been named to represent Artiste.

Artiste has conducted business with Copiers for several years. Copiers alleges that it sold Artiste a copy machine and that Artiste has failed to pay the money owed on the contract. Artiste and Copiers are unable to agree on a settlement out of court or through any alternative dispute resolution methods, which are discussed in Chapter 4.

Copiers files a lawsuit against Artiste in state court. Normally the paperwork is physically delivered to the clerk of the court either in person, by messenger, or by mail. Many courts allow electronic filing, file transfers through the Internet, or in some instances via CD-ROM using an Internet browser interface. Because Copiers filed the suit, Copiers is the plaintiff and Artiste is the defendant. Lawyers represent each party.

Pleadings and Process. A **pleading** is a document written by one of the parties to the lawsuit and sent to the other party (or parties) and to the court so it can be included in the judge's case file, which is a public record. The purpose of a pleading is to provide information to the other party, to seek information from the other party, or to seek a judicial ruling. Any person who is a party to a lawsuit typically has the opportunity to **plead** (present) his case before a trial court. The following are the more well-known pleadings:

- Complaint or petition
- Answer or response
- Counterclaim
- Reply to counterclaim
- Cross-claim
- Answer to cross-claim
- Third-party complaint
- Third-party answer

We briefly examine each of these types of pleadings. Some of these pleadings are discussed in more detail later in this section. A **complaint** is filed by the plaintiff and sets out the legal and factual basis for the suit. For some types of legal action, the plaintiff files a **petition**. For example, in some states, a person who is seeking a divorce files a petition instead of a complaint. A statute or the court rules determine the name of the pleading to be filed in the court.

If the defendant is served with a complaint, he will file an **answer** to the complaint that sets out the defendant's position on the lawsuit. If a *petition* were filed, the defendant files a *response* to the petition.

A **counterclaim** is essentially another lawsuit filed within the original lawsuit by the defendant seeking damages against the plaintiff. For example, Geoffrey sues for injuries received when Sean's automobile ran a red light and crashed into Geoffrey's automobile. Sean files a counterclaim against Geoffrey because Geoffrey allegedly attacked Sean with a tire iron after the accident. Since a counterclaim, in effect, is a lawsuit, the plaintiff must file a **reply** to the counterclaim setting out his defenses.

A **cross-claim** is brought by one defendant against a codefendant. Normally a cross-claim comes from the same facts that are the basis for the plaintiff's complaint. For example, an airplane crashes. In a subsequent lawsuit, the airline, the airplane manufacturer,

LEGAL HIGHLIGHT

The Friday Conference

On Friday mornings, promptly at 9:30 A.M., a buzzer summons the nine justices of the United States Supreme Court to an all-day meeting. Entering the conference room, each justice shakes hands with the other eight, a ritual started in the 1880s to symbolize harmony. The nine justices are William H. Rehnquist, chief justice of the United States (1972), John Paul Stevens (1975), Sandra Day O'Connor (1981), Antonin Scalia (1986), Anthony M. Kennedy (1988), David H. Souter (1990), Clarence Thomas (1991), Ruth Bader Ginsburg (1993), and Stephen G. Breyer (1994).

A custom started in 1907 is that no one else is allowed in the room—no law clerks, no secretaries, no pages, no security personnel—once the door is shut. The junior justice takes care of the coffee, answers the door (should anyone dare to knock), and handles all messages and documents.

The justices have assigned seats based on seniority. The chief justice sits at the east end of the table, and the senior associate justice sits at the west end. Behind each justice is a cart that holds her or his books and papers. The volumes of the *United States Reports*, containing every decision made by the body since its first decision, line the walls.

The Friday conference has two purposes: to vote on the cases already argued during the week and to select new cases for the Court to review. Only a few cases make it to the Discuss List. Every justice has already screened each case, so the cases are processed quickly. Of the cases originally on the Discuss List, rarely more than six survive to be heard by the Court. During these conferences, each justice tries to persuade the others to her or his point of view. In effect, the other justices serve as a jury. It is this persuasion process that eventually produces the consensus for a coherent Court decision.

Although much is known about the procedure of the Friday conference, the heart of the conference—the exchange of ideas and arguments among the justices—is not revealed. The justices customarily destroy their conference papers and they rarely talk about the sessions.[a]

---

[a] Additional informational about the justices of the United States Supreme Court can be found at the Oyez Project at Northwestern University's U.S. Supreme Court Multimedia Database web site at <http://oyez.nwu.edu/oyez.html>.

---

and various builders of parts of the airplane are sued. The defendant airplane manufacturer may file a cross-claim against the codefendant engine manufacturer because the engine was defective. When the codefendant, the engine manufacturer, is sued, it files an answer to set out its defenses in this case. Whenever a cross-claim is filed, the other party should file an answer to the cross-claim.

A **third-party complaint** is filed when another party, who was not an original party to the lawsuit, is sued. Once the third-party complaint is served, the new defendant files an answer. For example, a customer purchases a hamburger from a restaurant, bites into it, and breaks his tooth. He finds a drill bit in the hamburger. He lets the restaurant manager know about this problem, but the manager refuses to settle the case. The manager claims that he purchases prepared hamburger patties in large quantities from a wholesaler. The restaurant merely cooks the hamburger patties. The customer sues the restaurant, not the wholesaler, because the customer does not have a contractual relationship with the wholesaler. The restaurant files a third-party complaint against the wholesaler. The wholesaler should file an answer to the third-party complaint.

Process is a document that comes from the court and is signed by the judge or other judicial official, such as the clerk of the court. The actual document subject to process goes through three steps: it is issued, served, and filed.

A judge or other judicial officer issues a process document that orders a person affiliated with a case to take some action. A copy of the process is served on the person by a process server—usually a marshal or sheriff, but sometimes an authorized private party. In most states a party to the lawsuit personally cannot serve any papers involved with that suit. The process server files the process by returning it to the court case file, having noted when, where, and how the piece of process was served.

The following is a partial list of documents that are known as process:

- A **summons** informs the defendant of the claim brought by the plaintiff.

- A **subpoena** requires the attendance of a witness at a hearing.

- A **subpoena** *duces tecum* requires that evidence be brought to court by its custodian.

- **Writit of attachment**
- **Writ of garnishment**
- **Writ of execution**

{ These three writs are used to assist a party in the collection of a person's claim. These writs are discussed in detail in Chapter 14.

A complaint is one type of pleading, whereas a summons is one type of process. In our case, Copiers' lawsuit (or action) against Artiste will start when Copiers' lawyer files a complaint. The complaint is filed with the clerk of the trial court in the proper venue, which is the appropriate geographic area. In our case, Copiers will file the lawsuit in the superior court located in Maricopa County, Arizona. The court then issues a summons to the defendant.

The complaint informs Artiste of the reason for which it is being sued. The summons notifies Artiste of the time and place where it must file an answer or response.

The complaint contains (1) a statement alleging the facts necessary for the court to take jurisdiction, (2) a short statement of the facts necessary to show that Copiers has been harmed by Artiste and that Copiers is entitled to a remedy, and (3) a description of the remedy that Copiers seeks. Exhibit 3–4 illustrates a typical complaint.

The complaint states that Copiers is a duly organized corporation within the state and that Artiste also is a duly organized corporation of the state. Next, the facts are recited: Artiste agreed to purchase the copier, and it has not paid the monies it owes for the copier. The complaint goes on to state that Copiers is entitled to $15,000 to cover the cost of the copier.

After the complaint has been filed, Lakin, on behalf of Artiste, will be served a summons and a copy of the complaint by a process server, certified mail, or electronically. In most states, Lakin is allowed to voluntarily accept service. The service of a summons and complaint is the only time a pleading is served by a process server. Usually other pleadings, such as an answer, are sent by the parties to each other and to the court. Delivery is by mail, messenger service, or electronic transfer.

A typical summons is shown in Exhibit 3–5. A summons notifies Artiste that it is allowed to prepare an answer to the complaint.

A copy of the answer must be filed with the court and sent to the plaintiff's attorney within a specified time period, usually twenty to thirty days after the summons has been served. If Artiste does not file an answer within the time period, Copiers may obtain a **default judgment**. A default judgment occurs when the defendant fails to file the answer or **response** within the specified amount of time. In a default judgment, the defendant automatically loses the lawsuit.

Choices Available after Receipt of the Summons and Complaint.

Once the defendant is served with the summons and a copy of the complaint, the defendant should file a responsive pleading or motion. This filing must be done within the stipulated time period.

Among the defendant's choices are to file (1) a motion to dismiss, (2) an answer containing any affirmative defenses, (3) a counterclaim, (4) an answer containing both affirmative defenses and a counterclaim, or (5) any of these documents as well as a crossclaim or a third-party complaint. If the defendant does nothing, a default judgment may be entered against him or her. An exception is made for military personnel under the Soldiers and Sailors Civil Relief Act of 1943. A person serving on active duty is entitled to request the court to **stay**, that is, stop, the proceedings until the person is able to return and defend against the lawsuit.

Motion to Dismiss. If the defendant decides to challenge the plaintiff's complaint, the defendant can present to the court a **motion to dismiss**, also called a **demurrer**. The motion to dismiss contends that even if the facts presented in the complaint were true, no legal reason exists to go further with the suit and no need exists for the defendant to file an answer. If, for example, Copiers' complaint alleges facts that exclude the possibility of any breach of contract by Artiste, it can move to dismiss. If its motion were granted, Artiste is not required to file an answer.

If the court grants the motion to dismiss, the judge is saying that the plaintiff has failed to state a recognized cause of action. The plaintiff generally is given time to correct the problem and to file an amended complaint.

If the plaintiff does not file an amended complaint, a judgment is entered against the plaintiff solely on the basis of the pleadings. The plaintiff will not be allowed to bring suit on the same matter again.

If the court denies the motion to dismiss, however, the judge is indicating that the plaintiff has stated a recognized cause of action, and the defendant is given an extension of time to file a further pleading. If the defendant does not file an answer, normally a default judgment will be entered for the plaintiff.

Answer and Counterclaim. If the defendant chooses not to file a motion to dismiss or files a motion to dismiss that is denied, he must file an answer with the court. In most answers, the defendant admits to part of the allegations (such as admitting venue), denies other parts of the complaint (such as denying any breach of contract), and sets out any defenses.

If Artiste admits all of Copiers' allegations in its answer, a judgment will be entered for Copiers. If Artiste denies Copiers' allegations, the matter proceeds to trial. Artiste may admit the facts but deny owing the money; in which case, no actual trial of the facts will take place.

A trial's purpose is to determine the facts. If no facts are in dispute, the judge hears only arguments on the legal issues in this case, the legal determination of whether Artiste breached the contract. If a breach of contract occurred, Artiste owes the money. Artiste can prevail in the case, however, by successfully raising an affirmative defense.

Artiste can admit the truth of Copiers' complaint but raise new facts that may result in the action's dismissal. This action is called an **affirmative defense**. For example, Artiste could admit liability but would avoid judgment by stating that the time period for raising the claim had passed. If proven, the judge would dismiss Copiers's complaint based on the statute of limitations.

Artiste may take the following tactic. Artiste files an answer that admits to the purchase of the copy machine. Artiste then alleges as an affirmative defense that Copiers' copy machine failed to perform properly and that Artiste was forced to rent a similar copy machine from another supplier. This allegation is called, appropriately, a counterclaim. If Artiste files a counterclaim, Copiers must answer it with a pleading, normally called a reply, that has the same characteristics as an answer.

Discovery. Before a trial begins, the parties can use a number of procedural devices to obtain information and to gather evidence about the case. Copiers, for example, should establish that Artiste received the copier and should determine the reason for neglecting payment. If Artiste alleges the reason to be the copier's malfunction, Copiers would want to determine the specific malfunction and whether renting a replacement was necessary. The process of obtaining information from the opposing party or from witnesses is known as **discovery**.

Discovery includes gaining access to witnesses, documents, records, and other evidence. The rules governing discovery are designed to make sure that a witness or party is not harassed unduly, that privileged material is safeguarded, and that only matters relevant to the case at hand are subject to the discovery.

Discovery serves several purposes. It preserves evidence from witnesses who might not be available to testify at the trial or whose memories will fade as time passes. It also establishes a witness's testimony so that the witness's credibility can be challenged at trial if that testimony changes.

If discovery reveals that both parties agree on all the relevant facts, a motion for a **summary judgment** may be made. A summary judgment means that one side requests a decision from the judge. The party making the request for the summary judgment writes legal arguments, called legal briefs, and may make oral arguments to the judge as to the reasons for which the party should prevail based on the law.

The other side may oppose the request for summary judgment or may make its own request for a summary judgment. The judge reviews the pleadings filed in the case and the legal briefs to decide if a summary judgment should be granted. To warrant a summary judgment no relevant facts can be at issue. If relevant facts are disputed, a trial is the means to resolve the dispute. A summary judgment can be issued if only the law is being contested.

If one party finds that the opponent's case is too strong to challenge, discovery can lead to an out-of-court settlement. Even if the case does go to trial, discovery prevents surprises by providing parties access to evidence that might otherwise be hidden. Also, discov-

LEGAL HIGHLIGHT
Singing the Courthouse Blues

When they appeared at a concert in Portland, Oregon, on November 9, 1981, the Beach Boys—Al Jardine, Bruce Johnston, Mike Love, and Dennis Wilson—were provided security by off-duty deputies. Three of these deputies—Fred Byler, Donald Kerr, and Kevin McVicker—later sued the Beach Boys for $5.4 million. The deputies claimed they were battered and falsely imprisoned when they tried to take photographs of the musicians.

The Beach Boys were served properly with a summons and a copy of the complaint at another concert that they were playing in Portland in February 1983. No appearance was made, and no answer was filed. In August 1984 a default judgment was entered against the Beach Boys for $5.4 million. Each deputy was granted an award of $300,000 in general damages and $1.5 million in punitive damages. That award was upheld in December 1985 by a judge in the Multnomah County Circuit Court.

The lesson: Never ignore a summons and complaint because you may be held fully liable for the amount of damages alleged in the plaintiff's complaint.

Rules governing the service of a summons vary. Usually service is made by handing the summons and complaint to the defendant personally or by leaving these documents at either the defendant's residence or place of business.

When the defendant cannot be reached, special rules sometimes permit serving the summons by publishing it in the newspaper or by leaving it with a designated person, such as the secretary of state. If service is obtained in this manner, the court usually will not have personal jurisdiction over the defendant but will have authority over the defendant's property located within the court's jurisdiction.

---

ery serves to narrow the issues so that trial time is spent examining those issues.

Discovery can involve the use of *depositions, interrogatories,* or both. A **deposition** is sworn oral testimony by the opposing party or any witness that is recorded by a court reporter. The person being deposed appears before a court reporter to be placed under oath. The person answers questions asked by attorneys from both sides. A court reporter records and later transcribes the questions and answers.

Today, depositions may be videotaped. Even satellite transmissions are used to allow busy witnesses to stay at their jobs while answering questions for attorneys a continent away.

Interrogatories consist of a series of written questions normally sent to the opposing party. That party, with the aid of an attorney, prepares written answers that are then signed under oath.

Parties are obligated to answer questions even if the answers involve the disclosure of information from their records and files. Uniform interrogatories for specific types of cases, such as automobile accidents, have been developed to make the process more efficient.

Other discovery procedures exist. A party may file a **request to produce**, which requires the other party to make available the physical evidence that it has in its possession. For example, if the defendant claims it paid a debt by a check, a request to produce the check may be sought by the plaintiff.

Requests for physical or mental examination often are used in cases, such as automobile accidents, if the health of one of the parties is at issue. If the plaintiff is seeking monetary damages for injuries, the defendant may request that the plaintiff submit to an examination by the defendant's doctor to determine the type and extent of the injuries.

Dismissals and Judgments before Trial. Following the pleadings and discovery process, either party can file pretrial motions. The use of motions can shorten a lawsuit or avoid a trial. In fact, most lawsuits never come to trial. Numerous procedural avenues are available for resolving a case without a trial. Usually, the defendant attempts to have the case dismissed through the use of pretrial motions.

Either party may move for a summary judgment after discovery is completed. Artiste, for example, can

Exhibit 3–4 A Typical Complaint

IN THE SUPERIOR COURT OF THE STATE OF ARIZONA
IN AND FOR THE COUNTY OF MARICOPA

ACME COPIERS, INC., an Arizona corporation;	)))	No. _____
Plaintiff,	))	COMPLAINT (Contract)
ARTISTE LOGIN PRODUCTS, INC., an Arizona corporation	)))	
Defendant.	)))	

COMES NOW, the Plaintiff, ACME COPIERS, INC., by and through its attorney, I. M. Goodguy, and for its cause of action against the Defendant claims and alleges as follows:

I

The Defendant, ARTISTE LOGIN PRODUCTS, INC., is a duly organized corporation under the laws of the state of Arizona. The said Defendant caused events to occur within Maricopa County, Arizona, which gave rise to this Complaint. The Plaintiff is a duly organized corporation within the State of Arizona.

II

The Defendant, ARTISTE LOGIN PRODUCTS, INC., contracted with the Plaintiff to purchase a copy machine for $15,000.00. The copy machine was delivered by Plaintiff to the Defendant. Plaintiff then billed the Defendant on May 15, 2001, in the amount of $15,000.00. No payments have been received, which conduct constitutes breach of contract by the Defendant, ARTISTE LOGIN PRODUCTS, INC.

III

Plaintiff has made all demands or performed all other acts necessary to mature or accelerate the aforesaid amount. The Defendant is liable for the Plaintiff's reasonable attorney fees under Arizona Revised Statutes, Section 12-341.01.

WHEREFORE, Plaintiff respectfully demands judgment against Defendant as follows:
1. For the sum of $15,000 as compensatory damages.
2. For reasonable attorney fees under Arizona Revised Statutes, Section 12.341.01, plus Court costs in bringing this action.
3. For interest on all said sums from May 16, 2001, until paid.
4. For such other relief as the Court deems just and proper.

DATED this _____ day of January, 2002.

I. M. GOODGUY
2001 N. Winning Trial Lane
Tempe, Arizona 85281
Attorney for Plaintiff

Exhibit 3–5   **A Typical Summons**

IN THE SUPERIOR COURT OF THE STATE OF ARIZONA
IN AND FOR THE COUNTY OF MARICOPA

ACME COPIERS, INC., an Arizona corporation;	)	NO. _____
	)	
Plaintiff,	)	SUMMONS
	)	
vs.	)	
	)	
ARTISTE LOGIN PRODUCTS, INC.,	)	
an Arizona corporation,	)	
	)	
Defendant.	)	
_____	)	

WARNING: THIS IS AN OFFICIAL DOCUMENT FROM THE COURT THAT AFFECTS YOUR RIGHTS. READ THIS CAREFULLY. IF YOU DO NOT UNDERSTAND IT, CONTACT A LAWYER FOR HELP.

FROM THE STATE OF ARIZONA TO: PAUL L. LAKIN, statutory agent for ARTISTE LOGIN PRODUCTS, INC.

    1. A lawsuit has been filed against you. A copy of the lawsuit and other court papers are served on you with this Summons.

    2. If you do not want a judgment or order taken against you without your input, you must file an answer to a Response in writing with the Court, and pay the filing fee. If you do not file an answer or Response, the other party may be given the relief requested in his or her Petition or Complaint. To file your Response or Answer, take or send the Answer or Response to the Office of the Clerk of the Superior Court, 201 West Jefferson Street, Phoenix, Arizona 85003-2205, or the office of the Clerk of the Superior Court, 222 East Javelina Drive, Mesa, Arizona 85210-6201. Mail a copy of your Response or Answer to the other party at the address listed on the top of this Summons.

    3. If this Summons and the other court papers were served on you by a registered process server or the Sheriff, within the State of Arizona, your Response or answer must be Pled within TWENTY (20) CALENDAR DAYS from the date you were served, not counting the day you were served. If this summons and the other papers were served on you by a registered process server or the Sheriff outside the State of Arizona, your Response must be filed within THIRTY (30) CALENDAR DAYS from the date you were served, not counting the day you were served. Service by a registered process server or the sheriff is complete when made. Service by Publication is complete 30 days after the date of the first publication.

WARNING. If you signed an Acceptance/Waiver of Service, you must file your Response of answer within 60 days from the date the Notice and Request to Accept Service was sent to you. You should see a lawyer to help you make sure that you have complied with the Service and Response of Answers rules.

    4. You can get a copy of the court papers filed in this case from the Petitioner's attorney at the address at the top of this paper or from the Clerk of the Superior court at the address listed in Paragraph 2 above.

    5. Requests for reasonable accommodation for persons with disabilities must be made to the office of the Judge or Commissioner assigned to the case five days before your scheduled court date.

SIGNED AND SEALED this date:

_____
MICHAEL K. JEANES
Clerk of Superior court

By _____
Deputy Clerk

bring in the sworn statement of a witness that Artiste did not purchase a copier or that Copiers has served the wrong person. Unless Copiers can bring in other evidence raising the possibility that Artiste was the purchaser, Artiste will be entitled to dismissal on a motion for summary judgment. Motions for summary judgment can be made before a trial but will be granted only if the lack of factual disputes is truly obvious.

Before a judge will grant a pretrial motion that would avoid a trial, he or she must determine that no genuine issues of fact exist in the case. The only question must be one of law. Only a fact finder, a jury or a judge sitting alone (if the parties do not want a jury), can decide the facts of the case. If the judge denies the summary judgment, the case proceeds to trial.

Pretrial Hearing. Either party or the court can request a **pretrial hearing**, sometimes called a conference. Usually the hearing follows discovery and consists of an informal discussion among the judge and the opposing attorneys.

The hearing serves to identify and narrow the subject matter that is in dispute and to plan the course of the trial. The pretrial hearing is not intended to compel the parties to settle their case before trial, although judges may encourage them to settle out of court if circumstances suggest that a trial would be a waste of time.

The Trial. A trial procedurally consists of several steps from start to finish. It results when the parties are unable to reach a settlement outside of court. Although many lawsuits are filed, about 95 percent of these are settled out of court, mainly because of the time and expense of trying a case. Furthermore, of those cases that finally do reach trial, about 97 percent are resolved at the trial court level. Relatively few trial court decisions are appealed.

Jury Selection. A trial can be held with or without a jury. Most federal trials are held without a jury. Either party may request a jury, but many cases are tried without one. If there is no jury, the judge determines the truth of the facts alleged in the case. In most states and in federal courts, one of the parties in a civil trial must request a jury; otherwise the right to a jury is waived. Remember, when a person is suing for monetary damages, he or she is entitled to a jury. If the lawsuit is for equitable relief, no jury is allowed. See Chapter 1 on the differences between courts of law and courts of equity.

If a party or parties request a jury, the jury members are selected from a panel of citizens who have been ordered by the court to jury duty. The jury panel members (prospective jurors) are subject to *voir dire* (questions) from the judge and from the attorneys for the parties. The questions are asked to determine if any potential jury member has a bias toward one side, has any connection with the parties, or is unable to serve for the length of the trial. In significant cases, attorneys may use a psychologist or jury consultant to help them select jury members. Jurors who are selected to hear the case are paid a small daily fee and mileage. Normally, the losing party pays these costs.

As a result of the questions asked during *voir dire,* prospective jury members may be dismissed from serving on a jury for a particular trial. For example, if a prospective jury member admits that she has read about the case in the newspaper and has formed an opinion about it, the juror may be **challenged for cause.** A challenge for cause means that one party objects to a particular prospective jury member for a justifiable reason. Unlimited challenges for cause are allowed for each party.

A **peremptory challenge** occurs when a juror is dismissed without a stated reason. The number of peremptory challenges allowed varies from state to state but usually is around three. Each side is limited to the same number of peremptory challenges. These challenges, however, must be exercised with caution, because excluding minorities is unconstitutional.

In the case between Copiers and Artiste, both parties want a jury trial. After the jurors are selected, they are impaneled and sworn in. Then the trial is ready to begin.

Opening Statements. Both attorneys are allowed to make opening statements concerning the facts that they expect to prove during the trial. The plaintiff's attorney gives the first opening statement, followed by the defendant's opening statement. Opening statements are not evidence.

Rules of Evidence. Formal rules of evidence adopted by the courts ensure a fair hearing. The judge rules on the admissibility of all evidence, which must be *material, relevant,* and *reliable.* For example, Copiers cannot introduce evidence that Lakin has been married five times, has fifteen children, and was convicted of jaywalking twenty years ago because none of this infor-

LEGAL HIGHLIGHT

Attorney-Client Privilege, or What You Cannot Tell Your Attorney

Our judicial system has long recognized the attorney-client privilege. This privilege protects communications between a lawyer and a client so that the lawyer may represent the client with full knowledge of all the facts. These private conversations cannot be disclosed in court without the client's consent. A major exception to this rule exists, however.

Communications by the client that she or he is about to engage in a crime can be disclosed in court if the discussion occurs prior to the wrongful act. For example, a conversation with a lawyer in which a client sought advice about how to hide assets fraudulently before filing bankruptcy would not be a privileged conversation. This communication could be introduced into evidence against the client in a subsequent trial. In other words, the attorney-client privilege applies to conversations that occur after the wrongdoing. It does not allow persons to include their attorneys in making plans to carry out crimes and then claim the attorney-client privilege regarding what was said during the planning sessions. Attorneys who do not report such conversations are ethically impaired and are subject to criminal prosecution as accessories to the crime.

---

mation is material or relevant to the issue of whether Artiste purchased and paid for the copier.

Cases are decided by both direct and circumstantial evidence. *Direct evidence* shows the existence of facts in question without the need for additional evidence. A witness may testify, for example, that she saw Lakin using the copier at Artiste's main office. *Circumstantial evidence* consists of facts or circumstances from which the existence or nonexistence of a fact at issue may be inferred. Proof that Artiste mailed out 100,000 copies of an advertisement produced on a copy machine would be circumstantial evidence that the copier was functioning properly.

Information can be kept out of the trial if it qualifies as one of several types of exceptions, such as *hearsay evidence or privileged information*. **Hearsay evidence** is out-of-court information given by someone other than the witness to prove the truth of a contested fact. For example, as a witness for Copiers, Jose may be asked while he is on the stand to testify that he had a conversation with Liz, Lakin's neighbor, who said that Lakin told her that he was "going to get the copier for Artiste without having to pay for it." Liz's words, as quoted by Jose, are hearsay. The proper person to call as a witness would be Liz, who can testify as to her own conversation with Lakin.

Information also can be kept out of a trial if it can be categorized by the court as **privileged information**. By recognizing a privilege, the court protects a relationship in which confidential communication is very important. The best example of privileged information is the attorney-client relationship. Most communications between a person and her or his lawyer cannot be disclosed in court or anywhere else. Only the client may waive this right. This privilege encourages full communication between lawyers and clients so that attorneys can represent their clients to the best of their abilities during legal proceedings.

The common law has long recognized the physician-patient privilege, the husband–wife privilege, and the priest-penitent privilege. Other privileges are based on rules adopted by the court or by statute, such as the accountant-client or the media reporter-informer privilege. During the past decade, many exceptions to the privilege rules have been made by statutory provisions or court rules.[3]

Now that we have examined some rules of evidence, it is time for the trial to begin.

Plaintiff's Case. Since Copiers is the plaintiff, it carries the burden of proving its case. After opening statements, Copiers' attorney calls the first witness for the plaintiff and then examines the witness in what is called direct examination. After Copiers' attorney has

---

[3] The Federal Rules of Civil Procedure and the Federal Rules of Evidence can be found at <http://law.cornell.edu>.

finished, the witness may be cross-examined by Artiste's attorney. After cross-examination, Copiers' attorney has an opportunity to ask the witness further questions, called redirect examination.

When both attorneys have finished with the first witness, Copiers' attorney calls the succeeding witnesses in its case. Each witness is first examined by Copiers' attorney and then is subject to cross-examination by Artiste's attorney (and redirect, if necessary). Witnesses normally do not hear each other testify to prevent collusion or to prevent the tainting of the evidence being presented.

The rules of evidence govern the types of questions that the attorneys can ask and the way in which they can be asked. After the last of the plaintiff's witnesses has been examined, the plaintiff rests its case.

Defendant's Case. Artiste's attorney then presents the evidence and witnesses for its case. Witnesses for the defense are called and examined, and the attorney for Copiers has a right to cross-examine them. Artiste's attorney has the right to redirect each witness. Evidence favorable to Artiste is introduced. After all evidence has been presented and all witnesses dismissed, Artiste rests its case.

When the defendant's attorney has finished the presentation of evidence, the plaintiff's attorney can present, within certain bounds, additional evidence to refute the defendant's case in a rebuttal. The defendant's attorney can meet that evidence in a rejoinder.

Burden of Proof. During any trial, the plaintiff has the burden of proof, which is a measure of the quality of evidence presented by the plaintiff. Two standards of proof are used in civil courts, while only one standard is used in criminal courts. When thinking of the burden of proof, think of the scales of justice held by the Statue of Justice.

The burden of proof differs for each of the two types of civil courts, courts of law and courts of equity. For example, Copiers sues in a court of law seeking monetary damages. Copiers' burden of proof is to establish its case by a **preponderance of the evidence**. The plaintiff presents enough evidence that the defendant has not overcome, such that the scales of the Statue of Justice are tipped slightly toward the plaintiff.

In a court of equity, Copiers seeks an equitable remedy. Copiers is required to prove its case with a higher degree of evidence, sometimes called **clear and convincing evidence**. The plaintiff must present

more evidence than needed by a preponderance of the evidence, but less than that needed in criminal cases. The plaintiff must prove its case with evidence that goes beyond a well-founded doubt. The scales of the Statue of Justice are tipped clearly toward the plaintiff.

In a criminal case, however, the prosecution must prove the defendant guilty **beyond a reasonable doubt**. The jury must be *fully* convinced the defendant committed the crime, not that he is probably guilty or is likely guilty. The scales of the Statue of Justice do not need to tip all the way toward the prosecution, but nearly all the way.

Motions for Directed Verdicts. After the plaintiff's case has been presented, the defendant's attorney may ask the judge to direct a verdict on the grounds that the plaintiff has failed to present a sufficient case for jury consideration. Thus, there can be only one verdict as a matter of law—for the defendant. This *motion for a directed verdict* rarely is granted at this stage of the trial.

After the defendant's case has been presented, either attorney may move for a directed verdict. If the judge determines that the evidence presented by either side is so persuasive that a reasonable jury could only decide for that party, the motion will be granted. Typically, these motions are denied, and the case proceeds to a jury verdict.

Closing Arguments. After both sides have rested their cases, each attorney presents a closing argument, urging a verdict in favor of her client. The plaintiff has the burden of proof and therefore is the first party to present its closing argument. The defendant follows and makes its closing argument. The plaintiff then may rebut the defendant's closing argument.

Jury Instructions and Deliberations. The judge instructs the jury (if it is a jury trial) in the law that applies to the case. The instructions to the jury are called *charges*. Then the jury retires to the jury room to deliberate and deliver a verdict (that is, to make and present the decision).

Jury Verdict and Judgment. In *Copiers v. Artiste,* the jury will have to weigh the evidence and not only decide the case but also, if it finds for the plaintiff, decide the amount of money owed. The jury delivers its verdict, which is converted into a judgment once the judge signs the document that names the prevailing party and the amount to be paid.

Motion for a Judgment Notwithstanding the Verdict (J.N.O.V.). After the jury returns the verdict, a motion for a judgment notwithstanding the verdict (j.n.o.v.) can be filed with the trial judge to overturn the jury's verdict. This motion gives the judge the opportunity to decide as a matter of law that after consideration of all the evidence, the jury erred in its decision. This motion usually is denied by the trial judge. If granted, however, a judgment will be entered for the party filing the motion.

Motion for New Trial. At the end of the trial, the losing party can move to set aside the adverse verdict and to have a new trial. The motion will be granted if the trial judge is convinced, after looking at the evidence, that the verdict was in error. A new trial also can be granted on the grounds of newly discovered evidence, misconduct by the participants during the trial, or judge's error.

The Appeal. A notice of appeal must be filed within the prescribed time. If Copiers is the losing party at the trial and decides to appeal, Copiers becomes the **appellant** (the party appealing the case to a higher court) and Artiste becomes the **appellee** (the party defending the appeal).

Copiers' attorney will file the record on appeal with the court of appeals. The appeal contains (1) the pleadings, (2) a transcript of the trial testimony and copies of the exhibits, (3) the judge's rulings on motions made by the parties, (4) the arguments of counsel, (5) the instructions to the jury, (6) the verdict, (7) the post-trial motions, and (8) the judgment or order being appealed.

The state usually requires the person appealing, here Copiers, to post a bond, that is, to pay money or property as one of the steps to file the appeal. If the person appealing prevails at the appellate court, the money is returned. If the person loses the case, the money is paid over to the court or to the other party, depending on law, as reimbursement for the expenses incurred.

Appellate courts do not hear any evidence. Their decision concerning a case is based on the abstracts, the record, and the briefs. The attorneys can present oral arguments, after which the case is taken under advisement. When the court has reached a decision, the decision is written. The writing contains the opinion (the court's reasons for its decision) and the rules of law that apply.

In general, the appellate courts do not reverse findings of fact unless the findings are unsupported or contradicted by the evidence. Rather, these courts review the record for errors of law. If the reviewing court believes that an error was committed during the trial or that the jury was instructed improperly, the judgment will be reversed. Sometimes the case will be remanded for a new trial. Most decisions of the lower court are affirmed, resulting in enforcement of that court's judgment.

Enforcement of Judgments. Once a judgment has been finalized, the party who has been awarded the judgment wants to be able to collect or enforce it. Several procedures exist for the successful party to enforce the judgment against the losing party, if it does not comply. These procedures are discussed in Chapter 14.

Attorneys' Fees and Other Costs

A lawsuit involves a number of expenses. The parties must pay court costs of filing fees, service of process fees, discovery costs, expert witness fees, and fees for the court reporter. These costs are in addition to possible attorneys' fees.

Attorneys' Fees

In our judicial system, people can represent themselves, but that option is not recommended. Most people involved in a lawsuit hire an attorney. Three basic ways to pay attorneys are by the hour, by the type of work performed, or on a contingency fee basis. Fees per hour depend on the location and type of work being performed. Generally, fees range from $75 to $500 per hour. Contracts, probate, and defense are types of work for which lawyers normally charge by the hour.

Lawyers also can charge for the type of work performed, such as for a standard will. An attorney drafts the will based largely on standard clauses that are stored on the computer and arranges for the clients to sign the will in front of witnesses. The attorney may charge a flat rate of $150 for anyone who needs only the standard-form will. Another common variation of a flat fee is a law firm's pricing by units of work. For example, a firm may charge $500 for the preparation of an initial complaint involving a simple commercial problem or may charge $10 per question to answer interrogatories.

Some attorneys are hired on a contingency fee basis. If the plaintiff is successful at trial, she pays a percentage of the judgment to the attorney. Normally this percentage is one-third of the judgment. The plaintiff is not responsible for compensating the attorney if the case is lost. The plaintiff is responsible, however, for paying all the court costs, such as filing fees and discovery costs.

Contingency fee arrangements are used particularly in negligence lawsuits, such as those involving an automobile accident. The plaintiff retains a lawyer by agreeing to pay the lawyer one-third of any recovery made through settlement or from any judgment in the plaintiff's favor if the lawsuit goes to trial. Normally the defendant who caused the accident is represented by attorneys hired by the defendant's insurance company. These attorneys are paid by the hour, whether the defendant prevails or loses the lawsuit.

Other Costs

In any lawsuit, one of the most expensive procedures is that of conducting discovery. Sometimes the cost of discovery is more than the amount being litigated. Some law firms make it a standard practice, in both large and small cases, to request from the opposing side answers to a thousand or more written interrogatories. Depositions are scheduled for witnesses who have only minimum knowledge of the facts. The end result is a delay in trials because of the time required for discovery. These delays increase costs.

To correct this situation, several state supreme courts have adopted two measures: limited discovery and full disclosure. With limited discovery, the depositions are restricted to the parties and, sometimes, essential witnesses. The length of a deposition is limited to a maximum of four to six hours. The number of expert witnesses for each issue is limited to one per side. An expert witness is a specialist in a particular field and is able to testify about matters relating to her expertise at trial. Finally, only a limited number of interrogatories are allowed, usually thirty to fifty questions.

All parties are required to fully disclose evidence, even when that evidence might be damaging to them. To ensure compliance, the court penalizes the party failing to fully disclose by not allowing its witnesses and exhibits to be presented during the trial.

The federal court system is experimenting with full disclosure between the parties. In the following case, the court orders each party to disclose to the other side the information that it was going to use in trial without waiting for discovery procedures to take place.

Case 3.4

Sierra Club, Lone Star Chapter v. Cedar Point Oil Company, Inc.

United States Court of Appeals, Fifth Circuit, 1996
73 F.3d 546
http://www.ca5.uscourts
.gov/opinions/pub/94
/94-20461-cv0.htm

BACKGROUND AND FACTS Cedar Point was a Mississippi corporation that owned drilling rights in the Cedar Point field (the field), located in Galveston Bay, Texas. Cedar Point drilled its first oil well and began producing oil and gas from this well.

Cedar Point discharged the produced water (water that comes from the well) into Galveston Bay at approximately the same time that it began production from the well. The produced water contained, *inter alia*, barium, benzene, zinc, chlorides, sulfate, bicarbonate, ammonia, naphthalene, phenolic, radium, oil, and grease. This discharge continued through the trial in 1994, excepting when the discharge was temporarily suspended between April and August 1992. Throughout this period, the average daily discharge ranged between 500 and 1,200 barrels per day.

In a 1992 letter, Sierra Club informed Cedar Point that the discharge of produced water without a National Pollutant Discharge Elimination System (NPDES) permit violated the Clean Water Act (CWA). Further, Sierra Club planned to seek monetary penalties and an order enjoining Cedar Point's unpermitted discharges.

Sierra Club filed a lawsuit against Cedar Point in 1993. In its complaint, Sierra Club requested (1) a judgment declaring that Cedar Point's unpermitted discharges of produced water into Galveston Bay violated the CWA, (2) a permanent injunction prohibiting future unpermitted discharges, and (3) penalties for past unpermitted discharges. The district court immediately entered an Order for Accelerated Discovery, requiring the parties to make certain disclosures without waiting for discovery requests. This order directed that the parties disclose at least ninety days prior to trial the expert testimony that they would offer at trial.

Sierra Club then filed a motion for partial summary judgment on the issue of Cedar Point's liability under the CWA. The district court entered an order granting Sierra Club's motion for partial summary judgment. Specifically, the court found as a matter of law that Cedar Point had discharged pollutants without an NPDES permit, in violation of the CWA.

Sierra Club also filed a motion to strike Cedar Point's designation of experts that it would offer at trial. In this motion, Sierra Club alleged that Cedar Point had failed to comply with that part of the district court's discovery order requiring "written reports prepared and signed by the witnesses which included a complete statement of all opinions to be expressed and the basis and the reasons therefor." Specifically, Sierra Club complained that the reports submitted by Cedar Point were so inadequate that Sierra Club would be substantially harmed if the court allowed these witnesses to testify. The court granted Sierra Club's motion to strike Cedar Point's experts, finding that Cedar Point had failed to comply with its discovery order. Cedar Point appealed.

Circuit Judge KING

. . . .

With respect to the importance of Cedar Point's witnesses, it is clear that the bulk of their expected testimony concerned the degree of harm caused by Cedar Point's discharge of produced water. Although the district court made findings regarding harm to the environment in assessing the civil penalty against Cedar Point, the court based the amount of the penalty only on the economic benefit accruing to Cedar Point from the violation. Therefore, the stricken testimony ultimately proved to be unimportant to Cedar Point's case.

As to any prejudice to Sierra Club that would result from allowing Cedar Point's witnesses to testify, we note that Sierra Club did receive more detailed information from three of the witnesses in the form of rebuttal reports. While these disclosures were made approximately two months before trial, Sierra Club should have received most of this information in initial expert disclosures a month earlier. Such a delay would have likely resulted in some prejudice to Sierra Club. While a continuance would have given Sierra Club more time to review the late disclosures, such a measure "would neither punish [Cedar Point] for its conduct nor deter similar behavior in the future."

Finally, Cedar Point's reasons for failure to comply with the district court's discovery order are not persuasive. That harm to the environment would be an issue in this lawsuit was clear from the filing of the action in April 1993. Cedar Point had over nine months to solicit experts and prepare reports on this issue by the February 1, 1994 deadline. Regardless of the specificity of Sierra Club's complaint and initial disclosures, Cedar Point should have been able to produce more information regarding its defense of lack of harm than it did in its initial expert disclosures.

In light of Cedar Point's failure to adhere to discovery deadlines and the fact that the expected testimony ultimately proved to be relatively unimportant, we find that the district court did not abuse its discretion in striking Cedar Point's experts and excluding their testimony.

. . . .

DECISION AND REMEDY Cedar Point did not follow the order of the court about discovery. Because of its disregard of the order, the court did not allow any of the experts to testify on behalf of Cedar Point. As the court noted, "[A] violation of an order is a violation of an order regardless of the reasons therefor."

CRITICAL THINKING: ETHICAL CONSIDERATION Which stakeholders did Cedar Point ignore and how were they impacted by the actions of Cedar Point? See Chapter 2 or the inside front cover to learn about stakeholders.

The Judiciary

On center stage in any trial or appeal is the judge, the person responsible for overseeing the proceedings and for making the final decision in the case. The following sections discuss the selection procedures for the state and federal judiciary.

State Judicial Selection Procedures

Judicial selection varies from state to state. All judges, however, are selected either by election or by merit for a specific term, usually four to six years.

Many states still elect judges to the bench. Opponents of this process claim that it introduces politics into the judiciary. Supporters, however, claim that elections make the judiciary accountable to the public.

Judicial merit selection systems were created as an alternative to elections to ensure a more independent judiciary. Under a judicial merit selection system, applicants apply for an opening on the bench. After a committee reviews the applications, several names are sent to the governor, who then appoints one person from the list.

Judges who are appointed under the merit system stand for **retention** at regular elections. To stand for retention means that the judge's name appears on the ballot unopposed. If the judge is retained, he or she continues on the job. If the judge is not retained, a new judge is selected through the judicial merit selection system.

Federal Judicial Selection Procedures

When a vacancy occurs in the federal court system, U.S. senators and others recommend candidates for the position to the president. No formal requirement, such as being a lawyer, exists for a person who wants to serve as a judge at the federal level. The process starts when the president nominates a person for the vacancy from the list of candidates. The name is sent to the U.S. Senate, which either confirms or denies the appointment.

A federal judge holds office for as long as he or she exhibits good behavior. Since a federal judge is rarely impeached, confirmation is, in effect, a lifetime appointment.

U.S. Magistrate Judges

The concept of a magistrate was established in the federal judiciary with the Judiciary Act of 1789. Today, a U.S. magistrate judge is a special jurisdiction judge. He or she holds a position created by the Federal Magistrates Act of 1968. A magistrate is now officially called a magistrate judge.

A magistrate judge is a judicial officer appointed by the federal district court to assist in administering some of its functions. The magistrate judge has the authority to conduct many pretrial proceedings and to try minor federal criminal offenses and certain civil cases. For example, a person arrested for speeding in a national park would fall under a magistrate judge's jurisdiction.

Different Legal Systems in Foreign Trade

Procedures to enforce an individual's legal rights internationally differ greatly from country to country. Today most European countries, including those formerly in the Eastern Bloc, operate under the civil law system. The civil law system is based on statutes that can be traced back to the Roman emperor, Justinian 1, in A.D. 500.

Under the civil law system, if no statute covers a given topic, the judge acts more like an attorney in developing a case. The legislature—or, in some countries, the executive—is the dominant force in a civil law system. A civil law judge cannot create law, as judges do under the common law system.

The common law system developed in England and is now the legal system in many of the former English colonies such as Australia, Nigeria, and the United States. Under the common law system, the judge is neutral and independent of the parties suing before the court. The judge makes law that must be followed. The legislature also adopts statutes, but in the United States these statutes are subject to judicial interpretation.

Other countries, such as Iran and Saudi Arabia, follow Islamic law. These countries have adopted commercial law codes, but these laws must be interpreted in light of the Koran, a religious document similar in comprehensiveness to the Bible, and by the Sharia, which interprets the Koran. These interpretations have not been changed in nearly a thousand years. Non-Islamic businesspeople must be sensitive to religion's role in Islamic countries.

Businesspeople must appreciate that different cultures have different ways of making, deciding, and applying laws. In addition, the laws may be applied differently to foreigners than to natives before the courts. Foreign legislative and judicial bodies often operate differently from those of the American legal system.

Any country in the world community may utilize the **International Court of Justice (ICJ)**. Located at the Hague in the Netherlands, the ICJ is the principal judicial organ of the United Nations. The ICJ does not handle private disputes between citizens, such as commercial disputes, but matters between countries, which may involve individual citizens.

The ICJ decides cases submitted by U.N. members and renders opinions on legal questions at the request of authorized international organizations. The court is composed of fifteen judges elected by the U.N. General Assembly and the Security Council. Judges serve a nine-year term, with one-third of the judges elected every three years. The jurisdiction of the court depends on the consent of the nations that are the parties to the cases before it. The ICJ has jurisdiction over a sovereign nation only if, and only to the extent that, the nation has agreed that the ICJ shall have jurisdiction covering that particular factual situation.

LEGALLY SPEAKING

How to Find an Attorney

How do you find a competent attorney when you need one? The best method, and the oldest one, is to ask your friends and acquaintances. A good attorney has a good reputation. Word-of-mouth recommendations, even in this age of high technology, still are very reliable.

The Yellow Pages of your telephone directory provide a second source. Most attorneys specialize in a certain legal area, such as real estate, bankruptcy, or taxation. Many lawyers indicate their bar specialty in advertisements. A licensed attorney can place her or his name under most specialty headings without having passed any special examinations and without having experience in that particular field. You will have a better chance of finding a knowledgeable attorney if you identify a bar-certified lawyer who is listed only under the heading of the specialty that you need.

Most local bar associations have a referral service. Attorneys register their area of expertise with the bar association. You can have an initial interview with these attorneys for a small fee.

Finally, certain books, such as the *Martindale-Hubbell Law Directory*, often available in local libraries, list attorneys and their specialties.[a] They list the lawyer's specialty, age, gender, and years of practice; the schools from which the lawyer was graduated; and a list of the partners in the law firm.

A good practice is to speak with several attorneys before deciding to retain one. It is very important that you and the attorney have a good working relationship. Ask about the attorney's fees and other costs involved, the time required to resolve the case, whether the case will go to court or be settled, and the anticipated settlement terms. When you interview a lawyer, be prepared with a list of questions, just as you would for any other business appointment.

The following is a list of methods by which you might find a lawyer:

Checklist for Finding a Lawyer

✔ Check with friends and acquaintances who might have had a similar legal problem. Ask for the name of their attorney and whether they were satisfied with the representation. If they were dissatisfied with the attorney's services, find out the name of the opposing attorney.

✔ Look in the Yellow Pages of your telephone directory under the area of expertise that you need.

✔ Call the state or local county bar to obtain names of lawyers who are certified in that special area or who handle a large number of cases in that area of the law.

✔ Go to your local library and look in directories that list attorneys by their specialties.

Before you retain an attorney, clarify payment procedures and have them reduced to a signed agreement.

[a] The *Martindale-Hubbell Law Directory* is available on the web at <http://www.martindale.com>.

Chapter Summary

Before a court can act, it must have jurisdiction over the person or the property to be acted on. The court may have *in personam* jurisdiction (personal jurisdiction) of a person or business. *In rem* jurisdiction or *quasi in rem* jurisdiction provides the court with jurisdiction over property located within its jurisdiction.

Within the United States, there are at least fifty-two separate court systems including one for each of the fifty states, for the District of Columbia, and for the federal government. The U.S. Constitution provides for the Supreme Court and any other federal courts as Congress shall designate. Congress has created the federal system with at least one federal district court in each state and U.S. courts of appeal to handle their appeals. To fall under the jurisdiction of the federal courts, a case must involve either a federal question or diversity of citizenship involving $75,000 or more in controversy.

Actions begin by filing a complaint and having a summons issued by the court. Once these are served on the defendant, the defendant must file an answer within a specific time period or have a default judgment rendered against her. The defendant also may bring a counterclaim against the plaintiff, which, in turn, requires a reply. During the course of the lawsuit, either party may bring appropriate motions.

Prior to trial, discovery occurs by either oral depositions or written interrogatories. The plaintiff carries the burden of proof at the trial. The plaintiff always introduces evidence first. Once both parties have presented all the evidence, the case is submitted to the jury for a verdict or to the judge if there is no jury.

The jury or judge is the trier of fact. The losing party may appeal the decision. The reviewing court usually will not reverse the trial court's decision unless an error of law occurred in the trial process.

Filing a lawsuit involves many different types of expenses. These costs involve attorneys' fees, filing fees, service of process fees, discovery costs, expert witness fees, and fees for the court reporter. An attorney may be paid by one of three methods. The attorney may charge by the hour or by the type of work performed. In some types of cases, the attorney is paid on a contingency fee basis; thus, if the plaintiff is not successful at the trial, the attorney does not receive any compensation. If the plaintiff prevails at the trial, the attorney is paid based on a percentage of the judgment under a contingency fee contract.

Two methods are used to select state judges: election or merit. Federal judges are nominated by the president and are confirmed by the senate for a term of good behavior.

Using the World Wide Web

The United States Supreme Court has its own web page that contains information concerning its history, visiting the Court, and other related sites. Supreme Court cases are available for web site publication immediately upon finalization by the Court. The cases are also published in unofficial form on a number of web sites including Findlaw and media home pages.

Each federal court of appeals, specialized courts, and district courts has its own web site. The content varies for each court. To access the district courts, use the web site for the Federal Judiciary home page.

Finding the Law on the Web

Federal Judicial Center
    http://www.fjc.gov
Federal Judiciary home page
    http://www.uscourts.gov/
Judiciary Now: The Latest News and Features
    http://www.uscourts.gov/judnow/index.html
Federal Judiciary home page links
    http://www.uscourts.gov/links.html
Supreme Court of the United States
    http://www.supremecourtus.gov/

First Circuit Court of Appeals
    http://www.uscourts.gov/allinks.html#all
Second Circuit Court of Appeals
    http://www.uscourts.gov/allinks.html#all
Third Circuit Court of Appeals
    http://www.uscourts.gov/allinks.html#all
Fourth Circuit Court of Appeals
    http://www.uscourts.gov/allinks.html#all
Fifth Circuit Court of Appeals
    http://www.uscourts.gov/allinks.html#all
Sixth Circuit Court of Appeals
    http://www.uscourts.gov/allinks.html#all
Seventh Circuit Court of Appeals
    http://www.uscourts.gov/allinks.html#all
Eighth Circuit Court of Appeals
    http://www.uscourts.gov/allinks.html#all
Ninth Circuit Court of Appeals
    http://www.uscourts.gov/allinks.html#all
Tenth Circuit Court of Appeals
    http://www.uscourts.gov/allinks.html#all
Eleventh Circuit Court of Appeals
    http://www.uscourts.gov/allinks.html#all
D.C. Circuit Court of Appeals
    http://www.uscourts.gov/allinks.html#all

U.S. Court of Appeals for the Federal Circuit
http://www.uscourts.gov/allinks.html#all
U.S. Court of International Trade
http://www.uscit.gov/
U.S. Court of Appeals for the Armed Forces
http://www.armfor.uscourts.gov/
U.S. Court of Federal Claims
http://www.law.gwu.edu/fedcl/
United States Sentencing Commission
http://www.ussc.gov/
U.S. Tax Court
http://www.ustaxcourt.gov/

Chapter Web Sites

State courts
http://www.ncsc.dni.us/
or
http://www.courts.net/
Court TV
http://courttv.com
Oyez Project, Northwestern University's
U.S. Supreme Court Multimedia Database
http://oyez.nwu.edu/oyez.html

Federal Rules of Civil Procedure and Federal
Rules of Evidence
http://law.cornell.edu
Martindale-Hubbell Law Directory
http://www.martindale.com

Web Activities

3–1 Look at Exhibit 3–3 and determine in which federal court of appeals district your state is located. Once you have determined which district is appropriate, refer to the federal court web sites listed previously and find the web address. Go to the web address and determine if the federal district court for your state or area publishes its decisions on the Internet.

3–2 You are driving and listening the radio. During the news broadcast, you hear that the supreme court for your state has just made a ruling concerning a local business. Find out if your state court system publishes its opinions on the Internet. Does the court have its own web site?

Key Terms

adversary system
affirmative defense
answer
appellant
appellate jurisdiction
appellee
beyond a reasonable
doubt
challenge for cause
clear and convincing
evidence
complaint
concurrent jurisdiction
counterclaim
courts of appeal
cross-claim
default judgment
demurrer

deposition
discovery
diversity of citizenship
case
due process clause
exclusive jurisdiction
federal question case
full faith and credit clause
general jurisdiction
hearsay evidence
in personam (personal)
jurisdiction
in rem jurisdiction
International Court of
Justice (ICJ)
interrogatories
jurisdiction
limited jurisdiction

long-arm statute
motion
motion to dismiss
original jurisdiction
peremptory challenge
petition
plead
pleading
preponderance of the
evidence
pretrial hearing
privileged information
process
quasi in rem jurisdiction
reply
request for physical or
mental examination
request to produce

res judicata
response
retention
stay
subject matter jurisdiction
subpoena
subpoena *duces tecum*
summary judgment
summons
third-party complaint
venue
voir dire
writ of attachment
writ of *certiorari*
writ of execution
writ of garnishment

Questions and Case Problems

3–1 Court System The U.S. court system has two types of courts: courts with original jurisdiction and those with appellate jurisdiction. Describe the differences between the two systems.

3–2 Jurisdiction Discuss the differences among *in personam* jurisdiction, *in rem* jurisdiction, and *quasi in rem* jurisdiction.

3–3 Federal Jurisdiction Discuss the two types of lawsuits heard in federal courts.

3–4 Appellate Review Discuss the most common method of appellate review exercised by the Supreme Court.

3–5 Civil Procedure Discuss the differences between pleadings and process.

3–6 Judiciary In state judicial systems, judges serve specific terms in office, whereas federal judges serve for a term of good behavior. Compare the two systems. Based on constitutional and public policy grounds, which system seems better?

3–7 Jurisdiction Marvin, a resident of Alabama, was walking near a busy street in Birmingham when a large crate fell off a passing truck and hit him. Marvin received numerous injuries that resulted in large medical expenses and a great deal of pain and suffering. He lost six months of work. He wants to sue the trucking firm for $300,000. The firm's headquarters is in Mississippi, although the company does business in Alabama. Should Marvin bring his lawsuit in an Alabama state court, a Mississippi state court, or a federal district court located in Alabama or Mississippi? Explain your answer.

3–8 Jurisdiction In late 1993, Mid–America Tablewares, Inc., decided to produce and sell a dinnerware line to accompany its Harvest Festival table linen line. In May 1994, Mid-America entered into a contract with Mogi Trading Company, Ltd., whereby it was to provide dinnerware for Mid-America. Mogi was a Japanese corporation with its main place of business in Japan. It was in the business of contracting for the manufacture of ceramic dinnerware from several manufacturers. Prior to entering the contract, the parties exchanged a considerable number of communications and one visit was made by Masaichi Tsuchiya, a Mogi representative, to Mid-America's place of business. In one exchange, Mid-America emphasized the importance of complying with the Food and Drug Administration's (FDA) lead regulations. Tsuchiya faxed a response, discussing the lead issue, and specifically represented that Mogi's goods always met FDA standards. Shortly after Mogi purchased the Harvest Festival dinnerware from a manufacturer, it was shipped to Mid-America. In July 1994, the FDA determined that the dinnerware had unacceptably high lead levels and thereby exceeded FDA regulatory guidance levels. Upon being informed of the FDA's test results, Mid-America stopped selling it and began the process of recalling all the dinnerware. Mid-America sued Mogi in U.S. District Court, invoking the court's diversity jurisdiction. Mogi claimed that the court lacked. What was the result and why? [*Mid-America Tablewares, Inc. v. Mogi Trading Co.*, 100 F.3d 1353 (7th Cir. 1996)]

3–9 Jurisdiction Rudzewicz, an experienced and sophisticated businessperson, signed a twenty-year franchise contract in 1979 with Burger King Corporation to operate a restaurant in Michigan. He obligated himself to pay $1 million over the twenty-year period. At first business was steady, but when a recession hit, patronage declined, and Rudzewicz fell behind in his payments. After extended negotiations, Burger King filed a lawsuit in 1981. Burger King is a Florida corporation with its main offices in Miami. The franchise contract provided that the franchise relationship was established in Miami and governed by Florida law. All fees and notices were to be sent to the Miami headquarters. Rudzewicz claimed that he was a Michigan resident, that he had not been to Florida, that the claim did not arise in Florida, and that, therefore, the district court lacked personal jurisdiction. Should the case be dismissed in Florida? Explain your answer. [*Burger King Corp. v. Rudzewicz,* 471 U.S. 462, 105 S. Ct. 2174, 85 L. Ed. 528 (1985)]

3–10 Internet A popular rallying point of politicians is that the United States suffers from a litigation explosion. On the Internet, go to the Institute of Civil Justice, a part of the Rand Corporation, and access the Frequently Asked Questions (FAQs) page. What is the finding of the Institute of Civil Justice as to whether we are experiencing a litigation explosion in the United States? The web site is <http://www.rand.org/centers /icj/faqs/index.html>.

All disputes (if unhappily any should arise) shall be decided by three impartial and intelligent men, known for their probity and good understanding, two to be chosen by the disputants, each having the choice of one, and the third by those two, which three men thus chosen shall, unfettered by law or legal constructions, declare their sense of the testator's intention, and such decision is, to all intents and purposes, to be binding on the parties as if it had been given in the Supreme Court of the United States.

Last Will and Testament
George Washington, 1732–1799
First president of the United States of
America, 1789–1797

Discourage litigation. Persuade your neighbors to compromise whenever you can. Point out to them how the nominal winner is often a real loser—in fees, expenses, and waste of time. As a peacemaker the lawyer has a superior opportunity of being a good man. There will still be business enough.

"Notes for a Law Lecture," *The Collected Works of Abraham Lincoln*, edited by Roy P. Basler, Vol. II (July 1, 1850), p. 81
Abraham Lincoln, 1809–1865
Sixteenth president of the United States of
America, 1861–1865

Outline

Ethical Consideration

Full Disclosure in Arbitration?

A homeowner signed a contract with a builder to build a new home. A dispute arose between the homeowner and the building contractor. Among the many items under dispute, the homeowner claimed that the contractor failed to install below-surface drains as specified in the building plans. She came to you because she wanted to file a lawsuit against the contractor.

You reviewed the contract between the builder and your client. A clause in the contract required that all disputes be resolved by arbitration.

Arbitration is a formal procedure used by parties to resolve disputes. Used in place of a lawsuit, arbitration is a nonjudicial way to quickly and inexpensively resolve disputes. Each party submits its respective evidence in the matter to an impartial third party, called an arbitrator.

As you prepared for the arbitration hearing, you come across an old memorandum in the homeowner's handwriting that could be interpreted as acknowledging that she knew the drains had not been installed correctly and that she had relieved the contractor of liability for the drainage system in exchange for some additional work on the new house. When you talk with the homeowner, she states that it is the only copy, and she is sure that the contractor has forgotten about it because it was written during a particularly hectic part of the construction project.

You are aware that discovery procedures prior to arbitration hearings are either nonexistent or are so limited in scope that you probably will not have to involuntarily provide this document to the other side. If this matter were before a regular court, you most likely would be required to turn over a copy of this document to the attorney representing the contractor. Do you have any duty to supply this document to the other side prior to the hearing or at least to present it at the proceeding? Use the ethical model presented in Chapter 2 and reprinted on the inside front cover to develop your answer.

Introduction

Your World Wide Web (WWW) business, Artiste Login Products, Inc., has been involved in several lawsuits during the past few years. You have discovered that lawsuits are unwieldy in terms of money and time for your business. As a litigant, your business had to expend money on attorneys' fees, court fees, and evidence development.

The taxpayers, however, pay a majority of the costs because the court fees you paid as a litigant did not cover the actual cost of running the judicial system, such as paying for the construction and maintenance of the courthouses and the salaries of the court personnel, including the judges, clerks, and bailiffs. The time from the filing of a lawsuit to the final disposition of the case always is uncertain and usually is measured in years. As a result, the memories of the witnesses fade and evidence may be destroyed or lost.

Furthermore, as long as the dispute was in litigation, you discovered that you often harbored negative feelings toward the opposing party in litigation and the judicial system. Litigation is a stressful ordeal. What you really wanted to be able to do was carry on business with the opposing party while the dispute was being resolved quickly and inexpensively.

You decide to explore methods to resolve disputes that are less expensive and more expeditious than litigation. You find that the various advocates of **alternative dispute resolution (ADR)** all share the same basic goal: a speedy and just determination of the dispute at a reasonable cost to both parties.

Advocates of Alternative Dispute Resolution

Today, the judiciary is one of the strongest advocates of ADR procedures. The late Warren E. Burger, former chief justice of the United States, advocated the development of "mechanisms that can produce an acceptable result in the shortest possible time, with the least possible expense and with a minimum of stress on the participants."

Average citizens' rights are compromised when they must spend thousands of dollars and several years in litigation to obtain a decision, especially for routine cases, such as those involving an automobile accident.

More often than not, the case is settled literally in front of the courtroom door after considerable expense, frustration, and years in the judicial system.

The business sector is another strong proponent of alternative dispute resolution procedures. Businesspersons need expeditious justice at a reasonable cost. They often need to be able to maintain a business relationship with the opponent while resolving a particular dispute. Most disputes between businesses involve a contractual problem. People in business accept that disputes are inevitable. Even when a written contract is drawn carefully, problems will arise over the interpretation of a clause or over a disputed set of facts. Disputes over manufacturing delays, merchandise quality, contract performance, and other such misunderstandings are bound to arise.

Once a dispute occurs, most businesspersons prefer to resolve the dispute quickly, privately, inexpensively, and informally. Maintaining a business relationship while involved in litigation is very difficult, if not impossible. To preserve goodwill, most businesspersons are in favor of alternative dispute resolution procedures that will be fair, inexpensive, and quick, but that also will arrive at a just result.

The public has a great interest in reducing the caseload handled by the judiciary. Most cases in court are routine in nature and rarely involve great legal issues. Like businesspersons, the public wants fair, inexpensive, and quick procedures to settle routine legal problems. The field of ADR is evolving, and parties facing disputes may create new forms of ADR. The next sections look at the various types of ADR.

Negotiation, Conciliation, and Mediation

The most common form of ADR is negotiation, which is the foundation for conciliation and mediation. Arbitration, minitrials, and the use of private judges are more formal procedures that result in a decision. We first discuss the three informal types of ADR: negotiation, conciliation, and mediation.

Negotiation

Negotiation is the process in which two or more persons meet to discuss their differences and attempt to arrive at a settlement acceptable to both. Negotiation is a technique used to resolve a dispute, not to win an argument. Although reasonableness cannot be ensured by using negotiation, people can use it to engage in joint problem solving through cooperative behavior and to arrive at a mutually acceptable agreement.

All parties should win in a successful negotiation. If only one party gains and the other loses completely, the loser has no vested interest in making sure that the agreement will work. In fact, it is human nature to try to sabotage a forced agreement. Negotiation is both a skill that can be learned and an art form to be practiced.

Negotiation is an integral part of all alternative dispute resolution procedures. It is not, by itself, an ADR procedure in any formal sense. No ADR procedure, however, could exist without negotiation. In fact, the act of filing a lawsuit may in itself be a negotiating technique. Negotiation is by far the best dispute resolution technique because the parties arrive at a solution that they design themselves.

Negotiation Skills. As important a skill as negotiation is, many people are inexperienced at it. People generally have poorly developed negotiating skills. Primary or secondary schools rarely teach bargaining or negotiating and these skills often are not addressed even at the college or university level.

American businesses at the retail level have disregarded negotiation skills that could be valuable in purchasing and selling. To set a price rather than spend time negotiating a price is more efficient and less costly. The quick purchase of an item frees the buyer to spend his time performing other tasks. Yet while the modern business world values efficiency, other cultures value and develop the skills of social contact and bargaining that go with negotiations. This personal contact is especially useful when businesses deal with one another.

For example, the price of clothing at a department store, food at a grocery store or restaurant, or a night's stay in a motel is rarely subject to negotiation in the American culture. However, because very few laws set the price of any service or product today, prices for these items can be negotiated legally. Even though we, as a society, rarely take advantage of this freedom, the price of products and services is subject to negotiation unless a law prohibits it.

Negotiating skills are necessary in the business world. For example, a customer purchases merchandise, becomes dissatisfied with it, and decides to return it. The customer would like a full cash refund. The businessperson must decide whether to accept the merchandise back and, if the merchandise is returnable, whether to offer credit toward the purchase of additional products from the store or a full refund. Both parties want different results. But to settle this situation, both parties should expect to agree to less than their initial expectation.

When Negotiation Occurs. Negotiation may occur at any stage of a dispute. If a lawsuit has resulted, this period ranges from the moment the customer purchases the merchandise to the time immediately before the judge renders a decision. In fact, sometimes negotiation of a settlement will occur even after a case has been tried and the judge has entered a judgment.

Most cases filed in any court system are settled through negotiation by the attorneys. Comparatively few cases are litigated fully to the point at which a judge or jury makes the decision. Good-faith negotiation is a necessity; without it, the judicial system would collapse, even if only one-fifth of the lawsuits filed actually went to trial.

Conciliation

Conciliation occurs whenever a third party successfully gets conflicting parties to accept an agreement. A conciliator does not take an active part in the negotiations but rather attempts to limit all parties' passions and negative rhetoric. Conciliation is one method for obtaining a negotiated settlement from the parties.

Although conciliation is not used as extensively in this country as in other cultures, it is part of the federal labor law and is used widely in labor disputes. Conciliation is used in many states in divorce actions. When a divorce is filed, one of the parties may request a conciliation hearing, which is similar to marriage counseling.

Mediation

Conciliation brings parties together so that they may reach a settlement through negotiation. A conciliator takes no active role in the negotiation. In **mediation**, an impartial third person, called a mediator, also tries to persuade the parties to discuss their issues and come to a resolution.[1]

If the parties cannot agree on the issues, the mediator will not take an active role in helping the parties come to an agreement. The mediator has no formal position and can be discharged at any time by either party. The mediator does not have the power to make a decision or to force the parties to accept any suggestions or recommendations. Only when the parties come to a final settlement of their differences is mediation successful.[2]

Early mediation intervention allows for a quick solution to the problem before the positions taken by the parties become polarized. Mediation is a first step that allows the parties to proceed to arbitration or even to a lawsuit if they cannot work out their differences. Often a contract requires that money be deposited to cover the expenses of arbitration or litigation in case a dispute should reach that stage. Mediation does not require the setting aside of these funds. Thus, the parties have another incentive to attempt to resolve their differences using this process. Mediation today is available through the Internet.[3]

Judges can use mediation in cases being litigated. A judge in a pretrial conference attempts to bring the two parties together in a negotiated settlement and in doing so is using mediation. The Better Business Bureau uses mediation techniques when it handles complaints between businesses and customers. It attempts to bring the two parties together to reach a settlement of their differences. The Magnuson-Moss Warranty Act of 1975 authorizes mediation when a dispute occurs between a consumer and a business over a malfunctioning consumer product.

The Federal Mediation and Conciliation Service (FMCS) provides experienced mediators who serve in disputes between labor and management. If direct negotiations between labor and management on a labor contract break down, the FMCS sends mediators to mediate the dispute. If the parties still are unable to reach an agreement, a strike usually occurs.

Newspapers and radio and television stations may have teams devoted to resolving disputes that their readers or listeners have with a business. Often a person

---

[1] For an excellent discussion of mediation go to <http://www.freeadvice.com/law/559us.htm>.

[2] Several companies offer mediation and other alternative dispute resolution procedures. One of the largest is JAMS, which can be found at <http://www.jamsadr.com/>.

[3] Go to the Mediation Information & Resource Center to see how mediation works on the Internet. The address is <http://www.mediate.com/>.

Hurricane Andrew Whips Up ADR

On August 24, 1992, Hurricane Andrew's fury laid a path of destruction in Florida. By any measure, Hurricane Andrew was the most costly storm ever. In its aftermath, building owners, lenders, and insurance companies surveyed the damage. Building owners filed 700,000 claims with their insurance companies.

In one case the homeowner, now homeless, filed his claim with his insurance carrier. The insurance adjuster surveyed the damage and filed the report with the company, which acted quickly to hire a contractor to start rebuilding the home. The homeowner did not trust the insurance company, however, and demanded his own builder.

Litigation seemed likely until Florida created a new program called Alternative Procedures for Resolution of Disputed Claims Arising from Hurricane Andrew. Florida's Department of Insurance renovated an office building containing ten mediation rooms for the program. Computers from the Insurance Department and the American Arbitration Association accessed each other to track the progress of cases. Mediators were trained to handle the specialized requirements of the hurricane program.

Each party brought to the mediation all of its documents, photographs, and occasionally architects and contractors. Representatives from the Department of Insurance and the attorney general's office were on site for legal and procedural clarifications. Routinely homeowners asked these state representatives to sit in on the mediation sessions. Most cases involved damaged property for which the claim had been denied or only partial payment was granted. Each party presented its side to the mediator. The mediator met with each party separately and acted as a go-between with the parties until, it was hoped, a settlement could be reached. Sometimes the parties preferred to remain in the conference room until the conflict was resolved.

Not all claims involved the simple scenario of homeowner versus insurance company. One case involved a building with fourteen apartments, each unit insured separately. Thus, the mediation involved fourteen separate claims with fourteen separate policies with several insurance companies. Mediation resolution proved to be cheaper and achieved results faster than the traditional court system.

Source: Adapted with permission from "AAA Hurricane Claims Mediation Program," *Claims Forum* 7, no. 1 (February 1993): 1, 6.

---

will contact the media to report a problem. A reporter from the media will contact the business with whom the customer has a dispute. Because the media have extensive resources and are very visible, reporters often can contact the person within the business who has the power to resolve the dispute. To avoid bad publicity, most businesses are willing to participate when approached by the media.

Arbitration

Arbitration is a procedure in which the parties to a dispute submit the dispute to an impartial third person, called an **arbitrator**. An arbitrator frequently specializes in arbitrating disputes in a particular area, such as real estate or labor. This person is selected by the parties to make a decision based on evidence that they both submit. The arbitrator's decision is usually binding.[4]

Any and all types of disputes can be arbitrated. Most arbitration situations arise as a result of commercial, construction, employment, insurance, labor, international transactions, and security disputes.[5]

On the surface, arbitration seems to be similar to the judicial system, with a third person resolving the

[4] The Free Advice web site covers arbitration in great detail: <http://www.freeadvice.com/law/557us.htm>.
[5] VGIS Communications, Inc., maintains a web site at <http://www.seclaw.com/centers/arbcent.shtml>. The name they use on this web site is SEC LAW.com. They provide a source and rules for conducting arbitration involving disputes between customers and their security brokers.

dispute between opposing parties. Major differences do exist, however. Let's compare the two systems.

Comparisons between Arbitration and the Judicial System

Few studies comparing arbitration and the judicial system have been made. The Institute for Civil Justice, however, which was established within the RAND Corporation, has developed data from its studies of the judicial system.

The institute compared arbitration with the judicial system on the basis of six factors: financial costs, time costs, privacy, formality, selection of the decision maker, and the choice of forum. The studies found that on the basis of these six factors, arbitration offers many advantages over traditional judicial procedures.

Financial Costs.
The first comparison between arbitration and the judicial system involves the monetary cost. Government expenditures for running the judicial system vary widely. The cost of a jury trial, including judge, jury members, court reporter, bailiff, clerk, and secretary, averages about $8,300 in California. In Los Angeles County the cost is higher at $10,500 for a jury trial. Perhaps because of these costs, only about 1 percent of civil lawsuits filed in all of California results in a jury trial. In Florida the cost is much less, around $3,000 for a jury trial. At a daily cost of $2,700 to use a federal court, the cost of the average federal trial is more than $10,800.

In spite of this cost, the plaintiff obtains a money judgment in only 57 percent of cases in which the defendant disputes liability. The average judgment over the twenty-year period studied by the institute was $84,000.

The RAND study, however, discovered that one-fourth of the jury verdicts awarded less than $8,000. In one-half of the cases, the judgments were for less than $21,000. Only in 19 percent of the cases did the plaintiff equal or exceed the $84,000 average judgments. Ten percent of the judgments were for more than $181,000, and only 1 percent exceeded $1 million. The plaintiffs in automobile accident cases received the smallest judgments; more than 50 percent were under $15,000. Thus, most of the money went to only a few plaintiffs.

Consider that in one-fourth of the cases decided, the cost to the public of the trial was more than the amount recovered by the plaintiff, even though, of course, not all types of lawsuits should be judged strictly by the cost. In terms of the sheer numbers of cases filed on routine matters (such as automobile accident cases), however, many advocate a better method of resolving the dispute between the two parties.

The costs of alternative dispute resolution procedures also range widely, but all are on the lower end of the cost scale. The average cost of a private arbitration is estimated to be as low as $275. If the arbitration is private, the cost is paid by the disputing parties, not the taxpayers. More than 100,000 cases are arbitrated each year, and the number is increasing.

Time Costs.
The second comparison between arbitration and the judicial system is the cost factor measured in time. Extremes exist in the processing time of a case, which is measured from the date a lawsuit is filed to the date of its final disposition. In Arizona, this period is less than twelve months. In Connecticut, in contrast, the courts were backlogged beyond a five-year period, with more than 60,000 tort cases alone waiting for trial. Half of these cases were pending before the courts in just four cities.

In Los Angeles County, a forty-one-month delay exists from the time of filing to the time of final disposition. This time lag exists even though judicial arbitration is required. In the same county, only 10 percent of the cases filed ever go to trial. Forty percent of the cases were disposed of by the court, and 50 percent either were settled or dropped by the litigants.

Reasons for Time Lag. Why is the time lag so long in a lawsuit? During a lawsuit, a continuing debate takes place between the attorney representing the plaintiff and the attorney representing the defendant. For example, in a personal injury case, the plaintiff's attorney argues that she has little reason to encourage delay. An injured plaintiff must receive and pay for medical care and is often out of work while recovering.

In many cases, the plaintiff's attorney receives compensation from the amount recovered on behalf of the client based on a contingency fee agreement. Therefore, it is in the attorney's best interest to dispose of the case quickly. A practice has developed, however, that once the plaintiff's medical condition has stabilized and the attorneys have finished the discovery stage, each attorney waits for the other attorney to act because neither wants the other attorney to think he or she is afraid of litigating the case.

Unless the judge forces the case to move along, it stalls at this stage until the plaintiff's attorney or the court sets the trial date. Even if the trial date is set early in the case, it will be affected by a rule most courts have: that a lawsuit (including criminal proceedings) must go to trial within a specific time period. As cases pile up, many are in danger of going beyond that time period. Thus, those cases take preference on the trial calendar.

Both sides have a tendency to polarize their positions as the case is being processed through the court system. As the case proceeds, the attorneys for the plaintiff and the defendant evaluate the evidence. Quite often one attorney will make an offer to settle the case. The other attorney will consider the settlement offer and make a recommendation to the client. The party must weigh the settlement offer (that is, the given amount of money paid now) against the potential of winning or losing more in a trial at a later time.

Typically, the first offer is rejected and a counteroffer is made. Between each offer there is usually a waiting period. Only when faced with the decision of actually preparing for trial is a settlement seriously pursued, and even then attorneys usually wait to see if the judge will force early case preparation. A judge can force early case preparation by controlling the court calendar, refusing to allow continuances (postponement) of the case, limiting discovery to a reasonable level, and promoting pretrial settlement conferences.

ADR Time Periods. Statistics on the time it takes for alternative dispute resolution procedures are hard to find because of the wide range of procedures that may be used. The time spent in the court system, however, may be contrasted with the time spent in arbitration, which is a specific type of ADR procedure. In private arbitration, the average commercial case takes 145 days from the time of the filing until the arbitrator makes the decision.

California has two types of judicially mandated arbitration: voluntary and court ordered. Those litigants who volunteer to have their lawsuits arbitrated have a decision within seven months. Those litigants who are ordered by the court to have their cases arbitrated wait twenty-two months for a decision. Thus, in California either type of arbitration is faster than the judicial system.

Privacy Factor. A third comparison between arbitration and judicial procedures is privacy. Civil court procedures become public record. Anyone can observe many of the pretrial and all of the trial procedures. As a result, information that people or businesses would prefer to keep private is available for anyone to read. The disclosure factor becomes critical when a business must reveal trade secrets, budget planning, marketing strategies, or other sensitive information in court.

Most alternative dispute resolution procedures are private and not open to the public. Nonjudicial procedures allow for confidentiality of most information, whereas judicial proceedings, by law, rarely are closed to the public.

Formality. A fourth comparison between the two is the difference in formality. A judicial proceeding is very formal in nature. The judge wears a black robe and his entry into the courtroom is announced in a formal manner by the bailiff. Only attorneys and the litigants are allowed beyond the railing that separates the public area from the formal courtroom area.

Courtroom decorum has developed through the centuries and is strictly adhered to by judges. During the trial itself, court rules and the rules of evidence are closely followed. Although the rules have a definite purpose, their application often seems meaningless and confusing to the litigants.

Alternate dispute resolution procedures are informal in their setting. This informality allows the parties to be more relaxed, reducing stress from the level that the parties feel in a courtroom. Do not confuse an informal setting with a sloppy or inadequate presentation of material, however. As in a courtroom, the better prepared the parties in alternative dispute resolution procedures are in presenting their cases, the better the chance of resolving the dispute in a manner acceptable to both sides.

Selection of the Decision Maker. A fifth comparison is the selection of the decision maker. In the judicial system, the parties have very little control over which judge is selected for their case. Most alternative dispute resolution procedures allow the participants to have a say in deciding on the decision maker. When people have a voice in choosing the decision maker, they usually are more ready to accept his or her final decision.[6]

[6] Many professional arbitrators have sites on the Internet. For example, Stephen R. Marsh maintains a web site at <http://adrr.com/> where he explains quite well the differences between arbitration and mediation.

LEGAL HIGHLIGHT

Code of Ethics for Arbitrators

Arbitrators operate under a code of ethics. The people who act as arbitrators undertake a serious responsibility to the public, as well as to the parties involved. If the arbitrators do not discharge their duties in good faith and in a diligent manner, the whole system becomes suspect, and the public could lose faith in arbitration.

The American Arbitration Association (AAA) is one of many private organizations that educates, promotes, researches, and provides the administrative framework for those parties wanting to use ADR methods. The AAA developed the following seven canons in the code of ethics:

1. The arbitrator will uphold the integrity and fairness of the arbitration process.

2. If the arbitrator has an interest or relationship that is likely to affect her or his impartiality or that might create an appearance of partiality or bias, it must be disclosed.

3. An arbitrator, in communicating with the parties, should avoid impropriety or the appearance of it.

4. The arbitrator should conduct the proceedings fairly and diligently.

5. The arbitrator should make decisions in a just, independent, and deliberate manner.

6. The arbitrator should be faithful to the relationship of trust and confidentiality inherent in that office.

7. In a case for which a board of arbitrators is used, each party may select an arbitrator. The arbitrator must ensure that she or he follows all the ethical considerations in this type of situation.

Choice of Forum. A sixth comparison is the choice of the forum (place of litigation or hearing). The parties in a lawsuit have little control over where their case will be heard. The judicial system has limited the right of the parties to "forum shop."

Arbitration allows the disputing parties the opportunity to select a common forum in advance. This selection opportunity is important, particularly when there are business arrangements between the parties in more than one state.

Because the disputing parties are not subject to a court system, they can decide the best place to hold the arbitration hearing. Some organizations that offer alternative dispute resolution services operate in many or all of the states, and a few even have offices in other countries. As a result, the disputing parties are not restricted by the jurisdictional limits that they would encounter in a court system.

American Arbitration Association

The **American Arbitration Association (AAA)**[7] was founded in 1926 as a private, not-for-profit organ-

ization as an outgrowth of two earlier arbitration associations. Within both associations were two groups that held different philosophies concerning arbitration. One group was made up of business leaders and trade association executives. They viewed arbitration as a businessperson's court, much like the trade and guild courts of the Middle Ages. The other group was composed of attorneys who, although they believed in arbitration, also believed in the fundamental concepts of due process and fairness.

To satisfy these two groups, the AAA adopted as its purpose "to foster the study of arbitration in all of its aspects, to perfect its techniques under arbitration law, and to advance generally the science of arbitration for the prompt and economical settlement of disputes." Besides the administration of arbitration, the AAA's other functions include education, promotion, and research into the uses of arbitration for settling all types of disputes. Its slogan is "Speed, Economy, and Justice." AAA's performance has shown repeatedly that justice does result when there is speed and economy. The AAA handles more than 90,000 cases annually and maintains thirty-six offices throughout the United States.

---

[7] The web page for the American Arbitration Association is <http://www.adr.org/>.

Federal Legislation

Congress passed the **Federal Arbitration Act (FAA)**[8] in 1925 and, by doing so, declared a federal policy fa-

voring arbitration. The act withdraws the states' power to require a judicial forum to resolve disagreements if the parties have agreed by contract to solve disputes by arbitration. In the following case the Supreme Court upholds the intent of Congress to have the parties abide by their contract when it requires the arbitration of any subsequent disputes.

[8] A copy of the Federal Arbitration Act is at <http://www.adr.org/>. Use the search icon to find the FAA.

Case 4.1

Allied–Bruce Terminix Companies, Inc. v. Dobson

Supreme Court of the United States, 1995
513 U.S. 265, 115 S. Ct. 834, 130 L. Ed. 2d 753
http://www.supct.law
.cornell.edu/

BACKGROUND AND FACTS The Gwins owned a house in Birmingham, Alabama. In 1987, they purchased a lifetime "Termite Protection Plan" (Plan) from the local office of Allied-Bruce Terminix Companies, a franchise of Terminix International Company. Both Allied-Bruce Terminix and Terminix International were multistate businesses and shipped materials interstate.

The Plan promised to protect the house against termites, to provide periodic reinspections, to provide further treatment as necessary, and to repair up to $100,000 worth of damage caused by new termite infestations. The Plan also contained an arbitration clause. Alabama had a state statute that made written, predispute arbitration clauses invalid and unenforceable in court, although the rest of the contract would be enforceable. Parties to a contract could agree to arbitration only after a dispute arose.

In the spring of 1991, the Gwins were to sell their house to the Dobsons. Prior to the transfer of title, Allied-Bruce reinspected the house and certified the house to be free from termites. Immediately after the house was sold and Termite Protection Plan transferred to the Dobsons, the house was found to be swarming with termites. Allied-Bruce attempted to treat and repair the house, but the Dobsons found Allied-Bruce activities inadequate. They sued the Gwins, Allied-Bruce, and Terminix in state court.

Allied-Bruce and Terminix asked the court to dismiss the lawsuit because the contract had an arbitration clause. Under the clause, the dispute was to be submitted to arbitration. Both the trial court and the Alabama Supreme Court refused to dismiss the lawsuit and both enforced the Alabama statute that made written predispute arbitration clauses unenforceable. The case then was appealed to the United States Supreme Court.

The basis of the appeal is Article I, Section 8, Clause 3, of the U.S. Constitution, which is the interstate commerce clause. Section 2 of the Federal Arbitration Act provides that a contract with an arbitration clause involving commerce is valid, irrevocable, and enforceable in court. Since both Allied-Bruce and Terminix were interstate businesses, they wanted the lawsuit dismissed and the arbitration clause enforced. The issue is whether the Federal Arbitration Act would preempt state law, prohibiting predispute arbitration clauses when the contract involved the interstate commerce clause.

Justice BREYER delivered the opinion of the Court.

. . . .

The Federal Arbitration Act, § 2, provides that a "written provision in any maritime transaction or a contract *evidencing* transaction *involving* commerce to settle by arbitration a controversy thereafter arising out of such contract or transaction shall be valid, irrevocable, and enforceable, save upon such grounds as exist at law or in equity for the revocation of any contract." 9 U.S.C. § 2 (emphasis added).

. . . .

> . . . [Section] 2 gives States a method for protecting consumers against unfair pressure to agree to a contract with an unwanted arbitration provision. States may regulate contracts, including arbitration clauses, under general contract law principles, and they may invalidate an arbitration clause "upon such grounds as exist at law or in equity for the revocation of *any* contract." 9 U.S.C. § 2 (emphasis added). However, states may not decide that a contract is fair enough to enforce all its basic terms (price, service, credit), but not fair enough to enforce its arbitration clause. The Act makes any such state policy unlawful because that kind of policy would place arbitration clauses on an unequal "footing," directly contrary to the Act's language and Congress's intent.

DECISION AND REMEDY The Court found that the Federal Arbitration Act preempted the Alabama state law that invalidated arbitration clauses in contracts. The subject matter of the contract, however, must involve interstate commerce before the Federal Arbitration Act can preempt state law. The arbitration clause in the Plan was upheld, and the case was returned to the lower court to have the lawsuit dismissed.

CRITICAL THINKING: PUBLIC POLICY Why are Congress and the United States Supreme Court supportive of arbitration?

State Legislation

The **Uniform Arbitration Act**[9] was drafted by the National Conference of Commissioners on Uniform State Laws[10] in 1955. The American Bar Association[11] has approved it. The act is designed to make legislation on arbitration more uniform throughout the country. The act covers standards of procedure and rules to be used in the arbitration process. It also provides for judicial enforcement of the agreements to arbitrate.

The stated purpose of the act is to "validate voluntary, written arbitration agreements, make the arbitration process effective, provide necessary safeguards, and provide an efficient procedure when judicial assistance is necessary." This act has been adopted in thirty-four states and the District of Columbia. (See Exhibit 4–1.) The states that have not yet adopted the act normally follow many of the procedures suggested by it.

Arbitration occurs in one of two settings: *judicial* or *contractual*. The following sections discuss these two settings.

Judicial Arbitration

Compulsory (court-mandated) arbitration is called **judicial arbitration**. In some courts, after the parties have started a lawsuit, they can volunteer to have their case arbitrated, and the judge will issue an order to that effect. Even if the parties do not volunteer, they may be ordered by the judge to submit their case to arbitration.

In some jurisdictions, cases under a certain amount, such as $50,000, must be arbitrated. The types of civil disputes required to be submitted to arbitration are those in which money damages are sought. The arbitrator is appointed by the judge overseeing the lawsuit.

The actual hearing for a compulsory arbitration is the same as if the arbitration were a contractual one. No judge or jury is involved, and the arbitrator does not submit a written decision that sets out the reasons for the decision. Instead, only an award is issued, which is similar to a judgment.

In the hearing, the parties may use depositions, interrogatories, and certified documents to save the cost of a person's testifying at the hearing. Because the time spent to resolve the case is shorter than if the case went to court, the attorneys' fees usually are less.

The following case involves a dispute that went to arbitration. The court had to decide whether a party to a judicial arbitration was required to cooperate in a meaningful manner.

---

[9] A copy of the Uniform Arbitration Act, which currently is under revision, is at <http://www.law.upenn.edu/bll/ulc/ulc_frame.htm>.
[10] The National Conference has a web page at <http://www.nccusl.org/>.
[11] The web page for the American Bar Association in <http://www.abanet.org/>.

Case 4.2

Casino Properties, Inc. v. Andrews

Supreme Court of Nevada, 1996

911 P.2d 1181, 112 Nev. 132

BACKGROUND AND FACTS David DelRossi, his wife, four children, and adult niece, Andrews, stayed in two adjoining rooms at the Hacienda Resort Hotel and Casino (Hacienda) in Las Vegas for a week. The assistant hotel manager, O'Donnell, reviewed a computer report that indicated that the bill for the rooms exceeded DelRossi's credit card limit.

O'Donnell made several attempts to reach DelRossi to discuss payment terms but was unsuccessful. O'Donnell then ordered the security guards to perform a "lock-out" on both rooms. A lock-out is a procedure whereby the security guards lock the guest out of the room and deny the guest access to his personal belongings therein. This forces the guest to come to the front desk to pay his bill.

The security guards successfully locked out DelRossi's room and then attempted to do the same on the second room where Andrews and all of the children were staying. The security guard informed Andrews that there was a problem with the bill and that he was to escort her to the front desk so that she could straighten out the problem. Andrews refused to go because one of the children was ill and the others were allegedly near hysteria due to the guard's intrusion into the room.

Despite Andrews' concerns, the security guard forced Andrews to accompany him to the front desk, but he allowed the children to remain in the room. At the front desk, Andrews told O'Donnell that she was not responsible for the payment of the bill, and O'Donnell eventually located DelRossi, who paid the bill in full.

DelRossi sued the Hacienda for negligent and intentional infliction of emotional distress, invasion of privacy, and failure to provide protection from its abusive employees. The case was sent to judicial arbitration.

DelRossi's attorney delivered his pre-arbitration statement in a timely fashion to Hacienda. Hacienda, on the other hand, refused to share information about its employee and security handbooks and only supplied a statement one day before the arbitration hearing. Hacienda made O'Donnell, a key witness, available for questioning via telephone instead of in person.

The arbitrator awarded DelRossi $15,000 plus attorney's fees. Hacienda filed a motion (request) for a trial *de novo* (new trial). The district court held that Hacienda failed to defend the arbitration action in good faith, thereby waiving its right to request a trial *de novo*.

Hacienda filed this appeal. The Nevada Supreme Court reached a unanimous decision. The decision was written by the whole Court and not by one judge. Such an opinion is called *per curiam*.

PER CURIAM

The purpose of Nevada's Court Annexed Arbitration Program "is to provide a simplified procedure for obtaining a prompt and equitable resolution of certain civil matters." In *Gilling v. Eastern Airlines, Inc.,* a federal court dealing with the issue of good faith participation in arbitration equated "good faith" with "meaningful participation," and determined that if the parties did not participate in a meaningful manner, the purposes of mandatory arbitration would be compromised. We agree with this proposition and conclude that appellants did not defend the case in good faith during the arbitration proceeding because they did not participate in a meaningful manner.

The purposes of . . . mandatory arbitration are "to provide the parties with a quick and inexpensive means of resolving their dispute while, at the same time, reducing the court's caseload."

DECISION AND REMEDY Because Hacienda had failed to participate in a meaningful manner, the arbitrator's award of $15,000 plus attorney's fees in favor of DelRossi was upheld.

CRITICAL THINKING: PUBLIC POLICY The Seventh Amendment preserves the right to a jury trial. If a person does not participate in a judicial arbitration, should a person be denied the right to a jury trial? Please discuss fully.

Contractual Arbitration

The **contractual agreement to arbitrate** may be reached before or after the dispute arises. The parties may include a future dispute arbitration clause in their initial contract, ensuring that they will submit any future disputes to arbitration. If a dispute arises, the party making the complaint serves the Demand for Arbitration notice on the opposing party. (See Exhibit 4–2.)

If the parties fail to include an arbitration clause in the contract, however, when a dispute arises they still may agree mutually to submit the problem to arbitration. This agreement is called a Submission to Dispute Resolution and is signed by both parties. (See Exhibit 4–3.)

The two requirements for voluntary arbitration are that the agreement must be entered voluntarily and the agreement must be in writing to be enforceable in a court. Initially, this second requirement may seem to contradict the first. It is necessary, though, because even when there is a written agreement to arbitrate, one of the parties may refuse to participate in the arbitration

proceedings or may file a lawsuit, as in the *Allied-Bruce Terminix* case. The other party may request that the court order the first party to arbitrate. An oral agreement to arbitrate will not suffice. The written agreement is required because that agreement forfeits the parties' right to trial as guaranteed by the federal Constitution. The Seventh Amendment preserves the right to a trial by jury for civil cases at common law exceeding $20.

The modern view is that arbitration is binding on the parties once they have agreed to it. This agreement is called **binding arbitration**. In other words, a legal action cannot be brought if the parties have agreed to submit a controversy to arbitration. The arbitration procedures must be utilized to the fullest extent prior to filing a court action. The only exception would be when both parties refuse to arbitrate after initially agreeing to it.

If one party refuses to arbitrate, the other party may file a lawsuit and seek a court order to compel arbitration. The only defense is that there was no written agreement to arbitrate. The court will order arbitration

Exhibit 4–1 States that Have Adopted the Uniform Arbitration Act

Alaska	Indiana	Missouri	South Carolina
Arizona	Iowa	Montana	South Dakota
Arkansas	Kansas	Nebraska	Tennessee
Colorado	Kentucky	Nevada	Texas
Delaware	Maine	New Mexico	Utah
District of Columbia	Maryland	North Carolina	Vermont
Florida	Massachusetts	North Dakota	Virginia
Idaho	Michigan	Oklahoma	Wyoming
Illinois	Minnesota	Pennsylvania	

Exhibit 4–2   Sample Demand for Arbitration

American Arbitration Association
Commercial Arbitration Rules

To institute proceedings, please send two copies of this demand *and the arbitration agreement,* with the filing fee as provided in the rules, to the AAA. Send the original demand to the respondent.

DEMAND FOR ARBITRATION

DATE: _____

TO: Name _____

Address _____
(of the Party on Whom the Demand Is Made)

City and State _____   ZIP Code _____

Telephone (   ) _____   Fax _____

Name of Representative _____
(if Known)

Representative's Address _____

Name of Firm (if Applicable) _____

City and State _____   ZIP Code _____

Telephone (   ) _____   Fax _____

The named claimant, a party to an arbitration agreement contained in a written contract, dated _____ _____ and providing for arbitration under the Commercial Arbitration Rules of the American Association, hereby demands arbitration thereunder.

THE NATURE OF THE DISPUTE:

THE CLAIM OR RELIEF SOUGHT (the Amount, if Any):

DOES THIS DISPUTE ARISE OUT OF AN EMPLOYMENT RELATIONSHIP?   ☐ Yes   ☐ No

TYPE OF BUSINESS CLAIMANT _____   Respondent _____

HEARING LOCALE REQUESTED _____
(City and State)

You are hereby notified that copies of our arbitration agreement and this demand are being filed with the American Arbitration Association at its _____ office, with a request that it commence administration of the arbitration. Under the rules, you may file an answering statement within fifteen days after notice from the AAA.

Signed _____   Title _____
(May Be Signed by a Representative)

Name of Claimant _____

Address (to Be Used in Connection with This Case) _____

City and State _____   ZIP Code _____

Telephone (   ) _____   Fax _____

Name of Representative _____

Name of Firm (if Applicable) _____

Representative's Address _____

City and State _____   ZIP Code _____

Telephone (   ) _____   Fax _____

☐ **MEDIATION** is a nonbinding process. The mediator assists the parties in working out a solution that is acceptable to them. If you wish for the AAA to contact the other parties to ascertain whether they wish to mediate this matter, please check this box (there is no additional administrative fee for this service).

Form C2-3/99

Source: Reprinted with permission of the American Arbitration Association.

Exhibit 4–3   **Sample Submission to Dispute Resolution**

American Arbitration Association
SUBMISSION TO DISPUTE RESOLUTION

Date: _____

The named parties hereby submit the following dispute for resolution under the _____
_____ Rules* of the American Arbitration Association.

Procedure Selected: ☐ Arbitration   ☐ Mediation Settlement
                             ☐ Other _____
                                         (Describe.)

FOR INSURANCE CASES ONLY:

_____   _____ to _____   _____
Policy Number   Effective Dates   Application Policy Limits

_____   _____
Date of the Incident   Location

Insured: _____ Claim Number: _____

Name of Claimants	**Check if a minor.**	**Amounts Claimed**
_____	☐	_____
_____	☐	_____

Nature of Dispute and/or Injuries Alleged (Attach additional sheets if necessary.):

Place of Hearing: _____

We agree that, if binding arbitration is selected, we will abide by and perform any award rendered hereunder and that a judgment may be entered on the award.

To Be Completed by the Parties

_____	_____
Name of Party	Name of Party
_____	_____
Address	Address
_____	_____
City, State, and Zip Code	City, State, and Zip Code
( ) _____	( ) _____
Telephone Fax	Telephone Fax
_____	_____
Signature†	Signature†
Name of Party's Attorney or Representative	Name of Party's Attorney or Representative
_____	_____
Name of Firm (if Applicable)	Name of Firm (if Applicable)
_____	_____
Address	Address
( ) _____	( ) _____
Telephone Fax	Telephone Fax
_____	_____
Signature† (may be signed by representative)	Signature† (may be signed by representative)

Please file three copies with the AAA.

*If you have a question as to which rules apply, please contact the AAA.
†Signatures of all parties are required for arbitration.

Source: Reprinted with permission of the American Arbitration Association.

and stay (stop or delay) any other proceeding if it is presented with a contract that has an arbitration clause. An arbitration agreement is a contractual obligation into which the parties have voluntarily entered. The terms are enforced provided that they are legal and consistent with public policy. Although the court may order both parties to arbitrate, the parties themselves voluntarily agreed to the initial contract clause to submit disputes to arbitration.

Contractual Arbitration Procedure

Just as a lawsuit follows a series of steps, so does arbitration. Some parts of an arbitration procedure are similar to those of a judicial proceeding, whereas other parts are unique to arbitration. The terms that describe the process are peculiar to arbitration.

Tribunal Administrator.
The American Arbitration Association maintains offices around the country. The regional office has the responsibility of providing a **tribunal administrator**. This person manages the administrative matters and all communications between the parties and the arbitrator. The advantage is that the administrative burden of managing details and arrangements is not placed on the arbitrator, who may be located some distance from the parties and the place of the hearing. The arbitrator will be in direct communication with either of the parties only at the hearing. This arrangement prevents one side from making arguments, presenting evidence, or making suggestions to the arbitrator without allowing the other side an opportunity to be heard as well.

Selection of the Arbitrator.
Parties determine the method of appointing arbitrators in the arbitration agreement. Because it is a contractual arrangement, the arbitration agreement can specify the procedure to be followed in selecting an arbitrator. In the judicial system, this control cannot be exercised in selecting a judge. Usually, the parties must accept whichever judge is assigned to their case.

Generally, the parties do not have the foresight to include the method of selecting the arbitrator in the contract. In business arbitrations under $50,000, the American Arbitration Association directly appoints the arbitrator. In larger cases, between $50,000 and $1 million, the parties agree to an arbitrator. Each party re-

ceives a prepared list of proposed arbitrators who have expertise on the disputed topic. Each party chooses and prioritizes several names from its list. Each party then sends its list to the tribunal administrator for comparison to see which arbitrators are mutually acceptable and their order of preference. Finally, an arbitrator is agreed on by the parties. In large, complex disputes of more than $1 million, a panel of arbitrators usually is selected.

Preparation for the Hearing.
The parties determine a mutually convenient day and time for the hearing. Written notice of the hearing is provided to each party by the tribunal administrator. Each side should prepare for the hearings as it would for a trial. All documents and papers to be submitted into evidence are assembled and ordered logically. Proper arrangements are made if the arbitrator needs to visit a place for an on-the-spot investigation.

Before the hearing, all witnesses should be interviewed by each party. Each party should study the case from the opposition's viewpoint so that the opposition's evidence and arguments can be addressed. If a transcript of the hearings is needed, arrangements are made with the tribunal administrator for a court reporter to be present.

The Hearing.
An arbitration proceeding is very similar in form to a trial but does not quite take on the adversarial tone of a trial. A cooperative attitude is necessary for effective arbitration. Ordinary rules of courtesy and decorum are encouraged. Exaggeration, overemphasis, concealing of facts, and use of legal technicalities to disrupt or delay the hearing are discouraged.

Each party presents its case to the arbitrator in an orderly and logical manner. Just as in a trial, each side starts with a clear, concise opening statement. The complaining party usually presents first, telling the arbitrator its view of the dispute and the remedy it seeks. The second party then makes its opening statement. Both parties present documents and other materials to the arbitrator. If there are witnesses, they are examined to help each party establish its case. Finally, each side makes a closing argument. The closing argument includes a summary of the evidence, a refutation of the points made by the opposition, and a concluding argument to influence the arbitrator's decision. Following the closing arguments, the arbitrator declares the hearing closed.

The arbitrator hears the controversy and determines the decision based on the evidence produced, even if one party fails to appear, as long as the party received notification of the hearing. Either party to the case may have an attorney present, but representation is not required. Witnesses can be compelled to appear at an arbitration hearing through the use of subpoenas. The hearing can be adjourned to another time if the first meeting is not sufficient to hear all evidence.

The Award. The arbitrator must make her decision within thirty days after the hearing. If two or more arbitrators hear the case, the majority decision is binding, unless the parties agree beforehand that only a unanimous decision will be binding. The arbitrator's decision, or **award**, is based on the facts presented at the hearing.

Once the award is made, the arbitrator cannot change it. Only if the parties both agree to reopen the proceedings and restore power to the arbitrator can the award be changed. The award merely states which party prevailed and, when appropriate, the amount awarded. No supporting reasons are given. The award is final and binding on the parties. If the arbitration has been court ordered, the award is submitted to the court. Once the court accepts the award, it becomes the same as a judgment.

The Appeal. The following are the grounds on which the losing party may appeal an award in contractual arbitration:

1. The award was obtained through corruption, fraud, or other misconduct by the arbitrator.
2. Misconduct or partiality was exhibited by the arbitrator.
3. The arbitrator exceeded her or his powers.
4. The arbitrator refused to postpone the hearing or to hear evidence material to the controversy, which substantially prejudiced the rights of one of the parties.

5. The parties did not have a written arbitration agreement, and the issue of whether to take the dispute to arbitration was not determined in a court action to compel arbitration.

If the court does find one of these five grounds applicable to the case, it orders either a rehearing in front of the same arbitrator or a new hearing with a different arbitrator. The court has the right to modify the award under the following circumstances:

1. A miscalculation of figures was evident.
2. A mistake in the description of any person or property referred to in the award was evident.
3. The facts determined by the arbitrator were not those submitted to arbitration.
4. The award was not in the proper form.

A court is not allowed to modify an award in contractual arbitration on any other grounds.

In judicial arbitration, however, either party may appeal to the court. Normally, no grounds are required for the appeal other than that the appealing party does not accept the decision of the arbitrator. The appeal is treated by the court as a completely new case, and a trial *de novo* will be ordered. A trial *de novo* means that the decision of the arbitrator is not binding and the parties start over again. The case proceeds as a lawsuit, as it normally would have, if the arbitration never happened.

In the next case, the court had to decide whether to uphold a contractual arbitration agreement between a labor union and the employer. The two parties agreed to arbitrate employment issues that did not necessarily involve monetary claims. In most arbitration agreements, involve only questions of monetary damages and not equitable decisions. In this case, the parties broadened the scope of the arbitrator to include an equitable remedy.

Case 4.3

Eastern Associated Coal Corporation v. United Mine Workers of America

Supreme Court of the United States, 2000

531 U.S. 57, 121 S. Ct. 462, 148 L. Ed. 2d 354

BACKGROUND AND FACTS Eastern Associated Coal Corp. (Eastern), the employer, and United Mine Workers of America, the union, were parties to a collective-bargaining agreement with arbitration provisions. The clause to arbitrate provided that the arbitrator's decision was final. The arbitration agreement specified that in order to discharge an employee, Eastern must prove it had "just cause." Otherwise, the arbitrator would order the employee reinstated.

James Smith, a union member, worked for Eastern as a part of a road crew, a job that required him to drive heavy truck-like vehicles on public highways. As a truck driver, Smith was subject to Department of Transportation (DOT) regulations (the Testing Act) requiring random drug testing of workers engaged in "safety-sensitive" tasks.

In March 1996, Smith tested positive for marijuana. Eastern sought to discharge Smith. The union asserted Smith's rights under the arbitration clause. The arbitrator found that Smith's positive drug test did not amount to "just cause" for discharge. The arbitrator's award ordered Smith's reinstatement, provided that Smith (1) accept a suspension of 30 days without pay, (2) participate in a substance-abuse program, and (3) undergo drug tests at the discretion of Eastern (or an approved substance-abuse professional) for the next five years.

Between April 1996 and January 1997, Smith passed four random drug tests. But in July 1997, he again tested positive for marijuana. Eastern again sought to discharge Smith. The union again went to arbitration, and the arbitrator again concluded that Smith's use of marijuana did not amount to "just cause" for discharge, in light of two mitigating circumstances. First, Smith had been a good employee for seventeen years. Second, Smith made a credible and "very personal appeal under oath . . . concerning a personal/family problem which caused this one time lapse in drug usage."

The arbitrator ordered Smith's reinstatement provided that he (1) accept a new suspension without pay, this time for slightly more than three months; (2) reimburse Eastern and the union for the costs of both arbitration proceedings; (3) continue to participate in a substance-abuse program; (4) continue to undergo random drug testing; and (5) provide Eastern with a signed, undated letter of resignation, to take effect if Smith again tested positive within the next five years.

Eastern appealed the arbitrator's award to the federal district court, which upheld the arbitrator's award. Eastern appealed to the court of appeals, which ordered the award to be enforced. Eastern appealed this decision to the U.S. Supreme Court.

Justice BREYER delivered the opinion of the Court.

. . . .

Eastern claims that considerations of public policy make the arbitration award un-enforceable. In considering this claim, we must assume that the collective-bargaining agreement itself calls for Smith's reinstatement. That is because both employer and union have granted to the arbitrator the authority to interpret the meaning of their contract's language, including such words as "just cause." . . . They have "bargained for" the "arbitrator's construction" of their agreement. And courts will set aside the arbitrator's interpretation of what their agreement means only in rare instances. Of course, an arbitrator's award "must draw its essence from the contract and cannot simply reflect the arbitrator's own notions of industrial justice." . . . "But as long as [an honest] arbitrator is even arguably construing or applying the contract and acting within the scope of his authority," the fact that "a court is convinced he committed serious error does not suffice to overturn his decision." . . .

. . . .

We believe that these expressions of positive law embody several relevant policies. As Eastern points out, these policies include Testing Act policies against drug use by employees in safety-sensitive transportation positions and in favor of drug testing. They also include a Testing Act policy favoring rehabilitation of employees who use drugs. And the relevant statutory and regulatory provisions must be read in light of background labor law policy that favors determination of disciplinary questions through arbitration when chosen as a result of labor-management negotiation.

The award before us is not contrary to these several policies, taken together. The award does not condone Smith's conduct or ignore the risk to public safety that drug use by truck drivers may pose. Rather, the award punishes Smith by suspending him for three months, thereby depriving him of nearly $9,000 in lost wages, it requires him to pay the arbitration costs of both sides; it insists upon further substance-abuse treatment and testing; and it makes clear (by requiring Smith to provide a signed letter of resignation) that one more failed test means discharge.

The award violates no specific provision of any law or regulation. It is consistent with DOT rules requiring completion of substance-abuse treatment before returning to work, for it does not preclude Eastern from assigning Smith to a non-safety-sensitive position until Smith completes the prescribed treatment program. It is consistent with the Testing Act's 1-year and 10-year driving license suspension requirements, for those requirements apply only to drivers who, unlike Smith, actually operated vehicles under the influence of drugs. The award is also consistent with the Act's rehabilitative concerns, for it requires substance-abuse treatment and testing before Smith can return to work.

. . . .

We recognize that reasonable people can differ as to whether reinstatement or discharge is the more appropriate remedy here. But both employer and union have agreed to entrust this remedial decision to an arbitrator. We cannot find in the Act, the regulations, or any other law or legal precedent an "explicit," "well defined," "dominant" public policy to which the arbitrator's decision "runs contrary." We conclude that the lower courts correctly rejected Eastern's public policy claim.

DECISION AND REMEDY The Court upheld the arbitrators' award. Both parties had agreed in advance to arbitration. Therefore, the award was binding.

CRITICAL THINKING: PUBLIC POLICY Why should a person or business be held to a contractual arbitration agreement?

Differences

The following nine differences exist between a judicial arbitration and a contractual arbitration:

1. Under the contract arrangement the proceedings are private, but they are public for a judicial arbitration.

2. Under judicial arbitration full discovery rights are preserved, whereas discovery usually is very limited under the contract arrangement.

3. Subpoena power is preserved fully under the court arbitration, whereas none exists in the contract arrangement unless provided by statute. A subpoena is issued by a court, not ordinarily by an arbitrator.

4. The rules of evidence apply in a judicial arbitration but not in the contract arrangement.

5. The award is binding under the AAA arbitration rules, whereas in the judicial arbitration the award is binding only if it is not appealed. Judicial

arbitration cannot be binding, because the Seventh Amendment to the Constitution guarantees the right to a jury trial.

6. Appeal rights are preserved fully in a judicial arbitration. If an appeal is granted, the parties have a right to a trial in the court. Under the AAA arrangement, the arbitrator's decision is binding and final. Appeals may be made only on very limited grounds.

7. In the judicial arbitration setting, the arbitrator is usually an attorney with little or no arbitration experience, selected at random from the legal community. Under the contractual arrangement, the arbitrator is selected because of subject matter expertise.

8. The cost to the client is less under the contract arrangement, because no lawsuit is filed. Under the judicial arrangement the cost is more, because the case is pending before the courts. The cost, however, usually is less than that of a full court trial.

9. The stress on the parties is greater under judicial arbitration because the case is already in the court system. The stress is reduced under the contract arrangement because the arbitration has been agreed to by both parties.

Disadvantages of Arbitration

Although arbitration has many advantages, it also has inherent disadvantages when compared with a judicial proceeding. These seven major disadvantages need to be considered.

1. In most cases the arbitrator's award cannot be appealed except on the five grounds previously listed. Those grounds involve the lack of an arbitration agreement or involve the conduct of the arbitrator. The award itself cannot be appealed even though the arbitrator misapplied the law, as we will see in the next case. A judgment made by a court, in contrast, is appealable if the law is misapplied.

2. Arbitration lacks full discovery and full disclosure requirements. (See Chapter 3.) In arbitration,

discovery is very limited. Information disclosure is not even required.

3. The formal rules of evidence used in a courtroom trial do not apply in arbitration. These rules were developed to ensure justice to all parties. At times, evidence rules are technical, but they do promote fairness when presenting evidence. Evidence in court, for example, cannot be based on gossip or prejudices and must include relevant material. Often an arbitrator will hear evidence that would not be allowed in a court under its strict rules of evidence. The arbitrator must be careful to consider only evidence that has a bearing on the case.

4. A party may agree to arbitration without realizing it. Many times an arbitration clause is buried in the fine print within a contract. Even if the party were to read and understand the arbitration clause, he still may be coerced to agree to arbitration because the clause may appear in all contracts used by a particular industry.

5. A party usually is unaware of an arbitrator's background. All arbitrators have biases or prejudices.

6. Arbitrators tend to compromise when making awards rather than making clear-cut decisions for one party. Judicial decisions most often decide for or against one of the parties based on the case's merits.

7. After arbitration, future parties lose the use of prior written decisions as precedent. Written judicial opinions are one of the foundations of American law.

In summary, a person who agrees to arbitration waives the right to a jury trial, the right of appeal, and other protections of due process that are mandatory in the judicial setting. The arbitration proceeding is conducted privately. No written record exists, as is required for judicial proceedings. Finally, the person requesting the arbitration has the same burden of proof as for a trial. Without adequate discovery proceedings, the plaintiff may have a more difficult time proving her case before an arbitrator.

The next case illustrates the power of an arbitrator's award and the party's inability to appeal.

Case 4.4

Hembree v. Broadway Realty and Trust Company, Inc.

Court of Appeals of Arizona, 1986
151 Ariz. 418, 728 P.2d 288

BACKGROUND AND FACTS Broadway Realty and Trust Company, Inc., sold Hembree a home. The purchase contract had an arbitration clause requiring arbitration of any controversy or claim between the parties. The home had a defective roof. The case was arbitrated, and an award was given to Hembree based on breach of implied warranty, that is, a warranty imposed by law. The decision was appealed on the basis that (1) the arbitrator acted beyond his scope of authority and (2) the law of implied warranty should not have been applied. The trial court confirmed the award, and Broadway Realty appealed.

Chief Judge HATHAWAY

. . . .

I. SCOPE OF AUTHORITY . . . [T]he superior court will not confirm an arbitrator's award if the arbitrator exceeded his authority. An arbitrator's powers are defined by the agreement of the parties. The contract between appellees and appellants states that arbitration will be available for any controversy or claim "arising out of or *relating to this contract*" (emphasis added). . . . [O]nce an implied warranty comes into existence by reason of the circumstances of the sale, the law conceives such a warranty as being a term of the contract. Appellants argue that appellees' implied warranty claim does not arise out of or relate to "this contract." The gist of appellant's argument is that implied warranty can only apply to the sale of a home by a builder/vendor, and since appellant is a developer/vendor, the arbitration clause does not encompass this breach of implied warranty allegation. Appellants' argument, however, is legal rather than jurisdictional. The dispute between these parties relates to the sale of the home and the allegedly defective roof. In their lawsuit, appellees alleged a number of theories including implied warranty. Whether or not that theory was viable under these circumstances was a legal question for the arbitrator. The dispute, however, clearly arose out of and related to this contract for the sale of a home. Therefore, we find the arbitrator was within his authority in addressing the implied warranty claim.

II. MISTAKE OF LAW As stated above, appellants argue that parties who are not builders may not be held liable for breach of an implied warranty of habitability. It is settled case law that upon application to confirm an arbitration award, the superior court may not inquire as to whether errors of law were made by the arbitrator in reaching his decision. The power of this court is likewise severely circumscribed. Therefore this court may not review whether or not the arbitrator was correct in his application of the law. . . .

DECISION AND REMEDY The court upheld the award of the arbitrator. Although noting that the arbitrator might have been mistaken as to the legal issues on the implied warranty, the court held that it could not inquire into legal errors made by an arbitrator.

CRITICAL THINKING: PUBLIC POLICY When a trial judge, trained in the law, makes an error of law, her or his decision can be reversed on appeal. Why should the award based on an error of law made by an arbitrator, who is not trained in the law, not be appealable?

CyberLaw

Online ADR

Business is conducted worldwide and naturally legal conflicts will arise that require physical travel to resolve these disputes. Depending on the amount in controversy, travel may be simply too expensive and time consuming. Web sites exist that employ different alternative dispute resolution methods.[12] The most common methods used are mediation and arbitration. The cases submitted to online services tend to be those involving routine claims where only the amount of the claim is in dispute.

One party to the dispute contacts an online service, which, in turn, notifies the other party. If both parties are willing, settlement discussions may take place via e-mail, chat conference rooms, and faxes. The only requirement is for the parties to be online during the mediation session. The parties are not bound by anything said during these sessions.

Each side sends in an offer to settle the case to a secure, password-protected site. A party can check the site to see the status of the case. Each side is allowed to submit a limited number of offers, usually three. This method forces each side to evaluate the case in a realistic manner.

Just as in face-to-face discussions, in online mediation, the mediator has no authority to make a binding decision. It is only binding when all parties agree to be bound by the decision they reach. Mediation is a voluntary process that any participant may end for any reason. Until the parties agree to be bound, no one is bound.

Although a cost is associated with this type of online service, it is far less expensive than litigating a dispute. Approximately 85 percent of the cases submitted to mediation over the web have been settled.

[12] These firms have web addresses: Cybersettle <http://www.cybersettle.com>; National Arbitration and Mediation Corp. <http://www.clicknsettle.com>; U.S. Settlement Corp. <http://www.ussettle.com>; Onlinemediators <http://www.onlinemediators.com>; Internet Neutral <http://www.internetneutral.com>; and the Mediation Information and Resource Center <http://www.mediate.com>. These sites often offer more conventional ADR services.

Other Forms of ADR

New forms of alternative dispute resolution are being developed constantly. Most of them blend the concepts underlying conciliation and mediation. The following sections examine a few of the more recent developments in ADR.

Hybrid Mediation and Arbitration (Med/Arb)

Commercial agreements today use a hybrid system of combining mediation and arbitration, called **med/arb**, to resolve disputes. If a dispute arises, mediation is used first. The mediator will attempt to help the parties to find their own solution to the problem. Meeting with the parties separately, the mediator tries to bring the parties to agreement. The effect is to guide the parties to a resolution by building momentum in that direction. The resolution is an agreement mutually reached by the disputing parties.

If the parties fail to resolve their differences by mutual agreement, the next step is arbitration. The arbitrator's award is binding on both parties. Arbitration, in effect, is a forced solution.

A modified med/arb procedure is often used by automobile manufacturers when customers have disputes with dealerships. The arbitrator's award is binding on the dealership but is not binding on the customer, who can file a lawsuit if dissatisfied with the arbitrator's solution. A combination of mediation and arbitration is used extensively in the construction industry.

Exhibit 4–4 summarizes the distinctions among the various dispute resolution procedures discussed thus far.

Fact Finding

Used in complex commercial disputes, **fact finding** is an investigative process in which an independent third party investigates the issues and makes findings of fact. Courts use fact finders when confronted with a highly technical and involved fact situation requiring a high degree of expertise in a given area.

Frequently, a fact finder's role is solely that of making a recommendation. Having an independent person to determine certain facts often assists parties in reaching a settlement. If nothing else, the conclusions reached by the fact finder indicate to the parties the probable result of judicial litigation. This indication

Exhibit 4–4

Dispute Resolution Process Comparison Chart

Distinguishing Features	ADR PROCEDURE		COURT PROCEDURE	
	Voluntary Arbitration	Contractual Arbitration	Court-ordered/Judicial	Court Litigation
Dispute types	Any negotiable matter in the civil area	Civil matters of any type or complexity, unless prohibited by law, but only what parties provide for/agree to in writing	Civil matters for monetary relief only; usually a limit on the monetary amount of the claim	Civil and criminal cases heard; money damages and equitable remedies available
Private or public proceedings	Private	Private	Public	Public
Discovery rights	None provided by statute	Usually none or very limited under arbitration statutes; parties can provide for/agree to discovery in writing	Full rights as available under law or statute	Full rights as available under law or statute
Subpoena power	None provided by statute	Arbitrator has power to issue subpoenas in accordance with arbitration statutes; enforcement power rests with the court	Court has power to issue and enforce subpoenas	Court has power to issue and enforce subpoenas
Formal rules of evidence	None provided by statute	Do not apply unless provided by statute or unless parties provide for/agree to in writing	Do apply as provided for by statute and by court rules of procedure	Do apply as provided by statute and by court rules of procedure
Decision maker	The parties; the mediator facilitates further negotiations and settlement by the parties	An impartial arbitrator selected and/or empowered by the parties, who has special subject matter expertise	An impartial attorney usually chosen by the parties	A judge appointed by the court or an impartial jury chosen by the parties
Decision finality and enforcement	Verbal or written statement agreement may be enforceable through a judicial process	Final binding; enforceable by an appropriate court upon the entering of a judgment upon the award	Final and binding, unless appealed; if not appealed, enforceable by the court upon the entering of a judgment based upon the award	Final unless reversed on appeal
Appeal rights	Only available through a judicial process	Usually very limited under arbitration statutes unless parties provide/agree otherwise	Trial de novo (new trial) and full appeal rights as available under law	Full appeal rights as available under law
Relative speed from initiation to settlement or decision (not including appeal time)	Fastest (days to months); settlement occurs in 60 to 90% of cases mediated, depending on the type of case surveyed	Faster or fast (weeks to year); settlement occurs in 50% of cases submitted to AAA arbitration; parties can agree how fast or slow process will be	Fast (months to year); settlement occurs in 50% of these cases; the percentage of cases going to trial de novo is unknown	Slowest (one year to several years); settlement occurs in 95% of all civil cases, generally right before trial date
Who pays cost?	Parties	Parties	Taxpayers and parties	Taxpayers and parties

Source: American Arbitration Association.

LEGAL HIGHLIGHT

The Women at Hooters

On April Fool's Day, 1983, Hooters Restaurant was incorporated by the Hooters Six: L. D. Stewart, a painting contractor; Gil DiGiannantonio, a liquor salesman; "Uncle Billy" Ranieri, a retired service station owner; Ed Droste, a real estate executive; Dennis Johnson, a brick mason by trade; and Ken Wimmer, a partner in the painting business with L. D. Strange group. They wanted a restaurant with finger foods and 1950s and 1960s music.

The name Hooters came from comedian Steve Martin's comedy sketch. The creative menu and the irreverent humor combined with beautiful and vivacious young women, known as the Hooters Girls, to make the first restaurant so popular that within ten years it expanded across the country. But amid all the fun, there was a dark side.

Annette Phillips was employed as a bartender by Hooters in Myrtle Beach, South Carolina. She sued Hooters under Title VII of the Civil Rights Act alleging sexual harassment and a hostile work environment. Among the allegations were that she and other employees had to play sexually degrading games to determine to which restaurant area they would be assigned. She also alleged that Hooters managers exposed their genitals and underwear to female employees, and one manager offered bounty money to anyone who would find reasons to "write up" less attractive female employees, in order to fire them. It was alleged that the final straw was when the brother of the principal owner sexually harassed her by grabbing and slapping her buttocks. After appealing to her manager for help and being told to "let it go," she quit her job.

Prior to her resigning from her position with Hooters, she signed an arbitration agreement, known as the Hooters Rules. After the lawsuit was filed, Hooters requested the court to dismiss the case and send it to arbitration, an agreement which Phillips had agreed to.

But wait, said the court to Hooters. The Hooters Rules when taken as a whole, however, were so one sided that their only possible purpose was to undermine the neutrality of the proceeding. The rules required the employee to provide the company notice of her claim at the outset, including "the nature of the Claim" and "the specific act(s) or omissions(s) which are the basis of the Claim." Hooters, on the other hand, was not required to file any responsive pleadings or to give the plaintiff any notice of its defenses. Additionally, the employee was required to provide the company with a list of all witnesses with a brief summary of the facts known to each. The company, however, was not required to reciprocate.

The Hooters Rules also provided a mechanism for selecting a panel of three arbitrators that was crafted to ensure a biased decision maker. The employee and Hooters each selected an arbitrator, and the two arbitrators in turn selected a third. Sounds fair until the employee found out that both the employee's arbitrator and the third arbitrator had to be selected from a list of arbitrators created exclusively by Hooters. Thus, Hooters had control over the entire panel and the rules placed no limits whatsoever on whom Hooters could put on the list. Under the rules, Hooters was free to devise lists of partial arbitrators who have existing relationships, financial or familial, with Hooters and its management. In fact, the rules did not even prohibit Hooters from placing its managers themselves on the list. Further, nothing in the rules restricts Hooters from punishing arbitrators who rule against the company by removing them from the list.

The court struck down the Hooters Rules and wrote the following:

> Given the unrestricted control that one party (Hooters) has over the panel, the selection of an impartial decision maker would be a surprising result. Nor is fairness to be found once the proceedings are begun. Although Hooters may expand the scope of arbitration to any matter, "whether related or not to the Employee's Claim," the employee cannot raise "any matter not included in the Notice of Claim." Similarly, Hooters is permitted to move for summary dismissal of employee claims before a hearing is held whereas the employee is not permitted to seek summary judgment. Hooters, but not the employee, may record the arbitration hearing "by audio or videotaping or by verbatim transcription." The rules also grant Hooters the right to bring suit in court to vacate or modify an arbitral award when it can show, by a preponderance of the evidence, that the panel exceeded its authority. No such right is granted to the employee.

In addition, the rules provide that upon 30 days notice Hooters, but not the employee, may cancel the agreement to arbitrate. Moreover, Hooters reserves the right to modify the rules, "in whole or in part," whenever it wishes and "without notice" to the employee. Nothing in the rules even prohibits Hooters from changing the rules in the middle of an arbitration proceeding.

We hold that the promulgation of so many biased rules—especially the scheme whereby one party to the proceeding so controls the arbitral panel—breaches the contract entered into by the parties. The parties agreed to submit their claims to arbitration—a system whereby disputes are fairly resolved by an impartial third party. Hooters by contract took on the obligation of establishing such a system. By creating a sham system unworthy even of the name of arbitration, Hooters completely failed in performing its contractual duty.

Phillips would have her day in court. By not creating a ethical and fair arbitration agreement, Hooters lost its case.[a]

[a] *Hooters of America, Inc. v. Phillips*, 173 F. 3d 933 (1999).

---

by itself often helps the parties to reach a negotiated settlement.

A recent example was the appointment of Harvard law professor Lawrence Lessig as a special master (fact finder) by the trial judge in the Microsoft antitrust lawsuit by the Department of Justice. Microsoft objected to his appointment because of his alleged bias. The court of appeals suspended him from the case. If he had remained, he would have advised the judge on the legal issues affecting the lawsuit.

Minitrial

A **minitrial** is another voluntary procedure in which all parties must agree to its use. The primary purpose of a minitrial is to resolve questions of fact and law in complex, commercial disputes. It may be used in addition to fact finding.

No judge presides over a minitrial. Instead, the parties agree on an adviser. Normally, the adviser has had considerable experience with the subject matter that is the basis of the dispute. The parties determine the amount of authority that the adviser can exercise.

On being appointed, the adviser establishes an abbreviated discovery process that requires exchanging the documents, exhibits, written arguments, and names of witnesses that will be used by the parties. On conclusion of the discovery phase, the adviser meets with the parties, issues rulings on discovery matters, and attempts to resolve procedural questions.

Cases are settled more easily when all parties know the facts. When parties have full knowledge of the facts and the legalities that the case entails, the parties are better able to reach a settlement. Minitrials attempt to expedite discovery of the facts.

Another advantage of the minitrial is the confidentiality of its procedures. Many businesses prefer to withhold some information from the general public. The minitrial provides a procedure that limits the amount of information made public.

Minitrials have been used in cases of patent infringement, product liability, unfair competition, and antitrust violations. The minitrial is not considered an appropriate mechanism for cases involving constitutional law issues. It also is not appropriate for cases involving a large number of parties or legal questions.

Private Judge

A few states, particularly California, will allow the parties in a dispute to hire a **private judge**, called a referee. Normally, the referee is retired from the judiciary. The parties obtain a referee with expertise in the subject matter of the litigation. The referee is given the full powers of a judge, except the power to find someone in contempt of court.

The procedure is the same as that of a regular courtroom proceeding. The proceedings take place before the referee, no jury is allowed, and all trial procedures and rules of evidence are followed. A record is maintained for appeal purposes. The formality and judicial nature of this procedure differentiate it from arbitration.

The advantage of a private judge is that the parties are not controlled by the local court calendar. The case will be heard prior to cases filed earlier, because it will not be heard by the judges in the local court system.

LEGAL HIGHLIGHT

Electrical Companies Zap the Media

Three electrical utility companies (the plaintiffs) were building the William H. Zimmer Nuclear Power Plant. They contracted with General Electric Company (GE) to do construction work in the plant. A dispute occurred, and three electrical companies brought a lawsuit against GE for breach of contract. From the outset of this litigation, the parties recognized the need for confidential treatment of many documents. They stipulated that these documents would not be released. This agreement was confirmed by a court order.

The court required this case to be heard in a minitrial, the results of which were not binding on the parties. The proceeding was closed to the general public. The local news media objected to the closed hearing and filed a lawsuit to enforce their First Amendment rights of freedom of the press. In the meantime, the minitrial was held and the case was settled without going to a formal trial. In the media lawsuit, the judge refused to modify the original order, and the docu-

ments were not released to the news media. The news media appealed.

The U.S. Court of Appeals upheld the trial judge's order. The appeals court held that restrictions could be placed on information release when an alternative dispute resolution (ADR) proceeding is used.

Some types of ADR procedures, including minitrials, have been used for a little more than a decade. A conflict arises, however, between the right of access by the press and the public policy that encourages the use of ADR procedures. The court concluded that the law should favor the ADR proceeding.

If public access were allowed by the media, parties to lawsuits would have little incentive to try to settle the case in an ADR procedure. The public has no right to observe negotiations leading to a traditional case settlement. Thus, the public has no right to papers and other information used in an ADR proceeding that leads to a settlement.

This procedure allows expeditious treatment of the case before a referee who has both experience as a judge and special expertise in the subject matter.

The parties pay most, if not all, of the costs for this type of litigation. It can be expensive and is, therefore, available only to parties who can afford it. Because of this expense, the use of private judges has been criticized as creating a legal system for the wealthy that may result in a dual system of justice (that is, one for the rich and one for the less advantaged). The wealthy can have their cases decided rather quickly before judges with specialized experience, who devote full time to their cases, whereas the thousands of other parties to lawsuits must wait months and often years before their cases reach the court calendar.

Recently, relatively low-cost alternative private courts have been created as for-profit businesses. These private courts allow both parties to determine the hearing dates, location, presiding judge, and whether the judge's decision is binding. Each party is charged a

filing fee, as well as a set fee for each half-day hearing session. Obviously, the longer the hearing, the more costly the procedure becomes.

Short Trial

A few states have develop a blend between arbitration and a judicial trial. This procedure is called a short trial. The idea is to retain the jury format but have it binding on all parties. The number of jurors is reduced to no less than four. If three members out of the four agree, then that is the verdict. Before the trial, the parties agree that they will not appeal the decision of the jury.

All trials are only one day with each side having two hours to present evidence. These trials may be placed in between normal litigation whenever the court has a free day. People called for jury duty like this procedure because they only have to be in court one day. The parties like this approach because they get their day in court within months instead of years.

Partnering

Partnering is a process using team decisions to prevent or solve problems as they arise in large construction projects. The decision to include a clause mandating the partnering process is made during the contract negotiations. This process does not serve as a substitute for the contract. Instead, partnering attempts to create a sound working relationship.

In partnering, key decision makers from each contracting party and a neutral facilitator meet in retreats and workshops before the job starts. The individuals become acquainted with one another. The workshop allows each to learn the priorities, needs, and interests of the other project partners.

Partnering creates a framework for team building and requires good communication, trust building, working through problems, exploring options, and creating solutions. The idea is to prevent disputes or, if a dispute does arise, to resolve it as quickly as possible. Partnering implements the total quality management principles to which all parties should dedicate themselves in order to build a quality project. The partners meet on both a regular and an as needed basis throughout the construction period.

The costs of the partnering meetings and of the neutral facilitator are part of the project. By preventing disputes that might otherwise result in costly delays and lawsuits both partners save money. A problem solved costs less than a problem that is ignored or passed off to another party to the contract.

Partnering has been so successful in the construction industry that businesses are inserting partnering clauses in long-term supply contracts, purchasing contracts, and other nonconstruction contracts. Partnering is not really an alternative dispute resolution process but rather is an effective management tool that uses ADR methodology.

International Consideration

Arbitration in International Situations

Judicial procedures are used frequently in the United States to resolve disputes at all levels. Some cultures consider the need to resolve a dispute in court to be a personal failure. Thus, many international contracts provide for mediation, arbitration, or both.

The world community favors alternative dispute resolution procedures over the judicial forum. The **United Nations Convention on the Recognition and Enforcement of Foreign Arbitral Awards**,[13] commonly called the **New York Convention**, has been signed by seventy-three countries, including the United States, Canada, and Mexico. This convention allows the enforcement of arbitrated awards in any of the signature countries. Thus, international business associates may have disputes decided by arbitration. That arbitral award may be enforced in the country where the loser resides.

Additionally, the United States, Mexico, and ten Latin American countries have signed the **Inter-American Convention on International Commercial Arbitration (Panama Convention)**.[14] In this agreement, the twelve countries agree to submit their disputes of commercial transactions to arbitration.

With the North American Free Trade Agreement (NAFTA) now in effect, trade among the United States, Canada, and Mexico has steadily increased. The contracts negotiated among businesses should consider including mandatory mediation or arbitration clauses. Drafters of the contracts can look to many sources for model clauses, including those recommended

by the United Nations or the American Arbitration Association.

The **United Nations Commission on International Trade Law (UNCITRAL)**[15] has developed model arbitration clauses. The commission has rules for use in arbitration related to international trade, known as UNCITRAL Model Law on Commercial Arbitration.[16]

The American Arbitration Association follows international arbitration rules. These rules have provisions to determine the place and language of the arbitration, to authorize arbitrators to issue interim orders, and to appoint independent experts if necessary. Both arbitration and mediation provisions can be included in international commercial contracts.

Several organizations worldwide handle arbitration matters. The American Arbitration Association and the United Nations Commission on International Trade Law have already been mentioned. The London Court of International Arbitration[17] and the International Chamber of Commerce[18] (located in Paris, France) are among the other better known organizations. The Danish Institute of Arbitration is a permanent arbitration institution that has been in existence in Copenhagen ever since 1894. This organization has assisted in the settlement of numerous conflicts of a varied nature and accumulated a considerable fund of knowledge on arbitration procedures and the establishment of arbitration tribunals.[19]

---

[13] See the web site at <http://www.uncitral.org>.
[14] See the web site at <http://www.oas.org/>.

[15] See the UNCITRAL web site at <http://www.uncitral.org>.
[16] The Model Law is found at <http://www.jus.uio.no/lm/un.arbitration.model.law.1985/>.
[17] See the London Court of International Arbitration web site at <http://www.lcia-arbitration.com/>.
[18] See the International Chamber of Commerce web site at <http://www.iccwbo.org/>.
[19] The Danish Institute of Arbitration is located at <http://www.denarbitra.dk/>.

LEGALLY SPEAKING

Arbitration of Disputes Involving "Lemons"

You have purchased your first new automobile. On the way home, it suddenly stops. This event is just the beginning of your nightmare. After twelve trips to the dealership in a six-week period, you realize that you own a true lemon. Here are some steps to consider.

✔ Check to see if your contract requires arbitration for any problems that arise.

✔ Check to see if your state has a "lemon law." Usually, a modified arbitration procedure is authorized. If your vehicle meets the criteria for the lemon classification, you may be entitled to a replacement automobile or to an appropriate cash refund. If you are dissatisfied with the

arbitrator's decision, you can take your case to court. The automobile manufacturer, however, is bound by the decision. Make sure you follow the statutory provisions.

✔ Check to see if the dealer will agree to arbitration if the contract is silent on the matter and if your state does not have a lemon law.

If these options are not available, check to see if filing a lawsuit against the manufacturer and dealer is worth the time and expense to compensate you for your loss. You know, however, that this option would be very expensive, and months or years could pass before you finally have your day in court.

Chapter Summary

The judicial system is overburdened with litigation that results in long and expensive delays from the time of filing a complaint to the case conclusion. The judiciary, businesspersons, and the public have a real interest in finding alternatives to formal court procedures. These alternative dispute resolution procedures include negotiation, conciliation, mediation, arbitration, med/arb, fact finding, minitrials, hiring of private judges, short trials, and partnering.

In negotiation, the parties to the dispute resolve their differences by engaging in cooperative behavior to arrive at an agreement acceptable to all. Successful negotiation is an important skill that is not often taught in schools. Negotiations can occur at any stage of a dispute.

Conciliation involves a neutral third party. The conciliator facilitates the negotiations between the parties to help them to arrive at a mutually acceptable agreement. The conciliator does not actively participate in the negotiations and does not impose a decision on the parties. The parties must reach an agreement on their own.

Mediation also involves a neutral third party who facilitates the negotiations between the parties. The mediator helps the parties to negotiate their differences. The mediator has no power to make a decision. The parties must reach an agreement on their own.

In arbitration, the parties submit their dispute to an impartial third person. The arbitrator usually specializes in the subject area that the dispute is about. In 1925, Congress passed the Federal Arbitration Act, and federal policy favors arbitration. Arbitration is more favorable than litigation, having fewer financial costs, shorter time costs, maintenance of privacy, less formality, wider choice in decision-maker selection, and choice of the forum.

Arbitration occurs in one of two settings: contractual or judicial. A contractual agreement is voluntary and thus becomes binding arbitration. Many states require that lawsuits be sent to judicial arbitration when the amount requested is for less than a specified amount. If the parties agree with the decision of the judicial arbitrator, the case is settled. If one party disagrees, the case will be heard by the court.

Arbitration has seven disadvantages. First, the arbitrator's award cannot be appealed except on limited grounds. Second, arbitration does not have full discovery and full disclosure requirements. Third, the formal rules of evidence do not apply. Fourth, often people sign a contract without realizing that the contract has a binding arbitration clause. Fifth, the arbitrator's biases may not be known to the parties in the dispute. Sixth, arbitrators tend to compromise when making awards rather than to make a clear-cut decision. Seventh, since the reason for the award is not written, prior precedent is lost.

The field of ADR is evolving. Fact finding is an investigative process used in complex commercial disputes. Minitrials are used in courts where an adviser conducts an abbreviated discovery process. At the completion of discovery, the adviser helps the parties to reach a settlement. A few states allow parties to hire a private judge. The parties are able to hold the trial quickly rather than waiting for the case to be placed on the court calendar. Short trials are a combination of arbitration and judicial trials. Partnering is a process used in large construction projects to prevent disputes, or if a potential dispute develops, to resolve the matter quickly. Cybermediation is the use of web sites to be realistic about settlements concerning damage claims.

Using the World Wide Web

Registering a domain name is as simple as filling out a form and sending in the fees. Or is it? If the domain name you have selected has not been taken, generally there is no problem. But what if someone has taken the domain name? The Domain Name Dispute Resolution Service gives effect to the Uniform Domain Name Dispute Resolution Policy adopted by the Internet Corporation for Assigned Names and Numbers.

RAND Corporation is a not-for-profit organization that helps to improve public policy through research and analysis. The Institute for Civil Justice is a part of RAND Corporation that researches the civil justice system to make it more efficient and more equitable by supplying policymakers and the public with the results of objective, empirically based, analytical research. The institute has researched alternate dispute resolutions and provides information on the Internet and publications for purchase.

The Federal Trade Commission (FTC) has published a pamphlet in hardcopy and on the Internet concerning arbitration and mediation.

Go to the FTC site and answer the following questions:

- How would you find a dispute resolution program in your neighborhood?

- What questions should you ask about the program before you decide to use it?

- How should you prepare for an alternate dispute resolution program?

Finding the Law on the Web

Domain Name Dispute Resolution Service
http://www.arbiter.wipo.int/domains/index.html
RAND Corporation
http://www.rand.org/

Federal Trade Commission
http://www.ftc.gov/bcp/conline/pubs/general/dispute.htm

Chapter Web Sites

Free Advice
http://www.freeadvice.com/law/559us.htm
JAMS
http://www.jamsadr.com/
Mediation Information & Resource Center
http://www.mediate.com/
VGIS Communications, Inc.
http://www.seclaw.com/centers/arbcent.shtml
Stephen R. Marsh
http://adrr.com/
American Arbitration Association
http://www.adr.org/
Federal Arbitration Act
http://www.adr.org/
Allied-Bruce Terminix Companies, Inc. v. Dobson
http://www.supct.law.cornell.edu/
Uniform Arbitration Act
http://www.law.upenn.edu/bll/ulc/ulc_frame.htm
National Conference of Commissioners
on Uniform State Laws
http://www.nccusl.org/
American Bar Association
http://www.abanet.org/
Cybersettle
http://www.cybersettle.com
National Arbitration and Mediation Corp.
http://www.clicknsettle.com
U.S. Settlement Corp.
http://www.ussettle.com
Onlinemediators
http://www.onlinemediators.com

Internet Neutral
    http://www.internetneutral.com
Mediation Information and Resource Center
    http://www.mediate.com
United Nations Convention on the Recognition
    and Enforcement of Foreign Arbitral Awards
    (New York Convention)
    http://www.uncitral.org
InterAmerican Convention on International
    Commercial Arbitration (Panama Convention)
    http://www.oas.org/
United Nations Commission on International
    Trade Law (UNCITRAL)
    http://www.uncitral.org
Model Law on Commercial Arbitration
    http://www.jus.uio.no/lm/un.arbitration.model
    .law.1985/
London Court of International Arbitration
    http://www.lcia-arbitration.com/
International Chamber of Commerce
    http://www.iccwbo.org/
Danish Institute of Arbitration
    http://www.denarbitra.dk/

Federal Mediation and Conciliation Service
    http://www.fmcs.gov/
National Mediation Board
    http://www.nmb.gov/master.htm
Institute of Civil Justice (part of RAND Corporation)
    http://www.rand.org/centers/icj/faqs/ans11.html

Web Activities

4–1 Many organizations offer alternative dispute resolution assistance. One is the American Arbitration Association and the other is JAMS, The Resolution Experts. You are considering using one of these services for your business disputes. Compare the two web sites. Which web site is easier to use? Which site provides you with usable information that is easy to find? The American Arbitration Association is located at <http://www.adr.org/>. JAMS is located at <http://www.jamsadr.com/>.

4–2 The federal government has established laws governing labor relations and private businesses. Compare the Federal Mediation and Conciliation Service web site <http://www.fmcs.gov/> with the National Mediation Board <http://www.nmb.gov/> site. How are the two government agencies different?

Key Terms

alternative dispute
    resolution (ADR)
American Arbitration
    Association (AAA)
arbitration
arbitrator
award
binding arbitration
conciliation
contractual agreement to
    arbitrate

fact finding
Federal Arbitration Act
    (FAA)
InterAmerican
    Convention on
    International
    Commercial
    Arbitration (Panama
    Convention)
judicial arbitration
med/arb

mediation
minitrial
negotiation
partnering
private judge
tribunal administrator
Uniform Arbitration Act
United Nations
    Commission on
    International Trade
    Law (UNCITRAL)

United Nations
    Convention on the
    Recognition and
    Enforcement of
    Foreign Arbitral
    Awards (New York
    Convention)

Questions and Case Problems

4–1 Mediation Do you think that mediation should be used before a civil case goes to trial? If so, should the judge, who may be trying the case later, first serve as the mediator? What advantages and disadvantages do you see in such a situation?

4–2 Arbitration With a few exceptions, parties arbitrate their disputes because they have agreed to do so. Even with an agreement to arbitrate, one of the parties frequently changes his mind, deciding against arbitrating the dispute. Why do you think people want to avoid arbitration?

4–3 ADR You are the president of a medium-sized company that manufactures air conditioners. Recently you have noticed a substantial increase in legal expenses because of legal actions brought against your firm. Most, if not all, are brought by former employees and customers. In all cases, you believe the actions are not justified, but you want to decrease the cost of formal litigation. What types of cases would you allow to be handled through alternative dispute resolution procedures? What types of cases would you not allow to be handled through alternative dispute resolution procedures? Which alternative dispute resolution procedures would you use?

4–4 Arbitration Describe the advantages and disadvantages of arbitration over a judicial proceeding.

4–5 Arbitration The Southland Corporation is the owner and franchiser of 7-Eleven convenience stores. An arbitration clause within its franchise agreement requires arbitration for any controversy or claim arising from it. California has a franchise statute that allows legal actions to be brought in the courts. Some of the franchisees brought action against Southland Corporation based on violations of the California franchise law, along with other claims for fraud, misrepresentation, and breach of contract. Southland moved to force arbitration. What should the court hold? [*Southland Corp. v. Keating*, 465 U.S. 1, 104 S. Ct. 852, 79 L. Ed. 2d 1 (1984)]

4–6 Arbitration Alexander argues that he was discharged from his job because of his race. He had his case arbitrated but lost because the arbitrator found that Alexander's discharge was for just cause. Alexander appealed to a federal court to have the arbitration award overturned. On appeal, his ex-employer argued that Alexander had waived his rights under federal law to have the case heard by a court. Should Alexander have a new trial over the same issues and facts decided by the arbitrator? [*Alexander v. Gardner-Denver Co.*, 415 U.S. 36, 94 S. Ct. 1011, 39 L. Ed. 2d 147 (1974)]

4–7 Arbitration Lamar Byrd sold his medical practice and invested his $160,000 profit in securities through Dean Witter Reynolds, Inc. The value of his investments declined to about $60,000. Because of this, Byrd brought an action to recover his investment under federal and state laws. Numerous decisions held that actions under the federal law could not be subject to arbitration because of a federal statute. The question that Byrd presented to the United States Supreme Court was whether arbitration of the state law claims had to occur prior to any action taken concerning the alleged federal violations. What do you think was the result? Explain your answer. [*Dean Witter Reynolds, Inc. v. Byrd*, 470 U.S. 213, 105 S. Ct. 1238, 84 L. Ed. 2d 158 (1985)]

4–8 Arbitration Beers, while in Craft Warehouse's (Craft) store, was detained, then arrested by police for shoplifting. Beers was prosecuted and found not guilty. Afterwards, Beers' attorney wrote two identical letters to the store owner and store manager demanding $4,000 to settle plaintiff's claim for damages caused by the store's actions. Craft refused to settle. Beers filed two lawsuits seeking $4,000 for false imprisonment and $4,000 for malicious prosecution and attorney fees for each. The two lawsuits were consolidated and it was submitted to mandatory arbitration. The arbitrator awarded $4,000 and no attorney fees. The state statute required that in suits for $4,000 or less, reasonable attorney fees were to be awarded. Was the arbitrator correct in not awarding attorney fees? What was the result and why? [*Beers v. Jeson Enterprises*, 165 Or. App. 722, 998 P.2d 716 (Or. App. 2000)]

4–9 Arbitration AMF, Inc., and Brunswick Corporation compete nationally in the manufacture of bowling center equipment. In an earlier lawsuit, each of the two companies alleged that the other had advertised its products falsely. As part of the case settlement, AMF and Brunswick each agreed to submit to an advisory third party any further dispute involving an advertised claim to determine if there was valid support for the advertisement. The decision of the advisory third party was not binding on either party. Two years later, Brunswick advertised its new laminated bowling lanes as being superior to the wooden lanes AMF produced. AMF demanded that Brunswick's claims be submitted for independent validation by the advisory third party. Brunswick refused and argued that only binding arbitration clauses are enforceable. Is Brunswick's position correct? Why or why not? [*AMF Inc. v. Brunswick Corp.*, 621 F. Supp. 456 (D.C.N.Y. 1985)]

4–10 Internet The courts have embraced judicial arbitration with the stated goals of saving the courts time and money. The question arises as to whether judicial arbitration has accomplished this goal. What is the finding of the Institute of Civil Justice (which is a part of RAND Corporation)?

To find the answer, go to the Institute of Civil Justice, then to the Frequently Asked Questions (FAQs) page. Go to FAQ number 11, "Does alternative dispute resolution save time and money?" The specific web site address is <http://www.rand.org/centers/icj/faqs /ans11.html>.

Chapter 5

The Constitution and the Regulation of Business

The Constitution of 1789 deserves the veneration with which the Americans have been accustomed to regard it. It is true that many criticisms have been passed upon its arrangements, upon its omissions, upon the artificial character of some of the institutions it creates. . . .Yet, after all deductions, it ranks above every other written constitution for the intrinsic excellence of its scheme, its adaptation to the circumstances of the people, the simplicity, brevity, and precision of its language, its judicious mixture of definiteness in principle with elasticity in details.

The American Commonwealth, 3 vols. (London: Macmillan and Co., 1888), Vol. 1, p. 34
Viscount James Bryce, 1838–1922
British Ambassador to the United States of America, 1907–1913
Regius Professor of Civil Law, Oxford University

Outline

Ethical Consideration

Good Advertising?

You are the advertising manager for a local television station. You decide which commercials will be aired and when. You have just received a commercial for a lawyer in town. The commercial depicts a casually dressed man who looks into the television camera and announces firmly that he was an accident victim and that this lawyer "got me $155,000, even though the police report said that I was totally at fault." The next scene in the commercial shows another accident victim relaxing near a pool. This person states that the same lawyer recovered $1 million "from an insurance company that said I didn't even have a claim."

Although you are aware that freedom of speech is an important right, you are personally disgusted by this type of advertisement, which you believe has an insidious negative effect on the image of lawyers and on the judicial system as a whole. Should you reject or air the commercial? Use the ethical model presented in Chapter 2 and reprinted on the inside front cover to develop your answer.

Introduction

As a person with a World Wide Web (WWW) business, Artiste Login Products, Inc., you have given little thought to the U.S. Constitution. Why should you, as a businessperson, need to know and understand the U.S. Constitution and your state constitution?

First, the Constitution governs our personal and business lives as the supreme law in this country. All statutes passed by Congress or by a state legislature, all decisions made by judges in the federal and state courts, and all actions by the president or by the governor of a state must be in accordance with the Constitution. If a conflict arises between the state and federal constitutions, the U.S. Constitution prevails. The Constitution serves as a limitation on the power of the government.

Second, we must read the Constitution to understand court decisions and the reasons for which Congress acts or does not act in various situations. Third, every businessperson should appreciate the impact of the interstate commerce clause and other provisions affecting business contained in the Constitution.

Articles of the U.S. Constitution

The Constitution has two functions.[1] First, it creates the government. Second, it sets out an individual's rights in relation to that government.

The first three articles of the Constitution establish the framework for the federal government. Article IV gives direction to the states through the supremacy clause, the full faith and credit clause, and the privileges and immunities clause. Article V establishes the methods for amending the Constitution. Article VI ranks the order of the laws, giving highest priority to the Constitution itself and lowest priority to the laws of local government. Article VII, the last article, provides for the Constitution's ratification.

Separation of Powers Clause

The main body of the Constitution creates the federal government and establishes the three branches: the **legislative branch**, the **executive branch**, and the **judicial branch**. The rights, duties, and powers of the legislative branch are set forth in Article I. Article II creates the executive branch and establishes the powers of the president. The federal judicial system is created by Article III.

Each government's branch fulfills a separate function. Although no branch can exercise the authority of another branch, each branch has some power to limit the actions of the other two branches. This scheme creates a system of checks and balances, as mentioned in Chapter 1, so that no single branch can accumulate too much power.

For example, the executive branch is responsible for foreign affairs, but treaties with foreign governments require the advice and consent of the Senate. Congress has the power to tax, but the president can veto a tax bill. Congress determines the jurisdiction of the federal courts. The specific powers granted to Congress are listed in Article I, Section 8. Among those

[1] A complete copy of the constitution is found in Appendix A. Copies of the constitution may be viewed at <http://www.law.emory.edu/pub-cgi/usconwais> or at <http://wwwsecure.law.cornell.edu/constitution/constitution.overview.html>. The founding documents, such as the Declaration of Independence and different versions of the Constitution, can be seen at <http://www.constitution.org/cs_found.htm>. The Northwestern University web site has a multimedia database of Supreme Court decisions found at <http://oyez.nwu.edu/>. Cases can also be found at the Cornell Law School Legal Information Institute web site at <http://supct.law.cornell.edu:8080/supct/>.

powers are the power to regulate commerce, the taxing power, and the spending power.

Judicial Review. The Supreme Court exercises a power not specifically granted to it. This power is called the doctrine of **judicial review**, which allows the court to determine if acts of the other two government branches are in conflict with the mandates of the Constitution. Congress may pass, on rare occasions, a statute contrary to the Constitution, or the president may act, although rarely, counter to the Constitution. If the acts are in conflict, the Supreme Court can find them unconstitutional. The authority for judicial review is found in ancient English law.

The power of judicial review was first established in 1803 in the case of *Marbury v. Madison*. The Supreme Court determined that it had the power to decide whether a law passed by Congress violated the Constitution. Thus, the power of judicial review resides in the judicial branch and is part of the system of checks and balances. The following case creates the doctrine of judicial review.

Case 5.1

Marbury v. Madison

Supreme Court of the United States, 1803
5 U.S. (1 Cranch) 137,
2 L. Ed. 60
http://supct.law.cornell.edu
/supct/cases/name.htm

LANDMARK CASE

(Cranch was the second reporter of decisions and served from 1801 to 1815. The reporter of decisions is a Court position responsible for editing the Court's opinions and for supervising their printing and publication. During the time Cranch served, the Court issued oral opinions, which he wrote down. Cranch's reports were praised for their accuracy and clarity. The Court began to issue written opinions to supplement its oral opinions only for important cases during Cranch's service. Because Cranch was not paid, he was allowed to sell his reports to the public to earn a living. The U.S. Reports were published privately by different reporters of decisions who followed Cranch. In 1882, the U.S. Government Printing Office [GPO] assumed the duties of printing the Court's decisions. The GPO has republished these privately published decisions, citing the name of the reporter of decisions.)

BACKGROUND AND FACTS After George Washington[a] became President, a political division appeared between those who favored a strong federal government and those who favored a weak federal government. The Federalist Party, led by Alexander Hamilton[b] was in favor of a strong federal government and tended to reflect the views of the North and banking and manufacturing interests. The Democratic-Republican Party, led by Thomas Jefferson[c] favored a weak federal government, advocated states' rights, sought a strict interpretation of the Constitution, and represented the views of the South and farmers.

As a result of the national elections of 1800, President John Adams,[d] a Federalist, lost his bid for reelection to Thomas Jefferson, a Republican-Democrat. The political party controlling both the White House and Congress changed from the Federalist to the Democratic-Republican Party.

Believing that the Democratic-Republicans would weaken the national government, Adams, during the final hours of his administration, made fifty-nine midnight appointments to the judiciary. One way to extend political influence after leaving office was to appoint people to judiciary terms, since those terms last well beyond an administration. He hoped to pack the courts with loyal Federalists before Jefferson took office. Adams nominated William Marbury as a justice of the peace for Washington, D.C.

The U.S. Senate ratified Marbury's appointment, and Adams signed the commission. To make the appointment complete, the commissions had to be delivered to the appointee. Adams' secretary of state, John Marshall,[e] delivered forty-two of the fifty-nine appointments before he left office. After Jefferson became president, his newly appointed secretary of state, James Madison,[f] refused to deliver the commission to Marbury. Malbury, along with three others, decided to sue.

While Adams was still president, the Congress (dominated by the Federalists) passed a law (the Judiciary Act of 1789) concerning, in part, the issuance of a writ of *mandamus*, that is, a writ to enforce the performance of a public duty. The Judiciary Act required the United States Supreme Court to issue the writ, effectively making it a trial court. This statute greatly expanded the powers of the Supreme Court. It was on the basis of this new law that Marbury sued.

In an unusual turn of events, John Marshall had gone from being secretary of state under Adams to chief justice of the United States (appointed by Adams). Today, any judge would remove herself or himself from the case because of conflict of interest, but Marshall heard the *Marbury* case and wrote the following opinion, which still stands today.

Chief Justice MARSHALL delivered the opinion of the Court.

. . . .

The act to establish the judicial courts of the United States authorizes the Supreme Court, "to issue writs of mandamus, in cases warranted by the principles and usages of law, to any courts appointed or persons holding office, under the authority of the United States." The secretary of state, being a person holding an office under the authority of the United States, is precisely within the letter of this description; and if this court is not authorized to issue a writ of mandamus to such an officer, it must be because the law is unconstitutional.

. . . .

The question, whether an act, repugnant to the constitution, can become the law of the land, is a question deeply interesting to the United States; but, happily, not of an intricacy proportioned to its interest. It seems only necessary to recognize certain principles, supposed to have been long and well established, to decide it. That the people have an original right to establish, for their future government, such principles, as, in their opinion, shall most conduce to their own happiness is the basis on which the whole American fabric has been erected.

. . . .

It is emphatically the province and duty of the judicial department to say what the law is. Those who apply the rule to particular cases, must of necessity expound and interpret that rule. If two laws conflict with each other, the courts must decide on the operation of each.

So if a law be in opposition to the constitution; if both the law and the constitution apply to a particular case, so that the court must either decide that case conformably to the law, disregarding the constitution; or conformably to the constitution, disregarding the law; the court must determine which of these conflicting rules governs the case. This is of the very essence of judicial duty.

If, then, the courts are to regard the constitution, and the constitution is superior to any ordinary act of the legislature, the constitution, and not such ordinary act, must govern the case to which they both apply.

Those, then, who controvert the principle that the constitution is to be considered, in court, as a paramount law, are reduced to the necessity of maintaining that courts must close their eyes on the constitution, and see only the law.

This doctrine would subvert the very foundation of all written constitutions. It would declare that an act which, according to the principles and theory of our government, is entirely void, is yet, in practice, completely obligatory. It would declare that if the legislature shall do what is expressly forbidden, such act, notwithstanding the express prohibition, is in reality effectual. It would be giving to the legislature a practical and real omnipotence, with the same breath which professes to restrict their powers within narrow limits. It is prescribing limits, and declaring that those limits may be passed at pleasure.

. . . .

Thus, the particular phraseology of the constitution of the United States confirms and strengthens the principle, supposed to be essential to all written constitutions, that a law repugnant to the constitution is void; and that courts, as well as other departments, are bound by that instrument.

DECISION AND REMEDY   The Court held unconstitutional the provision of the Judiciary Act of 1789 that gave original jurisdiction to the United States Supreme Court to issue writs of *mandamus*. Thus, Marbury never became a justice of the peace.

COMMENT   Marshall was faced with a dilemma. If he exercised the authority given the Court by Congress to issue the writ of *mandamus* and thus ordered Madison, the new secretary of state, to deliver the commissions, Madison could refuse. The Court has no way to enforce its orders, because it has no enforcement machinery. The decisions of the Supreme Court even to this day rely on its moral authority. If Marshall did not issue the order, the secretary of state would be allowed to choose the acts that he would perform.

Marshall took another approach altogether. He found the act of Congress unconstitutional. The Constitution clearly delineates the cases over which the Court has original jurisdiction. The Constitution did not grant Congress the power to expand the Court's original jurisdiction as set out in Article III.

Because Congress did not have that power, the congressional act was declared unconstitutional by the Supreme Court. Marshall went on to say that Jefferson and Madison had acted incorrectly in refusing to deliver Marbury's commission, but the Supreme Court issued no order because it did not have the power to do so.

The Court's decision was a masterpiece of judicial navigation. Marshall avoided a confrontation with the president by not ordering him to do anything, found that the president had acted incorrectly, and firmly established the doctrine of judicial review. The case also illustrates that a situation revolving around an insignificant fact, such as an appointment of justice of the peace, can lead to a monumental judicial decision—in this case, the establishment of the doctrine of judicial review.

CRITICAL THINKING: POLITICAL CONSIDERATION   Discuss whether a judge should have the power to declare a statute unconstitutional when the act was passed by an elected legislative body and signed into law by either the president or a governor. Would your answer differ if the position of judge were elected or appointed? Can you find a recent case discussed in a newspaper or magazine in which a court declared a legislative act to be unconstitutional?

[a] George Washington (1732–1799), a Virginian, was the first president of the United States (1789–1797).
[b] Alexander Hamilton (1755–1804) from New York served as the first secretary of the treasury under President George Washington. Hamilton created the nation's central banking system.
[c] Thomas Jefferson (1743–1826) was from Virginia. He was elected as the third president of the United States (1801–1809). Jefferson and Adams died within hours of one another on July 4, 1826. Each died believing the other lived. They were the last two signers of the Declaration of Independence, signed fifty years earlier to the day.
[d] John Adams (1735–1826) from Massachusetts was elected as the second president of the United States (1797–1801).
[e] John Marshall (1755–1835) served as the fourth chief justice of the United States (1801–1835) appointed by President John Adams. In addition to deciding *Marbury v. Madison,* he also wrote the opinion of *McCullock v. Maryland* (1819), which decided that Congress had implied powers and that in a conflict between federal law and state law, federal law would prevail. See footnote 3 in this chapter.
[f] James Madison (1751–1836) from Virginia was elected as the fourth president of the United States (1809–1817). He was a Democratic-Republican.

LEGAL HIGHLIGHT

A Funny Thing Happened on the Way to Amend the Articles of Confederation

After winning independence from England, the original thirteen colonies created a government of states. This government was called the Confederation of the United States of America, a name used in the Declaration of Independence. The Articles of Confederation, adopted in 1781, created the confederation and set out the government powers.

Although a federal government existed, all the powers were held by the states. Unfortunately, the states did not work together. Each state based its decisions on its own best interests and not on the best interests of the unified thirteen colonies. Dissatisfaction arose, and in 1786, delegates from five states proposed that the Articles be reformed. Although reform was needed, many people vehemently opposed the idea of a strong central government. Nevertheless, the Congress, operating under the Articles of Confederation, called for a convention to amend the articles.

Seventy-four delegates were named to the convention. Fifty-five delegates from twelve states attended. Rhode Island disagreed with the procedure as a whole and sent no delegates.

The convention started on May 14, 1787, in Philadelphia. The delegates labored through a hot, humid Pennsylvania summer. Working secretly, they wrote guarded letters to friends and rarely spoke of the business at hand during their leisure hours.

Instead of amending the Articles of Confederation, the delegates drafted a completely new constitution that would replace the articles. The document created the strong central government so feared by many. Of the fifty-five delegates who started the work, forty-one were present when the convention ended on September 17, 1787. Only thirty-nine signed the document, the Constitution of the United States of America.

The Constitution then was submitted to the states. Before the Constitution could take effect, it had to be ratified by three-fourths of the states (nine out of thirteen). Heated debates in newspapers and in meetings followed. A series of newspaper articles that have become known as the *Federalist Papers*, written by James Madison, Alexander Hamilton, and John Jay, argued for the adoption of the Constitution.

After intense debate, the ninth state, New Hampshire, ratified the Constitution on June 21, 1788. Article VII of the proposed constitution stipulated that the Constitution would become effective (for those who ratified it) when ratified by nine states. By 1791, all thirteen states had ratified the Constitution. This document is now the oldest constitution in the world in continuous use. The genius of the writers lay in creating a mechanism that could translate theory into reality.

Many people observed that the Constitution listed no personal freedoms. Before ratifying the Constitution, a number of states made it clear that amendments containing the rights of the people in relation to the government would be necessary. The first ten amendments, known as the Bill of Rights, were adopted in 1791.

The Supreme Court still uses the doctrine of judicial review. When a congressional statute is challenged on the basis of constitutionality, the Court retains its power, as it has since *Marbury v. Madison*, to determine if Congress has exceeded its authority under the Constitution.

The United States Supreme Court has overturned fewer than 150 statutes during the past two centuries. In 1997, however, the Court overturned three statutes in one week.

The Commerce Clause

Congress has the power "to regulate Commerce with foreign Nations, and among the several States, and with the Indian Tribes" (Article I, Section 8). This clause is known as the **commerce clause**. No other clause in the Constitution has a greater impact on business. Because the federal government has the power to regulate commerce, the rules governing the movement of goods through the states are uniform.

Federal Regulation of Commerce. Congress holds the power to regulate any activity, interstate or intrastate, that substantially affects interstate commerce. For example, a federal regulation allows only a maximum number of acres of wheat to be grown. A farmer cannot plant more than the allowed acreage, even though the additional amount is for the farmer's own consumption. If enough farmers grew excess wheat for home consumption, they would reduce the overall wheat demand. A federal law must consider its cumulative effect on the entire economy. Thus, even one farmer may have a substantial economic effect on interstate commerce. If one farmer could grow excess wheat, others could too, and the goal of the federal regulation would be defeated.[2]

State Regulation of Commerce. States have a strong interest in regulating activities within their borders. States possess **police powers**, which give them

[2] *Wickard v. Filbert,* 317 U.S. 111, 63 S. Ct. 82, 87 L. Ed. 122 (1942), and <http://www.findlaw.com/casecode/supreme.html>.

the authority to regulate private activities in order to protect or promote the health, safety, morals, or general welfare of their citizens. For example, states have a strong interest in assuring the safety of privately owned trucks and automobiles using state highways in order to protect the rest of the traveling public.

Most state regulations place some burden on interstate commerce. When a state regulation encroaches on interstate commerce, the courts must balance the state's interest, reflected in the merits and purposes of the regulation, against the burden the regulation places on interstate commerce. A state law enacted pursuant to a state's police powers and affecting the health, safety, and welfare of local citizens, for example, carries a strong presumption of validity.

Because courts balance the interests between the state and federal governments, the outcome in a particular case cannot be predicted. The regulated activity, however, must involve commerce, that is, the exchange or trade of goods or property. The following case discusses whether the federal government could pass legislation under the commerce clause that attempts to prevent guns from being carried into public schools.

Case 5.2

United States v. Lopez

Supreme Court of the United States, 1995
514 U.S. 549, 115 S. Ct.1624, 131 L. Ed. 2d 626
http://supct.law.cornell.edu /supct/cases/name.htm

BACKGROUND AND FACTS Congress passed the Gun-Free School Zones Act of 1990. This statute made it a federal offense for any individual knowingly to possess a firearm in a school zone. Lopez was a twelfth-grade student who carried a .38 caliber handgun and bullets into his high school in San Antonio, Texas. Acting on an anonymous tip, school authorities confronted Lopez, who admitted to carrying the weapon.

Lopez was convicted of firearm possession in the federal district court, but the conviction was reversed by the court of appeals. The court held the statute to be invalid because it was beyond the power of Congress under the commerce clause. The federal government appealed to the United States Supreme Court.

Chief Justice REHNQUIST delivered the opinion of the Court.

. . . .

We start with first principles. The Constitution creates a Federal Government of enumerated powers. As James Madison wrote, "[t]he powers delegated by the proposed Constitution to the federal government are few and defined. Those which are to remain in the State governments are numerous and indefinite." This constitutionally mandated division of authority "was adopted by the Framers to ensure protection of our fundamental liberties." "Just as the separation and independence of the coordinate branches of the Federal Government serves to prevent the accumulation of excessive power in any one branch, a healthy balance of power between the States and the Federal Government will reduce the risk of tyranny and abuse from either front."

The Constitution delegates to Congress the power "[t]o regulate Commerce with foreign Nations, and among the several States, and with the Indian Tribes." . . .

. . . .

Consistent with this structure, we have identified three broad categories of activity that Congress may regulate under its commerce power. First, Congress may regulate the use of the channels of interstate commerce. ("'[T]he authority of Congress to keep the channels of interstate commerce free from immoral and injurious uses has been frequently sustained, and is no longer open to question.'") Second, Congress is empowered to regulate and protect the instrumentalities of interstate commerce, or persons or things in interstate commerce, even though the threat may come only from intrastate activities. ("[F]or example, the destruction of an aircraft or . . . thefts from interstate shipments.") Finally, Congress' commerce authority includes the power to regulate those activities having a substantial relation to interstate commerce, those activities that substantially affect interstate commerce.

. . . .

. . . The possession of a gun in a local school zone is in no sense an economic activity that might, through repetition elsewhere, substantially affect any sort of interstate commerce. Respondent was a local student at a local school; there is no indication that he had recently moved in interstate commerce, and there is no requirement that his possession of the firearm have any concrete tie to interstate commerce.

DECISION AND REMEDY The United States Supreme Court found that the possession of a gun by a student in a local school zone was not an economic activity that through repetition elsewhere would substantially affect interstate commerce. The statute was a criminal statute and by its own terms had nothing to do with commerce. The Supreme Court found that Congress had exceeded its authority.

CRITICAL THINKING: POLITICAL CONSIDERATION Without a special permit from the U.S. government, people can neither carry nor possess certain types of guns, such as a machine gun. Under this decision, does the possession of a machine gun violate the interstate commerce clause, and, if not, what is the federal government's authority to regulate these types of guns?

The Taxing Power

The **taxing power** comes from the constitutional clause that states that Congress has the "[p]ower to lay and collect Taxes, Duties, Imposts and Excises . . . but all Duties, Imposts and Excises shall be uniform throughout the United States" (Article I, Section 8). Imposts are taxes levied on imports. Excises are taxes placed on the sale or use of goods or service within a country and generally are paid by the buyer. For example, sales taxes are a form of excise tax.

All states must be treated equally for purposes of taxation. The courts examine whether Congress is actually attempting to regulate an area indirectly through taxation. If Congress is empowered to regulate an area, the tax is valid. If Congress attempts to regulate an area over which it has no authority, however, the tax law is void.

Federal taxes can be supported as a valid exercise of federal regulation. The Supreme Court has upheld statutes that impose taxation on income derived from both legal and illegal sources. For example, the Supreme Court has decided that taxes can be imposed on the transfer of firearms, on the transfer of marijuana, and on gambling income.

Taxing measures generally are found to be valid by the Supreme Court. The Court has held these tax laws to be within the national taxing power of Congress. Moreover, the Supreme Court has interpreted the commerce clause broadly to uphold various types of federal taxes imposed by Congress.

The Spending Power

Congress has the power "to pay the Debts and provide for the common Defense and general welfare of the United States" (Article I, Section 8). In other words, Congress can spend the monies collected under the taxing power. The **spending power** involves policy choices. Some taxpayers object to the government spending money on a particular program, such as Congress spending money to support national defense. It is, however, nearly impossible to object to specific government spending through the legal system because of the **standing to sue** requirement.

The doctrine of standing to sue requires a litigant to demonstrate a direct and immediate personal injury due to the challenged action. A litigant must show that the injury is related directly to the particular government spending program and that the court can give the litigant relief from the harm alleged. Rarely is a taxpayer directly harmed by any government spending program. As a result, the spending power seldom is challenged. Communicating directly with members of Congress is a more efficient method of influencing spending policies. The voters also can speak through the ballot box.

The Supremacy Clause

Article VI provides that the Constitution, laws, and treaties of the United States are "the supreme Law of the Land." This **supremacy clause** governs the relationship between the states and the federal government. When the Constitution specifically delegates a power to the federal government, any state law that conflicts with a federal law in that area is prohibited. If the conflict in the laws is taken to court, the state law will be rendered invalid. For example, only the federal government can coin money or pass naturalization laws.

In other areas, however, the state and federal governments may share powers; that is, they have **concurrent powers**. For example, bank robbery of a federally insured institution is both a state and federal crime.

Congress may choose to act exclusively in an area, but must do so under some provision of the Constitution. Congress has this power under the **preemption doctrine**. When Congress decides to exercise exclusive jurisdiction over a particular area, Congress is said to have preempted the area. The state government no longer holds authority to enact legislation in the preempted area. Congress will preempt an area that has national importance and where one uniform law is necessary. For example, the federal government has preempted the areas of aviation, labor, and nuclear power.

Congress rarely preempts an entire subject area by prohibiting state regulation. If a state law and a federal law conflict in an area of concurrent powers, and if the congressional intent is unclear, the courts must determine if Congress intended to exercise exclusive dominion over the given area.

Not all congressional powers are stated explicitly in the Constitution. Congress has the implied power under Article I, Section 8, to enact those laws necessary to carry out the enumerated powers vested in Congress and the government by the Constitution.[3]

---

[3] In *McCullock v. Maryland* (1819) the United States Supreme Court with John Marshall presiding as chief justice of the United States, had to decide whether Congress had the power to create the First Bank of the United States, a central bank, known in this century of the Federal Reserve Board.

Alexander Hamilton, secretary of treasury under President George Washington, had persuaded Congress to pass the statute creating the First Bank of the United States. Thomas Jefferson opposed it because the Constitution did not specifically create or authorize the creation of a central bank by the federal government. Hamilton argued that the federal government had implied powers to create a central bank. Hamilton's implied powers argument prevailed when the United States Supreme Court upheld the legislation that created the First Bank of the United States.

Chief Justice Marshall laid down two doctrines that prevail today. First, the implied powers doctrine. James McCullock, cashier of the Baltimore branch of the First Bank of the United States, refused to pay a tax imposed by Maryland on the bank. The court upheld the implied power of the Congress to create a bank, because Congress needed a bank to exercise its specific powers. The court ruled that Congress has implied powers in addition to those expressly set out in the Constitution. The decision was based on the section of the Constitution called the "necessary and proper" clause (Article I, Section 8). This clause gives Congress power "to make all laws which shall be necessary and proper" to carry out its other powers.

Second, the doctrine that federal power must prevail over state power in case of conflict. The tax was declared unconstitutional because it interfered with an instrument of the federal government. Chief Justice Marshall stated that the American people "did not design to make their government dependent on the states."

Federalism is the organizational system of the U.S. government. Under this system, state governments share powers with the federal government. Neither the state nor the federal government is superior to the other except within the particular area of authority granted to it by the Constitution.

Federalism appreciates that society is best served by distributing various functions among local governments and the national government depending on which government is best able to perform each function. For instance, the federal government can best handle national defense and foreign relations, whereas state and local governments are best able to handle domestic relations, probate, and traffic violations. Exhibit 5–1 depicts this division of powers.

Full Faith and Credit Clause

Article IV, Section 1, reads, "Full Faith and Credit shall be given in each State to the public Acts, Records, and judicial Proceedings of every other State." The Constitution requires every state, through the full faith and credit clause, to recognize and enforce the judgments and other public actions of sister states. For example, if you obtain a divorce in one state, all other states must recognize your divorce.

Limitations do apply. For instance, if the original court did not have jurisdiction, the judgment may be challenged in the state where the plaintiff tries to enforce the judgment.

Privileges and Immunities Clause

Article IV, Section 2, provides that "the citizens of each State shall be entitled to all Privileges and Immunities of Citizens in the several States." As a result of the **privileges and immunities clause**, one state cannot discriminate against the citizens of another state solely on the basis of their residency.

Limitations on this clause have been developed by the courts during the past 200 years. A state may pass a statute that protects "legitimate local interest." Under this protection, state-supported colleges and universities may charge higher tuition to nonresident students than to resident students. The justification is that the state's residents pay taxes that support the public university system.

Bill of Rights and the Other Amendments

The Bill of Rights was added to the Constitution in 1791.[4] Most of the first ten amendments contain specific protections for persons from the federal government. Guarantees provided by the Bill of Rights include the following:

1. The First Amendment protects religion, speech, press, assembly, and redress of grievances.
2. The Fourth Amendment offers provisions regarding arrest and unreasonable search and seizure.
3. The Fifth Amendment provides:
   a. protection from **double jeopardy**. A person cannot be tried by the same level of government more than once for the same crime.
   b. freedom from **self-incrimination**. A person cannot be forced to testify against herself or himself.
   c. right to due process. A person has the right to timely notice of a trial and to a fair hearing.
4. The Sixth Amendment guarantees the rights to a speedy and public trial by jury, to an attorney, to confront witnesses, and to cross-examination in criminal prosecutions.
5. The Seventh Amendment preserves the right to a jury trial in civil suits.
6. The Eighth Amendment provides for bail and prohibits cruel and unusual punishment.

Fourteenth Amendment

Passed after the Civil War (1861–1865), the Fourteenth Amendment applies to actions by state government. It includes a due process clause, similar to the one in the Fifth Amendment, that requires states to provide their residents with due process.

The Fourteenth Amendment also includes an **equal protection clause**, not found in any other part of the Constitution. The equal protection clause prohibits any state government from favoring one class of people at the expense of another. The Fifth Amendment's due

---

[4] Go to the following web address to find other sites that discuss the Constitution and its amendments: <http://www.constitution.org/cs_found.htm>.

Exhibit 5–1   **The American Federal System: Division of Powers between the Federal Government and the State Governments**

Powers Granted by the Constitution and Amendments

FEDERAL GOVERNMENT	FEDERAL AND STATE GOVERNMENTS	STATE GOVERNMENTS

Implied

"To make all laws which shall be necessary and proper for carrying into execution the foregoing powers, and all other powers vested by this Constitution in the Government of the United States, or in any Department or Officer thereof."

(Article I, Section 8:18)

Concurrent

- To levy and collect taxes
- To borrow money
- To make and enforce laws
- To establish courts
- To provide for the general welfare
- To charter banks and corporations

Reserved to the States

- To regulate intrastate commerce
- To conduct elections
- To provide for public health, safety, and morals
- To establish local governments
- To ratify amendments to the federal constitution

Enumerated

- To coin money
- To conduct foreign relations
- To regulate interstate commerce
- To levy and collect taxes
- To declare war
- To raise and support military forces
- To establish post offices
- To establish courts inferior to the Supreme Court
- To admit new states

Powers Denied by the Constitution

Federal

- To tax articles exported from any state
- To violate the Bill of Rights
- To change state boundaries

Federal and State

- To grant titles of nobility
- To permit slavery
- To deny citizens the right to vote

State

- To tax imports or exports
- To coin money
- To enter into treaties
- To impair obligations of contracts
- To abridge the privileges or immunities of citizens or deny due process and equal protection of the law

LEGAL HIGHLIGHT

Twenty-Seven of 10,000 Proposed Amendments

The delegates to the constitutional convention held in 1787 in Philadelphia did not believe that any protections of individual freedoms should be included in the document. Basically, the constitution should create the government, nothing more. Very shortly after the proposed constitution was circulated among the states, it became evident that the people had other ideas. Indeed, they demanded constitutional protections for the people against actions by the federal government.

More than 10,000 amendments have been proposed during the past 200 years. The first 10 amendments came as a package and were adopted in 1791, but only 17 amendments were added between 1798 and 1995. Of those 17 amendments, one canceled an earlier one; the Twenty-first Amendment repealed the Eighteenth Amendment on liquor prohibition.

One early proposed amendment intended to use the Constitution to prohibit the act of dueling. Another, which would have been the Thirteenth Amendment, attempted to prohibit Congress from abolishing slavery; ironically, the Thirteenth Amendment that eventually was adopted abolishes slavery.

More than 200 proposed amendments attempted to stop the Civil War. More recent proposals include the Equal Rights Amendment, the Right to Life Amendment, the Term Limits Amendment, a Balanced Budget Amendment, and the Anti-Flag-Burning Amendment.

---

process clause prevents the federal government from favoring a particular group of people.

Over a long series of cases, the Supreme Court adopted the **doctrine of selective incorporation**. Under this doctrine, the Court selectively has taken parts of the first ten amendments and applied them to the states using the Fourteenth Amendment as the basis. For example, the Fourth Amendment clause against unreasonable searches and seizures now applies to the states. If a case has not been decided, the individual protections granted by the Bill of Rights apply only to the federal government's actions and not to those of the state governments.

Specific protections found in the First, Fourth, Fifth, Sixth, Seventh, and Eighth Amendments now apply to the states. One exception is the right to a grand jury found in the Fifth Amendment. The Supreme Court found that the states can use methods other than indictment by a grand jury to bring to trial those accused of crimes.

Delegated Powers

The Tenth Amendment delegates certain **enumerated powers** to the federal government and reserves all other powers to the states or to the people. This amendment limits the power of the federal government by stating that "the powers not delegated to the United States by the Constitution, nor prohibited by it to the States, are reserved to the States respectively, or to the people." The federal government has no powers apart from those specified in the Constitution. The U.S. government holds only enumerated powers because it can exercise only those powers that are expressly or implicitly granted to it.

The term *expressly* was not included in the Tenth Amendment. *Expressly*, however, appeared in the Articles of Confederation in a similar provision. Because of this omission, the federal government can find implied federal powers. Thus, the Constitution implicitly allows the federal government to take necessary action to follow through on the specific powers granted to it. Or to take action in areas that did not exist when the Constitution was adopted, such as the areas of aviation and nuclear power.

The following U.S. Supreme Court case discusses a number of constitutional issues. The commerce clause and the Tenth Amendment are discussed in this edited case.

Case 5.3

Reno v. Condon

Supreme Court of the United States, 2000
528 U.S. 141, 120 S. Ct. 666,
145 L. Ed. 2d 587

BACKGROUND AND FACTS Congress passed the Driver's Privacy Protection Act of 1994 (DPPA or Act). This Act regulates the sale by state motor vehicle departments (DVMs) of personal information contained in drivers' licenses and motor vehicle registration records. Congress found that many States sold this personal information to individuals and businesses. Those sales generated significant revenues for the States. The DPPA also regulates the resale of this information.

The DPPA's ban on disclosure of personal information does not apply if drivers have consented to the release of their data. States must obtain a driver's affirmative consent to disclose the driver's personal information for use in surveys, marketing, solicitations, and other restricted purposes.

The DPPA's prohibition of nonconsensual disclosures is also subject to a number of statutory exceptions. The DPPA requires disclosure of personal information concerning matters of motor vehicle or driver safety; theft; emissions; motor vehicle product alterations, recalls, or advisories; performance monitoring of motor vehicles and dealers by motor vehicle manufacturers; and removal of nonowner records from the original owner records of motor vehicle manufacturers to carry out the purposes of the Anti-Car Theft Act, the Automobile Information Disclosure Act, and the Clean Air Act. South Carolina law conflicted with the DPPA's provisions.

Under that law, the information contained in the State's DMV records was available to any person or entity that filled out a form listing the requester's name and address and stating that the information would not be used for telephone solicitation.

Following the DPPA's enactment, South Carolina and its attorney general, Condon, filed suit alleging that the DPPA violated the Tenth and Eleventh Amendments to the U.S. Constitution. The district court concluded that the Act is incompatible with the principles of federalism inherent in the Constitution's division of power between the states and the federal government. The Court of Appeals for the Fourth Circuit affirmed, concluding that the Act violates constitutional principles of federalism.

Chief Justice REHNQUIST delivered the opinion of the Court.

. . . .

We of course begin with the time-honored presumption that the DPPA is a "constitutional exercise of legislative power."

The United States asserts that the DPPA is a proper exercise of Congress' authority to regulate interstate commerce under the Commerce Clause, U.S. Const., Art. I, § 8, cl. 3. The United States bases its Commerce Clause argument on the fact that the personal, identifying information that the DPPA regulates is a "thin[g] in interstate commerce," and that the sale or release of that information in interstate commerce is therefore a proper subject of congressional regulation. We agree with the United States' contention. The motor vehicle information which the States have historically sold is used by insurers, manufacturers, direct marketers, and others engaged in interstate commerce to contact drivers with customized solicitations. The information is also used in the stream of interstate commerce by various public and private entities for matters related to interstate motoring. Because drivers' information is, in this context, an article of commerce, its sale or release into the interstate stream of business is sufficient to support congressional regulation.

. . . .

But the fact that drivers' personal information is, in the context of this case, an article in interstate commerce does not conclusively resolve the constitutionality of the DPPA. . . .

. . . .

South Carolina contends that the DPPA violates the Tenth Amendment because it "thrusts upon the States all of the day-to-day responsibility for administering its complex provisions," and thereby makes "state officials the unwilling implementors of federal policy." South Carolina emphasizes that the DPPA requires the State's employees to learn and apply the Act's substantive restrictions, . . . and notes that these activities will consume the employees' time and thus the State's resources. South Carolina further notes that the DPPA's penalty provisions hang over the States as a potential punishment should they fail to comply with the Act.

We agree with South Carolina's assertion that the DPPA's provisions will require time and effort on the part of state employees, . . .

. . . .

. . . [T]he DPPA does not require the States in their sovereign capacity to regulate their own citizens. The DPPA regulates the States as the owners of databases. It does not require the South Carolina Legislature to enact any laws or regulations, and it does not require state officials to assist in the enforcement of federal statutes regulating private individuals. We accordingly conclude that the DPPA is consistent with the constitutional principles. . . .

As a final matter, we turn to South Carolina's argument that the DPPA is unconstitutional because it regulates the States exclusively. The essence of South Carolina's argument is that Congress may only regulate the States by means of "generally applicable" laws, or laws that apply to individuals as well as States. But we need not address the question whether general applicability is a constitutional requirement for federal regulation of the States, because the DPPA is generally applicable. The DPPA regulates the universe of entities that participate as suppliers to the market for motor vehicle information—the States as initial suppliers of the information in interstate commerce and private resellers or redisclosers of that information in commerce.

. . . .

DECISION AND REMEDY The court found that the DPPA regulation was involved with interstate commerce and, therefore, the sale or release of that information in interstate commerce was a proper subject of congressional regulation. The court went on to declare that the statute was not a violation of the Tenth Amendment.

CRITICAL THINKING: POLITICAL CONSIDERATION Why do you think the federal government should ever pass this type of a law?

Bill of Rights in a Business Context

The Bill of Rights guarantees persons certain protections. Does the Bill of Rights protect only individuals or does it also protect businesses?

A business may be conducted by one person operating under her own name or under a fictitious name. Other types of businesses are conducted by partnerships or by corporations. Corporations and some types of partnerships exist in the eyes of the law as legal entities separate from the individuals that own them.

A **legal entity** can sue and be sued in a court, pays taxes, and holds title to property. Thus, a legal entity includes individuals and various forms of business. As a legal entity, businesses are entitled to some of the same rights and privileges as an individual. The United States Supreme Court has held that since many of the amendments use the word *person* instead of *citizen* (which is used in other parts of the Constitution), illegal (undocumented) aliens and business entities are protected by many constitutional provisions.

The Supreme Court recognizes business entities as persons in very specific areas of the Constitution. In other areas, however, business entities do not qualify for constitutional protection. The following sections discuss portions of the First, Fourth, Fifth, and Fourteenth Amendments.

First Amendment

The First Amendment to the Constitution states:

Congress shall make no law respecting an establishment of religion, or prohibiting the free exercise thereof; or abridging the freedom of speech, or of the press; or the right of the people peaceably to assemble, and to petition the government for redress of grievances.

This section will examine two areas from the First Amendment: freedom of speech and freedom of religion.

Freedom of Speech

Our forebearers believed that the ability to generate and then to exchange ideas allowed for the development of a free and open society. Armed with knowledge, a citizen has the capability of making better decisions.

Although the First Amendment requires Congress (as well as state governments because of the Fourteenth Amendment) to avoid regulating free speech, a business can control speech. For example, the owners of a professional basketball team can require a player to stand when the national anthem is played prior to the game. Another example is that a business can restrict the passing out of flyers for an employee's personal pursuits, such as soliciting for a charity.

Speech is broadly defined as communication, and includes oral, written, and symbolic speech. Speech can be categorized as *protected speech, partially protected speech*, and *unprotected speech*. These categories deter-

mine whether speech can be restricted and regulated by the government.

Protected Speech. **Protected speech** cannot be restricted or regulated in any manner by the government, thus allowing a full exchange of ideas to take place. Political speech is an example of protected speech.

In this country's early years, Congress passed a statute forbidding any criticism of the president. The statute was later repealed. Today, such a law would never be passed because it is clearly unconstitutional. Another example is the case that involved the burning of the nation's flag in front of the building where a national political convention was meeting. The act of flag burning was protected as symbolic speech in a case decided by the United States Supreme Court. This decision has led to efforts by Congress to adopt a constitutional amendment prohibiting burning or otherwise defacing the nation's flag.

Partially Protected Speech. **Partially protected speech** cannot be regulated by the government, but it can be restricted as to time, place, and manner. Two types of speech that fall into this category include *offensive speech* and *commercial speech*.

Offensive Speech. Offensive speech (without obscenity) is protected speech. Offensiveness alone does not justify suppression; however, restriction as to time, place, and manner must be reasonable. For example, speakers who use offensive speech may be restricted to a portion of a public park where they may speak freely. Thus, the offensive speech is restricted, but not regulated.

The Federal Communications Commission (FCC) may restrict offensive language on broadcast television to late-night time periods when children generally are not watching. Broadcast television is beamed over public air waves, which the government regulates. Cable television, however, is not subject to such restrictions, since cable companies own the cable that delivers the medium. Cable may carry shows that cannot appear on broadcast television because of their offensive nature.

Over a period of decades, the federal government created and built what is now known as the Internet. Its use, however, was very restricted. With the demise of the Union of Soviet Socialist Republics in 1989, the government lifted its restrictions and by 1995 had basically turned over control of the Internet to private enterprise.

In 1993, the World Wide Web, one part of the Internet, was created. The WWW makes information accessible to laymen in a variety of formats. Some examples include graphic user interfaces (GUIs), such as interactive text, still photographs, moving videos, streaming videos (such as listening to a congressional debate in real time), telephony (a telephone-like connection that may use live video), push technology (instead of the user's going to the server located at another site, push technology "pushes" the information to your hard drive when the site is opened, with the information always updated), just to name a few services.

The WWW was very successful and attracted many businesses. Businesses that publish and sell sexually explicit material were quick to take advantage of the lack of regulations on this new medium.

Congress, concerned over the explosion of sexually explicit material, passed the Communications Decency Act (CDA) of 1996. After President William J. Clinton signed the bill into law, a lawsuit was immediately filed. This case was eventually appealed to the United States Supreme Court to determine if the CDA violated the First Amendment. The following case is the decision from the Supreme Court.

Case 5.4

Reno v. American Civil Liberties Union

Supreme Court of the United
States, 1997
521 U.S. 844, 117 S. Ct. 2329,
138 L. Ed. 2d 874
http://www.findlaw.com
/casecode/supreme.html

BACKGROUND AND FACTS Congress passed the Communications Decency Act in 1996, which became law upon the president's signature. The CDA sought to protect minors from harmful material on the Internet.

One section criminalized the "knowing" transmission of obscene or indecent messages to any minor under the age of eighteen. Providers, which are located both within and outside the United States, were to restrict minors' access by requiring proof of age, such as a verified credit card or an adult identification number. Immediately after the CDA became law, twenty parties filed suit.

A three-judge panel sitting on the district court heard the case. Based on the Act's special review provisions, the case was appealed directly to the United States Supreme Court.

Justice STEVENS delivered the opinion of the Court.

. . . .

Sexually explicit material on the Internet includes text, pictures, and chat and "extends from the modestly titillating to the hardest-core." These files are created, named, and posted in the same manner as material that is not sexually explicit, and may be accessed either deliberately or unintentionally during the course of an imprecise search. "Once a provider posts its content on the Internet, it cannot prevent that content from entering any community."

. . . .

. . . Neither before nor after the enactment of the CDA have the vast democratic fora of the Internet been subject to the type of government supervision and regulation that has attended the broadcast industry. Moreover, the Internet is not as "invasive" as radio or television. The District Court specifically found that "[c]ommunications over the Internet do not 'invade' an individual's home or appear on one's computer screen unbidden. Users seldom encounter content 'by accident.'" It also found that "[a]lmost all sexually explicit images are preceded by warnings as to the content," and cited testimony that "'odds are slim' that a user would come across a sexually explicit sight by accident."

. . . .

The vagueness of the CDA is a matter of special concern for two reasons. First, the CDA is a content-based regulation of speech. The vagueness of such a regulation raises special First Amendment concerns because of its obvious chilling effect on free speech. Second, the CDA is a criminal statute. In addition to the opprobrium and stigma of a criminal conviction, the CDA threatens violators with penalties including up to two years in prison for each act of violation. The severity of criminal sanctions may well cause speakers to remain silent rather than communicate even arguably unlawful words, ideas, and images. As a practical matter, this increased deterrent effect, coupled with the "risk of discriminatory enforcement" of vague regulations, poses greater First Amendment concerns than those implicated by the civil regulation reviewed in *Denver Area Ed. Telecommunications Consortium, Inc. v. FCC.*

. . . .

We are persuaded that the CDA lacks the precision that the First Amendment requires when a statute regulates the content of speech. In order to deny minors access to potentially harmful speech, the CDA effectively suppresses a large amount of speech that adults have a constitutional right to receive and to address to one another. That burden on adult speech is unacceptable if less restrictive alternatives would be at least as effective in achieving the legitimate purpose that the statute was enacted to serve.

In evaluating the free speech rights of adults, we have made it perfectly clear that "[s]exual expression which is indecent but not obscene is protected by the First Amendment."

. . . .

The breadth of the CDA's coverage is wholly unprecedented. Unlike the regulations upheld in [previous cases], the scope of the CDA is not limited to commercial speech or commercial entities. Its open-ended prohibitions embrace all nonprofit entities and individuals posting indecent messages or displaying them on their own computers in the presence of minors. The general, undefined terms "indecent" and "patently offensive" cover large amounts of nonpornographic material with serious educational or other value. Moreover, the "community standards" criterion as applied to the Internet means that any communication available to a nation-wide audience will be judged by the standards of the community most likely to be offended by the message.

. . . .

We find . . . [the government's] argument singularly unpersuasive. The dramatic expansion of this new marketplace of ideas contradicts the factual basis of . . . [the government's] contention. The record demonstrates that the growth of the Internet has been and continues to be phenomenal. As a matter of constitutional tradition, in the absence of evidence to the contrary, we presume that governmental regulation of the content of speech is more likely to interfere with the free exchange of ideas than to encourage it. The interest in encouraging freedom of expression in a democratic society outweighs any theoretical but unproven benefit of censorship.

DECISION AND REMEDY The government was enjoined from enforcing the criminal sections of the Act, that is, to knowingly transmit obscene or indecent messages to minors. The Act's content-based blanket restrictions on speech abridged the freedom of speech protected by the First Amendment.

CRITICAL THINKING: PUBLIC POLICY Why should communications over the Internet be treated differently from communications made through radio and broadcast television over which the government does exercise control through the Federal Communications Commission?

Many organizations are dedicated to the concept of freedom of speech. These organizations are found on the Internet. One of the more prestigious ones is the Freedom Forum,[5] which "is a nonpartisan, international foundation dedicated to free press, free speech and free spirit for all people." The foundation pursues its priorities through conferences, educational activities, publishing, broadcasting, online services, fellowships, partnerships, training, research, and other programs. The Freedom Forum funds only its own programs and related partnerships. Unsolicited funding requests are not accepted.

Operating programs by the Freedom Forum are the Newseum at the Freedom Forum World Center headquarters in Arlington, Virginia, the First Amendment Center at Vanderbilt University in Nashville, Tennessee, the Media Studies Center in New York City, and the Pacific Coast Center in San Francisco. The Freedom Forum also has operating offices in Cocoa Beach, Florida; Buenos Aires; Hong Kong; Johannesburg; and London.

The Cyberspace Law Institute (CLI) is involved with freedom of speech along with other cyber problems.[6] The CLI has posted many papers written about cyber issues. The American Civil Liberties Union is involved with freedom of speech issues and also has a web presence.[7]

Commercial Speech. In the past, the United States Supreme Court distinguished between an individual's freedom of speech versus freedom of speech in the commercial area. For example, political speech could not be restrained, but commercial advertising was subject to government control. This view continued until the case of *Virginia State Board of Pharmacy v. Virginia Citizens Consumer Council, Inc.*[8] This case, along with several others, challenged a legal ban on advertising the price of prescription drugs. The Court held, "It is clear . . . that speech does not lose its First Amendment protection because money is spent . . . as in a paid advertisement."

After this case, several cases arose confronting the issue of commercial speech, that is, advertising. One of the leading cases was *Bates v. State Bar of Arizona*[9] The state bar of Arizona refused to allow any attorney to advertise services or the price of those services. Advertising was considered unprofessional. Two attorneys advertised, quoting prices for routine legal work. The advertisements did not include anything that might commonly be called trade puffing. Because of this advertisement, the state bar of Arizona suspended the attorneys from practicing law. The United States Supreme Court held that the attorneys' freedom of speech had been violated.

Eventually, additional problems concerning restrictions on professional advertising confronted the United States Supreme Court. Can the government place restrictions on professional advertising? In the following case, the United States Supreme Court discusses commercial speech.

[5] The Freedom Forum's web address is <http://www.freedomforum.org/first/welcome.asp>.
[6] The Cyberspace Law Institute's web site is <http://www.cli.org/>.
[7] The American Civil Liberties Union's web site is <http://www.aclu.org>.

[8] *Virginia State Board of Pharmacy v. Virginia Citizens Consumer Council, Inc.* 425 U.S. 748, 96 S. Ct. 1817, 48 L. Ed. 2d 346 (1976), and <http://www.findlaw.com/casecode/supreme.html>.
[9] *Bates v. State Bar of Arizona,* 433 U.S. 350, 97 S. Ct. 2691, 53 L. Ed. 2d 810 (1977), and <http://supct.law.cornell.edu/supct/cases/name.htm>.

Case 5.5

Florida Bar v. Went For It, Inc.

Supreme Court of the United States, 1995
515 U.S. 618, 115 S. Ct. 2371, 132 L. Ed. 2d 541
http://www.findlaw.com/casecode/supreme.html

BACKGROUND AND FACTS Rules of the Florida Bar prohibited personal injury lawyers from sending targeted direct-mail solicitations to victims and their relatives for thirty days following an accident or disaster. In March 1992, G. Stewart McHenry and his wholly owned lawyer referral service, Went For It, Inc., filed this action for declaratory and injunctive relief in the U.S. District Court, challenging these rules as violative of the First and Fourteenth Amendments to the Constitution.

McHenry alleged that he routinely sent targeted solicitations to accident victims or their survivors within thirty days after accidents and that he wanted to continue doing so in the future. Went For It, Inc., also wanted to contact accident victims or their survivors within thirty days of accidents and to refer potential clients to participating Florida lawyers. The district court entered summary judgment for the plaintiffs, and the Eleventh Circuit affirmed the lower court.

Justice O'CONNOR delivered the opinion of the Court.

. . . .

Constitutional protection for attorney advertising, and for commercial speech generally, is of recent vintage. Until the mid-1970s, we adhered to the broad rule that, while the First Amendment guards against government restriction of speech in most contexts, "the Constitution imposes no such restraint on government as respects purely commercial advertising." In 1976, the Court changed course. In *Virginia Bd. of Pharmacy v. Virginia Citizens Consumer Council, Inc.*, we invalidated a state statute barring pharmacists from advertising prescription drug prices. . . .

In *Virginia Bd.*, the Court limited its holding to advertising by pharmacists, noting that "[p]hysicians and lawyers . . . do not dispense standardized products; they render professional services of almost infinite variety and nature, with the consequent enhanced possibility for confusion and deception if they were to undertake certain kinds of advertising."

One year later, however, the Court applied the Virginia State Board principles to invalidate a state rule prohibiting lawyers from advertising in newspapers and other media. In *Bates v. State Bar of Arizona* the Court struck a ban on price advertising for what it deemed "routine" legal services: "the uncontested divorce, the simple adoption, the uncontested personal bankruptcy, the change of name, and the like." . . .

Nearly two decades of cases have built upon the foundation laid by *Bates*. It is now well established that lawyer advertising is commercial speech and, as such, is accorded a measure of First Amendment protection. . . . Mindful of these concerns, we engage in "intermediate" scrutiny of restrictions on commercial speech, analyzing them under the framework set forth in *Central Hudson Gas & Electric Corp. v. Public Service Comm'n of N.Y.* Under *Central Hudson*, the government may freely regulate commercial speech that concerns unlawful activity or is misleading. Commercial speech that falls into neither of those categories, like the advertising at issue here, may be regulated if the government satisfies a test consisting of three related prongs: first, the government must assert a substantial interest in support of its regulation; second, the government must demonstrate that the restriction on commercial speech directly and materially advances that interest; and third, the regulation must be "'narrowly drawn.'"

. . . We have little trouble crediting the Bar's interest as substantial. On various occasions we have accepted the proposition that "States have a compelling interest in the practice of professions within their boundaries, and . . . as part of their power to protect the public health, safety, and other valid interests they have broad power to establish standards for licensing practitioners and regulating the practice of professions."

. . . .

Under *Central Hudson's* second prong, the State must demonstrate that the challenged regulation "advances the Government's interest 'in a direct and material way.'" . . .

. . . .

. . . After scouring the record, we are satisfied that the ban on direct-mail solicitation in the immediate aftermath of accidents, . . . targets a concrete, nonspeculative harm.

. . . .

Passing to *Central Hudson's* third prong, we examine the relationship between the Florida Bar's interests and the means chosen to serve them.

. . . .

. . . The Bar's rule is reasonably well-tailored to its stated objective of eliminating targeted mailings whose type and timing are a source of distress to Floridians, distress that has caused many of them to lose respect for the legal profession.

Respondents' second point would have force if the Bar's rule were not limited to a brief period and if there were not many other ways for injured Floridians to learn about the availability of legal representation during that time. Our lawyer-advertising cases have afforded lawyers a great deal of leeway to devise innovative ways to attract new business. . . .

DECISION AND REMEDY The Court believed that the Florida Bar's thirty-day restriction on targeted direct-mail solicitation of accident victims and their relatives withstood scrutiny under the three-part test that was devised for this context. The bar had a substantial interest both in protecting injured Floridians from invasive conduct by lawyers and in preventing the erosion of confidence in the profession that such repeated invasions have engendered.

CRITICAL THINKING: POLITICAL CONSIDERATION What restrictions should apply to professional advertisement? Please provide examples and discuss fully.

Although commercial speech is protected by the First Amendment, advertisements must not be deceptive, misleading, or fraudulent. In addition to advertising their services, businesses also may want to establish their positions on various social, political, trade, and economic issues.

At times, determining whether a business's intention is to advocate a public or political position or to use commercial speech is difficult. For example, a bank that opposes a referendum that would allow a graduated personal income tax wants to spend money to present its views to the public. A business has as much right to publicize its views as an individual, even though these views promote the business's own profit. Moreover, the public is enriched by being exposed to all views, whether they are those of an individual or of a business.

Unprotected Speech.
Unprotected speech is not protected by the First Amendment. During the past two centuries, six types of speech have been denied protection: dangerous speech, fighting words, speech that incites violence or revolution, defamatory speech, obscenity, and child pornography.

Dangerous speech is that which endangers the public. An example provided by the United States Supreme Court is yelling "Fire" in a crowded theater when in fact no fire exists. That word can create a stampede of people, thus placing others in harm's way.

Fighting words are intended to provoke a violent or hostile response from an ordinary person. Usually this type of speech is aimed at an individual.

Defamation is discussed in greater detail in Chapter 8. It is defined as the act of making an untrue statement that impinges on the integrity or character of another person or corporation. Historically, defamation has never been protected by the First Amendment. During the civil rights movement of the early 1960s, the *New York Times* printed articles of a defamatory nature against an elected southern official. When the official brought suit against the newspaper, the United States Supreme Court held that public officials seeking to recover for defamation relating to their performance of official duties must prove **actual malice**.[10] Actual malice means that a statement must be made with the knowledge that it is false or with reckless disregard of whether or not it is false.

---

[10] *New York Times Co. v. Sullivan,* 376 U.S. 254, 84 S. Ct. 710, 11 L. Ed. 2d 686 (1964), and <http://supct.law.cornell.edu/supct/cases /name.htm#Case_Name-N-O>.

The First Amendment covers public figures and officials. A public official is a person who is elected or appointed to government service. A public figure is a person, such as an actor or an athletic coach, who seeks public recognition or a person who is thrust into the limelight, such as a person accused of a crime or a survivor of an airplane crash.

As seen in the case of *Reno v. American Civil Liberties Union*, discussed previously, obscene speech and child pornography are not protected by the First Amendment. Obscene speech is defined by the United States Supreme Court as speech that (1) appeals to the prurient interest, (2) depicts sexual conduct in a patently offensive way, and (3) lacks serious literary, artistic, political, or scientific value. An example is child pornography that uses children for sexual purposes.

The problem with the freedom of speech lies in establishing limits. We all favor freedom of speech for ourselves; however, we also recognize potential reasons to limit others' freedom of speech. Should the American Nazi Party be allowed to hold a parade in a predominantly Jewish neighborhood? Should anti-nuclear demonstrators be allowed to block nuclear plant entrances?

Freedom of speech limitations have varied over the years. More than 200 years after the 1791 adoption of the First Amendment, society still is defining freedom of speech and limits that should be placed on that freedom.

Freedom of Religion

The government can neither establish any religion nor prohibit the free exercise of religious practices. Any government action, federal or state, must be neutral toward religion. An individual statute, however, may impact religion. As long as it does not promote or place a significant burden on religion, the statute is constitutional.

Sunday closing laws, for example, forbid the performance of certain business activities on Sunday. The closing laws have been found to be constitutional because the government has a legitimate interest in providing workers a day of rest. Although closing laws originally were religious in character, they have taken on the secular purpose of promoting workers' health and welfare. Even though closing laws admittedly facilitate Christian attendance at religious services, the United States Supreme Court has viewed this effect as

an incidental, not a primary, purpose of Sunday closing laws. Today, the few closing laws that remain generally allow businesses to be open on Sunday, so long as they do observe a day of rest.

Title VII of the Civil Rights Act of 1964 prohibits government and private employers and unions from discriminating against individuals because of their religion. Instead, businesses must accommodate their employees on the basis of religious beliefs.

The United States Supreme Court addressed this issue in *Estate of Thornton v. Caldor, Inc.*[11] The Court held that a Connecticut statute granting employees the absolute right not to work on their Sabbath had the effect of advancing religious practices in violation of the establishment clause of the First Amendment. The establishment clause prohibits the government from establishing a religion. The Connecticut type of statute discriminated against employees who might want a day off during the weekend for secular reasons.

In *Trans World Airlines, Inc. v. Hardison*,[12] the United States Supreme Court reviewed the case of a former airline clerk who brought a lawsuit against the airline and the union, claiming religious discrimination. The clerk sought to have Saturday, his Sabbath, off. Neither the union nor the airline could work out a solution to the problem because the clerk had low seniority, and those of higher seniority also wanted Saturdays off. Eventually he was fired for refusing to work on Saturday. The Supreme Court held that the airline and the union had made reasonable efforts to accommodate the clerk's religious beliefs and that the proposed solutions to his problem worked an undue hardship on the airline, the union, and his fellow employees. The operation of the seniority system was agreed to by both the airline and the union. As long as the seniority system did not have a discriminatory purpose, it was not an unlawful employment practice, even though the operation of the seniority system was discriminatory in its effect.

[11] *Estate of Thornton v. Caldor, Inc.,* 472 U.S. 703, 105 S. Ct. 2914, 86 L. Ed. 2d 557 (1985), and <http://www.findlaw.com/casecode/supreme.html>.
[12] *Trans World Airlines, Inc. v. Hardison,* 432 U.S. 63, 97 S. Ct. 2264, 53 L. Ed. 2d 113 (1977), and <http://www.findlaw.com/casecode/supreme.html>.

Fourth Amendment

The Fourth Amendment reads as follows:

The right of the people to be secure in their persons, houses, papers, and effects, against unreasonable searches and seizures, shall not be violated, and no Warrants shall issue, but upon probable cause, supported by Oath or affirmation, and particularly describing the place to be searched and the persons or things to be seized.

Search and Seizure

Before any governmental agency can search a place, that agency must obtain a search warrant from the court. The Supreme Court has found some exceptions, such as limited searches of automobiles or places where a suspect may reach for a weapon. Also excluded is the right of the government to search persons coming into the country. The search warrant must be based on **probable cause**. Probable cause requires law enforcement officials to have objective evidence that would convince a neutral magistrate that the proposed search is justified.

The warrant must specifically describe the place to be searched and the persons to be arrested or the items to be seized. General search warrants are prohibited. For example, a general search through a person's belongings is impermissible. The officer executing a search warrant has no authority to extend the search beyond that described in the warrant.

Constitutional protection against searches and seizures is important to businesses and professionals. With increased federal and state regulation of commercial activities, frequent and unannounced government inspection to ensure compliance with the law would be extremely disruptive.

In *Marshall v. Barlow's, Inc.,*[13] the Supreme Court held that government inspectors have no right to enter business premises without a warrant. In that case, the purpose of the law (Occupational Safety and Health Act of 1970) was to provide a safe workplace. If the business was found to be in violation of the government requirements, the government could impose fines for violations. Businesses have a right to require the government to obtain a warrant from a neutral magistrate before conducting a search. This case is discussed in greater detail in Chapter 6.

Right of Privacy

The right of privacy is not spelled out in the Constitution or the Bill of Rights. This right was initially advocated by Samuel D. Warren and Louis D. Brandeis[14] in an 1890 article in the *Harvard Law Review*. They argued that an individual has a personal right to be left alone. In 1965, the United States Supreme Court finally recognized the right to privacy as a constitutional right.

The basis of this right is found in the Fourth Amendment, which states that people should "be secure in their persons, houses, papers, and effects, against unreasonable searches and seizures." The right of privacy implies more than the right to be protected against unreasonable searches and seizures. The right includes a zone of privacy that protects against government intrusion, particularly against electronic eavesdropping and inspections by administrative agencies. Other protections include government prohibition against the release of your social security number, tax records, or census information unless statutory authority exists.

Although the states have passed many privacy statutes that prohibit information release by third persons, very few federal statutes on this topic have been passed. For example, little federal legislation exists protecting the privacy of your bank, credit card, telephone, employment, medical, or insurance records.

One exception is a federal law that prohibits a video store's disclosure of your videotape rental or purchase records. The statute was passed as the result of Judge Robert Bork's nomination hearing for the Supreme Court in 1987 before the U.S. Senate. During those proceedings, a local newspaper published a list of videos that Bork rented. Congress's reaction to the published list was to pass the 1988 Video Privacy Protection Act.

Many privacy rights issues have come to light because of the Internet. One of the foremost nonprofit organizations that campaigns for the right of privacy is the Center for Democracy and Technology (CDT).[15]

[13] *Marshall v. Barlow's, Inc.,* 436 U.S. 307, 98 S. Ct. 1816, 56 L. Ed. 2d 305 (1978), and <http://www.findlaw.com/casecode/supreme.html>.

[14] Louis Dembitz Brandeis (1856–1941) served as associate justice of the Supreme Court of the United States from 1916 to 1939.
[15] The Center for Democracy and Technology has a web site at <http://www.cdt.org>.

LEGAL HIGHLIGHT

So Where Is My Royalty?

Moving day comes, and off you go to your new residence. Of course, you filed a change-of-address form with the U.S. Postal Service. You also filed change-of-address forms with your insurance company, magazines, and everyone else who needs to know you moved. In your new mailbox, you find welcoming letters containing advertisements for local services. People even come to your front door to welcome you.

Off you go to your new supermarket, where you are offered membership in a frequent-buyer-bonus program. You sign up because items are discounted for club members, and for every $500 of purchases you will receive a gift. While at the market, you purchase a toaster oven and four frozen diet-food dinners. Once home, you fill out and mail in the product warranty for your toaster oven. You rip the proofs of purchase from the four diet-food containers, fill in your name and address for the $1 back on product purchase, and mail it all in.

You then call the 800 telephone number to learn how to cook your frozen dinners. After popping the frozen dinners into the toaster oven, you call the 900 telephone number to check on tomorrow's weather report. You use your cordless telephone to tell your best friend that you will be out of town for the next three days. You telephone your travel agent and request airline, hotel, and car rental reservations. Finally, you grab your laptop computer, log on, and use e-mail to check into work. You send an e-mail message to your coworker, in which you complain about the boss's bad attitude. You get on the Internet, go to a grocery store web site and order goods that are heavy in nature, such as gallons of water, boxes of soap, and cleaning materials. Your Internet provider provides you service at a cheaper rate if you allow it to track your Internet activities.

Are these activities protected from legal or illegal snoopers? The only possibly illegal "snooping activity"

is listening in on cordless or cellular telephone calls. The Postal Service sells the millions of address changes it receives to direct marketers. The product warranty form asks for lots of personal information. This information is logged into computer banks and resold. The dollar-off coupon information also is resold to other marketers, who now know that you are on a diet.

Although it has been illegal under federal law since 1986 to listen to cordless phone conversations, no way exists yet to know when someone is listening. The manufacture, import, sale, or possession of scanners, electronic devices that monitor or listen, was not made illegal until 1995. If a thief were listening, she or he would know that you would be gone for three days. If a break-in occurs, your laptop computer certainly is a target. After all, it probably contains more personal information about you and your business.

The airline computer reservation system has your travel plans and that information is resold to direct marketers. And those 800 and 900 numbers all have caller ID (identification); that is, when you call in, your telephone number shows up on the computer screen. That is more information about you to be sold. How about your e-mail messages? Employers legally can screen your e-mail. A survey shows that more than one-fifth of employers do monitor e-mail. And what about the electronic ordering from the grocery store? The store has electronically collected information about you and can now sell it. At least the Internet provider was upfront and honest about the lower rate in exchange for giving up your privacy.

Virtually no government regulation exists in the privacy area to protect you from having all this information about you placed in data banks and then being resold. The question is this: If all these people are making money from information generated by you, why aren't you receiving royalties?

Its mission statement states that it "works to promote democratic values and constitutional liberties in the digital age. With expertise in law, technology, and policy, CDT seeks practical solutions to enhance free expression and privacy in global communications technologies. CDT is dedicated to building consensus among all parties interested in the future of the Internet and other new communications media."

CyberLaw

Privacy

The World Wide Web has stirred serious concerns about privacy. Recently, Georgetown University prepared a report to the Federal Trade Commission on the privacy topic. They sampled of 361 dot.com addresses from a total of 7,500 top web sites used by consumers.

The survey revealed that 98.8 percent of the sites collected at least one type of personal information; 56.8 percent collected information about gender, zip codes, and other demographic information; and 56.2 percent collected both personal identifying and demographic information. These statistics are just one indication as to the use of private information.

Personal and demographic information often is placed in a data bank. This information then is sold to companies seeking to market products and services to individuals or businesses.

The real problem is that this personal information is collected and sold without the consent of the consumer. For example, Toysrus.com used a marketing service from a marketing company called Coremetrics to assist in evaluating information about visitors to the Toysrus.com site. Coremetrics used technology, such as web bugs and cookies, to track a visitor's whereabouts online as the visitor surfed the web. The problem that developed was that Toysrus.com had no control over what Coremetrics did with this information. After several legal actions, Toysrus.com terminated its relationship with Coremetrics.

How do you protect your privacy on the Internet? First, do not reveal personal information inadvertently. Do not give your name, address, and other personal information unless you really want to. If you meet a person on the Internet remember that you do not really know this person.

Watch out for "cookies." A cookie is placed on your computer without your knowledge to collect information about the all the web sites you visit, the time spent on the web site, if you return to that web site on a different visit, and whether you make any purchases.

Do not use your computer at work for personal reasons. Most companies have a policy against this. Your employer has a right to monitor the information on the company's computer at your workstation. This right includes monitoring your e-mail and which web sites you visit.

Do not respond to spammers. Spammers send unsolicited bulk e-mail usually to thousands of persons. Forget about clicking on the remove line. This just verifies your web address and you will not be removed from their list.

You may want to review privacy policies of a business that sells on the Internet. Most legitimate businesses have written policies about privacy that you may review before doing business with them. They will inform you whether your name or identity will be given to another company.

Even then you cannot rely on the company's assurances about never selling private information. Toysmart.com was a company that made such assurances. When the company was about to go into bankruptcy, it tried to sell its database, which contained the customer's credit card numbers along with the ages and names of children. A suit was filed by the FTC on behalf of consumers. The case was resolved when the majority shareholder (Disney Corporation) paid $50,000 for destruction of the database.

Fifth Amendment—Self-Incrimination

The Fifth Amendment guarantees against forced self-incrimination by stating that no person "shall be compelled in any criminal case to be a witness against himself." The federal government cannot force an accused person to confess or to give any evidence that might be used against him in any criminal prosecution.

The Fourteenth Amendment's due process clause incorporates the Fifth Amendment provision against self-incrimination and protects an accused from any illegal action by the state government. Accused people, however, have this protection only for themselves. They may be forced to testify against others.

The Fifth Amendment's guarantee against self-incrimination extends only to natural people (humans) and not to legal entities. Corporations and partnerships are legal entities and, as such, they do not have the protection of that Fifth Amendment clause. When the court orders these organizations to produce their records, they must comply, even if the evidence is incriminating.

What are the rights of businesspeople when they turn over incriminating papers to an accountant or lawyer? This question is answered in the following case.

Case 5.6

Fisher v. United States

Supreme Court of the United
States, 1976
425 U.S. 391, 96 S.Ct. 1569,
48 L.Ed.2d 39
http://www.findlaw.com
/casecode/supreme.html

LANDMARK CASE

BACKGROUND AND FACTS Two taxpayers were under investigation for possible civil or criminal liability under the federal income tax laws. One taxpayer obtained from his accountants certain documents relating to the accountants' preparation of the tax returns and transferred these documents to his attorneys.

The Internal Revenue Service attempted to obtain these documents by serving summonses on the taxpayer's attorneys. The attorneys refused to comply, based on their client's Fifth Amendment rights against self-incrimination and the attorney–client privilege.

Justice WHITE delivered the opinion of the Court.

In these two cases we are called upon to decide whether a summons directing an attorney to produce documents delivered to him by his client in connection with the attorney–client relationship is enforceable over claims that the documents were constitutionally immune from summons in the hands of the client and retained that immunity in the hands of the attorney.

. . . .

. . . [P]etitioners' appeal raised only their Fifth Amendment claim, but they argued in connection with that claim that enforcement of the summons would involve a violation of the taxpayers' reasonable expectation of privacy and particularly so in light of the confidential relationship of attorney to client. . . .

. . . .

All of the parties in these cases . . . have concurred in the proposition that if the Fifth Amendment would have excused a taxpayer from turning over the accountant's papers had he possessed them, the attorney to whom they are delivered for the purpose of obtaining legal advice should also be immune from subpoena. Although we agree with this proposition, we are convinced that . . . it is not the taxpayer's Fifth Amendment privilege that would excuse the attorney from production.

The relevant part of that Amendment provides:

"No person . . . shall be compelled in any criminal case to be a witness against himself" (emphasis added).

The taxpayer's privilege under this Amendment is not violated by enforcement of the summonses involved in these cases because enforcement against a taxpayer's lawyer would not "compel" the taxpayer to do anything—and certainly would not compel him to be a witness against himself. The Court has held repeatedly that the Fifth Amendment is limited to prohibiting the use of "physical or moral compulsion" exerted on the person asserting the privilege. In *Couch v. United States*, we recently ruled that the Fifth Amendment rights of a taxpayer were not violated by the enforcement of a documentary summons directed to her accountant and requiring production of the taxpayer's own records in the possession of the accountant. We did so on the ground that in such a case "the ingredient of personal compulsion against an accused is lacking."

Here, the taxpayers are compelled to do no more than was the taxpayer in *Couch*. The taxpayers' Fifth Amendment privilege is therefore not violated by enforcement of the summonses directed toward their attorneys. . . .

. . . .

Confidential disclosures by a client to an attorney made in order to obtain legal assistance are privileged. As a practical matter, if the client knows that damaging information could more readily be obtained from the attorney following than from himself in the absence of disclosure, the client would be reluctant to confide in his lawyer and it would be difficult to obtain fully informed legal advice. However, since the privilege has the effect of withholding relevant information from the fact finder, it applies only where necessary to achieve its purpose. Accordingly it protects only those disclosures—necessary to obtain informed legal advice—which might not have been made absent the privilege. This Court and the lower courts have thus uniformly held that preexisting documents which could have been obtained by court process from the client when he was in possession may also be obtained from the attorney by similar process following transfer by the client in order to obtain more informed legal advice. . . . It is otherwise if the documents are not obtainable by subpoena *duces tecum* [subpoena used to obtain evidence in the hands of another] or summons while in the exclusive possession of the client, for the client will then be reluctant to transfer possession to the lawyer unless the documents are also privileged in the latter's hands. . . .

. . . .

A subpoena served on a taxpayer requiring him to produce an accountant's work papers in his possession without doubt involves substantial compulsion. But it does not compel oral testimony; nor would it ordinarily compel the taxpayer to restate, repeat, or affirm the truth of the contents of the documents sought. Therefore, the Fifth Amendment would not be violated by the fact alone that the papers on their face might incriminate the taxpayer, for the privilege protects a person only against being incriminated by his own compelled testimonial communications. The accountant's work papers are not the taxpayer's. They were not prepared by the taxpayer, and they contain no testimonial declarations by him. . . .

. . . .

Whether the Fifth Amendment would shield the taxpayer from producing his own tax records in his possession is a question not involved here; for the papers demanded here are not his "private papers[.]"

DECISION AND REMEDY The Supreme Court held that nontestimonial (evidence that is not oral) business records not prepared by the taxpayer that are in the custody of third parties, including lawyers and accountants, must be surrendered when a search warrant is issued for them.

CRITICAL THINKING: LEGAL CONSIDERATION Discuss whether personal business records prepared solely by the taxpayer should be required to be surrendered. Explain.

Fifth and Fourteenth Amendments— Due Process Clause

Under our Constitution, no person shall be deprived "of life, liberty, or property, without due process of law." This clause is contained in both the Fifth and the Fourteenth Amendments and thus is applicable to both the federal and state governments.

Due process is a basic principle that requires fairness in the government's dealing with persons. Because the Supreme Court interprets this clause on a case-by-case basis, it has generated more cases than any other clause in the Constitution. Most of the basic rights discussed in this chapter are applicable to both government and private employers. But because the Fifth and Fourteenth Amendments apply explicitly to both federal and state governments, public employees have more due process rights than private employees.

The due process clause has two aspects: procedural and substantive. **Procedural due process** requires that safeguards be taken before any government decision can be made to take a person's life, liberty, or property.

Substantive due process focuses on the content, or substance, of legislation. Every statute, regulation, and government act must comply with the Constitution. Otherwise, substantive due process is violated.

For example, Congress passes a statute imposing a $1-million fine and mandatory five-year prison term without a trial on any university professor who appears as an expert on a television news program. This law would be unconstitutional on both substantive and procedural grounds. A court would invalidate this legislation because it abridges freedom of speech, a violation of the First Amendment. A denial of substantive due process requires a court to overrule any state or federal law that violates the Constitution. Procedurally, the law is unfair because the penalty is imposed without giving the accused a chance to defend her or his actions. A court will invalidate any statute or court decision that lacks procedural due process.

Equal Protection Clause

The equal protection clause in the Fourteenth Amendment is specifically addressed to state governments; it sets out that a state may not "deny to any person within its jurisdiction the equal protection of the laws." The United States Supreme Court used the due process clause of the Fifth Amendment to apply the equal protection guarantee to actions of the federal government. Equal protection means that the government must treat similarly situated individuals in a similar manner.

The government has created a number of protected classes, each of which can be categorized into one of three levels of protection. Receiving the highest level of protection are the classes of race, religion, national origin, and color. If discrimination is alleged by a person falling into one of these classes, the courts use the **strict scrutiny test**.

This test has two requirements that must be met before this type of discrimination is allowed: (1) a compelling governmental interest and (2) use of the least restrictive means available to satisfy that interest. For example, in the 1970s Iranians occupied the U.S. Embassy in Iran. In partial response to this crisis, all Iranians in the United States who were not U.S. citizens were ordered to report to the U.S. government. This requirement would meet the elements of the strict scrutiny test, even though international visitors from other countries were not required to report. Most government regulations involving protected classes, however, fail.

When a person alleges discrimination based on gender or age, the courts use the **intermediate scrutiny test**. This test requires that there be (1) an important governmental objective and (2) a substantial relationship between the means and the end before the court will approve discrimination on the basis of gender or age. For example, sixteen-year-olds are not allowed to purchase tobacco or alcohol products. The governmental objective is to keep minors from harmful substances and one method is to prohibit them from purchasing tobacco and alcohol. Thus, this discrimination is lawful. If the government prohibited anyone over age thirty from being employed as police officers, however, the first requirement would not be met, because no important governmental objective could be stated.

If a person complains about discrimination on the basis of economic discrimination or any other government classification that does not involve a protected class, the courts use the **rational basis test**. The two requirements of this test are (1) a legitimate governmental interest and (2) a rational relationship between the governmental interest and the means used to accomplish that interest. For example, a state government passed a law requiring everyone in the front seats of motor vehicles to use their seat belts. The courts have upheld such laws. The governmental interest is to protect motor vehicle occupants from serious injuries resulting in the need for medical treatment, often hospitalization, and time off from work. The seat belt law is a rational means to achieve the goal of lessening or preventing harm. Most regulation of businesses comes under the rational basis test.

International Consideration

Must a Court Recognize a Foreign Judgment?

Over the decades, the United States Supreme Court has implemented various well-recognized principles of international law, including those of comity, the act of state, and sovereign immunity.

Comity means courtesy or a willingness to grant a privilege, not as a matter of right but out of deference and goodwill. The principle of comity means that one nation recognizes the legislative, executive, or judicial acts of another nation. This doctrine is not based on any international legal obligations but rather on respect for the laws of another country. Under the principle of comity, a judgment from a foreign country is enforceable within the courts of the United States.[16] The foreign judgment must be based on having proper jurisdiction. The effect of comity is similar to the full faith and credit clause of the Constitution, which requires states to recognize the judgments coming from sister states.

The **act of state doctrine** means the courts cannot interfere with the acts of another nation within its boundaries. The effect of this doctrine is that U.S. courts normally are precluded from hearing cases in which a sovereign nation has expropriated or confiscated the assets of an American business.

Expropriation occurs when a government seizes privately owned goods or a privately owned business for a proper public purpose and awards just compensation. A **confiscation** occurs when the other country takes the privately owned goods or business without a proper public purpose and with no award of just compensation. The only exception to the principle regarding an act of state is when a treaty exists between the two countries that allows for a legal action in the United States.

In 1976, Congress passed the Foreign Sovereign Immunities Act (FSIA), which codifies the doctrine of sovereign immunity. **Sovereign immunity** means that a person cannot sue the government without its permission. For the purposes of this doctrine, a "foreign state" includes both the state and any agency of the foreign state, such as a state-owned bank.

The FSIA exclusively governs the circumstances under which an action may be brought against a foreign state in a U.S. court. Attachment of a foreign nation's property, for example, is provided for by the FSIA. Attachment is a court order to bring the debtor's (in this case the foreign state's) property under the control of the court during the lawsuit.

One of the primary purposes of the FSIA is to ensure that federal courts, rather than the Department of State, determine claims of foreign sovereign immunity. By removing the claims to federal court, the Department of State is relieved from political pressures to make diplomatic decisions that might be legally correct but politically unpopular. For example, a foreign ship or its cargo may be attached under a court order.

Section 1605 of the FSIA establishes the major exceptions to the jurisdictional immunity of a country. A foreign state is under the jurisdiction of the courts of the United States when the foreign government has waived its immunity. The foreign country also is under the jurisdiction of the courts when the action is based on a commercial activity carried out by the foreign nation within the jurisdictional limits of the United States.

---

[16] Chapter 4 described how the New York Convention requires nations that have signed the convention to recognize foreign arbitration awards. The principle of comity refers to judgments coming from courts.

LEGALLY SPEAKING

Stopping Employee Theft

You are the security officer for a large private business that is not unionized. Lately, you have noticed big increases in lost inventory. This type of loss indicates that employees are pilfering items. You have no idea who these employees may be, how many are involved, or if a criminal ring has infiltrated your company. After considering this problem, you decide to develop the following checklist:

✔ Notify all employees that telephone conversations will be monitored. Conversations are monitored routinely in most large businesses.

✔ Install discreetly hidden video cameras to monitor employees' activities in the warehouse and docking area to discover theft from the inventory.

✔ Scan voice mail and e-mail.

✔ Check lockers and desks occasionally since the business owns them. Employees should be notified that such checks may be conducted with and without the employees' knowledge or permission to detect employee misconduct. Personal belongings may not be searched.

Chapter Summary

The U.S. Constitution is the oldest active constitution in the modern world. It has lasted so long because our founders had the insight to produce a document that accomplishes three major objectives. First, the Constitution creates three branches of government, each independent of the other but with the ability to limit the powers of the other two branches through a system of checks and balances.

Second, the Constitution creates a central government that is supreme, but that derives its power from the states. Federalism is the basic structure of our government. Certain powers are given to the federal government, whereas other powers are shared with the states. The Constitution delegates certain powers or rights, called enumerated powers, to the federal government. For example, the commerce clause of the Constitution allows the federal government to regulate all interstate and foreign commerce. Any commerce, considered cumulatively, which has a substantial economic effect, is considered interstate commerce and subject to regulation. Occasionally, conflicts arise between federal and state law. The federal law is upheld under the Constitution's supremacy clause.

Third, the Constitution guarantees the people certain basic rights that neither local nor federal governments can abridge. The first ten constitutional amendments, called the Bill of Rights, set out these rights in detail. These amendments have particular applications to business. For example, under the First Amendment, commercial speech is protected as long as it is not false, deceptive, or misleading. The Fourth Amendment protects businesses from illegal search and seizures in the absence of a valid warrant. Business entities, however, are not protected from self-incrimination under the Fifth Amendment.

Businesses are protected by the due process clause in the Fifth and Fourteenth Amendments. The distinction between substantive and procedural due process is that procedural due process involves the methods used in protecting legal rights, while substantive due process involves protecting the basic legal rights themselves. The equal protection clause applies to both federal and state governments, which must give equal protection of the laws to all people.

Using the World Wide Web

Remember the documents you were supposed to have read in high school civics: the Magna Carta, the Declaration of Independence, the Articles of Confederation, and the Constitution? Today, with only a few keystrokes, people can access those documents on the Internet.

The National Archives and Records Administration provides a variety of interesting documents on its web pages. Its American Originals web page offers video clips and text that provide a glimpse of our past. Here are some web sites.

Finding the Law on the Web

National Archives and Records Administration
http://www.nara.gov
American Originals web page
http://www.nara.gov/exhall/orginals/original.html
Magna Carta
http://www.nara.gov/exhall/charters/magnacarta/magmain.html
Magna Carta and its American legacy
http://www.nara.gov/exhall/charters/magnacarta/magintrp.html
Declaration of Independence
http://www.nara.gov/exhall/charters/declaration/decmain.html
U.S. Constitution
http://www.nara.gov/exhall/charters/consitution/conmain.html
Bill of Rights
http://www.nara.gov/exhall/charters/billrights/billmain.html
Biographies of the fifty-five Founding Fathers
http://www.nara.gov/exhall/charters/constitution/confath.html
Louisiana Purchase
http://www.nara.gov/exhall/originals/loupurch.html
Electoral College
http://www.nara.gov/nara/fedreg/ec/echmpge.html

Chapter Web Sites

U.S. Constitution
http://www.law.emory.edu/pub-cgi/usconwais
or

http://www.secure.law.cornell.edu/constitution/constitution.overview.html
or
http://www.constitution.org/cs_found.htm
U.S. Supreme Court multimedia database, Northwestern University
http://oyez.nwu.edu/
Supreme Court cases at the Legal Information Institute, Cornell Law School
http://supct.law.cornell.edu:8080/supct/
Marbury v. Madison
http://supct.law.cornell.edu/supct/cases/name.htm
Wickard v. Filbert
http://www.findlaw.com/casecode/supreme.html
United States v. Lopez
http://supct.law.cornell.edu/supct/cases/name.htm
Reno v. American Civil Liberties Union
http://www.findlaw.com/casecode/supreme.html
Freedom Forum
http://www.freedomforum.org/first/welcome.asp
Cyberspace Law Institute
http://www.cli.org/
American Civil Liberties Union
http://www.aclu.org
Virginia State Board of Pharmacy v. Virginia Citizens Consumer Council, Inc.
http://www.findlaw.com/casecode/supreme.html
Bates v. State Bar of Arizona
http://supct.law.cornell.edu/supct/cases/name.htm
Florida Bar v. Went For It, Inc.
http://www.findlaw.com/casecode/supreme.html
New York Times Co. v. Sullivan
http://supct.law.cornell.edu/supct/cases/name.htm#Case_Name-N-O
Estate of Thornton v. Caldor, Inc.; Trans World Airlines, Inc. v. Hardison; and *Marshall v. Barlow's, Inc.*
http://www.findlaw.com/casecode/supreme.html
Center for Democracy and Technology
http://www.cdt.org/
Fisher v. United States
http://www.findlaw.com/casecode/supreme.html
University of Wuerzburg
http://www.uni-wuerzburg.de/law/
National Archives and Record Administration
http://www.nara-gov/exhall/charters/constitution/conqa.html

Web Activities

5–1 Go to the site <http://www.uni-wuerzburg.de/law/>, which is located in Germany, and click on the United Kingdom. What type of constitution does the United Kingdom have?

5–2 How did the Magna Carta influence the writing of the U.S. Constitution? Go to the National Archives and Records Administration's web site at <http://www.nara.gov/>. Go to the Exhibit Hall to find the link to the Magna Carta.

Key Terms

act of state doctrine
actual malice
comity
commerce clause
concurrent power
confiscation
defamation
doctrine of selective
    incorporation
double jeopardy

enumerated powers
equal protection clause
executive branch
expropriation
federalism
intermediate scrutiny test
judicial branch
judicial review
legal entity
legislative branch

partially protected
    speech
police powers
preemption doctrine
privileges and immunities
    clause
probable cause
procedural due process
protected speech
rational basis test

self-incrimination
sovereign immunity
spending power
standing to sue
strict scrutiny test
substantive due process
supremacy clause
taxing power
unprotected speech

Questions and Case Problems

5–1 Judicial Review Discuss the doctrine of judicial review.

5–2 Constitutional Rights A business has a backlog of orders. To meet its deadlines, management is considering running the firm seven days a week, eight hours a day. What issues of constitutional law should management consider in making this decision? Can management terminate an employee for refusing to work more than forty hours a week? Can management terminate an employee for refusing to work on a religious holy day?

5–3 Commerce Clause Unlike all other states in the West and Midwest, Iowa prohibited by statute the use of sixty-five-foot double-trailer trucks on its highways for safety reasons. The use of fifty-five-foot trailer trucks and sixty-foot double-trailer trucks was allowed. Consolidated Freightways, a Delaware corporation, owned sixty-five-foot double-trailer trucks. These trucks, which carried commodities, could not use the interstate highways that passed through Iowa. Consequently, Consolidated filed suit, alleging that Iowa's statutory scheme unconstitutionally burdened interstate commerce. Does Consolidated have a valid case? Explain your answer. [*Kassel v. Consolidated Freightways Corp. of Delaware,* 450 U.S. 662, 101 S. Ct. 1309, 67 L. Ed. 2d 580 (1981)]

5–4 Preemption A Wisconsin statute prohibits people or firms that have violated the National Labor Relations Act (NLRA) three times within a five-year period from conducting business with the state. For this reason, Gould, Inc., was not allowed to conduct business with the state. The NLRA has substantive requirements that conflict with the Wisconsin statute. Is this statute constitutional under the supremacy clause or displaced by the NLRA? [*Wisconsin Department of Industry v. Gould, Inc.,* 475 U.S. 282, 106 S. Ct. 1057, 89 L. Ed. 2d 223 (1986)]

5–5 Commercial Speech Puerto Rico passed a statute and regulations restricting casino gambling advertisements that were aimed at Puerto Rican residents. The operator of one casino filed a lawsuit to have these restrictions declared null and void as violating freedom of speech. Puerto Rico claimed "substantial governmental interest" that the restrictions on such advertising "directly advance[d]." How would you hold in this situation? [*Posadas de Puerto Rico Associates v. Tourism Co. of Puerto Rico,* 478 U.S. 328, 106 S. Ct. 2968, 92 L. Ed. 2d 266 (1986)]

5–6 Civil Rights A motel owner who refused to rent rooms to African Americans, despite the Civil Rights Act of 1964, brought an action to have the act declared unconstitutional. The motel owner alleged that Congress, in passing the act, had exceeded its power to regulate commerce. The statute was upheld. What legal arguments were used to validate it? [*Heart of Atlanta v. United States,* 379 U.S. 241, 85 S. Ct.348, 13 L. Ed. 2d 258 (1964)]

5–7 Privileges and Immunities In the early 1970s, an oil pipeline was built across Alaska. In 1972, the Alaska legislature passed an act that became known as the Alaska Hire. The act had a provision requiring the employment of qualified Alaska residents over non-residents. To qualify for the preference, a person had to have lived in Alaska for one year. The reason for the act was to reduce unemployment. Some individuals, who wanted jobs but who did not qualify for preference as Alaska residents, brought suit, challenging the act under the privileges and immunities clause. Who should win this case—the plaintiffs seeking jobs or Alaska seeking to reduce unemployment? Explain. [*Hicklin v. Orbeck,* 437 U.S. 518, 98 S. Ct. 2482, 57 L. Ed. 2d 397 (1978)]

5–8 Separation Clause The plaintiffs, Americans United for Separation of Church and State, Inc., as taxpayers, brought an action to challenge a conveyance of land from the Department of Health, Education, and Welfare (HEW) to Valley Forge Christian College, the defendant. The plaintiffs alleged that such a conveyance violated the establishment clause of the First Amendment. The district court dismissed the complaint on the ground that the plaintiffs lacked standing to sue. What was the result on appeal? [*Valley Forge Christian College v. Americans United for Separation of Church and State, Inc.,* 454 U.S. 464, 102 S. Ct. 752, 70 L. Ed. 2d 700 (1982)] (Note that HEW was later divided into two separate departments, the Department of Education and the Department of Health and Human Services.)

5–9 Interstate Commerce New Jersey enacted a law prohibiting the importation of most wastes into the state. Some of the landfill operators in New Jersey, however, had agreements with out-of-state residents to dispose of their solid and liquid waste. Philadelphia brought an action claiming that this statute violated the commerce clause because it discriminated against interstate commerce. New Jersey asserted that its statute was justified because its landfills were inadequate to dispose of its own waste, and importation had a significant and adverse potential effect on the environment. Is this state regulation of interstate commerce permissible? [*Philadelphia v. New Jersey,* 437 U.S. 617, 98 S. Ct. 2531, 57 L. Ed. 2d 475 (1978)]

5–10 Internet Who first created the name that eventually would become "United States of America"? Go to the National Archives and Records Administration web site at <http://www.nara.gov/exhall/charters/constitution/conqa.html>. The answer appears within the first few questions.

Chapter 6 Administrative Agencies and the Regulation of Business

The rise of administrative bodies probably has been the most significant legal trend of the last century and perhaps more values today are affected by their decisions than by those of all the courts, review of administrative decisions apart. They also have begun to have important consequences on personal rights. . . . They have become a veritable fourth branch of the Government which has deranged our three-branch legal theories as much as the concept of a fourth dimension unsettles our three-dimensional thinking.

Federal Trade Commission v. Ruberoid Co. 343 U.S. 470, 487; 72 S. Ct. 800, 810; 96 L. Ed. 2d 1081, 1094 (1952)

http://www.findlaw.com/casecode /supreme.htm

Outline

Ethical Consideration

Conflicts between Freedom of Speech and Ethics

You are a government employee working for the Nuclear Regulatory Agency. Already overwhelmed with requests for various reports, you have received still another request. A congressional committee needs information on the training level required for personnel who work in the various reactors around the country. You have no idea when you will have time to write this report. The agency requires all congressional inquiries to be answered within ten working days. You do not even know how to obtain this information, because the agency does not require that it be kept.

As often happens, you are visited by a lobbyist from a company involved in the manufacture of nuclear power plants. She wants to discuss some pending legislation. In the course of the conversation, you explain your dilemma, and she volunteers to find the information for you. You know that obtaining information from lobbyists is a common practice and that their information generally is reliable.

Should you accept or decline this offer? Use the ethical model presented in Chapter 2 and reprinted on the inside front cover to develop your answer.

Introduction

Generally, when people think about law enforcement, they think about the courts. Actually, few people ever see the inside of a courtroom for any offense more serious than a traffic violation. In contrast, you will be dealing with a number of administrative agencies on behalf of your online business, Artiste Login Products, Inc. For example, the federal and state labor agencies, safety agencies, and taxing agencies are but a few of the agencies that regulate businesses. Your online business will have to comply with a myrid of administrative rules issued by these agencies.

Congress and state legislatures create administrative agencies to enforce specific statutes that they have passed. For example, the Internal Revenue Service en-

forces the tax laws passed by Congress. Administrative agencies are called regulatory agencies or bureaucracies. These three terms are used interchangeably.

Today's business decisions are constrained both by congressional statutes and by the interpretation and enforcement of those statutes through rules made and enforced by administrative agencies. The study of the powers, procedures, and practices of these administrative agencies is called administrative law.

Since the late 1960s, the regulation of business has shifted dramatically from the courts' applying statutory and common law to resolve problems to the more direct and comprehensive controls of administrative agencies. The current constraints placed on business transactions by regulatory authorities greatly impact the economy. (See Exhibit 6-1 which shows how administrative agencies fit into the organizational structure of the federal government.)

This chapter first will review the areas of business that administrative agencies regulate. Second, it will describe the features embodied in administrative agencies that allow them to handle problems more effectively than the legislature or the courts. Third, it will discuss the Administrative Procedure Act, its amendments, and the three types of power of an administrative agency: quasi-legislative, quasi-judicial, and quasi-executive. Fourth, it will discuss the constitutional, statutory, and judicial limits of an administrative agency's power. Fifth, it will review the deregulation process.

Areas of Regulation

Administrative agencies handle two areas of public concern: *economic regulation* and *public welfare*. An example of economic regulation is the Federal Reserve Board, which regulates the banking industry. Public welfare, in turn, is divided into two parts: protection programs and entitlement programs. A protection program is one that protects the public, usually in the health and safety areas. An **entitlement program** is a program that administers benefits to which a person is entitled, such as social security, which is discussed in more detail later. (See Exhibit 6–2 for some examples of various types of regulations.)

Economic Regulation

Economic regulation covers three basic areas. First, administrative agencies issue approvals for certain types

Exhibit 6-1 Organization Chart of the Government of the United States

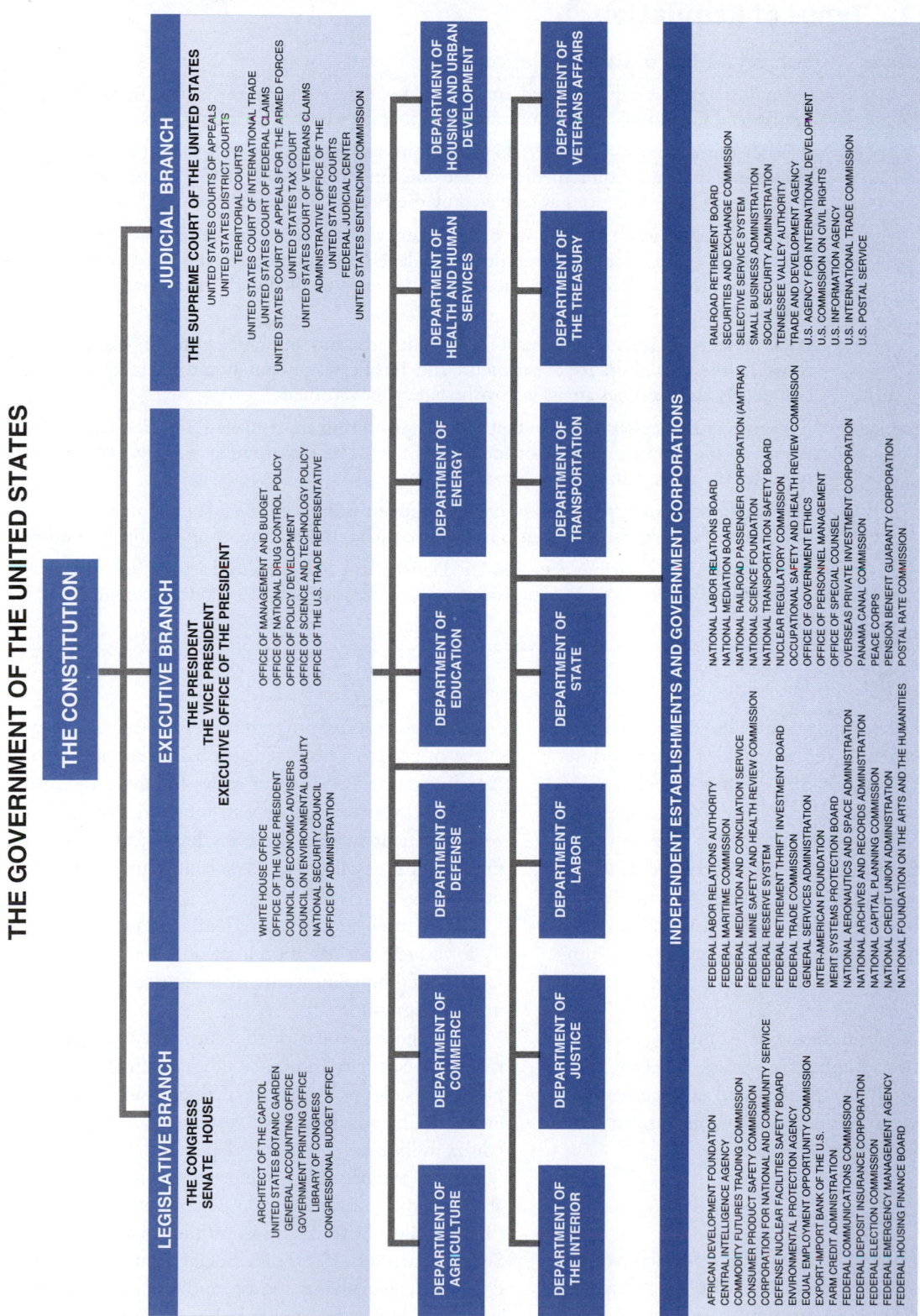

THE GOVERNMENT OF THE UNITED STATES

THE CONSTITUTION

LEGISLATIVE BRANCH

THE CONGRESS
SENATE HOUSE

ARCHITECT OF THE CAPITOL
UNITED STATES BOTANIC GARDEN
GENERAL ACCOUNTING OFFICE
GOVERNMENT PRINTING OFFICE
LIBRARY OF CONGRESS
CONGRESSIONAL BUDGET OFFICE

EXECUTIVE BRANCH

THE PRESIDENT
THE VICE PRESIDENT
EXECUTIVE OFFICE OF THE PRESIDENT

WHITE HOUSE OFFICE
OFFICE OF THE VICE PRESIDENT
COUNCIL OF ECONOMIC ADVISERS
COUNCIL ON ENVIRONMENTAL QUALITY
NATIONAL SECURITY COUNCIL
OFFICE OF ADMINISTRATION

OFFICE OF MANAGEMENT AND BUDGET
OFFICE OF NATIONAL DRUG CONTROL POLICY
OFFICE OF POLICY DEVELOPMENT
OFFICE OF SCIENCE AND TECHNOLOGY POLICY
OFFICE OF THE U.S. TRADE REPRESENTATIVE

JUDICIAL BRANCH

THE SUPREME COURT OF THE UNITED STATES

UNITED STATES COURTS OF APPEALS
UNITED STATES DISTRICT COURTS
TERRITORIAL COURTS
UNITED STATES COURT OF INTERNATIONAL TRADE
UNITED STATES COURT OF FEDERAL CLAIMS
UNITED STATES COURT OF APPEALS FOR THE ARMED FORCES
UNITED STATES TAX COURT
UNITED STATES COURT OF VETERANS CLAIMS
ADMINISTRATIVE OFFICE OF THE
UNITED STATES COURTS
FEDERAL JUDICIAL CENTER
UNITED STATES SENTENCING COMMISSION

DEPARTMENT OF AGRICULTURE

DEPARTMENT OF COMMERCE

DEPARTMENT OF DEFENSE

DEPARTMENT OF EDUCATION

DEPARTMENT OF ENERGY

DEPARTMENT OF HEALTH AND HUMAN SERVICES

DEPARTMENT OF HOUSING AND URBAN DEVELOPMENT

DEPARTMENT OF THE INTERIOR

DEPARTMENT OF JUSTICE

DEPARTMENT OF LABOR

DEPARTMENT OF STATE

DEPARTMENT OF TRANSPORTATION

DEPARTMENT OF THE TREASURY

DEPARTMENT OF VETERANS AFFAIRS

INDEPENDENT ESTABLISHMENTS AND GOVERNMENT CORPORATIONS

AFRICAN DEVELOPMENT FOUNDATION
CENTRAL INTELLIGENCE AGENCY
COMMODITY FUTURES TRADING COMMISSION
CONSUMER PRODUCT SAFETY COMMISSION
CORPORATION FOR NATIONAL AND COMMUNITY SERVICE
DEFENSE NUCLEAR FACILITIES SAFETY BOARD
ENVIRONMENTAL PROTECTION AGENCY
EQUAL EMPLOYMENT OPPORTUNITY COMMISSION
EXPORT-IMPORT BANK OF THE U.S.
FARM CREDIT ADMINISTRATION
FEDERAL COMMUNICATIONS COMMISSION
FEDERAL DEPOSIT INSURANCE CORPORATION
FEDERAL ELECTION COMMISSION
FEDERAL EMERGENCY MANAGEMENT AGENCY
FEDERAL HOUSING FINANCE BOARD

FEDERAL LABOR RELATIONS AUTHORITY
FEDERAL MARITIME COMMISSION
FEDERAL MEDIATION AND CONCILIATION SERVICE
FEDERAL MINE SAFETY AND HEALTH REVIEW COMMISSION
FEDERAL RESERVE SYSTEM
FEDERAL RETIREMENT THRIFT INVESTMENT BOARD
FEDERAL TRADE COMMISSION
GENERAL SERVICES ADMINISTRATION
INTER-AMERICAN FOUNDATION
MERIT SYSTEMS PROTECTION BOARD
NATIONAL AERONAUTICS AND SPACE ADMINISTRATION
NATIONAL ARCHIVES AND RECORDS ADMINISTRATION
NATIONAL CAPITAL PLANNING COMMISSION
NATIONAL CREDIT UNION ADMINISTRATION
NATIONAL FOUNDATION ON THE ARTS AND THE HUMANITIES

NATIONAL LABOR RELATIONS BOARD
NATIONAL MEDIATION BOARD
NATIONAL RAILROAD PASSENGER CORPORATION (AMTRAK)
NATIONAL SCIENCE FOUNDATION
NATIONAL TRANSPORTATION SAFETY BOARD
NUCLEAR REGULATORY COMMISSION
OCCUPATIONAL SAFETY AND HEALTH REVIEW COMMISSION
OFFICE OF GOVERNMENT ETHICS
OFFICE OF PERSONNEL MANAGEMENT
OFFICE OF SPECIAL COUNSEL
OVERSEAS PRIVATE INVESTMENT CORPORATION
PANAMA CANAL COMMISSION
PEACE CORPS
PENSION BENEFIT GUARANTY CORPORATION
POSTAL RATE COMMISSION

RAILROAD RETIREMENT BOARD
SECURITIES AND EXCHANGE COMMISSION
SELECTIVE SERVICE SYSTEM
SMALL BUSINESS ADMINISTRATION
SOCIAL SECURITY ADMINISTRATION
TENNESSEE VALLEY AUTHORITY
TRADE AND DEVELOPMENT AGENCY
U.S. AGENCY FOR INTERNATIONAL DEVELOPMENT
U.S. COMMISSION ON CIVIL RIGHTS
U.S. INFORMATION AGENCY
U.S. INTERNATIONAL TRADE COMMISSION
U.S. POSTAL SERVICE

Source: *U.S. Government Manual*, 1999–2000, Washington, DC (Government Printing Office, 1999),
p. 22.

EXHIBIT 6–2   Types of Regulation

Type of Regulation	Subject Matter of the Regulation
Advertisements	Cigarette, cigar, and liquor advertisements and sexually explicit material are controlled by the Federal Communications Commission as it applies to the broadcast media.
Contracts	Private contracts must follow certain regulations, such as the format for interest-rate disclosures, language requirements, and the consumer's right to rescind a contract within three days in some situations as regulated by the Federal Reserve Board.
Disclosure	Disclosure regulations issued by various regulatory agencies require health and nutritional information on food labels, fuel consumption labels on automobiles, and warning labels on dangerous products. Information about securities must be filed with the Securities and Exchange Commission.
Licensing	Bank charters are issued by the state banking departments; insurance business charters are issued by the state insurance departments; and certificates of operation to railroads, trucking companies, and bus lines are issued by the federal government.
Materials and processes	Materials and processes for some types of manufacturing are regulated. The Food and Drug Administration can ban the use of additives in food. The Environmental Protection Agency regulates the use and disposal of hazardous chemicals.
Quotas	The importation or exportation of certain products is limited. The sale of computer components to terrorist countries is not allowed. The importation of oil is subject to quotas.
Standards	Standards are set by various agencies. The Department of Agriculture sets the standards for meat and poultry. The Federal Aviation Administration sets the standards for airplane certification.

of businesses or their equipment. The Federal Aviation Administration (FAA), for example, certifies airlines and airports for operation and certifies specific aircraft for airworthiness. Second, administrative agencies regulate securities and financial businesses. The Securities and Exchange Commission regulates the securities industries. Third, some business activities are entirely subject to regulation, such as the broadcast media, which are regulated by the Federal Communications Commission (FCC).

Other agencies have regulatory powers that regulate all types of businesses. For example, the Equal Employment Opportunity Commission (EEOC) has responsibility for all compliance and enforcement activities that work to eliminate discrimination in business, labor unions, and government.

Public Welfare

For regulation purposes, the term **public welfare** refers to protection and entitlement programs that benefit the public at large. Its jurisdiction is not limited to government aid to lower income people.

The protection programs protect the health and safety of people. The Occupational Safety and Health Administration (OSHA) provides for the public welfare of all by ensuring safety in the work area. All citizens benefit if workers have a safe workplace because time and money losses as a result of injuries and death decrease.

With an entitlement program, the applicants qualify for a program based on a set of criteria. If a person meets certain qualifications, he is entitled to participate in the program.

The most popular of the entitlement programs is the Social Security Insurance program. Employed people are taxed on a portion of their wages for Social Security. The administrative costs for this program that covers millions of people are 1 percent.

Social Security has three programs: retirement, disability, and life insurance. If a person retires and meets the eligibility criteria, she is entitled to receive Social Security benefits. If she dies, Social Security pays benefits to her surviving spouse and minor children. If someone becomes disabled, he can receive Social Security benefits during the period of disability.

Social Security benefits are not based on income. Millionaires may receive Social Security if they have contributed to it during their working days; however, they must pay income taxes on it.

Features of Administrative Agencies

Several features allow regulatory agencies to deal with problems more effectively than the legislature can. First, because an agency regulates only a specific subject matter area, it develops expertise in that area and adopts detailed regulations. The legislature authorizes an agency to develop the detailed logistics needed to implement and monitor all of the policies it establishes.

Second, a regulatory agency consists of a very well developed hierarchy. A government employee will work for a particular agency for long periods of time, if not for his entire career. The employee is promoted and rewarded within that structured bureaucracy. In contrast, the legislature consists of elected representatives and thus has little continuity in its personnel.

Third, an agency has more flexibility than the legislature. If an industry wants Congress to pass a law, the process is tedious and the results are tenuous at best. In contrast, Congress has granted agencies the authority to change regulations in a quick and efficient manner. Some regulations are redrafted by an agency as soon as it sees the need for the change. Other regulations take longer to change because of the requirement to hold formal, public hearings. Even under this requirement, however, an agency's procedure for adopting or amending regulations is faster than it takes Congress to adopt, amend, or delete a statute.

Despite these advantages, the growth of administrative agencies has been criticized by those who believe that agency growth has limited the ability of elected officials to effect change. In the past, the legislative and executive branches of government held political power and influence. This power, however, has shifted to the bureaucracy. Thus, to a substantial degree, quasi-permanent, unelected, nonpartisan administrative officials wield political power and influence. The administrative agencies now are recognized by some as the fourth branch of the government. (See Exhibit 6–3, which shows the distribution of federal employees for the years 1989, 1995, and 1998.)

The Nature of Administrative Agencies

Administrative agencies are the primary interpreters and enforcers of congressional statutes. Created by Congress, an agency derives its authority from its enabling legislation. Four types of agencies can be created: line agencies, independent agencies, government agencies, and quasi-official agencies.

Line Agencies, Independent Agencies, Government Agencies, and Quasi-Official Agencies

An agency under the direct control of the president is known as a **line agency** or as an **executive agency**. A line agency is headed by one person, who is appointed by and serves at the pleasure of the president but who must be confirmed by the Senate. "At the pleasure of" means that the president can release an appointed person at any time, with or without a good reason. For example, the appointee, although doing a good job, may become a political embarrassment because of public statements. The president may request the person's resignation or fire him.

The members of the president's cabinet head the line agencies. For example, the secretary of the Department of Labor (a line agency) is a cabinet member who serves at the president's pleasure. Exhibit 6–4 shows a sample line agency's structure.

Congress also establishes administrative agencies independent of the legislative and executive branches. An agency that is freestanding from the president and Congress is known as an **independent agency**. The Federal Trade Commission (FTC) and the National Aeronautics and Space Administration (NASA) are examples of independent agencies.

These agencies usually are headed by a commission whose members are appointed by the president and confirmed by the Senate. Commissioners do not serve at the pleasure of the president as do line agency appointees. The president cannot remove them unilaterally. A commissioner can be impeached and if the Senate convicts the person, she is removed from office.

A commission ranges in size from three to fifteen people; the number is determined by Congress. Each commissioner is equal to the others. The chair of the commission runs the daily operations.

EXHIBIT 6–3   Distribution of Employees in the Federal Government

Branch of Government	1989	1995	1998
Government (total)	2,875,866	3,123,731	2,789,495
Legislative (total)	39,710	37,690	30,474
Judicial (total)	15,178	21,090	31,742
Executive Departments (total)	1,716,970	2,065,038	2,727,279
Agriculture	129,139	122,062	105,664
Commerce	48,563	45,091	50,041
Defense	960,116	1,075,437	717,901
Education	7,364	4,696	4,677
Energy	21,557	17,130	16,156
Health and Human Services[a]	155,662	122,250	59,813
Housing and Urban Development	16,964	13,544	10,063
Interior	77,357	77,545	72,434
Justice	56,327	79,667	122,759
Labor	23,400	18,125	15,894
State	23,497	25,327	24,713
Transportation	72,361	65,615	64,859
Treasury	124,663	152,548	140,873
Veterans Affairs	228,285	245,992	240,398
Independent Agencies (total)[b]	1,102,122	997,511	1,070,245
Environmental Protection Agency	14,715	15,590	18,787
Equal Employment Opportunity Commission	3,515	2,743	2,571
Federal Deposit Insurance Corporation	3,520	9,031	7,778
U.S. Postal Service	660,014	826,886	871,467

[a] Changes are sizable because the Social Security Administration separated from the DHHS to become an independent agency in April 1995.

[b] Includes agencies not shown separately.

Source: *Statistical Abstract of the United States,* Washington, DC (Government Printing Office, 1999), p. 362.

When appointing people to the commission, the president is required to be bipartisan, which means that both political parties must be represented. The length of service on the commission varies from agency to agency. Each member is appointed for a specific time period. All terms are staggered, however, and are longer than the four-year presidential term.

Congress creates a **government agency** to administer a quasi-business venture. *Quasi* is a Latin word meaning "as if," so the government agency administrates a program as if it were a private business. These agencies have three similar elements: (1) Each conducts a business-like activity that (2) produces revenue to continue its own existence and, as a result, (3) needs greater flexibility than usually is given to other types of agencies. The major government agencies are the Tennessee Valley Authority (TVA), the Federal Deposit Insurance Corporation (FDIC), the Pension Benefit Guaranty Corporation, and the U.S. Postal Service.

A **quasi-official agency** is created by Congress but does not have the same authority as other agencies. These agencies must publish notices and information in the *Federal Register*.[1] The members of the agency are appointed by the president, subject to Senate approval. The quasi-official agencies are Legal Services Corporation,[2] National Railroad Passenger Corporation (Amtrak),[3] and the Smithsonian Institution.[4]

CyberLaw

The Internal Revenue Service

Thanks to Congress, every federal administrative agency receives funds to create and support its own web site. Eventually, all of the state and local administrative agencies will have a web presence. One federal agency touches all business situations: the Internal Revenue Service (IRS).

The IRS looks for ways to cut its costs; thus, it is very involved with electronic filing of returns and providing the public electronic access to forms and online instructions on when to use and how to prepare the various IRS forms. One of the first electronic methods used was the touch-tone telephone. For example, one of the standard forms all businesses must file is Form 941, the employer's quarterly federal tax return reporting the amount of wages paid and the amount owed to the IRS for monies withheld for income tax, Federal Insurance Contributions Act (FICA) (Social Security), and Medicare. By filing Form 941 over the telephone, a business can save approximately two-thirds of the time that would have been expended if the business had filed the form by mail. A business must request a special tax package allowing it to access the system known as 941 *TeleFile*. The business then uses a touch-tone telephone to dial an 800 number listed in the tax package. A voice-processing system prompts users to make the necessary entries using the telephone key pad. The system repeats each entry to verify its accuracy and to allow mistakes to be corrected immediately. At the end of the telephone call, a confirmation number is issued to the caller as proof of filing.

Another method of filing a return is to use a personal computer. The business first obtains off-the-shelf tax preparation software. The business applies for a Personal Identification Number (PIN) by completing the Letter of Application included in the software. The business files the Letter electronically using a third-party transmitter. The third-party transmitter will batch other Letters of Application and electronically transmit the batch to an IRS center. The IRS will send the business a PIN by mail. The PIN is used in lieu of the business filer's signature.

The goal of the IRS is to increase the use of electronic filing by requiring large businesses to file electronically. For example, partnerships with more than 100 members can only file electronically.

A business or individual may obtain any necessary tax forms over the Internet. In the past, little-used forms were not distributed widely. Those needing a little-used form had to drive to an IRS center to physically obtain the form. Every form the IRS has is now available for downloading on its web site.[5]

Enabling Legislation

Most administrative agencies are created when Congress passes an **enabling act**. This act creates the agency; sets out its structure; gives it the authority to make rules, investigate problems, and adjudicate cases; and defines any other powers that it will have. Congress decides whether the agency will be a line agency in the executive branch, an independent agency, or a quasi-official government agency.

Congress controls the agencies. First, Congress creates and defines the agency's powers. Second, the Senate confirms the appointments of the head of the agency and the commissioners. Third, although the president sends the budget to Congress, only Congress, through its constitutional ability to tax and spend, controls agency appropriations. Fourth, Congress may reorganize or abolish the agency. Congress has passed deregulation legislation, and some agencies have been abolished.

After an agency is created, it must adopt a **general policy statement.** The statement sets out, in broad terms, that particular agency's philosophy and its mission and objectives. For example, the general policy statement for the FTC reads that "[i]t is responsible for

---

[1] The *Federal Register* is a component of the National Archives and Records Administration. The *Federal Register* publishes public laws, presidential documents, and administrative regulations and notices. The *Federal Register* has a web site at <http://www.nara.gov/fedreg>.
[2] The Legal Services Corporation's web site is found at <http://www.lsc.gov/>.
[3] Amtrak's official web page is <http://www.amtrak.com/>.
[4] The Smithsonian's web page is found at <http://www.si.edu/>.

[5] The Internal Revenue Service's web site is <http://www.irs.ustreas.gov/>.

Exhibit 6–4   A Line Agency: Department of Commerce

DEPARTMENT OF COMMERCE

Source: *U.S. Government Manual, 1999–2000*, Washington, DC (Government Printing Office, 1999), p. 22.

the administration of a variety of statutes which, in general, are designed to promote competition and to protect the public from unfair and deceptive acts and practices in the advertising and marketing of goods and services."[6]

The statement must be politically astute. It must satisfy both the political atmosphere that created the agency and opponents who might desire to curb its powers or abolish it outright. In 1995, Congress abolished the Interstate Commerce Commission and threatened to close the Department of Commerce and abolish the National Oceanic and Atmospheric Administration.

The authority of different agencies occasionally overlaps. The courts allow this overlapping provided that the agencies' actions are consistent with their respective enabling statutes.

Administrative Procedure Act

The **Administrative Procedure Act (APA)**[7] of 1946 standardized many agency practices and now governs procedures by which all federal agencies must conduct their business. The APA does allow for differences among the agencies, however, because each agency's enabling act differs.

The APA sets out the procedures that an agency must follow when making rules, when acquiring and investigating information, and when adjudicating. The APA ensures that the agency adheres to constitutional requirements.

Three Areas of Power

Administrative agencies have three prime responsibilities: to make rules, to acquire and act on information, and to judge cases. These activities are carried out using the agency's legislative, executive, and judicial powers. Any one agency may possess a combination of all three types of power. These powers really are quasi-powers. For example, an agency with quasi-legislative power does not have the actual power to pass legislation. Only Congress has legislative power. The agency does, however, have the power to adopt rules that are very similar to legislative power, thus, the name quasi-legislative power.

Agencies are able to promulgate rules that have the effect of law (a **quasi-legislative function**). They have policing powers to ensure compliance with those rules by acquiring information through record keeping and investigations (a **quasi-executive function**). They prosecute violators, render judgments, and impose penalties in an administrative hearing (a **quasi-judicial function**). Congress, however, has not given all three powers to every agency.

Quasi-Legislative Function. An administrative agency's quasi-legislative function operates in a manner similar to a legislative body. The administrative agency adopts and publishes rules so that the public knows how to conduct its business when dealing with the items regulated by the agency. For example, if the Environmental Protection Agency (EPA) establishes rules on how to dispose of asbestos found in a building, any contractor who agrees to remodel a building containing asbestos must follow those rules or face penalties.

Purpose of Rule Making. A rule adopted by an administrative agency is like a statute passed by Congress. A rule is designed to implement, interpret, or prescribe an agency's law, policy, or practice. When an agency announces a broadly applicable, prospective policy, the agency uses the mechanism of a rule. Based on future standards of conduct rather than a past or current act, a rule is more appropriate and efficient than applying regulations in a case-by-case approach.

Ministerial Powers. Ministerial powers implement an administrative act in a prescribed manner and do not involve the exercise of judgment, discretion, or policy-making. These powers are a very important part of an agency's activities. The only contact most members of the public have with an agency occurs when it is exercising its ministerial powers. For example, when a person visits a Social Security office or goes to its Internet site for information, the agency uses its ministerial powers. Often, a business will request an agency's opinion as to whether an action contemplated by the business will be legal under a certain regulation. The agency gives an opinion and offers the business informal advice.

Misinformation. The public relies on the agency to provide correct information. Based on that information, individuals and businesses carry out plans, knowing that their action complies with the agency rules.

[6] 16 C.F.R. § 0.1 (1995 edition).
[7] The Administrative Procedure Act is found at the Legal Information Institute web site at <http://www4.law.cornell.edu/uscode/5/ch5.html>.

What happens, however, if an agency employee provides inaccurate information? Public policy dictates that an agency is not bound by, or liable for, incorrect information given by its employees. The real meaning of this policy is that a person cannot successfully sue the government.

Why is an agency not liable for the misinformation given by an employee? If it were, an agency could assume powers that Congress had not authorized nor did Congress want the agency to have. If the agency were held liable, the courts would be ordering government money to be spent in a manner not authorized by Congress. Under the Constitution, only Congress has the power to appropriate money.

The agency also is responsible for spending the public monies entrusted to it in accordance with the law. Even if one individual is devastated by incorrect information given by the agency, the government's duty is to the public and to the protection of the public's trust and monies.

The agency rules are available to the public through the *Federal Register*. The courts have held that ignorance of an agency's rules or reliance on the agency's information is no excuse for an individual to not know, not understand, or not comply with those rules. A person may be able to alleviate the harshness of the penalty that results from ignorance of the law, however, if she fits into one of the following categories:

1. Congress can authorize an agency to stand behind the advice it gives in specific situations. For example, the Internal Revenue Service may issue a binding-opinion letter to a business about a question on a specific tax issue. The IRS must stand by the advice provided in that type of letter.

2. A person may incur a debt to the government because he relied on incorrect information given by an agency employee. The harmed person is not able to sue the government, but may ask the government to forgive the debt based on hardship and poor advice.

3. A person who has been harmed by incorrect advice provided by a government employee also may apply to Congress for a private bill of relief. The person's congressional representative drafts and submits a bill to Congress to compensate the person for the government's error. This route is long, difficult, and not often successful.

Discretionary Rule-Making Powers. Congress has authorized administrators to formulate rules and guidelines under a general (discretionary) authority granted to administrative agencies. For example, the commissioner of Social Security has the discretionary authority to make rules that specify those eligible for Medicare benefits. This rule-making authority, authorized by Congress, grants quasi-legislative powers to administrators.

The three types of agency rules are *procedural rules, interpretive rules,* and *substantive rules.* **Procedural rules** govern an agency's internal practices. An agency inherently has the power to determine its own governance. In accordance with the APA, procedural rules must be published in the *Federal Register*. An agency must follow its own procedural rules. A court may overturn any action that violates a procedural rule.

Remember that an agency is created by a statute. An **interpretive rule** allows the agency to interpret the statute that it is charged with administering. When an agency issues an interpretive rule, the only public action it must take is to publish the rule in the *Federal Register*. For example, the Federal Reserve Board is charged with enforcing the Truth-in-Lending Act. The Federal Reserve Board published in the *Federal Register* an interpretation of the criteria for determining when a late charge would be considered a finance charge. No prior notice or opportunity to comment was given to the public. An agency's definition of a term is considered an interpretive rule.

A **substantive rule** is based on a specific statutory authority to issue rules that create and manage programs. All rules that are not procedural or interpretive in nature are deemed substantive. APA procedural requirements for rule making vary, depending on whether an agency engages in *informal rule making* or *formal rule making.*

Informal and formal rule making are applied when an agency adopts a substantive rule. In **informal rule making**, the agency must publish notice of the proposed rule, give interested people an opportunity to participate in the rule making, and incorporate in the rule a concise, general statement of its basis and purpose. Informal rule making is frequently referred to as notice-and-comment rule making.

In **formal rule making**, an agency must conduct a hearing before it can adopt a rule. The parties for and against the rule are entitled to present their case or objection, to submit oral and documentary evidence, to

LEGAL HIGHLIGHT

"Governmentese" and Plain English

The contorted language used by regulators has jokingly been called "governmentese." For instance, in the 1970s, the Occupational Safety and Health Administration published standards concerning the ability of a ladder to hold a "live load unit ascending and descending the ladder with additional weights." Translated, this passage was referring to a person—the "live load unit"—climbing up and down a ladder with something in his hand. Regulators now are required to write in plain English. Here is the Consumer Product Safety Commission's description of a book of matches.

§ 1202.3 Definitions.

In additional to the definitions given in section 3 of the Consumer Product Safety Act (15 U.S.C. §2052), the following definitions apply for the purpose of this standard:

(a) "Bookmatch" means a single splint, with a matchhead attached, that comes from a matchbook.

(b) "Bridge" means the matchhead material held in common by two or more splints.

(c) "Broken bridge" means a bridge that has become separated.

(d) "Caddy" means a package of two or more matchbooks wrapped or boxed together at a production plant.

(e) "Comb" means a piece of wood, paper, or other suitable material that has been formed into splints, that remain joined at their base, and that are designed to have matchheads attached to their tips.

(f) "Cover" means the paperboard or other suitable material that is wrapped around and fastened to the comb(s).

(g) "Friction" means the dried chemical mixture on the matchbook cover used to ignite the bookmatch.

(h) "Match" means a single splint with matchhead attached.

(i) "Matchbook" means one or more combs with matchheads attached and a cover that is wrapped around and fastened to those combs.

(j) "Matchhead" means the dried chemical mixture on the end of a splint.

(k) "Splint" means the support for the matchhead or that portion normally held when using the bookmatch.

§ 1202.4 Matchbook general requirements.

A matchbook shall meet the following general requirements:

(a) The friction shall be located on the outside back cover near the bottom of the matchbook.

(b) The cover shall remain closed without external force.

(c) No friction material shall be located on the inside of the cover where possible contact with the matchheads may occur during ordinary use.

(d) There shall be no bridge(s) or broken bridge(s).

(e) No matchhead in the matchbook shall be split, chipped, cracked, or crumbled.

(f) No portion of any matchhead shall be outside the matchbook cover when the cover is closed.

(g) No part of a staple or other assembly device for securing the cover and combs shall be within or touching the friction area.

(h) A staple used an assembly device for securing the cover and combs shall be fully clinched so that the ends are flattened or turned into the cover.

§ 1202.5 Certification.

Certification shall be in accordance with section 14(a) of the Consumer Product Safety Act (15 U.S.C. 2063(a)). Under this provision, manufacturers and private labelers of products subject to safety standards must certify that their products conform to the standard, based on either a test of each product or on a reasonable testing program.

§ 1202.6 Marking.

(a) The manufacturer's or private labeler's name and city or a symbol which will identify the name and city shall appear on the matchbook. In addition, every private labeler must label the matchbook with a code which enables it to identify, if requested, the manufacturer of the product.

(b) Boxes or cartons in which two or more caddies are shipped shall be marked "For safety, store in a cool, dry place."

Source: 16 C.F.R. §§1202.3–1202.6. Ch. II (1-1-97 edition).

present witnesses, and to conduct examinations of the various witnesses who testify before the agency. Although the parties do not have a right to an attorney, most parties employ an attorney to represent them. In many respects, a formal rule-making hearing is similar to a trial.

Agency rules have the same legal effect as a statute. In other words, these rules become law. Ignorance of these rules is no excuse when a person is accused of violating an administrative rule. These rules are made available to the public in the *Federal Register* and in the *Code of Federal Regulations*.[8] Once a rule has been adopted, the agency later can rescind it.

Judicial Function.
Any problems that a person has with an agency usually can be resolved within the agency's administrative courts. The ability of the administrative agency to resolve internally most of the disputes that arise relieves the judicial court system of many cases. Not all agencies have this function, however.

Purpose of Adjudication. Administrative agencies develop policy through adjudication, as well as through rule making. *Adjudication* is another term for a decision from a court or from an agency's administrative court. Adjudication often is appropriate when a decision relates to specific facts and to particular parties or when an agency is not ready to announce a rule and wants to take a more cautious, case-by-case approach. The number of decisions each year is substantial.

Rule making is a legislative power, whereas adjudication is a judicial power. Agencies use either rule making or adjudication, depending on the circumstances. If the future consequences of conduct are to be prescribed and the application will be general, rule making is proper. If liability is to be determined based on present or past acts concerning a specific individual, the case is subject to adjudication.

Administrative Law Judge. An administrative agency adjudicates an individual case in a hearing conducted by an administrative law judge (ALJ) assigned to the agency. As an employee of the agency, an ALJ is not a member of the federal judiciary. The ALJ is authorized to perform a

variety of judge-like functions in the judicial hearing. The ALJ issues subpoenas, administers oaths to witnesses, conducts hearing conferences, regulates the conduct and course of the hearing, rules on admissibility of evidence, and makes other procedural rulings.

Outside the hearing, an ALJ may not talk with anyone on any issues before the administrative law court so as to remain as insulated as possible from external influences. After the hearing, the ALJ issues a decision with the findings and conclusions that support it, similar to a court judgment.

Procedures for Administrative Adjudication. A case begins with the issuance of a complaint to a business or person when the agency believes a violation of a particular regulation has occurred. After a complaint is served on an alleged wrongdoer, the party has an opportunity to answer. Eventually, the complaint is heard by an administrative law judge, who conducts the hearing, rules on motions, and decides both the facts and the law. In an agency hearing, an accused party has no right to a jury.

The hearing is conducted in a manner similar to a trial, but a hearing is more informal. The rules of evidence that apply in a judicial trial are not strictly followed in a hearing. For example, many agencies can determine whether hearsay evidence can be used in hearings. Hearsay is evidence that does not come from the witness's personal knowledge, but from information that the witness has heard another person say. Evidence based on hearsay testimony is not allowed in a judicial trial. If the agency rules, however, allow hearsay evidence, the ALJ must allow a witness to testify as to what another person said.

Either before or during the hearing, the party and the government can enter into an informal settlement process. The parties also can agree to a **consent decree**. A consent decree is an agreement that is signed by the ALJ so that the agreement carries the court's sanction.

When the parties cannot come to an agreement, a hearing will be held. The ALJ, after considering all the evidence and the law, issues an *order*. An **order** is the final disposition of the case and is similar to a court judgment. The order is subject to review by the head of the administrative agency.

After the hearing, the party that lost the case may appeal. Most agencies have an appeal route built into the administrative system. The party must follow all administrative review procedures. This process is called the **doctrine of exhaustion of remedies**. This doc-

---

[8] Web sites for the Code of Federal Regulations are at <http://www.nara.gov/fedreg> and <http://www.access.gpo.gov/nara/cfr/cfr-table-search.html>.

trine is deeply rooted in history and provides a reasonable balance between a person's and the government's rights. Only after a person has exhausted all administrative remedies may the case be appealed to the judicial courts for review.

As will be discussed later, the courts uphold the administrative agency's decision when there is **substantial evidence** on the record to support the order. Substantial evidence is defined in a negative way by the courts; that is, the administrative agency's decision must not be clearly erroneous or unsupported by credible evidence. As discussed in Chapter 3, civil cases have two burdens of proof. In a court of law, the plaintiff proves its case by the preponderance of the evidence. In a court of equity, the plaintiff proves its case by clear and convincing evidence.

Executive Function. Through the executive function, administrative agencies can ensure that their rules are followed.

Acquisition of Information. The bureaucracy is an information-gathering instrument of the government. Information acquisition enables an agency to become an expert on the subject matter it regulates.

Most of the information that an agency gathers is obtained voluntarily. On occasion, information must be obtained through compulsion. Agencies gather information in one of three ways: record keeping and periodic reports, subpoena power, and power to conduct physical inspections. The first method obtains information through voluntary cooperation, whereas the latter two methods use compulsion to obtain the information.

Record Keeping and Requirements. Federal agencies that regulate businesses require those businesses to maintain specific records and to make periodic mandatory reports based on those records. For example, a whiskey manufacturer must maintain records for the Bureau of Alcohol, Tobacco, and Firearms. This information allows the agency to study problems and to promulgate, amend, or delete rules as necessary.

Investigatory Powers. Other executive functions performed by an administrative agency are investigations and prosecutions. When performing these functions, an agency follows procedural rules prescribing its conduct.

Sometimes an agency fails to take any action on a complaint. The following case concerns the refusal of an administrative agency to conduct an investigation.

Case 6.1

Center for Auto Safety v. Dole

United States Court of Appeals, District of Columbia Circuit, 1987
828 F. 2d 799

BACKGROUND AND FACTS The National Traffic and Motor Vehicle Safety Act of 1966 states that if the secretary of transportation makes a determination that a safety-related defect exists, the secretary, through the National Highway Transportation Safety Administration (NHTSA), must order the manufacturer to recall and remedy the defect. The Center for Auto Safety alleged that between 1966 and 1979, defects in automatic transmissions built by the Ford Motor Company caused cars to disengage from "park" and to roll without warning.

A 1982 NHTSA investigation ended without a final determination on the existence of a defect because NHTSA and Ford entered a settlement agreement that required Ford to notify owners about the possibility of a defect. NHTSA explicitly reserved the right to commence a new proceeding on the alleged defect if additional acts warranted. In March 1985, the Center for Auto Safety petitioned NHTSA to reopen the hearing because of additional evidence. The NHTSA administrator denied the petition after reviewing the administrative record. She was not convinced that a final defect determination would be warranted even if a further investigation were undertaken. The Center for Auto Safety appealed the denied petition. The district court denied the review, and the center appealed.

Chief Judge WALD

. . . .

While this court cannot, and should not, second-guess the agency's safety determinations, this court can and should assure that the agency has some factual support for those safety determinations. Making sure that the agency's stated reason for denying an enforcement petition is in truth the lack of a "substantial safety issue" guarantees that the responsible administrative agency has given at least minimum amount of consideration to the citizens whose safety Congress has entrusted to the agency.

Our holding then is this: When Congress grants citizens the right to petition administrative agencies for enforcement of an issue of public safety, and the relevant substantive statute sends out no identifiable signals on the availability or scope of judicial review of an agency's denial of that petition, but the agency has bound itself by a legal rule to grant the petition unless it makes a finding of "no reasonable possibility" of a safety defect, then a petitioner is entitled under the APA to judicial review of a decision denying the petition to assure that the agency had some factual support for its "no reasonable possibility" finding. In such circumstances, the arbitrary or capricious standard of review in . . . the APA functions as usual, and is not limited to examining merely the stated reasons for the agency's decision. Therefore, . . . we hold that NHTSA's determination that no "reasonable possibility" of a safety-related defect exists in this case is subject to judicial review on the basis of the evidence that the Administrator had before her when she made her decision.

DECISION AND REMEDY The court reversed the district court's decision and remanded the case to the district court. The court of appeals held that the Motor Vehicle Safety Act allows judicial review of NHTSA decisions, even those denying a citizen's petition. The district court has the "reasonable possibility" standard with which to review the decisions. The reviewing court must examine the administrative record in order to make its decision.

CRITICAL THINKING: JUDICIAL CONSIDERATION Under what circumstances should the courts require an administrative agency to conduct hearings after the agency has determined a hearing to be inappropriate? Discuss fully.

Enforcement Powers. Enforcement powers also are delegated to agencies. All final orders issued by an ALJ may result in civil or criminal penalties if violated. These penalties are enforceable unless a reviewing court reverses the agency's decision.

Failure to comply with the penalties is treated like any other violation of the law. In most cases, violations are considered to be a civil matter. For example, the agency requires the installation of pollution control equipment by electrical utility companies to control the pollution created by burning coal, but Ace Electric Company fails to comply by the deadline. The ALJ may impose civil penalties, such as fines, on businesses or individuals that fail to comply with the agency's rules.

The following case examines a business's right to a jury trial when the ALJ might levy fines as punishment against it.

Case 6.2

Atlas Roofing Co. v. OSHA

Supreme Court of the United
States, 1977
430 U.S. 442, 97 S. Ct. 1261,
51 L. Ed. 2d 464
http://www.findlaw.com
/casecode/supreme.html

BACKGROUND AND FACTS Two firms were cited by Occupational Safety and Health Administration (OSHA) inspectors for having unsafe workplaces. The first firm was cited for failing to have the sides of trenches shored and was fined $7,500. The second firm was cited for failing to have roof-opening covers installed to prevent accidents. The fine was $600. Both firms appealed the fines.

The firms had a hearing before an ALJ, who affirmed the findings of the OSHA inspectors. The fine of $7,500 was reduced to $5,000. The second fine was affirmed at $600. Both firms appealed to the court of appeals, challenging the constitutionality of OSHA's enforcement procedures. The court of appeals affirmed the decision of the ALJ and found the enforcement procedures to be constitutional. Both firms appealed to the United States Supreme Court. The defendants argued that they were entitled to a jury trial under the Constitution.

Justice WHITE delivered the opinion of the Court.

. . . .

We granted the petitions for writs of *certiorari* [requests for review] limited to the important question whether the Seventh Amendment prevents Congress from assigning to an administrative agency, under these circumstances, the task of adjudicating violations of OSHA. . . .

The Seventh Amendment provides that "[i]n Suits at common law, where the value in controversy shall exceed twenty dollars, the right of trial by jury shall be preserved. . . ." The phrase "Suits at common law" has been construed to refer to cases tried prior to the adoption of the Seventh Amendment in courts of law in which jury trial was customary as distinguished from courts of equity or admiralty in which jury trial was not. . . . Petitioners claim that a suit in a federal court by the Government for civil penalties for violation of a statute is a suit for a money judgment which is classically a suit at common law . . . and that the defendant therefore has a Seventh Amendment right to a jury determination of all issues of fact in such a case. . . .

. . . [W]hen Congress creates new statutory "public rights," it may assign their adjudication to an administrative agency with which a jury trial would be incompatible, without violating the Seventh Amendment's injunction that jury trial is to be "preserved" in "suit at common law." Congress is not required by the Seventh Amendment to choke the already crowded federal courts with new types of litigation or prevented from committing some new types of litigation to administrative agencies with special competence in the relevant field. This is the case even if the Seventh Amendment would have required a jury where the adjudication of those rights is assigned to a federal court of law instead of an administrative agency. . . .

More to the point, it is apparent from the history of jury trial in civil matters that fact finding, which is the essential function of the jury in civil cases, was never the exclusive province of the jury under either the English or American legal systems at the time of the adoption of the Seventh Amendment; and the question whether a fact would be found by a jury turned to a considerable degree on the nature of the forum in which a litigant found himself. Critical fact finding was performed without juries in suits in equity, and there were no juries in admiralty [a field of law dealing only with maritime legal problems], nor were there juries in the military justice system. The jury was the fact finding mode in most suits in the common-law courts, but it was not exclusively so: Condemnation was a suit at common law but constitutionality could be tried without a jury[.] . . .

Thus, history and our cases support the proposition that the right to a jury trial turns not solely on the nature of the issue to be resolved but also on the forum in which it is to be resolved. Congress found the common-law and other existing remedies for work injuries resulting from unsafe working conditions to be inadequate to protect the Nation's working men and women. It created a new cause of action, and remedies, therefor, unknown to the common law, and placed their enforcement in a tribunal supplying speedy and expert resolutions of the issues involved. The Seventh Amendment is no bar to the creation of new rights or to their enforcement outside the regular courts of law.

DECISION AND REMEDY The decision of the court of appeals was affirmed, and the fines for both firms were upheld. More important, the Supreme Court found that Congress had the power to create statutory rights without providing that juries be available to decide facts. Congress is free to create new methods to resolve problems between disagreeing parties.

CRITICAL THINKING: JUDICIAL CONSIDERATION Discuss fully why a person or a business should be denied a jury trial when confronted with being sanctioned for wrongful conduct.

Limitations on Administrative Agencies' Powers

Most limitations on administrative agencies' powers arise from one of three sources: (1) the Constitution, (2) congressional statutes, and (3) judicial review. Constitutional limitations typically relate to administrative agency behavior. Any procedural inadequacies are subject to judicial review.

Major Constitutional Limitations

The Constitution provides the most important limitations on administrative agency actions. Although most constitutional rights, such as due process and unreasonable search and seizure, are regarded primarily as individual rights, businesses also have some constitutional rights.

Both procedural and substantive due process protect businesses against arbitrary, capricious, and unreasonable administrative agency actions. Substantive due process applies when issues arise that involve property or other rights affected by government. Procedural due process focuses on notice and hearing procedures. In most cases people or businesses must be given prior notice of any hearing that might directly affect them.

Enforcement of due process rights through the Fifth and Fourteenth Amendments, however, follows a double standard. Whenever government action directly affects economic activity, courts usually find it to be constitutional. In contrast, courts generally are suspicious of government actions that might limit basic human freedoms.

Fourth Amendment Limitations. The Constitution protects people from unwarranted intrusions into their personal privacy. In civil and criminal cases, businesses also are protected from unreasonable searches. The Fourth Amendment has been used to prohibit building inspectors from looking for building code violations against the desires of the owner of the premises when the inspectors have no warrant. An agency, however, may make an unannounced inspection of those businesses that traditionally have been heavily regulated, such as the alcoholic beverage industry, the firearm industry, the fishing industry, and the meat-packing industry.

In the case that follows, the United States Supreme Court held that government safety inspectors must have a warrant to make a routine inspection of work areas in a private business.

Case 6.3

Marshall v. Barlow's, Inc.

Supreme Court of the United States, 1978
436 U.S. 307, 98 S. Ct. 1816,
56 L. Ed. 2d 305
http://www.findlaw.com
/casecode/supreme.html

LANDMARK CASE

BACKGROUND AND FACTS Prior to this case, inspectors of the Occupational Safety and Health Administration (OSHA) were not required to obtain permission to enter the work areas of firms under OSHA's jurisdiction. OSHA's rules authorized inspections without a search warrant. In 1975, an OSHA inspector entered the customer service area of Barlow's, Inc., an electrical and plumbing installation business. After showing his credentials, the inspector informed the president and general manager, Barlow, that he (the inspector) would be conducting an inspection of the business's working areas.

On inquiry, Barlow learned that no complaint had been received about his company. The inspection simply resulted from random selection. The inspector had no search warrant. Barlow refused to permit the inspector to enter the working area of his business, relying on his rights guaranteed by the Fourth Amendment.

OSHA filed suit in the U.S. District Court. The court issued an order compelling Barlow to admit the OSHA inspector for purposes of conducting an occupational safety and health inspection. The OSHA inspector, now armed with a court order, went back to Barlow's, Inc. Barlow again refused him admission.

This time, Barlow went to the same district court, seeking an injunction to prohibit the inspector from making a warrantless search on the ground that the OSHA inspection violated the Fourth Amendment. This time the district court ruled in Barlow's favor. The district court held that the Fourth Amendment required a warrant for the search involved and that the authorization for warrantless inspections under the OSHA statute was unconstitutional.

A permanent injunction against such searches or inspections was entered on Barlow's behalf. A permanent injunction is a final court order granting relief, in this case forbidding the OSHA inspector from conducting any further searches or inspections of Barlow's premises. The Supreme Court granted a writ of *certiorari* after OSHA challenged the validity of the injunction.

Justice WHITE delivered the opinion of the Court.

. . . .

The Warrant Clause of the Fourth Amendment protects commercial buildings, as well as private homes. To hold otherwise would belie the origin of that Amendment, and the American colonial experience. . . .

. . . [U]nless some recognized exception to the warrant requirement applies, . . . a warrant [is required] to conduct the inspection sought in this case.

. . . Certain industries have such a history of government oversight that no reasonable expectation of privacy could exist for a proprietor over the stock of such an enterprise. Liquor and firearms are industries of this type; when an entrepreneur embarks upon such a business, he has voluntarily chosen to subject himself to a full arsenal of governmental regulation.

. . . The element that distinguishes these enterprises from ordinary businesses is a long tradition of close government supervision, of which any person who chooses to enter such a business must already be aware. . . .

The clear import . . . is that the closely regulated industry . . . is the exception. . . .

. . . .

The critical fact in this case is that entry over Mr. Barlow's objection is being sought by a Government agent. Employees are not being prohibited from reporting OSHA violations. What they observe in their daily functions is undoubtedly

beyond the employer's reasonable expectation of privacy. The Government inspector, however, is not an employee. Without a warrant he stands in no better position than a member of the public. What is observable by the public is observable, without a warrant, by the Government inspector as well. The owner of a business has not, by the necessary utilization of employees in his operation, thrown open the areas where employees alone are permitted to the warrantless scrutiny of Government agents. That an employee is free to report, and the Government is free to use, any evidence of noncompliance with OSHA that the employee observes furnishes no justification for federal agents to enter a place of business from which the public is restricted and to conduct their own warrantless search.
. . . .

Whether the Secretary proceeds to secure a warrant or other process, with or without prior notice, his entitlement to inspect will not depend on his demonstrating probable cause to believe that conditions in violation of OSHA exist on the premises. Probable cause in the criminal law sense is not required. For purposes of an administrative search such as this, probable cause justifying the issuance of a warrant may be based not only on specific evidence of an existing violation but also on a showing that "reasonable legislative or administrative standards are conducting an . . . inspection are satisfied with respect to a particular [establishment]."

A warrant showing that a specific business has been chosen for an OSHA search on the basis of a general administrative plan for the enforcement of the Act derived from neutral sources such as, for example, dispersion of employees in various types of industries across a given area, and the desired frequency of searches in any of the lesser divisions of the area, would protect an employer's Fourth Amendment rights. We doubt that the consumption of enforcement energies in the obtaining of such warrants will exceed manageable proportions.
. . . .

. . . The authority to make warrantless searches devolves almost unbridled discretion upon executive and administrative officers, particularly those in the field, as to when to search and whom to search. A warrant, by contrast, would provide assurances from a neutral officer that the inspection is reasonable under the Constitution, is authorized by statute, and is pursuant to an administrative plan containing specific neutral criteria. Also, a warrant would then and there advise the owner of the scope and objects of the search, beyond which limits the inspector is not expected to proceed. These are important functions for a warrant to perform, functions which underlie the Court's prior decisions that the Warrant Clause applies to inspections for compliance with regulatory statutes. We conclude that the concerns expressed by the Secretary do not suffice to justify warrantless inspections under OSHA or vitiate the general constitutional requirement that for a search to be reasonable a warrant must be obtained.

DECISION AND REMEDY The Supreme Court upheld the permanent injunction. OSHA inspections conducted without warrants are unconstitutional when the business to be inspected is not one that otherwise is regulated by close government supervision.

CRITICAL THINKING: PUBLIC POLICY CONSIDERATION In this case, the United States Supreme Court articulated a different standard than that used for criminal law when seeking a search warrant. Explain reasons for which a different warrant-procurement process should be applied for criminal law and administrative agency searches.

LEGAL HIGHLIGHT
No Jargon, Please!

The Social Security Administration mails more than 200 million letters a year to people receiving disability and retirement benefits. Most letters routinely inform the person that the amount they receive will be increased or decreased because of an adjustment.

Some letters, however, are written by the bureaucratic monster. For example, one woman received a letter stating, "We are sending you a check for $0. This is money due to you for December 4, 1990. You should receive this check no later than [a blank space]. After that, you will receive your regular check of $0 around the first day of each month." In other words, her claim for disability had been denied. Other Social Security recipients who have grave illnesses have been sent forms suggesting that they find part-time work.

The Social Security Administration now has a writing standard requiring notices to be written at the sixth-grade reading level, to contain no jargon, to have an average of fifteen to twenty words per sentence, and to be written in a "courteous, personal, non-threatening tone."

Fifth Amendment Applications. Under the Fifth Amendment, a person cannot be forced to testify against himself in a criminal case. The Supreme Court has held that a business, however, is not a person within the meaning of the Constitution, and thus a business is ineligible for protection under this Fifth Amendment clause.

Administrative agencies may require businesses to create and maintain records. Because a business is not a person, these records are not included under the self-incrimination clause and, therefore, may be disclosed in criminal or civil cases. These types of business records become, in effect, quasi-public records. Because the agency requires the business to maintain these records, the agency can inspect these records to ensure the accuracy of the reports it receives periodically.

Although these records are quasi-public, the disclosure requirement is not tantamount to public disclosure. Businesses legitimately have secrets concerning their products or services. They may have secret marketing strategies or trade secrets, as well as sensitive personal records.

Congress provides protection in two ways. First, the enabling act specifically may prohibit records from being made public and may prohibit the agency's employees from disclosing certain information. Second, in 1966, Congress passed the Freedom of Information Act. Although this act promotes information access and availability to the public and individuals, certain information is restricted from disclosure. This act will be examined in detail in the next section. In short, business records are protected from public disclosure under restricted circumstances.

Liability of Agencies and Federal Employees. Occasionally, an agency's employee violates a person's constitutional rights, for which the individual federal employee can be held personally liable. For example, agents, while searching a house without a warrant, tear down walls looking for hidden drugs. In this case, the individual agents may be held liable in a court of law by the people whose rights were violated.

The agency, however, cannot be held liable for any constitutional rights violations by its agents. An agency cannot authorize the constitutional violations of persons. To allow an agency to be held liable for the actions of its agents who act in an unconstitutional manner would create a potentially enormous financial burden on the federal government. More important, the deterrent effect would be lost if the victim had a choice of suing the agency or the employee. The victim would choose the agency to sue because it has more money than an individual employee. If the employee knew that the chances of being sued were slim because the agency would be held liable, prospective violators would be undeterred.

Congressional Statutes

When Congress creates an agency, its statutory scheme includes congressional limitations on that agency. Although certain general rules apply to all agencies, a person dealing with a specific agency must be aware of these congressional limitations. Some statutes amend the Administrative Procedure Act and thus affect all agencies. Other statutes apply only to one agency.

Freedom of Information Act.

The **Freedom of Information Act (FOIA)** is an amendment to the Administrative Procedure Act. All administrative agencies are subject to the FOIA, which makes all information held by federal agencies available to the public. Exemptions do exist, however, if information falls within certain categories.

Information may be disclosed under the FOIA in one of three ways. First, the *Federal Register* publishes information, such as agencies' policy statements and procedural and substantive rules. Second, agencies must make available for public inspection and copying certain information not printed in the *Federal Register*. Reprints of the opinions of administrative law judges, public statements, interpretive rules, staff manuals, and directives are sold to the public for a nominal fee. Third, if the information is not published under either of these methods and it is not exempt, each agency has established reasonable procedures for the public to follow when requesting a copy of that information. The **Electronic Freedom of Information Act** makes it possible for the public to have free electronic access to these documents on the Internet without having to make a formal request under the Freedom of Information Act.

The significant exempt categories are those that contain information in the following areas: information relating to national defense or foreign policy, internal personnel rules, information protected by another statute that prohibits disclosure, business trade secrets and privileged or confidential business information, and any information that violates personal privacy. Even though certain information may be classified in one of the exempt categories, the agency is not prohibited automatically from disclosing that information. The FOIA gives the agency discretion as to whether to disclose the information.

When an agency decides not to disclose information under the FOIA, the agency must disclose its reasons to the requester. After exhausting the administrative remedies, the requester has the right to file a lawsuit in district court to force the agency to disclose the information.

The agency has the burden of proof to support its action. The burden of proof is the obligation of a party to the case to demonstrate to the court that the evidence favors that party's side. The agency proves its case by substantial evidence in order to support the decision. If an agency has established substantial evidence, a district or an appellate court will not reverse it. The administrative decision will not be set aside unless it is clearly erroneous or unsupported by any credible evidence.

Privacy Act.

The **Privacy Act** is a 1974 amendment to the Administrative Procedure Act. The Privacy Act protects only individuals who are citizens or legal aliens. By statutory definition, business entities are not covered.

Agencies accumulate tremendous amounts of information on individuals. If a person requests all of the information that an agency has, the agency must provide it. The information maintained must be correct, accurate, and current. If this information is stale, inaccurate, or incomplete, the individual can make corrections.

The Privacy Act does not require an agency to disclose information it has on an individual under certain circumstances. For example, if a person is being investigated for a crime, the investigating agency does not have to disclose that an investigation is ongoing even if the individual requests it.

The agency cannot disclose information that it has on an individual to others unless the conditions of the Privacy Act are met. For example, if information is requested from an agency on a particular person, the agency cannot provide that information because it is protected under the Privacy Act. No exceptions to the act exist for newspapers. The following case demonstrates the relationship between the Privacy Act and the Freedom of Information Act.

Case 6.4

U.S. Department of Defense v. Labor Relations Authority

Supreme Court of the United States, 1994

510 U.S. 487, 114 S. Ct. 1006, 127 L. Ed. 2d 325

http://www.findlaw.com /casecode/supreme.html

BACKGROUND AND FACTS   Two local unions requested that several federal agencies provide the name and home address of employees who worked at the agencies. The federal agencies supplied the names and work stations but refused to release home addresses.

Congress allows federal employees to be unionized. The federal agency that reviews the relationship between unions and government agencies is the Federal Labor Relations Authority (the Authority). When the agencies refused to supply the home addresses, the unions appealed the denial to the Authority.

The Authority determined that the home addresses were to be released to the unions. The agencies appealed the determination. In this case, the United States Supreme Court reviewed the relationship between the Privacy Act and the Freedom of Information Act.

(The relationship between unions and government agencies is governed by the Authority. The relationship between unions and workers for private employers is governed by the National Labor Relations Board [NLRB].)

Justice THOMAS delivered the opinion for a unanimous Court.

. . . .

Petitioners contend that the Privacy Act prohibits disclosure. This statute provides in part:

> "No agency shall disclose any record which is contained in a system of records by any means of communication to any person, or to another agency, except pursuant to a written request by, or with the prior written consent of, the individual to whom the record pertains, unless disclosure of the record would be . . . (2) required under section 552 of this title [FOIA]."

The employee addresses sought by the unions are "records" covered by the broad terms of the Privacy Act. Therefore, unless FOIA would require release of the addresses, their disclosure is "prohibited by law," and the agencies may not reveal them to the unions.

We turn, then, to FOIA. As we have recognized previously, FOIA reflects "a general philosophy of full agency disclosure unless information is exempted under clearly delineated statutory language." Thus, while "disclosure, not secrecy, is the dominant objective of [FOIA]," there are a number of exemptions from the statute's broad reach. The exemption potentially applicable to employee addresses is Exemption 6, which provides that FOIA's disclosure requirements do not apply to "personnel and medical files and similar files the disclosure of which would constitute a clearly unwarranted invasion of personal privacy."

. . . .

The principles that we followed . . . can be applied easily to this case. We must weigh the privacy interest of bargaining unit employees in nondisclosure of their addresses against the only relevant public interest in the FOIA balancing analysis—the extent to which disclosure of the information sought would "she[d] light on an agency's performance of its statutory duties" or otherwise let citizens know "what their government is up to."

The relevant public interest supporting disclosure in this case is negligible, at best. Disclosure of the addresses might allow the unions to communicate more effectively with employees, but it would not appreciably further "the citizens' right

to be informed about what their government is up to." Indeed, such disclosure would reveal little or nothing about the employing agencies or their activities.
. . . .

Finally, respondents contend that our decision creates an unnecessary and unintended disparity between public and private sector unions. While private sector unions assertedly are entitled to receive employee home address lists from employers under the National Labor Relations Act, as interpreted by the National Labor Relations Board, respondents claim that federal sector unions now will be needlessly barred from obtaining this information, despite the lack of any indication that Congress intended such a result. We do not question that, as a general matter, private sector labor law may provide guidance in parallel public sector matters. This fact has little relevance here, however, for unlike private sector employees, federal employees enjoy the protection of the Privacy Act, and that statute prohibits the disclosure of the address lists sought in this case. To the extent that this prohibition leaves public sector unions in a position different from that of their private sector counterparts, Congress may correct the disparity.

DECISION AND REMEDY The Supreme Court held that the agencies were correct in not supplying the home addresses to the unions. A distinction exists between public and private employees. A union in the private sector is entitled to employees' home addresses. Government employees, however, enjoy the protection of the Privacy Act, so their home addresses are not releasable. The Freedom of Information Act did not allow disclosure of this information.

CRITICAL THINKING: PUBLIC POLICY CONSIDERATION Discuss fully why the rules for releasing government employees' home addresses to the unions differ from rules regulating the release of private-sector employees' home addresses.

Equal Access to Justice Act. An individual or a small business lacks the financial resources to defend against an unjustified action by a governmental agency. In 1982, Congress passed the **Equal Access to Justice Act**. An administrative law judge or a court may award legal fees (limited to $75 an hour), expert witness fees, or reasonable costs of studies and engineering reports to individuals or small businesses. These fees are awarded if the judge decides that the government agency was substantially unjustified in bringing the action.

The act applies to individuals whose net worth does not exceed $2 million and to small for-profit and not-for-profit organizations with no more than 500 employees and a net worth of no more than $7 million. This act allows an ordinary person to challenge an incorrect legal position held by the government.

Sunshine Act. The **Sunshine Act** of 1976 also amended the Administrative Procedure Act. This act prohibits agencies from holding secret meetings. An agency must give notice of the time and place of its meetings and provide an agenda. Even though not all meetings are open to the public, a meeting notice must be posted indicating that the meeting is open or closed. The Sunshine Act prevents secret, not closed, meetings.

If a person believes that an agency erred in its decision to close a meeting, the person can sue the agency in district court. The court may grant an injunction against future violations of the Sunshine Act. The court, however, may not overturn any action taken by the agency behind closed doors solely because the Sunshine Act was violated. Overturning the action taken by the agency must be based on other legal grounds.

Regulatory Flexibility Act. In 1980, Congress amended the Administrative Procedure Act with the **Regulatory Flexibility Act**. This act takes into account the differences among the various businesses subject to regulation. In particular, a regulation may have a different effect on a small business than it has on a large corporation. The act requires a special regulatory flexibility agenda to be printed in the *Federal Register* twice a year, in April and October. An agency must publish in the regulatory flexibility agenda a list of all rules that the agency is considering during the next few months. The rules listed are the ones likely to have a significant economic impact on small businesses.

Sunset Laws

Each of the statutes discussed previously was passed by Congress as separate statutes. **Sunset laws** are included in a variety of statutes that created specific agencies. A sunset law sets an automatic expiration date for the agency in order to force regular legislative review. In the past, some administrative agencies have outlived their purpose or usefulness but continued to exist because the agency's enabling act had not been repealed.

Today, for an agency to continue, Congress must take affirmative action to retain the agency. Knowing that Congress periodically evaluates it, the agency is more likely to be responsive to the public will. At reviewing time, Congress can make known its concerns about the agency by manipulating its budget or by threatening to reorganize or dismantle it.

Judicial Review

Administrative decisions can be appealed to the courts because the judiciary has the power and the duty to interpret the law. Congress's province is to formulate legislative policy, to mandate programs and projects, and to establish their relative national priority. Once Congress has exercised its legislative power by creating a new administrative agency and providing it a mandate, the agency then administers the law, and the judiciary interprets and enforces it.

In a judicial review of an agency's decision, the court reviews whether the person appealing has exhausted the administrative remedies as discussed previously. Failure to exhaust administrative remedies is the most common reason for dismissing a case. If administrative remedies are exhausted, the court determines whether the agency has any authority to make these specific rules.

Congress delegates broad discretionary powers over a specialized subject matter to each administrative agency. As a result, a court gives **judicial deference** to agency decisions. Judicial deference means that the court does not reverse an agency action unless the court finds that the agency violated a condition set out by the Administrative Procedure Act.

The court considers the record created by the administrative agency. This record resembles a court record and contains all the evidence and testimony provided during the administrative hearing. The court upholds the agency's decision if substantial evidence, as discussed previously, supports the decision. The court also determines whether the delegation from Congress was appropriate. If the agency has rule-making authority, the court must determine whether the agency exceeded its authority. For example, the Securities and Exchange Commission does not have the authority to adopt rules involving civil rights. In the following case, the court had to decide whether the administrative agency had exceeded its rule-making authority.

Case 6.5

Food and Drug Administration v. Brown & Williamson Tobacco Corporation

Supreme Court of the United States, 2000
529 U.S. 120, 120
S. Ct.1291,146 L. Ed. 2d 121
http://www.findlaw.com
/casecode/supreme.html

BACKGROUND AND FACTS In 1995, the Food and Drug Administration (FDA) published a proposed rule concerning the sale of cigarettes and smokeless tobacco to children and adolescents. The rule was designed to reduce the availability and attractiveness of tobacco products to young people. A public comment period followed, during which the FDA received more than 700,000 submissions, more than "at any other time in its history on any other subject."

In 1996, the FDA issued a final rule entitled "Regulations Restricting the Sale and Distribution of Cigarettes and Smokeless Tobacco to Protect Children and Adolescents." The FDA determined that nicotine is a "drug" and that cigarettes and smokeless tobacco are "drug delivery devices," and therefore it had jurisdiction under the Food, Drug, and Cosmetic Act (FDCA) to regulate tobacco products as marketed. The FDA found that tobacco products " 'affect the structure or any function of the body' " because nicotine "exerts psychoactive, or mood-altering, effects on the brain" that cause and sustain addiction, have both tranquilizing and stimulating effects, and control weight.

The FDA found that the manufacturers, through their advertising, intended to induce consumers to use tobacco products "predominantly or nearly exclusively" in obtaining these effects. The statements, research, and actions of the manufacturers revealed that they had designed cigarettes to provide pharmacologically active doses of nicotine to consumers. Finally, the FDA concluded that cigarettes and smokeless tobacco were "combination products" because, in addition to containing nicotine, they include device components that deliver a controlled amount of nicotine to the body.

A group of tobacco manufacturers, retailers, and advertisers filed suit challenging the regulations. They moved for summary judgment on the grounds that the FDA lacked jurisdiction to regulate tobacco products as customarily marketed, the regulations exceeded the FDA's authority, and the advertising restrictions violated the First Amendment. The district court granted respondents' motion in part and denied it in part. The court held that the FDCA authorizes the FDA to regulate tobacco products as customarily marketed and that the FDA's access and labeling regulations are permissible, but it also found that the agency's advertising and promotion restrictions exceeded its authority. The case was appealed.

The Court of Appeals for the Fourth Circuit reversed, holding that Congress had not granted the FDA jurisdiction to regulate tobacco products. Examining the FDCA as a whole, the court concluded that the FDA's regulation of tobacco products would create a number of internal inconsistencies. Various provisions of the Act require the agency to determine that any regulated product is "safe" before it can be sold or allowed to remain on the market, yet the FDA found in its rule-making proceeding that tobacco products are "dangerous" and "unsafe." Thus, the FDA apparently banned tobacco products, a result the court found clearly contrary to congressional intent.

This apparent anomaly, the Court of Appeals concluded, demonstrates that Congress did not intend to give the FDA authority to regulate tobacco. Importantly, the FDA consistently stated before 1995 that it lacked jurisdiction over tobacco, and Congress had enacted several tobacco-specific statutes fully cognizant of the FDA's position. In fact, the court reasoned, Congress had considered and rejected many bills that would have given the agency such authority. The case was then appealed to the United States Supreme Court.

Justice O'CONNOR delivered the opinion of the Court.

Considering the FDCA as a whole, it is clear that Congress intended to exclude tobacco products from the FDA's jurisdiction. A fundamental precept of the FDCA is that any product regulated by the FDA—but not banned—must be safe for its intended use. Various provisions of the Act make clear that this refers to the safety of using the product to obtain its intended effects, not the public health ramifications of alternative administrative actions by the FDA. That is, the FDA must determine that there is a reasonable assurance that the product's therapeutic benefits outweigh the risk of harm to the consumer. According to this standard, the FDA has concluded that, although tobacco products might be effective in delivering certain pharmacological effects, they are "unsafe" and "dangerous" when used for these purposes. Consequently, if tobacco products were within the FDA's jurisdiction, the Act would require the FDA to remove them from the market entirely. But a ban would contradict Congress' clear intent as expressed in its more recent, tobacco-specific legislation. The inescapable conclusion is that there is no room for tobacco products within the FDCA's regulatory scheme. If they cannot be used safely for any therapeutic purpose, and yet they cannot be banned, they simply do not fit.

. . . .

In adopting each statute, Congress has acted against the backdrop of the FDA's consistent and repeated statements that it lacked authority under the FDCA to regulate tobacco absent claims of therapeutic benefit by the manufacturer. In fact, on several occasions over this period, and after the health consequences of tobacco use and nicotine's pharmacological effects had become well known, Congress considered and rejected bills that would have granted the FDA such jurisdiction. Under these circumstances, it is evident that Congress' tobacco-specific statutes have effectively ratified the FDA's long-held position that it lacks jurisdiction under the FDCA to regulate tobacco products.

. . . .

DECISION AND REMEDY The Court found that the Food and Drug Administration had no authority to regulate tobacco. It was determined that Congress had to act to give the FDA authority in this area.

CRITICAL THINKING: PUBLIC POLICY Almost everyone recognizes the danger of tobacco. Why do you think the Court refused to uphold the FDA concerning this great health-destroying problem?

Deregulation

Congress and the president have imposed restraints on agencies by limiting the number of ineffective or potentially harmful rules they can make. In 1978, President Jimmy Carter issued an order requiring agencies to determine the impact of regulations on the economy. The order was issued with an eye to deregulation. Every president since then has worked to make government work more efficiently by abolishing or combining agencies and deregulating businesses.

President Carter's administration, although in office for only four years, made dramatic strides toward deregulation. Deregulation can mean either the elimination of specific agencies or the elimination of specific programs within agencies in order to reduce government regulation. Congress passed many deregulatory acts that took effect after President Ronald Reagan took office. The deregulation occurred mainly in the agencies responsible for economic regulation.

President Reagan issued two executive orders that further limited administrative regulations. These executive orders had several purposes: to establish regulatory priorities, to increase the accountability of agency officials, to provide for presidential oversight of the regulatory process, to reduce the burdens of existing and future regulations, to minimize duplication and conflict of regulations, and to enhance public and congressional understanding of the regulatory objectives.

Each agency must submit annually to the Office of Management and Budget a statement of its regulatory policies, goals, and objectives for the coming year. The agency also must submit information concerning all significant regulatory action under way or planned. Each agency must prepare a regulatory impact analysis of major rules. These executive orders apply only to the agencies in the executive branch and not to independent agencies. Many independent agencies, however, have chosen to comply voluntarily.

To make the government more available to the public, Congress and the president have mandated that all government resources be published on the Internet. The intent is that in the future, the government will not print much information in a hardcopy format since it will be available electronically.

International Consideration

Use of Administrative Law in Assisting International Transactions

The United Nations[9] has developed various administrative agencies to help it function. The six major agencies created to carry out the United Nations' work are (1) the General Assembly, (2) the Security Council, (3) the Secretariat, (4) the Economic and Social Council, (5) the International Court of Justice, and (6) the Trusteeship Council. Other agencies help the United Nations carry out its mission. These include the United Nations Development Program; the United Nations Educational, Scientific, and Cultural Organization (UNESCO); and the United Nations International Children's Emergency Fund (UNICEF).

The United Nations also has developed an international civil service based on administrative rules. Civil service employees are government workers who are not elected or appointed. They are hired, promoted, and dismissed in accordance with rules based on professional standards.

The civil service standards allow administrative hearings to be held when the employee believes the rules have not been applied properly in his or her case. These hearings are held to interpret these rules and develop case law. Decisions based on these hearings protect employees from such arbitrary actions as dismissal because of alleged national disloyalty. The United Nations civil service rules are only one example of an international organization that has many administrative agencies.

[9] The web page for the United Nations is <http://www.un.org/>.

LEGALLY SPEAKING

Facing Zoning Problems

You want to open a small video rental store that offers movies that appeal to college students. You find a perfect location with low monthly rent near the dormitories and other student housing. Before signing the lease, however, your prospective landlord insists that you contact the local municipal zoning agency to make certain that this type of business activity is permitted.

Wanting to open the store as soon as possible, you go to the proper city office and discover that the zoning ordinance does not allow the rental of products, only the sale of products. You ask whether there are any exceptions to this ordinance. The zoning official states that you can either (1) obtain a use permit or a variance to the zoning ordinance or (2) attempt to have the city council change the zoning ordinance.

This venture is your first contact with administrative law. To obtain a variance or use permit, you must submit an application to the zoning board. A

zoning board usually is made up of citizens who are appointed to the board. The job of the board is to determine the acceptable use of property within a particular area, such as a city. The board determines in which areas multifamily dwellings (apartments), light industry, parks, and so on are allowed.

An appointed official will review your application and either grant or deny it in a summary manner. If your application is denied, you have a right to appeal the official's decision to a board of adjustment. Normally, the members of the board of adjustment are appointed by the elected officials, either the members of the city council or the mayor. If the board of adjustment denies your request, you then can take your appeal to the judicial system. In some states you would appeal to the city council.

You also may try another administrative route. You can file a petition for a zoning change with the city planning department. The department will make a recommendation to the planning and zoning commission. This commission also is appointed by elected officials. Unlike the board of adjustment, which has the power to make a final administrative decision, however, the actions of the planning and zoning commission are simply advisory to the city council. Once a recommendation is made, it must be adopted by the city council, which acts in a legislative manner when deciding zoning issues.

You probably should file a petition for a change because the ordinance seems to be rather arbitrary in excluding rental businesses but allowing commercial sales. No doubt the restriction was just an oversight when the ordinance initially was adopted and it needs to be changed.

When you are interested in starting a business you should first check with local authorities about the following possible problems:

✔ *Zoning* Does the zoning law allow the operation of this type of business at your location?

✔ *Signs* What type of signs will be allowed on the premises? An important consideration is whether you can advertise your business on the premises.

✔ *Handicapped Accessibility* Make certain that the building has appropriate facilities for persons with disabilities.

✔ *Hazardous Material* Make certain no prior tenants have left hazardous material on the premises.

Chapter Summary

Administrative agencies handle two areas of public concern: economic regulation and public welfare. Economic regulation takes several forms. An agency may control entry into the marketplace by controlling license procedures, setting rates, or setting standards. Public welfare includes the protection of the public, as well as entitlement programs. Public welfare has two meanings; the broad meaning covers regulation that is for the benefit of the public at large. The secondary meaning covers programs for lower income people. Entitlement programs, such as Social Security, benefit those people who meet the programs' eligibility requirements.

Federal regulatory agencies have several features that allow them to deal with certain problems more effectively than the legislatures or the courts. First, an agency develops expertise in a particular area. Second, a regulatory agency consists of a very well developed hierarchy that helps to ensure continuity of personnel and experience. Third, an agency has more flexibility than the legislature.

When an agency is under the direct control of the president, it is known as a line agency and is headed by a member of the president's cabinet. Congress also has established independent agencies, which are freestanding from the president and from Congress. Government agencies are created by Congress to administer a quasi-

business venture. Quasi–official agencies also are created by Congress but lack the same authority as official agencies.

Administrative agencies engage in three prime areas of activity: they make rules, they acquire and act on information, and they judge cases. These activities are carried out through the quasi-legislative, quasi-executive, and quasi-judicial powers that agencies possess. The Administrative Procedure Act (APA) standardized procedures that agencies must use when exercising their powers. In addition, agencies must not violate a person's constitutional rights.

The APA has been amended several times. The Freedom of Information Act makes all the information held by federal agencies available to the public unless the information falls within an exempt category. The Electronic Freedom of Information Act makes it possible for the public to have free electronic access to these documents on the Internet.

The Privacy Act protects U.S. citizens and legal aliens but not corporations. A person is entitled to see personal information that an agency has concerning him or her. The Equal Access to Justice Act allows recovery of legal fees and court costs by individuals and small businesses when an agency initiates an unjustified action. The Sunshine Act prohibits agencies from holding secret, not closed, meetings. If the topics do not qualify under the closed meeting rules, the meeting must be open.

The Regulatory Flexibility Act takes into account differences in the way a regulation affects a small business versus a large business. The rules that affect small businesses must be published in the *Federal Register.*

The sunset acts are not part of the APA but are included in the statutes that create the agencies. A sunset act sets an automatic expiration date for the agency.

Actions taken by administrative agencies can be appealed to the courts. The courts investigate first whether the authority delegated by Congress to that agency is valid. If a court finds that the agency has the

authority to act, the court then determines if the agency has exceeded its properly delegated authority.

Because an agency is given broad discretionary powers over a specialized subject matter, a court gives judicial deference to agency decisions. To reverse an agency action, a court must find that the agency violated a condition set out by the Administrative Procedure Act.

Deregulation has taken place since the late 1970s. Two executive orders limit administrative regulations of line agencies. Each agency must submit to the Office of Management and Budget each year a statement of the goals of the upcoming year and set out major planned programs. Each agency also must prepare a regulatory impact analysis of its major rules.

Using the World Wide Web

Congress requires the federal executive agencies and independent agencies to maintain Internet sites. Information about Congress also is available on the WWW. The web pages for agencies, although not uniform, generally are easy to use. One of the easiest ways to access administrative agencies is through the Library of Congress Internet Resource Page, titled Official U.S. Executive Branch Web Sites found at <http://lcweb.loc.gov/global/executive/fed.html>.

Finding the Law on the Web

Official U.S. Executive Branch Web Sites
    http://lcweb.loc.gov/global/executive/fed.html
Federal Web Locator, Center for Information Law
    and Policy, Information Center at Chicago–Kent
    College of Law, Illinois
    http://www.infoctr.edu/fwl/
U.S. Senate
    http://www.senate.gov/
U.S. House of Representatives
    http://www.house.gov/
White House
    http://www.whitehouse.gov
U.S. Department of Agriculture
    http://www.usda.gov/
U.S. Department of Commerce
    http://www.doc.gov/

U.S. Department of Defense
    http://www.defenselink.mil/
U.S. Department of Education
    http://www.ed.gov/
U.S. Department of Energy
    http://www.doe.gov/
U.S. Department of Health and Human Services
    http://www.os.dhhs.gov/
U.S. Department of Housing and Urban Development
    http://www.hud.gov/
U.S. Department of the Interior
    http://www.doi.gov/
U.S. Department of Justice
    http://www.usdoj.gov/
U.S. Department of Labor
    http://www.dol.gov/
U.S. Department of State
    http://www.state.gov/
U.S. Department of Transportation
    http://www.dot.gov/
U.S. Department of Treasury
    http://www.ustreas.gov/
U.S. Department of Veterans Affairs
    http://www.va.gov/
Library of Congress
    http://lcweb.loc.gov/
Library of Congress, THOMAS, Legislative Information
    on the Internet
    http://thomas.loc.gov/

Chapter Web Sites

Federal Trade Commission v. Ruberoid Co.
 http://www.findlaw.com/casecode/supreme.html

Federal Register
 http://www.nara.gov/fedreg

Legal Services Corporation
 http://www.lsc.gov

Amtrak
 http://www.amtrak.com/

Smithsonian
 http://www.si.edu/

Internal Revenue Service
 http://www.irs.ustreas.gov/

Administrative Procedure Act
 http://www4.law.cornell.edu/uscode/5/ch5.html

Code of Federal Regulations
 http://www.nara.gov/fedreg

or
 http://www.access.gpo.gov/nara/cfr
 /cfr-table-search.html

Atlas Roofing Co. v. OSHA
 http://www.findlaw.com/casecode/supreme.html

Marshall v. Barlow's, Inc.
 http://www.findlaw.com/casecode/supreme.html

*U.S. Department of Defense v. Labor Relations
 Authority*
 http://www.findlaw.com/casecode/supreme.html

*Food and Drug Administration v. Brown & Williamson
 Tobacco Corporation*
 http://www.findlaw.com/casecode/supreme.html

United Nations
 http://www.un.org/

National Historic Preservation Program
 http://www.achp.gov/

National Trust for Historic Preservation
 http://www.nthp.org

U.S. General Accounting Office
 http://www.gao.gov

The White House Office of Management and Budget
 http://www.whitehouse.gov/omb/

Holly Farms Corporation v. National Labor Relations Board
 http://www.findlaw.com/casecode/supreme.html

Web Activities

6–1 The federal government has many programs that are not all that well known. One program is the program to save historic buildings, the neighborhoods, and landscapes. Congress established a program directed at federal government agencies to establish policies and procedures for historic preservation. See the National Historic Preservation Program web site at <http://www .achp.gov/>. Congress also chartered the National Trust for Historic Preservation as a private, nonprofit organization dedicated to historic preservation. Visit the National Trust for Historic Preservation at <http://www .nthp.org/>. Compare these two web sites. How is the National Historic Preservation Program different from the National Trust for Historic Preservation? When was each program established? How can businesses become involved in historic preservation?

6–2 Compare the General Accounting Office (GAO) with the Office of Management and Budget (OMB). The GAO is found at <http://www.gao.gov/>. The OMB is found at <http://www.whitehouse.gov/omb/>.

Key Terms

Administrative
 Procedure Act (APA)
consent decree
doctrine of exhaustion of
 remedies
economic regulation
Electronic Freedom of
 Information Act
enabling act

entitlement program
Equal Access to Justice
 Act
executive agency
formal rule making
Freedom of Information
 Act (FOIA)
general policy statement
government agency

independent agency
informal rule making
interpretive rule
judicial deference
line agency
order
Privacy Act
procedural rule
public welfare

quasi-executive function
quasi-judicial function
quasi-legislative function
quasi-official agency
Regulatory Flexibility Act
substantial evidence
substantive rule
sunset law
Sunshine Act

Questions and Case Problems

6–1 Separation of Powers Find the authority in the U.S. Constitution for government to establish administrative agencies.

6–2 Fourth Branch of Government Administrative agency law has been described as the government's "headless fourth branch." What does this expression mean? Explain why you agree or disagree with this terminology.

6–3 Substantial Evidence An appellate court will affirm the findings of the administrative law judge when those findings are supported by "substantial evidence on the record." When an administrative agency conducts a quasi-judicial hearing, it records all the evidence and testimony presented at the hearing. The Federal Trade Commission (FTC) accused the Adolph Coors Co. of engaging in certain price-fixing agreements in violation of the Sherman Antitrust Act. After a hearing, the FTC concluded that Coors had in fact engaged in illegal price fixing. Substantial evidence was presented at the hearings in support of the findings. Coors also presented substantial evidence that it had never entered into price-fixing arrangements. Should an appellate court uphold the FTC's findings? [*Adolph Coors Co. v. Federal Trade Commission,* 497 F.2d 1178 (10th Cir. 1974)]

6–4 Procedural Due Process An agency must provide notice and a hearing before it can deprive a party of his or her property or rights. New York State and New York City officials administered various federally assisted welfare programs. Some welfare recipients filed a complaint in court alleging that the state and city terminated, or were about to terminate, the aid without prior notice and a hearing, thereby denying the plaintiffs due process of law. The state and the city, however, adopted procedures, posted notice, and had a hearing after these suits were brought. Does the failure to provide a welfare recipient with a notice of termination before the aid is stopped violate procedural due process? [*Goldberg v. Kelly,* 397 U.S. 254, 90 S. Ct. 1011, 25 L. Ed. 2d 287 (1970)]

6–5 Judicial Review Holly Farms engaged in poultry operations. Broiler chickens are birds destined for human food markets. Holly Farms hatched 1,400 broiler chicks at its own hatcheries and immediately delivered the chicks to the farms of independent contractors. The contractors then raised the birds into full-grown broiler chickens. Holly Farms paid the contract growers for their services

but retained title to the broilers and supplied the food and medicine necessary to their growth. *Live haul* means that the chickens were alive while being transported. The live-haul crews, typically comprised nine chicken catchers, one forklift operator, and one live-haul driver, traveled in a flat-bed truck from Holly Farms' processing plant to the independent growers' farms to retrieve the chickens. The union filed a representation petition with the National Labor Relations Board (NLRB). The union sought an election in a proposed local union that included live-haul crews. Over Holly Farms' objection, the NRLB approved the new local union, ruling that the live-haul workers were employees protected by the National Labor Relations Act (act) rather than agricultural laborers excluded from the act's coverage by another section of the act. The NLRB ordered Holly Farms to bargain with the union. The NLRB's ruling was appealed by Holly Farms. Was the decision of the NLRB upheld on appeal? Give reasons for your answer. [*Holly Farms Corporation v. National Labor Relations Board,* 517 U.S. 392, 116 S. Ct. 1396, 134 L. Ed. 2d 593, (1996); <http://www.findlaw .com/casecode/supreme.html>]

6–6 Acquisition of Information Congress passed the Marine Mammal Protection Act (MMPA) to protect porpoises during commercial fishing operations. Captains of fishing boats can take porpoises only if the captains allow government observers to board and accompany vessels on regular fishing trips either to do research or to observe and collect data on the fishing operations for enforcement proceedings by the National Marine Fisheries Service. These inspectors collect data on the captains' fishing practices for later inclusion in any quasi-judicial proceeding against the captains if they have failed to follow the government regulations. The captains of two fishing vessels object. You are the judge. On what will you base your decision as to whether government scientific observers should be required to be aboard the fishing vessels? Will your decision differ if the fishing boat is out for one day or for a six-month trip? [*Balelo v. Baldridge,* 724 F.2d 753 (9th Cir. 1984)]

6–7 Exhaustion of Remedies The medical board started a proceeding against Davis, a medical doctor, for alleged violations of the Medical Practice Act. Davis challenged the proceeding, claiming that it was unconstitutional. The administrative law judge (ALJ) declined to rule on the constitutional claim. Before the hearing was held, Davis filed a lawsuit on the issue on which the ALJ had refused to rule; that is, that provisions within the Medical Practice Act were unconstitutional. The district court dismissed the case and held that Davis had failed to exhaust his administrative remedies. The hearing was held two years later and Davis's license was revoked. After the revocation, Davis now tries to appeal the dismissal of his original lawsuit in district court, claiming that the act was unconstitutional and that the trial court should not have dismissed his action. Is Davis correct in trying to revive his first lawsuit? Or should his appeal be dismissed because he needs to file a new lawsuit challenging the board's final recommendation that his license be revoked? [*Davis v. Robinson,* 871 P.2d 582 (Utah App. 1994)]

6–8 Due Process The claimant testified that her employer's vice-president continually made comments of a sexual nature to her against her wishes and that this conduct caused her to resign from her job. A hearing was held before the Industrial Claims Board to determine whether she should receive unemployment benefits. At the hearing she introduced into evidence her personal diary, which included entries concerning the incidents. The employer introduced conflicting evidence and objected to the introduction of the diary. The hearing officer offered to allow the employer additional time to review the diary, but the employer did not request a continuance (postponement). The board awarded unemployment benefits to the claimant. The employer appealed the decision to the court, claiming that it did not have a fair hearing. Do you believe that the employer was correct? Why or why not? [*QFD v. Industrial Claim Appeals Office,* 873 P.2d 32 (Colo. App. 1993)]

6–9 Procedures for Administrative Adjudication This case involved hearsay evidence. Evidence based on hearsay generally is not allowed because hearsay evidence does not come from the witness's own knowledge, but is based on what the witness heard someone else say. Evidence comes from a witness's own knowledge. Hause, while riding his motorcycle, was weaving erratically across two lanes of traffic. A police sergeant stopped Hause and smelled alcohol on his breath. The sergeant called a deputy officer to the scene. The deputy performed a sobriety check. The sergeant then left. Hause then told the deputy that he had between four and seven vodka and grapefruit drinks. The deputy asked Hause if he were feeling the effects of the vodkas. Hause said, "You bet I do." The blood test came back showing a blood alcohol level twice as high as the law allowed. Hause's driver's license was revoked. He requested a hearing to reinstate his license. At the hearing, the hearing officer allowed the deputy to testify as to what the sergeant said he had seen. Hause objected, alleging that these statements were hearsay. The hearing officer, however, overruled the objection. The hearing officer heard other evidence in the case, such as the blood alcohol test evidence and Hause's testimony that he may well have been weaving. The Motor Vehicle Department did not reinstate Hause's license. Hause appealed. Should the revocation of Hause's license be upheld? Why or why not? [*Hause v. MVD,* 873 P.2d 374 (Or. App. 1994)]

6–10 Internet Go to the web site for the IRS at <http://www.irs.ustreas.gov/>. The IRS has posted Tax Information for Businesses. Go to the Small Business Corner. What information is available to you to start your own business?

Chapter 7

The Regulation of Business through Criminal Law

Small crimes always precede great ones. Never have we seen timid innocence pass suddenly to extreme licentiousness.

Jean-Baptiste Racine, 1639–1699
French dramatic poet and historiographer

Outline

Ethical Consideration

Beyond the Insurance Policy

You are the president of Shop'n Serve Mini Markets, a regional chain of all-night minimarkets. Several months ago, an armed robber threatened a clerk's life in one of your stores. Although the clerk was not harmed physically, he was severely traumatized.

The company's medical policy allows for 20 hours of psychological counseling. Since the robbery, the employee has already used the 20 hours and still is too afraid to return to work. The therapist has recommended a regimen of treatment that will exceed 100 additional hours. The employee does not have the money for the supplementary sessions. Should the company pay for the additional treatment? Use the ethical model presented in Chapter 2 and reprinted on the inside front cover to develop your answer.

Introduction

At first, the subject of criminal law may seem out of place in a discussion of the legal environment of business. You own an online business, Artiste Login Products, Inc., and you run your business in an honest and ethical manner. You, like most businesspeople, are basically honest and truthful and your integrity is beyond question. Certain business activities, especially economic and environmental ventures, that once were considered legal are deemed to be criminal today. Both Congress and state legislatures have regulated specific business activities by passing criminal statutes.

An example of an economic venture that was lawful, but now is criminal in nature, is the securities laws. By 1911, a few state legislatures regulated the sale of stock (shares in a corporation) through criminal statutes. Two decades later, the federal government passed the first federal statute, the Securities Act of 1933, regulating the sale of new stock. Today, stockbrokers, accountants, lawyers, businesspeople, and others operate under these laws and suffer criminal penalties when these laws are violated.

Before discussing specific criminal acts, the distinction between civil and criminal law needs to be ad-

dressed. When a person has been harmed, she brings a civil lawsuit against the person who allegedly caused the harm. If the plaintiff wins the lawsuit, she usually obtains a monetary award.

When there is a violation of criminal law, only the government—city, county, state, or federal—can prosecute the accused person. All criminal actions are brought in the name of the government, for example, The *United States of America v. John Doe, Defendant*. The defendant must have violated a specific law, for which a punishment generally is prescribed. The accused may be incarcerated, fined, or both. The harm here is not to a specific individual but to society as a whole.

The same wrongful act may give rise to both criminal and civil litigation. For example, a person who intentionally kills another is guilty of the crime of murder. He also is liable to the victim's estate for the civil tort of wrongful death.

Two major differences exist between a criminal trial and a civil trial. First, the burden of proof differs. In Chapter 3, the various types of burdens of proof were discussed. A criminal trial requires a higher burden of proof, beyond a reasonable doubt, than in the two types of civil cases. In a court of law, the burden of proof is met by preponderance of the evidence, and in a court of equity, the burden is met by clear and convincing evidence.

Second, the Fifth Amendment right against self-incrimination does not apply in a civil case. With the exception of these two issues, the procedures involved in a criminal and a civil action are similar in many respects.

This chapter will discuss the classification of crimes and the elements of crimes in general. It will focus then on criminal activities that apply directly to the business world.

Classification of Crimes

A crime is classified as a *felony, misdemeanor*, or *petty offense*, according to its seriousness. Some states may use other terms for petty offense, such as civil offense. The definitions of these classifications vary greatly among the states and the federal government.

A **felony** is more serious than a misdemeanor or a petty offense and is punishable by imprisonment in a federal or state penitentiary for more than one year, by

LEGAL HIGHLIGHT

Ponzi or Pyramid, It Is Still a Criminal Scheme

Ponzi, pyramid, multilevel marketing plans, network marketing, or matrix marketing—many are the criminal schemes to part a fool from her money. Just who was Ponzi and how do these plans work?

Charles Ponzi developed a loan investment system that has become known as the Ponzi scheme. In 1903, at age twenty-one, he immigrated to the United States from Italy. Working at various low-paying jobs, he finally stumbled on a money-raising scheme. He promised people who invested money with him 50 percent interest on their money if he could keep it for thirty days and 100 percent if he could keep if for ninety days.

By word of mouth, news of this fantastic investment spread. People invested large sums of money, and Ponzi paid the first people with the money coming in from the later investors. More than $250,000 a day rolled in, and soon his worth grew to more than $8.5 million. Given time, he could no longer pay everyone what they had been promised. After millions were lost, he eventually was tried, convicted, and served five years in prison. He died in a charity ward in Brazil in 1949.

Today, similar scams exist. The criminal operator contacts people by mail, telephone, and now through the Internet. In 1997, the Federal Trade Commission (FTC) charged that Fortuna Alliance marketed a pyramid scheme through its home page on the World Wide Web and with printed materials.

Using fabulous earnings claims, Fortuna Alliance induced tens of thousands of consumers in more than sixty countries to pay between $250 and $1,750 to join the plan. Fortuna Alliance claimed that members would receive more than $5,000 per month in profits as others enrolled in the plan. The company provided members with advice for recruiting others to join the pyramid, both through direct contact and by setting up their own web sites.

Closed down in the same year by the FTC, it was estimated that more than 95 percent of the people who invested in Fortuna Alliance would have lost money had the scheme continued. The FTC and Fortuna Alliance entered into a consent agreement. Under the agreement terms, Fortuna Alliance set aside $2.8 million to make full refunds to the consumers. Bookkeeping and monitoring provisions were included to allow the FTC to track compliance with the settlement terms.

As for the victims in the sixty countries in which Fortuna Alliance had operated via the Internet, the FTC used legal counsel in London, Belize, and Antigua for the foreign litigation. The Department of Justice's Office of Foreign Litigation was instrumental in reaching settlements for the foreign actions.

Because this is a consent judgment for settlement purposes only, the defendant did not admit to a law violation. Consent judgments have the force of law after they are signed by a judge.

Source:<http://www.ftc.gov/opa/9702/fortuna4.htm>. See the FTC web page for information and publications concerning a variety of wealth-building schemes. The FTC web page is <http://www.ftc.gov>.

---

a fine, or even by death. The Model Penal Code[1] distinguishes among the following four types of felony, based on their seriousness:

1. Capital offenses are punishable by death.
2. First-degree felonies are punishable by a maximum penalty of life imprisonment.
3. Second-degree felonies are punishable by a maximum of ten years' imprisonment.
4. Third-degree felonies are punishable by up to five years' imprisonment.

These classifications set the maximum penalties. The actual sentence delivered by the judge to the convicted defendant usually is less than the maximum penalty authorized.

[1] Model codes are drafted by the National Conference of Commissioners on Uniform State Laws, which was discussed in Chapter 4. To avoid the potentially wide variety of statutes on a particular topic that could result from each state trying to draft its own legislation, the model code provides a single statutory scheme. The model code is sent to the fifty states for possible adoption into statute. A state may choose to adopt all or part of the model code, to modify parts of it, or to not adopt any part of it at all.

A **misdemeanor** is a crime punishable by a fine, by confinement for up to one year, or both. People convicted of misdemeanors are incarcerated in a city or county jail instead of in a state penitentiary. Disorderly conduct and trespassing are common misdemeanors. Misdemeanors generally are tried in city or other lower courts, whereas felonies are tried in state or federal courts that have general jurisdiction.

A **petty offense** often is not classified as a crime but as a civil matter. These offenses include many traffic or building code violations. Even for petty offenses, a guilty party may be incarcerated for a few days, fined, or both. The burden of proof for a petty offense is normally a preponderance of evidence, not beyond a reasonable doubt.

Crimes also can be classified according to their nature. For example, there are crimes against the person (murder, assault, rape), crimes against property (theft, burglary, arson), and crimes against the government (perjury, which is lying under oath). These classifications are used to group crimes within a statutory code.

The criminal code is structured to punish acts. The criminal code defines the criminal elements, the levels of seriousness, and the minimum and maximum punishments that can be imposed by the judge on the convicted defendant.

Criminal Statutory Law

Originally, criminal acts were defined by the judiciary under the common law instead of by legislative statutes. Today, all crimes are based on statutes. Judges, however, still use the original common law definitions when interpreting these criminal statutes.

Each criminal statute prohibits a certain behavior. The statute sets out the specific elements of the crime. The prosecutor must prove each element of the crime before a person can be convicted. Most crimes require an act of commission; that is, a person must do something to commit a crime. In some cases, an act of omission can be a crime, but only if the person has failed to carry out a legal duty. Failure to file a tax return is an example of an omission that is a crime.

Criminal statutes are interpreted narrowly by the courts; that is, the courts limit their application. Courts take into consideration the statutory language, the legislative history, and the statute's purpose in order to determine the prohibited type of behavior. In the following case, the United States Supreme Court interpreted a criminal statute passed by Congress.

Case 7.1

Posters 'N' Things v. United States

Supreme Court of the United States, 1994
511 U.S. 513, 114 S. Ct. 1747, 128 L. Ed. 2d 539
http://supct.law.cornell.edu

BACKGROUND AND FACTS Lana Christine Acty (one of the petitioners) formed Posters 'N' Things, Ltd. (another petitioner). The corporation operated three businesses: a diet-aid store, an art gallery, and a general merchandise outlet called World Wide Imports.

The police had information that World Wide Imports was selling drug paraphernalia. The officers obtained a search warrant; executed it on the petitioner's business premises; and seized various items, including pipes, bongs, scales, roach clips, and drug diluents. They also seized catalogs and advertisements describing products sold by the petitioner. The advertisements offered products such as "Coke Kits," "Free Base Kits," and diluents sold under the names "PseudoCaine" and "Procaine."

Both petitioners (Acty and Posters 'N' Things) were convicted of using an interstate conveyance (a vehicle, usually a motor vehicle, such as an automobile or truck) as part of a scheme to sell drug paraphernalia and conspiring to commit that offense. Acty also was convicted of aiding and abetting the manufacture and distribution of cocaine, investing income derived from a drug offense, money laundering, and engaging in monetary transactions with proceeds from unlawful activities. Acty was sentenced to imprisonment for nine years, to be followed by a five-year term of supervised release, and was fined $150,000. Posters 'N' Things was fined $75,000. The case was appealed to the U.S. Court of Appeals, which affirmed all convictions.

The United States Supreme Court accepted jurisdiction only over the conviction of using an interstate conveyance as part of a scheme to sell drug paraphernalia. The federal statute involved is the Mail Order Drug Paraphernalia Control Act. Acty argued that the statute was vague as to the definition of drug paraphernalia and that the act required specific intent (*scienter,* which means "guilty knowledge"). In other words, the prosecutors had to prove that Acty specifically knew that the products would be used for illegal drug activity by the individual purchasers.

Justice BLACKMUN delivered the opinion of the Court.

. . . .

Congress enacted the Mail Order Drug Paraphernalia Control Act as part of the Anti-Drug Abuse Act of 1986. As originally enacted, and as applicable in this case, the statute provides:

"It is unlawful for any person—

(1) to make use of the services of the Postal Service or other interstate conveyance as part of a scheme to sell drug paraphernalia;

(2) to offer for sale and transportation in interstate or foreign commerce drug paraphernalia; or

(3) to import or export drug paraphernalia."

[It] provides that anyone convicted under the statute shall be imprisoned for not more than three years and fined not more than $100,000.

[It] does not contain an express scienter requirement. Some courts, however, have located a scienter requirement in the statute's definitional provision, which defines the term "drug paraphernalia" as "any equipment, product, or material of any kind which is primarily intended or designed for use" with illegal drugs. Petitioners argue that the term "primarily intended" in this provision establishes a subjective-intent requirement on the part of the defendant. We disagree, and instead adopt the Government's position that establishes objective standards for determining what constitutes drug paraphernalia.

The objective characteristics of some items establish that they are designed specifically for use with controlled substances. Such items, including bongs, cocaine freebase kits, and certain kinds of pipes, have no other use besides contrived ones (such as use of a bong as a flower vase). Items that meet the "designed for use" standard constitute drug paraphernalia irrespective of the knowledge or intent of one who sells or transports them. Accordingly, the "designed for use" element does not establish a scienter requirement with respect to sellers such as petitioners.

The "primarily intended . . . for use" language presents a more difficult problem. The language might be understood to refer to the state of mind of the defendant (here, the seller), and thus to require an intent on the part of the defendant that the items at issue be used with drugs.

. . . .

. . . [W]e do not think that the knowledge standard in this context requires knowledge on the defendant's part that a particular customer actually will use an item of drug paraphernalia with illegal drugs. It is sufficient that the defendant be aware that customers in general are likely to use the merchandise with drugs. Therefore, the Government must establish that the defendant knew that the items at issue are likely to be used with illegal drugs. . . .

Finally, although the Government must establish that the defendant knew that the items at issue are likely to be used with illegal drugs, it need not prove specific knowledge that the items are "drug paraphernalia" within the meaning of the statute. It is sufficient for the Government to show that the defendant "knew the character and nature of the materials" with which he dealt.

DECISION AND REMEDY The Court found that the Mail Order Drug Paraphernalia Control Act, which bans the sale of drug paraphernalia, was not vague. The prosecutors did not have to show that the defendant specifically knew the products would be used for illegal drugs by the individual purchasers. Acty could be convicted, because she knew in a general way that the merchandise would be used with illegal drugs.

CRITICAL THINKING: PUBLIC POLICY Discuss whether a business that sells flower vases be prosecuted for selling an item that could be used as a bong. Define society's distinction between drug paraphernalia and items that are primarily used for non-illegal drug purposes.

Constitutional Safeguards

The criminal justice system operates on the premise that it is far worse for an innocent person to be punished than for a guilty person to go free. A person is innocent until proven guilty beyond a reasonable doubt. The procedures of the criminal legal system are designed to protect individual rights and to preserve the presumption of innocence.

Criminal law brings the weighty force of the government, with all its resources, to bear against the individual. The Constitution provide safeguards for all persons, including those accused of crimes. The United States Supreme Court has ruled that most of these safeguards apply not only in federal courts, but also in state courts by virtue of the Fourteenth Amendment's due process clause.

In past years, the U.S. Supreme Court has been active in interpreting these constitutional rights. The case of *Miranda v. Arizona*[2] established that the police must advise suspects of their constitutional rights prior to interrogation. Suspects must be warned prior to any questioning that they have the right to remain silent, that anything they say can be used against them in a court of law, that they have the right to the presence of an attorney, and that if they cannot afford an attorney one will be appointed for them prior to any questioning. The *Miranda* case has been criticized over the years. The United States Supreme Court recently upheld the *Miranda* warnings in the following case.

[2] 384 U.S. 436, 86 S. Ct. 1602, 16 L. Ed. 2d 694 (1966), or go to the findlaw.com site at <http://www.findlaw.com/scripts/getcase.pl?navby=case&court=US&vol=384&page=436>.

Case 7.2

Dickerson v. United States

Supreme Court of the United States, 2000
530 U.S. 428, 120 S. Ct. 2326, 147 L. Ed. 2d 405

BACKGROUND AND FACTS Petitioner Dickerson, under indictment for bank robbery and related federal crimes, moved to suppress a statement he had made to the Federal Bureau of Investigation, on the grounds he had not received the *Miranda* warnings before being interrogated. The federal district court granted his motion, and the government appealed.

The Fourth Circuit reversed the trial court and in doing so acknowledged that Dickerson had not been given his *Miranda* warnings. It held, however, that the federal statute was satisfied because his statement was voluntary. The federal statute provided that a confession could be used if it were voluntary. The Fourth Circuit concluded that *Miranda* was not a constitutional holding and that, therefore, Congress could by statute have the final say on the admissibility question. The United States Supreme Court granted a writ of *certiorari*.

Chief Justice REHNQUIST delivered the opinion of the Court.

In *Miranda v. Arizona*, we held that certain warnings must be given before a suspect's statement made during custodial interrogation could be admitted in evidence. In the wake of that decision, Congress enacted 18 U.S.C. § 3501, which in essence laid down a rule that the admissibility of such statements should turn only on whether or not they were voluntarily made. We hold that *Miranda,* being a constitutional decision of this Court, may not be in effect overruled by an Act of Congress, and we decline to overrule *Miranda* ourselves. We therefore hold that *Miranda* and its progeny in this Court govern the admissibility of statements made during custodial interrogation in both state and federal courts. . . . .

DECISION AND REMEDY The Court refused to reverse its holding in *Miranda v. State of Arizona*. All law enforcement officers must give the standard warnings before questioning the accused.

CRITICAL THINKING: POLITICAL CONSIDERATION Over the decades since *Miranda* was first decided, many people have argued that the *Miranda* warnings have resulted in guilty persons being set free without any negative consequences of their criminal behavior. Why should law enforcement officers be required to give these warnings? Why did the U.S. Supreme Court not change this requirement after so much criticism of the original decision?

Criminal Procedure

A criminal prosecution differs procedurally from a civil case in several respects. These differences reflect the efforts at safeguarding the individual's rights against the state.

Before a warrant for arrest can be issued, *probable cause* must exist for believing that the individual in question has committed a crime. **Probable cause** is defined as a substantial likelihood (not just a possibility) that the individual has committed a crime. Sometimes arrests may be made without a warrant when there is no time to get one. The action of the arresting officer, however, still is judged by the standard of probable cause.

Individuals must be formally charged with committing specific crimes before they can be brought to trial. Two ways are used to bring a person to court: the use of grand jury or the action of a magistrate.

A grand jury is made up of sixteen to twenty-four members who are citizens in the court's jurisdiction.

The court assembles the grand jury to hear evidence and to determine if an accused should be charged with a crime. This charge is called an **indictment** when issued by a grand jury. Once indicted, the accused can be tried for his crimes in court.

A magistrate is similar to a judge but has less authority. If the magistrate determines that a person should be tried for criminal acts, the charge is contained in a **bill of information**. Some states use other judicial officers, instead of magistrates, such as justices of the peace, to perform these functions.

At the trial, the accused person has to prove nothing. The entire burden of proof is on the prosecution (the government). The prosecution must show that, based on all of the evidence, the defendant is guilty beyond a reasonable doubt.

A jury can come to one of two decisions: guilty or not guilty. Either the prosecution has or has not met its burden of proof. Contrary to media jargon, a verdict of not guilty is different from a statement of the defendant's innocence. It merely means that the prosecution

LEGAL HIGHLIGHT

Ford and the Pinto

Ford designed the Pinto to compete with Volkswagen, a German automobile manufacturer whose name translates into "People's Car." The Pinto was to be an efficient, economical automobile.

In an effort to keep the costs down, a decision was made not to include an $11 safety improvement that would have lessened the likelihood of an automobile fire in case of collision. For years following the Pinto's introduction, injury and wrongful death lawsuits totaled more than $1 billion. Ford lost several civil lawsuits and made headlines when a judgment for negligence was awarded against it for $128.5 million, later reduced to $2.5 million.[a]

In 1980, Ford went on trial on criminal charges brought by the state of Indiana for reckless homicide as a result of the deaths of three people. Reckless homicide is a crime in which the accused is aware of and consciously disregards substantial and unjustifiable risk. The jury did not believe that Ford had acted recklessly or intentionally. Ford was found not guilty, but only after spending $1 million to defend itself.

[a] *Grimshaw v. Ford Motor Co.,* 119 Cal. App. 3d 757, 175 Cal. Rptr. (1981).

---

failed to present enough evidence to the court to prove the accused guilty beyond a reasonable doubt.

Courts have complex rules about the types of evidence allowed and procedures for presenting that evidence, especially in jury trials. These rules are designed to ensure that evidence in the trial is relevant, reliable, and not unfairly prejudicial to the defendant. The defense attorney cross-examines the government's witnesses who present evidence against the attorney's client in an attempt to show that witnesses' testimony is unreliable. Of course, the government also may cross-examine witnesses presented by the defense.

Basic Elements of Criminal Responsibility

The two requirements for many crimes are criminal intent (***mens rea***) and criminal conduct (***actus reus***). Thinking about embezzling funds or about stealing a computer program may be morally wrong, but these thoughts in themselves are not criminal until they are translated into action. A person can be punished for attempting to commit a crime, but only if she takes substantial steps toward the criminal objective, as will be discussed later in this section.

Criminal Intent

The Model Penal Code recognizes four categories of *mens rea*:

1. *Purpose* What did the accused intend to do? What was his conscious objective?

2. *Knowledge* Did the accused act knowingly with respect to the result?

3. *Recklessness* Did the accused act in such a wanton manner—that is, with knowledge and conscious disregard—that she created a considerable and unjustifiable risk to others?

4. *Negligence* Did the accused act so negligently—that is, deviate so substantially from the standard of care that a reasonable person would exercise under the circumstances—that he created a substantial and unnecessary risk to others?

In most cases, a wrongful mental state is required along with the wrongful act to establish criminal liability. In these cases, the mental state of the accused is important in determining the degree of wrongfulness of the crime. For example, the same criminal act that causes the death of another can be committed by different defendants with varying mental states.

One person may kill in cold blood with premeditation, called murder in the first degree. A second person may kill in the heat of passion, which is voluntary manslaughter. A third person may kill as the result of negligence. This killing is involuntary manslaughter, such as when someone dies as a result of extreme carelessness involving an automobile.

In each of these situations, the law recognizes a different degree of wrongfulness and the punishment differs accordingly. The greater the degree of *mens rea,* the more reprehensible the crime and, thus, the greater the punishment.

Criminal Conduct

Some statutes require no criminal intent, only criminal conduct. For example, a person shoots a rifle in the air to help the neighborhood celebrate the new year. The person intends no harm. Her conduct, however, the shooting of a rifle, violates a statute, and that conduct constitutes the crime.

Some criminal statutes target business and employee behavior in particular by requiring not criminal intent, but only criminal conduct by the business. These statutes avoid the old legal problem which says that a business cannot form a mental intent and, therefore, cannot be guilty of a crime.

Likewise, the statutes apply to individuals responsible for business management. For example, a person owns a restaurant that sells beer and wine. An employee sells beer to a person below the legal drinking age. The owner can be criminally charged with providing liquor to a minor.

The following case involves a statute that does not require *mens rea*.

Case 7.3

United States v. Park

Supreme Court of the United States, 1975
421 U.S. 658, 95 S. Ct 1903,
44 L. Ed. 2d 489
http://www.findlaw.com
/scripts/getcase.pl?navby=case
&court=US&vol=421&page=
658

LANDMARK CASE

BACKGROUND AND FACTS The defendant was the president of Acme Markets, Inc. Acme, a large national food chain, employed 36,000 employees and operated 874 retail outlets, twelve general warehouses, and four special warehouses. During 1970, Acme's president received a letter from the Food and Drug Administration (FDA) concerning rodents in a Baltimore warehouse where his firm stored a considerable amount of food. The rodents adulterated the food, making it unfit for consumption. The vice president in charge of the warehouse responded to the FDA letter.

In 1971 and 1972, similar conditions were observed. The defendant did not have direct control over the Baltimore warehouse but was convicted on five counts of causing adulteration of food that had been bought and sold in interstate commerce. He was fined $50 for each of the five convictions under the Federal Food, Drug, and Cosmetic Act.

Chief Justice BURGER delivered the opinion of the Court.

. . . .

The Act does not . . . make criminal liability turn on "awareness of some wrongdoing" or "conscious fraud." The duty imposed by Congress on responsible corporate agents is, we emphasize, one that requires the highest standard of foresight and vigilance, but the Act, in its criminal aspect, does not require that which is objectively impossible. The theory upon which responsible corporate agents are held criminally accountable for "causing" violations of the Act permits a claim that a defendant was "powerless" to prevent or correct the violation to "be raised defensively at a trial on the merits." If such a claim is made, the defendant has the burden of coming forward with evidence, but this does not alter the Government's ultimate burden of proving beyond a reasonable doubt the defendant's guilt, including his power, in light of the duty imposed by the Act, to prevent or correct the prohibited condition. Congress has seen fit to enforce the accountability of

responsible corporate agents dealing with products which may affect the health of consumers by penal sanctions cast in rigorous terms, and the obligation of the courts is to give them effect so long as they do not violate the Constitution.
. . . .

Although we need not decide whether this testimony would have entitled respondent to an instruction as to his lack of power had he requested it, the testimony clearly created the "need" for rebuttal evidence. That evidence was not offered to show that respondent had a propensity to commit criminal acts[;] its purpose was to demonstrate that respondent was on notice that he could not rely on his system of delegation to subordinates to prevent and correct unsanitary conditions at Acme's warehouses, and that he must have been aware of the deficiencies of this system before the Baltimore violations were discovered. The evidence was therefore relevant since it served to rebut respondent's defense that he had justifiably relied upon subordinates to handle sanitation matters.

DECISION AND REMEDY   Even though the defendant had no actual criminal intent, he still was convicted of a crime. For conviction, only the wrongful conduct of producing adulterated food that was in interstate commerce was required.

CRITICAL THINKING: MANAGERIAL POLICY   Assume that you are a high-level executive in a major corporation that employs more than 20,000 people. The company manufactures a toxic product that, if misused, could result in criminal prosecution of the top executives. Discuss fully how you would protect the corporation and yourself from criminal prosecution.

Attempts and Conspiracies

Two separate offenses can occur prior to a planned criminal act. One is called an *attempt*. The other is called a *conspiracy*.

A person can plan a crime and commit an **overt act**, that is, any act toward committing the crime, but not commit the crime. Legally, the overt act is considered to be an **attempt** to commit the crime. For example, a person plans to rob a bank, buys a gun, steals a getaway car, drives to the bank, and enters it. After yelling "Holdup," however, the person turns around and flees the scene. The crime, the bank robbery, was unsuccessful, but the person is guilty of attempted bank robbery.

A **conspiracy** arises when a person agrees (conspires) with one or more persons to commit a crime. They plan the crime and perform overt acts. Whether or not the crime is carried out, the people are guilty of conspiracy to commit a crime. In the previous bank robbery example, if two or more people plan the robbery and purchase guns (the overt act) to carry out their plan, they are guilty of conspiring to commit bank robbery.

Crimes Affecting Business

Crimes can be committed against businesses and businesses can commit crimes. Criminal offenses are divided into three general areas: crimes against property, white-collar crimes (generally committed by individuals), and crimes committed by businesses. These distinctions are artificial, but they assist in studying specific offenses. For example, crimes listed in the "White-Collar Crimes" section that follows can be committed not only by individuals, but also by businesses. Conversely, crimes listed in the section under "Crimes Businesses Can Commit" also can be committed by individuals.

Offenses against Property

Businesses are often victims of crimes against property. This section examines the following offenses against property: (1) burglary, (2) larceny, (3) robbery, and (4) arson.

Burglary. **Burglary** is defined as entering into or remaining in another's building with the intent to commit a crime. For example, Ace breaks into a warehouse and intends to steal a truckload of videotape recorders. Before he can load his truck, the burglar alarm goes off and he flees the scene. Ace is guilty of burglary because he broke into the premises and intended to commit the felony of theft. Aggravated burglary, which is defined as burglary with the use of a deadly weapon or burglary of a dwelling, receives a heavier penalty.

Larceny. A person's wrongful or fraudulent taking and carrying away of another's personal property is **larceny.** Generally, the person also must intend to deprive the owner of his property permanently. Many business-related larcenies entail fraudulent conduct, that is, actions by the criminal that deceive the victim, the businessperson. Generally, the place from which physical property is taken in a larceny is immaterial, although statutes usually prescribe a stiffer sentence for property taken from buildings, such as banks or warehouses.

As society has become more complex, the definition of property often arises. In most states, property that is subject to larceny statutes has been expanded. Stealing computer programs may constitute larceny even though the programs consist of magnetic impulses. Trade secrets can be subject to larceny statutes. The acts of stealing the use of telephone wires with a blue box device or theft of cellular telephone codes are subject to larceny statutes. Often special larceny statutes cover the theft of natural gas or electricity.

Robbery. **Robbery** is defined as taking another's personal property from his person or in his presence by force or intimidation, with the intent to deprive him of it permanently. The use of force or intimidation is necessary for an act of theft to be considered a robbery.

While robbery involves force or intimidation, larceny does not. Therefore, picking pockets is larceny, not robbery.

Typically, states impose more severe penalties for aggravated robbery (robbery with the use of a deadly weapon). Liquor stores, all-night convenience stores, and banks are especially vulnerable to robbery.

Arson. The intentional, willful, and malicious burning of another's building (and, in some states, of personal property) constitutes the crime of **arson**. Arson statutes apply to the burning of all kinds of buildings. If arson results in a person's death, the arsonist can be charged with murder.

Every state has a special statute that covers burning a building to collect insurance. If Akin owns an insured apartment building that is falling apart and burns it himself or pays someone else to set fire to it, Akin is guilty of arson to defraud insurers. Of course, the insurer pays no claim when insurance fraud is proved.

White-Collar Crime

White-collar crime is defined by the Department of Justice as a nonviolent offense involving corruption, deceit, or breach of trust. This type of crime generally is committed by individuals. More than 30 percent of the criminal filings in federal district courts involve white-collar crimes.

The large range of white-collar crimes includes receiving stolen goods, forgery, obtaining goods or money by false pretenses, embezzlement, use of the mails to defraud, and computer crimes.

Receiving Stolen Goods.
In the crime of **receiving stolen goods**, the recipient of the goods does not need to know the true identity of the owner or of the thief. All that is necessary is that the recipient knows or should have known that the goods were stolen. This knowledge implies an intent to deprive the owner of those goods.

Forgery.
The fraudulent making or altering of any writing that changes the legal liability of another is **forgery.** If Smith signs Gomez's name without authorization to the back of a check made out to Gomez, Smith has committed forgery. Forgery also includes changing trademarks, falsifying public records, counterfeiting, and altering any legal document.

Most states have a special statute, often called a credit card statute, to cover the illegal use of credit cards. Thus, the state's attorney can prosecute a person who uses a forged credit card for violating either the general forgery statute or a statute specifically targeting credit card forgeries.

Obtaining Goods or Money by False Pretenses.
The crime of **obtaining goods or money by false pretenses** consists of obtaining title to another's property by an intentionally false statement of a past or existing fact with intent to defraud another. Statutes covering such illegal activities vary widely from state to state. Almost all states have created a separate crime prohibiting the giving of a no-account or insufficient funds check with the intent to defraud.

In 1984, Congress passed the **Trademark Counterfeiting Act**, which makes dealing in goods or services under a counterfeit trademark a federal crime. The federal **False Statement Act** provides that intentionally making a false statement to the U.S. government to obtain a monetary return is a crime.

Embezzlement.
The fraudulent conversion of another's property or money by a person in lawful possession of that property is **embezzlement**. Typically, this crime involves an employee who fraudulently appropriates money. Banks and other businesses face this problem when officers of the business or accountants "jimmy" the books to cover up the fraudulent conversion of money for their own benefit.

Embezzlement is not larceny because the wrongdoer does not physically take the property from the possession of another. It is not robbery because the thief uses no force or intimidation.

Whether the accused takes the money from the victim or from a third person is immaterial. If, as the comptroller of a large business, Saunders pockets a certain number of checks from third parties that were given to her to deposit into the account of another company, she has committed embezzlement.

Another version of embezzlement occurs when the owner of a property provides payment to a contractor specifically to pay various people who have worked on the owner's building. A contractor who does not use the money for this purpose commits a special form of embezzlement called **misapplication of trust funds**. The funds are entrusted to the contractor for a specific purpose and that trust is violated. The fact that the accused may intend to replace the embezzled property eventually is not a sufficient defense.

Use of the Mails to Defraud.
Use of the mails to defraud the public is a federal crime. Illegal use of the mails involves (1) mailing a writing for the purpose of executing a scheme to defraud or (2) an organized scheme to defraud by false pretenses. For example, if Daniel Webster mails an advertisement offering for sale

a cure for baldness that he knows to be fraudulent, he can be prosecuted for use of the mails to defraud.

Computer Crimes. Governments and businesses have used computers since the 1940s. The real explosion of computers for government, business, and home use, however, began in the late 1970s and continues in the 2000s. Computer crimes are an unfortunate result of this widespread use.

Computer crimes can be delegated to three groupings. The first type is the sabotage of the computer or its programs. This type of crime is committed by a disgruntled current or former employee or by a hacker using the telephone or cable wires or through the Internet. The second type is computer or software theft. These activities fall into the category of crimes against property.

The third type involves computers being used to commit a wide range of crimes. Computers can commit crimes in record time—as little as three milliseconds. Detection often is difficult. Companies, and even the government, have discovered multimillion-dollar electronic thefts, but only after a significant period of time. Some electronic thefts include causing a computer to write extra paychecks, to transfer monies, or to shave cents off interest accounts and place the money into personal accounts.

The law involving computer crime is still developing. To counter the rising computer crime activity, Congress has passed two statutes. The **Counterfeit Access Device and Computer Fraud and Abuse Act**[3] was passed in 1984. This act makes it a federal crime to access a computer with a counterfeit or unauthorized card or device with the intent to obtain (1) restricted federal government information, (2) financial records from financial institutions, and (3) consumer files from consumer reporting agencies. The **Electronic Communications Privacy Act**[4] was passed in 1986.

Under this act, it is a federal crime to intercept an *electronic communication* at the point of or during transmission, when transmitted through a router or server, or after receipt by the intended recipient. An electronic communication includes any electronic transfer of signals, writings, images, sounds, data, or intelligence of any nature. Under these statutes, any unauthorized person who seeks entrance into another's computer systems, including electronic mail, computer-to-computer data transmissions, remote computing services, and private video conferences, commits a crime.

The statutes also prohibit the establishment of bulletin boards that list the passwords of individuals or businesses. They apply to governmental computers, computers of federally insured institutions, cellular car telephones, and computer access that crosses state lines. The penalties vary but can be as much as ten years in prison plus a $100,000 fine.

The full extent of computer crime in business is not known. Firms victimized by computer crime rarely publicize the fact. They are afraid that their customers will doubt the accuracy of their computer-generated material.

Trials of apprehended computer criminals are rare. The affected business usually allows the case to be plea-bargained instead of going to a trial. A plea bargain occurs when the defense attorney negotiates with the prosecutor that the accused will plead guilty in return for something, such as pleading guilty to a lesser crime or a statement by the prosecutor to the judge for a lighter sentence. Sometimes, for fear of publicity, the business will not even report the crime and may be blackmailed into giving the person who committed the crime a reference for another job.

CyberLaw

Fraud

The new frontier for criminal fraud activity is the World Wide Web (WWW). Government prosecutors have obtained a number of convictions for computer fraud.

In one type of fraud, a person offers an item for sale, but the seller uses various fictitious names and addresses. A buyer sees an item on a web site and sends in a payment. The purported seller accepts the payment, but no merchandise is sent. In a variation, the seller

[3] The Counterfeit Access Device and Computer Fraud and Abuse Act is found in two code sections at the Legal Information Institute. The prohibition against access devices is found at <http://www.law.cornell.edu:80/uscode/18/1029.html>. The prohibition concerning computers is at <http://www.law.cornell.edu:80/uscode/18/1030.html>. You can start your search at the Cornell University law site at <http://www.law.cornell.edu/>.

[4] The Electronic Communications Privacy Act is found at the Legal Information Institute under the section on Unlawful Access to Stored Communications at <http://www.law.cornell.edu:80/uscode/18/2701.html>. You can start your search at the Cornell University law site at <http://www.law.cornell.edu/>.

LEGAL HIGHLIGHT

The Barbie Doll Web Caper

Americans lose $40 billion a year to fast-talking swindlers on the other end of the telephone. Other swindlers use the World Wide Web. Ripoffs are as varied as the imagination.

Debbie Ann Amyot, who lives in Maryland, collects Barbie dolls. While surfing the web, she came across an advertisement for the sale of a "mint" collection of ninety-five Barbie dolls in their original boxes. The advertisement further stated that the dolls and boxes were all in "collector's condition." Intrigued, Ms. Amyot e-mailed and also telephoned the seller, Mary Jean Cain, who lives in Georgia. Ms. Amyot agreed to purchase the entire doll collection for $6,140. Ms. Amyot mailed the check. After Ms. Cain received the check, she shipped the doll collection.

Upon Barbie's arrival, Ms. Amyot joyously opened the box to see her new purchase. Joy turned to dissatisfaction when she saw only thirty-six dolls in poor condition, contained in boxes that were also in poor condition. She called Ms. Cain and requested to return the dolls. Ms. Cain terminated all contact with Ms. Amyot and had her telephone disconnected.

Disgusted and infuriated, Ms. Amyot complained to the police. Eventually, Ms. Cain was charged in Maryland with one count of theft by deception of property with a value over $300.[a] Ms. Cain moved to dismiss the charge on the ground that Maryland lacked territorial jurisdiction. The issue before the Court of Appeals of Maryland was whether it had jurisdiction over Ms. Cain in Georgia. The court started its decision with this statement:

This case appears to present a cutting-edge issue, because it involves a prosecution for theft by means of

deception across state lines perpetrated partly via the Internet. But in reality, the case turns on principles developed by common-law courts long ago, in connection with business done by mail.

The court held that it did have jurisdiction under the following well-established doctrine:

The principle that an accused, acting from outside a jurisdiction through an innocent agent inside the jurisdiction, is liable to prosecution in the jurisdiction, has often been applied in cases in which the innocent agent is a common carrier, and the accused acts through the common carrier by inducing a victim to deliver property to the common carrier, to be shipped from inside to the accused outside.

In other words, the accused, Ms. Cain, acting from outside Maryland, is liable for prosecution in Maryland because she induced Ms. Amyot to deliver property, her check, to a common carrier, the U.S. Post Office, which delivered the check outside of Maryland, in this case to Georgia.

Although a new technology was used to commit a potential scam, the tried-and-true legal rules still apply. This case was limited as to whether the Maryland court had jurisdiction over an out-of-state accused. Remember that the previous facts are the prosecution's version. Since Ms. Cain has not been tried or convicted, she has the presumption of innocence.

---

[a] *State v. Cain*, 360 Ms. 205, 757 A.2d 142 (2000).

---

sends merchandise, but it is not what was ordered. Or the items sent are different than what the seller represented.

Sometimes goods are placed on an auction web site, such as eBay. Although it is against the auction house rules, the seller bids on the item to drive up the price, making the ultimate price paid by an authentic buyer artificially high. The seller also can use an alias to

post a message on the seller's page at the auction house stating that the seller (posing as a buyer) was completely satisfied with prior dealings. This posted information is seen by other legitimate prospective buyers and gives them false confidence about the seller.

Other cases involve counterfeit merchandise, such as counterfeit Beanie Babies. On a web auction house, a seller posts for sale a number of hard-to-find Beanie

Babies. A buyer makes a winning bid, but when the merchandise arrives, the Beanie Babies are reproductions or knock-offs, instead of authentic items.

The sellers are not the only ones who perpetuate fraud. A buyer can win a bid on an auction house web site, then pay for it by using a stolen credit card.

Investment schemes also use the WWW to entice consumers to invest in nonexistent funds. The investment company promises to pay high rates of return with no risk. The company is vague about the nature of the investment, while stressing the rates of return. Many of these investment company offerings are really Ponzi schemes. The company normally operates the scam for a short time, takes in the investment money, quickly spends the money, then closes down before the scam is detected.

Anyone who surfs the web has seen advertisements to correct credit. Many companies operate legitimate businesses. Others, however, are fronts for criminals. The business requires the consumer to make an up-front payment to straighten out her poor credit record. The consumer then discovers that the company has done nothing. The consumer cannot get her money back and the only recourse left is to complain to the police.

Another type of fraud, the vacation ripoff, starts when the consumer receives an electronic certificate congratulating the person on winning a fabulous *free* vacation. The winner is required, however, to pay a handling fee. Often, the vacationer ends up on a cruise ship that looks more like a tug boat. The hotel accommodations are often shabby, and the advertised ocean view, golf course, and tennis courts are miles away.

Fraud also snares businesses. For example, a business receives a sales pitch to purchase a bulk e-mail list that includes millions of addresses. The addresses are loaded into the purchaser's computer. A sales letter is designed and is attached to the bulk e-mail list. The business sends the letter to the list of addresses. The problem is that the sending of bulk e-mail (also called *spamming*) probably violates Internet service provider (ISP) agreements and can result in the ISP shutting down the business's web site. The consequences might be even greater. Several states have laws regulating the sending of unsolicited commercial bulk e-mail. Businesses need to check their state laws before using bulk e-mail lists.

In the past, all of these scams were (and still are) committed the old-fashioned way: via the mails and

telephones. The technology-savvy criminal uses the web to snare victims. The adage "when something seems too good to be true, it probably is" is still true today. Consumers and businesses must stay alert to possible criminal scams.

Crimes Businesses Can Commit

Criminal statutes do not specify corporate crimes. *Corporate crimes* is a generic term that covers crimes that businesses or businesspersons commit. Many times criminals pose as businesspeople and use the business to commit crimes. During the past decades, criminal liability has expanded beyond the traditional types of crimes.

Businesses are held criminally liable for antitrust violations, such as fixing prices on goods or services, failing to issue and trade stock in accordance with securities laws, failing to meet safety standards set by statute, or failing to pay taxes. Business managers, such as officers and directors, who are in a position to prevent the crime may be prosecuted and, if found guilty, can be fined, incarcerated, or both.

Businesses are responsible criminally for the conduct of their employees. The Model Penal Code recognizes that a business can be guilty of a criminal offense through the actions of its employees if one of three situations occurs. First, the legislative purpose of the statute in question is to impose criminal liability on a business for its employees' acts when those acts are committed within the scope of employment. Second, the business has a legal statutory duty to perform a specific function, such as keeping accurate accounting records, and it fails to perform that function. Third, the criminal act is authorized, requested, dictated, performed, or recklessly tolerated by the higher levels of business management.

Businesses need to be aware of the following criminal areas: offenses under the Racketeer Influenced and Corrupt Organizations Act (RICO), violations of the Foreign Corrupt Practices Act, bankruptcy fraud, money laundering, regulatory offenses, obstruction of justice, and currency offenses. The following sections review each of these areas.

RICO Crimes. Congress passed an amendment to the Organized Crime Control Act of 1970, known as the **Racketeer Influenced and Corrupt Organizations**

Act (RICO)[5] of 1970. The policy behind the amendment intended to control organized crime's investments in legitimate business and to force forfeiture of any profits resulting from criminal activity. Any offenses that violate this statute are called RICO crimes.

RICO has two major sections: criminal and civil. Many states have followed the federal example and have adopted "little RICOs" that are similar to the federal statute.

Criminal RICO. The criminal provisions in RICO require a "pattern of racketeering activity" that is defined as two or more racketeering acts within ten years of each other. Generally, racketeering means extorting money by threat or engaging in an illegal profit-making enterprise.

The statute lists more than fifty specific federal crimes that constitute racketeering acts under RICO. These racketeering acts include mail fraud, wire fraud, fraud in the sale of securities, bankruptcy fraud, extortion, interstate transportation of stolen property, arson, murder, gambling, robbery, and drug dealing. A conviction of any two of these offenses within a ten-year period can lead to a conviction under RICO's criminal provisions. If convicted, a person is subject to a $25,000 fine, twenty years in prison, and forfeiture of all property obtained through the criminal activity to the federal government.

Civil RICO. In addition to RICO's criminal provisions, Congress also included civil provisions. Civil RICO lawsuits can be brought in a civil court of law by either the government or a private party, which can be a business or a person. The purpose behind RICO's civil provisions is simple: The government has insufficient resources to prosecute every RICO violation. This statute allows private individuals who have been harmed to sue.

The person bringing a civil RICO action must have been harmed by a business's illegal actions. In addition to proving the harm suffered, the plaintiff must show the court evidence that the business committed two RICO violations within the last ten years. The person does not need to show that the business was

convicted in criminal court of the RICO violation. Civil RICO cases have been filed against firms, such as General Motors, Merrill Lynch, American Express, and Prudential Insurance Company of America.

The penalties that the court can impose are the unique part of civil RICO. If the party is unable to prove the defendant's two prior RICO violations, the plaintiff receives only the amount of the damages proven. If the person is able to prove the two prior RICO acts, the person is entitled to treble damages, which equal the amount of the actual damages multiplied by three.

The penalties that the court can impose differ for a case brought by a private party than for a case brought by the government. The government can seek penalties that include *divestiture, dissolution,* or *reorganization* of the business, as well as seeking an injunction (a court order to prevent an action) against future racketeering activities. **Divestiture** means to take away from the defendant something of value, such as illegally gained profits or property used in the commission of the crime. **Dissolution** is the drastic measure the state takes to terminate the business entity so that it no longer exists. **Reorganization** means that the business's structure or management is restructured in a manner that will prevent its future participation in such criminal acts.

Although each year the number of lawsuits filed under RICO statutes increases, the chance of a business being sued under RICO still is very slight. In 1989 less than one-half of 1 percent of the federal courts' entire caseload involved RICO allegations. Even so, many groups, including manufacturers, various chambers of commerce, and certified public accountants, wanted the law changed. In the late 1980s, legislation was moving through Congress to lessen substantially RICO's impact when the scandal with the savings and loan associations became public. Congress quickly and quietly let the proposed change to the statute drop in an effort to appear strong against business crime.

In the following case, the United States Supreme Court considerably broadened RICO's effect. Injured parties are not required to show a prior criminal conviction against the defendant or even a distinct racketeering injury before bringing a civil lawsuit. The following case involves the crime of **bribery** (offering something of value in return for official action).

---

[5] The RICO statutes can be found at <http://www4.law.cornell.edu:80/uscode/18/1961.shtml>.

Case 7.4

H. J. Inc. v. Northwestern Bell Telephone Co.

Supreme Court of the United
States, 1989
492 U.S. 229, 109 S. Ct. 2893,
106 L. Ed. 2d 195
http://www.findlaw.com
/scripts/getcase.pl?navby=case
&court=US&vol=492&page=
229

BACKGROUND AND FACTS Customers, including H. J. Inc., instituted an action against Northwestern Bell Telephone Company, alleging that the company had paid numerous bribes to the Minnesota Public Utilities Commission to have the utility rates raised unreasonably. Plaintiffs sought an injunction and triple damages under RICO.

Both the trial court and the Eighth Circuit Court of Appeals held that all of the bribes were committed in furtherance of a single scheme. RICO requires at least two racketeering acts before the plaintiff can prevail in the civil lawsuit.

Justice BRENNAN delivered the opinion of the Court.

The Racketeer Influenced and Corrupt Organizations Act (RICO or the Act), . . . 18 U.S.C. §§1961-1968, . . . imposes criminal and civil liability upon those who engage in certain prohibited activities. Each prohibited activity is defined . . . to include, as one necessary element, proof either of "a pattern of racketeering activity" or of "collection of an unlawful debt." Racketeering activity is defined in RICO to mean "any act or threat involving" specified state-law crimes, any "act" indictable under various specified federal statutes, and certain federal "offenses," . . . but of the term "pattern" the statute says only that it "requires at least two acts of racketeering activity" within a 10-year period. . . . We are called upon in this civil case to consider what conduct meets RICO's pattern requirement.
. . . .

RICO provides for drastic remedies: conviction for a violation of RICO carries severe criminal penalties and forfeiture of illegal proceeds, . . . and a person found in a private civil action to have violated RICO is liable for treble damages, costs, and attorney's fees.
. . . .

In *Sedima S.P.R.L. v. Imrex Co.*, this Court rejected a restrictive interpretation . . . that would have made it a condition for maintaining a civil RICO action both that the defendant had already been convicted of a predicate [based upon] racketeering act or of a RICO violation, and that plaintiff show a special racketeering injury. In doing so, we acknowledged concern in some quarters over civil RICO's use against "legitimate" businesses, as well as "mobsters and organized criminals." . . . But we suggested that RICO's expansive uses "appear to be primarily the result of the breadth of the predicated offenses, in particular the inclusion of wire, mail, and securities fraud, and the failure of Congress and the courts to develop a meaningful concept of 'pattern'"—both factors that apply to criminal as well as civil applications of the Act. . . . Congress had done nothing in the interim further to illuminate RICO's key requirement of a pattern of racketeering; and as the plethora of different views expressed by the Courts of Appeals since *Sedima* demonstrates, . . . developing a meaningful concept of "pattern" within the existing statutory framework has proved to be no easy task.

. . . Congress had a more natural and common sense approach to RICO's pattern element in mind, intending a more stringent requirement than proof simply of two predicates, but also envisioning a concept of sufficient breadth that it might encompass multiple predicates within a single scheme that were related and that amounted to, or threatened the likelihood of, continued criminal activity.
. . . .

Whether the predicates proved establish a threat of continued racketeering activity depends on the specific facts of each case. Without making any claim to cover the field of possibilities—preferring to deal with this issue in the context of concrete factual situations presented for decision—we offer some examples of how this element might be satisfied. A RICO pattern may surely be established if the related predicates themselves involve a distinct threat of long-term racketeering activity, either implicit or explicit. Suppose a hoodlum were to sell "insurance" to a neighborhood's storekeepers to cover them against breakage of their windows, telling his victims he would be reappearing each month to collect the "premium" that would continue their "coverage." Though the number of related predicates involved may be small and they may occur close together in time, the racketeering acts themselves include a specific threat of repetition extending indefinitely into the future, and thus supply the requisite threat of continuity. In other cases, the threat of continuity may be established by showing that the predicate acts or offenses are part of an ongoing entity's regular way of doing business. Thus, the threat of continuity is sufficiently established where the predicates can be attributed to a defendant operating as part of a long-term association that exists for criminal purposes. Such associations include, but extend well beyond, those traditionally grouped under the phrase "organized crime." The continuity requirement is likewise satisfied where it is shown that the predicates are a regular way of conducting defendant's ongoing legitimate business (in the sense that it is not a business that exists for criminal purposes), or of conducting or participating in an ongoing and legitimate RICO enterprise.

DECISION AND REMEDY The Supreme Court returned the case to the district court for trial. The Supreme Court held that in order to prove a pattern of racketeering activity, the plaintiffs must prove two elements. First, at a minimum, two related racketeering acts must have been committed. Second, these acts must amount to, or threaten to continue the likelihood of, criminal activity. In other words, a plaintiff does not have to prove two separate, unrelated criminal acts. In the case at hand, each act of bribery was a separate criminal act that fit into a pattern of racketeering.

CRITICAL THINKING: PUBLIC POLICY The RICO statute was passed in an attempt to control organized crime. Why are such companies as American Express, General Motors, Merrill Lynch, and other legitimate businesses prosecuted under the RICO statute?

Extortion. **Extortion** is a white-collar crime in which a public official misuses his office to force monetary or property payment from another so that the official will carry out his official duties. Often an extortionist threatens or uses actual force or induces fear. In the past, extortion was committed only by public officials, for example, a restaurant paying a health inspector to provide a passing inspection. If the restaurant did not pay, the inspector would close it down for failing the health inspection.

Extortion commonly is called a crime of bribery. Some states limit bribery to public officials receiving money or property for doing their official duty. Other states have broadened the definition to include both public officials and private individuals. In those states, bribery and extortion are the same. In the private sector, extortion/bribery includes kickbacks and payoffs from an individual working for one company to an individual working for another. The payments are made for various reasons; for example, to obtain proprietary information, to cover up an inferior product, or to secure new business.

In the following case, a public official accepted $7,000 in cash but did not demand the money. The question is, did this acceptance constitute extortion?

Case 7.5

Evans v. United States

Supreme Court of the United States, 1992

504 U.S. 255, 112 S. Ct. 1881, 119 L. Ed. 2d 57

http://www.findlaw.com /scripts/getcase.pl?navby=case &court=US&vol=504&page= 255

BACKGROUND AND FACTS Evans (the petitioner) was an elected member of the Board of Commissioners of DeKalb County, Georgia. During the period between March 1985 and October 1986, the Federal Bureau of Investigation (FBI) investigated allegations of public corruption in and around Atlanta, particularly in the area of property rezoning.

An FBI agent, posing as a real estate developer, talked on the telephone and met with Evans on a number of occasions. Virtually all of those conversations were recorded on audiotape or videotape. In those conversations, the agent sought Evans's assistance in an effort to rezone a twenty-five-acre land tract for high-density residential use. On one occasion, the agent handed Evans cash totaling $7,000 and a check for $1,000 payable to his campaign. Evans reported the check, but not the cash, on his state campaign financing disclosure form. He also did not report the $7,000 on his 1986 federal income tax return.

Evans was indicted on one count of extortion and one count of failure to report income. He was convicted by a jury on both counts. He appealed the extortion conviction because he had not demanded or requested the money, and he had not conditioned the performance of any official act upon its receipt. The Court considered whether the taking of the $7,000 cash and the $1,000 campaign contribution was extortion.

Justice STEVENS delivered the opinion of the Court.

. . . .

Petitioner argues that the jury charge with respect to extortion allowed the jury to convict him on the basis of the "passive acceptance of a contribution." He contends that the instruction did not require the jury to find "an element of duress such as a demand," and it did not properly describe the *quid pro quo* [act] requirement for conviction if the jury found that the payment was a campaign contribution.

We reject petitioner's criticism of the instruction, and conclude that it satisfies the *quid pro quo* requirement because the offense is completed at the time when the public official receives a payment in return for his agreement to perform specific official acts; fulfillment of the *quid pro quo* is not an element of the offense. We also reject petitioner's contention that an affirmative is an element of the offense of extortion "under color of official right" and need be included in the [jury] instruction. . . . We hold today that the Government need only show that a public official has obtained a payment to which he was not entitled, knowing that the payment was made in return for official acts.

DECISION AND REMEDY The Court upheld Evans's extortion conviction. The Court held that an affirmative act of inducement by a public official, such as a demand, is not an element of the offense.

CRITICAL THINKING: PUBLIC POLICY Discuss whether the payment amount should be considered when establishing the crime of extortion. If so, what amount given to a politician should be regarded as criminal if the payer requests no favors? Explain.

Foreign Corrupt Practices Act.   Until the 1970s, bribery of foreign officials to obtain business contracts rarely, if ever, was discussed. Indeed, payments in cash or in-kind benefits to government officials for such purposes were considered normal business practice, although not necessarily legal.

A business might make cash payments to a foreign official so the business would be awarded lucrative contracts or so the foreign government would keep competitors out. In-kind benefits involve the exchange of property or services instead of cash. For example, instead of paying the official in cash, an all-expenses-paid week to attend the Super Bowl activities is provided. As a result of documented cases of U.S. businesses bribing corrupt dictators, Congress in 1977 passed the **Foreign Corrupt Practices Act (FCPA)**.

The FCPA consists of two major parts. The first part prohibits all U.S. companies and their directors, officers, shareholders, employees, or agents from offering bribes to foreign government officials for which the purpose is to obtain or retain business for the U.S. company.

The second part of the FCPA applies to all businesses registered with the Securities and Exchange Commission (SEC), even if the business operates only in the United States. It requires all registered companies to keep detailed records that "accurately and fairly" reflect the company's financial activities. These companies must have an accounting system that provides "reasonable assurance" that all transactions entered into by the company are accounted for and are legal. In fact, the second part has nothing to do with bribery or foreign corrupt practices. This part of the FCPA is directed toward accountants and financial officers because previous bribes often were concealed in business financial records.

Employees are prohibited from making false statements to accountants. No one can make false entries in any record or account. Violations of the act may result in a fine of up to $1 million and the incarceration of convicted officers or directors for a maximum of five years. Those officers and directors also can be fined up to $10,000, which cannot be paid with company funds.

Federal Sentencing Guidelines.   The federal *Sentencing Guidelines for Organizations*[6] enacted in 1991 gave both profit and nonprofit businesses an incentive to police themselves. Under these guidelines, any organization that has a compliance program will receive greatly reduced penalties than if no program is in place. A company must monitor and audit its records and accounts. The systems must be reasonably designed to detect criminal conduct by all employees.

Bankruptcy Fraud.   The U.S. Constitution, Article I, Section 8, provides all persons protection from creditors through **bankruptcy**. It has two goals: (1) to forgive the overwhelming debts owed by a person and (2) to distribute the debtor's assets to the creditors.

The federal **Bankruptcy Reform Acts** of 1978 and 1994 govern bankruptcy law. This act is discussed in more detail in Chapter 14. **Bankruptcy fraud** takes place when a person involved in bankruptcy misleads the bankruptcy court. The following are examples of white-collar crimes that can be perpetrated during a bankruptcy proceeding.

False Claims of Creditors.   Creditors are required by the bankruptcy law to file their individual claims against a debtor who is in bankruptcy proceedings. A creditor who files a false claim commits a crime. For example, your friend and you agree that she will file a false claim in bankruptcy court against your assets. The claim is for payment for engineering work that was never done. When your friend is successfully paid, she returns the money to you. You both have committed federal bankruptcy fraud.

Transfer or Concealment of Property.   Prior to bankruptcy proceedings, a debtor has an incentive to transfer assets to favored parties before or after the petition filing for bankruptcy. For example, a company-owned automobile worth $15,000 can be sold at a bargain price of $1,000 to a trusted friend or relative.

Closely related to the crime of fraudulent transfer of property is fraudulent concealment of property. The number of ways in which debtors fraudulently, but cleverly, have concealed assets would require several books to outline.

Scam Bankruptcies.   In a **scam bankruptcy**, perpetrators swindle creditors by purchasing goods in advance while planning a bankruptcy proceeding. The perpetrators purchase a legitimate business that sells highly movable goods, such as jewelry or electronic home

---

[6] Information on the federal *Sentencing Guidelines for Organizations* can be found at <http://www.corporatecompliance.com/> and at <http://www.ussc.gov/>.

entertainment equipment. *Movable goods,* as the term is used here, refers to personal property that can be sold easily but cannot be traced easily. The scam begins when the swindlers pose as new owners of a business and purchase numerous items on credit from a seller. The swindlers pay off initial debts quickly.

This activity continues until the creditors are willing to offer larger and larger amounts of credit to the new owners. Finally, the swindlers order a very large amount of merchandise on credit. They sell the goods immediately at whatever price is necessary to unload the merchandise quickly for cash. Then the swindlers close down the business and disappear. Of course, the business is bankrupt. The amount that those creditors will recover typically is very small and the scam operators are nowhere to be found.

Regulatory Offenses. Congress has created administrative agencies that regulate businesses, such as the Occupational Safety and Health Act, the Environmental Protection Act, the Securities Exchange Commission, and the Food and Drug Administration. These agencies were discussed in detail in Chapter 6.

Administrative agencies enforce statutes that have civil provisions. In the past decade, more violators have been assessed civil and administrative penalties than prosecuted criminally under the provisions of some statutes. In an administrative hearing, the burden of proof is less, no right to a jury exists, and settlements can be reached more easily. At the same time, administrative penalties may amount to more than $1 million a day per violation.

If an agency finds that a business has committed egregious criminal acts, the agency may refer the case to the Department of Justice for prosecution. The Department of Justice is the federal agency that has criminal jurisdiction. Administrative agencies do not have the authority to prosecute criminal cases.[7]

Obstruction of Justice. Executives may be prosecuted for destroying or hiding business records, such as e-mails, required under a subpoena by a grand jury, a court, or an investigative agency. The crime of obstruction of justice is independent of any other criminal vi-

olation. Even if a business is guilty of no other criminal act, it can be found guilty of obstruction of justice.

Currency Offenses. Criminals hide their illegally gained money by using schemes involving currency. Many types of crimes involve the hiding or misuse of currency, ranging from the violent world of narcotics trafficking to the crime of income tax evasion. To make it harder for criminals to deal in currency, Congress passed two separate laws; one statute is aimed at money laundering and the second makes currency reporting mandatory. The following sections describe these two laws.

Money Laundering. Criminals can use legitimate businesses to make it appear that money gained from illegal activities was earned through legal business activities. Criminals operate small businesses that generate cash flow, such as fast-food restaurants or dry cleaners. Such an operation can conduct business, but in reality serves as a front for the deposit of large amounts of cash through business accounts. This is one type of money laundering.

Congress made money laundering a crime by passing the **Money Laundering Control Act**. The act covers not only cash transactions, but also wire transfers of money, including transactions over the Internet.

Currency Transaction Report. A federal statute requires that financial institutions and businesses file a **Currency Transaction Report (CTR)** with the Internal Revenue Service under two different circumstances. First, a bank is required to file a CTR when it suspects criminal activity by a customer who is involved in a financial transaction of $1,000 or more. For example, if a customer does not appear to have a business and makes only cash deposits into his account, the bank may suspect criminal activity.

Second, when a single transaction or a series of related transactions of cash amount to more than $10,000,[8] the merchant or financial institution must file a CTR. Cash is broadly defined by the statute to include currency, cashier's checks, bank drafts, traveler's checks, and money orders. Regular checks are not included in

---

[7] The Department of Defense does have criminal jurisdiction over military service members, but it is beyond the subject matter of this book on the legal environment of business.

[8] The U.S. Treasury Department has proposed that when any money transaction over $750 is transferred out of the country by nonbanking institutions, such as a check-cashing store or a credit card issuer, like Visa, MasterCard, or American Express, the institution should be required to report it in order to stem money-laundering activities.

LEGAL HIGHLIGHT

Cybercrime

Cybercrime refers to crimes committed using high technology, for instance, a computer with a modem connected to the Internet. Add a cellular telephone and a cryptographic manual and the criminal has all the necessary tools. Online crimes cost the 40 million Internet users around $350 million per year. Here are some examples.

White-Collar Crime

Nearly every white-collar crime can be committed using technology. Hackers can break into computers holding sensitive information, such as a bank computer, change the codes, and transfer money to the hacker's bank account. They can change criminal files located on police computers. It is estimated, however, that about 80 to 85 percent of computer crime losses are committed by insiders. Most businesses suffer losses not to hackers, but to disloyal employees.

Espionage

Spies can work from the comfort of their computer rooms. No one has to break into the business office to photograph strategic plans of the company. Business research materials and passwords are available in computer files. With the correct key strokes and the right software, a business spy can break into the business victim's computer system. In a nanosecond, the files are copied and the thief logs off. Or the thief can leave a program on the computer that logs everything the computer does. The thief then reenters the computer later to check it.

Theft

Analog cellular telephones leave an electronic fingerprint when used. Thieves station themselves near airports or other busy areas to capture those fingerprints by the hundreds and immediately sell the numbers. The result is that the cellular telephone user receives a bill from the telephone company that can run to hundreds of thousands of dollars. Thieves can also break into a business telephone system, steal its long-distance access code, and, again, when the bill arrives it might document hundreds of thousands of dollars worth of telephone calls that have been made illegally.

These are but a few crimes that take advantage of high technology. Businesses need to install a security system to keep hackers out and to monitor their employees. Passwords and codes need to be treated as top secret. Sloppy security measures allow the criminal access to the businesses' confidential and secret information.

For more information, see The National Fraud Information Center web site located at <http://www.fraud.org> and the Better Business Bureau web site at <http://www.bbb.org>.

---

this area because they are in the banking system, where suspected illegal transactions can be documented.

A person purchases a house for $100,000 and pays for it with eleven cashier's checks, each made out in the amount of $9,090.90. The real estate broker must file the CTR, because the series of transactions contributed to one purchase, even though no single cashier's check was $10,000 or more. The act covers real estate brokers, insurance brokers, stock brokers, and all types of retailers, such as automobile, truck, airplane and motorcycle dealers; boat dealers; jewelers; antique dealers; home entertainment businesses; and travel agents, to name a few.

Defenses

The prosecutor bears the burden to prove to a jury (or judge, if both the prosecutor and the defense agree to no jury) that the accused is guilty beyond a reasonable doubt. The accused, however, has no responsibility to put on a defense; the government must respect the protection that the Constitution guarantees every defendant. For example, the government cannot torture a confession from a person because the Fifth Amendment protects people from being forced to testify against themselves. The constitutional protections are found in the Fourth, Fifth, Sixth, and Eighth Amendments.

Other defenses exist that a person or business may use if accused of a criminal act. Some of these are of historical origin and others have been created by statute.

Double Jeopardy

The Fifth Amendment to the U.S. Constitution provides that: "[N]or shall any person be subject for the same offense to be twice put in jeopardy of life or limb." This clause prevents both more than one prosecution and more than one punishment for the same offense by the same level of government.

A problem occurs, however, when different crimes are committed at the same time. For example, a person holds up a store with a gun. In doing so, the criminal forces the clerk move to the other side of the store and then takes $1,000 from the cash register. These simple facts involve several crimes: armed robbery, grand theft, assault with a deadly weapon, and even possibly kidnapping. The kidnapping occurred when the clerk was forced to move without consent.

To determine whether a single act constitutes a violation of more than one distinct statutory provision, the court must determine whether each provision requires separate proof of wrongdoing. For example, in the previous situation grand theft is established by the taking of $1,000, whereas assault with a deadly weapon is proven through the use of a gun.

The Constitution was designed to prevent double jeopardy, that is, the defendant's being tried twice by the same level of government. A person, however, can be convicted in both state and federal court for the same wrongful conduct. A person who commits a robbery at a national bank, for example, may be prosecuted in both federal and state courts.

Double jeopardy requires the case to have reached a final conclusion. A case is not final, for example, if it is appealed to higher courts or if the jury could not reach a verdict. Such a jury is referred to as a hung jury.

In the following case, the United States Supreme Court was confronted with the problem of whether double jeopardy should apply when property had been forfeited to the government under a civil procedure. The government had seized the defendant's property under civil law and prosecuted him for his conduct under criminal law.

Case 7.6

United States v. Ursery

Supreme Court of the United States, 1996
518 U.S 267, 116 S. Ct. 2135, 135 L. Ed. 2d 549
http://supct.law.cornell.edu

BACKGROUND AND FACTS Michigan police found marijuana growing adjacent to Guy Ursery's house and then discovered marijuana seeds, stems, stalks, and a growlight in his house. The U.S. government instituted civil forfeiture proceedings against the house, alleging that the property was subject to forfeiture because it had been used for several years to facilitate the unlawful processing and distribution of a controlled substance (marijuana).

Ursery ultimately paid the United States $13,250 to settle the forfeiture claim in full. Shortly before the settlement was completed, Ursery was indicted for manufacturing marijuana. A jury found him guilty, and he was sentenced to sixty-three months in prison. He appealed his conviction, alleging that the forfeiture of his house and the conviction violated his Fifth Amendment rights. The Sixth Court of Appeals reversed his conviction, holding that it violated the double jeopardy clause of the Fifth Amendment.

Chief Justice REHNQUIST delivered the opinion of the Court.

. . . .

. . . First, in light of our [previous] decisions . . . and the long tradition of federal statutes providing for a forfeiture proceeding following a criminal prosecution, it is absolutely clear that *in rem* civil forfeiture has not historically been regarded as punishment, as we have understood that term under the Double Jeopardy Clause. Second, there is no requirement in the statutes that we currently review that the

Government demonstrate scienter in order to establish that the property is subject to forfeiture; indeed, the property may be subject to forfeiture even if no party files a claim to it and the Government never shows any connection between the property and a particular person. Though both [statutes] contain an "innocent owner" exception, we do not think that such a provision, without more indication of an intent to punish, is relevant to the question whether a statute is punitive under the Double Jeopardy Clause. Third, though both statutes may fairly be said to serve the purpose of deterrence, we long have held that this purpose may serve civil as well as criminal goals. Finally, though both statutes are tied to criminal activity, . . . this fact is insufficient to render the statutes punitive. It is well settled that "Congress may impose both a criminal and a civil sanction in respect to the same act or omission." By itself, the fact that a forfeiture statute has some connection to a criminal violation is far from the "clearest proof" necessary to show that a proceeding is criminal. We hold that these *in rem* civil forfeitures are neither "punishment" nor criminal for purposes of the Double Jeopardy Clause.

DECISION AND REMEDY The United States Supreme Court found that the government has the authority to confiscate property under the civil law and to criminally prosecute the wrongdoer. These two government actions do not violate the Fifth Amendment's guarantee against double jeopardy.

CRITICAL THINKING: MANAGEMENT ISSUE Although this case does not involve a business, the principle is applicable to business situations. If you hired a person who was caught selling marijuana from a company vehicle or on the business property, what are the potential outcomes? Discuss how to control your employees' conduct to protect your company property from forfeiture.

Self-Defense

The **self-defense** doctrine gives a person the absolute right to defend his person. People may use deadly force if they are afraid for their own life or that of another. The fear must be based upon a reasonable belief that death or great physical harm is imminent if they do not use force.

Deadly force may not be used, however, except in response to the threat of deadly force. For example, if a person is involved in a fight in which both parties are of equal physical condition, neither party has a right to use a weapon on the other. A person also cannot use deadly force in protecting her property except when confronted with threat of deadly force. In other words, a person has no right to shoot another who is, for example, siphoning gas from her vehicle.

Entrapment

On occasion, the police or other government agencies have actively encouraged a defendant to participate in a criminal act. This encouragement is referred to as en-

trapment. For an accused to use this defense, he must fully admit to committing the crime. The jury must decide if the government agent's active pressures or suggestions precipitated the crime or if the crime would have occurred anyway. In other words, the entrapment occurs if the defendant was not predisposed to committing the crime.

Incapacity

One of the most common defenses is that a defendant lacks the mental ability to be held responsible for her actions. This defense is defined differently from one state to another. Most states excuse criminal conduct if the defendant lacks the capacity to differentiate between right and wrong.

A few states follow the irresistible-impulse theory, which means that, in spite of recognizing the wrongness of an act, the defendant could not control his actions.

Many states have adopted statutes that allow a jury to find a person mentally incompetent. Under these statutes the defendant is placed in a mental hospital, but upon her recovery must serve the full sentence for the criminal act.

In the case of John Hinkley, who attempted to assassinate President Ronald Reagan, the law at that time imposed upon the government the burden of proving that Hinkley was sane. Hinkley's long history of mental illness prevented the government from meeting that burden, so Hinkley was found not guilty. He was hospitalized, however, for his mental condition. The law was changed so that the government no longer has to prove that the defendant is sane. A defendant may defend herself by proving that she is insane.

Intoxication

Intoxication involves the voluntary consumption of either alcohol or drugs, legal or illegal. Although a person cannot drink two beers, commit a crime, and then claim that his intoxication caused the crime, the very heavy consumption of either drugs or alcohol may serve as a defense for a crime that requires *mens rea*. For example, a person consumes a quart of whiskey and then picks a fight with and kills another person. Can intoxication be used as a defense?

Intoxication may be a defense against a first-degree murder charge, but it probably would be an insufficient defense for manslaughter. First-degree murder requires intent to take another person's life. Manslaughter requires reckless conduct on the part of a person that results in the death of another. The question would be whether the person was so intoxicated that she could not form the intent.

International Consideration

The World Community versus International Criminals

International criminal law as a definitive body of law is very limited in scope, but it is a growing area. In 1951, the United Nations drafted a proposal for an international criminal court that has been revised in light of international narcotics trade and terrorism. Political considerations, constitutional prohibitions, and divergent cultural backgrounds have kept the proposal in various stages of draft form.

The U.N. Committee on Crime Prevention and Control has adopted various resolutions, including recommendations that the United Nations conduct criminal justice surveys more often, promote technical cooperation in crime prevention and criminal justice, redress the victims of crime and human rights violations, and address illicit drug production and trafficking. It has drafted five model treaties covering prevention of crimes that infringe on cultural heritage, extradition, mutual assistance, and transfer of supervision of foreign offenders.

The United Nations has several agencies working in the area of illicit drugs. The Commission on Narcotic Drugs is responsible for placing drafts and resolutions concerning illicit drugs before the U.N. General Assembly. The U.N. Division of Narcotic Drugs (DND) provides practical, technical, and scientific assistance to member states. It also operates the Drug Abuse Assessment System, which enables the DND to analyze drug abuse data at national, regional, and international levels and to facilitate worldwide cooperation.

The International Narcotics Control Board assesses the adverse national security aspects of drug trafficking. It also studies the direct threat to political institutions and economies from the illicit production, trafficking, and abuse of drugs and escalating drug-related violence.

Economic crime is a relatively new category of crime, and the policies of various nations on this topic remain divergent thus far. The United States was the first country to define antitrust activities, such as monopolies or unfair competition, as both a criminal and a civil offense. Over the decades many other countries have come to recognize antitrust activities as criminal acts, but still other nations officially encourage businesses to participate in antitrust activities. Even the United States now allows some forms of antitrust activities by businesses when they have dealings overseas.

Extradition is the delivery of an accused or convicted person to the country in which the crime allegedly occurred. It has been a political topic for centuries. For extradition to be required, a treaty outlining the extradition rules must exist between the two countries involved. Often these treaties provide that a person cannot be executed if extradited or that a person cannot be extradited if accused of a political crime. What constitutes a political crime, however, is a matter of definition. Defining what is a domestic political crime is difficult for a country internally, let alone for two nations striving to reach an agreement on extradition rules.

LEGALLY SPEAKING

Bad Checks

All states have a statute that makes it a crime to write a check against a closed account or one with insufficient funds. Many times these crimes constitute a felony, and a defendant, if convicted, is sentenced to prison. Each year, businesses lose millions of dollars because of bad checks. Following are some of the ways in which a business might reduce these losses.

✔ Most bad checks are written on new accounts. If the printed number on the check's upper right-hand corner is low or handwritten, this could signal that the check might not be good.

✔ A business should never accept a postdated check, even though a postdated check is legal. To convict a person of writing bad checks requires proof that the defendant, at the time of giving the check, intended to defraud the business. When a merchant accepts a postdated check, she acknowledges that currently the account lacks sufficient funds to cover the check. In effect, the merchant grants credit by accepting a postdated check. The check cannot be dishonored until the date on the check, which makes it very difficult to prove fraudulent intent at the time that the check was written.

✔ The employee of a business always should look closely at a check to confirm that the written and numerical amounts match. The person writing the check may write a number different from the figure on a check. If the figures do not match, a bank should not honor the check and return it to the business. Check processors, however, review hundreds of checks an hour and often look only at the numbers; they may not take time to verify that the words written out match. Generally, the figure written in words is the amount legally posted to the bank account.

✔ Merchants should require government-issued identification with a picture, such as a driver's license, for identification of the check writer. Merchants also should record the identifying driver's license number on the check. Both of these actions will help if a trial results.

✔ Forged checks may be spotted in several ways. First, each geographic area has a specific two-digit Federal Reserve number that appears twice on the check: as the first two digits of the nine-digit series at the bottom and as the denominator of the fraction at the upper right. If these are inconsistent, the check is not drawn on a bank. A businessperson should know the Federal Reserve number for his area. Second, the nine-digit number has a special magnetic ink that has a dull finish. Third, checks should have one perforated edge. Most forgers use a regular paper cutter that leaves all four sides of the check smooth.

✔ A businessperson should never threaten the check writer with criminal prosecution after receiving a bad check. Making such a threat could result in the merchant's being charged with extortion. The crook might go free and the businessperson might end up serving time! If the businessperson believes that a crime has taken place, she should report it to the police or to the county or district attorney's office.

Chapter Summary

Criminal law affects the business community in many ways. An act may constitute both a criminal and a civil wrong. When criminal conduct occurs, society is harmed. All criminal actions are brought in the name of the government, for example, *United States of America v. John Worthless*. Many criminal acts also give rise to a civil action by the injured party.

Crimes may be classified as felonies, misdemeanors, and petty offenses. A person convicted of a felony may serve a sentence of one year or more in a state or federal prison, be fined, or be put to death. A person convicted of a misdemeanor may serve less than one year in a local jail, be fined, or both. If convicted of a petty offense, a person usually is fined.

When a person is charged with a crime, the government must prove the defendant guilty beyond a reasonable doubt. The Constitution guarantees protection for individuals and businesses accused of crimes.

Historically, most crimes require both criminal intent (*mens rea*) and criminal conduct (*actus reus*). Many crimes require only criminal conduct and not criminal intent. This requirement allows businesses incapable of criminal "intent" to be convicted of crimes. Attempts and conspiracies might occur prior to a planned criminal act. Even if a crime is not committed, people can be charged with an attempt to commit the crime or with engaging in a conspiracy with another for the purpose of committing the crime.

Some important crimes that affect business are offenses against property, such as burglary, larceny, robbery, and arson. White-collar crimes are nonviolent offenses involving corruption, deceit, or breach of trust committed by individuals. A few types of white-collar crimes include receiving stolen goods, forgery, obtaining money or goods by false pretenses, embezzlement, use of the mails to defraud, computer crimes, and extortion.

Businesses also can commit crimes. More types of business actions may be regarded as criminal because of the expanding definition of criminal acts. Businesses are subject to the Racketeer Influenced and Corrupt Organizations Act (RICO), the Foreign Corrupt Practices Act (FCPA), bankruptcy fraud, regulatory offenses, and obstruction of justice.

RICO has both criminal and civil provisions. A business that has committed more than two acts of racketeering in ten years may be prosecuted criminally and may be liable for treble damages to the injured party in a civil lawsuit. Racketeering acts involve more than fifty federal statutes and consist of criminal activity such as mail fraud, wire fraud, fraud in the sale of securities, bankruptcy fraud, extortion, interstate transportation of stolen property, arson, murder, gambling, and robbery.

The FCPA consists of two parts. The first part forbids bribe payment to foreign officials. The second part requires businesses to establish and maintain accounting procedures.

Bankruptcy fraud is a crime in which a business perpetuates a fraud on a federal bankruptcy court. These acts typically consist of creditors' false claims, property transfer or concealment, and scam bankruptcy.

Regulatory offenses are committed by businesses when they violate regulatory statutes. Even though some offenses are civil, an administrative agency can impose large fines. Other offenses are criminal but must be prosecuted by the Department of Justice.

Obstruction of justice means interference with court procedures. These offenses usually include business record destruction or concealment in violation of court orders.

Using the World Wide Web

A number of sites are available to the public to look at the activities of law enforcement. Here are a few to get you started.

Finding the Law on the Web

U.S. Department of Justice home page
http://www.usdoj.gov/

U.S. Department of Justice criminal division
http://www.usdoj.gov/criminal/criminal-home.html

Department of Justice Computer Crime and Intellectual Property Section (CCIPS)
http://www.usdoj.gov/criminal/cybercrime/index.html

Federal Bureau of Investigation
http://www.fbi.gov/

The FBI's Ten Most Wanted List
http://www.fbi.gov/wanted.htm

Criminal law and procedure at the Cornell
Law School site
http://www.law.cornell.edu/topical.html

Statistics covering criminal law
http://www.ojp.usdoj.gov/bjs/

Florida State University, Criminal Justice Links
http://www.criminology.fsu.edu/cj.html

American Civil Liberties Union (ACLU)
http://www.aclu.org/issues/criminal/hmcj.html

Justice Information Center
http://www.ncjrs.org/

Georgetown University Law Center
http://www.ll.georgetown.edu/

National White Collar Crime Center (NW3C)
http://www.nw3c.org

Chapter Web Sites

FTC v. Fortuna Alliance
http://www.ftc.gov/opa/9702/fortuna4.htm

Federal Trade Commission
http://www.ftc.gov

Posters 'N' Things v. United States
http://supct.law.cornell.edu

Miranda v. Arizona
http://www.findlaw.com/scripts/getcase.pl?navby=
case&court=US&vol=384&page=436

United States v. Park
http://www.findlaw.com/scripts/getcase.pl?navby=
case&court=US&vol=421&page=658

Counterfeit Access Device and Computer Fraud and
Abuse Act of 1985
Prohibition against access devices:
http://www.law.cornell.edu:80/uscode/18/10
29.shtml
Prohibition concerning computers:
http://www.law.cornell.edu:80/uscode/18/10
30.shtml

Start search at Cornell School of Law site
http://www.law.cornell.edu

Electronic Communications Privacy Act of 1986.
This act is under Unlawful Access to Stored

Communications
http://www4.law.cornell.edu/uscode/18/2701
.html

Racketeer Influenced and Corrupt Organizations Act
(RICO)
http://www4.law.cornell.edu:80/uscode/18/1961
.shtml

H. J. Inc. v. Northwestern Bell Telephone Co.
http://www.findlaw.com
or
http://www.findlaw.com/scripts/getcase.pl?navby=
case&court=US&vol=492&page=229

Evans v. United States
http://www.findlaw.com
or
http://www.findlaw.com/scripts/getcase.pl?navby=
case&court=US&vol=504&page=255

Federal *Sentencing Guidelines for Organizations*
http://www.corporatecompliance.com/
and
http://www.ussc.gov/

National Fraud Information Center
http://www.fraud.org

Better Business Bureau
http://www.bbb.org

United States v. Ursery
http://supct.law.cornell.edu

Free Advice, search
http://www.freeadvice.com/law/6063us.htm

Free Advice, arrest
http://www.freeadvice.com/law/606us.htm

U.S. Department of Justice (DOJ) topical index
http://www.usdoj.gov/topical.html

Web Activities

7–1 Does a police officer have the authority to search
your automobile if you are stopped for speeding? Can
the police officer search you if you are not driving but
when you are a passenger in the automobile? Go to the
Free Advice web site at <http://www.freeadvice.com
/law/6063us.htm>.

7–2 When does an arrest occur? Go to the Free Advice
web site at <http://www.freeadvice.com/law
/606us.htm>.

Key Terms

actus reus	Currency Transaction	indictment	Racketeer Influenced
arson	Report (CTR)	larceny	and Corrupt
attempt	dissolution	*mens rea*	Organizations Act
bankruptcy	divestiture	misapplication of trust	(RICO)
bankruptcy fraud	Electronic	funds	receiving stolen goods
Bankruptcy Reform Acts	Communications	misdemeanor	reorganization
bill of information	Privacy Act	Money Laundering	robbery
bribery	embezzlement	Control Act	scam bankruptcy
burglary	extortion	obtaining goods or	self-defense
computer crime	extradition	money by false	Trademark
conspiracy	False Statement Act	pretenses	Counterfeiting Act
Counterfeit Access	felony	overt act	use of the mails to
Device and	Foreign Corrupt	petty offense	defraud
Computer Fraud and	Practices Act (FCPA)	probable cause	white-collar crime
Abuse Act	forgery		

Questions and Case Problems

7–1 Procedure Civil trials and criminal trials follow essentially the same format. There are, however, several important differences between them. In criminal trials, the defendant must be proved guilty beyond a reasonable doubt, whereas in civil trials, the defendant need only be proved guilty by a preponderance of the evidence. Explain possible reasons for this difference.

7–2 Crime Types The following situations are similar (all involve the theft of Jean's television set), yet three different crimes are described. Identify the three crimes and explain their differences.

  a. While passing Jean's house one night, Sam sees a portable television set left unattended on Jean's lawn. Sam takes the television set, carries it home, and tells everyone that he owns it.

  b. While passing Jean's house one night, Sam sees Jean outside with a portable television set. Holding Jean at gunpoint, Sam forces her to give up the set. He then runs away with it.

  c. While passing Jean's house one night, Sam sees a portable television set in a window. Sam breaks the front door lock, enters, and leaves with the set.

7–3 Elements Two basic elements needed to convict a person of most crimes are criminal intent and criminal conduct. Define these terms and discuss how each applies to the following:

  a. Embezzlement
  b. Forgery
  c. Arson

7–4 RICO Compare civil RICO with criminal RICO.

7–5 Civil RICO The plaintiff, Sedima, and the defendant, Imrex, entered into a joint-venture agreement in which Imrex would provide electronic components to Sedima. They were to split the net proceeds when Sedima sold the product. Although $8 million in orders were processed, Sedima became convinced that Imrex was inflating the bills and cheating Sedima out of profits. Sedima filed a lawsuit alleging RICO claims based on mail and wire fraud, because Imrex allegedly had used the mails and wires to overbill Sedima. Imrex's defense was that it had never been criminally convicted of a RICO violation. Must Sedima prove that Imrex was or could have been criminally prosecuted in order to recover civil damages under RICO? Explain. [*Sedima S.P.R.L. v. Imrex Co.,* 473 U.S. 479, 105 S. Ct. 3275, 87 L. Ed. 2d 346 (1985)]

7–6 Type Joseph Russello committed arson on a building that he owned. Prior to being charged and convicted, he collected the insurance on the building. What type of crime has Russello committed under these circumstances? Explain. [*Russello v. United States,* 464 U.S. 16, 104 S. Ct. 296, 78 L. Ed. 2d 17 (1983)]

7–7 Arson Faulknor was a seaman on the ship *Zemindar.* One night, while on duty, Faulknor went in search of the rum that he knew the ship was carrying. He found it and opened one of the kegs. Because he was holding a match at the time, he inadvertently ignited the rum and set fire to the ship. At the trial, it was determined that even though he had not intended to set fire to the rum, he had been engaged in the unlawful act of stealing it. Does Faulknor's theft of the rum make him criminally liable for setting fire to the ship? Explain. [*Regina v. Faulknor*, 13 Cox Crim. Cas. 550 (Ireland 1877)]

7–8 Forfeiture John Bennis was arrested after the police observed him engaged in a sexual act with a prostitute in his automobile in Detroit, Michigan. He was convicted of gross indecency. The state of Michigan brought a civil action against John and his wife Tina, who jointly owned the automobile, to have it declared a public nuisance and forfeited to the state. Tina objected because she did not know of her husband's activities and asserted that if the automobile was forfeited she was entitled to one-half of its value. The automobile was an eleven-year-old sedan purchased by the Bennises for $600. Who prevails and why? [*Bennis v. Michigan,* 526 U.S. 442, 116 S. Ct. 994, 134 L. Ed. 2d 68 (1996)]

7–9 Constitutional Rights Rushton's twelve-year-old neighbor notified the sheriff's office that Rushton had been growing marijuana at his house. The sheriff had time to obtain a search warrant; however, he did not obtain it because of overtime costs to pay his deputies to prepare and review the warrant application and to find the county attorney or justice of the peace, neither of whom were readily available that night. After Rushton went to bed, the sheriff and four deputies knocked at the door. Rushton's wife admitted them into the home. Without giving the *Miranda* warnings, a deputy interrogated Rushton, who implied that he was growing marijuana. He asked if he needed a lawyer, but his question was not answered. The sheriff obtained Rushton's signature on a search consent form. Based on the consent form, the officers conducted the search and seized eighteen plants and other material. Was it necessary for the sheriff to give the *Miranda* rights in order to use Rushton's statements against him in a criminal trial? Explain. [*State v. Rushton,* 870 P.2d 1355 (Mont. 1994)]

7–10 Internet In what topics is the U.S. Department of Justice (DOJ) currently interested? The DOJ has a topical index at <http://www.usdoj.gov/topical.html>.

Unit II Business and Private Law

I am charmed with many points of the Turkish law; when proved the authors of any notorious falsehood, they are burned on the forehead with a hot iron.

Lady Mary Wortley Montagu, 1689–1762
English writer

Outline

Ethical Consideration

Media's Responsibility When Reporting about Families of Public Figures

Senator Big Success had a teenage son, Small Success. The son, who otherwise had a spotless record, recently was arrested for shoplifting some small items from a grocery store. When he was arrested, Small Success had ample money in his wallet to pay for the items. He told the police that he had come into the store without the intent to steal. He said that he was tired of the pressure to live up to the many expectations placed on him because of his father's prominence and that, while in the store, he had a sudden whim to do something "bad." The items he took were of an insignificant monetary value. The city attorney decided not to prosecute out of respect for the senator and because the store was paid in full for the items.

You are the editor of the *Morning Glory*, the local newspaper. One of your reporters wants to write up this story focusing on the failure of celebrities and politicians to take the time to be good parents who teach their children right from wrong. Although you have no problem running stories about Senator Big Success, who is a public figure, you consider the fairness of putting such a public spotlight on the actions of his young son. In addition, by bringing up the city attorney's decision not to prosecute, the story might force the prosecution of Small Success, resulting in negative publicity and a blemish on his record. Do you let your reporter go ahead with the story or assign her to another project? Use the ethical model presented in Chapter 2 and reprinted on the inside front cover to develop your answer.

Introduction

Tort is a French word for "wrong." Society is interested in protecting its members' personal physical safety and in preventing property damage. Tort law provides remedies for acts that cause harm. Society also recognizes intangible interests in things, such as per-sonal privacy, family relations, reputation, and dignity. Tort law provides remedies for the invasion of these protected interests, too.

Tort law is a part of the civil law. Injured parties may file civil lawsuits in an attempt to seek compensation for their injuries. An act that is a tort also can be a crime. Thus, criminal law and tort law overlap. For example, Cal drives an automobile while under the influence of alcohol. He runs a red light and has an accident that wrecks a truck owned by your online business, Artiste Login Products, Inc. Your employee, Pat, was injured. Cal has committed a crime, driving under the influence of alcohol, and has committed a tort, negligent driving. You have to decide whether your online company will retain an attorney and sue Cal in a civil court. The local prosecuting attorney will decide whether to prosecute Cal for any criminal acts, such as driving under the influence of alcohol, running a red light, and reckless driving.

Some tort actions result solely in civil lawsuits with no criminal prosecution. The burden of proof in a criminal action is higher (beyond a reasonable doubt) than the burden of proof in a civil tort case (by a preponderance of the evidence). *Preponderance* means that the plaintiff presented the greater weight of the evidence, which was more convincing than that presented by the defendant. Thus, Cal might be found not guilty of a crime but may be found liable in a civil lawsuit for injuries to Pat and for the damage caused to the truck owned by your online company.

This chapter will examine those situations where tort law imposes liability on a person or business.

Types of Torts

Torts are divided traditionally into three categories. **Intentional torts**, as the name implies, are injuries caused by intentional acts. For example, when a movie star hits a photographer, he commits the intentional tort of assault and battery. **Negligence** consists of harm caused by careless acts or failure to perform a legal duty. Most automobile accidents are the result of negligence.

Strict liability requires the person causing the harm to compensate the injured party without regard to fault. Generally, this liability is imposed by law. A person who harbors wild animals is strictly liable for any harm they may cause. The following sections examine these three types of torts in more detail.

Intentional Torts

An intentional tort arises from an act that the defendant consciously performs. She either intends to harm another or knows with substantial certainty that injury to another could result. The intent to perform the act is this tort's distinguishing element. The actual nature of the damage ultimately caused is irrelevant in determining wrongdoer's intent.

For example, if Sean intentionally pushes Lil and she falls to the ground and breaks her arm, it does not matter that Sean never intended to break Lil's arm. Sean did intend to push Lil, and that in itself is a tortious act of battery. Sean is liable for the consequences, including injury to Lil's arm. If the push had been accidental, no intentional tort would exist.

Liability might be imposed for negligent conduct, however. Intentional torts are subdivided into two categories: wrongs against the person and wrongs against property. Further discussion of some specific intentional torts follows.

Wrongs against the Person

Intentional torts against a person include *assault, battery, false imprisonment, infliction of mental distress, invasion of privacy, defamation* (including *disparagement of goods, slander of title*, and *defamation by computer*), and *fraud* or *deceit*. If the person suffers an injury as a result of any of these torts, the term *personal injury*, or PI, applies.

Assault and/or Battery. An intentional act (that is not excused or allowed on grounds of self-defense or defense of others) that creates in another person a reasonable, imminent apprehension or fear of harm is an **assault**. If the harm results from physical contact and the victim experienced apprehension, either before or after the physical contact, **battery** occurs.

For example, Foster threatens to hit Heise with a baseball bat during an argument. The threat is an assault. Taking this example one step further, if Foster strikes Heise and she sees the strike coming, an assault and battery has occurred, because Heise has apprehension. On the other hand, assume Foster had not threatened Heise, but instead hits her with the baseball bat, rendering her unconscious. When she wakes up in the hospital, she has fear. A battery occurred because of the unlawful physical contact and the apprehension, even though the apprehension arose after the blow.

Physical injury does not have to occur. Receiving an unwelcome kiss or being escorted from a person's apartment with your arms pinned can constitute an assault, battery, or both.

False Imprisonment. **False imprisonment**, frequently associated with false arrest, is the intentional confinement or restraint of a person without justification and the interference with the person's ability to move about freely. Physical barriers, physical restraints, or threats of physical force can constitute intentional confinement. For false imprisonment to apply, it is essential that the person being restrained resist the restraint. A person is under no duty to risk personal harm in trying to escape, however.

Almost all states have adopted **merchant protection legislation** that allows a merchant to detain any suspected shoplifter, provided that reasonable cause for suspicion exists and that the detention is executed in a reasonable way. Merchants thus are given statutory protection from being sued successfully for false imprisonment. Because the loss to business from shoplifting is estimated to exceed $10 billion a year, this protection is important for businesses.

The following case first provides a discussion of whether an employer can be liable to an employee for false imprisonment. Second, the court discusses whether a business is protected under the merchant protection statute.

Case 8.1

Fermino v. Fedco, Inc.

Supreme Court of California, 1994

7 Cal. 4th 701, 872 P.2d 559, 30 Cal. Rptr. 2d 18

BACKGROUND AND FACTS Fermino was employed as a jewelry department sales-clerk at Fedco, Inc. The store's personnel manager summoned her to a windowless room and interrogated her about an alleged theft of $4.95.

The store's loss prevention manager and two security agents joined the personnel manager. One security agent told Fermino that a customer and an employee, who were waiting in the next room, had witnessed the theft. She was told that the interrogation could be handled in two ways: the "Fedco way" or the "system way." The "Fedco way" was to award points each time she denied her guilt. When she reached fourteen points, she would be handled the "system way," that is, handed over to the police. After each of Fermino's repeated and vehement denials, the security agent said "one point." The loss prevention manager "hurled profanities" and demanded that she confess.

Fermino's repeated requests to leave the room and to call her mother were denied. She was physically compelled to remain in the room for more than one hour. At one point she walked toward the door of the interrogation room in an attempt to leave. One security guard, however, threw up his hand and gestured her to stop. Finally, Fermino became hysterical and broke down in tears. At this point the guards admitted no one was waiting to testify against her. Finally they told her that they believed her and that she could leave.

Fermino filed a lawsuit for unspecified physical injuries, shock and injury to her nervous system, and intentional and negligent infliction of emotional distress. She claimed that the false imprisonment resulted from a method of interrogation that was approved company policy.

The trial court dismissed her lawsuit, and the appellate court affirmed the dismissal. The Supreme Court of California decided to hear the appeal. The court had to decide whether Fermino could sue Fedco in a civil action for the intentional tort of false imprisonment.

In making its decision, the court considers the merchant protection statute. This law requires the merchant to act in a reasonable way when dealing with a customer suspected of shoplifting. The court uses the merchant protection legislation as an analogy to determine if the employer acted in a reasonable manner when dealing with its employee. The court uses the term *compensation bargain* to mean "employment."

Justice MOSK

The crime of false imprisonment is defined by [the] Penal Code as the "unlawful violation of the personal liberty of another." The tort is identically defined. [T]he tort consists of the " 'nonconsensual, intentional confinement of a person, without lawful privilege, for an appreciable length of time, however, short.' " That length of time can be as brief as 15 minutes. . . .

The only mental state required to be shown to prove false imprisonment is the intent to confine, or to create a similar intrusion. Thus, the intent element of false imprisonment does not entail an intent or motive to cause harm; indeed false imprisonments often appear to arise from initially legitimate motives.

Merchants who detain individuals whom they have probable cause to believe are about to injure their property are privileged against a false imprisonment action. The detention itself must be carried out for a reasonable time and in a reasonable manner. Thus, this court upheld a 20-minute detention of a department store customer who store personnel had probable cause to suspect was in the process of stealing merchandise, and who was being held until the police arrived. This common law privilege has been codified [in the] Penal code: "A merchant may detain a person for a reasonable time for the purpose of conducting an investigation in a reasonable manner whenever the merchant has probable cause to believe the person to be detained is attempting to unlawfully take or has unlawfully taken merchandise from the merchant's premises." . . .

. . . .

We agree that all reasonable attempts to investigate employee theft, including employee interrogation, are a normal part of the employment relationship. It is also true that all such reasonable interrogation or voluntary confinement cannot be regarded as false imprisonment and is not actionable. . . .

. . . What is implicit in Fedco's position, then, is that there are certain "reasonable" false imprisonments, that may be considered a normal part of the employment relationship, distinguished from "unreasonable" false imprisonments that are either motivated by illegitimate ends or that employ disproportionate means. But a "reasonable" false imprisonment is oxymoronic. False imprisonment is, by definition, an unreasonable and indeed criminal confinement. . . . When an employer forcibly and criminally deprives an employee of her liberty, even as a means to otherwise legitimate ends, it steps outside its "proper role." . . .

. . . .

. . . We do not deny the right of an employer to reasonably detain an employee suspected of theft, and indeed to discharge an employee—consistent with the employee's contractual or other employment rights—if he or she refuses to cooperate with a reasonable investigation. But the question whether Fedco's actions were reasonable, justifiable, or privileged goes to the factual question whether its actions constituted false imprisonment—a question we cannot and do not resolve on the pleadings. Once it is determined, however, that a false imprisonment has indeed taken place, then such action cannot be said to be a normal aspect of the employment relationship, however legitimate its initial justification, any more than an assault on an employee can be brought within the scope of the exclusivity rule by claiming it was motivated by the need for employee discipline. We conclude therefore that false imprisonment committed by an employer against an employee is always outside the scope of compensation bargain.

. . . [W]e conclude that plaintiff has stated a cause of action for false imprisonment. [The] plaintiff here has pleaded that she was held against her will by her employer for an appreciable time under threat of force and threat of arrest for an apparently ill-founded reason.

DECISION AND REMEDY The court reversed the decisions of the two lower courts. The court held that an employee does have a right to sue the employer when she has been falsely imprisoned. False imprisonment, by California statute, is an unlawful violation of an individual's personal right. The court discussed that a merchant is protected by statute against false imprisonment claims if customers are restrained in a reasonable manner when the merchant believes that shoplifting has occurred.

Similarly, an employer may investigate employee theft by reasonable investigative methods or by voluntary confinement. In this case, Fedco had not used reasonable methods to investigate this case when Fermino was held under threat of force and threat of arrest. Because Fermino had not volunteered to be confined, her imprisonment became illegal.

CRITICAL THINKING: MANAGERIAL CONSIDERATION A merchant is allowed by statute to use reasonable restraint against a customer if he believes that a theft has occurred. Define the point at which a reasonable restraint becomes unreasonable.

Infliction of Mental Distress. People have a right to be free from imposed mental distress. The tort of **infliction of mental distress** is defined as a party's intentional act that amounts to extreme and outrageous conduct resulting in another person's severe emotional distress. For example, a creditor telephones Paul every hour during the night in an attempt to collect a debt. As a result, Paul suffers intense mental anxiety. The courts have found such acts by the creditor to be extreme and outrageous conduct that exceeds the bounds of decency accepted by society. The person committing these acts may be liable in a tort action. These acts also may be in violation of the Fair Debt Collection Practices Act, which is described in Chapter 14.

Invasion of Privacy. Closely allied to infliction of mental distress is the separate tort of the invasion of a person's privacy. A lawsuit based on **invasion of privacy** does not involve injury to a person's property or character but rather concerns an intentional invasion of a person's intangible right to be left alone. The use of two-way mirrors in women's fitting rooms that allow the store manager and others to observe women changing clothes has led to liability under this tort. The unauthorized commercial use of a person's picture is another example of invasion of privacy, as is publishing information about a person on the Internet without permission.

Defamation. **Defamation** occurs when someone makes false and malicious statements to others about another person or business. This tort, discussed in Chapter 5 under free speech, imposes a general duty on all people to refrain from making defamatory statements about others. Breaching this duty verbally is the tort of **slander**. Breaching it in writing is the tort of **libel**.

The basis for the tort of defamation is the publication of one or more statements that hold up an individual or business to contempt, ridicule, or hatred. Publication means that the defamatory statements are made to, or within the hearing of, people other than the defamed party.

In the case of a writing, the publication occurs when a third person reads a defamatory document without the consent of the person who is defamed. If Thompson writes Andrews a private letter accusing him of embezzling funds, that letter does not constitute libel unless someone reads it without the consent of Andrews. If Peters calls Gordon dishonest, unattractive, and incompetent when no one else is around, that act does not constitute slander. Because neither message was communicated to a third party, neither qualifies as defamation.

Disparagement of Goods, Slander of Title, and Defamation by Computer. These torts involve defamation of a business or its products. A false statement made about a business's product is a tort called **disparagement of goods**. An example of goods' disparagement would be a salesperson lying about a competitor's product.

Defaming the title (proof of ownership) that a business has to its property may prevent a business from selling the property. The tort that outlaws this is called **slander of title**.

Erroneous information from a computer about a business's credit standing or reputation can impair that business's ability to obtain credit. If the computer information's owner fails to correct erroneous information in a timely manner, the company may be liable to the victim. This tort is called **defamation by computer**. The company also is responsible under the Fair Credit Reporting Act, discussed in Chapter 14, for reporting correct information.

In recent times, libel actions have involved agricultural products. Many farmers and ranchers have convinced state legislatures to pass food-libel laws.[1] One provocative case involved Oprah Winfrey. Winfrey stated on national television that many cattle sold in the United States had the potential to cause "mad cow" disease. The Texas Beef Group brought an action against her. The appellate court held in her favor stating that she had a right of free speech. Other states, however, have similar laws. In Colorado, you commit a crime if you disparage even a lemon. The future of these statutes is still yet to be determined.

Defenses. A person who is sued for defamation may assert several defenses. First, truth is normally a complete defense against a defamation charge. For example, in the scenario given previously, let's say Thompson publishes his letter stating that Andrews was an embezzler. If Andrews had been convicted in court for embezzlement, truth would be Thompson's defense to any defamation lawsuit.

Second, under the defense of **privilege of immunity**, even if the statement were false, no action can be

---

[1] The Coalition for Free Speech posts a collection of agricultural libel laws at <http://www.cspinet.org/foodspeak/>.

LEGAL HIGHLIGHT

McHamburger v. McVeggies

McDonald's®, a corporation worth millions, sued Helen Steel and Dave Morris, vegetarian activists, for libel in a London court. Ms. Steel, who worked part time in a pub, and Mr. Morris, an unemployed postman, were among five activists sued in 1990. Three apologized, but Ms. Steel and Mr. Morris decided to fight.

It all began in 1985 when a group decided to expose the nutritional reality behind McDonald's products. They circulated leaflets, criticizing McDonald's practices, such as meat purchasing practices and employment practices. Undercover private investigators, hired by McDonald's, infiltrated the activist group. The corporate spies took notes of the meetings, befriended the activists, stole letters from the group, and determined where they lived. Later these investigators would testify for McDonald's.

Libel laws in England are very strict and differ from those in the United States. In the United States, a plaintiff who is a public official (like the president or a congressperson) or a public figure (such as an actress or a business) must prove that the defendant published a story with the knowledge that it was false or with a reckless disregard of the truth. This high standard makes libel a very difficult case to prove. In England, the defendant has the burden of proving the truth of her statements. Furthermore, although the poor in England have access to legal aid, public legal assistance is not available in libel cases.

The trial began on June 28, 1994, and ended on December 13, 1996, lasting 313 court days. The previous record for a libel trial was 101 days. More than 130 witnesses testified, generating 40,000 pages of documents and 20,000 pages of transcripts. Mr. Justice Rodger Bell of the High Court in the Royal Courts of Justice presided over the trial. Mr. Justice Bell did not allow a jury, ruling that the central issues were too complex and scientific for a jury to follow.

In a David and Goliath battle, Ms. Steel and Mr. Morris, both inexperienced in the courtroom, dressed casually, often wearing denim, while Mr. Richard Rampton, the attorney for McDonald's and a Queen's Counsel, dressed formally in his wig and robe. (To be a Queen's Counsel indicates that the attorney is among the top 10 percent of the legal profession in England.) Ms. Steel and Mr. Morris often prepared for the day's trial while riding the Underground (subway) and waited a week to obtain trial transcripts when the price decreased.

Judge Bell ruled in favor of McDonald's on most of the issues and granted a judgment of $98,000 against Ms. Steel and Mr. Morris. He did find that certain aspects of the leaflet were truthful. He found that McDonald's had paid lower wages and had sent workers home early to further lower their wages, had treated chickens cruelly, and had exploited children through advertising.

Estimates place the cost of the trial to McDonald's at $16 million dollars (the price of about 6.8 million Big Macs) and caused worldwide unfavorable publicity. As far as collecting the judgment against Ms. Steel and Mr. Morris, McDonald's announced that it did not intend to pursue collection procedures. After all, their joint income was less than $12,500 a year. The case resulted in international media coverage; a book, *McLiable: Burger Culture on Trial* (Macmillan, 1997); and a British television documentary. A World Wide Web (WWW) home page on the Internet contains a history along with documents.

And where is that leaflet that caused this great stir? It is accessible on the WWW, of course. Well, at least a shorter version is—in seven languages and as PDF files, of which two million were circulated in five years.

You can view the legal documents and other information on this case at <http://www.mcspotlight.org/case/index.html>. The verdict is located at <http://www.mcspotlight.org/case/trial/verdict/verdict0_sum.html>.

brought against the speaker or writer. The two types of privileged communications are *absolute* and *qualified*. In general, these privileges are granted if some important and overriding social value in sanctioning a person's conduct exists, even though the conduct may result in defamation.

Absolute privilege applies to judicial and legislative proceedings, but only when relevant to the activities of either governmental body. For example, statements made by an elected representative on the floor of Congress are absolutely privileged communications. These same statements, if made in a different arena, such as a newsletter or a press conference, are not privileged.

Qualified privilege is a common law concept based on the philosophy that a person's right to know or to speak is of equal importance to another person's right not to be defamed. For the communication to have a qualified privilege, the plaintiff must show that the privilege was abused in order to recover.

Examples of a qualified privilege are found in recommendation letters and in employee evaluations. Generally, if a person communicates in good faith and limits publication to those who have a legitimate interest in the communication, the statement falls within the qualified privilege.

Fraud or Deceit.
The tort of **fraud** or **deceit** involves (1) a misrepresentation of material facts, (2) the intent to deceive or the reckless disregard of the facts' truthfulness, (3) the knowledge that the facts are false, (4) the victim's justifiable reliance on these facts, and (5) damages. Sometimes failure to disclose material facts is a form of deceit.

For example, a homeowner knows that the roof has started to leak even though it is not evident. The house is for sale. The owner should inform any potential buyer of this latent (hidden) defect. If he fails to disclose this fact to a potential buyer, the seller may be held liable under the tort of fraud for any future damages that the buyer suffers as a result of the leaky roof.

Wrongs against Property

Intentional torts that are wrongs against property include *trespass*, *conversion*, and *nuisance*. In these types of torts, the property is said to be damaged.

Trespass to Land.
Any time a person enters onto another's land or causes something to enter onto the land or to remain there without consent or privilege, a tort of trespass to land has been committed. Once someone has been established as a trespasser, certain rights, duties, and privileges flow to both the owner and the trespasser. Some of these follow.

1. A trespasser is liable for any damage that she causes to the property.

2. A trespasser can be removed from the premises by use of nondeadly reasonable force without the property owner's being liable for assault, battery, or both.

3. The trespasser generally assumes the risks of the premises (that is, a trespasser cannot complain of personal injuries that occur as a result of the condition of the premises). This rule, however, does not permit the owner to lay traps. The owner may be required to post warnings on the property. Under the attractive nuisance doctrine, young children are exempt from assuming the risks of premises if the condition of the premises attracts them to it (such as a swimming pool or large sand piles on construction sites).

Trespass to Personal Property.
Trespass to personal property, such as an automobile, is similar to trespass to real property. In either type of trespass, a trespasser claims an intent to use the property rather than ownership interest.

A person's single act can result in two types of legal action. For example, a person takes an automobile without the intent to permanently keep it, but to drive to another city where eventually the car is abandoned. The trespasser did not intend to keep the automobile, but only to temporarily use it without the owner's permission. The trespasser can be charged with the crime of joy riding and may be civilly sued by the automobile owner for trespass to personal property.

Conversion.
Whenever personal property is taken from its rightful owner or possessor and placed in the service of another, the tort of **conversion** occurs. Conversion is the civil side of crimes related to stealing. A store clerk who steals merchandise from the store commits the crime of embezzlement and the tort of conversion at the same time. Of course, when conversion occurs, the lesser offense of trespass to personal property usually occurs as well.

LEGAL HIGHLIGHT

Secondary Smoke—Is It Battery?

Are smokers committing the tort of battery when they expose others to their cigarette, cigar, or pipe smoke? Battery requires the touching of another person against that person's will. Typical battery involves hitting or physically touching a victim. Does secondary (drifting) smoke constitute battery? That is the question that courts are deciding based on scientific evidence.

Drifting smoke is the smoke that floats to the non-smoker. The smoke is detected by the nose and is inhaled into the body. Once breathed in by the nose, the smoke travels through bronchi to the lungs. While the smoke is in the bronchi, it burns the cilia, the tiny hairs that act as filters in the bronchi. Finally, the smoke moves to the alveoli (air sacs in the lungs). From the alveoli, the absorbed smoke enters the nonsmoker's bloodstream. Inside the body, this absorbed smoke competes with oxygen; thus, the heart and lungs must work harder to carry sufficient oxygen to the cells.

Externally, drifting smoke can cause watery eyes, congested nasal passages, and excruciating headaches. In various studies the Environmental Protection Agency, the Centers for Disease Control and Prevention, and the National Institutes of Health have linked the inhalation of secondary smoke to lung cancer, allergies, and other ailments in nonsmokers.

Drifting smoke appears to make smoke-sensitive people ill. Courts in California, Ohio, and Georgia have found that secondary smoke satisfies the touching requirement for the tort of battery. Other states require that the smoker know that the nonsmoker is allergic to smoke or that the smoker deliberately aimed the smoke at another person for battery to occur. Will lawsuits be expanded so that anyone near a smoker may proceed with an action if the smoker continues smoking after being requested not to smoke?

If the initial taking of the property was unlawful, trespass has occurred. If the initial taking of the property was lawful, but the property, however, has been retained beyond the time period agreed to, then the retention of that property is conversion. Even if the initial taking of the property had been permitted by the owner, failure to return the property may be conversion. For example, you lend a friend the use of your car over the weekend. Two weeks later he has not yet returned the car. Although he initially possessed the car with your permission, he is now liable to you for conversion.

Nuisance. A person can commit a tort through the unreasonable use of his own property. A **nuisance** is an improper activity (that may involve the use of a person's own property) that interferes with another's enjoyment or use of his property. Nuisances can be either public or private. This topic is discussed in detail in Chapter 24.

A **public nuisance** disturbs or interferes with the public in general and is generally a crime. A **private nuisance** interferes with the property interest of a limited number of individuals and is a tort. Reasonable limitations on property use prevent the owner from unreasonably interfering with the health and comfort of neighbors or with their right to enjoy their own private property.

For example, Rick cannot keep chickens in his townhouse because this would constitute a nuisance, even if no city ordinances prohibited such activity. Lin cannot set up a speaker system in her backyard and play rock-and-roll or symphonic music at a volume that disturbs her neighbors. Lin's act also may be a crime (public nuisance) if, for instance, a city ordinance specifies that no sound exceeding 100 decibels shall be audible within 100 feet of another's property between 11 P.M. and 7 A.M.

Negligence

Intentional torts involve a particular mental state. In negligence, however, the perpetrator neither intends to bring about the consequences of the act nor believes that the consequences will occur. The perpetrator's conduct merely creates the risk of such consequences. Without the creation of a risk, negligence cannot occur. The risk, moreover, must be foreseeable in that a reasonable person would anticipate the risk and guard against it.

Many of the actions discussed in the section on intentional torts would constitute negligence if they were committed carelessly and without intent. For instance, carelessly bumping into someone who then falls and breaks an arm constitutes negligence. Likewise, carelessly (as opposed to intentionally) flooding another's land constitutes negligence. In a sense, negligence describes a way of committing a tort rather than constituting a distinct category of torts.

Negligence occurs when a person is injured or her property is damaged because someone else's conduct falls below the required duty of care. Negligence requires three elements: (1) breach (failure) of duty of care, (2) injury, and (3) causation. Various defenses may be available to a person accused of negligence.

Breach of Duty of Care

The first element of negligence, breach of duty of care, can be determined based on a two-part question:

1. Is there a duty of care?
2. Did the defendant's action breach (fail to live up to) that duty?

Tort law recognizes several standards for the duty of care, depending on the particular situation. First, the standard of care may be measured by an **objective standard of care**, one of reasonableness, known as the "reasonable person" standard. In determining if a tort has been committed, the courts ask. "How would a reasonable and prudent person have acted in the same or similar circumstances?"

The reasonable person standard is objective. Reasonableness does not necessarily describe the way in which a particular person would act; it describes society's judgment as reflected by a jury as to the way in which people should act in the same situation. If the reasonable person existed, he would be careful, conscientious, even-tempered, and honest. This hypothetical, reasonable person frequently is discussed in law.

Many times the standard of care is determined by the profession, industry, or business. Trade and professional organizations often determine the standard of care. The government may set the standard of care, such as when the government requires a recall of defective products.

Innkeepers and common carriers, such as motels and trucking firms, are held to a higher standard of care than that of reasonableness. For example, if your baggage is lost by an airline, you are able to recover damages up to an amount set by the government without proving negligence. If the passenger needs higher coverage than that, the passenger can purchase insurance coverage.

Excluding common carriers and innkeepers, the injured person must prove that the business did not act in a reasonable manner. In the following case, the court reviews the standard of care based on a reasonable and prudent business owner.

Case 8.2

Moultrie v. Consolidated Stores International Corporation

District Court of Appeal of Florida, First District, 2000
764 So. 2d 637

BACKGROUND AND FACTS Mrs. Moultrie and her two sons went to Big Lots Store #505, owned by the defendant Consolidated Stores International Corporation (Consolidated), to buy a vacuum cleaner. Mrs. Moultrie walked down an aisle of the store to the back wall, to an area where vacuum cleaners were displayed.

Mrs. Moultrie pointed to a vacuum cleaner she wanted her son to take down from the shelf. When her son reached up to get the vacuum cleaner, Mrs. Moultrie took a step backward to give him more room. As she did so, she tripped and fell on an empty wooden pallet that had been left in the aisle. The pallet was approximately six inches in height.

Mrs. Moultrie acknowledged that if she had looked to the right and left sides of the floor as she traversed the aisle of the store, she would have seen the pallet. Mrs.

Moultrie explained that when she enters any store, she assumes the aisles are clear and does not examine them for obstructions.

Consolidated filed a motion for summary judgment alleging that the pallet was an open and obvious condition and, due to the open and obvious nature of the pallet, she could not recover for her injuries. At the hearing conducted on the motion for summary judgment, Consolidated's counsel argued that a storekeeper is entitled to assume that a customer will perceive that which would be obvious to him upon the ordinary use of his senses.

Moultrie urged the pallet was not open and obvious, because "open and obvious" denotes knowledge of the existence of the condition or activity and an appreciation of the danger it involves. The trial court granted Consolidated's motion for summary final judgment, presumably persuaded that the pallet that resulted in Mrs. Moultrie's injury constituted an open and obvious condition. Consolidated is the appellant and Mrs. Moultrie is the appellee.

JOANOS, J.

. . . .

The well settled principles governing motions for summary judgment provide: "[t]o establish entitlement to a summary judgment, the moving party must demonstrate conclusively that no genuine issue exists as to any material fact, even after all reasonable inferences are drawn in favor of the party opposing the summary judgment." . . . On review of the trial court's grant of summary judgment, this court must resolve all doubts as to the existence of a genuine issue of material fact against the moving party. . . .

In actions involving premises liability, a "business invitee is one who is 'invited to enter or remain on land for a purpose directly or indirectly connected with business dealings with the possessor of the land.'" A business owner owes an invitee a duty—to use reasonable care in maintaining the premises in a reasonably safe condition and to give the plaintiff timely notice and warning of latent and concealed perils, known to the defendant or which by the exercise of due care should have been known to him, and which were not known by plaintiff or which by the exercise of due care could not have been known by him.

In this vein, an owner is entitled to assume the invitee will perceive that which would be obvious to the invitee through the normal use of his senses, and is not required to give the invitee notice or warning of an obvious danger.

Known or Obvious Dangers. A possessor of land is not liable to his invitees for physical harm caused to them by any activity or condition on the land whose danger is known or obvious to them, unless the possessor should anticipate the harm despite such knowledge or obviousness. In [a previous case] the supreme court instructed: "'In any case where the occupier [of land] as a reasonable person should anticipate an unreasonable risk of harm to the invitee notwithstanding his knowledge, warning, or the obvious nature of the condition, something more in the way of precautions may be required.'"

At the core of the duty element is the requirement that each defendant who creates a risk must exercise prudent foresight whenever others may be injured as a result of the risk. Thus, "duty exists as a matter of law and is not a factual question for the jury to decide." "As to duty, the proper inquiry for the reviewing court is whether the defendant's conduct created a foreseeable zone of risk, not whether the defendant could foresee the specific injury that actually occurred."

When we view all favorable inferences in favor of appellants, application of the foregoing principles to the record in this case shows that appellee created a foreseeable zone of risk by leaving an empty wooden pallet in the aisle of its store. The height of the pallet was such that it might not fall within the line of vision of adult invitees who entered the Big Lots Store to purchase items placed on counters and shelves. Further, the diagram sketched by appellant at the request of appellee's counsel shows the pallet was in a main aisle of the store, placed to the left side, rather than centered in the aisle. In these circumstances, we believe reasonable persons could differ as to whether the wooden pallet was open and obvious.

The cases cited by appellee involving uneven pavement, traffic bumps, and steps within business premises or residences, were decided in favor of the respective defendant on the ground that the conditions were a matter of common knowledge or every day life. Such is not the case here. Although appellee argued the pallet was "open and obvious," appellee has not asserted, nor could it do so, that it is customary or common practice for relatively large, empty wooden pallets to be placed in store aisles, with no elevated pennant or other type of warning device to alert customers or store employees of its presence.

. . . .

DECISION AND REMEDY The facts did not present a condition which was so open, obvious, and ordinary that it could be held as a matter of law that the pallet did not constitute a foreseeable risk of harm to individuals either patronizing or working in the store. Rather, there appeared to be material issues of fact as to whether the pallet was "open and obvious" and, if so, whether the defendant should have anticipated that, as a general rule, adult shoppers do not focus on the floor of a store aisle when moving toward merchandise they propose to buy. The motion for summary judgment was reversed and the case was returned to the trial court for a trial.

CRITICAL THINKING: PUBLIC POLICY Why should there be any legal difference when a person falls because of a crack in the sidewalk versus falling due to an item being left in an aisle?

A second standard of care may be imposed by a statute. Everyone driving a vehicle, for example, has a **statutory duty** not to proceed through an intersection when the traffic light is red. Reasonableness is not relevant under this standard of care.

For example, a person receives a traffic ticket for running a red light. He may tell the judge that at 3 A.M. he was rushing his pregnant wife to the hospital, that he stopped at the red light, that he looked both ways and determined that no cross traffic was coming from either direction, and that he then proceeded through the signal. The judge in his wisdom may dismiss the ticket. If the driver struck someone in the intersection, however, reasonableness as to his action could not suffice as a defense in the civil case. The statutory duty to stop at the red light is the standard of care. Because someone was harmed, he would be liable in civil court for the harm he caused, even though the judge does have the discretion to dismiss the ticket.

Injury

The plaintiff must suffer some loss, harm, wrong, or invasion of a protected interest to recover damages for a negligent act. The reason for the requirement of injury is obvious. Without an injury, the plaintiff lacks damages for which the defendant is required to compensate.

A defendant pays compensation in an effort to make the plaintiff "whole" again. Essentially, the purpose of the tort of negligence is to compensate the victim for legally recognized injuries resulting from the wrongdoer's acts. The intent is not to punish those acts.

Causation

Causation is the last element necessary to prove negligence. If a person breaches her duty of care, that breach must cause damage, and the person's negligent act must be linked closely with the damage for the person to be liable. The courts have limited the monetary amount of a person's liability if her negligent act is not wholly responsible for the resulting harm.

In deciding whether there is causation, the court must address two issues. First, was the act the cause in fact? Did the injury occur because of the defendant's act or would it have occurred anyway? Causation in fact usually can be determined by the "but for" test: but for the wrongful act, the injury would not have occurred.

If Carl carelessly leaves a campfire burning and the fire burns down the forest, causation in fact exists. The forest would not have burned but for Carl's negligent act. Therefore, Carl may be liable for the damages he caused.

If Carl carelessly leaves a campfire burning, but it burns out, and lightning causes a fire that burns down the forest, there is no causation in fact. In both examples, there is a wrongful act (Carl's leaving the campfire burning) and there is damage. In the second example, however, no causal connection exists between the wrongful act and the damage. Thus, Carl is not liable.

The second issue answers this question: Was the act the *proximate cause* of the injury? **Proximate cause** is the reasonable, causal relationship between the defendant's unreasonable conduct and the plaintiff's injury or damage. The purpose of proximate cause is to limit the defendant's liability as a result of his misconduct.

How far should a defendant's liability extend for a wrongful act that was a substantial factor in causing injury? For example, Carl's fire not only burns down the forest, but also sets off an explosion in a nearby ammunition plant that levels the entire plant, destroys the marshmallow factory located next door, and severely damages houses and businesses in the nearby community. Should Carl be liable to the ammunition plant owners, the marshmallow factory owners, and the people harmed in the nearby community?

The limitations on a person's liability are the issue when the courts consider proximate cause. Proximate cause is a question of public policy. The courts must ask whether the connection between an act and an injury is strong enough to justify imposing liability.

The courts use **foreseeability** as the test for proximate cause. If the act's consequences or the victims' harm were unforeseeable, no proximate cause exists. Carl was negligent, but for how much is he liable? How far along the chain of events could Carl reasonably foresee? In the next case, the court reviews the issue of foreseeability.

Case 8.3 — LANDMARK CASE

Palsgraf v. Long Island Railroad Company

Court of Appeals of New York, 1928
248 N.Y. 339, 162 N.E. 99, 1928 N.Y. LEXIS 1269, 59 A.L.R. 1253
http://www.wooster.edu/economics/js/law_archive/Palsgraf.html

BACKGROUND AND FACTS Palsgraf, plaintiff, was standing on a platform of the Long Island Railroad Co., defendant, after buying a ticket to go to Rockaway Beach. A train stopped at the station, bound for another place. Two men ran forward to catch it. One of the men reached the platform of the car without mishap, though the train was already moving. The other man, carrying a package, jumped aboard the car, but seemed unsteady, as if about to fall. A guard on the car, who had held the door open, reached forward to help him in, and another guard on the platform pushed him from behind.

He dropped the package and it fell to the rails. It was a small-sized package, about fifteen inches long, and was covered by a newspaper. In fact it contained fireworks, but there was nothing in its appearance to give notice of its contents. The fireworks exploded when they fell. The shock of the explosion toppled some scales at the other end of the platform, many feet away. The scales struck the plaintiff, causing injuries.

Judge CARDOZO, Ch.

. . . .

The conduct of the defendant's guard, if a wrong in its relation to the holder of the package, was not a wrong in its relation to the plaintiff, standing far away. Relatively to her it was not negligence at all. Nothing in the situation gave notice that the falling package had in it the potency of peril to persons thus removed. Negligence is not actionable unless it involves the invasion of a legally protected interest, the violation of a right. . . . "Negligence is the absence of care, according to the circumstances." . . .

A different conclusion will involve us, and swiftly too, in a maze of contradictions. A guard stumbles over a package which has been left upon a platform. It seems to be a bundle of newspapers. It turns out to be a can of dynamite. To the eye of ordinary vigilance, the bundle is abandoned waste, which may be kicked or trod on with impunity. Is a passenger at the other end of the platform protected by the law against the unsuspected hazard concealed beneath the waste? If not, is the result to be any different, so far as the distant passenger is concerned, when the guard stumbles over a valise which a truckman or a porter has left upon the walk? . . .

. . . The range of reasonable apprehension is at times a question for the court, and at times, if varying inferences are possible, a question for the jury. Here, by concession, there was nothing in the situation to suggest to the most cautious mind that the parcel wrapped in newspaper would spread wreckage through the station. If the guard had thrown it down knowingly and willfully, he would not have threatened the plaintiff's safety, so far as appearances could warn him. His conduct would not have involved, even then, an unreasonable probability of invasion of her bodily security. Liability can be no greater where the act is inadvertent.

Negligence, like risk, is thus a term of relation. Negligence in the abstract, apart from things related, is surely not a tort, if indeed it is understandable at all. Negligence is not a tort unless it results in the commission of a wrong, and the commission of a wrong imports the violation of a right, in this case, we are told, the right to be protected against interference with one's bodily security. But bodily security is protected, not against all forms of interference or aggression, but only against some. One who seeks redress at law does not make out a cause of action by showing without more that there has been damage to his person. If the harm was not willful, he must show that the act as to him had possibilities of danger so many and apparent as to entitle him to be protected against the doing of it though the harm was unintended. . . .

The law of causation, remote or proximate, is thus foreign to the case before us. The question of liability is always anterior to the question of the measure of the consequences that go with liability. If there is no tort to be redressed, there is no occasion to consider what damage might be recovered if there were a finding of a tort. We may assume, without deciding, that negligence, not at large or in the abstract, but in relation to the plaintiff, would entail liability for any and all consequences, however novel or extraordinary. There is room for argument that a distinction is to be drawn according to the diversity of interests invaded by the act, as where conduct negligent in that it threatens an insignificant invasion of an interest in property results in an unforseeable invasion of an interest of another order, as, e.g., one of bodily security. Perhaps other distinctions may be necessary. We do not go into the question now. The consequences to be followed must first be rooted in a wrong. . . . .

DECISION AND REMEDY The Court found that the plaintiff in a legal action for negligence must show that the act as to that person had possibilities of danger so many and apparent as to entitle him to be protected against the harm. In other words, the damages or injuries must have been foreseen when there was a breach of duty of reasonable care owed to the plaintiff.

CRITICAL THINKING: PUBLIC POLICY Why does the law require that damages must be foreseeable when there is a breach of reasonable care by one person to another? Why should a person who causes a loss not be liable for the full damages that may result?

Res Ipsa Loquitur

Some types of accidents occur only when someone is negligent. For example, you are walking on a sidewalk next to a building that is under construction. Pedestrians are allowed to walk there. Suddenly, a hammer falls from the building and strikes you on the shoulder and breaks several of your bones. This accident normally occurs only as a result of someone's negligence. But you have no idea who lost the hammer or why it fell from the building.

The doctrine of ***res ipsa loquitur*** (the thing speaks for itself) is used in these types of cases. This doctrine applies under the following conditions:

1. The event that caused the damage must not occur in the absence of negligence.
2. The conduct of the plaintiff or any other third party could not have caused the event.
3. The defendant owes the plaintiff a duty of reasonable care.

In the case just mentioned, the event of the hammer falling happens only as a result of someone's negligence. Neither you nor any other third party caused the hammer to fall. The construction company owed a duty of reasonable care to protect the pedestrians in the street below from harm. The area where you walked should have been covered. Additionally, the hammer should not have been in a position where it could fall to the street. Instead, it should have been anchored by a cord so that it could not have fallen.

The plaintiff cannot prove negligent conduct by the defendant because the plaintiff lacks access to all the information. Instead of trying to prove negligence, the plaintiff can prove the elements of *res ipsa loquitur*. The burden of proof shifts to the defendant to prove itself not negligent. In this case, the defendant may try to prove that an act of God caused a violent wind to rip the hammer from its secured place, causing it to fall to the street.

Defenses to Negligence

Defenses to negligence are (1) *superseding or intervening forces,* (2) *assumption of risk,* and (3) *contributory negligence* and (4) *comparative negligence.* We will look at each of these defenses.

A superseding or intervening force may break the causal connection between a wrongful act and injury to another. If so, it cancels the wrongful act. For example, Jed takes his automobile to a mechanic to repair his brakes. After repairing the brakes and replacing the tires, the mechanic fails to tighten bolts. Jed is driving along when he hears a terrible rattle coming from the automobile. As he is stopping his car along the shoulder of the freeway, the wheel comes off. Just then a drunk driver hits the car, injuring Jed. The drunk driver is an intervening force and may break the connection between the mechanic's negligent act and the damage to Jed and his automobile that resulted from the accident.

A plaintiff who voluntarily enters into a risky situation, knowing the risk involved, is barred from legal recovery. This defense is called **assumption of risk**. For example, a driver who enters an officially sanctioned automobile race accepts the risk of being killed or injured in a crash. The driver has assumed the risk of injury. Knowledge of the risk and voluntary assumption of that risk are the two requirements for this defense that disallow any recovery.

All individuals are expected to exercise a reasonable degree of care in looking out for themselves. In some jurisdictions, an injured person who has failed to exercise such care over herself is prevented from recovery for injury resulting from negligence. The defense of

LEGAL HIGHLIGHT

McDonald's Hot Coffee Case

Early one cold February morning in 1992, Mrs. Liebeck, age seventy-nine, and her grandson went to the drive-through window at the local McDonald's® where she ordered coffee. She rarely went to a fast-food restaurant; thus, this was a new experience for her. Her grandson parked the car so that she could add cream and sugar to her coffee. She placed the styrofoam cup between her knees to remove the plastic lid. When she pulled up on the plastic lid, the hot coffee spilled into her lap.

The sweatpants she was wearing held the hot coffee next to her skin. She suffered third-degree burns (a burn that goes completely through the skin) over 6 percent of her body, including her inner thighs, buttocks, and groin areas. She was hospitalized for eight days where she endured skin grafting and other medical treatments.

She sought to settle the case for $20,000, but McDonald's refused, so she filed a lawsuit. During discovery, McDonald's revealed that more than 700 claims had been filed by people who had been burned between 1982 and 1992. Some of them had suffered third-degree burns, similar to Mrs. Liebeck's burns.

McDonald's served its coffee between 180 and 190 degrees Fahrenheit, approximately 20 degrees higher than the industry standard. The McDonald's quality assurance manager testified that a burn hazard exists with any food or liquid above 140 degrees. He also admitted that coffee served at 180 degrees or more was unconsumable since it would burn the mouth and throat.

Experts for Mrs. Liebeck testified that liquids above 180 degrees will produce third-degree burns in two to seven seconds. If a 155-degree liquid were spilled, the extent of the resulting burn would be decreased significantly. In other words, Mrs. Liebeck would have suffered some burning if the coffee had been 155 degrees, but she would have avoided the serious third-degree burns.

McDonald's argued that many buyers intended to drink the coffee at work or home, even though its own customer survey indicated that buyers intended to drink the coffee while driving. McDonald's asserted that customers know that coffee is hot, but admitted in court that most did not know that they could suffer third-degree burns. The company also admitted that the warning statement "Hot" printed on the cup actually served as a reminder and not a warning that third-degree burns could result, since the customers were not informed of the hazard of serious burning.

In an on-camera interview after the verdict, one juror stated that when she was selected to hear the case, she thought the case was silly, but agreed to keep an open mind. She changed her mind after she heard the testimony of the various witnesses. The jury awarded Mrs. Liebeck $200,000 in compensatory damages, but reduced it to $160,000 because the jury found her to be 20 percent at fault for the spill. The jury also awarded her $2.7 million in punitive damages, which equals about two days of McDonald's coffee sales. The court later reduced the punitive award to $480,000 (three times the compensatory damages), but stated that McDonald's conduct was reckless, callous, and willful.

contributory negligence is available when both parties have been negligent and their combined negligence has contributed to cause the injury. When the plaintiff sues a defendant for the tort of negligence to recover damages, the defendant can assert that the plaintiff was contributorily negligent. When the defendant proves that the plaintiff also contributed to the accident by being negligent, the plaintiff will not be allowed to recover damages from the defendant.

The modern legal trend is moving away from the assumption of risk and contributory negligence defenses. Instead of allowing these defenses to completely prevent a plaintiff from recovering in a negligence lawsuit, an increasing number of states allow recovery based on the doctrine of **comparative negligence**. This doctrine enables computation of both the plaintiff's and the defendant's negligence. The plaintiff's damages are reduced by a percentage that represents the degree of his contributing fault. In some states, comparative negligence is used to reduce damages when the assumption-of-risk doctrine applies.

For example, Mario is driving his automobile. Although it is equipped with safety belts, he is not wearing his. Mario approaches an intersection with a green light. Peter, approaching in his car from the opposite direction, turns left in front of Mario's automobile. The cars collide, and Mario is thrown from his automobile and severely injured.

Subsequently, Mario files a lawsuit against Peter alleging negligence. Peter defends by using the comparative negligence defense. Through expert witnesses, Peter shows the jury that Mario's nonuse of his seat belt is a factor that the jury may use to reduce Mario's claim to damages. Mario may not recover damages for the full extent of his injuries. His failure to wear a safety belt was an act of negligence that contributed to the extent of his injuries. Data demonstrate that motorists suffer fewer and less severe injuries from accidents when they wear seat belts.

Strict Liability

The final category of torts is called strict liability, or liability without fault. Negligent torts involve an act that departs from a standard of care and causes an injury. Under the doctrine of strict liability, liability for injury is imposed for reasons other than fault.

When a person engages in abnormally dangerous activities, that person will be liable under strict liability if any harm occurs to others. An abnormally dangerous activity has three characteristics:

1. The activity involves potentially serious harm to persons or to property.
2. The activity involves a high degree of risk that cannot be guarded against completely by exercising reasonable care.
3. The activity is not performed commonly in the community.

Strict liability is applied because of the activity's extreme risk. Although an activity, such as blasting with dynamite, is performed with all reasonable care, innocent people still risk injury; thus, unless a person voluntarily and with knowledge enters a posted work site in which blasting work is being carried out, the dynamiter is liable for any damage to property or injury to a person caused by the blasting.

Because of the risk of harm, public policy requires that the person engaged in the dangerous activity be held liable for injuries caused by the activity. Responsibility is imposed because of the activity's nature, not because any fault exists. It is reasonable to require the person engaged in the activity to carry insurance or otherwise to be prepared to compensate anyone who suffers harm.

Applications of the strict liability principle are found in workers' compensation acts and in the area of product liability. Product liability is discussed in Chapter 11. In workers' compensation and product liability, either the employer or the manufacturer bears the liability as a matter of public policy. Such liability is based on two factors:

1. The employer and manufacturer are better able to bear the cost of injury than the injured person because they can spread it out to society through an increase in the cost of goods and services. For example, a toy manufacturer normally would sell a toy to a million customers for $20. The price can be raised to $21 (an increase of 5 percent) in order to pay for the liability claims ($1 million) for injuries to customers.
2. The employer and manufacturer profit from their activities and, therefore, as a matter of public policy, should bear the cost of injury as an operating expense.

Specific Torts Related to Business

The following torts have a direct application to the business environment:

1. Wrongful interference with a contractual or business relationship,
2. Infringement of trademarks, trade names, patents, and copyrights, and
3. Theft of trade secrets.

Wrongful Interference with a Contractual or Business Relationship

In an **intentional interference with a contractual or business relationship** case, the plaintiff must prove

LEGAL HIGHLIGHT
Mass Torts

The media often talk about mass torts. In a mass tort, an act has harmed a number of plaintiffs, with the number sometimes in the hundreds or even thousands.

A specific mass tort often gives rise to a class-action lawsuit. In this type of lawsuit, a large number of people each have a claim against the same defendant arising out of the same wrongful act allegedly committed by the defendant. In a class-action suit, the judge allows one or more plaintiffs to represent the class in a lawsuit against one or more defendants. Once a court has certified a class-action suit, the eventual case disposition binds all the parties. Some examples of class-action suits involving mass disasters include the following cases.

In 1981, the skywalks in the Hyatt Regency Hotel in Kansas City collapsed, killing more than 100 people and injuring hundreds more. The federal court certified two class-action suits. The claims were eventually settled.

A. H. Robins manufactured the Dalkon Shield, an intrauterine device (IUD), from 1971 to 1974. Between 1974 and 1986, more than 12,000 women filed damage suits. Robins went into bankruptcy court in 1986. More than 130,000 claims eventually were filed with the bankruptcy court against Robins.

In 1980, a fire swept through the lobby of the MGM Grand Hotel in Las Vegas, Nevada, killing 84 hotel guests and injuring more than 500. In addition to helicopters from the Las Vegas area, helicopters from a U.S. Air Force reserve unit located in Phoenix, Arizona, responded. The final settlement was in excess of $205 million.

In 1992, Pfizer, Inc., established a $500-million settlement plan to compensate 55,000 people or their estates who received defective heart valves. The valves had a history of fracturing, resulting in patients' trips to emergency rooms. Some people died as a result of the fracturing.

Businesses should monitor their activities to prevent or lessen these catastrophic events. It is cheaper to have a risk management program than to pay substantial damages.

For more information about mass torts you may want to visit the Rand Corporation web site covering this area of interest. It may be found at <http://www.rand.org/publications/RB/RB9021/RB9021.word.html>.

---

that the defendant intentionally induced the breach of a valid contractual or business relationship, not merely that the defendant reaped the benefits of the broken relationship. For example, Alicia has a one-year contract to deliver to Eat-Rite Restaurants all the doughnuts Eat-Rite requires for its breakfast menu. Frank's Doughnut Hole had unsuccessfully bid for the contract earlier. Frank's offers Eat-Rite a special price, much lower than Alicia's, if Eat-Rite will change suppliers immediately. Frank's further offers to pay for any costs Eat-Rite incurs in making the change. Eat-Rite breaks its contract with Alicia.

Based on this scenario, Frank's will be liable for wrongful interference with a contractual relationship. Suppose, however, that Frank's merely advertises a special price and further states that it will beat any valid price offered by a competitor. Eat-Rite reads the advertisement, breaks its contract with Alicia, and con-

tracts with Frank's Doughnut Hole. Although Frank's will reap the benefits of Eat-Rite's breach of contract with Alicia, Frank's will not be liable for the tort of wrongful interference with a contractual relationship.

The best known case of wrongful interference is *Texaco v. Pennzoil*.[2] The Getty family wanted to sell its business, Getty Oil Company. After negotiations, the chief executive officer (CEO) of Pennzoil reached an oral agreement with the representatives of Getty Oil for the two companies to merge. Both sides shook hands. Even though this contract involved millions of dollars, the law did not require this type of contract to be in writing to be enforced in court. The CEO for Pennzoil flew to New York that evening. The next day he heard that Texaco had purchased Getty Oil.

[2] 1729 S.W.2d 768 (Tex. Ct. App. 1987).

Pennzoil sued Texaco for wrongful interference with Pennzoil's contract with Getty Oil. The trial jury found that Texaco had wrongfully interfered with the planned merger (the contract) between Pennzoil and Getty Oil Company. The jury found that the three elements required for a wrongful interference with a contractual relationship were present. These requirements follow:

1. A valid contract existed between Pennzoil and Getty.

2. Texaco knew that this contract existed.

3. Texaco intentionally induced the breach of the contract by Getty, resulting in an economic or pecuniary gain.

The trial judgment was the largest in U.S. history, $7.53 billion in actual damages and $3 billion in punitive damages.[3]

Infringement of Trademarks, Trade Names, Patents, and Copyrights

A **trademark** is a distinctive mark, motto, device, or implement that a manufacturer stamps, prints, or otherwise affixes to its goods. For example, Corel® WordPerfect®, a software word-processing program, is a registered trademark of Corel Corporation. The trademark identifies and vouches for the origin of goods on the market.

Trademarks are filed with the U.S. Patent and Trademark Office.[4] Trademarks may be registered prior to use or after the trademark has been used. Legal protection is afforded to businesses that have made the effort and spent the time and money to develop a trademark. Clearly, if a person uses another's trademark, consumers will be misled into believing that the goods are genuine instead of what they really are—counterfeit goods. The law seeks to avoid this kind of confusion.

A **service mark** is similar to a trademark, but is used by the service industry to distinguish the services of one business from those of another. For example, each airline has a particular mark or symbol associated with its name. Titles or character names used in radio and television frequently are registered as service marks.

An example of a service mark is Price Waterhouse's Mind & Muscle℠.

Once a trademark or service mark has been registered with the federal government, the registering firm is entitled to its exclusive use for marketing purposes. Whenever another intentionally or unintentionally copies a trademark or service mark to a substantial degree or uses it in its entirety, the trademark or service mark has been infringed. The trademark need not be registered with the government in order to be granted protection from the tort of trademark infringement. Registration does furnish proof of the date of inception of its use, however.

A **patent** is a government grant that conveys and secures to an inventor the exclusive right to make, use, and sell an invention for twenty years. Patents for a lesser period are given for designs, as opposed to inventions. For either a regular patent or a design patent, the applicant must demonstrate to the satisfaction of the U.S. Patent Office that the invention, discovery, or design is genuine, novel, useful, and not obvious in light of the technology of the time. A patent holder provides notice to all that an article or design is patented by placing on it the word Patent or the abbreviation Pat. plus the patent number.

If a firm uses a device that is substantially similar to someone else's patented device, the tort of patent infringement exists. Patent infringement may exist even though only some features or parts of an invention are copied.[5]

A **copyright** is a right granted by statute to the author or originator of literary or artistic productions and computer programs. Works created after January 1, 1978, automatically receive statutory copyright protection for the life of the author plus seventy years. An idea, however, cannot possibly be copyrighted. What is copyrightable is the particular way in which an idea is expressed.

Whenever the form of expression of an idea is copied, an infringement of copyright has occurred. The infringement neither has to be exactly the same as the original nor must the original be reproduced in its entirety. If a substantial part of the original is reproduced, a copyright infringement exists. Limited copying is permitted under the "fair use" doctrine. The following case shows how the fair use doctrine has been applied in the music field.

---

[3] The case was settled in 1988 for $3 billion. On the day of the payment, Texaco completed its reorganization and emerged from twelve months of bankruptcy proceedings.

[4] The U.S. Patent and Trademark Office's web page is <http://www.uspto.gov>.

[5] Patents are used in international business. The status of European patents is available at the European Patent Office at <http://www.european-patent-office.org/>.

Case 8.4

Campbell v. Acuff-Rose Music, Inc.

Supreme Court of the United States, 1994
510 U.S. 569, 114 S. Ct. 1164, 127 L. Ed. 2d 500
http://supct.law.cornell.edu /supct/html/92-1292.ZO.html

BACKGROUND AND FACTS Roy Orbison and William Dees coauthored "Oh, Pretty Woman" and assigned their rights in the song to Acuff-Rose Music, Inc., in 1964. Acuff-Rose copyrighted the song in that same year.

Luther R. Campbell, Christopher Wongwon, Mark Ross, and David Hobbs are known collectively as 2 Live Crew, a popular rap music group. In 1989, Campbell wrote a song entitled "Pretty Woman," which he intended, based on its comical lyrics, to satirize the original work. On July 5, 1989, 2 Live Crew's manager wrote to Gary Teifer of Opryland U.S.A., Inc., and Acuff-Rose, informing him that 2 Live Crew intended to parody "Oh, Pretty Woman." Full credit would be given to Orbison and Dees as owners and authors. Acuff-Rose would be paid the rate required by statute for the song's use. Teifer responded on July 17, denying the license because "we cannot permit the use of a parody of 'Oh, Pretty Woman.'"

On July 15, two days before Teifer's letter, 2 Live Crew released its version of "Pretty Woman" on record albums, tapes, and compact discs, all entitled *As Clean As They Wanna Be*. Both the compact disc cover and the compact disc itself acknowledged Orbison and Dees as the authors of "Oh, Pretty Woman" and Acuff-Rose as the publisher.

Almost a year later, after nearly a quarter of a million copies of the recording had been sold, Acuff-Rose sued 2 Live Crew and their record company, Luke Skywalker Records, for copyright infringement, among other allegations. Acuff-Rose contended that the lyrics of "Oh, Pretty Woman" as sung by 2 Live Crew "are not consistent with good taste or would disparage the future value of the copyright."

Moving for summary judgment, 2 Live Crew argued that "Pretty Woman" was a parody that constitutes fair use under the Copyright Act. The district court granted the summary judgment, which was appealed. The court of appeals reversed the action of the district court and found that the rap group's parody was not fair use of a copyrighted song. Campbell filed a writ of *certiorari* with the Supreme Court of the United States. The writ was granted.

Justice SOUTER delivered the opinion for a unanimous Court.

. . . .

It is uncontested here that 2 Live Crew's song would be an infringement of Acuff-Rose's rights in "Oh, Pretty Woman," under the Copyright Act of 1976, but for a finding of fair use through parody. . . .

The germ of parody lies in the definition of the Greek *parodeia*, . . . as "a song sung alongside another." Modern dictionaries accordingly describe a parody as a "literary or artistic work that imitates the characteristic style of an author or a work for comic effect or ridicule," or as a "composition in prose or verse in which the characteristic turns of thought and phrase in an author or class of authors are imitated in such a way as to make them appear ridiculous." For the purposes of copyright law, the nub of the definitions, and the heart of any parodist's claim to quote from existing material, is the use of some elements of a prior author's composition to create a new one that, at least in part, comments on that author's works. If, on the contrary, the commentary has no critical bearing on the substance or style of the original composition, which the alleged infringer merely uses to get attention or to avoid the drudgery in working up something fresh, the claim to fairness in borrowing from another's work diminishes accordingly (if it does not vanish), and other factors, like the extent of its commerciality, loom larger. Parody needs to mimic an original to make its point, and so has some claim to use the creation of its victim's (or collective victims') imagination, whereas satire can stand on its own two feet and so requires justification for the very act of borrowing.

. . . .

While we might not assign a high rank to the parodic element here, we think it fair to say that 2 Live Crew's song reasonably could be perceived as commenting on the original or criticizing it, to some degree. 2 Live Crew juxtaposes the romantic musings of a man whose fantasy comes true, with degrading taunts, a bawdy demand for sex, and a sigh of relief from paternal responsibility. The later words can be taken as a comment on the naivete of the original of an earlier day, as a rejection of its sentiment that ignores the ugliness of street life and the debasement that it signifies. It is this joinder of reference and ridicule that marks off the author's choice of parody from the other types of comment and criticism that traditionally have had a claim to fair use protection as transformative works.

. . . .

It was error for the Court of Appeals to conclude that the commercial nature of 2 Live Crew's parody of "Oh, Pretty Woman" rendered it presumptively unfair. No such evidentiary presumption is available to address either the first factor, the character and purpose of the use, or the fourth, market harm, in determining whether a transformative use, such as parody, is a fair one. The court also erred in holding that 2 Live Crew had necessarily copied excessively from the Orbison original, considering the parodic purpose of the use. We therefore reverse the judgment of the Court of Appeals and remand for further proceedings consistent with this opinion.

Appendix A to the Opinion of the Court

"Oh, Pretty Woman" by Roy Orbison and William Dees
Pretty Woman, walking down the street,
Pretty Woman, the kind I like to meet,
Pretty Woman, I don't believe you, you're not the truth,
No one could look as good as you
Mercy
Pretty Woman, won't you pardon me,
Pretty Woman, I couldn't help but see,
Pretty Woman, that you look lovely as can be
Are you lonely just like me?
Pretty Woman, stop a while,
Pretty Woman, talk a while,
Pretty Woman give your smile to me
Pretty Woman, yeah, yeah, yeah
Pretty Woman, look my way,
Pretty Woman, say you'd stay with me
Cause I need you, I'll treat you right
Come to me baby, Be mine tonight
Pretty Woman, don't walk on by,
Pretty Woman, don't make me cry,
Pretty Woman, don't walk away,
Hey, O.K.
If that's the way it must be, O.K.
I guess I'll go on home, it's late
There'll be tomorrow night, but wait!
What do I see

Is she walking back to me?
Yeah, she's walking back to me!
Oh, Pretty Woman.

Appendix B to the Opinion of the Court

"Pretty Woman" as Recorded by 2 Live Crew
Pretty woman walkin' down the street
Pretty woman girl you look so sweet
Pretty woman you bring me down to that knee
Pretty woman you make me wanna beg please
Oh, pretty woman
Big hairy woman you need to shave that stuff
Big hairy woman you know I bet it's tough
Big hairy woman all that hair it ain't legit
'Cause you look like 'Cousin It'
Big hairy woman
Bald headed woman girl your hair won't grow
Bald headed woman you got a teeny weeny afro
Bald headed woman you know your hair could look nice
Bald headed woman first you got to roll it with rice
Bald headed woman here, let me get this hunk of biz for ya
Ya know what I'm saying you look better than rice a roni
Oh bald headed woman
Big hairy woman come on in
And don't forget your bald headed friend
Hey pretty woman let the boys
Jump in
Two timin' woman girl you know you ain't right
Two timin' woman you's out with my boy last night
Two timin' woman that takes a load off my mind
Two timin' woman now I know the baby ain't mine
Oh, two timin' woman
Oh pretty woman

DECISION AND REMEDY 2 Live Crew's "Pretty Woman" was an infringement on the copyright of the original and was a violation of the copyright laws unless the song was a parody under the fair use exception. The Supreme Court found that "Pretty Woman" was a parody. The Court remanded the case to be heard by the district court as to whether there is a threat of harm to the Acuff-Rose market for "Oh, Pretty Woman" by the parody version sold by 2 Live Crew.

Amici curiae (friends-of-the-court) briefs were filed in this case. People are allowed by the court to file *amici curiae* briefs to provide the court information, even though they are not party to the lawsuit. In this case, the entertainment industry split between the two sides. Dolly Parton, Michael Jackson, and the Nashville Songwriters' Association supported Acuff-Rose's position. On the other side, *Mad* magazine, the Capitol Steps, and television shows, such as *Comedy Central*, *Saturday Night Live*, and *Monty Python*, sided with 2 Live Crew.

CRITICAL THINKING: PREVENTIVE LAW Plagiarism is the unauthorized use of another's work and presenting it as one's own work. Discuss the difference between a parody and plagiarism.

Theft of Trade Secrets

Those processes or items of information that are neither patented nor patentable are nevertheless protected by law against a competitor's appropriation. Businesses generally protect their trade secrets by having all employees who use the process or information agree in their contracts never to divulge the trade secret. If a salesperson tries to solicit the company's customers for noncompany business or if an employee copies the employer's unique method of manufacture, she has appropriated a trade secret and also has broken a contract—two separate wrongs.

When a thief steals confidential data, his crime is also a tort called **theft of trade secrets**. This theft occurs when a business, for instance, wrongfully taps into a competitor's computer. The victim can sue the thief in a civil court for damages.

CyberLaw

Cyber Liability

Buying and selling on the Internet is now a part of daily business. In addition to the everyday risks businesses face, however, doing business on the Internet presents new risks. Business losses are incurred as the result of viruses, hackers, power outages, and electronic problems. If a business's web page is not available, the business cannot place orders or receive orders and can suffer additional losses.

Businesses usually keep their records on a computer, thus, they need to be prepared for computer crashes during which data could be lost. All businesses need to back up their data frequently. Without the data, businesses cannot file the mandatory government reports with the various governmental agencies, pay current bills, or collect on the accounts receivable.

Businesses need to protect confidential information collected by their customers. Liability may result if the business makes an unauthorized disclosure of a customer's private information to third parties. Often e-businesses will post their privacy statements on their web page to notify customers that any information collected will be placed in a database. As such, the database is an asset that may be sold. If the e-business has informed its customers, the e-business will not have liability unless a statute requires the e-business to keep specific information confidential.

Defamation suits can be filed as a result of postings of untruthful statements in e-mails, web sites, chat rooms, or bulletin boards. Many businesses have guidelines to prevent defamation lawsuits.

Many insurance companies exclude coverage for cyber liability. If a business needs coverage, it must purchase specific coverage to cover cyber losses. Several insurance companies offer broad coverage for any potential loss from cyberspace while other companies offer limited coverage. When a company has a web business, it needs to consider purchasing a business interruption policy or lost income policy.

Damages

People who have been harmed may choose to file a lawsuit against the person who caused the damages. The following sections review the different types of damages that may be sought.

Damages for Intentional Tort

An intentional tort occurs when a person intentionally harms another. In a previous example, if Greene deliberately hits Levy's car intending to harm her, Levy can sue for compensatory damages and for pain and suffering, but also for **punitive damages**.

Punitive damages are quasi-criminal in nature. Many intentional torts are also crimes. The criminal system lacks the resources to process effectively all of these types of crimes, so most states allow the plaintiff to seek punitive damages in a civil lawsuit. Instead of being based on the amount of harm the plaintiff has endured, these damages are based on the defendant's worth and the amount of wrongful conduct. As the name implies, punitive damages are intended to punish the defendant for his intentional tort and to prevent others from committing a similar act.

The question arises as to whether the amount of punitive damages should be related to the type of intentional act committed. The United States Supreme Court answered this question in the following case.

Case 8.5

BMW of North America, Inc. v. Gore

Supreme Court of the United States, 1996

517 U.S. 559, 116 S. Ct. 1589, 134 L. Ed. 2d 809

http://supct.law.cornell.edu /supct/html/94-896.ZS.html

BACKGROUND AND FACTS In 1983, BMW of North America, Inc. (BMW) had a nationwide policy to repair and sell as new the cars that were damaged in the course of manufacture or transportation. The dealers were advised that repairs had been made only when repair costs exceeded 3 percent of the suggested retail price.

Gore purchased a black BMW sports sedan for $40,750.88 from an authorized BMW dealer in Birmingham, Alabama. He drove the car for nine months without noticing any flaws in its appearance. To make it look "snazzier than it normally would appear," he took the car to "Slick Finish," an independent detailer. Slick Finish detected that the car had been repainted.

In fact, the top, hood, trunk, and quarter panels had been repainted in BMW's vehicle preparation center in Brunswick, Georgia. The original damage apparently had been caused by acid rain exposure during transit between the manufacturing plant in Germany and the preparation center. Because the $601.37 cost of repainting Gore's car was only about 1.5 percent of its suggested retail price, BMW did not disclose the damage or repair to the Birmingham dealer. Testimony by a former BMW dealer placed the value of a repainted car at 10 percent below that of a car that had not been repainted.

Gore sued BMW, alleging that BMW's intentional failure to disclose that the car had been repainted constituted suppression of a material fact. He sued for $500,000 in compensatory and punitive damages, and costs. The jury found BMW liable for compensatory damages in the amount of $4,000. The jury also assessed $4 million in punitive damages based on a determination that the nondisclosure policy constituted "gross, oppressive or malicious" fraud. BMW appealed.

The Alabama Supreme Court upheld the punitive damage award, but found that the jury had improperly calculated the amount and thus reduced the punitive damages to $2 million. BMW appealed the Alabama Supreme Court's decision.

Justice STEVENS delivered the opinion of the Court.

. . . .

Punitive damages may properly be imposed to further a State's legitimate interests in punishing unlawful conduct and deterring its repetition. In our federal system, States necessarily have considerable flexibility in determining the level of punitive damages that they will allow in different classes of cases and in any particular case. Most States that authorize exemplary damages afford the jury similar latitude, requiring only that the damages awarded be reasonably necessary to vindicate the State's legitimate interests in punishment and deterrence.

. . . .

Perhaps the most important indicium of the reasonableness of a punitive damages award is the degree of reprehensibility of the defendant's conduct. As the Court stated nearly 150 years ago, exemplary damages imposed on a defendant should reflect "the enormity of his offense." This principle reflects the accepted view that some wrongs are more blameworthy than others. Thus, we have said that "nonviolent crimes are less serious than crimes marked by violence or the threat of violence." . . .

In this case, none of the aggravating factors associated with particularly reprehensible conduct is present. The harm BMW inflicted on Dr. Gore was purely economic in nature. The presale refinishing of the car had no effect on its performance or safety features, or even its appearance for at least nine months after his purchase. BMW's conduct evinced no indifference to or reckless disregard for the health and safety of others. To be sure, infliction of economic injury, especially when done intentionally through affirmative acts of misconduct or when the target is financially vulnerable, can warrant a substantial penalty. But this observation does not convert all acts that cause economic harm into torts that are sufficiently reprehensible to justify a significant sanction in addition to compensatory damages.

DECISION AND REMEDY The Court overturned the $2 million award, which the Court noted to be 500 times Gore's actual harm. The Court refused, however, to set out a mathematical formula for calculating punitive damages. Instead, the Court held that the amount of punitive damages must be proportionate to the type of wrong inflicted on the victim.

CRITICAL THINKING: PUBLIC POLICY Should the Court have established a mathematical formula to provide clearer legal guidelines? Explain.

Damages for Negligence

Levy is driving her car through an intersection on a green light. Greene, approaching the same intersection, fails to stop at the red light, striking Levy's car and injuring her. She is taken to the hospital for treatment of her injuries. Levy decides to file a lawsuit to seek two types of damages: *compensatory damages* and *damages for pain and suffering.*

Compensatory damages reimburse the plaintiff, Levy, for the expenses she incurred resulting from the accident. Typically, such costs include hospital bills, doctors' bills, physical therapy bills, and lost wages during the period for which her personal injuries made her unable to work. Compensatory damages also cover the car repair bills, which are called *property damages.* These costs can be calculated relatively easily using the bills submitted.

Damages for pain and suffering are not as easy to quantify. These damages are awarded to compensate Levy who has endured pain and suffering caused by the automobile accident.

Both compensatory damages and damages for pain and suffering are determined by the amount of harm that Levy has suffered. Levy proves the amount of injury incurred through documents, such as medical and hospital bills. Levy can also put forth evidence as to the amount of pain and suffering she has endured. If the case is not settled and proceeds to trial, the jury will decide the amount to be awarded for both types of damages.

Current Tort Controversy

During President George Bush's term in office (1989–1993), the Council on Competitiveness[6] targeted the legal system for "unrestrained litigation" that has exacted a "terrible toll" on the U.S. economy. The cost, it charged, deterred U.S. manufacturers from product innovation, impeded competition with foreign companies, and cost consumers up to $300 billion.

In 1998, Congress considered bills that would place a cap on pain and suffering, as well as punitive damages; force the loser to pay all the court costs and attorneys' fees for the prevailing party; and abolish the contingent fee system. This fee payment system allows plaintiffs to arrange to pay an attorney a percentage of the damages awarded. This percentage usually ranges from 20 to 50 percent, depending on the case's difficulty. The attorney receives payment only if recovery of damages occurs. Do the facts verify that a problem really exists?

State courts handle more than 98 percent of all litigation in the United States. A study conducted by the National Center for State Courts (NCSC) showed that 98 million new cases were filed, of which 17.3 million were civil cases. Civil cases were defined as all contract cases, estate and probate matters, small claims court filings, and domestic relations cases. The actual number of

[6] The Council on Competitiveness' web site is at <http://www.compete.org/>.

LEGAL HIGHLIGHT

Thou Shall Not Steal

Internet theft is becoming commonplace. Specifically targeted is software that is stored on computers with Internet access. Many programs and photographs are freeware, donated by their producers for users to copy. Other software is copyrighted. Yet people have taken this copyrighted software and stored it in bulletin boards for others to copy at will without paying fees.

For example, Massachusetts Institute of Technology (MIT) computers were used to establish a computer bulletin board called Cynosure, which was in operation for nearly three months. While Cynosure was connected to the Internet, more than $1 million worth of copyrighted software was copied from it. When MIT discovered the bulletin board, it contacted the Federal Bureau of Investigation (FBI), which had already been notified by MIT students and was investigating the case. Eventually, criminal charges were filed against the twenty-year-old student operator of Cynosure, but the charges were later dropped.

The Internet is an international public computer network accessible by an estimated 60 million users and growing at the rate of 10 percent per month. Software companies want the government to investigate and criminally charge software pirates. These companies contend that billions of dollars of revenue are being lost annually by this type of illegal copying.

Other people contend that software piracy is a civil rights issue and that such information should be freely available to all. Copyrighted Internet material includes newsletters, music programs, photographs, and books, in addition to software. Criminal charges, it is argued, merely serve to stifle information transmission on the network. The courts will decide these issues.

---

tort cases filed in a recent year was 447,374, less than half of 1 percent of all cases filed. Included in the tort filings were all motor vehicle cases, which make up the majority of tort cases.

When the NCSC compared the tort filings with previous years, it found these to be increasing at more modest rates than in previous years. The NCSC concluded that tort filings were not increasing at a faster rate than other major categories of civil filings.

The NCSC findings were consistent with research conducted by the University of Wisconsin Law School, which examined twenty years of federal court data. It identified the major change to be a great increase in lawsuits among corporations. Most national and multinational business lawsuits are filed in the federal courts.

The RAND Corporation's Institute for Civil Justice conducted a similar study. It surveyed 70,000 individuals who had been injured. Most had been injured on the job or in motor vehicle accidents. Ten percent received compensation through the court system. Only a few people injured through defective products sought compensation through litigation.

The Council on Competitiveness contended that the United States has 70 percent of the world's lawyers. This figure is based on the number of lawyers in England, Germany, Japan, Wales, and the United States. A recent study that compared figures for 100 countries showed the United States as ranking 35th and having only 9.4 percent of the world's 7.3 million lawyers.[7]

The message from the Council on Competitiveness is not borne out by the facts. Various studies have demonstrated that the tort system is operating effectively. Yet, the argument over tort reform continues into new century. If any tort reform is needed, it must be based on facts, not perceived inequities.

[7] R. August, "The Mythical Kingdom of Lawyers," *American Bar Association Journal* 78 (September 1992): 72.

International Consideration

Combining Criminal and Civil Law

Differences exist between the common law system used in the United States and the civil law system used in Europe. For example, a drunk driver causes an accident that harms a person. In this situation, driving while under the influence of alcohol is both a tort and a crime. In the common law system, the lawsuit for the tort is handled separately from the criminal prosecution in the court system. The victim of a tort must file the lawsuit, while the government exclusively pursues the criminal prosecution.

The civil law system allows great latitude in compensating victims of wrongful acts. For example, the French civil law code, which is followed by a large number of countries, reads "every human act that causes damages to another obliges the one through whose fault it has occurred to pay damages." The French code allows the courts to combine civil and criminal proceedings. The victim of a drunk driver is represented by an attorney in criminal proceedings. In the same procedure, the court determines if the drunk driver is guilty of the crime of driving under the influence of alcohol. If the driver is found guilty, the judge imposes the sentence. Additionally, the judge has the authority to calculate civil liability on the victim's behalf.

Some jurisdictions in the United States take the same approach. For example, a person is assaulted and sustains injuries. After the criminal is convicted, the judge has the authority to order the defendant to pay the victim's expenses, such as medical costs, hospital bills, and lost income. But the statutes do not allow the judge the authority to order payment for pain and suffering. This is one example in which the differences between the common law system and the civil law system are lessening.

LEGALLY SPEAKING

Duties Owed to the Insurance Company

Insurance provides protection for businesses. If the business sustains a loss, the insurance reimburses the business for part or all of its losses, based on what type of coverage was purchased. A business should consider these three types: property insurance, product liability insurance, and motor vehicle and aircraft insurance.

Property insurance has two components. Property insurance covers the business premises for potential losses from disasters, such as fire, tornadoes, and hurricanes. Usually, damage from floods and earthquakes is not included in the basic coverage and must be covered specifically by additional insurance.

Property insurance also covers liability for a business's legal duty or obligation. This type of insurance covers the liability the business owes to a person injured as a result of a negligent act of the business. For example, a person slips, falls, and is injured on the business's premises as a result of the business's negligent act (allowing the floor to be dirty and slippery). A business also may purchase business interruption insurance. This insurance compensates the business for profit loss for the time period during which it is unable to function, such as after a fire.

Product liability insurance provides liability coverage if a business's manufactured or sold item harms someone or damages property. Not all losses or damages lead to liability, however. This topic is covered in more detail in Chapter 11.

Motor vehicle and aircraft insurance consists of three types: liability coverage, collision coverage, and comprehensive coverage. If a business employee, within the scope of her duties, negligently harms someone or damages property while using the business-owned motor vehicle or aircraft, the liability portion of the insurance will cover the claims. If the business's motor vehicle or aircraft is damaged, the collision portion covers vehicle or aircraft repair or replacement. The comprehensive coverage will repair or replace the business's vehicle or aircraft that was damaged as an act of God or that has been stolen.

Insurance policies generally have deductibles that range from $50 to millions of dollars. For example, a typical deductible for automobile insurance is $250. The insured (the person purchasing the insurance) pays the first $250 dollars of any damage. If the damage exceeds $250, the $250 must be paid by the insured before the insurance company pays the excess. Insurance premiums are based on the insured's prior losses.

The policy requires the insured to report all losses, including out-of-pocket losses. For example, a business employee has an accident that results in $100 worth of damage to its automobile. The business pays for the repair, but does not report the repair cost to its insurance company. By not informing the insurance company, the business has breached a term in its insurance policy.

Another reason for which a business has a duty to report any losses promptly to the insurance company is that prompt notification allows the insurance company to immediately investigate the circumstances surrounding the loss. The insurance company can send an investigator to view the scene of the loss and to take photographs. Potential witnesses can be interviewed while their memories are fresh.

Cases have been filed in which the initial damages appeared to be minor, but months later an injured party filed a lawsuit for thousands of dollars. By that time the insurance company cannot adequately prepare a defense. Because of these situations, if the business fails to report the accident, and thus breaches the terms of the insurance contract, the insurance company has the right to decline to represent the business in the lawsuit or to pay any judgment rendered against the business.

To be in a better position in dealing with the insurance company, the business should take the following actions before any loss occurs. Keep insurance policies in a safe-deposit box or safe place. One person should review the policies annually to ensure that the business is receiving the best coverage for the amount of premiums being paid. Photographs or videotapes of all property should be taken and placed in a safe place. A detailed inventory with receipts should be kept and updated on a regular schedule. Funds should be set aside to cover the deductible and other expenses in case of a disaster. Finally, the information should be stored on computer disks or tapes that are kept off the business premises so if the premises are damaged, the information needed to substantiate a claim with the insurance company will be available.

A business should take the following actions whenever a loss occurs:

✔ Immediately contact the business's insurance agent by telephone and follow that contact with written notification.

✔ If possible, make temporary repairs to prevent further loss. For example, place a tarp over the holes on the roof created by high winds.

✔ Collect all business records that have not been destroyed. These records include canceled checks, receipts, invoices, computer disks, and contracts that confirm the amount of the losses.

✔ Contact all witnesses to the accident or event creating the loss. Detailed notes of conversations need to be taken and kept in a safe place. Photographs or videotapes of the destroyed property or the accident scene need to be taken and safely stored.

✔ Prepare a detailed inventory of destroyed personal property.

✔ Download daily all business records from the computer, remove the backup disks or tapes from the business site, and keep them in a safe place.

Chapter Summary

A tort is a wrong committed by a person that inflicts injury to another or damage to his property. Tort law is part of the civil law. A person can commit a wrong that is both a crime and a tort. First, intentional torts are injuries caused by intentional acts. Second, negligence is a tort under which careless acts can result in liability. Third, strict liability is imposed by law without regard for fault.

Intentional torts are wrongs against a person or a business, such as assault and battery, false imprisonment, infliction of mental distress, invasion of privacy, defamation (disparagement of goods, slander of title, and defamation by computer), and fraud. Intentional torts also can be wrongs against property, such as trespass to real and personal property, conversion, and nuisance. All of these actions are based on the concept that the person or property was intentionally harmed.

The concept underlying negligence is that the defendant did not intend to harm another, but through her carelessness, a person was injured or property damage occurred. The first element of negligence is a breach of the duty of care. This duty is the objective standard of care that we all owe one another. The duty of care is breached when someone fails to act as a reasonable and prudent person would act when confronted with similar circumstances or fails to act in accordance with the duties defined by statutes. The second requirement of negligence is that an injury or damage has taken place. The last requirement is causation, in other words, did the breach of the duty of care cause the damages?

A limiting factor to liability based on negligence is the doctrine of foreseeability—could the defendant foresee the injury or damages to persons in the plaintiff's position when he or she breached the duty of care? Defenses to negligence include superseding intervening forces, assumption of risk, contributory negligence, and comparative negligence.

Strict liability is based on the idea that certain dangerous activities automatically create liability if damages or injuries result. The law imposes this liability because of public policy.

Certain torts apply only in a business situation. For example, a business cannot wrongfully interfere with other businesses' contractual or business relationships. A business can never infringe on another's trademark, patent, or copyright, nor use another's trade secrets without incurring liability for infringement.

Using the World Wide Web

The WWW has a variety of information on it concerning patents and trademarks. Both domestic and international sites are available for research. Consider the following pertinent web sites.

Finding the Law on the Web

U.S. Trademark Act
http://www.law.cornell.edu/lanham/lanham.table.html

Trademark Manual of Examining Procedure
http://www.uspto.gov/web/offices/tac/tmep/

Data interchange services information under the World Intellectual Property Organization (WIPO)
http://www1.uspto.gov/web/offices/cio/trm/TM-10.htm

Trademark Acceptable Identification of Goods and Services Manual
http://www1.uspto.gov/web/offices/tac/doc/gsmanual/

American Bar Association, section on tort and insurance practice.
http://www.abanet.org/tips/home.html

Find Law site to search all state statutes and cases
http://www.findlaw.com/casecode/state.html

Georgetown University Law Center web site for torts
http://www.ll.georgetown.edu/lr/rs/torts.html

Chapter Web Sites

Coalition for Free Speech, Food Speak
http://www.cspinet.org/foodspeak/

MacDonald's case
http://www.mcspotlight.org/case/index.html

MacDonald's verdict
http://www.mcspotlight.org/case/trial/verdict/verdict0_sum.html

Palsgraf v. Long Island Railroad Company
http://www.wooster.edu/economics/js/law_archive/Palsgraf.html

Rand Corporation
http://www.rand.org/

Rand Corporation, mass torts
http://www.rand.org/publications/RB/RB9021/RB9021.word.html

U.S. Patent and Trademark Office (PTO)
http://www.uspto.gov/

European Patent Office
http://www.european-patent-office.org/

Campbell v. Acuff-Rose Music, Inc.
http://supct.law.cornell.edu/supct/html/92-1292.ZO.html

BMW of North America, Inc. v. Gore
http://supct.law.cornell.edu/supct/html/94-896.ZS.html

Council on Competitiveness
http://www.compete.org/

Law Information Institute
http://www.law.cornell.edu/

Web Activities

8–1 Torts are always in the news. Go to Find Law web site at <http://www.findlaw.com>. Click on the button titled Legal News. Once on the Legal News site, scroll down until you find the section on torts. What torts are in the current news?

8–2 Mass torts occur in modern society. What two features distinguish mass torts from other product liability cases? Why are mass torts so difficult to resolve? Go to the Rand Corporation web site at <http://www.rand.org/publications/RB/RB9021/RB9021.word.html>.

Key Terms

absolute privilege
assault
assumption of risk
battery
causation
comparative negligence
compensatory damages
contributory negligence
conversion
copyright
damages for pain and
 suffering

deceit
defamation
defamation by computer
disparagement of goods
false imprisonment
foreseeability
fraud
infliction of mental
 distress
intentional interference
 with a contractual or
 business relationship

intentional tort
invasion of privacy
libel
merchant protection
 legislation
negligence
nuisance
objective standard of care
patent
private nuisance
privilege of immunity
proximate cause

public nuisance
punitive damages
qualified privilege
res ipsa loquitur
service mark
slander
slander of title
statutory duty
strict liability
theft of trade secrets
tort
trademark

Questions and Case Problems

8–1 Comparison Compare and contrast intentional and unintentional torts.

8–2 Copyright Rural Telephone Service provides telephone service and telephone directories to rural communities in Kansas. Feist Publications, Inc., is a publishing company that specializes in area-wide telephone directories covering a much larger geographical range than Rural Service. The Feist directories are distributed free of charge. Both companies compete for Yellow Pages advertising. Feist approached Rural and offered to pay for the right to use its White Pages. Rural refused. Feist then used them without Rural's consent. Is this a violation of the Copyright Act? Provide reasons to support your answer. [*Feist Publications, Inc. v. Rural Telephone Service,* 499 U.S. 340, 111 S. Ct. 1282, 113 L. Ed. 2d 358 (1991)]

8–3 Conversion Mr. and Mrs. Bhattal checked into the Grand Hyatt–New York. Shortly after arriving at their room with their luggage, they left to have lunch. They remembered to lock the door. On returning to their room, they discovered that their luggage was missing. As a result of a computer error made at the front desk, the Bhattals' luggage had been taken from their room and sent to the airport, along with the luggage of the previous occupants of the room, who were crew members of a Saudi Arabian airline. The Bhattals' luggage was never recovered. The Bhattals sued for conversion and intentional infliction of mental anguish. Who should prevail? Explain. [*Bhattal v. Grand Hyatt–New York,* 563 F. Supp. 277 (1983)]

8–4 Negligence Bigbee, the plaintiff, was in a telephone booth on Century Boulevard in the area of Los Angeles, California. Looking up, he saw an automobile coming toward him and realized that it was going to hit the telephone booth. He attempted to flee, but the door to the booth jammed, trapping Bigbee inside. Roberts, the driver of the automobile, was intoxicated. Evidence showed that the telephone booth had been demolished by an automobile crash twenty months before. Bigbee sued the driver and the businesses that served the driver alcoholic beverages. The case was settled as to those defendants. Bigbee also sued Pacific Telephone and Telegraph Company for negligence and strict liability for the design, location, installation, and maintenance of the telephone booths. Pacific Telephone was granted a summary judgment that, in effect, dismissed the case. Bigbee appealed. What result and why? [*Bigbee v. Pacific Telephone and Telegraph Co.,* 34 Cal. 3d 49, 665 P.2d 947, 192 Cal. Rptr. 857 (1983)]

8–5 Intentional Tort Over a ten-year period, a series of break-ins occurred at a farm home that was used to store miscellaneous items. No one lived in this home during that time period. The couple who owned it decided to place a 20-gauge shotgun in such a manner that it would discharge when the interior door was opened. Katko knew that the place was unoccupied and believed it to have been abandoned. Katko kept a collection of old bottles from the surrounding area. In search of bottles, he decided to enter the house by removing a panel covering a window that had no glass. He looked around the inside of the house for old bottles. When he pulled the interior door open to leave, the gun went off and injured his leg severely. He was convicted later of misdemeanor larceny and paid a fine. He sued the owners for his leg injury. Should he prevail? Explain. [*Katko v. Briney,* 183 N.W.2d 657 (Iowa, 1971)]

8–6 Negligence K-Mart Enterprises sold a rifle to William Knuck, who was a heavy marijuana user and was under indictment for a felony. Federal law prohibits the sale of any firearm to such a person. K-Mart was supposed to question potential customers about marijuana use or felony indictments prior to a sale. This was not done. William Knuck's brother, a heroin addict and alcoholic, took the rifle while drunk and assaulted his estranged wife and a police officer. The police officer brought a negligence action against K-Mart, which defended on the grounds of intervening circumstances. Discuss whether K-Mart was successful. Why or why not? [*K- Mart Enterprises v. Keller,* 439 So. 2d 283 (Fla. Dist. Ct. App. 1983)]

8–7 Negligence Charles and Patricia Keas were on vacation when their nineteen-year-old daughter, Kimberly, had a visitor, Kenneth Maxwell, at her parents' home, where she lived. After consuming alcoholic beverages, Kimberly became angry, grabbed a knife, and stabbed Kenneth to death. His estate brought a lawsuit against Kimberly's parents based on negligence because the parents failed to prevent their daughter from gaining access to alcohol when they knew, or should have known, that she was addicted to it. Were the parents negligent? Why or why not? Explain your answer. [*Maxwell v. Keas,* 639 A.2d 1215 (Pa. Super. 1994)]

8–8 Negligence Charles and Esther Kveragas rented a motel room at the Scottish Inns in Knoxville, Tennessee. That night, three intruders kicked open the door, shot Charles, injured Esther, and robbed them of $3,000. The Kveragases filed a lawsuit alleging that the motel owners failed to adequately provide for the motel guests' safety. The room was equipped with a hollow-core door that fit poorly into the door frame. The only door lock was incorporated into the handle, a grade-three lock, although a security chain also was provided. The plaintiffs had both locked and chained the door. A single kick applied to the door, however, opened it.

Dead-bolt locks, which are considerably stronger than the type of lock employed at this motel, and other security devices were easily available and in use throughout the motel industry. A dead-bolt lock could have withstood the force that was applied to the door. The trial court directed the jury to return a verdict for the defendants, which the jury did, on the grounds that the motel owners and operators had no duty to protect their guests from sudden criminal acts. The plaintiffs appealed. Should the jury had been given the right to determine negligence? Why or why not? [*Kveragas v. Scottish Inns, Inc.,* 733 F.2d 409 (1984)]

8–9 Negligence William H. Jordan was the principal of a middle school in Tulsa, Oklahoma. He brought an action for negligence against a local newspaper that had published a "letter to the editor" falsely attributed to him. The letter, on school stationery and enclosed in a school envelope, contained racist statements. Jordan claimed that he did not write the letter, did not sign the letter, and did not know anything about the letter until it was published. Jordan admitted that he was a public figure. Was the newspaper negligent in publishing the letter without verifying its authenticity? Does Jordan's position as a public figure have any bearing on the decision? Why or why not? (*Hint:* Refer to the sections on public figures in Chapter 5.) [*Jordan v. World Publishing Co.,* 872 P.2d 946 (Okl. App. 1994)]

8–10 Internet The U.S. government is sued often for committing torts. According to the statute, how will the United States be treated? Is the United States liable for punitive damages? Go to the Law Information Institute at <http://www.law.cornell.edu/uscode/28/2674.shtml>.

Chapter 9

Contract Formation

> *An acre of performance is worth the whole world of promise.*
>
> *Familiar Letters, 1650*
> J. B. Howell, 1594–1666

Outline

Ethical Consideration

Finders Keepers: Is There an Obligation to Disclose When a Deal Is Unfair?

You love to shop at garage sales and have found many good bargains in the process. You stop at one home with many items displayed on the lawn. A young boy greets you and tells you that he found these items in an old trunk in the attic. He tells you that he is earning spending money for the family's summer vacation.

As you browse through the offerings, you pick up a small box with a variety of items in it, including an old baseball. As you idly finger the baseball, you turn it over and cannot believe what you see. Trying to act nonchalant, you take a second look and now are sure that this baseball was signed by Babe Ruth.

You know that this baseball is worth a lot of money. When you ask how much the boy wants for the junk in the box, he asks you if five dollars would be too much. Do you tell him about the Babe Ruth baseball or simply pay the five dollars and walk away? Use the ethical model presented in Chapter 2 and reprinted on the inside front cover to develop your answer.

Introduction

People and businesses enter into and perform millions of contracts daily. A **contract** is an agreement between two or more parties that can be enforced in a court of law or a court of equity. In the legal environment of business, questions and disputes about contracts arise daily. Answering those questions and resolving those disputes are the essence of contract law.

The legal framework provides the stability and the structure within which businesses can plan and carry out their contracts. When adverse business conditions occur, a businessperson cannot rely on good faith that the other party to the contract will perform simply out of a sense of duty. The enforceability of contracts in courts of law and equity ensures the promised performance or entitles the person harmed to some form of relief.

You and your employees in your online business, Artiste Login Products, Inc., need a working knowledge of contract law because the fundamental method of exchanging goods, services, property, and money is accomplished through contracts. You need know how to negotiate with your suppliers and customers. Once you and the other party have come to an agreement, you need to know how to draft contracts or have a company attorney who can. Contract law is a complicated topic that can be reviewed only briefly in a legal environment course.

This chapter will discuss the sources of commercial law, the Uniform Commercial Code (UCC) and its effect on contract law, contract formation, and some contractual terms and elements.[1]

Comparing Torts with Contracts

The previous chapter discussed tort law. Occasionally, tort law and contract law arise out of the same set of facts. Torts, such as fraud and misrepresentation, can originate within a contract's context. A tort also results when someone intentionally interferes with an existing contract.

Contract and tort, however, are different branches of law. Contract law exists to enforce legally binding agreements between parties; tort law is designed to vindicate social policy. Contract law exists to protect promises that have been made, whereas tort law exists to protect people from certain kinds of harms.

Conduct that breaches a contract becomes a tort when it also violates a specific principle of tort law. Beside fraud and misrepresentation, a major tort action tied directly to contract law is the tort of intentional interference with contractual relationships. This tort arises when a third party intentionally causes or attempts to cause a contract party to breach a contract. The laws of torts and contracts overlap in such an action.

---

[1] A general overview of contract law can be found on the Internet at <http://www.law.cornell.edu/>. Once there, go to the very end of the material and type in contracts. It will then give you an overview of contract law. Another web address that will give you a considerable amount of information on contract law is <http://www.freeadvice.com>.

Sources of Commercial Law

Commercial or business law is the body of law that governs commercial transactions. Commercial law covers such topics as contracts, partnerships, corporations, and agencies. Many principles of commercial law developed centuries ago from what was known as the **law merchant**.

The Law Merchant

The Magna Carta (which means the Great Charter) is a charter granted in 1215 by King John to the barons at Runnymede, England. The Magna Carta is regarded as the foundation of the U.S. Constitution. One chapter particularly made special provisions for merchants, stating that all merchants should "have safe and secure conduct, to go out of, and to come into England, and to pass as well by lands as by water, for buying and selling by the ancient and allowed customs."

A system of mercantile courts developed in England and throughout Europe long before the advent of the common law courts. These mercantile courts administered the law merchant, which set out the rules that governed the contract process. These rules evolved from merchants' customs. The merchants themselves administered these mercantile courts.

The law merchant was important during the Middle Ages, during which time the fair, or market, was the primary commercial event. As the merchant traveled from place to place, he reasonably could be assured that the law would be similar, no matter where he conducted his business. The law merchant became part of the common law and eventually was incorporated into U.S. law.

Codification of Commercial Law

From its very beginning, the United States adopted the English common law, which covered commercial transactions. When early U.S. commerce was just developing, many gaps in the body of this law existed. States took opposing positions on many commercial issues, leaving New York's businesspeople, for example, uncertain as to Connecticut's law. Over the years, both the legal and the business professions realized the necessity for uniform laws covering commercial transactions.

To achieve this uniformity, the legal profession, through the National Conference of Commissioners on Uniform State Laws[2] in conjunction with the American Law Institute (ALI), developed uniform codes of commercial law. Once a uniform code is completed, it is sent to each state. The state may choose to adopt the uniform code completely, may change parts of it to make it compatible with local law, or may choose not to consider or adopt the uniform code. Today, these codes are continually being developed to correspond with changing business needs. Of all the uniform codes, the most important to businesses is the **Uniform Commercial Code (UCC)**.

Uniform Commercial Code

During the 1930s, to create uniform commercial laws, some members of Congress proposed a statutory scheme that would cover all interstate commercial transactions. The bills never were passed. Congress cannot control intrastate commerce, because the Constitution gives the individual states control over business conducted within their respective borders. The National Conference and the ALI began work on the Uniform Commercial Code in 1942. In 1952, they completed the first draft of a uniform act that would apply to both intrastate and interstate transactions. All fifty states, the District of Columbia, and the Virgin Islands have adopted the Uniform Commercial Code, which has been updated several times.[3]

The UCC consists of these articles:

1. General Provisions.
2. Sales.
2A. Leases.
3. Negotiable Instruments.
4. Bank Deposits and Collections.
4A. Funds Transfers.
5. Letters of Credit.
6. Repealer of Bulk Transfers.
7. Warehouse Receipts, Bills of Lading and Other Documents of Title.

---

[2] One web page for the National Conference of Commissioners on Uniform State Laws is found at <http://www.law.upenn.edu/bll/ulc/ulc_frame.htm>.

[3] Louisiana has adopted only Articles 1, 3, 4, and 5 of the Uniform Commercial Code.

8. Investment Securities.

9. Secured Transactions; Sales of Accounts and Chattel Paper.

10. Effective Date and Repealer.

11. Effective Date and Transition Provisions.

The UCC generally does not cover transactions involving real estate or personal services, such as house purchases or employment contracts. The code remains closely consistent with the basic principles of commercial law that derived from the law merchant and common law, yet it expands and comprehensively orders these principles to modernize, clarify, and standardize the rules.

The UCC also clarifies the legal relationship of the parties in modern commercial transactions. The code is designed to help determine the intentions of the parties to a commercial contract and to give force and effect to their agreement. Businesspeople are assured that their contracts, if validly entered into, will be enforced. In turn, this assurance encourages further business transactions.

A court, when reviewing a contract case, looks first to the contract's subject matter. Once the court determines the subject matter, it reviews any applicable statutes, such as the UCC. If no statute exists, the principles of common law apply.

Of the articles that make up the UCC, only three, Article 2 (Sales), Article 3 (Negotiable Instruments), and Article 9 (Secured Transactions; Sales of Accounts and Chattel Paper) significantly impact contractual situations. This chapter covers the common law, statutes, and several provisions of Article 2, Sales. Discussions of Articles 3 and 9 follow in subsequent chapters.[4]

Contract Terms

A contract is an agreement between two or more parties to perform—or to refrain from performing—some act now or in the future. When valid, this agreement is enforceable. A contract is based on a promise, but not all promises are legally enforceable. A contract is cre-

ated when there is an *offer* and an *acceptance* of that offer along with several other requirements.[5]

An **offer** is a promise that can be met with **acceptance** (a return promise) or with **rejection**, that is, the person receiving the offer refuses it. Every offer involves at least two parties. The **offeror**, or the party making the offer, promises to do—or not to do—an act. The **offeree** is the party to whom the offer is made and who has the power to accept or reject the offer. If the offeree accepts (by performing an act or by returning a promise), the contract is formed because promises have been exchanged. The offeree's rejection terminates the offer.

During the offer stage, negotiations occur. Negotiations may take years, as in the purchase of a large land tract, or may be over quickly, as in the decision to purchase a soft drink.

CyberLaw

Electronic Contracts

Electronic commerce (e-commerce) involves electronic contracts (e-contracts) using one of two methods. First, closed networks are used among businesses. For several decades, business-to-business (B2B) contracts have used the electronic data interchange (EDI). Second, the World Wide Web (WWW) open environment allows both business-to-consumer (B2C) contracts and B2B contracts to exist.

EDI was created in the 1960s when large department stores, such as Sears and J.C. Penney, were expanding rapidly. Dealing with hundreds of suppliers for hundreds of thousand types of goods, the paperwork for the purchaser and supplier was overwhelming. Necessity drove the purchaser to look for a more efficient method. Each retailer decided on a computer system and had software designed for the system. Each retailer used standard contract forms and these forms were placed on the computer. The suppliers to each retailer adapted their business practices and used computers that were compatible with the purchaser.

If a supplier dealt only with one purchaser, the supplier had efficiencies built in because the computer

---

[4] Many contracts contain standard clauses. Contracts involving the sale of goods under the Uniform Commercial Code generally contain these clauses. You can find some of these on the Internet at <http://lectlaw.com/formb.htm>.

[5] As you may have determined, contract law is rather complicated. If you should have a specific question, one of the best sources for an answer is <http://www.findlaw.com/>.

LEGAL HIGHLIGHT

The Tow Truck and Mud Wrestling

Ron's car got stuck in the mud in a swampy area behind a local bait shop in rural Maryland. He called a tow truck to haul the car out of the mud and then went fishing. The tow truck came and it too got stuck in the mud. The driver contacted another tow truck, which promptly got stuck in the mud as well. The two drivers called a third tow truck, which also got stuck.

A bulldozer was called in. It too got stuck in the mud. Next called was a construction company. Through the efforts of four dump trucks, the company constructed a dirt road. With a solid base in place, the

bulldozer, the three tow trucks, and Ron's car were rescued from the mud.

The bill was $4,740. Who shall pay? Ron agreed to pay for one tow truck. The first tow truck driver contended that Ron told him to get the car out and that Ron's father would pay for it. Ron's father said, "No way."

As in many cases of this type, the dispute was settled out of court. Only the parties know how it ended. All in all, it was a muddled contract case.

---

system replaced the labor-intensive paperwork. If a supplier did business with a number of purchasers, a major problem arose. The supplier needed to purchase a number of computer systems in order to be compatible with the different computers and software systems of the various purchasers. For example, a wholesale dress supplier may sell to ten different purchasers. The supplier needed a number of different computer systems to communicate with all ten purchasers. The suppliers needed a better method.

Suppliers and purchasers held a series of meetings and agreed on a set of standards that became the electronic data interchange. The EDI has an internationally agreed set of standards under UN/EDIFACT (United Nations Electronic Interchange for Administration, Commerce and Trade).[6] EDI transactions represent a paperless business information exchange that is independent of either business partner's unique business processes, computer software, or hardware. EDI provides flexibility, but does not impose the requirement of common hardware, software, business processes, or terminology on the diverse participants, only common data usage and transmission formats.

As stated on the UN/EDIFACT web page, implementing EDI is not a goal in and of itself. The adoption of EDI should be a part of a larger effort to improve

business practices. When EDI is used to replace paper while leaving the existing business processes in place, it brings benefits, including reduced data entry and mailing costs, more accurate information, faster communications, and decreased paperwork and reproduction. Fully exploiting the EDI potential, however, requires reengineering the business to bring about the greater advantages of

- faster processing of actions;
- availability of timely and accurate data for decision makers;
- lower personnel requirements; and
- a responsive environment that supports innovations, such as direct vendor delivery, flexible manufacturing, rapid distribution, and central pay.

Businesses form contracts by communicating electronically among their respective computers. EDI allows parties to send standardized forms, such as purchase orders, invoices, and shipping notices back and forth. EDI has become both a convenient and an efficient substitute for transmitting conventional paper documents between parties.

Terms Used with Contracts

Contract law uses specific terms to describe various contractual situations. Three sets of terms describe the contract's formation, the contract's enforceability in court, and the contract's performance.

---

[6] UN/EDIFACT can be found at <http://www.unece.org/trade/untdid/>.

Formation. The following terms define the various situations under which a contract is formed.

Bilateral and Unilateral Contracts. A **bilateral contract** is a "promise for a promise." A bilateral contract is created when the offeror makes an offer (promise) and wants the offeree to give his acceptance in the form of a return promise to perform. The offeree's return promise is the acceptance. Most contracts are bilateral.

For example, Miguel offers to sell his residence to Katrina for $100,000. When Katrina agrees (gives a return promise) to purchase Miguel's residence at that price, a bilateral contract results. In a sale of land, a statute (called the statute of frauds) requires that for the contract to be enforceable in a court of law, this type of contract must be in writing.

Whether a contract is bilateral or unilateral depends on the offeror's requirement of the offeree in accepting the offer. If the offeror's promise requires the offeree to complete the performance with a return act (and not with a promise), the contract is called a **unilateral contract**. The person making the promise wants the other person to perform an act in return. An example is the reward situation. A person offers a cash amount for the return of a lost dog, as indicated by the following ad. The person offering the reward requires action (the return of Useless), not a promise.

$500 REWARD
for return of two-year-old female border terrier.
Responds to name Useless.
Call 480-555-5555

Express and Implied Contracts. In an **express contract**, the terms of the offer and the acceptance are specifically stated, either orally or in writing. If the terms are not exactly set out, but are implied, a valid contract exists that is called an **implied-in-fact contract**. Implied contracts are created by the parties' conduct. When individuals act as if a contract were made, even though no words were spoken or written to that effect, the law implies a contract. For example, when a person visits the doctor's office to be treated for a cold, the person, by her conduct, agrees to pay for the doctor's services.

Formal and Informal Contracts. Statutes set out the provisions for a **formal contract**, requiring it to be in a special form to be valid. All formal contracts must be written, but not all written contracts are classified as formal contracts. An example of a formal contract is a bail bond to obtain someone's release from jail. Other examples are negotiable instruments and letters of credit (see Chapter 12). If the contract is not a formal contract, it is classified as an **informal contract**. Today, most contracts are either oral or written informal contracts.

Quasi-Contracts. Occasionally, a person is unjustly enriched at the expense of another. No express contract exists, and no conduct occurs to imply a contract, yet for one individual to be enriched at the expense of the other is unjust. The law will imply a promise to pay. This type of conduct creates a contract by operation of law, an **implied-in-law contract** (more commonly called a **quasi-contract**).

In a quasi-contract, the parties make no promise by word or conduct, but the law will impose a promise on the party who benefited. To recover, the plaintiff needs to prove three elements. First, a benefit was conferred on the defendant by the plaintiff. Second, the defendant appreciated or knew of the benefit. Third, the acceptance or retention by the defendant of the benefit was done under circumstances that unjustly enriched the defendant at the expense of the plaintiff.

A quasi-contract is distinguishable from an implied-in-fact contract. An implied-in-fact contract is a true contract made between the parties and is enforceable in court. In contrast, only a court can declare that a quasi-contract exists, because it is a legal fiction. The court creates a quasi-contract (that is, a fictional contract) for reasons of social policy, that is, to prevent a person from being enriched unjustly at the expense of another.

The following example shows a situation in which the court can grant the remedy of a quasi-contract. Joel, a salesperson, returns home at 10 A.M. to find a work crew ready to paint his house. He knows that they are supposed to paint his neighbor's house. He says nothing and leaves. When he returns to his house at 5 P.M., the house is painted. Under a quasi-contract, the painting company's remedy is to sue Joel for a reasonable amount for the paint job. He has received a benefit and to retain that benefit without paying for it would be unjust. Joel had a chance to stop the painting and he failed to do so. Until he pays, he has been unjustly enriched at the expense of the paint company. The following case represents another application of the doctrine of quasi-contract.

Case 9.1

Petrie v. Le Van

Missouri Court of Appeals,
1990

799 S.W.2d 632

BACKGROUND AND FACTS The Petries purchased a house from Le Van. The deed to the house was transferred on September 24, 1986. Unknown to either party, a severe storm had damaged the roof the night before the deed was recorded in the Petries' name. Because the title to the house was still in Le Van's name, only he could have a homeowner's insurance policy in case the house suffered any property damage.

The Petries asked Le Van to make a claim against his homeowner's insurance policy. The insurance company issued Le Van a check in the amount of $2,176.22. He refused to turn the money over to the Petries, who had made the roof repairs at a cost in excess of the $2,176.22. The Petries filed this lawsuit against Le Van, claiming that Le Van was unjustly enriched.

When a person unfairly holds money or property that belongs to another, the person who holds the money or property is said to hold it in trust for the real owner. The court uses the term *constructive trust* to describe a remedy when unfairness is involved, because the court constructs the trust.

Judge SHANGLER

. . . .

A person who has been unjustly enriched at the expense of another is required to make restitution to the other. The principle against unjust enrichment emerged against the grain of the common law forms of action then available for remedy and with the aid of the restitution devices of the equity court. The common law courts overcame this limitation on remedies imposed by the forms of action through the fiction of quasi contract. The law gave to a plaintiff against a defendant under an obligation, from the ties of natural justice, to refund, an action as if it were upon a contract. The equity courts independently developed restitution remedies against unjust enrichment. The fiction of constructive trust was used in cases of fraud or breach of fiduciary duty to reach the gains that, in conscience, belonged to another by treating the fraudulent procurer as a trustee. The constructive trust also became the means for restitution from one unjustly enriched by the mistake of another, even though the mistake was not induced by fraud or misrepresentation.

. . . .

The right to restitution for unjust enrichment presupposes: (1) that the defendant was enriched by the receipt of a benefit; (2) that the enrichment was at the expense of the plaintiff; (3) that it would be unjust to allow the defendant to retain the benefit.

. . . .

In that assessment, it is not the power of equity to order specific performance, injunction, or some variant of equitable conversion by contract as to the insurance proceeds that is invoked. It is equitable principle and good conscience that govern. In this case, it is the equitable principle against double recovery that disallows Le Van from retention of both the insurance proceeds and the full purchase price of the property and that good conscience requires that Le Van pay over to the Petries. If Le Van may keep the proceeds of the insurance and also the full purchase price, he has a windfall. Le Van is compensated for that which he did not lose and the Petries pay for that which they did not receive.

DECISION AND REMEDY The court found that Le Van was enriched at the expense of the Petries. The trial court was directed to enter a judgment in the amount of $2,176.22 against Le Van.

CRITICAL THINKING: LEGAL CONCEPTS In the last chapter you reviewed the concept of tort law, including the tort of conversion. Discuss whether the plaintiff should have sued under the quasi-contract theory or under the tort theory of conversion.

Enforceability. Another way to describe contracts is according to their enforceability by a court, using the terms *valid, voidable*, and *unenforceable contracts* or *void agreements*. A **valid contract** meets the elements required for the contract to be enforced in a court. These elements are discussed in detail in the next section.

In a **voidable contract**, one party to the contract is bound, but the other party may disaffirm (or avoid) it. For example, a **minor** (a person under a specified age, generally under age eighteen) has the right to disaffirm contracts, that is, she can avoid performing the contract. Occasionally, both parties may have the right to disaffirm the contract, such as when two minors have entered into a contract.

An **unenforceable contract** is one that started out as a valid contract, but for some legal reason, now cannot be enforced in court against the other party. In other words, statutes forbid the courts to enforce the contract. Consider, for example, a person entering into a valid contract to buy a stereo system on credit. Later the person goes into bankruptcy and the contract debt is discharged (forgiven) by the bankruptcy court. The valid contract has been converted into an unenforceable contract by the bankruptcy statute as applied by the bankruptcy court. Now the creditor cannot sue the debtor to collect the money owed on the contract because it has been discharged.

The term *void contract* is an oxymoron (a combination of contradictory words). If a contract is void, the law will not enforce the agreement. For example, if the purpose of a contract is illegal, it is a **void agreement**. In these cases, the word *agreement* is used because, by definition, a contract is legal.

Performance. Contracts can be described based on the performance status of each of the parties—*executed* versus *executory* contracts. These terms can apply in two situations. First, they can refer to the contract's status, considered as a whole. An **executed contract** is a fully

performed contract. An **executory contract** has not been performed.

Second, these terms can refer to the state of performance by one party in relation to the other. For example, Ann hands over a textbook to a friend with the understanding that she will receive twenty dollars for it. Ann's performance is fully executed, whereas the friend's performance is executory. In this case, the contract is partially performed. Because the contract still is not fully performed, it is an executory contract. Exhibit 9–1 summarizes the contract terms covered in this section.

Elements of a Contract: Part 1

All legally enforceable contracts must satisfy these requirements:

1. *Offer* An offer is a promise. An offer must be made by the offeror to the offeree.

2. *Acceptance* An acceptance is the return promise or act. The offeree either makes a return promise or performs the act requested in the offer. The offer and acceptance constitute mutual assent.

3. *Consideration* Consideration is the main reason for entering the contract. Two elements form consideration. First, the promises must be bargained for and exchanged. Second, the promises must have legal value. The consideration must be legally sufficient to support the offer and acceptance so the contract will be enforceable in court.

4. *Capacity* The parties must have the legal ability (capacity) to form a contract.

5. *Legality* The subject matter of the contract must be legal for the contract to be enforceable in court.

6. *Writing* Some types of agreements must be in writing to be enforceable in court.

Exhibit 9–1 Contract Terms

Contract Formation

1. The manner by which the offeree is required to accept the offer determines this classification of contract.
   a. *Bilateral* A promise for a promise.
   b. *Unilateral* A promise for an act (completed act is acceptance).

2. The parties' manner of expression determines this classification of contract.
   a. *Express* Formed by words (oral, written, or both).
   b. *Implied-in-fact* Formed by the conduct of the parties.

3. A court decision determines this classification of contract.
   a. *Quasi-contract* Imposed by law to prevent unjust enrichment.

4. The form determines this classification of contract.
   a. *Formal* Required by law to be in special written form to be valid.
   b. *Informal* No special form is required; may be oral or written.

Enforceability

1. *Valid* The contract has the necessary contractual elements of offer, acceptance, consideration, parties with capacity, and a legal purpose. It can be enforced in court.

2. *Voidable* A contract exists, but one party, by law, has a defense to avoid performing its contractual obligation. That party can elect to perform its obligation and can enforce the contract against the other party.

3. *Unenforceable* A contract exists, but it cannot be enforced by either party in a court because of a legal defense.

4. *Void* No contract exists. The agreement cannot be enforced in court.

Performance

1. *Executed* A fully performed contract.

2. *Executory* A contract not performed.

3. *Partially executed* A contract not fully performed by one or both parties.

The first three elements are discussed in this chapter. The last three are examined in Chapter 10.

Requirements of the Offer

An offer is a promise to do—or to refrain from doing—some specified thing now or in the future. Three elements are necessary for an offer to be effective: (1) *objective intent* by the offeror to be bound by her offer; (2) terms of the offer must be *reasonably definite*; and (3) offer must be *communicated* to the offeree. For a valid contract to exist, an offer must have been made.

Intent. An offeror must objectively intend to be bound by her offer. Objective intent is determined from the words and actions of the parties as interpreted by a reasonable person. In a dispute, an offer is interpreted as the expectation of a reasonable and prudent person if she heard or read the offeror's promise. Contract law is not concerned with the subjective (secret) intent of the offeror, that is, the offeror's real intent. The issue, instead, is whether the offeror intends to be bound by her offer if the offeree accepts it. Statements made in obvious anger, jest, or excitement do not meet the objective intent test.

Definite. An offer must have reasonably definite terms so that the parties can specifically determine the acts necessary to perform their part of the contract. If a dispute arises, a court must be able to determine if the promises by the parties have not been performed and, if so, to decide on an appropriate remedy.

Even prior to the adoption of the Uniform Commercial Code, the courts were reluctant to declare a contract invalid based on indefiniteness of the terms if, during the trial, the evidence showed the clear intention of both parties to enter into the contract. The courts try to substitute reasonable terms wherever possible to resolve ambiguous or missing terms.

LEGAL HIGHLIGHT
Opera, Dinner, and Court?

In San Francisco, Bill, a certified public accountant, asked Ann to join him in attending the opera and for dinner afterward. They agreed to the date three months in advance of the date of the opera. Late on the afternoon of the performance date, Ann called Bill to break the date because her old boyfriend was in town. Since Ann notified him so late in the afternoon, Bill was unable to find anyone else to accompany him. Bill decided to get even.

He sued Ann for breach of contract in small claims court. He requested the court to grant him the following damages:

the cost of one opera ticket,

one-half of the mileage cost to purchase and pick up the ticket in advance, and

the cost of his time to find someone to take in her place.

The small-claims court dismissed Bill's case, stating that a promise to go on a date was not a legally enforceable contract. Social promises are not legally enforceable. Life is not always fair.

UCC Article 2, Sales, covers the sale of all goods. Article 2 of the UCC liberalized the requirement of definiteness. Under the UCC, even though one or more of the contract's terms were not agreed to, a court may enforce a contract for the sale of goods. If the parties clearly intended to make a contract, and if a reasonably certain basis exists for giving an appropriate remedy, the court will supply or clarify the missing terms [UCC 2-204(3)].

The missing terms are provided in some of the following ways. If the price is omitted, the court imposes the reasonable price at the time the goods were delivered [UCC 2-305(1)]. If the place of delivery is unspecified, the court requires delivery at the seller's (not the buyer's) home or business [UCC 2-308(a)]. If the shipment or delivery time is ambiguous, the court establishes a reasonable deadline following the contract formation [UCC 2-309(1)]. If the payment time is unspecified, the court makes the payment due at the time and place of delivery [UCC 2-310(a)]. This section means that unless the purchaser arranged to pay for the goods on credit, she must pay in cash (currency or check) at the delivery time and place.

Communication. The third requirement for an effective offer is communication. A person cannot agree to a contract without knowing that the contract exists. Suppose Jones advertises a reward of $100 for the return of her lost dog. Garcia, not knowing of the

reward, finds the dog and returns it to Jones. Garcia cannot recover the $100 in a court, because he did not know that it was offered and, therefore, no contract existed to be enforced. Jones may still give the reward to Garcia, but a court will not force Jones to do so.

Exhibit 9–2 summarizes the requirements for an effective offer.

Termination of the Offer

An effective offer provides the offeree the power to transform that offer into a contract by accepting it. This power of acceptance, however, does not continue forever. Either an action by one of the parties or an operation of law can cancel an offer.

Termination of the Offer by Action of a Party.
An action of one of the parties can end the offer by (1) *revocation* of the offer by the offeror, (2) *rejection* of the offer by the offeree, or (3) *counteroffer* by the offeree. In determining a contract's validity, a court must determine if the offer is still open.

Revocation of the Offer by the Offeror. **Revocation** is the offeror's withdrawal of the offer. Even if the offeror promises to keep the offer open, she can inform the offeree of the revocation before the offeree accepts. The offeror revokes the offer in one of two ways. First, the offeror specifically repudiates the offer. For example,

Exhibit 9–2   Requirements for an Effective Offer

1. *Intent* The offeror must have shown a serious, objective intent to become bound by the offer.

2. *Definite* The terms of the offer must be sufficiently definite to be ascertainable by the parties or by a court. Under the UCC, the court can supply missing terms if the parties clearly intended to make a contract for the sale of goods and if a reasonably certain basis exists for giving an appropriate remedy [UCC 2-204]:
   a. *No price* Reasonable price at time of delivery [UCC 2-305(1)].
   b. *No delivery place* Seller's place of business or, if none, seller's home [UCC 2-308(a)].
   c. *No time set to ship or deliver* Reasonable time after contract is formed [UCC 2-309(1)].
   d. *No time set for payment* Money to be paid on delivery [UCC 2-310(a)].

3. *Communication* The offer must be communicated by the offeror to the offeree.

---

the offeror says, "I withdraw my offer of October 17." Second, the offeror acts in a manner inconsistent with the offer. In this case, the offeror makes an offer to sell a clock to Gabriel. The next day, while Gabriel is deciding, the offeror sells the clock to Amanda.

The offeror, however, must inform the offeree of the revocation before the offer is accepted. If the revocation follows the offeree's acceptance, the revocation normally is ineffective. A valid contract already has been formed because an acceptance usually is effective at the time it is made. Most states follow the general rule that a revocation is effective only on the offeree's actual knowledge of the revocation.

For example, an offer is made on April 1. When the offeree accepts the offer on April 3, a contract is formed. If the offeror sends a revocation on April 2 that is delivered to the offeree on April 4, the revocation is not effective. If the revocation had reached the offeree on April 2, however, *before* the offer was accepted, the offer would have been terminated.

Although most offers are revocable, certain offers can be made irrevocable. Three common types of irrevocable offers are (1) those involved in *option contracts*, (2) *firm offers* under the UCC, and (3) offers made irrevocable by virtue of *promissory estoppel*. Thus, in a contract dispute, the court must consider whether this type of offer is revocable.

Option Contracts. An **option contract** is a separate contract that removes the offeror's right to revoke the offer for the time period specified in the option. If an offeror promises to hold an offer open for a specific time period, and the offeree pays for the promise, an option contract has been created. If no time is specified, a reasonable period of time is implied.

For example, Beverly plans to purchase twelve acres at a prime location. She needs time to determine if she can obtain financing. If she cannot obtain financing, she does not want to buy the property. Beverly pays the landowner $1,000 to give up his right to sell the land to someone else and to take the property off the market for a specified time period, such as 180 days. An option contract has been created. During the 180 days, the landowner cannot revoke his offer to Beverly. At the end of the 180 days, the option expires. If she does not obtain financing, Beverly is not obligated to purchase the land under this option contract.

Firm Offers. A **firm offer** is a modification of an option contract and applies only to offers involving the sale and purchase of goods. Created by the UCC, a firm offer occurs when a **merchant** (a person who regularly deals in a particular type of goods) makes a written, signed offer to buy or sell goods and indicates in the offer that the offer is irrevocable. The merchant's offer is irrevocable even though the offeree does not pay any consideration [UCC 2-205]. The offer remains open for the stated time period. If the time is unspecified, the offer remains open for a reasonable period that cannot exceed three months.

Promissory Estoppel. Estoppel means "to bar, to impede, or to stop." **Promissory estoppel** means that the offeror cannot revoke the offer if the offeree changes his position by relying on the promises made in the offer. In such cases, revocation is considered unjust to the offeree.

For example, Dan (the offeree) owns a grocery business and the store building. Big Chain (the offeror) offers him a manager's position in a new store that it plans to build but tells Dan that he must sell his business and store building to be hired as manager. Relying on this offer, Dan sells his business and store building. Big Chain then revokes its offer, saying that it no longer plans to build its store, and thus does not plan to employ Dan. Had the offer not been made, Dan still would have his store building and grocery business. Dan has a case based on promissory estoppel. Big Chain cannot revoke its offer because the offeree, relying on the offer, changed his situation.

Rejection of the Offer by the Offeree. An offeree may reject the offer, in which case the offer ends. A rejection, by conduct or by words, shows an intent not to accept the offer and terminates the offer. Rejection is effective as a termination of the offer when the offeror learns of the rejection.

For example, Mary offers to sell her used personal computer printer to David for $450. On May 1, David responds that the offer appears to be a little high and asks Mary to lower her price. Mary cannot treat these words as a rejection, because David's words did not indicate an intent not to accept but merely an inquiry as to whether Mary would modify her offer. Mary, however, refuses to modify her offer. On May 3, David

mails a rejection letter to Mary. Before Mary receives David's letter, David calls Mary and accepts her offer. Because Mary received David's call accepting the offer before she received his letter of rejection, the contract is valid and enforceable.

Counteroffer by the Offeree. A **counteroffer** is a rejection of the original offer that, at the same time, constitutes a new offer. Any subsequent attempt by the offeree (now the offeror) to accept the expired offer is construed as a new offer, giving the original offeror (now the offeree) the power of acceptance.

Suppose Arnold offers to sell his computer to Dale for $1,000. Dale responds, "Your price is too high. I offer to purchase your computer for $650." Dale's response is termed a counteroffer because it constituted a rejection. The counteroffer ended Arnold's offer to sell at $1,000 and, at the same time, created a new offer by Dale to purchase at $650.

Exhibit 9–3 illustrates the relationship reversals of offeror and offeree when a counteroffer is made.

The following case involves a counteroffer. When trying to settle a case before proceeding to trial, attorneys will make offers and counteroffers, such as in this case.

Exhibit 9–3   The Dynamics of a Rejection and Counteroffer

Case 9.2

Beck v. Shrum

Missouri Court of Appeals,
2000
18 S.W.3d 8

BACKGROUND AND FACTS   Lillian L. Shrum, defendant, appeals from a judgment and order granting a *motion to enforce settlement* in favor of Betty Anne Beck, plaintiff. The issue on appeal is whether Shrum's $7,500 offer had been rejected by a counteroffer.

The case is for personal injuries arising out of an automobile accident involving Shrum and Beck. Prior to trial, Susan Horowitz (Horowitz) represented Defendant Shrum. On the day set for trial, the trial court granted Horowitz's *motion to withdraw*, and Crystal Smith (Smith) entered her appearance for defendant. James Whitney, Jr. (Whitney) remained Plaintiff Beck's counsel at all times.

At the hearing on the *motion to enforce settlement*, Whitney and Smith advised the trial court of the following. After the petition and answer were filed, a pretrial settlement conference was held. At this conference, Beck wanted $50,000. Shrum's insurance company offered to settle the case for $7,500. At some point after the settlement conference, Whitney told Horowitz that "If I could get $15,000 I could maybe talk [Plaintiff] into settling, although [Plaintiff] had never given [Whitney] any indication of another figure for which [Plaintiff] would settle." After talking with Shrum's insurance company, Horowitz indicated that "They couldn't, but the $7,500 was still available." Horowitz did not appear at the hearing because she was on maternity leave.

Whitney knew that Smith was reassigned to the case six days before the hearing. Four days before the hearing, Smith was present at Whitney's office for another matter. At that time, Whitney said to Smith, "If I could get a little more money, I could settle it. . . ." Smith indicated that she would talk to the appropriate people, and Whitney replied, "How about ten thousand, some more money will settle it." After this conversation, Whitney spoke with Beck, and she agreed to accept the $7,500 if she could not get more money.

While going through security at the courthouse with Smith on the day of the hearing, Whitney accepted the $7,500 offer of settlement. Smith replied, "I don't know how that you can do that, because you made a demand of ten." After calling Shrum's insurance company, Smith told Whitney that the company said, "There wasn't $7,500 on the table" because the offer had been rejected when Whitney said, "[I]f you can get me ten, we can make this thing go away." In granting plaintiff's *motion to enforce settlement*, the trial court took "judicial notice of the custom and practice that an offer is on the table until it is withdrawn, and the attorney is advised that it is withdrawn."

SHERRI B. SULLIVAN, Judge

. . . .

The basic elements of a contract are offer, acceptance and consideration. Any acceptance that includes new or variant terms from the offer amounts to a counteroffer and a rejection of the offer, which may become open again only if renewed by the offeror. However, although a request for a change or modification of a proposed contract made before an acceptance thereof amounts to a rejection of it, a mere inquiry as to whether the offeror will alter or modify its terms, made before acceptance or rejection, does not amount to a rejection. *Jaybe Construction Co. v. Beco, Inc.,* (concluding that the following statement was an inquiry: "The plaintiff stated that the bid to the state was a 'close' one, and if possible the plaintiff would like to have the defendant 'shave' its figure. . . ."); *Foster v. West Pub. Co.,* (concluding that the following statement, made subsequent to certain suggestions by the speaker, was an inquiry: "This, I say, would be my idea of a square deal; but, if you are not disposed to take the same view, I suppose there is nothing for me to do. . . ."). Consequently, if the offer has not been withdrawn, it may be accepted within a reasonable time to create a binding contract.

The issue, then, is whether Whitney's discussion with Smith at his office constituted an inquiry or a counteroffer. Both Smith and Whitney testified that Whitney used conditional language, i.e. "if," in the discussion. The language is not a clear rejection of the original offer, but rather it inquires about a larger amount of money while still keeping the original offer under consideration. Therefore, because the $7,500 offer had not been withdrawn and because Whitney made an inquiry about $10,000, not a counteroffer, his acceptance of the $7,500 offer at the courthouse created a binding contract.

DECISION AND REMEDY The court found that the mere inquiry as to whether the insurance company was willing to pay more to settle the case was not a rejection of the original offer. The original offer was never withdrawn prior to acceptance.

CRITICAL THINKING: PREVENTIVE LAW How can defendants protect themselves in similar situations?

Mirror-Image Rule. At common law, the **mirror-image rule** requires the offeree's acceptance to match the offeror's offer exactly. In other words, the acceptance must mirror the offer. Any change in, or addition to, the original offer's terms automatically ends that offer and constitutes a counteroffer. The original offeror (now the offeree) can accept the counteroffer's terms, creating a valid contract. The acceptance is effective when sent unless otherwise stated.

UCC Rules Modify Mirror-Image Rule. The mirror-image rule causes considerable problems in commercial transactions for the sale of goods. Commercial sellers and buyers use standard forms. When goods are bought and sold, buyers usually use standard purchase order forms. Sellers usually accept goods on their standard confirmation forms. Slight variations in terms between these two forms violate the mirror-image rule. Again, the acceptance is effective when sent unless otherwise stated.

Because these two forms can vary to some degree, confusion can result. For example, the confirmation form contains a requirement that any disputes must be submitted to arbitration (see Chapter 4), whereas the purchase order form does not address this topic. Such a conflict is referred to as the "battle of the forms." Under the common law's mirror-image rule, no contract results when terms in the standardized forms contradict terms of the offer. In the commercial world of contracting for the sale and purchase of goods, the mirror-image rule was too rigid and did not reflect business practice.

If, however, a contract falls under the UCC's rules concerning the sale of goods, and both parties are merchants, the contract is formed when the offeree "accepts" the offer, even though the terms of the acceptance (the confirmation form) modify or add to the terms of the original offer [UCC 2-207(1)]. When the contract is between merchants, the new terms become part of the contract automatically. For example, if the confirmation form requires disputes to be arbitrated, this new term becomes part of the contract, unless an exception exists.

The UCC created three exceptions to this rule as it applies to merchants [UCC 2-207(2)]. The first exception occurs if the offer clearly requires the acceptance to be the same as the offer with no variations [UCC 2-207(2)(a)]. The purchase form can include a statement ("Acceptance to be on these terms only.") that any additional terms in the confirmation order will not become part of the contract.

Second, if the acceptance's new or changed terms materially change the offeror's duties, the new terms in the confirmation order will not be part of the contract [UCC 2-207(2)(b)]. In the example, the issue is whether submitting disputes to arbitration materially alters the offeror's right to a judicial court hearing. If so, the arbitration clause addition does not become a part of the contract.

The third exception applies when the offeror reads the new or changed terms. The offeror must object to (reject) those terms within a reasonable time period [UCC 2-207(2)(c)].

When one or both parties to the contract are nonmerchants, the UCC has a different rule. In these cases, the contract is formed according to the offeror's terms, not according to the additional acceptance terms. The additional terms are considered to be proposals to the newly formed contract.

The Drafting Committee for Uniform State Laws has recommended a change to the UCC 2-207 for merchants and nonmerchants. Under the proposed modification, the new terms in the purported acceptance do not at any time become part of the contract unless the offeree proves that the offeror agrees to the terms or that the offeror knew or had reason to know of the inconsistent terms and did not object to them. If adopted, the proposed rule will eliminate the problem of the battle of the forms that now exists between the buyer and the seller.

Termination of the Offer by Operation of Law.

Operation of law is a broad concept used by the court or statute to impose rights or liabilities on a party to a contract without any action taken by the party. The offeree's power to accept the offer and to form a contract can be ended by operation of law.

Four types of operation of law can end the offer: lapse of time, destruction of the offer's specific subject matter, either party's death or incompetence, and the offer's illegality. Often an offer will have a time limitation stated. For example, this offer ends at 12:00 P.M., noon, Pacific Standard Time, tomorrow. At 12:00:01 the offer has terminated. If no time is stated, the offeree has a reasonable time within which to accept. A reasonable time can vary from a few seconds, such as on a stock market, to over a year in a slow-selling real estate market.

The remaining three ways may occur between the time the offer is made and before the offer is accepted or rejected. The subject matter of the offer may be destroyed between the time the offer was made, but before it was accepted or rejected. If so, the offer is terminated. For example, you offer to purchase the stock car that won a national race. The owner of the stock car takes it on a final tour of the United States. While showing off the car at a race track, the driver hits the wall at a tremendous speed. The car bounces off with parts flying everywhere. The driver has few injuries, even though the car is destroyed, thereby terminating the offer.

Either party may die or become mentally incompetent after an offer is made. The offer is terminated unless the offer is irrevocable, such as an option contract or a firm offer. The last type of operation of law occurs after an offer has been made. The legislature passes a statute or a court declares the subject matter of the offer to be illegal, thereby ending the offer. For example, Congress passes a law making it illegal to sell computer chips to terrorist countries. Any outstanding offers to sell computer chips to a firm in a terrorist country ends by operation of law.

Exhibit 9–4 summarizes the ways in which an offer can be terminated.

Exhibit 9–4 Termination of an Offer

1. *By acts of the parties:*
   a. *Revocation* Unless the offer is irrevocable, it can be revoked by the offeror at any time before acceptance without liability. The revocation is effective when received by the offeree. Irrevocable offers are (i) option contracts, (ii) a merchant's firm offer [UCC 2-205], or (iii) when an offer becomes irrevocable because of promissory estoppel.
   b. *Rejection* Accomplished by words or actions that demonstrate a clear intent not to accept or consider the offer further. A rejection is not effective until known by the offeror.
   c. *Counteroffer* A rejection of the original offer and a new offer constitutes a counteroffer.

2. *By operation of law:*
   a. *Lapse of time* The offer terminates (i) at the end of the time period specified in the offer or (ii) if no time period is stated in the offer, at the end of a reasonable time period.
   b. *Destruction* The offer terminates when the specific subject matter of the offer is destroyed. Destruction automatically terminates the offer.
   c. *Death or mental incompetence* If either party dies or becomes incompetent, the offer is terminated, unless the offer states it is binding on the deceased or incompetent party's heirs or the offer is irrevocable.
   d. *Illegality* If the court or a statute makes the subject matter of the offer illegal after the offer has been made, that supervening illegality terminates the offer.

Acceptance

Acceptance is an offeree's voluntary agreement to the terms of the offer and is usually indicated by either words or conduct. The acceptance must be unequivocal and communicated to the offeror.

Except in certain circumstances, only the person to whom the offer is made, or that person's authorized agent, can accept the offer and create a binding contract. Part of the offer identifies the offeree as one of the offer's conditions. For example, Jones offers to sell his motorcycle to Hanley. Hanley rejects the offer, but Hanley's friend, Smith, attempts to accept the offer. No contract is formed.

Silence as an Act of Acceptance.

Ordinarily, silence does not constitute acceptance, even if the offeror states, "By your silence and inaction you will be deemed to have accepted this offer." An offeree carries no burden of performing some act in order to reject an offer unless the offeree has accepted a "duty to speak" by agreement or the offeree solicited the offer.

Book and video clubs have a contract with their members. The clubs will automatically send a book or video selection unless the member returns a card indicating that she does not want the selection in the upcoming month. Silence acts as an acceptance because the contract between the club and the member establishes silence as an acceptance method. These clubs fall under the Federal Trade Commission's **Negative Option Rule**, which requires the clubs to give members enough time to respond if they want to decline the monthly selection.

Communication of Acceptance.

At common law, whether the offeror must be notified of the acceptance depends on the nature of the offer. In a unilateral contract, generally it is not necessary to notify the offeror because the act of acceptance is evident [see, however, UCC 2-206(2)]. The offer calls for the full performance of the act. Acceptance is not completed, therefore, until the act has been fully performed. In the example used previously to illustrate a unilateral contract, the contract is complete only when someone returns the lost dog for the reward.

In a bilateral contract involving real property or services, the offeree must communicate the acceptance to the offeror. The acceptance takes the form of a promise (not an act), and the contract is formed when the return promise (the acceptance) is made (rather than when the act is performed).

The acceptance is effective when sent by the same manner in which the original offer was made. For example, if the offer is sent by e-mail, the acceptance, if sent by e-mail, is effective when sent, even though the offeror never receives the e-mail containing the acceptance. This rule is known as the **mailbox rule**.

The offer can state the method to be used to return the acceptance. For example, the offer is made by mailing it to the offeree who is instructed to e-mail back the acceptance. If the offeree uses a method of communication authorized by the offeror, the acceptance is effective when sent. If the offeror states no specific method of responding, such as by mail, the rule is to mail the acceptance. The acceptance will be effective when mailed.

Under the UCC, an offer may be accepted in any manner and by any medium reasonable under the circumstances [UCC 2-206(1)(a)]. This is a practical rule for business transactions and the acceptance is effective when sent. Under this rule, a contract can be formed even if the offeror never receives the message of acceptance.

The UCC also provides that an order to buy goods may be treated as either a bilateral or a unilateral contract. The offer to buy goods can be accepted by a promise to ship the goods (bilateral contract) or by an actual shipment of the goods (unilateral contract) [UCC 2-206(1)(b)]. For example, Shirts Galore, Inc., receives a purchase order to ship two dozen red shirts to Burton's Men Store, Inc. Shirts Galore can accept by promptly shipping the red shirts to Burton's. If Shirts Galore does not have the red shirts to ship but will have them in three days, Shirts Galore can send a FAX (the acceptance) to Burton's that the shirts will be shipped. If Shirts Galore sends the red shirts as promised, the contract is completed. If Shirts Galore, however, sends blue shirts, Shirts Galore is in breach of contract because it shipped nonconforming goods.

Exhibit 9–5 summarizes the requirements for contract acceptance.

Genuineness of Mutual Assent

The offeror and the offeree must have a meeting of the minds, called **mutual assent**. In other words, the offer made by one party must be the offer accepted by the other party. The terms of the offer must be the terms of

Exhibit 9–5   Acceptance of a Contract

1. Agreement can be made only by the offeree or the offeree's authorized agent.
2. Terms must be unequivocal.
   a. *Mirror-image rule* Under the common law, terms of acceptance must be same as terms of offer.
   b. *UCC rule* A definite acceptance of an offer is not a counteroffer, even if new terms modify the terms of the original offer [UCC 2-207]. If either party is a nonmerchant, additional terms are proposals for addition to the contract but not part of it. Between merchants, the additional terms become a part of the contract, with these exceptions:
      i. Offer limits acceptance to its terms [UCC 2-207(2)(a)].
      ii. New terms materially change offer [UCC 2-207(2)(b)].
      iii. New terms are rejected [UCC 2-207(2)(c)].
3. Acceptance of a bilateral offer can be communicated to the offeror by an authorized mode of communication and is effective upon dispatch. Unless the mode of communication is expressly specified by the offeror, the following methods are implicitly authorized:
   a. The same or a faster mode than used by the offeror.
   b. By mail, when the two parties are at a distance.
   c. Under UCC 2-206(1)(a), in acceptance of offers for the sale of goods, any medium that is reasonable under the circumstance.
4. Under UCC 2-206(1)(b), an offer to buy goods for prompt shipment means:
   a. the offer can be accepted by shipment of conforming goods, and
   b. the offer can be accepted by promise to ship. The shipper can send conforming or nonconforming goods. If nonconforming goods are sent, the shipper is in breach of contract for failing to ship conforming goods in accordance with the contract.

---

the acceptance. Mutual assent means that both sides contract for the same item or service.

Factual disputes occur when a meeting of the minds was apparent, but in reality the parties did not reach an understanding. No genuine assent exists as to the contract terms when fraud, misrepresentation, certain forms of mistake, *duress,* or *undue influence* take place. A party to the contract can use these situations to prove to the court why he should not be ordered to perform the contract.

Fraud and Misrepresentation. When fraud occurs, the injured party can void the contract. The five requirements that establish fraud are as follows:

1. A misrepresentation of a material fact exists.
2. The guilty party makes the contract with the knowledge that the material fact is false or with reckless disregard as to its truthfulness.
3. The guilty party intends to deceive.

4. The innocent party justifiably relied on the misrepresentation.
5. The innocent party has suffered damages.

Fraud is difficult to prove because the other party's knowledge and wrongful intent must be established. Because of the difficulty in proving fraud, many injured parties sue for **misrepresentation** instead. To establish a claim for misrepresentation, one need not prove that the guilty party intended to deceive or had knowledge of falseness. Obviously, this makes misrepresentation much easier to prove but may result in a lesser remedy. The court usually awards greater damages if fraud is proved.[7] The following case discusses fraudulent misrepresentation.

---

[7] Recent acts of fraud are posted on the Internet. Go to <http://www.lectlaw.com/tcos.html> and look for the heading "Swindles, Scams, & Rip-offs." Posted are a long list of phony scams ranging from fraudulent student scholarships to living trusts.

Case 9.3

Richardson v. Hardin

Supreme Court of Wyoming,
2000
5 P.3d 793

BACKGROUND AND FACTS The Richardsons were planning a move from Jackson to Cody. They were looking for a house large enough to accommodate their family. They also wanted a place large enough that they could keep horses. Mrs. Richardson viewed the Hardins' home on two occasions. Mrs. Hardin was home on both occasions. At neither time did Mrs. Hardin make any statements that influenced Mrs. Richardson's decision to purchase the home.

Because homes were in short supply, Mrs. Richardson offered to purchase the home for the asking price of $107,000 before her husband had the opportunity to see the home. The Hardins accepted the offer. The Hardins signed and returned the Richardsons' offer along with the property condition statement that had not been seen by the Richardsons before this time.

The buy/sell contract was a standard form that contains language advising buyers that they are accepting the house "as is, where is" without any reliance on any representations of the sellers. The buyers were informed that buy/sell contract was a legally binding document and that the buyers might, therefore, want to consult with legal counsel before signing. Mrs. Richardson testified that she read and understood the contract before she signed it. The Richardsons were also aware that they had a right to inspect the property prior to closing and that the right of inspection also allowed them to void the sale if the inspection was unsatisfactory.

After moving into the home, the Richardsons discovered foundation defects. They hired a civil engineer to inspect the house and report on his findings. The engineer reported that the foundation had failed and the failure would continue to degrade, ultimately to the point of collapse. The engineer attributed the problem to the presence of expansive clays around the exterior of the basement foundation. He also noted that the basement floor was severely buckled, indicating the presence of expansive clays under the floor as well. He reported that he did not see any possibility of being able to repair the foundation and believed the only option was to remove the home from the foundation, reconstruct a completely new foundation designed for the soil conditions, and reset the home. He was concerned that the problems were known to the previous home owners because he had found some caulking in the cracks behind the paneling.

The Richardsons asserted that they did not have the property inspected because, after the buy/sell contract was formed, Mrs. Richardson asked Mrs. Hardin about whether she had ever had any problems with the home. The Richardsons claim that Mrs. Hardin answered that she had never had any problems with the home and that she was sad to leave it. The Richardsons insisted that they were defrauded by this statement because the Hardins had settling problems in 1981 that Mrs. Hardin failed to mention. The Richardsons also claimed that the property condition statement misrepresented the condition of the home when the answer "no" was checked in response to the inquiry about whether concealed cracks existed in the foundation walls or floors.

The Hardins contended that, at the time the floor was carpeted and the paneling was installed, the only cracks present were normal hairline cracks expected in normal settling and that they caulked the walls because they originally intended to paint the basement. They also asserted that, as required by the property condition statement, they provided the present description and condition of the property as they knew it to be.

The Richardsons filed suit, alleging fraudulent misrepresentation. The defendants filed a motion for a summary judgment. The district court granted the defendants' motion, finding that the Richardsons "failed to meet their burden of clear, unequivocal, and convincing evidence on summary judgment." The district court also found that the Richardsons "failed to prove any reliance upon a representation in purchasing the home and further failed to prove that any misrepresentation, if any existed, was intentional."

MACY, Justice

. . . .

To succeed on a claim of fraudulent misrepresentation, three elements must be established: First, the buyer must prove by clear and convincing evidence that the seller misrepresented a material fact; second, the buyer must establish that he relied upon the misrepresentations in entering into the contract and that such reliance was reasonable; and third, the buyer must demonstrate that he suffered injury as a result of his reliance upon the misrepresentation. With regard to the reasonable reliance element, this Court has recognized that the false representation must occur prior to the execution of the contract which is sought to be avoided or under which damages are sought to be recovered.

Our review of the record discloses that the representations at issue occurred after the contract had been formed. It is undisputed that the defendants did not make any representations to the Richardsons until after May 27, 1993—the date the parties executed the buy/sell contract.

We addressed a similar situation in [another case], where we held that any misrepresentations made after the buy/sell contract was executed could not be the basis of actionable fraud.

The documentation before the district court might well create a triable issue as to whether the misrepresentations which are complained of actually occurred, but this issue of fact cannot interfere with our affirmance of the district court's grant of the summary judgment. Even if such misrepresentations of fact did occur, they were made after the contract had been executed. As a matter of law such misrepresentations cannot form the basis of actionable fraud because they could not serve as an inducement to the buyers in entering into the contract.

DECISION AND REMEDY The court agreed with the district court that the Richardsons had failed to meet their burden of establishing by clear, unequivocal, and convincing evidence that they relied upon false representations in entering into the buy/sell contract.

CRITICAL THINKING: PREVENTIVE LAW Discuss methods the defendants could have taken to protect themselves from having to defend this action.

Mistake, Duress, and Undue Influence. Mistakes occur in two forms. A **unilateral mistake** is made by only one of the contracting parties. A **mutual mistake** is made by both of them.

Unilateral Mistake. A unilateral mistake does not affect the contract, which is still valid and enforceable, unless the mistake is so obvious that the other party recognized or should have recognized it. A person cannot take unfair advantage when she knows or should have known that the other party is mistaken.

For example, a court was faced with this set of facts. Jean ran a retail camera store. Jim, a salesperson for a printing company, obtained an order from Jean for re-turn address labels. Jean needed 4,000 labels. She, however, was busy at the time she filled out the form and inadvertently wrote "4,000 m.m." in the blank quantity space. The initials *m.m.* to a person who uses cameras is millimeter, which is a unit of measurement used when taking photographs. Jean was used to writing "m.m." after numbers and did not realize her mistake. Jim looked at the order but did not recheck it with Jean. He returned to the office elated that he had a sale for four million million (four trillion) labels. Neither he nor his company had ever had such a large order. In fact, a special printing run was made and a freight company made the delivery. The usual method of sending labels to the customer is by mail. Two trucks backed up to Jean's business and the drivers asked where to unload the four trillion labels. Jean refused to accept delivery because she wanted only 4,000 labels. In this case, the court held that Jim should have known that Jean had made a unilateral mistake because of the unusual nature of the order. He easily could have telephoned Jean to recheck the order before going to the trouble and expense of having the labels printed and delivered. The court ruled that Jean did not have a contract to purchase four trillion labels.

In contrast, had Jean filled out the form for "4,900" labels (with intent only to order 4,000), the burden of her unilateral mistake would fall on her, and she would be held liable for the purchase of 4,900 address labels. The mistake would not have been obvious. Thus, Jim would not have been held responsible for recognizing it.

Mutual Mistake. No contract is formed in the case of a mutual mistake under two circumstances: (1) when the parties disagree as to the identity of the contract's

subject matter or (2) when they are mistaken as to the existence of the subject matter. If one of these two conditions occurs, a meeting of the minds has not occurred, and a court will not find a binding contract. If a court finds, however, that a mutual mistake has occurred as to the value of the contract's subject matter, the contract generally will be fully enforceable against both parties.

For example, Gary contracts to sell Kathy a painting for $5,000. Both believe the painting's artist to be Tory, but they learn, instead, that the artist is Lori. Because the mutual mistake affected the subject matter's identity, there is no meeting of the minds and neither can enforce the contract. Had the mistake been related to the value—not the artist—of the painting, the contract would have been fully enforceable.

In the following case, the court was confronted with the issue of whether the jury should have been instructed about the requirement for a meeting of the minds.

Case 9.4

Flo-Products Co. v. Valley Farms Dairy Co.

Court of Appeals of Missouri, 1986
718 S.W.2d 207

BACKGROUND AND FACTS The plaintiff, Flo-Products Company, gave a telephone quote of "fifteen thirty-six," for certain cylinders to be used in the defendant's dairy packaging machine. The defendant's maintenance supervisor testified that the oral quote was "fifteen thirty-six," which he thought was $15.36. The cylinders were shipped to the defendant and billed at $1,536. The defendant refused to accept delivery because of the price discrepancy.

Flo-Products sued Valley Farms. The trial court did not instruct the jury to consider whether the parties had ever achieved a meeting of the minds. The plaintiff won a judgment in the trial court. Valley Farms appealed because the court did not instruct the jury concerning the meeting-of-the-minds element.

Judge DOWD

. . . .

. . . The jury was instructed . . . to find for plaintiff if they believe[d] plaintiff furnished the cylinders at defendant's request and that the charges for the cylinders were reasonable. Defendant requested the court to instruct the jury that "meeting of the minds" was a necessary element of plaintiff's case but the court refused the instruction.

Defendant alleges the trial court erred in refusing to give defendant's requested instruction on "meeting of the minds."

. . . "Meeting of the minds" is a necessary element to the making of a contract[.] . . . [A] meeting of the minds' as to price was a controverted [disputed] issue. For a verdict-directing instruction in favor of plaintiff to be acceptable, it must require the jury to find all the necessary elements of plaintiff's case except for uncontroverted facts. It is reversible error for an instruction to assume or ignore a controverted fact.

The discrepancy in the parties' understanding of the price term remained a controverted fact throughout the trial. Plaintiff Flo-Products Co. chose to submit its case to the jury[.] . . . [T]he jury [is required] to find for plaintiff if they believe: 1) Defendant requested plaintiff to furnish the goods, 2) Plaintiff furnished the goods to defendant, and 3) Plaintiff's charges were reasonable. Instructing the jury . . . under these circumstances resulted in a directed verdict for plaintiff without the only controverted issue of the case ever being before the jury.

DECISION AND REMEDY The trial court erred in not giving the jury an instruction on the requirement that the parties must have a meeting of the minds to have a valid contract. The discrepancy in the parties' understanding of the price remained the contested issue throughout the trial, yet the jury never made a decision on these contested facts. The trial court's judgment was reversed and the case was remanded to the trial court.

CRITICAL THINKING: PUBLIC APPLICATION Assume you are a jury member who was impaneled to hear this case. Assume that the jury was not provided the jury instruction that you knew to be tantamount to the decision. Discuss how you would vote as to the defendant's liability and discuss the arguments you would make to the other jury members.

Duress. **Duress** occurs when one party is forced into the contract by fear. The courts allow the party who was under duress to rescind the agreement. For example, if Piranha Loan Company threatens to harm Chang unless he signs over to Piranha his $10,000 car in order to secure a $100 loan, Piranha is guilty of using duress, so Chang could rescind the agreement.

Duress may involve the threat of physical or economic harm, such as the loss of a job. The threatened act must be wrongful or illegal. When a party is threatened with physical harm, any agreement signed while the party is subject to such a threat is void (that is, it is without any legal effect). When a person signs an agreement under threat of economic harm, the person may choose to carry out the agreement or to disaffirm it.

Undue Influence. **Undue influence** arises from special kinds of relationships in which one party can greatly influence another party, thus overcoming that party's free will. Minors and elderly people are often under the influence of close relatives. If, for example, Shady influences an elderly person who is under his legal care to enter into a contract that benefits Shady, undue influence has been exerted.

Undue influence can arise from a number of fiduciary (founded on trust) or confidential relationships, such as attorney–client, doctor–patient, guardian–ward, parent–child, husband–wife, or trustee–beneficiary. The essential element of undue influence is that the party of whom advantage is being taken does not, in reality, exercise free will when entering into the contract. This contract is voidable by the person who was unduly influenced.

Exhibit 9–6 summarizes the defenses that a party to a contract can use to contest mutual assent.

Consideration

The third requirement of a legally enforceable agreement is **consideration**. Consideration is divided into two elements: (1) one party must exchange something of legal value for the other's promise, and (2) the parties must bargain for and exchange the promises. Legal value may consist of a return promise or a performance.

Requirements of Consideration. To create a binding contract, the elements of consideration not only must exist but also must be legally sufficient. To be legally sufficient, consideration for a promise must be

Exhibit 9-6   Problems of Assent

Fraud

When fraud occurs, usually the innocent party can enforce or avoid the contract at his option. The five elements necessary for a court to find fraud follow:

1. Misrepresentation of a material fact exists.
2. Contract is made with knowledge that the fact is false.
3. Contract is made with the intent to deceive.
4. Innocent party justifiably relies on the misrepresentation.
5. Innocent party is damaged.

Misrepresentation

The elements in preceding items 2 and 3 are not required for the court to find misrepresentation. Usually in misrepresentation cases, the innocent party can rescind the contract but cannot seek damages.

Mistake

Unilateral Generally, the mistaken party is bound by her mistake and the other party can enforce the contract unless the other party knows or should have recognized the mistake.

Mutual When a mistake made by both parties involves the identity or existence of the contract's subject matter, either party can avoid performing the contract.

Duress

Duress is defined as forcing a party to enter an agreement under fear induced by a threat (for example, the threat of violence or economic pressure). The party forced to enter the contract can rescind the agreement.

Undue Influence

Undue influence arises from special relationships, such as fiduciary or confidential relationships, in which one party's free will has been overcome by the undue influence exerted by the other party. Usually, the contract is voidable.

---

legally detrimental to the **promisee**—the one receiving the promise—or legally beneficial to the **promisor**—the one making the promise. In every bilateral contract, each party (offeror and offeree) is treated as both a promisor and a promisee because each makes a promise. Neither *legal detriment* nor *legal benefit* is synonymous with actual economic detriment or benefit.

Note the language change from *offeror* and *offeree* to *promisor* and *promisee*. The former two words describe the parties during the contract formation. Once the parties exchange promises, they become the *promisor* and *promisee*.

Legal detriment occurs when a person does, or promises to do, something that he had no prior legal duty to perform or when the person gives up a legal right. Conversely, **legal benefit** occurs when a person obtains something that he had no prior legal right to obtain. In most cases, each party to a contract suffers a legal detriment and receives a legal benefit.

For example, Fine Gravel Company owns and mines a gravel pit. The land owned by Fine Gravel is adjacent to a school, but the actual mining takes place on the land furthest from the school. The school is one mile away from the mining site. After many years, Fine Gravel decides to mine within a few hundred yards of the school. It also plans to build a road for its trucks next to the school fence. The school board objects because of the danger to the children and the noise that the construction will produce. The school board offers $150,000 to Fine Gravel Company to refrain from building the road and from mining near the school. The gravel company agrees. The consideration flowing from the gravel company is the promise to refrain from an act that it is legally entitled to do, that is, to earn profits by mining gravel. The consideration flowing from the school board to Fine Gravel is the promise to pay a sum of money that it is not otherwise legally required to pay. In other words, the school board's legal benefit was the maintenance of conditions conducive to learning near the school grounds. Its legal detriment was to pay $150,000. The benefit to Fine Gravel was the $150,000. Its legal detriment was to give up the right to build the road and the right to mine land that it owned.

In the following case, one of the classics of contract law, the court found that refraining from certain behavior at the request of another was sufficient consideration to support a promise to pay a sum of money.

Case 9.5

Hamer v. Sidway

Court of Appeals of New
York, Second Division, 1891
124 N.Y. 538, 27 N.E. 256

LANDMARK CASE

BACKGROUND AND FACTS William E. Story, Sr., was the uncle of William E. Story II. In the presence of family members and guests at a family gathering, Story, Sr., promised to pay his nephew $5,000 to refrain from drinking, using tobacco, swearing, and playing cards or billiards for money until he reached the age of twenty-one.

The nephew agreed and fully kept his promise. When he reached age twenty-one, he wrote his uncle that he had kept his part of the agreement and was entitled to $5,000. The uncle replied by letter that he was pleased with his nephew's performance and that he was keeping his nephew's promised money in the bank to earn interest. The nephew agreed that his uncle should keep the money according to the terms and conditions of the letter.

The uncle died about twelve years later without having paid his nephew any part of the $5,000 or interest. Sidway, the executor of the uncle's estate (the defendant in this action), did not want to pay the $5,000 plus interest to the nephew, claiming that the nephew had not given valid consideration for the promise. In the meantime, the nephew sold his interest (his right to collect the $5,000 if the court ruled in his favor) to Hamer. Hamer sued Sidway to collect the $5,000. The court disagreed with the executor and reviewed the doctrine of detriment-benefit as valid consideration under the law.

Justice PARKER

. . . The defendant contends that the contract was without consideration to support it, and therefore invalid. He asserts that the promisee, by refraining from the use of liquor and tobacco, was not harmed, but benefitted; that which he did was best for him to do, independently of his uncle's promise—and insists that it follows that, unless the promisor was benefitted, the contract was without consideration—a contention which, if well founded, would seem to leave open for controversy in many cases whether that which the promisee did or omitted to do was in fact of such benefit to him as to leave no consideration to support the enforcement of the promisor's agreement. Such a rule could not be tolerated, and is without foundation in the law. The exchequer chamber [a type of court] in 1875 defined "consideration" as follows: "A valuable consideration, in the sense of the law, may consist either in some right, interest, profit, or benefit accruing to the one party, or some forbearance, detriment, loss, or responsibility given, suffered, or undertaken by the other." Courts "will not ask whether the thing which forms the consideration does in fact benefit the promisee or a third party, or is of any substantial value to any one. It is enough that something is promised, done, forborne, or suffered by the party to whom the promise is made as consideration for the promise made to him. In general a waiver of any legal right at the request of another party is a sufficient consideration for a promise." . . . Now, applying this rule to the facts before us, the promisee used tobacco, occasionally drank liquor, and he had a legal right to do so. That right he abandoned for a period of years upon the strength of the promise of the testator that for such forbearance he would give him $5,000. We need not speculate on the effort which may have been required to give up the use of those stimulants. It is sufficient that he restricted his lawful freedom of action within certain prescribed limits upon the faith of his uncle's agreement, and now, having fully performed the conditions imposed, it is of no moment whether such performance actually proved a benefit to the promisor, and the court will not inquire into it; but, were it a proper subject of inquiry, we see nothing in this record that would permit a determination that the uncle was not benefitted in a legal sense. . . .

DECISION AND REMEDY The court ruled that the nephew had provided legally sufficient consideration by giving up smoking, drinking, swearing, and playing cards or billiards for money until the age of twenty-one and, therefore, he was entitled to the money promised him. In the late 1800s, when this case took place, a minor could legally do these things.

Under the doctrine of detriment-benefit, the court looks at the party who suffered a detriment (harm) and the party who received a benefit (right). In this case, the nephew suffered a detriment of giving up his rights to drinking, smoking, swearing, and playing cards or billiards for money. The uncle received the benefit of the satisfaction that his nephew was not engaging in these activities.

COMMENT The *Hamer v. Sidway* case is a good illustration of the distinction between a benefit to the promisor and a detriment to the promisee. Here the court did not inquire as to whether a benefit flowed to the promisor but required only that a legally sufficient detriment to the promisee occurred.

CRITICAL THINKING: LEGAL APPLICATION This chapter covers the basic concepts of legal consideration. The key to understanding legal consideration is to recognize a bargain for exchange and a legal sufficiency of consideration. The most difficult aspect of determining these is identifying the detriment and benefit that occurred as applied to each party. In buying your textbook for this course from the local bookstore, you were involved in a contract. Explain the benefit and detriment of each party to this contract.

Although the previous case was decided more than 100 years ago, the principal rule on consideration remains the same. To have consideration each side must have a legal detriment and each is entitled to a legal benefit. Sometimes, in spite of the appearance that each side has made a binding promise, actually the promise cannot be found. These are called **illusory promises**. The following current case in the employment law area was decided on the basis of consideration.

Case 9.6

Gibson v. Neighborhood Health Clinics, Inc.

United States Court of Appeals, Seventh Circuit, 1997
121 F.3d 1126
http://www.kentlaw.edu/7circuit/1997/aug/96-2652.html

BACKGROUND AND FACTS Gibson, who had previously been employed by Neighborhood Health Clinics (NHC), was rehired by NHC on December 22, 1994. On December 30, at which time Gibson had not yet returned to work, NHC held a meeting to present employees with a new Associates Policy Manual (Manual), and to require employees to sign a new Associates Understanding (Understanding). Gibson was not required to attend the meeting and, in fact, did not.

The Understanding included the following language:

I agree to the grievance and arbitration provisions set forth in the Associates Policy Manual. I understand that I am waiving my right to a trial, including a jury trial, in state or federal court of the class of disputes specifically set forth in the grievance and arbitration provisions on pages 8–10 of the Manual.

The opening two paragraphs of the Manual included the following language:

Neighborhood Health Clinics reserves the right at any time to modify, revoke, suspend, terminate, or change any or all terms of this Manual, plans, policies, or procedures, in whole or in part, without having to consult or reach agreement with anyone, at any time, with or without notice. . . .

. . . [W]hile Neighborhood Health Clinics intends to abide by the policies and procedures described in this Manual, it does not constitute a contract nor promise of any kind. Therefore, employees can be terminated at any time, with or without notice, and with or without cause.

The arbitration provisions were not part of the terms of employment during Gibson's previous tenure with NHC. She reported to work on January 9, 1995, and met with NHC's personnel director, Chris Baxter, who handed Gibson a stack of papers to sign, including insurance and tax forms. The Understanding was among those papers. Baxter told her that all employees signed the form so that complaints about time off could be settled through a grievance procedure.

Baxter did not give Gibson the Manual referenced in the Understanding at that time, but was only able to locate a copy later that day, at which time Gibson received it. Although she signed the Understanding, Gibson never signed the Manual.

NHC fired Gibson on April 6, 1995. Gibson filed a federal lawsuit alleging sex and disability discrimination. NHC moved to dismiss Gibson's complaint because she had agreed to submit any disputes to arbitration. The district court agreed, concluding that the Manual in connection with the Understanding created an enforceable arbitration agreement, and granted the motion to dismiss. In addition, because Gibson failed to abide by the deadline for submitting her claim to arbitration, the dismissal effectively foreclosed her ability to obtain redress.

Circuit Judge FLAUM

. . . .

It is a basic tenet of contract law that in order for a promise to be enforceable against the promisor, the promisee must have given some consideration for the promise. Consideration is defined as bargained for exchange whereby the promisor (here Gibson) receives some benefit or the promisee (here NHC) suffers a detriment. Thus, in order for Gibson's agreement to be enforceable, there must be detriment to NHC or benefit to Gibson that was bargained for in exchange for Gibson's promise to arbitrate all disputes.

Often, consideration for one party's promise to arbitrate is the other party's promise to do the same. In the present case, however, NHC cannot point to its own promise to arbitrate in order to make enforceable Gibson's promise to do likewise. The Understanding contains no promise on NHC's part to submit claims to arbitration. It is worded entirely in terms of Gibson's obligation to submit her claims to arbitration (using phrases such as "I agree" "I understand" "I am waiving"); it contains no promise on NHC's part. In order for a contract to be enforceable, both parties must be bound by its terms.

. . . .

. . . Nor was Gibson's promise to submit claims to arbitration supported by consideration in the form of NHC's promise to hire her or to continue to employ her, or by its reasonable reliance on her promise. An initial offer of employment may constitute consideration for an employee's promise, such as a covenant not to compete. However, NHC's offer of employment to Gibson was not made in exchange for her promise to arbitrate, for she had already been hired at the time she made the promise. Once again, the element of bargained for exchange is lacking. An employer's specific promise to continue to employ an at-will employee may provide valid consideration for an employee's promise to forgo certain rights. . . . In the present case, however, NHC never made a promise to continue Gibson's employment in exchange for her promise to submit claims to arbitration. That is, it never communicated to her that if she signed the Understanding she could continue to work there, and that if she did not her status would be uncertain. It is true that NHC continued to employ her. Yet when an employer has made no specific promise, the mere fact of continued employment does not constitute consideration for the employee's promise. . . . Finally, while in the employment context it has been held that one party's partial performance in reliance upon the other party's promise may be sufficient consideration to make the promise enforceable, there is no indication in the present case that NHC was induced to rely on Gibson's promise. It had made its decision to hire her prior to her agreeing to the terms of the Understanding, and there is no evidence that its decision to continue to employ her following her signing of the Understanding (on the day she returned to work) was based upon her agreeing to the terms contained therein. We therefore conclude that Gibson's promise to submit her claims against NHC to arbitration did not give rise to an enforceable contract.

DECISION AND REMEDY The court found that, although Gibson had agreed to arbitration, NHC had not made any promise in exchange. The language in the Manual made it look as if NHC had made a promise when, in fact, it had not. This language is called an *illusory promise*.

COMMENT Other federal district courts have reached similar decisions in other employee arbitration clause cases that are similar to these facts. The Equal Employment Opportunity Commission (EEOC) has concluded that employees' agreements to waive their rights under the Americans with Disabilities Act and Title VII of the Civil Rights Act are invalid as a matter of public policy. The EEOC's position, however, has not been tested in court. Most courts, however, will uphold the arbitration clauses if anything has been provided in exchange for signing, such as a day off. Further, some courts have allowed people to be fired when they refused to sign a post-hire arbitration clause. Chapter 23 provides additional information about the Americans with Disabilities Act, Title VII of the Civil Rights Act, and the Equal Employment Opportunity Commission.

CRITICAL THINKING: LEGAL APPLICATION When an employer requires its prospective or current employees to sign an arbitration clause giving up their rights to sue the employer in the judicial system, can an employee argue that he signed the contract under economic duress, that is, he signed the arbitration clause as a condition of being hired? Explain.

Consideration is important when settling a disputed debt, or **unliquidated debt**. If the parties reach an amicable settlement for an unliquidated debt, the debt, at that point, becomes liquidated. A **liquidated debt** is one that is not disputed. Legal consideration comes into play whenever an unliquidated debt becomes liquidated.

For example, Steve is in his automobile when Brandon's truck strikes it in the rear. Steve suffers a whiplash injury, resulting in great pain and suffering. Steve believes that he should recover at least $100,000

for his automobile damage, injury, and pain and suffering. Brandon's insurance company believes that $2,000 is adequate to cover Steve's injury and to repair his automobile. To avoid a lawsuit, both parties agree that Steve will receive $10,000. Legal consideration is present in this case. Steve's legal detriment is giving up his legal right to sue for $90,000 more. His benefit is the settlement increase of $8,000. The reverse is true for Brandon. His benefit is Steve's reduced request from $100,000 to $10,000. His legal detriment is to pay $10,000 instead of $2,000. The debt was unliquidated originally but became liquidated when the parties reached a settlement.

In addition to parties experiencing bargaining difficulties involving unliquidated debts, problems concerning consideration often arise when a prior duty under an existing contract exists. The prior existing debt rule applies to resolving this problem. Every loan is due on demand unless the parties have an agreement that indicates a specific repayment arrangement. Payment on demand means that you can demand repayment at any time.

For example, let's assume that you loan a friend $100. When you see your friend at a football game, you ask him for the $100, but he insists that he only has $25. He offers to pay you the $25 if you will forget about the remaining $75. You know that your friend is unemployed and you probably will never recover the money that you loaned to him. As a result, you accept the $25 from him. The next day you find out that your friend won a $1 million lottery. You go to your friend and ask for the remaining $75, but your friend refuses to pay it, contending that the $25 payment discharged the remaining $75 he owed you. If you filed a lawsuit, a court would find in your favor. Your agreement to accept $25 in return for discharging the remaining $75 lacked legal consideration. Your friend owed you a liquidated debt of $100 and cannot discharge it by paying only $25. By paying you $25, your friend did not suffer a legal detriment, because he was under a prior legal duty to pay you the full $100. You did suffer a legal detriment by giving up $75, but you did not obtain a legal benefit because you were entitled to $100 and not just $25. Each person must obtain a legal benefit and must suffer a legal detriment. The fact that your friend won the lottery is irrelevant as to whether your friend still owed you the $75. Once the friend had money to repay the loan, you are legally justified to collect the $75. Without the lottery winnings, the $75 is merely uncollectible.

A different result occurs when the agreement involves the sale of goods instead of a loan. According to UCC 2-209, a contract involving the goods can be modified and does not need additional consideration to be binding. For example, you order lamps from a manufacturer for your furniture store at $75 per lamp. Later, you discover that one of your competitors sells a similar lamp to the general public for $60. You contact the manufacturer and explain that your competitors are selling a similar lamp for $60. The manufacturer and you reach an agreement that you will pay only $30 per lamp. The second agreement is enforceable because it involves a modification to a contract for the sale of goods. Neither party provided any new consideration to support this second agreement. You suffered no legal detriment, because you were obligated to pay $75 per lamp. The manufacturer received no legal benefit, because you already were obligated to purchase the lamps. UCC 2-209 exempts this type of modification from requiring new consideration and from the prior existing debt rule.

Adequacy of Consideration. Adequacy of consideration refers to a bargain's fairness. A court normally will not question the consideration's adequacy if it is legally sufficient. If a person buys an item at too high a price, she may have buyer's remorse, but the court will not set the contract aside unless a reason, such as fraud or mistake, exists.

Exhibit 9–7 summarizes the legal elements of consideration. The next chapter discusses the other elements of a contract and possible defenses against enforcing a contract.

Exhibit 9–7 Elements of Consideration

1. *Legal value* Does not mean economic value.
   a. *Legal detriment* To promisee, who promises to do (or refrain from doing); no prior legal duty to perform (or to refrain from performing).
   b. *Legal benefit* To promisor.
2. *Bargained for and legally sufficient* The promisee's performance or promises to perform must be given in exchange for the promisor's promise. Adequacy of consideration relates to how much consideration is given and whether a fair bargain is reached. Courts inquire into the adequacy of consideration (if the consideration is legally sufficient) only when fraud, undue influence, or duress may be involved.

International Consideration

Variations in Terms of Sale When Dealing Internationally

For international commerce to thrive, governments must establish standard contract criteria. For example, should contracts be in writing and, if so, what constitutes "in writing"? Does a videotape, DVD (digital versatile disc), CD (compact disc), e-mail, or a fax qualify for a writing, or is the term limited to conventional hard copy? People who negotiate, draft, and adopt treaties and conventions confront many problems of this type.

The **United Nations Commission on International Trade Law (UNCITRAL)**[8] developed model laws that cover commercial transactions. These codes include the 1974 **Convention on the Limitation Period in the International Sale of Goods**.[9] This convention established unified rules for determining the statute of limitations in a lawsuit. It attempted to reconcile the differences between the common law and the civil law approaches of various countries. The maximum period within which a party to an international sales contract for goods can bring a lawsuit is four years.

In 1980, the **Convention on Contracts for the International Sale of Goods (CISG)** was adopted. The 101-article document is structured in a manner sim-ilar to UCC, Article 2, Sales. The United States and many of the major trading nations ratified this convention. The rules provide guidance for contract formation, performance, warranty provisions, interpretation, and remedies.

In many Western countries, in a sale of goods, the price often is left open. This practice allows the market to set the price when the vendor delivers the goods. The market price is assumed to be the reasonable price. Some non-Western nations require that sellers state the price within a detailed written contract. The CISG has adopted the market price for an open-price sale (the price was not settled when the contract was signed), unless the parties put in their contract some other method of setting the price.

The CISG establishes the time period for acceptance. This period begins at the moment the seller hands the telegram for dispatch; on the date shown on the seller's letter; or if no date appears, then on the postmarked date. If the seller makes the offer by telephone, telex, or other means of instantaneous communication, the period begins at the time the offer reaches the offeree. The acceptance is effective when it reaches the offeror. The contract is made at the moment an offer's acceptance becomes effective. Note that the time when the acceptance becomes effective according to the CISG is very different from the time established in the UCC. Under the UCC, the acceptance is effective when it is sent under most conditions.[10]

[8] The United Nations Commission on International Trade Law is found at <http://www.uncitral.org/>.

[9] Documents on International Sale of Goods and Related Transactions are found at <http://www.uncitral.org/english/texts/sales/index.htm>.

[10] More information about international contract law can be found at the Pace University School of Law site at <http://cisgw3.law.pace.edu/>.

LEGALLY SPEAKING
Making Sure You Are Insured

A common problem that businesses confront involves the handling of consumer complaints about the provided product or service. For example, you go to Jim Onest Insurance Agency to purchase automobile liability insurance coverage. Onest obtains the necessary information to bind your vehicle for coverage and records this information in his computer. You pay the initial premium and leave his office. Shortly after you leave, a power failure causes the computerized information to be lost.

As you drive down the street, you overlook a stop sign and collide with a vehicle that had the right of way. No personal injuries are sustained, but extensive property damage occurs to the other vehicle. You contact Onest to inform him of the accident. He attempts to verify coverage but cannot do so because the information in the computer has been lost. He forgets about your check and informs you that you have no coverage.

This simple example illustrates some of the aspects of contract law. When you went to the insurance agency, you made an offer to purchase insurance, which Onest accepted. Legal consideration was present because the promises were bargained for and exchanged. Each party received a legal benefit and suffered a legal detriment. Lack of capacity or having an illegal contract is not at issue here. Most states do not require this type of contract to be in writing to be enforceable. You have proof of this contract in your canceled check. By not recognizing your contract, Onest has breached it.

You should have done several things, however, to protect yourself and avoid a lawsuit. While you were in Onest's office, you should have

✔ obtained the specifics of who, what, when, where, and how much;

✔ obtained the name of the company that was insuring you;

✔ obtained the policy number; and

✔ requested a receipt instead of relying on your check as your receipt and later remembering to keep the check as evidence that you purchased the policy.

Chapter Summary

In today's basic contract law, the old law merchant has been replaced by uniform laws that the states may adopt. The most important is the Uniform Commercial Code (UCC). UCC Article 2, Sales, covering the sale of goods, is an important article for contract law.

Contracts are divided into three elements: formation, enforceability, and performance. The following terms describe the types of contract formation: unilateral and bilateral contracts, express and implied–in–fact contracts, quasi-contracts (implied–in–law contracts), and formal and informal contracts. Contract enforceability can be described as valid, voidable, or unenforceable. Some types of agreements are void, such as illegal contracts.

A contract's performance status is either executed or executory. To have a valid and enforceable contract, the parties must ensure that the following items are present:

1. *Offer* An offer must be made.

2. *Acceptance* An acceptance must be given by return promise or by an act.

3. *Consideration* Promises must be bargained for and exchanged, have legal value, and be legally sufficient to support the offer and acceptance.

4. *Capacity* The parties must have the legal capacity to form a contract.

5. *Legality* The contract's subject matter must be legal.

6. *Writing* Certain agreements must be in writing to be enforceable.

An offer and an acceptance represent the concept of mutual assent or a meeting of the minds. To have a valid offer:

1. the offeror must have an objective intent to contract

2. the terms must be reasonably definite (the UCC liberalizes this rule), and

3. the terms must be communicated.

An offer may be terminated by revocation, rejection (including a counteroffer), or operation of law.

Acceptance is a voluntary act by which the offeree agrees to the offer's terms. Silence normally does not constitute acceptance. The UCC includes specific rules as to when a contract acceptance is valid for the sale of goods. Sometimes an offer and an acceptance create an appearance of a meeting of the minds, but, in reality, mutual consent has not been given because of fraud, mistake, duress, or undue influence.

Legal consideration has two elements: legal value and bargained-for and exchanged promises. The courts normally are not concerned with the adequacy of consideration, only with the fact that the consideration promised is sufficient. Two rules that help to resolve problems with consideration are the unliquidated debt rule and prior existing debt rule. The unliquidated debt rule states that when a debt is disputed and a settlement is reached, the debt is no longer disputed. The debt now becomes a liquidated debt.

Under the prior existing debt rule, a party cannot make a partial payment on a debt to discharge the whole debt. The party did no more than it had already agreed to do; that is, pay the whole debt. If the contract involves the sale of goods, UCC 2-209 allows the contract to be modified without any additional consideration. The newly modified contract can be enforced in court even though no new consideration was involved.

Using the World Wide Web

The federal government has developed several initiatives to promote and develop electronic commerce. The Federal Electronic Commerce Program "coordinates, monitors, and reports on the development of Electronic Commerce (e-commerce) within the Federal Government." E-commerce is the preferred way of doing business with the federal government.

Federal agencies are buying and paying for most products and services electronically. Universities and research centers can seek grants and deliver reports online. Citizens are using smart cards to receive a range of benefits. Suppliers have real-time access to government business opportunities. Federal government buyers find what they need using electronic catalogs.

E-commerce is doing business electronically through the exploitation of the web to improve commerce. E-commerce uses many core technology tools, the web, electronic data interchange (EDI), electronic mail (e-mail), electronic funds transfer (EFT), electronic benefits transfer, electronic catalogs, credit cards, smart cards, and other techniques. The growing availability of sophisticated technology and easy-to-use web tools is helping e-commerce flourish throughout government.

The Defense Logistics Agency (DLA) is the buying agent for all branches of America's military service and a number of other federal civilian organizations. DLA annually purchases and distributes nearly $11 billion of food, clothing, electronics, medical supplies, construction supplies, spare parts, and fuel. Its Defense Contract Management Command supervises contracts and provides contract administration services for more than 360,000 contracts per year—worth more than $900

billion-by private companies for military services and federal organizations. The DLA uses the web to make routine purchases, thus saving the taxpayers money.

E-Commerce Guide features a comprehensive list of links to hundreds of World Wide Web sites and resources devoted to the evolving electronic commerce industry.

Finding the Law on the Web

Federal Electronic Commerce Program
    http://www.ec.fed.gov/
Defense Logistics Agency
    http://www.dla.mil/
E-Commerce Guide
    http://e-comm.internet.com/

Chapter Web Sites

Legal Information Institute
    http://www.law.cornell.edu/
Free Advice
    http://www.freeadvice.com
'Lectric Law Library, Business & General Forms
    http://lectlaw.com/formb.htm
National Conference of Commissioners on Uniform
    State Laws
    http://www.law.upenn.edu/bll/ulc/ulc_frame.htm
'Lectric Law Library Lawcopedia
    http://www.lectlaw.com/tcos.html
FindLaw
    http://www.findlaw.com/
United Nations Electronic Data Interchange
    http://www.unece.org/trade/untdid/

Gibson v. Neighborhood Health Clinics, Inc.
   http://www.kentlaw.edu/7circuit/1997/aug
   /96-2652.html
United Nations Commission on International Trade Law
   http://www.uncitral.org/
International Sale of Goods and Related Transactions
   http://www.uncitral.org/english/texts/sales
   /index.htm
Pace University School of Law
   http://cisgw3.law.pace.edu/
'Lectric Law Library, Forms Room
   http://www.lectlaw.com/form.htm
eBay
   http://www.ebay.com/

Web Activities

9–1 Most students attend college with the help of some form of student aid. In most cases, the aid comes in the form of student loans. A student loan is a type of contract. If you have more than one student loan, you might consider consolidating the loans. The advantages of consolidation are provided at <http://www.lectlaw.com /form.htm>. Click on the "Reference Room," then go to "Consumer Issues & Protection." There you will find the topic of consolidating student loans with the federal direct loan program. What are the advantages of consolidating your student loans?

9–2 Business-to-consumer auction sites are often subject to fraudulent activities. What steps has the popular auction site, eBay, taken to protect purchasers? What steps can you as a purchaser take to protect yourself? Go to eBay's web site at <http://www.ebay.com/>, click on "Services," scroll down to "Safe Harbors."

Key Terms

acceptance	executory contract	mirror-image rule	revocation
bilateral contract	express contract	misrepresentation	undue influence
consideration	firm offer	mutual assent	unenforceable contract
contract	formal contract	mutual mistake	Uniform Commercial
Convention on	illusory promise	Negative Option Rule	Code (UCC)
Contracts for the	implied-in-fact contract	offer	unilateral contract
International Sale of	implied-in-law contract	offeree	unilateral mistake
Goods (CISG)	informal contract	offeror	United Nations
Convention on the	law merchant	operation of law	Commission on
Limitation Period in	legal benefit	option contract	International Trade
the International Sale	legal detriment	promisee	Law (UNCITRAL)
of Goods	liquidated debt	promisor	unliquidated debt
counteroffer	mailbox rule	promissory estoppel	valid contract
duress	merchant	quasi-contract	voidable contract
executed contract	minor	rejection	void agreement

Questions and Case Problems

9–1 Type James is confined to his bed. He calls a friend who lives across the street and offers to sell her his watch next week for $100. If his friend wants to accept, she is to put a red piece of paper in her front window. The next morning, she places a red piece of paper in her front window. Is this contract bilateral or unilateral? Explain.

9–2 Consideration Ingram started to work for Central Adjustment Bureau, Inc. (CABI). A week after starting work, his supervisor gave him an employment contract to sign. The contract contained a provision that restrained him from competing against CABI if he quit the company. He signed the contract because he was told that he would be fired if he did not sign it. Seven years later, he quit and started a competing business. CABI sued Ingram to prevent him from competing. Ingram defended on the basis that the contract lacked consideration because he signed it after he was working. Who prevailed and why? [*Central Adjustment Bureau, Inc. v. Ingram*, 678 S.W.2d 28 (Tenn. 1984)]

9–3 Undue Influence Conrad purchased a farm in 1945 for $23,500. He had thirteen children. In 1975, he conveyed his farm to his eldest son for the same amount as he had paid, although the farm was currently worth about $150,000. At the time of the conveyance, Conrad, at age eighty-two, was in extremely poor health and had been hospitalized often for various ailments. Eventually, a person called a conservator was appointed by a court to take care of Conrad's affairs. Conrad, through his conservator, filed a lawsuit to rescind the conveyance of the farm. At the trial, the eldest son testified that his father trusted and relied on him. Should this conveyance be set aside? If so, why? [*Schaneman v. Schaneman*, 206 Neb. 113, 291 N.W.2d 412 (1980)]

9–4 Offer–Acceptance The Olivers mentioned to Southworth, a neighbor, that they planned to sell off some of their ranch land. Southworth expressed interest in purchasing the property and later notified the Olivers that he had the money available to buy it. The Olivers told Southworth that they would let him know shortly about the details concerning the sale. The Olivers later sent a letter to Southworth—and (unknown to Southworth) to several other neighbors—giving information about the sale including the price, the property location, and the amount of acreage involved. When Southworth received the letter, he sent a letter to the Olivers "accepting" their offer. The Olivers stated that the information letter had not been intended as an "offer" but merely as a starting point for negotiations. Southworth brought suit against the Olivers to enforce the "contract." Did a contract exist? Explain. [*Southworth v. Oliver*, 284 Or. 361, 587 P.2d 994 (1978)]

9–5 Offer–Acceptance James desired to sell some timber that he owned. He sent notices to numerous potential buyers for bids (offers) for the timber. Eames responded by submitting the highest bid. James, however, refused to go through with the transaction, and Eames sued. Describe potential legal arguments for both James and Eames. [*Eames v. James*, 452 So. 2d 384 (La. App. 1984)]

9–6 Duress Laemmar was an employee of J. Walter Thompson Co. During the years of his employment, he purchased shares of common stock from the company. Laemmar's stock was subject to repurchase by the com-

pany if Laemmar's employment were terminated for any reason. The company's officers and directors decided to increase their control and demanded that Laemmar and several other employees sell their stock back to the company or lose their jobs. Although Laemmar did not want to sell his stock, he did so in order to keep his job. The officers and directors made no physical threats or suggestions of physical harm to Laemmar. Later, Laemmar instituted a lawsuit to rescind his sale of the stock on the basis of duress. Can Laemmar rescind? Explain. [*Laemmar v. J. Walter Thompson Co.*, 435 F.2d 680 (7th Cir. 1970)]

9–7 Misrepresentation Campbell (the plaintiff) was a high school dropout and was employed as a sheetmetal worker before he entered into negotiations with the defendant, Southland Corp., to purchase a 7-Eleven convenience store franchise. Southland Corp. operated more than 7,000 convenience stores. Southland Corp. required Campbell to prepare a business plan showing that he needed to receive a monthly income of $3,400 to meet both business and personal expenses. Southland Corp. did not inform Campbell that the store's average monthly income was $1,340, but Southland Corp. did inform Campbell that the average net income in his approximate location ranged from $1,400 to $3,100 per month. After operating the store for nineteen months, Campbell's store was below the franchise agreement's net worth requirement. Southland Corp. terminated Campbell's franchise (contract). Campbell filed a lawsuit alleging misrepresentation. The trial judge granted Southland Corp.'s motion for summary judgment because the projected profits were opinions and opinions normally do not constitute fraud. Should the judge's decision be upheld? Explain your decision. [*Campbell v. Southland Corp.*, 871 P.2d 487 (Or. App. 1994)]

9–8 Offer–Acceptance Treece, the defendant, was a vice president of Vend-A-Win, Inc., a corporation that was in the business of distributing punchboards (a gambling device). The Washington State Gambling Commission was investigating various aspects of gambling. Treece spoke before the commission on behalf of Vend-A-Win's application for a temporary license to distribute punchboards. During his appearance, which was televised, he stated, "I'll pay a hundred thousand dollars to anyone to find a crooked board. If they find it, I'll pay it." The statement brought laughter from the audience. Barnes, the plaintiff, watched a television news report of Treece's statement and also read a newspaper account. Barnes telephoned Treece, asking him if his statement was serious. Treece restated that he meant it and that the money was being held in escrow. Barnes was in possession of two crooked punchboards. Following Treece's instructions, Barnes brought one of the punchboards into Vend-A-Win's offices for inspection. He turned the other board over to the Washington State Gambling Commission. Treece and Vend-A-Win each refused to pay Barnes. Barnes filed a lawsuit. What result and why? [*Barnes v. Treece*, 15 Wash. App. 437, 549 P.2d 1152 (1976)]

9–9 Misrepresentation Alabi wanted to ship $15,000 in currency to his cousin in London, England. He shipped frequently with DHL Airways, Inc., and had been given a supply of DHL's shipping documents to use. He asked DHL twice about obtaining insurance coverage in the amount of $15,000, but DHL informed him that the maximum coverage was for $10,000. Alabi filled out the shipping documents. Under the goods description, he wrote "documents regarding school bills," and he placed $15,000 in currency into the package. Alabi took the package to DHL for shipment, but the $15,000 never reached his cousin. DHL would not have accepted the package for shipment if it had known that the package contained currency. Alabi brought a lawsuit against DHL. DHL defended on the basis that Alabi had misrepresented his package's contents and that DHL could not inspect every package that it accepted. Who should prevail? Explain your answer. [*Alabi v. DHL Airways, Inc.*, 583 A.2d 1358 (Del. 1990)]

9–10 Internet The federal government is active in engaging and promoting electronic commerce. What are the key goals of the federal electronic commerce program? Go to <http://ec.fed.gov/>, then scroll to Federal EDI Standards.

Chapter 10

Contract Defenses and Remedies

If a man owe a debt and Adad, the storm god, inundate his field and carry away the produce, or, through lack of water, grain has not grown in the field, in that year he shall not make any return of grain to the creditor, he shall alter his contract tablet, and he shall not pay the interest for that year.

> Code of Hammurabi
> Hammurabi
> Sixth ruler of the First Amorite dynasty of
> Babylon, reigning 1792–1750 B.C.

Outline

Ethical Consideration

The Value of a Handshake: The Statute of Frauds as a Sword

You have been graduated from college and landed your first job. After working for a while, you saved enough money for a down payment on a new sports car and decide to sell your old Peugeot, which served you well while you were in college. You place an advertisement in the newspaper asking $3,000 for the car, expecting to sell it for around $2,500.

The advertisement generates interest and you invite a prospective buyer to your home to examine the car. After the buyer looks at the car, she offers you $2,700. As a recently divorced, single mother of four children, she needs the car for her family. As you shake her hand in acceptance of her offer, you hear the telephone ring.

The person on the telephone tells you that he is calling from his cellular telephone across the street. He came to buy the car, and as he drove up, he saw you shake hands with the first buyer. He wants the car and offers you $3,000 in cash. When you tell him that you already have agreed to sell the car, he reminds you that the agreement is not legally binding because you have not put anything in writing or signed over the owner's certificate of title. He then says that he will pay an extra $200 above the $3,000 if you sell the car to him. He needs it for a movie.

To whom should you sell the car? Use the ethical model presented in Chapter 2 and reprinted on the inside front cover to develop your answer.

Introduction

The online company you own, Artiste Login Products, Inc., will engage in many contracts. A company that produces a variety of art products has a number of suppliers, such as the one that provides the raw materials for bronze and steel sculptures or the plastic materials for furniture. A number of your products are sold to retail stores. These commercial customers will purchase small items in volume for resale. In the previous chapter, you studied the first three elements of a binding contract:

offer, acceptance, and consideration. This chapter explains the other two elements: legal capacity and legality.

A defense to a contract is a legal excuse for which a person does not have to perform her promise. The last two requirements for a contract, legal capacity and legality, can be used as affirmative defenses to a contract. The chapter also includes discussion of the other potential defenses, such as the **statute of frauds** (which states that the contract must be in writing to be enforced in court).

The previous chapter discussed the relationship between the two original parties to a contract. This chapter examines a third party's involvement with the contract. A third party can purchase rights and obtain defenses in the original contract. In a gift situation, a third party may be given rights in the original contract.

Although most contracts are discharged as fully performed, other ways to discharge contracts exist. Finally, the types of damages and the remedies that a person may request in a lawsuit when a party to a contract has been harmed are reviewed.

Elements of a Contract: Part 2

The last two elements of a contract are legal capacity and legality. These two elements can also be used as a defense. This section also examines the statute of frauds requirement for some types of contracts.

Legal Capacity

Legal capacity, the competence (or legal ability) of the parties, is the fourth requirement for a valid contract. In most contracts, both parties have full legal capacity to enter into a contract, to perform the contract, and if they fail to perform, to have the contract enforced against them in a court of law. When a court judges a party to be mentally incompetent and appoints a guardian over him, however, no legal capacity exists. Such a person has no legal capacity to form a contract and any contract into which he enters is void.

Limited competence exists when one or both parties are minors, are intoxicated, or are mentally incompetent, but not officially judged to be mentally incompetent by a court. These parties have full and legal capacity to enter into a contract, but, if they so desire, they can avoid liability under the contract. This type of contract is said to be voidable. Most litigation in this area involves the contracts of minors.

For contractual purposes, the **age of majority** (when a person is no longer a minor) varies from state to state. For the sake of discussion, this text will use eighteen years as the age at which a person becomes an adult. The general rule of law is that a minor can enter into any contract that an adult can enter into, provided that the contract is not one prohibited by law. A contract prohibited by law in most states, for example, is that a person under twenty-one years of age may not purchase alcoholic beverages.

Minors can enter into contracts and they also have the right to **disaffirm** (to avoid) their liabilities under the contracts, subject to certain exceptions, such as necessaries (that is, goods or services needed for the sustenance of the minor, such as food, clothing, or shelter). A minor may disaffirm a contract at any time prior to age eighteen or during a reasonable period of time thereafter.

If, however, by the time the minor becomes an adult (or a reasonable period of time thereafter), she has failed to disaffirm an executed contract, the contract is ratified. A minor, on reaching the age of majority, has no legal responsibility to act on executory contracts. The minor's inaction, however, does not constitute **ratification** (adoption) of the executory contract. Ratification is the act of accepting and giving legal force to a contract. Only after minors reach adulthood can they ratify contracts made when they were minors.

A contract to purchase necessaries may not be totally disaffirmed by a minor. The rule applicable to contracts for the purchase of necessaries is that the minor is liable to the other contracting party for the reasonable value of the goods or services actually used. This purchase imposes on the minor a quasi-contractual liability to pay for purchases needed to fulfill the minor's basic needs if no parent or guardian is willing and able to furnish the required necessity.

Under Article 2 of the Uniform Commercial Code (UCC), dealing with the sales of goods, a minor cannot recover goods that she sells to an adult once the adult purchaser transfers them to a third party who is a bona fide purchaser (a good-faith purchaser for value). The new buyer needs to know that the items he buys in good faith will not be taken as the result of a dispute between the seller and a minor from whom the seller purchased the item.

For example, Mary Minor, who is sixteen, owns a car, which she sells to Al Adult. Al drives the car for six months and then sells it to Ellie Elder. Mary Minor decides she wants the car back. Mary Minor could disaffirm the contract with Al Adult, but Mary Minor cannot recover the car from Ellie Elder, who purchased the car in good faith.

When disaffirmance occurs, the adult must return the item to the minor. If the property itself cannot be returned, the adult must pay the minor its equivalent value. If both parties to the contract are minors, each has a right to disaffirm it.

When disaffirmance occurs, the minor also must return whatever he received and still possesses as a result of the contract. In most states, the minor's duty of restoration is only to return goods (or other consideration). If the minor meets this condition, he is not liable for depreciation or nonwillful damage to the goods. In the following case, for example, a minor was not liable for damages to an automobile.

Case 10.1

Swalberg v. Hannegan

Court of Appeals of Utah, 1994

883 P.2d 931

BACKGROUND AND FACTS In 1990, Hannegan, the defendant, contracted to purchase Swalberg's 1974 Ford truck for $2,500. The fact that Hannegan was a minor apparently was not discussed when the parties entered into the contract. Swalberg, an adult, made no allegation that Hannegan misrepresented his age. Hannegan paid Swalberg $640 on the sale date and agreed to pay the balance of $1,860 three months later.

Rather than paying the balance, however, Hannegan disaffirmed the contract on the basis of his minority. Swalberg filed a complaint asking that the contract be enforced or, in the alternative, that the truck be returned and that defendant be held responsible for the reasonable value of his use of the truck or for its depreciation amount while in defendant's possession. Thereafter, while Hannegan was still a minor, Swalberg gained possession of the truck.

Swalberg filed a motion for summary judgment. Swalberg argued that when Hannegan disaffirmed the contract, he did not properly restore the truck since he purchased it for $2,500 and returned it in a condition worth only $700. The trial court granted Swalberg's motion and awarded him $1,160, which was the remaining balance minus the value placed on the truck in its returned condition. Hannegan appealed the trial court's order.

Judge BENCH

. . . .

The dispositive issue on appeal is whether a minor who disaffirms a contract is required to restore the full value of the property received under the contract. Defendant argues that Utah law does not require a disaffirming minor to restore the other party to his or her precontractual status. We agree. Utah Code Ann. § 15-2-2 (1986) provides:

> A minor is bound not only for the reasonable value of necessities but also for his contracts, unless he disaffirms them before or within a reasonable time after he obtains his majority and restores to the other party all money or property received by him by virtue of said contracts and remaining within his control at any time after attaining his majority.

This statute requires only that the property remaining within the minor's control be returned to the other party. The trial court held, however, that defendant was required to return the property in its original condition or be liable for the difference in value. This holding is clearly contrary to the provisions of this unamended nineteenth century statute, as interpreted by controlling Utah case law.

DECISION AND REMEDY By state statute in Utah, the disaffirming minor must only return the property remaining within his or her control. The court allowed the minor to effectively disaffirm the underlying contract without restoring the property to its precontract condition. The Utah state legislature can amend the statute to require a minor to restore property to its precontract condition.

CRITICAL THINKING: PRACTICAL APPLICATION Discuss what steps the plaintiff could have taken to have prevented this legal action.

What happens if a minor lies about his age? The states have not been uniform in handling this troublesome area. The courts have created four different approaches.

Under the traditional view, the minor still may disaffirm the contract because the lack of capacity cannot be forfeited by misstating one's age. The adult who contracts with a minor who has lied can suffer severe consequences because the minor can return to the adult only the remains of the item purchased, if anything is left.

The second approach also allows the minor to disaffirm, but the items must be returned to the adult. The third approach allows the minor to disaffirm, but the minor is liable for fraud. The fourth method of handling this problem does not allow the minor to disaffirm the contract.

Legality

The fifth requirement is legality. A contract encompasses the performance of a legal act by each party. An agreement is illegal if either its formation or its performance is criminal, tortious, or otherwise opposed to public policy.

The reasoning for this requirement is quite simple. If a civil court requires a person to perform a contract that involves the commission of an illegal act, a criminal court could punish that person for committing a crime as a result of a civil court order. This result is not only illogical, but it defies public policy against the courts being party to a crime.

Generally, an illegal agreement is void. Neither party has rights against the other when the agreement's purpose is illegal. The following subsections discuss areas in which the courts have found illegality.

Licenses. Most businesses need some type of license from the government to operate. Licenses can be divided into two categories: regulatory or revenue raising.

Regulatory licensing statutes govern the qualifications of the person or business to conduct specific types of operations. Real estate and construction licenses are examples. If a person lacks this type of license, normally any business contract that she enters into is declared null and void. If an unlicensed pool builder constructs a swimming pool, for instance, the homeowner is not required to pay for it, because the agreement is void.

A good business practice is to verify that the person or business is properly licensed before contracting with it. Most states have established a consumer recovery fund. A consumer may recover damages from the fund if a licensed business fails to perform appropriately. States, however, generally do not protect consumers who have dealt with an unlicensed business.

Revenue-raising licensing statutes, as the name implies, establish licensing requirements solely to raise money. For example, most states have a sales tax. To ensure that the sales tax is collected and remitted to the state department of revenue, the state requires businesses to secure a sales tax license. The state can monitor a business to ensure that it collects the sales tax on its gross receipts and then forwards the monies to the state.

If a business fails to obtain a revenue-raising license, the state can take action against the business. Generally, if a business fails to obtain the appropriate revenue-raising license, however, the lack of the license has no effect on contracts into which the business may enter.

Usury. **Usury** is the charging of a higher interest rate than the law allows for a loan of money. In a few states, usury is a crime. Usury statutes set the maximum interest rate that may be charged for loaning money. Any higher interest rate is considered usurious.

For example, if a state usury statute sets the interest rate at 24 percent per annum, any rate above 24 percent is usurious and illegal. Any creditor charging above 24 percent may be forced to forfeit both principal and interest. Most states have modified the harsh consequence of total forfeiture of both principal and interest. Today, a business that charges a usurious rate may forfeit all interest but not principal. Other states merely require the forfeiture of the interest amount deemed to be usurious.

Many states abolished usury laws or set a very high interest rate in response to economic conditions of the 1970s and 1980s. In the 1990s, after dropping the usury laws, some states readopted the usury laws because of abuses by some businesses. Federal law sets a 40 percent maximum rate. Any rate higher is considered to be loan sharking or extortion.

Blue Sky Laws. **Blue sky laws** were passed by states to prevent fraud in investment sales. These laws apply to the sale of securities within a state, that is, intrastate sales. The basic purposes are to prevent dishonest sales practices and to require full, truthful disclosure. Chapter 20 covers this topic in more detail.[1]

Restraints of Trade. Competition is the basis of the U.S. economic system. First, common law, later followed by state and federal laws, prohibits many trade restraints. For example, if Haught owns a shopping center and agrees with O'Brien, who operates a record store, not to allow any other record stores in the mall, this agreement is void because it is in restraint of trade.

A restraint-of-trade agreement is normally void by itself. Some restraints, however, can become part of a

---

[1] Do not confuse blue sky laws with blue laws. Blue laws were statutes that forbid contracts from being created on Sundays. In 1610, Virginia passed the first statute. It stated that "Every man and woman shall repair in the morning to the divine service and sermons preached upon the Sabbath day, and in the afternoon to the divine service, and catechising, upon pain for the first fault to lose their provision and the allowance for the whole week following; for the second, to lose the said allowance and also to be whipt; and for the third to suffer death."

contract in two situations: in a sale of a business contract or in an employment contract.

When a business is sold, one of its major assets is the seller's goodwill, especially for a small business. The business's value diminishes significantly if the seller opens a new business near the original one.

Trade-restraint situations that involve employment contracts are not as easily defendable. In this case, the employee signs a contract agreeing not to compete against the employer following termination of the employment relationship.

Courts have upheld both types of restrictions, if they are reasonable as to time and geographical area. The theory behind these restrictions is that they allow the buyer and the employer to protect their valuable property rights.

Other trade restraints may be illegal under the Sherman Act, the Clayton Act, and other federal or state antitrust statutes. Chapter 21 discusses these acts.

Unconscionable Bargain. The law has long been concerned about the power balance between a strong party in relationship to a weak party in a contract. Chapter 1 discussed the concept of equity. Equity is applied by the courts to obtain fairness in these types of contracts.

The UCC adopted the concept of equity to the sale of goods in Section 2-302, which deals with **un-conscionable contracts**. The legal test for unconscionability is whether, in the light of the general commercial background and the business needs of the particular trade or case, the clauses in the contract are so one-sided as to be harsh and shocking to the conscience of the court under the circumstances. A court may refuse to enforce a contract or a provision of a contract if it is found to be unconscionable.

For example, a school purchases catsup in large quantities. A provision in the sales contract requires the school to reject each shipment within ten days if the goods fail to meet the contract specifications. After the rejection period passes, the school finds a catsup shipment to be contaminated. This contamination could only be discovered through microscopic analysis of the catsup bottles after the shipping container had been opened. In this case the court would find the ten-day rejection clause to be unconscionable.

In the following case, the court was faced with determining whether a contract was unconscionable. In the facts, there is discussion as to the truth-in-lending law. This federal statute requires that all financial costs and percentage rates be disclosed to a consumer. The truth-in-lending law will be covered in more depth in Chapter 14.

Case 10.2

Lozada v. Dale Baker Oldsmobile, Inc.

United States District Court, Western District of Michigan, 2000

91 F. Supp. 2d 1087 (W.D. Mich.)

BACKGROUND AND FACTS Plaintiffs Nancy Lozada, Bob Warren, A. D. Christian, and Jeanne Uwamaliya were all customers of Dale Baker Olds. They sought to purchase motor vehicles on credit. Because of their respective credit histories, Dale Baker Olds salesmen determined that plaintiffs would not be eligible for conventional auto financing. As a result, the salesmen referred plaintiffs to the Dale Baker Olds special finance department, which, in turn, after the contracts and notes were signed, sold these to Consumer Finance Corporation (CFC).

After selecting a vehicle, each plaintiff was introduced to Assistant Special Finance Manager Stormie Moore to complete the necessary documentation to obtain credit to finance their vehicles in the sub-prime credit market. At that time, each plaintiff was presented with and signed a Retail Installment Contract, which contained disclosures of the annual percentage rate, finance charge, amount financed, total sale price, and payment schedule. Those disclosures were contained under the heading "TRUTH IN LENDING DISCLOSURES" and placed immediately above the signature line.

While plaintiffs were shown the retail installment contracts at the time they signed them and while those installment contracts contained disclosures, plaintiffs were not given a copy of the contracts or disclosures until some days after they signed their agreements. Plaintiff Lozada received a copy ten days after signing the document. Plaintiff Warren received a copy two days after signing the document. Plaintiff Christian received a copy fifteen days after signing.

On the basis of this history, plaintiffs contended that Dale Baker Olds failed to make the disclosures required by the Truth-in-Lending Act (TILA) and the relevant regulations promulgated by the Federal Reserve Board pursuant to its authority under the TILA. Plaintiffs contended that CFC, as assignee of Dale Baker's contract with plaintiff Christian, was liable both under the federal and state statutes and under the terms of the contract. CFC moved to compel arbitration in accordance with the contract. The arbitration clause was written in very small print on the front of the contract.

HILLMAN, Senior District Judge

. . . .

In order to determine whether a contract is procedurally unconscionable, the court typically considers the relative bargaining power of the parties, their relative economic strength, the alternative sources of supply, "in a word, what are their options?" Having reviewed the verified allegations of the complaint, I am persuaded that plaintiffs have adequately alleged that inclusion of the arbitration provision was procedurally unconscionable.

In their complaint, plaintiffs allege that at the time of signing, Christian, like other consumers managed by the special finance department, was hurried to sign and had no reasonable opportunity to review the agreement. The complaint further alleges that Dale Baker Olds did not provide a copy of the contract to Christian at the time of signing. In fact, Christian was not given copies of any paperwork until two weeks after he had signed and after financing had been finalized through CFC. Plaintiffs further allege that such treatment resulted from the admitted practice of the special finance department to refuse to provide the customer with a copy of the retail installment contract until the contract had been purchased from Dale Baker Olds by a third-party finance company. As a consequence of both circumstances, plaintiffs contend that Christian did not and could not freely accept the arbitration provision.

I conclude that plaintiff has adequately alleged that the arbitration provision at issue was procedurally unconscionable. . . . Where a contract is prepared by one party and offered for rejection or acceptance without opportunity for bargaining under circumstances in which the party cannot obtain the desired product or service except by acquiescing in the form agreement, Michigan courts will conclude that the contract is adhesive and therefore procedurally unconscionable. . . .
. . . .

Further, the consumer protection statutes under which this action was brought were specifically designed to protect unsophisticated consumers from unscrupulous creditors. . . . A party seeking to remedy a contract's failure to comply with legislation designed in part to prevent unconscionable contracts has articulated a sound basis for asserting procedural unconscionability.

Finally, while print size alone would not warrant a finding of procedural unconscionability, the fact that the arbitration clause was written in the smallest print on the front of the contract is somewhat suggestive of procedural unconscionability.

Taken together, I find that plaintiffs have sufficiently alleged . . . unconscionability in the formation of the agreement to arbitrate. . . .

. . . .

DECISION AND REMEDY The court found that the plaintiffs' complaint would not be dismissed and refused to order arbitration. The court determined that the arbitration clause was unconscionable because of the manner in which it was formed when the contract was entered.

CRITICAL THINKING: PRACTICAL APPLICATION In Chapter 4 you studied arbitration and how the courts give great leeway to enforce arbitration clauses. Why do you think the judge in this case decided that this arbitration provision would not be enforced?

Statute of Frauds

Certain valid contracts, by statute, must be in writing to be enforceable by a court. This statute is called the *statute against the perpetuation of fraud*, or the *statute of frauds* for short.

The writing must be signed by the person against whom it is being enforced. Even without this statute, good business practice requires a written contract.

The statute of frauds varies from state to state. The following major types of business contracts must be in writing:

1. Contracts involving land interests, such as leases and sales.

2. Contracts that, by their terms, cannot be performed within one year from the date that the contract was formed.

3. **Collateral contracts** are express written contracts made by a third person (called a guarantor) in addition to the original contract. A third person (guarantor) makes the same promise to pay a debt or to perform a duty to one party (the creditor) on the original contract if the debtor is unable to do so. A collateral contract between the guarantor and the creditor parallels the original contract between the creditor and the debtor.

4. Contracts for the sale of goods priced at $500 or more, under the UCC.

The UCC requires that contracts involving the sale of goods for the price of $500 or more be in writing and signed by the party against whom enforcement is sought [UCC 2-201(1)]. But if the signed writing is insufficient because it omits or incorrectly states a term, the contract is still valid up to the amount or quantity of goods stated in the writing.

The UCC, however, allows enforcement of oral contracts under the following three conditions:

1. If an oral agreement involving goods exists between merchants and if one of them sends the other a written confirmation, the confirmation is the written evidence of the oral contract. The receiver has ten days to provide its written objection. If this objection is not sent, the terms of the oral contract are enforceable and are presumed to be the terms contained in the written confirmation. The contract is binding on both parties, even though both parties did not sign it.

2. Under the UCC, courts may enforce oral contracts up to the amount of payment made or up to the quantity of the goods received and accepted by the buyer.

3. The UCC allows a court to enforce an oral contract up to the amount that a party admits to in court or in court documents.

For example, Sean orally agrees to pay $5,000 for furniture from a furniture store. Although the furniture is delivered, Sean does not pay for it. Or the facts may be the other way around. Sean may have paid for the furniture, but the store refuses to deliver it.

Under the second condition, if Sean has paid the store $5,000, the court can order the store to return the $5,000 or order the furniture to be delivered. Sean can purchase furniture from another store, and if he has to pay more, he can recover the $5,000 plus the additional costs.

Now assume the $5,000 was to pay for two rooms of furniture, $3,000 for the living room and $2,000 for the den. If the store delivers the living room furniture, the oral contract is enforceable up to the amount of the goods received and accepted by Sean, that is, the $3,000.

Exhibit 10–1   Contracts Covered by the Statute of Frauds

Contracts to Guarantee the Debt of Another	*Application* Applies only to express written contracts made between the guarantor (third party) and the creditor who is a party in the original contract. The contract terms of the collateral contract make the guarantor secondly liable for the debt of the debtor who is a party of the original contract. The original contract is between the creditor and the debtor. The collateral contract is between the creditor and the third party guarantor who promises (guarantees) to pay the debt or to perform the duty of the debtor in the original contract if the debtor is unable to pay the debtor or to perform the duty.
Contracts Involving an Interest in Real Estate	*Application* Applies to any contract for an interest in real estate, such as sale or lease.
Contracts with Terms That Cannot Be Performed within One Year	*Application* Applies only to contracts that are impossible to perform fully within one year from the date of the contract's information.

Contracts for the Sale of Goods Priced at $500 or More	1. *Application* Applies only to the contract for the sale of goods when the purchase price (excluding taxes) is $500 or more [UCC 2-201(1)].
	2. *Exceptions*
	   a. Between merchants, where one sends a written confirmation and the recipient does not object in writing within ten days [UCC 2-201(2)].
	   b. Admission under oath of an oral contract [UCC 2-201(3)(b)].
	   c. Partial performance by buyer's payment or possession creates an enforceable contract up to the amount paid or quantity possessed [UCC 2-201(3)(c)].

Exception to Contracts Otherwise Unenforceable under the Statute of Frauds	*Memorandum* Written evidence of an oral contract signed by the party against whom enforcement is sought. Generally, the writing must name the parties and identify the contract's subject matter. In the sale of goods, the quantity must be stated. In the sale of real estate, the contract requires a land description and price. Exceptions exist under each section.

In another scenario, Sean fails to pay for the furniture. When the furniture store sues him, he files a response that he had an oral agreement to pay $5,000. Under the third condition, this written response is his admission in writing; the court can enforce the agreement up to $5,000, the amount Sean has admitted. Or, if he files a response that does not make any admissions, but he gives testimony in the trial and admits to the agreement to pay $5,000, the court can enforce the agreement.

Other parts of the oral contract remain unenforceable. Exhibit 10–1 summarizes the contracts covered by the statute of frauds.

Last, the UCC allows enforcement of oral contracts that involve specially manufactured goods, such as furniture specifically made to fit a particular house or golf clubs custom made for a person. Goods of this type are not suitable for sale to others in the ordinary course of business. In the following case, the court examines the requirements of specially manufactured goods.

Case 10.3

Contours, Inc. v. Lee

Intermediate Court of Appeals
of Hawai'i, 1994
874 P.2d 1100 (Haw. App.)

BACKGROUND AND FACTS   DiGrandi was the president of Contours, Inc., a custom furniture manufacturer. During a meeting between DiGrandi and Lee, they agreed in writing that DiGrandi would make and deliver several pieces of furniture for $18,000. Lee paid $3,000 down.

Lee needed the furniture seven days before December 5 for several large parties he planned to host in December. If the furniture were not delivered on time, Contours agreed to pay Lee $500 for each day delivery was delayed. Minor oral modifications to the original contract reduced the total price from $18,000 to $15,000.

Although work on a dining room table was incomplete, Lee requested that it be delivered by December 5 before his parties with the understanding that Contours would pick it up after the parties for the final finish. After the parties were held, Contours attempted on several occasions to pick up the furniture so it could complete the work required for the final finish, but Lee refused to surrender it. Contours brought a lawsuit to recover $12,000. The trial court reduced this sum by $3,500 because of Contour's seven-day delay in delivering the finished furniture.

Chief Judge BURNS

. . . .

The original contract was in writing. The subsequent oral modification of the contract canceling the order of some goods and changing the order for the remaining goods cannot be enforced against Lee absent an exception to the relevant statute of frauds. Thus, the question is whether the circuit court was right when it implicitly concluded that the oral modifications of the written contract were enforceable. In the absence of an essential finding of fact, we cannot answer this question.

Hawai'i's Uniform Commercial Code, Hawai'i Revised Statutes (HRS) chapter 490 (1985), states in relevant part as follows:

> § 490:2-201 Formal requirements, statute of frauds. (1) Except as otherwise provided in this section a contract for the sale of goods for the price of $500 or more is not enforceable by way of action or defense unless there is some writing sufficient to indicate that a contract for sale has been made between the parties and signed by the party against whom enforcement is sought or by his authorized agent or broker.
>
> . . . .
>
> (3) A contract which does not satisfy the requirements of subsection (1) but which is valid in other respects is enforceable.
>
> (a) If the goods are to be specially manufactured for the buyer and are not suitable for sale to others in the ordinary course of the seller's business and the seller, before notice of repudiation is received and under circumstances which reasonably indicate that the goods are for the buyer, has made either a substantial beginning of their manufacture or commitments for their procurement.

. . . .

As used in HRS § 490:2-201(3)(a), the term "specially manufactured," refers to the nature of the particular goods in question and not to whether the goods were made in an unusual, as opposed to the regular, business operation or manufacturing process of the seller. That the seller may be in the business of manufacturing custom designed and made goods does not necessarily preclude his goods from being deemed "specially manufactured" within the meaning of this exception. The crucial inquiry is whether the manufacturer could sell the goods in the ordinary course of his business to someone other than the original buyer. If with slight alterations the goods could be so sold, then they are not specially manufactured; if, however, essential changes are necessary to render the goods marketable by the seller to others, then the exception does apply.

DECISION AND REMEDY The court of appeals sent the case back to the trial court to determine if the furniture manufactured by Contours was specially manufactured goods. If the furniture were specially manufactured goods, the statute of frauds, as found in the Uniform Commercial Code, was satisfied.

CRITICAL THINKING: POLITICAL QUESTION Recently, Great Britain repealed the statute of frauds; thus, no longer must contracts be in writing. Discuss whether the United States should do likewise.

Parol Evidence Rule. The **parol** (oral) **evidence rule** also is known as the best evidence rule because the courts will not allow into evidence any oral statements made prior to or at the time of a written contract's signing. The courts believe that the best evidence is the written contract. Oral evidence cannot change or add to a fully integrated contract.

This rule does allow for some oral testimony. For example, oral testimony can explain terms or clarify ambiguities in the contract. Parol evidence may be used to show misrepresentation, fraud, duress, undue influence, mistake, and lack of contractual capacity. Oral testimony also can clarify typographical or clerical error that, when corrected, allows the court to reform the contract to the true intentions of the parties.

CyberLaw

Federal Electronic Signatures Act and Uniform Electronic Transactions Act

The Electronic Signatures in Global and National Commerce Act was signed into law by President William J. Clinton. This law attempts to eliminate legal barriers to using electronic technology to form and sign contracts, collect and store documents, and send and receive notices and disclosures. Consumers must affirmatively consent to doing business electronically. The act provides that no contract, signature, or record shall be denied legal effect solely because it is in electronic form. This statute allows businesses to contract electronically online in buying and selling their products.

The act does not apply to court proceedings, wills, trusts, mortgage foreclosures, and other similar types of documents. Specific concerns were raised by consumers, so the act does not apply to insurance and utility cancellation and termination notices.

The statute does not state what a signature must be. Congress did not want to limit new technology, so it declined to provide a definition. States are allowed to define what a signature is by state statute. More likely, the state governments will follow the federal act and not provide a statutory definition. The definition of a signature will be left to technology and what the contracting parties agree to accept as a signature. What concerns the parties is authenticating the signature. In the future, computers may be configured with slots like an automated teller machine (ATM) machine to slide a card through or even possibly the computer could scan a person's eye to authenticate the signature.

The National Conference of Commissioners on Uniform State Laws has issued a draft called the Uniform Electronic Transactions Act for states to consider adopting as law. This proposed act was issued (1) to facilitate electronic transactions consistent with other applicable law; (2) to be consistent with reasonable practices concerning electronic transactions and with the continued expansion of those practices; and (3) to effectuate its general purpose to make uniform the law with respect to electronic business.[2]

---

[2] The Uniform Electronic Transactions Act may be found at <http://www.law.upenn.edu/bll/ulc/ulc_frame.htm>.

LEGAL HIGHLIGHT

Faxes and the Feds

Need to drum up business? Why not fax to hundreds or thousands of potential customers at a time? Faxing takes time, but the results may be worth it. If faxes are sent locally, the only cost is the recipient's fax paper. If faxes are sent long distance, the cost is low because of the short time needed to send the fax. But wait a minute!

Have you read your friendly federal statutes lately? In 1992, Congress passed a law prohibiting the sending of unsolicited faxes and requiring the sender to remove from a fax list anyone who requests removal. Congressional members had been inundated with complaints from outraged constituents who had to bear the cost of unsolicited faxes. Even congressional offices were tired of receiving commercial faxes. Congress had the power to act and it did.

The Federal Communications Commission (FCC) oversees the law. Penalties are rare, but when numerous complaints are filed against a company, either the FCC or the state attorneys general can pursue the issue in court.

Faxes can be sent when the sender has established a business relationship with the recipient. The relationship can start when the recipient inquires or applies to, or requests a fax from, the sender. The recipient can request to be removed from the list at any time.

A business can run into problems, first, if the business is not aware of the law and sends multiple pages of unsolicited faxes repeatedly that start to annoy the recipient. An angry recipient may file a complaint with the FCC. Second, the business may be lax in removing names from the fax list when requested to do so. Again, complaints can be filed with the FCC against the business.

Based on the fax-restricting laws, should businesses expect Congress to forbid the spamming of electronic mail (e-mail)? Spamming is the sending of unsolicited e-mail (also called junk e-mail) to thousands, even hundreds of thousands of recipients at a time. When businesses abuse consumers, Congress often reacts. If Congress has prohibited unsolicited faxes, is the prohibition of electronic spamming coming soon?

Other Contractual Issues

After the original parties to a valid contract meet all contract requirements, other problems may arise. First, third parties may have rights based on the contract even though they did not participate in its original formation. Second, if a contract dispute arises, the parties need to know the available remedies.

Assignments and Delegations

Sometimes people who are not directly connected with the initial contract become involved in it. A third party (someone who was not an original party) can acquire an interest in a contract by assuming the rights or duties arising from it. An original party to a contract can transfer its rights or duties to a third person after making the original contract.

Each party to the contract has rights and duties. One party has the right to the performance that the other party promised. The transfer of the rights of a party to a contract to a third person is known as an **assignment**. The original party is known as the **assignor**. The third party who takes the assignment is known as the **assignee**. The assignee takes the place of the original party to the contract. If the original party to the contract has a defense to the contract against the assignor, the defense may also be used against the assignee.

For example, Nancy contracts to purchase a computer for $4,000. She promises to pay Computer Company $200 a month. Computer Company (the assignor) assigns the right to receive the $4,000 to Finance Company (the assignee). Now Nancy must pay the $200 a month to Finance Company until she pays the full $4,000 to complete her performance on the contract. Nancy has a defense for failing to pay if the computer does not work or if Computer Company used fraud to induce Nancy into the contract. Those defenses also may be used against the assignee, Finance Company.

Exhibit 10–2   Assignment and Delegation

Assignment   An assignment is the transfer of rights under a contract to a third party. The rights of the assignor (the person making the assignment) may be ended and the assignee (the person to whom the rights are assigned) now has a right to demand performance from the other original party to the contract.

Generally, all rights are assignable except where the law prohibits this, where the contract prohibits assignment, or where the assignment would materially alter or increase the duties of the original party to the contract.

Delegation   A delegation is the transfer of duties under a contract to a third party. The delegate (the third party) assumes the obligation of performing the contractual duties previously held by the delegator (the one making the delegation).

Some duties cannot be delegated because they are personal or because their delegation is prohibited by contract.

Each party to a contract has a duty to perform. The transfer of duties to another person is called a **delegation**. A contractual duty can be delegated to someone else to perform unless the duty of performance is personal and must be performed by the original party. For example, Enrique has an automobile for sale. Carrie wants to buy the automobile and assume the note. The note is the evidence of the amount loaned to Enrique to purchase the automobile. Enrique is under a duty to repay the note, but his duty can be delegated to Carrie if she is financially qualified to assume the note. Now she is primarily liable on the note, but Enrique is still liable if Carrie fails to pay the note. A person who owes a duty is not relieved of the duty if he delegates the duty to someone else to perform.

If the contract performance is personal in nature, the duty cannot be delegated. For example, Wong contracts with Happy, the Clown, to perform at Wong's birthday party. Happy cannot delegate this duty to another entertainer, such as the Scottish Bag Pipers Band, without Wong's consent. These contracts are for services and are not assignable because one person's service may be very different from another's. The payment for the services is assignable.

Exhibit 10–2 summarizes third-party rights.

The following case reviews an assignment clause in a contract.

Case 10.4

Parrish Chiropractic Centers v. Progressive Casualty Insurance Company

Supreme Court of Colorado, 1994
874 P.2d 1049 (Colo.)

BACKGROUND AND FACTS Colorado has an automobile no-fault insurance law. A no-fault law permits each driver in a traffic accident to collect insurance money from her or his own insurance company regardless of whose fault the accident is.

The defendant, Progressive Casualty Insurance Company, issues insurance policies under Colorado's automobile no-fault law. The personal injury protection (PIP) insurance policy issued by Progressive has the following clause: "Interest in this policy may not be assigned without our written consent." Progressive is the insurer and the patients are the insureds.

The plaintiff, Parrish Chiropractic Centers, P.C. (Professional Corporation), treated many patients injured in automobile accidents who held PIP policies issued by Progressive. Parrish required its patients to sign an assignment of insurance benefits agreement. An assignment in this case means that the patients authorized Progressive to pay the insurance benefits directly to Parrish (instead of paying the benefits to the patients) under the patients' PIP policies.

Progressive routinely honored such assignments until it changed its business practice from paying Parrish the insurance benefits to paying the patients. The reasons were that (1) treatment with Parrish, on average, took considerably longer and was more expensive than other chiropractors, and (2) the purported assignments of benefits violated the express terms of the policy and, consequently, were void from the beginning. Under the previous assignment method, both Progressive's and the patients' abilities to control the treatment frequency and costs provided by Parrish were diminished.

Under the new system, Progressive paid the PIP benefits directly to the patients and Progressive refused to honor any more assignments sent by Parrish. Although the patients received the insurance benefits, some failed to pay their chiropractic fees as they were supposed to. Parrish filed this lawsuit to recover its unreimbursed chiropractic fees. Parrish lost in both lower courts. The courts held that the assignments to Parrish were invalid as a matter of law in light of the express provision in the policies. If either court had upheld the assignments, Progressive's obligation under the insurance contract would have been materially changed. Parrish appealed to the Colorado Supreme Court.

In its opinion, the court discusses what is called a *chose in action* (a right that can be enforced by a lawsuit). If the insured is entitled to receive benefits and the insurance company does not pay the insured, she or he can sue the insurance company for the benefits. Whoever is entitled to the benefits has a chose in action, that is, a right to sue to enforce the right to receive those benefits. If the benefits have been assigned, then the third person has the chose in action. The assignment, in this case, is a transfer of the entitlement to the insurance benefits from the patient to the medical provider. The assignment is a chose in action.

Assignments were made by the patients directing Progressive to pay their benefits to Parrish. If Progressive fails to pay Parrish, Parrish has the right to file a lawsuit to receive the benefits under the assignment. Generally, public policy supports the transfer of choses in action, but exceptions exist. This court discusses one of those exceptions.

Justice MULLARKEY

. . . .

Contract rights generally are assignable, except where assignment is prohibited by contract or by operation of law or where the contract involves a matter of personal trust or confidence. Where the contract in question specifically prohibits the assignment of rights or interests under the contract without the consent of one or more of the contracting parties, any purported assignment without such consent will not be enforced.

. . . .

A distinction traditionally has been made, however, between an assignment of an insurance policy before a loss has occurred and the assignment of the benefits due to the insured after a loss. Non-assignment clauses are strictly enforced against attempted preloss transfers of the policy itself, because assignments before loss involve a transfer of a contractual relationship and, in most cases, would materially increase the risk to the insurer. By contrast, assignments of post-loss benefits are usually found to be valid regardless of any non-assignment clause in the policy. This rule is explained by the fact that (1) post-loss assignments of the benefits due under the policy are viewed as transfers of a chose in action and public policy favors the free alienability [transferability] of choses in action, and (2) such assignments would not materially increase the insurer's risk or obligation under the policy. . . .

Having set forth the general rules regarding non-assignment clauses in insurance policies, we now turn to an important exception to those rules. In recent years, several courts have concluded that non-assignment clauses in group health care contracts are enforceable against post-loss assignments to health care providers of the insured's right to receive benefits under the policy. . . .
. . . .

. . . To hold otherwise would be to force Progressive to deal with parties with whom it has not contracted, regardless of the fact that its policy contains an express contractual provision requiring its prior consent to any assignment of interests in the policy. The public policy of this state does not dictate such a result.

Accordingly, we reject Parrish's argument that a non-assignment clause in an insurance policy is unenforceable as a matter of law against post-loss assignments of policy benefits.

DECISION AND REMEDY The Supreme Court of Colorado also held that Parrish was not a third-party beneficiary of the PIP insurance contract. The insurance policy specifically forbade an assignment without Progressive's approval. Thus, the purported assignment to Parrish was not enforceable. Parrish was not obligated under any statute or by contract to treat Progressive's insureds. Parrish was merely an incidental beneficiary of Progressive's policy.

CRITICAL THINKING: PUBLIC POLICY Discuss whether any contract should be assignable.

Third-Party Beneficiaries

Third-party beneficiaries fall into two general categories: *intended beneficiaries* and *incidental beneficiaries*. A person's inclusion in one or the other category depends on whether the original parties, at the time of contracting, intended to benefit a third person. If so, that party is an **intended beneficiary**. If not, the party is an **incidental beneficiary**. For example, commuters on a train are the incidental beneficiaries of the contract between the union and the railroad.

An intended beneficiary generally is either a *creditor beneficiary* or a *donee beneficiary* (although, in some situations, the intended beneficiary may not fall under the heading of either creditor or donee). A **creditor beneficiary** purchases the right to receive money owed under the contract. For example, you owe Alice $100. You are hired to work at a music performance, for which you will earn $100. You request your employer to pay the $100 to Alice instead of to you. Alice is a creditor beneficiary of your contract for services with the music company.

A person is a **donee beneficiary** when the main purpose of the contract is to give a gift to him, even though he is not a party to the contract. The best example is the standard life insurance contract. The contract is between the life insurance company and the insured, but the party who is designated to receive the insurance proceeds after the insured dies is the donee beneficiary.

What rights does a creditor or donee beneficiary have? Generally, an intended beneficiary may bring a lawsuit on the contract, but an incidental beneficiary may not.

The following case examines whether a hospital was the third-party beneficiary of an agreement between two other parties.

Case 10.5

Sisters of St. Joseph of Peace, Health, and Hospital Services v. Russell

Supreme Court of Oregon, 1994
867 P.2d 1377, 318 Or. 370

BACKGROUND AND FACTS The defendant, Russell, broke his arm and back while at work at a logging mill. The plaintiff, Sisters of St. Joseph of Peace, Health, and Hospital Services, dba (doing business as) Sacred Heart General Hospital, provided medical treatment to Russell. He was uncertain as to who his employer was at the time of the injury.

For that reason he filed four separate workers' compensation claims against four purported employers. At a workers' compensation hearing, the referee held that the employer was insured by Aetna Casualty & Surety Company for workers' compensation purposes. Aetna appealed. While the decision was pending, all four purported employers and their insurance carriers entered into a disputed claim settlement (DCS) agreement with Russell that Aetna would be the insurance carrier. Russell and Aetna dismissed the appeal.

Sacred Heart was not compensated under this agreement and sued Russell and Aetna. Russell testified at the trial that he only agreed to pay the hospital for the treatment that saved his life. Although the jury found that Russell did not have to pay the hospital, it held that Aetna was responsible for paying Russell's hospital bill.

The appeals court reversed the trial court's decision and held that Aetna's liability depended on whether Russell was liable to the plaintiff. The hospital appealed the case, claiming that it was the beneficiary of the DCS between Russell and Aetna and that, therefore, Aetna should pay Russell's hospital bill.

Justice GRABER

. . . .

In this case, plaintiff gave medical care to Russell. Plaintiff billed Russell for that medical care. In other words, at the time the DCS agreement was signed, plaintiff had given something of value to Russell and was asserting that Russell had a duty to pay for it. In those circumstances, plaintiff was a creditor beneficiary of the DCS agreement if the parties intended that contract to benefit plaintiff. To determine whether Aetna and Russell intended to benefit the hospital, we must examine the DCS agreement.

. . . .

. . . Paragraph 5 absolved the four purported employers and their insurers of any further responsibility for Russell's "disputed and denied conditions excepting, however, the terms [that] this agreement provide[,] the parties agree that the sums heretofore set forth to be the sole responsibility of the carrier Aetna Casualty & Surety Company."

. . . .

Paragraph 5 of the DCS agreement . . . makes "*the sums* heretofore set forth" "the sole responsibility of the carrier Aetna" (emphasis added). One of those sums is stated to be *the full and exact dollar amount of plaintiff's bills* for Russell's care. . . . Paragraph 6 refers to the medical providers, including plaintiff, as Russell's "creditors." As a whole, the paragraph suggests that the parties to the DCS agreement recognized that Russell's medical expenses . . . were, in fact, owed.

DECISION AND REMEDY The court upheld the jury's verdict that Aetna was responsible for paying Russell's hospital bill. It found Aetna liable because Sacred Heart was a creditor beneficiary under the various provisions of the DCS agreement between Russell and Aetna.

CRITICAL THINKING: PREVENTIVE LAW Assume there are four separate employers on a construction site. Assume further an employee, such as Russell, is shared by the four employers over a period of time. Russell works on various problems, keeps track of his time, and is paid by each of the four employers separately. He is injured. Discuss whether the employers can avoid a lawsuit such as the one that occurred here.

Discharge

A contract usually is discharged because it has been fully performed, but contracts also can be discharged in other ways. The following examines the discharge of a contract by performance and then reviews other methods of discharge.

Discharge by Performance

In most cases, a contract is fully performed and is discharged. For example, when you purchased your textbook, you paid the store the price marked on the textbook and you left the store with the book. Assuming the textbook is complete and appropriately printed, the contract was fully performed.

Some contracts, because of their basic nature, cannot always be fully performed. Construction contracts involving many blueprints and other specifications often are not completely performed in every last detail. Even though minor deviations may exist, the contract may be discharged by substantial performance. A door to a classroom may be off by an eighth of an inch from the original plans. This minor deviation does not mean that the contract is breached. The contract has been discharged by substantial performance.

To have substantial performance, the contract must not have been intentionally breached and the performance must be close to that required by the contract. In the case of an intentional material breach, the contractor is not entitled to damages from the property's owner. If the performance were substantial, the contractor would be entitled to payment under the contract terms, less the damages the owner incurred.

Discharge by Agreement

If the contract were fully performed, the parties may agree to discharge the contract. Businesspeople can agree to settle claims or to discharge debts. The following agreements are frequently used: (1) accord and satisfaction, (2) covenant (agreement) not to sue, and (3) novation. See Exhibit 10–3.

Accord and Satisfaction. **Accord and satisfaction** involves a debtor's offer to settle a debt owed to the creditor that is different from the original contract and the creditor's acceptance of the debtor's offer. An accord is the agreement in which the parties decide to modify their contract or to settle a disputed debt. Satisfaction takes place when the accord, that is, the agreed performance, has been completed. At that point, the accord and satisfaction are completed and the debtor's obligation is discharged.

Covenant Not to Sue. A **covenant not to sue** is a contract between the two parties agreeing that one person waives his right to sue, usually, in return for a settlement. For example, Brian is involved in an automobile accident caused when Kay failed to stop at a red light.

Exhibit 10–3   **Discharge of a Contract by Agreement**

1. *Accord and satisfaction* The agreement by one party to a contract to perform, and the other party to accept, something different from that which was originally agreed, in satisfaction of the original contract. The agreement is the accord. The execution of the agreement is the satisfaction.

2. *Covenant not to sue* An agreement not to sue on a present, valid, and enforceable claim.

3. *Novation* A valid contract that substitutes a new party for one of the original parties, thereby, discharging the original contract and the previous party.

Kay offers Brian $500 to release her from any further liability resulting from the accident. Brian believes that the repair to his car will be less than $400 and signs the release, which includes a covenant not to sue.

Later Brian discovers that the repair to his car will cost $600. Can Brian collect the balance of $100? The answer is no. The covenant not to sue limits Brian's recovery to $500 and he no longer has the right to file a negligence lawsuit.

Novation. A **novation** is a contract whereby an outside party is substituted for one of the party's to the original contract. A common type of novation occurs when a debtor is completely discharged from the contract and another debtor is substituted. The discharged debtor (an original party to the contract) no longer is liable under the original contract.

For example, you sell your home to Joe and Jan Johnson. As part of the contract, the Johnsons assume (take over) your payments on the mortgage note. Without a novation, you will still be liable if the Johnsons do not pay because you signed the original mortgage note. If the mortgage company agrees to substitute the Johnsons for you, however, a novation has occurred. The Johnsons now are liable; you are discharged from liability on the original mortgage note.

Discharge by Operation of Law

A contract may be discharged by operation of law. If the terms of the contract were altered by one party without the knowledge of the other party, the contract may be discharged because the parties had no meeting of the minds on the modified part of the contract.

If one party breaches a contract, the harmed party must file a lawsuit during the time period established in a statute of limitations. When the time period during which the harmed party could have sued has passed, the contract is discharged.

The following are several reasons for which a contract may become impossible to perform.

1. If one party dies or becomes mentally incompetent and that person's performance is essential to the contract's completion.

2. If the specific subject matter of the contract is destroyed, making it impossible to perform.

3. If one of the parties goes into bankruptcy and receives a discharge from the court.

Remedies and Damages

Breach of contract is a party's failure to perform a duty as promised in the contract. Once the defendant fails to perform or performs inadequately, the plaintiff can choose one or more of several remedies.

A remedy, in contract law, is the relief provided for a plaintiff when the defendant fails to perform and therefore breaches the contract. A remedy enforces a right. Strictly speaking, the remedy is not a part of a lawsuit. It is the end result of the lawsuit. In breach of contract cases, the normal remedy is money damages. Occasionally, the plaintiff is able to request an equitable remedy, such as rescission, restitution, specific performance, or reformation. Let's look at the two types of remedies, legal and equitable.

Legal Remedies

One party breaches the contract. The other party has not breached the contract, but has suffered economic harm and has the right to seek the legal remedy of money damages in a court of law. The money compensates the nonbreaching party (the plaintiff) for the losses incurred because the breaching party (the defendant) failed to perform the promises made in the contract. The harmed party's position is reinstated as if the contract had been fully performed.

When possible, the nonbreaching party has a duty to mitigate (lessen or reduce) the amount of damages. For example, if a person has been wrongfully fired from a job, he has a duty to seek similar employment within the same area, that is, to try to mitigate the damages. If the new job pays less than the previous job, the person can seek damages. By obtaining a new job, the former employee has mitigated the damages. The person cannot remain unemployed without seeking a job and then file a lawsuit for all the damages incurred since the firing. He is not obligated to take a job, however, that is very different from the previous job; an accountant does not have to take a housekeeper's position. The previous employer has the right to argue that the former employee made insufficient attempts to lessen the damages and, therefore, is entitled to only a portion of the damages requested.

The three most common types of damages sought in a breach of contract case are compensatory damages, consequential damages, and liquidated damages.

Discussion of the differences among these types of damages follows.[3]

Compensatory Damages.

The injured party seeks **compensatory damages** to make up for the monetary loss caused to her because the other party breached the contract. The economic injury must arise directly from the contract breach.

For example, Betty had a contract with Les to purchase 100 silicon chips for $250 per chip. Les breaches the contract by refusing to complete the sale. Betty purchases the 100 chips at $265 per chip. The compensatory damages that Betty can seek are $15 per chip or $150 for the contract. Compensatory damages place the injured party, as nearly as possible, in the position in which she would have been if the contract had been performed.

Consequential Damages.

Consequential damages, in contrast, are foreseeable damages resulting from special circumstances beyond the contract itself. The damages arise not directly from the contract breach, but as a consequence of it. The damages must have been foreseeable and the breaching party must have known of the special circumstances.

The court awards consequential damages in addition to compensatory damages. Consequential damages are also called special damages. If foreseeable, a business's lost profits that result from a breach of contract are an example of special damages.

The following example includes both compensatory and consequential damages. TV Manufacturer contracts to sell for $40,000 wide-screen digital television sets with full Dolby sound to Visual Systems. The delivery date is December 1. Visual Systems plans to resell the television sets immediately and to make a profit of $15,000. TV Manufacturer is aware of Visual Systems' resale plans. On November 25, TV Manufacturer notifies Visual Systems that the television sets will not be delivered and that the contract has been canceled. Visual Systems purchases equivalent televisions from another manufacturer for $50,000. Visual Systems can sue TV Manufacturer for compensatory damages in the amount of $10,000, the difference between the open market price, $50,000, and the contract price, $40,000 (plus any costs incurred because of the breach). In addition, Visual Systems is entitled to consequential damages for any foreseeable loss that it can prove, which in this illustration would be lost profits. TV Manufacturer, however, must know at the time of contracting that, if it breaches the contract, it is responsible for any profit loss.

Liquidated Damages.

Liquidated damages are the amount of damages that the parties establish in a clause contained in the written contract. The parties agree to the amount in advance in case one party breaches the contract.

Liquidated damage clauses are very common in the construction industry. The contractor promises to complete a building on a specified date. In the event it fails to complete the project on time, the contractor agrees to pay the owner a specific sum for every day the project is not completed.

The court upholds liquidated damage provisions if the damages meet two requirements. First, the amount of liquidated damages must be difficult to assess at the time the contract is signed. Second, the damages specified in the contract must bear some reasonable relationship to the actual damages incurred. A liquidated damage clause is declared null and void if it does not satisfy both requirements.

The amount of damages contained in the liquidated damages clause cannot be so large that it is punitive in nature. Punitive damages are not awarded in a breach of contract case.

Equitable Remedies

The most common equitable remedies available to a nonbreaching party are rescission and restitution, specific performance of a contract, and reformation of a contract. Equitable remedies are available in unusual circumstances.

When a rescission of a contract is ordered, the parties are restored to their original positions before the contract was made. Rescission is available when fraud, mistake, duress, or failure of consideration occurs. When a contract is rescinded, each party returns all money or items received back to the other party under the contract. The return of the items is called **restitution**. Restitution prevents unjust enrichment.

---

[3] You can review the different types of damages at <http://www.freeadvice.com/law/5183us.htm>. If this web site does not respond, go <http://www.freeadvice.com> and then click on contract law under the icon for general practice.

The remedy of specific performance of a contract is not often allowed. If money damages would be an inadequate remedy because the contract involves land or unique personal property, the court may grant the equitable remedy of specific performance. Each party is ordered to perform the specific promises in the contract. Specific performance is inappropriate for contracts relating to personal services.

Contract reformation occurs when the contract needs to be rewritten (reformed) because of errors in the written document. The court orders the contract to be reformed in accordance with the parties' true, original intentions.

Exhibit 10–4 summarizes the remedies available for a breach of contract.

Exhibit 10–4 Remedies for Breach of Contract

Equitable Remedies

Recission and Restitution	1. *Recission* An action to cancel the contract and return the parties to the positions they occupied prior to the transaction. Available when fraud, mistake, duress, or failure of consideration is present.
	2. *Restitution* When a contract is rescinded, both parties must make restitution to each other by returning goods, property, or money previously conveyed. Restitution prevents the unjust enrichment of the defendant.
Specific Performance	Requires the performance of the act promised in the contract. Only available in special situations, such as in contracts for the sale of unique goods or land, and where monetary damages would be an inadequate remedy. Specific performance is not available as a remedy in contracts for personal services.
Reformation	Corrects or rewrites a written contract to conform with the original intention of the parties.

Legal Remedies

Damages	A legal remedy designed to compensate the nonbreaching party for the loss of the bargain. By awarding money damages, the court tries to place the parties financially in the position they would have occupied had the contract been fully performed. The nonbreaching party frequently has a duty to mitigate damages incurred. The three broad categories of damages are:
	1. *Compensatory damages* Compensate the nonbreaching party for economic injuries actually sustained and proven to have arisen directly from the breach of contract.
	2. *Consequential damages* Result from special circumstances beyond the contract itself. These damages flow only from the consequences of a breach. The defendant must know at the time of the contract the existence of the special circumstances. Thus, these damages are foreseeable as a breach of the contract. The breaching party knows that the nonbreaching party will suffer two types of damages, compensatory damages and the additional loss of consequential damages.
	3. *Liquidated damages* Compensate the nonbreaching party by setting out the amount of damages in the contract. First, the amount of damages must be difficult to determine at the time the contract is signed. Second, the amount of liquidated damages must be reasonable in relationship to the actual damages and cannot be punitive in nature.

International Consideration

Selling Goods Internationally

As discussed in Chapter 9, the United Nations Convention on Contracts for the International Sale of Goods (CISG)[4] is a comprehensive document that covers all aspects of the sale of goods. Articles in the CISG cover the delivery of the goods and the handing over of the shipping documents or warehouse receipts so that the buyer can take possession of the goods.

The seller must deliver goods of the quantity, quality, and description required by the contract. The seller is liable when the goods fail to conform. The buyer must inspect the goods promptly and give notice of any problems with conformity within a reasonable time period. The buyer loses the right to rely on the lack of conformity if he does not give the seller notice within two years after the goods were "actually handed over to the buyer."

The remedies under the CISG are money damages, avoidance of the contract, and specific performance. The last remedy rarely is allowed in contracts for the sale of goods under U.S. law unless the item is unique, such as the Hope diamond.

---

[4] CISG is found at <http://www.uncitral.org/>.

LEGALLY SPEAKING

Contractual Capacity

A businessperson may become involved with parties who lack contractual capacity (such as minors or those judged to be mentally incompetent) in several ways. For example, a minor might earn millions of dollars on a successful recording and need to invest this money, or a person who has had a successful business career but now has Alzheimer's disease may be unable to manage his own affairs.

In all states, procedures exist to appoint a person to manage these assets. This person is called either a *guardian* or a *conservator*. In many states, the appointed guardian arranges for the personal care of the incompetent person, whereas an appointed conservator manages the protected party's assets. The same person may serve in both roles or two different people may be appointed.

Before appointment, the conservator must post a bond with the court in the amount of the total assets that she will manage. If no bond is posted, all assets must be held in restricted, fully insured bank accounts. The conservator can remove funds from these restricted accounts only by specific court order. In states that have not established the concept of a conservator, the appointed person, or guardian, handles both the protected person's personal care and finances.

The following are some steps you can take to protect yourself when dealing with individuals with impaired capacity to contract.

✔ Determine if the guardian or conservator has been privately or court appointed. If this person has been privately appointed, you should exercise care. If you know or should have known that the guardian was embezzling monies and using the funds for her personal benefit, you will be required to return anything that the dishonest guardian paid or gave you.

✔ If the guardian or conservator has been court appointed, he will have the court documents reflecting the appointment. You should make copies for your business files.

✔ Verify that the person has authority to enter into this particular contract with you on behalf of the protected party by requesting to see the court order or the document called a power of attorney. The person may have restricted authority.

Chapter Summary

The first three elements of a binding contract, offer, acceptance, and consideration, were described in Chapter 9. The last two elements are legal capacity and legality.

Parties to a contract must have the capacity to contract. Minors and most mentally incompetent people can enter into contracts, but these contracts are voidable at their option. A minor is liable for necessary items, but only to the extent of the reasonable value of the property or services actually used. When disaffirmance occurs, a minor must return any items even though they are in poor condition. If a court determines a person to be mentally incompetent, the contracts made after the court's judgment are void.

A valid contract must have a legal object or subject matter. The general rule is that an illegal agreement is void. In addition, the law requires certain contracts to be in writing to be enforceable.

Contractual rights and duties can be transferred to a third person through assignment of the rights or delegation of the duties. Third parties may be given benefits under a contract. Beneficiaries are either incidental or intended beneficiaries. An intended beneficiary can be categorized as a creditor beneficiary or a donee beneficiary.

Contracts can be discharged by acts or by agreement, such as full performance, accord and satisfaction, covenant not to sue, or novation. Contracts can be ended by operation of the law, which is the unilateral alteration of a written contract, the expiration of the statute of limitations, discharge by bankruptcy proceedings, or impossibility of performance because of a party's death or insanity or because of the destruction of the contract's subject matter.

When a party breaches his contractual commitments, he is liable for the damages caused. The injured party may recover through the equitable remedies of rescission and restitution, specific performance, or reformation, or through the legal remedy of money damages.

Using the World Wide Web

Various web sites provide information on electronic commerce. The American Institute of Certified Public Accountants (AICPA) has broken new ground by assuring that web sites offering electronic commerce meet standards of consumer information protection, transaction integrity, and sound business practices. In 1997, the AICPA and the Canadian Institute of Chartered Accountants introduced the CPA WebTrust℠ seal, which CPAs will be able to use to ensure consumers that web sites bearing the seal are trustworthy and reliable with regard to confidential consumer information.

The United Nations (UN) has developed a model law on electronic commerce that is being submitted to members of the UN for their signature. The federal government also has developed initiatives concerning electronic commerce. The following table provides more web addresses.

Finding the Law on the Web

United Nations Commission on International Trade Law (UNCITRAL) Model Law on Electronic Commerce
http://www.uncitral.org/

A critical examination of the commercial development of the World Wide Web as a commercial medium and a market place is found at this Israeli site
http://techunix.technion.ac.il/~orena/ec/
AICPA site
http://www.aicpa.org/
Legal Information Institute at Cornell Law School, general information on contracts
http://www.law.cornell.edu/topics/contracts.html

Chapter Web Sites

Uniform Electronic Transactions Act
http://www.law.upenn.edu/bll/ulc/ulc_frame.htm
FreeAdvice
http://www.freeadvice.com
Contracts for the International Sale of Goods
http://www.uncitral.org/
Martindale-Hubbell, a division of Reed Elsevier Inc.
http://www.lawyers.com
Internet Legal Resource Guide
http://www.ilrg.com/
Better Business Bureau
http://www.bbb.org/complaints/BBBautoLine.html

Web Activities

10–1 You decide to purchase a new home. All purchases of real estate are based on contract law. Martindale-Hubbell maintains web pages that assist the general public to find lawyers. Among the topics listed is real estate. Go to <http://www.lawyers.com> and click on "More Areas of Law." Go to the web page that covers general topics of interest. Click on real estate and find the two-page information sheet on how the law of contracts affects real estate. Summarize the information.

10–2 Your business, Artiste Login Products, Inc., needs information on legal forms for a basic agreement. Go to Internet Legal Resource Guide at <http://www .ilrg.com/> and click on ILRG Legal Forms Archive. Once there, scroll to Basic Agreements and click on General Agreement. What is the disclaimer concerning these forms? Do you understand the general agreement? Explain what the general agreement really states.

Key Terms

accord and satisfaction	collateral contract	donee beneficiary	restitution
age of majority	compensatory damages	incidental beneficiary	statute of frauds
assignee	consequential damages	intended beneficiary	unconscionable contract
assignment	covenant not to sue	liquidated damages	usury
assignor	creditor beneficiary	novation	
blue sky law	delegation	parol evidence rule	
breach of contract	disaffirm	ratification	

Questions and Case Problems

10–1 Restrictive Covenant A major corporation requires you to sign a contract as a condition of your employment. The contract contains a clause stating that you cannot compete directly or indirectly with the employer for a period of one year after your termination. Are these provisions legal? Why or why not? Does this type of covenant constitute duress?

10–2 Unconscionable Bargain Ahern, the plaintiff, called Knecht, the defendant, to repair her central air-conditioning unit. On April 19, Knecht installed a new blower assembly and motor. On May 30, Knecht rendered more service. On June 23, the unit was not cooling, and Ahern called Knecht again. He repeated the same work previously performed but failed to fix the cooling problem. He charged $762. The next day Ahern called another repair shop, which fixed the unit for $72. Ahern sued Knecht, alleging that his charges were outrageously exorbitant and unconscionable. Who should prevail and why? [*Ahern and Knecht*, 563 N.E.2d 787 (Ill. App. 2 Dist. 1990)]

10–3 Mistake Leydet entered into a written contract with the city of Mountain Home for delivery of treated wastewater over a twenty-year period to irrigate his farmland. Delivery started in 1982 and Leydet paid. The city was never capable of delivering the amount set out in the contract and Leydet could never use more than that

which the city delivered from 1982 to 1987. A drought for two years, 1988 and 1989, prevented the city from delivering the amount of water contracted. Leydet sued, seeking damages. The city defended that the drought excused it from fully performing on the contract. Any other steps taken would have been prohibitively expensive. Thus, performing was impracticable, and nonperformance was excused. Who should prevail and why? [*Leydet v. City of Mountain Home*, 812 P.2d 755 (Idaho App. 1991)]

10–4 Accord and Satisfaction Six Industries, Inc., was a general contractor for the construction of an insurance building. Six Industries entered into a subcontract with Kirk Williams Co. for heating and air-conditioning installations in the building. As a standard practice on projects of this size, the contract between the parties was changed by formal written change orders on several occasions. Near completion of the building, Six Industries submitted two last change orders. Kirk Williams refused to sign or complete the change orders because it claimed that Six Industries had delayed the project to Kirk Williams's detriment. Six Industries issued a check to Kirk Williams for $14,850.04. On the check, the following language appeared: "Endorsement and/or negotiation of the check constitutes a full and complete release of Six Industries, Inc., and acknowledges full payment of all monies due."

Kirk Williams received the check and the bookkeeper deposited it. Kirk Williams tried to return the money alleging that he was owed more money. Six Industries asserted that the depositing of the check was accord and satisfaction. Was there an accord and satisfaction through the cashing of the check? Explain. [*Kirk Williams Co. v. Six Industries, Inc.,* 11 Ohio App. 3d 152, 463 N.E.2d 1266 (1983)]

10–5 Capacity In 1982, Webster Street Partnership, Ltd. (Webster) entered into a lease agreement with Matthew Sheridan and Pat Wilwerding. Webster was aware that both Sheridan and Wilwerding were minors. Both tenants were living away from home, believing that the landlord would allow them to return home at any time. Sheridan and Wilwerding paid the first month's rent, but then failed to pay the rent for the next month and vacated the apartment. Webster sued them for breach of contract. They claimed that the lease agreement was voidable because they were minors. Who will prevail in court and why? [*Webster Street Partnership, Ltd. v. Sheridan,* 220 Neb. 9, 368 N.W.2d 439 (1985)]

10–6 Liquidated Damages Vrgora, a general contractor, entered into a contract with the Los Angeles Unified School District (LAUSD) to construct an automotive service shed and specifically enclosed room outfitted with an electronic vehicle performance tester. The contract provided for liquidated damages in the amount of $100 per day if the project was not completed within 250 days. Vrgora was responsible for purchasing and installing the tester. A dispute between the tester's manufacturer and Vrgora arose. The manufacturer finally delivered the tester over six months later. As a result, Vrgora completed the project several months late. LAUSD now wants Vrgora to pay $20,700 in damages for failing to complete the contract within 250 days. Who should prevail and why? [*Vrgora v. Los Angeles Unified School District,* 152 Ca. App. 3d 1178, 200 Cal. Rptr. 130 (1984)]

10–7 Mistake Alchem, an Israeli corporation, manufactures and sells lightweight, small-sized, halogenated aerosol fire extinguishers. Alchem entered into a contract with the company Gerard owned that made Gerard its exclusive distributor outside of Israel. A contract condition required the approval of the Underwriters Laboratories (UL). A UL approval in the United States is an indication of safety, quality control, and reliability. UL approval is essential if the product is to be marketed in the United States, because most U.S. purchasers require it, but it means very little, if anything, outside the United States. The process of obtaining UL approval takes a long time, ranging from a minimum of three to a maximum of fifteen years. After seven years, Alchem still had not obtained UL approval. Naturally, Gerard sold no extin-

guishers in the United States. Alchem, however, did sell some fire extinguishers in distributorship areas outside the United States, where UL approvals were not required even though Alchem had given Gerard exclusive dealership in those areas. Gerard sued Alchem. Alchem argued that Gerard could have sold the product outside the United States, and by not doing so, it had acted in bad faith. Gerard argued that it did not have a duty to sell any products prior to UL approval. Which company is correct? Was there a mutual mistake? Explain your answer. [*Gerard v. Almouli,* 746 F.2d 936 (2d Cir. 1984)]

10–8 Unconscionable Nelson owned a business known as Pacific Equities, which was involved in locating persons to whom various businesses owed money or property. Panorama City, Inc., was attempting to locate a Richard Hodge who owned $50,000 worth of its stock because of a corporate restructuring. Nelson investigated and found that Hodge was deceased and that his widow had remarried. Nelson notified her that she had assets of $50,000 but refused to provide any details until she signed an agreement assigning 50 percent of the net value of the assets to him. Although she signed, she now refuses to pay the fee, arguing that 50 percent is unconscionable. Do you agree with her or with Nelson? Why? Support your answer. [*Nelson v. McGoldrick,* 871 P.2d 177 (Wash. App. Div. 2 1994)]

10–9 Enforceability The Palermos orally agreed to purchase carpet, other floor-covering materials, and bathroom tile from Colorado Carpet Installation. All of these items were to be, but never were, installed by Colorado Carpet. A dispute occurred between the Palermos and Colorado Carpet. Colorado Carpet brought a lawsuit against the Palermos. The Palermos denied that they had ever ordered anything other than the bathroom tile. At the trial, the Palermos took the position that this was a contract for the sale of goods over $500 and, as such, would be unenforceable under the UCC. Colorado Carpet took the position that the contract was for the sale of services and outside of the UCC, and that the oral contract was enforceable. Who should prevail and why? [*Colorado Carpet Installation v. Palermo,* 668 P.2d 1384 (1983)]

10–10 Internet Many states have lemon car laws. The national Better Business Bureau has a BBB AutoLine. This service does not handle cases that fall under state lemon car laws, which are aimed at disputes between the car owner and the dealership. The BBB AutoLine offers an arbitration service that attempts to resolve disputes between consumers and automobile manufacturers involving alleged defects in a vehicle's material or workmanship. Once the arbitrator renders a decision, what two options are available to the consumer and what happens under each option? See the web site at <http://www.bbb.org/complaints/BBBautoLine.html>.

Chapter 11

Sales Law and Product Liability

To things of sale, a seller's praise belongs.

Love's Labour's Lost, 1598
William Shakespeare, English classical writer,
1564–1616

Outline

Ethical Consideration

Safe Products—at What Cost?

You are the president of a company that manufactures a popular motorcycle called Distance Runner. Although you compete with several giant corporations in the motorcycle market, your highly successful innovative designs, including a gas tank with double the normal capacity, have made your company very profitable. Although your bike is relatively safe, you are aware that in case of an accident, the large-capacity gas tank is more likely than a normal gas tank to rupture, leading to spilled gas that could cause a fire. The owner's manual discloses this danger in bold print.

A confidential internal report indicates that 5 percent of your motorcycles will probably be involved in accidents. If a fire erupts from a ruptured gas tank, it will probably cause the cyclist's death. Generally, these accidents are caused when the driver exceeds the speed limit and loses control of the motorcycle. The report suggests that if the tank were reduced in size and made safer, the risk of rupture could be reduced to 1 percent. The increased cost of the motorcycle and the loss of the large-capacity gas tank, however, would probably reduce your sales by 20 percent.

This large reduction would force you to lay off a significant number of your employees and might jeopardize your company's future. Do you continue to make Distance Runner with its large-capacity tank or do you change the construction of the gas tank? Use the ethical model presented in Chapter 2 and reprinted on the inside front cover to develop your answer.

Introduction

The last two chapters examined contract law, along with a few basic provisions regarding the sale of goods. This chapter will discuss many sections of the Uniform Commercial Code (UCC), Article 2, Sales. Each section (sometimes called a provision) of the UCC establishes the rules on a particular topic.[1] Article 2 governs the sale of goods and has been adopted into statutory form by every state. The sale of services is governed by federal and other state statutory provisions and common law.

The sale of real property generally is governed by state law and common law. When examining a contract, first determine the subject matter of the contract as goods, services, or real property. That determination of the contract's subject matter will indicate the set of statutes to research or whether to look to the common law.

You own a company called Artiste Login Products, Inc. Artiste will be involved in many contracts for the sale of goods, services, and real property. As you read the text and the cases, notice that Article 2 provisions tend to protect the interests of the buyer over those of the seller. The laws covering the sale of services or the sale of real property, in contrast, follow common law, which tends to favor the seller.

Instead of purchasing goods, Artiste may be better off financially if it leased goods. For example, Artiste may prefer to lease an automobile. UCC Article 2A provides legal guidance in the lease of goods. It basically treats the long-term lease of goods in the same manner as a sale. Article 2A has been adopted by a number of states.

This chapter examines specific contract and warranty sections of Article 2. It addresses the definitions of various terms under the UCC. Then the chapter wraps up with a discussion on the legal theories of product liability.

Theory of the Uniform Commercial Code

The UCC provides guidance to parties who are involved in a contract for the sale and purchase of goods. The drafters of the UCC wanted it to be a practical guideline for businesspeople to use. The code is flexible enough to provide for expansion of commercial practices under the court's interpretation, whereas the statutory aspects provide a stable framework.

The UCC respects the principle of the freedom of contract. The parties to the contract may make whatever arrangements suit them. The obligations of good faith, diligence, and reasonableness are the standards set by the UCC for the courts to use when reviewing a contract. Many UCC sections include the words "unless otherwise agreed," indicating that the parties may set their own terms.

[1] The Uniform Commercial Code is constantly being reviewed. For current provisions and suggested modifications, go to <http://www.law.upenn.edu/bll/ulc/ulc_frame.htm>.

If the parties fail to include certain terms in the contract, the UCC encourages application of the rules of a particular trade to fill in the missing terms or to guide a court in interpreting a clause. This principle is called **usage of trade** [UCC 1-205]. A baker's dozen, for example, means thirteen items, not twelve. A contract for the sale of a baker's dozen of jelly-filled rolls means a purchaser expects thirteen rolls in the box.

The UCC also defers to the parties' previous **course of dealing**. In other words, the previous conduct between the parties of a contract establishes a basis for understanding and interpreting their expressions in the current contract and their other conduct [UCC 1-205]. Here again, the UCC honors the principle of freedom of contract.

If the parties fail to include a term in the contract and no trade usage rule exists, the parties may turn to the UCC to provide guidance for filling in the omission. In Chapter 9, for example, you learned that if the contract fails to provide for the place of delivery, the UCC establishes it to be the seller's place of business or, if the seller has none, the seller's home.

Often the sheer number of UCC rules seems overwhelming. Remember, however, that most rules are based on common sense. When you purchase a new automobile, for example, you pick it up at the car dealership (seller's place of business). If you were to purchase a used automobile from a private party, you would go to the seller's home to take delivery of the automobile, because the UCC states that if the seller does not have a business, the place of delivery is the seller's home [UCC 2-308]. Under the UCC, you also are free to agree that the automobile will be delivered at a place other than the seller's place of business or home.

A merchant is a person who deals in goods and hold itself out as having knowledge or skill peculiar to the practices or goods involved in the contract. A contract "between merchants" means that both parties to the contract have the knowledge or skill of merchants [UCC 2-104]. Merchants are subject to special rules under the UCC. This chapter will not cover all of these rules, but you should be aware that under certain circumstances, special rules for merchants do exist.

Goods

Under UCC 2-105, **goods** are defined as all things that are movable at the time they are identified to a specific contract. Goods also include growing crops and the unborn young of animals, plus any other items that may be severed from real estate by the seller. Money, negotiable instruments, and investment securities are not classified as goods.

Identification

Goods must exist and be identified to the contract. The terms *existing* and *identification* have separate meanings under the UCC. Existing means that the goods have been manufactured and are currently in a tangible form. **Identified goods** are existing goods that have been identified to a particular contract. Often in a store, an appliance will have a sign saying, for example, "SOLD to Mr. & Mrs. J. B. Flick." This existing good, the appliance, has been identified to a particular contract. Identification can be made in any manner to which the parties explicitly agree.

For parties who fail to place in their contract the manner in which the identification will occur, the UCC provides guidelines [UCC 2-501]. If the goods exist, the contract automatically identifies them when the contract is made. If you purchase a coat in a store, the coat exists and the contract identifies it at the time you purchase it.

May the seller substitute other goods once the seller has identified particular goods to the contract? The UCC does allow the supplier to substitute other goods until it notifies the buyer that specific goods have been identified to this contract.

When a seller goes into bankruptcy, identification becomes very important if creditors have competing claims to goods. If the buyer has paid the purchase price of the goods and the merchant files bankruptcy within the following ten days, then the buyer may obtain the goods identified to the contract in preference to other creditors. Generally, if the goods have not been identified to a specific contract, the buyer has no preference to the goods or the money paid for the goods with respect to other creditors or the seller's bankruptcy estate.

Risk of Loss

The seller retains the risk of loss until he has completed all duties with respect to the goods under the contract. (The risk of loss will be covered in more detail later in this chapter.) As long as the seller has a risk of loss, he has the right to obtain insurance to protect himself against such risk. Likewise, the buyer has an insurable risk in the goods once they exist and are identified to the contract. The reason for the UCC rules concerning the manner of identifying the goods is to determine the party who has an insurable interest in the goods.

Future Goods

A contract also may be made for the sale of goods that do not yet exist. This agreement is called a **contract for future goods**. After these goods are manufactured, they are identified to the contract when they are shipped, marked, or otherwise designated by the seller as the goods belonging to this particular contract.

Title

Three concerns arise around the issue of the title (proof of ownership) to goods. The first is **warranty of title**. A warranty is a promise that a particular statement of fact is true. In this case, it indicates the truth of the seller's statement that it has good title. (Later in this chapter warranties will be discussed in detail.) The second issue concerns when the title passes from the seller to the buyer. The third problem involves voidable titles; that is, when is the title subject to legal challenge?

Warranty of Title

The UCC requires sellers to warrant that they have good title to the goods they sell [UCC 2-312]. To **warrant** means to promise that the facts stated in the contract are true. The supplier guarantees the truth regarding the type of title it has. Perhaps the seller has only a half-interest in the goods, and the other half-interest is owned by someone else. Thus, the seller can only sell her half-interest. The seller also must fully disclose any liens held against the goods, unless this disclosure is exempt by law.

Liens are discussed in the next chapter. A creditor is entitled to place a lien against the title of the goods. The creditor lends money to the debtor–seller to purchase the goods originally. The creditor has an interest in ensuring that the debtor–seller repays the loan. If the debtor–seller fails to repay the loan, the creditor has the legal right to have the item repossessed and sold to repay the loan.

The creditor also wants to make sure that the original buyer notifies the creditor if the goods are resold. A lien, which is recorded in a government office, provides notice to other lenders (creditors) that the buyer has already borrowed money from a previous creditor and that the creditor has a legal interest (to be repaid) in particular items. If the item is to be sold, the seller must notify the creditor of the pending sale, thus giving the creditor the ability to protect its interest. When the item is sold, the seller repays the creditor, and the seller is entitled to the rest of the money. The following case involves a warranty of title in the sale of an automobile.

Case 11.1

Boyer v. Trinity Universal Insurance Co.

Court of Appeal of Louisiana, 1990
564 So. 2d 384 (La. App. 3d Cir.)

BACKGROUND AND FACTS Edward J. Cop purchased a 1982 BMW from Sunbelt Auto Imports, Inc., and received a Louisiana certificate of title. Cop sold the BMW to Wade B. Randolph, who likewise obtained a Louisiana title. Randolph sold the BMW to James Boyer, who also secured a Louisiana title. Approximately two years later, Reimer-Oberst, a German BMW dealership, repossessed the vehicle. Reimer-Oberst claimed that it had never been paid for the BMW and had never released the original title.

Boyer reported this situation to his insurance company, Trinity Universal Insurance Company, filing a claim to be reimbursed for the cost of the BMW. Failing to reach a negotiated settlement, Boyer sued Trinity. Trinity in turn sued Randolph. The trial court granted a judgment in favor of Boyer against Trinity. The court dismissed the action by Trinity against Randolph. Trinity appealed.

Judge KNOLL

. . . .

We first look at the legal relationship between Boyer and his immediate predecessor in title, Randolph. A seller is bound to two principal obligations, that of delivering and that of warranting the thing which he sells. The warranty respecting the seller has two objects: the buyer's peaceable possession of the thing sold, and the second is the hidden defects of the thing sold, or its redhibitory vices.

The peaceable possession of a buyer is disturbed when he is evicted from the totality or a part of the thing purchased, due to the right or claims of a third person. Moreover, Civil Code Article 2501 defines the buyer's warranty against eviction:

> "Although at the time of the sale no stipulations have been made respecting the warranty, the seller is obliged, of course, to warrant the buyer against the eviction suffered by him from the totality or part of the thing sold, and against the charges claimed on such thing, which were not declared at the time of the sale."

Louisiana law is clear that an evicted buyer is entitled to the restitution of the purchase price from the seller.

. . . .

We now turn our attention to Trinity's indemnity [reimbursement] claim against Randolph. In *Bewley Furniture Co., Inc. v. Maryland Casualty Co.*, the Louisiana Supreme Court characterized indemnification as follows:

> "It has long been held in Louisiana that a party not actually at fault, whose liability results from the faults of others, may recover by way of indemnity from such others. The cases have referred to this imposed liability variously as technical, constructive, vicarious and derivative.
>
> . . . .
>
> The rule of indemnity . . . is founded upon the general obligation to repair the damage caused by one's fault and the moral maxim that 'no one ought to enrich himself at the expense of another.'"

Applying this jurisprudence to the case *sub judice* [case before the court], we find that Trinity, who was found vicariously liable to Boyer under its contract of insurance, sought indemnification from Randolph on the basis that the cause of Boyer's eviction was Randolph's defective title to the BMW. Under this analysis, it is clear that Randolph was the real party at fault, and ultimately should bear the burden for Boyer's loss. Therefore, we find that the trial court clearly erred when it failed to grant Trinity's third-party demand for indemnification against Randolph.

DECISION AND REMEDY The court found that the insurance company was liable to Boyer, who lost his vehicle. The court allowed the insurance company to recover from Randolph, who had sold the BMW to Boyer, for breach of warranty of title.

CRITICAL THINKING: PRACTICAL APPLICATION How can a purchaser of a motor vehicle protect herself or himself in case the title is not valid?

Passing of Title

Passing of title from the seller to the buyer and passing the risk of loss for the goods from the seller to the buyer are not the same thing. Different rules apply as to when a purchaser comes into title and when it assumes risk of loss. The UCC deals with these issues between the seller and buyer in terms of their performance under the contract.

The buyer and seller always can agree as to when the title passes from the seller to the buyer. Most of the time, the parties fail to consider title possession when making a contract. In the absence of an agreement as to when the title passes, UCC 2-401 outlines several situations, which will be discussed in the following sections. Title cannot change from the seller to the buyer, however, prior to the identification of the goods to a particular contract [UCC 2-401(1)].

Shipping Contracts. When goods must be moved, title passes at the time the seller completes his duty with respect to the goods' physical delivery. The shipping contracts used most are **free on board**, **point of shipment** (designated as **F.O.B.**); and **free on board**, **destination** (**F.O.B. destination**). In an F.O.B. situation, if the contract requires the seller to ship ten computers to the buyer, the title passes to the buyer at the time and place that the seller physically delivers the goods to the shipper for the shipment [UCC 2-401(2)(a)].

If the contract, however, requires the ten computers to be shipped and delivered to the buyer's place of business, the title changes when the shipper **tenders** (offers) delivery of the computers at the buyer's location. This example is that of an F.O.B. destination contract. The act of the shipper notifying the buyer that the goods are ready to be delivered is called the tender of the goods. Think of the word *tender* as meaning "to offer." The shipper tenders (offers) the goods for delivery to the buyer at the buyer's location [UCC 2-401(2)(b)]. Exhibit 11–1 summarizes the various types of transportation contracts.

Documents of Title. If the goods do not require shipment, two scenarios may occur. The first scenario between a seller and a buyer involves documents of title. No documents of title are involved in the second scenario. Let's look at these two situations.

When a transportation company or a warehouse is involved, the seller must provide the buyer a *document of title* [UCC 2-401(3)(a)]. A **document of title** is a paper representing ownership in the goods. The two most common documents of title are the *bill of lading* and the *warehouse receipt*. Exhibit 11–2 summarizes various types of documents of title.

A **bill of lading** indicates title to goods in the transportation industry. A **warehouse receipt** indicates title to goods stored by a distributor.[2]

A business uses a bill of lading in the following manner. A manufacturer ships 100 crates of DVD players by truck from City A to a distributor's warehouse located in City B. The shipping company prepares a bill of lading. One copy accompanies the goods while the manufacturer receives the other copies. The manufacturer sends one copy to the distributor, which takes the paperwork to the shipping company's office in City B. The bill of lading is a document of title, indicating the distributor's right to possession of the DVD players.

A warehouse receipt is used in the following situation. The distributor stores videotapes in its warehouse. The buyer, a store that rents and sells videotapes at the retail level, purchases a number of videotapes from the distributor. The distributor provides the store manager with a warehouse receipt. The manager drives to the warehouse located ten miles away, where she presents the warehouse receipt to the warehouse clerk. The warehouse receipt is a document of title that provides proof that the holder is entitled to possession of the videotapes. The clerk turns the videotapes over to the store manager. Title passes to the store manager on the passing of the warehouse receipt.

But what happens if no documents of title control the goods that a third party holds? Title passes at the time and place of contracting once the goods are identified to the contract [UCC 2-401(3)(b)]. In the previous situation, suppose that the seller has no document of title controlling the videotapes. The seller calls the warehouse, provides the buyer's description to the attendant, and authorizes the warehouse to release the videotapes to her. Here, title passed when the buyer contracted with the seller to purchase the videotapes.

---

[2] An example of a bill of lading and how to complete one is found at <http://www.showtrans.com/bl.htm>.

Exhibit 11–1 Types of Transportation Contracts

I. *Point-of-shipment contract*

    A. Seller has duty to:
        1. Contract with a transportation company.
        2. Deliver the goods to the transportation company.

    B. Buyer has the duty to pay shipping costs.

    C. Terms:
        1. Free on board (F.O.B.) [UCC 2-319(1)(a)]. Term used in ground or air transportation.
        2. Free alongside (F.A.S.) [UCC 2-319(2)]. Term used in marine transportation.
        3. F.O.B. vessel, car, or other vehicle [UCC 2-319(1)(c)]. The seller, at its own expense and risk, must load the goods on board. After loading, the goods are treated as F.O.B.

    D. Most contracts are point-of-shipment contracts.

II. *Destination contract*

    A. Seller has duty to:
        1. Contract with a transportation company.
        2. Deliver the goods to the transportation company.
        3. Pay for shipment to the destination.
        4. Retain the risk of loss and the right to insure.

    B. Terms:
        1. Free on board, destination (F.O.B. destination) [UCC 2-319(1)(b)].
        2. Cost, insurance, and freight (C.I.F.) [UCC 2-320(1)].
        3. Cost and freight (C. & F.) [UCC 3-320(1)].
        4. Ex-ship [UCC 2-322]. Requires delivery from a ship which has reached the named port of destination. Risk of loss shifts to buyer once the goods are unloaded from the ship. At that time, buyer must pay seller unless other arrangements have been made.
        5. No arrival, no sale [UCC 2-324]. If the conforming goods do not arrive, no sale has been made.

Exhibit 11–2 Documents of Title

A document of title represents ownership in the goods. The paper or document represents that the person in possession or named in the document has the right to receive, hold, and dispose of the goods listed on the document of title. The document of title may be negotiable or nonnegotiable. Chapter 12 discusses negotiability.

  I. *Warehouse receipt* A warehouse receipt is need to retrieved goods stored in a warehouse [UCC 1-201(45) and UCC 7-201 through 7-210].

  II. *Documents of title* Documents of title used when the goods are transported [UCC 1-201(6) and UCC 7-302 through 7-309].
    A. *Bill of lading* Used in motor vehicle or rail transportation.
    B. *Air bill, air consignment note, or airway bill* Used in air transportation.
    C. *Marine bill* Used in ocean or marine transportation.

III. *Miscellaneous documents of title*
    A. *Bill of sale* Method of transferring ownership in goods.
    B. *Certificate of title* Method of transferring ownership in goods. Used in titles for motor vehicles.
    C. *Deed* Method of conveying ownership in real property.

If the buyer rejects the goods or otherwise refuses to perform, and if the title has passed to the buyer, the title now revests (returns) to the seller. This revestment occurs by operation of law and is not considered a sale [UCC 2-401(4)].

Voidable Title

Although the original seller can reclaim the goods from the buyer if the buyer committed an illegal act, what happens if the buyer resells the goods to an unsuspecting third party? In three situations, the new buyer in the ordinary course of business may obtain valid title if she has no knowledge of the illegal conduct of the original buyer.

In the first situation, assume that an original buyer pays for a lamp with a check that eventually is dishonored by the bank because of insufficient funds. The lamp is in the possession of the buyer. If the buyer sells the lamp to an innocent purchaser who has no knowledge of the bad check, the new buyer obtains valid title to the lamp.

In the second situation, title can be transferred if the seller mistakes the buyer's identity and turns over possession of the goods to an impostor. For example, Judy Pivon, who has excellent credit, places an order to purchase a dining room set from you. You turn over the dining room set to an impostor, thinking she is Judy Pivon. The impostor sells the dining room set to a third party, who knows nothing about this fraudulent transaction. The new purchaser has valid title. Your only recourse is to locate the imposter and bring a civil legal action against her. You may also file a criminal complaint against the imposter with the local prosecuting attorney's office.

In the third situation, the seller, instead of the original buyer as set out in the previous two situations, is the one who creates the problem. If a person leaves goods with a business that sells similar merchandise, the UCC allows the business to transfer valid title. For example, Larry takes his lawn mower in to be repaired. The repair shop also sells new and used lawn mowers. The shop accidentally sells Larry's lawn mower to a person who has no knowledge that Larry owns it. That purchaser has valid title to Larry's lawn mower. Larry, however, can bring a civil action against the repair shop if it fails to reach a settlement with him.

The reasoning behind the three rules is simple. When there are two innocent parties, the person who could have controlled the loss will incur the loss. Review the examples in this section and note that this underlying principle applies to each [UCC 2-403]. The following case emphasizes this position.

Case 11.2

Firoz Jaliwala v. Five Oceans Gem Corp.

United States Court of Appeals, Seventh Circuit, 1994
33 F.3d 56

BACKGROUND AND FACTS Jaliwala entrusted jewels to Morton Dock, who sold some of the jewels from his own account to the partnership of Five Oceans Gem Corp. and to Bretislav Stasny. Dock later was indicted for this act and committed suicide before he could be arrested. Five Oceans and Stasny turned their remaining inventory of Jaliwala's gems over to the Federal Bureau of Investigation (FBI). This suit determined whether Jaliwala or Five Oceans Gem Corp. had superior title to the gems. The lower court found that Five Oceans Gem Corp. was entitled to the gems. Jaliwala appealed.

Circuit Judges EASTERBROOK, MANION, and KANNE

. . . .

The UCC provides that a dishonest merchant to whom goods have been entrusted may convey good title to a purchaser "in ordinary course of business." UCC § 2-403(2). Thus the question for trial was whether the partnership bought the gems from Dock, a merchant, "in ordinary course of business." The district judge answered yes. The principal contrary argument is that the partnership got the gems at such a low price—a steal, Jaliwala says—that the transaction must have been outside the ordinary course. But there was conflicting evidence about the price Jaliwala himself paid for the gems and the amount he expected to obtain for them—a conflict that depends in part about the meaning of coded price sheets and in part about just how many of Jaliwala's jewels the partnership bought (the district court found that the partnership bought fewer carats than Jaliwala thinks, implying a higher price per carat). There was also a conflict about the extent to which the transaction conformed to business norms. Jaliwala emphasizes that it was conducted quickly with a stranger; the district court observed that the partners checked Dock's references and found him reputable before buying from him, and that they kept good records and retained unsold jewels in the original envelopes (unlikely steps if the buyers were suspicious about the legitimacy of the transaction). When evidence and inferences cut both ways, the decision of the trier of fact is, as a practical matter, conclusive.

DECISION AND REMEDY The court found that the trial court applied the law correctly to the situation; that is, property left with another who sells similar items and who sold the goods to a third party did pass valid title. The major issue confronting the court was whether the sale was in the ordinary course of business. Evidence conflicted as to that issue. The trial court found that the gems were sold in the ordinary course of business, which was upheld by the appellate court.

CRITICAL THINKING: PRACTICAL APPLICATION Assume that your bicycle is stolen while you are in class and that it was sold to a person in the ordinary course of business who had no knowledge of the theft. The law very clearly allows you to obtain possession of it once you discover its location. Discuss whether the rule should differ when you take the same bicycle to a repair shop that also sells bicycles in the ordinary course of business and the shop sells it to an innocent purchaser. In both situations, your bicycle was wrongfully taken from you, but in one case you can get your bicycle back while in the other case you cannot.

Risk of Loss

At one time, the question of title ownership was of prime importance in determining the party who incurred the risk of loss. The old rule was that the party in possession of the title also was responsible for the goods in the event that they were damaged. Today, that rule is no longer valid.

A buyer and seller always can bargain over which carries the risk of loss in the event that the merchandise is damaged or destroyed. Normally, the parties bargain over price, quality of goods, shipment terms, and credit terms. Seldom do they consider the consequences of merchandise damage or loss.

If risk of loss is not covered in the agreement, the Uniform Commercial Code supplies the rules as to who bears the loss. These rules were drafted with the view that whoever purchased insurance would assume the risk of loss. This underlying principle applies even in situations in which the buyer or seller breached the contractual obligations.

In the absence of contract breach by either the buyer or seller, and if the contract does not require the seller to deliver the goods to a particular place, the risk of loss passes to the buyer when the seller delivers the goods F.O.B. to the carrier. This rule holds even when the goods are shipped on the basis of **collect on delivery (C.O.D.)**. When goods are sent C.O.D., the delivery company collects from the buyer the money owed for the goods when it delivers them. If the buyer does not pay for the goods, the delivery company returns the goods to the seller. If the seller must deliver the goods at a particular destination (F.O.B. destination), the risk of loss passes to the buyer when the goods are tendered. The buyer is entitled to take delivery on payment [UCC 2-319].

If a third person holds the goods and there is a document of title, the risk of loss transfers to the buyer on

LEGAL HIGHLIGHT

The Midas Touch

Advanced technology makes the recovery of treasures from ships sunk centuries ago possible. Who has title to these riches? Is it the person who studies the ship's history; makes the careful calculations; finances the project; risks her or his life to search underwater; and recovers the gold, silver, and artifacts? Or is it the original owner, or even the government? Consider the Spanish galleon, *Nuestra Señora de Atocha*, which sunk off the Marquesas Keys in 1622 while en route to Spain, heavily laden with $250 million in cargo (contemporary value). Or consider the U.S. flagged, *SS Central America*, sailing from San Francisco carrying three tons of gold (worth $1 billion today), lost in 1857 during a hurricane off the South Carolina coast.

The law was not clearly established when cases involving these sunken ships reached the courts. In the case of the Spanish galleon, the court ruled that the persons who recovered the treasure could treat the treasure as abandoned and thus had valid title. The rule applied is called the *American rule*. The court noted that under the *English rule,* the treasure would belong to the U.S. government.

In the case of the *SS Central America*, thirty-nine insurance companies claimed ownership of the gold because they paid the claims of the original owners after the ship was lost. Factors beyond the owners' control caused the ship to be destroyed and the cargo to be lost, but the owners never abandoned the gold because salvage attempts were made over the years. Under salvage laws, the insurance companies showed that title was never divested (changed or withdrawn).

At times, the courts protected the rights of the original owner while compensating the party who recovered the cargo. The courts base these decisions, called *salvage law,* on the principle of equity. The person taking the risk to recover the cargo is paid a reasonable amount (based on the difficulty and hazardousness of the salvage efforts), whereas the owner retains title and ownership. The salvagers of the *SS Central America* spent $30 million to recover $22 million in gold. As a result of this expenditure, the court allowed the salvagers possession of most of the gold. The insurance companies shared only a small part of the return.

receipt of the document of title. If there is no document of title, the risk of loss passes to the buyer when the seller informs the third person of the sale [UCC 2-509(2)].

In all other cases, if no breach of contract is involved, and if the seller is a businessperson, the risk of loss transfers to the buyer when the buyer takes possession of the goods. If the seller is not in business, the risk of loss transfers to the buyer on the tender of delivery [UCC 2-509(3)]. Assume that you purchase a desk at a yard sale, but because you rode to the sale on your bicycle, you must leave the desk to procure transportation. The seller, who is not a merchant, tells you that you can have immediate delivery of the desk. You bicycle home to get your automobile. While you are gone, a rainstorm occurs, and lightning strikes your desk. In this situation, you hold the risk of loss. If the seller had been a merchant, however, she would have retained the risk of loss.

What happens when either the buyer or the seller breaches her contractual obligation? If the seller ships goods in a condition that allows for the buyer to reject them, the risk of loss remains with the seller [UCC 2-510(1)]. Many times a buyer accepts goods inconsistent with the original order and later revokes the acceptance. In that event, the buyer looks first to its insurance company for reimbursement of its losses and may look to the seller to pay the rest of the loss if the insurance does not pay the total amount lost [UCC 2-510(2)].

The seller may look to the buyer when goods have been identified to the contract, but the buyer repudiates the contract and the goods are later damaged. In such cases, the seller, to the extent of any deficiency in the seller's insurance coverage, may treat the risk of loss as the buyer's responsibility for a commercially reasonable length of time [UCC 2-510(3)].

Other delivery terms affect risk of loss. For example, **cost, insurance, and freight (C.I.F.)** indicates that part of the purchase price includes insurance during transportation. In this situation, the insurance company holds the risk of loss once the goods are shipped until the buyer is tendered delivery. If the contract is **cost and freight (C.&F.)**, the rules of F.O.B. contracts apply [UCC 2-320]. C.I.F. and C.&F. shipment terms are used predominantly with international sales.

The following case is an example of a C.&F. contract in which a loss was sustained. The court had to decide who would bear the risk of loss.

Case 11.3

Rheinberg Kellerei GmbH v. Brooksfield National Bank of Commerce Bank

United States Court of Appeals, Fifth Circuit, 1990
901 F.2d 481 (5th Cir.)

BACKGROUND AND FACTS In January 1986, J & J Wine, a U.S. company, ordered a shipment of wine from a German firm, Rheinberg Kellerei GmbH, through an importer, Frank Sutton & Company. (The "GmbH" designation means "Gesellschaft mit beschrankter Haftung," or "company with limited liability." GmbH is a common form of corporate organization in Germany and is similar to the "Inc." designation in the American corporate system.)

J & J Wine arranged for payment to be made through Edekabank in Germany and Brooksfield National Bank of Commerce Bank in San Antonio (NBC Bank). When Rheinberg shipped the wine from Germany to Houston, the shipping company delivered the paperwork, called a bill of lading, evidencing the shipment.

Rheinberg took the paperwork, retained copies for its files, and sent the rest of the bill of lading along with a letter of collection (a letter that requests the bank to collect the money) and invoices to Edekabank in Germany, which then forwarded all the paperwork to NBC Bank. If J & J Wine made its payment to NBC Bank, the copies of the bill of lading and invoices would be released to J & J Wine, which then could take the copies to the Port of Houston to accept the wine delivery. In the meantime, NBC Bank would forward the payment to Edekabank, which then would pay Rheinberg.

The International Chamber of Commerce's International Rules for Collection governs the enforcement of a letter of collection. These rules were binding on NBC Bank when it agreed to accept a letter of collection.

The letter of collection instructed NBC Bank to notify Sutton in case of any difficulty with payment. J & J Wine did not pay the amount due but asked NBC Bank to wait while J & J Wine raised the money for payment. NBC Bank did not notify Edekabank or Sutton regarding J & J Wine's request for time and its failure to pay.

The wine arrived at the Port of Houston on March 31, but NBC Bank did not receive notice. Because J & J Wine did not take delivery of it, the wine sat, exposed, at Houston harbor in metal containers until it deteriorated completely. U.S. Customs agents eventually sold it at auction. J & J Wine subsequently went out of business, and Rheinberg never received payment for the wine. NBC Bank still held the bill of lading. Rheinberg sued NBC Bank, alleging that it had negligently failed to inform Rheinberg of J & J Wine's failure to pay and that, as a result, the wine had spoiled at the Houston harbor. The district court found that NBC Bank was not liable. Rheinberg appealed.

Circuit Judge GARZA

. . . .

NBC Bank presented the letter of collection and the other documents to J & J Wine for payment on March 27,1986, before the wine had arrived and before the payment was due. Rheinberg Kellerei argues that, regardless of whether NBC Bank knew when the wine had arrived, once NBC Bank presented the documents, it had a duty to inform Edeka of any problem in collecting J & J Wine's payment. We agree. . . .

The letter, which is the primary source of responsibility in this case, instructs NBC Bank to notify Sutton "in case of any difficulty of lack of payment." The district court found that section demanded notice only if there were a "lack of payment or failure to pay." Likewise, NBC Bank emphasizes that the trigger for notice is a lack of payment.

What the court below and NBC Bank ignore is the word "difficulty." The letter did not instruct NBC Bank to notify Sutton only if there were a default, or a failure to pay, or a lack of payment. Rather, NBC Bank was called on to act also if there were any difficulty in collecting payment. And the request that NBC Bank hold the letter while J & J Wine sought financing certainly posed a difficulty in collection. Once NBC Bank knew that J & J Wine had asked for time to come up with the money, it should have notified Sutton in accordance with the letter's instructions.

. . . .

State law governs the measure of damages in a case such as this one. [T]he relevant standard [is] "the seller may recover, together with any incidental damages under the next section, the price (1) of goods accepted or of conforming goods lost or damaged . . . after risk of their loss has passed to the buyer." Risk of loss had passed to J & J Wine when the goods arrived at Houston harbor and were available for J & J Wine to take delivery. The district court found that because the wine was exposed for such a long period in Houston harbor, it was " 'over cooked' and had deteriorated, lost its original flavor, freshness, was flat and should not be sold into the market that it was intended." Since the goods were so damaged, Rheinberg Kellerei is entitled to the contract price plus the unpaid freight costs.

NBC Bank is entitled to a credit for the net proceeds of any resale of the damaged wine. Customs agents sold the wine at auction, but we have no evidence before us of the price paid or the net amount remaining after customs fees, wharfage, and the costs of the auction were paid. For that reason, we remand this case to the district court for the limited purpose of calculating that net amount. After finding that net amount, the district court should enter judgment for Rheinberg Kellerei for the contract price plus freight charges, less the net proceeds of the customs auction.

DECISION AND REMEDY NBC Bank had a duty to notify Edekabank or Sutton when J & J Wine asked for more time when presented with the letter of collection. The duty arose from the letter of collection to NBC Bank, which required it to notify Sutton if J & J Wine had any difficulty in paying. By NBC's remaining silent, neither Sutton nor Rheinberg had the opportunity to rescue the wine before it spoiled under the hot Houston sun.

CRITICAL THINKING: PREVENTIVE LAW Many commercial transactions use printed forms. Discuss steps the bank could have taken to protect itself in this case.

Trial Sales

In addition to the usual method, goods can also be sold using one of two types of contract clauses. The first type is called a **sale on approval** [UCC 2-326(1)(a)]. When the clause is inserted in a contract, no sale occurs until the potential purchaser is satisfied. If the potential purchaser is not satisfied, the goods are returned to the owner. For example, you want to buy a helicopter. Using this clause, you could use the helicopter for a reasonable time period. If you approve, the owner sells the helicopter to you. If the helicopter does not meet your approval, you return it to the owner. All sales on approval agreements are made to the ultimate consumer.

The second type of clause is called a **sale or return** [UCC 2-236(1)(b)]. This clause is used when the buyer is also a reseller; that is, the buyer purchases the goods for resale. Books and magazines are usually sold under a sale or return clause. If the purchaser does not resell the goods, it can return them to the original seller.

Under either one of these circumstances, the question arises as to which party, the seller or the buyer, has the title and risk of loss. When the goods are sold with a sale-on-approval clause, the seller retains the title and risk of loss until the buyer approves of the goods and the sale is complete. When the goods are sold with a sale-or-return clause, the buyer has actually purchased the items, so the title and risk of loss transfer to the buyer. If the buyer needs to return any items, such as unsold magazines, the title and risk of loss transfer back to the seller.

Performance

Normally, the parties to a contract negotiate the terms of its performance. As we have seen, the UCC supplies many of the necessary terms when the parties neglect to cover certain details. The UCC also assists both the seller and the buyer by providing them with certain rights when the contract neglects to address a particular issue.

Rights of Buyer and Seller

The buyer and seller have several rights. First, a buyer has a right to inspect goods before accepting or paying for them. The buyer can make certain that the goods conform to the specifications established in the contract. In some cases, such as when the goods are sent C.O.D., the buyer can inspect the goods only after paying. The buyer then has a right to revoke his acceptance if the breach of contract substantially impairs the value of the goods [UCC 2-513].

Second, the UCC allows both parties the right to obtain adequate assurance for further performance. Each party to a contract expects the other person to perform fully. At times, one party may doubt the other person's ability to perform fully. As long as this concern is based on good faith and fair treatment of the other party, the buyer or seller can request further assurances of full performance.

For example, you have ordered 100,000 computer chips from Johnson Industries. In a recent trade jour-

nal, an article implies that Johnson's quality control has not been fully effective and that many defective chips have resulted. You could insist that Johnson post a performance bond prior to your acceptance of future chips. Johnson would be required to purchase a performance bond from a bonding company. The bond requires the bonding company to pay you should Johnson fail to perform the contract by selling you inferior chips.

In another example, you have granted credit to a buyer, but later discover that the buyer is considering filing for bankruptcy. At that point, you could decide to send future shipments C.O.D. or you could request payment before shipment [UCC 2-609].

Impracticability

At the time of contracting, the parties believe that certain conditions exist that will allow the seller to perform fully on the contract. In some situations, when the seller cannot deliver certain products as promised because of factors beyond the seller's control, the UCC allows allocation of the goods by the seller to the buyer in any manner that is fair and reasonable. For example, a seller contracts to provide a unique type of wheat to the buyer. A storm destroys most of the crop. The UCC allows allocation of the wheat among all of the purchasers, so that one buyer could not insist on complete performance.

Another example of impracticability occurs when a contract requires that construction be completed within a certain time frame. Factors beyond the contractor's control, such as not having electrical power to the site, can delay the completion of the building by several weeks. The court takes these types of factors into consideration when determining whether a breach of contract has occurred. When a court finds impracticability, no breach of contract has occurred. At the time of contracting, however, the event that now makes the contract impracticable must have been unforeseeable [UCC 2-615].

Remedies

In the event that the other party to a contract for the sale of goods breaches its contractual obligations, the same basic rules govern your rights as in the breach of an ordinary contract, as discussed in Chapter 10. The next section identifies the parties' specific rights when a breach occurs. Keep in mind, however, that the rules

What Happens When Your New Software Crashes Your Computer?

Shopping at your local computer store, you notice a bin of programs on compact disc (CD). Enticed by the advertising material on the box, you purchase the CD. You think the new program will be great. You take it home and install the software on your computer. It crashes your computer and you must reinstall all of your programs. What can you do about this? Can you obtain a refund? Can you collect damages for the many hours it takes to reinstall your other software?

Anyone owning a computer for any length of time has been confronted with these types of problems. The sellers deny liability because you accepted their licensing agreement when you installed the software. The software included a provision that there is no liability on behalf of the supplier if something goes wrong.

The computer industry is attempting to provide suppliers with more defenses against consumers. A proposed provision for the UCC is Article 2B. This provision states that when you purchase a program you are not purchasing a product, only the right to use the program, which is a license. If you are not purchasing goods, then the consumer protection laws are not applicable.

But until Article 2B is passed by individual state legislatures, most courts hold that when you purchase a program at a store you are purchasing a product. Under the UCC, you have a right of inspection under Section 2-513. If you promptly revoke your acceptance of the goods, you are able to obtain a return of your purchase price.

Often when you reinstall software, you need to contact the supplier to obtain assistance and sometimes you must pay a fee for assistance. This fee is an incidental expense that is recoverable under UCC 2-715. You cannot, however, recover for your time spent to reinstall the software.

What about the software you download from the World Wide Web? In this instance, there is no physical product, just digital product. When you start the download process, you must click on an agreement that almost no one reads. Your click signifies that you agree with it; that is, the warranty disclaimer becomes effective. The terms in the disclaimer favor the seller and can be used against you in a legal dispute. In other words, you have no rights because you waived them with a click.

---

are very similar to those that apply to the breach of an ordinary contract.

Remedies of Buyers

Assume that you ordered 100,000 bushels of wheat to be delivered in sixty days from Growers Market. You agreed to pay the current market price for the day on which you entered into your contract. Since then, however, the market price increased substantially. Because of this, Growers notifies you that it will not send you the 100,000 bushels of wheat. What are your rights?

Wheat is a type of product that easily is purchased on the open market. Thus, you can secure what is called **cover**. That is, you can obtain goods similar to those required by the contract from other available sources. You then may recover from the original seller the difference between the contract and current mar-

ket price, plus incidental or consequential damages [UCC 2-711, 2-712].

Incidental damages include items, such as costs for transportation, reasonable charges, and expenses or commissions incurred in connection with obtaining cover. Consequential damages include loss of business profits if your business closes because of the seller's breach. For consequential damages to be available, the supplier must have known at the time of contracting that if it were to breach the contract, your business would close as a result [UCC 2-712, 2-713, 2-715].

Occasionally, the courts will force a seller to perform the contract. This order for specific performance occurs if the goods are unique or if obtaining cover is impossible. For example, one of the best indicators of the overall state of the economy is the health of the construction industry. Concrete is a construction item that normally is available. When the economy is expanding quickly, a shortage of concrete may exist. Concrete production takes large investments in capital goods and plants. Starting a new plant is not very easy or quick. Under certain conditions, a concrete manufacturer might refuse to deliver the amount of concrete for which it contracted. This refusal may be an attempt to secure a higher price from you. You can bring action in court seeking specific performance of this manufacturer to deliver the concrete if you cannot obtain cover from any other reasonable source. If specific performance is impossible, the court may award you appropriate damages [UCC 2-716].

Remedies of Sellers

The major problem that a seller confronts is nonpayment for goods that the buyer accepts. In this situation, the seller is entitled to be paid the contract price.

A more complicated problem occurs when the buyer refuses the goods and repudiates the contract. Normally, the seller may recover the difference between the market price and the unpaid contract price together with incidental damages, less any expenses saved by the buyer's breach. If this rule fails to place the seller in as good a position as if the contract had been performed, the measure of damages is the profit, including overhead, that the seller would have earned if the buyer had fully performed the contract, plus any incidental expenses [UCC 2-708].

A third kind of problem occurs when the seller cannot sell the goods identified to the contract at a reasonable price in the market. In this situation, the measure of damages is the contract price [UCC 2-709].

The next case discusses some of the problems in awarding damages to a seller.

Case 11.4

In re S.N.A. Nut Company v. Haagen-Dazs Company

United States Bankruptcy Court, Northern District Illinois, Eastern Division, 2000
247 B.R. 7, 41 U.C.C. Rep. Serv. 2d 834

BACKGROUND AND FACTS The debtor, S.N.A. Nut Company (SNA), filed a lawsuit against the Haagen-Dazs Company, Inc. (HD), alleging that SNA and HD entered into five contracts for the purchase and sale of specially manufactured nut products to be used in HD's ice cream. SNA alleged that after the bankruptcy petition was filed, HD breached five contracts. SNA sought damages in the amount of $981,866 for breach of all five contracts. HD is a division of the Pillsbury Company, a Delaware corporation.

The business relationship between SNA and HD began in 1984 when HD first purchased pecans from SNA. In later years, HD expanded its purchases from SNA to include other nut and candy products. HD and SNA worked together to develop several of these nut and candy products, including the product known as "coated macadamia brittle." SNA produced all finished goods for HD according to HD's specifications and instructions.

SNA did not manufacture all of the HD goods at once because of freshness concerns. HD supplied SNA with usage forecasts and SNA manufactured in response to these forecasts. The forecasts helped SNA set minimum inventory levels for HD products. To ensure that it did not run short of HD products, SNA usually produced more than the forecast called for.

As HD's plants needed ingredients manufactured by SNA, the plant managers would call. Arrangements would be made for delivery to the appropriate plant. SNA did not ship goods to HD unless HD called. The goods had a limited shelf life because they were perishable and would become rancid after too much time elapsed. HD would only accept goods within ninety days of the date on which they were boxed. Eventually, HD's annual purchases from SNA rose as high as $9 million.

After filing for bankruptcy SNA did have temporary problems suppling almonds. Rich, an employee of SNA, informed Reider, an employee of HD, that SNA's almond problems were temporary. The inventory sheets also clearly indicated that SNA was producing almonds and that its stock was growing. Reider never called Rich to ask about almond availability and Rich never again told Reider to seek alternate suppliers because SNA could not make the goods.

ERWIN I. KATZ, Bankruptcy Judge

. . . .

The parties agree that this action is governed by Article 2 of the Uniform Commercial Code.

. . . .

B. Contract Breach

. . . .

SNA claims that HD breached [the] contracts by failing to purchase all the goods contracted for. If a party to a contract fails to perform its contractual obligations when they become due, then that party is in breach. HD does not dispute that it failed to order or accept the goods which it contracted to purchase. SNA has thus met its burden of proving that HD breached the five contracts.

. . . .

2. SNA's Tender of the Goods

HD claims that SNA never tendered delivery of the goods contracted for and therefore, that HD had no duty to accept or pay for the goods. . . . Once the seller tenders the goods, the buyer is obligated to accept and pay for them according to the contract. To prove tender, a party must show only that it notified the other party that it was ready and willing to deliver the goods. . . .

It is very clear that, as part of a course of dealing established over many years, SNA did not deliver goods to HD unless and until HD ordered them. It is also clear that HD stopped ordering releases under the contracts at issue before completing its performance under the terms of those contracts.

. . . .

HD argues that SNA did not have the full contract balance of finished goods on hand at the time the contracts expired. However, the evidence of the parties' course of dealing shows that SNA manufactured in response to HD's needs.

. . . .

SNA tendered the goods and HD was obligated to accept and pay for them. HD was not excused from performance. . . .

D. Damage Calculations and Defenses

As to those finished goods that SNA was able to sell, SNA seeks only to recover the difference between the resale price and the contract price. SNA seeks only the difference between the purchase price and the resale price on raw materials; it has subtracted the amount of finished goods these raw nuts would have yielded from the total of goods neither manufactured nor taken. . . .

Under the UCC, remedies are to be liberally administered; the injured party should be put in a position as good as if the breaching party had fully performed its obligations. The UCC provides several remedies for a seller when the buyer has breached a contract. SNA seeks damages [for] . . . the profit that it would have made from HD's full performance under UCC § 2-708(2). . . .

. . . .

SNA argues that UCC § 2-708(2) is the proper measure of its damages because the goods at issue were manufactured specially for HD and had little or no value to anyone else.

. . . .

. . . [M]any courts have held that damages under UCC § 2-708(1) are inadequate for specially-manufactured goods that cannot be resold. Whether goods are specialty items is a question of fact. Such goods have no readily accessible market from which to determine market price. A formula basing damages on the difference between market price and contract price is without meaning in the context of a contract for a specialty item which has no market. A market must be a real market in which a sale of the goods would substantially mitigate the seller's damages. If the goods are specially-manufactured goods, then damages under UCC § 2-708(2) should be awarded.

The goods at issue were specially-manufactured goods. They were made for HD only, using HD's recipes and specifications. There was no market for the goods; the testimony was undisputed that no other food processor used nuts prepared according to HD's recipes. Thus, UCC § 2-708(2) is the proper measure of SNA's damages. SNA is entitled to recover the profits it would have earned had HD performed, including overhead, plus incidental damages, plus costs incurred, less proceeds from the goods it resold.

. . . .

DECISION AND REMEDY The court concluded that HD breached five contracts with SNA. The court found that the total amount owed to the plaintiff was $921,978.49.

CRITICAL THINKING: PREVENTIVE PROCEDURE One major business problem is how to protect your interest when a customer or supplier goes into bankruptcy. You will be covering bankruptcy law in Chapter 14. One thing that does occur whenever a person or business files for bankruptcy is the issuing of an automatic stay or order. This stay restricts you from doing anything against the property of the debtor. You sometimes cannot bring legal action against the debtor and you forfeit your rights to garnish or attach assets. In other words, you cannot use your normal legal procedures to protect your interest against a bankrupt person. Then why should you still have to be involved contractually with a bankrupt debtor?

CyberLaw

Taxes

In 1999, Congress passed the Internet Tax Freedom Act, which placed a three-year moratorium on state and local taxes on Internet access or on electronic commerce. Congress also declared no new federal taxes would be imposed during the same time period. The act created the Advisory Commission on Electronic Commerce to examine the impact of the imposition, collection, and administration of taxes on electronic commerce in other countries and the United States and the impact on global economy.

State and local governments depend heavily on sales tax revenue. As more tax-exempt sales are made over the Internet, state and local governments stand to lose a portion of their income. More than 7,500 juris-

dictions in the United States impose a sales tax. It is not the sheer volume of jurisdictions, but the complexity of the various tax codes that present a real challenge to those selling goods and services over the Internet.

If all 7,500 jurisdictions imposed taxes on web sales, the growth of the web and electronic commerce would be significantly impacted. Therein lies the conflict. State governments depend on sales taxes as a substantial portion of their income. If sales over the Internet are not taxed, state revenues will drop. Additionally, retailers located in the state pay taxes; thus, their products are by necessity priced higher than the same product sold over the web by a business that does not pay sales tax. Sales on the web and electronic commerce are new and growing and the imposition of numerous sales taxes could stifle growth.

To try to solve the problem, more than thirty-five states have come together to review the state sales tax system. They have created the Streamlined Sales Tax Project (SSTP). The project's main goal is simplification. Although this goal sounds easy, it contains many challenges. Some simplification strategies with which the project is concerned are as follows:

- Uniform exemptions (a buyer, such as a hospital, may be exempt from taxes in one state, but not in another). The purchaser would provide a standard set of information that identifies the purchaser and the reason for the exemption.

- Uniform definitions (sandals may be taxed as shoes in one state, but not in another). The project is creating a uniform definition of key terms (sale, gross receipts, delivery, tangible personal property) and developing uniform definitions for commonly exempt items, such as food and clothing.

- Uniform taxing source laws (ability to determine which jurisdiction has right to tax) and limiting tax rate changes (state and local governments frequently change rates).

- Uniform number of remittances per month, uniform electronic funds transfer formats, and uniform rule on remittances due on a legal holiday.

- Uniform tax return and standardized remittance form (if a multiseller has registered, it should have a uniform tax form to file and a standardize form to make remittance filings to a number of taxing entities).

- Centralized registration (currently multistate sellers must register separately in each state).

The states must be neutral in imposing any tax. The tax on products or services must be the same without regard to the method of sale. A sales tax system cannot provide an advantage to a supplier based solely on whether the sale was made in a store or online. These reforms should reduce the transaction costs to both storefront sellers and online sellers.

The National Governors Association (NGA) has a web page on the project.[3] The Electronic Commerce Association (ECA) can provide additional information.[4]

[3] National Governors Association's (NGA) discussion of the project is at <http://www.nga.org/internet/equality.asp>.
[4] The Electronic Commerce Association's (ECA) web page is at <http://www.ecassociation.org/pub.htm>.

Product Liability

When a product malfunctions, the buyer can seek remedies under the legal theories of negligence, strict liability, and breach of warranty. The remainder of this chapter looks at these theories and discusses the liability that a business may incur when a malfunctioning product harms someone.

Increasingly, the courts are combining tort law and contract law when the lawsuit involves products that malfunction and cause injuries. Consumers buy beer, medicine, microwave ovens, hair dryers, sporting goods, automobile tires, and thousands of other items with the complete faith that the product is designed properly, is manufactured for its intended use, is safe for consumption, and is labeled correctly. The Product Safety Commission, however, reported 21,600 deaths and 30 million consumer-product-related injuries from defective products in a recent one-year period.

How should the losses from injury and death because of defective products be allocated? The distribution of these losses makes up an area of the law called **product liability**. It does not fit squarely into any one body of law.

Common law rules of torts and contracts once set the parameters of product safety, but the common law standards applicable to product liability vary greatly from state to state. The Uniform Commercial Code provides the courts some degree of uniformity when determining potential liability for products through warranty law.

Historical Development

A long-established rule holds that the seller of goods has a duty to exercise the care of a reasonable person in ensuring that the goods are safe for the buyer. In the past, courts enforced this rule by using negligence as a basis for liability.

When applying negligence principles to product liability, however, earlier courts required **privity of contract**. The privity requirement meant that the injured party who sued for negligence also had to prove that a contract existed, that is, that she had bought the defective item from the defendant. This requirement imposed a hardship on the injured. For example, a family member used and was injured by a defective item that another family member had purchased. The injured family member could not recover because he was not in privity of

LEGAL HIGHLIGHT

Bridgestone/Firestone and Ford

In 2000, Bridgestone/Firestone recalled 6.5 million of its ATX, ATX II, and Wilderness AT tires. Before the recall, the National Highway Traffic Safety Administration (NHTSA) received more than 1,400 complaints, including reports of 88 deaths and at least 250 injuries all linked to the ATX, ATX II, and Wilderness AT tires.

Bridgestone/Firestone was a supplier of tires to Ford Motor Company. Ford used these tires on its Ford Explorers, which are sport utility vehicles (SUVs). Most SUVs have a high center of gravity that can cause them to overturn at a higher rate than other motor vehicles. A driver of a Ford Explorer would lose control when the tire tread separated, causing blowouts. Most of the accidents frequently occurred in hot weather and at high speeds.

Initially, Bridgestone/Firestone claimed that these accidents happened because the customer was not inflating the tires properly. To lower the center of gravity, Ford had recommended a lower level of air than what Bridgestone/Firestone had recommended. The chief executive officer of Bridgestone/Firestone, Masatoshi Ono, however, accepted full responsibility for the events.

When the media reported that Bridgestone/Firestone had recalled tires as early as two years previously in other countries, Congress became interested. Apparently Bridgestone/Firestone, when contacted by Ford to report the foreign recalls, replied that it was not required under recall regulations to report foreign recalls.

The publicity led to both the Senate and the House of Representatives holding hearings. Congressional representatives also contacted the Department of Justice to see if any criminal action could be taken because of the failure to notify the government and the failure of both companies to protect their customers and the motoring public. Dozens of product liability actions were filed against Bridgestone/Firestone and Ford in both the United States and in foreign countries.

---

contract with the seller. The consumer suffered a disadvantage as a result of the privity of contract rule because only the purchaser could sue, not the ultimate injured consumer, such as a family member or a gift recipient.

This same requirement, found in contract and warranty law, made contract, warranty, and tort laws insufficient in protecting consumers from unsafe products. Because of the privity requirement, the ultimate consumer frequently was not protected. The courts eventually resorted to the law of torts, specifically negligence, and abandoned the privity requirement. Yet negligence, too, proved inadequate in protecting the consumer because the manufacturer could avoid liability by proving that it had exercised reasonable care in producing the goods.

A new theory was developed to deal with the dilemma of the injured, but uncompensated victim. The common law extended the theories of contracts and torts, finally blending them to develop a cohesive doctrine known as strict liability. Under the doctrine of strict liability, an injured plaintiff can recover even when the manufacturer exercised reasonable care.

Product Liability Based on Negligence

As discussed in Chapter 8, negligence is defined as failure to use that degree of care that a reasonable, prudent person would have used under similar circumstances. The manufacturer of a product must exercise due care to ensure that the product is safe to be used as intended. Due care must be exercised in designing the product, in selecting the materials, in using the appropriate production process, in assembling and testing the product, and in placing adequate labeling to warn consumers about dangers of which an ordinary person might not be aware. The manufacturer's duty of care extends to the inspection and testing of items that are used to make the final product that is sold.

The defendant-manufacturer can defend itself by proving its use of due care in the manufacture of its product. The plaintiff's major burden is to tie the defendant-manufacturer's failure to exercise due care to the injury. Between the time that a product is manufactured and the time that the plaintiff uses the product, numerous events involving different people take place.

A retailer, for example, often must assemble a product before it can be sold to the consumer. If a manufacturer can show that any such event caused or contributed to the injury, it will assert that it has no liability because of this intervening cause. Other defenses exist, but their application varies from state to state.

Defenses discussed in Chapter 8 are assumption of risk, contributory negligence, and comparative negligence. For example, a person plugs an electric cord into an outlet, then plugs the other end into the electrical cord of a lawn mower that has a bare metal pushbar. If the person tries to mow wet grass, he may be electrocuted. The bare metal pushbar may be a negligent design, but mowing a wet lawn may be contributory negligence.

Likewise, any time a plaintiff misuses, modifies, or alters a product, the manufacturer can claim that the plaintiff contributed to the cause of her injuries. The defense is that the plaintiff's comparative negligence offsets the manufacturer's negligence.

Product Liability Based on Strict Liability

In early English history, a person whose conduct resulted in the injury of another was held liable for damages, even if he had not intended to injure anyone and had exercised reasonable care. Around 1800, the courts abandoned this approach in favor of the fault approach (negligence), in which the act became a tort only if the defendant was wrong or blameworthy in some respect. Dissatisfaction with the product liability cases led to a return to the English doctrine of strict liability in the United States.

Requirements of Strict Product Liability.
The difference between negligence and strict liability is that negligence evaluates the conduct of a supplier, processor, or manufacturer, whereas strict liability focuses entirely on the product's condition. The five basic requirements for strict product liability follow:

1. The defendant must sell the product in a defective condition.
2. The defendant must be engaged in the business of manufacturing that product.
3. The product must be unreasonably dangerous to the user or consumer because of its defective condition.
4. The defective condition must be the proximate cause of injury or damage.

5. The goods must not have been substantially changed from the time at which the product was sold to the time at which the injury was sustained.

In any action against a manufacturer or seller, the plaintiff has no obligation to show the reason or manner in which the product became defective. The plaintiff, however, must show that, at the time the injury was sustained, the product's condition was essentially the same as it was when it left the defendant-manufacturer.

In addition, all states have extended the strict liability protection to bystanders who are people near to, but not using, the defective item when they are injured by it. The injured party no longer is required to be a consumer or user of the product.

Most courts allow the application of the strict liability doctrine to cases even when no personal injuries have occurred. When a defective product only causes property damage, the seller also may be liable under the theory of strict liability.

The *Restatement of Torts*, 3rd Edition, takes a slightly different approach on product liability cases. Its position is succinct; if a product is defective, there is liability. A defective product may be the result of a manufacturing error, design defect, or inadequate warnings. A manufacturing defect is one where the product departs from its intended design, even though all possible care was exercised in the preparation and marketing of the product. A design defect is one where the foreseeable risks of harm posed by the product could have been reduced or avoided by the adoption of a reasonable alternative design. Inadequate warnings exist when the foreseeable risks of harm posed by the product could have been reduced or avoided by the provision of reasonable instructions. The *Restatement, 3rd Edition*, expands strict liability to include all product liability based on defects or faulty information.

In the following case, the court reviews the use of an expert witness. This type of witness is one who appears in court to testify about his expertise as applied to the facts in a case. In this case, the witness used his expertise to address management's attitude toward safety by using documentary evidence. This type of evidence applies to any type of writing, whether public or private. Here, the expert witness used documents generated by the defendant to show that management knew that the product was unsafe but decided against correcting the defect because of cost considerations.

Case 11.5

Grimshaw v. Ford Motor Co.

Court of Appeal of California, Fourth District, 1981
119 Cal. App. 3d 757, 174 Cal. Rptr. 348

LANDMARK CASE

BACKGROUND AND FACTS In November 1971, the Grays purchased a new 1972 Pinto hatchback. The Grays had trouble with the car from the beginning. They returned the car for repairs a number of times, for problems including excessive gas and oil consumption, automatic transmission downshifting, lack of power, and stalling. A heavy carburetor float caused the stalling and excessive fuel consumption.

On May 28, 1972, Mrs. Gray and thirteen-year-old Richard Grimshaw set out on a trip in the Pinto, which was then six months old and had 3,000 miles on it. While on the freeway, Mrs. Gray was driving at sixty miles per hour (which was legal in 1972). As she approached a major exit ramp with congested traffic, she moved from the outer fast lane to the middle lane of the freeway. Shortly after this lane change, the Pinto stalled and coasted to a halt in the middle lane. It was later established that the carburetor float had become so saturated with gasoline that it suddenly sank, opening the float chamber and causing the engine to flood and stall. The Pinto erupted into flames when it was rear-ended by a car proceeding in the same direction. Mrs. Gray suffered fatal burns, and Grimshaw suffered severe and permanently disfiguring burns on his face and entire body.

Grimshaw and Mrs. Gray's heirs, the plaintiffs, sued Ford Motor Company, the defendant. Following a six-month jury trial, verdicts were returned in favor of the plaintiffs. The court awarded the Gray family $559,680 in compensatory damages. It awarded Grimshaw $2,516,000 in compensatory damages and $125 million in punitive damages. The trial court reduced the punitive damages to $3.5 million. Ford appealed the judgment on seven major grounds.

Acting Presiding Justice TAMURA

Ford seeks reversal of the judgment as a whole. . . .

In the ensuing analysis (ad nauseam) of Ford's wide ranging assault on the judgment, we have concluded that Ford has failed to demonstrate that any errors or irregularities occurred during the trial which resulted in a miscarriage of justice requiring reversal.

. . . .

[Court's discussion of expert witness who was a former Ford employee]

A party offering an expert witness is enticed to examine him "as to his qualifications and experience so that the full weight to be accorded his testimony will become apparent." Such examination "should not be limited by narrow and stringent rules." It was therefore within the court's discretion to permit plaintiffs to elicit from Mr. Copp testimony as to when he left Ford and why. Evidence as to why he left Ford was part of the background information concerning the witness's professional experience which would assist the fact finder in determining the weight to be given to his testimony. While the evidence may also have tended to enhance the witness's credibility, the purpose of permitting a party producing an expert to question him as to his educational background, training, and experience in his area of expertise is not only to establish "the competency of the witness to the satisfaction of the court, but also for the purpose of making plain the strength of the witness's [sic] grounds of knowledge and the reason for trusting his belief." Therefore, the fact that the evidence may have enhanced the witness's credibility did not render it inadmissible.

. . . .

. . . The fact that Ford fired a high ranking engineering executive for advocating automotive safety was indicative of Ford management's attitude towards safety in automobile production and was thus relevant to the issue of malice [intent to harm someone deliberately]. It had a tendency in reason to prove that Ford's failure to correct the Pinto's fuel system design defects, despite knowledge of their existence, was deliberate and calculated. Ford's argument that firing Mr. Copp in 1976 for speaking out on safety does not reasonably tend to show that Ford disregarded safety in designing the Pinto some five years earlier lacks merit. The evidence was not that Mr. Copp first took his stand on safety in 1976; he testified that he had been outspoken on auto safety during all the many years he worked for Ford.

Ford complains that since Mr. Copp was permitted to testify to the circumstances surrounding this termination, Ford was compelled to cross-examine him to show that the reason for his dismissal was unexplained absences from work and unsatisfactory work performance; that if the court had not permitted Mr. Copp to give his version of the reason for termination, Ford would have had little or no reason to examine him about his retirement and plaintiffs would not have been able to adduce rehabilitation testimony [testimony that restores the witness's credibility (believability)] highly prejudicial to Ford. The record discloses that Mr. Copp testified only briefly concerning the circumstances of his early retirement from Ford but that on cross-examination Ford engaged in extensive questioning to show that the reason for his termination was not his safety views but unsatisfactory work and absenteeism. Plaintiffs thereafter introduced rehabilitating testimony. Mr. Copp was permitted to testify to his campaign for automotive safety during his entire period of employment with Ford, including a conversation he had with Henry Ford II on the subject, his testimony before a United States Senate Committee concerning the Chevrolet Corvair's unsafe design and his role in exposing Ford's conduct in connection with the emission control program. Ford argues that but for the court's erroneous initial ruling and its consequent cross-examination on the reason for Mr. Copp's retirement, the damaging rehabilitation evidence would not have come in. Since we find no error in the court's initial ruling and since Ford has not advanced any independent reason why the rehabilitating evidence should have been excluded, Ford's complaint concerning the prejudicial nature of that evidence must be rejected.

. . . .

[Court's discussion of documentary evidence]

Ford contends that the court erroneously admitted irrelevant documentary evidence highly prejudicial to Ford. We find the contention to be without merit.

(1) Exhibit No. 125:

Exhibit No. 125 was a report presented at a Ford production review meeting in April 1971, recommending action to be taken in anticipation of the promulgation of federal standards on fuel system integrity. The report recommended . . . deferral from 1974 to 1976 of the adoption of "flak suits" or "bladders" [equipment that would protect the fuel tank and prevent fires] in all Ford cars, including the Pinto, in order to realize a savings of $20.9 million. The report stated that the cost of the flak suit or bladder would be $4 to $8 per car. The meeting at which the report was presented was chaired by Vice President Harold MacDonald and attended by Vice President Robert Alexander and occurred sometime before the 1972 Pinto was placed on the market. A reasonable inference may be drawn from the evidence that despite management's knowledge that the Pinto's fuel system could be made safe at a cost of but $4 to $8 per car, it decided to defer corrective measures to save money and enhance profits. The evidence was thus highly relevant and properly received.

. . . .

(2) Exhibits Nos. 95 and 122:

Ford urges that a report (Exhibit No. 95) and a motion picture depicting Ford's crash test No. 1616 (Exhibit No. 122) should have been excluded because they were irrelevant and highly prejudicial to Ford in that they showed that in a 21.5-mile-per-hour crash of a 1971 Pinto prototype into a fixed barrier the fiber neck of the fuel tank separated allowing fluid to spill from the tank, whereas no such filler neck separation occurred in the Gray vehicle. Under the test for ascertaining relevancy of evidence to which we have previously alluded, we find no abuse of discretion in the court's ruling. Not only did the filler neck separation show the vulnerability of the Pinto fuel system in a 21.5-mile-per-hour fixed barrier test, but crash test No. 1616, as Ford conceded, resulted in a puncture of the fuel tank from the exposed bolt heads on the differential housing. Thus, the exhibits showed the defect in the Pinto's gas tank location and design, the hazard created by the protrusions on the differential housing, and, in addition, they served as evidence of Ford's awareness of those defects. Exhibit Nos. 95 and 122 were properly received in evidence.

. . . .

Ford contends that Grimshaw's counsel committed prejudicial misconduct in referring to Ford's executives meeting in the "glass house" and deciding to approve the Pinto's fuel tank design with knowledge that it was unsafe and would result in the loss of many lives. Ford argues that although there was evidence that the corporate headquarters of Ford was referred to as the "glass house" there was no evidence of management meetings held there in connection with the Pinto design. The record contains substantial evidence from which it reasonably may be inferred that Ford's management knew that the Pinto was unsafe but nevertheless decided not to alleviate the problem because of cost considerations, and thus that those decisions were made in Ford's corporate headquarters.

DECISION AND REMEDY The court of appeals, in a forty-one-page opinion, found against Ford on every issue on appeal. The trial court's judgment was affirmed.

CRITICAL THINKING: ETHICAL MANAGEMENT DECISION MAKING Discuss whether the top officials of Ford took into consideration the possible injuries or death to users of their vehicles when deciding whether to install the flak suit or bladder at a cost of $20.9 million. When should profits versus customer protection be considered in manufacturing a product?

Duty to Warn

A business has a duty to warn when it knows or should have known of any hazards associated with the product use when these hazards are not obvious, reasonably apparent, or as well known to the user as to the manufacturer or seller. Courts use this duty to warn in deciding product liability cases based either on strict liability or on negligence theories.

One example of a manufacturer's duty to warn involved a can of hair spray that contained butane. When the hair spray was used close to a flame, the butane gas would explode, which, in turn, caused serious injuries. In one case, the jury awarded $1.5 million because the container lacked any meaningful warnings. Sellers of a product need to place a conspicuous warning on the product to attempt to limit this form of liability.

Defenses to Strict Product Liability. The courts allow the defenses of assumption of the risk and comparative negligence.

When the defendant uses assumption of risk as a defense, it must show (1) that the plaintiff voluntarily proceeded while recognizing the risk, (2) that the plaintiff knew and appreciated the risk created by the defect, and (3) that the plaintiff's decision to undertake the known risk was unreasonable. The doctrine of comparative negligence also applies in these three situations.

The traditional defense of contributory fault, although frequently used in negligence cases, has been rejected by the courts in strict tort liability actions. Because strict liability assumes that the product manufacturer could foresee the danger, in principle, negligence and the defense of contributory negligence are immaterial in an action based on that theory.

Product Liability Based on Misrepresentation

Misrepresentation occurs when a business misrepresents a material fact concerning the character or quality of the good being sold. The seller is liable for physical harm to the consumer if the consumer justifiably relied on the misrepresentation.

The misrepresentation does not depend on the seller's negligence or whether the seller was committing fraud. The consumer can be anyone who uses the good, not just the item's buyer. For example, an automobile manufacturer advertises that its windshield glass is shatterproof. A driver is injured when a stone strikes the windshield and it shatters. The manufacturer is liable to the driver whether or not the driver purchased the automobile.

Product Liability Based on Warranty

A warranty is the seller's assurance to the buyer that goods meet certain standards. If the goods fail to meet those standards, the warranty is breached, and the defendant-seller is liable. The UCC designates several types of warranties that can arise: express warranties [UCC 2-313], implied warranties of merchantability [UCC 2-314], and implied warranties of fitness for a particular purpose [UCC 2-315].

Express Warranties. A seller can create an **express warranty** by making representations concerning the quality, condition, description, or performance potential of the goods. Express warranties arise when a seller suggests the following:

1. The goods conform to the seller's affirmation of fact or promise. (Such affirmations are usually promises made during the bargaining process through such statements as "These drill bits will easily penetrate stainless steel without dulling.")

2. The goods conform to their description. (For example, the description states that "Crate contains one 150-horsepower diesel engine," or the contract calls for delivery of a "camel hair coat.")

3. The goods conform to a sample or model.

To create an express warranty, the seller's promise must become part of the basis of the bargain. If the seller merely makes a statement that relates to the value or worth of the goods or makes a statement of opinion or recommendation about the goods, no express warranty is created.

For example, a seller claims, "This is the best used car to come along in years; it has four new tires and a 350-horsepower engine just rebuilt this year." The seller has stated several facts that create a warranty: The automobile has an engine; it is a 350-horsepower engine; the engine was rebuilt this year; there are four tires on the automobile; and the tires are new.

The seller's opinion that it is "the best used car to come along in years" is known as "trade puffing" and creates no warranty. Trade puffing is the expression of an opinion by a seller that is not made as a representation of fact. A statement relating to the value of the goods, such as "It's worth a fortune" or "Anywhere else you'd pay $10,000 for it," normally, will not create a warranty.

Implied Warranties. Implied warranties are created by law from the facts of the case and are not expressly stated by the parties.

An **implied warranty of merchantability** automatically arises in every sale of goods made by a merchant who deals in goods of that kind. A retailer of ski equipment makes an implied warranty of merchantability every time it sells a pair of skis. A neighbor selling skis at a garage sale does not make this type of implied warranty, because the neighbor is not a merchant.

Goods that are merchantable must be reasonably fit for the ordinary purposes for which such goods are used. They must be comparable to the quality of similar goods on the market. The goods must be adequately packaged and labeled and conform to their labels.

Some examples of nonmerchantable goods include light bulbs that explode when switched on, pajamas that burst into flames on slight contact with a stove burner, high heels that break off during normal use, or shotgun shells that explode prematurely.

The implied warranty of merchantability also imposes liability on the merchant for safe product performance. Whether the merchant knew of, or could have discovered, a defect that makes the product unsafe makes no difference. Merchants, however, do not absolutely insure against all accidents arising in connection with the goods. For example, a bar of soap remains merchantable even though a user can slip and fall by stepping on it.

The **implied warranty of fitness for a particular purpose** arises when any seller (merchant or nonmerchant) knows the particular purpose for which a buyer will use the goods and knows that the buyer is relying on the seller's skill and judgment to select suitable goods. A "particular purpose of the buyer" differs from the "ordinary purpose for which goods are used" (merchantability). Goods can be merchantable but still not fit for a buyer's particular purpose. For example, house paints suitable for outside wooden siding are not suitable for painting over stucco walls.

A contract can include both a warranty of merchantability and a warranty of fitness for a particular purpose, which relates to a specific use or to a special situation for which a buyer intends to use the goods. For example, a merchant-seller recommends a particular pair of shoes, knowing that a customer wants mountain-climbing shoes. The buyer purchases the shoes, relying on the seller's judgment. If the shoes were not only improperly made, but were also unsuitable for mountain climbing, the seller has breached both the warranty of merchantability and the warranty of fitness for a particular purpose. Exhibit 11–3 summarizes the three warranty types covered by the Uniform Commercial Code.

Disclaimers or Defenses against Implied Warranty Liability

The Uniform Commercial Code permits a seller to disclaim implied warranties or to defend under certain conditions against implied warranty liability. Some of these disclaimers and defenses follow:

1. The seller (manufacturer) can specifically disclaim either or both implied warranties. To specifically disclaim any implied warranty of fitness, the disclaimer must be in writing and conspicuous. The UCC gives an example: "There are no warranties which extend beyond the description on the face hereof." To specifically disclaim the implied warranty of merchantability, the disclaimer can be oral or written. It must, however, "mention merchantability" and, if in writing, must be conspicuous [UCC 2–316(2)].

2. The seller can disclaim both implied warranties by selling the goods with expressions such as "with all faults" or sold "as is" [UCC 2–316(3)(a)].

3. A defense may be available to the seller if the buyer actually examines the goods. The defense is that the buyer accepts responsibility for any defect it finds or should have found [UCC 2–316(3)(b)].

4. Implied warranties can be excluded or modified by usage of trade, previous course of performance, or previous dealings between the parties [UCC 2–316(3)(c)].

Exhibit 11–3   Three Warranties under the UCC

Type	How Created
Express warranty [UCC 2-313]	1. An affirmation of fact or promise, or 2. A sale by description, or 3. A sample shown as conforming to a finished product.
Warranty of merchantability [UCC 2-314]	1. The seller is a merchant, and 2. The seller deals in goods of the kind.
Warranty of fitness for a particular purpose [UCC 2-315]	1. The buyer's particular purpose or use must expressly or implicitly be known by the seller, and 2. The buyer must purchase in reliance on the seller's selection.

Because of the availability of these defenses and disclaimers, implied warranties may offer limited advantage to a buyer in seeking recovery under the warranty theory of product liability.

Magnuson–Moss Warranty Act. The **Magnuson–Moss Warranty Act** of 1975 is designed to prevent deception in warranties by making them easier to understand. The act is enforced by the Federal Trade Commission (FTC). To some degree, the Magnuson–Moss Warranty Act modifies the UCC warranty rules regarding consumer sales transactions. The UCC remains the primary statute of warranty rules for commercial (business-to-business) transactions.

No seller must give a written warranty for consumer goods. If a seller chooses to make an express written warranty, however, and the cost of the consumer goods is more than $10, the warranty must be labeled as "full" or "limited." In addition, if the cost of the goods is more than $15 (under FTC regulation), the warrantor must disclose certain information fully and conspicuously in a single document in "readily understood language." These disclosures include the name and address of the warrantor, what specifically is warranted, enforcement procedures for the warranty, any limitation on warranty relief, and the fact that the buyer has legal rights.

Although a **full warranty** may not cover every aspect of a product, the aspects that it does cover ensure some type of buyer satisfaction in case the product is defective. Full warranty requires free repair or replacement of any defective part. If a part cannot be repaired within a reasonable time, the consumer can choose either a refund or a replacement without charge. The full warranty frequently has no time limit.

A **limited warranty** arises when the written warranty fails to meet one of the minimum requirements for a full warranty. If damage to the product or unreasonable consumer use caused the problem with the product, the warrantor is released from the service obligation under either type of warranty.

When a sales contract grants an express warranty, the Magnuson–Moss Warranty Act prevents sellers from disclaiming or modifying the implied warranties of merchantability and fitness for a particular purpose. Sellers can impose a time limit on the duration of an implied warranty. Such time limits, however, must correspond to the duration of the express warranty.

Federal Preemption in Product Liability Cases. Congress has passed legislation requiring that information be disclosed when certain products may be unsafe. The question presented is whether these statutes preempt state laws under the supremacy clause of the U.S. Constitution.

The problem of exemption has confronted the courts, for example, in deciding cases concerning the health hazards in smoking tobacco products. Congress has passed legislation that requires health and safety warnings on all tobacco products and restricts the advertising of these products. The tobacco industry has taken the position that these federal statutory provisions preempt all state laws that might create liability. The following case discusses preemption by the federal government and several different theories of product liability.

Case 11.6

Cipollone v. Liggett Group, Inc.

Supreme Court of the United States, 1992
505 U.S. 504, 112 S. Ct. 2608, 120 L. Ed. 2d 407
http://supct.law.cornell.edu/supct/html/90-1038.ZO.html

LANDMARK CASE

BACKGROUND AND FACTS Rose Cipollone began smoking in 1942 and died of lung cancer in 1984. Before she died, she brought a lawsuit against the manufacturers of tobacco products based on several theories. First, the manufacturers had breached express warranties contained in their advertising, because they failed to warn consumers about smoking hazards. Second, the hazards had been fraudulently misrepresented to consumers. Third, the manufacturers conspired to misrepresent or conceal material facts that deprived the public of medical and scientific information about smoking. Cipollone's son continued the litigation after his mother's death.

In 1965, Congress enacted the Federal Cigarette Labeling and Advertising Act, which mandated warnings on cigarette packages, but barred the requirement of such warnings in cigarette advertising. In 1969, Congress enacted the Public Health Cigarette Smoking Act of 1969, which amended the 1965 act in several ways. First, the 1969 act strengthened the warning label, in part by requiring a statement that cigarette smoking "is dangerous" rather than that it "may be hazardous." Second, it banned cigarette advertising on television and radio. Third, it required warnings in advertisements. Fourth, it modified the preemption provision by prohibiting states from passing legislation with respect to advertising or promotion of cigarettes when the packages conformed to federal law.

The question presented to the Supreme Court was whether the 1965 and the 1969 statutes prevented any lawsuits against cigarette manufacturers because the statutes preempted any state laws on the subject of advertising. Section 5 is the provision that the Court considers in this portion of its discussion.

Justice STEVENS delivered the opinion of the Court.

. . . .

Breach of Express Warranty

[Cipollone's] claim for breach of an express warranty arises under [New Jersey statute] which provides:

> "Any affirmation of fact or promise made by the seller to the buyer which relates to the goods and becomes part of the basis of the bargain creates an express warranty that the goods shall conform to the affirmation or promise."

[Cipollone's] evidence of an express warranty consists largely of statements made in respondent's advertising. . . .

A manufacturer's liability for breach of an express warranty derives from, and is measured by, the terms of that warranty. Accordingly, the "requirements" imposed by an express warranty claim are not "imposed under State Law," but rather imposed by the warrantor. If, for example, a manufacturer expressly promised to pay a smoker's medical bills if she contracted emphysema, the duty to honor that promise could not fairly be said to be "imposed under state law," but rather is best understood as undertaken by the manufacturer itself. While the general duty not to breach warranties arises under state law, the particular "requirement . . . based on smoking and health . . . with respect to the advertising or promotion [of] cigarettes" in an express warranty claim arises from the manufacturer's statements in its advertisements. In short, a common law remedy for contractual commitment voluntarily undertaken should not be regarded as a "requirement . . . imposed under State law" within the meaning of § 5(b). . . . .

Fraudulent Misrepresentation

. . . .

Section 5(b) pre-empts only the imposition of state law obligations "with respect to the advertising or promotion" of cigarettes. [Cipollone's] claims that [defendants] concealed material facts are therefore not pre-empted insofar as those claims rely on a state law duty to disclose such facts through channels of communication other than advertising or promotion. Thus, for example, if state law obliged [defendants] to disclose material facts about smoking and health to an administrative agency, § 5(b) would not pre-empt a state law claim based on a failure to fulfill that obligation.

Moreover, [Cipollone's] fraudulent misrepresentation claims that do arise with respect to advertising and promotions (most notably claims based on allegedly false statements of material fact made in advertisements) are not pre-empted by § 5(b). Such claims are not predicated on a duty "based on smoking and health" but rather on a more general obligation—the duty not to deceive.

. . . .

Conspiracy to Misrepresent or Conceal Material Facts

[Cipollone's] final claim alleges a conspiracy among [defendants] to misrepresent or conceal material facts concerning the health hazards of smoking. The predicate duty underlying this claim is a duty not to conspire to commit fraud. For the reasons stated in our analysis of [Cipollone's] intentional fraud claim, this duty is not pre-empted by § 5(b) for it is not a prohibition "based on smoking and health" as that phrase is properly construed. Accordingly, we conclude that the 1969 Act does not pre-empt [Cipollone's] conspiracy claim.

To summarize our holding: The 1965 act did not pre-empt state law damages actions; the 1969 Act pre-empts [Cipollone's] claims based on a failure to warn and the neutralization of federally mandated warnings to the extent that those claims rely on omissions or inclusions in [defendants'] advertising or promotions; the 1969 Act does not pre-empt [Cipollone's] claims based on express warranty, intentional fraud and misrepresentation, or conspiracy.

DECISION AND REMEDY The Supreme Court held that the 1965 act did not pre-empt state law damages actions, because Cipollone had started smoking prior to the act. The 1969 act also did not preempt her claims based on express warranty, intentional fraud and misrepresentation, or conspiracy.

CRITICAL THINKING: PUBLIC POLICY Discuss whether the federal and state governments should regulate a product that is used by a large segment of the population.

International Consideration

Product Liability in the European Union

A major U.S. trading partner is the European Union (EU). The EU has rules that apply to U.S. businesses when products are bought from and sold to the EU.

In 1985, the Council of the European Communities adopted the Product Liability Directive, which addresses problems caused by malfunctioning of products. All member countries of the EU, except France, Ireland, and Spain, adopted this directive.

Article I summarizes its purpose: "The producer shall be liable for damage caused by a defect in his product." Although the directive terminated no prior theories in product liability cases, it did create a new and uniform system in pursuing cases that involve a malfunctioning product. The directive attempts to eliminate economic barriers that may inhibit the free transfer of goods so that all businesses in the EU handle product liability issues consistently.

The directive's primary objective is to compensate consumers for death or injury. It allows recovery for damages to certain noncommercial property, but excludes damage to the product itself. Prior law or the United Nations Convention on Contracts for the International Sale of Goods covers the issues of damages to the product or to commercial property. Pain and suffering compensation is not covered by the directive.

The Product Liability Directive covers damage claims between 500 and 70 million Euros (European currency). All actions must be brought within three years from the time the plaintiff learns of or reasonably could have learned of the injury, defect, and producer identity and within ten years after the product was placed into circulation.

Although several aspects of the directive are similar to the strict liability doctrine in the United States, the directive grants the injured consumer additional rights. Under strict liability in the United States, the injured person must prove that the product is "unreasonably dangerous." Under the directive, the consumer only needs to show the product to be defective. Article 6 defines this requirement as "not providing the safety which a person is entitled to expect, taking all circumstances into account, including: (a) the presentation of the product; (b) the use to which it could reasonably be expected that the product would be put; and (c) the time when the product was put into circulation." The directive creates a "consumer expectation test." In addition, privity is no longer required to bring an action.

An action can be maintained against a producer, which is interpreted very broadly to include (1) the manufacturer of the finished product or any component, the producer of any raw materials, or any person who presents himself as the producer by trademark; (2) any importer of a product for sale, rental, or leasing; and (3) any product supplier, if the producer is unknown. Agricultural products are excluded unless a member state agrees to cover these products.

The directive does allow the producer defenses. The directive contains no comparative negligence defense, but it does allow recovery to be reduced by the consumer's contributory negligence. It allows the defenses of (1) state-of-the-art, (2) state of scientific and technical knowledge, (3) compliance with member state design or production regulations, and (4) the development risks defense. A defendant may have the additional defenses that he did not put the product into circulation, that the defect did not exist at the time it was placed into commerce, or that no intent to produce the item for commercial purposes existed.

The European Council of Ministers has adopted the Product Safety Directive. . This directive's importance is that it established a high standard of protection for the safety and health of persons by requiring member states to permanently monitor marketed products to ensure that no unacceptable risks occur. Provisions exist for the testing, recalling, and banning of unsafe products. Other directives promote the health and safety of specific consumer products. All of these directives assist consumers in purchasing safe products and in granting them fair compensation if they should be injured.

LEGALLY SPEAKING

When a Retailer Becomes Liable

You are the chief executive officer for a chain of stores that sells retail toys and hobby supplies. Your market segment is older children and adults. Your firm purchases inventory directly from manufacturers throughout the world; it does not manufacture products.

Recently, one of your competitors lost a case and was held liable for $1.5 million involving a miniature radio-controlled automobile kit. The customer had bought a kit, which exploded because of a short circuit. The customer suffered severe eye damage.

Your firm sells the same type of product and you become concerned that your firm might be confronted with a similar case. You sampled your product and found no similar problem. You wonder, however, about legal theories that might surface in this type of case.

You contact your attorney for general information about product liability, and to your surprise, she lists several different legal theories that could be used. As a retailer, you may be liable to the consumer even though you did not manufacture or package the product.

First, a plaintiff may bring action based on a breach of express warranty because the product must conform to the description on the box or to the model that you use for demonstration purposes.

Second, a plaintiff may rely on the theory of breach of the implied warranties of merchantability and of fitness for a particular purpose.

Third, a plaintiff may base a lawsuit on the legal theory of strict liability. This theory applies whenever a product is unreasonably dangerous and causes an injury.

Fourth, an action for negligence might be brought. Normally, however, this would be used against the manufacturer.

Fifth, fraud might exist if you intended to deceive the customer about a material fact. To be liable, you must make the deception with the knowledge of its falsity, and the customer must rely on your deceit, which must, in turn, cause his or her injury.

How can you limit your potential liability? One way is to buy liability insurance. Insurance costs, however, have greatly increased during the last few years. Currently, your firm is a self-insured organization, which means your firm carries no insurance to protect itself from legal action, and has decided to assume this potential liability.

What else can you do to provide your firm with maximum protection in the absence of insurance coverage? You might consider these legal routes.

✔ Use disclaimer agreements. Obtain from each customer a signed written statement disclaiming any liability for your firm. This approach might be applicable to a small service business, such as a go-cart track. Some courts, however, have held these types of agreement to be against public policy. In other states, courts decide these agreements on a case-by-case basis and only uphold them when the agreements are entered into at arm's length and when the bargaining power between the parties is on a somewhat equal basis. The liability disclaimer does not prevent a consumer who was not the original purchaser from filing a lawsuit. As a practical matter, disclaimer agreements offer little protection for most retail concerns.

✔ Use the Uniform Commercial Code. Under the UCC, a retailer can bring the manufacturer into the lawsuit when the lawsuit is brought for breach of warranty. The manufacturer must either defend the lawsuit or be bound by the court decision. The practical effect is that the manufacturer ultimately is held liable.

Note, however, that this provision applies only to warranties, not to strict product liability. Remember, too, that because your firm purchases inventory from international sources, enforcing a judgment against a manufacturer outside the United States on inventory bought in Asia, South America, or other parts of the world may be impossible.

✔ Purchase insurance. In spite of high insurance rates, insurance may be the only reliable method of protecting your firm. The cost of this protection is passed on to the consumer in the form of higher prices.

In other words, no foolproof method exists to protect retail businesses from lawsuits brought by consumers based on malfunctioning products.

Chapter Summary

The Uniform Commercial Code provides rules that govern the sale of goods. Often the buyer and seller neglect to provide details in their contracts. When a court examines the agreement in a lawsuit, it first determines if particular rules of the trade exist or if the parties have a history of prior dealings in order to supply missing terms. If neither exists, the court applies the UCC rules.

For the court to apply any of these rules, the goods must be existing and identified to this particular contract. Placing the customer's name on an existing item is one way to identify goods. Other UCC rules apply to future goods.

Title to goods is important. Unless excluded by specific terms of the contract or by circumstances, the seller always warrants that it has good title and that the goods have no liens against them. The UCC established specific rules as to the point at which the title is transferred from the seller to the buyer. Under certain circumstances, the seller with a voidable title may transfer a valid title to a bona fide purchaser in the ordinary course of business.

The UCC sets out rules that determine whether the seller or the buyer carries the risk of loss when not specified in the contract. In addition, the buyer has the right to inspect goods on delivery. When the goods are sent by the method of collect on delivery (C.O.D.), the buyer loses this right.

Sales contracts can use two types of clauses that affect the passing of title and the shifting of the risk of loss. The first is sale on approval. The buyer is the consumer of the goods. The sale is complete when the buyer approves the goods. Once the goods are approved, the title and the risk of loss shift from the seller to the buyer. The other type is called sale or return. With this contract, the buyer purchases the goods for resale in its business. At the sale's completion, the buyer has the title and risk of loss. If the buyer is unable to sell the items, the buyer can return the items to the seller. Upon return of the items, the seller regains the title and has the risk of loss.

If either side believes that the other may not perform on its promise, the UCC provides for adequate assurances for future performance. The buyer's or the seller's doubt as to whether the other side will perform must be based on good faith and fair dealing. The UCC provides rules for performance and for breach of contract by either party.

Product liability causes specific legal problems for a business. Several legal doctrines apply when a product malfunctions. Negligence can apply, but the difficulty is establishing the point when the breach of the duty of care occurred. Under limited circumstances, strict liability may be used. Warranties provided by the seller, such as an express warranty, implied warranty of merchantability, or implied warranty of fitness for a particular purpose, also may provide the basis for liability.

Using the World Wide Web

In 1994, President William J. Clinton signed a new policy on U.S. access to space. The U.S. National Space Transportation Policy, NSTC-4, guides the government efforts to develop a lower cost, reliable launch capability in order to further the commercialization of space. The Department of Commerce keeps a variety of statistics on business.

The International Chamber of Commerce has developed Incoterms, which are standard commercial terms. These terms are used in international sales to define the responsibilities of buyer and seller in contracts.

Finding the Law on the Web

U.S. National Space Transportation Policy
    http://www.hq.nasa.gov/office/codez/nstc4.html
Uniform Commercial Code
    http://www.law.cornell.edu/ucc/
U.S. Department of Commerce, Economics and
    Statistics Administration (ESA)
    http://www.doc.gov/bureaus/econ.htm
International Chamber of Commerce, Guide to
    Incoterms
    http://www.iccwbo.org/

Chapter Web Sites

Uniform Commercial Code, current provisions and
   suggested modifications
      http://www.law.upenn.edu/bll/ulc/ulc_frame.htm
Bill of lading
      http://www.showtrans.com/bl.htm
National Governor's Association, discussion on equality
      http://www.nga.org/internet/equality.asp
Electronic Commerce Association
      http://www.ecassociation.org/pub.htm
Cipollone v. Liggett Group, Inc.
      http://supct.law.cornell.edu/supct/html
      /90-1038.ZO.html
Free Advice
      http://www.freeadvice.com/
U.S. Census Bureau
      http://www.census.gov/
Department of Commerce, Space
      http://www.ta.doc.gov/space

Web Activities

11–1 You have purchased an automobile that has repeated problems. What can you do after you have made
reasonable attempts to have it repaired?

   Most states have lemon laws covering automobiles.
Most of the statutes are directed toward new vehicles,
although some states have provisions for used ones. Go
to <http://www.freeadvice.com/>, go to "General
Practice" and click on "Lemon Law." How do you
demonstrate that your car is a lemon?

11–2 The U.S. Constitution requires a census every ten
years. The U.S. Census Bureau web page is <http://
www.census.gov/>. How do businesses benefit from the
information gathered by the U.S. Census?

Key Terms

bill of lading	document of title	identified goods	privity of contract
collect on delivery	express warranty	implied warranty of	product liability
(C.O.D.)	free on board,	fitness for a particular	sale on approval
contract for future goods	destination (F.O.B.	purpose	sale or return
cost and freight (C.&F.)	destination)	implied warranty of	tender
cost, insurance, and	free on board, point of	merchantability	usage of trade
freight (C.I.F.)	shipment (F.O.B.)	limited warranty	warehouse receipt
course of dealing	full warranty	Magnuson-Moss	warrant
cover	goods	Warranty Act	warranty of title

Questions and Case Problems

11–1 Strict Liability Kerly stands on a street corner,
waiting for a ride to work. Beyer has just purchased a
new car manufactured by Able Motors. Beyer is driving
down the street when suddenly the steering mechanism
breaks, causing Beyer to run over Kerly. Kerly suffers
permanent injuries. Beyer's total income per year has
never exceeded $15,000. Kerly files suit against Able
under the theory of strict liability in tort. Able pleads no
liability, because (1) due care was used in the manufacture of the car and (2) Able is not the manufacturer of
the steering mechanism (Smith is). What is the outcome
of Kerly's lawsuit?

11–2 Privity Baxter manufactures electric hair dryers.
Garza purchases a Baxter dryer from her local Ace
Drugstore. Green, a friend and guest in Garza's home,
has taken a shower and wants to dry her hair. Garza tells
Green to use the new Baxter hair dryer. As Green plugs
in the dryer, sparks fly out from the motor and continue
to do so as she operates it. Despite this, Green begins to
dry her hair. Suddenly, the entire dryer ignites into
flames, severely burning Green's scalp. Green sues Baxter
on the basis of the torts of negligence and strict liability.
Baxter denies liability, particularly because Green did not
purchase the dryer. Discuss the validity of Green's actions and any defense claimed by Baxter.

11–3 Negligence Beech Aircraft Corp. manufactured airplanes. Executive Beechcraft, Inc., owned, operated, and maintained airplanes, one of which was manufactured by Beech Aircraft. One part was to be installed in only one way. If installed backwards, the part would cause the plane, once airborne, to crash. No markings on the part indicated the correct way to install the part. The part, once installed, looks the same whether installed correctly or backwards, but the part functions differently. A plane did crash after Executive Beechcraft installed the part backward. Everyone on board, including Nesselrode, was killed. Nesselrode's estate brought action against Beech Aircraft. Beech Aircraft argued that it was not at fault because it had not installed the part. Was it correct? Explain. [*Nesselrode v. Executive Beechcraft, Inc.,* 707 S.W.2d 371 (Mo. 1986)]

11–4 Strict Liability Ford Motor Co. manufactured and distributed the Ford Cortina, which had only a cardboard shield separating the fuel tank from the passenger compartment. Nanda suffered severe disabling burns when the gas tank in his car exploded upon being struck in the rear by another car. Nanda filed a strict liability action against Ford Motor Co. Discuss who should prevail and why. [*Nanda v. Ford Motor Co.,* 509 F.2d 213 (7th Cir. 1974)]

11–5 Proximate Cause A two-year-old child lost his leg when he became entangled in a grain auger on his grandfather's farm. The auger had a safety guard that prevented any item larger than four and five-eighths inches from contacting the machine's moving parts. The child's foot was smaller than the openings in the safety guard. Was such an injury reasonably foreseeable? Explain. [*Richelman v. Kewanee Machinery & Conveyor Co.,* 59 Ill. App. 3d 578, 375 N.E.2d 885, 16 Ill. Dec. 778 (1978)]

11–6 Strict Liability Larry Colvin, an ironworker, was setting a steel truss on a concrete column while in a squatting position. He reached above his head to pull himself up. He grabbed an I-beam, known as a purlin, eight or ten feet long, that was not yet welded into place. The purlin failed to support Colvin's weight and he fell. The plans for the building called for the purlins to be over forty feet long, but only seven conformed to that length. The remaining purlins were substantially shorter and were welded together to serve their purpose as spacers between the trusses and the roof. Red Steel Co. supplied the purlins. Discuss whether Red Steel is strictly liable for Colvin's injury due to the short length of the purlin. [*Colvin v. Robert E. McKee, Inc.,* 671 S.W.2d 556 (Tex. Civ. App., Dallas 1984)]

11–7 Acceptance Block and Co., Inc., a mail-order business, entered into a contract with Alden Press, Inc., for Alden to print 125,000 copies of a catalog. Later Block discovered that the catalog covers with Block's address labels were fading. Alden Press attempted to resolve the problem, but Block believed that the entire catalog had to be reprinted. Block had Alden Press mail out 20,000 catalogs in spite of the defect because Block had no other choice in order to stay in business. Block ordered catalogs from another source and refused to pay anything to Alden Press. Alden alleged that the catalogs had been accepted. Explain how you would decide this case. [*Alden Press, Inc., v. Block and Co., Inc.,* 527 N.E.2d 489 (Ill. App. 1 Dist. 1988)]

11–8 Risk of Loss Petrosol International, Inc., a wholesale marketer of petroleum products, sold 10,000 barrels of propane to Commonwealth Petroleum Co. This gas was stored in an underground storage facility called the Lake Underground Storage when the title to the propane transferred from Petrosol to Commonwealth. Commonwealth notified the Lake Underground Storage of the transfer and that it owned the propane. Although Commonwealth would not move the gas immediately, they could move it over the next six months. During that period, a wall in the Lake Underground cavern collapsed and the propane was lost. Under these conditions, who should stand the risk of loss—Petrosol or Commonwealth? Did this type of sale involve an F.O.B. contract? Explain your answer. [*Commonwealth Petroleum Co. v. Petrosol International, Inc.,* 901 F.2d 1314 (6th Cir. 1990)]

11–9 Risk of Loss Morauer contracted with Deak & Co., Inc., to purchase several bags of silver and gold coins. The purchase occurred in Washington, D.C., which requires a sales tax. Morauer and Deak decided that Deak would send the coins to Morauer's residence in Maryland to avoid the sales tax. Deak sent the coins by registered mail. At the time of shipment, the seller's insurance would cover any loss. More than two years later, Morauer took an inventory and discovered that half of the shipment had been lost. By that time, the U.S. Postal Service had destroyed its records, and the seller's insurance had expired. Who should assume this loss? Explain. [*Morauer v. Deak & Co., Inc.,* 26 UCC Rep. (D.C. Super. Ct. 1979)]

11–10 Internet Commercial business is growing in outer space. The U.S. Department of Commerce is involved in space development for commercial purposes. What are the two tracks of the national policy on commercial space? Go to the Department of Commerce web site at <http://www.ta.doc.gov/space>. What are the five areas of commercial space?

Negotiable Instruments and Secured Transactions

We promise according to our hopes, we perform according to our selfishness and our fears.

> *Maximes,* 1665
> Duke Francois de la Rochefoucauld, VI,
> 1613–1680
> French classical author

Outline

Ethical Consideration

Legally Right but Morally Wrong: The Dilemma of the HDC

You are the branch manager of Bell Savings Bank and Trust. The bank stock is owned by local people, some of whom rely on the dividends for a major portion of their income. Bell Savings is more than 100 years old and has a good community reputation.

As the manager, you look for ways to generate income for Bell. On behalf of Bell Savings, you purchase twenty promissory notes from Rosta's Computer Services, Inc., a company that sells computers to small businesses. The manager of Rosta's Computer Services informs you that these promissory notes represent well-paying accounts from its business customers that have purchased computer equipment. You examine the notes and find them in proper order. Bell Savings purchases the notes at the usual discounted price, that is, an amount less than the principal on the note.

Bell Savings receives payments on a regular basis for two months. Within four months, however, your collection manager informs you that many of the notes are in default. When Bell contacted these customers regarding their lack of payments, they told the collection manager that they had not received the promised computer equipment and therefore refused to pay for it. The customers were contacted individually and there does not appear to be any collusion among the disappointed customers. You try to contact Rosta's Computer Services, but find its telephone disconnected. The post office has no forwarding address.

Bell Savings is a holder in due course (HDC) on the notes. To be an HDC means that the holder has the legal right to enforce payment on the notes through a lawsuit. The only defense the note signers, here the customers, have is to identify a physical error in the note itself. In this case, the notes are in proper order and have nothing wrong with them.

As bank manager, you recognize that the customers have received nothing for the notes, and the bank, unknowingly, may be part of a scam. Rosta's Computer Services apparently committed a fraud. Both the bank and the customers, however, are the innocent parties. Under the HDC doctrine, Bell Savings has the right to collect the principal and interest on the customers' notes by filing a lawsuit. The court will order the customers to pay the principal and interest as promised in their notes, even though they received nothing in return. Some of the small businesses may be forced out of business if they must pay.

Is the HDC doctrine ethical in this situation? Should the bank enforce collection on the notes? Use the ethical model presented in Chapter 2 and reprinted on the inside front cover to develop your answer.

Introduction

Contracts are essential for the existence of a market economy. Many contracts are completed simply by the exchange of an item for money. For example, you have a business, Artiste Login Products, Inc. This business will need to purchase raw materials to create sculptures, to purchase a studio and an office building, and to purchase computer equipment, such as servers, modems, and software. When Artiste purchases office supplies, it pays the seller in cash. In situations involving large sums, such as the purchase of real property and buildings, contracts are used and money is borrowed.

In the purchase of real estate, Artiste will obtain a loan. In this situation, Artiste is a debtor. The creditor that lends Artiste the money with which to make the purchase needs to ensure that the loan will be repaid. Artiste will sign a note and a lien. The note reflects the amount of money borrowed, whereas the lien allows the creditor to repossess the real property if Artiste fails to repay the loan. This example reflects two areas of the law that have developed over the centuries: *negotiable instruments* and *secured transactions*.

Negotiable instruments are specialized written documents signed by the debtor acknowledging a debt. These documents contain either an unconditional promise or an order to pay a fixed sum of money either on demand or at a specified future time.

Negotiable instruments have a very long history, originating before the age of Hammurabi, king of

Babylon, at about 1750 B.C. In thirteenth-century Europe, traveling merchants used some form of negotiable instruments because of the problems of transporting and guarding gold and silver. In the early 1700s, the English Parliament adopted the first statutes on negotiable instruments that formed the foundation for the current law on negotiable instruments in the United States.

Today, in the United States, the Uniform Commercial Code (UCC), Article 3, entitled Negotiable Instruments, establishes the law of negotiable instruments. Most states adopted the original UCC into statute between twenty and thirty years ago. Article 3 worked very well to meet business problems.

Over time, with the changes in technology and business practices, however, deficiencies became apparent. Article 3 was revised, and these revisions have been adopted in most states. Discussions of these changes have been integrated into the material in this chapter.

A **secured transaction** is a business arrangement that secures loan repayment. If the debtor fails to make payments on the loan, the creditor can repossess the debtor's item that secures the loan. Secured transactions date back to Roman times (753 B.C. to 476 A.D.) and are nearly as old as negotiable instruments.

A secured transaction involves two steps. In the first step, the creditor extends money or credit to the debtor. The debtor and the creditor generally sign a contract or negotiable instrument in which the debtor agrees to repay the money.

The second step entails the security agreement, in which the debtor promises in writing to give up her specific property (personal or real) to the creditor if the debtor fails to repay the debt. This written promise forms the secured transaction (agreement). If the debtor defaults on the loan (fails to make an agreed payment), the creditor can repossess and sell the debtor's property, using the proceeds to reduce the debt's balance.

Creditors file the secured transaction documents in a public office. The public filing notifies the public of the creditor's lien against the item. The lien remains until the debtor repays the note, at which time the creditor files a release of the lien in the same public office. The law of secured transactions appears in the Uniform Commercial Code, Article 9, entitled Secured Transactions; Sales of Accounts and Chattel Paper.

Often the banking system handles negotiable instruments and secured transactions. For example, **checks** (drawn on a bank by a depositor ordering the bank to pay money to a payee) are an integral part of the banking system. People deposit funds into and withdraw funds from their banking accounts using checks. The law on deposits and collections appears in the UCC, Article 4, entitled Bank Deposits and Collections.

This chapter will review some of the more important provisions of the law concerning negotiable instruments, the banking system, and secured transactions. Each of these very complex topics can be reviewed only briefly in a legal environment textbook.

Functions of Negotiable Instruments

Negotiable instruments have the dual purposes of substituting for currency and serving as a credit device. Currency includes legal coins and paper money bills.

A Substitute for Currency

The financial system lacks sufficient currency to meet all of society's needs. For centuries, negotiable instruments have served as a substitute for currency and they still do so today. Few Americans actually use currency to purchase an automobile, a residence, or a business entity. People use negotiable instruments because they are convenient and safe.

A Credit Device

Negotiable instruments are one method by which credit is extended to debtors. When a creditor lends money to a debtor, the creditor needs evidence that a loan has been made. The debtor usually must sign a document that reflects the principal amount of the loan, the interest rate, repayment date and terms, and other clauses that the creditor may use to protect itself.

Requirements for Negotiable Instruments

An instrument is either *negotiable* or *nonnegotiable*. A nonnegotiable instrument is usually a contract. Both the form and content determine whether an instrument is **negotiable**. For an instrument to be negotiable, it must meet these criteria.

1. Be in writing and signed [UCC 3–103(a)(6), UCC 3–103(a)(9)].

2. Be an unconditional promise or order to pay a fixed amount of money [UCC 3–104(a)].

3. Be payable to **"bearer"** (person who has physical possession of the instrument) or to "order" at the time it is issued [UCC 3–104(a)(1)].

4. Be payable on demand or at a definite time [UCC 3–104(a)(2)].

Each of these requirements needs to be reviewed separately. The UCC revised Article 3 contains the law that applies.

In Writing and Signed

Negotiable instruments must be written on something that is portable and permanent, so that they can be freely transferred. The transfer of an oral promise to a third party would entail the danger of fraud and difficulty in determining liability. A written negotiable instrument sets out the amount of liability, is portable and permanent, is freely transferable, and is used as a substitute for currency.

The person creating a negotiable instrument must sign it for it to become negotiable, but extreme latitude is granted in determining the definition of a signature. A signature includes any symbol used by the party with the intention of authenticating the instrument. Various symbols can be used in lieu of the traditional written signature. Initials, an X, or a thumb print will suffice if a person intends it to be a signature.

Unconditional Promise or Order to Pay a Fixed Amount of Money

A negotiable instrument must include an unconditional order or unconditional promise to pay a fixed amount of money. A mere acknowledgment of the debt, which might logically imply a promise, is insufficient for making the instrument negotiable. For example, an IOU (I owe you) is a written document that literally says "I owe you money," but it is not negotiable because it only acknowledges indebtedness.

The payment terms must be included in the writing on the face of a negotiable instrument. Excluding interest rates that are determined by an outside source, the party who holds the negotiable instrument must be able to determine its terms by looking only at the instrument. The terms cannot be conditioned on an event or agreement [UCC 3–106]. The instrument cannot be controlled by events beyond the instrument itself. If the **holder** (person who has possession of the negotiable instrument) of an instrument must investigate to determine if its conditions occurred, its use as a substitute for currency would be reduced significantly.

Negotiable instruments may refer to collateral that secures debt repayment. This reference does not make the promise unconditional. Many negotiable instruments also reference another writing to clarify the parties' rights concerning acceleration of payments or prepayment of the debt [UCC 3–106].

An instrument may be payable with or without an interest rate. A stated interest rate may be fixed or variable. The variable rate, however, derives from external data, such as a given bank's prime rate or the Federal Reserve discount rate. Reference to this external data is allowed in a negotiable instrument to set the variable interest rate.

If the instrument provides for interest, but the amount of interest payable cannot be determined from the description, interest is payable at the **judgment rate** in effect at the place of the instrument's payment and at the time interest first accrues [UCC 3–112]. Judgment rate is an interest rate set by statute and used when the parties have failed to set the interest rate.

A negotiable instrument must set a requirement to pay a fixed amount of money, which normally is payable in U.S. dollars. If the instrument allows payment in foreign money, it may be paid either in foreign money or in an equivalent amount of dollars calculated by using the current bank-offered *spot rate* at the place of payment for the purchase of dollars on the day on which the instrument is paid [UCC 3–107]. A **spot rate** is the exchange rate in effect between currencies at the time and place at which the exchange is made.

An instrument cannot be stated in terms of value of goods or services because it would be too difficult to ascertain the market value. For example, if the value in a ten-year negotiable instrument were stated in computer chips, determination of a Pentium chip's value today would be difficult to compare with its value in ten years.

Payable to Order or to Bearer

One function of a negotiable instrument is to be used as a substitute for currency; thus, freedom to transfer the instrument is an essential requirement. A negotiable instrument requires that it be "payable to order" or "payable to bearer" or words to that effect. These words acknowledge that another person, unknown at the time that the instrument is made and who is not the original payee, may eventually be the owner of the negotiable instrument.

Except on checks, these words or their equivalents must appear on both the three-party order-to-pay instruments and the two-party promise-to-pay instruments. Except on checks, if these words are absent or deleted, the instrument is nonnegotiable and, therefore, is only assignable. It is governed by contract law, which the chapter addresses later.

Under revised Article 3, a check is still a negotiable instrument, even if the words "payable to order" or "payable to bearer" have been deleted. In the past, people marked out these words when writing a check. Without these words, the check became a nonnegotiable instrument and destroyed the possibility of anyone being a **holder in due course** (that is, a person who not only has possession of the negotiable instrument, but also holds a special status in the eyes of the law concerning it; holders in due course are discussed later in this chapter). The new provisions ensure that a person who accepts a check in good faith and for value will become a holder in due course.

An instrument that states "payable to order" and that names a specific person as recipient is often referred to as **order paper**. When no specific person is designated, so that the instrument essentially is payable to any person holding (bearing) the paper, it is called **bearer paper** [UCC 3-109].

Payable on Demand or at a Definite Time

A negotiable instrument must be payable on demand or at a definite time. Clearly, the person responsible for paying the negotiable instrument must know when she must pay. For an interest-bearing instrument, a person must know the exact interval during which the interest will accrue in order to determine the present value of the instrument.

The instrument's very nature may indicate that it is payable on demand [UCC 3-108]. For example, a check, by definition, is payable on demand. Negotiable time drafts, in contrast, are payable at a definite time that is specified on the instrument's face [UCC 3-108].

The person responsible for paying the negotiable instrument is under no obligation to pay until the specified time has arrived or elapsed.

Types of Negotiable Instruments and Parties to Negotiable Instruments

Revised Article 3 lists the types of negotiable instruments in UCC 3-104. These types are divided into two instrument categories: two-party and three-party instruments. The following sections examine these different negotiable instruments.

Two-Party Instruments

A *promise to pay* is a two-party negotiable instrument between the *maker* and the *payee*. A **maker** is the person who signs and *issues* an instrument and who promises to pay a certain sum of money to a **payee**, that is, the person to whom an instrument is made payable. To **issue** means to deliver the instrument for the first time. The maker's signature must appear on the face of the promissory instrument for the maker to be liable. The maker is a debtor, usually of the payee (who is the creditor).

Generally, two-party instruments are used by people as credit devices. The two-party instruments are *promissory notes* and *certificates of deposit*.

Promissory Notes. A **promissory note** is a written promise to pay (other than a *certificate of deposit*) made between two parties, the maker and the payee.

A promissory note, commonly referred to as a note, can be made payable at a definite time or on demand. A promissory note must be payable to bearer or "payable to the order of" a payee. Banks and other financial institutions that lend money commonly use notes to document a loan of money to borrowers (the debtors).

For example, Foster wants to purchase an automobile, but needs to borrow money to finance the purchase. When Foster borrows from a financial institution, the First National Bank of Anywhere, he signs a promissory note. In the note, Foster promises to repay the money he owes. Exhibit 12–1 illustrates a sample promissory note.

Exhibit 12–1 A Sample Promissory Note

PROMISSORY NOTE

$ __6,000.00__   Anywhere, Iowa __April 30,__ 20.__01__   Due __April 30, 2002__

_____**Sixty days**_____ after date for value received, the undersigned jointly and severally promises to pay to the order of _____**THE FIRST NATIONAL**_____ ____**BANK OF ANYWHERE**____ at its office at Mississippi Boulevard and Missouri Road, Anywhere, Iowa, $_____**Six Thousand** Dollars with interest thereon from date hereof at the rate of – __14__ – percent per annum (computed on the basis of actual days and a year of 360 days.) Interest is payable beginning on __April 30, 2001__. This note is due and owing one year from date.

SIGNATURE __*Ed Foster*__

PAYEE

MAKER

Various types of credit transactions involve the use of notes. Often, the name of the loan type appears in the title of the note. For example, a promissory note to repay money lent to purchase real property is called a **mortgage note**, that is, a note secured by a mortgage.

A mortgage note contains two legal concepts: the note (the negotiable instrument) and the secured transactions (the mortgage). A mortgage is a type of secured transaction whereby the debtor agrees to repay money that the creditor lent on the note in order to purchase real property, such as a house and its surrounding land. If the debtor fails to repay on the note, the creditor initiates a legal procedure to take the property, sell it, and use the proceeds to pay the remainder owed on the note. Although the note is not the mortgage, the note notifies others that payment on it is secured (or backed up) by a mortgage.

Similarly, a **collateral note** (a note secured by some type of collateral) indicates that the creditor lent money to the debtor to purchase personal property. The item purchased, such as an automobile, is used to secure the repayment. The automobile serves as collateral to the note. If the debtor fails to pay, the creditor repossesses the collateral, here, the automobile.

An **installment note** is a note payable by installments, such as when you pay for a computer over a twenty-four-month period. If the computer serves as collateral to secure repayment, the note may be called a **collateral installment note.**

Certificates of Deposit. A **certificate of deposit (CD)** evidences a loan made for a specific period of time by a person to a bank; in return, the bank agrees to repay the principal with interest. Certificates of deposit are either negotiable or nonnegotiable instruments. Most large CDs ($100,000 or more) are negotiable. Their negotiable status allows them to be sold, to be used to pay debts, or to serve as security (collateral) for a loan.

For example, Ross goes to Citizen's Bank, where he has an account, to purchase a certificate of deposit. In buying the CD, Ross lends the bank his money and the bank pays him interest. Ross is considering the purchase of one of three lake lots within the next six months and may need the CD as a down payment. Therefore, Ross wants the CD to be payable to bearer. Citizen's Bank signs the certificate of deposit as a maker and issues it to Ross, but makes the CD payable to bearer. Ross can now make a down payment to the contractor or the architect with the bearer CD. Exhibit 12–2 shows a sample certificate of deposit.

Exhibit 12–2   A Sample Certificate of Deposit

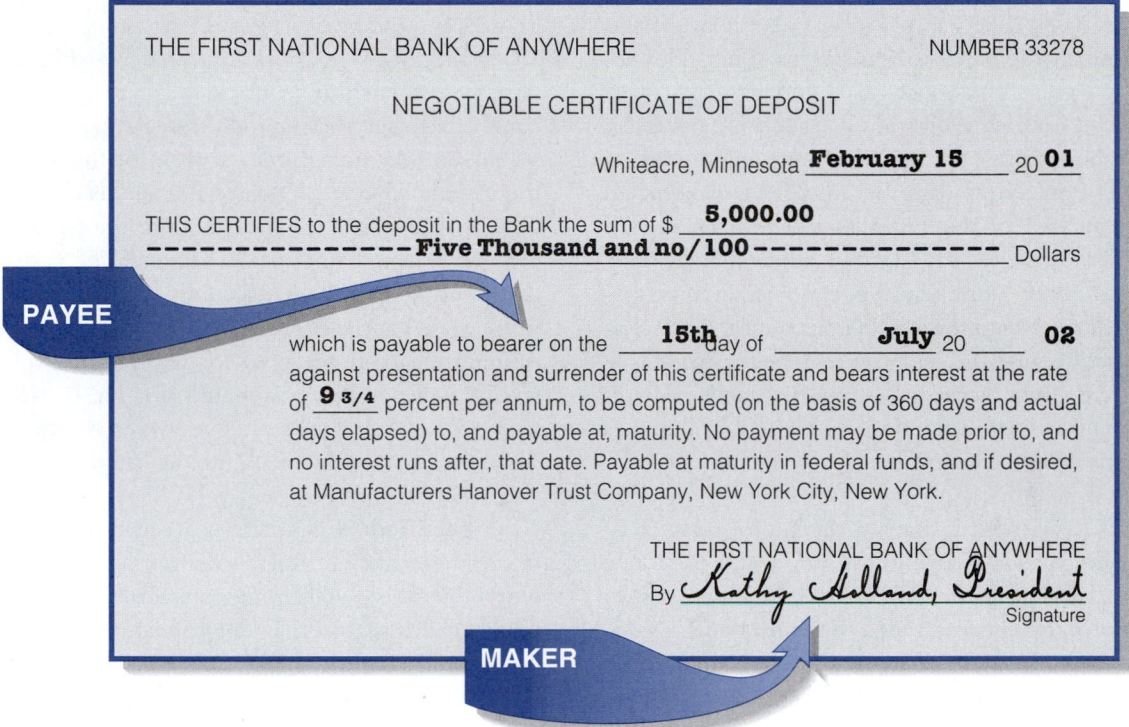

THE FIRST NATIONAL BANK OF ANYWHERE   NUMBER 33278

NEGOTIABLE CERTIFICATE OF DEPOSIT

Whiteacre, Minnesota **February 15**   20 **01**

THIS CERTIFIES to the deposit in the Bank the sum of $ _____ **5,000.00** _____
– – – – – – – – – – – – – – –**Five Thousand and no/100**– – – – – – – – – – – – – – Dollars

PAYEE

which is payable to bearer on the _____ **15th** day of _____ **July** 20 _____ **02**
against presentation and surrender of this certificate and bears interest at the rate
of **9 3/4** percent per annum, to be computed (on the basis of 360 days and actual
days elapsed) to, and payable at, maturity. No payment may be made prior to, and
no interest runs after, that date. Payable at maturity in federal funds, and if desired,
at Manufacturers Hanover Trust Company, New York City, New York.

THE FIRST NATIONAL BANK OF ANYWHERE
By *Kathy Adland, President*
Signature

MAKER

Three-Party Instruments

An *order to pay* is a three-party negotiable instrument. The three parties are the drawer, drawee, and the payee. The **drawer** is the person who creates and signs an instrument that orders the **drawee** to pay a certain sum of money to the payee. The drawer's signature must appear on the order instrument's face. That way, the drawee can authenticate the signature and then follow the exact order. If the drawee disobeys the order, it can be held liable. The drawee is a debtor of the drawer (who is the creditor).

Generally, three-party instruments are used by people in lieu of currency. All three-party instruments fall into the general category of drafts. Checks, cashier's checks, certified checks, and traveler's checks are specialized forms of drafts.

Drafts. A **draft** is an unconditional written order by the drawer to the drawee to pay money to the payee. The drawer can make the instrument payable to him-

self. For example, you can make a check payable to yourself. The drawer "orders" the instrument to be paid by the drawee to the payee. The drawer does not "make a promise to pay," which is the language used in instruments between two parties.

The draft represents a debt owed by the drawee to the drawer that has been made either by agreement, such as an agreement between a depositor and a bank, or through a debtor-creditor relationship. Two types of drafts are *time drafts* and *sight drafts*.

A **time draft** is a draft that is payable at a definite future time. A **sight draft**, also called a **demand draft**, is payable on sight (on demand). When the holder presents a sight draft for payment, such as a share draft used by a credit union, the drawee must pay it. Insurance companies use sight drafts to pay claims.

In the business world, a **trade acceptance** is a form of draft used to pay for goods. For example, each fall, Travis Lake Fabrics sells $50,000 worth of fabric to Quilts Plus, Inc., on terms requiring payment in ninety days on a time draft. One year later, Travis Lake needs cash, so it draws a type of time draft called a trade acceptance that orders Quilts Plus to pay $50,000 to the order of Travis Lake Fabrics ninety days hence. Travis Lake presents the paper to Quilts Plus. Quilts Plus accepts by signing the paper's face and returning it to Travis Lake Fabrics. Quilts Plus's acceptance creates an enforceable promise to pay the instrument when it comes due in ninety days. Because Travis Lake needs cash, it can take the trade acceptance to a bank and sell it in order to raise the cash. Travis Lake can sell the trade acceptance in the commercial money market more easily than it can assign the $50,000 account receivable as a contract because the trade acceptance is a negotiable instrument. Trade acceptances are the standard credit instruments in sales transactions. Exhibit 12–3 illustrates a sample trade acceptance that is a time draft.

Checks. A depositor draws a check on a bank or financial institution, ordering it to pay a sum of money on demand to a payee [UCC 3-104(f)]. The person who writes the check is called the drawer and is a depositor in the bank on which the check is drawn. The person to whom the check is payable is the payee. The

bank on which the check is drawn is the drawee. If Dominic writes a check against his checking account to pay for his boat, he is the drawer, his bank is the drawee, and the boat seller is the payee.

Other forms of checks are recognized by revised Article 3. A **cashier's check** is a draft in which the bank is both the drawer and drawee. A person goes to a bank and deposits money with it for the amount of the cashier's check, plus a fee for this service. A bank officer issues the check, authorizing the payee to receive the check's amount on demand. The payee then draws on the bank's own account, instead of on a private person's account. Because it is drawn on a bank, a cashier's check is accepted for many transactions for which a personal check would not be. Because the bank is both the drawer and the drawee, payment is assured (unless the bank goes into bankruptcy before the check clears).

A **certified check** carries a certification that the drawer has sufficient funds to cover payment. A **traveler's check** is a draft from a financial institution. This type of check requires a countersignature and is payable on demand at or through a bank. A traveler's check can be used around the world in lieu of currency if the trav-

Exhibit 12–3   A Sample Time Draft—Trade Acceptance

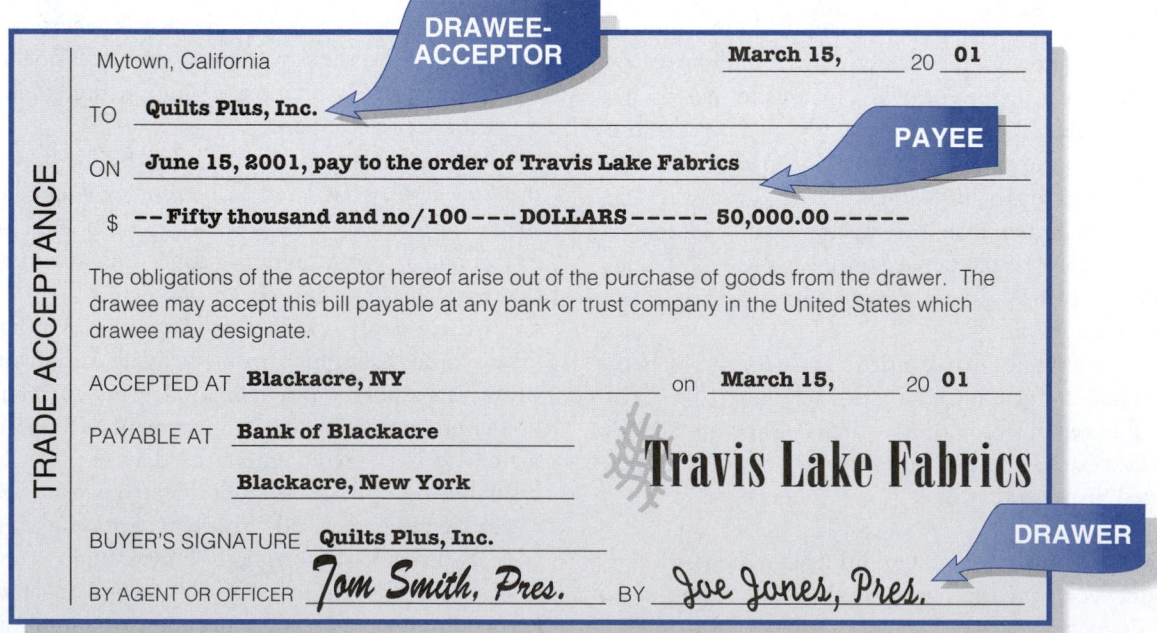

eler's check is issued in the local currency. For example, a traveler may be unable to purchase a toy in a London store if her traveler's checks are issued in dollars. The traveler's checks need to be issued in pounds sterling to be accepted in a London store.

A check is the most commonly used three-party instrument. For example, Marilyn Hicks has a checking account at the First National Bank of Anywhere. She plans to pay for her new automobile by check. She signs the check as the drawer and issues it to A-1 Car Company, the payee. On the check's face, she orders the drawee, First National Bank of Anywhere, to pay the amount written on the check's face to the payee, A-1 Car Company. Exhibit 12–4 shows a sample check.

Signature Liability of Makers, Acceptors, and Drawers

A maker is primarily liable on a note or CD. A drawee-acceptor is primarily liable on a draft [UCC 3-412 and UCC 3-413(a)]. An **acceptor** is a drawee that, by its signature, agrees to pay the drawer's instrument.

The instrument is presented by the payee, holder, or drawer to the drawee for payment, and the drawee accepts the instrument. When a maker or acceptor is primarily liable, the maker or acceptor must absolutely pay the face amount of the instrument, assuming that no real defense exists (see later section titled *Defenses*).

On a draft, a drawer is secondarily liable. To hold the drawer absolutely liable on its signature, the holder must properly present the instrument (for example, for a domestic check, within ninety days of date of issue) to the drawee. The drawee may dishonor (not pay) the instrument because the drawer has insufficient funds in the account, has closed the account, or the drawee may have made an error by dishonoring the draft.

If the drawee rightfully dishonored the instrument (insufficient funds), the drawer is liable to the holder. If the drawee wrongfully dishonored the instrument, the drawee is liable to the drawer. The holder must provide the proper notice of dishonor to the drawer in order for the drawee to be held liable. The holder is not obliged to notify a drawer of a check that the check has been dishonored because the law presumes that the drawer knows the balance in the checking account.

Exhibit 12–4   A Sample Check

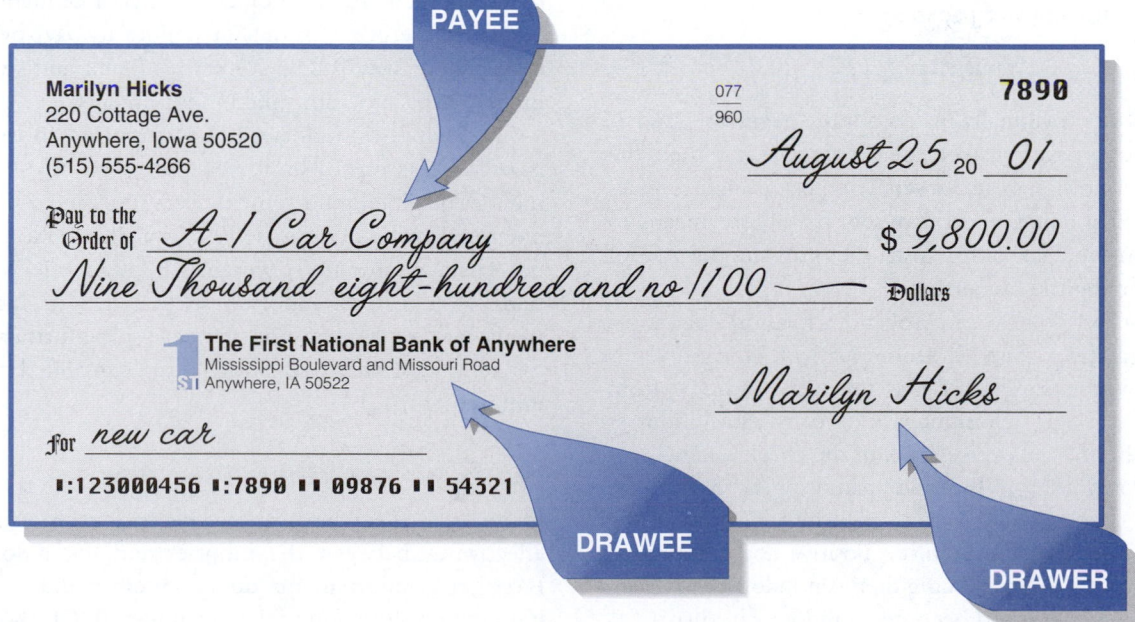

Discharge from liability on an instrument can come from payment, cancellation, or material alteration. If the drawer or maker pays the instrument, it is discharged [UCC 3-602]. The payee or holder may cancel the instrument by intentionally marking it paid (when in fact it has not been paid) or by intentionally destroying it [UCC 3-604]. If the instrument has been materially altered as previously discussed, liability on the instrument may be totally or partially discharged [UCC 3-407].

Indorsements

If negotiable instruments are used as a substitute for currency, a method to transfer ownership of an order instrument from the payee to a third person must exist. This transfer method is simple. The payee indorses (signs) the instrument on the back (or on another document permanently attached to the negotiable instrument) and delivers it to another person. Indorsements are required whenever the instrument being negotiated is classified as order paper.

The indorsement should be identical to the name that appears on the instrument. The payee or *indorsee* whose name is misspelled can indorse with the misspelled name, the correct name, or both. The payor can require both signatures [UCC 3-204(d)].

The following text first deals with the parties to an indorsement. Then it looks at various types of indorsements and signature and transfer liabilities. Finally, it will discuss a bearer paper.

Indorsers and Indorsees

The drawer originally makes out the negotiable instrument to a payee or to bearer. If a payee is named, the payee becomes an **indorser**. The person who receives the instrument is the **indorsee**. To indorse means to sign on the back of the instrument for the purpose of transferring the ownership.

For example, Marie Holland, a medical doctor, receives a check for $125 from a patient. Holland wants to purchase some software for her computer from Positive Logic Computer Company. She indorses (signs her name) on the back of the check and delivers it to Positive Logic. Holland's name appears both as the payee on the check's front and the indorser on the check's back. As the indorsee, Positive Logic is entitled to the $125. Positive Logic then can indorse the check to someone else and become an indorser in turn.

Four categories of indorsements are recognized: *blank*, *special*, *qualified*, and *restrictive*. Exhibit 12–5 contains examples of these various indorsements.

Blank Indorsements

A **blank indorsement** occurs when a payee or a previous indorser signs his name on the back of the negotiable instrument. If a payee merely signs his name without naming a new payee, it becomes a blank indorsement.

When Marie Holland, in the previous example, indorsed the check on the back with her name, she gave a blank indorsement (see Exhibit 12–5). The check becomes bearer paper that anyone can cash. A person should never indorse a check or other negotiable instrument in blank until she is ready to transfer ownership of that instrument.

Special Indorsements

A **special indorsement** is when the payee or previous indorser signs his name on the back of the negotiable instrument, but names a new payee. For example, Joe Jones receives his paycheck for $400. He wants to purchase a $400 printer from Wang. He can indorse "Pay to Wang, Joe Jones" (see Exhibit 12–5). When Joe Jones named a new payee, he made a special indorsement.

Qualified Indorsements

The blank or special indorser guarantees payment of the instrument to the holder or any subsequent indorser in the event of default (failure to pay) by the maker or drawee [UCC 3-415(b)]. Blank and special indorsements are unqualified indorsements.

In contrast, an indorser uses a **qualified indorsement** to disclaim or limit any liability to this instrument. A qualified indorsement commonly includes the notation "without recourse." The qualified indorser is not guaranteeing any payment, although title is still transferred from the indorser to the holder. An instrument with a qualified indorsement can be further negotiated. See Exhibit 12–5 for a sample qualified blank indorsement.

Restrictive Indorsements

Under revised Article 3, **restrictive indorsements** are effective as between the indorser and the indorsee. Restrictive indorsements do not prevent the further transfer or negotiation of the instrument [UCC 3-206].

Types of restrictive indorsements are conditional indorsements ("pay to Rosemary Porter on condition of her delivery of her blue truck at 100 Green Street by August 7, 2001"), prohibiting indorsements ("pay to Regina Hildaga only"), and trust indorsements ("pay to Katherine Burns in trust for David Burns").

A common type of restrictive indorsement is one that makes the indorsee (almost always a bank) a collecting agent of the indorser. For example, "for deposit only" is a very common indorsement (see Exhibit 12–5). This type of indorsement has the effect of locking the instrument (usually a check) into the bank collection process.

Indorsements, Signature and Transfer Warranty Liability

Blank, special, and restrictive indorsements are unqualified indorsements. That is, the indorser guarantees payment of the instrument in addition to transferring title to it. Unless an indorser can claim a valid defense against the holder demanding payment, the indorser is liable to the instrument's holder.

The indorser may be liable either on the basis of its signature (guaranty of payment) or on breach of warranties that the indorser made when transferring the instrument. When an indorser's signature makes the indorser liable, the liability is called *signature liability*.

Signature Liability. For signature or contractual liability, the blank and special indorsers have secondary liability. Liability based on a signature is dependent on three things:

1. The instrument was properly presented to the person with the responsibility of paying it.
2. The instrument was dishonored.
3. The indorser received timely notice of dishonor [UCC 3-415(a)].

Proper presentment requires the holder to present the instrument to the party responsible for its payment (for example, a note is presented to the maker), in a proper manner (for example, a check at the drawee's bank or at the holder's bank goes through a clearinghouse), on or before the instrument's due date [UCC 3-501].

Most improper presentments result because the holder fails to present the instrument within the appropriate time period. Time instruments must be presented on or before the due date. Demand instruments

(other than domestic checks) must be presented within a reasonable period after date of issue. To hold a blank or special indorser liable for its signature on a domestic check, the holder must present the check to the bank for payment within thirty days of the indorser's indorsement [UCC 3-415(e)].

Dishonor usually occurs when the party responsible for payment fails to pay upon presentment. Once the instrument is dishonored, the holder must notify (in any reasonable manner) any secondary party that the holder intends to hold liable.

A bank must provide this notice before midnight of the banking day following receipt. Those other than a bank must provide the notice within thirty days after the instrument is dishonored [UCC 3-503(c)]. Should the holder fail to make proper presentment or to provide the blank or special indorser proper notice of dishonor, the indorser is completely discharged from signature liability [UCC 3-415(c)].

Transfer Warranty Liability. When indorsers receive consideration (something of value as opposed to receiving a gift) from the transferee, the indorsers make five transfer warranties [UCC 3-416(a)]. These warranties cover all of the instrument's subsequent holders. The five warranties follow:

1. The warrantor is entitled to enforce the instrument.
2. All signatures on the instrument are authentic and authorized.
3. The instrument has not been altered.
4. The instrument is not subject to a defense or claim that can be asserted against the warrantor.
5. The warrantor has no knowledge of any insolvency proceeding commenced with respect to the maker or acceptor or, in the case of an unaccepted draft, the drawer.

In the case of checks, the indorser cannot disclaim these warranties. The claimant, within thirty days after it has reason to know of the breach and the identity of the warrantor, must notify the warrantor of the breach. If the warrantor receives late notification, it is discharged to the extent of any loss caused by the notification delay.

Should any of these warranties be breached at the time of the indorser's transfer, a subsequent holder can hold the indorser liable. This action is independent of

Exhibit 12–5 **Indorsements**

A. Checks

Checks deposited must be indorsed in a specific area on the back side of each check. The entire indorsement (whether a signature or a stamp), along with any other indorsements, identification information, driver's license number, etc., must fall within 1½ inches of a check's trailing edge. As you look at the front of a check, the trailing edge is the left edge. When you flip the check over, all indorsement information must be within 1½ inches of the edge.

B. Other negotiable instruments

On the other types of negotiable instruments, an indorsement may legally be placed anywhere.

A Sample Blank Indorsement

A Sample Qualified Blank Indorsement

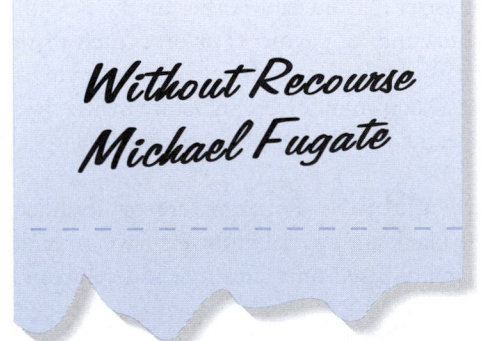

Marie Holland

Without Recourse
Michael Fugate

A Sample Special Indorsement

A Sample Restrictive Indorsement

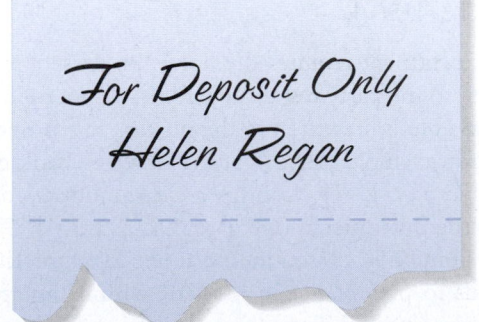

Pay to Wang
Joe Jones

For Deposit Only
Helen Regan

presentment and notice of dishonor (signature liability). Even if the holder improperly presents the instrument, a holder could sue for breach of warranty.

A bearer also can transfer an instrument and thus make the same transfer warranties as an indorser. The extent of liability, however, is that these warranties only flow to the bearer's immediate transferee, not to all subsequent holders.

A qualified indorser, who receives consideration, also makes transfer warranties. These warranties are the same as those made by a blank, special, or restrictive indorser, and these warranties also flow to all subsequent holders.

Holders and Holders in Due Course

Negotiable instruments can be held by one of two transferees: the holder or the holder in due course (HDC). Legally, the two have very different rights.

Holder

A holder is a person who is in possession of an instrument that is payable to bearer or payable to an identified person [UCC 1-201(20)]. A holder is one of three people.

First, the holder may be the original payee. Second, if the payee has transferred the negotiable instrument to another, that person (also called the transferee) is a holder. Third, a person in possession of a bearer instrument is likewise a holder. (A bearer instrument is made out to cash or bearer, or has been converted from order paper to bearer paper by a blank indorsement. Bearer instruments are discussed in more detail later in the chapter.)

All three of these types of holders have the status of an assignee of a contract right. As an assignee, the holder obtains only those rights that its predecessor-transferor had in the instrument. If a conflicting, superior claim or defense to the instrument exists, a holder cannot collect payment.

The holder is usually, but not necessarily, the negotiable instrument's owner. For example, Valdez takes a check made payable to him. He indorses the check on the back in blank, anticipating that he will deposit the check in his bank in the afternoon. He misplaces the check and someone steals it. The thief is a holder under the law. Even though, obviously, she is not the owner, the thief can legally transfer the check (a bearer instrument because of Valdez's blank indorsement) to another person, and that person can collect the money. This third person now becomes the holder.

Holder in Due Course

A holder in due course is a special-status transferee of a negotiable instrument. An HDC has a very special and protected standing within the law. If a holder has acquired the instrument in a manner that meets the UCC requirements, the holder transforms its position from that of ordinary holder to that of holder in due course.

An HDC normally is immune to any defenses (excuses) asserted by the drawer or maker against paying the instrument. As discussed later in this chapter, the Federal Trade Commission has modified the HDC doctrine as it applies to consumer transactions.

The law protects an HDC because negotiable instruments are currency substitutes. People who accept negotiable instruments as currency substitutes must have some protection. The law, therefore, does not allow the drawer or maker many reasons to avoid paying the instrument that he signed.

Under revised Article 3, in order to become an HDC, a holder of a negotiable instrument must meet six requirements. The holder must take the instrument

1. for value;

2. in good faith;

3. without notice that it is overdue or defective;

4. without notice that the instrument contains an unauthorized signature or has been altered;

5. without notice of any claim to the instrument; and

6. without notice that any party has a real defense, such as illegality, lack of legal capacity, duress, fraud in the inducement, discharge in bankruptcy, or material alteration [UCC 3-302(a) (2)].

The chapter discusses real defenses later. The underlying requirement for achieving the status of a holder in due course is, of course, that the person must first be a holder of the instrument.

Value. An HDC must give value for the instrument [UCC 3-303]. A person who receives an instrument as a gift or who inherits the instrument has not met the requirement of value. In these situations, the person remains an ordinary holder and does not possess the rights of an HDC.

The concept of value in the law of negotiable instruments differs from the concept of consideration in the law of contracts. For example, under contract law, a promise to pay a debt that the person already owes is not consideration. A holder who takes an instrument in payment of a prior debt, however, has given value.

Likewise, an executory promise (a promise to perform or pay in the future) is valid consideration to support a contract but does not constitute value to qualify a holder as an HDC. A holder takes the instrument for value only to the extent that the consideration actually has been performed or paid. For example, Lori makes out a check for $500 payable to Rory on Sunday. Rory needs funds but cannot cash Lori's check until Monday. Rory negotiates the check to Gary, who pays Rory $200 in cash and promises to pay Rory the balance on Friday, when he gets his paycheck. Gary has provided value in the amount of $200, so he can only qualify as an HDC for that amount.

Good Faith. An HDC must accept the instrument in good faith. The purchaser-holder must act honestly in the process of acquiring the instrument. Good faith is defined as honesty in fact in the conduct or the transaction concerned [UCC 1-201(19)].

The good-faith requirement applies only to the holder. Whether the transferor acts in good faith is immaterial. Thus, a person who in good faith takes a negotiable instrument from a thief can be an HDC.

Without Notice. A person who acquires an instrument knowing, or having reason to know, that it is defective in any one of the following ways forfeits the HDC protection. This protection is lost when an instrument

1. is overdue,
2. has been dishonored,
3. has an unauthorized signature,
4. has been altered, or
5. has any real or personal defenses that might be raised.

A check is presumed to be overdue if the holder fails to present it for payment within ninety days of its issue [UCC 3-304(a)(2)]. A person should examine the instrument before taking it to see if anything is wrong with it (any erasures or words crossed out) and to see if the time for payment has passed.

If nothing is wrong with the face of the instrument, and the person acquiring the instrument has no knowledge of any defect concerning the instrument, the person becomes an HDC. If the acquiring person is an HDC and she demands payment on the instrument, the instrument must be paid. The following case discusses this issue.

Case 12.1

Commerce Bank v. Rickett

Superior Court of New Jersey, Appellate Division, 2000
329 N.J. Super. 379, 748 A.2d 111

BACKGROUND AND FACTS On January 5, 1998, defendant Bruce Rickett, individually and trading as Rick's Auto Sales, presented a check to Commerce Bank, N.A. (the Bank), issued to him on January 3, 1998, by DeSimone Auto, Inc. (DeSimone), in the amount of $12,000, for deposit into Rickett's checking account with the Bank. The Bank credited Rickett's account and shortly thereafter allowed him to draw against same.

The check, dated January 3, 1997, but actually issued on January 3, 1998, was drawn on DeSimone's account at the Bank of Gloucester County for payment of a 1997 Buick LeSabre motor vehicle. The understanding between Rickett and DeSimone was that the check would not be presented for payment if the motor vehicle was damaged. Shortly after issuance of the check, DeSimone inspected the vehicle and found frame damage. DeSimone telephoned Rickett, advising him to pick up the vehicle and return the check. DeSimone returned the vehicle to Rickett, who accepted it. Thereafter, DeSimone issued a "stop payment" on the check.

Contrary to their agreement, Rickett had already presented the check for payment on January 5, 1998, and drawn against it. The check was returned by the Bank of Gloucester County to the Bank as unpaid on January 13, 1998. The amount charged back to Rickett's account by the Bank was $11,016.48.

The Bank filed a complaint against both Rickett and DeSimone, seeking the amount charged back to Rickett's account. Rickett could not be located by the Bank. As to DeSimone, the Bank asserted that it was a "holder in due course" and, therefore, entitled to payment from DeSimone.

DeSimone contended that the erroneous date of "January 3, 1997" placed the Bank on notice that the check might have been overdue, and, accordingly, the Bank could not be a holder in due course because "holder-in-due-course" status attaches at the time the transaction is made. The trial court granted a motion for summary judgment filed by the Bank and DeSimone appealed.

NEWMAN, J. A. D.

. . . .

In granting summary judgment in favor of the Bank in the amount of $11,016.48, Judge Supnick found that the Bank was a holder in due course, largely relying on the fact that DeSimone had admitted that the check was actually issued on January 3, 1998, not January 3, 1997, and on the Bank's proof that "checks presented for negotiation are often misdated in the first few days of a new year with the prior year still being written on the check." . . .

On appeal, DeSimone contends that the application of N.J.S.A. 12A:3-302a(2) negates the Bank's status as a holder in due course. That section reads as follows:

a. Subject to subsection c. of this section and subsection d. of 12A:3-106, "holder in due course" means the holder of an instrument if:

the holder took the instrument for value, in good faith, without notice that the instrument is overdue or has been dishonored or that there is an uncured default with respect to payment of another instrument issued as part of the same series, without notice that the instrument contains an un-authorized signature or has been altered, without notice of any claim to the instrument described in 12A:3-306, and without notice that any party has a defense or claim in recoupment described in subsection a. of 12A:3-305.

DeSimone asserts that the "January 3, 1997" date on the face of the check made it "overdue." N.J.S.A. 12A:3-304 provides, in relevant part:

a. An instrument payable on demand becomes overdue at the earliest of the following times:

. . . .

(2) if the instrument is a check, 90 days after its date [.]

DeSimone also cites to N.J.S.A. 12A:3-113, which provides, in pertinent part:

a. An instrument may be antedated or postdated. The date stated determines the time of payment if the instrument is payable at a fixed period after date.

DeSimone reasons that, because the check was dated January 3, 1997, and deposited in early January 1998, the Bank had actual notice that the check was overdue, as defined by the ninety-day period for checks set forth in N.J.S.A. 12A:3-304a(2), and was therefore not a holder in due course under N.J.S.A. 12A-3:302a(2). DeSimone also construes N.J.S.A. 12A:3-113a to mean that the fact that the check was dated January 3, 1997, establishes the check's "date" as

January 3, 1997, automatically rendering the check overdue when it was deposited on January 5, 1998.

DeSimone's reliance on N.J.S.A. 12A:3-113a to support its argument that January 3, 1997 must be viewed as the check's "date" for purposes of determining whether the instrument was overdue . . . is misplaced. N.J.S.A. 12A:3-113a refers to an instrument payable at a fixed period of time. A check does not fit within that definition, but rather is a demand instrument. Accordingly, N.J.S.A. 12A:3-113a is inapplicable.

The issue presented is whether, pursuant to N.J.S.A. 12A:3-304a(2), a check becomes overdue ninety days after the date on the face of the check or ninety days after its date of issue. We construe N.J.S.A. 12A:3-304a(2) to mean that a check becomes overdue ninety days after the date it is actually issued. To interpret N.J.S.A. 12A:3-304a(2) otherwise is impractical and inconsistent with other provisions in the Code.

Pazol v. Citizens Nat'l Bank of Sandy Springs is factually similar. There, a check that bore the date "January 4, 1963" was deposited on or about January 9, 1964. The drawer entered a stop-payment order, but the payee–depositor was permitted to withdraw its full value before the depositary bank received notice that the check had been dishonored. The payor bank refused to transfer funds, and the depository bank sued the drawer for the value of the check. The drawer sought a general demurrer on the ground that the depository bank had actual notice that the check was overdue based on the date on the face of the instrument and that it could not claim to be a holder in due course. The court rejected this argument, ruling that, although the date on an instrument is presumed to be correct, "this presumption is not conclusive, and may be overcome by parol evidence that it was in fact made on another date[.]"

The reasoning of the *Pazol* court is persuasive. Here, the Bank has established that the date on the face of the check was incorrect by DeSimone's admission that the check was actually issued on January 3, 1998. Accordingly, the Bank was a holder in due course, as DeSimone only challenges that status on the ground that the Bank had notice that the check was overdue.

. . . .

DECISION AND REMEDY DeSimone was found to be improvident in issuing an otherwise facially valid check for the full price of an uninspected vehicle. The Bank did not bear the loss because DeSimone was careless in filling out the instrument. It was admitted that the check was actually issued on January 3, 1998, thus making the Bank a legitimate holder in due course.

CRITICAL THINKING: LEGAL THEORY Discuss why a person should be held liable when he or she has been defrauded.

The case would have culminated differently if a contract had been involved. The following section specifically addresses the differences between a contract assignment and a negotiable instrument's negotiation.

Assignment or Negotiation

Once issued, a negotiable instrument can be transferred by assignment or by negotiation. The critical distinction is that with an assignment, the contract rights are assigned to a third party who has the status of an assignee and who has no better rights than the transferor-assignor.

A negotiable instrument is negotiated to a third person who, if he has the status of an HDC, can have better rights than the transferor. Again, because negotiable instruments substitute for currency, a person who accepts an instrument must be reasonably certain that she can collect on it free from any defenses that may be asserted against the holder of a normal contract assignment.

Assignment

Assignment is a transfer of rights under a contract. Recall from Chapter 10 that, under general contract principles, a transfer by assignment from an assignor (the original party to the contract) to an assignee (the person buying the contract right) gives the assignee only those rights that the assignor possessed.

Any defenses to the contract that can be raised against the assignor also can be raised against the assignee. A nonnegotiable instrument cannot be negotiated but can be assigned. Furthermore, when a transfer fails to qualify as a negotiation, it becomes an assignment.

Negotiation

Negotiation is the transfer of a negotiable instrument in a manner such that the transferee becomes a holder [UCC 3-201]. The holder minimally receives the previous possessor's rights [UCC 3-203(b)]. Unlike an assignment, a transfer by negotiation allows for a holder to become a holder in due course and to receive more rights in the instrument than the prior possessor [UCC 3-306].

Negotiating Order Paper.
Order paper initially names a specific payee, who then can indorse the instrument. Two steps required to negotiate (transfer) order paper are indorsement and delivery.

For example, the Transco Company issues a payroll check "to the order of Wang." Wang takes the check to the supermarket, signs her name on the back (a blank indorsement), gives it to the cashier (a delivery), and receives currency. Wang has negotiated the check (an order instrument) by a blank indorsement and delivery to the supermarket. The supermarket is now an HDC because it accepted the check for value, in good faith, and without noticing any problems with the check.

Negotiating Bearer Paper.
Bearer paper is negotiated by delivery alone. No indorsement is necessary [UCC 3-201(b)].

In an earlier example, Marie Holland indorsed a check in blank. Let's say that she delivers the check to Ross Matthews. Ross goes to the drawee bank to cash the check. In theory, since the check is now a bearer instrument, he should be able to present the check and the bank should pay him the amount of the check. The bank, however, may require Ross to indorse the check. Technically, however, this indorsement on the back is not required for negotiation. The bank may require it for purposes of identification and of verification that Ross received the money [UCC 3-501(b)(2)]. The use of bearer paper involves more risk through loss or theft than does the use of order paper.

Assume that Bob Brown writes a check "payable to cash" and hands it (a delivery) to Mary Maack. Brown negotiated the check (bearer paper) to Maack by delivery alone. Maack places the check in her wallet, which subsequently is stolen. The thief possesses the check. At this point, negotiation has not occurred because delivery must be voluntary on the part of the transferor. If the thief "delivers" the check to an innocent party who pays the thief the amount on the check, negotiation will have occurred. All rights to the check will be passed absolutely to that party, and Maack will lose all rights to recover the proceeds of the check from the innocent party [UCC 3-305(c)]. Of course, she can recover her money from the thief if the thief can be found.

Converting Order to Bearer Paper and Vice Versa.
The maker or drawer controls whether the instrument has a named payee (order paper) or whether a bearer (bearer paper) is entitled to payment. If it is order paper, the payee's indorsement determines whether the instrument continues as order paper or converts to bearer paper. A blank indorsement converts the order paper to bearer paper [UCC 3-205(b)], while a special indorsement continues the paper as order paper.

Bearer paper may be converted to order paper if the back of the paper has a special indorsement. For example, a check originally payable to "cash" is bearer paper and is negotiated by delivery. If the check subsequently is indorsed "pay to Jones," it must be negotiated as order paper (by indorsement and delivery), because it names a specific payee [UCC 3-205(a)].

Defenses

Defenses by a party to avoid payment fall into two general categories: *real defenses* and *personal defenses*. **Real defenses** prevent payment to all holders of a negotiable instrument, including an HDC. **Personal defenses** prevent payment to an ordinary holder of a negotiable instrument [UCC 3-305].

Real Defenses

Real (or universal) defenses are valid against all holders, including HDCs or holders who take an instrument through an HDC. (A holder who does not qualify as an HDC but who derives title through an HDC acquires the rights and privileges of an HDC [UCC 3-203(b)]. This is sometimes referred to as the *shelter principle*.) The following are several real defenses.

Forgery. Forgery of a maker's or a drawer's signature cannot bind the person whose name is used unless that person ratifies (formally confirms) the signature [UCC 3-401 and UCC 3-403(a)].

Fraud in Execution. A person may be deceived into signing a negotiable instrument, such as when a person believes that she is signing something other than a negotiable instrument (for example, a receipt). This deception is called *fraud in execution*.

For instance, a consumer unfamiliar with the English language signs a paper presented by a salesperson as a request for an estimate. In fact, it is a promissory note. Even if the note were negotiated to an HDC, the consumer may have a valid defense based on the real defense of fraud in execution. This defense cannot be used if a reasonable person would not or should not have been deceived as to the character of the instrument being signed.

Alteration. An alteration is material if it changes the contract terms in any way. Examples of material alterations include changing the number or relations of the parties, or adding to or removing from the writing after the instrument is signed [UCC 3-407(a)].

A material alteration is a complete defense against an ordinary holder, but is at best only a partial defense against an HDC. A holder cannot recover anything on an instrument that has been materially altered [UCC 3-407(b)]. If the original terms are altered, such as the amount payable, prior to the HDC purchasing the instrument, the HDC can collect the original amount from the maker or drawer. If the instrument is incomplete and later completed in an unauthorized manner prior to the HDC purchasing the instrument, the alteration cannot serve as a defense against an HDC. Furthermore, the HDC can enforce the instrument up to the amount written [UCC 3-407(c)].

Bankruptcy. When a debt that is represented by a negotiable instrument is discharged (forgiven) in bankruptcy, that discharge is an absolute defense against paying the instrument to either a holder or an HDC. The purpose of bankruptcy is to settle and forgive all of the solvent's debts [UCC 3-305(a)(1)].

Operation of Law. When illegal conduct renders an instrument void, payment to either a holder or an HDC is dismissed. If a person were declared mentally incompetent by state proceedings, any instrument issued by that person thereafter would be null and void. The instrument is void from the beginning (time of issue) and unenforceable by any holder or an HDC [UCC 3-305(a)(1)].

Extreme duress is another defense. When a person signs and issues a negotiable instrument under extreme duress, such as an immediate threat of force or violence (for example, at gunpoint), the instrument is void and unenforceable by any holder or HDC [UCC 3-305(a)(1)].

Personal Defenses

All other defenses that are valid in a contract setting, such as breach of contract, breach of warranty, misrepresentation, mistake, undue influence, and economic duress, are considered personal defenses. These defenses are invalid against an HDC but valid against an ordinary holder.

For example, Penny wants to install a digital widescreen television for the patrons at her bar. Penny agrees to purchase the television for $2,800 from an acquaintance, Slick. Slick, knowing his statements to be false, tells Penny that the television is only six months old and is in good working order. In addition, he tells Penny that he owns the television free and clear of all claims. Penny pays Slick $500 in cash and issues a negotiable promissory note for the balance. As it turns out, Slick still owes the original seller $500 on the television purchase, and the television is subject to a security interest (lien) filed by the original seller in the appropriate state office. In addition, the television is three years old. Penny can refuse to pay the note if it is held by an ordinary holder, such as Slick in this case. If Slick has negotiated the note to an HDC, however, Penny must pay the HDC. Of course, Penny can then sue Slick. (Penny cannot use the Federal Trade Commission rule described in the next section because she owns a business and therefore does not qualify as a consumer.)

Federal Limitations on Holder-in-Due-Course Rights

A Federal Trade Commission (FTC) rule has severely limited the preferential position enjoyed by an HDC in a *consumer credit transaction*. A **consumer credit transaction** occurs when a consumer enters into a contract to purchase an item and at the same time receives credit from the seller or financial institution to purchase the item. The consumer signs a note promising to pay for the item. Payment by check is exempt as a credit transaction for purposes of this FTC rule.

Prior to the FTC rule, the law giving preferential treatment to an HDC worked a severe hardship on consumers. For example, Ron, a consumer, buys a new digital wide-screen television for his home from Shady TV Dealers for $2,500. Ron signs a promissory note to pay for the television. The payee is Shady TV Dealers. Shady sells the note (negotiates it) at a discounted amount to Better Bank. The bank, having paid value, having taken the note in good faith, and having taken it without notice of any problems, qualifies as an HDC. Ron discovers that the television is defective and never will work properly. This defect is a personal defense and, naturally, he wants to withhold payments for the TV. The note, however, is held now by the bank, an HDC. Prior to the FTC rule, Ron would have to pay the bank on the note. In the past, the defenses Ron had on the contract for the purchase of the defective television were valid only against Shady TV Dealers, not the bank.

Today, under the FTC rule, when a note is part of a consumer credit contract, the note must include a warning to any holder who may qualify as an HDC that the note holder is subject to all contract defenses that the original purchaser may have against the original seller. In other words, in a consumer credit contract, personal defenses are valid even when the holder would otherwise qualify as an HDC. With the warning included, Ron can use the FTC rule as a defense against both Shady TV Dealers and Better Bank.

Accord and Satisfaction Doctrine

As discussed in Chapter 10, a contract can be discharged through the doctrine of accord and satisfaction. Most commonly this doctrine is applied to checks.

Assume that a definite dispute exists between two parties over exactly how much is owed. The debtor can settle the dispute by sending the creditor a check with a notation of "in full settlement" or "payment in full." These words indicate that a debtor is attempting to settle a disputed debt. When the creditor cashes the check, an accord and satisfaction results. The creditor cannot bring a lawsuit to recover the remaining debt.

This law worked well when checks were handled manually and the creditor could control the cashing of the check. In the modern world, large businesses handle thousands of checks daily. The creditor's employees rarely see checks because electronic equipment processes them. A check is cashed before the creditor has any actual knowledge of the terms written on it. Only after the check has cleared the bank does the creditor find out about the notice because the debtor refuses to pay any more and references the terms on the check.

Revised Article 3 provides businesses with two protections. First, the creditor can send the debtor a conspicuous statement requiring her to communicate with a designated person, office, or place in case of a dispute. Delivery of this notice frees the creditor from being bound by any communication sent by the debtor unless it is sent to the specified location. Any check sent with the "paid in full" notation, therefore, is effective only if it is sent to the specified address and the check is then cashed.

Second, even if the business fails to send this notice, it can escape the settlement if it refunds the amount of the check within ninety days of cashing the check. These changes assist businesses confronted with an honest dispute [UCC 3-311].

Checks and the Banking System

Checks are the most common kind of negotiable instrument regulated by the Uniform Commercial Code. Checks, credit cards, debit cards, and charge accounts are rapidly replacing currency as a means of paying for goods and services. Approximately 62 billion

LEGAL HIGHLIGHT

Bounce a Check, No Bank Account

For decades, it was easy to open a bank account. When you applied for a new checking account, the new bank did not review your prior check-writing history or note if you wrote checks that bounced.

This attitude has now changed. When you apply for a checking account at a new bank, your prior history is reviewed. For example, if you bounced a check or if your bank paid a check and you did not immediately reimburse the bank, then your bank may have reported you to ChecSystems and may close your account.

ChecSystems is a national database company that more than 80 percent of U.S. banks have joined. Once a bank decides to send a person's name into this database, it remains on the negative list for five years. The

result of having your name in this database is that you will be denied the ability to open another checking account during the next five years. The banking community is not interested in handling customers who bounce checks, do not immediately repay an overdraft, or do not keep their payments on the bank credit cards current.

Consider the difficulty of not being able to write or cash checks. You would be forced to use to a check-cashing service. These services normally charge 5 to 10 percent of the amount of the check being cashed. Utilities, house payment, groceries, and other bills would need to be paid in cash or with money orders or certified checks.

---

personal and commercial checks are written each year in the United States. Checks are more than a daily convenience. "Checkbook money" is an integral part of the economic system. A check is a credit instrument treated like cash by the industry.

The Bank–Customer Relationship

Article 4 of the UCC governs modern bank deposit and collection procedures. This article governs the relationships of banks with one another as they process checks for payment. It also establishes a framework for deposit and checking agreements between banks and their customers.

The provisions of Article 3 of the UCC establish the extent to which any party is liable on a check. A check can fall within the scope of Article 3 as a negotiable instrument and also is subject to the provisions of Article 4 while it is in the course of collection. In the case of a conflict between Articles 3 and 4, Article 4 controls [UCC 4-102(a)]. Exhibit 12–6 shows the collection route that a check takes from the time it is issued until it returns to the drawer.

Customer Duties

A checking account holder has a duty to examine the monthly statements and canceled checks for forgeries

with reasonable promptness. When the customer's negligence substantially contributes to a forgery, the bank is not obliged to credit the customer's account for the forged check amount.

"Reasonable promptness" means within a few days, but no more than thirty. The court applies comparative negligence rules if a forgery is discovered. If the customer fails to examine the statement or fails to notify the bank of forged checks, the withdrawals from the customer's account based on the forged checks become the customer's responsibility after thirty days [UCC 3-406 and UCC 4-406]. If the checkbook is left where a thief could easily find it, the court may find the customer negligent even if the forged check is discovered within thirty days.

Duties of the Bank

A commercial bank serves its customers primarily in three ways. The bank

1. honors checks for the withdrawal of funds deposited in the customer–drawer's account,

2. accepts deposits in currency and collects checks written to or indorsed to its customers that are drawn on other banks, and

3. honors stop-payment orders.

Exhibit 12–6   A Sample Route of a Check

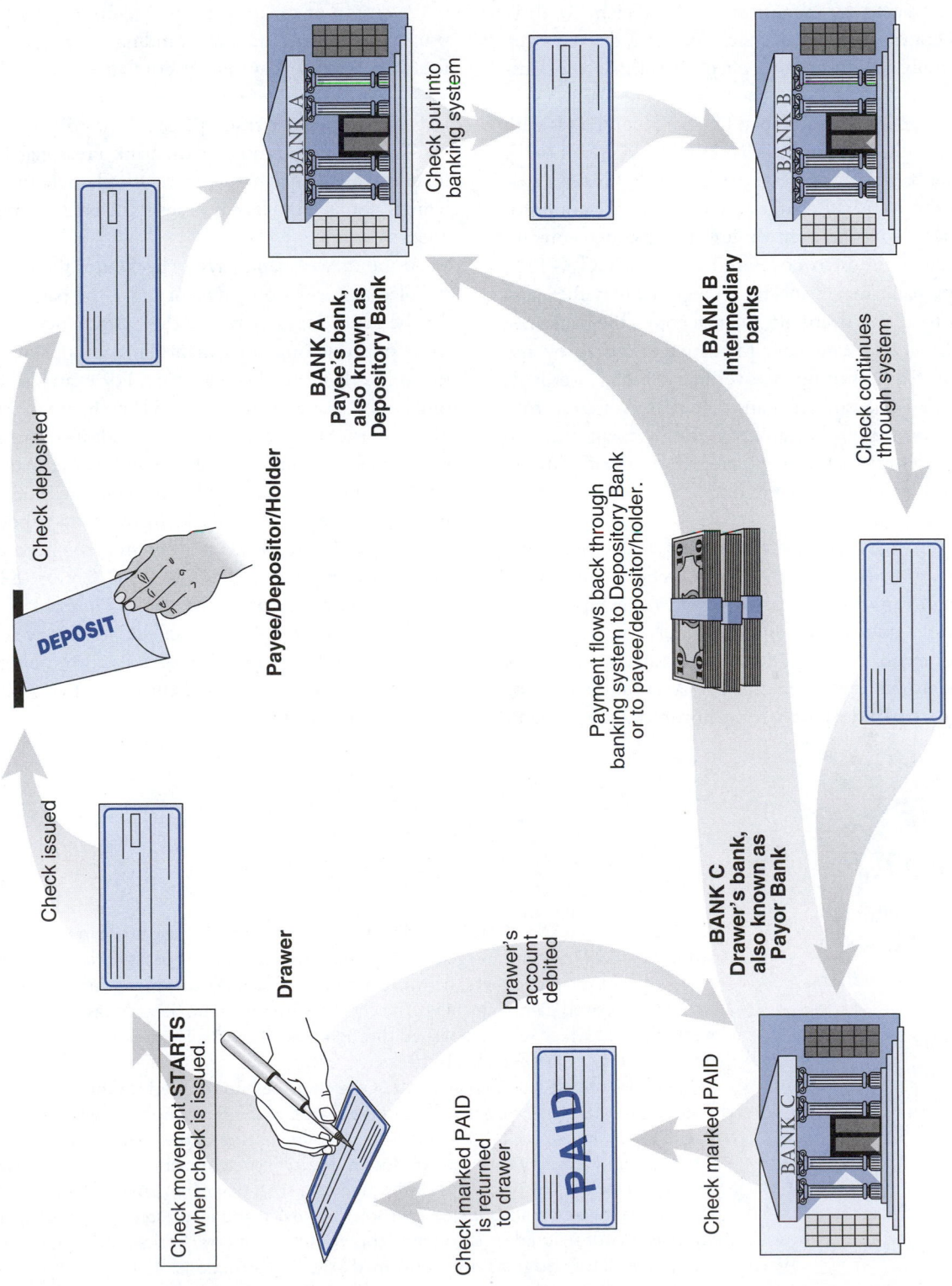

Honoring Checks. When a commercial bank provides checking services, it agrees to honor the checks written by its customers if sufficient funds in the account cover each check. When a drawee bank wrongfully fails to honor a check, it is liable to its customer-drawer, not to the check holder, for damages resulting from its refusal to pay. The bank contract is with customer-drawer, not the check holder [UCC 4-401].

The bank may agree to accept overdrafts for a customer. An overdraft charges the customer's account for the check amount, even though the account contains insufficient funds to cover the check [UCC 4-401]. Once a bank makes special arrangements with a customer to accept overdrafts to an account, the bank may be liable to the customer for damages caused by any wrongful dishonoring of overdrafts. Today, overdrafts are treated as customer loans that charge interest from the day on which the bank pays the overdraft until the customer deposits funds to cover the overdraft plus the fees for handling the overdraft.

Honoring Stop-Payment Orders. Only a customer can order the bank to pay a check, and only a customer can order the bank to stop a check payment. This right does not extend to holders (such as payees or indorsees) because the drawee-bank's contract is limited to its customer-drawers. A customer cannot issue a **stop-payment order**, however, on a cashier's or teller's check because they are not issued on the customer's account.

A customer can give a stop-payment order orally, usually by phone, and it is binding on the bank for fourteen calendar days unless confirmed in writing. A written stop-payment order is effective for six months, unless renewed in writing [UCC 4-403(b)].

The customer must give the bank a reasonable time to effect a stop-payment order. Until such time, the bank is not liable to its customer if the bank honors the check.

If the drawee bank pays a check after the customer has filed a proper stop-payment order, the bank is liable for the actual loss suffered by the customer-drawer because of the wrongful payment. This amount might be much less than the check amount. For example, JoAnn orders six plants priced at $50 each from Frank's Greenhouse. She pays Frank $300 in advance. Frank delivers only five plants and tells JoAnn that the sixth plant will be delivered in six months. JoAnn immediately stops payment on her $300 check. Inadvertently, the bank honors the $300 check over her stop-payment order. JoAnn can only establish a loss of $50 ($300 − $250 = $50) because she received five plants. The bank is liable for only $50 for the plant that she did not receive.

The bank has a duty to inform its customers of the requirements for a stop-payment order. The next case deals with this issue.

Case 12.2

Seigel v. Merrill Lynch, Pierce, Fenner & Smith, Inc.

District of Columbia Court of Appeals, 2000
745 A.2d 301

BACKGROUND AND FACTS The events giving rise to this case arose in January and February of 1997. Plaintiff Seigel, a Maryland resident, traveled to Atlantic City, New Jersey, to gamble. While there, he wrote a number of checks to various casinos and, in exchange, received gambling chips. The checks were drawn on Seigel's cash management account, which was established through Merrill Lynch. There were sufficient funds in the account to cover all of the checks.

Seigel eventually gambled away all of the chips he had received for the checks. Upon returning to Maryland, Seigel discussed the status of the outstanding checks with Merrill Lynch, informing his broker of the gambling nature of the transactions and his desire to avoid realizing the apparent losses. Merrill Lynch informed Seigel that it was possible to escape paying the checks by placing a stop-payment order and liquidating his cash management account. Seigel took this advice and instructed Merrill Lynch to close his account, liquidate the assets, and not to honor any checks drawn on the account. Merrill Lynch agreed and confirmed Seigel's instructions.

Many of the checks were subsequently dishonored and are not part of this case. Merrill Lynch, however, accidently paid several of the checks totaling $143,000, despite the stop- payment order and account closure. Merrill Lynch then debited Seigel's margin account to cover the payments.

Seigel brought suit in the District of Columbia against Merrill Lynch, alleging breach of contract, negligence, and breach of trust, demanding a return of the $143,000 plus interest. Seigel argued that D.C. Code § 16-1701 precluded enforcement of the checks as a void gambling debt, or in the alternative that New Jersey law prohibited the enforcement of the checks, and that therefore Merrill Lynch had no rights by way of subrogation as a defense to its payment over the stop-payment order.

Merrill Lynch denied the applicability of the D.C. statute or any relevant New Jersey law. It contended that it stood in the shoes of the casinos to whom valid and enforceable checks were given, and therefore the plaintiff had not suffered any actual loss as a result of the payment of the checks. The trial court dismissed the complaint.

STEADMAN, Associate Judge

. . . .

We begin with an examination of the statutory scheme relating to stop-payment orders, because we believe these provisions are determinative of this appeal. The relevant sections are found in the Uniform Commercial Code as enacted in the District of Columbia, and in particular D.C. Code §§ 28:4-403 and 28:4-407. The basic right of the depositor to stop payment on any item drawn on the depositor's account is set forth in section 28:4-403(a). However, liability on the bank for payment over a stop-payment order is far from automatic. On the contrary, section 28:4-403(c) provides: "The burden of establishing the fact and amount of loss resulting from the payment of an item contrary to a stop-payment order or order to close an account is on the customer."

This provision, which places the burden on the customer to show actual loss, is reinforced by the extensive rights of subrogation given to the payor bank by section 28:4-407. Under that section, as to the drawer or maker (that is, the depositor), the bank is subrogated both to the rights of "any holder in due course on the item" and to the rights of "the payee or any other holder of the item against the drawer or maker either on the item or under the transaction out of which the item arose." As a leading authority on the Uniform Commercial Code has noted, this section "contemplates that the bank will use its subrogation rights primarily to defend against a suit by the customer to recover payment."

As applied to the facts here, then, Seigel is required to bear the burden of establishing that he in fact suffered a loss as a result of the payment of the checks. In assessing whether any such loss was actually incurred, Merrill Lynch must be treated as the subrogee of any rights of the casino payees against Seigel. As the payee of a dishonored check, the casino would have a prima facie right to recover its amount from Seigel as drawer, . . . and the burden would be on Seigel to establish any defense he might assert on the instrument. Seigel asserts two such defenses: duress and illegality. We turn to an examination of those defenses.

Seigel first argues that the casinos would have no right to enforce the checks even under New Jersey law because he is a compulsive gambler. He contends that enforcement of checks by a casino against a compulsive gambler would run counter to New Jersey's Casino Control Act, or against the common law, and therefore the checks are invalid. . . . Nothing in the New Jersey Casino Control Act, however, specifically prohibits the cashing and redemption of checks made by "compulsive gamblers." . . .

With regard to Seigel's common law argument, it appears to be true that intoxication, duress, and unconscionability may, in certain circumstances, be valid defenses to the enforcement of gambling contracts in New Jersey. However, compulsive gambling, in and of itself, is not a defense to a contract action in New Jersey. Rather, the facts of a particular transaction may reveal "some overreaching or imposition resulting from a bargaining disparity between the parties, or such patent unfairness in the contract that no reasonable person not acting under compulsion or out of necessity would accept its terms." . . . The question, therefore, is whether Seigel has set forth adequate facts to raise a genuine issue regarding the enforceability of the checks in light of his alleged compulsion and duress flowing from that disorder.

The entirety of appellant's duress argument emanates from a single sentence in his affidavit: "For years I have had [a] gambling problem." If not ambiguous, the statement is conclusory. . . . Appellant fails to produce any evidence in the record, specific or otherwise, regarding his problem and its relation to any unconscionable duress in the transactions at issue. . . . The record—even when viewed in the light most favorable to Seigel on whom the burden of proof rests—simply does not present a genuine disputed issue of fact as to whether the contracts evidenced by the checks were made under duress, and therefore unenforceable. . . . We therefore conclude that Seigel's assertion that the checks would be unenforceable in New Jersey fails.

Seigel also invokes the fact that these checks were given in order to obtain chips with which to gamble, and cites us in particular to D.C. Code . . . . Modeled after the English "Statute of Anne," 9 Anne, 14, § 1 (1710), that section provides that:

> A thing in action, judgment, mortgage, or other security or conveyance made and executed by a person in which any part of the consideration is for money or other valuable things won by playing at any game whatsoever, or by betting on the sides or hands of persons who play, or for the reimbursement or payment of any money knowingly lent or advanced for the purpose, or lent or advanced at the time and place of the play or bet, to a person so playing or betting or who, during the play, so plays or bets, is void.

. . . .

. . . [E]ven if payment had been stopped [in D.C.], the casinos could have enforced the checks in New Jersey, where the transaction was entered into. Merrill Lynch therefore, under the Code scheme, conceptually has the same right. Furthermore, even if there were a problem in asserting jurisdiction over Seigel in New Jersey, Maryland would have provided an appropriate forum for enforcing the checks. The highest Maryland court has squarely held that because there is no longer a strong public policy against gambling per se, but only against illegal gambling, the doctrine of *lex loci contractus* [the local law on contracts] prevails in full, and that therefore Maryland courts will enforce gambling debts if legally incurred in a foreign jurisdiction.

. . . .

DECISION AND REMEDY The court concluded that Seigel failed to establish that he ultimately suffered any actual loss as a result of the payment of the checks by Merrill Lynch.

CRITICAL THINKING: LEGAL CONCEPTS Do you think it is fair for a bank or other financial institution not to be liable when they have disregarded a stop-payment order?

Paying on Forged Signatures. Signatures of the drawer, maker, or indorser occasionally are forged. Forgery is common with checks. A forged drawer's signature on a check has no effect legally, as a general rule [UCC 3-406]. Banks require the customer's signature on a signature card. Banks, which process thousands of checks each hour, rarely compare the signature on the check with the signature card. The bank is still responsible, however, for determining if the signature on a customer's check is genuine.

Occasionally a forged check will be processed and paid. The general rule is that the bank must recredit the customer's account when it pays on a forged signature. The customer has duties to the bank, however. If the customer's negligence contributed to the forgery or if the customer breached his duty to discover and report the forgery to the bank, the bank is not liable for those forged checks. The following case involves a situation in which the customer failed to check her monthly statement regularly.

Case 12.3

Mansi v. Gaines & Sterling National Bank & Trust Company of New York

Supreme Court, Appellate Division, Second Department, 1995
216 A.D.2d 536, 628 N.Y.S.2d 804

BACKGROUND AND FACTS Mansi, the plaintiff, alleged that substantial sums of money were removed from her accounts with the Sterling National Bank & Trust Company of New York (Sterling). This removal was allegedly accomplished by a fraudulent power of attorney and by forged checks. Mansi sought compensatory damages, punitive damages, and attorneys' fees. Mansi submitted an affidavit from a handwriting expert stating that the signatures on eighteen checks were apparently forgeries.

Sterling acknowledged that it honored the eighteen checks but claimed that, pursuant to the bank's business practices, nine of those checks and the respective account statements had been forwarded to Mansi more than one year before she filed the lawsuit. With respect to the remaining nine checks, Sterling asserted that Mansi's claims were barred by UCC 4-406 because Mansi failed to inform Sterling about the nine checks until thirty days had passed.

Sterling noted that at a deposition Mansi stated that she did not review her monthly bank statements. She acknowledged in her answer to interrogatories that she had failed to examine canceled check copies for more than one year. Sterling submitted evidence that its practice was to check the signature on every check filed against the customer's signature card. Portions of the affidavit from Mansi's handwriting expert worked against her when the expert stated that the checks in question bore signatures that were apparently "written by another person who attempted to simulate her signature" and thus were not obvious forgeries.

Judges SULLIVAN, PIZZUTO, SANTUCCI, and GOLDSTEIN

. . . .

Although the evidence in the record indicated that the appellant honored 18 checks which may have been forged, liability with respect to nine of those checks was barred by UCC 4-406(4) since the plaintiff did not report the alleged fraud within one year after those checks and the bank statements with respect thereto were made available to her.

With respect to the remaining nine checks, liability was barred by UCC 4-406(2)(b) since it was established that the plaintiff failed to exercise reasonable care to examine her bank statements and the plaintiff failed to submit any evidence that the appellant failed to exercise ordinary care in paying the items.

DECISION AND REMEDY Mansi lost her lawsuit because she failed to review her bank statements for more than one year. She might have been able to recover if she could have proven the bank to be negligent. In this case she was unable to do so.

CRITICAL THINKING: PREVENTIVE LAW What steps should a business take to prevent this problem?

The Impostor Rule, the Fictitious Payee Rule, and the Dishonest Employee Rule.

The *impostor rule*, the *fictitious payee rule*, and the *dishonest employee rule* deal with a basic theft by using a check. The theft can be carried out in three different ways. The following three examples illustrate these. The problem is to determine who bears the burden of loss created by the theft.

Impostor Rule. The **impostor rule** involves a theft by an impostor. Sanchez works as a consultant for ABC Distributing Company, but it does not pay her immediately for the work she performed. Ivana Imp goes to ABC Distributing Company and represents herself to be Sanchez. ABC Distributing Company issues a check to Ivana Imp made out to Sanchez. She indorses the check by forging Sanchez's name and deposits the check into her own bank account. Shortly thereafter, Ivana Imp withdraws cash from her account and disappears.

Fictitious Payee Rule. A **fictitious payee rule** involves a theft by an employee who creates a fictitious payee. In one scenario, Fred Fact, an employee, has the authority to make and sign his employer's checks. Fred Fact makes checks out to a fictitious payee, endorses the checks, and deposits them into his own account.

In a second scenario, Fred Fact lacks the authority to sign checks because Fred Fact's employer signs the checks. Fred Fact again makes out the checks to a fictitious payee. If, while he is signing checks, the employer asks about the fictitious payee, Fred Fact tells a good story about the payee's being either an employee or a business with which the employer deals. Again, Fred Fact deposits these checks into his own account.

Dishonest Employee Rule. The **dishonest employee rule** involves a theft by an employee working in the employer's business operations. For example, Dirk Dishonest works in business operations and has the

authority to indorse negotiable instruments, to process instruments for bookkeeping purposes, to prepare and process instruments for issue in the employer's name, and to perform other acts on his employer's behalf. Dirk Dishonest indorses his employer's signature on a check made payable to the employer. Instead of depositing the check into the employer's account, he deposits the check into his own account.

Discussion of the Three Rules. In the business world, these three wrongdoers, Ivana Imp, Fred Fact, and Dirk Dishonest, have harmed others and are ultimately liable under the law. In many cases, by the time these people are identified, they are either long gone or under arrest. More important, however, these people often have no money to repay the victims.

These three scams are operated similarly. The wrongdoer cashes the checks or deposits them in his or her bank account. Only the manner in which the check is obtained differs. Once deposited, the check is sent through the banking system until the drawee bank finally pays it. The problem becomes who will bear the burden of the loss.

Revised Article 3 of the UCC states that the forged signature is as effective as the valid signature of the drawer, payee, or indorser. The bank, which in good faith paid the instrument, is not liable. In other words, the forged signature is binding on the drawer. The bank that cashes the check is not liable to pay a second time.

In the impostor theft, ABC Distributing was the drawer and, through its negligence, contributed to the forged indorser's signature. ABC Distributing could have verified that Ivana Imp either was Sanchez or had the authority to act on behalf of Sanchez. Even so, Ivana Imp victimized ABC Distributing. The innocent parties are the drawer, ABC Distributing, and the bank that paid the check. ABC Distributing, even though a victim, had the best opportunity to prevent the fraud. If the bank paid the check in good faith, the bank will not be liable. In the end, ABC Distributing paid on the check to Ivana Imp and also must pay Sanchez, to whom it still owes money [UCC 3-404].

In the case of the fictitious payee theft, the two innocent parties are the employer and the bank. The employer, even though a victim, should know its employees and creditors and should have verified Fred Fact's representations. The rule is that the forged indorsement is effective as the payee's indorsement. The bank paid the check in good faith and will not be liable. In the end, the employer paid on a check made out to a nonexistent party [UCC 3-404].

In the dishonest employee theft, the employer trusted the employee and is responsible for the employee's dishonest actions. The rule is that the forged indorsement is effective as the indorsement of the payee (employer). The bank paid the check in good faith and is not liable. In the end, the employer must bear the loss [UCC 3-405].

These simple rules have a major exception. Under revised Article 3, the comparative negligence rule may apply when a bank pays on a check with a forged signature. If the bank fails to exercise ordinary care in paying the check that results in a loss, the loss is allocated between the drawer, payee, or indorser, who are each partially at fault, and the bank that is also negligent.

Courts decide to apply the comparative negligence rule on a case-by-case basis. In any of the three previously discussed cases, if the bank failed to exercise ordinary care in paying the check and that failure contributed to the loss, ABC Distributing or either employer could assert comparative negligence against the bank. If the bank is at fault, it will have to pay part or all of the loss.

In the following case, the court was confronted with losses caused by a dishonest employee. The court had to determine whether the bank or the employee would be responsible for the losses.

Case 12.4

Globe Motor Car Co. v. First Fidelity Bank

Supreme Court of New Jersey, Law Division, Essex County, 1993
273 N.J. 388, 641 A.2d 1136

BACKGROUND AND FACTS   The plaintiff, Globe Motor Car Company, was an automobile dealership located in Fairfield, New Jersey. Globe had an agreement with First Fidelity Bank to finance Globe's inventory. Globe promised to repay the loan upon selling a motor vehicle.

The office manager, John Gallo, handled most of Globe's day-to-day finances. Gallo embezzled over $1.5 million from his employer over a three-year period. On many occasions, Gallo simply retained money paid to Globe. He purchased a vehicle for his own use instead of depositing the proceeds to pay off the bank loans owed on the cars being traded in. On other occasions, Gallo made himself and others the payees on checks signed in blank by the owner. As the embezzlement progressed, Gallo forged the owner's signature to checks payable to himself and others.

To conceal his activities, Gallo removed checks made out to him from the monthly checking account statement. He also made out fake certificates of deposit and falsified monthly bank reconciliations. The plaintiff claimed that the bank should reimburse all funds paid on these forgeries.

J.S.C. FUENTES

. . . .

Gallo frequently committed the fraud by filling in checks signed in blank by one of plaintiff's officers. Other times, Gallo would forge the signatures and fill in the rest of the check. Ordinarily a bank cannot charge a forged check to the depositor's account but rather it must pay out of its own fund. However, the bank is **relieved from liability where its payment of the forged check is caused by the negligence of its depositor and where the bank is free from negligence.**

The law as to who absorbs the loss in an embezzlement scheme involving a bank and its depositor is well-settled and logically sound. Where a check is signed in blank by the maker and is given to a dishonest employee who fills it in, the loss normally falls upon the depositor, not the bank. Under such circumstances, the signature is deemed to be genuine and the check bears no evidence on its face that payment was not intended. In this case, as between the bank and the depositor, the loss should be borne by the one whose act enabled the wrongdoer to commit the fraud.

. . . .

Generally, a very high degree of care should be exercised by the drawer of a negotiable instrument to safeguard it from every reasonable likelihood of alteration. The depositor has a duty to promptly examine and compare the returned checks with the record of payments made. The discharge of that duty should promptly dispel alterations or discrepancies and prevent the successful commission of continuous frauds by exposing the first irregularity.

. . . .

Here since Globe gave Gallo checks signed in blank with no entry as to payee or amount, plaintiff bears the loss. As observed . . . "where blanks are filled or an incomplete instrument is otherwise completed, this section . . . [places] the loss upon the party who left the instrument incomplete. . . ." And "this result is intended even though the instrument was stolen from the maker or drawer and completed after the theft."

As to the forgeries, a number of decisions have addressed the question of a bank's liability in case of forgery by the depositor's employee. In some states where the employer has entrusted the examination of his account to the dishonest employee who is in a position to conceal the fraud, the bank is nevertheless held liable. Others, including New Jersey, have held that the employer of a dishonest employee is liable even if that very employee is entrusted with examining the accounts.

. . . .

Ultimately, fault must lie with the employer, the person or persons who presumably carried out the necessary background checks and maintained the most significant day-to-day contact with the dishonest employee. The employer that hires a thief must suffer the consequences of his or her misjudgment.

DECISION AND REMEDY The court found that the employer of a dishonest employee is liable when the employer signs blank checks and allows the employee to fill in the payee and the amounts. The employer had to absorb the loss when the same employee forged the employer's signature.

CRITICAL THINKING: MANAGEMENT ISSUE Discuss steps a business should take to prevent this type of loss.

Electronic Funds Transfer Systems

The present basis of the payment-collection process is the check. Banks, however, are finding these billions of pieces of paper increasingly difficult to cope with.

Electronic funds transfer (EFT)[1] systems assist banks by removing the mountains of paperwork formerly necessary to transfer money.

[1] The terms *electronic funds transfer* (EFT) and *electronic transfer of funds* (ETF) are used interchangeably in business and government.

An EFT system has the following components:

1. *Automated teller machines (ATMs).* Located conveniently and connected online to the bank's computers, these machines receive payments on loans, receive deposits for or dispense cash from checking or savings accounts, and make credit card advances.

2. *Point-of-sale systems.* Located in the merchant's store and connected online to the bank's computers, a point-of-sale system immediately debits the customer's checking account and transfers the funds to the merchant's account.

3. *Automatic payments and direct deposits.* Advance authorization allows regular electronic fund transfers from an account (for the automatic payment of bills) or into an account (for direct deposit, such as an automatic payroll deposit).

4. *Telecommunications systems.* A customer can order, by computer or telephone, money transfers to and from his or her accounts or for bill payment.

5. *Automatic clearinghouses.* Clearinghouses record customer entries in the form of electronic signals, eliminating check use. Businesspeople use clearinghouses for recurrent payments, such as payroll, Social Security, or pension funds.

ETF technology, however, has aroused some serious consumer concerns. With the speed of the transmissions, issuing stop-payment orders becomes difficult. Precisely because transmissions are electronic, fewer paper records are available. Electronic systems allow more opportunities for an unauthorized person to tamper with an account, with a resulting decrease in privacy. The time between the writing of a check and its deduction from an account (the float time) is lost.

A Bank's Liability in EFTs. Federal statutes, such as the Electronic Fund Transfer Act (EFTA), govern electronic funds transfers that customers operate by telephone or by the presentation of a debit card to merchants when making purchases. The information concerning the consumer's rights under federal law must be given to every customer who opens an EFT account.

Banks provide a monthly statement for every month in which a customer electronically transfers funds. Otherwise, they provide statements every quarter. The statement indicates the amount and date of the transfer, the names of the retailers involved, the location or identification of the terminal, the fees, and an address and telephone number for inquiries and error notices. The bank furnishes receipts for transactions made through computer terminals, but it is not obliged to do so for telephone transfers. The customer has the duty to reconcile his receipts against the statements.

Article 4A. Banks, other financial institutions, and the federal government electronically transfer between $1 billion and $2 trillion on any given day.

The UCC, Article 4A, Funds Transfers, sets out a comprehensive scheme that covers the bank's relationship with the fund's originator and with the payee. Typically, the originator sends money via electronic transfer through the bank to the customer (payee). This procedure is accomplished through a **payment order**, which deletes money from the originator account and inserts it into the payee's account. Most states have adopted Article 4A.

Transfer of Funds by the Federal Government

The federal government has a big stake in electronic fund transfers. The U.S. Treasury issues millions of checks annually to pay government debts (accounts payable) and it also receives millions of checks from those who owe debts to the United States (accounts receivable). In the future, the government will issue payment and receive funds by electronic transfer.

The Debt Collection Improvement Act (DCIA) of 1996 requires the Department of Treasury to issue rules concerning the electronic payment and collection of funds. This initiative is known as "Electronic Funds Transfer" or "EFT '99." The initiative's first goal is to convert all federal government payments to electronic form.

Federal payment recipients, such as those receiving Social Security, who have an account at a financial institution automatically receive their Social Security payments electronically. The DCIA includes vendors, Medicare recipients, welfare recipients, and veterans.

Recipients without an account at a financial institution who would face financial hardship if they received their payments electronically are eligible for a waiver, which allows them to receive paper checks. For those people without a regular bank account who certify that they have physical disabilities or confront geographic barriers (such as living overseas in a remote area), the payments are transmitted electronically to special accounts, electronic transfer accounts (ETAs), that permit ATM and point-of-sale access. The agency issuing the payment has the discretion to issue waivers, such as in the case of certain one-time payments, or if the recipient is residing in a foreign country.

Any business that paid more than $20,000 in employment taxes during 1997 is required file its payment electronically to the Internal Revenue Service or face a 10 percent penalty.

The government cited several reasons for phasing out checks in favor of electronic payments:

1. Electronic payments are safer, faster, easier, and less expensive to process than those made by paper check. Paper checks can be lost, stolen, damaged, or delayed.

2. Each year, individuals, businesses, and the government lose an estimated $65 million dollars as a result of forgery, theft, and counterfeiting of government checks.

3. Problems with electronic payments can be resolved quickly. For example, a lost or stolen paper check can take two weeks to replace, while an electronic transfer problem can be traced and corrected within a single day.

4. Electronic payment will save the federal government as much as $100 million a year in processing costs and postage fees. The U.S. Treasury is able to make an electronic payment for less than two cents, compared with the average cost of forty-three cents per paper check. More information about this rule is available on the Internet.[2]

CyberLaw

Electronic Checks

Electronic checks are used by many consumers to order merchandise. An electronic check works in several ways. One way is for the customer, Artiste Login Products, Inc., to create an account with an online electronic check business, Virtual Monies. Instead of a signature that authenticates a paper check, Artiste and Virtual Monies agree that the verification is Artiste's e-mail address. Artiste now has an account on which it may draw.

Artiste needs to purchase office supplies, finds what is needed with an online merchant, and fills out the online purchase order. Artiste also supplies the merchant with the account number with Virtual. The merchant forwards the essential information to Virtual, including the account number, the dollar amount, and the date and time of the purchase. Virtual sends an e-mail to Artiste to confirm the purchase. Artiste must respond before the purchase can be completed. Once Artiste replies, Virtual forwards an electronic check to the office supply merchant. The merchant receives the check, which is printed on a laser printer equipped with magnetic toner that will capture the bank account number and routing information on the check, dollar amount, date and time, and the check serial number. The check can be deposited in the same manner as a paper check. Notice that no encryption mechanism was used because the verification was the e-mail.

In another variation, Artiste creates an account with a merchant. Artiste sends a copy of an Artiste check to the merchant who takes all the pertinent information and returns the void check to Artiste. The merchant now has an electronic copy of the customer's check. When the customer places an order, the merchant must e-mail Artiste a "check stub." Artiste must reply to the e-mail authorizing the order. The merchant takes the check information, the transaction amount, and initiates an Automated Clearing House (ACH) debit. The debit is processed electronically through the ACH Network. Artiste's bank statement contains all the information from the electronic check, just as if it were a paper check.

The Electronic Payment Association (NACHA)[3] is a not-for-profit trade association. Some of its activities include developing operating rules and business practices for the Automated Clearing House Network,[4] and facilitating the adoption of electronic payments for e-commerce, electronic bill payment and presentment (EBPP), financial electronic data interchange (EDI), international payments, electronic checks, electronic

---

[2] See the U.S. Department of Treasury's web site under Regulations and Policy at <http://www.fms.treas.gov/eft>.

[3] Electronic Payment Association's (NACHA) web page is <http://www.nacha.org>.

[4] Automated Clearing House information is available at <http://www.fms.treas.gov/ach/index.html>.

benefits transfer (EBT), and student lending. NACHA represents more than 12,000 financial institutions and more than 600 members in its seven industry councils and corporate affiliate membership program. The ACH Network serves 20,000 financial institutions, 2.5 million businesses, and 100 million people.

The Board of Governors of the Federal Reserve System[5] is removing barriers to the development of electronic check presentment. These efforts include reducing legal barriers to the electronic collection or return of checks, while protecting consumers who want to use paper checks. The board is developing and implementing technical standards for the exchange of electronic checks and for check imaging. The Federal Reserve is partnering with the banking industry to encourage businesses to use and accept electronic checks.

Secured Transactions

The concept of a secured transaction is as basic to modern business practice as the concept of credit. Few purchasers (manufacturers, wholesalers, retailers, or consumers) have the resources to pay with currency for major goods. Lenders rarely lend money to a debtor based solely on the debtor's promise to repay the debt. Sellers and lenders simply require a guarantee of repayment to minimize the risk of loss from nonpayment.

To minimize the risk of loss, the creditor often requires the debtor to provide some type of security. When this security takes the form of personal or real property that the debtor owns or in which the debtor has a legal interest, the transaction becomes known as a *secured transaction,* more commonly called a *lien.*

Business today relies heavily on secured transactions. State laws generally allow secured creditors access to certain types of property that is generally exempt from collection when the creditor collects on a loan. These exemption laws exist to protect debtors. Under federal bankruptcy laws, secured creditors have a favored position over unsecured creditors should the debtor become bankrupt.

The underlying philosophy of secured transaction laws deals with two of the creditor's major concerns should the debtor default on the obligation. First, the

debt will be satisfied from specific property (collateral) of the debtor. Second, the creditor's position in the property will have priority over other creditors' and purchasers' claims to that specific collateral (property).

The provisions covering secured financing are found in the revised Article 9 of the UCC, which most states have adopted. Revised Article 9 applies to any transaction that intends to create a security interest in personal property. Transactions involving real property are excluded [UCC 9-109]. Exhibit 12–7 shows a sample security agreement.

Creating a Security Interest

For a creditor to become a secured party, the creditor must be provided by the debtor with a security interest in the debtor's collateral. A creditor must meet three requirements to have an enforceable security interest.

First, unless the creditor has possession of the collateral, the creditor must have a written security agreement signed by the debtor. The security agreement must describe the collateral reasonably so that it can be identified. A description of collateral as "all the debtor's assets" or "all the debtor's personal property" does not reasonably identify the collateral [UCC 9-108].[6]

The form of a written security agreement has been modified by the Revised Article 9. Prior to these changes, the security agreement had to be in written form and signed by the debtor. Now it has to be authenticated. This change was made to encompass the filing and transmission of both tangible and intangible records. Authentication includes signing, executing a symbol, or using some type of electronic encryption method that indicates that the debtor desires to be bound [UCC 9-102 (a)(7)].

Second, the creditor must have given something of value to the debtor. Normally, the value given by a secured party is in the form of a direct loan or involves a commitment to sell goods on credit.

Third, the debtor must have rights in the property used as collateral; that is, the debtor must have some ownership interest or right to obtain possession of that collateral. The debtor's rights can represent either a current or a future legal interest in the collateral. For example, a retail seller-debtor can give a secured party a security interest, not only in existing inventory

[5] The Board of Governors of the Federal Reserve System's web page is <http://www.federalreserve.gov>.

[6] A financing statement may state that it "covers all assets or all personal property" [UCC 9-504].

Exhibit 12–7 A Sample Security Agreement

SECURITY AGREEMENT

June 30, 2001
Date

William M. Smith	1306 37th Street	Des Moines	Polk	Iowa
Name	No. and Street	City	County	State

(hereinafter called Debtor) hereby grants to   **Janet Johnson Appliance Corporation**

706 Grand Avenue		Des Moines	Polk	Iowa
No. and Street		City	County	State

(hereinafter called Secured Party) a security interest in the following property (hereinafter called the Collateral):

One 1998 Zenith 27" screen television set, Serial No. AZ22478

to secure payment and performance of obligations identified or set out as follows (hereinafter called the Obligations)

$50.00 per month for the next 60 months to be paid on the first day of every month

beginning on the first day of August, 2001.

Default in payment or performance of any of the Obligations or default under any agreement evidencing any of the Obligations is a default under this agreement. Upon such default Secured Party may declare all Obligations immediately due and payable and shall have the remedies of a Secured Party under the Iowa Uniform Commercial Code.
Signed in triplicate.

William M. Smith
Debtor

Janet Johnson Appliance Corporation

By *Janet Johnson, President*

SECURED PARTY

---

owned by the retailer, but also in future inventory that the retailer will acquire.

Once these requirements are met, the creditor's rights are said to "attach to" the collateral. Attachment means that the creditor has an enforceable security interest against the debtor. The attachment of the security interest in the collateral establishes the rights and liabilities of the debtor and creditor with respect to the collateral [UCC 9-203].

Perfection

Even though the creditor's security interest has attached to the debtor's property, the secured creditor must take steps to protect its claim to the collateral over claims that third parties may have to the same property. The third parties may be other secured creditors, general creditors, trustees in bankruptcy, or purchasers of the collateral. The procedures to protect the creditor's

rights are called **perfection**. There are three methods of perfection:

1. *Upon attachment.* If there is a *purchase-money security interest* agreement in consumer goods (goods used or bought primarily for personal, family, or household purposes), perfection occurs automatically upon creation of the security interest without a filing and without the secured party's taking possession. A purchase-money security interest agreement secures payment of the unpaid balance of the purchase price that is given to the creditor by the consumer when he or she purchases consumer goods. Other forms of collateral may be perfected only by an attachment. For example, a person dies owing a hospital for hospital care. The person's heir who will inherit the estate makes an assignment to the hospital. This assignment is a perfected security interest without filing.

2. *On possession.* A secured party's possession of a debtor's collateral is notice of a possible lien and, thus, perfection. For example, a deposit at a financial institution like a certificate of deposit can only be perfected by possession [UCC 9-312].

3. *On filing.* The most common method is for the secured party to file the relevant document with the appropriate government office. In the sale of goods, the most common document is called a **financing statement** [UCC 9-310]. A creditor files a financing statement on a UCC-1 form. A financing statement is a document signed by the debtor that briefly describes property used as collateral in a security agreement. This document does not create the security interest, but is filed in a public office to notify the public that a security interest exists in the described personal property. Under prior law, the general rule required the financing statement to be filed where the collateral was located. Revised Article 9 requires that it be recorded in the state of an individual's residence. If there is only one place of business, the financing statement should be recorded in that state. The major change affects a debtor that does business in several locations. In that situation, the creditor must record the financing statement in the state where the business was created, such as the place of incorporation.

As a general rule, the party that perfects its lien has first priority rights to the collateral. One type of purchaser, however, prevails regardless of a secured party's perfection and despite the fact that the purchaser knows of the secured party's interest at the time of purchase. This type of purchaser is anyone who purchases goods in the ordinary course of business [UCC 9-320(A)].

For example, Last Chance Bank has a perfected security interest in the inventory of Gary's retail TV store. Joan purchases a TV set from Gary, subject to Last Chance Bank's perfected security interest. Joan takes the TV set free of Last Chance Bank's security interest (if Gary goes into default, Last Chance Bank cannot repossess the TV from Joan), even if Joan knew of the loan at the time of sale.

In the following case, the court was confronted with the issue of whether a buyer of a motor home, which was sold under *consignment*, could defeat the interest of a prior secured party. A **consignment** occurs when an owner of goods turns them over to a person in the business of selling this type of goods and who agrees to sell the goods in the ordinary course of business. The consignee does not take title to the goods because the original owner (consignor) retains title.

Case 12.5

Schultz v. Bank of the West, C.B.C.

Supreme Court of Oregon, 1997

325 Or. 81, 934 P.2d 421

BACKGROUND AND FACTS In 1987, defendants (the Muirs) bought a motor home. In 1988, the Muirs borrowed money from Bank of the West (Bank), which took a secured interest (lien) in the motor home. The Bank also perfected its right by filing the lien in the appropriate government office.

Gateleys' Fairway Motors (Gateleys) was in the business of selling motor homes. In 1992, the Muirs contracted with Gateleys to sell the motor home on consignment. Gateleys sold the motor home to plaintiffs, the Schultzes.

Gateleys failed to notify the Schultzes that the motor home was being sold on consignment or that a security interest was attached to it. Gateleys failed to pay any of the sale money to the Muirs and, subsequently, filed for bankruptcy.

After learning of the Bank's security interest, the Schultzes brought this action, seeking a declaration that they owned the motor home free of the security interest. The trial court granted summary judgment in plaintiffs' favor. The Bank appealed, and the Oregon Court of Appeals reversed the trial court, holding that the Bank's security interest remained in force. The Oregon Supreme Court accepted review of the case.

Justice GILLETTE

. . . .

Whether or not a buyer takes goods free of a prior perfected security interest is governed by Article 9 of the Uniform Commercial Code (the UCC). The specific question for decision here is whether plaintiffs are entitled to the special protection afforded to consumers by UCC section 9–307 (codified as ORS 79.3070(1)). That section provides in part:

> "A buyer in ordinary course of business as defined in ORS 71.2010(9) . . . takes free of a security interest created by the seller even though the security interest is perfected. . . . "

The cross-referenced section, ORS 71.2010(9), defines "buyer in ordinary course." It provides:

> " 'Buyer in ordinary course of business' means a person who in good faith and without knowledge that the sale to the person is in violation of the ownership rights or security interest of a third party in the goods buys in ordinary course from a person in the business of selling goods of that kind but does not include a pawnbroker."

If plaintiffs can show that they come within the terms of ORS 79.3070(1), they own the motor home free of the Bank's security interest. To do so, the parties here agree that plaintiffs must show two things: (1) They were a "buyer in ordinary course" when they bought the motor home from Gateleys, and (2) the seller of the motor home was the one who created the security interest.

. . . .

1. Were plaintiffs buyers in the ordinary course of business?

As always, in construing an Oregon statute, this court's task is to discern the intent of the legislature. In doing so, this court looks first to the text and context of the statute. Here, the relevant text from ORS 71.2010(9) states that a buyer in ordinary course "*buys* . . . from a *person* in the business of selling goods of that kind." (Emphasis added.) Clearly, the plaintiffs bought from Gateleys, which was in the business of selling goods of that kind. But does the text require that the "person in the business of selling goods" *have title* to the specific goods that the buyer buys, *i.e.,* be the "seller" of the goods. This inquiry is important, because Gateleys disposed of the Muirs' motor home on consignment—it did not have title.

The text does not require that the "person" from whom the goods are purchased have title. This is clear, first, from the text itself. Use of the word, "person," instead of "seller" in a law as carefully crafted as the UCC is a conscious choice. That choice recognizes that there will be those who hold out goods for sale who do not have title, e.g., consignees such as Gateleys, in circumstances in which the stability of the marketplace would be undermined if good faith purchases from those parties were not valid. This point is made even more clear by the textual exclusion of "pawnbroker"—a special kind of consignee—from the definition. Finally, the text of ORS 71.2010(9) recognizes that a sale to a buyer in ordinary course may be "in violation of the ownership rights . . . of a third party." Any ownership rights in a third party would mean that the "person in the business" did not have title to the goods. Thus, the text of ORS 71.2010(9) indicates that "person" does not mean "seller."

. . . .

2. Was the security interest created by the seller?

We now turn to ORS 79.3070(1). It provides that "[a] buyer in ordinary course of business . . . takes free of a security interest created by the seller even though the security interest is perfected and even though the buyer knows of its existence." Here, the Muirs created the security interest, but plaintiffs' dealings were with Gateleys. In order to prevail, plaintiffs must show that, in spite of the fact that they dealt with Gateleys, the Muirs were "the seller" for the purposes of this provision. In our view, that issue turns on whether the seller is the party whose title to the goods was transferred.

On its face, the text is not decisive, because it does not say whether, for the purpose of the provision, the concept of "seller" is limited to the party with legal title to the goods or whether, instead, the seller is simply the party that physically performs the exchange of goods for money with the buyer. Context, however, answers the question. As we have noted elsewhere, ORS 72.1060(1) provides that "[a] 'sale' consists in the passing of title from the seller to the buyer for a price." Nothing in ORS 79.3070(1) suggests that this definition, which specifically states that it is the seller who transfers title, is inapplicable. We hold that "seller," as that term is used in ORS 79.3070(1), refers to the legal owner of the goods purchased by a buyer in ordinary course. Gateleys, with whom plaintiffs dealt, did not itself transfer title to the goods. Thus, it was not the "seller," for the purposes of ORS 79.3070(1). The true seller of the motor home was the party that ultimately parted with title—the Muirs. And, because the Muirs created the security interest, plaintiffs took the motor home free of the Bank's security interest.

. . . .

DECISION AND REMEDY The Oregon Supreme Court found that a person may obtain title to goods that are sold on consignment even though the title owner is not in the business of selling such goods. Because the consignee was in the business of selling the goods, UCC 9- 320 is satisfied, and the buyer in the ordinary course of business will obtain clear title to the goods.

CRITICAL THINKING: LEGAL ANALYSIS Two justices drafted a strong dissent to the decision. They basically argued that the title holder was not in the business of selling motor homes. Therefore, UCC 9-320 was not applicable. Do you agree with the majority opinion or with the two dissenters?

Default

Article 9 of the UCC defines the rights, duties, and remedies in case a debtor defaults on a secured loan. When a debtor defaults, a secured creditor can protect its claim to the collateral by enforcing its security interest by a court judgment, by foreclosure, or by any other available judicial process [UCC 9-609].

Secured Party's Remedies. A secured party's remedies can be divided into two categories. First, a secured creditor can forgo its security interest and proceed to a court judgment on the debt. Once the

secured party has the judgment, it can use the judgment to take other assets of the debtor to satisfy the judgment debt. This procedure is used when the secured collateral's value has been greatly reduced below the debt amount, such as a wrecked automobile, and the debtor has other assets available to satisfy the debt.

Second, a secured creditor can take possession, called *repossession*, of the collateral covered by the security agreement [UCC 9-609]. On **repossession**, the secured party can retain the collateral covered by the security agreement for partial or complete satisfaction of the debt [UCC 9-620] or can resell the goods and

LEGAL HIGHLIGHT

Do I Still Owe on the Car?

People often overextend themselves financially. For example, Katie had an executive position with a large corporation, earning $60,000. She purchased a new car for $40,000. After paying a $10,000 down payment, she took a seven-year loan for the remaining $30,000. Four years later, she is downsized out of a job with several hundred other managers. Katie still owes $10,000 on the loan. Unable to meet the loan payments, she decides to return the car to the bank.

If the bank is able to sell the car for $10,000 plus costs of the resale, Katie owes nothing. If the bank sells it for more, she receives the surplus since she is the car owner. Unfortunately, banks often sell cars in this type of situation for less than the amount still owed to the bank. If the bank can obtain $4,000, it can go to court to obtain a deficiency judgment (that is, a judgment for the amount still deficient for the contract to be paid in full) for $6,000.

Returning the car to the bank fails to relieve Katie of her bank debt. If Katie is unable to repay the remaining $6,000, she may be forced to go to bankruptcy court to have her debts forgiven.

apply the proceeds toward the debt. The sale must be conducted in a commercially reasonable manner [UCC 9-610].

The creditor's rights and remedies under the UCC are cumulative. Therefore, if a secured creditor is unsuccessful in enforcing its rights by one method, it can pursue another method. The UCC does not require the secured creditor to choose between remedies, that is, between a lawsuit to obtain a judgment and repossession of the collateral.

The secured party has the right to take peaceful possession of the collateral on default. As long as no breach of the peace occurs, the secured party can simply repossess the collateral. Otherwise, the secured party must resort to the judicial process [UCC 9-609].

The definition of a breach of the peace is of prime importance to both parties, for such an act can open the secured party (the party repossessing) to tort liability. The UCC fails to define breach of the peace, so the parties must look to the state laws to determine it.

In most states, the secured party must obtain the collateral without breaking and entering, committing assault or battery, or trespassing. Generally, the creditor or the creditor's agent must receive permission to enter a debtor's home, garage, or place of business. For example, if an automobile is the collateral on a defaulted loan and the repossessing party walks onto the debtor's premises, proceeds up the driveway, enters the vehicle

without entering the garage, and drives off, this probably will not amount to a breach of the peace. In some states, however, an action for wrongful trespass could be the debtor's basis for filing a breach-of-the-peace lawsuit. Thus, most car repossessions occur when the car is parked on a street or in a parking lot.

Proceeds from the Disposition of Collateral.
If the secured party sells the collateral on the debtor's default, proceeds from the collateral sale are applied in the following order. First, the creditor's reasonable expenses stemming from the retaking, holding, or sale preparation are paid. These expenses can include reasonable attorneys' fees and legal expenses. Second, the balance of the debt owed to the secured party is satisfied.

Third, written demands for subordinate security interests that were received prior to the completion of distribution of the proceeds are paid. Subordinate security interests are for loans that are second or third liens on the property. Second, third, or even fourth liens are so named for the position they occupy after the first (senior) lien. When the collateral is sold, the first lien holder is paid first. If any money is left, the second lien holder is paid. Each subordinate lien holder is paid in turn as long as the money lasts [UCC 9-615].

For example, Bill buys an expensive antique automobile—one that is known to appreciate in value—and signs a security agreement. He has the car loan nearly paid, but borrows more money by using the equity in the car as collateral for another loan from Bank B to start a small business. Unfortunately, the business fails, and Bill defaults on the original car loan and on the second (business) loan. When the creditor repossesses the car and sells it, first the costs of the whole process of repossession are paid. Next the original loan balance is paid. Finally, the second (business) loan balance from Bank B is paid, assuming that the business loan secured party (Bank B) gave written notice [UCC 9-615].

Any surplus is paid to the debtor. If the loan balances are not paid, the creditor may go to court and obtain a deficiency judgment (a judgment for the amount still deficient to have the contract paid in full).

Termination

When a debtor pays a debt, the secured party must send a termination statement to the debtor. If the secured party filed a lien, it must file the **termination statement** in the same place at which the original financing statement was filed.

The termination statement shows that the debt has been paid. If the secured party fails to file a termination statement at the proper time, the secured party may be liable to the debtor for $500. Additionally, the secured party is liable for any loss caused to the debtor for its failure to file the appropriate release-of-debt documents [UCC 9-625].

International Consideration

So You Want to Sell Overseas: How Do You Get Your Money?

The United States has signed the **United Nations Convention on International Bills of Exchange and Promissory Notes.**[7] Basically, the convention covers both orders to pay and promises to pay. Bills of exchange were developed during the Middle Ages. Article 3 of the UCC, Negotiable Instruments, does not use the term *bill of exchange*; it instead uses the term *draft*.

Bills of exchange and bills of lading are commonly used in international trade. Common carriers, such as ocean vessels, airline companies, and railroad companies, use bills of lading to keep track of goods being shipped. The shipping company issues a multipart bill of lading. One part stays with the goods and another part is turned over to the seller. Whoever controls the seller's copy of the bill of lading controls the goods. The seller's bill of lading is surrendered to the transport company before the buyer takes possession of these goods. How does the buyer obtain possession of the seller's bill of lading?

A bill of exchange is essentially like a check, but it is not drawn on a bank. The seller draws it on the buyer. The drawer (seller) signs the bill of exchange ordering the drawee (buyer) to pay the money to the payee (usually a financial institution). The seller sends the seller's copy of the bill of lading and the bill of exchange to its financial institution, typically a bank. The seller's bank forwards the documents to the buyer's bank, which notifies the buyer that the documents are available to be picked up. The buyer accepts (pays for) the bill of exchange and in return receives the bill of lading. The buyer then can obtain possession of the goods from the transportation company. The buyer's bank sends the money, minus a service fee, to the seller's bank.

The UN convention provides unified rules on this complex topic. Whereas the Western world has had centuries of experience in this field, many developing countries have not. This convention provides guidance and ensures uniformity for the creation, interpretation, and performance of bills of exchange and promissory notes.

Normally, a letter of credit that is issued by a financial institution is associated with the transaction just described. Letters of credit will be discussed in more detail in Chapter 13. The rules covering letters of credit are based on treaties. The International Chamber of Commerce originally adopted the **Uniform Customs and Practices for Documentary Credits (UCP)**[8] in the 1930s. The UCP has since been modified to reflect changes in business. The UCP has many provisions involving letters of credit.

---

[7] The United Nations Convention on International Bills of Exchange and Promissory Notes site at <http://www.uncitral.org/en-index.htm>.

[8] Uniform Customs and Practices for Documentary Credits (UCP) is found at <http://www.uncitral.org/english/texts/payments/mlict.htm>.

LEGALLY SPEAKING

The Problem with Postdating a Check

On Wednesday, Sally sees an advertisement to join a health club. The advertisement states "Today only for one-half price." After work she stops by to check out the club. A salesperson shows her all the club features and reminds her of the one-half price sale. Payday is Monday, five days away, but Sally wants to join at the bargain rate. The salesperson agrees to accept a postdated check and assures Sally that the check will not be deposited until Monday.

When Sally arrives home on Tuesday after work, she receives a notice from her bank that her account is overdrawn. Two minutes later, the health club calls concerning her bounced check. On Wednesday, she checks with the bank and finds that the postdated check was deposited on the previous Thursday. The health club threatens Sally with criminal action. Has Sally committed a crime?

Most people believe that postdating or antedating a check is illegal. The truth is that no date is required on a check to make it negotiable, because it is a demand instrument. Thus, to postdate or antedate a check is not illegal. The act of postdating or antedating the check becomes illegal when the drawer intends to defraud the payee by failing to have the money to cover the check in his or her account. Fraud is difficult to prove under these circumstances, however. As you may remember from Chapter 9, to prove fraud, you must prove an objective intent to deceive at the time of the act. Intent is difficult to prove with a postdated check.

In Sally's case, the district attorney will not prosecute because the date on the face of the check clearly shows that the funds would be available on Monday. If Sally can show that the money (her paycheck) was in the account on Monday, the district attorney cannot show intent to deceive.

Many payees, such as the health club, will require that a date be inserted on the check because under UCC 4-404, a check is "stale" if it is not presented to the bank for payment within six months from the check's date. Thus, after six months, the bank can refuse to pay the check in good faith. To ensure that the bank will pay the check, the payee may require that the date be filled in.

If Sally lives in a state that has adopted the revised Article 3 of the UCC, she must give the bank advance written notice that she is writing a postdated check. If she fails to give the bank written notice, it may honor the check. If she provides written notice, the bank must honor Sally's request to hold payment on the check before the date. Otherwise, the bank is liable to Sally for problems that arise.

The lessons Sally learned include the following:

✔ Never write a postdated check.

✔ Never rely on the oral assurances of a salesperson.

Chapter Summary

Negotiable instruments serve two purposes: substituting for currency and serving as a credit device. Two major types of negotiable instruments are promises to pay, which are two-party instruments, and orders to pay, which are three-party instruments. The two-party instruments have a maker who signs and issues an instrument with a promise to pay a certain sum of money to a payee. The three-party instruments have a drawer who creates an instrument that orders the drawee to pay money to the payee.

Revised Article 3 of the UCC lists the types of negotiable instruments: promissory notes, certificates of deposit, drafts, checks, cashier's checks, teller's checks, traveler's checks, and money orders (which are checks). All of these instruments fall into one of two categories: two-party instruments or three-party instruments. For these instruments to be negotiable, they must meet four requirements. A negotiable instrument must be (1) in writing and signed by the maker or drawer, (2) an unconditional promise or order to pay a fixed amount of money, (3) payable to bearer or to order at the time it is issued, and (4) payable on demand or at a definite time.

To negotiate these instruments, a payee indorses (signs) on the instruments' back and delivers it to another person. The payee who signs the back becomes an indorser, and the person who receives the instrument is called the indorsee. A bearer is any person who physically possesses an instrument that either is payable to anyone without designation or is indorsed in blank.

Negotiable instruments are held by either a holder or a person who becomes a holder in due course (HDC). The holder may be the original payee or one who has taken a negotiable instrument from another person. A holder takes the negotiable instrument subject to all of the defenses that the maker or the drawer has against paying the instrument. A holder has the status of an assignee of a contract right.

An HDC has a special status, however, and is protected by the law. The only defense the maker or drawer has against paying the instrument held by an HDC is a real defense, that is, when something is wrong with the instrument itself. Defenses based on the contract cannot be used against an HDC. To become an HDC, the person must accept the instrument (1) for value, (2) in good faith, (3) without notice that the instrument is overdue or defective, (4) without notice that the instrument contains an unauthorized signature or has been altered, (5) without notice of any claim to the instrument, and (6) without notice that any party has a real defense.

The Federal Trade Commission limits the rights of an HDC to have the instrument paid. In consumer transactions, every contract must carry a warning that the holder has no greater rights to be paid than the original party to the contract. One way a contract is discharged is through the doctrine of accord and satisfaction. In the past, a dispute could be settled if the debtor sent the creditor a check with a notation of "payment in full" or similar words. The creditor in the modern business world would fail to notice the notation in time to return the check uncashed to keep the dispute alive. Today, the creditor must designate a special office to which a check with such a notation must be sent. Even if a creditor fails to supply an office address, the business can refund the check's amount within ninety days of cashing it to avoid closure on settlement.

The UCC recognizes four types of indorsements: blank, special, qualified, and restrictive. A blank endorsement occurs when the payee merely endorses the instrument on the back. When the holder names another person to whom the instrument is negotiated, the signature on the back is called a special endorsement. Blank and special indorsers who have received consideration from the transferee make five transfer warranties: (1) The warrantor is entitled to enforce the instrument, (2) all signatures on the instrument are authentic and authorized, (3) the instrument is unaltered, (4) the instrument is free from a defense or claim that can be asserted against the warrantor, and (5) the warrantor has no knowledge of any insolvency proceeding commenced with respect to maker or acceptor or, in the case of an unaccepted draft, the drawer. A qualified indorsement disclaims or limits an indorser's liability on paying the instrument. A restrictive indorsement is a conditional indorsement and often is used to place a check in the bank collecting process.

A maker, acceptor, or certifier has primary liability on an instrument. This means that this person absolutely must pay the instrument's face amount. A drawer, however, has secondary liability to pay because the drawer orders the drawee to pay. Once the drawee accepts the instrument, the drawee has primary liability. An instrument is discharged by payment, cancellation, or material alteration.

The UCC governs the relationship between a bank and its customers. The bank has a duty to pay checks drawn on a customer's account, to accept deposits, and to honor stop-payment orders. The customer must check his or her statements every month and check for forged signatures on checks.

The banking system has been revolutionized by electronic funds transfer systems, which include ATMs, point-of-sale systems, automatic payments and direct deposits, telecommunications systems, and automatic clearinghouses. Federal laws govern many aspects of electronic funds transfers.

When a merchant extends credit or makes a loan, the merchant wants to ensure debt repayment. The merchant will have the debtor use her or his property as collateral to secure repayment of the monies owed. A secured transaction also is called a lien. The creditor has two major concerns: (1) if the property used as collateral is sold, the amount of money raised from the sale will pay the debt; and (2) the creditor's debt will have priority over the claims of other creditors to, and purchasers of, the collateral.

The creditor (secured party) needs to perfect its security interest to protect its claim in the collateral over other creditors' claims. Three methods of perfection are recognized: (1) attachment, (2) possession, and (3) filing documents (usually a financing statement) in the appropriate public office. If the debtor defaults on the loan payment, the secured party can ignore its interest in the property and proceed to a lawsuit for judgment. The secured party can take possession of the collateral to satisfy the debt or to resell the goods and apply the proceeds toward the debt.

The proceeds of the collateral sale are applied (1) to the reasonable expenses of selling the collateral, (2) to satisfy the debt owed to the secured party, and (3) to pay subsequent subordinate security interests if any proceeds are still on hand. Once the debt has been paid, the secured party must file a termination statement in the same public office as the original document evidencing that the security interest had been filed.

Using the World Wide Web

Negotiable instruments and secured transactions are covered by state statutes. If your state government has a web site for statutes, you should be able to find the statutes dealing with negotiable instruments and secured transactions.

Finding the Law on the Web

Internal Revenue Service
  http://www.irs.ustreas.gov/
Bearer Depository Receipts
  http://www.lectlaw.com/filesh/bbg06.htm
Swift v. Tuson
  http://www.allrise.com/procedure/cases/41US1.html
The Militia Watchdog, Idiot Legal Arguments
  http://www.militia-watchdog.org/suss7.htm

Chapter Web Sites

U.S. Department of Treasury, Financial Management
    Service, electronic funds transfer
  http://www.fms.treas.gov/eft
Electronic Payment Association (NACHA)
  http://www.nacha.org
Automated Clearing House Network
  http://www.fms.treas.gov/ach/index.html
Board of Governors of the Federal Reserve System
  http://www.federalreserve.gov
United Nations Convention on International Bills of
    Exchange and Promissory Notes
  http://www.uncitral.org/en-index.htm

Uniform Customs and Practices for Documentary
    Credits (UCP)
  http://www.uncitral.org/english/texts/payments
  /mlict.htm
Internal Revenue Service
  http://www.irs.ustreas.gov/prod/index.html
Internal Revenue Service, check and money order
    information
  http://www.irs.ustreas.gov/bus_info/tax_pro
  /irm-part/part05/35406a.html
Uniform Commercial Code, Biddle Law Library,
    University of Pennsylvania Law School
  http://www.law.upenn.edu/bll/

Web Activities

12–1 Go to the Internal Revenue Service's web page at <http://www.irs.ustreas.gov/prod/index.html>. Scroll to the bottom and click on "Tax Info for Business." Scroll down to the "Tax Professionals' Corner." Scroll down to "Director of Practice, Enrolled Agent Program." What is an enrolled agent and how does a person become an enrolled agent?

12–2 Go to the Internal Revenue Service's web page at <http://www.irs.ustreas.gov/bus_info/tax_pro/irm-part/part05/35406a.html>. You will be on a page entitled "Chapter 6, Types of Seizures and Seizures in Special Cases." Scroll down to "[5.10] 6.8 Checks and Money Orders" and click. What happens to checks or money orders that are seized? What happens if the check is returned for lack of a personal indorsement? Can the financial institution impose a return check penalty?

Key Terms

acceptor
bearer
bearer paper
blank indorsement
cashier's check
certificate of deposit (CD)
certified check
check
collateral installment
   note
collateral note
consignment
consumer credit
   transaction
demand draft
dishonest employee rule

draft
drawee
drawer
electronic funds transfer
   (EFT)
fictitious payee rule
financing statement
holder
holder in due course
   (HDC)
impostor rule
indorsee
indorser
installment note
issue
judgment rate

maker
mortgage note
negotiable
negotiable instrument
order paper
payee
payment order
perfection
personal defense
promissory note
qualified indorsement
real defense
repossession
restrictive indorsement
secured transaction
sight draft

special indorsement
spot rate
stop-payment order
termination statement
time draft
traveler's check
trade acceptance
Uniform Customs
   and Practices for
   Documentary Credits
   (UCP)
United Nations
   Convention on
   International Bills of
   Exchange and
   Promissory Notes

Questions and Case Problems

12–1 Negotiable Instrument The following is written by Gloria Natale on the back of an envelope: "I, Gloria Natale, promise to pay to Perry Wilson or bearer $1,000 on demand." Is this note a negotiable instrument? Please explain fully.

12–2 Check Jeff draws a check for $1,500 made payable to the order of Kelley. Jeff turns the check over to Kelley. Kelley owes her landlord $500 in rent and transfers the check to her landlord with the following indorsement: "For rent paid. [Signed] Kelley." Kelley's landlord has contracted to have Eric repair the electrical wiring in several apartments. Eric insists on immediate payment. The landlord transfers the check to Eric without indorsement. Later, in order to pay for the electrical supplies at Supply Store, Eric transfers the check with the following indorsement: "Pay to Supply Store, without recourse. [Signed] Eric." Supply sends the check to its bank indorsed "For deposit only. [Signed] Supply Store."

   a. Classify each of these indorsements.
   b. Was the transfer from Kelley's landlord to Eric without indorsement an assignment or a negotiation? Explain.

12–3 HDC Mansfield issues a ninety-day negotiable promissory note payable to the order of Eastwood. He leaves the note's amount blank, to be filled in by

Eastwood when the price of the diamond that Mansfield plans to buy from Eastwood is determined. Mansfield orally authorizes Eastwood to fill in the blank, but the amount is not to exceed $10,000. Eastwood, without authority, fills in the note in the amount of $200,000 and thirty days later sells the note to the First National Bank for $16,000. Eastwood does not buy the diamond and leaves the state. First National Bank had no knowledge that the instrument was incomplete when issued or that Eastwood had no authority to complete the instrument in an amount over $10,000. Does the bank qualify as a holder in due course? If so, for what amount? Explain fully.

12–4 HDC On April 1, Jesse draws a check payable to George for $4,000 to remodel Jesse's house by June 15. George indorses the check in blank to Ronald on July 2 as payment for fireworks that George was buying from Ronald. On July 3, Ronald attempts to cash the check. The bank refuses to pay the check. Ronald tries to collect the amount of the check from Jesse. Jesse claims that his defense—that George never remodeled the house—is valid against Ronald. Ronald claims that the check must be honored because he is an HDC. Who is correct? Explain fully.

12–5 HDC A business advertises freezers, offering purchasers the incentive of the right to purchase frozen food, including meat, at substantial discounts. You visit the business and discover that the cost of the freezer is twice the cost offered by other retailers, but you can finance the freezer by signing a promissory note and security agreement. The business promises that upon signing the documents, you are entitled to purchase all the meat you need over the next year for only ninety-nine cents a pound. You decide to purchase the freezer and sign the documents. The next day, the retailer takes the note to the local bank. The bank purchases the note at a 5 percent discounted rate, which means that the bank purchases the note at 5 percent less than its face value (the principal). The bank sends you a notice that it now holds the note and that you should make your payments to it. The freezer arrives a week later and it works. When the meat arrives, however, it is spoiled. Can you stop making payments to the bank until the retailer supplies edible meat? Explain.

12–6 Stop Payment and HDC Chafont Industries manufactured an automotive product. Kutner Buick was an automobile dealer. Chafont Industries and Kutner Buick maintained a close relationship because Kutner Buick was wholly owned by Jules Kutner, and Chafont Industries was wholly owned by Jules's son, Jerome. Jerome negotiated with Stuart Crawford concerning the possible distributorship purchase. During the negotiations, Jerome made a number of false representations to Crawford who was not aware of the falsity. Crawford issued a cashier's check drawn in the amount of $50,023, which he mailed to Jerome. Later, Crawford discovered the fraud. Crawford instructed his lawyer to try to stop payment. Jerome indorsed the cashier's check and delivered it to Kutner Buick. Kutner Buick deposited the check into its bank account. Jerome then filed for bankruptcy. Crawford's bank was caught in a legal bind. The bank was obliged to pay a cashier's check, but it could not disobey the judicial restraining order that prohibited payment. The bank did not pay the check. Who should be entitled to the proceeds of this check and why? [*Bankers Trust Company of Western New York v. Crawford*, 781 F.2d 39 (1986)]

12–7 Check Money Mart Check Cashing Center, Inc., cashed a paycheck for an employee of Epicycle Corp. Epicycle had placed a stop payment on this check because of claims it had against the employee. Was Money Mart required to verify the check's validity before cashing it? Explain. [*Money Mart Check Cashing Center, Inc. v. Epicycle Corp.*, 667 P.2d 1372 (Colo. 1983)]

12–8 Repossession Wade purchased an automobile that was financed by Ford Motor Credit Co. Wade fell behind in her monthly payments. The vehicle was repossessed from Wade's driveway at 2 A.M. by a Ford Motor Credit agent. Wade testified that she heard a car burning rubber, looked outside, and saw that her vehicle was missing. No other confrontation occurred. Wade claims that this repossession was a breach of the peace and was wrongful. She sought damages from Ford Motor Credit, whereas Ford Motor Credit sought $2,900 as a deficiency. Was this repossession wrongful? Was Ford Motor Credit entitled to a deficiency judgment? [*Wade v. Ford Motor Credit Co.*, 8 Kan. App. 2d 737, 668 P.2d 183 (1983)]

12–9 Risk Trans World Airlines, Inc. (TWA), entered into a sale and lease-back agreement with Connecticut National Bank (CNB). TWA sold ten aircraft to CNB for $312 million and then leased them back. The transaction's purpose serves to increase cash flow. In the contract, TWA agreed to pay back $100 million on January 31, 1991. The Persian Gulf conflict in early 1991, however, resulted in decreased air travel and increased oil prices. This curtailed TWA's cash flow, rendering TWA unable to pay the $100 million on January 31. CNB filed a lawsuit for the return of the aircraft. TWA argued that CNB should not repossess the aircraft because the Persian Gulf conflict was an intervening cause excusing TWA from its agreed performance. Who should prevail, and why? [*Connecticut National Bank v. Trans World Airlines, Inc.*, 762 F. Supp. 76 (S.D.N.Y. 1991)]

12–10 Internet Article 9 of the UCC is under review with the possibility of revision. As a businessperson, you would like to comment on a particular section that is being revised. Go to <http://www.law.upenn.edu/bll/>, which is the Biddle Law Library, University of Pennsylvania Law School's web site. Scroll down to "NCCUSL" (National Conference of Commissioners on Uniform State Laws) and click. Find a section in Article 9 that is under consideration for revision. Analyze the proposed changes and write a paragraph comparing the old section with the proposed new section.

The manufacturer who waits in the woods for the world to beat a path to his door is a great optimist. But the manufacturer who shows his "mousetraps" to the world keeps the smoke coming out of his chimney.

O. B. Winters, 1892–1940
American advertising man

Outline

Ethical Consideration

Monitoring Conditions of Foreign Employees

As the president of a large clothing manufacturer, you recently returned from visiting several suppliers in Asia. Some of the suppliers treated their workers well. Others, however, took unfair advantage of their employees based on your ethical standards.

In some locations, you saw young children and pregnant women performing strenuous work. These workers are paid much less than workers in the United States. Often, they are paid below the minimum wage set in their own countries. Their work generates a substandard living wage. Work hours range from twelve to fifteen hours day, seven days a week. Employers lock the workplace doors during working hours, so that if a fire were to break out, the workers would be trapped inside. The plants were filthy and inadequately ventilated. The smell of strong dyes and other pungent odors permeated the air.

You discuss the situation with upper-level management at your firm. Some of the managers agree that the conditions are terrible. They argue that the company needs to monitor the suppliers more closely. The company, however, needs to keep the product cost down to remain competitive in the global marketplace. Other managers argue that each nation must develop its own standards for employment protection, minimum wage, and child labor laws.

Should you try to monitor the working conditions of your suppliers or simply look for the cheapest manufacturing costs for your products? Use the ethical model presented in Chapter 2 and reprinted on the inside front cover to develop your answer.

Introduction

Since World War II, businesses have become increasingly multinational. Commonly, U.S. businesses have investments or manufacturing plants in various foreign countries and foreign countries have operations in the United States. Because the exchange of goods, services, and ideas on a global level is common, the business-person must have some familiarity with the laws pertaining to international business transactions.

International law consists of a body of laws that legally bind otherwise independent nations. No sovereign nation can be compelled against its will to obey an external law. Nations, however, can and do voluntarily agree to be governed in certain respects by international law to facilitate international trade and commerce. A nation's laws fundamentally control the relationship between its international business activities (conducted within its borders or conducted by the nation's businesses outside its borders) and the nation's international agreements.

This chapter explores the sources of the international business laws, the sources of the U.S. international business laws, the agencies responsible for implementing these laws, the statutes affecting international businesses, and international business transactions. The International Considerations sections at the end of each chapter (except this one) provide further information.

Sources of International Law

International, regional, and national laws regulate businesses engaged in international commerce. International law has evolved in three ways: through international customs, through agreements that have the force of law, and through international organizations and conferences. Agreements are developed either by the nations themselves gathering together or by international agencies to which various nations belong.

International Customs

International customs have evolved among nations in response to their relations with one another. The United Nations International Court of Justice defines international custom (customary law) as "evidence of a general practice accepted as law." Customary law serves as an independent form of law. This definition's application, however, is subject to challenge on a case-by-case basis. The courts must decide, for example, when a particular custom has evolved into a general practice that constitutes a law.

Agreements

Instruments used to bring about an international agreement include a *treaty* or *compact*, a *convention*, a *protocol*, or an *executive agreement*. A **treaty**, or **compact**, is a written international agreement between two or more nations, governed by international law and authorized by each nation's supreme power.

When a country is a party to multiple treaties, conflicts may arise. Under the auspices of the United Nations, the **Vienna Convention on the Law of Treaties**[1] was adopted in 1969 and became legally enforceable in 1980. The entire body of the law of treaties is codified by this convention. It covers issues such as the legal difference between treaties and other types of agreements, constitutional limitations on treaty-making powers, terminology, legal designation of parties, and general rules that apply to interpreting treaties.

A **convention** is a code adopted by an international organization, such as the United Nations. The organization circulates the draft convention (or code) among the organization's members, with the hope that it will be adopted by those members.

A **protocol** is an official agreement, but it does not have the force of a treaty. The document reflects issues on which the diplomats agree.

The last important type of international agreement is the **executive agreement** into which a head of state (the executive) enters on reaching an agreement with another head of state. The creation of an executive agreement is simpler and faster than that of a treaty, which is used for more complicated problems. The U.S. Constitution fails to provide for an executive agreement, but the device has a long history in the diplomatic world.

These various types of international agreements affect international business relationships and cover a multitude of areas, such as *exporting, importing, quotas,* and *tariffs*. **Exporting** is the selling of goods manufactured in, and sent (exported) from, the domestic country to a foreign country. **Importing** is the buying of goods manufactured in a foreign country, which are then brought (imported) into the domestic country.

A **quota** limits the quantity of goods to be imported. For example, the United States at one time had a quota on the number of automobiles that could be imported from Japan. This quota was designed to protect the domestic automobile manufacturers. Other items subject to quotas include silicon chips and high-technology electronic equipment.

A **tariff** is a tax placed on imported goods. No equivalent tax exists for the same type of domestic goods. A tariff generally is assessed on either an *ad valorem* basis or a flat-rate basis. An *ad valorem* tariff is based on a percentage of the value of the imported goods. A flat-rate tariff may be based on a unit, such as a barrel of oil. It also may be based on weight, such as a tariff assessed on each ton of material that is imported, such as steel.

International Organizations

More than 3,100 governmental international organizations exist around the world, of which 300 or more deal with economic matters. These organizations normally form as a result of an international agreement.

The organizations or agreements fall into five classifications. First, the United Nations has an array of organizations, the duties of which range from keeping the peace to addressing health concerns. The United Nations operates out of three locations. It is headquartered in New York City; the UN International Court of Justice is located at The Hague in the Netherlands; and the UN European office and several specialized agencies operate out of Geneva, Switzerland.

The second type of organization or agreement includes economic organizations or agreements, such as the World Bank,[2] the International Monetary Fund (IMF),[3] the General Agreement on Tariffs and Trade (GATT), and the Organization for Economic Co-operation and Development (OECD).[4] Third are the regional organizations, such as the European Union (EU),[5] the Association of Southeast Asian Nations (ASEAN),[6] the Andean Common Market (ANCOM),[7]

---

[1] All of the entire provisions of the Vienna Convention on the Law of Treaties are available at <http://www.ifs.univie.ac.at/intlaw/konterm/vrkon_en/html/doku/treaties.htm#1.0>.

[2] The World Bank is found at <http://www.worldbank.org/>.
[3] The International Monetary Fund can be found at <http://www.imf.org/>.
[4] The OECD's home page is <http://www.oecd.org/>.
[5] The fifteen member states of the European Union are Austria, Belgium, Denmark, Finland, France, Germany, Greece, Ireland, Italy, Luxembourg, the Netherlands, Portugal, Spain, Sweden, and the United Kingdom. The home page for the EU is <http://europa.eu.int>.
[6] The six member states of ASEAN are Brunei, Indonesia, Malaysia, Republic of the Philippines, Singapore, and Thailand. Some information about ASEAN is available through the International Monetary Fund at <http://www.imf.org/external/np/sec/decdo/asean.htm>.
[7] The five member states of ANCOM are Bolivia, Colombia, Ecuador, Peru, and Venezuela.

the Gulf Cooperation Council,[8] and the Asian-Pacific Economic Cooperation forum (APEC).[9]

Fourth, specialized commodity agreements exist for products like jute, sugar, or cotton. Fifth, specialty agreements and organizations exist that are very narrow in scope, such as the World Intellectual Property Organization, which deals with copyright and patent issues or the American-Mexican Boundary Treaty Act of 1972.

World Trade Organization

After World War II, the United States and other nations recognized the need to avoid the economic mistakes that followed World War I and helped to fuel World War II. Having fought two world wars within a forty-year period, the nations were determined to prevent another war and to build relationships.

Negotiations among these nations started in 1947 and led to the **General Agreement on Tariffs and Trade (GATT)**, originally signed in 1948. The eighth and latest GATT agreement, called the Uruguay Round,[10] was ratified by the United States in 1995. The Uruguay Round created the **World Trade Organization (WTO)**.[11] This organization replaced the old small GATT organization and the agreements reached under the WTO have replaced the GATT agreements.

The WTO has three purposes: (1) to help trade flow as freely as possible by removing trade barriers and making the rules transparent and predictable, (2) to serve as a forum for trade negotiations, and (3) to administer the dispute-resolution system. The WTO is an international organization that administers the GATT.

The People's Republic of China (China) and the Russian Federation are the only nations with major economies that have not joined the WTO. Both have started the process of joining.

The agreements reached under the WTO cover goods and, for the first time, also services (such as banking and insurance) and intellectual property (such as copyrights and patents). The WTO administers all of these agreements. The WTO facilitates the implementation of trade agreements by requiring full participation of all its member countries in one new trading system and by providing a permanent forum to discuss new issues facing the international trading system. The WTO system is available only to countries that (1) are contracting parties to GATT, (2) agree to adhere to the Uruguay Round agreements, and (3) submit schedules of market access commitments for industrial goods and services.

With the complicated trade agreements, disputes will arise. Under the WTO, disagreements are heard by the Dispute Settlement Body. After its decision is rendered, appeals may be made. Members must comply with its findings and rulings. The Dispute Settlement Body follows a strict timetable to prevent case backlog.

When trading with other member states, each country must abide by two nondiscrimination principles: *normal trade relations* and *national treatment*. **Normal trade relations (NTR)**[12] means equal treatment with the other countries granted NTR status, not favorable treatment. The importing country must handle imported goods from another nation the same as those from other NTR countries. The U.S. has granted China what is called Permanent Normal Trading Relations (PNTR), which means that although China is not a member of the WTO, China is treated by the U.S. for trading purposes as if it were a member.

National treatment means that the importing country must treat foreign goods just as it treats domestic goods; that is, once the imported goods clear customs, they become part of the domestic commerce. For example, dresses made in Mexico and imported into the United States must be treated the same as dresses made in the United States. No additional taxes may be attached because the dresses are made in another

---

[8] The six member states of the Gulf Cooperation Council are Bahrain, Kuwait, Oman, Qatar, Saudi Arabia, and the United Arab Emirates.
[9] The eighteen member states of APEC are Australia; Brunei Darussalam; Canada; Chile; People's Republic of China; Hong Kong, China; Indonesia; Japan; Republic of Korea (South Korea); Malaysia; Mexico; New Zealand; Papua New Guinea; Republic of the Philippines; Singapore; Chinese Taipei (Taiwan); Thailand; and the United States. The home page for APEC is <http://www.apecsec.org.sg/>.
[10] Since 1947, eight rounds have been completed. Rounds are named after the place where the talks started, this latest time in Uruguay. Negotiations lasted from 1986 to 1993. Between 1995 and 1996, 124 countries had signed the Uruguay Round.
[11] The home page for the World Trade Organization is <http://www.wto.org/>.

[12] For policy reasons, the WTO, followed by the U.S. Department of State, in 1998 changed the terminology from most-favored-nation status to normal trade relations.

country. GATT requires that if one nation grants a trade advantage to another country, it must grant that advantage to all other GATT members.

Occasionally, Congress passes a federal statute that directly opposes a foreign trade agreement that Congress has previously ratified. The courts must decide which act has priority. In most cases, the judicial system leaves it to Congress to determine which law should have priority. Problems also may arise when a treaty provision conflicts with state law. The following case confronts this issue.

Case 13.1

Brandt v. American Airlines

United States District Court,
N.D. California, 2000
2000 WL 288393

BACKGROUND AND FACTS According to the complaint, Brandt, the plaintiff, had a medical condition, myasthenia gravis, that causes unusual muscle weakness and slow movement. To treat the condition, Brandt takes medication, Mestonin, which must be consumed with food to reduce the medication's side effects. A common side effect of Mestonin is leg cramps.

Brandt purchased from American Airlines a round-trip ticket from San Francisco, to Winnipeg, Canada. The return flight took plaintiff on a longer path, starting in Winnipeg, to Calgary, Canada, to Dallas-Fort Worth, and finally back to San Francisco. Brandt boarded his flight from Winnipeg to Calgary at 10:30 A.M. (Central Time). At approximately 8 P.M. that same day, Brandt boarded American's Flight 1911 at the Dallas-Fort Worth Airport, the final connection of the trip.

Brandt occupied an aisle seat so that he could periodically stretch his legs to reduce cramping. Shortly after boarding, he called flight attendant Chambers to his seat. Explaining his medical condition and the need to have food with his medication, he stated that it was time for him to take his medicine and asked Chambers for a snack. Chambers stated that no food was available to coach passengers. After a period of time, plaintiff again requested food from defendant Chambers and was again denied.

As more time passed and the plane's departure appeared delayed, Brandt asked Chambers if he, Brandt, could temporarily deplane to purchase a snack with which to take his medication. Chambers denied this request even though the plane was still at the gate and plaintiff saw flight crew "and others" exiting and entering the plane. Shortly thereafter, Brandt went to the back of the plane and observed the flight crew eating prepared meals. Brandt asked if he could have some food, but Chambers replied that the meals were exclusively for the flight crew.

At approximately 9:30 P.M., the plane was still at the gate. Brandt stood up in the aisle next to his seat to stretch his legs and relieve some cramping. At about the same time, a passenger in the rear of the plane had struck his head on a television monitor and was being treated and prepared for deplaning. Chambers approached Brandt from the rear of the aircraft and Brandt requested an approximate departure time. According to the complaint, Chambers yelled back at Brandt to clear the aisle for a medical emergency and pushed him down into his seat as he was positioning himself to sit down. A few minutes later, Brandt observed a passenger "in no apparent distress" leave the plane carrying luggage.

Shortly thereafter, Chambers returned to Brandt's seat and "resumed shouting at him in an extremely agitated, out-of-control fashion," alleging that Brandt "had gotten in his way and had not obeyed his orders." A short time later, the pilot, Steve Clyatt (Clyatt), approached Brandt and, according to the complaint, began shouting at Brandt accusing him of causing trouble and not obeying the flight attendants' orders. Clyatt stated that if Brandt did not get off the plane immediately, Clyatt would have the police arrest Brandt for the federal crime of refusing to obey the flight attendants.

A few minutes later, Customer Service Manager Kathy Johnson boarded the plane. She spoke first with Clyatt, then with Brandt who explained his medical condition and need to eat food with his medication. The complaint alleges that other passengers sitting near Brandt informed Ms. Johnson that Brandt had done nothing wrong.

Brandt prepared to deplane "in order to avoid being arrested." As Brandt walked down the aisle toward the door, American Airlines made an announcement over the public address system that the "passengers who had caused the delay were now getting off," prompting several first class passengers to "sneer and hiss" at him.

Customer Service Representative Johnson and Passenger Service Manager Thomas Brown escorted Brandt into the terminal and apologized, saying that the incident was all a big mistake. Brandt was placed on a later flight to San Francisco, where, after explaining his medical condition, Brandt was given crackers and a glass of milk so that he could take his medicine. The flight arrived in San Francisco.

The complaint alleged ten state tort causes of action, as well as claims under the Air Carrier Access Act (ACAA). Thereafter defendants moved for judgment on the pleadings based on the Warsaw Convention.

ILLSTON, J.

. . . .

The Warsaw Convention (the "Convention") is a comprehensive international treaty governing the liability in "all international transportation of persons, baggage, or goods." . . . Articles 20 and 22 cap a carrier's liability at $75,000 per passenger and preclude all liability if the carrier has taken the measures, necessary or possible, to avoid the damage. . . . Article 25, on which plaintiffs base much of their argument, withholds the limited liability protections of Articles 20 and 22 from carriers who act "with intent to cause damage or recklessly and with knowledge that damage would probably result." Several of these basic and interdependent provisions are integral to the resolution of the case at hand.

A. Preemption of Claims Based On "Local" Law

Defendant asserts that plaintiffs' federal ACAA and state law claims are preempted by the Convention and, therefore, must be dismissed. Plaintiffs appear to concede that the Convention preempts these claims. Nonetheless, plaintiffs argue that because they have alleged that their claims arose from defendant's "wilful misconduct," under Article 25 of the Convention plaintiffs are permitted to bring claims based on state and federal law.

1. Preemption

In *El Al Israel Airlines v. Tseng*, . . . the Supreme Court addressed the issue of whether plaintiffs may bring state law claims when those claims are also covered by the Convention. The Court found that amended Article 24 was "clear" in its statement of "the Convention's preemptive effect." The Convention "precludes passengers from bringing actions under local law," even when they are unable to establish liability under the Convention . . . (holding that "Convention precludes a passenger from maintaining an action for personal injury damages under local law [even] when her claim does not satisfy the conditions for liability under the Convention"). The Court expressly decided that "[g]iven the Convention's comprehensive scheme of liability rules and its textual emphasis on uniformity, we would be hard put to conclude that the delegates at Warsaw meant to subject air carriers to the distinct, nonuniform liability rules of the individual signatory nations." Accordingly, if plaintiffs' claims are governed by the Convention, they may not also bring state law claims based upon the same allegations.

. . . .

. . . [T]he United States maintains a strong policy interest in favor of protecting persons within its borders from discriminatory treatment. However, the United States Supreme Court has recognized that the Convention's primary purpose was to secure "uniformity of rules governing claims arising from international air transportation." Allowing air carrier exposure to discrimination claims which do not conform to the requirements of the Convention would undercut the signatory nations' desire for uniformity and "the Convention's comprehensive scheme of liability," subjecting them to "unlimited liability under diverse legal regimes." Accordingly, the Court concludes that plaintiffs' ACAA cause of action is also preempted by the Convention.

2. Article 25's Effect on Limited Liability

Plaintiffs' primary argument is that, under the terms of Article 25 of the Convention, plaintiffs may base their claims solely on local law because they have alleged "wilful misconduct" by defendant American. After examining the language of the Convention, available authority, as well as recent amendments to the Convention, this Court finds that Article 25 does not entitle plaintiffs to base their claims on local state or federal law.

To show that an air carrier is liable for personal injuries under the Convention, a plaintiff must show that there was a physical injury caused by an "accident." . . .

. . . .

The Court therefore concludes that Article 25 does not give a plaintiff engaged in international travel at the time of the alleged injury an independent cause of action under local law when wilful misconduct is alleged.

. . . .

This interpretation is consistent with the Supreme Court's January 12, 1999, decision in *El Al Israel Airlines v. Tseng.* . . . In *Tseng*, the Court addressed an issue it had twice reserved in the past: the exclusivity of the Convention's cause of action for personal injury. The Court held that Article 24's limitation on the type of claim a passenger may bring under the Convention similarly restricts the ability of a plaintiff to bring a claim under local law. Should a plaintiff be unable to meet the Convention's personal injury claim requirements, the plaintiff is nonetheless precluded from filing suit based on local law; the Convention provides the sole cause of action and remedy.

DECISION AND REMEDY All claims that arise during international travel are preempted by the Warsaw Convention, which limits both the right to institute actions and the amount of recovery. A physical injury must occur and the total amount of recovery is limited to $75,000. If this case involved a fight within the United States, the result would have been different.

CRITICAL THINKING: POLITICAL ISSUE Why should there be different legal rights when you fly internationally versus flying within the United States?

Although this case did not involve any provision of the WTO agreements on goods, services, or intellectual property, the principle applied in the case would be valid in a similar disagreement. When an international agreement has preempted a particular area, no local government can adopt laws to the contrary.

U.S. Agencies Concerned with International Business

This section discusses the U.S. governmental agencies' regulation of international law. Let's look first to federal authority concerned with international law.

Federal Lawmaking Authority

The Constitution divides the lawmaking authority concerning international relations between the Congress and the president. Article I, Section 8, grants Congress the power "[t]o regulate Commerce with foreign Nations, and among the several States." During the past two centuries, the Supreme Court has reaffirmed Congress's authority to establish economic policy and to impose and collect taxes and duties.

Article I, Section 9, however, specifically forbids export taxes. Article II, Section 2, grants the constitutional right to make treaties to the president. The Senate, however, must ratify treaties by a two-thirds vote. During the last century, the president has predominantly dealt with international affairs.

Agencies Regulating International Trade

Four federal agencies and one special court handle trade policy and trade disputes.

Office of the U.S. Trade Representative.
Established in 1963, the **U.S. Trade Representative (USTR)**[13] is a cabinet-level official with the rank of ambassador, directly responsible to the president.

The formulation of trade policy for the United States starts in the office of the USTR, which is also responsible for all bilateral and multilateral trade negotiations. The USTR is the chief representative of the United States in all activities concerning GATT.

U.S. Customs Service.
The **U.S. Customs Service**,[14] established in 1789, is housed in the Department of the Treasury. The customs service assesses and collects customs duties, excise taxes, fees, and penalties owed on imported merchandise.[15] It detects and apprehends persons engaged in fraudulent practices designed to circumvent customs.

The customs service also enforces copyright, patent, trademark, and maskwork[16] provisions; quotas; and marking requirements for imported merchandise. It collects international trade statistics and cooperates with customs services in other countries.

International Trade Administration.
The **International Trade Administration (ITA)**[17] is part of the Department of Commerce (DOC). Created in 1980 by the secretary of commerce, the ITA promotes world trade and strengthens the international trade and investment position of the United States.

The ITA supports the trade policy negotiation efforts of the U.S. Trade Representative. It also promotes export trading companies and issues them certificates that provide limited exemptions from liability under the antitrust laws. These certificates are discussed later in the chapter.

International Trade Commission.
The **International Trade Commission (ITC)**[18] is an independent agency created in 1916. The ITC imposes tariff adjustments and import quotas for industries. It can authorize monetary assistance to workers and firms in industries adversely affected by imports.

The ITC has broad investigatory powers concerning (1) the volume of importation in comparison with domestic production and consumption; (2) the conditions, causes, and effects relating to competition of foreign industries with those of the United States; and (3) all other factors affecting competition between domestically produced and imported articles. The commission advises the president as to the probable economic effect on the domestic industry of any proposed trade agreement involving the increase, reduction, or elimination of a tariff.

[13] You can find more information about the U.S. trade representative at <http://www.ustr.gov/>.
[14] For more information about the U.S. Customs Service, see <http://www.customs.ustreas.gov/>.
[15] Duties of the U.S. Customs Service are found at <http://www.law.cornell.edu/uscode/19/>.
[16] Maskwork is discussed in more detail in Chapter 16. A maskwork is a series of related images, fixed or encoded, in a three-dimensional pattern on a computer chip.
[17] Information about the ITA may be found at <http://www.ita.doc.gov/>.
[18] A large amount of information about the ITC is available at <http://www.usitc.gov/>.

LEGAL HIGHLIGHT

NAFTA and the Free Trade Association of the Americas

Two important trade agreements in the Western Hemisphere are the North American Free Trade Agreement (NAFTA)[a] and the Free Trade Association of the Americas.

NAFTA

Created in 1993, the North American Free Trade Agreement joined the United States, Canada, and Mexico to form a free trade area. Canada is the largest trading partner of the United States, and Mexico ranks third. (Japan is second.) The agreement among the three countries involves 363 million people and $6.3 trillion in combined gross domestic product.

NAFTA's purpose is to eliminate trade barriers and to facilitate the cross-border movement of goods and services among the three countries. Customs administration within each country's jurisdiction will continue. Goods imported into the three countries must comply with each country's laws and regulations.

The section in NAFTA concerning trade between the United States and Mexico abolishes tariffs in stages. Over one-half of the tariff barriers were phased out in 1994. Textiles made from North American fabric or yarn currently are exempt from tariffs. Other duty-free items include manual typewriters, dry-cleaning equipment, elevators, and Christmas trees. In 1999, tariffs on items including plums, electric typewriters, malt liquor, two-door refrigerators, and station wagons were removed. At the ten-year point, apples, blenders, refrigerators, and new cars will be tariff-free. U.S. automobile manufacturers will no longer maintain new car production facilities in Mexico to sell in country. Finally, by 2009 tariffs on politically sensitive items will be the last to be eliminated. Examples of these are corn, peanuts, sugar, orange juice, powdered milk, tuna, and used cars.

In 1998, all United States–Canada trade became duty free. The United States–Canada Free-Trade Agreement of 1988 already had reduced the tariffs between these two countries. NAFTA superseded the 1988 agreement.

[a] All of the provisions of NAFTA can be obtained at <http://www.sice.oas.org/trade/nafta/naftatce.asp>.

NAFTA created the North American Made rules of origin to prevent non-NAFTA countries from funneling their goods into the U.S. market and from gaining access to the duty-free area. For example, toys imported from India into Mexico cannot be sent to the United States duty free under NAFTA, because a country outside of the duty-free area would benefit from entering the U.S. market duty free. Goods, in this case toys, made with materials or labor from outside the region, however, can qualify for NAFTA treatment if the goods undergo substantial transformation within NAFTA jurisdiction.

The three official languages of the NAFTA countries are English, French, and Spanish. For a product to be sold in the other two countries, its label must be in the language of the buyer country. Many companies print information in all three languages right on the item. Other manufacturers label the item in the appropriate language.

Prior to NAFTA, foreign ownership of financial services was either prohibited or severely restricted depending on the country. As a result of NAFTA, U.S., Canadian, and Mexican banks and securities firms can have 100 percent foreign ownership by firms from another NAFTA country. Firms may acquire 100 percent ownership in Mexican insurance companies. Investors from the three countries must be legally treated the same within each country.

Under NAFTA, U.S. trucking companies have been able to carry international cargo to the Mexican states contiguous to the United States since 1995 and has been able to service all of Mexico since 1999. U.S. companies will be able to buy Mexican trucking firms by 2003. Border crossing by commercial truck traffic has increased so much that new customs facilities are being built by the NAFTA countries to help expedite trade among them.

Before NAFTA, a traveller needed to purchase three tickets to travel through the three NAFTA countries, Canada to the United States, the United States to Mexico, and then within Mexico. Bus passengers now can purchase one ticket to travel from Canada to Mexico and vice versa. The passengers, however, still need to pass through customs and immigration checkpoints.

The U.S. and Mexican governments each invested $225 million in the new North American Development Bank. With these funds, the bank can borrow up to $3 billion from other sources to lend aid to communities hurt by NAFTA.

Two side agreements to NAFTA cover environmental standards and workers' rights. The Commission for Environmental Cooperation (CEC)[b] is located in Montréal (Québec), Canada. The CEC facilitates cooperation and public participation to foster conservation, protection, and enhancement of the North American environment. The U.S.-Mexico Border Environmental Commission is authorized to spend up to $8 billion from the North American Development Bank, the World Bank, and the Inter-American Development Bank on various environmental cleanup projects. Environmental problems include air and water pollution and contaminated soil. NAFTA can impose fines or trade sanctions when a country fails to enforce its own environmental laws.

The North American Agreement on Labor Cooperation[c] authorized the establishment of the Commission for Labor Cooperation to investigate plant closures and labor abuses. NAFTA can authorize fines or trade sanctions if a country fails to enforce its

worker safety standards, child labor rules, or minimum wage laws.

Free Trade Association of the Americas

The Free Trade Association of the Americas (FTAA)[d] has a long-term goal to unite all the countries of North America and Latin America into one free trade area, eliminating all tariffs. Originally, the FTAA planners outlined a twenty- to thirty-year time frame with unification by the year 2030. The time length was shortened considerably after President William J. Clinton (1993–2001) sent emissaries to Latin America in late 1994 to ask each leader what the United States could do that would be most beneficial to their country. One word summed up their collective thoughts: trade.

The Summit of the Americas was planned and held less than six weeks later, in December 1994, in Miami, Florida. For the first time in modern history, the leaders of both North and Latin American countries are marching to the same economic and political tune—open markets and democracy. The single common goal is to create by 2005 a thirty-four member Free Trade Association of the Americas that will stretch from the northern reaches of Canada to the southern tip of Chile.

[b] The home page for the Commission on Environmental Cooperation is <http://www.cec.org/>.
[c] Find the Northern American Agreement on Labor Cooperation at <http://www.naalc.org/>.

[d] The home page for the Free Trade Association of the Americas is <http://www.ftaa-alca.org/>. You can also find information through the Organization of American States' web site at <http://www.sice.oas.org/ftaa_e.asp>.

The ITC, upon petition by a harmed group, conducts investigations to determine if the increase in quantity of a particular import comprises or poses the threat of a serious injury to a domestic industry that produces a competitive article. If the commission finds that this situation, called *dumping* (examined later in this chapter, but for now it means selling below price), exists, it recommends to the president an action to redress the injury.

U.S. Court of International Trade. Established in 1890 and formerly known as the United States Tariff Commission, the **Court of International Trade**

(CIT)[19] became a court in 1980. The court has all the powers in law and equity of a federal district court. It reviews agency decisions involving dumping and *countervailing duty* matters.

A **countervailing duty** is an import tax equal to the grant extended to an exporter by its home country to encourage exportation or to assist the exporter in meeting competition. Countervailing duties are intended to eliminate the competitive advantage gained by government subsidization of foreign exporters.

[19] Additional information can be obtained at <http://www.uscit.gov/>.

The CIT hears all civil actions against the United States that arise from laws governing import transactions. This court also holds exclusive jurisdiction over civil actions resulting from import transactions that are commenced by the United States and that seek penalties for alleged fraud or negligence.

Statutes Regulating International Trade

Congress has the constitutional authority to pass legislation concerning international trade. The following subsections explain some of these federal statutes.

Export Administration Act

The **Export Administration Act** restricts the export of goods and technology in the military field when release of these would be detrimental to the United States. The Export Enhancement Act, which amends the Export Administration Act, liberalized the products that can be exported, stiffened penalties for violating the statute, and increased enforcement.

Under Export Administration Act, an exporter must determine if the products being considered for sale can be shipped to the specific country in which the exporter hopes to do business. For example, many exports to Cuba, North Korea, and Iraq are prohibited. If the act permits trade with a specific country, the exporter must determine if a license is required.

Two types of licenses exist: general and validated. The **general license** is really a misnomer. Many goods can be shipped to specific countries without an official license. The general license is more of a general authority to ship than an actual license. The Department of Commerce classifies foreign countries to indicate if goods being exported to a specific country require a general license.

A **validated license** helps the United States to enforce its foreign policy by restricting the sale of goods involved with high technology. This license prohibits certain types of goods from being shipped to countries of concern that may pose a military threat to the United States.[20]

The act authorizes keeping products within the United States when there is a short supply. During the Korean conflict (1950–1953), when copper was in short supply, its export was restricted.

The Export Administration Act controls exports even when the final product is produced outside of the United States. The act's jurisdiction depends on whether the final goods are manufactured either with technical data developed in the United States or with parts originating in the United States. For example, a computer made in South Korea from component parts from the United States, or based on technical information from the United States, must have a validated license when sold by the South Korean company to a buyer in the People's Republic of China. Export laws have extraterritorial applications.

One major problem that exporters face is determining whether their goods will be diverted from one country to another. For example, a U.S. exporter sells a product to Nigeria. Unknown to the exporter, the Nigerian business ships the product to Iraq. An exporter can be held liable if it should have known that the product could be sent to an embargoed area.

The penalties for violating the Export Administration Act are substantial. Fines can equal up to five times the value of the exports or $1 million, whichever is greater, for a willful violation. The businessperson responsible for the violation faces five years in prison, plus a $250,000 fine. The law allows for property forfeitures, civil penalties, and revocation of export license privileges.

The following case illustrates the implementation of this act when the defendant was involved in a diversion of goods to a banned country.

[20] In 2000, the U.S. Department of State replace the term "rogue state" with the term "country of concern." No official list of countries classified as rogue states existed, but it was commonly assumed to include Iran, Iraq, Libya, and North Korea. These states were believed to be sponsoring terrorism or developing nuclear, chemical, or biological weapons.

Case 13.2

United States v. Elkins

United States Court of
Appeal, Eleventh Circuit, 1989
885 F.2d 775

BACKGROUND AND FACTS This prosecution arose out of an investigation into the 1985 shipment of two Lockheed L-100-30 aircraft to Libya, which, at the time, was subject to strict export controls. Export licenses were required for the export of these two jets. Because of government restrictions on trade with Libya, no export licenses would have been granted to export these planes to Libya.

Elkins owned a company called Armaflex, Inc. He negotiated with Lockheed as a representative of Contrust, a West German oil exploration subsidiary controlled by Badir, a Libyan dealer. Lockheed preferred to sell the aircraft to Armaflex rather than to Contrust.

Elkins created a new corporation, AFI International, which represented Contrust in the negotiations. In negotiations with Lockheed, Elkins maintained that the airplanes were destined for the West African country of Benin. When Lockheed learned of Badir's involvement, Lockheed canceled the negotiations.

Elkins assured Lockheed that Badir represented a legitimate West German concern and that Badir was a Libyan expatriate antagonistic to the Libyan government. Based on this information, Lockheed resumed negotiations.

Elkins withheld from Lockheed the fact that the planes were to be modified with a midair refueling capability and were to be used by the Libyan Air Force. Elkins and Lockheed agreed on the sale of two L-100-30 planes and parts to AFI. The contract provided that AFI had the sole responsibility for obtaining a valid export license. Elkins made a net profit of $7 million.

Lockheed officials accompanied Elkins to the Department of Commerce to obtain an export license. The U.S. government officials knew that Contrust was owned by Libyans. Elkins explained that the planes were destined for Benin. At no time did Elkins inform government officials of the planned refueling modification. The Department of Commerce approved the export license. Lockheed delivered the planes to Benin. They were never seen in Benin again. One plane was found in Cairo. The plane's radio signal and operations manual indicated that the plane had been used by the Libyan Air Force.

Elkins, along with several other individuals, was indicted as a result of an investigation. Elkins was convicted of violating export restrictions. He received a fifteen-year prison sentence and was fined $6.6 million. A $100 special assessment also was imposed. Elkins appealed.

Circuit Judge JACKSON

. . . .

An indictment must set forth the elements of the offense in a manner which fairly informs the defendant of the charges against him and enables him to enter a plea which will bar future prosecution for the same offense. In this case, the indictment charged defendant with conspiracy to commit four substantive offenses against the United States. Although the fraud was charged as the object of the substantive offense of wire fraud rather than as the object of the conspiracy, defendant had clear notice that violations of the substantive offenses constituted fraud against the government. Conspiracy to violate the substantive offenses is conspiracy to defraud the government. Reading the indictment as a whole, we conclude that the indictment adequately charged defendant with conspiring to deprive the United States of its ability to control its foreign policy by concealing material facts from responsible government agencies.

We also conclude that the district court adequately charged the jury on conspiracy to defraud the United States. . . .

. . . The district court clarified and repeated this instruction as follows:

What must be proved beyond a reasonable doubt is that the accused planned knowingly and willfully to devise or intending to devise a scheme to defraud the United States of America and its executive agencies out of the right to implement its foreign policy and to conduct its affairs free from stealth, false statement, and fraud and that the use of the interstate wire or foreign wire communications were to be closely related to the scheme.

. . . Conspiracy to commit wire fraud against the United States contains all of the elements of conspiracy to defraud the United States. Conspiracy to commit wire fraud contains the additional element of use of wire transmission services in furtherance of the scheme to defraud.

. . . .

Defendant was sentenced to five years' imprisonment on the conspiracy conviction, and to a consecutive term of ten years' imprisonment and a $6.6 million fine on the export control violation conviction. Defendant also received a special assessment of $50 on each count. Defendant eventually makes one argument that his sentence violated the Eighth Amendment: "Because the harshness of Appellant's sentence far exceeds the sentences imposed in similar export prosecutions in the Northern District of Georgia and elsewhere, Appellant respectfully submits that this Court should conclude that his sentence is unconstitutionally disproportionate." A sentence is disproportionate for Eighth Amendment purposes if the punishment is grossly disproportionate when compared with the nature of the crime. . . .

In a variety of situations, life sentences with the possibility of parole have been held not to violate the Eighth Amendment. These sentences, five years for conspiracy and ten years for violating export control laws, certainly are not grossly excessive compared to the nature of the crime. Additionally, the ten-year sentence imposed for violating export control regulations is not grossly disproportionate to the sentences imposed in other federal jurisdictions for violations of the same federal laws. Defendant unlawfully sold $57 million worth of high technology aircraft equipment to an unfriendly nation. Although his sentence may have been longer than the sentences normally imposed for this offense, that fact alone does not mean it was grossly disproportionate. . . .

Defendant also challenges the fine imposed on count two. There may be circumstances where an excessive fine constitutes cruel and unusual punishment in violation of the Eighth Amendment. We need not identify those circumstances in this case. Defendant made a gross profit of $13,049,474, a net profit of $7,336,233, and an after-tax profit of $3,368,917 from the sale of these aircraft. Defendant's fine of $6.6 million was less than his gross profit and less than his net profit from the sale of these planes. Although a large amount, we hold that a fine representing an amount less than the net profit of an illegal transaction does not violate the Eighth Amendment absent a showing of severe, particularized hardship suffered by defendant.

DECISION AND REMEDY Elkins's conviction for conspiracy against the United States in violation of the Export Administration Act was upheld.

CRITICAL THINKING: MANAGEMENT CONSIDERATION Assume you are in the position of handling exports for your firm like the one involving Lockheed in the above case. Discuss the steps to take to protect your firm from selling products requiring a validated license to a foreign country that is on the list of possible military threats to this country.

Omnibus Trade and Competitiveness Act

In 1988, Congress passed an act to enhance the competitiveness of U.S. exports. The **Omnibus Trade and Competitiveness Act (OTCA)**[21] has four purposes: (1) to authorize the negotiation of reciprocal trade agreements; (2) to strengthen U.S. trade laws; (3) to improve the development and management of U.S. trade strategy; and (4) through these actions, to improve living standards in the world.

Under this act, Congress made it the highest priority to pursue a broad array of domestic and international policies. Congress resolved that maintaining a position of world leadership is in the national interest of the United States. This national policy established the importance of maintaining the vitality of the technological, industrial, and agricultural base of the United States. Working with the president, Congress, through the OTCA, developed a procedure, formerly called the *fast-track authority*, to use when dealing with other governments.

Trade Promotion Authority.
Trade promotion authority (formerly called fast-track authority) means that once the president has signed an agreement with another country or countries, Congress must either approve or disapprove of the agreement as signed. Congress cannot amend it. Article I of the Constitution gives Congress exclusive authority to set tariffs and to enact other legislation concerning international trade. Article II of the Constitution gives the president exclusive authority to negotiate international agreements. If the president negotiates a trade agreement that requires changes in U.S. tariffs or in other domestic laws, the trade agreement must be submitted to Congress for approval.

If trade promotion authority is not authorized, Congress can take one of four actions. First, Congress can approve the agreement with no amendments. Second, Congress can reject the agreement. Third, and the most common action, Congress can amend the negotiated agreement and then vote on its approval. Finally, Congress can take no action, and the president would abide by the agreement without formal approval from Congress. This last action allows the president to engage in politically sensitive agreements, such as arms control agreements. Congress does not want to formally approve the agreement, but its inaction frees the president to follow the agreement's terms.

In the past, the president would enter into a negotiated trade agreement with a foreign government and then send the agreement to Congress for approval. If approved, Congress would return the bill to the president for a signature. The trade agreement then was binding on the United States, although it did not become part of the domestic statutes.

Occasionally, the president was politically embarrassed when he made a trade agreement and then Congress either adopted the agreement with amendments or refused to adopt it. Foreign nations viewed the need for Congress's approval as "two shakes of the dice." When Congress failed to approve an agreement and passed amendments, the president was forced to reopen negotiations. Foreign countries took a dim view of this process because the original commitment was not honored. To remedy this problem, Congress enacted the former fast-track procedures for adopting trade agreements.

Congress first created fast-track authority in the **Trade Act** of 1974, which adopted the Tokyo Round of the General Agreement on Trade and Tariffs. Congress renewed fast-track authority in 1979, 1984, 1988, 1991, and 1993. With the various renewals, presidents have had fast-track negotiating authority continuously from January 1975 to April 1994 with only a brief lapse for eight months in 1988. Currently, fast-track authority has lapsed and Congress is debating as to whether to renew it as trade promotion authority.

Fast-track authority had three features. First, the president must consult extensively and coordinate with Congress throughout the negotiating process. Second, the president must notify Congress of his or her intention to negotiate and sign a trade agreement. Public notice of the anticipated trade agreement is published

---

[21] For more information see <http://av.yahoo.com/bin/query? p=omnibus+trade+and+competitiveness+act&b=41&hc=0&hs=0>.

LEGAL HIGHLIGHT

What Is a BEM?

BEM stands for Big Emerging Market. These markets are Argentina, Brazil, India, Indonesia, Mexico, the People's Republic of China, Poland, South Africa, South Korea, Taiwan, and Turkey.

These countries are expected to account for more than 44 percent of total global imports during the next twenty years, surpassing even Japan and Europe. In the next two decades, almost three-quarters of all global imports are expected to come from the BEMs and other developing countries, which will account for 26 percent. Keep your eyes on the BEMs for future growth.

---

in the *Federal Register.* Finally, Congress approves or rejects the agreement with no amendments. If the trade agreement is approved, it becomes law.

This authority provided the president with credibility to negotiate trade agreements while Congress retains its central role before, during, and after negotiations. This procedure reassures foreign governments that the president can deliver on promises made.

Both the North American Free Trade Agreement (NAFTA), which established a free trade zone among Canada, Mexico, and the United States, and the Uruguay Round of GATT were negotiated on the fast-track procedure. Each house of Congress could debate the merits of ratifying NAFTA and GATT, but no member of Congress could amend the legislation. Congress approved both NAFTA and GATT as ordinary bills of legislation, not as treaties, although this point is in litigation.

Two WTO agreements have fostered free trade. The 1997 Information Technology Agreement eliminated $600 billion in tariffs on 95 percent of the world's production of computers, telecommunications equipment, and semiconductors. The 1997 Basic Telecommunications Act opened up competition in the communications sector, ranging from satellites to submarine cables.

Export Trading Company Act

The **Export Trading Company Act** of 1982 resulted from legal difficulties arising from violations of antitrust laws by companies conducting business internationally. The act allows a business to file an application for a certificate of antitrust immunity with the International Trade Administration.

The application contains information based on the company's business plans. Once the administration grants the certificate, and as long as the company follows its business plan, the company is immune from antitrust prosecution by the Department of Justice.

Export-Import Bank

The **Export-Import Bank (Eximbank)**[22] provides financial assistance to exporting and importing firms. The primary type of assistance offered consists of the credit guarantees that Eximbank provides to commercial banks. Based on those guarantees, the commercial banks, in turn, make direct loans to exporting companies.

National Export Strategy

The **National Export Strategy** is an expanded and streamlined program to promote U.S. exports by the federal government. The strategy focuses on one central goal: to create a more efficient, effective, and customer-focused set of export promotion and export financing programs. The dynamic global marketplace has more than four billion customers. This market opportunity represents a challenge for U.S. firms able and willing to compete.

The four key elements of the National Export Strategy are the streamlining of programs, leveraging of resources, national allocation of resources, and removal of obstacles. To better assist businesses, the Department of Commerce (DOC) streamlined its export programs by combining its export promotion and trade finance specialists into a one-stop shop concept. The one-stop shop specifically refers to the Export Assistance Cen-

---

[22] The Export-Import Bank web page is <http://www.exim.gov/>. The statute establishing the bank is found at <http://www4law.cornell.edu/uscode/12/ch6A.html>.

ters,[23] a number of which have set up in various cities. Prior to the creation of the one-stop shop, an export or import business had to make its way through a myriad of government agencies to gather information, permits, or other necessary government documents before conducting business.

The DOC also is leveraging its key resources by establishing a national network of private-sector intermediaries to provide company-specific resources for small- and medium-sized businesses to ensure their long-term success. Government trade events are oriented toward firms preparing to export. In the future, government support will be withdrawn and these trade events will be privatized.

To allocate government resources rationally, the National Export Strategy developed an effective interagency process to aid businesses. For example, the Department of Commerce, the Department of Energy, and the Environmental Protection Agency have formed an interagency group to review strategies to boost environmental exports.

The last element of the National Export Strategy is to remove obstacles. The DOC identifies government regulations and other barriers to exporting. The DOC helps to remove identified barriers through reform or by suggesting legislation to Congress. Since 1994, the government's licensing and decision-making processes have removed most of the exporting obstacles. The National Export Strategy is helping to make the United States a global leader in exports for the twenty-first century.

Unfair Import Practices

Several unfair import practices can occur. The following subsections examine four types of unfair practices: (1) dumping; (2) infringement of copyright, trademark, and patent laws; (3) government financing of products, called subsidizing; and (4) the sale of gray-market goods.

Dumping

Dumping is the practice of selling goods in the buyer's country below the price charged for them in the seller's country. Its purpose is to drive out competition in the buyer's country. When material injury is sustained by a domestic industry, WTO allows additional duties to be added to equal the price discrepancy.

The **Trade Agreement Act** of 1979, based on the GATT Antidumping Code, regulates dumping in the United States. The International Trade Administration protects domestic industries against economic injury caused by the sale of foreign merchandise at less than fair value in the United States.[24]

The ITA ascertains the types of goods most likely to be sold at less than fair value. If a business believes itself to be injured, it files a complaint with the International Trade Commission. The ITC determines if a threat of material injury or actual material injury to the business exists because the imports are being subsidized or sold at less than fair value. If the ITC finds that dumping has occurred, import duties are assessed against the merchandise. The duties can remain in effect for three to five years after violations of the act have ceased.

Infringement

The ITC likewise is charged with investigating unfair competition methods, including infringement of copyright, patent, trademark, and maskwork laws. For example, a business located in a developing country produces copies of music tapes created by a U.S. recording company that holds the copyright to such works. This copying is done without permission and without paying royalties to the copyright holders. These tapes can be seized by the U.S. Customs Service on request from the ITC.

Subsidies

A third unfair import practice occurs when a government provides subsidies to its local export businesses. Subsidies take different forms, such as low-interest or interest-free loans, rebates on taxes earned from sales to foreign countries, or price guarantees to offset international currency fluctuations.

Any subsidy distorts the true movement of trade in the international community. The ITA is charged with protecting U.S. businesses from foreign businesses that receive subsidies when these subsidies constitute a material injury to an industry. A countervailing duty may

[23] If you would like additional information on the Export Assistance Centers located throughout the country and ways to obtain financing, see <http://av.yahoo.com/bin/query?p=Export+Assistance+Center&hc=0&hs=3&S=G>.

[24] Antidumping regulations are found at <http://ia.ita.doc.gov/newregs.htm>.

LEGAL HIGHLIGHT

APEC

The Asia-Pacific Economic Cooperation forum (APEC) was formed in 1989 as a loose gathering of Pacific Rim countries without a clear goal. By the end of 1994, APEC had become the most powerful economic region in the world. It represented 40 percent of the world's population and a combined gross regional product of about $14 trillion—more than half of the gross world product.

Eighteen countries are now members. APEC's goal was clear: the removal of trade barriers. The three members of NAFTA—Canada, Mexico, and the United States—belong to APEC.

APEC adopted the Bogor Declaration, which calls for the industrialized members of APEC to remove trade barriers by the year 2010. Free and open trade for both developed and developing countries is the goal set for 2020. APEC's trade liberalization efforts will complement and harmonize with those of the World Trade Organization created by GATT.

be imposed when the ITA determines that the exporting country is subsidizing a business.

Gray-Market Goods

The term **gray-market goods** refers to foreign-manufactured goods for which a valid U.S. trademark has been registered. The goods are purchased legally abroad and imported into the United States, but without the consent of the American trademark holder. The term *gray market*, which at times is used unfairly, implies a nefarious undertaking by the importer. A more accurate term for the goods is **parallel import**. This term is devoid of negative connotations. But *gray-market goods*, for better or for worse, has become the commonly accepted term for such goods.

Sometimes a company wants to stop the importation of products. In the following case, although a soap product was manufactured by a wholly owned foreign affiliate, the product was physically different from the American-made soap. The foreign-made products were then imported into the U.S. by an unrelated third party. Although the judge does not use the term *gray market*, the case involves a parallel import of a soap product.

Case 13.3

Lever Brothers Co. v. United States

United States Court of Appeals, District of Columbia Circuit, 1993
981 F.2d 1330

BACKGROUND AND FACTS Lever Brothers Company (Lever), an American company, and its British affiliate, Lever Brothers Limited (Lever UK), both manufacture deodorant soap under the "Shield" trademark and hand dishwashing liquid under the "Sunlight" trademark. The trademarks are registered in each country. The products were formulated differently to suit local tests. The U.S. version lathers more. The two soaps smell different. Unrelated third parties purchased the Lever UK-made Shield and Sunlight soaps and imported these products into the United States.

Numerous complaints about the product were filed by persons who had purchased the Lever UK products, thinking the soaps were the U.S. product. Lever wanted the U.S. Customs Service to stop these imports. Customs refused, because it had a regulation [found in the Code of Federal Regulation and cited in the case as 19 C.F.R. §133.21(c)(2)] that allowed the importation of goods with the same trademark if they were manufactured by a subsidiary company.

Lever Brothers sued the U.S. Customs Service and sought an order from the court to stop the importation of the gray-market goods that were physically different from the U.S. goods. This case does not involve a dispute between corporate affiliates. Neither Lever US nor Lever UK authorized the importation that the third parties conducted.

The district court heard the case. Lever appealed its decision. The court of appeals ruled in the case, called Lever I, and returned it to the district court. The district court found the U.S. Customs Service regulation to be in conflict with a statute, the Lanham Act, and ordered Customs to stop the importation of the Lever UK soaps. Customs appealed this second order to the court of appeals.

Circuit Judge SENTELLE

. . . .

Lever asserts that the unauthorized import of these foreign products has created substantial consumer confusion and deception in the United States about the nature and origin of this merchandise, and that it has received numerous consumer complaints from American consumers who unknowingly bought the British products and were disappointed.

Lever argues that the importation of the British products was in violation of section 42 of the Lanham Act, which provides that with the exception of goods imported for personal use:

> [N]o article of imported merchandise which shall copy or simulate the name of the [sic] any domestic manufacture, or manufacturer . . . or which shall copy or simulate a trademark registered in accordance with the provisions of this chapter . . . shall be admitted to entry at any customhouse of the United States.

. . . The United States Customs Service ("Customs"), however, was allowing importation of the British goods under the "affiliate exception" created by 19 C.F.R. § 133.21(c)(2), which provides that foreign goods bearing United States trademarks are not forbidden when "[t]he foreign and domestic trademark or tradename owners are parent and subsidiary companies or are otherwise subject to common ownership or control."

. . . .

There is a[n] . . . ultimately fatal weakness in Customs' position in this case. Section 42 on its face appears to forbid importation of goods that "copy or simulate" a United States trademark. Customs has the burden of adducing evidence from the legislative history of section 42 and its administrative practice of an exception for materially different goods whose similar foreign and domestic trademarks are owned by affiliated companies. At a minimum, this requires that the specific question be addressed in the legislative history and administrative practice. The bottom line, however, is that the issue of materially different goods was not addressed either in the legislative history or the administrative record. It is not enough to posit that silence implies authorization, when the authorization sought runs counter to the evident meaning of the governing statute. Therefore, we conclude that section 42 of the Lanham Act precludes the application of Customs' affiliate exception with respect to physically, materially different goods.

IV. Conclusion

For the foregoing reasons, we affirm the District Court's ruling that section 42 of the Lanham Act bars the importation of physically different foreign goods bearing a trademark identical to a valid U.S. trademark, regardless of the trademark's genuine character abroad or affiliation between the producing firms. Injunctive relief, however, is limited to the two products which were the subject of this action.

DECISION AND REMEDY The court found that the products were substantially different. Having the same or similar trademark caused consumer confusion. Congress wanted to avoid this. The court found that the U.S. Customs Service regulation conflicted with the Lanham Act, which banned foreign goods that bore a valid U.S. trademark but that were materially and physically different from the U.S. version of the goods. Because Lever Brothers asked that only two products (Shield and Sunlight) be banned from importation, that was all the district court banned.

CRITICAL THINKING: MANAGERIAL CONSIDERATION Discuss how the problem represented by this case could have been handled without going to court.

International Business Transactions

A business can be an exporter, an importer, or both. An exporter sells its goods overseas, whereas an importer buys products made in another country. Conducting business internationally involves a few more steps than does a domestic business transaction. Exporting is more complicated than importing. The following sections discuss some steps involved in developing first an export business, then later, an import business.

Developing an Export Business

Once a business decides to export its products or services, it must develop a master international business plan. Usually, a business devotes far more time and effort to establishing an overseas business within a foreign market than in developing a U.S. market for its products. Top management must make a long-term commitment to develop an export market.

Planned, orderly growth is necessary. In the beginning, a business should target only one or two geographic areas. It may need to modify its products to meet the regulations imposed by the importing country and the cultural preferences of the people who live there. Information concerning sales messages, warranties, and other important information must be printed in the language of the importing country.

The firm needs to establish contacts with government agencies and with businesspeople who are knowledgeable about the export business. These agencies and people include accountants, attorneys, consultants, **customs brokers** (licensed people who conduct customs business on behalf of others), financial institutions and lenders, **freight forwarders** (businesses that arrange the international transportation of goods), import or export companies, insurance agents, marketing and public relations services, translation and cross-cultural services, international organizations, port authorities, telecommunications systems, and government support resources.

Conducting Business. An exporter can conduct business internationally either indirectly or directly. The two indirect ways are by distributorship or by agent. The direct method is a contact between the exporter and the importer with no intermediary. The following sections discuss these three methods.

International Distribution Agreements. One cost-effective way to enter the international market, especially for small to medium-sized firms, is through a distributor. The distributor actually conducts the business overseas. A business must choose an overseas distributor with great care. The complications involved in overseas communications, transportation, and government regulations require the international distributor to act with greater independence than would a domestic counterpart.

The contract with an overseas distributor should be comprehensive and written in the languages of all parties involved. Some of the issues that should be covered include the amount of authority that the agent has, the amount of support that either party will provide, the specific products that are covered and their delivery and service terms, the geographic territory that the distributor will cover, the method of payment, and other essential terms.

LEGAL HIGHLIGHT

European Union and the European Community

What is the difference between the European Union (EU) and the European Community (EC)? Basically the EU is a political union rather than a legal one. Its ultimate objective is European integration by promoting economic and social progress. All nationals of the fifteen Member States are now citizens of the EU, which grants them certain rights, such as human rights protection. The EU is founded on international treaties among sovereign states, rather than on a constitution.

The main feature of the European Community is its community market. The citizens within these countries enjoy various freedoms, such as the free movement of goods, workers, services, capital, and payments. The EC also implements various policies, such as commercial, agricultural, competitive, and environmental policies.

The 1957 Treaty of Rome, which is the foundation treaty for the EU, originally created the former European Economic Community (EEC). In 1991, the Maastricht Agreement[a] (officially the Treaty on European Unity) was signed in Maastricht, the Netherlands. The Maastricht Agreement amends the Treaty of Rome by replacing the EEC with the European Community and by providing the basis for a political, monetary, and economic union.

The Maastricht Agreement created a single market among the fifteen EU countries' 375 million consumers and $7 trillion combined gross domestic product. The EU recognizes ten languages: English, Finnish, Flemish, French, German, Greek, Italian, Portuguese, Spanish, and Swedish.

[a] A complete copy of the Maastricht Agreement is found at <http://europa.eu.int/en/record/mt/top.html>.

Air passenger and cargo services are integrated. Citizens of the member states can travel freely within the EU by air, bus, train, or automobile. A traveler who enters the EU or who is a citizen of the EU does not need a passport and is exempt from customs when traveling within the EU.

International shippers have unified guidelines. Because the border controls have been abolished, millions of tons of cargo now move freely. Any EU air carrier can fly directly to any other EU member country instead of being required to land in each country along the way. The EU railways are integrated and a high-speed rail system throughout the EU is planned. All regulations for maritime traffic are integrated. An imposed 15 percent minimum value-added tax (VAT) frees businesses from overlapping taxation of profits.

The EU has integrated its banking, securities, investment services, and insurance sectors. U.S. businesses can open these services in any EU country, if they meet EU standards. Reciprocal national treatment is required by each of the EU countries. The country in which a business originates is called the home country. A firm may have branches or sell services in the other EU host countries.

Professional services can be offered across borders. The Mutual Recognition of Professional Qualifications for accountants, lawyers, and consultants allows these professionals to practice in other member states.

In the corporate area, however, no uniform decisions have been reached on any rules ranging from disclosure to accounting procedures. No uniformity on minimum wage legislation or layoff restrictions has been agreed on. Although much work lies ahead before the EU really is an integrated union, much has been accomplished during the past forty years.

The government controls over imports and exports need to be established in the contract, as well as any government restrictions that apply to the products. A clause that specifies if arbitration will be used and, if so, the identification of the arbitration provider should be negotiated. A statement should specify if the contract is assignable. The contract needs to state clearly that it is the sole applicable agreement.

The contract ending date needs to be defined, either by setting a date or by setting out the conditions that will terminate the contract. Any other grounds that will end the contract should be stated. The contract should provide the amount of notice that one party needs to provide to the other in order to end the contract, such as a thirty-day notice or a two-week notice. Finally, the contract should state the damages that can be sought, such as liquidated damages, and any limitations on the amount of damages.

International Agent. An **international agent** can help a business find buyers in another country. Unlike a distributor, which actually conducts business, an agent brings the seller (exporter) and the buyer (importer) together. The agent may live and work both inside and outside the United States.

The agent knows the businesspeople in the foreign country, visits the various firms, conducts trade shows, understands the culture, and speaks the language. The agent helps to set up the sales and subsequent contracts by representing the U.S. principal. The importer chooses to deal with an exporter (the U.S. principal) based on the agent's integrity and reputation.

Direct Contact. An exporter can have direct contact between the importer and itself. If all goes well, this contact results in a contract. Neither the exporter nor the importer is represented by an agent.

The exporter and the importer find one another through reputation, trade shows, or any number of other ways. They then negotiate and finally contract with each other directly. These contracts must be evaluated in view of the company's objective in entering the international marketplace.

Contracts Involved in Exporting. Whether a firm uses an agent or distributor, or deals directly with the importer, the export/import contract needs to be negotiated until all the details are completed. The traditional components of a contract, such as the price and types of goods, remain the same. Attorneys familiar with both business and international law, however, should be involved in drafting these contracts. The contract draft needs to be reviewed by all parties prior to reducing the contract to final form. Once the exporter and importer agree on the terms, they have a purchase/sell (export/import) contract.

Usually, this contract will refer to other contracts needed to complete the business transaction. The exporter faces the task of sending and delivering the goods overseas while ensuring itself that it will be paid by the importer. The importer needs assurances that the product delivered is the same as that promised in the contract.

Another type of contract pertains to the financing of the purchase/sell contract. In this contract, the buyer enters into a financing arrangement with a lending institution, whereby credit is extended to the buyer. Another contract involves people who facilitate exporting and importing, such as freight forwarders and customs brokers. The last type of contract concerns the export transaction documents. Each of these contracts is separate, but they all fit together to complete the total business transaction.

In comparison with domestic contracts, most international contracts involve more people and different means to bring a business deal to a successful conclusion. The following sections address additional clauses to be included in an export/import contract, various financing methods, export facilitators, and export transaction documents.

Clauses within an Export/Import Contract. Although the function of an export/import contract is the same as that of a domestic contract, additional clauses need to be included in international contracts. The following subsections describe provisions for consideration in an export/import contract: choice of law and forum, official-language clause, and risk-of-loss clause.

Choice of Law and Forum. The parties can write into the contract *choice-of-law* and *choice-of-forum clauses*. A **choice-of-law clause** selects the substantive law of a governmental body that will apply. For example, a Florida corporation contracts with a firm in London. The parties can insert a clause stating that Florida law will apply in case of a dispute. Many countries recognize the validity of the choice-of-law clause and will enforce it in their courts. Before entering into a transnational business contract, it is critical that both parties be familiar with the laws of the foreign countries involved.

If a choice-of-law provision is contained in the contract, it determines the law that will apply. It does not settle, however, where the lawsuit should be filed. A **choice-of-forum clause** designates the forum, or location, in which the case will be heard in the event of any dispute.

Complications occur when the parties are incorporated in different countries and are doing business in other countries. This type of situation complicates the decision as to where to file any court action. The following case considers some of these problems, including the place to file the lawsuit.

Case 13.4

Chiquita International v. Fresh Del Monte Produce

District Court of Appeal of Florida, 1997
690 So.2d 698

BACKGROUND AND FACTS Chiquita had a longstanding business relationship with a Philippine banana grower, Tagum Development Corporation (TADECO). TADECO provided Chiquita with vast quantities of bananas for Chiquita's Asian market.

At some point in the relationship, TADECO notified Chiquita that it would terminate their relationship. Sometime thereafter, Chiquita realized that TADECO had contracted with Del Monte to provide it with the bananas TADECO had previously sold to Chiquita.

Chiquita filed suit against Del Monte in the Circuit Court of Dade County for tortious interference with its contract and business relationship with TADECO. The complaint alleged that the tortious interference at issue occurred in Coral Gables, Florida. Among the defendants were several subsidiaries of Del Monte. Del Monte filed a motion to dismiss for *forum non conveniens*. The trial court granted the motion, which was appealed.

Judge SORONDO

. . . .

The Appellant/Plaintiff, Chiquita, appeals the dismissal of its complaint against Appellees/Defendants, Del Monte (collectively), on grounds of *forum non conveniens*.

. . . .

. . . [T]he Supreme Court of Florida [has] adopted the federal doctrine of *forum non conveniens*. The Court held that in reviewing a *forum non conveniens* motion, the courts must engage in a four-step analysis:

> [1] As a prerequisite, the court must establish whether an adequate alternative forum exists which possesses jurisdiction over the whole case. [2] Next, the trial judge must consider all the relevant factors of private interest, weighing in the balance a strong presumption against disturbing plaintiff's initial forum choice. [3] If the trial judge finds this balance of private interests in equipoise or near equipoise, he must then determine whether or not factors of public interest tip the balance in favor of a trial in [another] forum. [4] If he decides that the balance favors such a . . . forum, the trial judge must finally ensure that plaintiffs can reinstate their suit in the alternative forum without undue inconvenience or prejudice.

Chiquita argues that Del Monte failed to establish and the trial judge failed to properly find that an adequate alternative forum exists which possesses jurisdiction over the whole case, the first of the Kinney criteria. We agree.

Chiquita International Limited is a corporation organized under the laws of Bermuda. Fresh Del Monte Produce, N.V. is a corporation organized under the laws of the Netherland Antilles. Del Monte Fresh Produce Company is a corporation organized under the laws of the State of Delaware in the United States of America. Del Monte Fresh Produce International, Inc. is a corporation organized under the laws of Liberia.

Chiquita is headquartered in Cincinnati, Ohio. Del Monte Fresh Produce International, Inc. is headquartered in Monaco. Chiquita repeatedly asserts throughout its briefs that the other two Del Monte corporations referred to above are headquartered in Coral Gables, Florida. Although Del Monte clearly identifies the headquarters of Del Monte Fresh Produce International, Inc. in its appellate pleadings, it does not identify the corporate headquarters of the other two corporations. Regardless of where their "formal" headquarters may be, however, it is clear that Del Monte has a significant corporate presence in Coral Gables, Florida, where some of the companies' major executives are located. Indeed, as we have previously noted, the alleged plot to tortiously interfere with Chiquita's contract with TADECO was allegedly "hatched" in Coral Gables.

There is nothing in this record that even remotely suggests that a Philippine court would have subject-matter jurisdiction over four foreign corporations, none of which maintains a business presence in the Philippines, in a lawsuit which arises as a result of an intentional tort allegedly committed in Florida. We do not believe that Del Monte has established, as it must, that the country of the Philippines is an "adequate alternative forum" with jurisdiction over this case.

. . . .

In light of our conclusions concerning the first two of the Kinney criteria, it is clear that we do not find that the parties are in equipoise or near equipoise, as required by the third criterion, and consequently we do not proceed with the analysis.

DECISION AND REMEDY The court found that the Florida court had the proper jurisdiction to hear the case. The doctrine of *forum non conveniens* was not applicable.

CRITICAL THINKING: MANAGERIAL CONSIDERATION What additional provision should have been included in the contract between Chiquita International and TADECO to avoid this dispute?

Official-Language Clause. A clause in the contract should designate the official language to be used in interpreting the contract's terms. This clause promotes a clear and precise understanding of the contract's terms by each of the parties. For example, in a sale-of-goods contract, the basic contract of sale should include a legal definition of terms, the price and manner of payment, and a provision specifying the acceptable currency for payment.

Risk-of-Loss Clause. Transacting international business involves peculiar risks because thousands of miles often separate buyers and sellers. Sellers want to avoid delivering goods for which they might not be paid. Buyers want evidence that sellers have shipped goods. Specific clauses can dictate the exact moment when risk of loss passes from the seller to the buyer. In addition, a *force majeure* clause, which protects the parties from forces beyond their control (such as acts of God), also should be included.

Financing Methods. At least five different methods of financing exports are available for businesspeople: cash in advance, open account, factoring, forfaiting, and letter of credit. In choosing a financing method, the exporter tries to maximize cash flow, reduce transaction risks, and enhance competitiveness by offering flexible payment terms to the buyer.

When the seller and buyer are in different countries, two problems exist: (1) delivering the goods from the seller to the buyer and (2) ensuring payment from the buyer to the seller. Appropriate financing arrangements ensure that the seller receives payment for the goods sent and the buyer receives the goods.

Cash in Advance or Open Account. When the importer pays cash in advance for goods the importer takes a chance that the exporter will follow through on the sales contract by sending the quality and quantity of goods on the agreed delivery schedule.

The importer may establish an open account with the exporter. When the seller ships the goods, the exporter sends a statement to the importer as in a domestic credit situation. The problem with this arrangement is that the importer might not pay. The exporter would then have to bring legal action in a foreign country to obtain payment.

Factoring. A **factor** offers credit services. A factor who works for an exporter is known as the *export factor.*

When working for an importer, the factor is known as the *import factor*. The factor is placed legally between the seller and the buyer.

An exporter contacts an export factor for a credit check on the importer. The export factor requests credit information from an import factor through an international factors network. Once the importer's credit is approved, the exporter ships the goods and submits the invoice and transportation documents to the export factor, who in turn forwards all the documents to the import factor. The import factor assumes the credit risk and administration and collection of the payment from the importer. The exporter normally has no dealings with the import factor.

The financing arrangement with a factor works in the following manner. The factor pays the exporter, less a commission charge, when the receivables are due (or shortly thereafter), regardless of the importer's financial ability to pay. The cost of the factoring commission charge is fixed. It ranges generally between 1 and 3 percent, depending on the country, sales volume, and amount of paperwork involved. The factor then collects its money from the importer.

Small and medium-sized firms find factoring their export receivables to be the most hassle-free method of financing export sales and of collecting payment from the buyers. With export factoring, the exporter avoids tying up working capital and spending substantial amounts of time in administering accounts receivables. The following limitations, however, do exist:

- Factoring generally is available only to firms that have an established export market and want the flexibility of selling on open accounts.

- A factor does not handle a one-time transaction, because the factor requires access to a certain volume of the exporter's yearly sales.

- A factor works with short-term receivables of 30- to 180-day terms.

- Factors work only in developed countries, because those countries have established legal and financial systems.

- A factor assumes credit risk. The importer still has recourse to the exporter for disputes by the importer concerning merchandise (such as the quality or condition of the goods) and the terms of the contract of sale (such as the timeliness of delivery).

- Exporters working with a letter of credit often receive payment sooner than if they were working with collection factoring alone.

Traditionally, export factoring was limited to textiles, apparel, footwear, and carpeting sectors. U.S. factors now work with more diversified consumer products. Generally, an export factor does not work with an exporter that has a contract that involves capital goods of large projects because the repayment schedules stretch over several years. In some cases, a forfaiter may handle those types of projects.

Forfaiting. Like a factor, a **forfaiter** is in the business of supplying credit. The term *forfaiter* is derived from the French term *forfait*, meaning "having surrendered or relinquished rights to something." The exporter surrenders possession of the export receivables (usually guaranteed by a bank in the importer's country) by selling the receivables at a discount to a forfaiter in exchange for cash. The practice of forfaiting developed after World War II as a means of financing West German exports to Eastern bloc countries. These countries were short of hard currency, so forfaiting developed to extend medium-term financing.

In a typical forfaiting transaction, an exporter contacts a forfaiter before finalizing the transaction. Once the forfaiter commits to the deal and sets the discount rate, the exporter incorporates the discount into the selling price. Forfaiters usually work with promissory notes that are unconditional and easily transferable as debt instruments that can be sold on the secondary market.

Forfaiters, except when working with exporters of unquestionable creditworthiness, require a guarantee from a reputable commercial bank in the importer's country or sometimes a guarantee from the government itself. Typically, the guarantee consists of the guaranteeing bank's written endorsement directly on the notes. The guarantee eases the risks to the forfaiter when working with receivables from developing countries.

The exporter's contract with the importer typically involves capital goods, commodities, or large projects. The contract usually has medium- to long-term repayment periods, usually between six months and ten years. Because of high costs, many forfaiters refuse transactions of less than $250,000. Forfaiters often purchase receivables as a one-shot deal, without requiring an ongoing volume of business. Trade finance offices in banks handle many forfait transactions in which exporters already may be customers and have established a working relationship with the bank.

Forfaiting eliminates virtually all financial risk to the exporter. The exporter, however, still remains liable for the contract performance, such as quality of goods and timeliness of delivery. Forfaiting, however, has the following limitations:

- Forfaiting is unavailable for short-term financing of less than 180 days.

- Interest costs and commitment fees may be high.

- Transaction size usually is limited to $250,000 or more.

Export Factoring versus Forfaiting. From the exporter's viewpoint, both export factoring and forfaiting ensure that the exporter will be paid. In both cases, the exporter sells receivables to a third party at a discount for cash. The two methods differ significantly in these primary ways:

- Factors want access to a large percentage of the exporter's factoring business. Forfaiters will work on a one-transaction basis.

- Factors work only with short-term receivables (no greater than 180 days). Forfaiters work with medium- to long-term receivables (180 days to ten years).

- Payment terms tend reflect the type of product involved. Factors work mostly with consumer goods. Forfaiters work with capital goods, commodities, and large projects.

- Factors work in developed countries with strong legal and financial frameworks and where credit information is readily available. Most forfaiters operate in developing regions, even though the country's legal and financial structures are inadequate. Forfaiters usually require a bank guarantee or a guarantee from the developing country's government.

Letters of Credit. A **letter of credit** is an instrument issued by a lending institution in favor of a beneficiary, the exporter. The letter of credit substitutes the bank's creditworthiness for that of the importer, because the bank guarantees the exporter payment for the merchandise sold under the export/import contract.

A letter of credit ensures the seller that it will receive payment, while at the same time ensuring the buyer that payment will be held until the seller complies with the terms of the letter of credit. The letter, thus, protects both the buyer and the seller. If the documents presented by the seller comply with the terms of the letter of credit, the bank must honor the letter. The UN agreement on Uniform Customs and Practices for Documentary Credits[25] provides internationally honored rules, covering letters of credit.

Businesses often use two documents, *bills of exchange* and *bills of lading*, in connection with letters of credit. The **bill of exchange** normally is called a draft. A check is a form of a draft. A check, however, always is drawn on a bank, whereas bills of exchange are drawn on the buyer of the goods.

A bill of lading initially is issued by a common carrier, such as a railroad, trucking, airline, or marine shipping company. The bill of lading controls possession of the goods. (Bills of lading were discussed in Chapter 11.)

The common carrier delivers the bill of lading to the seller. Prior to shipment, the buyer obtains a letter of credit from its bank. In the meantime, the seller (drawer) prepares a bill of exchange naming the buyer as the drawee. The payee normally is the seller's bank.

The bill of lading, the bill of exchange, and the letter of credit are sent to the seller's bank, which in turn sends all three documents to the buyer's bank. The buyer's bank pays the bill of exchange under the terms of the letter of credit and provides the buyer with the bill of lading. The buyer's bank must pay the seller through the seller's bank when the seller complies with the terms of the letter of credit. The seller looks to the buyer's bank, not to the buyer, to be paid when the seller presents the documents required by the letter of credit. The buyer takes the bill of lading to the transportation company that has possession of the goods. With the bill of lading, the buyer obtains possession of the goods. The UN Convention on International Bills of Exchange and Promissory Notes[26] provides the rules in this area.

---

[25] The Uniform Customs and Practices for Documentary Credits was discussed in Chapter 12. More information is available at <http://www.uncitral.org/english/texts/payments/mlict.htm>.
[26] The UN Convention on International Bills of Exchange and Promissory Notes was discussed in Chapter 12. Its web site is at <http://www2.austlii.edu.au/~joseph/dfat/seldoc/1988/3614.html>.

Export Facilitators. Exporters may know their own business, but unless engaged in exporting on a large scale, most need assistance in navigating through the various government regulations. Exporters can hire consultants, but most exporters need expert help in the actual transaction. Two common export facilitators are freight forwarders and custom brokers.

Freight Forwarders. An exporter contracts with a freight forwarder to provide three services: freight arrangement, document handling, and information services. A freight forwarder buys cargo space with an airline or marine shipping company. Based on the exporter's needs, the forwarder may purchase either the entire space on a cargo airplane or ship or may combine the cargo with shipments from other exporters to obtain a lower cost based on a consolidated rate.

The basic documentation for shipping goods internationally is the same as for shipping goods domestically. The exporter supplies the freight forwarder with a commercial invoice and a packing list. The rest of the documentation needed to ship goods internationally varies from country to country. For example, alligator handbags entering the United States from Italy require a certificate indicating that the leather does not come from an endangered species. Goods entering Mexico from the United States require a certificate of origin indicating that they were actually manufactured in the United States.

The U.S. Customs Service and the Department of Commerce must be informed of products being shipped to safeguard U.S. interests and to provide trade statistics. An invoice is required by the destination country for the shipment to pass through that country's customs. The importer may require a quality certificate or an insurance certificate. The freight forwarder ensures that all required documentation accompanies the cargo.

The freight forwarder also has tracking and tracing abilities. It keeps the exporter and importer informed on the cargo's progress across international borders. Once the destination country is reached, the freight forwarder can follow the cargo's movement from the seaport or airport to the destination warehouse or to the importer directly. All appropriate documents accompany the shipment. Both the exporter and the freight forwarder retain copies.

Customs Broker. A customs broker is licensed to conduct customs business on behalf of others. The customs business concerns the entry and admissibility of products through customs and the classification and valuation of those products. The customs broker ensures that duties, taxes, or other assessed charges are paid. The service provides information to the exporter or importer on the cost of clearing merchandise through customs.

A customs broker may be licensed in several countries and may offer other services, such as freight forwarding services. For example, a customs broker may be licensed in both the United States and in Mexico and is authorized to advise clients of customs procedures in both countries. If the broker also handles freight forwarding, it can make transportation arrangements for cargo shipment. A broker can handle the document preparation needed for cargo shipment.

Export Transaction Documents. Many documents are required to export a product. Some documents are required because they are part of normal business procedures, such as shipment documents. The government requires others. The use of accurate and complete export documentation can avoid costly delays.

Shipment Documents. Shipment documents include the bill of lading, marine bill, or airway bill. Land carriers use a bill of lading, ocean carriers use a marine bill, and airlines use an airway bill. All three documents are virtually the same, but the name reflects the type of transportation. The documents establish the contract terms between the shipper (the freight forwarder) and the transportation company. These documents also represent the title to the goods. The contract details that freight is to be moved between two points for a specified price. Although the carrier provides the forms, the shipper prepares them. The bill of lading, marine bill, or airway bill serves as a document of title, a contract or carriage, and a receipt for the goods.

Another shipment document is a warehouse receipt. If the goods are not delivered directly to the buyer, the seller arranges for the goods to be sent to a warehouse. To claim the goods, the seller must send the warehouse receipt to the buyer.

Usually, the seller sends the warehouse receipt through a factor or bank, so the buyer must pay for the goods or have credit extended prior to the release of the warehouse receipt to the buyer. The buyer takes the receipt to the warehouse and claims the goods. A warehouse receipt may be issued prior to or after the goods have been shipped and may serve as a document of title.

LEGAL HIGHLIGHT

Ethics in International Sales

American businesses must consider the effects of selling their products in foreign markets. A product appropriate to the American market may be unacceptable in other countries. Marketing techniques should always be directed so that a company does not exploit a foreign economy. The following are some examples.

In the United States and the rest of the industrialized world, the consumption of tobacco has decreased in recent years. Meanwhile, the use of tobacco is increasing in developing countries. These countries' governments are very involved in tobacco sales, either through their ownership of the distributor or through their taxation of the products. Because this involvement provides these governments with a positive revenue flow, they refrain from discouraging tobacco use.

After the 1964 U.S. Surgeon General's Report, U.S. tobacco companies moved abroad, entering into marketing arrangements with foreign firms through business agreements and making direct investments in production facilities.

To this day, U.S. trade policy pressures countries, such as the People's Republic of China, to open their markets to our products, one of which is tobacco. U.S. tobacco companies compete for a share of the Chinese market, where the percentage of smokers has increased greatly during the past twenty years. As the number of smokers increased, the diseases associated with smoking likewise increased.

Did the tobacco companies employ ethical conduct in moving their production overseas or in trying to open new markets for tobacco? Is it up to foreign governments to regulate this area based on determining the good of their own citizens? Is it ethical, however, for the governments of poorer nations to use valuable foreign exchange on a product that poses serious health hazards? Should the foreign governments, instead, purchase products that would improve their health care standards? Should the U.S. government assist in tobacco sales to these countries for the purposes of balancing foreign trade and assisting U.S. producers?

Whereas tobacco use presents a clear health hazard, other products marketed overseas to developing countries would seem benign at first glance. For example, in this country, no major problems developed from the use of baby formula. In developing countries, serious problems arose. These problems centered on three issues.

First, many people in these countries are illiterate. The directions on the side of the box or package have little value to an unschooled consumer. Second, the foreign consumer often dilutes the formula, resulting in undernourished babies. Their mother's milk would have been less likely to cause malnourishment. Third, formula is made by adding water. In many developing countries, the poor quality of the water supply exposes infants to additional health hazards.

Should American companies sell potentially harmful products to developing countries? In these examples, the products themselves were not defective. What ethical responsibility does a business have to its foreign customers?

Invoices and Certificates. A packing list is sent with the goods to show the detailed contents of the package, such as the number and kind of items being shipped. The invoice shows the buyer and seller, the shipment and payment terms, and the product. The invoice and all packing lists, if more than one carton or item is sent, should conform.

As discussed earlier in this chapter, exportation of certain types of goods may require an export license. A shipper's export declaration (SED) is a form that must be filed with the U.S. Department of Commerce for any shipment valued at more than $500. An export declaration is a formal statement made to the collector of customs at a port of exit declaring the full particulars about the goods being exported. An example is that on an export declaration on computers being shipped overseas, exact information about the computers must appear.

A certificate of origin indicates where the product was actually produced or assembled. Every article of foreign origin imported into the United States must be marked with its country of origin in such a manner that the ultimate purchaser, for example, a person shopping for a business suit, can see it. The purpose is to allow the ultimate purchaser to decide if she or he would buy or refuse to buy the item. An agreement, such as NAFTA, may provide a uniform certificate of origin to be used by exporters in all member countries.

An insurance certificate verifies that coverage was purchased by the seller to protect against loss or damage while the goods are in transit. The exporter can arrange to obtain an open cargo insurance policy that the freight forwarder maintains. The open cargo policy allows the exporter to ship products over a specified time period, so long as the maximum amount of value specified in the insurance policy is not exceeded. The exporter need not purchase insurance for each shipment. The buyer may require a quality certificate to ensure that the product meets certain standards.

Developing an Importing Business

Like an exporter, an importer needs to develop its goals and objectives when deciding to import products. A business that intends to import products should perform a market analysis to determine the expected market demand, the expected repeat sales potential, and the existing and likely competition for marketing the same or similar products. The business should also evaluate the life expectancy, warranties, and quality of the product.

Because its product is located in another country, the importer needs to consider the logistics of import-ing the product. The U.S. government may have import restrictions. The Food and Drug Administration requirements must be met for food or plant products. Other products may need approval by other government agencies. The product may need to be repackaged in order to be sold at the retail level. U.S. specifications may differ from those of the exporting country, so the importer must determine if modifications need to be made. Transportation costs may be involved to move the goods from the seaport or airport to the final destination. Compliance with each of these steps increases the sales price.

The importer needs to know if the supplier is reliable and has supplies available to meet the importer's expected demand for the product. Once the product is in the United States, the importer must ensure that it meets U.S. safety and durability standards. The importer must consider the product's price, the order lead time needed, installation and maintenance requirements, and likely technical problems.

The importer also needs to determine the classification and duty rate for the imported goods. For this information, an importer refers to the Harmonized Tariff Schedule of the United States (HTSUS). Sometimes U.S. Customs disputes the classification of import goods. The proper classification is critical in determining the tariff rate that is applied to a particular product. Tariff or duty means a tax imposed on imported products. The problem of classification is discussed in the following case.

Case 13.5

Marubeni America Corp. v. U.S.

United States Court of Appeals, Federal Circuit, 1994
35 F.3d 530

BACKGROUND AND FACTS Marubeni America Corporation imported vehicles manufactured by Nissan in Japan. Nissan began to manufacture a vehicle named the "Pathfinder." This vehicle had two doors, two-wheel or four-wheel drive, and a body that consisted of one unit. This body was configured much like an ordinary station wagon in that it had rear seats that folded forward (but not flat) to create extra cargo space. The spare tire was housed within the cargo space or attached outside the vehicle on the rear hatch, depending on the model. The rear hatch operated like that of a station wagon. The vehicle, however, was built around a frame normally used for a truck. The cab portion from the front bumper to the frame was consistent with that of a truck.

The import duty on passenger vehicles was 2.5 percent, whereas the duty for trucks was 25 percent. U.S. Customs took the position that this vehicle was a truck. Marubeni America Corporation sued. The trial court reversed the position of U.S. Customs, and the government appealed.

Circuit Judge RICH

. . . .

The issue is whether the Pathfinder has been classified under the appropriate tariff provision. Resolution of that issue entails a two step process: (1) ascertaining the proper meaning of specific terms in the tariff provision; and (2) determining whether the merchandise at issue comes within the description of such terms as properly construed. The first step is a question of law which we review de novo and the second is a question of fact which we review for clear error.

The government asserts that the CIT [Court of International Trade] erred by applying improper and inconsistent standards, and that the Pathfinder is not primarily designed for the transport of persons based on the practice of Nissan and the industry.

. . . .

The two competing provisions of the HTSUS [Harmonized Tariff Schedule of the United States] are set forth below.

> 8703 Motor cars and other motor vehicles principally designed for the transport of persons (other than those of heading 8702), including station wagons and racing cars.
>   8704 Motor vehicles for the transport of goods.

There are no legally binding notes to these headings that are relevant to the classification of dual-purpose vehicles such as the Pathfinder; therefore, we need only look to the common meaning of the terms as they appear above.

. . . .

The government argues that "the correct standard to be utilized in determining the principal design of any vehicle must be its construction—its basic structure, body, components, and vehicle layout—and the proper question to be asked is whether that construction is uniquely for passenger transportation."

. . . .

. . . "[R]equir[ing] that the resulting product be uniquely constructed for the purpose of transporting persons," to the exclusion of any other use, is a constrictive interpretation of the terms with which we cannot agree.

There is nothing in the statute, legislative history, or prior Customs decisions that would indicate that "principally designed" refers only to a vehicle's structural design as asserted by the government. To answer the question, whether a vehicle is principally designed for a particular purpose, not uniquely designed for a particular purpose, one must look at both the structural and auxiliary design features, as neither by itself is determinative.

The government's exclusionary construction fails on another point. Heading 8703 HTSUS specifically includes "station wagons," which are not uniquely designed for transport of persons, rather, they are designed as dual-purpose vehicles for the transport of goods and persons. The Pathfinder, like a station wagon, is a vehicle designed with a dual-purpose—to transport goods and persons.

. . . .

The CIT also recognized that the Pathfinder was basically derived from Nissan's Hardbody truck, yet the Pathfinder was based upon totally different design concepts than a truck. The CIT correctly pointed out these differences and more importantly, the reasons behind the design decisions, including the need for speed and economy in manufacturing to capture the changing market, a market into which Nissan was a late entrant. Specifically, the designers decided to adopt the

Hardbody's frame side rails and the cab portion from the front bumper to the frame just behind the driver's seat so that they could quickly and economically reach the market. The front suspension system was also adopted from Nissan's truck line but the rear suspension was not. The fact that a vehicle is derived in-part from a truck or from a sedan is not, without more, determinative of its intended principal design objectives which were passenger transport and off road capability.

. . . Customs has drawn what appears to be a line between two door and four door versions of sports utility vehicles. . . . This line, classifying two door dual-purpose vehicles for the transport of foods while classifying the four door version as principally designed for transport of persons, appears to be arbitrary.

. . . Two door passenger cars are equipped with a seat slide mechanism that effectively slides the front seat forward to provide easier access to the rear seat. The doors of two door passenger cars are generally wider as well. The CIT found that the Pathfinder has both of these features so that passengers can be easily accommodated. Therefore, the two door Pathfinder accommodates passengers in the rear seat as well as two door passenger cars, if not as easily as four door sports utility vehicles. Consequently, the number of doors on a vehicle should not be determinative.

. . . .

We hold that the court applied the correct legal standards, and that the evidence of record supports the CIT's decision that the Pathfinder is principally designed for the transport of persons.

DECISION AND REMEDY The appeals court upheld the trial court's decision. The court found that the Pathfinder was principally designed for the transport of people, not cargo. In doing so it discussed the differences between a passenger car and a truck. The decision by the court was that the Pathfinder was a passenger vehicle and, as such, subject to the lower tariff rate of 2.5 percent.

CRITICAL THINKING: POLITICAL QUESTION Discuss why the import duty of an automobile would be ten times lower than that of a pickup truck.

The classification and duty rate can be determined based on the advice of the importer's customs broker and that of U.S. Customs officials. To avoid problems, the importer can obtain a written letter ruling from U.S. Customs determining the proper classification and duty rate for both current and prospective transactions. A **letter ruling**[27] is the official position of U.S. Customs with respect to a particular product. It is valid until revoked or modified.

A letter ruling prevents a later charge by U.S. Customs that the importer willfully or negligently misclassified the product, subjecting it to civil penalties, criminal punishment, or both. For example, does

sweetened molten chocolate in a tank truck qualify for the lower tariff rate of "Chocolate: Sweetened: in bars or blocks weighing ten pounds or more" or for the higher tariff rate of "Chocolate: Sweetened: in any other form"? A written letter ruling would prevent a dispute if the importer misclassified the product. In this case, an importer argued that its molten chocolate was in a block larger than ten pounds. Because the importer's chocolate was molten and not solidified, U.S. Customs prevailed in the lawsuit. The court held that the common meaning would be applied, that is, that bars or blocks meant solidified chocolate. The cost of the lawsuit and possible civil and criminal action could have been avoided if the importer had requested a letter ruling from U.S. Customs prior to the product's entry into the United States.

[27] Letter rulings are issued by many administrative agencies, such as the U.S. Customs Service or the Internal Revenue Service.

CyberLaw

Electronic Auctions

Electronic auctions help people and businesses buy and sell products using the World Wide Web. Most people are familiar with business-to-consumer (B2C) types of electronic auctions, such as eBay, which is the English-style auction. The English model is familiar because it is used by public auctions and people have seen it on television or in the movies. Businesses, however, use a business-to-business (B2B) auction model, which is the Dutch-style auction. This model is not familiar to most people because it is conducted privately. The two auction models are opposite in nature.

The B2C electronic auction uses the public network, the web. The auction house sets up an electronic auction business that is open to the public. Neither the buyer nor the seller is qualified. Because neither is qualified, fraud is inevitable so the electronic auction site provides some protections.

The site offers information on the site as to ways to protect against being defrauded, such as a seller making sure a check has cleared before sending items to a buyer. Buyers can purchase insurance in case the items have been stolen and placed on the web by the seller-thief. Remember, anytime a person believes he or she has purchased stolen merchandise, the person must notify the police. The sale was made electronically and the purchaser can be traced and charged with possession of stolen property. For example, you purchase a digital camera through an electronic auction site. The digital camera works fine, but has a plate attached saying "Property of State High School. ID # 55-555-55. If found, please return. Call 555-555-5555." Because you did not purchase the item from State High School and since the ID plate was not removed, you have an obligation to call. At some point, State High School will take inventory and discover that the camera was checked out to a student in the journalism department who cannot account for it. It does not take long to check the student's computers at school and at home to determine that you have the digital camera in your possession.

The seller sets the length of time the auction will last, usually four to seven days. Potential buyers can view the product and choose whether to bid. Usually, bidding starts not long before the end of the auction, commonly during the last hour. Anyone really wanting the item will wait to see the bids of others, then in the last fifteen to thirty seconds place a bid, leaving no time for someone to raise the price. The bid price will be higher than the previous bid, so the price goes up. Once the final bid is in, the winning bidder is obligated to purchase the item.

The B2B auction works in a totally different manner. These auctions are conducted on private networks, so the public is not able to see how they are conducted. A business, such as an automobile manufacturer, needs to build 10,000 automobiles. For example, at this particular auction, the manufacturer needs steel, composite materials, seats, and tires. Of course, the manufacturer wants to purchase these items at as low a price as possible.

In this type of auction, both the purchaser and the suppliers are prequalified. The purchaser must have the financial strength to make the purchases. Both domestic and international suppliers must be able to supply the materials in the quantities needed and be able to ship them in a timely manner. The purchaser may have its own network, such as Covisint,[28] the automotive Internet exchange formed by General Motors, Ford, DaimlerChrysler, Renault, and Nissan, or the purchaser may select an electronic house that specializes in B2B auctions, such as Free Markets.[29] Either way, the network is private.

A B2B auction is open from one to three hours. A supplier must bid and if it does not, the auction house will call. If the supplier still does not bid, the supplier is disconnected from the network and not allowed to participate or watch the rest of the auction. The auction works in the following manner. A supplier wants to sell its products to the purchaser and bids the sale

---

[28] Covisint is an independent company. The name Covisint (pronounced KO-vis-int), is a combination of the primary concepts of why the exchange was formed. The letters "Co" represent connectivity, collaboration, and communication. "Vis" represents the visibility that the Internet provides and the vision of the future of supply chain management. "Int" represents the integrated solutions the venture will provide as well as the international scope of the exchange.

The web allows a manufacturer's production schedule and any subsequent changes to be sent simultaneously and instantly throughout its entire supply chain. This real-time information results in less costly inventory at all levels of the supply chain and increases the ability to respond quickly to market changes. Purchasers and suppliers, regardless of their size and position in the supply chain are able to communicate with each other in a real-time, virtual way. The result is lower costs to both the buyer and seller.

[29] Free Markets is located at <http://www.freemarkets.com>.

price. A second supplier sees the bid and it also wants the contract, so the second supplier bids a lower price than the first bidder. As a result, the price of the products is reduced. Often the purchaser can save between 10 and 20 percent,, which translates to multimillions of dollars in savings to the purchaser.

In a B2B auction, the purchaser is not obligated to purchase. The purchaser will look at other things besides lowest price. Other factors are the location of the supplier (for instance, in another state or in another country), stability of transportation when shipping from another country, reputation of the supplier, and many other factors.

A B2C auction is commonplace and establishes as nearly a true market price as possible. A B2B auction is commonplace among businesses and aids in lowering costs to the purchaser.

LEGALLY SPEAKING

Increasing Sales through Exports

You are employed by a small company that has grown steadily and hopes to continue to increase sales substantially during the next year. Your firm is owned and managed by a family whose grandparents started it. Because you are the first person to be hired into a management position outside of "family," you believe you need to prove that you can increase profits by additional sales.

The family members tend to be hesitant in initiating new ideas. While in college, you studied aspects of international business, joined international organizations, and traveled overseas on vacation. You think that profits will increase, if the business exported overseas. You expect that initially the family members will oppose exporting, because they lack an understanding of international business procedures. You want to present as many arguments in favor of exporting as you can.

You stress that this country has only 5 percent of the world's customers. Your firm currently misses out on selling to 95 percent of its potential customers.

You also prepare answers to specific questions involving the areas of the world on which to concentrate. You prepare a paper on the required government documents, the means to finance the production of the additional products, and the methods of ensuring payment from foreign buyers.

You obtain much of this information from the federal government. The government lists the specialists in specific areas. These agencies can assist in arranging financing, determining potentially successful international business opportunities, obtaining customer leads, and advising in a number of aspects of international business. The Commercial Service of the U.S. Department of Commerce is one of the best sources of this type of information. This agency can become your business's international advocate.

The Commercial Service has a global network operation of more than 70 offices in the United States and more than 130 offices all over the world with 1,400 employees dedicated to serving American business firms. Through partnerships with other trade promotion organizations—public and private—the Commercial Service can offer your business comprehensive, customized solutions to international trade challenges.

The International Trade Administration, also located in the U.S. Department of Commerce, has created Export Assistance Centers located in most U.S. commercial centers. These centers assist with international market research, trade contacts, overseas contracts, export credit insurance, and short- and long-term financing.

Before you discuss the idea of exporting with the family members, however, you should research the following items:

✔ Study which countries offer the best opportunity for selling your company's products.

✔ Develop a marketing plan within the country or countries. Review from this chapter possible alternative plans.

✔ Discuss informally your ideas with local financial institutions to ascertain whether you can obtain their assistance in processing the appropriate financial documents to obtain payment for your product. In many small communities, the local bank lacks the resources or knowledge to assist in this area. You may have to contact a financial institution in a major commercial area to obtain this help.

✔ Prepare a pro forma statement indicating the total financial results of exporting.

✔ Stress to the family members the importance of international sales and that exporting is the future both for the firm and this country.

Chapter Summary

Growth in international business relations has led, in turn, to the development of international law. International law consists of a body of laws that are considered to be legally binding among otherwise independent nations. This legal area has developed through three methods: international customs, agreements that have the force of law, and international organizations and conferences. International customs consist of the relationship that nations have developed over the years with one another on particular legal matters. Agreements are reached either by nations acting independently, as in the signing of treaties, or through international organizations and conferences.

The U.S. Constitution grants authority to Congress and the president to regulate commerce with foreign nations. Several administrative agencies and one court assist in this regulation. Several statutory provisions control import and export activities. The Export Administration Act restricts exports to certain countries and requires licenses for the export of certain products to other countries. Violations of this act can result in long prison terms and substantial damages against the defendant.

The 1988 Omnibus Trade and Competitiveness Act strengthened the competitiveness of U.S. exports. It strengthened the fast-track procedure to expedite the ratification of trade agreements. The Export Trading Company Act and Export-Import Bank relate to import and export benefits for the United States.

Four unfair import practices can result in either goods forfeiture or additional import duties. These practices are dumping; infringement of copyright, patent, trademark, and maskwork laws; government subsidizing; and the sale of gray-market goods.

Exporting and importing involve more people and paperwork than domestic business transactions. To conduct business overseas, a firm may contact an importer directly, but this method is extremely risky. Usually, a business will use one of two indirect methods: either an international distribution agreement or an international agent. Financing also differs for financing imports versus financing domestically purchased products. The exporter needs assurances that it will receive payment, and the importer needs assurances that the product order will be delivered. Five common financing methods are cash in advance, open account, factoring, forfaiting, and letters of credit.

Because of the myriad of government regulations and customs rules and the complexity of shipping product procedures, the exporter may use the services of freight forwarders or customs brokers. These experts help the exporter with the paperwork needed (the export transaction documents) to ship the goods to the importer in a foreign country and to facilitate the goods passing through customs both in the United States and in the foreign country.

Once a business decides to import goods, it must abide by U.S. Customs Service rules. To determine the tariff (tax) to be paid, the importer must abide by the Harmonized Tariff Schedule of the United States. When the importer is unsure of the classification, it can request a letter ruling from U.S. Customs to prevent civil penalties, criminal punishment, or both.

Using the World Wide Web

A number of international organizations have web pages. These sites provide updated and in-depth information about the organization's activities, meetings, and reports. The European Union has a web site that allows a person to stay abreast of current activities.

The Organization of American States (OAS) is the world's oldest regional organization. It is the principal forum in the hemisphere for dialogue on political, economic, and social issues. Every country in the Americas is a member of the OAS. Its headquarters is located in Washington, D.C.

The United Nations has locations throughout the world. It has a well-developed web site. The countries that have the eight largest economies are called the Group of Eight (G-8). They are Canada, France, Germany, Italy, Japan, the Russian Federation, the United Kingdom, and the United States. The G-8 is often referred to as the G-7 (Group of Seven) when the Russian Federation does not attend.

Developments involving the North American Free Trade Agreement and the Free Trade Association of the Americas can be tracked using the web. The same is true of the web sites for the United Nations and the European Union.

These web sites open with a choice of languages. Choose the language you are most comfortable with and proceed to explore.

Finding the Law on the Web

Organization of American States
http://www.oas.org/
United Nations
http://www.unsystem.org/
Group of Eight (G-8)
http://www.library.utoronto.ca/g7/internat.htm
Group of Fifteen (G-15)
http://sittdec.org.my/g15/inframe.htm
Public Citizen, Global Trade Watch, North American Free Trade Agreement
http://www.citizen.org/pctrade/nafta/naftapg.html
International Court of Justice
http://www.icj-cij.org/
United Nations Commission on International Trade Law
http://www.uncitral.org/
Trade Compliance Center
http://mac.doc.gov/tcc/index.html
Trade agreements database
http://mac.doc.gov/TCC/DATA/index.html
Exporter's guides
http://mac.doc.gov/TCC/TCC2/GUIDES/index.html
Market access reports
http://www.mac.doc.gov/TCC/DATA/index_reports.html
World Trade Organization, latest proposed technical regulations
http://www.mac.doc.gov/TCC/TCC2/monitor/note_index.html
International members government procurement opportunities
http://www.mac.doc.gov/TCC/TCC2/igp/index.htm
Countries and regions
http://www.ita.doc.gov/ita_home/itacnreg.htm
Business holidays
http://tradeinfo.doc.gov/TicWeb/Business.nsf/b968bba91070548d852566c000681b52?OpenView
Foreign currency exchange rates
http://ia.ita.doc.gov/exchange/index.html

U.S. Customs Service's importing and exporting information
http://www.customs.ustreas.gov/impoexpo/impoexpo.htm
Findlaw's International Trade Law Web Guide
http://www.findlaw.com/01topics/25interntrade/database.html
Findlaw's Government Agencies Guide
http://www.findlaw.com/01topics/25interntrade/gov_agencies.html

Chapter Web Sites

Vienna Convention on the Law of Treaties
http://www.ifs.univie.ac.at/intlaw/konterm/vrkon_en/html/doku/treaties.htm#1.0
World Bank
http://www.worldbank.org/
International Monetary Fund
http://www.imf.org/
Organization for Economic Cooperation and Development
http://www.oecd.org/
European Union
http://europa.eu.int/
Association of Southeast Asian Nations
http://www.imf.org/external/np/sec/decdo/asean.htm
Asian-Pacific Economic Cooperation
http://www.apecsec.org.sg/
World Trade Organization
http://www.wto.org/
Office of the U.S. Trade Representative
http://www.ustr.gov/
U.S. Customs Service
http://www.customs.ustreas.gov/
Duties of the U.S. Customs Service
http://www.law.cornell.edu/uscode/19/
International Trade Administration
http://www.ita.doc.gov/
International Trade Commission
http://www.usitc.gov/
NAFTA
http://www.sice.oas.org/trade/nafta/naftatce.asp
Commission on Environmental Cooperation
http://www.cec.org/
Northern American Agreement on Labor Cooperation
http://www.naalc.org/
Free Trade Association of the Americas
http://www.ftaa-alca.org/

Organization of American States
http://www.sice.oas.org/ftaa_e.asp
U.S. Court of International Trade
http://www.uscit.gov/
Omnibus Trade and Competitiveness Act
http://av.yahoo.com/bin/query?p=omnibus+trade
+and+competitiveness+act&b=41&hc=0&hs=0
Export-Import Bank
http://www.exim.gov/
Statute establishing the Export-Import Bank
http://www4law.cornell.edu/uscode/12
/ch6A.html
Export Assistance Centers
http://av.yahoo.com/bin/query?p=Export
+Assistance+Center&hc=0&hs=3&S=G
Antidumping regulations
http://ia.ita.doc.gov/newregs.htm
Maastricht Agreement
http://europa.eu.int/en/record/mt/top.html
Uniform Customs and Practices for Documentary Credits
http://www.uncitral.org/english/texts/payments
/mlict.htm
UN Convention on International Bills of Exchange and
Promissory Notes
http://www2.austlii.edu.au/~joseph/dfat/seldoc
/1988/3614.html
Free Markets
http://www.freemarkets.com
Small Business Regulatory Enforcement Fairness Act
http://www.customs.ustreas.gov/impoexpo
/impoexpo.htm

Library of Congress' Country Studies/Area Handbook
Program
http://lcweb2.loc.gov/frd/cs/cshome.html
Central Intelligence Agency
http://www.cia.gov/
Trade Information Centers and Export Assistance Centers
http://www.ita.doc.gov/

Web Activities

13–1 You own the online business, Artiste Login Products, Inc., which is classified as as a small business. You are interested in exporting your products. Go to the U.S. Customs Service web page at <http://www.customs.ustreas.gov/impoexpo/impoexpo.htm>. Click on Small Business Regulatory Enforcement Fairness Act (SBREFA). Scroll down to Customs Reg/Fair Program heading. Scroll to the bottom of the second paragraph and click on the hyperlinked words "improving the trade's knowledge." On the first web page, explain the purpose of SBREFA. On the second web page, what information is available on exporting?

13–2 Your online business, Artiste Login Products, Inc., is investigating whether to export custom-made pottery, including dinnerware, overseas. Choose a country to which you would like to export your products. Compare the Library of Congress's web site <http://lcweb2.loc.gov/frd/cs/cshome.html> with the Central Intelligence Agency web site <http://www.odci.gov/>. Which site has better information for a business deciding whether or not to export?

Key Terms

bill of exchange	Company Act	Administration (ITA)	Trade Act
choice-of-forum clause	exporting	International Trade	Trade Agreement Act
choice-of-law clause	factor	Commission (ITC)	trade promotion
compact	forfaiter	letter of credit	authority
convention	freight forwarders	letter ruling	treaty
countervailing duty	General Agreement on	National Export Strategy	U.S. Customs Service
Court of International	Tariffs and Trade	national treatment	U.S. Trade
Trade (CIT)	(GATT)	normal trade relations	Representative
customs brokers	general license	Omnibus Trade and	(USTR)
dumping	gray-market goods	Competitiveness Act	validated license
executive agreement	importing	(OTCA)	Vienna Convention on
Export Administration Act	international agent	parallel import	the Law of Treaties
Export-Import Bank	international custom	protocol	World Trade
(Eximbank)	international law	quota	Organization (WTO)
Export Trading	International Trade	tariff	

Questions and Case Problems

13–1 Export You own a small manufacturing business and are considering exporting products to increase sales. Your major concern is receiving payment once the goods have been shipped. What methods are available to ensure that you receive payment? Explain how your choice of method would depend on the type of product that is sold. What other factors should you consider in making your final decision?

13–2 Imports XYZ, Inc., desires to import goods from a business in Haiti. It wants to be certain that the goods it receives are those that it ordered and that the goods are received in acceptable condition. The Haitian business wants payment if the goods are shipped. Describe the procedures that should be followed.

13–3 Conflict between Federal Law and a Treaty Congress passed a poultry inspection statute, called the Poultry Products Inspection Act (PPIA). The statute contained a provision mandating that all imported poultry products be subject to the same inspection, sanitation, quality, species verification, and residue standards applied to poultry products produced in the United States. The Department of Agriculture and the Food Safety and Inspection Services (Agency) adopted a regulation that required foreign producers to have inspection procedures "at least equal to" those applicable to local producers. The Mississippi Poultry Association, which represented the local poultry associations, took exception to the language "at least equal to" because it differed from statutory language of "be subject to the same" standards. The Agency took the position that this interpretation would place the regulation in violation of a GATT provision. Who prevailed? Explain your answer. [*Mississippi Poultry Association v. Madigan*, 992 F.2d 1359 (1993)]

13–4 Import Duty Sears, Roebuck & Co. imported from Japan electronic merchandise consisting of tuners, amplifiers, turntables, and dual cassette decks, as well as wooden racks. Its speakers were manufactured in the United States. Sears put these items into three boxes and sold them as the model 9291 stereo rack system. One box contained the speakers, one contained the rack, and the last contained the electronic merchandise. Sears took the position that this was an entire system that should be taxed at a 4.2 percent rate. The government argued that the three individual components should be taxed at different rates ranging from 4.2 to 7.7 percent. Testimony was given that all of the components were advertised and sold as one complete system. Most of the items, however, could be used with other products with little or no modification. Should these items be treated as one complete commercial entity or should they be taxed individually? Explain your answer. [*Sears, Roebuck & Co. v. United States*, 723 F. Supp. 805 (Ct. Int'l Trade, 1989)]

13–5 Antidumping and Countervailing Duty The plaintiffs represented the domestic prestressed concrete steel wire stand industry. They believed the wire stand manufactured in Spain, France, and Brazil was being subsidized by those governments and sued the foreign manufacturers. Prior to the court's ruling, the plaintiffs' domestic production increased steadily over several years and employment in the industry likewise increased. The International Trade Commission (ITC), based on this information, found that the importers' actions did not create a material injury to the domestic producers. The ITC did not apply the antidumping and countervailing duty provisions. The plaintiffs argued that their net profits had decreased because of the subsidies. Should the court reverse the findings of the ITC based on reduced profits? Support your reasons. [*American Spring Wire Corp. v. United States*, 590 F. Supp. 1273 (Ct. Int'l Trade, 1984)]

13–6 Country of Origin Uniroyal, Inc., exported to Indonesia leather and other materials that then were turned into the upper portion of shoes. These items were imported back into the United States, where they were attached to soles, polished, and sold under the trade name Sperry Topsiders. When they were imported back to the United States, the cartons were marked "Made in Indonesia," but the upper part of the shoe indicated no place of manufacture. The Customs Service refused to permit them to enter the United States on the grounds that they were not marked with the country of origin. The question presented to the court was whether the attachment of the soles and the polishing was a "substantial transformation" of the product that would require the plaintiff to have the top of each shoe marked as to the country of origin. What was the result and why? [*Uniroyal, Inc. v. United States*, 542 F. Supp. 1026 (Ct. Int'l Trade, 1982)]

13–7 International Agreement Charles T. Main International brought an action to recover assets that had been lost because of the shah's overthrow in Iran. To obtain the release of hostages, President Jimmy Carter signed an agreement to submit all claims by either Iran or the United States to binding arbitration. The plaintiff wanted to recover assets from Iran that had been frozen in the United States. Main claimed that the president's agreement, freezing Iranian assets, exceeded the president's authority and violated his company's constitutional rights because the freeze amounted to the taking of company property without just compensation. Explain the result. [*Charles T. Main International v. Khuzestan and Power Authority*, 651 F.2d 800 (1st Cir. 1981)]

13–8 Arbitration Mitsubishi Motor Corp. and Soler Chrysler–Plymouth entered a contract that required binding arbitration. A dispute occurred and Mitsubishi wanted to arbitrate it. Soler Chrysler–Plymouth claimed that Mitsubishi had violated the U.S. antitrust laws, which made the parties' contract illegal and thus not subject to arbitration. Who prevailed in this case? Explain. [*Mitsubishi Motor Corp. v. Soler Chrysler–Plymouth*, 473 U.S. 614, 105 S. Ct. 3346, 87 L .Ed. 2d 444 (1985)] (See Chapter 4, concerning arbitration.)

13–9 Import Hasbro Industries imported G.I. Joe action figures that could be manipulated. Hasbro adver-

tised G.I. Joe as a doll. G.I. Joe also appeared in doll collector books. Letters from purchasers referred to the figure as a doll. Hasbro requested U.S. Customs to classify the G.I. Joe action figures as "toy figures," that is, as a modern update of a toy soldier. This classification would allow G.I. Joe to be imported duty free (tax free). If classified as a doll, Hasbro would have to pay duties. The U.S. Customs office determined that the G.I. Joe action figures were dolls because the figures were individually named and provided with specific biographical information, thus inviting play. Because U.S. Customs found that the G.I. Joe action figures were not comparable to toy figures, G.I. Joe was subject to a tariff. Do you think that a G.I. Joe is a doll or a toy figure that should be imported duty free? Explain. [*Hasbro Industries v. United States*, 879 F.2d 838 (Fed. Cir. 1989)]

13–10 Internet Explain the difference between the Trade Information Centers and the Export Assistance Centers. Go to <http://www.ita.doc.gov/>.

Rights of Consumers, Debtors, and Creditors

Outline

Ethical Consideration

Can You Be Required to Have Credit Life Insurance?

You are the sole owner of both Fine Automobiles Dealership and Cheap Rates Insurance Company. When Fine Automobiles Dealership sells an automobile on credit, it requires all purchasers to acquire credit life, credit disability, and credit unemployment insurance. This type of insurance guarantees the monthly automobile payment in case of death, disability, or unemployment. Fine Automobiles Dealership has a serious, legitimate concern regarding continued payment of the automobile loan in case of death, disability, or unemployment. Under federal law, the cost of this insurance must be treated as an interest expense.

You require the Fine Automobiles Dealership sales force to recommend only Cheap Rates Insurance Company. Cheap Rates Insurance Company earns a substantial premium from selling this insurance. In fact, Cheap Rates Insurance Company has a low claim rate and a high income over expenses. Thus, Cheap Rates Insurance Company can pay its shareholders high dividends.

Is it ethical for Fine Automobiles Dealership to require such insurance from its credit customers through Cheap Rates? Is it ethical for Fine Automobiles Dealership to recommend to its customers only Cheap Rates Insurance Company rather than advising them to shop around to determine if Cheap Rates Insurance Company actually does provide the best coverage for the lowest rates? Use the ethical model provided in Chapter 2 and reprinted on the inside front cover to develop your answer.

Introduction

Your business, Artiste Login Products, Inc., deals with consumer credit on a daily basis. People send paper checks and money orders through the mail. They also use electronic checks. Most of your consumers, however, purchase online using a credit card through your secured web site.

Purchase on credit is a basic element of our business community. In the last fifty years, the United States has converted from a cash to a credit society. Consumer credit card use led this transformation. Consumer credit has increased from $2.5 billion at the end of World War II to $1.4 trillion by 2000. Major consumer products, such as automobiles, stereos, televisions, and furniture, are almost always purchased on credit. Consumer credit rests on two assumptions: the debtor's willingness to pay and the debtor's ability to pay.

By the mid-1960s, the tremendous increase in credit unfortunately had led to a rise in consumer abuse. Consumers were insufficiently informed about shopping comparatively for interest rates. They were misled into signing installment contracts. Few regulations protected consumers from harassment by debt collectors. They were denied access to their credit reports. Worst of all, the consumer had little recourse from computer billing errors. State law failed to adequately protect consumers.

The U.S. Congress became concerned and, in 1968, adopted the Consumer Credit Protection Act, which has been amended several times. These amendments are known by their popular names. In this chapter, the following acts will be discussed:

1. Consumer Credit Cost Disclosure Act, commonly known as the Truth-in-Lending Act
2. Fair Credit Billing Act
3. Fair Credit Reporting Act
4. Equal Credit Opportunity Act
5. Fair Debt Collection Practices Act

The Electronic Fund Transfer Act discussed in Chapter 12 also is part of the Consumer Credit Protection Act. The chapter will end with discussion of the rights of creditors and a review of some bankruptcy laws.

Consumer Credit Protection Act

The **Consumer Credit Protection Act (CCPA)** is the primary source of federal law covering credit transactions. Numerous federal agencies enforce the CCPA. Individual consumers also can use the act to protect their rights when a business fails to fully comply with the CCPA's provisions. The legal consequences vary for each provision violated, but both criminal and civil sanctions result if a business fails to comply.

Consumer Credit Cost Disclosure: Truth-in-Lending Act

During hearings in 1968, Congress discovered that financial institutions stated interest rates and the loan's total dollar cost in a variety of ways. Rates of interest were based on recognized, but varying, financial methods of calculation. No uniform method of stating an interest rate existed. Congress heard considerable debate as to whether charges for insurance, credit reports, discount points, and other items should be classified as interest charges. Prior to 1968, a consumer could not shop for credit because of the difficulties in comparing one lending institution's charges with another.

To resolve this problem, Congress passed the Consumer Credit Protection Act. Title I of the act is known as the **Consumer Credit Cost Disclosure Act**, more commonly called the **Truth-in-Lending Act (TILA)**. The TILA deals with deceptive credit practices and requires notice and disclosure to prevent sellers and creditors from taking unfair advantage of consumers. Through disclosure, the purchaser can compare more easily the available credit terms. The act applies to most consumer credit transactions.

Disclosure Requirements of the TILA.

The disclosure requirements apply to credit transactions in which a finance charge is imposed or in which payment is made in more than four installments. The most important information that a lender must disclose includes (1) the cash price; (2) the down payment or trade-in allowance, if any; (3) the unpaid cash price (the cash price minus the down payment) that is to be financed; (4) the **finance charge** (the total amount of interest and other charges, such as filing fees and insurance premiums); and (5) the **annual percentage rate** (the true rate of interest charged on a yearly basis) by which the finance charge is calculated.

The creditor also must tell the debtor the date on which the finance charge begins to accumulate; the number, amounts, and due dates of payments; the late-payment charges; and whether there is a prepayment penalty. A prepayment penalty is an amount that the debtor pays if he pays off the debt early. In the past, the prepayment penalty often was a substantial amount of the debt. For example, Harris borrows $5,000. He has paid back $4,000 in monthly installments. He now wants to pay the remaining $1,000 early in one last payment. To complete the loan payment, the prepay-

ment penalty is $2,000. In other words, he would have to pay a total of $3,000 in order to pay off the loan early. Today, many states ban prepayment penalties.

The provisions of the Truth-in-Lending Act apply to both sales and leases of personal and real property. Two key terms summarize the act's disclosure philosophy: finance charge and annual percentage rate. Armed with this information, the consumer can comparison shop for a loan or for credit.

The Federal Reserve Board issues the administrative rules that implement the TILA. Known as Regulation Z,[1] these rules include model forms for businesses to follow when selling goods. The forms, if used correctly by a business, fully comply with the statute. Exhibits 14–1 and 14–2 provide examples that come from the *Code of Federal Regulations*.

The **Consumer Leasing Act** requires full disclosure of all financial terms in consumer leasing contracts. The Federal Reserve Board's Regulation M governs this area. It requires disclosures to consumers similar to those required by Regulation Z.

Creditors Subject to the TILA.
The Truth-in-Lending Act applies to businesses that, in the ordinary course of their operations, lend money, sell on credit, or arrange for the extension of credit to consumers. The TILA protects only human debtors. Sales or loans made between two consumers do not come under the act's jurisdiction. Furthermore, business entities and governmental agencies are not protected by the act.

Transactions involving purchases of property (real or personal) for personal, family, household, or agricultural use come under the terms and provisions of the act if the amount being financed is less than $25,000. Transactions covered by the act typically include retail and installment sales, installment loans, car loans, home improvement loans, and certain real estate loans. Real estate loans of more than $25,000 on a debtor's residence are not covered by the act.

Penalties.
A creditor who fails to comply with the disclosure requirements may be liable to the consumer for any actual damages plus twice the amount of the finance charge and attorneys' fees. Damages may not exceed $2,000. The total liability for a class action is

[1] Regulation Z is located at <http://www4.law.cornell.edu/cfr/12p226.htm#start>.

Exhibit 14–1 Loan Model Form Supplied by the Federal Reserve Board

ANNUAL PERCENTAGE RATE The cost of your credit as a yearly rate.	FINANCE CHARGE The dollar amount the credit will cost you.	AMOUNT FINANCED The amount of credit provided to you or on your behalf.	TOTAL OF PAYMENTS The amount you will have paid after you have made all payments as scheduled.
%	$	$	$

You have the right to receive at the time an itemization of the Amount Financed.
❏ I want an itemization.   ❏ I do not want an itemization.

Your payment schedule will be:

Number of Payments	Amount of Payments	When Payments Are Due

Insurance
Credit life insurance and credit disability insurance are not required to obtain credit, and will not be provided unless you sign and agree to pay the additional cost.

Type	Premium	Signature	
Credit Life		I want credit life insurance.	Signature
Credit Disability		I want credit disability insurance.	Signature
Credit Life and Disability		I want credit life and disability insurance.	Signature

You may obtain property insurance from anyone you want that is acceptable to   (creditor)   . If you get the insurance from   (creditor)   . You will pay $ _____ .

Security: You are giving a security interest in:
❏ The goods or property being purchased.
❏ (Brief description of other property).

Filing Fees $ _____   Non-filing insurance $ _____

Late Charge: If payment is late, you will be charged $ _____ / _____ % of the payment.

Prepayment: If you pay off early, you
❏ may   ❏ will not   have to pay a penalty.
❏ may   ❏ will not   be entitled to a refund of part of the finance charge.

See your contract documents for any additional information about nonpayment, default, any required repayment in full before the scheduled date, and prepayment refunds and penalties.

e means an estimate

Source: 12 *Code of Federal Regulations,* Section 226, Appendix H–2, 2000.

Exhibit 14–2 **Credit Sale Model Form Supplied by the Federal Reserve Board**

ANNUAL PERCENTAGE RATE	FINANCE CHARGE	AMOUNT FINANCED	TOTAL OF PAYMENTS	TOTAL SALE PRICE
The cost of your credit as a yearly rate.	The dollar amount the credit will cost you.	The amount of credit provided to you or on your behalf.	The amount you will have paid after you have made all payments as scheduled.	The total cost of your purchase on credit, including your downpayment of $ _____
%	$	$	$	$

You have the right to receive at the time an itemization of the Amount Financed.
❏ I want an itemization.   ❏ I do not want an itemization.

Your payment schedule will be:

Number of Payments	Amount of Payments	When Payments Are Due

Insurance
Credit life insurance and credit disability insurance are not required to obtain credit, and will not be provided unless you sign and agree to pay the additional cost.

Type	Premium	Signature
Credit Life		I want credit life insurance. _____ Signature
Credit Disability		I want credit disability insurance. _____ Signature
Credit Life and Disability		I want credit life and disability insurance. _____ Signature

You may obtain property insurance from anyone you want that is acceptable to ____(creditor)____ . If you get the insurance from ____(creditor)____ . You will pay $ _____ .

Security: You are giving a security interest in:
❏ The goods or property being purchased.
❏ (Brief description of other property).

Filing Fees $ _____   Non-filing insurance $ _____

Late Charge: If payment is late, you will be charged $ _____ / _____ % of the payment.

Prepayment: If you pay off early, you
❏ may   ❏ will not   have to pay a penalty.
❏ may   ❏ will not   be entitled to a refund of part of the finance charge.

See your contract documents for any additional information about nonpayment, default, any required repayment in full before the scheduled date, and prepayment refunds and penalties.

e means an estimate

Source: 12 *Code of Federal Regulations,* Section 226, Appendix H-1, 2000.

$500,000 or 1 percent of the creditor's net worth, whichever is less.

The consumer has one year from the date of the violation to bring suit against a creditor who failed to provide the disclosure statement. A creditor who willfully and knowingly violates these provisions is liable criminally and may be fined $5,000, imprisoned for up to one year, or both. In addition, the debtor can rescind the transaction at any time up to three years from the date of the transaction.

Other Provisions of the CCPA

Over the years, Congress has added statutes to the CCPA's initial provisions. These provisions cover real estate improvements, credit and debit card usage, credit billing errors, equal credit opportunities, and debt collection practices.

Real Estate. A consumer wants to improve her residence. She enters into a contract with a creditor to borrow the money and, in turn, provides the creditor a security interest in the residence to secure payment for the improvement.

The TILA gives the consumer-borrower the right to rescind the contract by midnight of the third business day following the signing of the contract even though all disclosure provisions of the TILA have been followed. This protection is called the *three-day rescission rule*. A consumer must be given notice of this right to rescind along with the material disclosures of annual percentage rate, the finance charge, the amount financed, the total payments, and the payment schedule.

For example, Sandy wants to have a pool built. She signs a contract with Pool Company to have the pool built for $20,000. Sandy does not have $20,000, so she signs a note to repay the $20,000 and provides Pool Company a security interest in her home. If she fails to repay the note, Pool Company can go to court to force the sale of Sandy's house to recover the loan amount that has not been repaid. For a creditor to have this right, however, the contract must state clearly Sandy's right to rescind the contract within three business days after the signing of the contract. Further, it must include all disclosure requirements.

If Sandy rescinds the contract within the three business days, the security interest in her residence is void and she pays no finance charge. The Pool Company must return any money or property that it received (such as a down payment) and Sandy must return anything that she received (in this example, probably nothing). If the return is impracticable, the consumer must pay the reasonable value of what has been received.

The three-day rescission rule does not apply in two situations. The first involves an emergency situation in which the customer needs to have his home repaired immediately, as in the case of damage resulting from a fire or storm. The second situation concerns the purchase money lender. The rule does not apply to a creditor that lends money in order for a consumer to purchase a residence if the creditor takes a lien (mortgage). The following case illustrates the need for businesses to comply with the Truth-in-Lending Act requirements.

Case 14.1

Stutsman County State Bank v. Federal Deposit Insurance Corporation

United States Court of Appeals, Eighth Circuit, 2000
207 F.3d 464

BACKGROUND AND FACTS During a period of nearly two years beginning in August 1996, Stutsman assessed and collected a one-time processing fee for each credit account opened pursuant to a particular open-ended credit plan, without disclosing the processing fee in the Initial Disclosure Statement.

The parties stipulated, among other things, that the processing fees in question varied from $27 to $59 and that they cumulatively affected approximately 25,640 active accounts, for a total of approximately $1,470,938. Stutsman presented evidence to show that it had disclosed the processing fee in a script read to credit applicants over the telephone and in written credit approval letters and that a third party had generated and mailed the Initial Disclosure Statements pursuant to a contract with Stutsman.

The administrative law judge (ALJ) concluded that Stutsman had engaged in a clear and consistent pattern or practice of violations, requiring reimbursement of the affected customers under 15 U.S.C. § 1607(e)(1), and that waiver of the reimbursement requirement was not warranted under any of the exceptions in 15 U.S.C. § 1607(e)(2)(A)–(D) (the Truth-in-Lending statutes). Upon review of the ALJ's findings and recommendation, the Federal Deposit Insurance Corporation Board of Directors (Board) affirmed and adopted the ALJ's conclusions.

PER CURIAM

. . . .

We have carefully reviewed the ALJ's findings and recommendations, the Board's decision and order, the record on appeal, and the arguments of the parties. We deny the petition for review because the Board's factual findings are supported by substantial evidence on the record as a whole and because the Board has thoroughly examined the relevant data and has articulated a satisfactory explanation for its legal conclusions, including a rational connection between its findings of fact and the remedy imposed.

Stutsman's petition for review of the Board's decision and order is denied.

DECISION AND REMEDY Charging a fee for a consumer open credit account and not informing the consumer about the fee in writing prior to the credit being granted was a direct violation of the Truth-in-Lending Act and Regulation Z. The bank was required to make a full refund of these fees.

CRITICAL THINKING: MANAGERIAL CONSIDERATION As a bank manager, should you have been concerned about the letter of the law or its main purpose? Did the bank attempt to comply with the purpose of the law? Why then did the bank not prevail?

Credit Cards. The TILA has specific provisions that cover the issuance and use of credit cards.[2] First, an individual or a business must request that an initial credit card be sent. Any unauthorized use of an unrequested card cannot be charged to the named cardholder. Renewal credit cards, however, can be sent without a specific request.

Second, if a credit card is lost or stolen, $50 is the limit of the cardholder's liability for the unauthorized card use. The $50 limit is for each card, so if a consumer loses ten cards, the actual loss to the consumer could be $500.

Debit Cards. Debit cards are used to debit the customer's bank account immediately through the use of electronic transfer of funds. People often use debit cards at teller machines or in stores when making purchases. To use a debit card, the user must provide a PIN (personal information number) at the time of the transaction.

If a debit card is lost or stolen, the consumer is liable for an unauthorized transfer of up to only $50 if he takes reasonable steps to notify the financial institution within two business days after the loss or theft. After the two-day period, the consumer's liability increases to $500. If the consumer fails to report the card loss or theft or any unauthorized charges within sixty days, the consumer has unlimited liability. If a person is unable to notify the institution of a loss or theft because of extended travel or hospitalization, he has a reasonable time to notify the institution.

Fair Credit Billing Act. Even computers make errors on charge accounts. The experience of correcting these errors can be unnerving. An amendment to the TILA, the **Fair Credit Billing Act**, requires creditors to correct errors promptly and without damage to a person's credit rating. See Exhibit 14–3 for a sample notice of billing error rights.

---

[2] The Truth-in-Lending Act is found at <http://www.law.cornell.edu/uscode/15/1601.html>. The Federal Trade Commission has various consumer protection acts on its web site at <http://www.ftc.gov>.

Exhibit 14–3   **Sample Notice of Billing Error Rights**

BILLING ERROR RIGHTS

YOUR BILLING RIGHTS

KEEP THIS NOTICE FOR FUTURE USE

This notice contains important information about your rights and our responsibilities under the Fair Credit Billing Act.

Notify us in case of errors or questions about your bill.

If you think your bill is wrong, or if you need more information about a transaction on your bill, write us on a separate sheet at 1400 South Cactus Road, Swiftrace, California 99999-5555 or at the address listed on your bill. Write to us as soon as possible. We must hear from you no later than sixty (60) days after we send you the first bill on which the error or problem appeared. You can telephone us, but doing so will not preserve your rights.

In your letter, give us the following information:
Your name and account number.
The dollar amount of the suspected error.

Describe the error and explain, if you can, why you believe there is an error.
If you have authorized us to pay your bill automatically from your savings or checking account, you can stop payment on any amount you think is wrong. To stop the payment, your letter must reach us three (3) business days before the automatic payment is scheduled to occur.

Your rights and our responsibilities start after we receive your written notice.

We must acknowledge your letter within thirty (30) days, unless we have corrected the error by then. Within ninety (90) days, we must either correct the error or explain why we believe the bill was correct.
After we receive your letter, we cannot try to collect any amount you question, or report you as delinquent. We can continue to bill you for the amount you question, including finance charges, and we can apply any unpaid amount against your credit limit. You do not have to pay any questioned amount while we are investigating, but you are still obligated to pay the parts of your bill that are not in question.
If we find that we made a mistake on your bill, you will not have to pay any finance charges related to any questioned amount. If we didn't make a mistake, you may have to pay finance charges, and you will have to make up any missed payments on the questioned amount. In either case, we will send you a statement of the amount you owe and the date on which it is due.
If you fail to pay the amount that we think you owe, we may report you as delinquent. However, if the explanation does not satisfy you, write to us within ten (10) days telling us that you still refuse to pay. We must tell anyone we report you to that you have a question about your bill. We must tell you the name of anyone we reported you to. When the account is finally settled, we must tell anyone we report you to that the matter has been settled.
If we don't follow these rules, we can't collect the first $50 of the questioned amount, even if your bill was correct.

A person who believes that her charge account statement is in error must notify the creditor in writing with a statement explaining the perceived error. The customer must pay the undisputed amount while waiting for an answer from the business on the amount in question. Within thirty days, the creditor must acknowledge the inquiry and within ninety days the creditor either must correct the account or provide an explanation as to why the creditor believes the account to be correct. During this time, the creditor is not allowed to give an unfavorable credit report or to attempt to collect the amount in dispute.

LEGAL HIGHLIGHT

Earth Calling Computer, Earth Calling Computer, Do You Read Me?

When Congress considered passing the Fair Credit Billing Act, the members of Congress heard horror stories, such as the following, about computers that sent bills to consumers.

- A women in Yonkers, New York, bought furniture from Gimbels. One piece arrived damaged and beyond repair. The furniture piece was returned. The replacement piece did not match and was returned. After five months, the third piece had not arrived. The woman paid for the delivered pieces but not for the undelivered piece. The woman was in constant contact with the Gimbels credit department, but apparently the credit personnel failed to talk to the computer. The computer billed her for one year, then turned the unpaid bill over to a debt collection agency. The letter to her read, "The good things of life are obtainable by many people through their recorded credit reputation." In frustration, she wrote to the debt collection agency, three Gimbels executives, the attorney general for New York, the Federal Trade Commission, Consumers Union, Senator William Proxmire (Democrat, Wisconsin, who was holding hearings on the passage of the act), and the New York State Consumer Protection Board. She received replies from all except the debt collection agency and Gimbels.

- BankAmericard sent an unsolicited credit card to a man in the Bronx, New York. He never received the card because it was stolen. Despite his repeated efforts to inform the credit card issuer that these charges were not his, the computer continued sending him the bill, including interest and late payment charges.

- A couple from Monaghan, New York, ordered furniture from Macy's. They owed $1,217. Macy's twice delivered the wrong furniture. After ten months, Macy's finally delivered the correct furniture and the bill was paid. The couple was in contact with Macy's during this period, but the personnel failed to correct the computer. It billed them for finance charges for the ten months, plus 6 percent sales tax, although the sales tax in that area was only 3 percent. Finally, the couple wrote to the chairman of the board of Macy's. He expressed concern. Within three days, however, an attorney for Macy's called and gave them five days to pay the bill or be taken to court. They contacted the New York State Consumer Protection Board, which resolved the problem. In the meantime, they were denied a house loan because of this "unpaid" bill.

Fair Credit Reporting Act. At one time, consumers had no access to the contents of credit and investigative reports kept on them by credit reporting agencies. Consumers also had no control over the use of these reports. Inaccuracies, once reported, were almost impossible to uncover, much less to correct.

In 1970, Congress enacted the **Fair Credit Reporting Act**. Consumers are entitled, on request, to be informed of the nature and scope of a credit investigation, the kind of information that is compiled, and the names of people who will receive the report.

Any inaccurate or misleading material must be reinvestigated and, if not verified, removed from the file. Consumers have the right to include in the file

their own 100-word statement describing their position with regard to any disputed matters. The law also provides for updating information. Information more than seven years old must be deleted. Information regarding any bankruptcy more than ten years old must be removed.

The original act was modified in 1996 by the passing of the **Consumer Reporting Reform Act**.[3] This act requires all credit bureaus to make an employee, not recordings, available when a consumer calls

---

[3] The Consumer Reporting Reform Act is available at <http://www.ftc.gov/os/statutes/fcra.htm>.

the company. The credit bureaus must provide a toll-free number during normal working hours. The credit bureaus must verify the information within thirty days. Consumers must consent to a prospective or new employer obtaining their credit report. Before any personal medical information is released, the consumer must authorize it. Often, a consumer can receive a free credit report, but if there is a charge, the charge is less than $10.

A consumer credit reporting agency that fails to comply with the terms of the act can be held liable for actual damages, for punitive damages, and for attorneys' fees and court costs. The following case involved a credit reporting agency and one of its reports.

Case 14.2

Cushman v. Trans Union Corporation

United States Court of Appeals, Third Circuit, 1997
115 F.3d 220

BACKGROUND AND FACTS In the summer of 1993, an unknown person, possibly a member of Cushman's household, applied under her name for credit cards from three credit grantors: American Express (Amex), Citibank Visa (Citibank), and Chase Manhattan Bank (Chase). The person provided the credit grantors with Cushman's Social Security number, address, and other identifying information. Each company issued a credit card to that person in Cushman's name, and that person accumulated charges totaling approximately $2,400 on the cards between June 1993 and April 1994. These charges occurred without Cushman's knowledge.

In August 1994, a bill collector informed Cushman that Trans Union Corporation (TUC) was publishing a consumer credit report indicating that she was delinquent on her payments. Cushman notified TUC that she neither had applied for nor used the three credit cards in question, and suggested that a third party had fraudulently applied for, obtained, and used the cards.

In response, a TUC clerk called Amex and Chase to determine if the verifying information (such as Cushman's name, Social Security number, and address) in Amex's and Chase's records matched the information in the TUC report. The TUC clerk also asked if Cushman had opened a fraud investigation with the credit grantors. Because the information matched and because Cushman had not opened a fraud investigation, TUC published the information in its report.

Because TUC failed to contact Citibank, it deleted the Citibank entry from the report. TUC's investigations were performed by clerks who were paid $7.50 per hour and who were expected to perform ten investigations per hour. No evidence indicated that TUC obtained access to pertinent documents from the credit grantors that would enable TUC to perform a handwriting comparison.

TUC allowed Cushman the opportunity to complete and sign a form requesting that a special handling statement be placed on her report. A TUC employee testified, however, that the form would not have been used for a handwriting comparison had Cushman completed it. TUC advised consumers in Cushman's position to communicate and to complete signature verifications and fraud affidavits with the credit grantors.

When TUC sent Cushman a copy of the updated report still containing the Amex and Chase delinquencies, she sent a second letter to TUC reiterating her disagreement with the facts contained in the report and offering to sign affidavits for TUC to the effect that the delinquencies were not hers. TUC subsequently performed a reinvestigation identical to the first one. The credit report remained unchanged. At no time did TUC provide Cushman with a description of its reinvestigation procedures.

Cushman brought this action in the district court, alleging violations of the Fair Credit Reporting Act (FCRA). Subsequently, in April 1995, TUC verified the information with Citibank and placed the Citibank entry back onto Cushman's report. TUC notified Cushman of the reinsertion through her attorneys.

That September, Cushman, for the first time, disputed the delinquencies with the three credit grantors. A Citibank employee, comparing a handwriting sample provided by Cushman with the credit card application, determined that the card had been fraudulently obtained. The other two credit grantors came to a similar conclusion. TUC has since deleted the entries from Cushman's report.

By this time, TUC had been granted a summary judgment. Cushman appealed.

Circuit Judge COWEN

. . . .

As this Court recently wrote: The FCRA was enacted in order to ensure that "consumer reporting agencies adopt reasonable procedures for meeting the needs of commerce for consumer credit, personnel, insurance, and other information in a manner which is fair and equitable to the consumer, with regard to the confidentiality, accuracy, relevancy, and proper utilization of such information." The FCRA was prompted by "congressional concern over abuses in the credit reporting industry." In the FCRA, Congress has recognized the crucial role that consumer reporting agencies play in collecting and transmitting consumer credit information, and the detrimental effects inaccurate information can visit upon both the individual consumer and the nation's economy as a whole.

Title 15 U.S.C. § 1681i(a) provides in relevant part:

> If the completeness or accuracy of any item of information contained in [her] file is disputed by a consumer, and such dispute is directly conveyed to the consumer reporting agency by the consumer, the consumer reporting agency shall within a reasonable period of time reinvestigate and record the current status of that information unless it has reasonable grounds to believe that the dispute by the consumer is frivolous or irrelevant. If after such reinvestigation such information is found to be inaccurate or can no longer be verified, the consumer reporting agency shall promptly delete such information.

. . . .

. . . According to TUC, it is never required to go beyond the original source in ascertaining whether the information is accurate. This position has been rejected [by the courts].

. . . .

. . . [T]he plain language of the statute places the burden of reinvestigation on the consumer reporting agency.

. . . .

A reasonable jury weighing this evidence . . . could have rendered a verdict for Cushman. The jury could have concluded that after TUC was alerted to the accusation that the accounts were obtained fraudulently, and then confronted with the credit grantors' reiteration of the inaccurate information, TUC should have known that the credit grantors were "unreliable" to the extent that they had not been informed of the fraud. Similarly, the jury could have concluded that seventy-five cents per investigation was too little to spend when weighed against Cushman's damages. It was for "the trier of fact [to] weigh the[se] factors."

. . . .

DECISION AND REMEDY The district court abrogated its role by granting the motion to dismiss the action on behalf of the credit reporting company. The judgment of the district court, therefore, was reversed and the case remanded for a jury trial.

CRITICAL THINKING: POLITICAL CONSIDERATION Without this federal law, a consumer could still bring legal action for defamation against a credit reporting agency if inaccurate information were in a credit file. Why does the government require credit reporting agencies to verify information contained in their credit reports?

Equal Credit Opportunity Act. In 1974, Congress enacted the **Equal Credit Opportunity Act**,[4] which forbids certain forms of discrimination. If a person can repay a loan, she cannot be denied credit on the basis of race, color, religion, national origin, sex, marital status, age, or the fact that her income is derived from public assistance. Discrimination against a person by denying her credit on any of these bases is illegal. The civil liabilities for violation of this act include actual damages as well as punitive damages up to $10,000, plus attorneys' fees and court costs.

CyberLaw

Protecting Your Credit

Credit! Without good credit, businesses and people cannot borrow money to purchase a business, buildings, computer systems, vehicle, or any other large purchase. The ability to obtain credit requires a good credit history.

Any number of things can occur to adversely affect a credit rating. For example, you may not discover someone has stolen your identity until it is too late to stop the thief from using your good credit to obtain money or property. Or a former landlord might file an unfavorable report with a credit reporting firm. You would not know about this negative information in your credit report until you or your prospective creditors review your credit report.

How do lenders make a decision as to whether to lend money to a specific borrower? Most lenders use a scoring system. To obtain a good score, you need to have different types of accounts, for example, mortgages on your house and your business property, unsecured loans, or credit cards, and always pay them on time.

A lower score is not achieved solely because you pay your bills late or are delinquent. Having a large number of credit cards will lower your score. Inactive credit cards hinder your score. Credit cards used to pay other accounts will impede your score. A number of credit card accounts opened within a short period of time results in points being deducted from your score.

If you or your creditors check your credit report more than three times in a month, these actions negatively impact your score. Although you may have been shopping for lower rates for a loan, creditors view it as a precursor to credit delinquency. These actions of yours may be innocent. Creditors, however, view these actions negatively and use them as warning signs that you are about to abuse your credit.

You can check your credit report in a couple of ways. If you have Internet access, you can type in "free credit report." Numerous firms on the web offer free credit reports. Many will provide you with tips on correcting errors and mistakes. Often, you do not pay for this service for the first thirty days. If you are satisfied with their service, you can subscribe to the service primarily to have the company alert you if negative information is filed. Another way to check is to use the Federal Trade Commission's web site. The FTC has listed the major credit reporting bureaus. Each bureau charges a nominal fee to view your credit report.

Only you can protect your good credit rating. Check your credit report annually at a minimum. If the actions of others have impaired your credit report, you can then take immediate, corrective action.

Fair Debt Collection Practices Act. In 1977, Congress passed the **Fair Debt Collection Practices Act**. This act applies to anyone who is in the business of consumer debt collection for others (collection agencies). Even without federal statutory provisions, however, invasion of a person's privacy or intentionally causing a person emotional distress is illegal.

For example, under the Fair Debt Collection Practices Act, Ace, a debt collector, cannot contact

[4] The Equal Credit Opportunity Act is at <http://www4.law.cornell.edu/uscode/topn/>.

LEGAL HIGHLIGHT

Gossip, Gossip, Gossip

What type of information was placed in people's credit files prior to the passage of the Fair Credit Reporting Act?

Here are a few examples.

- A man who applied for automobile insurance was denied coverage. He later found this statement in his file: "Subject's son is a hippie type."

- A woman's application for automobile insurance was denied. In her file was a notation that she was a topless dancer who was divorced.

- A man who applied for life insurance was denied. In his record was a statement based on gossip from an unknown source that his former boss had "suspected him of taking money from the till." No charges had ever been filed.

- Another man was fortunate. His file contained the statement: "We learn of no connection with any Peace movement or other serversice [sic] type organization. He is regarded as a normal loyal american [sic]."

- A man who applied for life insurance was denied. His file included a false statement that he kept "unsavory company." A second statement, more than fifteen years old, said that he had destroyed property. The truth was that he had accidentally broken a neighbor's plate-glass window while playing softball. When he went to the credit bureau and told his story, the credit bureau agreed to correct his file for a fee. The fee to check out his story was $10 an hour, with a fifteen-hour minimum, payable in advance.

- A man in Atlanta had immigrated to the United States from his native Hungary. He arrived in the United States penniless and knowing little English. Twelve years later he had a thriving business. When he went to borrow money, however, he was denied credit again and again. Finally, he found that his record noted that he had been involved in a $200 lawsuit, had bad debts, had gone bankrupt, and had skipped town. In fact, he had a business, had lived in the same house for twelve years, had not been involved in a $200 lawsuit, had no bad debts, and had never filed for bankruptcy.

After two personal visits to the credit reporting bureau and letters to the Justice Department, the Federal Trade Commission, President Richard M. Nixon, and the man's hometown newspaper—and with lawyers talking directly to the credit reporting bureau—the man still failed to clear the false information from his file. The problem began in 1966. Finally, in March 1972, he was told that the incorrect information had been expunged from his file. When he applied for credit cards from Standard Oil and Sears in May 1972, however, credit was denied. Both companies cited the same source of their negative information: the credit reporting agency with which he had been fighting for years.

Dan, a debtor, before 8 A.M. or after 9 P.M. Repeatedly calling Dan on the telephone is prohibited. If Dan's employer has a policy against debt collectors contacting employees at work, the debt collector cannot call his place of employment. Ace can contact a third party one time for Dan's address, but cannot tell the third party that Dan owes a debt. Dan can write a letter advising Ace to stop communicating with him. If Dan notifies Ace that he has an attorney, the debt collector must make subsequent communications with Dan's attorney. The return address on Ace's postcards or envelopes must conceal that Ace is a debt collector. Ace cannot threaten to use physical violence and cannot threaten to harm Dan's reputation or property. He also must refrain from using obscene or profane language.

Ace cannot imply that he is collecting the debt under government authority and cannot wear a badge or uniform. Ace cannot claim to be an attorney unless admitted to practice law. Because Ace is not the original creditor, he must notify Dan that he is attempting to collect a debt and that any information that Dan provides may be used for that purpose. Ace must include this warning in any written correspondence to Dan. Ace cannot misrepresent that nonpayment of the debt will result in Dan's arrest or imprisonment. The threats of the seizure, garnishment, attachment, or sale of any of Dan's property or wages is forbidden unless Ace intends to file a lawsuit against Dan and informs Dan of the remedies that Ace may use to collect if it wins.

If a debt collector violates a provision of the act, the collection agency must pay actual damages plus additional damages up to $1,000 and attorneys' fees. The following case considers possible violations of the Fair Debt Collection Practices Act.

Case 14.3

Bass v. Stolper

United States Court of Appeals, Seventh Circuit, 1997
111 F.3d 1322
http://www.kentlaw.edu
/7circuit/1997/apr
/96-2113.html

BACKGROUND AND FACTS To pay for groceries, Joe Arsenault wrote a check in the amount of $156.94 to "Copps," a local supermarket. The check, which was subsequently dishonored by his bank because of insufficient funds, was drawn on an account that Arsenault held jointly with plaintiff Bass.

To collect on the check, Copps employed defendant law firm, Stolper, Koritzinsky, Brewster & Neider, S.C. (SKBN), which instituted collection activities against Arsenault under Wisconsin's civil recovery statute. SKBN's first three collection attempts, to which Arsenault did not respond, were in the form of collection letters addressed solely to Arsenault.

Its fourth collection letter, however, was addressed jointly to Arsenault and Bass. This letter, written and signed by defendant Kathy Leschensky, a nonattorney employee of SKBN, advised that she drafted and filed lawsuits in collections matters, and that she would "hold off taking any action for 7 days" if Arsenault or Bass would make arrangements to pay.

In response, Bass brought an action for statutory damages for defendants' failure to comply with the Fair Debt Collection Practices Act (FDCPA) in its collection letter. Among other complaints, Bass alleged that in the letter Leschensky misrepresented herself as an attorney in violation of the FDCPA and that the letter failed to include language specifically required by the act stating that the letter's purpose was to collect a debt and that any information received would be used solely in collection efforts. SKBN conceded before the district court that the letter lacked this required language.

The district court granted Bass's motion for a summary judgment by finding that (1) the act applies to collectors of dishonored checks and (2) the letter sent to Bass violated the act. In finding that the act applied, the district court reasoned that a consumer who issues a subsequently dishonored check has an obligation to pay it. That obligation to pay the check meets the act's definition of the term "debt." The defendants appealed.

Circuit Judge ESCHBACH

. . . .

. . . On September 20, 1977, premised on Congressional concern that state protections against questionable debt collection practices were insufficient, President Carter signed into law the Fair Debt Collection Practices Act as an amendment to the Consumer Credit Protection Act ("CCPA"). The primary goal of the FDCPA is to protect consumers from abusive, deceptive, and unfair debt collection practices, including threats of violence, use of obscene language, certain contacts with acquaintances of the consumer, late night phone calls, and simulated legal process.

. . . .

In the most general terms, the FDCPA prohibits a debt collector from using certain enumerated collection methods in its effort to collect a "debt" from a consumer. Because not all obligations to pay are considered "debts" under the Act, the definition of "debt" thus serves to limit the scope of the FDCPA. SKBN has conceded that the collection letter sent to Arsenault and Bass used one of the collection methods prohibited by the Act. Therefore, we face only the task of resolving the parties' dispute over the scope of the FDCPA, specifically whether the payment obligation that arises from a dishonored check constitutes a "debt" as defined in the FDCPA. Appellants' argument, that the FDCPA does not control the collection activities arising from worthless checks, rises and falls on its assertion that the only type of "debt" triggering application of the FDCPA is debt arising from an offer or extension of credit to the consumer. . . .

. . . .

A "debt," the collection of which is governed by the FDCPA, is defined in the Act as any obligation or alleged obligation of a consumer to pay money arising out of a transaction in which the money, property, insurance, or services which are the subject of the transaction are primarily for personal, family, or household purposes, whether or not such obligation has been reduced to judgment. Appellants would have us read into this definition the additional requirement that the debt flow from a specific type of consumer transaction—one involving the offer or extension of credit. However, we see no language in the Act's definition of "debt" (or any other section of the Act) that mentions, let alone requires, that the debt arise from an extension of credit. Nor do we find patent ambiguity in the definition of "debt." . . .

. . . .

On the contrary, the plain language of the Act defines "debt" quite broadly as "any obligation to pay arising out of a [consumer] transaction." . . .

DECISION AND REMEDY The court found that in the absence of an explicit statement showing that Congress intended a fraud exception to the Act, the wrong occasioned by debtor fraud was more appropriately redressed under the statutory and common law remedies that were already in place. The court held that the act did apply to lawyers collecting on bad checks.

CRITICAL THINKING: POLITICAL CONSIDERATION The result of this case is that a person who commits fraud by writing a bad check is still protected from debt collectors by federal law. Discuss whether a person who possibly even committed a crime by writing a bad check should ever be protected by law when an honest debt collector attempts to collect a debt.

Other Consumer-Oriented Laws

At the federal and state levels, a variety of consumer protection laws exist. These laws regulate a range of activities from the operation of dance studios and health clubs to used automobile sales and even funeral sales. The following sections discuss two major laws.

Uniform Consumer Credit Code

In 1968, the National Conference of Commissioners on Uniform State Laws promulgated the **Uniform Consumer Credit Code (UCCC)**. The UCCC has been controversial and only a few states have adopted it. It is a comprehensive body of rules governing the most important aspects of consumer credit. Sections of the UCCC, for example, focus on truth-in-lending,

LEGAL HIGHLIGHT

Women and the Credit Revolution

The Equal Credit Opportunity Act was passed in 1974. Until this act was adopted, most single working women could not obtain credit or buy homes or automobiles in their own names without a cosigner.

A woman whose marriage had ended either in divorce or by the death of her husband also could not obtain credit. A married couple's credit was maintained in the husband's name, even if only the wife worked. If the marriage ended, the woman had no credit rating. Financial institutions would deny her a loan, a credit card, or a bank card. Worse, if her former husband had good credit, it did not follow her; if he had a bad credit rating, it did follow her. Here are some more examples:

- A woman received $250,000 in a divorce settlement. From 1970 to 1972, she repeatedly applied for a bank card with a $500 limit; she was denied credit because she was divorced.

- In 1973, a married female attorney who had had a law practice for ten years, was denied a department store credit card in her own name.

- In 1969, a widow of six years received a credit card in her deceased husband's name after being denied credit in her own name.

Congress heard many similar stories. Recognizing that women had become a stable part of the nation's workforce, Congress passed the Equal Credit Opportunity Act.

As a side note, prior to this law, both single women and single men found it nearly impossible to purchase a house. Financial institutions determined single people to be unstable. Today, more than one-fourth of all houses, condominiums, and townhouses are sold to single people.

---

door-to-door sales, referral sales, and maximum credit interest rate ceilings.

The UCCC also addresses creditor remedies, including deficiency judgments. The UCCC applies to most types of sales, including real estate. It also covers installment loans, retail installment sales, and usury (charging more than the maximum rate of interest allowed by state law).

Real Estate Settlement Procedures Act

Congress passed the **Real Estate Settlement Procedures Act** in 1974. The act governs the purchase of a house and the borrowing of money to pay for it. The time between when the contract is signed by both the buyer and the seller and the time when the property is titled in the buyer's name is approximately six weeks. At time of settlement, the buyer and seller are informed of all the costs and resolve any problems.

After a person applies for a mortgage loan, the lender, within three business days, sends him a booklet prepared by the U.S. Department of Housing and Urban Development. The booklet outlines the appli-

cant's rights and explains settlement procedures and costs. The lender provides the buyer an estimate of most of the settlement costs within that three-day period. If the loan is approved, the lender must provide a truth-in-lending statement that shows the annual percentage rate on the mortgage loan.

Creditors' Rights

A creditor has the right to payment. When the debtor fails to fulfill his obligation to make timely payments, state laws establish procedures by which a creditor can secure debt payment or recovery of the goods for which the debt was incurred.

Writ of Execution

A debt must be past due in order for a creditor to commence legal action against a debtor. If the creditor is successful, the court awards the creditor a judgment against the debtor (usually for the amount of the debt plus any interest and legal costs incurred in obtaining the judgment). If the debtor still does not or cannot pay the judgment, the creditor can return to the court to obtain a writ of execution.

A **writ of execution** is an order, issued by a judge or the clerk of the court, directing the sheriff to seize and sell any of the debtor's nonexempt real or personal property that is within the court's geographic jurisdiction (usually the county in which the courthouse is located). **Nonexempt property** is property that the creditor can have seized from the debtor and sold. The proceeds of the sale are used to pay off the judgment and the costs of the sale itself. This procedure is known as a **judicial sale**. Any excess of the proceeds is paid to the debtor who owned the property.

At any time before the sale takes place, the debtor can pay the judgment and can redeem the nonexempt property. **Exempt property** is specifically named in statutes as property that can be kept by the debtor and is protected from the creditor. Such property may include the debtor's furniture and other essentials for living.

Attachment

A **writ of attachment** is a court-ordered seizure by which the sheriff takes the defendant's specified property into custody. The writ of attachment is normally a prejudgment remedy, requested by the creditor either when the lawsuit is filed or sometime after the filing, but before the entry of a final judgment. The remedy assists the creditor in collecting the debt owed if the judgment is made in the creditor's favor, because the sheriff, not the debtors, has custody of the property.

By statute, the restrictions and requirements concerning a creditor's right to attachment before judgment are very specific. The due process clause found in the Fifth and Fourteenth Amendments of the U.S. Constitution limits a court's power to authorize seizure of a debtor's property without notice to the debtor or a hearing on the facts.

To use attachment as a remedy, the creditor must follow certain procedures. He must file an affidavit with the court. An **affidavit** is a short written statement of facts given under oath and is used as evidence in a court. The affidavit states that the debtor is in default and states the statutory grounds under which attachment is sought. A bond must be posted by the creditor to cover court costs, the loss of the use of the goods as incurred by the debtor, and the value of the property attached.

When the court is satisfied that the creditor has met all the requirements, it issues a writ of attachment. This writ directs the sheriff or other officer to seize nonexempt property. If the creditor prevails at trial, the seized property then can be sold to satisfy the judgment.

Garnishment

A **garnishment** is a statutory procedure in which a debtor's property, currently in another's possession, is applied to the payment of that person's debts. For example, the wages owed to a debtor by his employer might be garnished. The court can issue a writ of garnishment for these wages, addressed to the employer, requiring that a portion of the employee's paycheck be paid to the creditor.

Garnishments are regulated by federal and state law. Congress determined that debtors needed some protection. Congressional hearings showed that the lack of laws protecting debtors encouraged lenders to extend credit to people who could not afford it. The federal law sets out the maximum amounts that can be garnished. Before the federal law was passed, many states allowed the creditor to garnish (that is, to take) the debtor's entire paycheck.

State laws today frequently set even lower limits on the amounts set by federal law. Federal agencies that try to collect debts, however, are not subject to the limits placed by the states. For example, when the Internal Revenue Service (IRS) tries to collect debts owed to it, it allows reasonable amounts for food, housing, housekeeping supplies, apparel and services, personal care products and services, and transportation. Federal law determines the amounts based on the debtor's location. Under these regulations the employee retains at least some of his paycheck.

An employer cannot discharge an employee for garnishment of his paycheck. If the debtor is fired, the employer may be fined $1,000, imprisoned for one year, or both.

In addition to the protections offered by federal or state statutes, the United States Supreme Court declared that a consumer has a right to a hearing before wages can be garnished. The following case established this right. This decision was based in part on the Constitution's due process clause.

Case 14.4

Sniadach v. Family Finance Corporation

Supreme Court of the United States, 1969
395 U.S. 337, 89 S. Ct. 1820,
20 L. Ed. 2d 349
http://www.thelawengine
.com

LANDMARK CASE

BACKGROUND AND FACTS Family Finance Corporation garnished Mrs. Sniadach's wages after it alleged that she failed to make timely payments on a loan. No trial or hearing was held to determine that Mrs. Sniadach had defaulted on the debt or that the garnishment was otherwise authorized. Her only notice was served on her at the same time that her wages were garnished.

Mrs. Sniadach contended that the finance company's failure to give her notice that the wages would be seized violated her right to due process. Both the trial court and the Wisconsin Supreme Court upheld the procedure allowed by Wisconsin law to garnish wages without prior notice to the consumer. Mrs. Sniadach took her case to the United States Supreme Court.

Justice DOUGLAS delivered the opinion of the Court.

[Family Finance Corporation] instituted a garnishment action against [Sniadach] as defendant and Miller Harris Instrument Co., her employer, as garnishee. The complaint alleged a claim of $420 on a promissory note. . . .

. . . .

. . . She . . . claims that the Wisconsin garnishment procedure violates that due process required by the Fourteenth Amendment, in that notice and an opportunity to be heard are not given before the . . . seizure of the wages. What happens in Wisconsin is that the clerk of the court issues the summons at the request of the creditor's lawyer; and it is the latter who by serving the garnishee sets in motion the machinery whereby the wages are frozen. They may, it is true, be unfrozen if the trial of the main suit is ever held and the wage earner wins on the merits. But in the interim the wage earner is deprived of his enjoyment of earned wages without any opportunity to be heard or to tender any defense he may have, whether it be fraud or otherwise.

Such summary procedure may well meet the requirements of due process in extraordinary situations. But in the present case, no situation requiring special protection to a state or creditor interest is presented by the facts; nor is the Wisconsin statute narrowly drawn to meet any such unusual condition. [Sniadach] was a resident of this Wisconsin community and in personam jurisdiction was readily obtainable.

. . . In this case, the sole question is whether there has been a taking of property without that procedural due process that is required by the Fourteenth Amendment. We have dealt over and over again with the question of what constitutes "the right to be heard" within the meaning of procedural due process. . . . [W]e said that the right to be heard "has little reality or worth unless one is informed that the matter is pending and can choose for himself whether to appear or default, acquiesce or contest." . . .

A prejudgment garnishment of the Wisconsin type is a taking which may impose tremendous hardship on wage earners with families to support. . . . Over and beyond that was the great drain on family income. As stated by Congressman Reuss:

> The idea of wage garnishment in advance of judgment, of trustee process, of wage attachment, or whatever it is called is a most inhuman doctrine. It compels the wage earner, trying to keep his family together, to be driven below the poverty level.

. . . .

The result is that a prejudgment garnishment of the Wisconsin type may as a practical matter drive a wage-earning family to the wall. Where the taking of one's property is so obvious, it needs no extended argument to conclude that absent notice and a prior hearing this prejudgment garnishment procedure violates the fundamental principles of due process.

DECISION AND REMEDY The Court ruled that the Wisconsin statute was unconstitutional. As a result of this decision, today a court must determine that a valid debt exists before wages can be garnished. The debtor also must receive proper notice and be offered a hearing before garnishment can take place.

CRITICAL THINKING: POLITICAL CONSIDERATION The case failed to discuss the issue of terminating employees if their wages are garnished. As discussed prior to this case, federal law does not allow businesses to terminate employees when their wages are garnished. Discuss whether the federal government should allow a business to terminate an employee when his or her wages are garnished.

Mortgage Foreclosure on Real Property

Chapter 12 reviewed the procedure by which a secured party (a creditor) repossesses personal property. The same basic format applies for the repossession of real property, with some differences. Liens on real estate have various names depending on the way in which the lien was created. For this discussion, the term *mortgage* is used since it is a familiar term.

Creation of the Mortgage. A real estate mortgage is a lien against the real property to secure payment of a loan given (usually) to secure the purchase of real property. For example, to purchase a house, Jane enters into a purchase agreement. She arranges with a lender to borrow money over a thirty-year period at a 9 percent interest rate. She signs a note with the lender in which she, the debtor-borrower, agrees to pay back the money in monthly installments to the creditor-lender during the next thirty years. At this point, the unsecured note is the only evidence of the debt. If Jane were to default on the note, the creditor could only sue her in court on the note.

The creditor wants something to back up the note, that is, the creditor wants a secured note (sometimes called a *mortgage note* as explained in Chapter 12). In real estate, the note is secured by a lien against the home (real property), called a **mortgage**. Jane, the debtor-borrower, creates a mortgage on the real estate and becomes the **mortgagor**. The creditor-lender is the beneficiary of the mortgage and is the **mortgagee**.

Default and Foreclosure. If Jane (the mortgagor or debtor-borrower) defaults by failing to pay the note, the real estate mortgage agreement provides that the mortgage company (the mortgagee or creditor-lender) can declare the entire loan due immediately. The mortgagee can have the loan paid by seeking a lawsuit called a **foreclosure**.

In this suit, the real estate that is covered by the mortgage is sold at a court-ordered sale (a foreclosure sale) under a writ of execution. If the proceeds of the sale are sufficient to cover both the costs of the foreclosure and the loan, any surplus is paid to the debtor. Jane is entitled to the surplus money because she owned the property. The creditor holds only a lien against her property. The creditor is entitled to have only the loan repaid and is not entitled to make a profit. The creditor only can collect the amount of the unpaid loan plus costs.

Deficiency Judgment. If, however, the sale proceeds are insufficient to cover the foreclosure costs and to repay the loan, in most states the mortgagee can seek to recover the difference from Jane (the mortgagor) by obtaining a *deficiency judgment*. A **deficiency judgment** represents the deficiency amount, that is, the difference between the loan along with the foreclosure costs and the amount actually received from the fore-closure sale's proceeds.

A deficiency judgment normally is obtained in a separate legal action that the creditor files after the foreclosure, because she only knows of a deficiency after the sale is complete. The creditor can recover the amount of the deficiency judgment from other property owned by the debtor.

Only nonexempt property (property that is subject to execution or garnishment) can be used to satisfy the deficiency judgment. In many states, the creditor cannot obtain a deficiency judgment at all against a debtor when the foreclosure involves the debtor's residence.

Between the time of default and the time of the foreclosure sale, Jane can redeem her property by paying the full amount of the loan still outstanding plus any interest and other costs that have accrued. In some states, Jane may even redeem her property within a statutory period after the judicial sale.

Protection for the Debtor

In most states, certain types of real and personal property are exempt from execution or attachment. Probably the most familiar of these exemptions is the **homestead exemption**. Each state permits the debtor to retain the family home, either in its entirety or up to a specified dollar amount, free from unsecured creditors or trustees in bankruptcy claims. The purpose is to ensure that the debtor will retain or be able to obtain some form of shelter. A homestead exemption, however, is not valid against a purchase-money lender.

For example, Dan owes Carey $40,000 as the result of a contract. The debt is the subject of a lawsuit. The court awards Carey a judgment of $40,000 against Dan. At some time before, during, or in some states even after the judgment has been awarded, Dan can file a homestead exemption. Dan's home is valued at $180,000, but he owes $30,000 on the purchase-money lender's mortgage. To satisfy the judgment debt, Dan's family home is sold at public auction for $175,000. Assume that the state law allows a homestead exemption of $125,000. The proceeds of the sale are distributed as follows.

1. The purchase-money lender is paid $30,000.
2. Dan is paid $125,000 as his homestead exemption.
3. Carey is paid $20,000 toward the judgment debt.
4. A $20,000 debt is still owed.

Carey now has a deficiency judgment for $20,000. This deficiency judgment can be satisfied from any other nonexempt property (personal or real) that Dan may have if allowed by state law.

Personal property that often is exempt from satisfaction of judgment debts includes the following:

1. Household furniture, such as beds, dining tables, and chairs, usually up to a specified dollar amount.
2. Clothing and certain personal possessions, such as family pictures, books, tools, and Bibles.
3. A vehicle for transportation (at least up to a specific dollar amount).

If Dan is unable to repay the rest of the $20,000, he may seek protection from his creditors. The following sections discuss **bankruptcies** (a debtor's public declaration that his bills or debts exceed his assets) and **reorganizations** (a plan formulated between a debtor and creditor under which the debtor pays a portion of his debts and is discharged of the remainder and under which the debtor can remain in business).

Bankruptcies and Reorganizations

The U.S. Constitution, Article I, Section 8, provides that

The Congress shall have power . . . To establish . . . uniform Laws on the subject of Bankruptcies throughout the United States.

Federal law governs bankruptcy proceedings. Congress passed the Bankruptcy Act, which has been amended over the decades. The Bankruptcy Act often is referred to as the Bankruptcy Code or just the code.

Bankruptcy courts are special federal courts. The U.S. court of appeals appoints bankruptcy judges for fourteen-year terms. Each federal judicial district has a **U.S. trustee** who monitors the administration of bankruptcy cases. Appeals of bankruptcy cases go to the Bankruptcy Appellate Panel or a federal district court before they can be heard by the appropriate U.S. circuit court of appeals.

Goals of Bankruptcy

Bankruptcy is designed to accomplish two main goals. The first is to provide relief and protection (a fresh start) to debtors who are deeply in debt and cannot recover financially without help.

The second major goal of bankruptcy is to provide a fair means of distributing a debtor's assets among all creditors. Although the bankruptcy acts are federal laws, state laws on secured transactions, liens, judgments, and exempt property play a role in federal bankruptcy proceedings.[5]

Bankruptcy Chapters

The Bankruptcy Code, comprised of several chapters, is contained in the United States Code. Chapters 1, 3, and 5 include general definitions and provisions governing the case administration, the creditors, the debtor, and the estate. These three chapters apply generally to all bankruptcies.

Several chapters set forth different types of bankruptcy relief. Chapter 7 provides for liquidations. Chapter 9 governs the adjustment of debts of a municipality. Chapter 11 allows for reorganizations of individual and business debtors. Chapter 12 provides bankruptcy relief for family farmers. Chapter 13 provides for the adjustment of debts for individuals with regular income.

Chapter 7, Liquidations. The most familiar type of bankruptcy proceeding is referred to as a *straight bankruptcy*. Put simply, a debtor in a **straight bankruptcy** lists her debts and turns her assets over to a trustee. The trustee sells the assets and distributes the proceeds to creditors. The debts then are discharged (forgiven) so that the debtor is relieved from the obligation to pay these debts.

Any person—defined here to include individuals, partnerships, and corporations—may be a debtor under Chapter 7. The term *corporation* as used here includes unincorporated companies and associations, as well as labor unions. Chapter 7 does not apply to railroads, insurance companies, banks, savings and loan associations, or governmental units. Other chapters of the Bankruptcy Act or other federal and state statutes apply to them.

[5] A good Internet link where you can locate answers to questions involving bankruptcy is <http://www.agin.com/lawfind/>. The American Bankruptcy Institute's web site contains information involving bankruptcy and legislative updates. The web address is <http://www.abiworld.org/>.

Bankruptcy Procedure. A straight bankruptcy begins when a debtor or creditors file a petition on the bankruptcy court's official forms. The debtor can file a voluntary petition, or unsecured creditors whose aggregate claims equal $5,000 or more can file an involuntary petition against the debtor. The petition lists both secured and unsecured creditors, their addresses, and the amount owed to each; states the debtor's financial affairs; and lists all of the debtor's property, including property that the debtor claims as exempt.

These official forms must be completed accurately, sworn to under oath, and signed by the debtor. To conceal assets or knowingly supply false information on these schedules is a federal crime and can result in the debtor's discharge in bankruptcy being denied.

The filing of a petition operates as an **automatic stay**, which stops or suspends all civil litigation against the debtor. In other words, creditors cannot start or continue legal actions against the debtor to recover claims against her, nor can creditors take any action to repossess the debtor's property. All actions against the debtor then must go through the bankruptcy court.

Trustees. A court-appointed trustee is distinguished from a U.S. trustee. The U.S. trustee is an administrative position within the bankruptcy court. A **regular trustee** (interim or permanent) is appointed by the court to represent the creditors.

The court appoints an interim trustee to preside over the debtor's property until the first meeting of creditors. At this first meeting, a permanent trustee is elected by the creditors. The trustee's principal duty is to collect the debtor's property, reduce it to money, and close up the estate as soon as possible, keeping in mind the best interests of all parties. Trustees are entitled to compensation for services rendered, plus reimbursement for expenses.

A trustee steps into the debtor's shoes and has specific powers to rescind the debtor's obligations. This power is called **avoidance**. Any reason that a debtor can use to obtain the return of his property can be used by the trustee as well. These grounds include fraud, duress, incapacity, and mutual mistake.

For example, Ben sells his boat to Frank. Frank gives Ben a check, knowing that he has insufficient funds in the bank account to cover the check. Frank has committed fraud. Ben can cancel the contract and recover the boat from Frank. If Ben has filed for bankruptcy, his trustee can exercise the same right to recover the boat from Frank.

The trustee's power of avoidance includes setting aside liens that are granted by statutes, called **statutory liens**, such as a landlord's lien. In some states, if the renter does not pay, the landlord can keep and even sell the tenant's personal property.

The trustee also can set aside **preferential payments**, that is, payments that the debtor made to favored creditors, but not to other creditors, within ninety days prior to the filing of the bankruptcy. Payments that the debtor made to an insider (a relative, partner, officer, or director) within one year can be set aside.

The same rules apply to a *preferential lien* that the debtor granted prior to filing bankruptcy. A **preferential lien** (as opposed to a statutory lien just mentioned) is one that the debtor made voluntarily, such as a lien placed on land that is owned free and clear, to enable a favored creditor to receive payments over the other creditors.

One reason the debtor would make a preferential lien is to gain favor with a creditor so that, after the bankruptcy, the creditor will continue to deal with the debtor. Another reason is to protect property by giving a preferential lien to a family member. The court, however, will not recognize the family member's property right because after bankruptcy, the family member could return the property to the debtor. These types of preferential liens operate to the detriment of the other creditors and are not allowed.

The purpose of setting these payments and liens aside is to ensure that all creditors are treated equally. The following case discusses a preferential lien that a trustee believed the bankrupt person made to a family member.

Case 14.5

In re Anderson

United States Bankruptcy
Court, 1994
165 B.R. 482 (Bkrtcy. D. Or.)

BACKGROUND AND FACTS Gerald and Ronald Anderson were the heirs to their mother's estate. Gerald misappropriated property from his mother's estate. Ronald was appointed as personal representative for the estate. A personal representative is appointed by the court to settle and distribute the estate's property. The estate sued Gerald in California. The court awarded the mother's estate a judgment in the amount of $1.8 million. Gerald then declared bankruptcy.

Gerald owned land in Arizona. Thus, Ronald proceeded to enforce the judgment in Arizona courts. Before the judgment was finalized in Arizona, Ronald, as personal representative, obtained a writ of attachment whereby a lien was placed on Gerald's Arizona real estate. The lien was dated January 10, 1992. On August 19, 1992, Gerald filed in federal court for bankruptcy. The trustee in bankruptcy sued the estate and Ronald. The trustee took the position that the real estate lien was a preferential lien to an insider, the mother's estate, and that therefore the lien should be set aside.

Bankruptcy Judge ALBERT E. RADCLIFFE

. . . .

The only issue presented to this court is whether Ronald W. Anderson, acting in his capacity as the personal representative of the probate estate of Dorothy Stewart Anderson, or such probate estate itself, was an insider of the debtor, when the lien attached to the property.

There are five elements to an action to avoid a transfer as preferential under [the Code]. The parties agree that all but one of those elements has been established. If the transfer occurs between ninety days and one year before the date of the filing of the petition, the transfer can be avoided, as a preference, only if the transferee was, at the time of the transfer, an insider.

[T]he Code defines four entities as "insiders" when the debtor is an individual:

"insider" includes—
(A) if the debtor is an individual—
    (i) relative of the debtor or of a general partner of the debtor;
    (ii) partnership in which the debtor is a general partner;
    (iii) general partner of the debtor; or
    (iv) corporation of which the debtor is a director, officer, or person in control;

The word "includes" as used in the definition is meant to be expansive. "Relative" is defined as:

. . . individual related by affinity or consanguinity within the third degree as determined by the common law, or individual in a step or adoptive relationship within such third degree.

The parties agree that when the transfer in question occurred, Ronald was acting only in his capacity as the personal representative of the probate estate. The plaintiff has sued Ronald in that capacity. Plaintiff admits that "If Ronald were being sued personally, he would clearly be an insider. . . . Being sued in his representative capacity, the defendant is actually the probate estate itself." Ronald agrees with this characterization. The real issue before the court then becomes whether the probate estate is an insider.
. . . .

Here, the defendant is the probate estate. It is true that it is the probate estate for Dorothy Stewart Anderson, the mother of the debtor. Its personal representative is Ronald, the debtor's brother. Either of these individuals would be per se insiders. Probate estates, however, are not listed within the Code's definition of insiders as set forth in [the Code].
. . . .

Though the probate estate could be an insider of the debtor if, in fact, the circumstances demonstrate . . . [a] type of closeness and degree of control . . . [but] in this case there was clearly an adversarial relationship between the defendant and the debtor.
. . . .

. . . [T]he probate estate of a relative is not included within the Code's definition of "insider." Given the hostility between Ronald, acting on behalf of the probate estate, and the debtor, which existed when the transfer occurred as well as the circumstances leading up to the Writ of Attachment, it is clear that the probate estate did not exercise sufficient control over the affairs of the debtor so as to render the probate estate an insider. Since the transfer occurred more than 90 days before the debtor filed his bankruptcy petition herein, the plaintiff may not avoid the lien as preferential.

DECISION AND REMEDY The court found that estates were not listed within the Code's definitions of insiders. The court found a clearly adversarial relationship between the estate and Gerald. The estate did not exercise sufficient control over Gerald's affairs to make the estate an insider.

CRITICAL THINKING: POLITICAL CONSIDERATION Discuss whether the law should treat insiders any differently from other creditors.

Exemptions. An individual debtor is entitled to choose to keep certain property as exempt from bankruptcy. An individual debtor can choose between the exemptions provided under the state law or federal law if the state law allows this choice. The following list shows some of the property exempt under federal law.

1. Equity interest in a debtor's residence up to $15,000.

2. One motor vehicle up to $2,400.

3. Household furnishings and apparel up to $8,000 with no more than one item worth more than $400.

4. Jewelry up to $1,000.

5. Professional books or tools of no more than $1,500.

6. Life insurance contracts.

7. Professionally prescribed health aids.

8. Miscellaneous property up to $800.

9. Social Security, profit-sharing, disability, alimony, and other funds for the support of the debtor or of his or her dependents.

10. Amounts paid to the debtor under a crime victim's law or wrongful death award, and amounts up to $15,000 (not including pain and suffering) for a personal injury.

Property Distribution. After reducing the debtor's assets to money, the trustee must pay the debts to those unsecured creditors who appropriately filed claims. Bankruptcy law establishes an order-of-priority list for certain classes of debts owed to unsecured creditors. Each class must be fully paid before the next class on the list is entitled to any proceeds.

If there is insufficient money to pay a class, the money is prorated among the creditors of that class, and all classes lower in priority receive nothing. If all classes are fully paid, any remaining balance goes to the debtor.

Examples of the order of priority among classes of unsecured creditors are as follows.

1. All bankruptcy costs (top priority).

2. Claims for unpaid wages, salaries, or commissions due to employees that were earned within ninety days of the bankruptcy petition (limited to $2,000 per employee).

3. Claims for funds that creditors prepaid to the debtor for goods or services that the debtor failed to deliver (limited to $900 per claim).

4. Certain taxes (and penalties) owed to government entities.

All of these creditors and others must be paid before any unsecured creditor receives proceeds from the debtor's estate.

Nondischargeable Debts. From the debtor's viewpoint, the primary purpose of a Chapter 7 liquidation is to obtain a fresh start through the **discharge** (excused from paying) of debts. In certain circumstances, however, a debt will not be discharged.

Debts that are not dischargeable include claims for back taxes accruing within three years prior to bankruptcy; claims against property or money obtained by the debtor under false representations; claims for alimony and child support; claims for certain student loans; and judgments or consent decrees awarded against a debtor for liability incurred as a result of the debtor's operation of a motor vehicle while legally intoxicated.

Discharges are granted only to "individuals" as debtors, not to corporations or partnerships. The latter may use Chapter 11 or, where appropriate, Chapter 12 bankruptcy proceedings.

Reaffirmation. A debtor can **reaffirm** (renew) his old debts through a reaffirmation agreement; that is, the debtor can agree to repay the debt. The debtor must agree to these repayments before he is granted a discharge.

The agreement must be filed with and approved by the court. The debtor must be counseled by his attorney and must file a declaration stating that the debtor knows the consequences of the voluntary agreement and that the agreement imposes no hardship on the debtor or on his dependents.

The debtor can rescind the agreement at any time prior to discharge or within sixty days of filing the agreement, whichever is later. This rescission period must be stated clearly and conspicuously in the reaffirmation agreement.

Chapter 11, Reorganizations. Chapter 11 reorganization is used most commonly by a corporate debtor. Essentially, in a reorganization the creditors and the debtor formulate a plan under which the debtor

Sears, Roebuck and Co. (Sears) has its own credit card system which is used by 60 million customers. The credit card operation is very profitable and in recent years has accounted for nearly one-half of Sears' net income.

Bankruptcies, in the meantime, have been climbing. In 1992, approximately 900,000 personal bankruptcies were filed. In 1999, more than 1,354,376 were filed.

These bankruptcies affected Sears' credit card business. Approximately 500,000 customers had charged over $400 million in merchandise between 1992 and 1997. During that time, Sears made 500,000 reaffirmation (repayment) agreements with bankrupt credit card customers. If the person signed the reaffirmation agreement and paid the debt down to a predetermined level, Sears then would extend a small line of credit, usually $500. This offer was very enticing to the bankrupt person because it helped her reestablish credit after bankruptcy.

When a person filed for bankruptcy, the creditors were notified. Sears then sent a nonlawyer representative to attend the public creditor meetings. The representative later approached the customer about repaying the Sears debt. Most reaffirmations followed this model.

A reaffirmation agreement must be filed with the bankruptcy court, which then must approve the agreement. Sears failed to file the reaffirmation agreements with the various bankruptcy courts.

A bankruptcy judge in Massachusetts discovered the reaffirmation plans when a bankrupt man requested that the Sears debt be discharged after he signed a reaffirmation agreement. Finding that Sears had failed to file or gain court approval of the agreement, the judge ordered a hearing.

Sears decided not to contest the allegations, to conduct an audit of its records from 1992 to 1997, and to return, with interest, money paid by customers whose reaffirmation agreements were not filed with the court. The cost: $400 million, plus a stain on its reputation as a good corporate citizen.

pays a portion of its debts and is discharged of the remainder. The debtor may continue in business. Proceedings may be initiated by either a voluntary or involuntary petition. A fast track for reorganization is provided for small businesses that have debts of less than $2 million and that are not engaged in owning or operating real estate.

The same principles that govern the filing of a Chapter 7 petition apply to Chapter 11 proceedings and to the court's entry of the order for relief. The automatic stay and adequate protection provisions previously discussed apply in reorganizations.

The debtor generally continues to operate its business as a "debtor in possession." The court may appoint a trustee to operate the debtor's business if it finds gross mismanagement of the business or if trustee appointment is in the debtor's best interests.

The debtor files a Chapter 11 plan that must be "fair and equitable." Classes of claims, such as those by secured and unsecured creditors, must be designated under the plan. The court provides the same treatment for each claim within a particular class. Once the plan has been developed, it is submitted to each class of creditors for acceptance. Each class is required to accept the plan.

The plan must be in the best interests of the creditors. On confirmation, the debtor receives a Chapter 11 discharge for all claims not protected under the plan. Those debts protected by the plan are paid in part according to the plan, but the remainder of those debts is discharged.

Chapter 13, Adjustment of Debts of an Individual with Regular Income.

The Bankruptcy Act provides for the formulation of plans to allow people with regular income to pay off their debts free from the harassment of creditors. Under these plans, people avoid the stigma of being adjudicated "bankrupt."

Who May File. Individuals (not partnerships or corporations) with regular income who owe unsecured debts of less than $250,000 and secured debts of less than $750,000 may take advantage of Chapter 13. The act includes individual business proprietors and individuals on welfare, Social Security, fixed pensions, or investment income. Many small business debtors can choose between filing a plan under either Chapter 11 or Chapter 13.

Several advantages of filing a Chapter 13 plan include that it is less expensive and less complicated than a Chapter 11 proceeding or a Chapter 7 liquidation. A Chapter 13 case can only be initiated by the voluntary filing of a petition by the debtor. Any eligible debtor who is presently in a Chapter 7 or Chapter 11 bankruptcy proceeding can convert it to a Chapter 13 case.

Bankruptcy Proceedings. When a debtor files a Chapter 13 petition, the automatic stay previously discussed takes effect. The debtor may propose a plan that provides for either full or partial payment of his debts. A Chapter 13 plan must provide for the turnover of the debtor's future earnings or income to the trustee as is necessary to carry out the plan. Full payment of all claims entitled to priority must be included in the plan.

The full payment is made by paying smaller amounts over a longer time period than would have been allowed under the original creditor–debtor agreement. Each claim within a particular class must be treated equally. Each secured debt, for example, must be paid in the same method as all other secured debts. The time for payment under the plan may not exceed three years, unless the court approves an extension. The plan, with extension, may not exceed five years.

The plan must be confirmed by the court as long as all of the debtor's projected disposable income will be applied to making payments. Disposable income is all income less amounts needed to support the debtor (and dependents), amounts needed to meet ordinary expenses to continue a business operation, or both.

The debtor must make "timely payments," which must begin under the proposed plan within thirty days after the plan has been filed. A debtor's failure to make timely payments or to commence payments within the thirty-day period allows the court to convert the case to a Chapter 7 liquidation or to dismiss the petition.

After completion of all payments under a Chapter 13 plan, the court discharges all debts for which the plan provided. Taxes, alimony, and child support debts cannot be discharged.

Even if the debtor fails to complete the plan because of circumstances beyond the debtor's control and if the property distributed by the plan was greater than would have been paid in a Chapter 7 liquidation, a hardship discharge may be granted. For example, if the debtor were seriously injured in an accident and became permanently disabled, the debtor's income would be severely reduced; therefore, he would be unable to complete the plan. In such a case, a discharge of the remaining debts might be granted.

Chapter 12, Adjustment of Debts of a Family Farmer with Regular Annual Income. The Family Farmer Bankruptcy Act defines a family farmer as one whose gross income is at least 50 percent farm dependent and whose debts are at least 80 percent farm related. The total debt must not exceed $1.5 million. A partnership or closely held corporation (at least 50 percent owned by the farm family) also can take advantage of this law.

A Chapter 12 filing is very similar in procedure to a Chapter 13 filing. The farmer-debtor must file a plan not later than ninety days after the order of relief. The filing of the petition acts as an automatic stay against creditors and co-obligor actions against the estate.

The plan's content and confirmation are basically the same as for a Chapter 13 filing. The plan can be modified by the farmer-debtor, but except for cause, must be confirmed or denied within forty-five days of the filing of the plan's filing. The plan must provide for payment of secured debts at the collateral's value. If the secured debt exceeds the collateral's value, the remaining debt is unsecured.

For unsecured debtors, the plan must be confirmed either if the value of the property to be distributed under the plan equals the amount of the claim or if the plan provides that all of the debtor-farmer's disposable income received in a three-year period (or longer, by court approval) will be applied to making payments.

Disposable income includes all income received less amounts needed to support the farmer-debtor and family and to continue the farming operation. Completion of payments under the plan constitutes the discharge of all debts for which the plan provided.

International Consideration

Consumer Credit Protection in Foreign Countries

The Organization for Economic Cooperation and Development (OECD) was started in 1961 as an intergovernmental institution for Western countries. Its aim is to achieve the highest sustainable economic growth and employment, to maintain financial stability, and to contribute to the expansion of world trade.

No direct equivalents to the consumer protections set out in this chapter, however, have been adopted in the international setting. In 1977, the OECD recognized the importance of consumer credit. A recommendation was made to its member countries to adopt internal legislation that includes the following protections.

Consumers should be provided with credit information through advertisements, a recommendation that is very similar to the Truth-in-Lending Act. The documents should clearly establish full disclosure of all credit terms. Legislation should provide for the consumer's privacy. Regulation of door-to-door sales, abolishment of the consumer holder-in-due-course concept, prohibition of unfair trade practices, and regulation of debt collection agencies are a few of the consumer protections recommended by the OECD. Notice that most of these provisions are already a part of the U.S. Consumer Credit Protection Act.

LEGALLY SPEAKING

The Proper Way to Grant Credit

You are a manager of a medium-sized manufacturing firm that sells predominantly to retail consumers. Your average sale is $2,500, which necessitates that your firm grant credit.

No problems arise when your customers pay in accordance with your agreement and your customers normally pay on time. You, however, must plan ahead to give your company the best position possible under federal and state laws in the event that a customer does not pay.

Before granting credit, you should take a number of steps.

✔ Obtain a detailed credit application that lists the consumer's assets and liabilities. Included on this form are the names and addresses of creditors and the consumer's relatives. The information about the relatives may help you to determine assets that are available for attachment, execution, or garnishment. It also may help you to locate the debtor, if he or she moves.

✔ Although you cannot require it, ask for a Social Security number. This information is helpful for identification purposes, especially when the consumer has a common name, such as Gomez, Nguyen, or Smith. With this information, you can verify credit information with reporting agencies or with the listed creditors.

If you will receive more than four payments, you must comply with the truth-in-lending laws.

✔ Use the forms drafted by the Federal Reserve Board and published in the *Code of Federal Regulations*. You will save time and conform with the law.

If your product is sold door to door, you must comply with federal law.

✔ State clearly in the contract the three-business-day cooling-off period.

✔ State clearly in the contract where the customer should send a revocation notice if she or he exercises that option.

If you sell personal property (goods), decide whether to secure your interest under the Uniform Commercial Code, Article 9. This procedure is covered in Chapter 12.

✔ Obtain a written security agreement signed by the debtor when the consumer-debtor has possession of the product.

✔ File a financing statement (UCC-1) with the appropriate public office to protect your interest.

If an account becomes delinquent, follow federal regulations when collecting.

✔ Establish a written policy concerning debt collection.

✔ Review the provisions of the Fair Debt Collection Practices Act.

✔ Investigate and respond to a debtor's inquiry if he or she contests a bill.

✔ Never threaten criminal prosecution, even if the debtor has committed a criminal act, such as giving a bad check or committing fraud on the credit application. These threats could be considered duress in a civil action and the threats themselves could result in you being charged with the crime of extortion.

✔ If you decide to hire a debt collection agency, write a contract with the collection agency that includes its agreement to conform with federal law.

At times, your firm will have to write off a debt as uncollectible and take a tax loss, if allowed. The old saying "You can't get blood out of a turnip" has application today. If the consumer is unemployed, is in prison, has a disability, or is suffering some other catastrophe, your firm should take the loss as soon as possible. In fact, if you have no losses on credit sales, possibly your credit policies are too rigid. Your firm might be able to increase sales by relaxing those policies.

You should be prepared for a debtor to file for bankruptcy. Having knowledge of the bankruptcy chapters available to the debtor and your rights as creditor under each chapter is important in establishing your credit policy.

Chapter Summary

The Consumer Credit Protection Act has five sections that apply directly to businesses and consumers. These sections may be summarized briefly as follows:

1. The Truth-in-Lending Act requires the disclosure of the price owed, the finance charges, and the annual percentage rate of interest for the privilege of paying off the debt over a period of time. It also allows a three-day cooling-off period for credit transactions involving liens on residences (except first liens). The Federal Reserve Board has prepared forms that allow businesses to comply with this act. Under this act, a consumer normally can incur no more than $50 of liability on a stolen or lost credit card for its unauthorized use.

2. The Fair Credit Billing Act was enacted to assist debtors in correcting billing errors. The law allows any debtor who believes that a billing statement is in error to notify the creditor in writing explaining the error. The debtor does not have to pay the disputed amount at that time. The creditor must acknowledge receipt of the error inquiry and within ninety days correct the account or justify to the debtor the reason for which the amount is correct.

3. The Fair Credit Reporting Act establishes certain rights for consumers. The consumer can obtain the information contained in the credit records. In the event that the debtor contests this information, the reporting agency must investigate and correct misinformation and/or allow the debtor to file explanations. Only information from the last seven years may be maintained. Information regarding bankruptcies over ten years old must be deleted from the record.

4. The Equal Credit Opportunity Act prohibits the creditor from discriminating against credit applicants based on race, color, religion, national origin, gender, marital status, age, or income receipt through public assistance.

5. The Fair Debt Collection Practices Act was adopted to protect consumers from overzealous collection agencies. Debt collectors must refrain from certain practices that would cause an invasion of the debtor's privacy and from the intentional infliction of emotional distress or duress.

Creditors use three judicial methods to try to collect on judgments owed them: writ of execution, writ of attachment, and writ of garnishment. Writs of attachment and execution are directed against nonexempt property in the debtor's possession. The writ of garnishment is directed against the debtor's property that is in the possession of a third party.

Chapters 7, 11, 12, and 13 of the Bankruptcy Code are of major importance to businesses. Chapter 7 allows a discharge of most debts. Chapter 11 provides for reorganization. Chapters 12 and 13 permit family farmers and individuals to readjust their debts with a payout plan over a three- to five-year period. Some debts are not dischargeable by bankruptcy. In addition, certain assets are exempt from bankruptcy by law, meaning that the debtor may keep these assets.

Using the World Wide Web

Founded by the U.S. Congress in 1913, the Federal Reserve is the central bank of the United States. Congress charged the Federal Reserve with providing the nation with a safe, flexible, and stable monetary and financial system.

As stated on its web page, "The Federal Reserve's duties fall into four general areas: (1) conducting the nation's monetary policy; (2) supervising and regulating banking institutions and protecting the credit rights of consumers; (3) maintaining the stability of the financial system; and (4) providing certain financial services to the U.S. government, the public, financial institutions, and foreign official institutions." The following web sites provide additional information about the Federal Reserve System and the Federal Reserve banks.

Finding the Law on the Web

Federal Reserve System
    http://www.clev.frb.org/fedlinks.htm
Federal Reserve Bank of Atlanta
    http://frbatlanta.org
Federal Reserve Bank of Boston
    http://www.bos.frb.org

Federal Reserve Bank of Chicago
   http://www.frbchi.org
Federal Reserve Bank of Cleveland
   http://www.clev.frb.org
Federal Reserve Bank of Dallas
   http://www.dallasfed.org
Federal Reserve Bank of Minneapolis
   http://woodrow.mpls.frb.fed.us
Federal Reserve Bank of New York
   http://www.ny.frb.org
Federal Reserve Bank of Philadelphia
   http://www.phil.frb.org/
Federal Reserve Bank of St. Louis
   http://www.stls.frb.org
Federal Reserve Bank of San Francisco
   http://www.frbsf.org

Chapter Web Sites

Regulation Z
   http://www4.law.cornell.edu/cfr/12p226.htm#start
Truth-in-Lending Act
   http://www.law.cornell.edu/uscoe/15/1601.shtml
Federal Trade Commission
   http://www.ftc.gov/
or
   http://www.ftc.gov/bcp/conline/pubs/buspubs
   /credempl.htm
Consumer Reporting Reform Act
   http://www.ftc.gov/os/statutes/fcra.htm
Equal Credit Opportunity Act
   http://www4.law.cornell.edu/uscode/topn/

Bass v. Stolper
   http://www.kentlaw.edu/7circuit/1997/apr
   /96-2113.html
Sniadach v. Family Finance Corporation
   http://www.thelawengine.com
Bankruptcy questions
   http://www.agin.com/lawfind/
American Bankruptcy Institute
   http://www.abiworld.org/
Secured credit cards
   http://www.freeadvice.com

Web Activities

14–1 Can you reestablish a good credit record after you have declared bankruptcy or have created a very poor credit record? Yes. Although it takes a long time to reestablish a good credit record, one way to start is to obtain a secured credit card. Go to <http://www.freeadvice.com> and scroll to "Bankruptcy Law" and click on "Credit Problems." Many credit issues are discussed including obtaining a secured credit card. What is a secured credit card? What are its advantages?

14–2 You are on a trip. You register at a hotel and use your credit card. You may run into the concept of credit card blocking. What is credit card blocking and how do you protect yourself? Go to the Federal Trade Commission's web page at <http://www.ftc.gov> and click on "Consumer Protection," then click on "Credit." At this web page, click on credit card blocking.

Key Terms

affidavit
annual percentage rate (ARP)
automatic stay
avoidance
bankruptcy
Consumer Credit Cost Disclosure Act
Consumer Credit Protection Act (CCPA)
Consumer Leasing Act
Consumer Reporting

Reform Act
deficiency judgment
discharge
Equal Credit Opportunity Act
exempt property
Fair Credit Billing Act
Fair Credit Reporting Act
Fair Debt Collection Practices Act
finance charge
foreclosure

garnishment
homestead exemption
judicial sale
mortgage
mortgagee
mortgagor
nonexempt property
preferential lien
preferential payments
reaffirm
Real Estate Settlement Procedures Act
regular trustee

reorganization
statutory liens
straight bankruptcy
Truth-in-Lending Act (TILA)
Uniform Consumer Credit Code (UCCC)
U.S. trustee
writ of attachment
writ of execution

Questions and Case Problems

14–1 Bankruptcy The East Bank was a secured party on a loan of $5,000 that it made to Sally. Sally later experienced financial difficulty. Creditors other than the East Bank petitioned her into Chapter 7 involuntary bankruptcy. The value of the secured collateral had decreased substantially. On sale, the debt to East Bank was reduced only to $2,500. Sally's estate consisted of $100,000 in exempt assets and $2,000 in nonexempt assets. After the bankruptcy costs and back wages to Sally's employees were paid, no funds remained for unsecured creditors. Sally received a discharge in bankruptcy. Six years later she decided to go back into business. By selling a few exempt assets and getting a small loan, she could buy a small but profitable restaurant. She went to East Bank for the loan. East Bank claimed that the balance of its secured debt was not discharged in bankruptcy. Sally signed an agreement to pay East Bank the $2,500, because the bank was not a party to petitioning Sally into bankruptcy. Because of this, East Bank made a new unsecured loan to Sally.

    a. Discuss East Bank's claim that the balance of its secured debt was not discharged in bankruptcy.

    b. Discuss the legal effect of Sally's agreement to pay East Bank $2,500 after the discharge in bankruptcy.

    c. If, one year later, Sally went into voluntary bankruptcy, what effect would the bankruptcy proceedings have on the new unsecured loan?

14–2 Credit Card Liability Green receives two new credit cards on May 1. One was solicited from the King Department Store. The other was unsolicited from Flyways Airline. During May, Green makes numerous credit card purchases from King, but she does not use the Flyways Airline card. On May 31, a burglar breaks into Green's home and steals both credit cards, along with other items. Green notifies the King Department Store of the theft on June 2, but she fails to notify Flyways Airline. Using the King credit card, the burglar makes a $500 purchase on June 1 and a $200 purchase on June 3. The burglar then charges a vacation flight on the Flyways Airline card for $1,000 on June 5. Green receives the bills for these charges and refuses to pay them. Discuss Green's liability in these situations.

14–3 Bankruptcy Procedures Prior to filing for bankruptcy, Bray made loan payments to his company's credit union through payroll deductions. Bray's employer continued to deduct the loan payments from Bray's paychecks after being notified of the bankruptcy petition. Is this a violation of the Bankruptcy Code? [*In re Bray*, 17 B.R. 152 (Bkrtcy. N. D. Ga. 1982)]

14–4 Fair Credit Reporting Act In 1976, Zeller and Samia jointly purchased a beach cottage. Zeller signed a note promising to pay Samia $3,333.33, which was his share of the $10,000 down payment. In 1985 the relationship between the two parties deteriorated. In 1986, Samia sued Zeller for the balance due on the note. In 1987, after Zeller failed to pay, Samia reported a charge-off of $11,000 (unpaid principal, interest, and costs) to Credit Data. A charge-off is a bookkeeping entry that occurs when a creditor believes a debt to be no longer collectible. As a result, two mortgage companies and a credit card company rejected Zeller's credit requests. Zeller filed an action alleging violations of the Fair Credit Reporting Act (FCRA) and sought actual and punitive damages. Did Samia's action of filing the charge-off with Credit Data violate the Fair Credit Reporting Act? Explain. [*Zeller v. Samia*, 758 F. Supp. 775 (D. Mass. 1991)]

14–5 Truth-in-Lending Two salespeople from Capitol Roofing visited the plaintiffs, Norman and Judy Cole, to sell them siding for their home. After a sales pitch, the salespeople estimated the cost to be $4,900. Before the salespeople left, the Coles signed a number of documents, including a work order, a home improvement retail installment contract, a security agreement and disclosure statement, a loan application, a notice of right to cancel, and a deed of trust. The only document the Coles fully read was the work order. They only saw the signature block on the other papers. The salespeople misrepresented to the Coles the real nature of the paperwork. The Coles were told that they had signed a work order, credit application, and insurance papers. Shortly thereafter, the Coles decided to hold off on the work so that they could obtain estimates from other companies. Mrs. Cole called Capitol Roofing the next morning and said they had decided to wait. She was told that the papers had been processed, the workers would be out at the end of the week, and she could do nothing. She went to work, and when she returned, she found the crew installing the siding. The contract was assigned by Capitol Roofing to United Companies Mortgage (UCM). The Coles experienced problems with the siding. After eleven payments, the Coles became frustrated and discontinued payment to UCM. They brought legal action to recover the payments that they did make. Did they prevail and why? [*Cole v. Lovett,* 672 F. Supp. 947 (1987)]

14–6 Truth-in-Lending Harold Grey signed an installment contract as payment for membership in European Health Spas, Inc. The disclosure documents that accompanied the installment loan contract were printed in regular type, with the exception of the following words, which were printed in capital letters: "FINANCE CHARGE," "ANNUAL PERCENTAGE RATE," and "MEMBER ACKNOWLEDGES THAT HE HAS READ AND RECEIVED A FILLED-IN SIGNED COPY OF THIS AGREEMENT." In addition, at the top of the disclosure statement, the words "NOTICE TO BUYER" were printed. Under federal truth-in-lending regulations, the words *finance charge* and *annual percentage rate* must be printed conspicuously in the truth-in-lending disclosure statements. Otherwise, the creditor is deemed in violation of the act. Discuss whether European Health spas met the requirement of conspicuousness. [*Grey v. European Health Spas, Inc.,* 428 F. Supp. 841 (D. Conn. 1977)]

14–7 Truth-in-Lending In the summer of 1972, Robert Martin applied for and was issued an American Express card. Approximately three years later, in April 1975, Martin gave his card to E. L. McBride, a business associate, and orally authorized McBride to charge up to $500 on it. Martin also wrote to American Express requesting that charges on his account be limited to $1,000. In June 1975, however, Martin received a statement from American Express indicating that the amount owed on his card account was approximately $5,300. Under the Truth-in-Lending Act, for how much will Martin be liable to American Express? [*Martin v. American Express, Inc.,* 361 So. 2d 597 (Ala. App. 1978)]

14–8 Fair Debt Collection Practices Act Telecredit Service Corp. is a computerized check authorization and purchase service. It purchases, on average, 608,959 dishonored checks a year. A customer writes a check to a merchant, who then verifies with Telecredit whether the customer previously has written bad checks. If the customer's record is clean, Telecredit authorizes acceptance of the check. If the check then is dishonored, Telecredit purchases the check and attempts collection of it. Holmes wrote a bad check for $315. Telecredit purchased the check and used various means to collect from Holmes. These procedures possibly violated the Fair Debt Collection Practices Act. Telecredit argued that it owned the check and thus was exempt from the act's restrictions. Is Telecredit subject to the act? Explain. [*Holmes v. Telecredit Service Corp.,* 736 F. Supp. 1289 (D. Del. 1990)]

14–9 Fair Debt Collection Practices Act Masuda, the plaintiff, incurred debts with a laboratory. When he failed to pay these debts, they were assigned to a collection agency, Thomas Richards & Company (TRC), the defendant. In attempting to collect the debt, TRC sent several letters requesting payment that its own employees signed. Kenneth N. Wolfe, attorney-at-law, signed other standard form letters, but they were not on his regular stationery. The attorney's letters provided TRC's address and telephone number. Wolfe had no knowledge of, and had not conferred with TRC concerning, Masuda's debt. Masuda hired an attorney who informed the defendant, TRC, to send any future communications through his office. TRC continued to send letters to Masuda. He instituted action under the Fair Debt Collection Practices Act. Did TRC's action violate the Fair Debt Collection Practices Act? Explain. [*Masuda v. Thomas Richards & Co.,* 759 F. Supp. 1456 (C.D. Ca. 1991)]

14–10 Internet Your advertisement for cashiers nets 100 applications. You want credit reports on each applicant. You plan to eliminate those with poor credit histories. What are your obligations? Go to the Federal Trade Commission web site, which addresses this question, at <http://www.ftc.gov/bcp/conline/pubs/buspubs/credempl.htm>.

Chapter 15 Consumer Protection

Caveat emptor: *Let the buyer beware.*

Latin maxim

Ethical Consideration

What You Do Not Know Can Bother You: Sharing Information from Warranty Cards

You own Global Electronics, a maker of electronic equipment. When Global Electronics sells a product, such as a television, it includes a warranty card. The card requests information regarding the purchaser's e-mail address, salary, profession, age, marital status, number of persons in the household, income, hobbies, and other personal information. Global Electronics uses some of the information for its own purposes, but this information also is placed into a database, which is sold. This information is used by direct-mail businesses, telemarketers, and Internet marketers, and for other purposes.

Customers who fill out the warranty cards may be unaware that your company will sell their personal information. Is it ethical to request this information on the warranty card and to sell the data without informing the customer? Would your answer differ if the customer were informed? Use the ethical model presented in Chapter 2 and reprinted on the inside front cover to develop your answer.

Introduction

Earlier chapters addressed ways in which the law attempts to protect consumers' interests. Courts, administrative agencies, and legislatures have outlawed certain business practices because they have been determined to be unfair or deceptive. This chapter discusses laws that attempt to control unfair and deceptive trade practices, to prevent misleading advertising, and to encourage the development of safe products.

Artiste Login Products, Inc., your web business, needs to be aware of federal and state consumer protection statutes. Often, these statutes stipulate civil and criminal penalties for failing to comply with the statutory requirements. The requirements may be as simple as disclosing information or disclosing it in a specific manner.

Consumer protection statutes promote both safety and fair dealing. They try to prevent injury to a person's body or damage to his property or economic well-being. Although some statutes provide a specific remedy if the consumer suffers an injury, consumer protection statutes aim to eliminate the harm itself. Many of these statutes provide no remedies for injured consumers. Redress for injuries suffered usually involves another area of the law, such as tort or contract law (covered in Chapters 8 through 11).

Artiste Login Products must assume the costs of complying with government regulations associated with consumer protection. Artiste, in turn, passes these costs of compliance on to its consumers in the form of higher prices for goods and services.

For every consumer protection statute, society poses three questions:

1. From what harm does the statute protect consumers?

2. Whom does the statute protect?

3. What is the cost of this protection?

Exhibit 15–1 lists statutes and regulations designed to protect consumers. This chapter will familiarize you with the nature and existence of some of the important statutes. Chapter 14, on credit regulation, explored the most significant legislation applicable to consumer financing.

Federal Trade Commission

Consumer protection, as we know it today, originated with the **Wheeler–Lea Act** of 1938, which gave the **Federal Trade Commission Act** a dual focus: to regulate anticompetitive business behavior and to provide consumer protection. The 1938 law amended the Federal Trade Commission Act, originally passed in 1914. Prior to 1938, courts aided only a few purchasers who sued sellers of defective goods by finding that the seller had breached a contract, had breached a warranty, or had violated a duty to the purchaser. As pointed out in Chapter 11, these claims often are difficult to prove.

The Wheeler–Lea amendment prohibited **"unfair or deceptive acts or practices,"** which enabled the Federal Trade Commission (FTC) to focus its attention on direct consumer protection. The amendment also gave the FTC the authority to monitor deceptive advertising practices. Under this amendment, the FTC

Exhibit 15–1 Consumer Protection Statutes and Regulations

Date	Popular Name	Purpose
		Advertising
1938	Wheeler–Lea Act	Amends the Federal Trade Commission Act (1914); prohibits deceptive and unfair trade practices.
1946	Lanham Act	Prohibits deceptive advertising.
1950	Oleomargarine Tax Repeal Act	Prohibits advertising that oleomargarine is a dairy product.
1969	Public Health Cigarette Smoking Act	Prohibits advertising of cigarettes on television.
1973	FTC Rules of Negative Options	Regulates advertisements for book and record clubs.
1988	Charity Games Advertising Act	Allows interstate advertising of gambling games if state run or for charitable purposes.
		Inspection and Certification
1906	Meat Inspection Act	Provides for inspection of meat.
1907	Wholesome Meat Act	Amends Meat Inspection Act.
1938	Food, Drug, and Cosmetic Act	Provides for inspection and regulation of food, drugs, and cosmetics.
1958	Food Additive (Delaney) Amendment to Food Drug, and Cosmetic Act	Requires that food additives not cause cancer and be safe.
1966	Hazardous Substances Act	Regulates hazardous substances
1968	Poultry Inspection Act	Provides for inspection of poultry.
1969	Child Protection and Toy Safety Act	Amends Hazardous Substances Act; bans toys that pose electrical, mechanical, or thermal hazards.
1972	Odometer Act	Regulates odometers.
1976	Medical Device Amendments	Requires premarket clearance of medical devices.
1976	Toxic Stubstances Control Act	Regulates certain chemical substances and mixtures.
1994	Hazardous Material Transportation Act	Requires inspection of hazardous materials during transportation.
		Labeling
1906	Jewelers' Liability Act	Prohibits stamping on gold or silver products with "U.S. Assay."
1939	Wool Products Labeling Act	Requires accurate labeling of wool products.
1951	Fur Products Labeling Act	Prohibits misbranding of fur products.
1953	Flammable Fabrics Act	Sets standards and requires labeling for flammable fabrics and products.
1958	Textile Fiber Products Identification Act	Requires accurate labeling of textiles.
1960	Hazardous Substances Labeling Act	Requires accurate labeling of hazardous substances.
1966	Fair Packaging and Labeling Act	Requires accurate names, quantities, and weights to be reported on packages.
1966	Child Protection Act	Requires childproof devices and special labeling.
1966	Cigarette Labeling and Advertising Act	Requires labels warning of possible health hazards.
1970	Poison Prevention Packaging Act	Requires labeling of poisonous household substances.
1986	Smokeless Tobacco Act	Requires conspicuous warnings on tobacco products.
1990	Nutrition Labeling Act	Requires labels on food packages to provide calories and other nutritional information.
		Sales and Warranties
1968	Interstate Land Sales	Requires full disclosure in interstate land sales.
1973	FTC Rule on Door-to-Door Sales	Regulates door-to-door sales contracts.
1975	Magnuson–Moss Warranty Act	Regulates warranties on consumer products.
1976	Real Estate Settlements Procedures Act	Requires disclosure of home-buying costs.
1980	FTC Rule on Vocational and Correspondence Schools	Regulates contracts with vocational and correspondence schools.
1984	FTC Rule on Used Cars	Regulates warranties in used car sales.
1994	Telemarketing and Consumer Fraud and Abuse Prevention Act	Regulates sales made over the telephone.

does not have to prove to the court that an advertising practice affected the competition. The definitions of the two words *unfair* and *deceptive* are left to the FTC. In general, any practice that would tend to mislead consumers is unfair or deceptive.

As a result of this amendment, the FTC has two bureaus: the Bureau of Competition and the Bureau of Consumer Protection. The Bureau of Competition handles the FTC's antitrust activities. The Bureau of Consumer Protection monitors advertising and labeling practices, investigates complaints, and prosecutes cases involving alleged unfair practices. Exhibit 15–2 shows the FTC's organizational structure.

Trade Regulation Rules

As an administrative agency, the FTC can adopt trade regulation rules. A **trade regulation rule** is a statement by the agency that has general applicability. The rule's effect is to implement the agency's law, policy, or practice. In other words, a rule has the force of law.

FTC trade regulation rules apply to an entire industry rather than to a particular seller. The commission can focus on an industry and formulate standards to which all businesses within that industry must conform. In the past, the FTC has investigated household detergents, appliances, office copiers, the title insurance business, the funeral industry, and car rental agencies. Other investigations included industries, such as transportation, health-care facilities, nursing homes, agriculture, and energy.

The FTC may institute an action against an alleged wrongdoer either in its administrative law court or in federal court. The FTC first tries to persuade a seller to stop an unfair or deceptive practice. This tactic is effective because most cases are settled by a consent decree. The seller and the FTC reach an agreement as to how the seller will conduct its business in the future. This agreement is finalized in the form of a consent decree whereby the seller consents to an order restraining the activity found by the FTC to be unfair or deceptive. A defendant-seller may be required to compensate injured buyers when the seller has violated an FTC rule or order.

If the FTC and the seller do not come to an agreement, the FTC may take the case to an administrative law court and request a **cease-and-desist order**. This order requires the seller-defendant to cease its activities and desist from undertaking those activities in the future. This type of order forces the seller to correct its business operations.

If unable to reach an agreement, the FTC may elect to take the case to a U.S. district court instead of bringing the case to the FTC's administrative law court. At the request of the FTC, the district court can grant an injunction to restrain or prohibit a particular practice. Fines for violations may amount to $10,000 per day. Any person or firm subject to an FTC order or rule may seek a review of the FTC's action in a U.S. court of appeals.

Additional orders that the FTC can issue include *affirmative disclosure orders, corrective advertising orders,* and *multiple product orders*. By issuing an **affirmative disclosure order**, the FTC requires the defendant to place affirmative disclaimers into future advertisements.

An affirmative disclaimer states the ways in which the product will not benefit the user. The disclaimers help to remedy past deceptive advertisements. For example, the FTC required the J. B. Williams Company to state in its future advertisements for Geritol that it would not benefit the great majority of people who suffer from tiredness. Geritol had advertised that it was effective for any illness for which tiredness was a symptom. The advertising was deceptive, according to the FTC, because tiredness is symptomatic of many illnesses—including cancer and diabetes—on which Geritol had no effect.

A **corrective advertising order** is very similar to an affirmative disclaimer, but it takes the remedy one step further. This order requires the defendant to place a statement in the advertisements to the effect that its past advertisements were false.

The FTC can order the words "contrary to prior advertising" to be placed in future advertisements if the defendant engaged in egregious and intentional deception. For example, Novartis Consumer Health produces Doan's pills. The product had been advertised as more effective than other painkillers for back problems. The FTC required the company to spend $8 million over one year in its advertising and packaging to state that "Although Doan's is an effective pain reliever, there is no evidence that Doan's is more effective than other pain relievers for back pain."[1]

Generally, if the FTC finds deceptive advertising, it requires the firm to refrain from making any further deceptive advertisements. In cases in which a firm sells multiple products, such an order may have little effect. If the FTC finds not only deceptive advertising but

---

[1] *Novartis Corporation v. Federal Trade Commission,* 223 F.3d 783 (2000).

Exhibit 15–2 **Organizational Structure of the Federal Trade Commission**

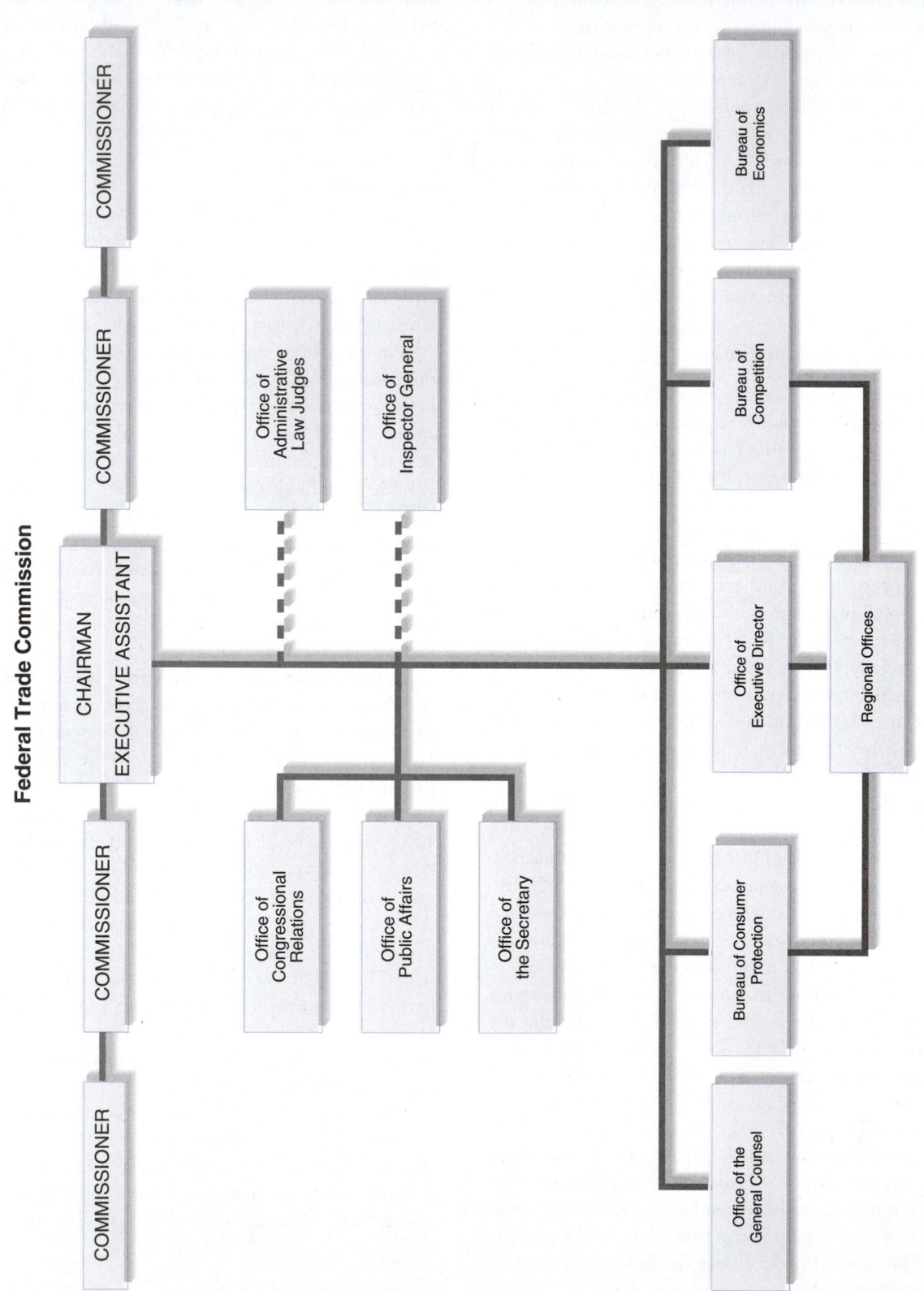

also a history of false advertising, it can issue a **multiple product order**. This order requires all future advertisements for all of the firm's products (or for all of the products in a certain category) to be accurate, not just advertisements for the original product that the firm falsely advertised. In the following case, the court of appeals reviews the power of the FTC to issue a multiple product order.

Case 15.1

Sears, Roebuck and Co. v. Federal Trade Commission

United States Court of
Appeals, Ninth Circuit, 1982
676 F.2d 385

BACKGROUND AND FACTS In the early 1970s, Sears formulated a plan to increase sales of its top-of-the-line Lady Kenmore dishwasher. The plan did not call for any reengineering of the dishwasher or other mechanical improvement. Rather, the plan fostered an image change for the Lady Kenmore, or in sales jargon, Sears sought to "reposition" the machine in the marketplace. The advertising objective was to change the consumer image from a "price" (economy) brand to that of a superior product at a reasonable price. Sears hoped that the machine would move from market leadership to market dominance as the market share increased.

Sears recognized that a dishwasher that eliminated the need to prerinse and prescrape dishes would attract new customers and command a premium price. It also knew that a machine's ability to clean dishes on the upper rack as thoroughly as those on the bottom rack would further attract new customers. Based on this knowledge, Sears prepared advertisements claiming that the Lady Kenmore "completely eliminated" the need for prescraping and prerinsing. The advertisements characterized the machine as the "freedom maker."

Advertisements for the Lady Kenmore appeared in print and on television throughout the country over a four-year period at a cost to Sears of roughly $8 million. During the first three years, Lady Kenmore unit sales rose 300 percent. The value of the company's total dishwasher sales rose from $73,470,000 in 1971 to $94,500,000 in 1973.

The "no scraping, no prerinsing" claim was false. Sears had no reasonable basis for asserting the claim. Furthermore, the owner's manual that customers received after purchasing the dishwasher contradicted the claim. A 1973 survey conducted for Sears found that more than half of recent Lady Kenmore purchasers disagreed with the proposition that the Lady Kenmore did not require prerinsing.

The FTC began an investigation of the advertisements in 1975. In 1977, the FTC issued a complaint, charging Sears and its advertising agency, J. Walter Thompson Company, with disseminating deceptive and unfair advertisements. After an extensive administrative hearing, the administrative law judge (ALJ) held Sears liable for deceptive and false advertising. The ALJ issued a multiple product order to Sears not to make any performance claims for any major home appliances without first possessing a reasonable basis consisting of competent and reliable tests. Further, it ordered Sears to keep records for three years. Sears sought review of the administrative law judge's order.

Judge REINHARDT

. . . .

A judgment regarding "reasonable relation" in multi-product order cases "depends upon the specific circumstances of the case." "[T]he ultimate question is the likelihood of the petitioner committing the sort of unfair practices [the order] prohibit[s][.]" We answer that question by first examining the specific circumstances present in a particular case. Then, giving due deference to the Commission's expertise and judgment, we determine whether there is a "reasonable relation" between those circumstances and the concern regarding future violations manifested by the Commission's order.

Where a fair assessment of an advertiser's conduct shows a ready willingness to flout the law, sufficient cause for concern regarding further, additional violations exists. Two factors or elements frequently influence our decision—the deliberateness and seriousness of the present violation, and the violator's past record with respect to unfair advertising practices. Other circumstances may be weighted, including the adaptability or transferability of the unfair practice to other products. The weight given a particular factor or element will vary. The more egregious the facts with respect to a particular element, the less important it is that another negative factor be present. In the final analysis, we look to the circumstances as a whole and not to the presence or absence of any single factor.

. . . .

. . . Sears states that advertisements concerning the other covered products, e.g., microwave ovens and trash compactors, are never related to those promoting dishwashers since dishwashers do not perform work similar to the work performed by the microwave ovens or trash compactors, and that, therefore, an order covering these functionally unrelated machines is inherently unreasonable. This argument misses the fundamental point that the Commission is concerned not with how machines work, but with how machines are sold. Thus, the correct question is not whether the machines function in similar ways but whether the machines could be sold with similar techniques. . . .

. . . .

. . . Under [the specific] circumstances, Sears' advertising campaign demonstrates "blatant and utter disregard" for the law. The Commission also considered petitioner's compliance record and concluded that is was "a wash." We see no reason to find otherwise.

Sears' advertisements were no accident or "isolated instance." Rather, they were part of an advertising strategy, with attendant slogans, adopted without regard to the actual performance of the advertised machines. As the Commission pointed out, the covered machines are major ticket items generally purchased infrequently by any particular person. For that reason, their profitability does not depend on repeat purchases as is the case with frequently purchased, low-cost items. A selling strategy based on this purchasing fact, e.g., the making of false and unsubstantiated performance claims as to a major ticket item, would be effective for a considerable period of time, with great benefit to the merchant but at great cost to consumers. This selling strategy could readily be transferred to the marketing of other machines in the home appliance category.

The prevention of "transfers" of unfair trade practices is a fundamental goal of the Commission's remedial work. Justice Brandeis, a draftsman of the 1914 legislation which created the Commission, made this point in *Federal Trade Comm'n v. Gratz*[.] Objecting to the Court's attempt to narrow the Commission's remedial authority, he expressed a view which has since become law.

> The purpose of Congress [in creating the Commission] was to prevent any unfair method which may have been used by any concern in competition from becoming its general practice. It was only by stopping its use before it became general practice that the apprehended effect of all unfair methods . . . could be averted.

It is not only pretermitting a "general practice" which is important here, however. The "transfer" to any other single major home appliance could well cause substantial damage to consumers prior to the time that the Commission could again investigate the Acts and obtain the evidence necessary to prove that a similar violation had occurred. By that time, it would be too late to protect the large number of consumers who, in reliance on the truthfulness of the advertised claims, had purchased a major home appliance which they expected to perform the advertised work for many years. This danger is particularly acute where national brands, like Sears' major home appliances, are involved and the advertising campaigns are both widespread and intensive.

In addition, if we were to deny "transfer prevention" authority to the Commission under these circumstances, unscrupulous merchandisers (and we do not imply that Sears falls in that category) might be encouraged to transfer unlawful but successful advertising techniques from product to product, leaving the Commission the job of instituting separate proceedings to secure new orders for each unlawfully advertised product. Because so drastic a limitation on the Commission's enforcement procedure would conflict with the Congressional intent described by Justice Brandeis, would consume enormous resources, and would afford no particular protection to lawful advertisements and little protection to consumers, the Commission need not wait until a "transfer" occurs before issuing multi-product orders in cases like the one before us. It may issue and enforce such orders to avert an "apprehended effect."

To prevent the false and unsubstantiated performance claims strategy from being used in connection with another major home appliance or from becoming Sears' general practice with respect to such appliances, the Commission deemed a broad order necessary. A judgment of this nature depends on detailed knowledge of the major home appliances business and its related advertising techniques. "[D]eceptive advertising cases necessarily require 'inference and pragmatic judgment.'" This sort of knowledge of the commercial world and the ability to make the type of judgment required lie in the realm of the Commission's greater expertise.

We note one other important Act. . . . [T]he order before us is not an all-products order. It is a limited order that applies only to 14 major ticket items. These 14 items constitute a small proportion of the total number of products sold by Sears.

In light of the flagrant and egregious nature of the violation found and the other circumstances present here, and giving the Commission's conclusions the required "great weight," we find no basis for substituting our judgment for the Commission's regarding the necessity for this multi-product order. We hold that the multi-product order is reasonably related to the petitioner's conduct, that a multi-product order is appropriate, and that the inclusion of the "performance claims" provision in that order is supported by the record before us and does not render the order overbroad.

DECISION AND REMEDY The court of appeals upheld the validity of the FTC's multiple product order covering all of Sears' major home appliances, including clothes washers, clothes dryers, disposals, trash compactors, refrigerators, freezers, ranges, stoves, ovens, and stereophonic consoles. As the court pointed out, the FTC's fundamental goal is to prevent the "transfer" of unfair trade practices from one product to another. Congress created the FTC to stop unfair practices before they became a general practice. Thus, the FTC has the power to issue multiple product orders.

CRITICAL THINKING: ETHICS Discuss whether a major corporation today would attempt a sales program similar to Sears' dishwasher advertisements of the 1970s.

Exemptions to FTC Regulation

The major exemptions to FTC trade regulation activities are those firms or industries that are regulated by local, state, or other federal authorities. For example, public utilities are regulated by state authorities. Thus, few public utilities are subject to the FTC's authority.

Industries directly regulated by federal agencies are also outside the scope of FTC investigations. For example, the securities markets are regulated by the Securities and Exchange Commission. Some exceptions exist for which both the FTC and another federal agency have the power from Congress to investigate the same industry. For example, the FTC enforces some credit protection statutes even though the Federal Reserve Board, the Federal Home Loan Bank Board, and other federal agencies regulate credit. Another example is that both the FTC and the Food and Drug Administration regulate the labeling of food and drugs.

These agencies have interagency agreements that set out each agency's specific duties and indicate which will have primary investigative and enforcement powers. Thus, only one federal agency handles the aspects of any given case, rather than two or more federal agencies competing and wasting resources by repeating investigation and enforcement procedures.

Deceptive Advertising

Through its focus on advertising, the FTC can investigate before an injury to consumers occurs. If the investigation uncovers deceptive advertising, the FTC can take the case to its administrative law court. If an advertiser challenges an FTC administrative court ruling in a judicial court, the FTC needs only to prove that the advertisement could deceive consumers, not that it actually did so. Evidence of consumer misunderstanding of the claims made in the advertisement usually is not offered.

The FTC has adopted a policy statement that sets out the guidelines as to the three elements of deceptive advertising.[2] First, the advertising must contain a representation, omission, or practice. Second, the representation, omission, or practice must be found likely to mislead consumers acting reasonably under the circumstances. Third, the representation, omission, or practice must be material (or significant). It also must be likely to mislead. An actual deception need not occur.

Advertisements are frequently challenged based on one of the following issues:

1. False statements or claims.
2. Failure to disclose important facts.
3. Statements that are less than the whole truth.
4. Unsupported claims.

False Statements or Claims

Misrepresentations about the quality, composition, origin, character, or availability of products are illegal. Such misrepresentations need not involve an explicit false statement or claim. An advertisement that creates a false impression is deceptive; no verbal or written statement is required. For example, a cosmetic company advertises a "rejuvenescence cream" that would rejuvenate and restore youth or the appearance of youth to the skin. Unfortunately, medical science knows that virtually nothing can restore skin youthfulness. This type of advertising is false and deceptive.

Failure to Disclose Important Facts

Silence may be considered deceptive when it represents a failure to disclose important facts. Some facts known to the seller are so important that they should be communicated to prospective buyers. Although the FTC does not require that every negative fact about a product be revealed, instances exist when the FTC requires an advertiser either to include additional information or to stop its advertising program.

Even if state law permits a practice (that is, a certain type of advertising or a certain wording used in advertising), an FTC ruling will preempt the state's determination of legality. In the following case, the court reviewed the FTC's allegation that the defendant engaged in deceptive advertising.

---

[2] The FTC regulations on Guides Against Deceptive Pricing are located at <http://www.ftc.gov/bcp/guides/decptprc.htm>.

Case 15.2

F.T.C. v. American Standard Credit Systems, Inc.

United States District Court,
C. D. California, 1994
874 F. Supp. 1080

BACKGROUND AND FACTS The Federal Trade Commission brought action against American Standard Credit Systems, Inc. (ASCS), and three of its directors. They were charged with committing deceptive acts and practices in connection with ASCS's marketing of VISA and Mastercards for the First National Bank of Marin (FNBM). The defendants hired a contractor to provide promotional materials. One of the advertisements follows.

ANYONE CAN QUALIFY
FOR VISA AND MASTERCARD

Separated? Divorced? Bankrupt?
Widowed? Military?

Bad Credit? No Credit?

No Problem!

Make the Call and Get the
Credit You Deserve NOW!

In reality, not everyone could qualify for an FNBM credit card. An applicant needed a minimum household income, could not have an open bankruptcy proceeding, and could not have had a charge-off on any secured bank credit card. A secured card requires the card holder to put money on deposit. If the person is unable to pay the credit card balance, the company that issues the credit card pays off the debt with the money on deposit. This transaction is called a charge-off. Further, an applicant had to deposit $300 as security on the card and $60 as an application fee. ASCS failed to disclose these facts to the public in its advertisements.

District Judge BAIRD

. . . .

The test for deception is whether "there is a representation, omission or practice that is likely to mislead the consumer acting reasonably under the circumstances."

Count 3 of Plaintiff's complaint is based on Defendants' alleged failure to disclose that consumers can only obtain a VISA or Mastercard by paying a processing fee and making a minimum deposit of $300. The undisputed facts show that consumers had to pay an application fee and had to make a minimum $300 deposit with FNBM to secure their line of credit. The facts also show that the advertising approved by ASCS failed to disclose this requirement. Therefore, it was not until after consumers paid $9.95 to call a "900" number that they learned of the application fee and the minimum deposit requirement.

These omissions were likely to mislead consumers acting reasonably under the circumstances as it is likely that many consumers would not have made the call had they known of these requirements. Therefore, the omissions were deceptive under § 5 of the FTCA [Federal Trade Commission Act].

Count 4 of Plaintiff's complaint is based on Defendants' alleged failure to disclose that consumers must meet certain minimum qualifying criteria to even apply for a VISA or Mastercard. The undisputed facts show that advertisements approved by ASCS included the statement "anyone [or everyone] can qualify" for an FNBM secured credit card. Furthermore, ASCS approved advertising promised that even people with past credit problems would be approved for an FNBM credit card.

However, not everyone could qualify for an FNBM credit card. From May 1989 through July 1991, FNBM had in existence credit granting criteria. For example, FNBM considered whether an applicant had a current, open bankruptcy proceeding, or a charge-off on any secured bank credit card in determining whether to approve an application. Furthermore, consumers had to have a minimum household income.

The representations made in ASCS approved advertising that anyone could qualify, even those with past credit problems, were likely to mislead the consumer acting reasonably under the circumstances. Therefore, these representations were deceptive under § 5 of the FTCA.

DECISION AND REMEDY The court found that by withholding material facts the defendants had violated the Federal Trade Commission Act. This nondisclosure constituted deceptive acts or practices. The test for deception is whether a representation, omission, or practice is likely to mislead the consumer about action reasonable under the circumstances. The failure to disclose requirements like an application fee, minimum deposit, and the fact that not all persons could qualify constituted deception.

CRITICAL THINKING: MANAGEMENT CONSIDERATION Discuss the difference between trade puffing (see the following text) and deceptive acts or practices.

Statements That Are Less Than the Whole Truth

Deception that involves stating less than the whole truth is the counterpart to failing to disclose important facts. Instead of omitting a material fact, the advertiser uses true statements out of context or in a way that deliberately misleads. A product that is "guaranteed for life," for example, usually means a guarantee for the consumer's life, not the product's. The FTC restrained the Parker Pen Company from making such guarantees after Parker revealed that it referred to the life of its pens in its lifetime guarantee.

Ocean Spray Cranberry Juice was required by a consent order to explain in future advertisements its statement that "Cranberry Juice Cocktail has more food energy than orange juice or tomato juice." Ocean Spray used "food energy" to mean—not vitamins or minerals—but calories.

Unsupported Claims

Firms must supply reasonable, scientific evidence to substantiate advertising claims. Otherwise, the advertisement makes unsupported claims. If a business claims its product to be faster or safer than similar products, sufficient testing must prove the claim's validity.

Certain statements are considered mere trade puffing rather than deceptive advertising. Trade puffing is an opinion stated by the seller of goods. For example, a manufacturer's statement that its product is "the best" would not be regarded as a product claim but merely as puffing. In contrast, a statement that a product lasts three times longer than comparable products must be supported by reasonable evidence. During the 1950s, one major cigarette company advertised that its cigarettes were "just what the doctor ordered." Today, this advertisement would be a violation of the law. The next case demonstrates the requirement that a product must live up to the claims made about it.

Case 15.3

Federal Trade Commission v. Pantron I Corporation

United States Court of Appeals, Ninth Circuit, 1994
33 F.3d 1088
http://caselaw.findlaw.com
/cgi=bin/getcase.pl?court=
9th&navby=case&f=3&vol=
33&invol=1088

BACKGROUND AND FACTS Pantron I Corporation (Pantron) marketed the Helsinki Formula (Formula), which supposedly arrested hair loss and stimulated hair regrowth in baldness sufferers. The Formula consisted of a conditioner and a shampoo and sold for $49.95 for a three-month supply. Pantron offered a full money-back guarantee to unsatisfied customers.

Pantron's advertisements (including late-night infomercials hosted by the *Man from U.N.C.L.E.,* Robert Vaughn) featured both Formula claims. The advertisements also represented that recognized scientific studies supported those claims.

In November 1988, the Federal Trade Commission (FTC) filed a suit in U.S. district court. The FTC's complaint alleged that the advertisements, which represented that the Formula was effective, were false and constituted an unfair or deceptive trade practice in violation of Sections 5 and 12 of the Federal Trade Commission Act and that no scientific evidence supported the claims.

The district court conducted a five-day bench trial (judge alone) in November 1989. The FTC presented various evidence to show that the Formula had no effectiveness (other than its placebo effect) in arresting hair loss or in promoting hair regrowth. Dr. Karl Kramer, a dermatologist and expert witness, testified that, based on his knowledge and review of the medical literature, he believed that the Helsinki Formula was useless in treating hair loss.

Dr. Elaine Orenberg corroborated Dr. Kramer's testimony. She stated that the studies on which Pantron relied (by Dr. Schreck-Purola and Dr. Pons) failed to satisfy the generally accepted scientific standards of being randomized, double blinded, and placebo controlled. The "placebo effect" means that even though a product has no inherent merit, it may have some effectiveness in treating the condition based on psychological or other unexplained reasons. For example, a patient who takes a sugar pill believing it to be a strong pain reliever may well experience some pain relief, even though the sugar pill is inherently worthless in treating pain. In this example, the sugar pill is a "placebo" and the relief experienced by the patient is the "placebo effect." Additional research, known as the Groveman study, determined that the ingredients in the Formula were ineffective in stopping hair loss and promoting hair regrowth. The Groveman study was a placebo-controlled, double-blinded, randomized study which appeared in the *Archives of Internal Medicine,* a peer-reviewed journal.

Pantron introduced evidence that users of the Helsinki Formula were satisfied that it was effective. Eighteen users testified that they had experienced hair regrowth or a reduction in hair loss. Pantron conducted a consumer satisfaction survey in late 1988. During routine sales follow-up calls, a Pantron representative interviewed a cross-section of 579 Helsinki Formula customers. The Pantron official who conducted the survey could not remember the questions that he asked and the company failed to record these questions. The survey data showed positive results ranging from 29.4 percent of those using the product for less than two months, to 70 percent of those using it for six months or more. Over half of the orders came from repeat purchasers, Pantron received very few written complaints, and less than three percent of the customers exercised their rights under the money-back guarantee.

Pantron introduced the results of Finnish studies, for which the Helsinki Formula was named, performed by Dr. Ilona Schreck-Purola. Her uncontrolled, unblinded, unrandomized, un-peer-reviewed study concluded that the Formula was effective in arresting excessive hair loss within two to four weeks and that it led to new hair growth in 60 percent of the subjects within four months.

The district court found no scientifically valid evidence that the Formula was effective for hair loss treatment or for inducing growth. The district court concluded that the FTC had marginally carried its burden of proof that Pantron's claims were false. The court refused to order monetary equitable relief because the FTC failed to establish that defendants' conduct caused actual deception and injury to consumers or that defendant knew or should have known such conduct to be fraudulent. The FTC appealed the district court's refusal to award any monetary equitable relief.

Circuit Judge REINHARDT

. . . .

The Federal Trade Commission brought this suit pursuant to sections 5(a) and 12 of the Federal Trade Commission Act. Section 5(a) of the Act declares unlawful "unfair or deceptive acts or practices in or affecting commerce" and empowers the Commission to prevent such acts or practices. Section 12 of the Act is specifically directed to false advertising. That section prohibits the dissemination of "any false advertisement" in order to induce the purchase of "food, drugs, devices, or cosmetics." It also provides that the dissemination of any such false advertisement is an "unfair or deceptive act or practice in or affecting commerce" within the meaning of section 5. The Act defines "false advertisement" as an advertisement, other than labeling, which is misleading in a material respect."

. . . .

The district court concluded that the F.T.C. failed to carry its burden of proving that Pantron's efficacy representations were false. It held that "[t]o prevail on its charge that defendant has misrepresented the efficacy of the 'Helsinki Formula,' the F.T.C. must prove that the product is wholly ineffective; i.e., that it does not work at all." The district court held that the F.T.C. had not satisfied its burden of proof. It concluded that, although Pantron's clinical studies did not conform to contemporary American scientific standards, they nevertheless showed that the Formula is effective in reducing hair loss in many people.

We hold that the district court erred in concluding that Pantron's representations regarding the Helsinki Formula's efficacy did not amount to false advertising. Although there was sufficient evidence in the record to support the district court's finding that use of the Helsinki Formula might arrest hair loss in some of the people some of the time, the overwhelming weight of the proof at trial made clear that any effectiveness is due solely to the product's placebo effect.

. . . .

Assessing this evidence, the district court concluded that the F.T.C. had failed to carry its burden of showing that the Helsinki Formula is "wholly ineffective." In essence, the district court held that, as a matter of law, a seller can represent that its product is effective even when this effectiveness is based solely on the placebo effect. We believe that the district court misapprehended the law.

. . . .

Because the district court's refusal to order monetary relief against the corporation was based on the application of erroneous legal principles, and because an application of the proper principles compels an order of monetary relief, we instruct the district court to order the Pantron Corporation to pay monetary equitable relief to the extent of its unjust enrichment.

DECISION AND REMEDY The court decided that for a seller to represent a product as "effective" when its efficacy resulted solely from a "placebo effect" was unlawful. The representation constituted a "false advertisement" under the Federal Trade Commission Act.

CRITICAL THINKING: POLITICAL APPLICATION Should the government interfere in advertisements if product use makes customers feel better, even though the product fails to accomplish the advertisements' claim?

Other Deceptive Practices

Every year complaints flow into the Federal Trade Commission office. By categorizing the complaints, the FTC can determine if patterns develop. Once a pattern of deception evolves, the FTC may issue rules to curb its practice. The following are a few of the more important regulations that the FTC has developed in order to protect the public.

Illegal Multilevel Marketing Schemes

Many legal multilevel marketing (MLM) programs similar to Amway exist. MLM programs survive by making money from product sales, not new recruits. In contrast, "pyramid schemes" reward participants for inducing other people to join the program; over time, the hierarchy of participants resembles a pyramid as newer, larger layers of participants join the established structure. As discussed in Chapter 7, these pyramids are called Ponzi schemes.

Pyramids are operated strictly by paying earlier investors with money tendered by later investors. No clear line separates illegal pyramid schemes from legitimate MLM programs. To differentiate the two, regulators evaluate the marketing strategy (e.g., emphasis on recruitment versus sales) and the percent of product sold compared with the percent of commissions granted. The following case is an example of a business conducting an illegal MLM operation.

Case 15.4

Federal Trade Commission v. Five-Star Auto Club, Inc.

United States District Court, S.D. New York, 2000
97 F. Supp. 2d 502

BACKGROUND AND FACTS The Federal Trade Commission enforces Section 5(a) of the FTC Act, 15 U.S.C. § 45(a), which prohibits unfair or deceptive acts or practices in or affecting commerce. The FTC filed suit against Five Star Auto Club, Inc., and other defendants alleging that they (1) made false and misleading earnings claims to consumers; (2) made false and misleading promises to consumers that their program offered "everyone the opportunity to drive their dream vehicle for free"; (3) provided others with the means and instrumentalities to make the same deceptive claims; and (4) failed to disclosed to consumers that Five Star's pyramid structure would not allow many of Five Star's participants to achieve the benefits promised by Defendants.

First, Defendants promised, both explicitly and by implication, that Five Star made it possible for everyone to drive their dream vehicle for free, or for no more than $100 per month. Second, Defendants claimed that Five Star participants could make a substantial income from the sale of Five Star memberships. Participants could join Five Star at three different levels: consultants, members, and members-consultants.

Consultants paid a $95 annual fee to Five Star. In exchange for their dues, consultants had the right to receive commissions from the sale of memberships, but did not have the right to participate in Five Star's Vehicle Incentive Program (VIP), Reverse Value Lease (RVL), or Buyers Assistance Program (BAP).

Members paid a $395 annual fee to Five Star and in exchange received the right to participate in the VIP, BAP, and RVL. (Members could not earn commissions.)

Member-consultants paid a $490 annual fee to Five Star and in exchange received all the benefits of both consultants and members.

The promise that Five Star made it possible for everyone to drive their dream car for free while earning a substantial income lies at the heart of the Five Star advertising scheme. The VIP is the vehicle through which Defendants claimed they could fulfill this promise. A letter to all new participants suggesting that they sell Five Star memberships by asking: "Would you be interested in driving a new car for just $100.00 per month under a new Lease Alternative? Keep it simple by asking them just one question."

To qualify for a VIP lease, Five Star participants were required to pay Five Star $100 per month starting on the 10th of the month after they joined the VIP program. Participants could join the VIP program at three different times. First, Defendants encourage VIP participants to start paying monthly dues on the 10th of the first month after enrollment. This option allowed member-consultants to start earning commissions on the sale of new memberships immediately. Second, VIP participants could start paying $100 per month on the 10th of the month following establishment of a complete primary group. Pursuant to this option, participants could not earn commissions on the sales necessary to establish their primary group. Third, VIP participants could wait until delivery of their VIP vehicle to start paying $100 per month. Under this option, participants would have to pay their own down payment, security deposit, and bank acquisition fees (estimated by Defendants at $2,000 to $4,000).

Both Five Star's VIP program and the promise of a substantial income were predicated on the receipt of these monthly dues. The $100 per month dues were the financial backbone of the Five Star program.

To qualify for a VIP lease, a consumer ("A" level) had to establish both a "primary group" and "secondary group" of new members. A member's primary group ("B" level) consisted of those new members whose memberships were purchased directly from the original member. The number of members required in a consumer's primary group depended on the cost of the desired vehicle. For example, in order to qualify to lease a $12,000 vehicle, a consumer had to directly sell three new memberships. To qualify to lease a $40,000 vehicle, a consumer had to sell twenty new memberships.

Additionally, a consumer participating in the VIP program had to establish a secondary group ("C" level) that was three times the size of his/her primary group in order to qualify to lease a vehicle for free or for $100 per month. The secondary group consisted of new members who purchased their membership either directly from the original participant or from an individual in the original participant's primary group.

A portion of the payments from a consumer's primary and secondary groups was supposed to be placed in escrow and used to prepay a twenty-four-month lease when the consumer had a sufficient number of participants in his/her primary and secondary groups. Money collected from individuals who were recruited at the B and C levels was to be used to pay for automobiles being leased for individuals who were at the A level.

To sustain the VIP program, it was imperative that VIP participants recruit new members who also participated in the VIP program and/or attempted to earn commissions. Specifically, even if 100 percent of the payments received by a participant's downline were placed in escrow, less commissions paid on those memberships, there would not be enough money placed in escrow to prepay for a VIP lease, unless at least a portion of that participant's downline was paying $100 per month VIP dues. Moreover, Five Star's program anticipated that a consumer's primary group would recruit the consumer's secondary group. The only incentive to recruit new members was to achieve a VIP lease and/or earn commissions; therefore, a consumer's primary group had to establish his/her own downline of recruiters.

Five Star promised to pay consultants a $100 commission for each new membership they sold directly. Additionally, consultants were promised a $20 per month commission for each $100 per month payment made by each member in their secondary group. This $20 commission increased to $40 when a consumer had twenty or more members in his/her secondary group.

Five Star's promotional materials focus on the theoretically large earnings that they claimed could be achieved through the $20 and $40 per month commissions. Defendants made numerous monthly earnings claims ranging from $180 per month to $80,000 per month.

These monthly commissions were dependent on participants' recruiting others who in turn would also attempt to recruit new members, because these commissions were to be paid only if a consumer's downline recruit participated in the VIP program (thus making the $100 per month payments from which monthly commissions are derived).

McMAHON, District Judge

. . . .

II. DEFENDANTS VIOLATED SECTION 5 OF THE FTC ACT

A. In order to establish that Defendants engaged in deceptive acts or practices in violation of Section 5 of the FTC Act, the Commission must demonstrate: (1) a representation, omission, or practice; (2) that is likely to mislead consumers acting reasonably under the circumstances; and (3) that the representation, omission, or practice is material.

B. It is not necessary to prove Defendants' misrepresentations were made with an intent to defraud or deceive, or were made in bad faith to establish a Section 5 violation.

C. The Commission has demonstrated by a preponderance of the evidence that Defendants violated Section 5 of the FTC Act by making the false and material claims that consumers participating in the Five Star program could "Drive [their] Dream Car for Free" and earn a substantial income. The Commission has also shown that Defendants violated the FTC Act by providing others with the means and instrumentalities to deceive others in order to perpetuate the Five Star scheme. The Commission has further demonstrated that Defendants violated the FTC Act by failing to disclose the material information that because of Five Star's structure, the vast majority of participants had not and could not achieve the promised car or income.

. . . .

A pyramid scheme is a mechanism used to transfer funds from one person to another. In the most extreme form of a pyramid scheme, there is no product or service; instead, people are motivated to join by promises of a certain portion of the payments made by those who join later and are placed in one's "downline." If enough additional people join the scheme, a given member could recoup his or her initial payment and even receive additional returns. But, by the nature of the scheme, those at the bottom of the structure at any given time will have lost money, and the number of consumers at the bottom who have lost money will grow exponentially as more people are recruited to join. Moreover, the required number of new members cannot, in fact, be recruited on a perpetual basis, causing the scheme to collapse of its own weight if it does not first falter when a significant number of members are unable to find enough people as gullible as themselves to recruit.

3. A legitimate multi-level marketing ("MLM") firm includes a system of distributing products or services in which each participant earns income from sales of a product to his or her downline and also from sales to the public. The

operative question is whether the revenues from sales of the goods and services to consumers is sufficient to cover the production costs or costs of the goods sold, the various marketing expenses, and the promised rewards for recruiting new participants. If the revenue from such sales is sufficient, there is no structural certainty of collapse.

4. Defendants claim that their "retail product" includes the "Buyer's Assistance Program" which was allegedly received by consumers who purchased Five Star memberships, as well as advantages in insurance, long distance rates, and the like. However, even under conditions most favorable to Defendants' position, sale of memberships/BAP was not sufficient to provide the promised rewards of a free car lease and substantial income.

5. Based on a thorough review of Five Star marketing material, the FTC's expert, Dr. Vander Nat, initially concluded that at least 90% of all participants would lose money and would not qualify for a lease. However, as Dr. Vander Nat explained, the higher the value of the car sought by the average participant, the greater the size of the bottom of the pyramid, and therefore the higher the percentage of participants who will lose money, and not receive their dream car.

6. Using the information available in the Five Star Netmark database, and some very conservative (i.e., pro-Defendant) assumptions, Dr. Vander Nat estimated that in fact 97.7% of all participants failed to qualify for a car, and that 95% of all participants lost money on the Five Star scheme. I find Dr. Vander Nat's testimony to be credible and I accept it.

. . . .

DECISION AND REMEDY The Defendants' failure to disclose the limitations of their marketing plan resulted in misleading their customers and violated the law in that this constituted an unfair or deceptive act or practice.

CRITICAL THINKING: MANAGERIAL ISSUE What modifications could Five Star have made to make them a lawful multilevel marketing company?

Bait and Switch

In some cases, the Federal Trade Commission has promulgated specific rules to govern advertising. One of its more important rules is called "Guides against Bait Advertising."[3] This rule is designed to prohibit bait-and-switch advertisements that specify a very low price for a particular item. The low price is the bait to lure the consumer into the store.

The salesperson then tries to switch the consumer to a more expensive item. According to the FTC guidelines, bait advertising occurs if the seller refuses to show the advertised item, fails to have adequate quantities of it available, fails to promise or to deliver the advertised item within a reasonable time, or discourages employees from selling the item.

Deceptive Comparisons

Deceptive comparative advertising is subject to the **Lanham Act** of 1946. This statute prohibits false descriptions about products or services when people are likely to be damaged by these deceptive advertisements. An inaccurate comparative advertisement is one in which the defendant makes false statements about either the quality or the price of its own product as compared with a competitor's product.

---

[3] The FTC regulations on bait and switch are located at <http://www.ftc.gov/bcp/conline/pubs/buspubs/ad-faqs.htm.>

The FTC has ruled that several forms of pricing are deceptive.[4] Stating the price of goods in a way that causes consumers to believe they are getting a bargain or a good deal, when in fact they are not, is unlawful. If the seller compares the current sales price with a higher regular price, the good actually must have been offered by that seller at the higher price in the recent past. It is deceptive to compare the retail price of goods with a "manufacturer's list price" that is not the usual and customary retail price in the area.

The FTC has issued guidelines for the offer of "free" merchandise.[5] If goods are offered "two for the price of one" or "buy one, get one free," the price charged for the two items must not exceed the regular price for the same single item. The seller cannot recover the free item's cost by marking up the regular price of the item to be purchased or by substituting inferior merchandise.

In the case that follows, the FTC charged Bristol-Myers Company with inaccurate comparative advertising for their Bufferin and Excedrin products.

[4] See the FTC's site on advertising on the Internet at <http://www.ftc.gov/bcp/conline/pubs/buspubs/ruleroad.htm>.

[5] *Free* is defined in the FTC regulations and can be found at <http://www.ftc.gov/bcp/guides/free.htm>.

Case 15.5

Bristol-Myers Company v. Federal Trade Commission

United States Court of Appeals, Second Circuit, 1984
738 F.2d 554

BACKGROUND AND FACTS Bristol-Myers Company (Bristol) petitioned the court of appeals to review an order issued by the Federal Trade Commission (FTC) made in respect to Bristol's advertising of its well-known analgesics, Bufferin and Excedrin. The order represented over ten years of agency work, formally commencing with the FTC's filing of complaints in February 1973 against Bristol and its advertising agencies concerning alleged violations of Sections 5 and 12 of the FTC act.

After a hearing, the FTC found that Bristol had misrepresented the analgesic superiority of Excedrin and Bufferin over competing products and further found that such superiority was not established by the use of phrases such as "scientific tests" and "medically endorsed." The FTC found that Bristol made seven false and deceptive claims of this nature. The FTC prohibited Bristol from making comparative establishment claims asserting the products' superior effectiveness without proof consisting of two or more adequate and well-controlled clinical investigations conducted in accordance with procedures that the order set forth in detail.

The FTC found that Bristol deceptively advertised that its products contained special ingredients even though other over-the-counter drug products commonly use the same ingredients. The FTC found that these special ingredient claims concealed that Bufferin and Excedrin were aspirin based. The deception was based on Bristol's emphasis on the unspecified analgesic ingredients.

Circuit Judge OAKES

. . . .

Whatever the merits [of] the argument that the use of such a presumption violates the First Amendment, it is clear that in this case the FTC made a factual finding, based on its investigation of Bristol's ads, that consumers viewing the ads would believe them to be making claims supported by a reasonable basis. It then found that lacking such a basis the ads were deceptive. A conclusion of this nature is "in the very realm of the Commission's greatest expertise—what constitutes deception in advertising. . . . As such the reviewing court must give the

Commission's findings 'great weight.'" We find the conclusion amply supported in this case.

. . . .

DECISION AND REMEDY Bristol had a history of deceptive practices. False claims that consumers are unable to evaluate for themselves and that encourage the unnecessary use of a potentially hazardous product constitute serious violations, which helped to justify the scope of the remedial order. The court found that the FTC had quite carefully worded its remedial order to suit the violations. The order was broad enough to protect the public while narrow enough to permit compliance without undue burden.

CRITICAL THINKING: MANAGEMENT CONSIDERATION Discuss the advertising a company should use when selling over-the-counter drugs.

Deceptive Testimonials and Endorsements

From its inception, the FTC has proceeded with vigor against deceptive testimonials and endorsements used to promote products. This advertising technique convinces consumers that someone other than the seller believes in the product's benefits. Film stars and athletes often endorse products. FTC guidelines require that the endorsements reflect the celebrity's honest opinion about the product. The endorser must be a product user.

If an advertisement represents that the endorser has superior expertise in judging the product, the endorser must have experience or training that qualifies her as an expert. If an advertisement represents that the endorser is a doctor, she must have a medical degree. Some advertisements contain dramatizations involving purported doctors or scientists. Because the public recognizes that these people are actors, these advertisements are allowed.

Telemarketing Fraud

The **Telemarketing and Consumer Fraud and Abuse Prevention Act** was adopted by Congress in 1994[6] as a result of widespread fraud carried out by persons who victimized consumers to the tune of $40 billion per year. The act requires the FTC to issue rules to prevent telemarketers from undertaking a pattern of unsolicited telephone calls that a reasonable consumer would consider coercive or abusive and in violation of a person's right to privacy.

The FTC sets the hours of the day and night when telemarketers can make unsolicited telephone calls. Anyone soliciting business via the telephone must disclose promptly and clearly to the person receiving the call that the call's purpose is to sell goods or services and must make other disclosures, including the nature and price of the goods and services. The FTC, attorneys general of individual states, and private persons may bring actions under this act.

Marketing Research

The FTC has not issued specific regulations about marketing research, but has issued a policy statement to guide marketing research firms.[7] The FTC believes that deceptively inducing consumers to provide personal information that they erroneously assumed would be kept confidential is unfair.

For example, the FTC prohibits businesses from using a secret or invisible code on a survey form or return envelope to identify the consumer who provided the information. The FTC did not find the code itself to be unfair and deceptive. A deceptive practice is to use a survey accompanied by a misleading promise of anonymity in order to obtain highly sensitive information about a consumer that otherwise would not have been disclosed. Use of any information for purposes other than those of the market survey is considered deceptive.

---

[6] For more information on the Telemarketing and Consumer Fraud and Abuse Prevention Act, go to <http://www.ftc.gov/bcp/conline/pubs/buspubs/tsr/introduc.htm>. The actual FTC rules are found at <http://www.access.gpo.gov/nara/cfr/waisidx_00/16cfr310_00.html>.

[7] Market surveys gather information on consumers. See a speech on consumer privacy at <http://www.ftc.gov/speeches/varney/priv&ame.htm>.

CyberLaw

Identity Theft

Advances in computer technology make it possible for detailed information about people to be compiled into a database so it can be shared more easily and cheaply than ever. In many respects, computer technology is good for society as a whole and individual consumers. For example, it is easier for law enforcement to track down criminals, for banks to prevent fraud, and for consumers to learn about new products and services. At the same time, as personal information becomes more accessible, individuals, companies, associations, and government agencies must take precautions to protect against the misuse of that information.

Although identity theft—where someone uses your name and personal information to obtain money or property—has been committed for decades, with the advent of the web, the incidents of identity theft have skyrocketed.

How does identity theft begin? Thieves can operate alone or an organized effort may be involved. A thief starts collecting information by co-opting your name, Social Security number, credit card number, or some other piece of your personal information for his or her own use. People leave these pieces of information laying around in abundant number.

Here are some ways to protect yourself:

- Do not freely use your Social Security number. Do not have your SSN on your driver's license request. Instead request the driver's license bureau to assign another number.

- Do not have your SSN printed on your checks along with your name and address.

- When you receive a credit card application and you do not intend to apply for the credit card, shred the application. If you do not destroy the application, someone could fill it in and receive the credit card that is issued in your name.

- When you pay with a credit card, make sure you receive the copy. Sometimes people leave the credit card receipts in the gasoline pumping station when purchasing gas. Fortunately, however, recently installed machines do not print out the credit card number. Or a consumer may accidently drop the credit card receipt instead of placing it in a safe place and keeping track of it.

- If you receive an e-mail request that appears to be from your Internet service provider (ISP) stating that your "account information needs to be updated" or that "the credit card you signed up with is invalid or expired and the information needs to be reentered to keep your account active," do not respond without checking with your ISP first.

Taking precautions to safeguard your personal information is time consuming. But trying to fight an identity thief is more than time consuming—it is emotionally draining. An ounce of prevention is worth a pound of cure in this situation.

The Federal Trade Commission[8] educates consumers and businesses about the importance of per-

---

[8] Go to the Federal Trade Commission's web site at <http://www.ftc.gov/>, then click on Consumer Protection.

LEGAL HIGHLIGHT

Telemarketing Fraud

Most telephone sales pitches are made on behalf of legitimate organizations offering bona fide products and services. Unfortunately, many telephone sales calls are frauds. Consumers lose more than $40 billion a year to telemarketing fraud. Fraudulent telemarketers and sellers can reach you in several ways, such as cold telephone calls, mail, or direct advertisements.

Cold Calls. A telemarketer telephones you at home. Your number is available from telephone directories, mailing lists, or "sucker lists." The latter refers to lists of consumers who have spent (read "lost") money purchasing fraudulent prize promotions or merchandise sales. These lists contain names, addresses, phone numbers, and other information, such as how much money was spent by people who have responded to telemarketing solicitations. "Sucker lists" are bought and sold by unscrupulous promoters. They are invaluable to scam artists who know that consumers who have been deceived once are vulnerable to additional scams.

Direct Mail. You receive a postcard announcing that you have won cash, an appliance, a diamond, or even an automobile. The postcard represents the items as free except for a small shipping fee. You are tempted to call the toll-free number to check on the prize. If you do, the salesperson will use persuasive sales pitches, scare tactics, and exaggerated claims.

You may be asked for your checking account number. Without your knowledge, the outfit you called sends a demand draft to your bank. A demand draft is similar to a check, but the customer's signature is unnecessary. A bank does not normally check for authorized signatures and pays the draft; you will only

discover the theft after your checks bounce or when you receive your monthly statement. In the meantime, the thief who has posed as a telemarketer changes locations. Remember to treat your checking account number as a secret.

Broadcast and Print Advertisements. You are reading the newspaper, watching television, or surfing the web. You see an advertisement for a product or a service that prominently features a telephone number. You make the telephone call in response to a television, newspaper, or magazine advertisement or a direct-mail solicitation. Even though these advertisements are usually placed by legitimate businesses, criminals also place advertisements. Although the advertisement appears legitimate, you still need to be cautious about buying or investing over the telephone.

Fight fraud by reporting scam artists to your state attorney general. Many states have a telephone fraud statute that makes this activity illegal. The federal Telemarketing Sales Rule provides local law enforcement officers with the power to prosecute fraudulent telemarketers when operating across state lines.

Additionally, you can file a complaint with the FTC. Contact the Consumer Response Center by phone: toll-free 1-877-FTC-HELP (382-4357); TDD: 202-326-2502; by mail: Consumer Response Center, Federal Trade Commission, 600 Pennsylvania Avenue, NW, Washington, DC 20580; or use the FTC's web page at <http://www.ftc.gov/> to file an online complaint. Although the FTC cannot resolve individual problems for consumers, it can act against a company if it sees a pattern of possible law violations.

sonal information privacy. Their web site contains updated information including government reports and congressional testimony, law enforcement updates, and links to other sites with helpful information about identity theft.

Other Consumer Protection Laws

Over the years, Congress has passed laws that provide consumers protection from abhorrent business practices. The following subsections examine the more significant of these statutes.

Fair Packaging and Labeling Act

The number of products that are prepackaged has increased significantly since 1950. The packaging often prevents the consumer from inspecting the product, so the label becomes the only source of information about the package's contents. The **Fair Packaging and Labeling Act (FPLA)**[9] was enacted by Congress in 1966 to give the Department of Commerce the authority to deal with this problem.

The FPLA applies to those who package or label any consumer commodity. It primarily focuses on items sold in supermarkets. Four provisions of the FPLA are mandatory:

1. The label must include the name and address of the manufacturer, packer, or distributor.
2. The front panel must indicate the net quantity.
3. The quantity must be listed in a specific manner.
4. If the quantity is stated as a specified number of servings, the size of each serving must be indicated.

These mandatory provisions enable the purchaser to compare competing products. The Department of Commerce, the Federal Trade Commission, and the Food and Drug Administration all issue rules under the FPLA. Other federal statutes that also apply to packaging and labeling include the Wool Products Labeling Act, the Fur Products Labeling Act, the Cigarette Labeling and Advertising Act, and the Flammable Fabrics Act.

Magnuson–Moss Warranty Act

Dissatisfaction with automobile warranties led Congress to pass the Magnuson–Moss Warranty Act of 1975.[10] This act, also discussed in Chapter 12, establishes standards for consumer warranties.

The act requires that every warranty disclosure contain certain information that is necessary for a consumer to determine the extent of the warranty and the method of enforcing it. If a warrantor refuses to honor the warranty, then the consumer can bring a legal action in either a state or federal court. The government also may bring a court action to prevent a manufacturer from continuing to issue deceptive warranties or for failing to comply with the act.

Food, Drug, and Cosmetic Act

The purpose of the Food and Drug Administration (FDA) is to protect the public from harm caused by food, drugs, cosmetics, therapeutic items, household substances, pesticides, poisons, and other consumer items. The FDA is part of the Department of Health and Human Services. Through its rule-making authority, the FDA attempts to ensure that food is safe, pure, and wholesome; that drugs and therapeutic items are safe and effective; that cosmetics are harmless; and that consumers are not exposed to excessive risks of injury.

The **Food, Drug, and Cosmetic Act** of 1938 prohibits the adulteration or misbranding of various items. The FDA informs the public through press releases about products that pose an imminent danger to health or products that grossly deceive the consumer. Warnings have involved soup, fish, cranberries, fireworks, and baby food.

Although numerous amendments to the act have been passed, none has been more important than the 1962 Drug Amendment. The amendment was adopted after a drug called thalidomide that caused numerous birth defects had been sold extensively in Europe. The 1962 Drug Amendment requires the Food and Drug Administration to follow certain procedures in approving new prescription drugs for marketing.

The FDA has been severely criticized throughout its history. Critics contend the agency takes too long to approve new drug applications, thus keeping the benefits of new scientific discoveries from the consumer for unreasonable periods of time. The FDA, however, now has established a fast track to allow drugs used to fight acquired immune deficiency syndrome (AIDS) to reach the market sooner.

Violations of the Food, Drug, and Cosmetic Act regulations can result in fines or imprisonment. In addition, plaintiffs who allege that they have suffered harm from an adulterated or misbranded product frequently bring civil lawsuits for damages. These plaintiffs generally introduce evidence that the defendant has violated an FDA rule or regulation.

---

[9] The Fair Packaging and Labeling Act is found at <http://www.law.cornell.edu/uscode/15/ch39.html>.
[10] An explanation of the Magnuson-Moss Warranty Act can be found at <http://www.ftc.gov/bcp/conline/pubs/buspubs/warranty/undermag.htm>.

LEGAL HIGHLIGHT

Fleecing the Small Business

Many schemes abound to defraud businesses, particularly small firms. Rarely do small businesses have the resources to verify sales pitches and they end up losing money on worthless products. The following anecdotes describe some of these frauds.

One scheme is to sell paper and toner for the office copier over the telephone. The caller asks the business for its copier type. The caller just happens to be overstocked with toner and paper for that specific model. The caller claims that the business will receive a very good deal if it purchases this oversupply over the telephone. Once the business agrees, the paper and toner are shipped collect on delivery (C.O.D.), which does not allow the business to inspect the products before paying for them. Later, when the business opens the boxes, it discovers that the poor quality of the paper and toner could ruin the copier and even void the copier warranty. The caller's name is either unknown or fake. The small business is stuck with an unusable product.

The advance loan fee fraud lures in businesses short on cash. A con artist places an advertisement in a local newspaper offering working capital loans at a favorable rate of interest. A business calls the number given and receives a loan application. To process the application, the business pays an origination fee of $1,000 to $2,000, which is submitted with the completed application. Several days elapse before the business attempts to track progress on the loan, at which time the business discovers the telephone number to be disconnected and the address to be a mail drop with no forwarding address.

Charitable solicitation schemes abound because many legitimate businesspeople support causes that help people (for example, research to cure cata-strophic diseases like cancer). A con artist will form a company with a name very similar to a legitimate charity or with a name that implies great charitable activities. Small businesses are solicited for donations. In reality very little, if any, of the funds are donated to any charitable cause beyond the con artist's own needs.

An uglier fraud is the blackmail trick. A supplier tells the purchasing clerk of ABC Corporation that he is sending the clerk an expensive television set because ABC Corporation is an outstanding customer. The supplier hopes that the clerk will continue to place large orders. The clerk receives the gift. Later, if the clerk fails to continue placing large orders, the supplier threatens to inform the employer about the clerk's accepting bribes.

The phony invoice scam occurs when a crook makes out a phony invoice for goods never delivered. She presents the invoice to the person in charge of paying the bills. Thinking that management ordered and accepted this item, the person pays the invoice. By the time the accounts payable department discovers that no order was made and the invoice is phony, the crook has disappeared.

Business opportunity frauds rip off the naive person. An advertisement placed in the newspaper's classified section offers the opportunity to buy a franchise or coin-operated machines. The sales pitch touts that you can be your own boss by owning your own business. Actually, the buyer gets very little, if any, monetary return on the hard work and money invested. The buyer needs to be very careful before investing in a franchise or in coin-operated machines.

Postal Fraud Statutes

Consumers purchase billions of dollars' worth of products through the mail each year. Of two federal statutes that prohibit mail fraud, one is criminal in nature and the other, civil. Violations of the criminal statute provide for imprisonment and fines.

The civil statute allows the postmaster general to return all mail addressed to, or mailed by, a promoter who has made a false representation. This procedure of intercepting the fraudulent seller's mail is effective in combating deceptive practices. In more serious cases, the postmaster can confiscate the mail instead of returning it. The postal regulations require that unordered merchandise have a clear and conspicuous statement indicating that the merchandise is a free sample. The promoter can take no action to persuade the consumer to pay for unordered merchandise later.

The following case was brought by the U.S. Postal Service to stop the defendants from using the mails to defraud consumers.

Case 15.6

United States v. Weingold

United States District Court,
New Jersey, 1994
844 F. Supp. 1560

BACKGROUND AND FACTS   Defendant Harold P. Weingold and seven corporate defendants were engaged in the business of direct-mail marketing. They were accused of creating and implementing eleven separate mail fraud schemes by using different names and mailing addresses to solicit orders for such items as procedures to win lotteries, a cosmic protector, and tarot cards.

Three of the promotions were titled respectively the Helen Archer promotion, the Paul Zax, Jr., promotion, and the Holy Trinity Society, Inc., promotion. For example, one solicitation letter from the Helen Archer promotion scheme read as follows.

> *Last night I had a vision about you. It was very powerful. Very vivid. I know for a fact you had won a very large cash prize (something like $211,721.06 or even more) and you were collecting your money from the Pennsylvania State Lottery Director, Mr Charles Kline! This will happen sometime before Friday, August 13, probably in the next several weeks! Every time I've had these visions before, it has always meant a BIG CASH PAYOFF for the person involved.*
>
> *It is very important that I speak with you right away (name of recipient). I will give you my private phone number. This is so important that I've made special arrangements with the phone company so you won't ever have to pay any long distance charges.*

Under oath, Helen Archer, a reputed psychic, acknowledged that the "vision" was about a sum of money, $211,721.06, and that no specific vision of the person to whom she was writing occurred. Instead, she would receive "an impulse" or "feeling" when running her fingers over a computer-generated commercial mailing list that the addressee was the recipient of the generalized vision of the money.

People who responded to the Archer solicitation received a postcard bearing a 1-800 telephone number. A person calling that number would receive a tape-recorded message that would instruct the caller to note and add together the numbers for the time of day, add together the numbers in her or his age, and add together the numbers of her or his Social Security number to obtain the caller's "lucky numbers." The defendants then had the names and addresses of callers and used that information in follow-up contacts to sell them products or services.

In the Paul Zax, Jr., promotion scheme, the solicitation letter specifically cited examples of lottery winners, who supposedly won the lottery because his "secret formula was used." One testimonial in the solicitation letter included the sixteen employees of the Barrington, Illinois, Police Department, representing that they won $8.3 million in the Illinois State Lottery using the Zax method. In fact, the winning individuals had not used the Weingold/Zax secret formula nor any lottery device.

Another scheme was the Holy Trinity Society, Inc., promotion scheme, which offered a personalized communication from a person named "Wilkerson" who told a tale of having received a pendant with the image of the Virgin Mary from an "old man." The pendant's "secret power" provided the old man with good fortune and now required him to pass it on to another person. Wilkerson claimed to be its current owner and offered to provide it to the recipients of the solicitation for the "token sum" of $20. Recipients were to receive at least one "miracle" within six months, or the money would be refunded.

The U.S. Postal Service (USPS) filed a suit in U.S. district court, seeking an injunction against the defendants to stop them from these types of sales schemes.

District Judge BASSLER

. . . .

To obtain injunctive relief . . . on the grounds of false representations . . . the United States Postal Service must show by a preponderance of the evidence that there is probable cause to believe that the defendants' schemes are "reasonably calculated to deceive persons of ordinary prudence and comprehension." A showing of intent to mislead is, therefore, necessary for the entry of a preliminary injunction.

. . . .

A showing of "probable cause" requires the Government to establish a set of facts which would cause a reasonably prudent and intelligent person to believe that a cause of action . . . exists.

. . . .

Weingold argues that if the solicitations are carefully analyzed there is no basis to conclude that they are misleading. For example, he claims that he did not misspeak when he wrote that the Barrington, Ill. Police Department used his "secret formula," because they, in fact, used the concept behind his formula—pooling; or again, when he said the Pope endorsed the Holy Trinity Pendant, because the Pope did, in fact, thank the Virgin Mary in a public address shortly after he was shot by a would-be assassin.

Weingold cannot hide behind a technical exegesis of consumer solicitations reminiscent of the philosophy of common law pleading. The solicitations must be read as a whole; isolated passages cannot provide immunity from all of the circumstantial evidence indicative of an intent to deceive.

. . . .

In their closing argument, defendants disingenuously argued that this case is about the "beliefs" of the defendants and members of the consuming public. The Government here is not trying to censor any beliefs; quite to the contrary, the Government's purpose here is to protect the public from deceptive solicitations. This case is not about the First Amendment, but about fraud. As the Third Circuit has recognized, defendants possess "no constitutional right to disseminate false or misleading materials."

. . . .

Because the Government has met its burden of proving probable cause to believe that the defendants' solicitations and promotions are intentionally vague, misleading, false, and in light of the precedents . . . , the Court will grant the Government's application for a preliminary injunction.

DECISION AND REMEDY The court determined that the government met the burden of proof because the solicitations were intentionally vague and misleading. The court determined that the letters were intended to deceive persons of ordinary prudence and comprehension.

CRITICAL THINKING: ETHICAL APPLICATION This chapter began with a Latin phrase that stated *caveat emptor:* Let the buyer beware. This maxim represented the law's philosophy for many years. Does the consumer bear any responsibility for buying into these types of schemes?

Mail-Order Houses

Mail-order houses, a growing industry, have annual sales exceeding $80 billion. Consumers buying from mail-order houses typically have less protection than those who purchase items in stores. Many mail-order houses are located in a different state from the purchaser, thus making it more costly for the customer seeking redress for grievances. The FTC and the U.S.

Postal Service share enforcement of the laws concerning mail-order houses.[11]

Negative option plans used by book, record, videotape, and compact disc clubs are regulated. Such plans require the member to return a card to decline merchandise to be sent. A negative option plan must disclose all of its terms, must notify the consumer of intent to send the product in enough time for the member to accept or reject, and must include a rejection form for the club member's use.

An FTC rule requires a mail-order house to ship ordered merchandise promptly. If the business is unable to ship the goods within thirty days, it must notify the buyer of her option either to cancel the order and receive a refund or to allow further shipment delay.

Interstate Land Sales Full Disclosure Act

During the 1950s and early 1960s, many older people invested their life savings in real estate, particularly in Florida and the Southwest. Much of this land was marketed through advertisements in magazines and newspapers, through mail and telephone solicitations, and by personal contact in booths set up near convention facilities. The purchasers rarely saw the parcel of land prior to signing the purchase contract and paying for the land. Later, they would discover that the land they had purchased was underwater or was years away from being ready for development.

The **Interstate Land Sales Full Disclosure Act**, passed in 1968 and administered by the Department of Housing and Urban Development (HUD), is intended to decrease the opportunities for fraud and deception that are inherent in these "sight unseen" sales. The Office of Interstate Land Sales Registration within HUD regulates the sale of undeveloped land for homesites. Regulations require developers to disclose fully their financial condition. These rules also govern advertising and sales practices.

Developers must file a registration statement with the agency before commencing sales. If the Office of Interstate Land Sales Registration determines that the disclosure is adequate, the developer can solicit sales. If the disclosure is inadequate, the developer must file additional information to gain approval.

Purchasers must receive a copy of the property report before signing a contract. The act applies to sales and leases of property in subdivisions, as well as to condominium units that will be uncompleted for two years after the purchase date. Congress used its power under the interstate commerce clause to pass this legislation. If the developer fails to follow the statute, the purchaser may be entitled to a full refund.

Consumer Product Safety Act

The **Consumer Product Safety Act** was passed in 1972 to protect consumers from unreasonable risk of injury from hazardous products.[12] The act is administered by the Consumer Product Safety Commission (CPSC), which has sweeping powers to regulate the production and sale of potentially hazardous consumer products. Consumer product safety legislation began earlier with a variety of statutes that sought to improve the safety standards in selected industries.

The act is very comprehensive. The CPSC is charged with regulating "any article, or component part thereof produced or distributed for sale to a consumer for use in or around a permanent or temporary household or residence, a school, in recreation or otherwise, or for the personal use, consumption or employment of a consumer." The CPSC also enforces the Refrigerator Safety Act, the Flammable Fabrics Act, the Child Protection and Toy Safety Act, the Poison Prevention Packaging Act, and the Hazardous Substances Labeling Act.

Congress has charged the CPSC with conducting research on product safety and with maintaining a clearinghouse that collects, investigates, analyzes, and disseminates injury data relating to the causes and possible prevention of death, injury, and illness associated with consumer products. Product manufacturers must inform the CPSC about events that cause injury or death.

The commission has the authority to establish construction standards, as well as performance standards, for the finished product and to issue adequate danger warnings. If the CPSC can isolate a consumer product that is extremely hazardous to consumers, it can ban the product's sale.

[11] The FTC regulations on mail-order houses can be found at <http://www.ftc.gov/bcp/conline/pubs/buspubs/mailordr/toc.htm>.

[12] The Consumer Product Safety Act is at <http://www.cpsc.gov/>. At this site you can obtain information about products that were recalled years ago. You may have an item in the attic or basement that was recalled and remains very dangerous. At this site you can report an unsafe product.

Door-to-Door Sales

Door-to-door sales are singled out for special treatment in the laws of most states and by FTC regulation.[13] The FTC regulation requires door-to-door sellers to provide consumers with a written notice of their right to cancel a sale within three business days. The seller must provide the buyer with a written form that can be filled in and mailed back to the seller exercising the right to cancel the contract. If the seller fails to follow these regulations, the customer can cancel within one year.

The door-to-door rule applies in addition to state statutes. Consumers are protected by the most favorable benefits of the FTC rule and of their own state laws. The Federal Trade Commission rule requires the seller to provide the notification in the same language in which the sale was negotiated.

This business type has a lengthy history of using high-pressure tactics (such as salesmen staying in the prospective customer's house all night talking until the customer signs) and other systematic consumer abuse (such as businesses sending encyclopedias with blank or missing pages). The special treatment also stems in part from the nature of the sales transaction. A door-to-door seller has the advantage of a captive audience because individuals cannot leave their own homes and hesitate to ask people to leave. Repeat purchases are less likely with door-to-door sales than they are in stores, because the seller has little incentive to establish goodwill with the purchaser. Furthermore, the buyer is unlikely to comparison shop for alternative products and their prices.

Miscellaneous Consumer Protection Statutes

A variety of other consumer protection statutes exist that will not be examined in depth here. Various state statutes prohibit unfair or deceptive acts or practices (UDAP statutes). These state laws provide private remedies to fight the wide range of consumer abuses. Every state has at least one UDAP statute. Most of these statutes were adopted during the mid-1960s to the mid-1970s. The following consumer areas are regulated by the FTC or other federal agencies and/or by the states' UDAP statutes.

Statutes cover subject matter ranging from automobiles to funeral homes. For example, the federal Odometer Act prohibits odometers from being rolled back. The FTC Used Car Rule governs the sales of used cars. State laws regulate towing company charges and collection procedures. Many other federal and state laws regulate such areas as mobile home sales, private vocational schools, insurance sales, solar energy equipment, hearing aids, health spas, dancing studios, and carpet sales.

This discussion of statutes and regulations barely taps the volume of consumer protection in force today from both the federal and state governments. As a direct result of consumer abuse by some businesses, all businesses and consumers now pay the price for this protection.

---

[13] The regulation on door-to-door sales is found at <http://www.ftc.gov/bcp/conline/pubs/buying/cooling.htm>.

International Consideration

Self-Regulation by Foreign Corporations

Consumer protection proposals originated in the late 1800s in Germany, the Netherlands, Sweden, and the United Kingdom before crossing the Atlantic to the United States. The debate over whether government regulation or business self-regulation is better continues. Over the decades, the European Union has taken a leadership role in this area.

The International Chamber of Commerce, an independent organization, has promoted self-regulation by developing voluntary codes of marketing practices for businesses. The goal is to avoid governmental regulation. In 1976, the Organization of Economic Cooperation and Development (OECD) adopted the "Guidelines on Multinational Enterprises." This document deals with issues of corporate disclosure and the liability of parent companies for their subsidiaries. No international organization to date specifically deals with consumer protection, however.

LEGALLY SPEAKING

Operating a Mail-Order Business

After much consideration, you start a new business. You believe the business should initially involve limited overhead. After reviewing numerous business opportunities, you decide to operate a mail-order business. You can operate it from your home during your spare time, thus limiting overhead expense.

A mail-order business's largest expense is advertising through magazines, catalogs, and brochures. You learn that, to be successful, you need repeat sales from satisfied customers based on your promotional materials. You also need to offer products that are not readily available in local stores. You decide to offer a line of "how-to" books that describe furniture construction, furniture refinishing, and general household repairs. You prepare advertisements to be placed in magazines and newspapers of general interest, such as, *Better Homes & Gardens* and *Readers Digest*. You also prepare a small catalog offering thirty-two different books or plans.

If you think that your business has no major involvement with federal or state laws, you are wrong. First, you must comply with the U.S. Postal Service regulations. If you advertise in a fraudulent manner by misrepresenting your products, the Postal Service will return your customers' mail, and the Department of Justice may bring criminal charges against you. You must make only claims that you can prove. For example, if you use customer testimonials, you must be able to prove to the Postal Service authorities that they are real. If you offer a money-back guarantee, any customer who is dissatisfied with your product must be given a full and prompt refund.

The actual mailing of your product is another problem. The Postal Service offers a book rate that is considerably lower than the first-class postal rate. At the book rate, however, you cannot include any advertisements for your other products with the books. Your product must be a book and not merely plans for the construction of certain prod-

ucts. If you fail to follow the Postal Service rules, your mailing will be returned to you or, worse, confiscated.

You also must follow the rules of the Federal Trade Commission. Your promotional material must make true claims, disclose important facts, state the whole truth, and explain unsupported claims. The FTC and the Postal Service cooperate in their investigations when fraudulent materials are involved.

If you decide to sell other products through the mail, you must comply with the regulations of other administrative agencies. For example, you must comply with the Fair Packaging and Labeling Act if your product has a label. The label must disclose at least the minimum required information. If you sell cosmetics through the mail, you must comply with the regulations of the Food, Drug, and Cosmetic Act.

As you can see, a simple business operated from your home can involve compliance with many federal laws and regulations. Some states have similar legal provisions. These laws are intended to protect the consumers, even though the laws may be troublesome and costly for business. The following is a checklist for mail-order business owners.

✔ Offer several products that allow repeat sales.

✔ Find the best magazines to ensure you a good response to your advertisements.

✔ Verify that the information and graphics contained in the advertisements are completely truthful. Make only claims that you can substantiate.

✔ Use more than one method to ship your product. If the postal service or other private carrier goes on strike, you can be out of business.

✔ Comply with all federal and state laws and regulations if you are selling a unique product.

Chapter Summary

Consumer laws protect the consumer from both financial and bodily harm. Costs associated with this protection eventually are paid by the consumer in the form of higher prices.

The Federal Trade Commission has the primary duty to prohibit "unfair or deceptive acts or practices." The Bureau of Consumer Protection carries out this responsibility by issuing trade regulations that apply to entire industries and by obtaining consent decrees or cease-and-desist orders.

The FTC regulates advertising that makes false statements or claims, fails to disclose important facts, does not relate the whole truth, or makes unsupported claims. The FTC also enforces rules against bait-and-switch advertisements. These advertisements entice a consumer with an alleged bargain. Then the salesperson attempts to convince the consumer to buy a more expensive product.

Other statutes that protect consumers include the Fair Packaging and Labeling Act, which requires certain information to be disclosed on any package that prevents the consumer from inspecting the product. The Food, Drug, and Cosmetic Act ensures that goods are safe, pure, and wholesome and that pharmaceutical products are therapeutic and not experimental. The U.S. Postal Service has the power to return or confiscate any mail that makes a false representation. The Interstate Land Sales Full Disclosure Act controls the sale of unimproved lots through interstate commerce. Finally, the Consumer Product Safety Act ensures the safety of products that are sold to the public.

Using the World Wide Web

The Federal Trade Commission has adopted many regulations to implement the statutes that it implements. More information is available at the following sites:

Finding the Law on the Web

Internet Privacy Study
http://www.ftc.gov/bcp/privacy/wkshp97/comments1/etrust/index.htm
Federal Trade Commission
http://www.ftc.gov/ogc/stats.htm
'Lectric Law Library Lawcopedia; summarizes numerous issues on consumer rights and protection
http://www.lectlaw.com//tcos.html

Chapter Web Sites

FTC regulations on Guides Against Deceptive Pricing
http://www.ftc.gov/bcp/guides/decptprc.htm
FTC v. Pantron I Corporation
http://caselaw.findlaw.com/cgi=bin/getcase.pl?court=9th&navby=case&f=3&vol=33&invol=1088
FTC regulations on bait and switch
http://www.ftc.gov/bcp/conline/pubs/buspubs/ad-faqs.htm

FTC's site on advertising on the Internet
http://www.ftc.gov/bcp/conline/pubs/buspubs/ruleroad.htm
FTC regulations defining free
http://www.ftc.gov/bcp/guides/free.htm
Information on Telemarketing and Consumer Fraud and Abuse Prevention Act
http://www.ftc.gov/bcp/conline/pubs/buspubs/tsr/introduc.htm
FTC rules on Telemarketing and Consumer Fraud and Abuse Prevention Act
http://www.access.gpo.gov/nara/cfr/waisidx_00/16cfr310_00.html
FTC policy statement on marketing research
http://www.ftc.gov/speeches/varney/priv&ame.htm
Fair Packaging and Labeling Act
http://www.law.cornell.edu/uscode/15/ch39.html
Magnuson-Moss Warranty Act
http://www.ftc.gov/bcp/conline/pubs/buspubs/warranty/undermag.htm
FTC regulations on mail-order houses
http://www.ftc.gov/bcp/conline/pubs/buspubs/mailordr/toc.htm
Consumer Product Safety Act
http://www.cpsc.gov/

FTC regulation on door-to-door sales
http://www.ftc.gov/bcp/conline/pubs/buying/cooling.htm
FTC information on multilevel marketing plans versus pyramids
http://www.ftc.gov/bcp/conline/pubs/alerts/pyrdalrt.htm
or
http://www.ftc.gov/bcp/conline/pubs/invest/mlm.htm
United States Postal Inspection Service web site for current frauds
http://www.usps.gov/websites/depart/inspect/

Web Activities

15–1 Not all multilevel marketing plans are illegal pyramids. Many of them are very legal and profitable. This is one type of business that a person can operate with limited financial investment. Many business opportunities, however, are scams. How can you tell the difference? Go to <http:www.ftc.gov/> and click on "Consumer Protection." Click on "Franchise and Business Opportunities" then click on "Multilevel Marketing Plans" to see what the Federal Trade Commission recommends.

15–2 Artiste Login Products, Inc., decides to advertise on its web site. Go to the Federal Trade Commission's web site at <http://www.ftc.gov>, click on "Consumer Protection," then click on "Advertising and Marketing on the Internet: The Rules of the Road." Scroll to the link that reads "Dot Com Disclosures: Information About Online Advertising." Are the rules for advertising different for web advertisements than from the usual media advertising? Summarize what a web designer must take into consideration. Does a web designer have any responsibilities for web advertisements?

Key Terms

affirmative disclosure order
cease-and-desist order
Consumer Product Safety Act
corrective advertising order

Fair Packaging and Labeling Act (FPLA)
Federal Trade Commission Act
Food, Drug, and Cosmetic Act

Interstate Land Sales Full Disclosure Act
Lanham Act
multiple product order
Telemarketing and Consumer Fraud and Abuse Prevention Act

trade regulation rule
unfair or deceptive acts or practices
Wheeler-Lea Act

Questions and Case Problems

15–1 Consumer Product Safety Act Joyce, who made toys at home, introduced a new line of homemade dolls. These stuffed dolls were especially appealing because they had real glass marbles for eyes. Three-year old Samantha received one of these marble-eyed dolls for her birthday. Samantha was captivated by the shiny marble eyes. Unfortunately, after a month of use, the glue holding the marbles on the face of the doll disintegrated to the point that Samantha was able to pull the marbles off, put one in her mouth, swallow it, and then choke on it. She was rushed to the hospital, where her stomach was pumped. Samantha's mother feels that Joyce, as the manufacturer, should be regulated by a federal agency. Which agency would regulate and under what act? What can the agency do to regulate the marble-eyed dolls?

15–2 False Advertising Monty advertises a fuel-saving device for automobile engines. The advertisement claims that the device is "an important unique invention," that "every car needs one," and that a typical driver will realize a significant improvement in fuel economy. Jane buys the device and installs it on her automobile. After six months, she checks her maintenance records and finds that she has realized no savings in fuel economy. Discuss fully any rights that Jane may have under consumer protection laws.

15–3 Medical Regulations IRONMED advertises that it can cure "tired blood." One television advertisement states that "If you often have a tired and run-down feeling and if you take vitamins and still feel worn out, remember, your trouble may be due to iron-poor blood.

Vitamins alone can't build up your iron-poor blood. But IRONMED can. Just two tablets daily contain seven vitamins, plus twice the iron in a whole pound of calves' liver. IRONMED starts strengthening your iron-poor blood in 24 hours."

Ron begins to take IRONMED daily. After six months, he feels the same-worn out and tired. Ron hears that most people feel tired not as a result of iron-deficiency anemia (iron-poor blood), but for a variety of other reasons that only medical tests can detect. Discuss fully Ron's rights under consumer protection laws. Fully discuss the potential actions of the specific federal agency that would regulate IRONMED.

15–4 Regulation of Food Baby Food, Inc., makes and sells a baby formula from which it has removed all the salt. Ann feeds her baby the infant formula but notices that after being on the formula for a while the baby is sick and weak. Although she takes the baby to a pediatrician, the baby dies six weeks later from a lack of salt. Ann checks the formula's label and sees that salt is a listed ingredient.

Later she learns through a magazine article that Baby Food, Inc., had removed the salt from the infant formula two years before her baby was born. The American Academy of Pediatrics Committee on Nutrition found that salt is absolutely necessary for a baby's nutrition. Discuss fully Ann's rights under consumer protection laws. Fully discuss the potential actions of any federal agency that regulates Baby Food.

15–5 Bait and Switch Goldberg entered the Manhattan Ford Lincoln-Mercury, Inc. (Manhattan) showroom to purchase a 1985 Lincoln Town Car, proposing to trade in his 1981 Volvo as part of the deal. Manhattan originally agreed to provide a $10,000 trade-in allowance, subject to appraisal and the sales manager's approval. Goldberg was to keep his Volvo until the Lincoln was ready. Because of slight damage to the Volvo, Manhattan reduced the trade-in allowance to $8,500. Goldberg insisted that the Volvo should not be subject to mechanical inspection at the time of delivery. Manhattan's sales manager refused to sign such a provision. Negotiations ended. Goldberg sued, claiming that each of these stages in negotiation for the used car constituted a "deceptive practice," as being a bait-and-switch situation. Was this a bait-and-switch situation? Why or why not? [*Goldberg v. Manhattan Ford Lincoln-Mercury, Inc.* 492 N.Y.S.2d 318, (1985)]

15–6 Deceptive Practices In the past, used automobile dealers commonly turned back the odometers on used cars. The federal Odometer Act allows a penalty in the amount of $1,500 for each occurrence. Ohio's attorney general brought action against Hughes Motors. The defense was based on the grounds that (1) the attorney general had no standing without naming the consumers as part of the lawsuit, and (2) no judgment could be entered unless the attorney general could prove actual loss. Was the defendant successful in its legal position? Explain. [*Celebrezze v. Hughes*, 18 Ohio 3d 71, 479 N.E.2d 886 (1985)]

15–7 Bait and Switch All-State Industries of North Carolina, Inc., which produced aluminum siding and storm windows, featured in advertisements "ADV," a lower cost aluminum. Following the training manual, however, All-State's salespeople always attempted to sell "PRO" grade to customers because of its better quality. The salespeople received no commission for selling ADV, but they received a substantial commission if they sold PRO. Was this an unfair trade practice of bait and switch? Explain. [*All-State Industries of North Carolina, Inc. v. Federal Trade Commission*, 423 F.2d 423 (1970)]

15–8 Safety Standards The Consumer Product Safety Commission proposed safety standards that mandated placing a warning on swimming pool slides. Research showed that there was one chance in ten million that a spinal injury could occur when using a pool slide. Would you consider a warning standard reasonably necessary? Does the use of a pool slide constitute an "unreasonable risk" of bodily harm? [*Aqua Slide N Dive Corp. v. Consumer Product Safety Commission*, 569 F.2d 831 (1978)]

15–9 Deceptive Comparisons American Home Products Corp. sold one of its products under the trade name Anacin. The company promoted Anacin by claiming that it consisted of a unique pain-killing formula far superior to that of similar products. In reality, Anacin was only aspirin. The Federal Trade Commission issued a cease-and-desist order after finding this claim to be deceptive. American Home Products appealed the decision. Was this trade puffing or was it deceptive advertising? Explain. [*American Home Products Corp. v. Federal Trade Commission*, 695 F.2d 681 (1982)]

15–10 Internet List several current frauds that the U.S. Postal Inspection Service warns against. Go to the United States Postal Inspection Service's site at <http://www.usps.gov/websites/depart/inspect/>.

Chapter 16 Property Law and Intellectual Property and Computer Law

Property, or the dominion of man over external objects, has its origin from the Creator, as his gift to mankind.

William Blackstone,1723–1780
English judge, author, and professor

Outline

Ethical Consideration

Joint Tenancy: Should the Property Always Go to the Survivor?

Your grandmother has passed away. You were close to your grandmother, who loved and trusted you and was proud of your many civic activities. You know that she loved all of her ten grandchildren. You call your grandmother's attorney, Ms. Rubio, who informs you and your family that your grandmother left a will naming the ten grandchildren as the beneficiaries to share her property equally. Ms. Rubio discloses that several years before, your grandmother heard in a lecture that the best way to avoid probate and to reduce attorney's fees was to hold property in joint tenancy. Ms. Rubio informs you that probate is a court proceeding that gathers the property of the deceased and redistributes it in accordance with a will or, if there is no will, then according to the state's statutes. Probate can be an expensive proceeding.

Based on this information, your grandmother placed her home, the main asset in her estate, in joint tenancy with you. You were unaware of your grandmother's actions. You are not totally surprised though because you are the oldest and most mature of the grandchildren.

Legally, the home passed to you at the moment of your grandmother's death. The other grandchildren are quite upset and believe that the value of the home should be placed in the estate. Do you keep the home as your sole property or do your sell it and divide the proceeds equally among your siblings and cousins? Use the ethical model presented in Chapter 2 and reprinted on the inside front cover to develop your answer. Disregard any tax issues that may arise.

Introduction

In our culture, individual rights and property rights are so interwoven that any discussion of one must include both. We place a premium on individual rights, but property rights also are protected whenever that protection does not conflict with individual rights.

The recognition of property rights allows Americans to have the economic system that exists today. Our business community exists based on the concept of property rights and the law that protects these rights. Business organizations own or control property that, with the addition of labor, produces a final product or service. The end result of any successful business is profit based on the sale of these products or services. Property rights are the foundation of our free enterprise system.

The Constitution specifically recognizes and protects property rights. The Fifth Amendment provides that "[n]o person shall be . . . deprived of life, liberty, or property, without due process of law; nor shall private property be taken for public use, without just compensation." Similar language is found in the Fourteenth Amendment: "No State shall . . . deprive any person of life, liberty, or property, without due process of law."

Artiste Login Products, Inc., your online business, has property rights recognized by both the federal and state governments. Artiste owns personal property, such as its computer system, and real property, such as its business building. How Artiste uses its property is regulated under the police power of government. This power is inherent to any government or sovereign to govern itself. In our country, police power is controlled and limited by these constitutional provisions.

The distinction between real property and personal property is important because different laws apply to each category. In particular, the law of taxation and the methods of property transfer vary depending on whether property is real or personal. This chapter addresses (1) the classifications of property, (2) property rights and ownership title, (3) real property, (4) methods to acquire ownership over personal property, (5) bailments, and (6) intellectual property law and its effects on computers.

Classifications of Property

Property is divided into these classifications: real or personal, tangible or intangible, and fixtures. The following sections discuss these different types of property.

Real and Personal Property

Real property (sometimes called real estate or realty) means the land surface, the airspace, those materials below the surface, and those items attached permanently to the land. **Personal property** is any item that is not land or attached permanently to land. Real property is conveyed by a **deed**. Personal property is sold by the use of a **bill of sale**, especially when transferring ownership of an expensive item.

At different times, the same article may be real property or personal property. For example, a growing tree is considered real property. When it is cut down and turned into lumber, the tree becomes personal property. The tree becomes real property again when it is transformed into a house frame.

Tangible and Intangible Property

All property is classified as tangible or intangible. **Tangible property** is visible and has physical existence, such as land, cattle, buildings, sheep, automobiles, or computers. **Intangible property** has invisible value. Examples are annuities, checks, copyrights, patents, common stock, debts, or bonds. The value of any of these properties is invisible. The rights these papers represent are recognized by the law.

Fixtures

A **fixture** is personal property that becomes so closely associated with the real property to which it is attached that the law views it as real property. Personal property becomes a fixture when it is attached to the realty by roots; embedded in it; or permanently attached by means of cement, plaster, bolts, nails, or screws. For ex-

ample, a tree and a rosebush grow in the ground at a nursery. Once they are dug out of the ground, they become personal property. A homeowner purchases the tree and the rosebush. When the homeowner plants them in the ground, they become fixtures because they are reattached permanently to real property.

Gravity even can be the method of attachment, if the item is large enough. A two-ton statue, for example, qualifies as a fixture. The fixture can be physically attached to real property, can be attached to another fixture, or can even be without any actual physical attachment to the land, as long as the owner intends the property to be a fixture.

Fixtures are included in the sale of land unless the sales contract provides otherwise. The sale of a house includes the land and the house and garage on it, as well as the cabinets, plumbing, and windows. These items are affixed permanently to the property; thus, they are considered part of it. Unless otherwise agreed, the curtains and throw rugs are not included. Items, such as drapes, metal storage units, and window-unit air conditioners, are difficult to classify. A contract for the sale of a house or commercial realty should indicate the items included or not included in the sale. State law may list items considered fixtures.

To determine if a certain item is a fixture, the court examines several elements. The following case emphasizes some of the problems surrounding fixtures.

Case 16.1

Vallerie v. Town of Stonington

Supreme Court of
Connecticut, 2000
253 Conn. 371, 751 A.2d 829

BACKGROUND AND FACTS Norwest and Vallerie brought an application for relief against the town of Stonington. They alleged that the tax assessor's October 1, 1994, and October 1, 1995, valuations of the property they owned were manifestly excessive and contrary to law.

The plaintiffs claimed that the tax assessor illegally valued the personal property of floating docks and finger piers as real property. If these items were not classified as real property, the plaintiffs would save a considerable amount in taxes. The trial court rejected the plaintiffs' claim, finding that the finger piers and floating docks were fixtures and, therefore, part of the real estate. The plaintiffs appealed.

PER CURIAM

. . . .

The plaintiffs do not quarrel with the trial court's legal conclusion that "[i]n determining whether the docks and [finger piers] are personalty or realty we must first look at whether the docks and [finger piers] are fixtures. If they are fixtures, the personalty becomes part of the property and they are considered realty. To constitute a fixture, we must look at the character of how the personalty was attached to real estate, the nature and adaptation of the docks and [finger piers] to the uses and purposes to which they were appropriated at the time the annexation was made, and whether the annexer intended to make a permanent accession to the realty. The character of the personal property attached to the real estate is determined at the time that the property is attached to the real estate.

The plaintiffs do, however, contest the trial court's determination that the docks and finger piers are fixtures. We consider that determination a conclusion of fact. "[W]here the factual basis of the [trial] court's decision is challenged we must determine whether the facts set out in the memorandum of decision are supported by the evidence or whether, in light of the evidence and the pleadings in the whole record, those facts are clearly erroneous."

We conclude that the trial court's determination that the floating docks and finger piers are real property was not clearly erroneous. The court found the following facts: "The docks have fresh water and electricity available to boats using the slips. The river has a depth of ten feet at the subject premises. The docks and the slips remain in the water throughout the year. The docks are used to get to the [finger piers] which contain the boat slips. The slips are on open water. The docks and slips float up and down with the tide but are kept in place with seventy to eighty pilings in the river. The docks are attached to bulkheads which are imbedded in concrete. The docks contain utility stanchions with lights that act as street lights. The stanchions also contain lines for water, electricity and telephone service. The water lines are turned off in the winter. There are a total of 133 slips attached to four docks. The docks are periodically removed, repaired and replaced. The economic life of a dock is about fifteen years.

. . . .

The trial court concluded that: "First, there was no evidence presented to us that the annexer ever claimed that the docks and [finger piers] were personalty as did Norwest when it acquired title in 1995. There was also no evidence presented that the annexer meant the docks and piers to be temporary structures. The main business conducted on the subject premises is that of a marina as a going concern. The marina business at the premises is structured on having docks and finger piers attached to the land by bulkheads and concrete walks, running out into the Pawcatuck River, containing stanchions providing amenities such as electricity and water to the slips, supported by pilings driven into the bed of the river. All of these factors cause us to conclude that the intent of the annexer was to make the docks and [finger piers] a permanent fixture to the land."

DECISION AND REMEDY The court concluded that the trial court applied the correct principles of law to the question before it. After examining the trial evidentiary record and exhibits, the Supreme Court of Connecticut concluded substantial evidence existed to support the trial court's factual findings that the docks and finger piers were real estate.

CRITICAL THINKING: LEGAL THEORY Why should society have the doctrine of fixtures?

Property Rights and Ownership Title

Property can be viewed as a bundle of rights. Some of these rights are possession, use, and the right to dispose of the property.

More than one person can hold the same property rights at one time. You may own, with another person, either personal or real property in one of four types of concurrent ownerships. The four types of concurrent ownerships are: (1) tenancy in common; (2) joint tenancy with right of survivorship, commonly called joint tenancy; (3) tenancy by the entirety; and (4) community property.

Tenancy in Common

Tenancy in common is co-ownership in which two or more persons own an undivided (equal or unequal) fractional interest in the property, but, on one tenant's death, that interest passes to his heirs. For example, a brother and sister, Michael and Laura, own a farm as tenants in common. Should Michael die before Laura, Michael's interest in the farm would become the property of Michael's heirs. If Michael sold his interest to Patricia before he died, Patricia and Laura would be co-owners as tenants in common. If Patricia died, her interest in the property would pass to her heirs who, in turn, would own the property with Laura as tenants in common.

Joint Tenancy with Right of Survivorship

In a **joint tenancy with right of survivorship**, two or more people own an undivided interest in either personal or real property. If a joint tenant dies, his interest transfers to the remaining joint tenants, not to his heirs. If Michael and Laura are joint tenants and Michael dies before Laura, the entire farm becomes Laura's property. Michael's heirs receive absolutely no interest in the real estate.

If, prior to Michael's death, he sells his interest to Patricia, Patricia and Laura become tenants in common. Michael's sale terminates the joint tenancy. Joint tenancy with right of survivorship can be terminated at any time by gift or by sale before the joint tenant's death. If either Patricia or Laura dies, her interest passes to her heirs, who would own the property as tenants in common.

Tenancy by the Entirety

Tenancy by the entirety is less common today than it used to be. Only a husband and wife can own property in tenancy by the entirety. Typically, it is created by a husband and wife purchasing property. It is distinguished from joint tenancy with right of survivorship because neither spouse can transfer his or her interest separately without the other's consent. Generally, the two must sell the property together. A divorce will end a tenancy by the entirety. Depending on the state in which the property is located, a divorce usually turns the estate into a tenancy in common.

Community Property

The type of ownership known as **community property** applies in Arizona, California, Idaho, Louisiana, Nevada, New Mexico, Texas, Washington, and Wisconsin. The community property laws apply only to the property of married couples. Each spouse owns an undivided one-half interest in most property acquired during the marriage.

Under this type of ownership, when a spouse dies, he or she can give his or her one-half community property interest to someone other than the other spouse through a last will and testament. The deceased, however, cannot deprive the other spouse of his or her own one-half interest.

Several exceptions exist. Property acquired prior to the marriage or property obtained by gift or inheritance during the marriage usually is not classified as community property, but rather as separate property.

Real Property

Real property[1] consists of land, buildings, plants, trees, subsurface and air rights, and fixtures. Whereas personal property is movable, real property is immovable.

---

[1] Interested in purchasing your first home? See the Internet site for the National Association of Realtors at <http://nar.realtor.com/ind_mn.htm>. You can obtain current information about purchasing a residence or other real estate at this site. If you want to conduct a preliminary search for a new home, see <http://www.realtor.com/>.

LEGAL HIGHLIGHT

Private Control

Charles H. Keating, Jr., was one of the major participants in the savings and loan scandals of the late 1980s. He was convicted of numerous counts of defrauding small investors by enticing them to buy high-risk bonds. He served time in prison before his convictions were over turned on appeal.

Before being convicted, Keating was involved with the antipornography movement. One investment his firm financed was a subdivision, called Estrella, located near Phoenix, Arizona.

Keating was so opposed to pornography that he placed in the Declaration of Covenants, Conditions, Restrictions and Easements (commonly called deed restrictions) for Estrella a provision restricting home-owners from having items in their homes that "depict, describe or relate to any Specified Sexual Activity or Specified Anatomical Area and that the Board, in its sole and absolute discretion, deems to be unacceptable or inappropriate due to the indecent or otherwise offensive nature or content." The homeowners association could come into a home and remove any book, picture, videotape, or similar item that the board found offensive.

After his conviction, the Estrella development went into bankruptcy. The restrictions were modified after the property was sold in bankruptcy to another developer. These deed restrictions were not in force long enough to have a lawsuit determine their legality.

Air and Subsurface Rights

The owner of real property has relatively exclusive rights to the airspace. Until ninety years ago, the right to airspace use was irrelevant. Today, cases involving air rights present questions, such as the right of airspace for high-rise buildings, the right of individuals and governments to seed clouds and produce artificial rain, and the right of commercial and private airplanes to fly over property. Flights over private land normally do not violate the property owners' rights unless the flights are low and frequent, causing a direct interference with the enjoyment and use of the land.

In many states, but not all, the owner of the surface of a piece of land is the owner of the subsurface. Subsurface rights can be extremely valuable because they include the ownership of minerals and, in most states, oil and natural gas.

Water rights also are extremely valuable, especially in the West. When the ownership is separated into surface and subsurface rights, each owner can pass title to his rights without the other's consent.

Ownership Interest in Real Property: Estates in Land

Ownership of property is an abstract concept that exists within the legal system. No one actually can possess or hold a piece of land, the air above, the earth below, and all the water contained on it. The legal system, therefore, recognizes certain rights and duties that constitute the ownership interest in real property. Rights of ownership in real property are called estates and are classified according to their nature, interest, and extent. Interests in real property are divided into two classifications: freehold estates and nonfreehold estates.

Freehold Estates. A **freehold estate** is one in which the owner holds the right to the land for an undetermined time period. The two classes of freehold estates are estates in fee and life estates.

Estates in Fee. The three major categories of estates in fee are **fee simple absolute** (the title to the land is held by the owner with virtually no limitations), **fee simple defeasible** (the title to the land is taken away automatically from the owner under certain conditions), and **fee simple subject to a condition subsequent** (the title to the land can be taken away by the original owners if a specified event occurs).

A fee simple absolute (generally called a fee simple) encompasses the greatest aggregation of rights, privileges, and power possible. The owner of a fee simple estate has the right to use the land for whatever purpose she sees fit, subject to two restrictions. First, laws prevent the owner from unreasonably interfering with another person's land. Second, the owner is subject to applica-

LEGAL HIGHLIGHT

Dino Dirt

The Black Hills Institute of Geological Research, Inc., collected and restored fossils for display in museums. In August 1990, Black Hills was excavating fossils in western South Dakota. Sue Hendrickson, a researcher working on the project, made an exciting discovery of a sixty-five-million-year-old tyrannosaurus rex fossil. The fossil is the largest, most complete, and best preserved and, therefore, the most valuable tyrannosaurus rex skeleton ever found. As a tribute to the person who found the fossil, it was named Sue.

Black Hills was excavating with permission on the ranch of Williams, a Native American. Since 1969, the ranch had been held in trust by the United States under federal law for the sole use and benefit of Williams. Two days after the discovery, Black Hills scientists began excavating Sue. Black Hills purchased from Williams the right to excavate Sue for $5000. After excavation, Black Hills moved the ten tons of bones to Hill City, South Dakota, where scientists began the laborious process of restoring the fossil.

In May 1992, however, federal officers seized Sue and moved her to the South Dakota School of Mines and Technology. The federal authorities contended that under the law the United States, not Williams, owned the property. Because the land was held in trust by the United States for Williams, he had no right to sell any real estate because he did not own the land. A lawsuit was filed.

The federal district court had to decide whether the fossils, before Black Hills excavated it, were personal property (Williams had a right to sell) or real property (he had no right to sell). If it were land within the meaning of the relevant statutes and regulations, the contract between Williams and Black Hills was void.

The court found that the fossil was real property. Sue Hendrickson found the fossil embedded in the land. Under South Dakota law, the fossil was an "ingredient" comprising part of the "solid material of the earth." The bones were a component part of Williams's land, just like the soil, the rocks, and what-

ever other naturally occurring materials made up the earth of the ranch. The fact that the skeleton was once a dinosaur that walked on the surface of the earth and the fact that a bone was protruding from the ground when Hendrickson discovered it, did not make the fossil personal property.

The salient point was that the fossil for millions of years had been an "ingredient" of the earth that the United States held in trust for Williams. The tyrannosaurus rex died nearly sixty-five million years ago and gradually became fossilized and incorporated into land that would eventually become land that was held in trust by the United States. Although the fossil became movable, personal property after a great deal of work to separate the bones from the dirt, at the time Hendrickson discovered the fossil, it was part of Williams's land and was subject to federal law. Because the U.S. government held the land in trust for Williams, it was decided to sell Sue, that is, convert an asset into money, at a public auction.

Later, Black Hills filed a lien in an attempt to recover $209,000 for the expenses it incurred in removing Sue from the Williams land. The court denied Black Hills the right to a lien on the basis that Black Hills had not acted in good faith in excavating the fossil.

Sue was sold at auction in October 1997 by Sotheby's[a] auction house in New York for $8.4 million to the Field Museum of Natural History[b] in Chicago, Illinois. Prior to the auction, experts estimated Sue would sell for no more than one million. Sue now is on public display in Chicago and has her own web site.[c]

---

[a] Sotheby's web site is found at <http://www.sothebys.com/>.
[b] The web site for the Field Museum of Natural History is located at <http://www.fieldmuseum.org>.
[c] Sue has her own web site at <http://www.fieldmuseum.org/sue/default.htm>. Since the tyrannosaurus rex was named after its discoverer, Sue Hendrickson, it is referred to in the feminine gender, although the scientists have not determined its gender.

---

ble zoning, building, and other regulations. A person can own a fee simple for an indefinite period, then can dispose of it by sale or gift.

The owner of a fee simple defeasible or of a fee simple subject to a condition subsequent estate has fewer rights than the owner of a fee simple. With a fee simple defeasible or a fee simple subject to a condition subsequent, the right of ownership can be taken away if specific conditions set out in the deed either occur or fail to occur.

For example, a conveyance from Lincoln "to Tex and his heirs as long as the land is used for a church" creates a fee simple defeasible. In this type of conveyance, Lincoln retains a partial ownership interest. As long as the specified condition occurs (the land is used for a church), Tex maintains other ownership rights. If the specified condition fails to occur (the land ceases to be used for a church), the land reverts (returns) to the original owner, Lincoln, or to his heirs. The interest that Lincoln retains is called a future interest, because if it arises, it will arise in the future.

A fee simple subject to a condition subsequent is very similar to a fee simple defeasible, but normally involves additional language in creating it. Added to the language in the previously discussed transfer to a church would be words such as "the grantor or his heirs shall have a right to reenter and take possession whenever the property is not used as a church."

Life Estates. A **life estate** is where the duration of the estate is measured by the life of one or more human beings. A life estate may be created, for example, by a conveyance of the land by the owner to another person (the life tenant) to occupy and use the land during his lifetime. The person granting the life estate has designated someone else (or the owner himself) as the future owner of the land, who holds the land in fee simple absolute after the life tenant. During the life estate, however, the life tenant has the same rights as a fee simple owner except that he must preserve the value of the land for the holder of the future interest.

Nonfreehold Estates. A **nonfreehold estate** occurs when a person can possess real estate without owning the property. This type of estate generally is treated as a personal interest and not as an interest in real property.

Nonfreehold estates commonly are called *leases* or *tenancies.* Leases are classified as (1) tenancy for years, (2) tenancy from period to period, or (3) tenancy at will. Another tenancy, called tenancy by sufferance, is not actually an estate, however.

Landlord-Tenant Relationship. Before looking at the types of tenancies, the landlord–tenant relationship must be defined. Many real property owners do not use their property themselves. Instead, others, called **tenants**, occupy and use the property under a **lease**. A lease is a contract by which the **landlord**—the owner—grants the tenant exclusive right to use and possess the land, usually for a specific time period. The tenant must pay rent and return the premises in good condition at the end of the lease period.

The landlord ensures that the tenant can possess the property at the time the lease period begins. The landlord must not have rented the premises to another or allow others to occupy and remain on the premises. The tenant is entitled to possess the premises in peace and without disturbance. Usually, the lease or state law determines the landlord's obligation to maintain and repair the premises. In absence of agreement, generally the tenant is liable for maintenance and normal repairs,

LEGAL HIGHLIGHT

Whose House Is This?

Edna Snowden of Sunset Beach, California, thought life estates were wonderful. She was the beneficiary of one. In 1928, Snowden moved in with Mrs. Mary Jane McKinley as live-in housekeeper and companion.

When McKinley died in 1946, her two sons inserted a clause into the deed that gave Snowden a life estate. She was to live in the house rent free. The owners of the house were to maintain all the utilities and provide whatever work was necessary to keep the place livable at no cost to her. She was sixty-eight years old at that time.

When she died in the early 1980s, at more than 100 years old, she had outlived the two sons and six more owners of the house. The last owner, a schoolteacher, was the first owner to live in the house for almost forty years.

Exhibit 16–1 Forms of Ownership of Real Property

Forms of Ownership	Types and Definitions
Concurrent ownership	1. *Tenancy in common* Each tenant owns an undivided fractional share of the property. Such interest can be conveyed without consent and, upon death, passes to tenant's heirs. 2. *Joint tenancy with right of survivorship* Each tenant owns an undivided share of the property. Such interest can be conveyed without consent, converting the interest to a tenancy in common. Upon death, interest passes to surviving joint tenant, not heirs. 3. *Tenancy by the entirety* Like a joint tenancy with right of survivorship between husband and wife in common law states. 4. *Community property* In those states that recognize community property, most property acquired during marriage by either or both spouses is owned equally by each spouse.

Freehold estate (held indefinitely)	1. *Estate in fee:*
	  a. *Fee simple absolute* Most complete form of ownership.
	  b. *Fee simple defeasible* Ownership ends automatically if specified condition occurs or fails to occur. Land reverts to original owner.
	  c. *Fee simple subject to a condition subsequent* Ownership may end if the specified condition occurs or fails to occur. Ownership continues in the current owner. Original owner must take affirmative action to reacquire the land.
	  d. *Life estate* A person owns the property during his or her lifetime. Upon death, the property reverts back to the grantor or to someone the grantor has selected.

Nonfreehold estates (possessory interests held for a specified period of time)	1. *Tenancy for years* Lasts for a period of time stated by an express contract. 2. *Tenancy from period to period* Period determined by frequency of rent payments; automatically renewed unless proper notice is given. 3. *Tenancy at will* For as long as both parties agree. No notice of termination is required. 4. *Tenancy by sufferance* Possession of land without any legal right.

and the landlord is liable for major repairs and improvements.

Types of Tenancies. A tenancy for years, a tenancy from period to period, and a tenancy at will involve the transfer of the right to possession from the landlord (lessor) to a tenant (lessee) for a specified time period. In every lease, the tenant has a qualified right to exclusive possession (qualified by the landlord's right to enter the premises for limited purposes, such as emergency repairs). The tenant can make appropriate use of the land, for example, to grow crops, but cannot injure the land by activities, such as cutting down timber for sale or pumping gas or oil.

A **tenancy for years** is created by express contract (which can sometimes be oral) in which the property is leased for a specified time period. For example, sign-ing a one-year lease to rent an apartment creates a tenancy for years. After the period specified in the lease ends (without notice), the right to the apartment's possession returns to the lessor.

A **tenancy from period to period** is created by a lease that does not specify the length of time for which it is to last, but does specify that rent is to be paid at certain intervals, usually monthly. This type of tenancy is renewed automatically for another rental period unless terminated.

Suppose a landlord rents an apartment to a tenant "for as long as both agree." In such a case, the tenant receives a leasehold estate known as a **tenancy at will**. At common law, either party can terminate the tenancy without notice. This type of estate usually arises when a tenant who has rented under a tenancy for years retains possession, with the landlord's consent, after the lease ends. Sometimes the tenant pays no rent, but acknowledges that the landlord owns the property. Quite often, this tenancy is converted to a tenancy from period to period, which then is renewed automatically and requires proper termination notice.

Whenever a tenancy for years, tenancy from period to period, or tenancy at will ends and the tenant retains possession of the premises without the owner's permission, a **tenancy by sufferance** is created. This tenancy is not a true tenancy and is not an estate, because it is created by a tenant's wrongfully retaining the possession of the property. The tenant is subject to immediate eviction. State statutes must be followed in eviction cases. The landlord files an eviction suit in court. Generally, an eviction action is heard by a judge shortly after the case is filed. State statutes provide that these types of suits will be given preference on the court calender.

Exhibit 16–1 summarizes the forms of ownership described in this section.

Transfer of Ownership

A number of methods exist by which real property ownership can pass from one person to another. These methods include (1) inheritance or will, (2) eminent domain, (3) adverse possession, and (4) conveyance by deed, including selling the property or giving it away.

Transfer by Inheritance or Will. When a person dies with a will, both real and personal property passes according to the will's terms. When the person dies without a will, the real and personal property passes to those relatives listed according to state statues. Any property held in joint tenancy with right of survivorship, however, passes to the remaining tenants outside the will.

Eminent Domain. Even when ownership in real property is fee simple, a superior ownership may limit that fee simple. Called **eminent domain**, the police power of the government allows it to condemn land for public use. The government can acquire real property as authorized by the Constitution and by state law whenever required by public interest.

For example, when a new public highway is to be built, the government must decide where to build it and how much land to condemn. The power of eminent domain generally is invoked through condemnation proceedings. After the government determines that a particular land parcel is necessary for public use, it brings a judicial proceeding to obtain title to the land. Then, in another proceeding, the court further determines the land's fair value, which usually equals its approximate market value. Under the Fifth Amendment, private property may not be taken for public use without just compensation.

In the following case, the United States Supreme Court had to decide whether a city had the right to require a landowner to dedicate part of her property in exchange for a building permit. "To dedicate" means that the city would have the right to use the dedicated property.

Case 16.2

Dolan v. City of Tigard

Supreme Court of the United States, 1994
512 U.S. 374, 114 S. Ct. 2309, 129 L. Ed. 2d 304
http://supct.law.cornell.edu /supct/html/93-518.ZO.html

BACKGROUND AND FACTS In 1973, the state of Oregon enacted a comprehensive land use management program, which required all Oregon counties and cities to adopt new comprehensive land use plans consistent with the statewide planning goals. Pursuant to the state's requirements, the city of Tigard developed and codified a comprehensive plan in its Community Development Code (CDC).

The CDC required property owners in the central business district to comply with a 15 percent open space and landscaping requirement. In effect, the structures and paved parking could cover no more than 85 percent of the land site. A transportation study identified congestion in the central business district as a particular problem, so Tigard adopted a plan for a pedestrian/bicycle pathway intended to encourage alternatives to automobile transportation for short trips. The CDC required any new development to advance this plan by dedicating land for pedestrian pathways.

Dolan owned a plumbing and electric supply store located in Tigard's central business district. The store had 9,700 square feet and sat on the eastern side of a 1.67-acre parcel. On the southwestern corner of the lot was Fanno Creek. The year-round flow of the creek rendered the area within the creek's 100-year floodplain virtually unusable for commercial development.

Dolan applied to the city planning commission for a permit to redevelop the site. She planned to build a new store twice the size of the existing one and to pave a parking lot. The existing store, located on the opposite side of the parcel, would be razed in sections as construction progressed on the new building. In the second phase of the project, Dolan proposed to build an additional structure on the northeast side of the site for complementary businesses and to provide more parking. The proposed expansion and intensified use were consistent with the city's zoning scheme in the central business district.

The commission required that Dolan dedicate the portion of her property lying within the 100-year floodplain for improvement of a storm drainage system along Fanno Creek and that she dedicate an additional fifteen-foot strip of land adjacent to the floodplain as a pedestrian/bicycle pathway. The amount of land required for this dedication was nearly 7,000 square feet, or roughly 10 percent of her land.

She could apply the dedicated property to her 15 percent open space and landscaping requirement mandated by the city's zoning scheme. Tigard would bear the cost of maintaining a landscaped buffer between the dedicated area and the new store. Dolan requested variances from the CDC standards, but her request was denied. She filed a lawsuit that she eventually appealed to the U.S. Supreme Court.

Chief Justice REHNQUIST delivered the opinion of the Court.

. . . .

The Takings Clause of the Fifth Amendment of the United States Constitution, made applicable to the States through the Fourteenth Amendment, provides: "[N]or shall private property be taken for public use, without just compensation." One of the principal purposes of the Takings Clause is "to bar Government from forcing some people alone to bear public burdens which, in all fairness and justice, should be borne by the public as a whole." Without question, had the city simply required petitioner to dedicate a strip of land along Fanno Creek for public use, rather than conditioning the grant of her permit to redevelop her property on such a dedication, a taking would have occurred. Such public access would deprive petitioner of the right to exclude others, "one of the most essential sticks in the bundle of rights that are commonly characterized as property."

On the other side of the ledger, the authority of state and local governments to engage in land use planning has been sustained against constitutional challenge. "Government hardly could go on if to some extent values incident to property could not be diminished without paying for every such change in the general law." A land use regulation does not effect a taking if it "substantially advance[s] state interests" and does not "den[y] an owner economically viable use of his land."

. . . .

. . . Under the well-settled doctrine of "unconstitutional conditions," the government may not require a person to give up a constitutional right—here the right to receive just compensation when property is taken for a public use—in exchange for a discretionary benefit conferred by the government where the property sought has little or no relationship to the benefit.

. . . .

. . . [B]ecause petitioner's property lies within the Central Business District, the Community Development Code already required that petitioner leave 15% of it as open space and the undeveloped floodplain would have nearly satisfied that requirement. But the city demanded more—it not only wanted petitioner not to build in the floodplain, but it also wanted petitioner's property along Fanno Creek for its Greenway system. The city has never said why a public greenway, as opposed to a private one, was required in the interest of flood control.

. . . .

Cities have long engaged in the commendable task of land use planning, made necessary by increasing urbanization particularly in metropolitan areas such as Portland. The city's goals of reducing flooding hazards and traffic congestion, and providing for public greenways, are laudable, but there are outer limits to how this may be done. "A strong public desire to improve the public condition [will not] warrant achieving the desire by a shorter cut than the constitutional way of paying for the change."

DECISION AND REMEDY The Supreme Court found that Tigard had violated Dolan's constitutional rights. The city had not carried its burden of demonstrating a reasonable relationship between the need for the dedication of private property for public use and the landowner's proposed development.

CRITICAL THINKING: PUBLIC POLICY Some owners of real property believe that their property should be used entirely at their discretion. For example, an owner may put a junkyard next to a luxury hotel. After all, the person owns the property. Should the government restrict a person's use of his or her own property without paying compensation to the owner?

Adverse Possession. **Adverse possession** is a means of obtaining title to land without a deed. Essentially, one person possesses the property of another in an open, hostile, notorious manner and for an uninterrupted statutory time period (ranging from three to thirty years, with ten years being most common). Called an adverse possessor, that person acquires title to the land and cannot be removed from the land by the original owner.

For example, Bill and Karen find an unoccupied house in the woods. They decide to occupy the house, find the owner, and buy it. After six months, they cannot find the owner. Because the land has two years of back taxes owed, they assume the owner has abandoned the property. Bill and Karen pay the back taxes and for ten years live on the property, fence in the property, remove trespassers, pay taxes and utilities, have mail and other items delivered to it, and invite guests to the house. Suddenly, the recorded title owner, Jerry, appears and demands that Bill and Karen vacate the premises. If Bill and Karen have possessed the property continuously for the required statutory period (assume ten years), they successfully can claim title by adverse possession. Their possession was open, exclusive as to the others (hostile), and without Jerry's permission.

After the adverse possessor meets all statutory requirements, a *quiet title action* may be filed in court. If granted, the court's judgment is recorded in the appropriate government office. A **quiet title action** decides who has title to the property; thus, this action settles a dispute over the title and places the title in the true owner's name. The adverse possessor records the judgment and holds title, just as if a conveyance by deed had been made.

Conveyance by Deed. Possession and land title generally pass from person to person by means of a deed, the written instrument of conveyance for real property. A deed is signed by a property owner to transfer title to another person. Deeds must meet certain requirements, such as being delivered from the grantor to the grantee and containing a full description of the property as well as, in some states, an acknowledgment of the grantor's signature by a notary public.

Several types of deeds are used today. The first is a **general warranty deed.** This type of deed provides the buyer the most protection against defects in the title to the land. The seller warrants, first, that he has the right and power to convey the title to the land. Second, the seller warrants that no liens or interests exist or, if they do, that they are listed and/or known to the buyer. Liens and interests include mortgages, tax liens, mechanics' liens, and easements and these usually are recorded in a public office. Third, the seller warrants that the buyer will have "quiet enjoyment" of the property, in other words, that no one with a better title will force the buyer from the property. These warranties apply to any adverse claims that may exist from the original grant from the government through the seller's ownership.

A second type of deed is the **special warranty deed.** The seller warrants only that he did nothing previously to lessen the real estate's value and does not warrant what prior owners have done.

The third type of deed is called a **bargain and sale deed**. This deed does not warrant or guarantee title, but it does convey the title to the purchaser.

The fourth type of deed, called the **quitclaim deed**, conveys less than other types of deeds. This deed transfers to the buyer whatever interest the grantor (who is not necessarily the seller) has, if any. This type of deed can clear interests, if any, in the property.

For example, a piece of reality is held in the name of the husband. The husband and wife separated. A prospective property buyer may want a warranty deed from the seller husband and a quitclaim deed from the wife. If the prospective buyer pays a nominal amount of money, the wife will sign a quitclaim deed transferring any interest she may have in the property. In many states, however, a quitclaim deed causes the title to be defective. A court action must clean up the rights of the parties involved. In those states, a person should use a bargain and sale deed instead of a quitclaim deed.

Recording Statutes.

Every state has a **recording statute**. The purpose of this type of statute is to provide prospective buyers with a way to check a property's history and to determine any outstanding interests, liens, judgments, or taxes that have been placed against the property's title. Recording a deed (or a lien) provides notice to the world that a certain person owns a particular parcel of real estate and notice

that a "cloud" may be on the title. This information is known as **constructive notice**. A buyer may not know about the recorded document, but the law presumes that the buyer has a knowledge of it, because these are public records.

Anything recorded against the property can act as a cloud on its title for persons interested in purchasing or lending money on it. Tax liens, mortgages, or judgment liens are clouds on the title. Recorded liens prevent owners from selling their land without paying creditors who have liens against the property. By recording your deed, you give the public notice that you are the true owner. In the case of recorded deeds, former owners are prevented from fraudulently conveying the land to other purchasers.

Nonpossessory Interests

Some interests in land do not include rights of possession. One important nonpossessory interest is an **easement**. An easement is the right to make limited use of another person's real property without actually possessing it. Often, an easement is called a right-of-way. The right to drive across another's property and the right to place water and sewage pipes, electrical and telephone wires, cables, or fiber optic lines on another's property are examples of easements. Easements can be created by deed, will, contract, or statute. Also, a person may obtain an easement similar to owning property by adverse possession. These easements are called **easements by prescription**.

Acquiring Ownership of Personal Property

Personal property ownership can be accomplished in a variety of ways. Rights can be acquired by possession, purchase, production, gift, will or inheritance, accession, or confusion.

Possession

If you have possession, you normally have ownership. A familiar adage is "Possession is nine-tenths of the law." In reality, this ownership concept is limited in its application. Possession is important in the following situations: wildlife, lost or mislaid property, and abandoned property. One example of acquiring ownership by pos-

LEGAL HIGHLIGHT

Rails to Trails

Listen as the train's lonesome whistle gives way to the biker's bell. A conversion is taking place that ranges from the Atlantic to the Pacific. Abandoned railroad lines are being converted to hiking and bicycling trails.

In the last half of the nineteenth century, railroad tracks were built across the nation. The land on which the railroad was laid was sometimes purchased outright, so the railroad paid a fee simple interest. In other areas, the railroad had an easement.

By 1916, the United States had the largest railroad system in the world with almost 3 million miles of track. The railroad reached the smallest villages, tying people together and moving products across the nation. By the 1960s, the railroad system gave way in part to a nationwide freeway system and to the airline transportation system. Both the trucking and airline industries offered cheaper rates for moving freight; thus, they took freight business from the railroads. People decided to travel by passenger automobiles or by airplanes. By the 1990s, less than half of the original 1916 rail system existed.

Slowly, the railroad system gave way. Some easements ended when the railroad line was abandoned. Other easements were broad enough so that when the railroad no longer used the land, the language in the easement allowed other public uses. Still other land reverted to the original grantor's heirs or to the current landowners. In other words, land dispersement arrangements were inconsistent across the nation. In the 1980s the federal government passed the Rails-to-Trails Act that allowed for the conversion of abandoned railroad property to trails. Across forty-nine states (Hawai'i being the exception) the Rails-to-Trails program converted 878 rail property to trails.

Rail-trails, as they are called, are skinny public parks that cross urban, suburban, and rural America. These rail-trails currently function as trails for hiking, bicycling, horseback riding, in-line skating, cross-country skiing, and wheelchair use.

Although rail-trails are popular with the public, owners of private land adjacent to them have successfully sued to prevent such conversions. In some situations, for example, if the easement were written in such a manner that the land reverted back to the land owner, a conversion can be stopped. Land owners argue that the trains traveled across the property at regular intervals and without stopping. Hikers and bikers, on the other hand, often stop and leave the trail, prompting trespassing and private property misuse, such as picking fruits from private orchards. Hundreds of people may pass by where an occasional train ran a decade ago.

But towns that were dying during the last decade also benefit from the boom that hundreds of travelers bring with them. Towns, counties, and states are working together to connect rail-trails. For more information, go to the Rails-to-Trails Conservancy, a nonprofit public charity web site at <http://www.railtrails.org>.

---

session is the capture of wild animals. Wild animals belong to no one in their natural state. The first person to take possession of a wild animal normally owns it. The killing of a wild animal amounts to assuming ownership of it. A commercial fishing captain, for example, acquires ownership over fish caught in the open seas.

Mislaid or Lost Property. Property voluntarily placed somewhere by the owner, then inadvertently forgotten is **mislaid property**. When mislaid property is found, the finder does not obtain title to, or possession of, the goods. Instead, the possessor of the place at which the property was mislaid becomes the property's caretaker because it is highly likely that the true owner will return. Suppose you leave your textbook under your chair after class. The textbook is mislaid property. If a school employee finds it, the school becomes responsible for the book's reasonable care.

Property that is not left voluntarily but is forgotten is **lost property**. In the absence of a statutory provision, a finder of lost property can claim title to the property against everyone, except the true owner. If the true owner demands that the lost property be returned, the finder must return it.

Abandoned Property. Property that the true owner intentionally discards is **abandoned property**. For example, garbage qualifies as abandoned property. Someone who finds abandoned property acquires title to it and such title is good against everyone, including the original owner. The lost property's owner, who eventually gives up any further attempt to find the lost property, frequently is held to have abandoned the property.

Purchase

Purchase is one of the most common means of acquiring and transferring personal property ownership. The purchase or sale of personal property (called goods) is covered in Chapter 11.

Production

Production, the fruits of labor, is another means of acquiring ownership of personal property. Nearly everyone in the United States today is involved in some sort of production. For example, writers, inventors, and manufacturers all produce personal property and thereby acquire title to it. If you are employed to produce an item, however, your employer will own the produced item.

Gifts

A **gift** is another common means of both acquiring and transferring ownership of personal property. A gift is a voluntary transfer of property ownership. It is not supported by legally sufficient consideration to make a contract, because the very definition of a gift is giving without consideration. A gift must be transferred or delivered in the present rather than in the future and the donor must intend to make a gift.

For example, suppose that your aunt, the donor, tells you, the donee, that she is going to give you a new Corvette for your next birthday. This statement is simply a promise to make a gift. Only when the Corvette or its keys are delivered to you is it considered a gift. Once the gift has been unconditionally delivered, it is irrevocable (cannot be taken back by your aunt).

Will or Inheritance

The law in our society requires that when a person dies (the decedent), title to the decedent's property must vest in (deliver full possession to) someone. The decedent can direct the passage of property after his death through the legal instrument known as a will, subject to certain limitations imposed by the state. If the person dies without a will, he is said to have died intestate. State law determines the distribution of his property among his relatives. If no relatives can be found, the property escheats (title is transferred) to the state.

In addition, a person can transfer property through a trust. The owner (settler) of the property transfers legal title to a trustee, who has a duty imposed by law to hold the property for the use or benefit of another (the beneficiary).

Accession

Accession means addition or increase, or coming into possession of a right. In property law, accession means that someone has added some improvement to a piece of personal property (owned by another) by either labor or materials. Generally, no dispute exists about ownership of the improved property after accession occurs, especially when the accession is accomplished with the owner's consent.

For example, Michio takes his Corvette to Corvette Customizing Garage. Michio wants a unique bumper placed on his Corvette. Michio simply pays the customizer for the value of the labor for improving his automobile. He retains title to the Corvette with the unique bumper.

Confusion

Confusion occurs when property of the same type, otherwise known as *fungible goods,* is mixed. **Fungible goods** are identical goods (the equivalent of other, like units) by nature or usage of trade. For example, a farmer takes his wheat crop to the grain elevator. Once the wheat is mixed with other farmers' wheat of like grade and quality, the ownership changes. The farmers become owners of the grain as tenants in common. The farmer now owns a percentage of the wheat in the grain elevator. No means or reason exists to separate the farmer's original grain from the other farmers' grain; thus, title can pass without the grain being removed from the elevator.

Bailments

A **bailment** is formed by the delivery of personal property, without transfer of title, by one person (called a **bailor**) to another (called a **bailee**), usually under an agreement for a particular purpose (for example, loan, storage, repair, or transportation). On completion of the purpose, the bailee must return the bailed property to the bailor or a third person, or dispose of it as directed. Individuals and businesses are affected by the law of bailments at one time or another.

Most bailments are created by agreement, but not necessarily by contract, because in many bailments not all of the elements of a contract, such as mutual assent or consideration, are present. For example, let's say you mislay your textbook, which is found by a classmate. Your classmate is a bailee, but not by contract, because

no mutual assent or legal consideration occurred. Similarly, if you loan your textbook to a friend so that your friend can read tomorrow's assignment, a bailment is created, but not by contract, because again mutual assent or legal consideration were not present. In contrast, many commercial bailments, such as the delivery of your suit or dress to the cleaners, are based on contract.

A bailment is distinguished from a sale or a gift. In a bailment, possession transfers without passage of title or without intent to transfer title. In a sale or gift, in contrast, title transfers from the seller or donor to the buyer or donee. The following case discusses a bailee's potential liability when the bailed property is stolen.

Case 16.3

United Truck Rental Equipment Leasing, Inc., v. Kleenco Corp.

Intermediate Court of Appeals of Hawai'i, 1996

929 P.2d 99

BACKGROUND AND FACTS Kleenco is in the business of providing commercial cleaning services. United is in the business of renting trucks to the general public. On January 2, 1988, Keith Sugioka (Sugioka), an employee of Kleenco at the time, rented a 1987 one-half-ton Toyota pickup truck (the truck) from United for eighteen days. Having the authority to do so, Sugioka signed a rental agreement (Agreement) for the truck on behalf of Kleenco. The truck was stolen while in Kleenco's possession after a Kleenco employee left the keys in the ignition of the unattended and unlocked truck. United brought suit against Kleenco for the truck's loss.

Kleenco filed a counterclaim that asserted that United's failure to inform Kleenco that it had no theft insurance on the truck constituted an unfair and deceptive trade practice under Hawai'i Revised Statutes, a breach of the implied covenant of good faith and fair dealing contained in the agreement, and fraud.

The court dismissed Kleenco's counterclaim and awarded judgment against Kleenco for $8,957.23. The court's judgment found that the defendant owed $7,500 for the truck, $550 for its use, plus other fees and costs. Kleenco appealed.

Judge ACOBA

. . . .

At common law, the rental of a motor vehicle creates a bailment for the mutual benefit of the parties. A bailment is "a delivery of personal property by one person to another in trust for a specific purpose, with an express or implied contract that the property will be returned or accounted for when the specific purpose has been accomplished or when the bailor reclaims the property." Because United's rental of the truck to Kleenco was a bailment for their mutual benefit, Kleenco, the bailee, was under a duty to "use ordinary care and diligence in the safeguarding of the bailor's property, and [it was] answerable for loss or injury resulting from failure to exercise such care, or for any loss or injury due to [its] negligence, or ordinary negligence." In that regard, "[t]heft is clearly one of the harms against which a bailee must protect." Therefore, under the rules of bailment,

Kleenco bore the risk of loss if it was negligent in its handling of the vehicle. However, the parties are free to enter into a contract to alter their common law duties "provided their agreement does not contravene public policy or violate a statute." The contract involved here was the Agreement.

The Agreement was United's standard rental form. It purportedly contained the entire agreement between the parties. The two relevant provisions on the front of the Agreement, the "collision waiver" and "full responsibility" provisions, are arranged in printed boxes.

The collision waiver provision stated the following:

Collision Waiver

By initialing, renter agrees to pay the sum of $_____ per day or fraction thereof additional and the renter will be responsible only for the first $_____ of damage (except cube box) provided vehicle is operated in conformity with rental agreement. Collision waiver does not cover overhead roof damage. Any damage to cube box is not in any way covered by this waiver.

Initial here x_____

The "full responsibility" provision located below the collision waiver provision stated the following:

Full Responsibility

By initialing, renter agrees to pay United Truck for all loss or damage to vehicle (regardless of negligence).

Initial here x_____

Sugioka did not initial or mark the "collision waiver" provision. Rather, he initialed the "full responsibility" provision as evidenced by the initials "K.S." on the "initial here" line.

. . . .

We agree that the term "collision" would not include "theft." However, we do not agree, as Kleenco urges, that the "full responsibility" obligation under the agreement did not render Kleenco liable in the event the truck was stolen while in its possession. For, examining the contract as a whole, we discern no ambiguity in the contract.

. . . .

The "full responsibility" clause setting forth Kleenco's responsibility "for all loss or damage" is also reiterated in the paragraph three statement that the renter is responsible for "all loss or damage whatsoever." Construing the contract as a whole, the plain meaning of these provisions is that under the Agreement, the renter was responsible for "all loss or damage" except to the extent of the "collision waiver" amount, and in that respect, only if the renter operated the vehicle in conformity with the provisions of the contract.

Therefore, if Kleenco had accepted the collision waiver option and not signed the "full responsibility" box, it would have been responsible for all losses and damages except for damages resulting from a collision (less the amount specified in the collision waiver provision). Because Kleenco did not accept the collision waiver, however, it was liable for all losses and damages including those resulting from a collision.

DECISION AND REMEDY The court upheld the judgment of the trial court except as to damages for loss of use. As to such damages, the court awarded only nominal damages because of the plaintiff's lack of proof.

CRITICAL THINKING: MANAGEMENT APPLICATION Under what circumstances should the renter be liable for an automobile or other vehicle if it is stolen while leased?

Once a bailment is created, the bailee has certain duties and rights concerning the bailed property. Exhibit 16–2 summarizes these rights and duties.

Intellectual Property Law and Computer Law

Intellectual property concerns the creative processes that flow from a person's mind. Inventions, such as the integrated chip or the jet engine, result from creative minds. Or the mind might produce a screenplay, a novel, or a song.

The U.S. Constitution recognizes these creative processes. Article I, Section 8, Clause 8, reads as follows:

> *To promote the Progress of Science and useful Arts, by securing for limited Times to Authors and Inventors the exclusive Right to their respective Writings and Discoveries.*

The federal government has exclusive jurisdiction in these areas.

Computer law is not a specific topic, but involves a wide range of statutes and common law. The federal and state governments have concurrent jurisdiction over various aspects of the subject known as computer law. State law generally covers contracts for computers, while patents on computer components are under exclusive federal jurisdiction.

A distinction must be made between **hardware** and **software** when discussing computers. Hardware is the equipment itself, such as the central processing unit, the video monitor, the keyboard, and the mouse.

Software is the programming involved with a computer system. The two basic kinds of software are system programs, which coordinate the computer's operation, and application programs, such as word-processing programs or spreadsheet programs, which solve particular user problems. Some authorities expand the software's definition to encompass, not only the programming, but also the advice, assistance, and counseling in loading the software onto the hardware.

The question for developers is whether a new creation of software or hardware should be copyrighted or patented. These decisions are covered under intellectual property law. The following sections discuss, first, intellectual property law, then, computer law.

Protection of Intellectual Property Rights

Intellectual property rights covers a wide range of materials, including those related to the computer industry. Although the computer was developed prior to World War II (1941–1945), the real market expansion slowly started in the late 1970s and early 1980s, with explosive growth in the late 1980s and 1990s. The personal computer (PC) became more affordable with the refinement of semiconductor chips and integrated circuits.

The law has evolved slowly, whereas the pace of technology has accelerated. Congress has amended patent, copyright, and trademark laws and passed new laws dealing with legal issues surrounding computer technology.

Patent Law. Patents are filed with the U.S. Patent and Trademark Office (PTO).[2] A patent provides the patent holder the exclusive right to make, use, and market an invention for a nonrenewable period of twenty years.

In 1981, the Supreme Court held that if a "claim containing a mathematical formula implements or applies that formula in a structure or process, which, when considered as a whole, is performing a function which the patent laws were designed to protect (e.g., transforming or reducing an article to a different state

---

[2] The web site for the U.S. Patent and Trademark Office is <http://www.uspto.gov>.

Exhibit 16–2   Rights and Duties of a Bailee

Rights
1. A bailee has the right to be compensated or reimbursed for keeping bailed property. This right is based in contract or quasi-contract.
2. Unpaid compensation or reimbursement entitles the bailee to a lien (usually possessory) on the bailed property and the right of foreclosure.
3. A bailee has the right to limit his or her liability. An ordinary bailee can limit risk, monetary amount, or both, provided that proper notice is given and the limitation is not against public policy. In special bailments, such as common carriers or innkeepers, limitations on types of risk usually are not allowed, but limitations on the monetary amount of risk are permitted by regulation.
4. The right of possession allows actions against third persons who damage or convert the bailed property and allows actions against the bailor for wrongful breach of the bailment.
5. The right to an insurable interest in the bailed property allows the bailee to insure and recover under the insurance policy for loss or damage to the property.

Duties
1. A bailee must exercise reasonable care over property entrusted to him or her. A common carrier (special bailee) is held to a standard of care based on strict liability unless the bailed property is lost or destroyed because of (a) an act of God, (b) an act of a public enemy, (c) an act of a governmental authority, (d) an act of a shipper, or (e) the inherent nature of the goods.
2. Bailed goods in a bailee's possession must be returned to the bailor or disposed of according to the bailor's directions.
3. A bailee cannot use or profit from bailed goods except by agreement or in situations where the use is implied to further the bailment purpose.

---

or thing), then the claim satisfies the [patent laws]."[3] This case set the stage for software to be patented.

Computer software now is patentable with the PTO. Although the PTO accepts software patents, these patents are subject to challenge and difficult to defend. Those who patent computer games have an easier time because the game is unique.

The algorithm (a sequence of steps designed for programming a computer to solve a specific problem) used in software is not patentable because an algorithm, like a law of nature, cannot be the subject of a patent. The software process itself can be patented even though some steps, such as the use of the algorithms within the software, are not novel or independently eligible for patent protection. The software must be viewed as a whole to show that it performs a function designed to be protected by the patent laws.

Copyright Law. The U.S. Copyright Office[4] issues copyrights. Copyrights are granted by the government to protect original works from being used by others without compensating the copyright holders.

The Constitution encouraged people to be creative by granting authors exclusive rights to their original compositions. These creative people earned royalties when others purchased their works. During the past two centuries, Congress has passed a number of statutes concerning copyrights.

Copyrights for original works are governed by the Copyright Act of 1976. A copyright is valid for the author's life plus seventy years. The Internet challenges the centuries-old traditions of copyright and royalties. Music is easily downloadable from the web, whereas previously the release of music was controlled and made available only in stores. The songwriter, the artist, and the music publishing company were assured of their royalties. Today, music and other copyrighted works are freely available on the Internet with no assurance of royalties.

Congress has struggled to pass laws that address the current copyright problems. The courts also need to protect the copyright holder, but at the same time must decide the extent of the copyright protection. In the following case, the court was confronted with the issue of whether a menu command hierarchy was covered by copyright laws.

---

[3] *Diamond v. Diehr,* 450 U.S. 175, 101 S. Ct. 1048, 67 L. Ed. 2d 155, 169 (1981).

[4] The U.S. Copyright Office is located at <http://lcweb.loc.gov/copyright/>.

Case 16.4

Lotus Development Corporation v. Borland International, Inc.

United States Court of Appeals, First Circuit, 1995
49 F.3d 807

BACKGROUND AND FACTS Lotus 1-2-3 is a spreadsheet program that enables users to perform accounting functions electronically on a computer. Users manipulate and control the program via a series of menu commands, such as "Copy," "Print," and "Quit," which users choose either by highlighting them on the screen or by typing their first letter. In all, Lotus 1-2-3 has 469 commands arranged into more than fifty menus and submenus.

After Borland's engineers had labored over its development for nearly three years it released its first Quattro program to the public in 1987. Borland's objective was to develop a spreadsheet program far superior to existing programs, including Lotus 1-2-3. In Borland's words, "[f]rom the time of its initial release . . . Quattro included enormous innovations over competing spreadsheet products."

The district court found, and Borland did not contest, that Borland included in its Quattro and Quattro Pro version 1.0 programs "a virtually identical copy of the entire 1-2-3 menu tree." Borland, however, copied none of Lotus's underlying computer code; it copied only the words and structure of Lotus's menu command hierarchy. Borland included the Lotus menu command hierarchy in its programs to make them compatible with Lotus 1-2-3, allowing spreadsheet users who were already familiar with Lotus 1-2-3 to switch to the Borland programs without learning new commands or rewriting their Lotus macros.

Lotus sued Borland for copyright violations. The district court held that Lotus held a copyright that included its menu command hierarchy and that Borland had infringed Lotus's copyright in Lotus 1-2-3. The district court then entered a permanent injunction against Borland, which it appealed.

Circuit Judge STAHL

. . . .

Borland argues that the Lotus menu command hierarchy is uncopyrightable because it is a system, method of operation, process, or procedure foreclosed from copyright protection by 17 U.S.C. § 102(b). Section 102(b) states: "In no case does copyright protection for an original work of authorship extend to any idea, procedure, process, system, method of operation, concept, principle, or discovery, regardless of the form in which it is described, explained, illustrated, or embodied in such work." Because we conclude that the Lotus menu command hierarchy is a method of operation, we do not consider whether it could also be a system, process, or procedure.

We think that "method of operation," as that term is used in §102(b), refers to the means by which a person operates something, whether it be a car, a food processor, or a computer. Thus a text describing how to operate something would not extend copyright protection to the method of operation itself; other people would be free to employ that method and to describe it in their own words. Similarly, if a new method of operation is used rather than described, other people would still be free to employ or describe that method.

We hold that the Lotus menu command hierarchy is an uncopyrightable "method of operation." The Lotus menu command hierarchy provides the means by which users control and operate Lotus 1-2-3. If users wish to copy material, for example, they use the "Copy" command. If users wish to print material, they use the "Print" command. Users must use the command terms to tell the computer what to do. Without the menu command hierarchy, users would not be able to access and control, or indeed make use of, Lotus 1-2-3's functional capabilities.

. . . .

In many ways, the Lotus menu command hierarchy is like the buttons used to control, say, a video cassette recorder ("VCR"). A VCR is a machine that enables one to watch and record video tapes. Users operate VCRs by pressing a series of buttons that are typically labelled "Record, Play, Reverse, Fast Forward, Pause, Stop/Eject." That the buttons are arranged and labeled does not make them a "literary work," nor does it make them an "expression" of the abstract "method of operating" a VCR via a set of labeled buttons. Instead, the buttons are themselves the "method of operating" the VCR.

When a Lotus 1-2-3 user chooses a command, either by highlighting it on the screen or by typing its first letter, he or she effectively pushes a button. Highlighting the "Print" command on the screen, or typing the letter "P," is analogous to pressing a VCR button labeled "Play." Just as one could not operate a buttonless VCR, it would be impossible to operate Lotus 1-2-3 without employing its menu command hierarchy.

. . . .

Original developers are not the only people entitled to build on the methods of operation they create; anyone can. Thus, Borland may build on the method of operation that Lotus designed and may use the Lotus menu command hierarchy in doing so.

DECISION AND REMEDY The court held that the Lotus menu command hierarchy was not copyrightable subject matter and, therefore, Borland did not infringe Lotus's copyright.

COMMENT This case was appealed to the U.S. Supreme Court, which came to a "nondecision" by a four-to-four vote. Four justices believed that the menu command hierarchy was not copyrightable, while the other four believed it to be copyrighted. Justice John Paul Stevens abstained.

Industry experts believe that more than $20 million was spent on litigating this case. The Supreme Court's decision has no effect. The result is that the First Circuit Court's decision is the leading opinion in the field. Although the First Circuit's opinion is not binding in any other federal circuit, these courts may adopt the First Circuit's position. As a result of the Supreme Court's inaction and Congress's failure to amend the Copyright Act, some experts believe that in the future, software developers may file for patents with the PTO.

CRITICAL THINKING: LEGAL CONSIDERATION The court seemed to differentiate between computer programs and macros, which are similar. But a computer program must create a macro. Do you think the court took that fact into consideration when it held that no copyright violation occurred?

Congress in 1984 passed the **Protection of Semiconductor Chip Products Act**. Products in the field of semiconductor chip production, which are called **maskwork**, were allowed to be copyrighted. A maskwork is a series of related images fixed or encoded in a three-dimensional pattern on the chip that are layered in a series, so that each image has a pattern. Imagine a film negative that is black on clear plastic. As it is processed into a picture, various layers of plastic with images are layered. Eventually, the final product, a colored photograph, is produced. Maskwork is a similar process. This application of copyright law protects the manufacturer from counterfeiters, a prevalent problem in the industry.

LEGAL HIGHLIGHT

What the Computer Knows about You

In two seconds, you can communicate with a person anywhere in the world, thanks to computers and satellites. In the past, you left a trail of paperwork as a result of your daily activities. Today, you leave an electronic wave of information as various computers monitor your daily activities.

At the job site, your arrival time in the parking lot is electronically noted. The time at which you turn on the computer at your workstation is logged. Your telephone calls are monitored not only for the content of your conversation, but also for the length of time to the second. Your pay is deposited electronically into your bank account, and preauthorized bills are paid.

Your travel agent's computer knows that you are taking a trip. It knows your name, address, telephone number, arrival and departure times, destination and arrival, meal preferences, whether you are traveling round-trip or one way, and whether you have excess luggage or are bringing your pet. It knows the rates charged and the time used in automobile rentals and hotel arrangements, your driver's license information, perhaps your Social Security number, and any special requests. The computer knows your credit card issuer, your card number, the expiration date, those authorized to sign, and the number of credit cards you have. It knows your passport number and places that you have visited outside of the United States.

Which information did you voluntarily disclose and which information was gathered with little knowledge or thought on your part? How long does this information remain in the various computer banks? Is this information destroyed or archived? Who accesses it: competitors who may gain access lawfully by purchasing it or the government, which may request information from parties who control it? How should businesses handle sensitive information? The loss of privacy will expand as more information is gathered and stored on computers.

The web allows all of this information to be gathered into large databases. Congress passed legislation to cover information gathered by companies on the web because of complaints by consumers. For example, a dot com called ToysSmart went into bankruptcy. The web site stated that any information gathered at the web site would not be sold or distributed. Once in

bankruptcy, however, the database was seen as an asset to be sold to help pay the creditors. The company placed an advertisement in the *Wall Street Journal*. The Federal Trade Commission, the attorneys general of forty-two states, and others sued ToySmart to keep it from divulging the data, which included names, addresses, and credit card numbers. The Walt Disney Co., a majority owner of ToySmart, paid $50,000 for the toy company to destroy its database. This action by Walt Disney Co., speaks to its high ethics, because the action was not taken for immediate monetary gain.

Another example, in 2000, Amazon, the online retailer, announced that it had changed its privacy policy. The policy printed on the its web site clearly stated, in fine print, that Amazon reserved the right to change its policy. The policy changed from not sharing any private information and not selling the information it collected to Amazon making the database available for purchase. Customers were not allowed to opt out of being in the database nor could they request specific information be deleted.

Congress adopted the opt-out method over the opt-in method for consumers. The opt-in method means that the customer's protected, unless it signs a permission form so the company that holds the information can sell it to a purchaser. The opt-out method operates in reserve. Any information held by the company is available for sale, unless the customer is proactive. The customer must request the form, sign the form, and return the form stating that he does not give permission to the company to sell any information it holds about him. In other words, the customers must know of their rights, then act on those rights.

The Electronic Privacy Information Center (EPIC)[a] is very active in this field. It has a number of publications on the topic of electronic privacy. After the change in Amazon's privacy policy, the EPIC ended its ties with Amazon. Amazon's old privacy policy and new privacy policy are available through the EPIC's web site.

---

[a] The Electronic Privacy Information Center's web page is at <http://www.epic.org/>.

The law also gave authority to the secretary of commerce to issue orders extending protection under the Semiconductor Chip Products Act to foreign governments. In the future, treaties and other agreements will be used to achieve international consensus in this area. In 1985, President Ronald Reagan (1981–1989) issued an executive order extending protection against unauthorized duplication of semiconductor chip products to foreign countries.

The Copyright Act was amended in 1990 by the **Computer Software Rental Amendments Act**, which allows a computer program's copyright holder to control the rental, leasing, or lending of the computer program after the first sale. Prior to the passage of this act, the exclusive right to sell a copy extended only to the first sale of the copy. After the first sale of a copy, the copyright owner did not have any control over the conditions of future sales.

Computer Law

When discussing the legal issues of computer hardware, the general principles of Uniform Commercial Code, Article 2, Sales, and Article 2A, Leases, will suffice. The Uniform Commercial Code (UCC) was previously discussed in Chapters 9 through 12. The sale and purchase of computer hardware is identical to the sale and purchase of many other types of personal property. The sale of hardware, which is a tangible, movable good, is covered by the UCC. Contracts for computer hardware are covered generally by state law.

The unique aspect of computer law involves software and semiconductor chips. These items are usually copyrighted or patented, as discussed previously, and, as such, are covered by federal laws. Once copyrighted or patented, software is sold to consumers.

Is the sale of software loaded on the hardware, such as a PC that is sold with a word-processing, spreadsheet, and database loaded, covered by general contract law or the UCC? Is software that is sold separately from a PC covered by general contract law or the UCC? The importance of this determination is that Article 2 gives very specific rights and obligations to both the buyer and the seller. If Article 2 fails to apply, basic contract law applies. Article 2 is more protective of the buyer, whereas common law tends to give more protection to the seller, for instance, under the doctrine of *caveat emptor* ("let the buyer beware").

The courts uniformly have held that when software is sold with or given with the sale of hardware, a sale of goods occurs. Thus, Article 2 of the UCC applies.

The problem occurs when software is sold separately. When the software is purchased from a store, the courts tend to treat it as a sale of goods because it is sold under a sales contract. What happens, however, when a program is written for a specific use instead of for common usage? Is this a sale of goods or the provision of a service?

The cases are divided on this issue. Logic dictates that this transaction would be considered a sale of a specialty good based on a transfer of a tape or disk. Under the law, the definition of goods is very broad and should encompass the sale of software.

Some cases hold, however, that the sale of software is a transaction involving service, not a sale of goods, since the program on the tape or disk is being sold. In those jurisdictions where these cases have been decided, the general principles of contract law are applied, and the protection given to buyers by Article 2 of the UCC is inapplicable.

A large segment of the computer software business involves transfer by either a lease or a license, but not by a sale. The UCC covers the leasing of goods in Article 2A, Leases. Forty-nine states have adopted Article 2A.

Article 2B treats a computer program as a license whenever there is a sale. This article is known as the Uniform Computer Information Act.

Software Warranties

The UCC applies to the transfer (sale or lease) of software; thus, specific warranties apply. In particular, the UCC defines an express warranty, the implied warranty of merchantability, and the implied warranty of fitness for a particular purpose. These warranties are covered in Chapter 11. Warranties provide the buyer-user specific rights that are unavailable through the common law. Often, the software agreement specifically states that no warranties apply. The question that courts now face is whether a manufacturer can sell these new products without warranties. If a state has enacted Article 2B, any software sold within the state does not carry any warranties.

E-Mail and Business

In 1994, 31 million people in the United States used electronic mail (e-mail). By 1997, there were 66 million, and by the year 2000 an estimated 107 million persons were using this means of communication. These users generated 812 billion messages in 1994, 2.7 trillion in 1997, and, by current calculation, at least 6.8 trillion messages were sent in 2000. E-mail continues to be a very important means of communication for both business and private persons.

E-mail's advantage is its speed and ease of use. E-mail misuse, however, may result in lawsuits. People routinely send informal messages by e-mail that they normally would not write. They regard e-mail as a temporary document rather than a permanent one that may be available for years to come.

People assume that once they hit the delete key, the e-mail message is destroyed, similar to shredding a piece of paper. But this misunderstanding is far removed from the actuality. Unless e-mail shredding software is installed on the storage server, e-mail may remain for years on a server where it is stored. Or the message may be moved to another area of the computer. When a user presses the delete key, the computer allows the area occupied by the e-mail to now be overwritten. Until overwritten, the message, however, can still be retrieved until a new message or document is saved over the same area of the hard drive. The average user cannot instruct the computer to overwrite a given area. The internal operation of the computer determines this procedure. Most deleted messages may be retrieved and possibly used against a business in the event a legal action is instituted.

Under federal and most state laws, e-mail is a discoverable document in the event of a lawsuit. The problem is that e-mail normally is kept informally, like other written business documents. To determine which messages were sent or which were received by e-mail can take numerous hours. Today's businesses should implement a retention policy that maintains important messages that may minimize liability and that may have legal importance at the time of a trial. If evidence is destroyed, the destruction allows the opponent to argue that the business knew of the evidence's potential relevance to the litigation. The best defense is to show the jury a formal retention policy that allowed the destruction of certain types of e-mail. For example, when Microsoft was sued by the U.S. Department of Justice, Microsoft had to supply all of its prior e-mails, many more than a decade old.

A business has potential civil and criminal liability when it uses e-mail. For example, if an employee sends child pornography by using the business's e-mail server, the business may have to defend itself in criminal court. At the very least, the business may lose a computer because the government may seize any computer used in the commission of a crime.

Another example is one where one employee uses the business's Internet access to download and send explicit pictures to another employee who finds the material offensive. This act can serve as the basis of a sexual harassment action against the business. Again, the best defense to these types of situations is to establish a written policy against them.

A continuing problem involves e-mail document ownership. Many employees regard their e-mail messages as private, like mail sent through the U.S. Postal Service and, as such, these e-mail messages should be unavailable to their employers. The courts have denied this argument, finding that e-mail belongs to the business and not the employee and, as such, the employee has no right to expect privacy. But what happens if the business tells its employees that their e-mail messages are private? The following case confronts this issue.

Case 16.5

Smyth v. The Pillsbury Company

United States District Court
(E.D. Penn.), 1996
914 F. Supp. 97

BACKGROUND AND FACTS Pillsbury Company, the defendant, maintained an electronic mail (e-mail) communication system to promote internal corporate communications among its employees. Pillsbury repeatedly assured its employees, including Smyth, the plaintiff, that e-mail communications would remain confidential and privileged. Pillsbury further assured its employees that their e-mail communications could not be intercepted and used against employees as grounds for termination or reprimand.

In October 1994, Smyth received certain e-mail communications from his supervisor over Pillsbury's e-mail system on his home computer. Relying on Pillsbury's assurances regarding its e-mail system, Smyth responded and exchanged e-mail messages with his supervisor. At some later date, contrary to Pillsbury's confidentiality assurances, Pillsbury intercepted Smyth's private e-mail messages made in October 1994. On January 17, 1995, Pillsbury notified Smyth that his employment was terminated effective February 1, 1995, for transmitting inappropriate and unprofessional comments over its e-mail system.

The statements to which Pillsbury objected included threats to "kill the back-stabbing bastards" in sales management and referred to the planned holiday party as the "Jim Jones Koolaid affair." The plaintiff brought this action based on wrongful discharge.

District Judge WEINER

. . . .

. . . [U]nlike urinalysis and personal property searches, we do not find a reasonable expectation of privacy in e-mail communications voluntarily made by an employee to his supervisor over the company e-mail system notwithstanding any assurances that such communications would not be intercepted by management. Once plaintiff communicated the alleged unprofessional comments to a second person (his supervisor) over an e-mail system which was apparently utilized by the entire company, any reasonable expectation of privacy was lost. Significantly, the defendant did not require plaintiff, as in the case of a urinalysis or personal property search to disclose any personal information about himself. Rather, plaintiff voluntarily communicated the alleged unprofessional comments over the company e-mail system. We find no privacy interests in such communications.

. . . [E]ven if we found that an employee had a reasonable expectation of privacy in the contents of his e-mail communications over the company e-mail system, we do not find that a reasonable person would consider the defendant's interception of these communications to be a substantial and highly offensive invasion of his privacy. Again, we note that by intercepting such communications, the company is not, as in the case of urinalysis or personal property searches, requiring the employee to disclose any personal information about himself or invading the employee's person or personal effects. Moreover, the company's interest in preventing inappropriate and unprofessional comments or even illegal activity over its e-mail system outweighs any privacy interest the employee may have in those comments. In sum, we find that the defendant's actions did not tortiously invade the plaintiffs privacy and, therefore, did not violate public policy.

DECISION AND REMEDY Smyth was unable to obtain relief for wrongful discharge based on his e-mail communications even though his employer assured him that the e-mail would remain confidential.

CRITICAL THINKING: MANAGERIAL CONSIDERATION Discuss whether it is ethical for an employer to contradict its stated position.

The Ever-Developing Field

In an ever-changing society, the concept of personal property, especially in the computer technology area, is expanding. Often, after a new type of property is developed, the courts and legislature must resolve problems that arise from it. For example, the courts have determined that to make illegal duplicate tapes of records, audiotape recordings, videotape recordings, computer programs, compact discs, and digital versatile (or video) discs (DVD) is a crime. The next question is this: Is the law broad enough to cover the developing problems of personal property in outer space, in space laboratories, or during very long space flights?

CyberLaw

Web Pages

The business world is facing major changes in selling goods and services over the coming years. Sales over the Internet have mushroomed during the last few years with no limit in sight. E-commerce is conducted through a business web site. To obtain a web address, a business must have a domain name, an electronic digital address used by computers. At the present time, between 20,000 to 30,000 names are being registered each day.

Until 1995, names were reserved on a "first come, first served" basis. Now a business must register its domain name through InterNIC, a registered service mark of the U.S. Department of Commerce.[5] Names are not registered directly with the InterNIC. Names are registered with one of the companies appearing in a Registrar Directory that is maintained by InterNIC. A registration is valid for two years and can be renewed every year for up to ten years.

The Internet Corporation for Assigned Names and Numbers (ICANN)[6] is a nonprofit international corporation to determine Internet policy including domain names. ICANN resolves questions involving domain disputes.

A business cannot hijack the name of another business entity. Court cases have established that when a business has a valid trademark, it cannot be used by another person as a domain name. Names can be registered if not already taken. The name must be used or someone may register it and use it. For example, if a travel business reserves a name which includes travel that is acceptable. Another business cannot reserve a name that includes travel, if travel is not part of that business.

---

[5] The InterNIC's web address is <http://rs.internic.net/>.
[6] The ICANN's web address is <http://www.icann.org>.

International Consideration

Protecting Your Assets and Ideas in Foreign Countries

The laws of the host country control investments in businesses and property. Many countries restrict foreigners from owning a majority interest in domestic businesses. Under the **Exon-Florio provision** of the Omnibus Trade and Competitiveness Act of 1988, the U.S. president can prevent the purchase by a foreign business of any U.S. firms, such as airline companies, telecommunications businesses, or defense industries, if the purchase threatens national security.

Some countries require foreign investors to go through a preapproval procedure. The potential investor must submit a proposal to a host country's government for evaluation. Various agencies review the proposal, which occasionally goes through up to 100 agencies, to determine if the potential investor meets government requirements. This procedure may take months, if not years. Ownership in private property is allowed only through a trust by which the foreign business owns up to 49 percent, while a domestic business owns the remaining 51 percent. Usually, these trusts have a limited ten-year period, after which time the trust must end or be renewed.

Other countries encourage international investments by offering preferences and incentives, particularly for high-technology industries. The Eastern European countries that had ties with the former Soviet Union encourage investments to bolster sagging economies. For example, Hungary in 1988 adopted the Investments of Foreigners in Hungary Act. This act encourages investments by streamlining an approval procedure, allowing profits to flow out of the country, providing contract guarantees, and allowing foreign managers. The Russia Federation (Russia) allows private land ownership by foreign businesses. Tax and other incentives are being used to encourage investment in Russia.

A business may protect its intellectual property, such as copyrights and patents, at the international level. The United States signed the **Universal Copyright Convention** in 1952 and the **Berne Convention for the Protection of Literary and Artistic Works** in 1988. The Universal Copyright Convention grants an author copyright protection in every country that has signed when he or she first publishes a work in one of the countries with the prescribed notice. Each country is bound to protect the work according to its laws. The Berne Convention similarly provides the citizens of any other member country the same copyright protections that it provides its own citizens.

As early as 1883, the United States and others were signatories to a treaty that provided the citizens of other countries the same rights to obtain a patent as were granted to the country's own citizens. This early treaty established the principle of right of priority. If a person applied for a patent in his or her own country and within a year applied for a patent in one of the other countries, the later application was considered as having been made on the same date as the one made in his or her own country.

The **Paris Convention for the Protection of Industrial Property** attempts to achieve uniformity in the patent area by having countries adopt a universal system of granting and recognizing patents. This convention also recognizes the principle of right of priority.

In 1998, the U.S. signed the **Digital Millennium Copyright Act (DMCA)**,[7] which implements two World Intellectual Property Organization treaties. The treaty limits liability of online service providers for copyright infringement. An exception is made under the treaty for making a copy of a computer program by activating a computer for purposes of maintenance or repair. Other provisions cover diverse issues, such as distance education, libraries, and webcasting of sound recordings.

The WTO fosters cooperative methods that allowed for negotiations of the global agreement on intellectual-property protection (TRIPS). All WTO members are committed to enact and enforce copyright, patent, and trademark laws.

---

[7] To see a copy of the Digital Millennium Copyright Act, go to the U.S. Copyright Office's web page at <http://lcweb.loc.gov/copyright>.

LEGALLY SPEAKING

Protecting Real Property

You decide to purchase a specific parcel of real property, which consists of several vacant buildings located in a suburban area on twenty acres of land. Because the property is rather isolated, numerous illegal intrusions into the buildings have been made by transients in order to stay a night or two and by youths for parties. These individuals have caused considerable damage to the buildings.

You consider several alternatives to deal with these occurrences: (1) placing guard dogs on the premises, (2) hiring a night watchperson, (3) setting up shotguns that would be triggered by a person touching a string close to the floor, or (4) simply letting these people use the premises until you find a tenant to lease the property.

You check with an attorney to identify the best alternative. The attorney tells you that the first alternative is not allowed. Many states, including yours, have adopted laws naming a dog's owner liable for bites when the owner knows the dog to be vicious.

The second alternative is possible. The use of a night watchperson is proper as long as he does not use firearms against trespassers. No one can shoot mere trespassers. Before a person can use deadly force, a clear danger to the shooter or another person must exist.

The third alternative is the worst choice. The property owner who sets up this type of gun arrangement is liable for criminal and civil charges if anyone is injured. According to longtime English and American laws, no one can protect property by this method.

The fourth alternative is also unfeasible. If a person, even a trespasser, is injured on your property by falling into a hole or tripping on debris, you may be liable. As the property's owner, you have certain legal duties toward others on the property. Many states require that you act as a reasonable and prudent person would under the same or similar circumstances. Other states require you to make the premises reasonably safe once you are aware that other people are using them.

What should you do? Here is a short list of items you should consider.

✔ Purchase sufficient liability insurance for any incidents that may occur on the property.

✔ Post "No Trespassing" signs prominently.

✔ Board up the buildings, making them very difficult for anyone to enter.

✔ Inform the police department about the situation and ask the police to watch the premises.

✔ Hire security guards if the expense can be justified.

These alternatives are the safest ones that a real estate owner may exercise.

Chapter Summary

Property rights are of prime importance to our society. In fact, the U.S. Constitution protects property rights.

These property classifications are recognized: real or personal, tangible or intangible, and fixtures. All property constitutes either real estate or personal property. Tangible property has physical existence, whereas intangible property consists of rights. Fixtures are items that are installed in real estate and that become part of the land.

A person may own real property with another person. These joint forms of ownership are tenancy in common, joint tenancy with right of survivorship, tenancy by the entirety, and community property. To own an interest in either tenancy by the entirety or community property, the joint owners must be husband and wife.

Different interests in real property are found in freehold and nonfreehold estates. A freehold estate provides a person ownership for an indefinite period. Freehold estates include the fee simple absolute, fee simple defeasible, fee simple subject to a condition subsequent, and life estates. The nonfreehold estates are leases that govern possessory rights to real property in the relationship between a landlord and a tenant.

Transferring all interest in real property occurs by will, by operation of law (eminent domain), by adverse possession, or by deed. Eminent domain is the right of the government to take a person's property. In doing so, however, the government must pay just compensation to the owner. Adverse possession means obtaining title to land (without a deed) by the adverse use of real property for a specified time period.

The seven ways to obtain personal property ownership are by possession, purchase, production, gift, will or inheritance, accession, and confusion.

Bailments concern the transfer of possession of personal property without transfer of title from the "owner" to another person. The bailment can be based on a contract or it can be gratuitous.

Intellectual property and computer law are growing areas of the law. Intellectual property covers patents and copyrights. An important question in computer law is whether transfer of a computer program entails a sale of goods or of service.

Using the World Wide Web

A number of web sites exist where you can find information concerning intellectual property law and computer law. Here are just a few.

Finding the Law on the Web

U.S. Patent Database
http://patents.uspto.gov/access/search-bool.html
Search for patent titles and abstracts and access to patent statutes, Title 35 of the U.S. Code
http://www.law.cornell.edu/uscode/35/
Search for alternate view of patents
http://www.bustpatents.com/
U.S. Patent and Trade Office, Index to Classification
http://patents.uspto.gov/CLASSES/classes.html
or
http://metalab.unc.edu/patents/index.html
Menu to U.S. and international legal materials
http://www.uspto.gov/web/menu/menu5.html
Copyright Office Electronic Registration, Recordation & Deposit System (CORDS)
http://lcweb.loc.gov/copyright/cords/
Copyright Act, Title 17 of U.S. Code
http://www.law.cornell.edu/uscode/17/
National Information Infrastructure, copyright issues
http://iitf.doc.gov/
National Information Infrastructure, copyright issues, opposition arguments, found at Digital Future Coalition
http://www.dfc.org/
Links to intellectual property law
http://www.law.emory.edu/FOCAL /intellectual.html
Copyright web site
http://www.benedict.com/
United Nations Computer Centre
http://www.unicc.org/

Chapter Web Sites

National Association of Realtors
http://nar.realtor.com/ind_mn.htm
National Association of Realtors
http://www.realtor.com/
Sotheby's
http://www.sothebys.com/
Field Museum of Natural History
http://www.fieldmuseum.org
Sue, the T-rex
http://www.fieldmuseum.org/sue/default.htm
Dolan v. City of Tigard
http://supct.law.cornell.edu/supct/html /93-518.ZO.html
Rails-to-Trails Conservancy
http://www.railstrails.org
U.S. Patent and Trademark Office (PTO)
http://www.uspto.gov
U.S. Copyright Office
http://lcweb.loc.gov/copyright
Electronic Privacy Information Center (EPIC)
http://www.epic.org/
InterNIC
http://rs.internic.net/
Internet Corporation for Assigned Names and Numbers (ICANN)
http://www.icann.org
Digital Millennium Copyright Act
http://lcweb.loc.gov/copyright
LegaldotNet
http://db.legal.net/ldn/welcome/query.cfm
National Archives and Record Administration (NARA)
http://www.nara.gov/exhall/nixonelvis/

Web Activities

16–1 Artiste Login Products, Inc., needs to lease a small commercial property that it owns. Go to LegaldotNet at <http://db.legal.net/ldn/welcome/query.cfm> and follow the instructions to login to the web site. Type in "lease." Find the information Artiste needs. You need to click on "thank you." The web site allows you to request free forms. Several files containing different leases will appear. Pick the lease you think is the most appropriate one for leasing Artiste's property.

16–2 Artiste needs to have some of its designs copyrighted. Go to the U.S. Copyright Office's web site at <http://lcweb.loc.gov/copyright/>. Go to "General Information" and click on "Copyright Basics." What works are copyrightable and how is a copyright secured?

Key Terms

abandoned property
accession
adverse possession
bailee
bailment
bailor
bargain and sale deed
Berne Convention for
    the Protection of
    Literary and Artistic
    Works
bill of sale
community property
Computer Software
    Rental Amendments
    Act
confusion
constructive notice

deed
Digital Millennium
    Copyright Act
    (DMCA)
easement
easements by prescription
eminent domain
Exon-Florio provision
fee simple absolute
fee simple defeasible
fee simple subject to a
    condition subsequent
fixture
freehold estate
fungible goods
general warranty deed
gift
hardware

intangible property
joint tenancy with right
    of survivorship
landlord
lease
life estate
lost property
maskwork
mislaid property
nonfreehold estate
Paris Convention for the
    Protection of
    Industrial Property
personal property
production
Protection of
    Semiconductor Chip
    Products Act

purchase
quiet title action
quitclaim deed
real property
recording statute
software
special warranty deed
tangible property
tenancy at will
tenancy by sufferance
tenancy by the entirety
tenancy for years
tenancy from period to
    period
tenancy in common
tenant
Universal Copyright
    Convention

Questions and Case Problems

16–1 Mislaid Property Sally goes into Meyer's Department Store to shop for the holidays. She becomes engrossed in looking over a number of silk blouses, when she suddenly realizes that she has a dinner engagement. She hastily leaves the store, inadvertently leaving her purse on a sales counter. Julie, a sales clerk at the store, notices the purse on the counter but leaves it there, expecting Sally to return for it. Later, when Sally returns, the purse is gone. Sally files an action against Meyer's Department Store for the loss of her purse. Discuss the probable outcome of her suit.

16–2 Leases Goodman contracted to lease an apartment near the campus from landlord Lopez for one year, with the monthly rent due and payable on the first of each month. At the end of the year, Goodman fails to

vacate the apartment and Lopez does not object. Goodman continues to pay the rent on the first day of the month and Lopez accepts it. Six months later, Lopez informs Goodman that the apartment has been leased to Green and that Goodman must vacate the premises by the end of the week. Goodman refuses to leave; Lopez threatens eviction proceedings. Discuss the parties' rights under these circumstances.

16–3 Mislaid Property Bill Heise is a custodian for the First Mercantile Department Store. While walking to work, Bill discovers an expensive watch lying on the curb. Later that day, while Bill cleans the store aisles, he discovers a wallet containing $500 with no identification. Bill turns over the wallet to his superior, Moe Frances. Bill gives the watch to his son Gordon. Two weeks later, Martin Avery, the watch's owner, discovers that Bill found the watch. Martin demands it back from Gordon. Bill then decides to claim the wallet with its $500, but Moe refuses to turn it over, denying that Bill is the true owner and contending that the money is really the store's property. Discuss who is entitled to the watch and who is entitled to the wallet containing $500.

16–4 Adverse Possession Harold was a wanderer until twenty-one years ago. At that time, he decided to settle down on a vacant three-acre piece of land, which he did not own. People in the area indicated to him that they had no idea who owned it. Harold built a house on the land, married, and raised three children while living there. He fenced the land, placed a gate with a sign, "Harold's Homestead," above it, and had trespassers removed. Harold now is confronted by Joe Moonfeld, who has a deed in his name as property owner. Joe orders Harold and his family off the property, claiming his own title ownership. Discuss who has best "title" to the property. What steps should Harold take to protect his property interest, if any?

16–5 Fixtures In 1973, Van Sickle moved his double-wide mobile home to a plot of land in Silver City, Iowa. He had the real estate landscaped, a foundation poured, concrete blocks set, and steel girders aligned on the blocks. After removing hitches and wheels, a crane set the mobile home on the foundation. The mobile home and the foundation were then hooked together. Over time, Van Sickle substantially modified his residence. It could not be moved as one unit, except by a house mover. Jedlicka owned the land. In 1977, Ford purchased the land from Jedlicka for $3,350. In 1982, Venard attempted to enforce a judgment against Van Sickle by attaching and forcing execution on the home. Ford brought this suit, claiming he owned Van Sickle's home. He requested an injunction to restrain Venard from enforcing the sale. Was he successful or not and why? [*Ford v. Venard*, 340 N.W.2d 270 (1983)]

16–6 Fixtures A mortgage was placed on a parcel of land. Afterward, the land owner constructed a grain storage facility there. It consisted of a number of steel structures bolted into concrete slabs that were partially embedded into the ground and which included fifty to sixty feet of underground tubing. Air was electronically pumped through the tubing to move grain from the dryer to several storage bins. To remove these structures would take about two weeks. The facility's owner defaulted on the mortgage. The mortgagee (creditor) filed an action to regain the property. The mortgagee argued that this facility was a fixture and should remain on the

land. Do you agree? Explain. [*Metropolitan Life Insurance Co. v. Reeves*, 223 Neb. 299, 389 N.W.2d 295 (1986)]

16–7 Common Ownership Paul was the owner of real estate located in Putnam County, Florida. In 1982, while Paul was living with Lucille, he executed a deed conveying the property to himself and Lucille as joint tenants with right of survivorship. In 1985, Paul and Lucille stopped living together. Three months later Lucille conveyed her interest in the property to her daughter, Sandra. What type of interest does Sandra possess in the property? Explain. [*Foucart v. Paul*, 516 So. 2d 1035 (Fla. Dist. Ct. App. 1987)]

16–8 Lost Property Danny Smith and his brother discovered a sixteen-foot boat lying beside a roadway in Alabama. Danny Smith informed the police, who immediately impounded the boat and stored it in a city warehouse. Although Smith acquiesced to the police action, he told the police that if the true owner failed to claim the boat, he wanted it. When the true owner failed to come forward, the police department refused to relinquish the boat to Smith and instead told Smith that it planned to auction it to the highest bidder on the city's behalf. Smith sued for custody of the boat. Because Smith never physically held the boat, but rather allowed the police to take possession, should Smith succeed in his claim to title as finder? Could Smith defeat a claim if the true owner sought to retake the boat? [*Smith v. Purvis*, 474 So. 2d 1131 (Ala. Civ. App. 1985)]

16–9 Fixtures A bank installed bank vault doors, night depository equipment, drive-up teller window equipment, and remote transaction systems. The city of Lansing taxed these improvements as real property. The bank took the position that it never intended these items to become part of the real estate. Who should win? Explain. [*Michigan National Bank, Lansing v. City of Lansing*, 293 N.W.2d 626 (1980)]

16–10 Internet On December 21, 1970, Elvis Presley met with President Richard M. Nixon (1969–1974) in the Oval Office located in the White House in Washington, D.C. During that meeting, the White House photographer took twenty-eight photographs. A photograph showing the two men shaking hands is the most requested photograph from the National Archives and Records Administration. For the first time, all of the photographs are available on the web at <http://www.nara.gov/exhall/nixonelvis/>. Are these photographs in the public domain or does a user need to make further inquiries as to the rights to use these pictures?

Unit III Business Formation

Chapter 17

Agency Law and Private Employment Law

> *Employment gives health, sobriety, and morals. Constant employment and well-paid labor produce, in a country like ours, general prosperity, content, and cheerfulness.*
>
> Daniel Webster, 1782–1852
> U.S. congressman (1813–1817, 1823–1827),
> U.S. senator (1827–1841, 1845–1850), and
> U.S. secretary of state (1841–1843, 1850–1852)

Outline

Ethical Consideration

The Hard Decisions Surrounding Medical Insurance

You own Sam's Clothing Store, which has been in business for more than twenty years. Your business is known in the community for its good employee benefits. One benefit is the group health insurance plan.

You have a very loyal workforce, including several employees who have worked for the clothing store since its inception. One of the longtime employees has severe medical problems that require very expensive procedures. Although he has been absent a little more than normal, he still performs his job. The cost of his medical bills, however, is beginning to affect the medical plan's cost. Your medical insurance broker informs you that if this employee continues on the medical plan, the rates for next year will increase significantly.

Your broker advises you to be prepared to pay significantly higher rates or to provide each employee with a specific sum of money to help offset the cost of private health insurance for which the broker will assist each employee to enroll. Although the broker's idea of letting each person find his or her own insurance appeals to your business sense, you know that individual medical insurance is very expensive.

You believe that the ill employee will be unable to purchase insurance. What course of action should you take? Use the ethical model presented in Chapter 2 and reprinted on the inside front to develop your answer.

Introduction

Agency law[1] is important because it permeates the entire legal system. Agency law defines the relationship between two parties in which one of them, called the **agent**, agrees to represent or act for the other, called the **principal**. The principal has the right to control the agent's conduct in matters entrusted to the agent.[2]

In **employment law**, the employer can control the time and place at which the employee will work and the type of work to be done. The employer is called the master and the employee is called the servant. If the employee is authorized to enter into contracts on behalf of the employer, the employee is acting in the capacity of an agent, and the employer is also the principal. Some states have moved away from the use of the terms master and servant because they are seen as insulting to employees.

The rules in agency law are relatively simple and straightforward, although the application of the rules to a specific problem is sometimes difficult. Both agency law and its counterpart, employment law, have evolved over the centuries. The basic concepts, however, remain consistent. This chapter will discuss agency law and the private employment law. Other laws that affect employment will be discussed in later chapters.

Your online business, Artiste Login Products, Inc., hires agents, employees, and independent contractors. Not only must you be aware of the different laws that apply to each category, but you also need to be alert to possible tax implications.

Background

The forerunners of agency law were the legal principles developed during Roman times relating to slave ownership. Even in ancient times, an owner was financially liable for the torts of his slaves. The reasoning was that if a person could increase his wealth through the services of slaves, he should be responsible for the slaves' acts.

This concept continued to develop through the Middle Ages. Eventually, a body of law governing the relationship of master and servant evolved. A master could be held liable for the servant's acts committed within the **scope of employment**, in other words, within the time and area of the work assignment. A servant could not enter into contracts on the master's behalf. The liability of a master, therefore, usually was

---

[1] At the web site for Law Com, <http://www.law.com/>, type in the word "agency." You will discover more than 1,100 articles on this subject.

[2] The 'Lectric Law Library has a good general discussion of agency law. You may access it at <http://www.lectlaw.com/d-a.htm>.

limited to tort damages. For example, the master was liable if a servant negligently harnessed a carriage and this negligence resulted in damages or injuries to another person.

Today, the same concept is applied to the employer–employee relationship. Under employment law, employers are responsible for the harm caused by the torts of their employees who act within the scope of their employment.

The Industrial Revolution, which started in the mid-1700s, created the need for many contractual relationships. The owners of new industrial plants entered into many contracts to keep the plants operating. The owners purchased raw materials in volume from several sources and sold the manufactured products over a wide territory to many people. No longer would the majority of contracts be between the individual who produced an item and the individual who purchased it.

People who owned industrial plants delegated the responsibility to enter into these contracts to individuals known as agents. By using agents, an owner (or principal) could conduct multiple business operations simultaneously in various locations. In addition, the owner of the industrial plant incurred liability on the contracts made on his behalf by the agents. As a result, the concept of agency law developed.

The underlying concept of the employer–employee and principal–agent legal relationship is summarized by a Latin phrase, *qui facit per atium facit per se*, which means "he [or she] who acts through another acts himself [or herself]." This phrase summarizes the theory that has served as the foundation of agency law from Roman times through today. If a person increases business profits through the use of other people, he or she should be liable for the actions of those people.

Formation of the Agency Relationship

Generally, no formalities are required to create an agency. The agency relationship can arise by one of several methods: agreement, ratification, or estoppel.

Agency by Agreement

Agency is a consensual relationship. The agency relationship is created when the principal agrees to have

the agent act on behalf of the principal. Most agency relationships are created in this manner.

Agency relationships can be based on oral express agreements. Good business practice, however, dictates that the agreement should be in writing. The agency relationship normally is a contractual one; thus, contract rules apply including the statute of frauds discussed in Chapter 10. This statute requires certain types of contracts to be in writing to be enforceable in a court. For example, the sale of any interest in real estate must be in writing; so, for instance, real estate listing agreements between the seller (principal) and the real estate broker (agent) must be in writing.

A common agency by agreement is a written document called a **power of attorney** that grants a person the authority to perform acts on your behalf, such as signing papers, opening accounts, or making purchases. Assume that you are purchasing a house and will be out of town when the actual purchase takes place. Your spouse needs to sign the papers on your behalf. You can grant your spouse the authority to sign your name to the papers by providing your spouse a power of attorney. Most states require this document to be signed by the principal in the presence of a government-sanctioned official, such as a notary public. A power of attorney is signed by the principal (you) granting the agent (your spouse, in this case) either unlimited authority to act on the principal's behalf or limited authority to perform specific acts. The agent is called an attorney-in-fact.

Agency by Ratification

On occasion, a person who is not in fact an agent, or who acts outside the scope of her authority as an agent, may make a contract on behalf of a purported principal. No authority from the alleged principal, either express or implied, is present when the professed agent makes the unauthorized contract.

If the principal later approves or affirms that contract by word or by action, an agency relationship is created by ratification. **Ratification** is determined by intent, and intent can be expressed by either words or conduct. Ratification binds the principal to the agent's acts and treats these acts or contracts as if the principal had authorized them. The principal must be aware of all material facts; otherwise, the ratification is not effective.

The principal's ratification can be either expressed or implied from the principal's words or conduct. The creation of the agency by ratification "relates back" to the time of the unauthorized act. By his acceptance, the principal acknowledges that the contract started at the time of the unauthorized act. The principal ratifies both the advantages and the disadvantages of the ratified contract or act.

For example, a person with no connection to an alarm business convinces a ninety-year-old widow to sign a contract for the installation of a burglar alarm.

He guarantees her that the company will pay any losses she may incur because of a burglary. When he presents the contract to the business and it agrees to install the system, it also must be bound by the guarantee made by the salesperson. If a burglary loss occurs, the business must pay the widow.

The following case decides if silence on the part of a purported principal can be construed as ratification.

Case 17.1

First National Bank of Shreveport v. Crawford

Court of Appeals of Louisiana, 1984
455 So. 2d 1209

BACKGROUND AND FACTS In 1974, Mrs. Crawford executed a power of attorney naming her daughter, Mrs. Howe, as her agent. She restricted the power of attorney to the agent borrowing money for Mrs. Crawford's benefit.

Mrs. Howe and her husband operated a dairy farm. Mrs. Crawford took no part in managing the dairy business and received no benefits from it. In 1980, the Howes experienced severe financial difficulties in operating their farm and needed to refinance their debt. A few days before the new loan for more than $2 million dollars closed, Mrs. Howe advised the attorney handling the transaction that she would sign the loan instruments as her mother's agent under the 1974 power of attorney so that her mother could avoid coming to town for the closing.

The attorney examined the power of attorney, approved it, and prepared the loan papers. Mrs. Howe acted as an agent for Mrs. Crawford in this matter without Mrs. Crawford's knowledge or consent. Mrs. Crawford testified at the trial that she knew nothing about the loan transaction. Mrs. Howe testified that she told her mother something about it approximately a month after the loan was closed, but her testimony as to the information she told her mother was vague and indefinite.

Mr. and Mrs. Howe were unable to pay the debt and went into bankruptcy. The bank sued Mrs. Crawford to collect the loan, alleging that Mrs. Crawford had ratified the agreement. The trial court entered a judgment for Mrs. Crawford. The bank appealed.

Judge HALL

. . . .

The bank argues that Mrs. Crawford, by her silence and inaction after being informed of the bank transaction, ratified the action of her agent in executing the note and mortgage, and is bound thereby regardless of the agent's original authority. The concept of ratification by a principal of an agent's unauthorized acts is recognized in two articles of the Civil Code:

[1] "The attorney cannot go beyond the limits of his procuration; whatever he does exceeding his power is null and void with regard to the principal, unless ratified by the latter, and the attorney is alone bound by it in his individual capacity."

[2] "The principal is bound to execute the engagements contracted by the attorney, conformably to the power confided to him."

"For anything further he is not bound, except in so far as he has expressly ratified it."

. . . .

The bank did not prove by a preponderance of the evidence that Mrs. Crawford knew and understood what her agent had done in this case. Mrs. Crawford denied knowing anything about the transaction until this suit was filed. Mrs. Howe's testimony was vague and indefinite as to what she told her mother about the transaction and when she told her. A clear intent to ratify the [loan] . . . cannot be inferred from the facts of this case. Ratification was not established.

DECISION AND REMEDY The court of appeals affirmed the trial court's judgment for Mrs. Crawford. The plaintiff must prove ratification by showing a clear and absolute intent to ratify the unauthorized act. Under these circumstances, in which the bank failed to prove Mrs. Crawford's knowledge of the loan, silence failed to indicate ratification.

CRITICAL THINKING: MANAGERIAL QUESTION Discuss the circumstances under which a financial institution should rely on a power of attorney.

Agency by Estoppel

An **agency by estoppel** occurs when a principal leads a third person to believe that another person is his agent. When the third person deals with the supposed agent, the principal cannot deny the agency relationship. In other words, the principal cannot claim the agency relationship does not exist. In these situations, the principal's actions create the appearance of an agency that does not in fact exist.

For example, Kona is in the insurance business and hires McGant as an agent to solicit and sell insurance. Kona advertises to the general public that McGant is his agent. After a period of time, Kona discovers that McGant is keeping some of the premiums paid in cash. Obviously, McGant is dishonest and probably has committed a criminal act. Kona fires McGant immediately, but Kona's advertisements still give McGant the appearance of being Kona's agent. If McGant should contract with an innocent third party after being fired, Kona will be estopped from denying that McGant was his agent. Kona represented McGant to the public as his agent, and an innocent purchaser relied on this representation. Kona, therefore, is not allowed to claim a lack of an agency relationship. To avoid possible future liability, Kona might publish notice that McGant is no longer Kona's agent and personally notify all previous customers who dealt with McGant of this fact.

Agency Relationships

Two types of agency relationships exist. The first is the principal–agent, including professional agents. The second is the employer–employee when the employee is also an agent.

The legal principles developed under either agency law or employment law have similar applications. A person can be both an employee and an agent at the same time. For example, a business may employ a person full time to analyze the real estate market. That person also may have the authority to negotiate the price of, and to purchase or sell, specific pieces of land. Because these two relationships, that is, employer–employee and principal–agent, easily can be intertwined, a clear application of separate legal principles sometimes is impossible.

Exhibit 17–1 summarizes the types of agency relationships recognized by law. Throughout the rest of this chapter, the terms *principal* and *agent* will include the terms *employer* and *employee,* unless otherwise stated.

Relationship between the Principal and Agent

The agent acts on behalf of, and instead of, the principal to negotiate, conduct, and contract business with third persons. The agent has **derivative authority**; that is, she derives the authority to carry out the principal's business from the principal and not from her own acts. The principal is liable to the third party for the agent's acts based on that contract.

Assume that Creative Music Corporation hires Bob, a booking agent, to negotiate and contract with the Super Jazz, the latest jazz group, for a series of appearances and television commercials endorsing Creative Music's products. Contracts made by Bob, the agent, within his authority, are binding and legally

Exhibit 17–1   Legal Relationships in Agency Law

Type of Legal Relationship	Definition
Principal–agent	An agent acts on behalf of, and instead of, the principal and uses a certain degree of his or her own discretion.
Employer–employee	An employee's (servant's) physical conduct is controlled or subject to control by an employer. An employee also can be an agent.

enforceable by Creative Music Corporation, the principal. The Super Jazz, the third party, also may enforce the contract against Creative Music Corporation. If Bob had no authority to represent Creative Music Corporation, he could not bind, on his own, Creative Music Corporation to a contract with the Super Jazz.

The authority must come from the principal. A principal is liable for acts of another only if the principal hires an agent or acts in such a way as to create an agency relationship.

Scope of Agent's Authority.
A principal's liability in a contract with a third party arises from the authority given to the agent to enter legally binding contracts on the principal's behalf. An agent's authority to act stems from one of the following sources:

1. Actual authority.
   a. Express (or specific).
   b. Implied (or inherent).
2. Apparent authority.

Even if an agent contracts outside the scope of her authority, the principal still may be liable by ratifying the contract, as discussed previously.

Actual Authority. An agent who acts on behalf of the principal either by agreement or by operation of law has **actual authority** that can be either express or implied. **Express authority** provides the agent specific instructions. Express authority can be granted orally or in writing. A written agency agreement is a good business practice. A well-drafted instrument clarifies the relationship for both the principal and the agent.

Even the best drafted agency agreement, however, does not cover every aspect of the agent's responsibili-

ties. These responsibilities are part of the agent's **implied authority**, sometimes called inherent authority. Often, implied authority is conferred by virtue of the customary practices of that particular agency. Implied authority may be inferred from the position the agent occupies. For example, in a department store, the manager of the men's clothing section has the implied authority to discount a shirt that has a spot on it.

An agent has implied authority for acts that are reasonably necessary for the agent to carry out her expressly authorized duty. For example, Cherri is employed by Dolly's Clothing to manage one of its stores. Dolly's Clothing has not expressly stated Cherri's authority to contract with third persons. The authority to manage a business, however, implies the authority to act as reasonably required in order to operate the business. Cherri's implied authority includes the right to contract with employees, buy merchandise and equipment, and advertise products sold in the store.

Apparent Authority. A principal makes a third party reasonably believe that a particular person is the principal's agent and has the authority to act on the principal's behalf. If the third party relies on the appearance of authority that the principal has apparently given to another person, the person is said to be an agent by **apparent authority**. This agency is based on the principle of **estoppel** (to bar, to impede, or to stop). The apparent authority is a substitute for actual authority when the principal instructs the agent not to perform certain duties even though the agent occupies a position that would appear to have such authority. The principal is stopped from saying that the person had no authority to act on the principal's behalf, even though the agent has no actual authority.

LEGAL HIGHLIGHT

Whose Agent Are You, Anyway?

Television advertisements for insurance may leave you with the impression that the insurance agent is your (the customer's) agent. Legally this is false. The agent represents the insurance company, the principal, not you. The insurance company, not you, pays the agent.

The same is true of travel agents. The travel agent sells you, the third party, a travel package on behalf of his or her principal, which may be a hotel or airline. The travel agent represents and is paid by the hotel or airline, not by you. If something goes wrong with a reservation that a travel agent makes at a hotel, and the clerk tells you that "your travel agent" made a mistake, you might politely inform the clerk that the travel agent is the hotel's agent, not yours. As the principal, the hotel is responsible for its agent's acts.

Real estate agents also confuse customers as to their principals. When you enter a real estate office wanting to buy a house and speak with a very nice real estate broker, remember that she or he earns a commission based on the house's selling price.

Today, in many states, the person representing the buyer must provide a statement that establishes any conflict of interest. Let's say that, you, the buyer, want to purchase a house for the lowest price. The agent's commission depends on the selling price, so he or she has a financial interest in your paying a higher price. The agent actually works for the seller, who pays the commission to both the real estate agent representing her and to the real estate agent representing you. The agent owes you a duty of good faith under state law to represent you when negotiating the price of the house.

Often today, a buyer hires a buyer's representative (another term for a buyer's agent) for a fee. The representative's check is independent of the house's price. The buyer then can be completely assured that the buyer's representative is looking out for the buyer. The bottom line is that, in most commercial transactions, only if you pay the person is he or she your agent.

Apparent authority often is considered to be title authority. That is, the authority exists by virtue of the person's business title—general manager, assistant manager, sales manager, and so on. It also depends on the size and scope of the business. For example, not all radio station managers have the authority to promote other station personnel. In a small station, the owner may retain the right to promote personnel, whereas in larger stations, the general manager may have that authority. A person may have apparent authority when no actual authority exists. In the previous example involving Cherri, if her supervisor told Cherri that she could not contract for advertising, Cherri still would have apparent authority to do so.

You need to determine the authority of the person with whom you contract. Does that person have au-

thority to enter into the contract which you propose? As indicated previously, a person's title is only one factor to consider. Statements by the agent alone do not create authority. A person may lie about his authority and be so convincing that you believe the person. You pay the false agent in the belief that the money will in turn be paid to the principal who owns the item you think you are purchasing.

The principal's actions determine the authority. The level of authority would be particularly important if you were a salesperson seeking orders for goods or services. You must ascertain the agent's authority to purchase your goods or services. The following case discusses the concept of implied or inherent authority.

Case 17.2

Menard, Inc. v. Dage–MTI, Inc.

Supreme Court of Indiana, 2000

726 N.E.2d 1206

BACKGROUND AND FACTS Dage-MTI, Inc. (Dage), was a manufacturing corporation that owned a thirty-acre parcel. Dage was governed by a six-member board of directors (Board) of which both Kerrigan and Sterling were members. In addition to being a Board member, Sterling had served as president of Dage for twenty years.

For many years, Sterling operated Dage without significant input from or oversight by the Board. During 1993, however, Kerrigan took steps to subject Dage's management to Board control.

In late October 1993, the Dage shareholders held a meeting. During the course of the meeting, Sterling first informed other directors that Menard, Inc. (Menard), owner of home improvement stores, had expressed interest in purchasing a thirty-acre parcel of land owned by Dage.

On October 30, 1993, Menard forwarded a formal offer to Sterling pertaining to the purchase of ten and one-half acres of the thirty-acre parcel. Upon receipt of the offer, Sterling did not contact Menard to discuss the terms and conditions of the offer. Instead, he forwarded the offer to all Dage directors with a cover note acknowledging that Board approval was required to accept or reject the offer. Ultimately, this offer was rejected. This rejection was communicated to Sterling and, although he viewed the offer to purchase favorably, he let the offer lapse. Later, he informed Menard's agent, Gary Litvin, that members of Dage's Board objected to various provisions of the offer.

On November 30, 1993, Sterling called Kerrigan and informed him that Menard would make a second offer for the entire thirty-acre parcel. Sterling presented a two-part proposed resolution to the Board that authorized Sterling to "offer and sell" the thirty-acre parcel. Sterling and Kerrigan discussed the offer and Sterling was told to change the "offer and sell" provision to "to offer for sale." He was instructed that he could only "offer" the thirty-acre parcel to Menard at a particular price. Additionally, Sterling was told that in soliciting offers for the thirty-acre parcel, he was not to negotiate the terms of a sale. Gorinsky, another lawyer hired by Kerrigan to represent his interests concerning Dage, reminded Sterling that any offer from Menard would require Board review and acceptance. He instructed Sterling to forward any offer to the Board for approval or rejection.

Finally, Sterling was told that if Menard submitted an agreement with the same objectionable provisions as the first offer, it would be rejected. Sterling agreed to follow the instructions of the Board. Based on the discussion, Sterling drafted a new resolution, which stated that he was authorized "to take such actions as are necessary to offer for sale our 30 acre parcel . . . for a price not less than $1,200,000."

Piccolo was a member of the board of directors and a financial consultant retained by Kerrigan. On December 6, 1993, Sterling informed Piccolo that Menard had agreed to make another offer. Piccolo reminded Sterling of his obligation to secure Board approval of the offer. Menard forwarded a second proposed purchase agreement to Sterling. This offer was for the purchase of the entire thirty-acre parcel for $1,450,000.

During a week-long series of discussions beginning December 14, 1993, and unknown to any other member of the Dage Board, Sterling negotiated several minor changes in the Menard agreement and then signed the revised offer on behalf of Dage. Menard also signed, accepting the offer. Under a paragraph of the agreement, Sterling, as president of Dage, represented as follows: "The persons signing this Agreement on behalf of the Seller are duly authorized to do so and their signatures bind the Seller in accordance with the terms of this Agreement." No one at Dage had informed Menard that Sterling's authority with respect to the sale of the thirty-acre parcel was limited to only the solicitation of offers.

Upon learning of the signed agreement with Menard, the Board instructed Sterling to extricate Dage from the agreement. Menard filed suit to require Dage to specifically perform the agreement and also for damages.

The trial court ruled in favor of Dage. The court of appeals affirmed, finding that Sterling did not have the express or apparent authority to bind the corporation in this land transaction.

SULLIVAN, Justice

. . . .

Two main classifications of authority are generally recognized: "actual authority" and "apparent authority." Actual authority is created "by written or spoken words or other conduct of the principal which, reasonably interpreted, causes the agent to believe that the principal desires him so to act on the principal's account." Apparent authority refers to a third party's reasonable belief that the principal has authorized the acts of its agent, it arises from the principal's indirect or direct manifestations to a third party and not from the representations or acts of the agent, . . .

"'Inherent agency power is a term used . . . to indicate the power of an agent which is derived not from authority, apparent authority or estoppel, but solely from the agency relation and exists for the protection of persons harmed by or dealing with a servant or other agent.'"

. . . .

We find the concept of inherent authority—rather than actual or apparent authority—controls our analysis in this case. Menard did not negotiate and ultimately contract with a lower-tiered employee or a prototypical "general" or "special" agent, with respect to whom actual or apparent authority might be at issue. Menard dealt with the president of the corporation, whom "'[t]he law recognizes . . . [as one of] the officers [who] are the means, the hands and the head, by which corporations normally act.'"

. . . .

Distilled to its basics, we find that Sterling had inherent authority here if: (1) first, Sterling acted within the usual and ordinary scope of his authority as president; (2) second, Menard reasonably believed that Sterling was authorized to contract for the sale and purchase of Dage real estate; and (3) third, Menard had no notice that Sterling was not authorized to sell the 30-acre parcel without Board approval.

. . . [T]he trial court entered findings of fact and conclusions of law. Having accepted the findings of fact, we review them to see if they will support a finding that Sterling had the inherent authority as president to bind Dage in this transaction.

As to whether Sterling acted within the usual and ordinary scope of his authority as president, the trial court found that Sterling, a director and substantial shareholder of Dage, had served as Dage's president from its inception; had managed the affairs of Dage for an extended period of time with little or no Board oversight; and had purchased real estate for Dage without Board approval. However, the trial court reached the conclusion that "[t]he record persuasively demonstrates that the land transaction in question was an extraordinary transaction" for Dage, which manufactures electronic video products. Thus, the court concluded that "Sterling was not performing an act that was appropriate in the ordinary course of Dage's business."

. . . .

Given that the trial court found that Sterling, as president of the company since its inception, had managed its affairs for an extended period of time with little or no Board oversight and, in particular, had purchased real estate for Dage in the past without Board approval, we conclude that Sterling's actions at issue here were acts that "usually accompany or are incidental to transactions which [he was] authorized to conduct."

Next, we must determine whether Menard reasonably believed that Sterling was authorized to contract for the sale and purchase of Dage real estate. While Sterling's apparent authority to bind Dage was "vitiated" by Menard's knowledge that the sale of Dage real estate required Board approval, this information did not defeat Sterling's inherent authority as Dage president to bind the corporation in a "setting" where he was the sole negotiator.

. . . [C]onsidering that the "agent" in this case is a general officer of the corporation (as opposed to an "appointed general agent" or "company general manager"), we find that Menard "should not be required to scrutinize too carefully the mandates of [this] permanent . . . agent . . . who [did] no more than what is usually done by a corporate president."

Here, the facts establish that Menard reasonably believed that Sterling was authorized to contract for the sale and purchase of Dage real estate. We begin with the premise that "'the acts of a corporation done through its officers are acts done per se.'" Next, we note that at all times "Sterling held himself out as president of Dage." In fact, "Sterling ha[d] served as president of Dage since its inception"; as noted in the preceding section, he was a substantial shareholder and member of the six-person Board of Directors; he had managed the affairs of Dage for an extended period of time with little or no Board oversight; and he had purchased real estate for Dage without Board approval. And although "early in the transaction, Sterling advised [Menard] that he was required to go back to his 'partners' to obtain authority to sell the entire thirty acres[, Sterling later] confirmed that he had the authority from his Board of Directors to proceed." . . . .

We also find it reasonable for Menard not to scrutinize Sterling's personal "acknowledge[ment] that he signed the agreement for the purchase and sale of the real estate by authority of Dage's board of directors." We believe this especially to be the case where (1) Sterling himself was a member of the Board, (2) the agreement contained an express representation that "[t]he persons signing this Agreement on behalf of the Seller are duly authorized to do so and their signatures bind the Seller in accordance with the terms of this Agreement," and (3) Menard was aware that Dage's corporate counsel, . . . was involved in the review of the terms of the agreement.

Finally, we consider whether Menard had notice that Sterling was not authorized to sell the 30-acre parcel without Board approval. The record does not indicate that Menard was aware of the existence of the consent resolution, much less that it limited Sterling's authority as president. Nor was there evidence that either the Board or Sterling informed Menard that Sterling's authority with respect to the sale of the 30-acre parcel was limited to only the solicitation of offers. . . . .

DECISION AND REMEDY The court found that a president of a closely held corporation had inherent authority to bind the company involving the sale of real estate. In an agency relationship, an agent has inherent authority that may subject his or her principal to liability. A president of a corporation has a considerable inherent authority to bind the principal, that is, the corporation.

CRITICAL THINKING: REASONING BEHIND THE LAW Why should there ever be implied or inherent authority in an agency relationship?

Professional Agents. A **professional agent** is in a business that handles contracts in a particular field. Often, the state government licenses professional agents to represent principals in contracts in those fields. Examples of professional agents are insurance agents, real estate brokers, travel agents, attorneys, and entertainment agents.

For example, because real estate brokers are licensed to represent a person who wants to sell his real property, a real estate broker is a professional agent. A "real estate agent" is actually a subagent of the real estate broker and only can represent a person through her employer, the real estate broker. A businessperson needs to learn the lines of authority in a particular business in order to determine the functions of professional agents.

The Employee as an Agent

The law defines an employee as one employed by the employer to perform services. The employer controls the employee's conduct. The employer establishes the time of work, the work to be performed, the location at which the work is performed, and other similar directions.

Agency law may apply under the right circumstances to the employer–employee relationship. The rules governing this relationship arose out of the impact of the Industrial Revolution and, more recently, social legislation. The impact of social legislation will be discussed in Chapters 22 and 23.

The employer–employee relationship is included in this chapter because frequently an employee is also an agent for her employer–principal. For example, Malini is employed by a large department store as a clerk in the jewelry section. When she stocks or straightens inventory, she is an employee. When Malini sells a bracelet, she is an agent who contracts with a customer on behalf of her employer, who is also the principal. In both cases, she is an employee. In contrast, a person employed as an electrician in the department store is strictly an employee and has no authority to transact business on the employer's behalf. The employer is liable, however, for negligent torts that the electrician commits on the job.

CyberLaw

Uniform Computer Information Transactions Act

A new uniform act, the Uniform Computer Information Transactions Act (UCITA), has been approved by the National Conference of Commissioners on Uniform State Laws. The UCITA, which focuses on computer information, has been passed by several states.

One part of the act is involved with electronic agents. The traditional contract concepts do not function when you have a computer program that sends automated responses to either requests for prices or quoting prices. The UCITA provides rules that validate electronic agents. A business is held liable for contracts entered into by its electronic agent.

Two electronic agents (one representing the purchaser and the other the supplier) may enter into a binding contract without any individual being involved. The agents are programmed to solicit bids for these goods and accept the lowest bid over the web. Electronic agents are used to purchase routine items from electronic catalogs available on the web.

Duties of Agents and Principals

Once the principal–agent relationship has been created, both parties have duties that govern their conduct. The agent owes to the principal a high **fiduciary duty**, that is, one based on trust and honesty and a duty to act with the utmost good faith. The principal, however, has very limited duties toward the agent, as will become apparent later in this chapter.

The Agent's Duty to the Principal

The duties that an agent owes to a principal are set out in the agency agreement and are imposed by law. Duties are also implied from the agency relationship itself. Duties exist between the principal and the agent, even if the principal's identity is disclosed to a third party. Generally, by operation of law, the agent owes the principal the following five duties: performance, loyalty, obedience, accounting, and notification.

The Duty of Performance.

An implied condition in every agency contract is the agent's agreement to use reasonable diligence and skill in performing the work. When an agent fails to perform the work in this manner, liability for breach of the agency contract can occur. In addition, the principal may be liable to a third party for any negligent act of the agent that occurs within the context of the contract.

For example, a principal hires a real estate broker to sell her house in California. A potential buyer asks how many square feet the house has. The real estate broker negligently answers "2,700 square feet," because he is too lazy to look up the precise footage and he considers himself to be good at guessing. When the buyer finds out that the actual size is 2,500 square feet, the principal is liable for the agent's negligent conduct, because the action is within the context of the contract. Of course, the agent is in turn liable to the principal if the buyer successfully collects money for damages against the principal.

The degree of skill or care required of an agent is that expected of a reasonable person under similar circumstances. Although this standard usually is interpreted to mean "ordinary care," if an agent has presented himself as possessing special skills (such as those of an accountant or an attorney), the agent is expected to exercise the skill claimed. Even if the agent is not paid, he must exercise the same degree of skill or care as a paid agent. Failure to do so constitutes a breach of the agent's duty. When an agent performs carelessly or negligently, then he also is liable in tort.

The Duty of Loyalty.

Loyalty is one of the most fundamental duties in a fiduciary relationship. The agent has the duty to act solely for the principal's benefit and not for her own interest or that of a third party. This fiduciary duty is owed only in one direction: from the agent to the principal.

For example, International Business Machines (IBM) has the right to appoint two sales agents to the same territory, unless IBM has specifically contracted with one agent for an exclusive territory. The IBM sales agent, however, has no right to represent more than one computer manufacturer.

An agent must refrain from any personal dealings that detract from the good of the principal. An agent employed by a principal to purchase property, for example, cannot buy that property for herself and then resell the property to the principal. Likewise, an agent employed to sell property cannot purchase the property without the principal's consent. In short, the agent's loyalty must be undivided. Otherwise, the agent has a conflict of interest with the principal.

If the agent would like to purchase the property, he must make full disclosure to the principal. If the principal allows the purchase after full disclosure, no conflict of interest arises. The agent's actions must strictly benefit the principal and must not result in any secret profit for the agent.

The Duty of Obedience.

When an agent acts on behalf of the principal, the agent has a duty to obey all lawful and clearly stated instructions from the principal. The agent violates this duty whenever she deviates from those instructions. If the circumstances merit it—for example, during emergency situations when the principal cannot be consulted—the agent may deviate from such instructions without violating this duty. Whenever the principal's instructions are not stated clearly, the agent can fulfill the duty of obedience by acting in good faith and in a reasonable manner under the circumstances.

The Duty of Accounting.

The agent has a duty to the principal to keep and make available an accounting of all property and money received and paid out on the principal's behalf. The principal is entitled to receive all gifts from third persons collected by the agent. For example, an airline gives the agent a gift for qualifying as a frequent flyer. Because the agent accumulated the mileage while traveling on business for the principal, the gift received by the agent belongs to the principal.

Commingling of personal and agency funds is not allowed. The agent has a duty to maintain separate accounts, one for personal funds and another for the principal's funds. Whenever a licensed professional, such as an attorney, real estate broker, or insurance agent, violates the duty to account, she may be subject to disciplinary proceedings by the appropriate regulatory institution. These proceedings are in addition to the agent's liability to the principal for failure to account.

The Duty of Notification.

A maxim in agency law is "All the agent knows, the principal knows." This expression refers to the duty of notification. The agent must notify the principal of all matters that come to his attention concerning the subject matter of the agency and that are within the agency's scope. When the agent notifies the principal, the principal has **actual knowledge**.

When the agent fails to notify the principal, the common law has adopted what is called a legal fiction, which means in this case, that whatever the agent knows, the principal also knows. A **legal fiction** is an assumption in law; in this case, the law assumes the principal has the same actual knowledge that the agent possesses. Under these circumstances, the principal is said to have **constructive knowledge** of the notice to an agent.

Regardless of the actual incident, the law treats this matter as if it had occurred according to the legal fiction version. Even if the agent has not relayed the information to the principal, the law assumes that the principal knew what the agent knew and holds the principal liable. If the agent failed to inform the principal, the agent generally is liable to the principal for failing to fulfill the duty of notification. The knowledge must have been obtained, however, within the scope of the agency. Serving legal papers on the building custodian does not give constructive notice to the employer.

Problems arise when an officer, director, or employee works for two separate businesses and is involved in a transaction that affects both employers. In the following case, the court was faced with several problems that arose when one person, who was a director and an officer in two different businesses, lent a pickup truck belonging to one business to the other.

Case 17.3

Williams v. State Medical Oxygen & Supply, Inc.

Supreme Court of Montana,
1994
874 P.2d 1225

BACKGROUND AND FACTS Brian Cloutier was an officer and director for Cay Enterprises and an officer and director for State Medical Oxygen & Supply, Inc. On behalf of Cay Enterprises, he had Craig Williams and five other teenagers, all employees of Cay Enterprises, move several truckloads of mattresses.

Cloutier arranged to have a State Medical pickup truck left at his home to be used for the job. He gave the keys to the pickup truck to one of the teenagers, who then drove it. He told the teenagers to move as many mattresses in each load as they could. Cloutier also instructed them not to sit on the tailgate of the pickup truck when moving the load. Cloutier provided no ropes or other items to secure the load.

Williams was sitting on top of a load of mattresses when the pickup truck turned a corner. He fell off the pickup truck and hit his head on the pavement. Williams suffered injuries as a result of this fall. He sued State Medical, as well as Cay Enterprises. State Medical prevailed against Williams, who appealed.

Justice NELSON

. . . .

In the instant case, the District Court ruled that the pickup was under the control of State Medical's officer, Cloutier, before he turned the keys over to the Cay Enterprises' employees. That being the case, it follows then, that because Cloutier had control over the pickup before he turned it over to Cay Enterprises' employees, he also had the power to prevent Cay Enterprises' employees from using the vehicle. Therefore, a question of negligent entrustment . . . remains. Was State Medical, through its officer and director, Cloutier, negligent at the time of providing the pickup to Cay Enterprises' employees, if it knew or should have known that Cay Enterprises' employees would likely use the pickup or conduct themselves in such a manner as to create an unreasonable risk of harm to others?

. . . .

The first principle holds, that an officer of a corporation, when acting within the course and scope of his employment, is an agent of the corporation when dealing with third parties.

. . . .

Turning to the second principle, imputing knowledge to two separate corporations which are dealing with one another through a common officer, we start with the premise that under Montana law, the knowledge of an agent is imputed to the principal. As a general rule, where there are two corporations, dealing with one another through a common officer, the question of whether one corporation is to be charged with notice of what is known to the agent by virtue of his relation to the other corporation depends on the circumstances of each case. "However, [a] common officer's knowledge of the affairs of one corporation will be imputed to the other when such knowledge is present in his mind and memory at the time he engaged in a transaction on behalf of such other corporation, or when such knowledge comes to him while acting for such other corporation in his official capacity, or while acting as an agent of such corporation, and within the scope of his authority. . . ."

Therefore, albeit he was going to supervise and manage the mattress moving project on behalf of Cay Enterprises, the knowledge Cloutier had regarding how he would manage and supervise the mattress moving project, at the time he turned control of the pickup over to the Cay Enterprises employees, must be imputed to State Medical.

DECISION AND REMEDY The court reaffirmed the law that a common officer's knowledge of the affairs of one corporation will be imputed to the other corporation when such knowledge is present in his mind and memory at the time he engages in a transaction on behalf of the other corporation.

CRITICAL THINKING: PREVENTIVE LAW Discuss which rules a business should have concerning the use of property by the directors, officers, or employees when the use is not for the business's benefit.

Principal's Duties to the Agent

The principal's duties to the agent are compensation, reimbursement and indemnification, cooperation, and safe working conditions. These duties may be set out in a contract or be implied by law.

The Duty of Compensation.
The principal must pay for the agent's services unless it is a *gratuitous agency* relationship. A **gratuitous agency** occurs when the agent performs services without compensation. Even though the agent may not be paid, she still owes the principal the duties of performance and loyalty, as discussed in the previous section.

The principal must agree to compensate the agent for his services before the agent is entitled to remuneration. When the amount of compensation is agreed on by the parties, the principal owes the duty to compensate the agent on completion of the specified activities. If no amount is agreed on, the principal usually pays either the reasonable value of the agent's service or can look to the customary amount of compensation for such services. For example, in the auction of horses, the auctioneer normally takes 10 percent commission.

The Duty of Reimbursement and Indemnification.
When an agent enters into a contract with a third party to purchase something, the principal, not the agent, has the ultimate duty to pay the third party. The principal may use one of several methods to pay the third party. The principal may arrange with the third party to pay her directly, the principal may advance

the funds to the agent to pay the third party, or the agent may pay the third party out of her own pocket.

In the last case, the principal then has the duty to reimburse the agent for expenses that the agent has incurred while performing her job for the principal. If an agent pays for other necessary expenses in the course of reasonable performance of agency duties, the principal has the duty to reimburse the agent.

The principal has an overlapping duty to indemnify (compensate) the agent for any losses that the agent suffers while performing her duties for the principal. For example, if the agent loses money while performing a contract, the principal must compensate the agent for those losses.

Agents can recover no expenses or losses incurred by their own misconduct or negligence. For example, if an agent has the principal's money on hand to pay a bill on time but negligently fails to pay it, the agent must pay the late penalty. The principal has no duty to reimburse the agent.

The Duty of Cooperation. A principal has a duty both to cooperate with and to assist an agent in performing her duties. The principal must do nothing to prevent such performance. For example, a seller hires a real estate broker to sell a house. The broker finds a buyer who is willing, able, and ready to buy the house. The seller-principal must cooperate with the agent, must sign the papers in a timely manner, and must do nothing to prohibit the buyer from proceeding with the purchase.

The Duty to Provide Safe Working Conditions. The principal must provide safe premises, equipment, and conditions for agents and employees. The principal has a duty to inspect working conditions and to warn agents and employees about unsafe areas. If the agent is also an employee (as in the case of a department store clerk), the employer's liability frequently is covered by workers' compensation insurance, which is the primary remedy for an employee's injury on the job.

If the employer has eleven or more employees, federal law requires the employer to display a poster on job safety and health protection in an area where employees gather, such as in a breakroom. The employer also must post a summary of the injuries and illnesses for that location and must post citations for violations of safety standards.

Liability of Principals and Agents to Third Parties

Because the agent deals with third parties, the following sections examine the rights of the third party. Both the principal and the agent may be liable to a third person based either on contract or tort law.

Principal's and Agent's Liability for Contracts

In their relationships with third parties, principals are classified as *disclosed, partially disclosed,* or *undisclosed.* A **disclosed principal** is a principal whose identity is known by the third party at the time at which he makes the contract with the agent. A **partially disclosed principal** is a principal whose identity is unknown by the third party, but the third party knows that the agent is acting for a principal at the time the contract is made. An **undisclosed principal** is a principal whose identity is totally unknown by the third party, and the third party has no knowledge that the agent is acting in any agency capacity at the time the contract is made.

Liability of Disclosed Principals. If an agent acts within the scope of his authority, a disclosed principal is liable to a third party for a contract made by the agent. In these situations, an agent has no contractual liability for the principal's or the third party's nonperformance.

Liability of Partially Disclosed or Undisclosed Principals. In most states, if the principal is partially disclosed or undisclosed, the principal and agent are both treated as parties to the contract. The third party can elect to hold either the partially disclosed principal or the agent liable if the contract is not performed.

If the principal is undisclosed, the agent is deemed to be dealing directly with the third party. Thus, for an undisclosed principal, the agent is liable as a party on the contract. Once the third party discovers that the previously undisclosed principal exists, the third party can elect to sue either the principal or the agent.

For example, Walt Disney Company decides to build another amusement park. Research shows that in a specific prime tourist area, the land needs for the new park will be met if Disney purchases five parcels of land. Disney, however, knows that if word gets out that it plans to purchase land, the price will be higher. Disney hires five different agents to make the five different land purchases. Disney is the undisclosed principal. The five agents make the purchases over the period of a year, each in his or her own name. The sellers relied on the individual agents' credit and reputation, not on that of Disney.

Because each agent has acted within the scope of his or her authority, the undisclosed principal, Disney, must perform in accordance with the contracts made by each of its agents. Even though Disney's identity was not disclosed to the sellers of each of the five properties, Disney must ensure that each of its agents can perform on the respective contracts with each seller. Disney can enforce contracts against each seller through the respective agent, if Disney decides to remain undisclosed. Or Disney may reveal that it is the principal and enforce the contracts in its own name as a disclosed principal. The seller, however, may bring a legal action against either Disney or the agent, but not both after the seller discovers Disney.

Warranties of the Agent

Occasionally, the agent either will lack authority for an action or will exceed the scope of her or his authority. When this situation occurs, the agent, not the principal, is liable to the third party. The agent's liability to the third party is based on a breach of **implied warranty of authority**, not on breach of the contract itself.

The agent can breach the implied warranty of authority by intentionally breaching the warranty or by making a good-faith mistake. The agent is liable if the third party relied on the agent's status.

In contrast, when the third party knows at the time the contract is made that the agent is mistaken about the extent of his authority, or if the agent indicates to the third party uncertainty about the extent of his authority, the agent is not liable personally for breach of warranty. In these situations, the third party recognizes an irregularity and should have checked further about the agent's authority.

Tort Liability

Tort liability was discussed in Chapter 8. Negligence occurs when a person commits an act that she could foresee as potentially causing harm to another. An intentional act occurs when a person intends to harm another. An agent or employee always is liable for her own torts and crimes.

The question arises: Is the principal or employer liable also for the negligent acts of the agent or employee? If the employee makes a misrepresentation to a third party, is the employer liable? Is the employer liable for the intentional torts of the employee?

In the following discussion, most references will be made to the employer–employee relationship, but the same rules apply to the principal–agent relationship. Three areas will be examined: negligence and the doctrine of *respondeat superior*, misrepresentation, and intentional tort.

Negligence and the Doctrine of *Respondeat Superior*. An employer may be liable for the negligent torts of the employee if the employee commits the torts within the scope of employment. The employer's liability is indirect because although the employer is not itself negligent, the employer is responsible for its employee's negligent acts. The employer is liable under the **doctrine of *respondeat superior***, which is Latin for "let the master answer." This theory imposes strict liability on the employer. Liability is imposed without regard to the personal fault of the employer for negligent torts committed by an employee in the course of employment.

For example, an employee works for a construction company. Part of her job is to drive the company pickup truck from one job site to another. One day the employee has a traffic accident by negligently turning left in front of an oncoming automobile. The employee is liable because she was negligent, but the company also is liable under the doctrine of *respondeat superior*.

An employer that knows or should have known that an employee is likely to commit torts is liable for the employee's acts even if the torts ordinarily would be considered outside the scope of employment. Of course, the employee is responsible for his torts. For example, a cookie manufacturer has many complaints about the actions of a salesman. The salesman goes to a grocery store, removes the competitors' products and pushes a store manager who objects. The manufacturer is liable for the salesman's assault and battery. The manufacturer knew or should have known about the employee's acts based on earlier complaints and taken steps to prevent any further acts by the salesperson.

When an employee departs from the employer's business to take care of personal affairs, is the employer liable? It depends. If the employee's activity is a substantial departure equivalent to an utter abandonment of the employer's business, the employer is not liable.

For example, Clint, a traveling salesperson, drives his employer's automobile to call on a customer for a possible sales order. On the way to the customer's place of business, Clint deviates one block from his usual route to mail a letter at the post office. As Clint approaches the post office, he negligently runs into Doug's parked vehicle. Clint's departure from the employer's business to take care of a personal affair is minimal. Clint is still within the scope of his employment, and Clint's employer is liable to Doug.

On the other hand, if Clint picked up a few friends for a party in another city and in the process negligently ran into Doug's vehicle, Doug normally could not hold Clint's employer liable. In this case, Clint's action entails more than a minimal departure from the scope of his employment. Only Clint would be liable in this case.

The court considers the following general factors in determining if an agent's particular tortious act occurred within the course or scope of employment:

1. Did the employer authorize the act?
2. What was the time, place, and purpose of the act?
3. Was the act commonly performed by the employee on behalf of the employer?
4. To what extent was the employer's interest advanced by the act?
5. To what extent were the employee's private interests involved?
6. Did the employer furnish the means or instrumentality (for example, a truck or machine) that caused the injury?
7. Did the employer have reason to know that the employee would do the act in question and had the employee done it before?
8. Did the act involve the commission of a serious crime?

The following case involves problems of defining the scope of employment.

Case 17.4

Clover v. Snowbird Ski Resort

Supreme Court of Utah, 1991
808 P.2d 1037

BACKGROUND AND FACTS Snowbird Ski Resort employed Zulliger as a chef at the Plaza Restaurant located at the base of the ski resort. The Mid-Gad Restaurant was located halfway up the mountain.

Zulliger's father was head chef at both restaurants. Zulliger's father instructed him to make periodic trips to the Mid-Gad to monitor its operations. Zulliger had made several inspection trips to the Mid-Gad. On one occasion, Snowbird paid him for the trip.

Snowbird preferred for its employees to ski to and from work. Part of Zulliger's compensation included season ski passes. Zulliger was asked to inspect the operation of the Mid-Gad prior to beginning work at the Plaza at 3 P.M.

Zulliger stopped at the Mid-Gad in the middle of his first run down the mountain. At the restaurant, he inspected the kitchen, talked to the personnel for twenty minutes, and ate a snack. He skied four runs before heading down the mountain to begin work.

On his final run, Zulliger jumped from a crest on the side of an intermediate run, a jump he had taken many times before. From this jump, a skier would become airborne because of the steep dropoff. It was impossible for skiers above the crest to see skiers below the crest. Snowbird knew the jump well. Snowbird ski patrol often instructed people not to jump from the crest. Furthermore, Snowbird posted a sign instructing skiers to ski slowly at this point in the run.

Zulliger ignored the sign and skied over the crest at a significant speed. Clover, who had just entered the same ski run from a point below the crest, was in Zulliger's path. As Zulliger jumped, he collided with Clover, who was hit on the head and severely injured.

Clover brought claims against Zulliger and Snowbird. The trial court, in a summary judgment, dismissed the claims against Snowbird by finding that as a matter of law, Zulliger was acting outside the scope of his employment at the time of the collision.

Chief Justice HALL

. . . .

Under the doctrine of *respondeat superior*, employers are held vicariously liable for the torts their employees commit when the employees are acting within the scope of their employment. Clover's *respondeat superior* claim was dismissed on the ground that as a matter of law, Zulliger's actions at the time of the accident were not within the scope of his employment. In a recent case, *Birkner v. Salt Lake County*, this court addressed the issue of what types of acts fall within the scope of employment. In *Birkner*, we stated that acts within the scope of employment are "those acts which are so closely connected with what the servant is employed to do, and so fairly and reasonably incidental to it, that they may be regarded as methods, even though quite improper ones, of carrying out the objectives of the employment." The question of whether an employee is acting within the scope of employment is a question of fact.

. . . .

. . . [T]here is evidence that the manager of both the Mid-Gad and the Plaza wanted an employee to inspect the restaurant and report back by 3 P.M. If Zulliger had not inspected the restaurant, it would have been necessary to send a second employee to accomplish the same purpose. Furthermore, the second employee would have most likely used the ski lifts and ski runs in traveling to and from the restaurant.

. . . .

Under the circumstances of the instant case, it is entirely possible for a jury to reasonably believe that at the time of the accident, Zulliger had resumed his employment and that Zulliger's deviation was not substantial enough to constitute a total abandonment of employment.

DECISION AND REMEDY The court found that a jury must decide whether Zulliger's actions were within the scope of his employment. His actions were not, as a matter of law, outside the scope of his employment with Snowbird. Clover will have her day in court.

COMMENT A similar incident occurred in 1997 in Vail, Colorado. An employee of a ski lift company left when his shift was over. Although an expert skier, he ignored poor snow conditions and safety precautions and was skiing too fast for the conditions. He collided with another skier who was killed as a consequence. In 2000, the expert skier was tried and convicted of negligent homicide.

CRITICAL THINKING: ETHICAL ISSUE A delivery person decides to go fishing while using the business vehicle. While driving to the lake, he causes an accident. Discuss whether the employer should be liable to the injured party.

Misrepresentation. Whenever a third person sustains losses because of the agent's misrepresentation, the principal is exposed to tort liability. The key to a principal's liability is whether the agent actually or apparently was authorized to make representations and whether such representations were made within the scope of the agency.

When a principal has placed an agent in a position to defraud a third party, the principal is liable for the agent's fraudulent acts. For example, Harmon is a loan officer for State Employees Credit Union. In the ordinary course of her job, Harmon approves and services loans and has access to customers' credit records. Harmon calls Lopez, a credit union member who has

LEGAL HIGHLIGHT

Good Credit Means a Job

Chapter 14 discussed credit reports and procedures to correct erroneous information that might be in a credit file. A credit report is a major tool on which businesses rely when considering the hiring of a new employee. Employers believe that the way in which a person handles his or her personal finances indicates his or her honesty and dependability. When a person has serious financial problems, he or she may be more likely to take advantage of the employment situation and abscond with cash, inventory, or trade secrets. Employers believe this even though no studies have justified this belief.

Some credit firms specialize in providing relevant information from a person's credit record. Stores Protective Association (SPA) assists many of the large retailers in hiring. It maintains records based on both its subscribers' information and public records.

SPA maintains records on all persons who are terminated for dishonesty by a subscriber. It preserves a copy of any written confession signed by the employee. If no written confession exists, the event causing the termination must have been videotaped or witnessed by at least two individuals, and SPA keeps these. SPA also researches public records for any convictions for felonies or criminal misdemeanors and places this information in the individual's file. It keeps the records for seven years, the maximum time allowed under the federal Fair Credit Reporting Act (FCRA). SPA must comply with the rules under the FCRA that require the applicant to give written permission for her or his credit file to be examined.

A good credit rating and clean criminal record, therefore, can affect people's careers.

an outstanding loan. Harmon falsely represents to Lopez that the credit union believes that he is about to default on his loan. She threatens to call in the loan (meaning that Lopez must pay the loan in full) unless he provides additional collateral, such as stocks and bonds. Lopez gives Harmon numerous stock certificates, which Harmon keeps in her own possession. She later uses them to make personal investments and loses money on all these investments.

The credit union is liable to Lopez for losses sustained on the stocks, even though the credit union had no direct role or knowledge of the fraudulent scheme. The principal (the credit union) placed the agent (Harmon) in a position that conveyed to third persons (such as Lopez) that Harmon had the authority to make statements and perform acts consistent with her position's ordinary duties. When an agent appears to act within the scope of the authority that the position of agency confers, but actually takes advantage of a third party, the principal who placed the agent in that position is liable. For example, if a security guard had told Lopez that the credit union required additional security for a loan, Lopez would not be justified in relying on that person's authority to make that representation. Lopez reasonably could expect, however, that the loan officer was telling the truth.

Intentional Torts. The employer may be liable for its employee's intentional torts when the employee commits those acts within the scope of employment. The employer's liability is based on one of four theories: (1) the employer was negligent in hiring or retaining the employee, (2) the employer is liable for certain types of employees' intentional torts, (3) the employer ratifies the intentional tort, or (4) the employer helps to commit the intentional tort.

In a previous section, we saw that an employer, even though it acted responsibly, could be held liable for the negligent acts of its agent or employee under the doctrine of *respondeat superior*. Usually, an employer is not responsible for the intentional torts of its employees. Third persons harmed by the intentional torts of an employee, however, may bring a legal action against the employer for negligence in hiring or supervising the employee.

The law allows negligent hiring actions even though the employee's wrongful act was outside the course or scope of his employment. The basis of these actions is that the employer knew or should have known that the employee was unfit, the employee caused the injury to another person, and a causal connection existed between the injury incurred and the employment of the employee.

Many laws restrict an employer from inquiring into a potential employee's background. An employer, however, will be held liable if it fails to make the proper background checks or if it failed to investigate and take appropriate action for reported incidents of wrongdoing. For example, in one case, a real estate firm employed a person who had been convicted of passing bad checks. The employer knew of the criminal record. The firm was held liable for negligence in hiring when the employee forged legal documents to obtain a commission from a client of the real estate firm. Another example concerns an apartment manager who murdered a child who was collecting money for her newspaper route. The apartment owner had not conducted an investigation of the manager before hiring him. An investigation would have disclosed that the manager had a history of molesting children and had served prison time. The court held the apartment owner liable for failure to use reasonable efforts to investigate the manager's background.

The employer may be held liable for an employee's intentional torts when the employee commits them within the scope of employment. This responsibility is imposed if the employer should have anticipated the intentional act. The employer's liability, however, is very limited in most states.

For example, Duffy's Tavern hires Vicious Vic as a bouncer, knowing that he has a history of arrests for assault and battery. While working one night within the scope of his employment, Vicious Vic ferociously attacks a patron who "looked at him funny." Duffy's Tavern will bear the responsibility for Vicious Vic's assault and battery, because it knew he had a propensity for committing such acts and because he committed this tort during the normal course of his job.

If the employer ratifies the intentional tort or participates in the intentional tort committed by the employee within the scope of employment, the employer is liable for the harm caused by the intentional tort. This liability is imposed directly because the employer directly engaged in or ratified the intentional act that harmed a third person.

For example, Dishonest John defrauds Widow Green by convincing her to sign a contract to sell her house by promising to trade her house for an ostrich farm located in the Nevada desert. She read that a person can make lots of money raising and selling ostriches. No such ostrich farm actually exists. Dishonest John takes the contract to his employer and explains the transaction in detail. The employer is a land developer who wants to tear down the house and, along with other land he has purchased that adjoins Green's land, he plans to develop a commercial center. John's employer agrees to the contract. By its agreement, the employer has ratified the contract. Green finds out that the ostrich farm does not exist and she sues both Dishonest John and his employer. This liability is imposed even when the original intentional act was committed by an employee.

Termination of the Agency Relationship

An agency can be terminated either by an act by one of the parties or by operation of law. Once the relationship between the principal and agent ends, the agent no longer has the right to bind the principal. The principal must notify third persons when the agency ends to stop an agent's apparent authority.

Termination by Act of the Parties

Usually, the agency agreement sets out the time period during which the agency relationship will exist. The agency ends when that time expires. If no definite time is stated, the agency continues for a reasonable time, depending on the circumstances and the nature of the agency relationship, and can be terminated at will by either party.

An agent can be hired to complete a particular objective, such as the purchase of a computer system for a business. The agency relationship automatically ends after the computer system has been purchased because the reason for the agency relationship no longer exists.

Parties can cancel (rescind) a contract by mutually agreeing to terminate the contractual relationship. For example, Leslie no longer wants Cisco to be her agent, and Cisco no longer wants to work for Leslie. Either Leslie or Cisco can communicate with the other the intent to end the relationship. Agreement to terminate the agency relationship effectively relieves each party of any further rights, duties, and powers inherent in the relationship.

Termination by Operation of Law

Mental incompetency or death of either the principal or the agent automatically and immediately terminates the ordinary agency relationship. Knowledge of the death is not required. For example, Cassie sends Marco to Mexico to purchase a rare coin. Before Marco makes the purchase, Cassie dies. Marco's status as an agent ends at the moment of death, even though Marco does not know that Cassie has died.

An exception to this rule applies to banks. The Uniform Commercial Code, Section 4-405, allows banks to honor checks up to ten days after their customers' death. A bank does not honor any payment of notes or drafts after death, however.

The durable power of attorney is another exception to the rule that an agency is terminated by the principal's incapacity. A durable power of attorney is specifically worded to allow the attorney-in-fact to act on behalf of the principal when he becomes mentally incapacitated.

When an agency's specific subject matter is destroyed or lost, the agency is terminated. For example, Priscilla employs Mark to sell her house. Prior to any sale, a hurricane destroys the house. Mark's agency and authority to sell Priscilla's house are both ended. In addition, when it becomes impossible for the agent to perform the agency's responsibilities lawfully because of war or because of a change in the law, the agency terminates.

When an event occurs that has an unusual effect on the subject matter of the agency so that the agent reasonably can infer that the principal will not want the agency to continue, the agency terminates. Sima hires Aaron to sell a tract of land for $1 million. Subsequently, Aaron learns that Disney Corporation plans a resort and theme park across the road and the land now is worth $5 million. The agency and Aaron's authority to sell the land for $1 million both are terminated.

Notice Required for Termination

When an agency terminates by operation of law because of a principal's mental incompetency, death, or some other unforeseen circumstance, no duty exists to notify third persons. If, however, the parties themselves have terminated the agency, the principal must inform any third parties who knew of the agency's existence that it is terminated.

The principal is expected to notify directly any third person who the principal knows has dealt with the agent. For third persons who have heard about the agency but have not dealt with the agent, constructive notice is sufficient. In other words, a notice should be published in a newspaper within the general area or in commercial journals for technical employees, stating that the principal no longer employs the agent. Until notice is given, the agent retains apparent authority for a reasonable length of time.

Independent Contractors

An **independent contractor** is not an employee, but may be an agent under certain limited situations. Two major issues arise with independent contractors. The first problem is liability; the second is responsibility for tax payment to the Internal Revenue Service. The tax issue is discussed later in the section titled *Employees or Independent Contractors?*

A person who hires an independent contractor is said to have "employed" the independent contractor. When the term *employment* is used in connection with an independent contractor, however, its meaning differs from the legal context of employer–employee. The employer of an independent contractor has no control over the details of the independent contractor's performance. Because the employer does not control the independent contractor, the employer normally is not responsible for the independent contractor's torts.

> *Restatement, Second, Agency, Section 2, defines an independent contractor as a person who contracts with another to do something for him but who is not controlled by the other nor subject to the other's right to control with respect to his physical conduct in the performance of the undertaking. He may or may not be an agent.*

The courts review many elements to determine whether a relationship is one of employer–employee or of employer–independent contractor. The following are some factors considered by the courts:

1. The extent of control exercised by the employer over the details of the work.
2. The type of job, business, or occupation involved and the amount of skill required to perform the job.

3. Who supplies the tools or equipment.

4. The length of employment.

5. The method of payment.

6. The tax returns filed by both parties.

The construction industry is a good example of an employer–independent contractor relationship. If an owner of raw land wants to build an office building, she hires a general contractor, who is responsible for building the office complex. The general contractor in turn hires subcontractors, such as electrical subcontractors or plumbing subcontractors, who are responsible for specific portions of the building.

The general contractor is an independent contractor, and the property owner does not control this professional's acts. The property owner has no contractual relationship with the subcontractors whom the general contractor hires; thus, the owner is not responsible for the subcontractors' acts. Some states by statute, however, have changed this rule. The statute makes the general contractor an agent for the owner (principal). When the general contractor enters into contracts with subcontractors, the general contractor acts as an agent for the owner, making the owner liable as the principal. Today, statutes govern the construction industry, but these general concepts still apply.

Consider this example. A property owner hires a real estate broker to negotiate a property sale. The owner not only contracted with an independent contractor (the real estate broker), but also established an agency relationship for the specific purpose of finding a third party who will enter into a contract to purchase the property.

A person retaining an independent contractor's services normally is not responsible for the tortious acts of the independent contractor, because of the lack of control over him. An employer is responsible for the acts of an independent contractor, however, when the independent contractor performs one of the employer's duties, as established by law. For example, a department store is liable when it hires an independent security agency to supply security and a security officer makes an illegal arrest for shoplifting. The store, along with the security agency, is liable to the victim. An employer is liable for acts of independent contractors when the activity involves ultrahazardous conduct, such as handling explosives.

Employees or Independent Contractors?

Workers' classification as employees or as independent contractors is significant for federal income tax and employment tax purposes. Employers withhold income, Social Security, and Medicare taxes from employees' wages to forward to the federal government. The same taxes are collected from independent contractors when they pay estimated taxes.

Workers' classification as employees or independent contractors is also significant for a variety of federal and state labor and worker protection laws. These laws cover only employees, not independent contractors. These protections include unemployment insurance, workers' compensation, wage and hour requirements, and family and medical leave requirements. Additionally, independent contractors have no rights to sick leave, vacation time, pension and profit benefits, and other common employee benefits.

The government rarely questions an employer's classification of a worker as an employee. When an employer hires workers as independent contractors, however, government agencies, especially the Internal Revenue Service (IRS), may challenge the decision. A common law test of the employer–employee classification focuses on whether the employer controls the result of the worker's services and the means by which the worker achieves that result.

In company audits, the Internal Revenue Service can reclassify independent contractors as employees. The employer then is liable for the full amount of income taxes and the employee's share of Social Security and Medicare taxes that it failed to withhold for all years open under the statute of limitations. In addition, the employer remains liable for the employer's share of Social Security, Medicare, and unemployment insurance taxes plus interest on these amounts. The Internal Revenue Service can also assess penalties.

The employer's liability for underwithholding can be abated to the extent that the employer demonstrates that the misclassified worker paid income, Social Security, and Medicare taxes. Data to support the determinations, unfortunately, often are difficult to obtain, especially when the worker no longer provides services to the employer.

After an IRS audit of Microsoft Corporation, the Ninth Circuit Court of Appeals in 1996 upheld a lower court's finding that Microsoft had misclassified workers as independent contractors. Before working for Microsoft, these workers signed agreements indicating knowledge of their responsibilities for paying the federal and state income taxes, Social Security and Medicare taxes, and for providing for their own benefits. The case involved software testers and technical manual writers. They worked for years doing the same kind of work as regular Microsoft employees. Because they were independent contractors, however, they could not participate in the company's stock-purchase plan and its tax-deferred 401(k) plan. The case was appealed by Microsoft, but the U.S. Supreme Court refused to grant the writ of *certiorari*. Notice that the Ninth Circuit's holding is the opposite of that of the DuPont case discussed in the section on *Employee Leasing*.

Employment Law

Federal and state statutes regulate many areas of private employment law. These statutes will be examined in Chapters 22 and 23. A body of common law exists in areas that are not regulated by various statutes. These areas include employment contracts and employee termination.

Employment Contracts

Employer–employee relationships are created by a contract. The contract provides the employer with the right to control the employee's conduct, workplace, work habits, and benefits enjoyed within the scope of employment. An employment contract is a mutual agreement between the employer and the employee. Basic contract rules apply. The parties can include any contract terms, as long as these terms conform with all statutes and public policy. For example, a contract today for an hourly wage of $1 violates the minimum wage rate set by the Fair Labor Standards Act and is illegal.

In some written employment contracts, employees agree that, should they ever leave their employment, they will not accept employment with a competitor. This clause in the employment contract is called a **covenant not to compete**. If the scope of the prohibition is reasonable in geographic area and duration, the covenant generally is enforceable.

Employee Leasing

A company known as a professional employer organization (PEO) operates in a manner similar to the personnel administration in large corporations. For a small business, the benefits of working with a PEO can be very attractive.

A PEO handles the myriad of details necessary to employing personnel, including payroll administration, income tax withholding, medical benefits, life insurance, disability insurance, workers' compensation, unemployment insurance, retirement plans, tax deferred retirement plans, and compliance with employment statutes and labor laws. The cost of using a PEO runs between 2 and 8 percent of the total payroll, that is in addition to the employer's regular costs.

The employer approves of the employee to be hired. The new hire is sent to the PEO, who hires the employee and processes all the paperwork. The PEO then leases the employee to the business employer. Each pay period, the funds are transferred from the employer to the PEO to cover wages, taxes, benefits, and fees. If the business decides to fire or lay off an employee, it notifies the PEO, which handles all the paperwork and payment of the final paycheck.

One benefit of using a PEO is that it can pool the employees of all its clients. With the larger pool, the PEO can negotiate lower insurance rates and can amortize the cost of benefit plans over a broader base.

The disadvantage of leasing employees is that the PEO may collapse. Some are poorly managed, while others operate fraudulently. In one case, several companies paid a PEO, but instead of distributing the payroll among the companies' employees, the money vanished along with the PEO operators. The company is still liable to pay these workers.

Any business considering using a PEO should take a number of steps. It should obtain a list of the PEO's clients and interview a large number of them to be sure that they are satisfied with the PEO's services. If the business interviews only a few clients, it may miss the clients who have had problems and fail to discover the PEO's weaknesses. The potential client along with its accountant should review the PEO's audited financial statement. If the PEO rushes to sign up a number of new clients, some of whom are risky, the PEO may weaken its financial base.

A business should determine if the PEO has a number of clients in the same field. When a PEO knows the industry, it may be able to help a client improve its operation. The PEO should be able to tailor its program to the company's needs, such as administrating a tax-deferred benefit plan.

A business should refuse a standard contract from the PEO. The contract should be tailored to the needs of the business and its employees. Two important contract items to watch for include (1) identifying the company responsible for certain duties, especially tax withholding, and (2) ensuring that the PEO retains liability under the contract. Any contract should be reviewed by an attorney specializing in employment law.

Why would a business use leased employees? First, the business is relieved of the paperwork that the government requires. Second, if the business provides benefits, the tax laws require that the benefits be offered to all employees, not just the managers. If the business retains a few managers, they may enjoy benefits, but the business is not obligated to provide these benefits to leased employees. Third, leased employees are less likely to organize into labor unions.

Although PEOs are unregulated in most states, approximately fifteen states now license PEOs. A national professional association is the Institute for the Accreditation of Professional Employer Organizations based in Bethesda, Maryland.

In 1997, the Fourth Circuit Court of Appeals ruled that the DuPont Co. was not liable to pay standard employee benefits to leased employees.[3] An engineer, who was leased to the company, performed the same work as DuPont engineers. He worked directly for DuPont, but was laid off in 1970. He signed a contract with a national employee-leasing firm and from 1975 to 1993, he worked for other construction companies that regularly worked for DuPont. On his income tax returns and on an unemployment-benefits application, he listed the employee-leasing firm as his employer. He worked for DuPont as a leased employee until his death. His widow was denied any benefits that she would have received had he been DuPont's direct employee. Notice that the outcome of this case differed from the independent contractor situation involving Microsoft discussed in the section titled *Employees or Independent Contractors?*

Difference between Independent Contractors and Leased Employees

Differences exist between leased employees and independent contractors. A leased employee is employed by a leasing firm and leased to another employer where the person actually works. The leasing firm handles all the paperwork, such as withholding all the income and

other taxes, and remits the taxes to the appropriate government agencies. Depending on the leasing arrangements, the leasing firm can establish a tax-deferred retirement plan and can purchase a health plan for the benefit of the leased employee. The leased employee usually works for long periods for one employer.

Independent contractors pay their own income and other taxes. They establish their own tax-deferred retirement plans and purchase their own health plans. Independent contractors can work for several employers at once and make their own time schedules. The less independence an independent contractor has, the more likely the IRS will find that an employment relationship exists and not an independent contractor relationship.

Modern View on Termination of Employees

If termination of the employment breaches the employment contract, the employee can seek damages. Most employment situations, however, are created without a written employment contract and are called **employment at will**. Employment at will can occur with a written contract if the employer retains the right to terminate the employee at any time either for a good reason or for no reason at all. An employee has no claim against the employer for the termination because an employee has no right to the job.

Employee-at-will situations have led to abuses by employers. Some states passed specific statutes to protect an employee from an arbitrary termination after he has been employed for a specified period of time. Specific grounds must be established before a person can be fired. States will not allow an employer to terminate an employee who, after being ordered to commit a crime, refuses to do so.

Other states without statutory provisions have attempted through the courts to create certain rights for employees. For example, in the absence of a contract an employee manual given to all employees may be interpreted to be the employment contract. If an employer establishes certain procedures in the manual, these procedures must be followed before an employee can be fired. Otherwise, the employer is liable for breach of contract.

Many states recognize that an implied covenant of good faith and fair dealing is inherent in every employment contract. In other words, the law requires a business to treat its employees fairly, as the next case shows.

[3] *Clark v. E.I. DuPont De Nemours,* 105 F.3d 646 (4th Cir. 1997).

Case 17.5

Huey v. Honeywell, Inc.

United States Court of
Appeals, Ninth Circuit, 1996
82 F.3d 327
http://www.law.vill.edu
/Fed–Ct/Circuit/9th
/opinions/9415748.htm

BACKGROUND AND FACTS Honeywell hired John Huey as an hourly employee to work in its shipping and receiving department. He consistently received high job performance ratings and letters of recommendation in recognition of his outstanding job performance.

Honeywell's hourly employees turned in time cards only when they worked more or less than forty hours a week. Huey's supervisor instituted a flextime policy allowing workers to work more or less than forty hours in any week as long as they made up the time. The human resources representative for the shipping and receiving department knew of this policy.

Honeywell's standards of employee conduct and disciplinary procedures were established in the company's personnel manual, but the manual was not distributed to its employees. Honeywell relied on its supervisors to inform its employees of the company's personnel manual and disciplinary procedures.

Honeywell's disciplinary procedures provided that Honeywell would give its employees a series of verbal and written warnings, along with opportunities to be heard and to improve before they were terminated. The disciplinary procedures further provided that employees be given the benefit of any doubts during the investigation of disciplinary charges; that any termination for violation of a company policy must be supported with documentation; and that discipline was to be mitigated when an employee violated a company policy in reliance on a supervisor's representation of that policy.

One provision in the personnel manual that Honeywell's supervisors routinely failed to relay to employees was the following disclaimer: "Employment at Honeywell, Inc., is voluntarily entered into and employees are free to resign at any time. Similarly, Honeywell may terminate the employment relationship where it believes it is in the Company's best interests. The policy statements contained in this manual do not intend to negate this principle." Acting in accordance with company practice, Huey's supervisor failed to communicate this disclaimer to Huey.

Huey was one of many Honeywell employees in the shipping and receiving department to utilize the flextime policy. In doing so, Huey never claimed or received payment for any hours which he did not actually work. Huey's coworkers informed Honeywell's personnel department that they suspected Huey of falsely reporting his time. Honeywell's security division conducted an investigation.

The comparison of Huey's gate and time records revealed five inconsistencies. One inconsistency was due to Huey's attendance at a work-related seminar. The other four inconsistencies were due to the flextime policy.

Huey was suspended, pending further investigation. Further investigation failed to include any discussions with Huey or his supervisor who had created the flextime. Rather than speaking with Huey, Honeywell hired a private investigation firm, Pinkerton, Inc., to investigate.

Pinkerton engaged in the following activities. It followed Huey on his way home from work; it established surveillance points at Huey's home; it videotaped Huey's activities; and at Honeywell's request, it obtained personal information relating to Huey, his wife, and other members of Huey's family.

Honeywell's management finally called Huey in for an interview two months later. Huey tried to explain that the discrepancies on his time card were due to the flextime policy, but he was told that the decision to terminate him had already been made. Huey was told at this meeting that he was officially terminated. No other employees in Huey's department were terminated or disciplined for utilizing the flextime policy.

The federal district court granted a judgment to Honeywell, Inc., and Huey appealed.

Judge FERGUSON

. . . .

Under Arizona state law, a contractual relationship between an employer and an employee with no specified duration is presumed to be "at-will" unless modified by the parties' representations or course of dealing. . . .

Three general exceptions to the at-will employment presumption have developed. First, the public policy exception to the at-will doctrine permits an at-will employee to recover for wrongful discharge upon a finding that the employer's conduct undermined an important public policy. Second, an exception based on contract law allows an at-will employee to recover for wrongful discharge upon proof of an implied-in-fact promise of employment for a specific duration. Such an implied-in-fact promise can be found in the circumstances surrounding the employment relationship, including assurances of job security in company personnel manuals or memoranda. Third, courts have found an implied-in-law covenant of "good faith and fair dealing" in employment contracts and have held employers liable in both contract and tort for breach of this covenant.

. . . .

The following actions by Honeywell created a material question of fact as to Huey's employment status as an at-will employee: (1) Honeywell developed written policies and a personnel manual adopting a progressive disciplinary program; (2) Honeywell relies on its supervisors to orally explain its personnel policies to other employees; (3) Honeywell's written policies and personnel manual were not distributed to its employees; (4) Although the personnel manual contained a disclaimer which stated that no portion of the manual was to be interpreted as altering Honeywell's at-will employment contracts, this waiver was not orally relayed to Huey and he was not given a copy of the manual; and (5) Huey was aware of other employees at Honeywell who were progressively disciplined, rather than terminated, for violating company policies.

. . . [I]f an employer does choose to issue a policy statement, in a manual or otherwise, and, by its language or by the employer's actions, encourages reliance thereon, the employer cannot be free to only selectively abide by it. Having announced a policy, the employer may not treat it as illusory. Honeywell clearly chose to issue a policy statement that it would practice progressive discipline by setting forth such a policy in its manual and relying upon its supervisors to relay this policy to other employees. Therefore, Honeywell may not treat this policy as illusory.

DECISION AND REMEDY The court reversed the granting of the judgment for the defendant and sent the case back for trial. The real question was whether Honeywell had followed its own procedures when it terminated Huey.

CRITICAL THINKING: MANAGERIAL CONSIDERATION Would you recommend that a business have a personnel manual? If so, what should be included in it? Should the employee be provided a copy? Should a business be able to terminate an employee for any reason?

Government Regulation of Employment Law

Many aspects of employment law today are controlled by government regulation. Federal and state laws govern the relationship between management and labor. Discrimination on the basis of gender, race, national origin, religious beliefs, and other invidious classifications is forbidden by statutes. We examine the government's role in employment law in Chapters 22 and 23.

International Consideration

Decision Making by Employees

U.S. companies operate in a fairly free environment concerning employee relations. Employees rarely serve on boards of directors or have input into the business decision-making process. Other countries, especially European countries and Japan, have a different attitude toward employees.

In other industrialized countries, a distinctive management style exists. Often a two-tiered board of directors governs the corporation. One level supervises the day-to-day activities, whereas the other deals with long-range planning. Substantial employee representation on the supervisory board of directors is required. Both boards of directors must agree to employee lay-offs.

American companies that invest in overseas businesses must adhere to the host countries' traditional and legal procedures affecting employee rights. Knowledge of those arrangements is essential to conducting business overseas.

LEGALLY SPEAKING

What You Should Do Before Hiring an Employee

As an employer, you can incur substantial liability for hiring the wrong person. This liability may be based on your employees' actions or your own negligence in hiring a person. The following are some items to keep in mind prior to hiring:

✔ The application form should cover at least the last seven years. Have the applicant sign an authorization form so that you can make a thorough background check—including prior employers, criminal records, educational records, and references.

✔ On the application form, request both months and years worked on prior jobs. A substantial gap between jobs may indicate that a person was incarcerated.

✔ Ignore arrests, but consider convictions.

✔ Investigate given references, including prior employers. Recognize that many prior employers will volunteer little information for fear of a defamation action.

✔ A credit report also can provide useful information. A poor credit rating may indicate that the person is under serious financial pressure, which, in turn, might result in her or him misappropriating property from the employer or third persons.

Chapter Summary

The body of law that conceals the private relationships within the employment sphere originates in the legal principles concerning slave ownership. During the Middle Ages, the principles expanded to cover the employer–employee relationship. With the Industrial Revolution, the law developed the concepts of principal and agent. The distinction between an employer–employee and principal–agent is that an employee enters into no contracts on behalf of his or her employer, whereas an agent does. The same rules generally apply to both relationships.

The concept underlying these relationships is summarized by the phrase here, which has been translated from the Latin: "He [or she] who acts through another acts himself [or herself]." If a company increases its business through the use of employees, the company is responsible for those employees' acts. An agency can be created by agreement, ratification, or estoppel.

Three types of agency relationships exist: (1) principal–agent, (2) employer–employee, and (3) employer's or principal's relationship with an independent contractor. In a relationship between the principal and agent, the agent has derivative authority to act on the principal's behalf. The agent's authority to act stems from one of the following two sources: (1) actual authority, whether express or implied, or (2) apparent authority.

When an employer and employee relationship exists, the employer can regulate the employee's conduct. An employee commonly acts as an agent for the employer. An independent contractor may be hired by an employer to do specific work or by a principal to assist with a contractual relationship with a third person. These relationships are sometimes unclear. The court reviews several factors to determine if a relationship is one of employer–employee or independent contractor.

The principal and agent each owe the other a set of duties. The agent owes the principal the duties of performance, loyalty, obedience, accounting, and notification. The principal owes the agent the duties of compensation, reimbursement and indemnification, cooperation, and safe working conditions.

In a contract situation, the principal may be a disclosed principal, a partially disclosed principal, or an undisclosed principal. The principal is liable on the contract when the principal is disclosed. If the principal is partially disclosed, both the agent and principal are liable. If the principal is not disclosed, the agent is liable. When the agent acts, she or he gives the implied warranty of authority; that is, she or he has the authority to act on behalf of the principal on the contract.

In a tort situation, the employer is liable for the negligent acts of the employee when those acts are committed within the scope of the employee's employment. Even though the employer has not acted negligently, the employer is liable for the employee's acts under the doctrine of *respondeat superior,* which is Latin for "let the master answer."

Normally the employer is not liable for an employee's intentional torts. Liability is expanding, however, in this area. The employer may be liable under one of four theories: (1) the employer was negligent in hiring or retaining the employee, (2) the employer is liable for certain types of employees' intentional torts, (3) the employer ratifies the intentional tort, or (4) the employer helps to commit the intentional tort.

An agency relationship can be ended by an act of the parties or by operation of law when either the principal or agent becomes mentally incompetent or dies, when an agency's subject matter is destroyed or lost, or when an event occurs that has an unusual effect on the agency's subject matter.

An employment relationship is a contractual agreement. Most types of employment are employment-at-will situations. An employee handbook may be the basis for a written contractual relationship. Although the employment relationship is a private one, the government controls some aspects. An employer cannot discriminate on the basis of gender, race, national origin, religious beliefs, and other invidious classifications. The government statutes also govern the relationship between management and labor.

Using the World Wide Web

A businessperson should be aware of the positions that the Internal Revenue Service takes on different issues. The IRS's web site has a list of publications which you can read online or download.

No web site exists specifically dedicated to agency law. The web sites that provide some information on agency and employment law are listed here.

Finding the Law on the Web

Cornell University
    http://www.law.cornell.edu/topics/agency.html
Internal Revenue Service, training materials for IRS examiners on worker classification
    http://www.irs.ustreas.gov/plain/bus_info /training.html

Internal Revenue Service
    http://www.irs.gov/
Internal Revenue Service, forms and publications
    http://www.irs.gov/forms_pubs/pubs/index.htm

Chapter Web Sites

Law Com
    http://www.law.com/
'Lectric Law Library
    http://www.lectlaw.com/d-a.htm
Huey v. Honeywell, Inc.
    http://www.law.vill.edu/Fed-Ct/Circuit/9th /opinions/9415748.htm
Employment
    http://www.freeadvice.com/

Web Activities

17–1 You worked for a company for ten years, before you were fired. What are your rights as to severance pay? Free Advice has information as to your employment rights and termination. Go to <http://www.freeadvice.com/> and click on "Firing." What are your rights upon being fired? Are you entitled to severance pay?

17–2 You are an employer. You are considering reclassifying your employees as independent contractors. You need to know the Internal Revenue Service (IRS) position on independent contractors. What are the three main categories that the IRS reviews? Give an industry example found at the bottom of the site.

Here are three ways to reach the same site:

a. Go to the IRS's web page at <http://www.irs.gov/>. Scroll to the bottom of the page (where the pictures are) and click on "Search." On the web page that comes up, type in "independent contractor." Scroll down and click on "Publication 15a, Employer's Supplemental Tax Guide; 2. Employee or Independent Contractor."

b. Go directly to the same by using this URL: <http://www.irs.gov/prod/forms_pubs/pubs/p15a04.htm>.

c. Go to the IRS's web page at <http://www.irs.gov> and click on "Forms & Pubs." On the page that comes up, click on "Publications Online." On the next web page, scroll down and click on "Publication 15A." Scroll down to "2. Employees or Independent Contractors."

Key Terms

actual authority	derivative authority	fiduciary duty	partially disclosed
actual knowledge	disclosed principal	gratuitous agency	principal
agency by estoppel	doctrine of *respondeat*	implied authority	power of attorney
agency law	*superior*	implied warranty of	principal
agent	employment at will	authority	professional agent
apparent authority	employment law	independent contractor	ratification
constructive knowledge	estoppel	legal fiction	scope of employment
covenant not to compete	express authority		undisclosed principal

Questions and Case Problems

17–1 *Respondeat Superior* Roy makes deliveries for a local pizza restaurant, driving the company car with the restaurant's telephone number printed on the side. One day, after a delivery, but while still on duty, Roy picks up three friends, who need a ride into the next town. Figuring that the restaurant is so busy that he will not be missed, he agrees to take them. While in the next town, Roy accidentally backs into Mr. Phillip's truck, putting a small dent in the truck's bumper. Because it is such a small dent and because Roy needs to get back to work, he leaves without writing a note to the truck's owner. When he arrives back at work, Tony, the restaurant's owner, is waiting for him. Mr. Phillip had been watching his truck from his apartment window. He saw the accident and the telephone number on the side of the car. When he called the telephone number, he reached Tony. Who is responsible for the cost of fixing Mr. Phillip's bumper? Explain.

17–2 Fiduciary Duty Peters hires Ahmed as a traveling salesperson. Ahmed not only solicits orders but also delivers the goods and collects payments from his customers. Ahmed places all payments in his private checking account and, at the end of each month, withdraws sufficient cash from his bank to cover the payments made. Peters is unaware of this procedure. Because of an economic slowdown, Peters tells his salespeople to offer 20 percent discounts on orders. Ahmed solicits orders, but he offers only 15 percent discounts, pocketing the extra 5 percent. Ahmed has lost no orders by this practice, and Peters rates him as one of his top salespeople. When Peters learns of Ahmed's actions, what are his duties and rights in this matter?

17–3 Employment Law Vijay, a pilot for the Big Canyon Tour Company, flies passengers into the canyon to photograph the view. During the past few years, Big Canyon has honored him with all but one of its outstanding employee service awards. The state legislature passes a law prohibiting all aircraft from flying below the canyon's rim. Wayne, the owner of Big Canyon Tour Company, tells the pilots to ignore the new law because the quality of the view without flying below the canyon's rim is poor. Vijay refuses to break this law even though he will lose his job if he fails to follow company orders. Vijay, an at-will employee, is fired. Is Vijay entitled to damages of any kind? Explain.

17–4 Scope of Employment Dependable Trucking Company has a contract with the U.S. Postal Service to haul mail from a large metropolitan area, Large City, to a small rural community, Small Town, six days a week. The communities are located 100 miles apart. A semi-truck that bears no insignia or logo hauls the mail. The semi-truck leaves Large City by 6 A.M., reaches Small Town by 8 A.M., and returns at 5 P.M. The driver receives payment for the two-hour trips and the layover time between 8 and 5. Small Town offers few diversions. After making the mail run on Monday and Tuesday a new driver has fully explored the town. On Wednesday, after dropping the trailer off at the Post Office, he drives the tractor to the nearest bar, located ten miles from town, and consumes ten beers. By 4:00 P.M. he starts the drive back to the Post Office. Five miles from Small Town, he fails to stop at a stop sign, and broadsides a car, killing the three occupants. Who is liable? Explain.

17–5 Agent On April 14, 1987, McCurley Chevrolet, Inc., sold a new Camaro to Rutz. Four days later she was involved in a collision and had the automobile towed back to McCurley Chevrolet. Rutz requested a written estimate for the repairs, but never received it. McCurley Chevrolet, however, submitted a written estimate to its insurance adjuster, who issued a check payable to both Rutz and McCurley Chevrolet in the amount of $7,114.48. The Camaro remained in the shop until June. Rutz was dissatisfied with the work and returned the vehicle numerous times until November. Finally, McCurley Chevrolet brought this action to recover compensation for the work on the Camaro. Rutz, who kept the insurance check, turned it over to the court, paying nothing to McCurley. The court awarded McCurley Chevrolet $3,657.24. Rutz appealed. The question facing the court was whether the insurance adjustor was Rutz's agent when he accepted the written estimate. If he were an agent, the full amount of

$7,114.48 should have been turned over to McCurley Chevrolet. What result and why? [*Bill McCurley Chevrolet, Inc. v. Rutz*, 808 P.2d 1167 (1991)]

17–6 Employment Law Sargent, a former bank auditor for Central National Bank & Trust Co., was fired for refusing to destroy or alter a report to the audit committee. Several statutes prohibited the acts that his superiors had allegedly urged him to commit. Sargent brought an action to recover for wrongful discharge. Who prevails? Explain. [*Sargent v. Central National Bank & Trust Co.,* 809 P.2d 1298 (Okla. 1991)]

17-7 Independent Contractor Hansen, nineteen years old and a professional driver, entered the Sunnyside Honda Fall Classic motocross race that was held in the city park. The promotor of the race, Squisher Racing, found sponsors, arranged prizes, hired employees to promote and conduct the race, and arranged with the city for the park rental. The city required the sponsor to provide medical services, and Squisher Racing complied by contracting with Tri-City Aid Service to provide those services. The flyers and posters advertising the race used Sunnyside Honda's logo and two telephone numbers, one of which was Honda's business phone. When a person called the telephone number, a Honda employee answered questions regarding the race. Honda received no money from the race, paid no employees involved in the race, and had no control over the race. Its benefit was the advertising value of sponsoring the race. Hansen broke his neck during the race and was paralyzed as a result. He was treated at the scene by volunteer emergency medical technicians from Tri-City Aid Service, who, he alleged, removed his helmet improperly and exacerbated his injury. Hansen sued Squisher Racing, Sunnyside Honda, the city, and Tri-City Aid Service. Who prevails? Explain. [*Hansen v. Horn Rapids O.R.V. Park*, 932 P.2d 724 (Wash. App. Div. 3 1997)]

17-8 Apparent Authority Alaska Mack Trucks of Fairbanks is a dealer and franchisee of Mack Trucks, Inc., of Allentown, Pennsylvania. As part of the franchise agreement, Mack permitted Alaska Mack to use the name "Mack." Alaska Mack was listed in the telephone directory under the heading "MACK TRUCKS"; the Mack bulldog was displayed on the Alaska Mack building; and the Mack logo was on Alaska Mack's posters, printed Mack brochures, and promotional materials. Furthermore, a distributorship agreement existed between Alaska Mack and Mack Trucks, Inc.; Mack provided training for the distributorship's employees; Mack engaged in national advertising programs and in joint advertising with the distributor; and Mack established sales quotas and required reports as to the use of the vehicles sold. The city of Delta Junction, Alaska, entered into a contract with Alaska Mack Trucks for a fire truck. Alaska Mack modified the truck to carry a 5,000-gallon gas tank. After delivery, the truck exceeded the specifications for total gross weight and it was dangerous to drive. The city brought action against Alaska Mack and Mack Trucks, Inc. Did Alaska Mack have apparent authority to act as an agent for Mack Trucks, Inc.? Did the act of modifying the truck exceed the possible limits of any apparent authority? Explain. [*City of Delta Junction v. Mack Trucks, Inc.,* 670 P.2d 1128 (Alaska 1983)]

17–9 Negligent Hiring Don went to the defendant's racetrack to pay a debt he owed to Bill, whom the defendant employed. Bill began a fight with Don, resulting in injuries to Don. Don brought legal action against the racetrack on the basis of negligent hiring. Bill had been involved in an earlier altercation that the defendant racetrack could have discovered if it had checked with the police department. No conviction occurred, however, because the other victim failed to prosecute. Bill held a license issued by the Oklahoma Horse Racing Commission. Is the racetrack liable for negligent hiring under these facts? Explain. [*Jackson v. Remington Park, Inc.,* 874 P.2d (Okla. App. 1994)]

17–10 Internet You are an employer who needs to know which of your employees are considered by the Internal Revenue Service (IRS) to be statutory employees. Go to the IRS's web page at <http://www.irs.gov> and click on "Forms & Pubs." On the page that comes up, click on "Publications Online." On the next web page, scroll down and click on "Publication 15, Circular E, Employer's Tax Guide." Scroll down to "2. Who Are Employees?" Scroll down to the heading "Statutory Employees." Who are the statutory employees? As an employer, do you have to pay Social Security, Medicare, and unemployment [Federal Unemployment Tax Act (FUTA)] taxes for them?

Chapter 18

Business Enterprises: Noncorporate Business Entities

> *It is a socialist idea that making profits is a vice. I consider the real vice is making losses.*
>
> Sir Winston Churchill, 1874–1965
> Prime Minister of Great Britain, 1940–1945, 1951–1955

Ethical Consideration

If I Am Only for Myself, What Am I Getting Out of a Limited Partnership?

You are a limited partner in High Return Real Estate Partnership. High Return owns several apartment buildings and is paying, as promised, a high rate of return to all of the limited partners.

You become suspicious of the lofty return, however, at a time when there appears to be a high vacancy rate in most apartment buildings. You do some investigation and find that, in fact, many of the apartments owned by High Return are vacant. You also determine that the buildings need significant repair. Neither the exteriors nor the interiors of the apartment buildings are being maintained. You talk with several of the tenants, who complain that High Return has neglected basic plumbing and electrical repairs.

You conclude that High Return, to keep up its image, has decided to forgo making repairs and, instead, to use its cash to pay investors. You believe that in only a matter of time this policy will ruin the properties being held by High Return and jeopardize the value of the partnership.

You approach the general partner and demand a return of your limited partnership investment. The general partner will return your money on the condition that you keep the information you know to yourself. Do you take your money on that condition? Use the ethical model presented in Chapter 2 and reprinted on the inside front cover to develop your answer.

Introduction

Many people consider owning a business at some point in their lives. You have been fortunate to start a web business, Artiste Login Products, Inc. Although a common belief is that business owners set their own hours, are their own bosses, and make a comfortable living, you know that it takes hard work and long hours. Unfortunately, the sad truth is that most small businesses fail.

Many reasons exist for the large number of failures among small businesses. These failures include a lack of planning, sufficient financing, effective marketing strategies, good management structures, appropriate accounting systems, and lack of appreciation of the legal issues. Statistics show that businesses employing fewer than twenty employees have almost 91 percent chance of failure in the first ten years.[1]

This chapter will examine five different forms of businesses: *sole proprietorship, partnership, limited partnership, limited liability company,* and *limited liability partnership.* A **sole proprietorship** is a business owned by one person. A **partnership** is a business that is run for profit in which two or more people have an undivided (and sometimes unequal) ownership interest. In a **limited partnership**, two or more people own the business. At least one person, called the **general partner**, has unlimited liability, whereas the **limited partner** has limited liability. This type of business entity often is used as an investment vehicle and for tax benefits.

A **limited liability company (LLC)** is very similar to a corporation in that it affords the owners limited liability, but the LLC can be treated as a partnership for tax purposes. The LLC has become one of the more popular forms of business entity in recent years. At least fifty jurisdictions recognize this form of organization today. The **limited liability partnership**, also known as a *registered limited liability partnership,* protects partners from personal liability for partnership debts. Otherwise, the limited liability partnership is treated as a regular partnership. This form has become popular with professional organizations, such as accounting and law firms.

The limited partnership, the limited liability company, and the limited liability partnership must be authorized by state statute. Sole proprietorships and general partnerships exist without any specific authorization of state law.

In 1994, the National Conference of Commissioners on Uniform State Laws issued the Revised Uniform Partnership Act, discussed later in this chapter. In 1996, the National Conference added the Limited Liability Partnership Act and Foreign Limited Liability

---

[1] The Edward Lowe Foundation is a not-for-profit organization dedicated to championing the entrepreneurial spirit in this country. It provides information, research, and education about entrepreneurships and financially assists new businesses. The web address is <http://www.lowe.org/programs/about.htm>. One of the major reasons for failure of a business is lack of funding and location. This site may assist you in these areas.

Partnership Act to the 1994 act. The Foreign Limited Liability Partnership Act applies to a partnership that is formed in one state and does business in another state.[2]

Comparing Business Enterprises

Knowing about the different forms of business entities helps a businessperson make decisions when starting a business. The four entities considered most often are the sole proprietorship, general partnership, limited partnership, and corporation. A corporation is by far the most complex business entity. Chapter 19 discusses corporations in detail.

In deciding which form to adopt, the business-person needs to consider the following factors:

- Difficulty of forming the organization
- Liability
- Tax considerations
- Continuity of existence and ability to transfer ownership
- Management and control
- Financing
- Licenses
- Location.

Each of these factors has legal, as well as business, ramifications. Examining each of these issues and making decisions about them will help the owner determine the business form that best suits his or her needs because each type of business organization has advantages and disadvantages.

Difficulty of Forming the Organization

Some business organizations are easier to create than others. A sole proprietorship is the easiest, because a person merely starts doing business. The person may have to obtain a business license from the state or city before starting a business. State governments do not have statutes regulating the formation of a sole proprietorship.

[2] The 'Lectric Law Library offers considerable information about different forms of business entities. This information is available at <http://www.lectlaw.com/bus.html>.

All state governments require a **fictitious name filing** if an owner decides to use a business name other than his own. A form is filed with the state, requiring the proprietor to give his real name and address, and then the fictitious name under which the business will be conducted. This filing notifies the public that a particular person is participating in this business. The state may refuse to grant the use of a particular fictitious name if it is the same or similar to a name already in use.

A general partnership similarly is easy to form. Two or more people simply conduct a business for profit. A person may even be in a partnership without realizing it. Again, besides obtaining a business license or filing for the use of a fictitious name, state governments do not mandate any legal formalities when creating a general partnership.

All states, however, set legal requirements for creating a limited partnership, limited liability company, limited liability partnership, or corporation. All of these business entities must file appropriate documents with some state agency, such as the secretary of state or a corporation commission.

Liability

Financial liability often stems from negligent acts of the businessperson. Perhaps a customer injured herself because the business failed to properly maintain and repair a stairwell or a product failed, resulting in product liability (discussed in Chapter 11).

Sole proprietors and general partners have unlimited liability. If the sole proprietor, partnership, or partner is sued successfully, the person who obtained the judgment seeks to have the judgment paid out of the business's assets and, if the judgment is not fully paid by business assets, then out of the sole proprietor's or general partner's personal assets. Hopefully, the business has insurance so the assets of the business or the personal assets of the owner are not needed.

Personal liability is limited in the case of a limited partnership, limited liability company, limited liability partnership, or corporation. Of these business forms, only the limited partnership is required to have at least one person, the general partner, who has unlimited liability. The liability of investors in the other entities is limited to the amount of their investment.

Personal liability is not limited, however, for people who hold professional licenses, such as lawyers, accountants, and medical doctors who commit malpractice (negligent acts in the professional practice). For example, in the practice of law, regardless of the type of business organization, the attorney has unlimited liability for negligence in handling a client's affairs. Professionals have limited personal liability for all other business matters.

Tax Considerations

A businessperson must consider the federal and state tax laws when deciding on the type of business organization. The income tax law usually is the most important. A business operated as a sole proprietorship receives no tax advantages. Because it is not a legal entity separate from the owner, it files no separate tax returns. The sole proprietor reports and pays the individual tax rate on the income earned.

Partnerships, limited partnerships, limited liability companies, and limited liability partnerships are subject to the income tax reporting laws, but generally do not pay income tax. Each must file an income tax informational return with the government. The income or deductions pass from the legal entity to the investor, who is subject to income tax laws.

A corporation is taxed as a separate entity on its income. In addition, stockholders who receive dividends are subject to individual income tax laws. Depending on the current tax laws and the amount of income involved, the income tax rates for individuals may be higher or lower than the tax rates for corporations (called C corporations under the federal tax laws). Federal tax laws currently allow corporations that meet specific guidelines, called S corporations, to qualify for various tax breaks. The tax status of corporations is discussed in more detail in Chapter 19. Some states have more favorable tax laws for businesses than other states.

Continuity of Existence and Ability to Transfer Ownership

A sole proprietorship usually exists as long as the owner is able to work. Once the person becomes incapacitated or dies, the business ends. Any sale of the business normally occurs only after a probate case is opened in court. Even if the owner is alive and capable, the business may be hard to sell for any number of reasons, including whether a market for this type of business exists. Often, only the business's assets are salable.

A partnership or a limited liability partnership dissolves whenever a new partner is added or a current partner dies or otherwise leaves the business. Although the partnership is technically dissolved, the business may continue under the new entity formed by the personnel change. A death of a member of a limited liability company or a limited partner does not automatically cause a dissolution of the entity.

Selling an interest in any of these organizations, however, may be difficult. The sale of corporate ownership, on the other hand, usually occurs by the selling of the owner's stock shares. If a corporation's shares are listed on a major stock exchange, the transfer of the shares is relatively easy because a structured market exists.

For a corporation that does not offer its shares on a stock exchange, selling the stock may be difficult. In this situation, people are often more willing to buy the corporation's physical assets rather than an ownership interest in the corporation. A purchaser may be reluctant to buy an ownership interest because of a corporation's outstanding liability. For example, an employee is at fault in an accident with a company automobile in January 1998. The corporation is sold in July 1998. A lawsuit is filed against the corporation in December 1999. The corporation is found liable in an amount that bankrupts it. If the person had purchased only the corporation's assets, she would not be liable for the harm caused by the automobile accident.

Management and Control

A sole proprietor has total management and control over his business. With a general partnership or a limited liability partnership arrangement, in absence of agreement, each partner has equal management and control as the other partners. Thus, each partner has one vote in management matters, regardless of the proportionate size of her partnership interest. Major problems can result if the partners disagree on business strategy.

In a limited partnership, the general partners have the responsibility of management and control. In a limited liability company, the matter of control is determined by the **operating agreement**. This document spells out the rights of the owners (called **members**) and **managers**.

In a corporation, the shareholders elect a board of directors, which, in turn, hires officers to manage the corporation's activities. The shareholders, through the election of the board of directors, control and manage the corporation.

LEGAL HIGHLIGHT

Refinancing Your Home: Is This the Way to Raise Capital?

You purchased your house for $85,000 several years ago. Over the years, you have added improvements that have increased the value of the house. Fortunately, the property values in general have increased in your town.

You locate a small business that you think would be a good investment. Your problem is that you have little cash to invest. Watching television, you see advertisements that explain the benefits of a home equity loan. Benefits range from low interest rates that are tax deductible to putting your hidden wealth, that is, your home equity, to good use now.

You apply for a home equity loan to purchase this business. The appraisal places the house's value at $235,000. According to the advertisement, the bank will lend you 100 percent of the equity at a 10 percent rate of interest. You decide to borrow $150,000.

You go to the bank and fully disclose that you intend to use this money to purchase a small business. The bank agrees to lend you the money without even asking for a business plan. You sign a negotiable note agreeing to repay the $150,000 at 10 percent over twenty years, and place a second mortgage on your house to secure the loan. As you sign the loan papers, the loan officer rushes you through the transaction and you fail to read all the documents. The papers include all the disclosures that the bank must make

under the federal home equity loan amendments to the Truth-in-Lending Act. Later that month you purchase the business for $150,000.

During the next three years, you deduct the interest paid on the $150,000, along with the interest on the first mortgage, on your federal individual income tax return. One day you receive in the mail greetings from the friendly Internal Revenue Service (IRS). You have been selected for a random audit on home deductions.

During your audit, the IRS auditor informs you that only the interest paid on the first $100,000 of the home equity loan was deductible. You must file amended income tax returns for the past three years, pay the taxes owed, plus interest, plus late payment penalties.

Feeling down and out, you return home to open a letter from your mortgage company. You find the interest rate has jumped from 10 to 14 percent. The 10 percent rate was effective for only the first thirty-six months of the loan. The interest rate is readjusted to the prevailing interest rate after the first three years and is subject to review every third year.

Your business did not borrow the money, therefore, it did not received any tax deductions for this loan. Is raising capital to purchase a business by mortgaging your home a good idea? What other methods of financing the purchase of a business are available?

Financing

A sole proprietor obtains loans based on his personal worth, which includes the business's assets. The same may be true of the other forms of organizations. If the business has a lengthy record, loans may be made on the strength of the business assets and abilities rather than on the creditworthiness of the individual investors. Some investors, like limited partners, will not sign personal guarantees; in this way, they limit their liability to their investment amount.

Corporations raise money by selling shares. A corporation also may obtain loans based on the strength of its assets and business record. A lending institution,

however, dealing with a new corporation or a corporation with few shareholders, may require the individual shareholders or officers to be personally liable for the corporate loans in case the corporation fails. For example, a ten-year-old corporation is owned by a family. The bank may require each shareholder personally to guarantee the corporation's operating line of credit.

Licenses

A businessperson must consider which licenses are needed to conduct business. Almost all states require some type of sales or use tax license, because a business must collect taxes from its customers, which, in turn, are remitted to the state. In addition, many businesses, such as insurance agents, real estate brokers, contractors, and pest exterminators, are subject to specific regulations. Sellers of regulated products, such as alcohol, guns, or explosives, are subject to regulations. Operators of businesses such as pawnshops, funeral homes, nursing homes, day-care centers, and food preparation businesses, require separate types of licenses. Most regulated businesses must obtain a specific license.

The importance of having a license cannot be overemphasized, especially when the purpose of the li-

censing statute is to regulate and not to raise revenues. Any contract entered into by an unlicensed individual, whose business is required to have a license, may be declared void by a court when the purpose of the statute is to regulate the business or profession. In addition, if an individual should conduct business without a license under these circumstances, he may face criminal prosecution and civil liability, including the inability to collect amounts owed on contracts that the business has completed. The following case reviews the reasons for which a license is required and the repercussions when a person fails to obtain one.

Case 18.1

W & N Construction Company, Inc. v. Williams

Supreme Court of South Carolina, 1996
322 S.C. 448, 472 S.E.2d 622

BACKGROUND AND FACTS W & N Construction Company contracted for and performed approximately $60,000 worth of commercial work at respondents' building in Seneca. After completion, W & N brought a mechanics lien action to collect an unpaid balance of $30,481.89.

In South Carolina, a person called a master handles this type of situation instead of a judge. The master found that the contract was illegal and unenforceable, because W & N was not a licensed general contractor. Prior to entering into this contract, W & N's license had been revoked when its secretary failed to pay its taxes.

FINNEY, C.J.

. . . .

It is illegal for general contractors who undertake construction in excess of $30,000.00 to do so without first obtaining a license in this state. Nothing in Chapter 11 of Title 40, however, specifically prohibits an unlicensed general contractor from bringing suit to enforce a contract entered into without a license. The master found, notwithstanding the absence of an express statutory prohibition against its maintenance of suit, that W & N had acted illegally in entering into the contract such that it was void and unenforceable. Accordingly, respondents were granted summary judgment.

In *Berkebile v. Outen*, we recognized the general rule that courts will not enforce a contract which is violative of public policy, statutory law, or provisions of the constitution. Similarly, the Court of Appeals recently held: It is a well-founded policy of law that no person be permitted to acquire a right of action from their own unlawful act and one who participates in an unlawful act cannot recover damages for the consequence of that act. This rule applies at both law and in equity and whether the cause of action is in contract or in tort.

A number of jurisdictions adopt the view that an unlicensed contractor may not recover on a contract even though the relevant licensing statute contains no express provision relating to the enforceability of the contract. The rationale is that such licensing statutes protect the public and to permit unlicensed contractors to circumvent licensing requirements by payment of a small fine would defeat the legislative intent. We concur with these authorities.

Accordingly, we affirm the ruling of the master.

DECISION AND REMEDY The plaintiff did not have a contractor's license, so any contract that the business entered into was null and void. In other words, the W & N Construction Company lost $30,000 because it lacked a license.

CRITICAL THINKING: POLITICAL CONSIDERATION Why have states passed legislation requiring construction companies to have a license?

Location

The location of the new business is an important decision, regardless of its form. Numerous legal restrictions may affect the location choice. When reviewing a prospective location, an owner should consider the business's visibility, including signs that promote the business. Most local ordinances control the size, location, and type of signs that a business can display.

Zoning laws are the classification, regulation, and restriction of property use by local government. Owners must be certain that the zoning regulations allow their type of business, along with appropriate signs, to be established in a particular location. Obtaining *use permits* and/or *variances* from local governmental bodies may be required. A **use permit** grants permission to operate a given type of business. A **variance** allows an exception to the zoning laws. Chapter 16 discussed other legal issues concerning property that relate to business.

CyberLaw

Web Businesses

All the *Fortune 1000* companies and many small businesses are on the World Wide Web, which connects more than 100 million people around the world. With new innovations being developed, the web assists both large and small companies to either start a business or increase the sales of established businesses. The web market is growing steadily.

Most business organizations are created under state law, even if they are strictly a web-based business. Many pitfalls await those establishing themselves on the web.

First, you need to select among the hundreds of Internet service providers (ISP) offering access to the web. The ISP needs to be stable, be able to support your needs, and be able to provide assistance. Second, you need a web designer to assist you in developing and designing your web page.

Once the web page is designed and developed, it needs to be publicized. You need to register your web page with an Internet search service that allows surfers to find it. For the search engines, you need to choose words that a customer might use. You can post your web site with news groups and also e-mail information about it to specific organizations that have a need for your web page. You can link your web site with permission to other web sites. You can always advertise your web URL in the traditional media, such as newspapers, other periodicals, radio, and other media.

Partnerships

The **Uniform Partnership Act (UPA)** establishes the law on general partnerships. The term "partnership" means general partnership. If a partnership agreement exists but omits certain matters, the UPA supplies the missing provisions. Most sections of the UPA have no application when the partners have made provisions in the agreement addressing that particular area.

A general partnership is defined as "an association of two or more persons to carry on as co-owners a business for profit" [UPA Section 6]. A partnership agreement is a contract. State statutes do not regulate the formation of a partnership.

Although most partnerships are formed pursuant to a partnership contract among the parties, a partnership also may arise as a result of the conduct of the parties. A sharing of profits from a business, for example, raises a presumption of a partnership [UPA Section 7(4)].

If the conduct of the parties leads third parties to believe that a partnership exists, a partnership may be found to exist legally by a court or an arbitrator. This association is known as a **partnership by estoppel** [UPA Section 16].

No law requires a partnership agreement to be in writing. A court will find that a partnership exists, if two or more people decide to operate a business as co-owners for profit.

Although a written document is not legally required, a partnership agreement should be prepared. Partners participate in a very close relationship that is not unlike a marriage. Both relationships are based on trust, confidence, and mutual reliance. Misunderstandings, frustrating situations, and disagreements are bound to occur. Through a written partnership agreement, many of these problems can be resolved before they escalate.

The statute of frauds (discussed in Chapter 10) requires the agreement to be in writing if the partnership is to last more than one year. Without a written agreement, the relationship is called a partnership at will, which means that it can be dissolved by a partner at any time.

A partnership is treated as a legal entity for certain purposes. For example, partnership property can be held and transferred in the partnership name [UPA Section 8]. In most situations, the partnership is treated as a collection of individuals. Property can be held and transferred in the name of the individual partners [UPA Section 10], the partners can each be sued individually [UPA Section 15], and the partners each have unlimited individual liability.

The **Revised Uniform Partnership Act (RUPA)** of 1994 was sent to state legislatures for possible adoption. At least twelve states have either adopted the new act completely or substantial parts of it. More states are expected to adopt the RUPA.

The RUPA includes major changes to current partnership law. One change is that a partnership is treated as an entity rather than as a collection of individuals. For some purposes though, such as the liability of individual partners and tax issues, the partnership is not treated as an entity. Property acquired by a partnership, however, is the property of the partnership and not of the partners individually. A creditor of the business must exhaust the assets of the partnership before seeking recovery against the personal assets of the individual partners. Partners are granted under the RUPA greater authority to contract on behalf of the partnership. Reference to the major provisions of the RUPA will be made in footnotes.

Partnership breakups also are changed under the RUPA. The term **dissociation** replaced dissolution, that is, the end of a relationship with the partnership. Two methods for partnership breakups are provided. One procedure allows the business to be terminated, whereas the other allows the business to continue. These proposed changes reflect methods by which businesses want partnerships to be treated by legislatures and the courts.

Capital Requirements and Funding of a Partnership

A partnership generally is funded through each partner's capital contributions. The partnership itself also may be able to obtain credit and loans based on its own creditworthiness and that of all of the partners. In addition, the partners may make loans to the partnership.

Partnership Management and Control

Each partner has an equal right to manage and control the partnership [UPA Section 18(e)] and to use partnership property for an appropriate purpose [UPA Section 25(2)(a)]. These rights can be altered by an agreement among the partners. Each partner is an agent for the partnership and for every other partner [UPA Section 9]. Each partner is in a fiduciary relationship with the other partners. Each partner has a fiduciary duty to act in good faith for the benefit of the partnership and to consider the mutual welfare of all partners. For example, unless an agreement states otherwise, a partner cannot engage in outside activities, such as holding a second job, when it involves the partnership's time.

The partners generally receive no compensation for their management of the partnership's business [UPA Section 18(f)]. Instead, the partners share in the business's profits. In the absence of an agreement, profits and losses are shared equally. If an agreement exists, profits and losses are shared in the proportion that the agreement establishes [UPA Section 18(a)]. The amount of the partners' capital contributions has no application in the sharing of profits and losses unless a contrary agreement has been made.

LEGAL HIGHLIGHT

Historic Perspective of Uniform Acts

The constitution of the American Bar Association (ABA), formed in 1878, established as one of its objectives the promotion of the uniformity of legislation among the states. To promote this goal, the ABA created a committee on Uniform Laws. The committee convened a study of interstate laws to achieve uniformity.

The study group's report showed almost unanimous agreement that "desired uniformity could be secured best by concurrent legislative action in the various states." This report led to the establishment in 1892 of the National Conference of Commissioners on Uniform State Laws.

Since its initial organization, the National Conference has drafted more than 200 laws on numerous subjects and various fields of law, many of which have been widely enacted. The National Conference recommends both uniform acts and model acts.

Uniform acts address matters that are appropriate for state legislation and have substantial interstate implication. An example is the transactions covering the sale of goods in Article 2 of the Uniform Commercial Code.

Model acts, on the other hand, cover subjects that only indirectly affect relationships among the states, but that involve problems common to many states, such as water rights. The National Commissioners specifically state that uniformity is unnecessary for model acts but "helpful if a state desires legislation on the subject."

The earlier part of this text addressed the Uniform Commercial Code. This chapter will discuss the application of several additional uniform acts. The next chapter will address the model corporation act.

The partners may agree to delegate day-to-day management responsibilities to one or more of the partners. Each partner, however, has one vote in management matters regardless of his capital contribution. A majority vote usually is required for such partnership decisions [UPA Section 18(b)].

The unanimous consent of all the partners, however, is required in matters significantly altering the nature of the partnership business or property. Other actions requiring the consent of all of the partners include an act by a partner that makes it impossible to carry on the partnership's business in the usual way, the disposition of the goodwill of the business, and the submission of a partnership dispute to arbitration [UPA Section 9(3)].[3]

Any act of a partner that appears to carry on the partnership's business as usual will bind the partnership

to that act. This principle does not apply when the partner has no authority and the person with whom the partner deals knows that the partner has no authority to act [UPA Section 9(1)].[4]

Liability of Old and New Partners

Each partner personally is liable for the entire amount of the partnership's debts. A partner is liable for any act by another partner, even if the act is wrongful, that results in liability for the partnership [UPA Section 13]. This liability exists because, when a partner acts, she acts as the partnership's agent. Such liability can result from either a contract or a tort [UPA Section 15]. A

---

[3] The RUPA follows a similar approach: A majority vote decides any act in the ordinary course of business or in the absence of an agreement, and a unanimous agreement is required for an act outside of the ordinary course of business or to amend the partnership agreement [RUPA § 401], but no provision of arbitration exists in the RUPA as it does in the UPA.

[4] Some conflict appears in this area under the RUPA. Section 301 states that each partner is an agent of the partnership. If the partner has no authority and the third party knows this, the third party cannot hold the partnership liable. Section 303 provides that a partnership may file a statement of partnership authority with a public official that can include limitations on the power of a partner. This seems to indicate that all persons dealing with a partnership must first check the recorded documents. Section 305 states, however, that a partnership is liable for any loss caused to a person when the partner acts in the ordinary course of business.

partner, however, is not liable for other partners' debts that are not connected with the business.[5]

In satisfying their claims based on partnership liabilities, creditors can look to the assets of the individual

partners after the partnership assets have been exhausted. If a person joins an existing partnership, his capital contribution is subject to the claims of prior creditors, but he is not liable personally for the prior debts of the partnership [UPA Section 17]. The new partner is liable personally for debts incurred after he joins the partnership, just as an original partner would be. The following case discusses a new partner's potential liability for debts of the partnership that he had joined.

---

[5] Under the RUPA, a creditor must first seek the partnership assets before seeking the assets of the individual partners. The liability of a partner is joint and several [RUPA §§ 306, 307].

Case 18.2

Citizens Bank of Massachusetts v. Parham-Woodman Medical Associates

United States District Court, E.D. Virginia, 1995
874 F. Supp. 705

BACKGROUND AND FACTS   Citizens Bank of Massachusetts and Parham-Woodman Medical Associates, a Virginia general partnership, entered into a construction loan agreement and a note dated April 30, 1985. The note, in the principal amount of $2 million, was to fund construction of a medical office building, Parham-Woodman's principal asset. Nilda R. Ante and Larry E. King were the general partners of Parham-Woodman when the construction loan agreement and the note were executed. Ante and King also executed a guaranty (guaranteeing repayment of the note) in favor of Citizen's Bank on April 30, 1985.

As contemplated by the documents, Citizen's Bank made advances from time to time during the building's construction. The advances as of June 3, 1986, totaled $1,457,123.15.

Dr. Richard L. Hunley, along with Joseph and Nada Tas, husband and wife, became general partners in Parham-Woodman on June 25, 1986. From July 2, 1986, through November 17, 1986, Citizen's Bank made eight additional advances in the amount of $542,876.85. Subsequently, Kenneth E. Brown became a general partner in Parham-Woodman.

The medical office building was built, and the partnership made numerous payments, but ultimately defaulted. On December 15, 1993, a foreclosure sale brought $912,000, which yielded net proceeds of $890,195.12 to Citizen's Bank.

Judgment was entered against Parham-Woodman in the amount of $1,218,244.98. The liability of Ante and King was eliminated by their respective bankruptcy discharges. The parties agreed that Brown had no personal liability for partnership debt. The court considered the liability of Richard L. Hunley and Joseph and Nada Tas.

District Judge PAYNE

. . . .

Resolution of the dispositive issue also requires consideration of the Uniform Partnership Act and its effect on the nature and extent of the liabilities of incoming partners. This necessitates an examination of the language of the Act, the intent of the Act's drafters and the interpretation of the Act by other jurisdictions.

Section 17 of the Act . . . makes an incoming partner liable for "all the obligations of the partnership arising before his admission," but provides that "this liability shall be satisfied only out of partnership property." Section 17 altered slightly the common law because, at common law, admission of a new partner dissolved the old partnership and created a new one. New creditors, then, were preferred over creditors of the old partnership when partnership assets were sought to cover unpaid partnership debts. To remedy this unfairness to creditors, drafters of the Act removed the preference with respect to partnership assets. "So as to preserve the present law as nearly as possible," however, and presumably to continue the common law's fair treatment of incoming partners, the drafters provided that for pre-existing debts, "liability of the incoming partner shall be satisfied only out of partnership property." . . . "It, therefore, results that existing and subsequent creditors have equal rights as against partnership property and the separate property of all the previously existing members of the partnership, while only the subsequent creditors have rights against the separate estate of the newly admitted partner."

Decisions before and after adoption of the UPA suggest the reason why the law restricts an incoming partner's personal liability, a restriction maintained by the Act. Specifically, where a partnership undertakes a debt before a new partner is made, "[t]he credit of [the] new member . . . does not enter into the consideration of the creditors of the old firm, and it would be manifestly unjust to hold the new partner liable." These decisions and the long-standing principle which they confirm support the view that a partnership obligation arises, within the meaning of Section 17, when the creditor extends the credit to the partnership. In this instance, that occurred on April 30, 1985 and not on the occasion when the bank disbursed each advance.

. . . .

DECISION AND REMEDY An incoming partner's personal assets are exempt from satisfying postadmission advances under a preadmission contract's terms. The court found that all of the partners were liable for the debt owed the bank, but that the liability of Kenneth E. Brown, Richard L. Hunley, Joseph Tas, and Nada Tas could be satisfied only with partnership assets.[a]

CRITICAL THINKING: LEGAL CONSIDERATION Should an incoming partner be treated any differently than an original partner or partners with respect to his or her financial responsibility?

[a] A similar result would occur under the RUPA § 306.

Duration and Termination of the Partnership

A partnership has indefinite duration, unless the partnership agreement states a specific time period. The members of the partnership may change; no person, however, can become a partner without the consent of all of the existing partners, unless the partnership agreement states otherwise [UPA Section 13(g)].

Ending a partnership is a three-step process: *dissolution, winding up,* and *termination.* **Dissolution** means that the partnership union is discontinued. The partnership business continues in order to proceed through the stages of winding up and termination. A new partner, a transfer of a partner's interest in the partnership, a partner's decision to withdraw, or unanimous consent by all the partners will dissolve the original partnership. A partnership also is dissolved if the business of the partnership becomes unlawful; if the business can only be carried on at a loss; if the partnership becomes bankrupt; if a partner dies, becomes mentally ill, or becomes bankrupt; or if a court orders a dissolution [UPA Sections 31 and 32].

Dissolution does not mean that the business is terminated automatically [UPA Section 30]. Depending on the circumstances, the business may continue, conducted by a new partnership entity.

When dissolution occurs and a new partnership is not formed, then **winding up** of the business takes place. All the partners must be notified. At this point, the partners no longer can create any new liabilities on behalf of the partnership. The only authority they maintain is to complete the transactions begun, but not yet finished, at the time of the dissolution and to wind up the business [UPA Section 35]. Winding up includes collecting and preserving partnership assets, paying debts, and accounting to each partner for the value of her partnership interest.[6]

Both creditors of the partnership and creditors of the individual partners can make claims on the partnership's assets. In general, partnership creditors have priority on the partnership's assets. Individual creditors have priority on the personal assets of the partners.[7]

When the business has been wound up, it is then terminated. In **termination**, the assets, if any, are distributed in the following order.

1. Debts owed to creditors other than partners
2. Debts owed to partners for loans made to the partnership
3. Amounts owed to partners for capital
4. Amounts owed to partners as profits [UPA Section 40].[8]

The following case discusses some of the problems that can arise when a partnership dissolves. Notice that the business mentioned in the case continued after dissolution.

---

[6] The RUPA recognizes that the dissociation of one partner who leaves the partnership does not dissolve the partnership. Many dissociations result in a buyout of the withdrawing partner's interest. A dissolution can result for these reasons: if the partnership was at will, was established for a specific time period, had a business that became illegal, could not make a profit, or encountered other similar occurrences [RUPA § 801].

[7] The Bankruptcy Code changed this rule. Thus, the RUPA partnership creditors share pro rata with the partners' individual creditors in the assets of the partners' estate.

[8] The RUPA does not have a similar list as in the UPA. The same theory applies, however, as to the distribution of assets and the payment of obligations [RUPA §§ 401, 807].

Case 18.3

Lange v. Bartlett

Court of Appeals of Wisconsin, 1984
121 Wis. 2d 599, 360 N.W.2d 702

BACKGROUND AND FACTS Art Lange and Bert Bartlett worked together installing swimming pools for several years on a part-time basis. In 1972, they verbally agreed to form the partnership "Pool Boys" and began operating the business full time. This arrangement continued until April 1975, when Lange told Bartlett that he wanted to dissolve the partnership.

Bartlett eventually offered Lange $3,000 in payment for Lange's share of the partnership. Lange refused this offer. Neither Bartlett nor Lange obtained an accounting, nor did Lange accept any money.

Between 1975 and 1978, Bartlett worked hard and as business increased, the partnership became more profitable. In 1978, Lange sued to recover his interest in the partnership, claiming that he was entitled to one-half of both the assets and the profits from the business subsequent to April 1975. The trial court entered a judgment that gave him one-half of the assets. Lange appealed, asserting that he was also entitled to one-half the profits.

Presiding Judge BROWN

. . . .

Before discussing the trial court's decision after trial, it is important for a clear understanding of this case to review the basic tenets of partnership law.

When a partner dies or retires, the partnership is dissolved. However, the partnership is not terminated upon dissolution; it continues until the wind-up of the partnership affairs are completed.

It is at this juncture, the point of dissolution, that the retiring partner makes an election. He can either force the business to "wind-up" and take his part of the proceeds, sharing in profits and losses after dissolution, or he can permit the business to continue and claim as a creditor the value of his interest at dissolution. The determination of whether the retiring partner consented to or acquiesced in the continuation of the business is a question of fact.

. . . Distinguishing . . . whether a wind-up or a continuation is at hand is critical simply because the settlement of the former partner's account differs depending on whether it is a wind-up or a continuation.

For instance, if a trial court determines that a business was engaged in a wind-up, the former partner receives the value of his or her interest at the date of liquidation or final settlement. . . . In other words, the outgoing partner shares in both profits and losses until termination. The former partner, therefore, does not take as a creditor. The outgoing partner gets a share of the profits, if any, only after all of the other creditors have been paid and only until termination. Termination is the point in time when all of the partnership affairs are wound up.

Continuation, however, effects a totally different settlement of the former partner's account. The outgoing partner can agree, at the time of dissolution, that the business will be continued. If the outgoing partner elects to allow the business to continue, then that partner has a second election—to receive either interest or profits from the date of dissolution—in addition to the value of his or her interest in the partnership. This "second election" can be made only by the former partner; it cannot be made by either the continuing partner or the trial court. The profits garnered from continuation are different from the profits at wind-up simply because, in a continuation, the outgoing partner is not responsible for the debts of the continuing partnership. The outgoing partner, instead, takes as a creditor.

. . . .

Finally, we reach a contention by Bartlett which is found to be a common complaint in partnership dissolution in our research of cases across the country. Bartlett strenuously argues that the business has greatly expanded since Lange left in 1975. He claims it is not the intent of the statutes to allow Lange to reap profits from aspects of the business which were not operating at the time of the partnership dissolution. Bartlett is incorrect. [The statute] states that the retiring partner may opt, in lieu of interest, for "profits attributable *to the use of his right in the property of the dissolved partnership. . . .*" (Emphasis added.) This figure may differ from year to year depending upon Bartlett's use of partnership property. Lange's partnership property includes not only the tangible assets but also any goodwill in the "Pool Boys" name and reputation prior to dissolution that would have contributed to the success of Bartlett's sauna, spa and hot tub business.

. . . .

We conclude that regardless of the expended effort on behalf of Bartlett, Lange is still entitled to a share of the partnership profit from the day of dissolution. However, a court can take into account the substantial labor and management services made by the continuing partner and deduct that amount before arriving at the figure of what profit is due the former partner.

DECISION AND REMEDY The trial court's judgment was reversed and the case was remanded for a new trial. Whenever a partner withdraws from a partnership, a determination must be made as to whether the partnership is in the stage of winding up with the expectation of termination or whether it is being continued. This is a question of fact to be determined based on the conduct of all partners.

CRITICAL THINKING: PRACTICAL APPLICATION What steps should Bartlett have taken to protect his interest when Lange left?

Limited Partnerships

A limited partnership consists of at least one general partner and one or more limited partners. The person who accepts the position of general partner agrees to manage the day-to-day activities of the business. Others want to invest while limiting their liability to the amount invested. The investing partners find a limited partnership attractive for two reasons. First, a limited partnership limits the liability of its limited partners to the amount of their contributions. Second, tax advantages exist. Tax benefits, especially in certain industries, such as oil and lumber, make limited partnerships attractive investments.

The limited partners, as such, are not bound by the obligations of the partnership and cannot have any day-to-day management responsibilities. The general partner or partners have total responsibility for the partnership's management and unlimited liability for its debts.

A limited partnership is only authorized by statute. Failure to comply with the statutory requirements changes the limited partnership into a general partnership. The **Uniform Limited Partnership Act (ULPA)** of 1916 and the **Revised Uniform Limited Partnership Act (RULPA)** of 1976, with 1985 amendments, include the current law on limited partnerships. The RULPA updated the original ULPA to resolve current problems with limited partnerships.

The ULPA and the RULPA require the limited partnership to file a certificate (see Exhibit 18–1) that becomes part of the public record. The certificate is similar to the articles of incorporation for a corporation. A partnership certificate contains basic information, such as the name, location, and business of the partnership; the name and residence of each partner (general or limited); the term for which the partnership will exist; and the amount of cash and property contributed by each limited partner.

In addition to the certificate of limited partnership, the partners often enter into a more detailed partnership agreement that is not filed as part of the public record, but that covers such items as each partner's share of the profits. The general partners normally share the profits and losses evenly, but may agree to other ratios.

Limited partners share the profits in accordance with the agreement. Limited partners, however, share in the losses of the limited partnership only up to the amount of their capital contribution.

Limited partnership interests are considered to be securities (like stock certificates or corporate bonds). First, one person (the limited partner) pays money to another (the general partner). Second, the money is invested in a common enterprise from which the investor is led to expect profits. Third, the profits arise primarily from the effort of people other than the investor. The issuance, sale, and transfer of a limited partner's interest, therefore, are subject to federal and state securities laws (discussed in detail in Chapter 20).

Sources of Funding for Limited Partnerships

The general and the limited partners contribute to the capital of the limited partnership and also may make loans to it. The partnership agreement may provide for additional contributions and voluntary or involuntary assessments of the partners after the partnership's formation. The liability of the limited partners is restricted to the amount of their contributions. The ability of the partnership to obtain loans from third parties will be based on the partnership's assets and the creditworthiness of the general partner or partners who have unlimited liability.

Control of the Limited Partnership

The control and management of the limited partnership is vested in the hands of the general partner. Control does not necessarily follow ownership interest, as it does in a corporation. A general partner may have a very small ownership interest, yet still retain the right to control the entity. Unless there is an agreement to the contrary, the general partner has absolute discretion as to when profit distributions are made.

Exhibit 18–1 Sample Certificate of Limited Partnership

CERTIFICATE OF LIMITED PARTNERSHIP

The undersigned, desiring to form a Limited Partnership under the Uniform Limited Partnership Act of the State of _____ , make this certificate for that purpose.

╱**1. Name.** The name of the Partnership shall be " _____
_____ ."

╱**2. Purpose.** The purpose of the Partnership shall be to [describe].

╱**3. Location.** The location of the Partnership's principal place of business is _____
_____ County, _____.

╱**4. Members and Designation.** The names and places of residence of the members, and their designation as General or Limited Partners, are:

_____	[Address]	General Partner
_____	[Address]	General Partner
_____	[Address]	Limited Partner
_____	[Address]	Limited Partner

╱**5. Term.** The term for which the Partnership is to exist is indefinite.

╱**6. Initial Contributions of Limited Partners.** The amount of cash and a description of the agreed value of the other property contributed by each Limited Partner are:

[Name]	[Describe]
[Name]	[Describe]

╱**7. Subsequent Contributions of Limited Partners.** Each Limited Partner may (but shall not be obliged to) make such additional contributions to the capital of the Partnership as may from time to time be agreed upon by the General Partners.

╱**8. Profit Shares of Limited Partners.** The share of the profits which each Limited Partner shall receive by reason of his contribution is:

[Name]	_____	%
[Name]	_____	%

Signed _____ , 20 _____

_____
_____
_____
_____

Signed and sworn before me, the undersigned authority, this _____ , 20_____.

Notary Public
_____ County, _____

The general partner has all of the rights and powers and is subject to all of the restrictions and liabilities of a partner in a general partnership. The general partner lacks the authority to act in a manner that contravenes the partnership certificate.

A limited partner has the same rights as any general partner to access partnership books and records; to have an accounting of the partnership business; to dissolve and wind up the partnership by court order; to receive the share of profits or compensation stipulated in the partnership certificate; and to have a return of her contribution on dissolution and distribution of the partnership assets, subject to the rights of creditors. Exhibit 18–2 illustrates the basic comparisons of a general partnership, a revised limited partnership, and a limited liability company.

Liability in Limited Partnerships

A limited partnership must have at least one general partner, who has unlimited liability. Most states now allow the general partner to be a corporation or a natural person.

Generally speaking, the limited partners' liability is limited to their capital contributions. This contribution also includes the amount of capital that limited partners have pledged to contribute, but have not yet actually paid.

Limited partners can lose their limited liability if they participate in the management and control of the partnership's business. If another party (often called a third party), however, has knowledge of the involvement, the limited partner can lose the limited liability protection. The third party that has a legal complaint against the limited partnership, which now has few or no assets, would look to see if a limited partner has participated in the management of the partnership. If so, then that limited partner loses the limited liability protection and is treated as a general partner with unlimited liability. Certain state statutes specify that the right of a limited partner to demand that the general partner be expelled from the partnership will not be considered as taking part in the control of the business.

The following case examines the question of whether a limited partner had lost his limited liability status. This case was decided under the ULPA.

Case 18.4

Gonzalez v. Chalpin

Court of Appeals of New York, 1990
564 N.Y.S.2d 702

BACKGROUND AND FACTS Chalpin hired Gonzalez to be the superintendent and maintenance worker at Excel Associate's apartment building. Excel was a limited partnership that had one individual general partner, Lipkin; one corporate general partner, Tribute Music, Inc., a valid corporation; and one limited partner, Chalpin. Chalpin was also Tribute's president, sole shareholder, and director. Gonzalez was not paid for much of the work he performed. He sued Chalpin individually, as well as Excel Associates and its limited and general partners, for breach of contract.

Judge BELLACOSA

. . . .

The general restriction on the liability of limited partners is not controlling here because, if the partner in addition to the exercise of [the partner's] rights and powers as a limited partner takes part in the control of the business, the limited partner becomes liable as a general partner . . . Chalpin cannot challenge the trial court's affirmed factual determination that he took part in the control of Excel's business. Instead, he attempts to skirt the individual and general responsibility imposed [by the law] by claiming that he acted at all times solely in his capacity as an officer of Tribute.

Irrefutably, individual liability should not be imposed on a limited partner merely because that person happens also to be an officer, director and/or shareholder of a corporate general partner. . . . But that is not this case. Moreover and conversely, a limited partner who takes part in the control of the limited partnership's business should not automatically be insulated from individual liability merely by benefit of status as an officer and sole owner of the corporate general partner. That is this case.

A limited partner who assumes such a dual capacity rightly bears a heavy burden when seeking to elude personal liability. For once a plaintiff meets the threshold burden of proving that a limited partner took an active individual part in effectuating the limited partnership's interests . . . , the fulcrum shifts. The limited partner in such a dual capacity must then, at least, prove that any relevant actions taken were performed solely in the capacity as officer of the general partner.

Defendant in this case failed to adjust to the shift and did not overcome the proof of involvement and responsibility for his actions undertaken in his individual capacity.

DECISION AND REMEDY The court rejected Chalpin's limited liability defense because he failed to prove that he acted only as an officer of the general partnership. He was held individually liable to Gonzalez.

CRITICAL THINKING: PREVENTIVE CONSIDERATION What actions could Chalpin have taken to avoid being held liable for the debts of the limited partnership?

Tax Consequences for a Limited Partnership

The limited partnership itself is not a taxable entity. The tax status of a limited partnership is the same as that of a general partnership, that is, both are pass-through organizations. The limited partnership makes an informational filing, reporting the allocation of profits and losses and other tax items to the various partners. Individual partners, both limited and general, report their allocated profits or losses on their own tax returns.

Profits and losses pass through the limited partnership to the individual partners before the income is subject to federal taxation. This arrangement is called **pass-through tax treatment**.

Because limited partnerships are used extensively as tax shelters, their tax status as partnerships often is challenged by the IRS. For federal income tax purposes, the IRS regulations provide that a limited partnership will be classified as a "partnership," rather than as "an association taxable as a corporation," if it possesses fewer corporate than noncorporate characteristics.

The IRS looks for six corporate-like characteristics.

1. Two or more associates.
2. Carrying on a business for profit.
3. Centralization of management.
4. Limited liability. The business's debts are limited to its assets, and creditors cannot look to the personal assets of the owners for payments.
5. Continuity of life. The business has unlimited life on its own and will continue in existence after the original shareholders or partners die.
6. Free transferability of interest in the business.

If a business entity lacks any two of these corporate characteristics, the IRS will classify it as a partnership rather than as a corporation for tax purposes. The two easiest characteristics to avoid are free transferability of interests and continuity of life. Nearly all limited partnership agreements and limited liability companies provide for a termination date and impose restrictions on transferability of interest to avoid two of the corporate characteristics. If they do not, they will be taxed as a corporation.

Limited Liability Companies

The limited liability company (LLC) is a hybrid form of business organization that provides the limited

Exhibit 18–2   Basic Comparison of Partnerships and Limited Liability Companies

Characteristic	General Partnership	Revised Limited Partnership	Limited Liability Company

Creation	• By agreement of two or more persons:
	   • Informal agreement (determined by actions of the people), or
	   • Formal written agreement.
	 • Purpose is to carry on a business as co-owners for profit.
		• Must be allowed by state law.
		 • Must file a certificate of limited partnership in the appropriate state office.
		 • By agreement of two or more persons.
		 • Partners (one or more general partners and one or more limited partners).
		 • Purpose is to carry on a business as co-owners for profit.
			• Must be allowed by state law.
			 • Must file articles of organization in the appropriate state office.
			 • Two or more persons.

Sharing of profits and losses	• By agreement.
	 • In absence of agreement:
	   • Profits and losses are shared equally by partners.
	   • If agreement covers only profits but not losses, then losses are shared in the same ratio as profits.
		• General partners by agreement.
		 • Limited partners:
		   • Share profits by agreement.
		   • Share losses only up to their capital contribution.
			• By operating agreement.

Liability	• All partners have unlimited personal liability.	• All general partners have unlimited personal liability. • Limited partners are liable up to the amount of their investment.	• All members are liable up to the amount of their investment.
Capital contribution	• No minimum or mandatory amount by law; the amount is set by agreement or actions.	• Set by agreement (cash, property, or past services) and any obligation, including future services.	• Set by agreement (cash, property, or past services) and any obligation, including future services.

(continued)

Exhibit 18–2 Basic Comparison of Partnerships and Limited Liability Companies (*continued*)

Characteristic	General Partnership	Revised Limited Partnership	Limited Liability Company

Management	• By agreement.
	• In absence of agreement, all partners have an equal voice.
		• General partners:
		  • By agreement or
		  • In absence of management clause in agreement, each has an equal voice.
		• Limited partners have no voice, or
		  • If they are active in management, they have general liability as general partners, if third party has knowledge of such involvement.
		  • Limited partner may act as an agent or employee of the partnership and vote on amending the certificate or sale or dissolution of the partnership.
			• Members may be the managers.
			• Members may hire outsiders as managers.

Duration	• By agreement.
	• Can be dissolved by the following:
	  • Action of partner (withdrawal).
	  • Operation of law, death, or bankruptcy.
	  • Court decree.
		• General partners:
		  • By agreement in the certificate.
		  • By withdrawal, death, or insanity of a general partner in the absence of the right of other general partners to continue the partnership.
		• Limited partner's death does not terminate the partnership, unless he or she is the only remaining limited partner.
			• By the articles of organization:
			  • Date set, and/or
			  • Any events that would cause a dissolution.
			• When fewer than two members remain.

Priorities (order) upon liquidation	• Outside creditors. • Partner creditors. • Capital contribution of partners. • Profits of partners.	• Outside creditors. • Partner creditors. • By agreement, amounts before withdrawal to which partners are entitled.	• Outside creditors. • Member creditors. • By the operating agreement.

liability protection of a corporation while retaining sufficient partnership characteristics to qualify for partnership status for federal income tax purposes. Nearly every state has a statute that authorizes the creation of LLCs. More important, the IRS recognizes LLCs.

The LLC form of organization was first developed in Germany and then spread to Latin America. Businesspeople from the United States traveling to Europe and Latin America eventually brought the concept home. In 1977, Wyoming was the first state to adopt legislation to allow this type of entity to cover mining leases. Businesspeople soon recognized the advantages of LLCs and the concept quickly expanded from mining leases to all types of businesses.

Once the IRS recognized this form of organization, states quickly adopted statutes authorizing it. Legislatures, wanting to encourage small businesses, had two goals for the LLC: (1) favorable tax treatment, as if the LLC were a partnership, and (2) limited owner liability, as if the LLC were a corporation.

The LLC differs from either a partnership or a corporation, but has aspects of both. The following sections look at the formation, tax treatment, management, limited liability, and continuity of existence of the LLC.

Formation of an LLC

A limited liability company is no more difficult to form than a limited partnership. All statutory provisions must be followed. Specific provisions vary from state to state. The owners of the LLC are called **members**. The **managers** of the LLC, those who manage the LLC from day to day, may be either the members or nonowners.

One or more persons must file the **articles of organization** and pay the appropriate fees at the designated public office. Exhibit 18–3 shows an example of the articles of organization for an LLC. Included within the articles are the name of the company, the date when the company will be dissolved, restrictions on trading the shares, whether the company will be managed by members or nonowners, the name and address of the statutory agent who receives legal papers, and other required information.

A limited liability company is required to use the words *limited liability company* or *limited company*, or the abbreviations LLC or LC. Many states forbid an LLC to use the following words and their abbreviations: association, corporation, or incorporated.

Tax Consequences

As discussed previously, partnerships and limited partnerships are not subject to federal income tax, even though they must file informational tax returns. The partnership passes income, credits, and losses through to its partners. The partners pay tax on the income received from the partnership.

Income generated by corporations is subject to what some call double taxation. The corporation must pay federal income tax on its taxable earnings. Part of the corporate income may be paid to shareholders as dividends. If the corporation pays dividends to the shareholders, they must report the dividends as income on their federal income tax returns.

The IRS allows small business corporations to apply for an S corporation tax status, which means that the corporation is treated as if it were a partnership for tax purposes. If the business meets all the IRS regulations, the corporation's income is not subject to federal income tax, although an income tax return must be filed. The income, credits, and losses may pass through the corporation to the shareholders. The income is subject to taxation when received by the shareholders. The income is taxed only once, just as it is in a partnership arrangement.

The IRS treats the LLC as a partnership instead of as a corporation if the LLC possesses no more than four of the six corporate-like characteristics discussed previously. The two attributes easiest to limit are continuity of life and free transferability of interests. The articles of organization can set an ending date for the LLC, and the operating agreement can restrict the transferability of interests.

The IRS has issued check-the-box regulations. On the income tax return filed by unincorporated associations, such as limited partnerships or limited liability companies, businesses can check a box indicating their partnership status.

Managing an LLC

A limited liability company is managed either by the members or by managers. The managers need not be members of the LLC. The members decide on the management.

If managed by members, the LLC has a management similar to that of a general partnership and is not considered to be centralized. If managed by nonowner

Exhibit 18–3 Sample Articles of Organization

STATE OF ARIZONA
OFFICE OF THE CORPORATION COMMISSION

WORLD AMUSEMENT, L.L.C.

ARTICLES OF ORGANIZATION

Pursuant to A.R.S. § 29–632 the undersigned states as follows:

1.   The name of the limited liability company is World Amusement, L.L.C.

2.   The address of the registered office in Arizona is 206 N. Campo Avenue, Phoenix, Arizona 85881, which is located in the county of Maricopa.

3.   The name and address of the statutory agent is John Lawyer, 100 East Loyola, Tempe, Arizona 85283.

4.   There are two or more members at the time the limited liability company is formed.

5.   The latest date on which the limited liability company is to dissolve is December 31, 2010.

6.   Management of the limited liability company is vested in a manager or managers. The names and addresses of each person who is a manager and each member who owns a twenty percent or greater interest in the capital or profits of the limited liability are:

    Hiley Banks   [x] member   [x] manager
    Shirley Banks   [x] member   [x] manager

Signed _____ Date _____

Signed _____ Date _____

The persons executing this document need not be members of the limited liability company at the time of formation or after formation has occurred.

I, John Lawyer, having been designated to act as Statutory Agent, hereby consent to act in that capacity until removed or resignation is submitted in accordance with the Arizona Revised Statutes.

_____
Statutory Agent

managers, the LLC may practice centralized management similar to that of a corporation.

The members' operating agreement establishes their rights and responsibilities as members. The operating agreement may indicate whether a member's interest can be transferred and, if so, the circumstances and method of transfer. The agreement can be as broad or as limited as the members decide.

Limited Liability

The limited liability company affords its members protection of their personal assets from the claims of the LLC's creditors. The members are liable only up to the amount that they invest. That investment may be in the form of contributed property, services, cash, or a promissory note to the LLC in exchange for an LLC interest. The members have greater protection than is offered to general partners in any type of partnership. As discussed previously, in a limited partnership, all general

partners have unlimited personal liability. In a general partnership, all partners are personally liable for business debts.

Continuity of Existence

One characteristic of a corporation is that it exists in perpetuity, unaffected by the death, retirement, insanity, or bankruptcy of its shareholders. One way to avoid being taxed as a corporation is to establish a termination date. On termination, if desired, the owners can merely form another LLC.

A problem occurs when a member dies. To keep the partnership aspect that qualifies the LLC for the pass-through tax treatment in the event of a death, the IRS requires an LLC to obtain an agreement not to dissolve signed by a majority of the remaining members and by all of the remaining managers.

The following case discusses limited liability companies and how they are treated as separate entities.

Case 18.5

Gebhardt Family Investment, L.L.C. v. Nations Title Insurance of New York, Inc.

Court of Special Appeals of Maryland, 2000
132 Md. App. 457, 752 A.2d 1222

BACKGROUND AND FACTS The Gebhardts purchased 31.6707 acres of land in Prince George's County on September 1, 1987. They simultaneously purchased title insurance from Nations Title Insurance of New York, Inc. The policy named Joseph and Faye Gebhardt as the insureds.

In 1995, the Gebhardts learned that someone else was paying property taxes on 4.75 acres of the property. They reported to Nations that there was a cloud on the title as to the 4.75 acres. They demanded that Nations correct the situation by negotiating a purchase from person alleging ownership and by obtaining a quitclaim to the 4.75 acres in favor of the Gebhardts.

On December 18, 1996, before the matter was resolved, and apparently to facilitate their estate planning, the Gebhardts executed a special warranty deed conveying all 31.6707 acres in fee simple to Gebhardt Family Investment, LLC, a limited liability company created under Virginia law. The Gebhardts were the sole members of the LLC. The deed stated that the LLC paid consideration of $160,990.00 for the property.

On November 13, 1997, the Gebhardts and the LLC sued Nations for breach of contract for failing to resolve the cloud on title. Trial was held on July 22, 1999, and the sole issue before the court was whether the Gebhardts and/or the LLC were insured under the title insurance policy. The parties apparently reached a settlement agreement as to the amount of damages that Nations would pay in the event that the court found there was coverage.

Joseph Gebhardt was the only witness called. He testified to the effect that he and his wife formed the LLC and conveyed the property in question to it as part of their estate planning. Gebhardt stated that they did not pay any consideration and the consideration of $160,990.00 recited on the deed was written so Virginia would transfer taxes from them as individuals to the LLC. Gebhardt added that he and his wife still owned the property and paid all of the taxes.

The title insurance policy issued by Nations to the Gebhardts in 1987 states, in pertinent part:

> *The coverage of this policy shall continue in force as of Date of Policy in favor of an insured so long as such insured retains an estate or interest in the land, or holds an indebtedness secured by a purchase money mortgage given by a purchaser from such insured, or so long as such insured shall have liability by reason of covenants of warranty made by such insured in any transfer or conveyance of such estate or interest, provided, however, this policy shall not continue in force in favor of any purchaser from such insured of either said estate or interest or the indebtedness secured by a purchase money mortgage given to such insured.*

Paragraph 2(a) of Conditions and Stipulations to Policy of Title Insurance. The policy defines "insured" as

> *the insured named [in the policy] and, subject to any rights or defenses the Company may have had against the named insured, those who succeed to the interest of such insured by operation of law as distinguished from purchase including, but not limited to, heirs, distributees, devisees, survivors, personal representatives, next of kin, or corporate or fiduciary successors.*

The court thus determined that the LLC was not insured under the policy because it obtained the property by way of purchase rather than by operation of law. It determined that the Gebhardts' coverage terminated when they conveyed the property to a separate entity. The court directed that judgment be entered in favor of Nations.

MARVIN H. SMITH, Judge

. . . .

The appellants argue that because the Gebhardts are the sole members of the L.L.C. the conveyance was, in effect, to themselves and they still retain an interest in the property within the meaning of Paragraph 2(a) of the policy's Conditions and Stipulations.

The argument is based on a misunderstanding of the nature of limited liability companies. It is widely recognized that:

> [t]he allure of the limited liability company is its unique ability to bring together in a single business organization the best features of all other business forms—properly structured, its owners obtain both a corporate-styled liability shield and the pass-through tax benefits of a partnership. General and limited partnerships do not offer their partners a corporate-styled liability shield. Corporations, including those having made a Subchapter S election, do not offer their shareholders all the pass-through tax benefits of a partnership. All state limited liability company acts contain provisions for a liability shield and partnership tax status.

. . . .

As the trial court recognized, when the Gebhardts conveyed their interest in the property to the L.L.C., they effected a "transfer from one entity or person to another." The Gebhardts and the L.L.C. are separate entities. The Gebhardts may not file suit in their own names on behalf of the L.L.C. Nor may they be held individually liable for wrongful conduct of the L.L.C. While the Gebhardts have an interest in the L.L.C., they no longer have an interest in the property. Rather, it is the L.L.C. that has the interest in the property. To hold otherwise would be to disregard the nature and viability of limited liability companies.

. . . .

By conveying the property under special warranty deed, moreover, the Gebhardts covenanted to protect the L.L.C. only against claims made "by, through, or under" the Gebhardts, as grantors. They did not warrant title against a claim of superior title made by someone else. There is no suggestion that the alleged cloud on title was created by any action or inaction on the part of the Gebhardts while the property was titled in their names. The Gebhardts thus transferred from themselves to the L.L.C. the problem of the cloud on title as to the 4.75 acres. Should the other persons claiming title to the 4.75 acres bring an action to quiet title, the L.L.C, rather than the Gebhardts, would be required to defend and the Gebhardts could not be held personally liable.

. . . .

The appellants admit in their brief that "[t]here has, as yet, been no monetary loss." They nevertheless contend that they suffered a loss in that "a title which has a known overlap cannot be said to be 'undamaged.'" Presumably, the appellants believe, as Mr. Gebhardt testified at trial, that such property is unmarketable. Assuming arguendo that there is a "known overlap"—and the record is unclear in that regard—the fatal flaw in this reasoning is that the Gebhardts successfully conveyed the entire property, including the 4.75 acres in question, to the L.L.C. by way of a special warranty deed. . . . If any loss is suffered because of the cloud on title, it will be suffered by the L.L.C., which was not an insured under the policy either before or after the conveyance.

DECISION AND REMEDY A limited liability company is a separate legal entity. The problem involving the cloud on title became the problem of the LLC and not the Gebhardts once the property was conveyed to it. The title policy only covered the Gebhardts and not the LLCs.

CRITICAL THINKING: LEGAL THEORY Assume for the moment that you own an LLC. You have a contract that restricts the transfer of the contract to another person or entity. The contract prohibits the LLC from transferring the contract from the LLC to you. Why does the law not allow you to combine your individual rights with the rights of the LLC when you are essentially the LLC?

Limited Liability Partnerships

Many states have passed legislation to permit the creation of limited liability partnerships (also called registered limited liability partnerships). The collapse of the savings and loan associations caused the need for this type of business entity.

When the savings and loan associations declared bankruptcy, injured people looked to the law firms and accounting firms of the savings and loan associations. People brought lawsuits against these firms to recover losses that had been incurred as the result of malpractice acts (negligent acts) by a partner in the law or accounting firms. Many of these organizations were general partnerships that were national or international firms with hundreds of partners. For example, a partner in Hong Kong could be held liable personally for negligent actions of a partner in California even though the partner in Hong Kong did not have any knowledge of the California partner's activities.

These organizations did not want to form corporations or limited liability companies because they would then be subject to the public reporting requirements of the Securities and Exchange Commission (SEC) and their finances would become public information. The solution was the creation of the limited liability partnership entity. This type of partnership has no general partners, so any judgment is limited to recovery from the partnership assets. If the judgment is for malpractice (negligence), recovery can be made from the partnership's assets and from the individual partner's assets who committed the malpractice. Currently, public disclosure of the partnership's business is not required. The SEC or the courts still must determine if this type of entity protects against information disclosure.

A state statute must authorize a limited liability partnership's creation. Normally these statutes require a public filing containing the name and the address of the partnership, the number of partners in the partnership, and a brief description of the business in which the partnership engages. If the partners follow the statutory provisions, they are not liable personally for the business's debts. In 1996, the National Conference of Commissioners on Uniform State Laws adopted proposed statutes on limited liability partnerships and foreign limited liability partnerships as part of the Uniform Partnership Act.[9]

---

[9] Family businesses can present unique problems. Some of these issues and how to solve them are discussed at the following web address: <http://www.fambiz.com/>. Occasionally, these problems develop because the family is using the wrong form of organization.

International Consideration

Business Entities Overseas

When a business decides to enter international markets, it must determine the type of organization to use overseas. Although a business can sell products through normal export procedures, it may need to establish a permanent office or staff in another country, especially if its products will be manufactured in the foreign country.

Most Western countries recognize two forms of organizations that provide limited liability to the owners. One form is called a *corporation for profit*, and the second is the *limited liability company*. Most countries require a minimum amount of capital to start and run the business. They require a larger amount of capital for a corporation than for a limited liability company. For example, Germany recognizes business entities that are similar to U.S. corporations and limited liability companies. In Germany, the creation of a limited liability company requires the investment of a minimum of 50,000 deutsche marks, whereas 100,000 deutsche marks are required for a corporation. Other countries of the European Union have similar provisions. Just as requirements for minimum amounts of capital investment vary among the fifty states, the amounts vary from one country to another in the European Union.

LEGALLY SPEAKING

Drafting a Partnership Agreement

You and a friend decide to go into partnership to sell a new product. The following are some of the considerations to be included in your written partnership agreement:

1. Names and addresses of the general partners and the designation of partnership status
2. Name of the partnership and address of the principal place of business
3. Character of the business
4. Duration of the partnership
5. Contributions of the partners:
   a. Form of contribution
   b. Interest on contribution
   c. Additional contribution requirements
6. Assets of the partnership:
   a. Identification of the assets
   b. Valuation of the assets
   c. Control of the assets and accountability for them
   d. Distribution of the assets
7. Duties of the partners
8. Distribution of profits and losses
9. Compensation, benefits, and expenses of the partners
10. Policy and management of the business
11. Accounting practices and procedures
12. Liability and insurance requirements
13. Indemnity clause (to compensate for loss or to reimburse expenses)
14. Changes in the partners by withdrawal, retirement, death, mental illness, bankruptcy, or admission of additional partners
15. Sale or assignment of the partnership interest
16. Arbitration provisions
17. Amendment provisions
18. Dissolution, winding up, and termination of the partnership
19. Date of the agreement
20. Signatures of the partners.

With a well-drafted agreement, you should also be able to answer the following questions, which frequently arise:

✔ What happens if one partner fails to spend the required time in the business? For example, what happens if your partner goes to Europe for a six-month vacation?

✔ What happens if one partner becomes disabled or dies?

(continued)

✔ How will the profits and losses be shared?

✔ What happens if the business requires additional capital?

✔ How much time should each partner spend doing partnership business?

✔ Who should sign the checks and make the deposits?

Chapter Summary

Six forms of business organizations exist: sole proprietorship, partnership, limited partnership, limited liability company, limited liability partnership, and corporation. Concerns in selecting a type of business entity include the difficulty in forming it, limited liability, tax considerations, continuity of existence, transferability, management and control, financing, licenses, and location.

The sole proprietorship is the most informal business organization. A business's sole owner has unlimited liability and the business may cease to operate upon the owner's death or incapacity. No tax advantages exist for this form of ownership. It does, however, give maximum control of the business to the owner.

A general partnership allows people to join together to operate a business. No formal requirements exist to create a general partnership. Each partner has an equal right to manage the business. In the absence of an agreement, partners share profits and losses equally. Partners have unlimited liability for the partnership's debts. If a partner dies, becomes incapacitated, or otherwise leaves the partnership, the partnership dissolves. Dissolution means that the partnership union is discontinued, but

the business continues through the stages of winding up and termination.

The limited partnership must be organized in accordance with statutory provisions. All limited partnerships must have at least one general partner who manages the business's operation and one limited partner. If a limited partner takes an active role in managing, that limited partner assumes unlimited liability for the business's debts. Otherwise, a limited partner's only liability is his or her capital contribution. In a limited partnership, the general partner has unlimited liability. Profits are shared in accordance with the limited partnership certificate. If a partner dies, the limited partnership is not dissolved.

Like the limited partnership, the limited liability company and the limited liability partnership must follow state statutes when they form. Limited liability companies are treated as a partnership for tax purposes if they do not have the characteristics of a corporation. Both the LLC and the limited liability partnership have limited liability, which means that the investor's liability is limited to the amount that the person invested.

Using the World Wide Web

Commerce Clearing House (CCH) Incorporated, a major publisher of business material, maintains one of the more informative web sites that covers the different forms of organizations and the problems in forming a new business. It details considerations important to starting or purchasing a business.

The Small Business Administration (SBA) maintains a web site to aid small businesses. You learn about the SBA and where its offices are located in the United States. The SBA maintains an online library.

Finding the Law on the Web

Commerce Clearing House (CCH) Incorporated
http://www.cch.com
Commerce Clearing House Incorporated, Tool Kit
http://www.toolkit.cch.com/scripts/soho_toc.dll
Small Business Administration (SBA)
http://www.sbaonline.sba.gov/
Small Business Administration, Learn About the SBA
http://www.sba.gov/aboutsba/
Small Business Administration, Library
http://www.sbaonline.sba.gov/library/
Nolo
http://www.nolo.com/

Chapter Web Sites

Edward Lowe Foundation
     http://www.lowe.org/programs/about.htm
'Lectric Law Library
     http://www.lectlaw.com/bus.html
fambiz.com
     http://www.fambiz.com/
Free Advice
     http://www.freeadvice.com/
National Institute of Standards and Technology,
     Malcolm Baldrige Award
     http://www.baldrige.org/
Small Business Administration, Office of the
     National Ombudsman, Your Rights to Fair
     Regulatory Enforcement
     http://www.sbaonline.sba.gov/regfair/rights.html

Web Activities

18–1 An excellent web site that provides information about starting a business is <http://www.freeadvice.com/>. You also can find information about partnerships. Both of these are listed under Business Law. Does your business need to file a fictitious name statement?

18–2 Every business wants to be a quality company. The Malcolm Baldrige Award is named after Malcolm Baldrige who served from 1981 to 1987 as secretary of commerce under President Ronald W. Reagan (1980–1988). Secretary Baldrige died while serving in office (1922–1987). Go to the Malcolm Baldrige Award web site for the winners' list at <http://www.quality.nist.gov/winners/winlist.htm>. Which LLC company earned the award in 1999 and why?

Key Terms

articles of organization
dissociation
dissolution
fictitious name filing
general partner
limited liability company
    (LLC)
limited liability
    partnership

limited partner
limited partnership
manager
member
operating agreement
partnership
partnership by estoppel
pass-through tax
    treatment

Revised Uniform
    Limited Partnership
    Act (RULPA)
Revised Uniform
    Partnership Act
    (RUPA)
sole proprietorship
termination

Uniform Limited
    Partnership Act
    (ULPA)
Uniform Partnership
    Act (UPA)
use permit
variance
winding up

Questions and Case Problems

18–1 Choice of Business Organizations Lisa, Amy, and Mary are college graduates. Lisa has an idea for a new product that she believes could make the three of them very wealthy. Her idea is to manufacture beer dispensers for home use. Her goal is to market them to consumers throughout the Midwest. Lisa's personal experience qualifies her to be both first-line supervisor and general manager of the new firm. Amy is a born salesperson. Mary has little interest in sales or management, but would like to invest a large sum of money that she has inherited from her aunt. Based on this information, which form of business organization should Lisa, Amy, and Mary consider adopting?

18–2 Limited Liability Assume that Mary, in Question 18–1, is willing to put her inherited money into the business, but that she wants no further liability should the beer dispenser manufacturing business fail. The bank will lend capital at a 9 percent interest rate, but only if certain restrictions are placed on management decisions. The restrictions are unsatisfactory to Amy and Lisa, so the two decide to bring Mary into the business instead of using the bank. Under these circumstances, discuss the types of business organizations best suited to meet Mary's needs.

18–3 Limited Liability The limited liability aspect of the corporation or limited partnership is one of the most important reasons that firms choose to organize as corporations or limited partnerships rather than as general partnerships or sole proprietorships. Limited liability means that if a corporation or limited partnership is unable to meet its obligations with corporate or partnership assets, creditors will not be allowed to look to the owners (stockholders) of the corporation or the limited partners to satisfy their claims. Assume that Lisa and Amy (from Question 18–1) do not have a wealthy friend like Mary who wants to go into business with them and that therefore they must borrow money from a bank to start their business. Lisa and Amy decide to incorporate. What do you think a bank will ask them to sign when they seek a loan? What effect does this bank loan have on the "advantage" of limited liability under corporations?

18–4 Partnership Able, Baker, and Carlton have formed a twenty-year partnership to purchase land, develop it, manage it, and then sell the property. The partnership agreement calls for the partners to devote full time to the business. Assume that each of the following events takes place:

a. After two years, Baker and Carlton agree that the partnership's working hours will be from 8:00 A.M. to 6 P.M. rather than the previously established schedule of 9 A.M. to 5 P.M. Able refuses to work before 9 A.M. and quits promptly at 5 P.M.

b. After two years, Able quits the partnership.

c. After two years, Able becomes insolvent.

d. After two years, Able dies.

Discuss fully which of these acts constitutes a dissolution and what types of liability, if any, Able faces.

18–5 Dissolution of Partnership Rosita and Jorge formed a partnership. At the time of formation, Rosita's capital contribution was $10,000 and Jorge's was $15,000. Later, Rosita made a $10,000 loan to the partnership when it needed working capital. The partnership agreement provides that profits are to be shared, with 40 percent for Rosita and 60 percent for Jorge. The partnership is dissolved by Jorge's death. At the end of the dissolution and winding up of the partnership, the partnership's assets are $50,000. The partnership's general creditor debts are $8,000. Discuss fully how the assets will be distributed.

18–6 Limited Partnership Zhang and Zook form a limited partnership, with Zhang as the general partner and Zook as the limited partner. Zook puts up $15,000.

Zhang contributes some office equipment that he owns. They properly file a certificate of limited partnership and begin business. One month later, Zhang becomes ill. Instead of hiring someone to manage the business, Zook takes over complete management himself. While Zook is in control, he contracts with Abba for a large sum of money. Zhang returns to work. Because of other commitments, the Abba contract is breached. Abba contends that he can hold Zhang and Zook personally liable if the amount owed him cannot be satisfied out of the assets of the limited partnership. Discuss this contention.

18–7 What Is a Partnership? Oddo and Ries entered into a partnership agreement in March 1978 to create and publish a book describing how to restore F-100 pickup trucks. Oddo was to write the book and Ries was to provide the capital. Oddo supplied Ries with the manuscript, but Ries was dissatisfied and hired someone else to revise the manuscript. Ries published the book, which contained substantial amounts of Oddo's work. Did Ries's actions constitute a dissolution of the partnership? Can Oddo require Ries to account formally for the profits on the book? Explain. [*Oddo v. Ries*, 743 F.2d 630 (9th Cir. 1984)]

18–8 Liability Southland Construction, Inc., brought action against Thomas Richeson, individually as an engineer, and also against his business, Richeson, LLC, for negligence and breach of contract in failing to design a wall in a manner conforming to professional engineering standards. As the general contractor for the apartment project, Southland hired the firm of Richeson, LLC, to design a retaining wall. Richeson, individually, drew the engineering drawings and signed them for his LLC. Southland alleged that the wall's design was inconsistent with proper procedures, resulting in its cracking. Southland spent $188,000 to repair the damaged wall. The trial court dismissed Richeson as an individual from the case and Southland appealed. Was only the LLC liable for the cracked wall or were both the LLC and Richeson liable? Explain your answer. [*Southland Construction, Inc. v. Richeson Corporation*, 642 So. 2d 5 (Fla App. 1994)]

18–9 Partnership by Estoppel Paramount Steamship Company owned the *Courtney D*, a seagoing vessel. Paramount Petroleum Corp. was in the oil business. Both companies belonged to the same shareholders, operated out of the same address, and had the same accountant. Receptionists at either company answered the telephones by saying "Paramount." The *Courtney D* required extensive repairs. Taylor Rental Center extended credit on equipment to make these repairs. When Taylor was not paid, it sued both Paramount corporations. Can both Paramount corporations be held liable under the theory of partnership by estoppel? Explain. [*Paramount Petroleum Corp. v. Taylor Rental Center,* 712 S.W.2d 534 (Tex. Ct. App. 1986)]

18–10 Internet Small businesses can run afoul of regulations issued by various administrative agencies. The Small Business Administration (SBA) has a web site that offers information to small businesses. One bureau in the SBA is the Office of the National Ombudsman. Its web site, entitled "Your Rights to Fair Regulatory Enforcement," found at <http://www.sbaonline.sba.gov/regfair/rights.html>, offers small businesses information on their rights. Agencies must establish policies for small businesses when they have violated a regulation. What should an agency include in its policy?

Chapter 19

Corporate Law and Franchising Law

> *A corporation is an artificial being, invisible, intangible, and existing only in contemplation of law.*
>
> *Dartmouth College v. Woodward,*
> **17 U.S. (4 Wheat.) 518, 4 L. Ed. 629, 1819**
> **Chief Justice John Marshall, 1755–1835**
> **Fourth chief justice of the United States of America, 1801–1835**

Outline

Ethical Consideration

Corporate Giving: Whose Money Is It? The Corporation's or the Shareholders'?

You are the president of a highly successful corporation. You believe that business leaders have a civic duty to take significant leadership roles in community affairs. Involvement as a community leader helps to promote the corporation, although the benefit is difficult to measure. In addition to taking time from your corporate duties to attend meetings and appear at functions, your office staff and management team support community activities. The corporation also donates significantly to public programs.

At a recent shareholders' meeting, several shareholders questioned your right as the president to use work time, corporate staff, and corporate funds to assist in community endeavors. They believe that you should use your "free time" for community work and donate to charities from your own assets. These shareholders believe that rather than the corporation donating time and money, it should pay larger dividends. They also believe that each shareholder should decide the charities, if any, they prefer the corporation to support. Do you continue your community involvement on corporate time and keep the corporate donation programs? Use the ethical model presented in Chapter 2 and reprinted on the inside front cover to develop your answer.

Introduction

The corporate form is the most important type of business organization in the United States. Although corporations are the most formal type, they offer many advantages over other forms of business entities.

A **corporation** is a separate legal entity owned by shareholders. Corporations generally are characterized by two or more persons carrying on a business for profit, with centralized management, continuity of existence, limited liability for the shareholders, and freely transferable shares.

The corporate organizational structure is well suited to a public offering of securities and a listing on a stock exchange. Any publicly offered securities are subject to federal and/or state securities laws, discussed in Chapter 20. Most corporations, the majority of which are small businesses, are not listed on any stock exchange.

In the past centuries, individuals owned most businesses. A person who wanted to create a corporation had to obtain a charter from the state legislature. Even in the early 1800s, states did not look fondly on corporations and placed many restrictions on them. During the twentieth century, the states became more flexible, not only in creating corporations, but in allowing corporations to conduct a variety of businesses.

Your decided to incorporate your online business, Artiste Login Products, Inc., because incorporation offers tax advantages and longevity for your business.

Ease of Formation

Corporations are formed under state law. Most states have adopted one of two model provisions into statutes. Some states use the **Model Business Corporation Act (MBCA)**, while others use the **Revised Model Business Corporation Act (RMBCA)**. No state has adopted all the original provisions in either act.

The MBCA was originally proposed in 1933 and modified in 1969. In response to demands for different forms of corporations and for simpler procedures, the RMBCA was issued in 1984. Most state legislatures, however, greatly modified the MBCA or RMBCA to reflect their respective state's history. Although the major provisions of the MBCA and RMBCA have been adopted by many states, the corporate statutes vary greatly from state to state. The following discussion references the RMBCA.

Incorporators are the people who start the corporation. They choose the state in which to charter their corporation. Most states allow a business to incorporate in one state but to locate its principal place of business elsewhere, as long as the corporation maintains a registered office in the state in which it is incorporated. A corporation is a **domestic corporation** in the state in which it originally incorporated. A corporation files as a **foreign corporation** in all other states in which it will do business. An **alien corporation** is one that comes from outside the United States to do business within the United States.

LEGAL HIGHLIGHT

The Model Business Corporation Act and the Revised Model Business Corporation Act

The Model Business Corporation Act (MBCA) is a codification of modern corporation law. A model statute is created with the understanding that it may need amendments or changes to reflect local interests, needs, or problems, but it is presented for various jurisdictions to draw on in forming their decisions concerning corporate law.

The MBCA first was published in its complete form in 1933 by the Committee on Corporate Laws of the American Bar Association. It was patterned after the Illinois Business Corporation Act of 1933. The act was drafted, in part, in response to the tumultuous history of corporations in the United States prior to that time. The corporate form of business organization is common today, but it was rare until after the Civil War (1861–1865). Until the late 1800s, the states granted the corporate status sparingly and only when the grant seemed necessary to procure some specific benefit for the community.

The corporate form was limited because people distrusted the sheer size of a corporation. People feared the disastrous effects on the community's economic life, because corporations embody a concentration of economic power. People believed that corporations could easily swallow up small individual businesses, could virtually enslave labor, and, thus, dominate the state.

Even when the use of the corporate structure eventually was permitted for more general business purposes, the states placed severe restrictions on the size and scope of its use. The states limited the scope of the corporation's powers and activities, established a maximum duration for corporations, and required state residence as a prerequisite to incorporation.

By the turn of the century, however, a number of states removed these safeguards from their incorpora-tion statutes to capture the significant revenue raised by charging fees to grant corporate charters. If a state had permissive corporate laws, more corporations would incorporate in the state. For example, New Jersey permitted a New York corporation to incorporate under New Jersey's more permissive laws and yet operate principally in New York.

The constant rivalry among the states competing for revenues and control created notable inconsistencies in corporate law among the states and substantial confusion in the courts.[a] The MBCA filled the need for uniformity in corporate law. Since 1933, the act as undergone several changes and last was revised and renumbered in 1969.

The Revised Model Business Corporation Act (RMBCA) of 1984 served as a convenient guide for the states to revise their respective state corporation acts. It was designed for use by both publicly held and closely held corporations and includes provisions for the rights and duties of shareholders, management, and directors. A number of states have amended their corporation laws, to a limited degree, based on the RMBCA.

Neither the revised and renumbered 1969 act nor the 1984 act has been adopted totally by any state. These acts, however, have influenced the codification of corporate statutes in most states. Considerable variation exists among the state statutes based on these two acts. When making a business decision, the corporation must rely on the individual state statutes and not on the model acts as published by the National Conference of Commissioners on Uniform State Laws.

---

[a] The intense competition among the states to attract corporate charters is vividly described by Justice Louis Brandeis (1856–1941), associate justice (1916-1939), in *Louis K. Ligget Co. v. Lee*, 288 U.S. 517, 548-564; 53 S. Ct. 483, 490-496; 77 L. Ed. 929, 944-953 (1933).

Incorporators look for favorable state corporate and tax codes and also consider the state's case law interpreting its corporate code. The more developed the state's law, the more the corporation can anticipate the legal consequences of its actions.

Incorporators frequently hire a **promoter**, who makes contacts for and takes preliminary steps to organize the corporation. Unless a promoter specifically limits his liability in the contract by requiring parties to look to the corporation yet to be formed, the promoter bears personal liability for all preincorporation contracts. These contracts can include the purchase or lease of land, contracts to construct buildings, the purchase of equipment and inventory, and even financing agreements with third parties. Even after the corporation forms, the promoter remains personally liable until the corporation, through its board of directors, assumes responsibility for the contracts by adopting them as contracts of the corporation.

Articles of Incorporation

The first step in formalizing a corporation's creation is a public filing. As part of the initial incorporation process, the incorporators must file **articles of incorporation** with a designated state office, such as the office of the secretary of state. Once the state approves the articles of incorporation, it issues a corporate charter. The charter may be a separate piece of paper issued by the state; most states today return the articles of incorporation stamped "incorporated" and the stamped articles serve as the charter.

The articles provide basic information about the corporation and serve as the primary source of authority for its future operations. The articles of incorporation are analogous to a constitution for the corporation. Specific requirements vary somewhat from state to state. Basically, however, the articles of incorporation include the following:

1. The name of the corporation
2. The purpose of the corporation, which may be stated in a general way in order to include all lawful business
3. The duration of the corporation, which is almost always perpetual
4. The date and time of the commencement of corporate existence, which usually starts with the filing of the articles with the secretary of state or which may be set by statute
5. The number of shares that the corporation has the authority to issue, which often includes a list of the various classes of shares, their rights and limitations, and the capital allowed to start business
6. The address of the corporation's registered office and the name of its registered agent in the state
7. The number of members on the first board of directors and, where required, their names

and addresses and the name and address of each incorporator
8. The shareholders' preemptive rights (the rights of existing shareholders to purchase newly issued stock to maintain their position of control and financial interest in the corporation, if any).

In many states, only one incorporator is required, and the incorporator may be a natural person, a corporation, a partnership, a limited partnership, or a limited liability company. The corporation's name must include the word *corporation, incorporated, company, limited,* or an abbreviation of one of these words. Exhibit 19–1 shows sample articles of incorporation.

Bylaws

After the charter has been issued, the corporation is formed. The incorporator or incorporators elect the board of directors. In many states, the board of directors may consist of only one person. The initial board then meets and, among other things, adopts the corporation's **bylaws**. The bylaws must conform with the state corporate code and its articles of incorporation.

If the articles of incorporation are considered to be equivalent to a constitution, the bylaws are equivalent to statutes. Just as the constitution (articles of incorporation) is the basic governing document and is hard to change, statutes (bylaws) carry out the constitution's guidelines and are easier to change.

The bylaws set forth the internal management rules for the corporation, typically including what constitutes a quorum (minimum number of members who must be present at a meeting in order to take valid actions), voting requirements for shareholders and directors, the requirements for election of the **directors** and **officers** and the terms for which each will serve, the officers' duties, and similar provisions.

Source of Funding

A corporation can raise money in several ways. The two most common are (1) to sell a part ownership in the corporation by issuing *equity securities* and (2) to borrow money by issuing *debt securities*.

A corporation commonly acquires funds by accepting offers to buy an interest in it. The corporation sends to the purchaser either paper or electronic stock

Exhibit 19–1 Sample Articles of Incorporation

State *of* Delaware
Certificate *of* Incorporation
A Stock Corporation

- **First:** The name of this Corporation is _____
_____

- **Second:** Its registered office in the State of Delaware is to be located at _____
_____ Street, in the City of _____
County of _____ Zip Code _____.
The registered agent in charge thereof is _____
_____
_____

- **Third:** The purpose of the corporation is to engage in any lawful act or activity for which corporations may be organized under the General Corporation Law of Delaware.

- **Fourth:** The amount of the total authorized capital stock of this corporation is
_____ Dollars ($ _____) divided into _____ shares of
_____ Dollars ($ _____) each.

- **Fifth:** The name and mailing address of the incorporator are as follows:
Name _____
Mailing Address _____
_____ Zip Code _____

- **I, The Undersigned,** for the purpose of forming a corporation under the laws of the State of Delaware, do make, file and record this Certificate, and do certify that the facts herein stated are true, and I have accordingly hereunto set my hand this _____ day of _____, A.D. 20_____.

BY: _____
(Incorporator)

NAME: _____
(Type or Print)

---

certificates that represent an ownership interest. Usually, an individual never sees the stock certificates, because they are held by the brokerage firm. This ownership interest in a corporation, represented by stock, is known as an **equity security**.

A corporation also may raise money by borrowing it. Often, a corporation issues **bonds** (which represent a long-term debt). Bonds may be secured by the business's assets or the bonds may be unsecured. Unsecured bonds are called **debentures**. Bonds are **debt securities** that represent a corporate obligation.

Equity Securities versus Debt Securities

Differences exist between equity securities (shares in the corporation) and debt securities (evidence of borrowed money). With an equity security, if the value of the shares increases, the shareholders can profit from the increased valuation as owners of the corporation. If the value of the shares decreases, the shareholders lose the equity and may even lose their entire investment.

A debt security is treated like any loan. With a debt security, the holder knows that he will receive interest paid at a specific rate, such as 10 percent, on the loan. If the corporation dissolves, the debt holders always have a higher priority for repayment than the equity holders when the assets are sold.

Equity Securities

Equity securities are represented by share certificates in a corporation. Equity securities represent ownership and, usually, voting rights. Over the centuries, a wide variety of equity securities have developed. Exhibit 19–2 lists most of the different types of equity securities. The following sections discuss two types of stock, common and preferred, in more detail.

Common Stock. The most commonly held equity security is common stock. The owners of **common stock** generally have the right to vote to elect directors; to amend the articles of incorporation; to

amend the bylaws, if the articles so provide; and to decide other major corporate matters. The shareholder also has a right to a share of the corporation's profits proportionate to the number of shares owned, if the board of directors declares a dividend. Common stock generally has no fixed dividend rate and does not carry with it any inherent right to have a dividend declared, even when the corporation is profitable.

On dissolution and liquidation of a corporation, the shareholders have a right to a proportionate share of the assets after the creditors' claims have been satisfied. Unless stock is redeemed (repurchased) by the corporation, the shares have an indefinite duration.

Preferred Stock. Although **preferred stock** generally is considered an equity security, from an investment standpoint it also bears certain similarities to a debt security. Preferred stock offers various designated

Exhibit 19–2 Types and Definitions of Equity Securities

Types	Definitions
Common stock	Owners of common stock receive the lowest priority with respect to dividends paid and to the distribution of assets on dissolution of the corporation.
Preferred stock	Shares of preferred stock have priority over common stock shares as to payment of dividends and distribution of assets on corporate dissolution. Dividend payments are usually a fixed percentage of the face value of the share.
Cumulative preferred stock	With this type of preferred stock, a required dividend not paid in a given year must be paid in a subsequent year before any common stock dividends are paid.
Participating preferred stock	Owners of participating preferred stock first receive agreed to dividends and then receive the same distribution of dividends that is paid on common stock.
Convertible preferred stock	Convertible preferred stock gives holders the option to convert their shares into a specified number of common shares either in the issuing corporation or, sometimes, in another corporation.
Redeemable (callable) preferred stock	Redeemable preferred shares are issued with the express preferred stock condition that the issuing corporation has the right to repurchase the shares as specified.
Authorized shares	Authorized shares are allowed to be issued by the articles of incorporation.
Issued shares	Issued shares are transferred to shareholders.
Outstanding shares	Authorized and issued shares that are still held by shareholders are outstanding shares.
Treasury shares	Treasury shares are authorized and issued but are not outstanding (reacquired by the corporation).
No par value shares	No par value shares are issued without any stated value. The price usually is fixed by the board of directors or the shareholders.
Par value shares	Par value shares are issued and priced at a stated value per share.

preferences that the articles of incorporation establish. Generally, payment of preferred stock dividends carries a preference over dividends paid to common stockholders and often pays dividends at a fixed rate.

When a corporation is dissolved and the assets sold and converted to money, preferred shareholders often have priority over common shareholders. If the corporation is not profitable and preferred dividends cannot be paid, some preferred stock, called **cumulative preferred stock**, carries the right to accumulate the unpaid dividend. This right means that if, in the future, a dividend is declared, the preferred stockholder receives the previous unpaid dividend before any common stockholders receive payment of dividends.

Preferred stockholders may or may not have voting rights on some corporate issues. Usually, voting rights are reserved strictly for common shareholders; if dividends have not been paid to the preferred shareholders, however, then they have a right to vote in many situations. On liquidation, the debt securities and other debts of the corporation are paid first. Then, depending on provisions in the articles of incorporation, the value of the preferred stock may be paid to its holders before holders of common stock receive any payments. Preferred stock dividends paid by the corporation are not deductible as an interest expense (treated as an equity security) for corporate income tax purposes.

A corporation must be careful not to sell more stock than is authorized in its articles of incorporation. In the following case, the officers and directors of the corporation were found liable after the corporation issued too many shares of stock.

Case 19.1

Agosta v. Southwest Breeders, Inc.

Court of Appeals of
Oklahoma, 1991
810 P.2d 377

BACKGROUND AND FACTS The articles of incorporation for Southwest Breeders Inc., allowed the corporation to issue no more than 50,000 shares of its stock at $1.00 per share. On March 31, 1986, Agosta purchased 15,000 shares.

Agosta later discovered that on December 27, 1985, the officers and directors of Southwest Breeders issued 1,370,000 shares at below-par value to themselves. These shares were clearly in excess of the amount allowed by the articles of incorporation.

Sometime after March 31, Southwest Breeders filed an amendment to its articles of incorporation with the secretary of state, which authorized it to increase the number of shares from 50,000 to 50 million. The state issued an amended certificate of incorporation.

Agosta filed suit to rescind the contract, seeking $6,000 in damages for purchase of the overissued stock. The trial court determined that the sale of the overissued stock to Agosta constituted a sale of nonexistent stock for which the directors were personally liable.

Chief Judge HUNTER

. . . .

A corporation whose capital is limited by its charter either in amount or in the number of shares, cannot issue valid certificates in excess of the limit prescribed. . . . Certificates of stock issued in violation of statute are wholly valueless and void, without regard to the intent of the parties to the overissue.
. . . .

Generally, officers of a corporation are not liable to third persons for corporate acts where they do not purport to bind themselves. . . . However, it is also true that officers and agents of the corporation may be held personally liable by the purchaser for a fraudulent issue of stock or stock issued in violation of the law. 18A [American Jurisprudence, 2d] Corporations, section 515, states, in part:

It is said that in authenticating and issuing certificates the officers represent that the stock is not spurious and is not invalid by reason of fraudulent or known acts or omissions of such officers, and such representations are addressed to whoever should thereafter purchase the certificate.

In this case, the participation of these officers by their acts in negotiating the sale of the stock and by signing the certificates represented to Agosta that the stock was valid and bound them by their false representations.

DECISION AND REMEDY The court found that the officers personally were liable for the over-issued stock that later was found to be invalid.

CRITICAL THINKING: MANAGEMENT CONSIDERATION In this case, the articles later were amended to allow the sale of a larger number of shares. Why then should the members of the board of directors be held personally liable when they would not have been liable if they sold the stock after the articles were amended?

Debt Securities

Different forms of debt exist, including secured bonds and debentures. Both represent a long-term commitment to repay the creditor. The loan is made to the corporation based on its ability to repay the debt. A secured bond or debenture does not carry with it any right to control the corporation's management and usually does not offer any voting rights on other matters.

These obligations earn interest at fixed or variable rates of interest that is payable regardless of the corporation's profitability. They mature at a specified date, when the corporation must repay the principal. Generally, owners of these obligations have first claim against the corporation's assets on its liquidation. The holder of secured bonds has first claim against the assets that have been pledged.

Liability

The corporate form of business entity is favored because liability is limited for shareholders, directors, and officers. Liability may stem from creditors' claims or from a judgment against the corporation. The limit on liability offered by a corporation is not absolute, however.

Liability of Shareholders

If a creditor has a claim against the corporation, the claim must be satisfied from corporate assets. As a general rule, the shareholder has limited liability to the extent of her investment in the corporation. In other words, shareholders can lose, at the most, the amount that they have invested in stock, but their personal assets are insulated from the corporation's liabilities.

In some circumstances, especially with smaller corporations, when the corporation obtains a loan or enters into a contract, the creditor may require, in addition to the corporation's liability, a personal guarantee from the shareholders or officers. A personal guarantee means, of course, that the guarantor's personal assets are at risk if the corporation fails to meet its obligations.

In some circumstances, a court may **pierce the corporate veil** (ignore the corporate structure) and look to the shareholders' personal assets to satisfy corporate obligations. Several reasons exist as to why this might occur. First, the shareholder may have ignored the corporation's existence by failing to comply with the corporate formalities, such as holding meetings of the board of directors or keeping corporate minutes. Second, the shareholder may have commingled personal and corporate assets. The corporation may be regarded as merely the alter ego of the shareholder (that is, one cannot distinguish between the shareholder and the corporation). Third, the shareholder

LEGAL HIGHLIGHT

Some Costs of Conducting Business

Starting a business can involve significant costs. As you consider the following costs, remember that these are only the basic ones.

1. *Lawyers' fees* Fees can range from a minimum of $250 to $25,000 or more if the business is a corporation that must meet securities law requirements before issuing stock.

2. *Filing fees* The fees for filing the incorporation papers can range from a few dollars to several hundred dollars. Often, businesses other than corporations (such as limited partnerships) must pay fees associated with the filing of appropriate forms in various state or federal offices.

Once a business has been established, ongoing costs are significant. A few of these costs follow:

1. *Employer's contribution to Social Security* Payment of the nonrefundable employer's contribution to the federal Social Security system for all employees is mandatory. A self-employed person must pay the equivalent of both the employer's and employee's Social Security contributions.

2. *Worker's compensation* All businesses must provide coverage for their employees in the event that they are injured on the job.

3. *Unemployment insurance taxes* Payment of state unemployment insurance taxes for all employees is mandatory in all states.

4. *Annual legal and accounting fees* Businesses must keep accurate books both for tax purposes and as a good business practice. The books should be audited by a certified public accountant (CPA). Audit costs can range from several hundred dollars to thousands of dollars. Various forms must be filed on a monthly, quarterly, and annual basis. Corporate records and minute books must be maintained, usually by an accountant or a lawyer. Annual fees for such services can run into hundreds or thousands of dollars.

5. *Retirement plans* Although no state requires a business to provide retirement plans for its employees, if the business adopts such a plan, it must comply with the applicable federal and state requirements.

---

initially may have *undercapitalized* the corporation to such an extent that creditors are unable to collect against the corporation. **Undercapitalization** means that the corporation has insufficient capital (money and property) for a successful operation unless it is a bona fide loan.

Fourth, the shareholder, rather than investing capital, may make a loan and take a security interest in the corporate assets. By loaning money to the corporation, the shareholder becomes a creditor and has the same

standing as outside creditors. The courts will not allow a shareholder to circumvent the other creditors of the corporation.

Finally, any evidence that the corporation was used to perpetrate a fraud, to circumvent the law, or to accomplish some illegal objective may lead a court to disregard the corporate existence. In the following case, the court had to decide whether to disregard the corporate entity (pierce the corporate veil) and hold the shareholders' personally liable.

Case 19.2

Autrey v. 22 Texas Services, Inc.

United States District Court,
S.D. Texas, 2000
79 F. Supp. 2d 735

BACKGROUND AND FACTS The plaintiffs are the Estate of J. D. Autrey and his surviving widow and son. Autrey was a resident of one of the defendants' nursing homes, Caldwell, until shortly before his death. He allegedly died as a result of the negligence of the nursing home staff and administration.

Among the many defendants are Caldwell; 22 Texas Services, L.P.; 22 Texas Services, Inc.; Arizona Partners, Inc.; Venture 22 Corporation (Venture 22); John H. Durham; John P. Durham; Carol Durham; and Christine Bogrette. The ownership and management of the Caldwell nursing home was very complicated. Caldwell was one of forty-nine nursing homes in Texas owned by 22 Texas Services, L.P., a limited partnership formed under the laws of Texas.

22 Texas Services, L.P., has one general partner, 22 Texas Services, Inc., a Pennsylvania corporation. The limited partners of 22 Texas Services, L.P., are John P. Durham, who owns a 30 percent interest, John H. Durham, with a 21 percent interest, and others. Under the limited partnership agreement, general partner 22 Texas Services, Inc., owns a 1 percent interest in 22 Texas Services, L.P., but is solely responsible for conducting the partnership business and for liabilities arising out of the partnership business. John H. Durham and Carol Durham are the sole shareholders of 22 Texas Services, Inc.

CCS, Caldwell's management company, is a limited partnership formed under the laws of Pennsylvania. CCS has one general partner, Arizona Partners, Inc. CCS's limited partners are John H. Durham, John P. Durham, Christine Bogrette, and others as well as Venture 22 Corporation, of which John H. Durham is the sole shareholder. According to the limited partnership agreement, Arizona Partners has a 1 percent interest in CCS, but is responsible for the partnership business and the liabilities arising out of the partnership business. John P. Durham and Bogrette are the sole shareholders of Arizona Partners.

Arizona Partners, Inc., and 22 Texas Services, Inc., were both incorporated under the laws of Pennsylvania. Tax records indicate that Arizona Partners, which lists its business address at 120 Gibralter Road, neither pays rent or expenses for repairs or maintenance nor does it spend any money on advertising. Arizona Partners had no cash assets in 1996 or 1997, and in 1997, it reported a net worth of $42,132.

Tax records indicate that 22 Texas Services, Inc., which like Arizona Partners lists its address as 120 Gibralter Road, pays no rent or expenses for repair or maintenance, has no employees or expenses for employees, and pays no costs for advertising. In 1997, 22 Texas Services, Inc., showed total assets of $54,955; in 1997, it showed a total loss of $80,399.

The trial court had to decide whether it was appropriate to pierce the corporate veil and hold defendants John H. Durham, John P. Durham, Carol Durham, and Christine Bogrette individually liable for the injuries suffered by Autrey and his family.

KENT, District Judge

. . . .

Under Pennsylvania law, there is a strong presumption against piercing the corporate veil. . . . Factors to be considered in disregarding the corporate form include—but are not limited to—undercapitalization, failure to adhere to corporate formalities, substantial intermingling of corporate and personal affairs, and use of the corporate form to commit a fraud. Additionally, Pennsylvania law has long provided that the corporate veil may be pierced if justice and public policy would be served. The primary concerns for courts deciding whether to pierce the corporate veil are determining whether equity requires that the shareholders' "traditional insulation" from personal liability be disregarded and discerning whether the corporate form is essentially a sham.

. . . .

1. Arizona Partners, Inc.

. . . In this case, it is undisputed that Arizona Partners, Inc. had, at the time of the incident underlying this action, a net worth of approximately $42,000. In 1996 and 1997, the company operated with virtually no liquid assets. At the same time, the corporation assumed one hundred percent of the liability for the operation of not only forty-nine nursing homes in Texas but of numerous other facilities across the United States. At the outset, the Court notes that this financial condition raises disturbing questions regarding whether Arizona Partners, Inc. was set up to be financially responsible to potential creditors.

. . . .

The corporate structure of Arizona Partners, Inc. also suggests that the corporate veil should be pierced. At the time of incorporation, Arizona Partners had no employees, office space, or expenses; consequently, the company paid no rent and spent no money on advertising. What is more, the Court finds it suspicious that Arizona Partners, Inc. apparently had nonfunctioning corporate officers. . . . Thus, if Plaintiffs can prove at trial that Defendants asserted control over the management and ownership of the Texas nursing homes owned by Arizona Partners, Inc., it would add credence to their claim that Arizona Partners, Inc. represents nothing more than a corporate sham benefitting Defendants, all of whom serve as the sole shareholders of Arizona Partners, Inc.

2. 22 Texas Services, Inc.

The other corporate entity involved, 22 Texas Services, Inc., owns forty-nine nursing homes and assisted living facilities in Texas. As the sole general partner in 22 Texas Services, L.P., it is entitled to only one percent of the partnership profits even though once the assets of the partnership are extinguished it assumes one hundred percent of the partnership's liability. The evidence indicates, however, that six months after formation the net worth of 22 Texas Services, Inc. was negative, as it had more than $54,000 in liabilities with no accompanying net assets. Also noteworthy is the fact that the company was incorporated with an initial capitalization of only $25,000. Just like Arizona Partners, Inc., 22 Texas Services, Inc. pays no rent, has no employees or expenses. Unlike Arizona Partners, Inc., however, 22 Texas Services, Inc. has not paid a dividend to its shareholders. Based on the nature and risk of the nursing home business, the Court notes that engaging in the ownership of forty-nine nursing homes while also maintaining no net assets appears to amount to nothing less than a disputable issue regarding undercapitalization—but as noted previously it does not definitively resolve the issue. On that basis and for the reasons explained below, the Court will allow a jury to determine whether to disregard the corporate form of 22 Texas Services, Inc. Accordingly, the Court finds that a fact issue exists concerning whether actions taken by 22 Texas Services, Inc. should be imputed to its shareholders, Defendants John H. Durham, John P. Durham, Christine Bogrette, and Carol Durham for liability purposes.

. . . .

3. Has an Injustice Occurred?

Having concluded that a material factual issue surrounds whether Arizona Partners, Inc. and 22 Texas Services, Inc. had been undercapitalized, the Court next must consider whether piercing the corporate veil will prevent fraud or injustice. The Court accepts for the purposes of this summary judgment motion Plaintiffs' argument that Defendants' alleged effort to avoid personal liability by creating sham corporate shields, if proven at trial, constitutes the type of injustice that would satisfy that element of the standard for piercing the corporate veil. Because Plaintiffs' have challenged the legitimacy of Arizona Partners, Inc. and 22 Texas Services, Inc. with a sufficient amount of evidence, the Court rejects, for the time being, Defendants' argument that the corporate veil cannot be pierced as a matter of law. On the other hand, Plaintiffs also have failed to forward enough evidence to conclusively show that the corporate forms should be disregarded. Accordingly, both Defendants' and Plaintiffs' Motions for Summary Judgment as to Piercing the Corporate Veil are DENIED.

. . . .

DECISION AND REMEDY The plaintiffs brought forth enough evidence that provided a basis for a reasonable jury to pierce the corporate veils of 22 Texas Services, Inc., and Arizona Partners, Inc. The court decided that this issue should be one for a jury to decide.

CRITICAL THINKING: MANAGEMENT CONSIDERATION One of the advantages to forming a corporation is that the owner has limited liability. Why should a court ever hold a person who is not a shareholder liable when there is a valid corporation?

Liability of Directors and Officers

The directors and officers of a corporation are fiduciaries of the corporation and of its shareholders. A fiduciary relationship is based on trust and confidence. Directors are elected by the shareholders to the **board of directors**. The board is responsible for the corporation's overall policies and management. The board of directors hires officers to implement the management's policy and to oversee the corporation's daily operations. Directors and officers have three principal duties: obedience, loyalty, and care.

Duty of Obedience. The duty of obedience requires directors and officers to follow all statutes and regulations that govern the corporation's business. Further, they must abide by any limitations established in the articles of incorporation and the bylaws. Case 19.1, *Agosta v. Southwest Breeders, Inc.*, provides an example of a situation in which officers failed to obey the articles of incorporation. In that case, officers personally were held liable for failing to obey the limitation set out in the articles.

Duty of Loyalty. All employees, officers, and directors owe a fiduciary duty to the corporation. This duty prohibits them from making any secret profits at the corporation's expense.

The corporate personnel cannot take advantage of information obtained concerning business contracts or involving the potential purchase by the corporation of real estate or other assets. They cannot purchase property, then sell it to the corporation without full disclosure. Upon leaving the corporation, they cannot use trade secrets obtained while they were involved with the corporation.

Duty of Care. Directors and officers also have the duty of care to the corporation. They must act (1) in good faith, (2) with the care of an ordinary prudent person in a comparable position and under similar circumstances, and (3) in a manner that is reasonably believed to be in the corporation's best interests. If a director or officer possesses special qualifications, such as certification as a public accountant, she must exercise the higher standard required by the professional designation.

Applications of Duties. Directors and officers must perform their duties in good faith and in a manner that they reasonably believe to be in the corporation's best interest. Although the officers and directors of the corporation are not guarantors of its success, they must perform their duties.

In performing their duties, they are entitled to rely on information presented by officers or employees of the corporation whom they reasonably believe to be reliable and competent in the matters presented. Directors of corporations that must register with the Securities and Exchange Commission (SEC) have a greater exposure to liability, because they are ultimately responsible for compliance with SEC rules.

Directors may not rely on information provided by officers and employees if the directors have knowledge or expertise that would make such a reliance unwarranted. Directors must diligently seek information. They must act with the care that a reasonably prudent person in a comparable position would use under similar circumstances. If a director complies with this standard, he will not be held liable simply for holding the position of director.

Directors and officers must deal honestly and in good faith in guiding the corporation. The law allows them wide latitude in making valid business decisions. The law will not hold directors and officers liable for honest errors in business decisions if they made these decisions with the correct motives and in good faith. This law is referred to as the **business judgment rule**. The decisions must be within the powers of the corporation and the resulting actions must be exercised with due care.

The test of the decisions made by directors and officers is objective. They must exercise the same degree of care that reasonably prudent people use in the conduct of their own business affairs to avoid personal liability. To satisfy this test, the directors and officers must act in good faith and on an informed basis. They must believe that their action was in the best interests of the corporation.

Directors must act in the best interests of the corporation as a whole, rather than on behalf of any individual or group of shareholders. Because they are fiduciaries, the directors and officers of a corporation may not usurp business opportunities that legitimately belong to the company itself. When a business opportunity would be of interest to the company, the directors or officers, in good faith, may take advantage of the opportunity only if the company is unable to do so and only if the directors or officers are not in direct competition with the company.

The business judgment rule has been reexamined by several courts because of mergers and buyouts of large corporations. The following case applied the business judgment rule.

Case 19.3

Paramount Communications, Inc. v. Time, Inc.

Supreme Court of Delaware, 1990

571 A.2d 1140

BACKGROUND AND FACTS In the early 1980s, the Time, Inc., executive board began considering expansion of Time's operations into the entertainment industry. By 1987, Time had established a special committee to consider and propose corporate strategies for the 1990s. First, Time wanted better control over the quality and price of the film products delivered to its subsidiaries, Home Box Office and Cinemax. Second, Time was concerned with the increasing globalization of the world economy.

By late spring of 1987, representatives from Time and Warner Brothers met to discuss the possibility of a joint venture. In July 1988, Time's board of directors met to consider expansion into the entertainment industry on a global scale and heard profiles for Warner, Disney, 20th Century Fox, Universal, and Paramount.

The board approved the strategic plan for Time's expansion. The board gave management the right to continue discussions with Warner about a possible merger. After extensive negotiations, on March 3, 1989, Time's board unanimously approved a stock-for-stock merger with Warner and a new name, Time-Warner, Inc.

On June 7, 1989, Paramount Communications, Inc., made a surprise all-cash offer to purchase all outstanding shares of Time for $175 per share. Time's stock rose the next day from $126 to $170 per share. After many meetings and negotiations, Time's board, on June 16, formally rejected Paramount's offer. At the same meeting, Time's board decided to acquire Warner for all cash for 51 percent of Warner's outstanding stock at $70 per share. This action did not require shareholder approval. To provide the funds, Time agreed to assume $7 billion to $10 billion worth of debt.

On June 23, Paramount raised its all-cash offer to $200 per share. On June 26, Time's board formally rejected this second offer. The board believed Paramount's offer to be inadequate and that the Warner transaction offered a greater long-term value for the stockholders. It also perceived Paramount's offer to be a threat to the "Time Culture" and its editorial freedom because Time would be the acquired company. During the negotiations with Warner and with Paramount, Time was adamant about preserving the "Time culture" and its editorial freedom.

Paramount and some of Time's shareholders instituted this lawsuit. In the lower court, the chancellor (judge) wrote a fifty-page opinion in which he refused to enjoin Time's purchase of Warner's stock. Paramount appealed.

Justice HORSEY

. . . .

The principal ground for reversal, asserted by all plaintiffs, is that Paramount's June 7, 1989 uninvited all-cash, all-shares, "fully negotiable" (though conditional) tender offer [offer to purchase] for Time triggered duties under *Unocal Corp. v. Mesa Petroleum Co.,* and that Time's board of directors, in responding to Paramount's offer, breached those duties. As a consequence, plaintiffs argue that in our review of the Time board's decision of June 16, 1989 to enter into a revised merger agreement with Warner, Time is not entitled to the benefit and protection of the business judgment rule.

. . . .

We turn now to plaintiffs' *Unocal* claim. We begin by noting, as did the Chancellor, that our decision does not require us to pass on the wisdom of the board's decision to enter into the original Time–Warner agreement. That is not a court's task. Our task is simply to review the record to determine whether there is sufficient evidence to support the Chancellor's conclusion that the initial Time–Warner agreement was the product of a proper exercise of business judgment.

. . . .

In *Unocal*, we held that before the business judgment rule is applied to a board's adoption of a defensive measure, the burden will lie with the board to prove (a) reasonable grounds for believing that a danger to corporate policy and effectiveness existed; and (b) that the defensive measure adopted was reasonable in relation to the threat posed. Directors satisfy the first part of the *Unocal* test by demonstrating good faith and reasonable investigation. We have repeatedly stated that the refusal to entertain an offer may comport with a valid exercise of a board's business judgment.

. . . .

Plaintiffs' position represents a fundamental misconception of our standard of review under *Unocal* principally because it would involve the court in substituting its judgment as to what is a "better" deal for that of a corporation's board of directors.

The usefulness of *Unocal* as an analytical tool is precisely its flexibility in the face of a variety of fact scenarios. *Unocal* is not intended as an abstract standard; neither is it a structured and mechanistic procedure of appraisal. Thus, we have said that directors may consider, evaluating the threat posed by a takeover bid, the inadequacy of the price offered, nature and timing of the offer, questions of illegality, the impact on constituencies other than shareholders, the risk of non-consummation, and the quality of securities being offered in the exchange.

. . . .

We turn to the second part of the *Unocal* analysis. The obvious requisite to determining the reasonableness of a defensive action is a clear identification of the nature of the threat. As the Chancellor correctly noted, this "requires an evaluation of the importance of the corporate objective threatened; alternative methods of protecting that objective; impacts of the 'defensive' action, and other relevant factors." It is not until both parts of the *Unocal* inquiry have been satisfied that the business judgment rule attaches to defensive actions of a board of directors. As applied to the facts of this case, the question is whether the record evidence supports the Court of Chancery's conclusion that the restructuring of the Time-Warner transaction, including the adoption of several preclusive defensive measures, was a *reasonable response* in relation to a perceived threat.

. . . Delaware law confers the management of the corporate enterprise to the stockholders' duly elected board representatives. The fiduciary duty to manage a corporate enterprise includes the selection of a time frame for achievement of corporate goals. That duty may not be delegated to the stockholders. Directors are not obliged to abandon a deliberately conceived corporate plan for a short-term shareholder profit unless there is clearly no basis to sustain the corporate strategy.

. . . .

We affirm the Chancellor's rulings as clearly supported by the record. Finally, we note that although Time was required, as a result of Paramount's hostile offer, to incur a heavy debt [$7 billion to $10 billion] to finance its acquisition of Warner, that fact alone does not render the board's decision unreasonable so long as the directors could reasonably perceive the debt load not to be so injurious to the corporation as to jeopardize its well being.

DECISION AND REMEDY Time prevailed in this case. A tender offer is made by a group of investors to purchase the stock of a particular company at a fixed price per share in order for the group to gain control over the company. In this case, the court found that Paramount's tender offer was reasonably perceived by Time's board to pose a threat to Time and that the board's response to that threat was reasonable. The court rejected the argument that the only corporate threat posed by an all-shares all-cash offer was the possibility of inadequate value. The threat was to the very life of "Time culture" and editorial freedom.

CRITICAL THINKING: MANAGEMENT CONSIDERATION Assume that you are a member of a board of directors for a large corporation. How would you protect yourself from potential liability because of your position?

Control

In theory, one of the characteristics of a corporation is centralized management. Directors set policy for the corporation and hire the officers to run the corporation on a day-to-day basis. An officer also can be a director of the corporation.

The usual officer positions are the president, at least one vice-president, the secretary, and the treasurer. Under the MBCA, a person may hold more than one office, but cannot serve as both president and secretary. Corporate officers can be removed by the board of directors at any time, with or without cause and without shareholder approval. A wrongful dismissal can result in liability for breach of contract. The RMBCA, however, does not require any specific officers and leaves it to the corporation to determine this issue.

Shareholders' Control

The shareholders elect the directors and have voting rights on major corporate matters, such as amending the articles of incorporation, deciding to merge or consolidate with another corporation, opting to sell all or substantially all of the corporate assets, or dissolving the corporation. The controlling shareholders, also called majority shareholders, own enough of the stock to control actions that the corporation will take through their voting rights. Minority shareholders have insufficient voting shares to control the corporation.

When transferring their shares, majority shareholders have a fiduciary duty to the corporation and to the minority shareholders, a duty similar to that of directors and officers. A controlling shareholder may dispose of his stock and receive a premium price for the ability to control. The controlling shareholder, however, may not sell control of the corporation if a reasonably prudent person would foresee the possibility of mismanagement by the purchaser.

Generally, in the absence of extraordinary circumstances, such as fraud or detriment to the corporation, courts hold that directors, officers, and controlling shareholders may buy and sell their shares without including, or even making disclosures to, minority shareholders.

Minority shareholders receive some protection through bylaws or restrictions stamped on the stock certificate. This protection may include requiring a majority shareholder, director, or officer to give notice of sale or purchase to minority shareholders, or providing the right of first refusal (to be discussed later) to purchase the shares being sold to the minority shareholders or the corporation.

Close Corporation Control

Shares of a **close corporation** are closely held by family members or by comparatively few persons. Close corporations often are referred to as *closed, closely held, family,* or *privately held corporations.* The members know one another personally. Because the number of shareholders is so small, frequently no trading market exists for these shares. In practice, these corporations operate like partnerships.

In a close corporation, the question of who controls the business is very important. To maintain control, it is said that a person always should try to obtain 51 percent, accept 50 percent, but should never accept 49 percent or less of common stock. In a close corporation, the board of directors can be one person. That person controls the corporation, because the board of directors appoints officers and establishes the budget, including the amount to be paid in salaries and fringe benefits.

Some rights are reserved to the minority shareholder. One is the right to receive information about the business's value if the minority shareholder sells her interest to the majority shareholder. The following case considers this problem.

Case 19.4

Van Schaack Holdings, LTD v. Van Schaack

Supreme Court of Colorado, 1994

867 P.2d 892

BACKGROUND AND FACTS The Van Schaack Corporation (VSC) owned 29,000 acres of Colorado farmland known as the Box Elder land. Mrs. Van Schaack owned 750 shares of VSC stock. She was not on VSC's board of directors but did receive the annual shareholder letter that included VSC's audited financial statements. In 1982, she wanted to sell her stock, the value of which was almost exclusively determined by the value of the land. She was interested in the present per-acre value and future events that might affect that value, particularly the new Denver International Airport, which would be located on or near the Box Elder land. One director told her that "no way" would the new airport be located on Box Elder land.

Mrs. Van Schaack did not know that at a VSC board of directors meeting in 1980, the board concluded that the Box Elder land would benefit from the relocation of the Denver airport, and by 1981, the board believed that 6,500 acres of Box Elder land would be condemned for the project. VSC sold some land in 1982 at $8,000 per acre. In 1983, VSC purchased 40 acres of land contiguous to its property for $2,750 per acre.

In 1983, Mrs. Van Schaack sold her stock for $1.5 million dollars at $2,000 per share. In 1985, Denver announced the relocation of the airport and the relocation of a major highway to a portion of the Box Elder land. In 1988, Mrs. Van Schaack sued, alleging a breach of fiduciary duty in connection with the sale of stock because the board misrepresented material facts and failed to disclose material facts relating to the value of the Box Elder land, the airport relocation, and the relocation of the highway. Although she was the largest individual stockholder, she was a minority stockholder because her 750 shares represented only 16 percent of the stock. The jury returned a verdict for her in the amount of $750,000. The judgment was appealed.

Chief Justice ROVIRA

. . . .

We have previously recognized that corporate directors owe a fiduciary duty to shareholders in exercising their responsibilities. This duty encompasses the requirement that directors of a corporation and its controlling shareholders act with an extreme measure of candor, unselfishness, and good faith in relation to remaining shareholders. In addition, it is widely recognized that the fiduciary duty imposed on corporate directors and officers dealing with minority shareholders is enhanced in the context of closed corporations.

The duties previously recognized in this jurisdiction applicable to corporate directors dealing with shareholders include exercise of complete candor with minority shareholders in the negotiation of stock transactions. In our view, this duty encompasses the obligation to fully disclose all material facts and circumstances surrounding or affecting a proposed transaction.

Imposition of such a duty is particularly justified in the context of closed corporations because shares of closed corporations are not publicly traded and information affecting the value of such shares is not generally known. While the value of publicly traded securities presumably reflects the marshalling and analysis of all information known by "the market," including information which is required to be disclosed under state and federal securities laws, a liquid and efficient market for shares of a closed corporation is, generally speaking, not available. Indeed, one commentator remarks that a closed corporation is, by definition, "a corporation whose shares are not generally traded in the securities markets."

. . . .

We hold, therefore, that it is a violation of a fiduciary duty for an officer or director of a closed corporation to purchase the stock of minority shareholders without disclosing material facts affecting the value of the stock, known to the purchasing officer or director by virtue of his position but not known to the selling shareholder.

. . . Thus, information is "material" if there is a "substantial likelihood that, under all the circumstances, the omitted fact would have assumed actual significance in the deliberations of the reasonable shareholder" and "would have been viewed by the reasonable investor as having significantly altered the 'total mix' of information made available."

DECISION AND REMEDY The court held that the board of directors of a closely held corporation must disclose material facts affecting the value of the corporate stock when purchasing the stock of a minority shareholder.

CRITICAL THINKING: MANAGERIAL CONSIDERATION Assume that you and four friends decide to form a corporation in which each one of you owns 25 percent of the business. As a minority shareholder, how would you protect your interests from the other shareholders?

Directors' Control

The board of directors is authorized to exercise all of the corporate powers, to manage the business, and to set the policy of the corporation. The directors' responsibilities include the declaration and payment of dividends to shareholders and the fixing of compensation for the officers and directors.

In larger corporations, the directors often serve on executive committees that handle management decisions between board meetings. Often, officers are also directors of the corporation and sit on many of the executive committees created by the board of directors. The board of directors delegates much of the responsibility for day-to-day management to the officers. Major policy, financial, and contract decisions involving the management of a corporation, however, cannot be delegated by the board of directors to the corporation's officers.

Transferability of Interest

Another characteristic of corporations is the free transferability of shares. The law generally recognizes an owner's right to transfer property except when valid restrictions on its transferability exist.

Restrictions are imposed by securities laws if the shares are registered with the Securities and Exchange Commission or if insiders (such as directors, officers, or controlling shareholders of the corporation), who have access to inside information, trade their securities on the basis of this information. Other restrictions may be imposed by contract, articles of incorporation, or bylaws.

Restrictions for Close Corporations

Within a close corporation, the need to provide restrictions on the transfer of common shares is greater than in other types of corporations. The interpersonal relationship of the principal shareholders of the close corporation is very intense. In many close corporations, a person spends more time with fellow shareholders than with his own family. This commitment requires mutual respect, trust, and understanding.

The possibility always exists that one of the principal shareholders may die, divorce, resign, or retire. Without restrictions on the transferability of shares, a remaining shareholder might find herself in business with the former associate's ex-spouse or heirs, or even with a stranger. The shareholder may find it impossible to work with, and to be associated closely with, these new parties.

The articles of incorporation or bylaws can restrict the transfer of shares in a close corporation by imposing the option of the right of first refusal. This option means that the shares to be transferred must first be offered for sale to the corporation or to the remaining shareholders. The corporation or shareholders have the first right either to buy or to refuse to buy the shares.

A procedure should be established to determine the price of the stock. For example, the articles of incorporation, the bylaws, or a shareholder agreement states that the corporation or remaining shareholders have a right to purchase the stock upon a shareholder's death, with the value of the shares to be determined by an independent appraiser.

Additionally, the corporation or remaining shareholders need to have the capability to buy the shares. Funds for the purchase of the stock can be provided by a life insurance policy taken out and paid for by the corporation on the shareholder's life.

Notice of Restrictions

Any restrictions on transferability (including the right of first refusal) must appear on the stock certificate. Some state statutes require that restrictions be placed in the articles of incorporation. If no such statute exists, restrictions should be stated in the bylaws and on the stock certificates.

The common law does not like restrictions on transferability. Because of this, the restrictions must be written in very specific language and follow the state law exactly. The articles or bylaws cannot restrict the transferability completely, but they may require the offering of shares to the other stockholders first and may establish a procedure to determine the value of the shares as discussed previously.

Taxes

The corporation, as a separate entity, is also a separate taxpayer. The corporation pays taxes on its earnings in the year earned. When the earnings are distributed to the shareholders as dividends, the shareholders are taxed on the dividends received. The corporation cannot deduct the payment of dividends from its revenue.

Losses are deducted by the corporation. Losses off-set corporate revenue rather than passing through to the shareholders to be deducted from their income for tax purposes.

One means of avoiding the double taxation, when the shareholders are also officers or employees of the corporation, is by paying them salaries rather than distributing dividends. Salaries are a deduction from revenue for the corporation. This deduction may be disallowed, however, by the Internal Revenue Service (IRS) if the salaries are held to be excessive or unreasonable.

Avoidance of Taxes

Shareholders can receive income in the form of dividends. Shareholders, rather than contributing all of their money to the capital of the corporation by purchasing shares, can become a creditor by lending capital to the corporation as a loan. The interest on the loan is a deductible item for the corporation, but the creditor must pay taxes on the interest received.

The IRS pays close attention to undercapitalization of corporations. Generally, a debt-to-equity ratio greater than three-to-one may be challenged by the IRS. This type of undercapitalization also endangers the shareholders' limited liability.

Only when the corporation's earnings are distributed to the shareholders as dividends does the shareholder pay tax. Often, the corporation will accumulate earnings rather than distribute them. The IRS rules, however, will impose a tax on the corporation for excessive accumulated earnings. The IRS rules encourage the distribution of earnings to shareholders rather than the retention of earnings not needed for the business.

S Corporation

The label **S corporation** refers to the tax status of a corporation, not to a type of corporation.[1] The promoters apply to the state for incorporation. Once the state creates the corporation, the shareholders determine if the corporation will apply to the IRS to become an S corporation.

S refers to the subchapter in the IRS statutes that set out the qualifications for meeting the S corporation

[1] See the following web site for corporation tax statistics: <http://www.irs.ustreas.gov/prod/tax_stats/corp.html>.

requirements. An S corporation is a voluntary tax status for a close corporation. The shareholders must elect to apply to the IRS for the S corporation status. If the corporation meets all the IRS requirements, the IRS will grant the S status. The S corporation will remain in that status as long as it meets the IRS regulations.

The S tax status allows the corporation to be treated as a partnership (yet retain the advantages of a corporation, such as limited liability) and to pass all losses and gains through the corporation to the individual shareholders without being taxed at the corporate level. In an S corporation, the profit is passed through to the shareholders for tax purposes regardless of whether it actually is distributed to them in the form of dividends.

To qualify, an S corporation may have no more than seventy-five shareholders. An S corporation can have only one class of stock. Only domestic corporations can qualify for this status. Many technical requirements must be met for a corporation to become and to maintain an S corporation status.

The IRS has the authority to audit an S corporation and to revoke the S corporation status if these conditions are not met. The IRS's audit can cover several previous years to determine the year when the corporation first failed to meet the conditions. The corporation then owes back taxes, interest, and late penalties. To maintain the S corporation status, the shareholders' agreement must provide that shares can be transferred only to qualified shareholders (many corporations, partnerships, trusts, and foreigners cannot be shareholders).

CyberLaw

International Taxes

Many complaints are heard that a person buying items on the web escapes paying sale taxes. As previously discussed in Chapter 11, states are losing a large source of revenue from sales taxes. One state, Maryland, attempted to obtain from businesses that sell on the Internet the names and addresses of customers and what they purchased to attempt to recover some of the lost revenue. The Internet Tax Freedom Act passed by Congress imposes a moratorium on state and local taxes for transactions on the web.

Today, we have a worldwide economy. The individual European countries and the European Union (EU) rely heavily on the value-added tax (VAT). It is a form of a sales tax imposed at every level of the sale of goods and services, from raw material to final disposal. The percentage varies from one country to another, but provides 44 percent of the Europe Union's budget. Luxembourg has the lowest VAT rate at 15 percent in contrast to Sweden and Denmark at 25 percent. EU firms must charge the VAT to other businesses in the EU, but the non-EU countries do not charge this tax. Luxembourg has requested permission to require the payment of this tax from any business whether or not it is an EU business. This proposal is currently under study by the Commission on Directives. The EU is the first to attempt to tax items purchased on the web.

Duration

Unless otherwise specified in the articles of incorporation, a corporation has perpetual existence. In theory, the death of a shareholder, director, or officer has no effect on the corporate entity. As a practical matter, in many close corporations, the death of the major shareholder, who happens also to be a director or an officer, effectively brings an end to the business, if not the corporation. In such instances, the estate of the deceased shareholder may attempt to find a buyer for the corporation to continue the operation. If a buyer cannot be found, the corporation may have to be dissolved.

A corporation may be *dissolved* and *liquidated*. To **dissolve** means that the corporation ceases its business, except those operations that are necessary to complete the termination of the business. **Liquidation** means that the assets are sold and converted to cash proceeds. The debts are paid and, if any proceeds remain, they are distributed to the shareholders.

The board and a majority of the shareholders adopt a resolution called the **articles of dissolution**. The corporation then proceeds in one of two ways. The corporation on its own may end its business and liquidate assets. Or the corporation may apply to the court to supervise the liquidation. The court has the power to appoint a receiver, who, with the powers and duties specified by the court, will end the business and liquidate the assets.

The articles of dissolution are filed with the state. A dissolved corporation continues to exist to liquidate its business. It must notify all creditors that it is dissolved.

The creditors have 120 days in which to file a claim. For unknown creditors, a corporation must publish the notice of dissolution in a newspaper of general circulation. All claims against the dissolved corporation are barred after five years. The prior shareholders are liable up to the amount they received from the dissolved corporation during this five-year period. Finally, the dissolved corporation ceases to exist.

Dissolution also can occur by means other than the voluntary filing of the resolution for articles of dissolution. For example, any of the following may result in dissolution:

1. An act of the legislature in the state of incorporation (such as making the activities of the corporation illegal)

2. Expiration of the time of existence specified in the charter without a renewal

3. A court decree through an action brought by the state attorney general when the actions of the corporation justify dissolution (such as procurement of the charter by fraud, abuse of corporate powers, abandonment of operations, or continued violation of criminal statutes)

4. Merger (a legal combination of two or more corporations by which one corporation is absorbed into the surviving corporation, thus dissolving the other corporation)

5. Consolidation (a combination of two or more corporations by which the corporations are joined to form a new corporation, dissolving the original corporations)

6. The nonpayment of taxes or annual fees owed to the state.

Franchising

The Federal Trade Commission defines a **franchise** as an arrangement between a **franchisor**, who owns a trademark, a trade name, or a copyright, and another person, known as the *franchisee*. The franchisor licenses the **franchisee** (the holder of the franchise) to use the trademark, trade name, or copyright in marketing the goods or services under specified conditions or limitations. Most franchisees are corporations, but ownership is not limited to the corporate form.

LEGAL HIGHLIGHT

Quality Standards

In 2001, the marketplace is more global, competition is tougher, and buyers demand higher quality standards than in the past. Regardless of the form of business chosen, management needs to be concerned with the quality of its products, services, and, indeed, the quality of the system that the company uses to conduct its business.

Businesses can look to one or both well-known quality measures, the Malcolm Baldrige award in the United States.[a] and the International Standards Organization (ISO) 9000 series standards originating in Europe.[b] Businesses can use the standards as guidelines to improve their own business.

The Baldrige award and the ISO 9000 registration differ in focus, purpose, and content. The focus of the Baldrige award is to enhance competitiveness. The award has three purposes: (1) to promote awareness and understanding of the importance of quality improvement to our nation's economy, (2) to recognize companies for outstanding quality management and achievement, and (3) to share information on successful quality strategies. The Baldrige award is a one-time event and not an ongoing process. A business can reapply and be awarded the Baldrige award a second time, but the two awards are separate.

The ISO 9000 series standards focus on enhancing and facilitating trade. The ISO 9000 standards consist of five separate standards found in ISO 9001 to 9005. These standards represent an international consensus on the essential features of a quality system to ensure the effective operation of any business, whether a manufacturer or a service provider, whether in the public or the private sector. A company applies to the ISO for registration. The application can be limited, such as for a product or a service, or can be for the total management system.

The company submits documents to be reviewed by the ISO registrar. A preassessment by the registrar identifies potential problems. Two to three auditors spend several days on the premises assessing the application. It the company meets the requirements, it will receive a registration. If the company does not receive the registration, it has a period to correct the problems found. After a company receives a registration, the ISO conducts periodic reaudits to verify conformity with the practices and systems registered. ISO 9000 registration ensures that the registrant's practices conform with its quality systems.

The two awards are not similar. The Baldrige award looks to continuous improvement in overall operations. ISO registration, on the other hand, looks to conformance with practices established in the registrant's own quality systems. More businesses are requiring that their suppliers evidence quality by being registered. Many businesses hold ISO registrations, and governments that are purchasing items often will not deal with a business that has not received its ISO registration. Quality can no longer be ignored.

[a] Information on the Baldrige award is at <http://www.nist.gov/public_affairs/results/res-qual.html>.
[b] Information on ISO is located at <http://www.iso.ch/>.

The franchise system also has been described as an organization composed of distributive units established and administered by a supplier as a means of expanding and controlling the market for its products. Each franchise dealer is a legally independent, but economically dependent, unit of the integrated business system. The individual franchisee operates as an independent business. It obtains affiliation advantages with the regional or national organization, however, which supplies the products, advertising, and other services.

The use of franchises has expanded rapidly in recent years. Between 1910 and 1940, franchising was used primarily in the automobile industry, sports, and the soft drink bottling industry. Now, franchises account for about 34 percent of all retail sales. The franchise pattern of business development is a particularly appealing form of capitalist enterprise, because it enables groups of individuals with small amounts of capital to become entrepreneurs.

Types of Franchises

The three types of franchises are the **distributorship franchise, business format franchise,** and **manufacturing or processing plant franchise**.

1. *Distributorship franchise* A manufacturing concern (the franchisor) licenses a dealer (the franchisee) to sell its product. The franchise outlets serve merely as conduits through which the trademarked goods of the franchisor flow. The trademark in a distributorship franchise represents the end product marketed by the system. Often, a distributorship covers an exclusive territory.

2. *Business format franchise* This franchise is the typical chain-style business for which the franchisor merely provides the trademark. The franchisee is responsible for the manufacture and sale of the end product. The franchisee operates under the franchisor's trade name and is identified as a member of a select group of dealers that engage in the franchisor's business. The franchisee generally must follow standardized operations methods. Often, the franchisor requires minimum prices and quality standards to be maintained. Examples of this type of franchise are McDonald's and most other fast-food chains.

3. *Manufacturing or processing plant franchise* The franchisor transfers to the franchisee the essential ingredients or formula to make a particular product. The franchisee then markets it on either a wholesale or retail basis in accordance with the franchisor's standards. Examples of this type of franchise are Coca-Cola and other soft drink corporations.

The Law of Franchising

The growth in franchise operations has outdistanced the law of franchising. The courts interpret franchising statutes when a state has them. If no acts have been adopted by the state, the courts apply general common law principles. Although the franchise agreement itself is a contract, the franchise relationship exhibits characteristics associated with agency and employment law, as well as ordinary contract law.

A franchise purchaser can suffer substantial losses if the franchisor fails to provide complete information regarding the franchisor–franchisee relationship, as well as the details of the contract under which the business will operate. Only a few states that have enacted legislation concerning franchising have included disclosure provisions.

California was the first state to enact a franchise disclosure law. This law serves as a model for other disclosure statutes. The California Franchise Investment Law identifies twenty-two items that must be disclosed in a registration filed with the state. Some of the items to be disclosed follow:

1. The name and business address of the franchisor
2. The business experience of any people affiliated with the franchisor
3. Whether any person associated with the franchisor has been convicted of a felony
4. A recent financial statement
5. A typical franchise agreement
6. A statement of all fees that the franchisee must pay
7. Other information that the commissioner of corporations may reasonably require.

When misrepresentation permeates a franchise operation's initial sale, the common law remedy of fraud provides inadequate relief. In most cases, the franchisee already has paid the franchise purchase price and also may have incurred substantial losses in the business's initial operating phases. The elements of fraud are exceedingly difficult to prove. The franchisee has a great burden to show that the franchisor's original offer was fraudulent.

The FTC Franchise Rule[2] of 1978 was promulgated in response to widespread evidence of deception and unfair practices in connection with the sale of franchises and business opportunity ventures. This rule requires that within a specified time, franchisors and franchise brokers (sellers of franchises) must furnish the information that prospective franchisees need to make an informed decision about entering into a franchise relationship. The rule establishes the circumstances under which a franchisor or broker can make claims

---

[2] To view the FTC Franchise Rule, go to <http://www.ftc.gov/bcp/franchise/netrule.htm>.

about the projected sales income or profits of existing or potential outlets. The rule also imposes requirements that concern the establishment and termination of the franchise relationship.

The Franchise Agreement

A contract defines the relationship between the franchisor and the franchisee. Each franchise relationship and each industry has its own characteristics, creating a broad range of details that a franchising contract may include. The following sections, however, define the essential characteristics of the franchise relationship.

Payment for Franchise. The franchisee ordinarily pays an initial fee or lump-sum price for the franchise license (the privilege of being granted a franchise). This fee is separate from the fees for various products that the franchisee purchases from or through the franchisor. In some industries, the franchisor relies heavily on the initial sale of the franchise to realize a profit. In other industries, the continued dealing between the parties brings profit to both.

In most situations, the franchisor receives a stated percentage of the annual sales or annual volume of business done by the franchisee. The franchise agreement also may require the franchisee to pay a percentage of advertising costs and certain administrative expenses incurred throughout the franchise arrangement.

Location and Business Organization. Typically, the franchisor determines the territory to be served by the franchise. The franchise agreement can specify whether the premises for the business must be leased or purchased outright. In some cases, construction of a building is necessary to meet the terms of the franchise agreement.

In addition, the agreement specifies whether the franchisor or the franchisee bears responsibility for supplying equipment and furnishings for the premises. When the franchise is a service operation, such as a motel, the contract often provides that the franchisor will establish certain standards for the facility and will inspect to ensure that the standards are maintained to protect the franchise name and reputation.

The business organization of the franchisee greatly concerns the franchisor. Depending on the terms of the franchise agreement, the franchisor may specify particular requirements for the business's form and capital structure. The franchise agreement can provide that certain standards of operation, such as sales quotas, quality considerations, or record keeping, must be met by the franchisee.

Furthermore, a franchisor may retain stringent control over the training of personnel involved in the operation and over administrative aspects of the business. Although the day-to-day operation of the franchise business normally is left to the franchisee, the franchise agreement can provide for whatever amount of supervision and control the parties desire.

One area of franchises that causes a great deal of conflict is the territorial exclusivity of the franchise. Many franchise agreements define the territory allotted to a particular franchise, but specifically state that the franchise is nonexclusive. Nonexclusivity allows the franchisor to establish multiple franchises in the same territory.

Price and Quality Controls. Franchises provide the franchisor with an outlet for the firm's goods and services. Depending on the nature of the business, the franchisor may require the franchisee to purchase products from the franchisor at an established price. A franchisor cannot set the prices at which the franchisee will resell the goods, because this violates state or federal antitrust laws. A franchisor can suggest retail prices but cannot insist on them. The franchisor can restrict the franchisee from selling above a maximum price, however.

Although a franchisor can require franchisees to purchase supplies from it, requiring a franchisee to purchase exclusively from the franchisor may violate state or federal antitrust laws. The implications of antitrust violations on territorial restrictions, restrictions on products sold, resale price fixing, and price discrimination are discussed in Chapter 21.

As a general rule, no question exists as to the validity of a provision permitting the franchisor to enforce certain quality standards. Because the franchisor has a legitimate interest in maintaining the quality of the product or service in order to protect its name and reputation, it can exercise greater control in this area than would otherwise be tolerated.

Termination of the Franchise Arrangement

The franchise's duration is negotiated between the parties. Generally, a franchise starts out for a short period, say, a year, so that the franchise and the franchisor can determine whether they want to stay in business with each other. The franchise agreement usually specifies that termination must be for cause, such as death or disability of the franchisee, insolvency of the franchisee, breach of the franchise agreement, or failure to meet specified sales quotas. Most franchise contracts provide that notice of termination must be given.

Much franchise litigation arises over termination provisions. Because the franchise agreement normally is a preprinted contract prepared by the franchisor, and the bargaining power of the franchisee rarely equals that of the franchisor, the termination provisions of contracts are generally more favorable to the franchisor. The lack of statutory and case law in this area affects the franchisee most keenly. Franchisees in automobile dealerships and gasoline stations have some statutory protection under the Automobile Dealers' Day in Court and the Petroleum Marketing Practices Acts.

The franchisee normally invests substantial time and money into the franchise operation to make it successful. Despite this fact, the franchisee may receive little or nothing for the business on termination. The franchisor owns the trademark and hence the business.

Franchisee's Relationship to Franchisor: Agent or Independent Contractor?

The mere licensing of a trade name does not create an agency relationship. The courts have determined that certain other factors in the franchisor–franchisee relationship may indicate the existence of an agency relationship:

1. The terms of the agreement create an agency relationship.

2. The franchisor exercises a high degree of control over the franchisee's activities.

3. A third person looking at the relationship between the franchisor and the franchisee would reasonably believe that an agency relationship exists.

4. The franchisor derives an especially great benefit from the franchisee's activities. The greater the benefit, the more likely an agency relationship will be found.

If these factors show a very close relationship between the franchisor and the franchisee, their relationship will be deemed to be that of an employer–employee or principal–agent in dealings with third parties. If the factors show a high degree of independence between the franchisee and the franchisor, the franchisee will be deemed an independent contractor.

The characterization of the relationship has tax implications and implications for the regulatory treatment of the business organization. In addition, if an agency relationship is found, the franchisor is liable for the franchisee's improper actions or injuries to third parties both in tort and in contract.

International Consideration

How to Expand without Investing

U.S. corporations often do business overseas through the use of licensing or franchising agreements. Licensing agreements can be divided into two categories: *patent licensing* and *know-how licensing*. With a **patent license**, the foreign licensee has access to and use of the patent, and the U.S. licensor receives the royalties. With **know-how licensing**, the U.S. licensor has a trade secret or knows how to use certain technology that no one else knows how to use. The U.S. business sells the foreign licensee the right to use the trade secret or know-how.

Franchising is a specialized form of licensing. The franchisor (supplier) licenses the franchisee (foreign firm) to use the franchisor's marketing knowledge, product, and services in exchange for fees. This agreement allows the franchisee to use the franchisor's trademark and copyrights. Examples include the International Hilton Hotel chain, McDonald's, and Coca-Cola.

Foreign companies can, of course, conduct business in the United States under the same arrangements. Examples include foreign automobile dealerships and distributorships of electronic equipment, such as computers, video cameras, and compact disc players.

LEGALLY SPEAKING

Choosing the Best Form of Business Organization

Your friend has developed a new oil filter for use in internal combustion engines that enables the engine to use the same oil up to ten times as long as is currently possible. She believes that a market exists for such a product, but being totally unfamiliar with business matters, she comes to you for advice.

After reviewing her developed materials and hearing her explanation of the product, you believe that the project is worth pursuing. The two of you would like to begin a business to produce and sell the product.

Good business practice would suggest that you consult an attorney before proceeding with your plans. A good business lawyer can discuss your goals with you, offer alternative courses of action to meet those goals, and evaluate the probable consequences of each alternative.

To take maximum advantage of the time spent with your attorney, you should prepare certain information. Be prepared to provide information on the assets that will be part of the business and in whose name the assets are currently held. You will transfer real property to the business and your friend may transfer patent or other rights. You will need to discuss the tax consequences of those transfers.

Both you and your friend also will want to collect information on your individual financial and tax statutes that may impact the decision about which form of business entity is appropriate for you. How much money will you need to bring to your business in order to carry it through the first year? You should have an idea as to how you will raise this money. Can you and your friend provide it personally from your savings or through a bank loan or will you bring in other equity investors? If you bring in other investors, the questions of liability and business control will become more complex. Even if you and your friend provide the capital, however, the issues of liability and control of day-to-day operations and long-term policy are critical.

You also must consider the degree of freedom with which your business's ownership interests can be transferred. Your friend may implicitly trust your business judgment, but would she accept being in business with your heirs if you should die? Would you proceed if she sold her interest in the business to a stranger without her technical skills? Perhaps both of you will want the option to buy the other's interest in the business in case of death. Alternatively, you both may want a right of first refusal if one of you decides to transfer your interest during your lifetime.

Obviously, the answers to these questions will impact the form of business organization that you should use. Be sure to consider these questions in advance. When you meet with the lawyer be prepared to

✔ Bring the cash flow projections, as well as tax and other relevant information to the meeting.

✔ Determine the assets that must be initially obtained and their cost.

✔ Consider actions if one of you should die or decide to leave the business.

✔ Decide whether limited liability is of prime importance to you both.

✔ Research methods to raise the initial funds required for this investment.

Chapter Summary

A corporation is the most formal type of business entity. The first step in formalizing a corporation is to file articles of incorporation with the appropriate state agency. Among the items included in this document are the name, address, and general purpose of the corporation, its duration, the number and classes of shares, the number of directors, and the names of the incorporators.

The next step is the adoption of bylaws by the board of directors. The bylaws control the business's internal operation. In addition, any business must have funds with which to operate. Funds are obtained by issuing securities. The two broad classes of securities are equity securities and debt securities.

The most frequently held equity securities are common stock and preferred stock. Debt securities are secured bonds and debentures. On dissolution, debt securities are paid ahead of equity securities.

Generally, in the absence of a personal guarantee, shareholders are immune from liability for the corporation's debts. If the corporation's business is not properly conducted, however, the courts may allow the corporate veil to be pierced to hold shareholders liable.

As long as directors and officers perform their fiduciary duties, they are not personally liable for the debts of the corporation. They, however, can be held liable for mismanagement in carrying out their responsibilities. Under the business judgment rule, they are protected from legal actions based on losses brought about by their making honest errors in business decisions.

The shareholders own the corporation and elect the board of directors. The board of directors establishes corporate policy and appoints the officers. All corporations must have officers who conduct the corporation's day-to-day activities. These officers are normally a president, at least one vice-president, a secretary, and a treasurer.

A corporation reasonably can limit the transferability of securities. The limitations also must be known (placed on the security) to the holder and prospective purchaser. Whenever a business decision is made, its effects on taxes must be considered. Special tax advantages occur if S corporation status is elected instead of the normal tax status of a corporation. All losses and profits pass through the corporation to the shareholders if a corporation elects to be taxed under the S corporation provisions of the Internal Revenue Code.

A franchise exists when one party owns a trademark, trade name, or copyright and another party contracts to use this right under specified conditions or limitations. Three different types of franchises have been developed: (1) distributorship, (2) business format, and (3) manufacturing or processing plant.

The law of franchising is developed through cases and through state and federal statutes. The Federal Trade Commission's disclosure rules specify information that must be given to all franchisees before they sign franchise agreements. This information enables franchisees to analyze the potential business success of the venture.

The franchise agreement establishes the rights of the franchisor and franchisee. Among the items that may be included are the required payments, the location of the business, the business organization of the franchisee, pricing and quality control provisions, and how the franchise can be terminated.

Using the World Wide Web

The state most famous for incorporating is the state of Delaware. More than 293,000 companies have incorporated within that state. Fifty percent of the corporations listed on the New York Stock Exchange have a Delaware charter and 60 percent of the *Fortune 500* likewise are organized in that state.

It is possible to incorporate in Delaware through the web. Different fees are charged depending on the form of organization and how fast the incorporation needs to be finalized. You will discover that it is very simple to create a corporation in Delaware.

Finding the Law on the Web

Court TV, different business forms
http://www.courttv.com
Delaware, forms
http://www.state.de.us/corp/index.htm
Maryland, articles of incorporation
http://www.dat.state.md.us/guide_for_close.html
Rhode Island, articles of incorporation
http://www.tug.org/articles.html

Chapter Web Sites

Internal Revenue Service, corporation tax statistics
http://www.irs.ustreas.gov/prod/tax_stats/corp
.html

Baldrige Award
http://www.nist.gov/public_affairs/results
/res-qual.html
International Standards Organization
http://www.iso.ch/
FTC Franchise Rule
http://www.ftc.gov/bcp/franchise/netrule.htm
Cornell University, Law Information Institute
http://fatty.law.cornell.edu/topics/state_statutes
.html#corporations
'Lectric Law Library
http://www.lectlaw.com/files/bul18.htm
Court TV, e-mail policy form
http://www.courttv.com/legalhelp/business
/forms/

Web Activities

19–1 Most statutory provisions for the incorporation of a business are located at <http://fatty.law.cornell.edu /topics/state_statutes.html#corporations>. Review your own state statutes to see what is required to incorporate.

19–2 You have a business that you want to sell. 'Lectric Law <http://www.lectlaw.com/files/bul18.htm>. What documents should you be prepared to present to a prospective purchaser?

Key Terms

alien corporation
articles of dissolution
articles of incorporation
board of directors
bond
business format franchise
business judgment rule
bylaws
close corporation
common stock
corporation

cumulative preferred
    stock
debenture
debt securities
director
dissolve
distributorship franchise
domestic corporation
equity securities
foreign corporation
franchise

franchisee
franchisor
incorporator
know-how licensing
liquidation
manufacturing or pro-
    cessing plant franchise
Model Business
    Corporation Act
    (MBCA)
officer

patent license
pierce the corporate veil
preferred stock
promoter
Revised Model Business
    Corporation Act
    (RMBCA)
S corporation
undercapitalization

Questions and Case Problems

19–1 Franchise Blake is interested in becoming a service station dealer. He contacts Esco Oil Company and obtains a franchise contract in which Esco agrees to furnish Blake with all gasoline, oil, and related products necessary to run the service station. In addition, Esco provides Blake with Esco signs and promotional material. A sign reading "Blake's Esco Service" is provided for the front of the station. In return for supplying all the necessary products, promotional materials, signs, and other services, Esco will receive a percentage of receipts on all products sold. Esco advertises that it stands behind its dealers. The relationship between Blake and Esco is challenged. Discuss whether the association is strictly a franchisor–franchisee relationship or a principal–agent (employer–employee) relationship.

19–2 Fiduciary Duty Morad, Thomson, and Coupounas were officers, directors, and shareholders of Bio-Lab. While serving as officers and directors of Bio-Lab, Morad and Thomson incorporated and operated a competing business, Med-Lab. Coupounas brought a suit on behalf of Bio-Lab against Morad, Thomson, and Med-Lab, alleging that they had usurped a corporate opportunity of Bio-Lab. Who prevails? Explain. [*Morad v. Coupounas*, 361 So. 2d 6 (1978)]

19–3 Board of Directors' Authority The Boston Athletic Association (BAA) is responsible for organizing the Boston Marathon. This activity is the corporation's principal business. The board of directors granted Cloney, the president, authority to negotiate and execute agreements to promote the marathon. Cloney entered into a contract with International Marathons, Inc. (IMI), as the exclusive promoter of the Boston Marathon. IMI was granted all rights, title, and interest to the exclusive use of the Boston Marathon and its logo. The board later learned of the exclusive contract. It brought a lawsuit to declare the contract void based on improper delegation of the board's authority. Should this contract be declared null and void? Explain. [*Boston Athletic Association v. International Marathons, Inc.,* 467 N.E.2d 58 (1984)]

19–4 Usurping Corporate Opportunity Klinicki and Lundgren founded Berlinair, a closely held Oregon corporation, to provide air transportation out of West Germany. Klinicki, who owned 33 percent of the company stock, was the vice-president and a director. Lundgren and his family owned 66 percent of Berlinair, and Berlinair's attorney owned the last 1 percent of stock. One of Berlinair's goals was to obtain a contract with BFR, a West German consortium of travel agents,

to provide BFR with air charter service. Later Lundgren learned that the BFR contract might become available. Lundgren then incorporated Air Berlin Charter Company, of which he was the sole owner, and bid for the BFR contract. Lundgren won the BFR contract for Air Berlin while using Berlinair working time, staff, money, and facilities without the knowledge of Klinicki. When Klinicki learned of the BFR contract, he filed a suit as a minority stockholder against Lundgren and Air Berlin for usurping a corporate opportunity. Should Klinicki recover against Air Berlin? If so, what damages should Klinicki be awarded? [*Klinicki v. Lundgren*, 67 Or. App. 160, 678 P.2d 1250 (1984)]

19–5 Personal Liability of Shareholder Salem Tent & Awning Company was a corporation in the business of renting awnings and tents. Dusty Schmidt came into the office to rent seven tents to cover his Christmas trees during the four weeks before Christmas. Although Schmidt and another person owned Western Oregon Christmas Trees, Inc., he signed the prepared invoice without indicating that he was part owner of this corporation or that the tents were for the business. The invoice stated "Renter is Responsible for Damages." Schmidt gave Salem Tent a $2,000 down payment check on which was printed "Western Oregon Christmas Trees." He gave no indication that a corporation existed. Schmidt received the tents and began to use them. A sudden storm destroyed several of the tents. When Schmidt refused to pay for the damaged tents, Salem Tent sued for damages. Are both Western Oregon Christmas Trees and Dusty Schmidt liable for this loss, or just one of them? Explain. [*Salem Tent & Awning Co. v. Schmidt*, 79 Or. App. 475, 719 P.2d 899 (1986)]

19–6 Fiduciary Duty to Shareholders Atlantic Properties, Inc., had only four shareholders, each of whom owned 25 percent of the capital stock. The by-laws required an 80 percent affirmative vote of the shareholders on all actions taken by the corporation. This provision had the effect of giving any of the four original shareholders a veto in corporate decisions. One shareholder refused to vote for any dividends for seven years although he was warned that his actions might expose the corporation to IRS penalties for unreasonable accumulation of corporate earnings and profits. The IRS did impose such penalties on the corporation. Can the dissenting shareholder be held personally liable for these penalties? [*Smith v. Atlantic Properties, Inc.*, 12 Mass. App. Ct. 201, 422 N.E.2d 798 (1981)]

19–7 Pierce the Corporate Veil The Harveys are a group of investors that includes five Harvey corporations along with partnerships and individuals, totaling eighteen in all. The five Harvey corporations entered into an agreement with Flynt Distributing Company, Inc., to distribute nationally various magazines published by the Harveys. After Flynt provided other services, the Harvey corporations refused to ship their publications for distribution and refused to pay for services that Flynt provided. Flynt showed that Leon and Alfred Harvey (1) were the only shareholders of the five corporations, were the only partners in the Harvey partnerships, and were individual investors; (2) dealt with the corporations, partnerships, and their individual investments as if all the businesses were one; and (3) converted the assets of the corporations and partnerships to their own use. The conversion of assets left the corporations undercapitalized. Flynt was awarded a $300,000 judgment but is unable to collect because of the undercapitalization. Discuss whether the court should pierce the corporate veil so that Flynt may collect its judgment. [*Flynt Distributing Co. v. Harvey*, 734 F.2d 1389 (9th Cir. 1984)]

19–8 Alter Ego Pacific Development, Inc., was incorporated in the District of Columbia for the purpose of international relations. Pacific's founder, president, and sole shareholder was Tongsun Park. He made all the corporate decisions. The board of directors played no significant role. Pacific purchased property. The purchase price was financed through Valley Finance, Inc., another of Park's wholly owned corporations. Valley placed a mortgage (lien) against the property to secure loan repayment. Park was a South Korean who improperly influenced Congress to provide economic and military aid to South Korea. His actions led to a scandal that involved members of Congress. A resulting IRS investi-gation of Park and his corporations revealed that he failed to pay his income taxes, and the IRS assessed $4.5 million in back taxes against Park. The IRS seized the property owned by Pacific by claiming that Pacific was merely an alter ego for Park. Because he totally controlled Pacific, the IRS claimed that it could set aside Pacific's corporate veil and use its assets to help pay off the $4.5 million. Valley claimed that the IRS improperly pierced Pacific's corporate veil. Pacific's property should not be used to pay off Park's personal debt of taxes to the IRS, but should be used to pay the debt owed to Valley. Should the corporate veil be pierced? Explain. [*Valley Finance, Inc., v. United States*, 629 F.2d 162 (D.C. Cir. 1980)]

19–9 Franchise Imperial Motors, Inc., has a franchise agreement with Chrysler. The agreement explicitly provided that Imperial would not have the exclusive right to purchase Chrysler cars for resale in a four-town area of South Carolina. Chrysler allowed another dealer to move into a new showroom seven miles from Imperial's location. Imperial brought legal action against Chrysler. Chrysler filed a motion for summary judgment, claiming that Imperial had not established a cause of action. Should the court grant this motion? Explain. [*Imperial Motors, Inc. v. Chrysler*, 559 F. Supp. 1312 (1983)]

19–10 Internet Regardless of the business form you adopt, you need to establish policies on a number of different topics. For example, there should be a policy on e-mail. Court TV has a web site that offers several different model forms. Does the model form on e-mail policy allow a person to use the business's e-mail server for personal use? Go to <http://www.courttv.com/legalhelp/business/forms/>. You will find a list of forms, one of which is a model form for an e-mail policy.

Unit IV Business and Government Regulation

Chapter 20

Securities Law

> *Corporations cannot commit treason, nor be outlawed nor excommunicated for they have no soul.*
>
> *Case of Sutton's Hospital (1625)*
> Sir Edward Coke, 1552–1634
> British jurist and politician, advocate of the supremacy of the common law

Outline

Ethical Consideration

Securities Disclosure Requirements: Do the Consumers Really Get the Information They Need?

You are a staff attorney assigned to prepare material for prospective investors in a limited partnership that will build and manage an office building. After coordinating the material, you are confident that you have satisfied the legal requirements for appropriate disclosure. You believe, however, that the documents are so complicated that few prospective investors will understand them. The market for office space is soft, and you, personally, would never invest in such a project.

You carefully bring your concerns to your supervising attorney. He reminds you, however, that your obligation is to make sure that the legal requirements are met. When you question him about the financial soundness of building an office building in this economy, he explains that the deal allows for the general partners to receive their money up front and, therefore, to benefit whether or not the deal is successful. The general partners are the clients and their interest is to be protected. Because this initial payout to the general partners is fully disclosed, all the legal requirements have been met.

You are dissatisfied with the explanation and perceive that the law firm is participating in a rather shady deal that will benefit the general partners at the expense of the innocent investors. Do you insist on a meeting with the law firm's senior partner in the hope that the firm will refuse to be a party to such a practice, or do you simply certify that the documents meet all legal requirements and remain silent? Use the ethical model presented in Chapter 2 and reprinted on the inside front cover to develop your answer.

Introduction

Not until the twentieth century did the government consider regulating securities. In 1911, the state of Kansas adopted the first law to regulate the sale of securities within the state (intrastate transactions). To pass the initial legislation, a member of the Kansas legislature claimed that promoters were so shrewd that they could sell anyone a "piece of the blue sky itself." Since then, statutes that regulate the sales of securities within a state have been called **blue sky laws**.

The devastating effects of the Great Depression (1929-1939) led Congress to hold hearings. These investigations tried to search out the causes of the financial system's collapse in 1929 so that legislation could be adopted to prevent another such disaster. These laws regulated securities, financial markets, business practices, and specific industries, such as stockbrokers.

The federal regulating body is the **Securities and Exchange Commission (SEC)**.[1] Federal statutes dominate in the regulation of securities. This chapter discusses the Securities Act of 1933, Securities Exchange Act of 1934, Securities Investor Protection Act of 1970, Foreign Corrupt Practices Act of 1977, Insider Trading Sanctions Act of 1984, Insider Trading and Securities Fraud Enforcement Act of 1988, Securities Enforcement Remedies and Penny Stock Reform Act of 1990, and Market Reform Act of 1990. Then it reviews more recent legislation passed by Congress: the National Securities Markets Improvement Act and the Private Securities Litigation Reform Act. Before these statutes can be examined, however, the definition of a security must be established.

When you formed your online business, Artiste Login Products, Inc., you were fortunate to have the money to purchase all the shares. As you read through this chapter, think about the legal aspects of taking the company public.

What Is a Security?

Stocks and bonds are two common types of securities that were reviewed in Chapter 19. A security, as defined in the Securities Act of 1933, is very broad, and its exact definition is unclear. The Courts have interpreted

---

[1] The Securities and Exchange Commission's web site is <http://www.sec.gov/>. An Internet site that covers most security laws is maintained by the University of Cincinnati College of Law. Its address is <http://www.law.uc.edu/CCL/>. Another site that offers investors, the judiciary, policymakers, and students a careful look into the workings of security litigation and, in particular, class action is one that Stanford University maintains. Its address is <http://securities.stanford.edu/about/caveat.html>.

LEGAL HIGHLIGHT

What Do Earthworms and Salvador Dali Prints Have in Common?

Earthworms Are Securities

Allen J. Gross sent out promotional newsletters on how to make money by purchasing an earthworm farm. The newsletter promised several things. First, growing instructions would accompany the earthworm farm. Second, the time involved to grow the earthworms was similar to that of raising a garden. Third, earthworms multiplied sixty-four times a year. Lastly, Gross would buy back at $2.25 per pound all bait-size earthworms produced.

Gerald Smith responded to the newsletter. Gross told Smith that the work required little time or effort, that Gross needed Smith's help in the common enterprise of supplying worms for the bait industry, and that Gross's agreement to repurchase guaranteed success. Smith purchased the earthworm farm.

Smith soon found that earthworms multiply eight times a year rather than sixty-four times a year. He could make a profit only if worms reproduced sixty-four times a year. The price of $2.25 was ten times greater than dictated by true market conditions. Gross could pay the $2.25 price only by selling worms to new worm farmers at inflated prices. In fact, little market existed for the earthworms in Phoenix, Arizona. Smith sued Gross.

The question facing the court was whether the sale of the earthworm farm was an investment contract type of security. The court found that it was. First, Smith invested money when he purchased the earth-

worm farm. Second, a common enterprise existed because Smith could receive the promised income only if Gross purchased the earthworm harvest and both Smith and Gross were dependent on others purchasing earthworm farms at inflated prices from Gross. Third, the profits came from the efforts of others. The effort required by Smith was minimal because of the promised high earthworm reproduction rate and the profit depended on Gross reselling the production to new earthworm farmers.

Salvador Dali Prints Are Securities

Some art galleries had sold fake Salvador Dali prints to customers for several years. Some of these galleries were boiler-room operations in which the seller called potential customers, telling them that they could own an affordable Dali print. The seller purchased the print for $25 to $50 and sold it to the victim for $1,500 to $2,500. The print, however, was really a reproduction and not a genuine limited-edition lithograph. The "Dali prints" were neither authorized nor supervised by Dali.

Although each victim was overcharged a relatively small sum, the total amount was staggering. In New York, a boiler-room operation was convicted of defrauding investors out of $1.3 million. Because the operation's owners had sold the Dali prints to victims over the telephone as investments, they were convicted of securities fraud.

this language expansively. A **security** is defined as (1) an investment of money or other consideration, (2) in a common enterprise, (3) with the investor expecting a profit, and (4) with the profit derived primarily through the efforts of a promoter or a third party other than the investor.

To meet this criterion, the investor must turn money over to another individual for investment purposes, which must be pooled with the capital of other investors so that each individual owns an undivided interest in the whole. The investor has no day-to-day

control over the enterprise. A security owner is passive. An officer or employee who owns stock in her company is considered to be a passive investor.

Securities are created by the issuing party, called the **issuer**, such as a corporation or limited partnership. They can be issued in unlimited amounts and at relatively little cost because the physical representation of a security is nothing more than a piece of paper that represents a financial interest. A security is not used or consumed. Rather, it is a type of currency traded in the "secondary market." A security in the secondary market is bought and sold by people who normally are not the security's issuers.

Securities are more vulnerable to price fluctuation than are other types of investments, such as automobiles or real estate. The economy, interest rates, and information concerning the business influences the value of a security. True, false, and misleading information about the business influences the security's price. This distinctive feature of securities makes it very easy for individuals or brokerage firms to misrepresent an investment's value. Securities laws attempt to protect investors by mandating full and truthful disclosure, by prohibiting fraud, and by prohibiting insider trading.

Securities laws have been applied to various transactions that traditionally have not been thought of as securities. In addition to the traditional stocks and bonds, courts have found investment contracts to be securities. Examples of investment contracts include the sale of interest in land involving orange and pecan groves, the sale of limited partnership interests, and investments in mink and chinchilla farms. The Legal Highlight entitled *What Do Earthworms and Salvador Dali Prints Have in Common?* provides more examples. The possibility that a business venture may be termed a security must be considered in every transaction, because the legal ramifications of engaging in the buying and selling of securities are far reaching. The next case illustrates this point.

Case 20.1

Reves v. Ernst & Young

Supreme Court of the United States, 1990
494 U.S. 56, 110 S. Ct. 945, 108 L. Ed. 2d 47
http://caselaw.findlaw.com/

BACKGROUND AND FACTS Farmer's Cooperative of Arkansas and Oklahoma (Co-op) is a 23,000-member agricultural cooperative. To raise money, it sold promissory notes payable on demand by the holder. The notes were not backed with any collateral and they were not insured. The Co-op marketed the notes as an investment program, advertising that more than $11 million in assets stood behind these investments. Several months later, the Co-op filed for bankruptcy, leaving 1,600 people holding notes worth a total of $10 million.

This litigation was instituted against the accounting firms including Ernst & Young for overvaluing a gasohol plant that was one of the biggest assets. The plaintiffs obtained a $6.1 million judgment in the trial court.

This judgment was overturned by the U.S. Eighth Circuit Court of Appeals on the basis that the 1934 Securities Exchange Act did not cover these demand notes. The act excluded, among other things, "any note . . . which has a maturity at time of issuance of not exceeding nine months." In other words, the debt, evidenced by a promissory note, paid before the end of nine months is not a security.

Justice MARSHALL delivered the opinion of the Court.

. . . .

This case requires us to decide whether the note issued by the Co-op is a "security" within the meaning of the 1934 Act. Section 3(a)(10) of that Act is our starting point:

> "The term 'security' means any . . . but shall not include currency or any note, draft, bill of exchange, or banker's acceptance which has a maturity at the time of issuance of not exceeding nine months." . . .

The fundamental purpose undergirding the Securities Acts is to eliminate serious abuses in largely unregulated securities.

. . . .

In discharging our duty, we are not bound by legal formalisms, but instead take account of the economics of the transaction under investigation. . . .

Congress' purpose in enacting the securities laws was to regulate investments, in whatever form they are made and by whatever name they are called.

. . . .

First, we examine the transaction to assess the motivations that would prompt a reasonable seller and buyer to enter into it. If the seller's purpose is to raise money for the general use of a business enterprise or to finance substantial investments and the buyer is interested primarily in the profit the note is expected to generate, the instrument is likely to be a "security." If the note is exchanged to facilitate the purchase and sale of a minor asset or consumer good, to correct for the seller's cash-flow difficulties, or to advance some other commercial or consumer purpose, on the other hand, the note is less sensibly described as a "security." . . . Second, we examine the plan of distribution of the instrument to determine whether it is an instrument in which there is common trading for speculation or investment. Third, we examine the reasonable expectations of the investing public: The Court will consider instruments to be "securities" on the basis of such public expectations, even where an economic analysis of the circumstances of the particular transaction might suggest that the instruments are not "securities" as used in that transaction. Finally, we examine whether some factor such as the existence of another regulatory scheme significantly reduces the risk of the instrument, thereby rendering application of the Securities Acts unnecessary. . . .

. . . .

. . . [W]e conclude that the demand notes at issue here fall under the "note" category of instruments that are "securities" under the 1933 and 1934 Acts. . . .

DECISION AND REMEDY Whether a promissory note is a security depends on the method by which it was issued. The Court established the four factors to be considered in making this determination and concluded that the notes in this case were securities.

CRITICAL THINKING: POLITICAL CONSIDERATION For many years prior to 1933, the philosophy of security law was to prosecute only those persons who committed actual fraud by intentional wrongful acts. Beginning with the passage of the Securities Act of 1933, the philosophy changed and many new statutes and rules were implemented to protect the investing public. With any regulation comes cost. Should laws protect the investing public or should investors perform their own investigations and take responsibility for their investment decisions?

The Securities Act of 1933

The first securities regulation statute enacted by Congress, the **Securities Act of 1933**,[2] has two aspects: the disclosure of information and the prohibition of fraud and deceit. This act often is referred to as the "truth in securities" law, because it requires full and truthful disclosure by companies issuing securities.

Every new issue of securities must be registered with the SEC, unless the security qualifies for an exemption, as discussed later. The 1933 act also forbids fraud and deceit in the distribution of the securities and applies even to securities not required to be registered. The statute was designed to prohibit various forms of fraud and to stabilize the securities industry by requiring that all essential information concerning the issuing of securities be made available to the investing public.[3]

---

[2] The Securities Act of 1933 is located at <http://www4.law.cornell.edu/uscode/15/ch2A.html>.

[3] A good web site that discusses security fraud is <http://www.securitieslaw.com/>.

LEGAL HIGHLIGHT
Plain English for Investing?

The Securities and Exchange Commission is making investing more understandable by requiring that information given to consumers be written in plain English. Mutual funds, stocks, and bonds often are sold with high-pressure tactics. Demystifying these investments is a challenge. The SEC created a task force to make recommendations.

The SEC task force addressed the lack of readability of prospectuses and other disclosure documents. Issuers, underwriters, and their lawyers created defensively written documents that utilized legal jargon and over inclusive disclosures. The task force found the language describing even basic information about the issuer's business to be "turgid," "opaque," and "unreadable." The result was that trivial issues sometimes received as much attention as material information and buried points significant to an investment decision. The task force recommended the following:

- The use of plain English principles in the organization, language, and structure of the prospectus's and other documents' cover pages, summary, and risk factors section. These sections should communicate the information clearly to investors.

- The use of pictures, logos, charts, graphs, or other design elements.

- The use of clear, concise paragraphs and sentences, using bulleted lists and short sentences, if possible.

- The avoidance of legal and highly technical business terminology.

- The definition of terms in a glossary when the meanings are unclear from the context.

The Office of Investor Education and Assistance wrote a book for businesses called *A Plain English Handbook: How to Create Clear SEC Disclosure Documents.* This book offers insights into those areas that the SEC considers important to be explained in plain English.

The SEC has a hotline to better serve the investing public. Callers can hear prerecorded messages on investing in general, finding investor's alert pamphlets, filing complaints, requesting SEC publications, accessing public records, and obtaining disciplinary information on brokers. The SEC encourages the public to report people believed to be violating any of the federal securities laws. By reporting suspected violations of the federal securities laws that may be occurring over the Internet or anywhere else, a future victim may be protected from losing her or his life savings.

Requirements of the Registration Statement

Businesses issuing a security, unless exempt, must file with the SEC a **registration statement** that provides important information, such as the names of directors and officers, as well as financial, economic, and other important information. Businesses must register the security before offering it to the public. In addition, businesses must provide investors with a **prospectus**, which is the document that is utilized to sell the security. The registration statement and prospectus supply sufficient information to enable unsophisticated investors to evaluate the financial risk involved. The prospectus must be written in plain English.[4]

The corporation's principal executive officer, principal accounting officer, principal financial officer, and at least a majority of the members of the board of directors must sign the registration statement. Signing the registration statement makes a person potentially liable for any errors or material omissions in it.

---

[4] The guidelines that SEC has promulgated concerning plain English are found at <http://www.sec.gov/consumer/plaine.htm>.

The SEC does not attempt to determine whether an investment is a good one. It only demands that sufficient information be available to a potential investor so that he can make an intelligent decision.

CyberLaw

EDGAR

The SEC is moving from paper document filings to electronic filings on the **Electronic Data Gathering, Analysis, and Retrieval (EDGAR)**[5] system. This system performs automated collection, validation, indexing, acceptance, and forwarding of submissions by companies that are required by law to file forms with the SEC.

The SEC requires some corporations to file certain documents electronically on EDGAR. For example, all 8-K, 10-K, 10-Q, and other similar documents must be filed electronically. As a result, the SEC has rid itself of much paperwork. Electronic filings allow the general public to view and search on the computer many of the documents filed by corporations.

Requirements of the Registering Corporation

Before filing the registration statement and prospectus with the SEC, the business can obtain an underwriter to monitor distribution of the new issue. A twenty-day waiting period after registration is mandated before any sale can take place. The SEC may extend this period, or the registration statement may require amendments that start the twenty-day period over again.

During this period, oral offers between interested investors and the issuer concerning the purchase and sale of the proposed securities may take place. The securities cannot be bought or sold legally, however. Exhibit 20–1 sets out the time periods for a new security.

During the waiting period, written advertising is allowed in the form of a **tombstone advertisement**. This advertisement is so named because it is outlined in black and resembles a tombstone. Such advertisements simply tell the investor where and how to obtain a prospectus. Normally, any other type of advertising is prohibited.

At this time, a **red herring prospectus**[6] (the preliminary prospectus) may be distributed. The name comes from the red legend printed across it, stating that the registration has been filed but has not become effective. The red legend indicates that the prospectus is not final and not yet approved by the SEC.

Once the registration process is complete, the registrant can issue stock. Two SEC rules help to make the process more efficient and cost effective, the simplified registration process and the shelf registration rules.

Regulation A, Simplified Registration Process.
Under **Regulation A**, a seller can sell up to $1.5 million in a one-year period with a simplified registration process. Regulation A does not place a limit on the number of purchasers.

Disclosure is not required if the offering is under $100,000. Any offering above $100,000 must disclose material information regarding the investment. The circular containing the information must be filed with the SEC ten days prior to the sale of the securities.

Regulation C, Rule 415, Shelf Registration.
Corporations with stock having a minimum value of $150 million may register the new security, but need not sell all the securities they have issued at the same time. Popularly called **shelf registration**, Regulation C, **Rule 415**, these securities are put "on the shelf" to be sold at a later time.

Once the registration is approved by the SEC, the only requirement is for the company to amend its registration in case of any major changes. This rule aids efficiency by reducing legal, accounting, and printing costs.

Misrepresentations in Registering with the SEC

A registration statement that contains material untruths or omissions makes the issuer liable for violation of the securities laws. In addition, all individuals who signed, were named, or participated in drafting the registration statement are liable. The **due diligence defense** is available to those who sign a false statement. A

---

[5] The EDGAR database of corporate information web site is <http://www.sec.gov/edgarhp.htm>.

[6] To see initial public offerings (IPOs) go to the Red Herring web site at <http://www.redherring.com>.

Exhibit 20–1 **Time Periods for a New Security under the Securities Act of 1933**

Time Period	Actions Allowed	Actions Not Allowed
Prefiling period	Preliminary work, such as consulting with the following: • Attorneys • Investment bankers • Accountants. Preliminary work, such as preparing paperwork for filing the following with the SEC: • Registration statement • Supporting documents. Preparing the preliminary prospectus. Publishing a notice setting out the following: • Name of issuer • Description of the security.	Must not offer the security for sale. Must not contract to sell the security. Must not generate publicity to excite the public about the future security.
Registration Statement and Supporting Documents Filed		
Waiting period, usually twenty days (SEC reviews registration statement and supporting documents)	Publishing or distributing information through the following: • Tombstone advertisements • Red herring prospectus • Notice of proposed offering. Oral offers are permitted.	Must not contract to sell the security.
SEC Approves Registration		
Posteffective period	Must try to sell all the newly registered securities. • Exemption: Shelf Registration [Rule 415]. Corporations having a minimum value of $150 million may place part of their new securities "on the shelf" to sell later. Securities may be both offered and sold. Final prospectus is issued. Final prospectus is sent before or with all sales or delivery of securities.	Must not have a red herring prospectus.

defendant who exercised "due diligence" in verifying the truth of the statement may escape liability for false statements made to the SEC. The issuer, however, cannot use the due diligence defense.

In the following case, the court found that the registration statement contained material false statements of fact and material omissions. The individuals who were involved in the issuance of the new securities attempted to use the defense of due diligence.

Case 20.2

Escott v. BarChris Construction Corp.

United States District Court, Southern District of New York, 1968

283 F. Supp. 643

LANDMARK CASE

BACKGROUND AND FACTS This lawsuit was brought by purchasers of BarChris Construction Corporation debentures (an unsecured bond) under Section 11 of the Securities Act of 1933. In 1961, BarChris filed a registration statement to issue the debentures with the Securities and Exchange Commission. The plaintiffs alleged that the registration statement contained material false statements and material omissions.

The defendants fell into three categories: (1) the people who signed the registration statement, (2) the underwriters (consisting of eight investment banking firms), and (3) BarChris's auditors, Peat, Marwick, Mitchell & Company. Included in the group of defendants who signed the registration statement were (1) BarChris's nine directors, (2) BarChris's controller, (3) one of BarChris's attorneys, (4) two investment bankers who were later named as directors of the BarChris Construction Corporation, and (5) numerous other people participating in the preparation of the registration statement.

BarChris grew from a bowling alley building company that started in 1946. The introduction of automatic pin-setting machines in 1952 sparked rapid growth in the bowling industry. BarChris benefited from this increased interest in bowling and its construction operations expanded rapidly. In 1960, BarChris installed approximately 3 percent of all bowling lanes built in the United States. BarChris's sales increased dramatically between 1956 and 1960, and the company was recognized as a significant factor in the bowling construction industry.

BarChris constantly needed cash to finance its operations, a need that grew more and more pressing as the operations expanded. In 1959, BarChris sold over half a million shares of its common stock to the public. By early 1961, it needed additional working capital and decided to sell debentures.

BarChris sold the debentures. Nevertheless, the proceeds from the sale of debentures provided only temporary relief, and soon it experienced increasing financial difficulties, which in time became insurmountable. By early 1962, BarChris began to fail. In October, BarChris filed for bankruptcy. By November, it defaulted on the interest due on the debentures.

The plaintiffs challenged the registration statement's accuracy. They also charged that the text of the prospectus—including many of the figures—was false and that material information had been omitted.

Judge MCLEAN

. . . .

Materiality

It is a prerequisite to liability under Section 11 of the Act that the fact which is falsely stated in a registration statement, or the fact that is omitted when it should have been stated to avoid misleading, be "material."

. . . .

The average prudent investor is not concerned with minor inaccuracies or with errors as to matters which are of no interest to him. The facts which tend to deter him from purchasing a security are facts which have an important bearing upon the nature or condition of the issuing corporation or its business.

Judged by this test, there is no doubt that many of the misstatements and omissions in this prospectus were material.

The "Due Diligence" Defenses

Section 11 (b) of the Act provides that:

> . . . "no person, other than the issuer, shall be liable . . . who shall sustain the burden of proof— . . . .
>
> (3) that (A) as regards any part of the registration statement not purporting to be made on the authority of an expert . . . he had, after reasonable investigation, reasonable ground to believe and did believe, at the time such part of the registration statement became effective, that the statements therein were true and that there was no omission to state a material fact required to be stated therein or necessary to make the statements therein not misleading."

Kircher

Kircher was treasurer of BarChris and its chief financial officer. He is a certified public accountant and an intelligent man. He was thoroughly familiar with BarChris's financial affairs. He knew the terms of BarChris's agreements. . . . He knew of the customers' delinquency problem. . . . He knew how the financing proceeds were to be applied and he saw to it that they were so applied. He arranged the officers' loans and he knew all the facts concerning them.

As to the rest of the prospectus, knowing the facts, he did not have a reasonable ground to believe it to be true. On the contrary, he must have known that in part it was untrue. Under these circumstances, he was not entitled to sit back and place the blame on the lawyers for not advising him about it. Kircher has not proved his due diligence defenses.

Trilling

Trilling's position is somewhat different from Kircher's. He was BarChris's controller. He signed the registration statement in that capacity, although he was not a director.

Trilling was not a member of the executive committee. He was a comparative minor figure in BarChris. The description of BarChris's "management" on page 9 of the prospectus does not mention him. He was not considered to be an executive officer.

Trilling may well have been unaware of several of the inaccuracies in the prospectus. But he must have known of some of them. As a financial officer, he was familiar with BarChris's finances and with its books of account.

As far as appears, he made no investigation. He did what was asked of him and assumed that others would properly take care of supplying accurate data as to the other aspects of the company's business. This would have been well enough but for the fact that he signed the registration statement. As a signer, he could not avoid responsibility by leaving it up to others to make it accurate. Trilling did not sustain the burden of proving his due diligence defenses.

Birnbaum

Birnbaum was a young lawyer, admitted to the bar in 1957, who, after brief periods of employment by two different law firms and an equally brief period of practicing in his own firm, was employed by BarChris as house counsel and assistant secretary in October 1960. Unfortunately for him, he became secretary and a director of BarChris on April 17, 1961, after the first version of the registration statement had been filed with the Securities and Exchange Commission. He signed the later amendments, thereby becoming responsible for the accuracy of the prospectus in its final form.

Although the prospectus, in its description of "management," lists Birnbaum among the "executive officers" and devotes several sentences to a recital of his career, the fact seems to be that he was not an executive officer in any real sense. He did not participate in the management of the company. As house counsel, he attended to legal matters of a routine nature.

It seems probable that Birnbaum did not know of many of the inaccuracies in the prospectus. He must, however, have appreciated some of them. In any case, he made no investigation and relied on the others to get it right. . . . As a lawyer, he should have known his obligations under the statute. He should have known that he was required to make a reasonable investigation of the truth of all the statements in the unexpertised portion of the document which he signed. Having failed to make such an investigation, he did not have reasonable ground to believe that all these statements were true. Birnbaum has not established his diligence defenses. . . .

Auslander

Auslander was an "outside" director, i.e., one who was not an officer of BarChris. He was chairman of the board of Valley Stream National Bank. . . . In February 1961 [he was asked] to become a director of BarChris. . . .

. . . .

Auslander was elected a director on April 17, 1961. The registration statement in its original form had already been filed, of course without his signature. On May 10, 1961, he signed a signature page for the first amendment to the registration statement which was filed on May 11, 1961. This was a separate sheet without any document attached. Auslander did not know that it was a signature page for a registration statement. He vaguely understood that it was something "for the SEC."

Auslander attended a meeting of BarChris's directors on May 15, 1961. At that meeting he, along with the other directors, signed the signature sheet for the second amendment which constituted the registration statement in its final form. Again, this was only a separate sheet without any document attached.

It is true that Auslander became a director on the eve of the financing. He had little opportunity to familiarize himself with the company's affairs. . . .

Section 11 imposes liability in the first instance upon a director, no matter how new he is. He is presumed to know his responsibility when he becomes a director. He can escape liability only by using that reasonable care to investigate the facts which a prudent man would employ in the management of his own property. In my opinion, a prudent man would not act in an important matter without any knowledge of the relevant facts, in sole reliance upon representations of persons who are comparative strangers and upon general information which does not purport to cover the particular case. To say that such minimal conduct measures up to the statutory standard would, to all intents and purposes, absolve new directors from responsibility merely because they are new. This is not a sensible construction of Section 11, when one bears in mind its fundamental purpose of requiring full and truthful disclosure for the protection of investors.

I find and conclude that Auslander has not established his due diligence defense.

Peat, Marwick

. . . .

Berardi was then about thirty years old. He was not yet a C.P.A. He had no previous experience with the bowling industry. This was his first job as a senior accountant. He could hardly have been given a more difficult assignment.

. . . .

Berardi had no conception of how tight the cash position was. He did not discover that BarChris was holding up checks in substantial amounts because there was no money in the bank to cover them. He did not know of the loan from Manufacturers Trust Company or of the officers' loans. Since he never read the prospectus, he was not even aware that there had ever been any problem about loans from officers.

. . . .

Accountants should not be held to a standard higher than that recognized in their profession. I do not do so here. Berardi's review did not come up to that standard. He did not take some of the steps which Peat, Marwick's written program prescribed. He did not spend an adequate amount of time on a task of this magnitude. Most important of all he was too easily satisfied with glib answers to his inquiries.

This is not to say that he should have made a complete audit. But there were enough danger signals in the materials which he did examine to require some further investigation on his part. Generally accepted accounting standards required such further investigation under these circumstances. It is not always sufficient merely to ask questions.

[T]he burden of proof is on Peat, Marwick. I find that that burden has not been satisfied. I conclude that Peat, Marwick has not established its due diligence defense.

DECISION AND REMEDY BarChris Construction Corporation itself, the signers of the registration statement, the debentures, the underwriters, and the corporations' auditors were held liable.

CRITICAL THINKING: MANAGEMENT CONSIDERATION While some of the accused persons in this case actively lied, how could the others have avoided liability?

Exemptions

A corporation can avoid the high cost and complicated procedures associated with registration by taking advantage of certain exemptions to the registration requirement. Two general types of exemption are allowed: *exempt transactions* and *exempt securities*.

Exempt Transactions. The 1933 Securities Act exempts three types of transactions involving new securities from the registration requirements. The three **exempt transactions** are *small offering exemptions, private offering exemptions,* and *intrastate offering exemptions.*

These exemptions are very broad; thus, an offering may qualify for more than one exemption. Although the sale may be exempt from registration, the SEC may require that a report be filed.

An exemption is available only for the current transaction and does not cover future transactions. The next transaction must either be registered or be exempt from registration in its own right.

Small Offering Exemptions. The SEC rules outline different types of **small offering exemptions**. These offerings by an issuer are not large enough for the federal government to regulate: (1) certain types of bank loans, (2) privately negotiated sales of securities to large institutional investors, and (3) business-venture promotions by a few closely related persons.

These offers involve a small amount of money or the securities are offered for sale in a limited manner. Small offering exemptions are covered by Regulation D and Section 4(f).

Regulation D. Regulation D of the 1933 act sets out exemptions from registration requirements if certain conditions are met. Regulation D distinguishes between an *accredited investor* and an *unaccredited investor*.

The **accredited investor** is not likely to need government protection in making its investment determinations. An accredited investor is one of the following:

1. An institutional investor, such as an insurance company, bank, credit union, or pension fund

2. The seller's directors and officers

3. An individual investor who has had an annual income of more than $200,000, or a husband and wife with annual income in excess of $300,000, for two consecutive years

4. An individual with a net worth of more than $1 million

5. Any corporation or charitable organization with total assets of more than $5 million.

An **unaccredited investor** does not meet the previously listed requirements for an accredited investor. The unaccredited investor is likely to need protection.

Regulation D, Rule 504. A noninvestment company does not engage primarily in the business of investing or trading securities. The Rule 504 exemption is for noninvestment companies that do not report to the SEC under the Securities Exchange Act of 1934. Under Regulation D, **Rule 504**, a noninvestment company can sell up to $1 million in securities that it issues in any one year without registration if the company does not advertise or make any general solicitations.

Although Rule 504 exempts the securities from registration, the seller must file a notice with the SEC. Resale of these securities is restricted. State law, however, may apply. Any amount between $500,000 and $1 million must be registered under the state securities registration law.

Regulation D, Rule 505. Under **Rule 505** of Regulation D, a private, noninvestment company may sell up to $5 million in securities in any one year to any number of accredited investors if the company does not advertise or make any general solicitations.

Unaccredited investors can make purchases, but the number of unaccredited investors is limited to thirty-five. If the sale involves any unaccredited investors, the seller must provide all investors with material information about the offering company, its business, and the securities before the sale. The issuer is not required to believe that each unaccredited investor "has such knowledge and experience in financial and business matters that he [or she] is capable of evaluating the merits and the risks of the prospective investment."

A notice of the sale must be filed with the SEC. This exemption applies to businesses, even if they are covered by the 1934 act.

Section 4(f). An issuer can offer to sell securities exempt from registration solely to accredited investors if the amount is no more than $5 million. No unaccredited investors can participate. No limit, however, is placed on the number of accredited investors.

The company cannot advertise or make any general solicitation for the sale of these securities. A notice of the sale must be filed with the SEC.

Private Offering Exemptions, Regulation D, Rule 506.

The federal government is not interested in regulating privately made offerings because the goal of the 1933 act is public protection. Thus, the SEC allows **private offering exemptions**.

Under **Rule 506** of Regulation D, a private, noninvestment company may offer an unlimited number of securities if they generally do not solicit or advertise them. An unlimited number of accredited investors can participate. No more than thirty-five unaccredited investors, however, can be involved.

The seller must determine if each unaccredited investor has enough knowledge and experience in financial and business matters to evaluate the merits and risks of the prospective investment. When there are unaccredited investors, the issuer must provide to all purchasers material information about itself, its business, and the securities before the sale.

A notice of the sale must be filed with the SEC. The Rule 506 exemption applies to businesses, even if they are covered by the 1934 act.

Rule 506 differs from Rule 505 in that Rule 506 requires the issuer to verify that each unaccredited investor has sufficient knowledge or experience to evaluate the risks and merits of the security.

Resales. Securities acquired under a previously discussed exemption cannot be resold without registration under the act, unless they requalify for an exemption. Rule 144A provides a safe harbor exemption for resales of such securities. A resale may activate registration requirements unless the seller complies with Rule 144 or Rule 144A. These rules are popularly called the **safe-harbor exemptions**.

Safe Harbor Exemption, Rule 144. **Restricted securities** are securities acquired in unregistered, private sales from an issuer. Some of the ways investors purchase restricted securities are though private placement offerings, Regulation D offerings, and employee stock benefit plans.

If a person has held the restricted securities for more than one year, the securities can be sold if the following conditions set in **Rule 144** are met. Current adequate public information about the issuer of the securities must be available, which can be found in the reports filed with the SEC under the 1934 Act. The amount allowed to be sold is based on a trading volume formula set out in Rule 144. A notice of sale must be filed with the SEC. Once these conditions are met, the seller is protected from SEC action by the safe harbor exemption.

Safe Harbor Exemption, Rule 144A. **Rule 144A** provides a safe harbor exemption for the sellers from the registration requirements of the Securities Act of 1933. The seller is reselling securities that at the time they were issued were not as the same class listed on a national securities exchange or quoted in a U.S. automated interdealer quotation system. These securities may be sold solely to qualified institutional buyers or registered broker–dealers purchasing as principals.

In general, a qualified institutional buyer is an institutional investor that in the aggregate owns and invests on a discretionary basis at least $100 million in securities of issuers that are not affiliated with the buyer. Registered broker–dealers need only own and invest at least $10 million of securities in order to purchase as a principal under Rule 144A. Accordingly, broker–dealers may purchase privately placed securities from issuers as principal and resell such securities to qualified institutional buyers under Rule 144A.

Intrastate Offering Exemptions, Rule 147. With **intrastate offering exemptions**, the federal government allows each state to regulate securities offerings within its boundaries. An intrastate offering must be made only to resident investors in one state by a seller that resides within that state.

The seller's principal office, 80 percent of its assets, and 80 percent of its gross revenues must be in the state. In addition, 80 percent of the proceeds of the offering must be used within the state. An offer made to an out-of-state resident may result in the cancellation of this exemption.

Exempt Securities. In addition to the exempt transactions, some types of securities are exempt from registration under the 1933 act. **Exempt securities** include securities issued by governments (state and federal). For example, a state government issues bonds to build a classroom building. These bonds are exempt from SEC registration. Banks, savings and loan associations, charitable organizations, and common carriers that are regulated by other federal laws are also exempt.

Corporations issue stock dividends or have stock splits. These types of securities are exempt. Exhibit 20–2 sets out in a chart these different types of exempt securities.

Liability under the 1933 Act

Violations of the Securities Act of 1933 may be dealt with by the Department of Justice (DOJ) filing a criminal action, by the SEC filing a civil action, or by a private party filing a lawsuit. Criminal charges can be filed by DOJ if the defendant has engaged in willful violations of the 1933 act. If convicted, the defendant faces up to five years in prison and a $10,000 fine.

Exhibit 20–2   Types of Securities Exempt under the Securities Act of 1933

Classification of Security	Types of Security
Based on the issuer	1. Securities issued or guaranteed by a government, such as a U.S. Treasury bond 2. Securities issued by a nonprofit, religious, or charitable organization
Regulated by other statutes	1. Securities issued by a bank or savings and loan association 2. Insurance policies and annuity contracts
No overriding public reason to require registration	Notes or drafts maturing in nine months or less

The SEC may file a complaint and seek an administrative hearing before an administrative law judge (ALJ). Prior to the ALJ's issuing a decision, the SEC and the accused may enter into a consent order, in which the accused agrees to discontinue its unlawful conduct. If the SEC and the accused are unable to reach an agreement, a hearing in an administrative law court can be held and the ALJ may issue a cease-and-desist order to prevent or stop illegal activities.

The SEC may seek an injunction or other relief, such as recovery of profits in a federal district court. The SEC may seek civil money damages ranging from $5,000 to $500,000. A private party who is the investor in a new security may bring an action against the company to recover for damages. The amount of recovery, however, cannot exceed the price paid for the securities.

The Securities Exchange Act of 1934

The primary purposes of the **Securities Exchange Act of 1934**[7] are (1) to ensure the integrity of stock and securities sold through national stock exchanges and over-the-counter markets, (2) to inform the investing public of the financial condition of a business, and (3) to protect the public from fraudulent activity. The 1934 act has six parts. First, it created the Securities and Exchange Commission.

Second, it provides for the regulation and registration of security exchanges where securities are bought and sold (such as the New York Stock Exchange), all broker–dealers that have interstate operations, and securities associations, such as the National Association of Securities Dealers (NASD). Third, the statute requires market surveillance. Today, the SEC uses computers to engage in market surveillance to regulate such undesirable market practices as fraud, market manipulation, and misrepresentation.

Fourth, similar to the 1933 act, the 1934 act establishes a requirement for registration and continuous disclosure by (1) any business with securities listed on any regulated securities exchange and (2) companies that have assets in excess of $5 million and 500 or more shareholders. The act applies to the exchange of securities issued by these companies. Fifth, the statute regulates the solicitation of proxies (written authorization given by a shareholder to a third party to vote the shareholder's stock). Finally, the statute prohibits insider trading.

Securities and Exchange Commission

The Securities and Exchange Commission is an independent regulatory agency. Congress delegated to the SEC administrative rule-making powers and the responsibility for administering the entire body of federal securities law, including the 1933 act.[8]

[7] The Securities Exchange Act of 1934 is located at <http://www4.law.cornell.edu/uscode/15/ch2B.shtml>.

[8] The SEC has a page for small businesses at <http://www.sec.gov/smbus1.htm>.

The SEC is composed of five commissioners who serve staggered five-year terms.[9] They are appointed by the president of the United States. No more than three members may be from the same political party.

Proxy Requirement

A **proxy** is written authorization empowering another person to act for the signer, in this case, at the shareholders' meeting. Before the meeting, the company sends the shareholders materials including a proxy solicitation. The 1934 act regulates proxy solicitation for voting. A company or person can solicit proxies from a number of shareholders in an attempt to concentrate voting power. The SEC reviews the procedures used in obtaining proxies. Its rules require that proposed proxy material be filed in advance for examination. In any solicitation, clear disclosures must be made on all matters on which shareholders are to vote. Shareholders must be afforded the right to vote a simple yes or no on each matter.

Insider Trading and Fraud

One of the most important parts of the 1934 act relates to **insider trading**. Corporate directors, officers, and key employees often obtain in advance inside information about matters that can affect the future market value of the corporate stock. This knowledge can give them a trading advantage over the general public and shareholders. Section 16 of the 1934 act prohibits insider trading.

The 1934 act protects investors by prohibiting fraud and manipulation of the markets. Section 10(b) of the 1934 act and Rule 10b-5, a regulation issued by the SEC that implements the statute 10(b), are the primary laws governing issues of fraud and manipulation.

Section 16. **Section 16** of the 1934 act covers directors, officers, and owners of more than 10 percent of the shares of any one class of stock of a company registered with the SEC. These people are designated as insiders who must file reports of their holdings and transactions with the SEC.

If an insider makes a purchase-and-sale or sale-and-purchase of stock within a six-month period that results in a profit, that profit is known as a short-swing profit. Congress made this kind of profit illegal.

The 1934 act authorizes the issuer (corporation that issued the shares) or a shareholder to file a lawsuit against those who have profited. Together or independently, the issuer and shareholder can sue those statutory insiders (officers, directors, or shareholders of 10 percent or more of the stock).

Section 16 is a strict liability statute; in other words, the plaintiff need only show that the action took place. The only proof needed is that an insider purchased-and-sold or sold-and-purchased shares within a six-month period. The damages are found by matching the highest sale-and-purchase or purchase-and-sale within any six-month period. In drafting the statute, Congress decided that the plaintiff did not need to prove that the person had used insider information for personal gain.

The SEC cannot pursue any action against those who have made a short-swing profit. Because violations of Section 16 are not crimes, the Department of Justice (DOJ) cannot file any criminal charges. The SEC, however, may refer any information it may have to the DOJ for possible criminal prosecution when the SEC suspects other types of insider trading violations in addition to the short-swing profit violations.

Section 10(b) and Rule 10b-5. One of the basic tools employed by the SEC to provide and promote investor protection is the prohibition of fraud.[10] The most widely applied section is **Section 10(b)** of the 1934 act which makes it unlawful:

> to use or employ, in connection with the purchase or sale of any security . . . any manipulative or deceptive device or contrivance, in contravention of such rules and regulations as the SEC may prescribe.

The SEC adopted **Rule 10b-5** to implement Section 10(b). This regulation makes it

> unlawful for any person, directly or indirectly, by use of any means or instrumentality of interstate commerce, or the mails, or of any facility of any national securities exchange to defraud or mislead anyone in the purchase or sale of any security.

---

[9] The five commissioners of the SEC have a web page at <http://www.sec.gov/asec/seccom.htm>. To see how the SEC is organized go to <http://www.sec.gov/asec/wwwsec.htm>. To find the regional offices of the SEC go to <http://www.sec.gov/asec/secaddr.htm>.

[10] The SEC has a page alerting investors to prior frauds and scams at <http://www.sec.gov/enforce/inva.htm>.

The antifraud rule applies to the purchase or sale of any security, regardless of how small or large the amount or whether it is a public or private offering. The exemptions discussed earlier under the 1933 act apply only to registration, not to the antifraud provisions. Section 10(b) and Rule 10b-5 cover virtually every transaction involving a security.

The 1934 act does not define the words *fraud* or *misrepresentation*. As a result, the SEC rules and the courts have broadly defined this offense. Violations generally fit into two categories: (1) insider trading cases and (2) claims arising from corporate misstatements or omissions (such as knowingly inflating earnings projections or manipulating financial records to show profits rather than a real loss) or arising from fraud and manipulation by brokers and dealers in trading stock.

The SEC refers to the DOJ those cases involving willful violations of Section 10(b). Violators, if convicted, face up to ten years in prison for each violation and a fine of $2.5 million when the violator is a corporation or $1 million when the violator is an individual.

The SEC may seek a cease-and-desist order to prevent or stop illegal activities. A consent order is obtained by the SEC when the defendant consents to stop its actions. Finally, the SEC may go to federal district court to seek an injunction to stop the defendant's activities.

Private parties may seek damages. They must have been purchasers or sellers trading shares at the same time as the violators.

The following case concerns a violation of Section 10(b) of a registered representative who worked for a brokerage house. The SEC sought an injunction from federal district court to against the trader and a cease-and-desist order from its administrative law court against the stockbroker. The court discusses **scienter** (guilty knowledge that is greater than simple negligence) by the registered representative.

Case 20.3

Graham v. Voss

United States Court of Appeals, District of Columbia Circuit, 2000
222 F.3d 994

BACKGROUND AND FACTS Voss is the owner and president of an independent discount brokerage firm, Voss & Co., Inc. (VCI). Graham was a registered representative, as well as VCI's cashier, back office assistant, and primary house broker. Graham's immediate supervisor, James Pasztor, was VCI's vice-president and SEC compliance officer.

One of the firm's house accounts was an account in the name of John Broumas. His troubles began when the stock market crashed in 1987. To cover his losses, he borrowed heavily and by May 1989 owed roughly $2 million in personal loans and $1 million in mortgages. Unable to borrow any more from banks, Broumas launched upon a scheme that the SEC described as "similar to check-kiting."

Broumas held a number of shares in stock of James Madison, Ltd. (JML), which was listed on the American Stock Exchange (AMEX). Broumas undertook a series of trades and arranged wash trades of JML stock among accounts in his own name and in the name of nominees whose accounts he controlled. Broumas directed these trades among at least twenty-five different brokerage accounts he controlled at fourteen different broker-dealers. In each case, he would instruct one broker to buy and another to sell a specified number of shares at a specified price, thus moving the stock from one of his (or his controlled) accounts to another. Neither broker was told by Broumas that the other account also belonged to or was controlled by him.

Broumas' stock was held in margin accounts where he had assess to the proceeds from a sale one day after the transaction was completed, but could wait at least five business days until the settlement date to pay for the corresponding purchase. When the settlement date arrived, Broumas sometimes executed another set of wash trades to obtain the funds he needed to make the payment—as if he were playing a fiscal version of "musical chairs." Between January 1989 and June 1990, Broumas effectuated 203 sets of wash trades in JML stock involving a total of 420 trades. Each trade typically involved the purchase and sale of between 3,000 and 12,000 JML shares.

Seventy-six of the directed trades were conducted by VCI; approximately sixty of those—an average of one every week-and-a-half—were executed by Graham who observed that Broumas "had a peculiar way of trading." Of the 100 house accounts she handled during this time, only Broumas directed trades, and only Broumas traded in such large quantities.

Because of Broumas' suspicious manner of trading, Graham undertook special precautions to protect her firm's financial interests. She knew that Broumas had financial problems, that he had bounced checks, and that he often owed money on his account. Graham discussed Broumas' "peculiar way of trading" with her supervisor, James Pasztor, and, as a safeguard, generally sought his prior approval for Broumas' trades—something she rarely did with respect to her other house accounts.

Eventually, a check Broumas had given VCI to pay for the purchase of JML shares was returned for insufficient funds. Pasztor restricted the account and told Graham that Broumas could not trade without cleared funds. Initially, Voss concurred, but after having lunch with Broumas, Voss told Pasztor that Broumas could continue to trade. Pasztor in turn informed Graham. Eventually, Broumas became unable to satisfy his margin calls and failed to pay for his last trade through VCI. Although the firm liquidated Broumas' account, it suffered a loss of over $60,000. Broumas filed for personal bankruptcy in early 1991.

In 1991, the SEC filed a complaint in district court alleging that Broumas violated the securities laws by executing wash trades in JML stock. Without admitting or denying the allegations, Broumas consented to a permanent injunction against future violations. Subsequently, Broumas pled guilty to utilizing a check-kiting scheme to meet margin calls.

In 1994, the SEC issued an administrative complaint against Graham, Voss, and Pasztor in connection with Broumas' trades. Graham was charged with willfully aiding and abetting Broumas' violations of the Securities Exchange Act of 1934, which prohibits the effectuation of wash trades. One section prohibits creating a false or misleading appearance of active trading in any security registered on a national securities exchange or creating a false or misleading appearance with respect to the market for any such security,

Pasztor and Voss were charged with failing reasonably to supervise Graham "with a view to preventing" the violations. The SEC subsequently found Pasztor liable for failure to supervise and sanctioned him with a three-month suspension.

The charges against Graham and Voss were heard before an Administrative Law Judge (ALJ), who found Graham and Voss liable on all charges, suspended them from association with any broker or dealer for two and three months, respectively, and ordered Graham to cease and desist from future violations. On appeal, the SEC affirmed the ALJ's holding that Broumas' wash trades violated section 10(b) and Rule 10b-5 because they operated as a fraud on (a) the market for JML stock by creating a deceptive appearance of market activity, and (b) the brokerage firms that were induced to pay him money they would not have paid had they known the sales were not bona fide. The Commission further affirmed the ALJ's findings that Graham aided and abetted Broumas, and that Voss failed reasonably to supervise and it upheld the suspensions. Graham and Voss petition for review of the Commission's order.

GARLAND, Circuit Judge

. . . .

Although variously formulated, three principal elements are required to establish liability for aiding and abetting a violation of section 10(b) and Rule 10b-5: (1)

that a principal committed a primary violation; (2) that the aider and abettor provided substantial assistance to the primary violator; and (3) that the aider and abettor had the necessary "scienter"—i.e., that she rendered such assistance knowingly or recklessly.

. . . .

The real question here concerns the third element of aiding and abetting liability: did Graham assist Broumas with the requisite scienter? We have held that knowledge or recklessness is sufficient to satisfy that requirement. We are satisfied that Graham acted with at least extreme recklessness in aiding Broumas' stock-kiting scheme.

The SEC did not hold Graham reckless merely for executing stock trades. Rather, during the course of executing some 60 trades, Graham noticed numerous suspicious circumstances. She observed that Broumas invariably specified the contra-broker for his trades, rather than using American Securities, the firm VCI typically contacted for over-the-counter trades in exchange-listed securities. Out of the more than 300 accounts with which Graham worked, only Broumas specified the contra-broker with whom to execute the trade, and only Broumas traded in such large volumes. He also detailed every aspect of the trade, including the specific employee at the contra-broker with whom he wanted Graham to speak. Graham testified that, as a result, she assumed Broumas controlled the shares in the accounts or at least "had connections" with them.

Perhaps most important, Graham recognized, and discussed with Pasztor, the fact that Broumas had "a peculiar way of trading." Although these were "big money trades" involving thousands of shares, and although he was repeatedly buying and selling and paying commissions on the transactions, Graham realized that Broumas was not making any money on the trades. This economically irrational trading was a large red flag.

. . . .

In her defense, Graham notes that she "stood to gain absolutely nothing from Broumas' scheme," since Broumas traded through a "house account" for which she did not receive commissions. It is true that lack of opportunity for personal gain may suggest lack of motive, which may in turn be relevant to the question of scienter. But the absence of commissions does not necessarily negate either motive or scienter. Graham may have gone along with Broumas' scheme (or hidden her head in the sand) to please her bosses or to keep her job. Or she may have done so merely because she was reckless, regardless of any motive to gain money or favor. Either way, the absence of commissions does not absolve her of responsibility. . . .

Graham also points to the fact that she sought and obtained approval for Broumas' trades from her immediate supervisor, James Pasztor, who told her they were "fine." She "left it up to my supervisor," she states, to "say that this was not allowed." And she argues that this reliance negates the scienter necessary for an aiding and abetting violation. . . .

The SEC rejected Graham's reliance defense, noting that she is an experienced professional who has an independent duty to use diligence "where there are any unusual factors." Registered representatives are "under a duty to investigate," and "red flags and suggestions of irregularities demand inquiry as well as adequate follow-up and review." Given the abundance of red flags here, it would be very hard to characterize Graham's conduct as anything but extremely reckless, regardless of the approvals she received from Pasztor.

DECISION AND REMEDY The Court upheld the SEC findings that Graham, a registered representative, violated section 10(b) of the Securities Exchange Act of 1934 and Rule 10b-5 by aiding and abetting Broumas in the fraudulent trading of stock. The Court concluded that Voss had failed reasonably to supervise Graham with a view to preventing the securities violations. The Commission's decision was found to be reasonable and supported by substantial evidence.

CRITICAL THINKING: MANAGERIAL CONSIDERATION What steps should VCI have taken to have prevented this problem?

Exhibit 20–3   Comparison of Disclosure Requirements

Disclosure	Securities Act of 1933	Securities Exchange Act of 1934
When is disclosure required?	When new securities are issued	Throughout the life cycle of the security
How often is disclosure required?	One-time disclosure	Periodic disclosure
How is disclosure made?	Filing with the SEC: 1. Registration statement 2. Prospectus	Filing with the SEC: 1. Form 10-K, annually 2. Form 10-Q, quarterly 3. Form 8-K, monthly when a special event occurs

---

Disclosure under Rule 10b-5. Any material omission or misrepresentation of material facts in connection with the purchase or sale of a security may violate Section 10(b) and Rule 10b-5. The key to liability is whether the insider's information is material.

Some examples of material facts under Rule 10b-5 that require disclosure are fraudulent trading in the company stock by a broker–dealer, a dividend change (whether up or down), a contract for the sale of corporate assets, a new discovery of a process or a product, a significant change in the firm's financial condition, or a takeover bid by another firm or individual. Exhibit 20–3 compares the disclosure requirements of the 1933 Securities Act with the Securities and Exchange Act of 1934.

The Supreme Court has expressly adopted the standard of materiality applicable to Section 10(b) and Rule 10b-5. According to this standard, an omitted fact is material if there is a substantial likelihood that its disclosure would be considered significant by a reasonable investor.

Timing of Disclosure under Rule 10b-5. Courts have struggled with determining when information becomes public knowledge. Clearly, when inside information becomes public knowledge, insiders should be allowed to trade without disclosure. Insiders should refrain from trading for a reasonable waiting period when the news is not readily translatable into investment action. Presumably, this time period gives the news time to filter down and to be evaluated by the investing public. What constitutes a reasonable waiting period, however, is not at all clear.

The following is one of the landmark cases interpreting Section 10(b) and Rule 10b-5. The SEC sued Texas Gulf Sulphur Company for issuing a misleading press release. The release misrepresented the magnitude and value of a mineral discovery.

Case 20.4

Securities and Exchange Commission v. Texas Gulf Sulphur Co.

United States Court of Appeals, Second Circuit, 1968
401 F.2d 833

LANDMARK CASE

BACKGROUND AND FACTS Texas Gulf Sulphur Company (TGS) drilled a hole on November 12, 1963, near Timmins, Ontario, Canada, which appeared to yield a core with exceedingly high mineral content. Because TGS did not own the mineral rights in the surrounding regions, it maintained secrecy about the core sample results. It undertook evasive tactics to camouflage the drill site and drilled a second hole. TGS completed an extensive land acquisition program and then began drilling this lucrative site. Rumors spread. By early April 1964, a "tremendous staking rush [was] going on."

On April 11, 1964, an unauthorized report of the extraordinary mineral find hit the papers. On April 12, TGS issued a press release that played down the discovery and stated that it was too early to tell if the ore finding would be significant.

The Securities and Exchange Commission (SEC) filed suit against TGS, which had issued a deceptive press release on April 22, 1964. The trial court judge held that the issuance of the press release was lawful, because it was not issued for the purpose of benefiting the corporation, and no evidence indicated that any insider used the information in the press release to personal advantage. Thus, it was not "misleading or deceptive on the basis of the facts then known." The SEC appealed.

Judge WATERMAN

. . . .

At 3 P.M. on April 12, 1964, evidently believing it desirable to comment upon the rumors concerning the Timmins project, TGS issued the press release quoted in pertinent part[:]

> Recent drilling on one property near Timmins has led to preliminary indications that more drilling would be required for proper evaluation of this prospect. The drilling done to date has not been conclusive, but the statements made by many outside quarters are unreliable and include information and figures that are not available to TGS. The work done to date has not been sufficient to reach definite conclusions and any statements as to size and grade of ore would be premature and possibly misleading. When we have progressed to the point where reasonable and logical conclusions can be made, TGS will issue a definite statement to its stockholders and to the public in order to clarify the Timmins project.

. . . .

. . . It does not appear to be unfair to impose upon corporate management a duty to ascertain the truth of any statements the corporation releases to its shareholders or to the investing public at large. Accordingly, we hold that Rule 10b-5 is violated whenever assertions are made, as here, in a manner reasonably calculated to influence the investing public, e.g., by means of the financial media, if such assertions are false or misleading or are so incomplete as to mislead irrespective of whether the issuance of the release was motivated by corporate officials for ulterior purposes. It seems clear, however, that if corporate management demonstrates that it was diligent in ascertaining that the information it published was the whole truth and that such diligently obtained information was disseminated in good faith, Rule 10b-5 would not have been violated.

. . . .

We conclude, then, that, having established that the release was issued in a manner reasonably calculated to affect the market price of TGS stock and to influence the investing public, we must remand to the district court to decide whether the release was misleading to the reasonable investor and if found to be misleading, whether the court in its discretion should issue the injunction the SEC seeks.

DECISION AND REMEDY The appellate court's judgment was favorable to the SEC. It determined that the information contained in the press release was material and violated Rule 10b-5. The questions of whether the press release was misleading and which remedies should be imposed were remanded to the trial court for decision. A trial court is bound to apply the law as enunciated by the court of appeals in making this type of decision.

COMMENT Texas Gulf Sulphur Company was not only sued by the SEC, but numerous civil actions for damages were brought against it by plaintiff-investors who had sold their TGS stock as a result of the deceptively gloomy press release regarding the corporation's mineral exploration. All these suits were settled in 1972. In a federal lawsuit filed against TGS some two years after the initial case, a court of appeals held that investors who had sold stock relying on the representations in the press release could recover damages from both the corporation and the officers who had drafted the release. The court went on to state that the proper measure of damages was the difference between the selling price and the price at which the investors could have reinvested within a reasonable time after they became aware of TGS's curative press release announcing the strike of 25 million tons.

The court held that a diligent and reasonable investor could have known the information within four days of TGS's curative press release. The investors who sold their stock more than four days after the second press release was made could not recover under the Securities Exchange Act by claiming that they had relied on the earlier, deceptive release.

CRITICAL THINKING: MANAGEMENT CONSIDERATION How would you have handled this situation if you were in TGS management?

Scienter Requirement under Rule 10b-5. Two elements of a Section 10(b) and Rule 10b-5 violation are required. The first is the use of a manipulative or deceptive device in connection with the purchase or sale of a security, in which a material fact has been misrepresented or omitted. Second, the act must have been committed with scienter. The additional requirement of scienter limited the broad application of Section 10(b) after the *Texas Gulf Sulphur* case. The first case to establish this criterion follows.

Case 20.5

Ernst & Ernst v. Hochfelder

Supreme Court of the United States, 1976

425 U.S. 185, 96 S. Ct. 1375, 47 L. Ed. 2d 668

http://caselaw.findlaw.com/

LANDMARK CASE

BACKGROUND AND FACTS First Securities Company, a brokerage firm, retained Ernst & Ernst, a Chicago accounting firm, to audit its books. In addition to the auditing, Ernst & Ernst prepared and filed the necessary reports of First Securities with the SEC. The president of First Securities, Leston B. Nay, manipulated a fraudulent scheme of investment in which Hochfelder and others invested their money. The scheme involved interest rates on low-risk escrow accounts. An escrow account is one in which money is deposited with an impartial third party. Unfortunately for Hochfelder and the other investors, these accounts never existed. For more than twenty years, Hochfelder continued unknowingly to place money into a nonexistent account, because he received official-looking statements.

Nay took the money for his own use. The escrow accounts never appeared in Ernst & Ernst's audits, so it failed to suspect Nay. When Hochfelder wanted his money, Nay committed suicide and left information describing the fraud. Hochfelder filed a lawsuit against Ernst & Ernst for aiding and abetting Nay's fraud. The district court granted a judgment in favor of Ernst & Ernst. The court of appeals reversed the decision. The United States Supreme Court reviewed the issue.

Justice POWELL delivered the opinion of the Court.

The issue in this case is whether an action for civil damages may lie under Section 10(b) of the Securities Exchange Act of 1934, and Securities and Exchange Commission Rule 10b-5, in the absence of an allegation of intent to deceive, manipulate, or defraud on the part of the defendant.

Petitioner, Ernst & Ernst, is an accounting firm. From 1946 through 1967 it was retained by First Securities Company of Chicago (First Securities), a small brokerage firm and member of the Midwest Stock Exchange and of the National Association of Securities Dealers, to perform periodic audits of the firm's books and records. In connection with these audits Ernst & Ernst prepared for filing with the Securities and Exchange Commission (Commission) the annual reports required of First Securities. It also prepared for First Securities responses to the financial questionnaires of the Midwest Stock Exchange (Exchange).

Respondents were customers of First Securities who invested in a fraudulent securities scheme perpetrated by Leston B. Nay, president of the firm and owner of 92 percent of its stock. Nay induced the respondents to invest funds in "escrow" accounts that he represented would yield a high rate of return. Respondents did so from 1942 through 1966, with the majority of the transactions occurring in the 1950s. In fact, there were no escrow accounts as Nay converted respondents' funds to his own use immediately upon receipt.

This fraud came to light in 1968 when Nay committed suicide, leaving a note that described First Securities as bankrupt and the escrow accounts as "spurious." Respondents subsequently filed this action for damages against Ernst & Ernst. . . . As revealed through discovery, respondents' cause of action rested on a theory of negligent nonfeasance [negligently failing to perform a required act]. The premise was that Ernst & Ernst had failed to utilize "appropriate auditing procedures" in its audits of First Securities, thereby failing to discover internal practices of the firm said to prevent an effective audit. The practice principally relied on Nay's rule that only he could open mail addressed to him at First Securities or addressed to First Securities to his attention, even if it arrived in his absence. Respondents contended that if Ernst & Ernst had conducted a proper audit, it would have discovered this "mail rule." The existence of the rule then would have been disclosed in reports to the Exchange and to the Commission by Ernst & Ernst as an irregular procedure that prevented an effective audit. This would have led to an investigation of Nay that would have revealed the fraudulent scheme. Respondents specifically disclaimed the existence of fraud or intentional misconduct on the part of Ernst & Ernst.

. . . .

Section 10(b) makes unlawful the use or employment of "any manipulative or deceptive device or contrivance" in contravention of Commission rules. The words "manipulative or deceptive" used in conjunction with "device or contrivance" strongly suggest that Sec. 10(b) was intended to proscribe knowing or intentional misconduct.

. . . .

. . . When a statute speaks so specifically in terms of manipulation and deception, and of implementing devices and contrivances—the commonly understood terminology of intentional wrongdoing—and when its history reflects no more expansive intent, we are quite unwilling to extend the scope of the statute to negligent conduct.

DECISION AND REMEDY The United States Supreme Court reversed the court of appeals and held that in the absence of scienter, no cause of action for fraud exists under Section 10(b).

COMMENT Scienter is generally defined as a mental state embracing the intent to deceive, manipulate, or defraud. The more difficult question is whether recklessness is enough to satisfy the scienter requirement. In certain areas of the law, recklessness is considered a form of intentional conduct, where conduct is so careless as to evince a total disregard for the welfare of others. This type of recklessness then creates liability.

CRITICAL THINKING: POLITICAL CONSIDERATION Under the 1933 Security Act, any person who signs a business's registration statement may be held liable for a material misstatement of fact or a material omission. An injured investor does not have to prove intent to deceive. Under the Security Exchange Act of 1934, however, a person must prove scienter, that is, must prove the intent to deceive. Should a difference in proof exist between a new issue of stocks versus stocks that have been issued and are now traded?

Persons Who Have a Duty under Rule 10b-5. The SEC prosecutes insiders who trade a security, based on nonpublic information, for personal financial benefit. The reasoning behind this rule is that an insider should refrain from using nonpublic information to his gain, because such actions are unfair to individual investors who lack such information and have no equal means of acquiring the information. The public will lose faith and stop investing if it believes that insiders have an unfair advantage. The courts and the SEC prohibit insiders from trading, unless information first is disclosed to the general public.

Insider trading rules cover not only corporate officers, directors, and majority shareholders, but also anyone having access to, or receiving information of, a nonpublic nature from an insider on which trading is based. People to whom material information is given are known as **tippees**. The person giving the information is known as the **tipper**.

Before liability can be imposed, a fiduciary duty is owed by the tipper to the regulated company to refrain from disclosing nonpublic information, and the tippee must know of this duty. Once this duty is established, both the tipper and the tippee are liable for any profits made by the tippee, in addition to other liabilities imposed by the 1934 act.

The test is determined by whether a fiduciary duty exists. For example, if someone receives information and passes it on to a family member, who in turn passes this information to another person, the second passing of information does not violate this rule. Merely being related to the person who is the insider does not create a fiduciary relationship. The family member who has no direct inside information can pass the information on to others.

Another legal theory creating liability based on insider information is misappropriation of information. For example, if a person finds out information from a newspaper columnist prior to an article appearing in the paper and trades on this information, the trading will create liability. Likewise, a person may obtain information without computer authorization and may trade on this information. This trading also is misap-propriation of information.

Whether the insider information results from an insider's breach of fiduciary duty, a tipper–tippee relationship, or a misappropriation of information, the penalties for insider trading are the same. The SEC may refer criminal charges to the DOJ for prosecution. The SEC may seek an order of **disgorgement**, which means that if the order were granted, the wrongdoer would be required to return the wrongfully obtained profits. Those who profit from insider trading lose all their profits under a disgorgement order. The SEC may also seek civil money penalties up to three times the amount of profit.

The following is a case dealing with insider trading. The government sued on a criminal basis, because the defendant made more than $4.3 million by using insider information.

Case 20.6

United States v. O'Hagan

Supreme Court of the United States, 1997
521 U.S. 642, 117 S. Ct. 2199, 138 L. Ed. 2d 724
http://caselaw.findlaw.com/

BACKGROUND AND FACTS Defendant James O'Hagan was a partner in the law firm of Dorsey & Whitney in Minneapolis, Minnesota. In July 1988, Grand Metropolitan, PLC (Grand Met), a company based in London, England, retained Dorsey & Whitney as local counsel to represent Grand Met regarding a potential purchase of the Pillsbury Company, headquartered in Minneapolis. Both Grand Met and Dorsey & Whitney took precautions to protect the confidentiality of Grand Met's plans. O'Hagan did not work on the Grand Met representation. Dorsey & Whitney withdrew from representing Grand Met on September 9, 1988. Less than a month later, on October 4, 1988, Grand Met publicly announced its offer to purchase Pillsbury stock.

On August 18, 1988, while Dorsey & Whitney still represented Grand Met, O'Hagan began purchasing call options for Pillsbury stock. Each option gave him the right to purchase 100 shares of Pillsbury stock by a specified date in September 1988. Later in August and in September, O'Hagan made additional purchases of Pillsbury call options. By the end of September, he owned 2,500 unexpired Pillsbury options, apparently more than any other individual investor. O'Hagan also purchased, in September 1988, some 5,000 shares of Pillsbury common stock, at a price just under $39 per share. When Grand Met announced its plan in October, the price of Pillsbury stock rose to nearly $60 per share. O'Hagan then sold his Pillsbury call options and common stock, making a profit of more than $4.3 million.

The Securities and Exchange Commission initiated an investigation into O'Hagan's transactions, culminating in a fifty-seven-count indictment. The indictment alleged that O'Hagan defrauded his law firm and its client, Grand Met, by using for his own trading purposes material, nonpublic information regarding Grand Met's planned purchase. According to the indictment, O'Hagan used the profits he gained through this trading to conceal his previous embezzlement and conversion of unrelated client trust funds. A jury convicted O'Hagan on all fifty-seven counts, and he was sentenced to a forty-one-month term of imprisonment. The appellate court reversed the convictions and the government appealed.

Justice GINSBURG delivered the opinion of the Court.

. . . .

Under the "traditional" or "classical theory" of insider trading liability, §10(b) and Rule 10b-5 are violated when a corporate insider trades in the securities of his corporation on the basis of material, nonpublic information. Trading on such information qualifies as a "deceptive device" under §10(b), we have affirmed, because "a relationship of trust and confidence [exists] between the shareholders of a corporation and those insiders who have obtained confidential information by reason of their position with that corporation." That relationship, we recognized, "gives rise to a duty to disclose [or to abstain from trading] because of the 'necessity of preventing a corporate insider from . . . tak[ing] unfair advantage of . . . uninformed . . . stockholders.'" The classical theory applies not only to officers, directors, and other permanent insiders of a corporation, but also to attorneys, accountants, consultants, and others who temporarily become fiduciaries of a corporation.

The "misappropriation theory" holds that a person commits fraud "in connection with" a securities transaction, and thereby violates 10(b) and Rule 10b-5, when he misappropriates confidential information for securities trading purposes, in breach of a duty owed to the source of the information. Under this theory, a fiduciary's undisclosed, self-serving use of a principal's information to purchase or sell securities, in breach of a duty of loyalty and confidentiality, defrauds the principal of the exclusive use of that information. In lieu of premising liability on a fiduciary relationship between company insider and purchaser or seller of the company's stock, the misappropriation theory premises liability on fiduciary-turned-trader's deception of those who entrusted him with access to confidential information.

The two theories are complementary, each addressing efforts to capitalize on nonpublic information through the purchase or sale of securities. The classical theory targets a corporate insider's breach of duty to shareholders with whom the insider transacts; the misappropriation theory outlaws trading on the basis of nonpublic information by a corporate "outsider" in breach of a duty owed not to a trading party, but to the source of the information. The misappropriation theory is thus designed to "protec[t] the integrity of the securities markets against abuses by 'outsiders' to a corporation who have access to confidential information that will affect th[e] corporation's security price when revealed, but who owe no fiduciary or other duty to that corporation's shareholders."

In this case, the indictment alleged that O'Hagan, in breach of a duty of trust and confidence he owed to his law firm, Dorsey & Whitney, and to its client, Grand Met, traded on the basis of nonpublic information regarding Grand Met's planned . . . offer for Pillsbury common stock. This conduct, the Government charged, constituted a fraudulent device in connection with the purchase and sale of securities.

. . . .

We agree with the Government that misappropriation, as just defined, satisfies §10(b)'s requirement that chargeable conduct involve a "deceptive device or contrivance" used "in connection with" the purchase or sale of securities. We observe, first, that misappropriators, as the Government describes them, deal in deception. A fiduciary who "[pretends] loyalty to the principal while secretly converting the principal's information for personal gain," "dupes" or defrauds the principal.

. . . .

DECISION AND REMEDY The court found that O'Hagan violated the law by failing to disclose his personal trading to Grand Met and Dorsey, which made his conduct deceptive within the meaning of Section 10(b) of the Securities Exchange Act.

CRITICAL THINKING: PRACTICAL APPLICATION Assume you are in a restaurant and overhear a conversation among several people about a planned merger of two large corporations. You check with your broker and from the information he tells you, you conclude that the information you overheard has not been publicly disclosed. You do not mention this to your broker. Can you use this information to buy stocks of either corporations?

Section 18. **Section 18** of the 1934 Securities Exchange Act requires publicly held corporations registered with the SEC to file periodic and intermittent reports.[11] The annual report, Form 10-K, is filed at the end of the corporation's fiscal period. Form 10-K must include audited financial statements, the business's current financial status, and its securities holdings.

The unaudited quarterly report, Form 10-Q, reflects any financial changes that have occurred since the last reporting period. Form 8-K is filed any time a material event occurs, such as a change in management control, a significant judgment against the company, or a bankruptcy. A material event is any occurrence that a reasonably prudent investor would want to know about in order to reevaluate its investment.

If private parties relied on the documents filed, they may sue for damages. The reports on which a private party can rely are the 10-K and 8-K reports and the proxy statements because these are audited and certified. The quarterly 10-Q report is unaudited, so it cannot be relied upon. A plaintiff who claims that she or he relied on the filed documents must prove four elements:

1. False or misleading statements or omissions were made
2. The plaintiff purchased or sold shares
3. The plaintiff relied on the statements
4. The defendant knew that the statements were false or misleading or that omissions occurred.

If the previous items are proven, the plaintiff is entitled to damages.

Other Securities Laws

Over the decades since the 1933 and the 1934 acts were passed, other laws governing securities have been passed. Congress adopted new statutes in reaction to various events that demonstrated a particular weakness in the original statute. The new laws strengthened the controls over the securities markets. Reviews of some of these laws follow.

The Securities Investor Protection Act of 1970

A series of stockbrokerage houses failed in the 1960s, leading Congress to amend the 1934 act to protect the consumer. The amendment created the **Securities Investor Protection Corporation (SIPC)**, which manages a fund that protects investors from the financial harm caused when stockbrokerage houses fail. The fund is similar to that administered by the Federal Deposit Insurance Corporation (FDIC), which protects bank depositors.

Foreign Corrupt Practices Act

The Foreign Corrupt Practices Act (FCPA) of 1977 also amended the 1934 act. Although part of the FCPA applies to corporations doing business in other countries, the rest of the act applies to all corporations registered with the SEC, whether or not they are engaged in foreign business.

The FCPA requires, for the first time, public corporations to maintain records that accurately reflect their financial activities. All corporations reporting under the 1934 act are required to have an internal accounting system to ensure accurate records.

The act attempts to prevent the concealment of illegal activities. Some activities were criminal acts even prior to the adoption of the FCPA. In the past, corporations engaged in acts that ranged from the purchasing of castles in Ireland for top management to the paying of millions to foreign officials to ensure lucrative contracts. These millions of dollars in payment were not disclosed to the shareholders or to the SEC.

The **Insider Trading Sanctions Act (ITSA)** of 1984 gives additional power to the SEC for violations of insider trading. This act applies to people who use nonpublic information and who purchase or sell through a national securities exchange or a registered broker–dealer. The SEC can recover up to three times the profit made in these situations. Any recovery goes to the government, not to parties who may have been injured by such activity.

In 1988, this act was amended by the **Insider Trading and Securities Fraud Enforcement Act**. The amendment enlarged the scope of people who have civil liability under the act, gave the SEC authority

---

[11] The SEC provides a short description of the most common corporate filings made with the SEC at <http://www.sec.gov/edgarhp.htm>.

LEGAL HIGHLIGHT

Crime and Punishment

Starting in the mid-1980s, federal prosecutors, acting mainly on tips, unearthed some of the largest insider trading scandals in U.S. history. Americans and Wall Street were shocked by the numerous revelations of insider trading that resulted in the prosecution of some of the most successful traders. The following is a partial list of these people, their activities, and their ages at the time of sentencing.

PAUL THAYER, 65. *History:* Thayer was a corporate director with a number of major corporations. During the time he served on those boards, he leaked inside information to his girlfriend and a stockbroker, who in turn earned $3 million from the tips. Thayer did not make any money. The Securities and Exchange Commission (SEC) brought civil and criminal charges. He pleaded guilty to obstructing justice because he lied to the SEC.

Sentence: In May 1985, Thayer was sentenced to four years in prison and fined $5,000. He also paid the government $550,000 as a fine for the profits earned by others through his tips.

DENNIS B. LEVINE, 34. *History:* Levine was an investment banker who worked on Wall Street. Through his contacts, he set up an information network of Wall Street sources at investment banks and law firms. He traded on insider information through an offshore bank account, from which he earned $12.6 million on stock trades. He pleaded guilty to insider trading, perjury, and tax violations. He was given a lighter sentence in view of his cooperation with authorities, which led SEC investigators to Ivan Boesky and others.

Sentence: In February 1987, Levine was sentenced to two years in prison and fined $362,000. He repaid $11.6 million.

ILAN K. REICH, 32. *History:* Reich is a lawyer who gave Levine information about his law firm's corporate clients that were planning major corporate moves. Reich stopped giving Levine information on two occasions. Despite this, Levine set aside $300,000 for Reich, who never claimed the money. Reich pleaded guilty to charges of securities fraud.

Sentence: In January 1987, Reich was sentenced to one year and a day in prison and five years' probation. He paid $485,000 to the SEC.

IVAN BOESKY, 55. *History:* Boesky was known as Mr. Arbitrage on Wall Street. He is by far the biggest investor to be caught trading with insider information. Dennis Levine provided much of his information. After cooperating with the SEC, Boesky pleaded guilty to one felony count.

Sentence: In November 1987, Boesky was sentenced to three years in prison. He served twenty-two months in the federal prison at Lompoc, California, and four months at a Brooklyn, New York, halfway house. He repaid the government $50 million in illegal profits, paid $50 million in civil penalties, and agreed to withdraw permanently from the securities business.

MICHAEL MILKEN, 43. *History:* An employee of Drexel Burnham Lambert, Inc., Milken assisted Boesky by keeping fraudulent records to hide securities that Boesky owned. He failed to disclose to Drexel the true price of stocks purchased and sold, with the profits going to his junk bond operation. (A junk bond is an interest-bearing certificate held without a security [lien] that funds takeovers of businesses and provides a higher interest than other types of bonds. It is a high-risk investment.) He pleaded guilty to six felonies.

Sentence: In November 1990, Milken was sentenced to ten years in prison, to pay $200 million in fines to the government, and to pay $400 million in restitution to defrauded investors. He has been barred for life from the securities industry.

DREXEL BURNHAM LAMBERT, INC. *History:* An established Wall Street firm, it hired Michael Milken, who eventually took over Drexel's junk bond operation. By 1988, Milken and Drexel had half of the $140 billion junk bond market. Drexel and Boesky agreed covertly to defraud clients by driving up the price of certain stocks. Drexel pleaded guilty to six felony counts of securities fraud.

Sentence: In December 1988, Drexel was ordered to pay $680 million in fines and restitution and agreed to fire Milken.

TOSHIHIDE IGUCHI, 45. *History:* Iguchi was a bond trader for Daiwa Bank, Ltd., a Japanese bank. He caused the bank to lose $1.1 billion over eleven years on speculative bond investments. He pleaded guilty to six counts of financial fraud and embezzlement and conspiracy.

Sentence: In December 1996, he was sentenced to four years in prison and ordered to pay $2.6 million in fines and restitution.

EDDIE ANTAR, 51. *History:* Antar fabricated inventory that overstated income and then had public relations firms publicize the profits. His firm was Crazy Eddie.

Sentence: In May 1996, he was sentence to five years after he plead guilty.

DONALD FERRARINI, 71. *History:* Ferrarini reported nonexistent revenues that made his company, Underwriters Financial Group, look profitable.

Sentence: He was convicted in May 1999, and was sentence to twelve years under the Insider Trading Sanctions Act of 1984.

JONATHAN LEBED, 15. *History:* Lebed made more than $272,000 in profit from Internet stock fraud manipulation. He purchased large blocks of microcap stock, then touted the stock on web message boards. He was the first minor against whom the SEC brought charges.

Sentence: In September 2000, he plead no contest and agreed to repay the money plus interest for a total of $285,000.

to reward informants in insider trading cases,[12] required securities firms to adopt specific policies and procedures to prevent insider trading, and increased criminal penalties. The award of treble damages against securities firms is available for failing to maintain a proper system of supervision to prevent and detect insider trading violations by employees.

Securities Enforcement Remedies and Penny Stock Reform Act of 1990

Congress enacted the **Securities Enforcement Remedies and Penny Stock Reform Act** of 1990 in response to the growing number of fraudulent activities discovered in the stock market. As its name indicates, the act has two major functions: to strengthen enforcement powers of the SEC and to regulate the penny stock market.

Penny Stock Reform. Low-priced stock, ranging in value from a few pennies to several dollars per share, was the subject of unscrupulous activity during the 1980s. Many investors lost money in this high-risk market. This act authorizes the SEC to adopt rules requiring securities dealers and brokers to provide potential investors with specific information about the penny stock prices and the risks involved in the volatile penny stock market.

Enforcement Remedies. The act grants the SEC (1) new authority to issue cease-and-desist orders and (2) expanded authority to impose civil money penalties. A cease-and-desist order is an administrative remedy that directs a person to refrain from engaging in further violative conduct. Cease-and-desist authority permits swift remedial action in response to illegal conduct without filing a lawsuit for a temporary restraining order in court.

The SEC is authorized to issue cease-and-desist orders against anyone who violates securities laws or who engages in activities that make it likely that a future violation of the securities laws will occur. The alleged violator is served notice and a hearing is held. If the SEC issues the cease-and-desist order, the person can file a lawsuit in federal district court for a judicial review of the order.

Prior to this act, the SEC had the authority to seek only an order of disgorgement. In the absence of a criminal prosecution or a private suit for damages, even though the wrongdoer deliberately violated the law, he or she did not risk monetary sanctions more severe than to return the illegal profit under an order of disgorgement. Violators did not have any personal risk because they were left in the same financial position as they had been prior to the wrongdoing. This act greatly expanded the SEC's authority to seek civil money penalties against wrongdoers. People who engage in wrongdoing are now placed at financial risk.

Penalties are applied to active violators of the securities laws. In one case, a broker–dealer failed to comply with the SEC's customer protection rule. The rule

---

[12] The SEC provides a page that offers a bounty to people who provide information on insider trading: <http://www.sec.gov/enforce/insider.htm>.

required the broker–dealer to maintain a separate account for a customer's fully paid or excess margin securities. A margin security account is used when the broker allows a customer to purchase securities on credit. The customer then pays the amount owed into the account. The broker–dealer failed to comply with this regulation simply because it was unwilling to devote the resources necessary to maintain separate accounts. Although the firm did not engage actively in a scheme to defraud, the customer was exposed to a serious risk of loss in the event that the broker–dealer house failed.

The SEC is authorized to impose civil money penalties, which provide a disincentive to engage in insider trading, market manipulation, and fraudulent financial reporting. These penalties also discourage those who want to maximize profits through cost reduction by failing to comply with the SEC regulations.

The **Market Reform Act** of 1990 addresses the stability of U.S. securities markets when extraordinarily volatile situations occur. In October 1987, the market fell 508 points in one day. At that time, the fall amounted to a 23 percent decline. This severe decline resulted in the Market Reform Act. One decade later, in October 1997, the stock market experienced its largest point one-day decline in history, a 554-point decline in the Dow Jones Industrial Average. Because the market was higher, this decline meant less than an 8 percent decline in stock prices.

Fundamental changes have occurred since the original securities acts were adopted in the mid-1930s. The marketplace has become increasingly institutional. Significant numbers of institutional portfolio managers utilize indexing strategies that trade the market as a whole (the index) through purchases of portfolios of securities rather than by making judgments on individual stocks. These strategies can cause extraordinary peak volume and volatility and can overwhelm the market's capacity. The Market Reform Act ensures the stability, resiliency, and integrity of the nation's securities markets by granting the SEC broader powers.

Limits are now set on program trading (computer-driven programs) that send sell orders when the market reaches certain benchmarks. In the event of a sudden, large movement in the price of securities (up or down), trading is suspended to control the stock markets until order has been restored.

The SEC prohibits manipulative practices related to market price levels and trading practices. The statute allows increased monitoring of risks posed to firms that are SEC regulated. For example, the financial failure of Drexel Burnham Lambert Group, Inc., affected its two principal regulated subsidiaries, Drexel Burnham Lambert, Inc., a registered broker-dealer, and Drexel Burnham Lambert Government Securities, Inc., a registered government securities dealer. Large traders are required to keep records and provide information to the SEC. Additionally, the Market Reform Act established a coordinated national system for the safe and accurate clearance and settlement of securities sales and purchases.

The **National Securities Markets Improvement Act** of 1996 significantly impacted state securities laws, especially those laws that regulate investment advisers and those laws governing the filing requirements of mutual funds. The act ended the dual regulation of investment advisers by providing the SEC authority over any adviser who manages $25 million or more of assets. Any advisor whose management load falls below this sum is now regulated by the individual states.

This act is particularly important for investment advisers who trade in mutual funds because they make up a large percentage of the market and are sold nationally. Today, if the SEC approves an issue for sale, the stock issuer is no longer required to have a second review at the state level. Issuers, however, still must pay fees to a state to be permitted to sell within that state. A state must impose requirements similar to those that the SEC requires regarding capital, margin, financial responsibility, making and keeping records, bonding, or operational reporting.

The **Private Securities Litigation Reform Act** of 1995 curtails lawsuits against businesses based on securities law violations. Numerous cases filed during the past decades were based on questionable grounds, forcing businesses to incur substantial costs and to expend considerable time in defending themselves.

The act places limits on private persons considering litigation. The act allows corporations to make statements or projections provided that they are identified as such in a document called a **forward-looking statement**. This statement must state that actual results may differ materially from the predictions. The corporation will be held liable, however, if it made the statements with actual knowledge of the information being false. Forward-looking statements are not authorized for initial public offerings.

The Private Securities Litigation Reform Act limits personal liability. Any damages awarded must be based on individual actual fault rather than on joint liability with others. Joint liability, however, is available in two instances.

First, when all defendants knew that the statements were false and that investors would be likely to rely on the false statements, the defendants can be held jointly liable. In this situation, all defendants can be held individually liable. Additionally, each defendant may be required to pay the judgment owed by the other defendants if those defendants disappear or are insolvent. The purpose for the policy is to protect the innocent investors and to maximize the penalty amount against a knowing wrongdoer. For example, the plaintiff is awarded $300,000. Defendant A is responsible for $200,000, and Defendant B is responsible for $100,000. Defendant A goes into bankruptcy and cannot pay any portion of the judgment. Defendant B, because of the fraud involved, must pay all of the $300,000.

Second, if the plaintiff has a net worth of less than $200,000 and one or more of the defendants cannot pay the judgment, the SEC can require the remaining defendants to pay up to 150 percent of the amount of their judgment to the plaintiff. For example, a plaintiff is awarded a judgment of $500,000. Defendant A is liable in the amount of $200,000, Defendant B is liable for $200,000, and Defendant C for $100,000. Defendant A goes into bankruptcy and cannot pay any of the $200,000. The SEC can require Defendant B to pay up to $300,000 and Defendant C up to $150,000 toward the $500,000 judgment.

The act requires the plaintiffs to certify that they purchased the security honestly, not merely to bring the lawsuit. Further, they must sign a document stating their willingness to represent all people in their similar position. These plaintiffs cannot accept any payment for serving as the representative beyond the award that everyone else in the class receives.

In a class action lawsuit, the plaintiffs are restricted in alleging a Racketeer Influence and Corrupt Organization Act (RICO) violation. The only time a RICO violation may be pursued by a class action suit is after a defendant has been criminally convicted of security laws violations.

State Securities Laws

All states have their own corporate securities laws that regulate the offering of and sale of securities within individual state borders. Since the adoption of the federal 1933 and 1934 acts, state and federal governments have regulated securities concurrently. Indeed, both acts specifically allow state securities laws. Certain features are common to all state blue sky laws. For example, they all have antifraud provisions, many of which are patterned after the federal law. Most state corporate securities laws regulate securities brokers and dealers.

Typically, these laws provide for the registration or qualification of securities offered or issued for sale within the state. Unless an applicable exemption from registration is found, issuers must register or qualify their stock with the appropriate state office.

A difference in philosophy exists among the state statutes. Many statutes are similar to the Securities Act of 1933 and mandate certain disclosures before the registration is effective. They may require a permit to sell the securities. Other statutes have fairness standards that a corporation must meet in order to offer or sell stock in the state. A few states require a **merit registration**, whereby the states review the registration for its merits rather than being restricted to reviewing it for disclosures only. The Uniform Securities Act (adopted in part by several states) was drafted to be acceptable to states with differing regulatory philosophies.

International Consideration

Attitudes toward Securities Regulations

At this moment, in some country around the world, a stock market is open, is doing business, and can be monitored from homes via personal computers and television. Each market is operated in accordance with the laws of its host country. No international agreements have been made regarding stock markets.

U.S. law has criminalized violations of the heavily regulated securities markets. Computers monitor the markets to ensure compliance with the laws. Other countries, however, differ in their attitudes toward securities regulation.

Japan has legislation prohibiting securities violations, but the government rarely enforces these laws. In the past, some large Japanese stockbrokerage houses reimbursed large traders in the stock market for losses that they incurred on recommended investments. The public revelation of this news eventually led to a change in the government and promises by the stockbrokers to treat large investors the same as small investors. The Japanese market is not as heavily regulated as the U.S. market.

Members of the European Union (EU) have different views of insider trading. Denmark, France, Great Britain, and Switzerland have insider trading prohibitions, whereas the rest of the member nations do not. Large profits have been made on international stock markets. *Caveat emptor* (let the buyer beware) applies to any U.S. investor in the overseas market.

In 1990, Congress passed the **International Securities Enforcement Cooperation Act**. It allows the SEC to cooperate with other countries to regulate security markets and transactions. The SEC has entered into memorandums of understanding with several foreign countries, allowing for the exchange of information among countries. An outgrowth of this statute was the creation of the **International Organization of Securities Commission**, which purpose is to cooperate to promote high standards in regulating to maintain just, efficient, and sound markets. It has four regional standing committees: Africa–Middle East, Asia–Pacific, European, and Interamerican. In carrying out its purpose, the commission established, among other programs, a set of international accounting standards.[13]

---

[13] For more information about the International Organization of Securities Commission go to <http://www.iosco.org/gen-info_01.html>.

LEGALLY SPEAKING

Purchasing and Selling Securities on the Web

More than 200 securities firms offer online brokerage services with an estimated ten million-plus online accounts. Not surprisingly, the online brokerage industry is experiencing growing pains. State and national securities regulators have been bombarded with complaints from investors stemming from much-publicized server outages, computer glitches, and fraud.

Many members of the public are currently or in the near future will be purchasing securities using web resources. If you decide to trade online, you need to thinking about the following items:

✔ Receive full disclosure, prior to opening your account, about the alternatives to buying and selling securities online if the online account is not functional. Have the broker explain how to obtain account information if you cannot access the firm's web site. Do not be in a hurry. Shop around before you pick an online brokerage firm and do your own investigation. Leading financial publications rate online brokers using criteria such as speed of execution and customer satisfaction.

✔ Understand that you probably are not linked directly to the market, and that the click of your mouse does not instantly execute the trade. Do not forget that technology can fail and that any system can be overwhelmed by demand. Remember that in volatile markets your order could be delayed and you may not get the price you want.

✔ Understand how the software works before you make your first trade; find out who to contact or a web site where you can make corrections if you make a mistake or have a problem.

✔ Receive information from the firm to substantiate any advertised claims concerning the ease and speed of online trading. Look beyond the slick advertising. Carefully read the customer account agreement. Know your rights.

✔ Search out information from the firm to see if it has had significant web site outages, delays, and other interruptions to securities trading and account access.

✔ Seek information before trading about entering and canceling orders (market, limit and stop loss) and the details and risks of margin accounts (borrowing to buy stocks).

✔ Determine whether you are receiving delayed or real-time stock quotes and when and how often your account information will be updated.

✔ Review the firm''s privacy and web site security policies and whether your name may be used for mailing lists or other promotional activities by the firm or any other party. Remember, these policies probably have a clause that allows the firm to change the policies such that information that is private today may be made available for sale after the change of policy.

✔ Receive clear information about sales commissions and fees and conditions that apply to any advertised discount on commissions.

✔ Know how to, and if necessary, contact a customer service representative with your concerns and request prompt attention and fair consideration.

✔ Contact your state or provincial securities agency to verify the registration/licensing status and disciplinary history of the online brokerage firm. Ask for the firm's CRD record to determine whether it has a regulatory disciplinary history. (CRD stands for Central Registration Depository, a computer database containing information on all registered brokers and brokerage firms in the United States.)

Chapter Summary

Securities are regulated by both federal and state authorities. A security can be something other than a stock or bond. It is any financial transaction in which an investor exchanges money for an interest in a common enterprise with the expectation of making a profit through the endeavors of the promoter or third party.

Two primary federal statutes have been adopted: the Securities Act of 1933 and the Securities Exchange Act of 1934. Both the 1933 and 1934 acts prohibit fraud in the issuance of securities and in the disclosure of information available to the investing public.

The 1933 act regulates new issues of securities and requires, prior to issuance, full disclosure of all material facts. This information is presented in a prospectus, which is based on the registration statement. The registration statement is filed with the Securities and Exchange Commission and must be signed by the corporation's principal executive officer, principal accounting officer, and principal financial officer as well as by a majority of the members of the board of directors. Any person signing the registration statement is personally liable if full and truthful disclosure of all material facts is lacking. Certain transactions and securities are exempt from the registration requirements of the 1933 act.

The Securities Exchange Act of 1934 regulates securities that are traded on national exchanges and securities extensively traded over the counter. In addition, this statute established the SEC.

Under Section 10(b) and SEC's Rule 10b-5, no individual may take advantage of insider information, whether a situation involves new securities or ones actively traded. Most insiders are either directors, officers,

key employees, or owners of 10 percent or more of the common stock. Rule 10b-5 applies, however, to both insiders and tippees. Any profits realized from inside information belong to the corporation. Substantial criminal penalties can be assessed.

Over the decades Congress has adopted other securities laws. The Securities Investor Protection Act of 1970 created the Securities Investor Protection Corporation. This corporation manages a fund that protects investors from financial harm, if their stock-brokerage house fails. The Foreign Corrupt Practices Act requires all corporations registered with the SEC to maintain records that accurately reflect their financial activities, to maintain internal accounting systems that ensure accurate records, and to prevent concealment of illegal activities.

The Insider Trading Sanctions Act of 1984 provides the SEC with additional powers to punish violations of insider trading. The Insider Trading and Securities Fraud Enforcement Act amended this act in 1988. The act enlarged the number of people who are liable for insider trading, provided the SEC authority to reward informants, required firms to adopt policies on insider trading, and increased the criminal penalties for SEC violations.

The Securities Enforcement Remedies and Penny Stock Reform Act of 1990 provided more regulation of the penny stock market and granted the SEC more enforcement remedies. The Market Reform Act of 1990 limited the stock market during volatile situations, placed limits on program trading, and prohibited additional manipulative practices.

Using the World Wide Web

Securities are offered over the Internet. The SEC allows businesses to reference its web site and include this statement: "Our SEC filings are also available to the public from our web site." Any registration statement filed with the SEC, however, must include all relevant information and cannot merely refer to the information at its web site.

The SEC offers many educational publications for consumers. You can call 1-800-SEC-0330 to order these. A number of these publications are available on its web

site. Some web sites for various trading organizations include those listed below.

Transparency International is an organization devoted to curbing national and international corruption. This organization supports the position that all information about a business be open (transparent) and available to the public. Openness helps to deter corruption and other criminal activity. Transparency International's web site has a list of nations considered to be bribe-takers and another list of nations considered to be bribe-givers.

Finding the Law on the Web

Cornell University, Legal Information Institute, popular names of statutes
http://www.law.cornell.edu/uscode/topn/

Securities and Exchange Commission, links to other sites
http://www.sec.gov/others.htm#oreg

Securities and Exchange Commission, consumer publications
http://www.sec.gov/consumer/online.htm

Transparency International
http://www.transparency.org/

American Stock Exchange
http://www.amex.com

Chicago Board Options Exchange
http://www.sec.gov/edgarhp.htm

Chicago Stock Exchange
http://www.chicagostockex.com

NASD
http://www.nasd.com/

New York Stock Exchange
http://www.nyse.com/

North American Securities Administrators Association
http://www.nasaa.org/

California Public Employees' Retirement System
http://www.calpers.ca.gov

Chapter Web Sites

Securities and Exchange Commission
http://www.sec.gov/

University of Cincinnati College of Law, covers most securities laws
http://www.law.uc.edu/CCL/

Stanford University, security litigation
http://securities.stanford.edu/about/caveat.html

Reves v. Ernst & Young
http://caselaw.findlaw.com/

Securities Act of 1933
http://www4.law.cornell.edu/uscode/15/ch2A.html

Securities fraud and investor protection
http://www.securitieslaw.com/

Securities and Exchange Commission, *Plain English Handbook*
http://www.sec.gov/consumer/plaine.htm

Securities and Exchange Commission's EDGAR database of corporate information
http://www.sec.gov/edgarhp.htm

Red Herring IPO site
http://www.redherring.com

Securities Exchange Act of 1934
http://www4.law.cornell.edu/uscode/15/ch2B.shtml

Securities and Exchange Commission, small business information
http://www.sec.gov/smbus1.htm

Securities and Exchange Commission listing of commission members
http://www.sec.gov/asec/seccom.htm

Securities and Exchange Commission organization
http://www.sec.gov/asec/wwwsec.htm

Securities and Exchange Commission regional offices
http://www.sec.gov/asec/secaddr.htm

Securities and Exchange Commission, frauds and scams
http://www.sec.gov/enforce/inva.htm

Ernst & Ernst v. Hochfelder
http://caselaw.findlaw.com/

United States v. O'Hagan
http://caselaw.findlaw.com/

Securities and Exchange Commission's bounty page for insider information
http://www.sec.gov/enforce/insider.htm

International Organization of Securities Commission
http://www.iosco.org/gen-info_01.html

'Lectric Law Library Reference Room
http://www.lectlaw.com/ref.html

Securities and Exchange Commission, most recent actions
http://www.seclaw.com/Welcome.shtml

Securities and Exchange Commission, consumer complaints
http://www.sec.gov/consumer/howoiea.htm

Web Activities

20–1 What happens when a security is either lost or stolen? The question is how to get a replacement for the security. Go to the 'Lectric Law Library Reference Room at <http://www.lectlaw.com/ref.html> and click on "Investments & Securities." On this page you will find a topic list. Click on "Replacing Lost/Stolen Securities Laws." How do you replace a lost or stolen security?

20–2 Select a business that is registered with the Securities and Exchange Commission. You need to know the most recent news that the federal government or the public companies have taken. Look up the company by going to <http://www.seclaw.com/Welcome.shtml> to find out what is happening with it.

Key Terms

accredited investor
blue sky law
disgorgement
due diligence defense
Electronic Data
    Gathering, Analysis,
    and Retrieval
    (EDGAR)
exempt security
exempt transaction
forward-looking
    statement
insider trading
Insider Trading Sanctions
    Act (ITSA)
Insider Trading and
    Securities Fraud
    Enforcement Act

International
    Organization of
    Securities
    Commission
International Securities
    Enforcement
    Cooperation Act
intrastate offering
    exemption
issuer
Market Reform Act
merit registration
National Securities
    Markets
    Improvement Act
private offering
    exemption
Private Securities
    Litigation Reform
    Act

prospectus
proxy
red herring prospectus
registration statement
Regulation A
Regulation D
restricted securities
Rule 10b-5
Rule 144
Rule 144A
Rule 415
Rule 504
Rule 505
Rule 506
safe harbor exemption
scienter
Section 10(b)
Section 16
Section 18

Securities Act of 1933
Securities Enforcement
    Remedies and Penny
    Stock Reform Act
Securities Exchange Act
    of 1934
Securities and Exchange
    Commission (SEC)
Securities Investor
    Protection
    Corporation (SIPC)
security
shelf registration
small offering exemption
tippee
tipper
tombstone advertisement
unaccredited investor

Questions and Case Problems

20–1 Requirement of Registration Maresh, an experienced geologist, owned certain oil and gas leases covering land in Nebraska. To raise money for the drilling of a test well, he undertook to sell fractional interests in the leases. He approached Garfield, with whom he had done business in the past. Garfield had mentioned that he would be interested in investing in some of Maresh's future oil ventures. Garfield had wide business experience in the stock market and in oil stocks. He believed that the investment in Maresh's gas leases could be lucrative. Based on Garfield's promise to wire the money promptly, Maresh began drilling. Soon after, when Maresh realized that the land was dry, Garfield claimed that he could rescind the agreement to invest, because the investment offered by Maresh was a security within the meaning of the Securities Act of 1933 and it had not been registered. Did Maresh offer a security within the meaning of the 1933 act? Explain. [*Garfield v. Strain*, 320 F.2d 116 (10th Cir. 1963)]

20–2 Possible False Statements Basic, Inc., was a publicly traded company primarily engaged in manufacturing chemical refractories for the steel industry. Combustion Engineering was in a similar business and was interested in acquiring Basic. In 1976, representatives

from both companies met to discuss a possible merger. In 1978, Basic made three public statements denying any merger negotiations. About one month after the last denial, Basic announced the merger. Plaintiffs had sold their stock after Basic issued its first denial. They brought action on the basis that directors had issued three false or misleading statements that violated Section 10(b) and Rule 10b-5. The defendants argued that the misstatements were immaterial and not a violation. How should the court handle this defense? [*Basic Inc. v. Levinson*, 485 U.S. 224, 108 S. Ct. 978, 99 L. Ed. 2d 194 (1988)]

20–3 Insider Chiarella was a printer who handled announcements of corporate takeover bids. Even though the documents concealed the target corporations' identities, he was able to deduce the names of the target companies. He purchased stock in target companies and sold the shares immediately after the takeover attempts were made public. He realized a gain of slightly more than $30,000 over fourteen months. The Securities and Exchange Commission investigated and Chiarella was convicted of insider trading. He appealed his conviction. What was the result? Explain. [*Chiarella v. United States*, 445 U.S. 222, 110 S. Ct. 1108, 63 L. Ed. 2d 348 (1980)]

20–4 Press Releases On September 1, 1971, Ecological Science Corp. issued a press release stating, in part, that it had renegotiated the terms of approximately $14 million in loans from its prime lender and that, under the renegotiated agreement, $4 million was due on demand and the remainder on a specified date. The press release, however, failed to mention that on the same date as the renegotiated loan agreement, an insurance and annuity association refused to provide the corporation with the $4 million loan that it had planned to use to repay the demand loan. Moreover, while discussing its European prospects in the press release, Ecological Science Corp. failed to mention the proposed transfer of voting control among its European subsidiaries. Has Ecological Science Corp. violated any of the provisions of the Securities Exchange Act of 1934? Explain. [*Securities and Exchange Commission v. Koenig*, 469 F.2d 198 (2d Cir. 1972)]

20–5 Insider Trading Emerson Electric Co. owned 13.2 percent of Dodge Manufacturing Co. stock. Within six months of the stock purchase, Emerson sold enough shares to a broker to reduce its holding to 9.96 percent of its former Dodge holdings. One week later (but less than six months after Emerson's initial purchase), Emerson sold its remaining shares of Dodge stock. The sole purpose of Emerson's initial sale of just over 3 percent of its Dodge stock was to avoid liability under Section 16 of the Securities Exchange Act of 1934, which prohibits short-swing trading. Assuming that Emerson made no profit on the initial sale of stock, but made substantial profits when it sold the remaining 9.96 percent of Dodge stock, must it return its profits on the sale? Explain. [*Reliance Electric Co. v. Emerson Electric Co.*, 404 U.S. 418, 92 S. Ct. 596, 30 L. Ed. 2d 575 (1972)]

20–6 What Is a Security? American Breeding Herds, Inc. (ABH), offered a cattle breeding plan, under which Ronnett contracted to buy thirty-six Charolais cows at $3,000 per head and a one-quarter interest in a Charolais bull at $5,000, totaling $113,000. The ABH agreement described itself as a "tax shelter program . . . unlike the purchase of securities such as stocks and bonds." Ronnett entered into the agreement based on investment advice from Shannon, an investment counselor. The cows were tagged and sent to an ABH approved breeding ranch. Ronnett signed a maintenance agreement and paid a monthly maintenance fee. Was the ABH plan a security? Should it have been registered under the securities law? Explain. [*Ronnett v. American Breeding Herds, Inc.*, 124 Ill. App. 3d 842, 464 N.E.2d 1202, 80 Ill. Dec. 218 (1984)]

20–7 Insider Dirks advised institutional investors on the financial merits of different insurance companies. A for-

mer officer of Equity Funding of America told Dirks that Equity Funding had fraudulently overstated many assets in its financial reports. While investigating this information, Dirks openly discussed the matter with reporters and a number of his clients. He did not own any shares. Some of his clients sold their stock based on information received from Dirks. The stock fell from about $26 a share to $15 a share in two weeks. The Securities and Exchange Commission (SEC) censured Dirks, contending that he was an insider or a tippee of an insider. Dirks appealed the censure. Should the SEC censure of Dirks be upheld? Explain. [*Dirks v. Securities and Exchange Commission*, 463 U.S. 646, 103 S. Ct. 3255, 77 L. Ed. 2d 911 (1983)]

20–8 What Is a Security? Adams devised a plan to sell "rabbit kits." For $7,200 per kit, a person would receive twelve female and two male rabbits that should produce 720 breeding females within a year. Part of the sales promotion was that Adams would be available for consultation. Also, Adams requested that all buyers join an association that would purchase pelts. Membership in the association was not part of the "rabbit kit." Adams controlled the association. The state of Florida claimed that Adams was selling an unlicenced security. Was Adams selling securities that should have been registered? Explain. [*Adams v. State*, 443 So.2d 1003 (Fla. Dist. Ct. App. 1983)]

20–9 Advertising vs. Financial Information Apple Computer developed and marketed the Lisa line of computers. The company promoted this new line of computers as if it would take over the computer market. This release was publicized in the major journals with the following quotation: "Lisa is going to be phenomenally successful in the first year out of the chute." Many critics pointed out that Lisa was not IBM compatible, that it experienced problems with software suppliers, and that it was very expensive. Lisa turned out to be a complete failure, causing a 75 percent drop in Apple stock. Purchasers of Apple stock brought an action against Apple for failure to disclose problems with Lisa. Who prevails? Explain. [*In re Apple Computer Securities Litigation*, 886 F.2d 1109 (9th Cir. 1989)]

20–10 Internet You are cruising the World Wide Web when you find an interesting web site at which you read about a company and its product. You believe that this company will be a good investment. You follow the instructions on the web site and purchase 500 shares. Six months later you conclude that you were defrauded. You decide to complain to the SEC. What happens to your complaint once it reaches the SEC? Go to <http://www.sec.gov/consumer/howoiea.htm>.

Every agreement concerning trade, every regulation of trade, restrains. To bind, to restrain, is of their very essence. The true test of legality is whether the restraint imposed is such as merely regulates and perhaps thereby promotes competition or whether it is such as may suppress or even destroy competition.

Board of Trade of the City of Chicago v. United States, 246 U.S. 231, 38 S. Ct. 242, 62 L. Ed. 683, 1918
Justice Louis Dembitz Brandeis, 1856–1941
Associate Justice, United States Supreme Court, 1916–1939

Outline

Ethical Consideration

Antitrust Laws and Medical Costs: A Help or a Hindrance?

You are a high-level administrator at one of the three large hospitals in a metropolitan area. The physicians on the hospital's staff are pressuring you to purchase a specialized laser surgery unit. If the hospital purchases this unit, the other two hospitals will purchase similar units to remain competitive. A feasibility study shows that one unit will service the community's needs. One reason for high health-care costs is the duplication of expensive, but often underutilized, high-tech equipment and services that the administration of each hospital believes it must provide to remain competitive.

If you could, you would have the administrators from the three hospitals in your area meet and work out a program in which distinct specialties and services would be allocated among the various hospitals. Units that earn money (such as maternity wards) and units that lose money (such as burn units) would be distributed so that each hospital could earn income. This system would reduce the need for each of the competing hospitals to acquire all of the latest equipment, would help ensure that the equipment purchased would be better utilized, and would reduce duplication of services.

You know that such a scheme violates the antitrust laws. Your local congresswoman is involved with health-care reform issues and favors hospitals working together to reduce the multiplicity of services and equipment. In a recent conversation with your congresswoman, you told her of your dilemma. She confidently told you that she is sure that hospitals will be exempted from the antitrust laws in a very short time. This exemption is included in proposed legislation.

You would like to meet with the other hospital administrators to study the feasibility of dividing up the specialties. If the study were completed in time, it would contain the type of information that could be submitted to U.S. House and Senate committees studying the problem of antitrust exemption for hospitals. Because no exemption now exists, however, you may be in violation of the antitrust laws if you meet with the other hospital administrators. Do you wait until hospitals legally are exempted from antitrust laws or do you meet with the other hospital administrators to conduct a study? Use the ethical model presented in Chapter 2 and reprinted on the inside front cover to develop your answer.

Introduction

To understand what *antitrust laws* are, we need to look at the definition of a trust, the history of how business trusts operated, and the antitrust statutes that countered these trusts.

Laws that regulate economic competition are referred to as **antitrust laws**. Their purpose is to prevent businesses from controlling the economy *through restraints of trade* and *monopolies*. During the last half of the nineteenth century, trusts controlled the economy. A **trust** is a legal entity that encompasses three parties, the *trustor,* the *trustee,* and the *beneficiary.* The **trustor** creates the trust and names the trustee and the beneficiary. The **trustee** holds title to property and manages the property for the benefit of one or more persons or businesses. The people who benefit are called the **beneficiaries**. The beneficiaries are entitled to income from the property.

After the Civil War (1861–1865), large corporations used trusts to eliminate competition. Corporations engaged in the same type of business combined together to create a trust. These corporations designated themselves as both the trustor and beneficiary and then also designated a trustee. Once the trust was created, the corporations transferred their stock to a trustee and received trust certificates in return. The trustee made decisions that fixed prices, controlled production, and determined the control of exclusive geographic markets for the entire industry. Corporations (the beneficiaries) participating in a trust no longer competed with one another. The trusts wielded such power that corporations outside the trusts were unable to affect the market. Basically, these corporations viewed their competitors as friends and their customers as enemies.

Through these trusts, businesses created economic arrangements either to create a *monopoly* or to *restrain trade*. Although **monopoly** is not defined in any statute, the courts find that a monopoly exists when a

658 •   Unit IV *Business and Government Regulation*

business has either exclusive control or nearly total control of the market share of a business aspect or even of a whole industry.

Restraints of trade (restraining the competition) are not defined by any statute either. The courts find a restraint of trade when businesses try to affect trade by substantially reducing competition. A business may act alone or with others. It does not need to try to achieve a monopoly; it merely needs to try to substantially reduce competition.

During the nineteenth century, trusts gained control of several major industries, including oil, cotton, whiskey, sugar, and linseed oil. Their activities constituted a monopoly in each geographic area. For example, Standard Oil Trust sold kerosene at a price below its own costs to drive smaller competitors out of business. Once its monopoly position was assured, Standard Oil raised prices to recoup the losses and reap monopoly profits. Whether the trust gained a monopoly or restrained trade, the overall effect was to end competition and to pass on higher prices to consumers.

During this time period, common law protected a business's freedom to enter a market and to conduct trade in any manner. The common law, however, was inadequate in dealing with abuses by the giant corporations and trusts conducting trade. The public became concerned that the trusts controlled an increasing number of industries through unfair methods. Some states attempted to control such restraints in trade by enacting statutes to outlaw trusts.

By the 1880s, the federal government recognized that restraints and monopolies were a national problem. Because state statutes have no jurisdiction over interstate trade abuses, the states could not handle these abuses. Congress needed to find a way to destroy the trusts without destroying free enterprise. Congress, therefore, passed a number of antitrust statutes. The most important statutes are the Sherman Act, the Clayton Act, and the Federal Trade Commission Act. All of these acts have been amended over the years. These statutes are enforced by the Department of Justice[1] and the Federal Trade Commission.[2] Exhibit 21–1 lists the major antitrust laws and provides a brief summary of each.

For more than a century, these antitrust laws have protected the competitive process that is the basis of a free market economy. The laws support a competitive marketplace that lowers prices and a free market that helps to maximize consumer choice. These statutes also stimulate innovation by discouraging anticompetitive conduct by businesses that defeats a free market economy.

Most trusts are legal, and their use flourishes today, particularly in estate planning. Trusts, today, may not form monopolies or restraints of trade as they did in the past. Although your web business, Artiste Login Products, Inc., conducts business in the competitive art world, you still need to be aware of antitrust laws. Artiste needs to avoid the common mistakes of price fixing, restraints of trade, and boycotts.

Sherman Act

In 1890, Congress enacted the Sherman Antitrust Act, today called the **Sherman Act**, to promote competition within the U.S. economy. The author of the legislation, Senator John Sherman (1823–1900),[3] argued that the Sherman Act did not announce a new principle of law, but simply applied well-recognized principles of the common law.

The Sherman Act was an attempt by Congress to end monopolies and restraints of trade. Sections 1 and 2 of the Sherman Act contain its main provisions:

Section 1. Every contract, combination in the form of trust or otherwise, or conspiracy, in restraint of trade or commerce among the several States, or with foreign nations, is hereby declared to be illegal [and is a felony punishable by fine and/or imprisonment]. . . .

Section 2. Every person who shall monopolize, or attempt to monopolize, or combine or conspire with any other person or persons, to monopolize any part of the

---

[1] The Department of Justice web site is <http://www.usdoj.gov/>. The Antitrust Division's web site is <http://www.usdoj.gov/atr/index.html>.
[2] The antitrust division of the Federal Trade Commission is located at <http://www.ftc.gov/ftc/antitrust.htm>. The antitrust guidelines are located at <http://www.ftc.gov/bc/guidelin.htm>.

[3] A Republican from Ohio, Senator Sherman served in the U.S. House of Representative (1855–1861) and U.S. Senate (1861–1877, 1881–1897), and served as secretary of the treasury under President Rutherford H. Hayes (1877–1881). Senator Sherman was the younger brother of famous Civil War (1861–1865) military leader for the Union, General William Tecumseh Sherman (1829–1891).

Exhibit 21–1 Major Antitrust Statutes and Amendments

Date	Name	Description	Enforcement	Civil	Criminal
1890	**Sherman Antitrust Act** (name later changed to Sherman Act)				
	Section 1	Bans contracts, combinations, and conspiracies in restraint of trade.	Department of Justice (DOJ) (civil and criminal)	DOJ sues for treble damages and injunctive relief on behalf of the U.S. when it has been harmed.	• Individuals: $350,000 fine and/or 3 years in prison. • Corporation: $10 million fine.
			State attorneys general (civil)	State attorney generals sue for treble damages and injunctive relief on behalf of respective states when they have been harmed.	
			Private parties (civil)	Private parties sue for treble damages and injunctive relief when they have been harmed.	
	Section 2	Bans monopolies, attempts to monopolize, and conspiracies.			
1914	**Clayton Act**				
1936	Section 2 Robinson-Patman Act	Price discrimination: Bans sellers from charging different customers different prices for the same goods where the effect may be to lessen competition substantially.	Department of Justice, state attorney generals, private parties	Same as above for DOJ, state attorney generals, and private parties.	Directors and officers liable if they had intent and knowledge and the action taken has an anticompetitive effect; $5,000 and/or one year (misdemeanor).
	Section 3	Bans exclusive dealing and tying arrangements that may lessen competition substantially.	Federal Trade Commission (FTC)	FTC may issue cease-and-desist order or enter into a consent order when the business agrees to the order.	
1950	Section 7 Celler-Kefauver Act	Bans mergers that may lessen competition substantially.			
1976	Hart-Scott-Rodino Antitrust Improvements Act	Requires premerger notification to DOJ and FTC.			
	Section 8	Prohibits interlocking directorships and officerships when business had $10 million in capital and profits, based on gross domestic product.			
1914	**Federal Trade Commission Act**	Created the Federal Trade Commission.	FTC	FTC may issue cease-and-desist order or enter into a consent order when the business agrees to the order.	None
	Section 5 (original)	Banned "unfair methods of competition in commerce."			
1938	Wheeler-Lea Act	Added words to above, "and unfair or deceptive acts or practices in commerce."			
1975	Magnuson-Moss Federal Trade Improvement Act	Section 5 now reads "Unfair methods of competition in or affecting commerce, and unfair or deceptive acts or practices in or affecting commerce, are declared unlawful."			

trade or commerce among the several States, or with foreign nations, shall be deemed guilty of a felony [and is similarly punishable].

Sections 1 and 2 Compared

Section 1 and Section 2 are relatively vague and cover different commercial activity. Congress left it to the courts to determine acts that violated the Sherman Act. The courts have continued to consider the meanings of these two provisions through the intervening decades.

These two main sections differ considerably from each other. Section 1 requires action by two or more people because, by definition, a person needs a cohort to combine or conspire. The essence of the illegal activity is the act of joining together. Section 2, on the other hand, applies both to an individual person and to several people because it states "[e]very person who . . ." therefore, conduct by one person can result in a violation of Section 2.

The cases brought to court under Section 1 of the Sherman Act differ from those brought under Section 2. Section 1 cases often concern the finding of an agreement (written, oral, or based on conduct) that leads to a restraint of trade. Section 2 cases deal with the structure of a monopoly that exists in the marketplace.

Section 1 focuses on restrictive agreements, that is, agreements that have a wrongful purpose, whereas Section 2 looks at the misuse of monopoly power in the marketplace. Both sections seek to curtail commercial practices that result in undesired pricing, collusion, and other restraints of trade. Any case brought under Section 2, however, already must hold the threshold or necessary amount of monopoly power.

The Sherman Act does not regulate a business's actions. The statute establishes ways in which a business should not act. In this sense, the statute is proscriptive rather than prescriptive and forms the basis for policing rather than for regulating business conduct.

Restraint of Trade, Section 1 Violations

The courts use two doctrines in deciding Sherman Act restraint of trade cases: the *rule of reason* and the *per se*

rule (only proof of the agreement's existence is required to prove the illegality). The courts have used these two rules during the past century when examining the activities of businesses.[4]

Business activities are first evaluated under the *per se* rule. If the business behavior is not classified as a *per se* violation, the courts evaluate it under the rule of reason.

Per Se Rule, Section 1 Violations

The United States Supreme Court, over the years, has determined that some types of restrictive agreements are inherently anticompetitive and are an unreasonable restraint on trade. Applying the **per se rule** has advantages. First, the government does not need to demonstrate the business's market power or the business practice's anticompetitive effect. Second, the defendant business cannot use any defense. If the government proves that the act took place, the defendant cannot have any excuse for committing the act. The *per se* rule eases administrative burdens, clarifies the behaviors that constitute illegal acts, and deters business behavior that is anticompetitive.

The *per se* restraints only serve to stifle competition. The *per se* rule applies to agreements made among horizontal competitors (those on the same level), such as competing retailers, wholesalers, or manufacturers. Three types of agreements to restrain trade are Section 1 violations of the Sherman Act and generally are illegal *per se: horizontal price fixing, horizontal market division,* and *group boycotts.* Group boycotts may involve both horizontal relationships and vertical relationships, such as a wholesaler dealing with a retailer.

Horizontal Price Fixing. **Horizontal price fixing** occurs when two or more potential competitors on the same level literally "fix" a "price" for their

---

[4] The Sherman Act does not define what actions are illegal. Congress left it to the courts to determine what is illegal. Many web sites have information about the different cases handed down over the years. The Antitrust Case Summary Browser created by Anthony D. Becker, Ph.D., is at <http://www.stolaf.edu/people/becker/antitrust/antitrust.html>. Yahoo! also has some interesting information. Go to <http://dir.yahoo.com/government/law> and type in antitrust. The American Bar Association maintains a web page on antitrust matters at <http://www.abanet.org/>. Search for antitrust.

goods or services. (Later this chapter will address how a manufacturer may fix a price to a retailer because the relationship between a manufacturer and a retailer is vertical.) Under the Sherman Act, an agreement to raise, depress, fix, peg, or stabilize the price of goods or services that are traded interstate is illegal *per se.*

The following case, *United States v. Socony-Vacuum Oil Co.*, is the first case in which price fixing was declared illegal *per se.*[5]

[5] Socony-Vacuum Oil Company was one of the companies in the Standard Oil Trust. Socony-Vacuum Oil Company and Standard Oil of New York became Mobil Oil Company. In 1999, Exxon Corporation and Mobil Oil Company merged into Exxon Mobil Corporation (ExxonMobil). For more history, see <http://www.exxon.mobil.com/>.

Case 21.1

United States v. Socony–Vacuum Oil Co.

Supreme Court of the United States, 1940

310 U.S. 150, 60 S. Ct. 811, 84 L. Ed. 1129

http://caselaw.findlaw.com/scripts/getcase.pl?court=US&navby=case&vol=310&page=150#150

LANDMARK CASE

BACKGROUND AND FACTS During the Great Depression, more oil was refined into gasoline than consumers could use. Major oil refiners kept ample storage facilities and had the capacity to distribute gasoline to retailers. Smaller, independent refiners lacked storage facilities and sold their gasoline at distressed prices on the "spot market" (a term used in the commodities market to mean current price) for immediate delivery to retailers. The glut of gasoline available in the spot market drove prices down.

The major oil companies embarked on a program of purchasing and storing the "distressed oil." The major companies agreed among themselves that each would buy distressed oil from a particular independent refiner. Although it appeared that the bidding and buying were based on the market price, the major companies, through their bidding, established a floor for gasoline prices that enabled them to prevent prices on the spot market from falling any lower.

Justice DOUGLAS delivered the opinion of the Court.

. . . .

The elimination of the so-called competitive evils is no legal justification for such buying programs. The elimination of such conditions was sought primarily for its effect on the price structures. Fairer competitive prices, it is claimed, resulted when distressed gasoline was removed from the market. But such defense is typical of the protestations usually made in price-fixing cases. Ruinous competition, financial disaster, evils of price cutting and the like appear throughout our history as ostensible justifications for price-fixing. If the so-called competitive abuses were to be appraised here, the reasonableness of prices would necessarily become an issue in every price-fixing case. In that event the Sherman Act would soon be emasculated; its philosophy would be supplanted by one which is wholly alien to a system of free competition; it would not be the charter of freedom which its framers intended.

The reasonableness of prices has no constancy due to the dynamic quality of business facts underlying price structures. Those who fixed reasonable prices today would perpetuate unreasonable prices tomorrow, since those prices would not be subject to continuous administrative supervision and readjustment in light of changed conditions. Those who controlled the prices would control or effectively dominate the market. And those who were in that strategic position would have it in their power to destroy or drastically impair the competitive system. . . .

. . . .

DECISION AND REMEDY The Supreme Court affirmed the judgment of the trial court that illegal price fixing took place when the oil companies agreed to purchase the distressed oil from the independent refiners. Each corporation was fined $5,000; each individual, $1,000. The Court held that to try to fix prices even though the prices seemed to be reasonable is an illegal *per se* violation of the Sherman Act.

CRITICAL THINKING: LEGAL APPLICATION Why did the Court not recognize that purchasing oil at a certain price was reasonable so that refiners could survive economically during the Great Depression?

Horizontal Market Division. Dividing a market (**horizontal market division**) for the sale of a specific product among competitors on the same level is a *per se* violation of the Sherman Act. Market division can be accomplished in many ways, all of which are illegal. The act restricts competitors from allocating among themselves exclusive geographic market divisions, customer allocations, or product types. Even though such agreements might seem reasonable, they eliminate competition.

A **territorial and customer division** operates in this basic fashion. Atec Computers, Bell Computers, and Chipper Computers, all wholesalers, compete against one another in the states of Kansas, Nebraska, and Iowa. Tired of the cut-throat competition, they divided up the territories. Atec sells products only in Kansas, Bell sells only in Nebraska, and Chipper sells only in Iowa. This concerted action reduces costs and allows all three (assuming that no other competition exists) to raise the price of the goods sold in their respective states.

The same violation would take place if they divided the customers instead of the geographic area, such as agreeing that Atec would sell only to institutional purchasers (school districts, universities, state agencies and departments, cities, and so on) in the three states, Bell only to wholesalers, and Chipper only to retailers.

In the following case, the Department of Justice filed an antitrust criminal action against one of the largest U.S. agricultural corporations. The case involved blatant price fixing, market division, and restrictions on production.

Case 21.2

United States v. Andreas

United States Court of Appeals, Seventh Circuit, 2000
216 F.3d 645 (7th Cir.)

BACKGROUND AND FACTS Archer Daniels Midland Co. (ADM), based in Decatur, Illinois, is an agriculture processing company. ADM's business involves nearly every farm commodity and the processing of commodities, such as lysine. ADM, the self-professed "supermarket to the world," is a behemoth in its industry with global sales of $14 billion in 1999 and 23,000 employees. ADM has a worldwide sales force and a global transportation network involving thousands of rail lines, barges, and trucks.

The Andreas family had long controlled ADM. Dwayne Andreas, a director and the former CEO, had built ADM into a worldwide agribusiness powerhouse. G. Allen Andreas was the board chairman and president. Defendant Michael D. Andreas was vice chairman of the board of directors and executive vice president of sales and marketing. Defendant Terrance S. Wilson was president of the corn processing division and reported directly to Michael Andreas. Defendant Mark E. Whitacre, the informant in this case, was president of its bioproducts division and answered directly to Michael Andreas.

Lysine is an amino acid used to stimulate an animal's growth and is sold to feed manufacturers who add it to animal feed. Lysine is a highly fungible commodity and sold almost entirely on the basis of price. Pricing depended largely on two variables: the price of organic substitutes, such as soy or fish meal, and the price charged by other lysine producers.

Until 1991, the lysine market was dominated by a cartel of three companies in Korea and Japan, which produced all of the world's lysine until the 1990s. The cartel periodically agreed to fix prices, which at times reached as high as $3 per pound. In 1989, ADM announced that it was building the world's largest lysine plant capable of producing two or three times as much lysine as any other plant. In 1991, ADM started production of lysine and immediately created chaos in the market, igniting a price war that drove the price of lysine down to about 70 cents per pound.

In 1992, Whitacre began working with Wilson. The two attended many meetings of the lysine producers. The first meeting was held in Mexico City, chosen in part because the participants did not want to meet within the jurisdiction of American antitrust laws. Between 1992 and 1995, representatives from the lysine businesses met in Paris, Vancouver, California, Hong Kong, and Hawaii.

At these meetings, the companies discussed price agreements and allocating sales volumes among the market participants, which was critical to raising the price. Without the agreement, the five members tended to cheat, resulting in the price of lysine dropping. The purpose of these meetings was disguised by fake agendas and a fictitious lysine producers trade association, so they could meet and share information without raising the suspicions of customers or law enforcement agencies.

In 1992, shortly after the Mexico City meeting, Whitacre began cooperating with the FBI in an undercover sting operation aimed at the price-fixing conspiracy. As a result, most of the meetings and telephone conversations involving Whitacre and other conspirators from 1992 through 1995 were taped. Whitacre made between 120 and 130 tapes for the FBI during the investigation by using recording equipment, tapes, and instruction provided by the government. FBI agents met with Whitacre more than 150 times during the investigation. Whitacre was told to record conversations relevant to the conspiracy, but not to record anything about ADM's legitimate business.

In 1995, the FBI raided the offices of ADM in Decatur. These raids ended the cartel. Criminal charges were brought against the three defendants.

The jury convicted the defendants, Michael Andreas and Wilson, of conspiring to violate Section 1 of the Sherman Act, which prohibits any conspiracy or combination to restrain trade. The court sentenced each defendant to twenty-four months in prison. The defendants appealed the length of their sentences.

KANNE, Circuit Judge

For many years, Archer Daniels Midland Co.'s philosophy of customer relations could be summed up by a quote from former ADM President James Randall: "Our competitors are our friends. Our customers are the enemy." This motto animated the company's business dealings and ultimately led to blatant violations of U.S. antitrust law. . . . The facts involved in this case reflect an inexplicable lack of business ethics and an atmosphere of general lawlessness that infected the very heart of one of America's leading corporate citizens. Top executives at ADM and its Asian co-conspirators throughout the early 1990s spied on each other, fabricated aliases and front organizations to hide their activities, hired prostitutes to gather information from competitors, lied, cheated, embezzled, extorted and obstructed justice.

. . . We find no error related to the convictions, but agree with the government that the defendants should have received longer sentences for their leadership roles in the conspiracy.

. . . .

C. Per Se Violations

. . . .

Violations of § 1 require evidence proving that the charged practice had the effect of unreasonably restraining trade under the "rule of reason," except in the limited cases referred to as per se violations. Per se violations are ones that "always or almost always tend to restrict competition and decrease output" such that the court may dispense with the requirement of economic evidence. Per se violations are "naked restraints of trade with no purpose except stifling of competition," and have been characterized as so "plainly anti-competitive" and lacking "any redeeming virtue" that they are presumed illegal under § 1. Courts apply per se treatment only after "considerable experience" with a particular business practice has inevitably resulted in a finding of anticompetitive effects. . . .

. . . .

The conspirators began discussing the volume limits at their first meeting in Mexico City when Wilson proposed the idea and explained its vital importance to the overall scheme to control the industry. . . . ADM and the others began haggling over how much each would be allowed to produce. This argument continued until Andreas and Yamada met in Irvine, and Andreas threatened to flood the market. . . . The conspirators left this meeting with an agreement that . . . ADM would sell 67,000 tons, with adjustments for expected growth in the market. This agreement constituted an output limitation, which long has been condemned as a per se violation of the Sherman Act. . . .

. . . .

. . . While market demand might not support the full production of . . . companies at a profitable price, this fact does not distinguish lysine from many other markets. ADM's entrance into the market may have resulted in oversupply and lower prices for consumers, but this does not grant a license to violate the antitrust laws.

. . . .

E. Sufficiency of the Evidence

Andreas next asks us to overturn the jury's verdict because there was insufficient evidence to support it. We will overturn a jury verdict "only if the record contains no evidence, regardless of how it is weighed, from which the jury could find guilt beyond a reasonable doubt." We view "the evidence in the light most favorable to the prosecution," and decide whether "any rational trier of fact could have found the essential elements of the crime beyond a reasonable doubt."

Andreas attended three meetings of the conspirators and served a vital role in the successful efforts to reach an agreement to implement the price-fixing and volume deals. The jury . . . heard Andreas threaten to flood the market if they did not agree. Evidence at trial indicated that the details of the plan were arranged by upper management, but that all sides recognized that their corporate superiors remained in control of the deal and would be called in to settle any unresolved disputes. . . .

Furthermore, Andreas directly supervised Wilson and Whitacre. They reported the results of the meetings to him, and he on more than one occasion coached them on what to say at an upcoming meeting. . . .

It would require a great leap of imagination to believe that Andreas knew nothing of the illegal deals on price and output carried out by his direct subordinates, yet happened to play a key role in Irvine and at subsequent meetings to facilitate those deals. . . . Based on the overwhelming evidence presented at trial, we cannot conclude that the jury acted irrationally in convicting Andreas of conspiring to restrain trade.

Finally, the Court has reviewed all of the evidence against Andreas and Wilson and can fairly characterize it as overwhelming. . . . The price fluctuated, and cartel members cheated each other when they could, but the evidence soundly supports a volume of commerce influenced by the conspiracy of at least $168 million. . . .

DECISION AND REMEDY The court found overwhelming evidence of antitrust activities, such as price fixing and restrictions on production, and upheld the convictions. This edited case focuses on only two defendants. The case involved ADM and a number of other corporate and individual defendants. The decision discussed at length the sentences of Andreas and Wilson. Each defendant originally was sentenced to two years and fined $350,000. Each lost their jobs with ADM. On remand, the trial court increased Andreas's sentence from two years to three years and Wilson's sentence from two years to two years and nine months. The U.S. Supreme Court refused to grant the writ of *certiorari*.

COMMENT One month before the scheduled sentencing of his son, Dwayne Andreas stepped down as chairman in 1999 after serving in that position since 1970. ADM was worth $100 million in 1970 and valued at his departure at $6.5 billion. As a result of its antitrust activities, ADM paid a civil penalty of $35 million, a criminal penalty of $70 million, and Canada fined ADM $11.4 million (U.S.). The estimated total of litigation costs and fines approached $350 million. The value of the common stock dropped $2.4 billion in the days after the raid in 1995.

Unbeknownst to ADM and the FBI, Whitacre was embezzling from ADM. This crime spree started prior to his involvement with the FBI, continued while he made the tapes for the FBI, and ended only after the FBI raids. In the end, he swindled ADM out of $9 million for which he was sentenced to serve nine years, along with two years and six months for his participation in the price-fixing scheme.

CRITICAL THINKING: PUBLIC POLICY The U.S. government would not have discovered these violations of antitrust laws without the cooperation and assistance of Whitacre who had failed to negotiate a grant of immunity when he agreed to cooperate. What policy should the U.S. government adopt concerning people who come forward with evidence of crimes?

Trade Associations. Businesspeople in certain types of associations must be careful to avoid engaging in actions that might be considered violations of the antitrust laws. For example, competitors often organize into **trade associations** to pursue common interests, such as lobbying Congress for favorable laws. These associations disseminate information, represent the members' business interests before governmental bodies, initiate joint advertising campaigns, and attempt to police their own industry.

These exchanges of information among related businesses pose special antitrust problems. Trade association activities are, by their very nature, joint actions and therefore subject to the antitrust laws.

Professional Associations. For many years, professionals were regarded as outside the scope of the antitrust laws because, it was thought, their activities did not involve trade or commerce. This assumption is no longer valid. **Professional associations** are similar to trade associations in that professionals join to pursue common interests.

Similar to trade associations, professionals must avoid engaging in actions that violate antitrust laws. For example, the Supreme Court held that a minimum fee schedule mandated by a bar association was price fixing. It also held that a maximum fee plan set by a medical association was price fixing.[6]

[6] *Arizona v. Maricopa County Medical Society,* 457 U.S. 332, 102 S. Ct. 2466,73 L. Ed. 2d 48 (1982).

LEGAL HIGHLIGHT

Can a University Violate Antitrust Laws?

Most people would consider universities to be outside the realm of antitrust laws. The Department of Justice (DOJ), however, charged nine Ivy League schools[a] with horizontal price fixing. In 1958, the nine schools formed the Ivy Overlap Group to determine collectively the amount of financial assistance to award to students. The students involved had been accepted and had applied for financial aid at two or more of these schools.

To qualify for federal financial aid, the students and their parents were required to disclose financial information to the College Scholarship Service (CSS). CSS processed this information and forwarded it to the U.S. Department of Education, which used the Congressional Methodology formula to determine the amount of aid that the schools expected the family to contribute. After the department determined the amount of family aid, it returned the information to the CSS, which, in turn, forwarded it to the nine schools.

The Ivy Overlap Group met annually to share the information received from CSS. The schools agreed to share financial information concerning candidates. Collectively, the group developed and applied a uniform analysis to determine needs for assessing family contributions. The only meaningful competition to the Ivy Overlap Group was Stanford University.

In 1991, DOJ alleged that the annual meeting involved horizontal price fixing and was in violation of Section 1 of the Sherman Act. It charged the Ivy Overlap Group with unlawfully conspiring to restrain trade by (1) agreeing to award financial aid exclusively on the basis of need, (2) agreeing to utilize a common

formula to calculate need, and (3) collectively setting the family's contribution, not on the Congressional Methodology, but on its own formula. The DOJ sought an injunction to stop the practice. Eight of the nine schools signed a consent decree with the DOJ. The schools did not admit wrongdoing, but agreed to stop sharing student information.

Massachusetts Institute of Technology (MIT), however, refused to sign the consent decree. In the trial, the federal district court found that the agreement among the universities was a *per se* violation of the Sherman Act and found MIT guilty of price fixing. On appeal, the U.S. Court of Appeals[b] reversed the decision. The court noted that financial aid to students was part of the process of determining tuition, which is a commercial transaction. The Ivy Overlap Group agreements, however, did not reduce any output of students, so the effect of the Overlap agreements differed from the normal economic agreements that fixed prices. In fact, the agreements promoted socioeconomic diversity at the member institutions. The appellate court remanded (returned) the case to the district court. In the retrial, the district court was to apply the rule of reason to determine if MIT, in fact, enhanced rather than restricted competition.

In 1992, Congress passed the Higher Education Amendment, which approved the concept of need-blind admissions and agreements among schools on general principles for determining student aid. The act prohibits discussion of individual aid.[c] This act would have ended the Ivy Overlap Group agreements in any event, because the act made these types of agreements illegal.

[a] The nine Ivy League universities are Brown University, Columbia University, Cornell University, Dartmouth College, Harvard University, Massachusetts Institute of Technology, Princeton University, the University of Pennsylvania, and Yale University.

[b] *U.S. v. Brown University*, 5 F.3d 658 (3rd Cir. 1993).
[c] Higher Education Amendments of 1992, Pub. L. No. 102-325, 91544, 106 Stat. 448, 837 (codified at 20 U.S.C. Ch. 28).

Group Boycotts. **Group boycotts** (concerted refusals by groups to deal with another) are a *per se* offense. A boycott often cuts off a firm's access to a supply, facility, or market that is necessary for the boycotted firm to compete. The boycotting businesses frequently possess a dominant position in the market-

place. Generally, this type of boycott cannot be justified as intending to increase the market's overall efficiency and to increase competition.

When two levels of the same industry are involved, the traders on one level agree to deal with businesses on another level. For example, the General Motors new retail automobile dealers agreed to boycott General Motors, the seller, to prevent it from selling cars to automobile discount outlets. The court found this agreement among the retail car dealers to be a *per se* violation of the antitrust law.

Only group boycotts are illegal, not all boycotts. A business can decide with which other businesses it will deal. A business legally may refuse to deal with a particular firm. The statute prevents agreements among businesses, not unilateral refusals by one business to deal with another.

For example, a newspaper's investigative reporter writes a series of articles on automobile dealers who use fraudulent means to sell automobiles. If one automobile dealership on its own withdraws its advertisements from the newspaper, this decision is legal. If the trade association for automobile dealers, comprised of the local competing automobile dealers, decides that none of its members will advertise in the newspaper, the decision is an illegal group boycott. If the newspaper suffers a drop in revenue that can be traced to the withdrawal of those advertisements, it has been economically damaged. In this situation, even though the group boycotted against

another industry, its purpose is to substantially reduce competition, so the action is illegal.

The Rule of Reason, Section 1 Violations

The **rule of reason** determines the anticompetitive acts that violate antitrust laws. When the business actions do not fall under the *per se* rule, the courts use the rule of reason. A court must review all the circumstances of a case to decide whether the defendant's practice created an unreasonable restraint on competition. Defendants can prove in court a procompetitive business justification for their acts. Defenses of this type of these defenses are discussed later in the chapter.

The next case, involving Standard Oil Company of New Jersey, is the most important early case interpreting the Sherman Act. The Supreme Court found the oil company guilty of violations of both Sections 1 and 2. Having determined that Congress could not have intended a literal interpretation of every restraint of trade in Section 1, the Court used a standard of reasonableness to analyze the oil company's conduct. This case is the first to set out the rule of reason.

Case 21.3

Standard Oil Co. of New Jersey v. United States

Supreme Court of the United States, 1911
221 U.S. 1, 31, S. Ct. 502, 55 L. Ed. 619
http://caselaw.findlaw.com /scripts/getcase.pl?navby= case&court=US&vol=221& page=1

LANDMARK CASE

BACKGROUND AND FACTS The government charged the Standard Oil Company of New Jersey [Standard Oil] and thirty-five other corporations, John D. Rockefeller, William Rockefeller, and five other individual defendants with a conspiracy alleged to have been formed around 1870. The government charged that the individual defendants organized the Standard Oil Corporation of Ohio and soon afterward became participants in an illegal plan to acquire substantially all of the oil refineries located in Cleveland, Ohio. Therefore, the government charged the original owners of the company with forming and participating in an illegal combination for the restraint and monopolization of all interstate commerce in petroleum products.

The government charged that a trust agreement existed in which the stock of more than forty corporations was held for the benefit of the members of the combination. The trial court voided the trust agreement as a restraint of trade and ordered the trust dissolved. It is questionable, however, if the trust actually was dissolved because the stock held by the trust apparently shifted among the companies, but ultimately was preserved in the same hands.

Chief Justice WHITE delivered the opinion of the Court.

. . . .

. . . The merely generic enumeration which the statute makes of the acts to which it refers, and the absence of any definition of restraint of trade as used in the statute, leaves room for but one conclusion, which is, that it was expressly designed not to unduly limit the application of the act by precise definition, but, while clearly fixing a standard, that is, by defining the ulterior boundaries which could not be transgressed with impunity, to leave it to be determined by the light of reason, guided by the principles of law and the duty to apply and enforce the public policy embodied in the statute, in every given case whether any particular act or contract was within the contemplation of the statute.

. . . .

[Referring] to the acts done by the individuals or corporations who were mainly instrumental in bringing about the expansion of the New Jersey corporation during the period prior to the formation of the trust agreements of 1879 and 1882, including those agreements, . . . we think no disinterested mind can survey the period in question without being irresistibly driven to the conclusion that the very genius for commercial development and organization which it would seem was manifested from the beginning soon begot all intent and purpose to exclude others which was frequently manifested by acts and dealings wholly inconsistent with the theory that they were made with the single conception of advancing the development of business power by usual methods, but which on the contrary necessarily involved the intent to drive others from the field and to exclude them from their right to trade and thus accomplish the mastery which was the end in view.

DECISION AND REMEDY The Supreme Court upheld the trial court's order to dissolve Standard Oil.

COMMENT This divestiture led to a reorganization of the oil business from which the Seven Sisters, as they became known, arose. Five were American companies. Three of these five companies were known as the Standard Oil Group (Exxon, Mobil, and Socal) because they retained many of the directors from Standard Oil and their principal shareholder was John D. Rockefeller. The other two American oil corporations were Gulf and Texaco. The sixth sister was a British company, British Petroleum. The seventh sister was an Anglo-Dutch company, Shell.

CRITICAL THINKING: POLITICAL CONSIDERATION Why not allow trusts that would control prices?

The Supreme Court in Standard Oil reasoned that Congress intended the Sherman Act to apply only to unreasonable restraints on trade that would result in monopolization. With this decision, the Court created the rule of reason. The Court rejected the idea that every business act should be illegal, regardless of its reasonableness. If the Court had not interpreted the act in this way, every conceivable business practice would have violated the Sherman Act.

Vertical Restraints. Vertical relationships involve the various levels of a particular supply chain. Manufacturers by necessity deal with wholesalers and retailers. Wholesalers deal with both manufacturers and retailers. Agreements that restrain trade involving firms at different levels of the production and distribution processes violate antitrust laws. These violations are called **vertical restraints** of trade.[7] These agreements, however, vary to such a degree that even to define the typical vertical arrangement is sometimes difficult.

Resale Price Maintenance. A **resale price maintenance agreement** is a contract to fix prices when a vertical relationship exists. For example, a wholesaler sells a product to a retailer. The wholesaler (the seller), however, wants to control the price at which the re-

[7] For an indepth discussion about vertical restraints go to <http://www.antitrust.org>.

tailer can sell the item, a tactic that is called vertical price fixing. The courts review these types of agreements under the rule of reason to determine if a violation of Section 1 of the Sherman Act has occurred.

In the following case, the Supreme Court reviewed a case involving a manufacturer (the seller) fixing the maximum price at which a product could be sold by its retailer (the buyer). Prior to the following case, vertical price fixing was thought to be illegal *per se*. Follow the Supreme Court's reasoning as it applies the rule of reason, and not the *per se* rule, to this case, which involved price fixing in a vertical relationship.

Case 21.4

State Oil Company v. Khan

Supreme Court of the United States, 1997

522 U.S. 3, 118 S. Ct. 275, 139 L. Ed. 2d 199

http://caselaw.findlaw.com /cgi=bin/getcase.pl?court= US&vol=000&invol=96-871

BACKGROUND AND FACTS Respondents, Barkat U. Khan and his corporation, entered into an agreement with petitioner, State Oil Company, to lease and operate a gas station and convenience store owned by State Oil. The agreement provided that Khan would purchase the station's gasoline supply from State Oil at the suggested retail price set by State Oil, less a margin of 3.25 cents per gallon. Under the agreement, Khan could charge any amount for gasoline sold to his station's customers, but if the price charged was higher than State Oil's suggested retail price, the excess was rebated to State Oil. Khan could sell gasoline for less than State Oil's suggested retail price, but any such decrease would reduce his 3.25-cents-per-gallon margin.

About a year after Khan began operating the gas station, he fell behind in the lease payments. State Oil then gave notice of its intent to terminate the agreement and began eviction proceedings in state court. At State Oil's request, the state court appointed a receiver to operate the gas station. The receiver operated the station for several months without being subject to the price restraints in Khan's agreement with State Oil. According to Khan, the receiver obtained an overall profit margin in excess of 3.25 cents per gallon by lowering the price of regular-grade gasoline and raising the price of premium grades.

Khan sued State Oil in the United States District Court, alleging in part that State Oil engaged in price fixing in violation of Section 1 of the Sherman Act by preventing him from raising or lowering retail gas prices. The district court found that the allegations in the complaint failed to state a *per se* violation of the Sherman Act because they failed to establish the sort of "manifestly anticompetitive implications or pernicious effect on competition" that would justify *per se* prohibition of State Oil's conduct. The district court held that Khan had not shown that a difference in gasoline pricing would have increased the station's sales, nor had he shown that State Oil had market power or that its pricing provisions affected competition in a relevant market.

The Court of Appeals for the Seventh Circuit reversed, finding that the agreement between Khan and State Oil did indeed fix maximum gasoline prices by making it "worthless" for Khan to exceed the suggested retail prices. After reviewing legal and economic aspects of price fixing, the court concluded that State Oil's pricing scheme was a *per se* antitrust violation under the Supreme Court ruling in the *Albrecht v. Herald Co.* case, which had been decided in 1968. The Supreme Court granted *certiorari*.

Justice O'CONNOR delivered the opinion of the Court.

. . . .

Although the Sherman Act, by its terms, prohibits every agreement "in restraint of trade," this Court has long recognized that Congress intended to outlaw only unreasonable restraints. As a consequence, most antitrust claims are analyzed under a "rule of reason," according to which the finder of fact must decide whether the questioned practice imposes an unreasonable restraint on competition, taking into account a variety of factors, including specific information about the relevant business, its condition before and after the restraint was imposed, and the restraint's history, nature, and effect.

Some types of restraints, however, have such predictable and pernicious anticompetitive effect, and such limited potential for procompetitive benefit, that they are deemed unlawful *per se*. *Per se* treatment is appropriate "[o]nce experience with a particular kind of restraint enables the Court to predict with confidence that the rule of reason will condemn it." Thus, we have expressed reluctance to adopt *per se* rules with regard to "restraints imposed in the context of business relationships where the economic impact of certain practices is not immediately obvious."

. . . .

We recognize that the *Albrecht* decision presented a number of theoretical justifications for a *per se* rule against vertical maximum price fixing. But criticism of those premises abounds. . . .

The *Albrecht* Court . . . expressed the concern that maximum prices may be set too low for dealers to offer consumers essential or desired services. But such conduct, by driving away customers, would seem likely to harm manufacturers as well as dealers and consumers, making it unlikely that a supplier would set such a price as a matter of business judgment. . . .

Finally, *Albrecht* reflected the Court's fear that maximum price fixing could be used to disguise arrangements to fix minimum prices which remain illegal *per se*. Although we have acknowledged the possibility that maximum pricing might mask minimum pricing, we believe that such conduct—as with the other concerns articulated in *Albrecht*—can be appropriately recognized and punished under the rule of reason.

Not only are the potential injuries cited in *Albrecht* less serious than the Court imagined, the *per se* rule established therein could in fact exacerbate problems related to the unrestrained exercise of market power by monopolist dealers. Indeed, both courts and antitrust scholars have noted that *Albrecht's* rule may actually harm consumers and manufacturers.

. . . .

In overruling *Albrecht,* we of course do not hold that all vertical maximum price fixing is *per se* lawful. Instead, vertical maximum price fixing, like the majority of commercial arrangements subject to the antitrust laws, should be evaluated under the rule of reason. In our view, rule-of-reason analysis will effectively identify those situations in which vertical maximum price fixing amounts to anticompetitive conduct.

DECISION AND REMEDY The United States Supreme Court overruled a case that had restricted a seller from setting maximum prices. Today, a seller of goods may set a maximum price for which a buyer, such as a wholesaler or retailer, may resell the item provided that the price is reasonable when considering all economic factors.

CRITICAL THINKING: ECONOMIC CONSIDERATION Assume Khan had agreed with other gasoline station operators to set a price below which none of them would sell gasoline. How would a court treat this example differently from its handling of the actual case?

Restrictions in the Vertical Distribution Process. The methods by which manufacturers market their products to wholesalers or retailers vary greatly. A manufacturer may sell directly to retailers or to wholesale distributors, who in turn resell to retailers. The manufacturer may even own the retail outlets where its products are sold.

Regardless of the arrangement selected, both the manufacturer and the retailer seek maximum profits. Some methods that increase profits violate the antitrust laws.

The manufacturer often imposes territorial restrictions on its retailers to prevent competition among themselves. This restriction creates a sales advantage for each retailer, because the desired product cannot be purchased anywhere else in the immediate area. Selling goods of the same make under territorial restrictions may result in less competition. Territorial and customer restrictions generally are lawful unless their use unreasonably restrains trade.

Manufacturers may attempt to prohibit wholesalers or retailers from reselling the products to certain classes of buyers, such as competing retailers, constituting consumer restrictions. See the Legal Highlight entitled Toys "Я" Us for a story in which the retailer controlled the manufacturer through a vertical agreement.

Monopoly Power, Section 2 Violations

The antitrust statutes do not define the term *monopoly,* but the accepted meaning is that of a business that exclusively controls a business aspect or even an entire industry. The courts determine if a monopoly exists on a case-by-case basis, considering, first, whether a firm has accumulated enough dominance in the marketplace that it has monopoly power. Second, the courts decide if the business accumulated its monopoly power through wrongful actions. The courts concern themselves with only those actions that are wrongful and have led to monopoly power.

To determine if a firm has monopoly power, a court must examine whether the firm has *market power.* **Market power** is determined if the firm's power is so great that it can force its decisions on others, based on structural analysis. Structural analysis involves two steps:

1. Define the market in which the firm's power should be evaluated.
2. Measure the extent of the firm's share of that market.

Structural analysis involves more than identifying a firm within a market and comparing its sales with those of its competitors. The court also determines the *relevant product market* and the *relevant geographic market.* The **relevant product market** evaluates the market for the product, its competition, and items that can be substituted for the product.

Relevant geographic market considers the area where the product is sold, the ease of transportation, and the distance that consumers will travel to purchase the product. The geographical area may be national, regional, or local. After determining these markets, the court compares the sales of the firms within these markets.

Although structural analysis is an inexact science, it is a tool used by the courts to support the inference that monopoly power exists. The court also considers any barriers to entry that may exist and whether acceptable substitutes for the firm's product are available.

Defining the Relevant Market

The relevant market is defined by considering information about the characteristics of the product, its substitutes, its competition, and the geographic area where the product is sold. Because the market share is extremely sensitive to the definition of relevant market, both sides in these cases take considerable care in assembling and presenting evidence to determine the market.

Product Market. Substitutes are available for most products. If General Motors raised the prices for its cars significantly, consumers would purchase more Fords or other brands. Courts would determine if General Motors' Cadillac division had monopoly power by considering the following questions: Should all cars sold in the United States be included in the computation of Cadillac's market share? Should only luxury cars be included? Do Japanese, Korean, Swedish, or German automobile imports compete with Cadillacs for sales? Although General Motors is the sole producer of Cadillacs, it will not have monopoly power as long as substitute products exist because market forces

LEGAL HIGHLIGHT
Toys "Я" Us

For several years, warehouse (also called discount) clubs sold toys at nearly two-thirds the price charged by retail toy stores. Toy manufacturers projected that these clubs would have 6 to 8 percent of the market. As the warehouse clubs gained market share, the retail toy chain outlets shrunk. Toys "Я" Us, the only national full-line toy chain, decided to take action.

A powerhouse in the toy business, Toys "Я" Us had 29 percent of the top ten toy makers' sales. With its buying power, Toys "Я" Us managed to pull all the major toy manufacturers, such as Hasbro and Mattel, into vertical agreements to restrict their sales to warehouse clubs.

Toys "Я" Us then orchestrated a series of horizontal agreements among the otherwise competing manufacturers to adhere to sales restrictions in the vertical agreements. Toys "Я" Us enforced the agreements by shopping at the competing warehouse clubs to see if the discount clubs sold products that were also offered in Toys "Я" Us stores. In addition, manufacturers would complain to Toys "Я" Us about competitors' products being sold in warehouse clubs. On finding a manufacturer's toys in a discount store, Toys "Я" Us would contact the manufacturer and threaten to stop buying its toy products. The manufacturer would then apologize and reaffirm the agreement to restrict sales to warehouse clubs.

As a result, Mattel, Hasbro, and other major toy manufacturers stopped selling to Price Club, Sam's,

B.J.'s and other discount clubs. Consumers shopping at a discount club could no longer find toys, forcing them to shop at retail toy stores and pay a higher price.

The Federal Trade Commission charged Toys "Я" Us with violations of the antitrust acts by engaging in both vertical and horizontal restraints of trade agreements. The commission found that Toys "Я" Us entered into vertical agreements with individual manufacturers and coordinated a horizontal agreement among the same manufacturers. The commission also found that in the areas where discount clubs and Toys "Я" Us competed, the toy prices were lower in the Toys "Я" Us stores than in those stores where no competitive discount clubs were located. The commission issued an order prohibiting Toys "Я" Us from entering into these types of agreements for five years.

The commission's order was appealed by Toys "Я" Us. The court of appeals held that substantial evidence existed to support the Commission's findings and also upheld the commission's order.[a]

The ironic part of this story is that when Toys "Я" Us became successful, retailers, such as department stores, tried to prevent toy manufacturers from selling to Toys "Я" Us because its prices were too low!

[a] *Toys "Я" Us, Inc. v. Federal Trade Commission*, 221 F.3d 928 (2000).

---

will keep the price of Cadillacs competitive with the price of substitute products.

Courts determine the relevant product market by defining the products that can be substituted for the product that is alleged to be dominating the market to the exclusion of competitors. In some cases, the product market is extremely wide. Including all cars sold in the United States in a measure of Cadillac's market share makes Cadillac's share relatively small. Measuring

Cadillac sales against the combined sales of cars and trucks decreases Cadillac's share even further. If only luxury cars are considered, Cadillac has a larger market share. Whenever monopoly power is alleged, courts must decide which products offer competition to the dominant product. The following case illustrates the process by which the court determined if a firm had an illegal monopoly.

Case 21.5

United States v. Aluminum Co. of America (ALCOA)

United States Court of Appeals, Second Circuit, 1945
148 F.2d 416

LANDMARK CASE

BACKGROUND AND FACTS The United States charged Aluminum Company of America (Alcoa) with monopolizing interstate and foreign commerce in the manufacture and sale of "virgin" aluminum ingot. The government contended that because Alcoa was the sole producer of virgin ingot in the United States, Alcoa had an unlawful monopoly. Alcoa contended that it was subject to competition from imported virgin ingot and from "secondary" ingot (recycled aluminum) and did not have monopoly power.

The district court found that Alcoa had a 33 percent share of the market, which included both the secondary material that had been salvaged from scrap and the new ingot. The lower court found for Alcoa. The court of appeals computed the market share differently and found that Alcoa had 90 percent of the virgin ingot market.

Judge HAND

. . . .

From 1902 onward until 1928 "Alcoa" was making ingot in Canada through a wholly owned subsidiary; so much of this [ingot was] imported into the United States it is proper to include with what it produced here. In the year 1912 the sum of these two items represented nearly ninety-one percent of the total amount of "virgin" ingot available for sale in this country. . . .

. . . .

We conclude therefore that "Alcoa's" control over the ingot market must be reckoned at over ninety percent; that being the proportion which its production bears to imported "virgin" ingot. If the fraction which it did not supply were the produce of domestic manufacture there could be no doubt that this percentage gave it a monopoly—lawful or unlawful, as the case might be. The producer of so large a proportion of the supply has complete control within certain limits.

DECISION AND REMEDY The court of appeals found that Alcoa had monopolized the aluminum industry by having a 90 percent share of the virgin ingot market, along with having an intent to acquire a monopoly of this market.

COMMENT The United States Supreme Court did not hear this appeal. The Court lacked a quorum because too many of the justices had been involved with the case before they were appointed to the Supreme Court. Congress passed a special statute to allow the Second Circuit Court of Appeals to hear the case.

CRITICAL THINKING: MANAGERIAL CONSIDERATION Would you, as a businessperson, want the government to use a broad or a limited definition of the relevant market power?

Geographic Market. The relevant geographic market usually is less difficult to determine than the relevant product market. If sellers within an area can raise prices or reduce the supply of products without quantities of lower priced goods quickly flowing into the area, the sellers have a separate geographic market for their products.

Geographic markets may be local, regional, or national. In determining a geographic market, the courts consider the mobility of both competing sellers and purchasers. The courts consider whether a buyer can easily purchase the goods at a lower price outside of the immediate area or whether a seller in another geographic area can ship goods easily into the area. Because consumers are willing to travel greater distances to make major purchases than to buy everyday necessities, courts determine the geographic market more broadly for sales of automobiles than for sales of milk.

Determining the Market Share

After defining the relevant product and geographic markets, the court can determine the percentage of the market held by any one firm. This percentage is the firm's market share, that is, the comparison of one firm's position with the positions of all other firms with which it competes. Monopoly power is a matter of degree. In the *Alcoa* case, 90 percent of the relevant market was sufficient for the court to conclude that Alcoa held a monopoly.

Courts have found that no monopoly exists when the firms control less than 65 percent of their relevant markets. In the *Alcoa* case, the court said that two-thirds of the relevant market would questionably constitute a monopoly, but that one-third of the market would not constitute a monopoly situation.

The courts attempt to determine if a firm holds such substantial power over a market that it can engage in actions not associated with natural growth to exclude competitors and to control prices. Market share is the measurement used to make that determination objectively.

Clayton Act

In 1914, Congress strengthened the federal antitrust laws by adopting the **Clayton Act**, which is aimed at specific monopolistic practices. The Sherman Act prohibits activities that eliminate competition or result in monopoly power, but it does not reach activities that *merely reduce* competition or *could lead to* monopoly power. The Clayton Act declares these specific activities to be illegal, even though these practices might not constitute the contract, combination, or conspiracy in restraint of trade necessary for a Sherman Act violation.

The important sections of the Clayton Act are Sections 2, 3, 7, and 8. Section 2 prohibits price dis-

crimination, Section 3 prohibits exclusive dealing agreements or tying arrangements, and Section 7 prohibits mergers when these arrangements tend to substantially lessen competition or create a monopoly. Section 8 prohibits interlocking directorships and officerships under specific circumstances.

Section 2, Robinson-Patman Act

The objective of Section 2 is to promote economic equality in the purchasing and selling of goods. Section 2, as originally passed, was very weak. In 1936, Congress passed the **Robinson-Patman Act**, which strengthened that section. The Robinson-Patman Act makes it illegal for any seller to discriminate in the prices charged for goods of the same quality to different purchasers.

Sales at differing prices must have an anticompetitive effect for a violation of the act to have occurred. If a seller engages in interstate commerce, it must sell goods of similar grade and quality to different competing purchasers.

The courts view sales of the same or similar goods at different prices to competing consumers (such as competing retailers) as **price discrimination** under Robinson-Patman. Price discrimination is unlawful even when the firm engaged in it does not have, and does not seek, monopoly power. Later sections discuss the three defenses to price discrimination.

Price discrimination can occur at two different levels, the primary level or secondary level. A primary level, or first line, price discrimination occurs when the seller of the goods uses price discrimination to drive its own competition out of business. A seller of goods is prohibited from gaining an unfair advantage over its competitor by offering a better price to (and thus discriminating among) different buyers for similar goods when the effect will substantially lessen competition or when it may create a monopoly. For example, Flour Mill offers flour at a lower price to all the large bakeries in the state than to small bakeries. All the large bakeries purchase from Flour Mill. This practice either drives competitors of Flour Mill out of business or allows them a smaller share of the market, because they sell only to the small bakeries.

A secondary level, or second line, price discrimination occurs when the purchaser of the goods uses price discrimination to drive other competitors out of business. Buyers are prohibited from using their economic power to obtain better prices from the seller to gain an economic advantage over their competitors. For example, Large Purchaser and Smaller Competitor are competitors. Large Purchaser uses its purchasing power to induce Supplier to sell to Large Purchaser at a lower price. Large Purchaser arranges more favorable payment terms and additional services, because of its large purchasing volume. Smaller Competitor suffers a competitive damage when it must purchase the goods at a higher price from Supplier. Additionally, Smaller Competitor is unable to arrange favorable payment schedules or additional services. Thus, Smaller Competitor must resell the goods at a higher price. Smaller Competitor loses business to Large Purchaser, because most customers prefer to buy the lower priced goods from Large Purchaser.

The following case, which involves both price fixing and price discrimination, discusses both the Sherman Act and the Robinson–Patman Act.

Case 21.6

Brooke Group Ltd. v. Brown & Williamson Tobacco Corporation

Supreme Court of the United States, 1993
509 U.S. 209, 113 S. Ct. 2578, 125 L. Ed. 2d 168
http://caselaw.findlaw.com /scripts/getcase.pl?navby=case &court=US&vol=509&page= 209

BACKGROUND AND FACTS In the mid-1980s, a market struggle erupted as a price war took place in the domestic generic cigarette market. Customers generally buy generic cigarettes because of their bargain prices. Brook Group, Ltd. (Liggett), whose prior corporate name was Liggett during the time of the price war, charged that to counter its innovative development of generic cigarettes, Brown & Williamson Tobacco Corporation introduced its own line of generic cigarettes and sold them below cost in an unlawful effort to stifle price competition. Liggett contended that Brown & Williamson violated the Robinson-Patman Act by offering discriminatory volume rebates to wholesalers to force Liggett to raise its own generic cigarette prices.

In 1980, prior to Liggett's introduction of generic cigarettes, also called black and whites, sales of generic cigarettes amounted to less than 1 percent of the domestic cigarette market. Cigarette manufacturing has long been one of America's most concentrated industries. For decades, six firms have dominated production: R.J. Reynolds, Philip Morris, American Brands, Lorillard, Liggett, and Brown & Williamson. R.J. Reynolds and Philip Morris, the two industry leaders, enjoyed respective market shares of about 28 and 40 percent at the time of trial. Brown & Williamson ran a distant third, its market share never exceeding 12 percent. Liggett's share of the market was even less, from a low of just over 2 percent in 1980 to a high of just over 5 percent in 1984.

The cigarette industry also has long been one of America's most profitable industries. For many years no significant price competition occurred among the rival firms. Prices for cigarettes increased in lockstep, twice a year, for a number of years, irrespective of the rate of inflation, changes in the costs of production, or shifts in consumer demand. The industry reaped the benefits of prices above a competitive level, though not through unlawful conduct that once characterized the industry.

By 1980, however, broad market trends worked against the industry. Overall cigarette demand in the United States declined with no immediate prospect of recovery as fewer people smoked. This decline in demand, coupled with the effects of nonprice competition, had a severe negative impact on Liggett. Its market share of over 20 percent had declined by 1980 to a little over 2 percent. With this meager share of the market, Liggett verged on going out of business.

In 1980, Liggett introduced a line of generic cigarettes that sold at a price roughly 30 percent lower than the full-priced, branded cigarettes. Liggett promoted these at the wholesale level by means of rebates that increased with the volume of cigarettes ordered. Liggett's black and whites were an immediate success, growing to over 4 percent of the total cigarette market by early 1984. By 1984, when Brown & Williamson entered the generic market, Liggett had 97 percent of the generic segment, which in turn accounted for a little more than 4 percent of domestic cigarette sales.

The growth of Liggett's generic cigarettes negatively impacted the other firms' profitable sales of branded cigarettes. Brown & Williamson was hardest hit because many of its consumers were sensitive to changes in cigarette prices. Although Brown & Williamson sold only 11.4 percent of the market's branded cigarettes, 20 percent of its customers switched to Liggett's black and whites. Losing volume and profits in its branded products, Brown & Williamson entered the generic cigarette market.

Because Liggett's and Brown & Williamson's generics were more or less fungible (interchangeable), wholesalers had little incentive to carry more than one line. Brown & Williamson not only matched Liggett's prices but beat them. At the retail level, the price of Brown & Williamson's black and whites was the same as Liggett's, but Brown & Williamson's volume discounts to wholesalers were larger. Brown & Williamson marketed its black and whites to Liggett's existing distributors as well as to its own full list of buyers, which included a thousand wholesalers who had not yet carried any generic products.

Liggett responded to Brown & Williamson's introduction of black and whites by increasing its own wholesale rebates. This action precipitated a price war at the wholesale level, in which Liggett five times attempted to beat the rebates offered by Brown & Williamson. At the end of each round, Brown & Williamson maintained a real advantage over Liggett's prices. Liggett filed this lawsuit.

The district court found that despite the price cutting and the volume discounts, the growth rate of generics was not slowing, and thus no injury to competition existed. Brown & Williamson, therefore, had no reasonable possibility of limiting the growth of the generic segment. The United States Court of Appeals for the Fourth Circuit affirmed.

Justice KENNEDY delivered the opinion of the Court.

. . . .

. . . Although we have reiterated that "'a price discrimination within the meaning of [this] provision is merely a price difference,'" the statute as a practical matter could not, and does not, ban all price differences charged to "different purchasers of commodities of like grade and quality." . . . By its terms, the Robinson-Patman Act condemns price discrimination only to the extent that it threatens to injure competition.

. . . .

If circumstances indicate that below-cost pricing could likely produce its intended effect on the target, there is still the further question whether it would likely injure competition in the relevant market. The plaintiff must demonstrate that there is a likelihood that the predatory scheme alleged would cause a rise in prices above a competitive level that would be sufficient to compensate for the amounts expended on the predation, including the time value of the money invested in it. As we have observed on a prior occasion, "[i]n order to recoup their losses, [predators] must obtain enough market power to set higher than competitive prices, and then must sustain those prices long enough to earn in excess profits what they earlier gave up in below-cost prices."

DECISION AND REMEDY The United States Supreme Court found that no violation of the Robinson-Patman Act occurred. Brooke Group had to show more than below-cost pricing and that Brown & Williamson would raise prices after Brooke Group had been eliminated from competing. Brown & Williamson had no reasonable prospect of recouping its losses because the other cigarette manufacturers would act to protect their market share.

CRITICAL THINKING: INTERPRETATION Although not included in this edited case, two terms, *oligopolistic market* and *predatory losses*, are used in this case and in many antitrust cases. Define each.

Section 3

Section 3 prohibits *exclusive dealing agreements* and *tying arrangements* when they substantially reduce competition or when they tend to create a monopoly. Under an **exclusive dealing agreement**, the seller of goods requires the buyer to promise not to handle the products of any of the seller's competitors. For example, an oil company requires its dealers to carry only its brand of products, such as gasoline, oil, parts, and batteries. This requirement is an exclusive dealing agreement and is illegal if it reduces competition or creates a monopoly.

A **tying arrangement** occurs when the supplier forces the buyer to purchase an unrelated item (the tied item). Usually, but not always, the tied item does poorly on its own in the marketplace. The tied item is often unwanted by the buyer, or the buyer believes it can purchase the tied item at a lower price. The supplier (seller) either wants to get rid of the tied item or may be profiting from it.

For example, Fast-Food Franchise requires its franchisees to purchase not only its secret recipe mix and specially designed cooking machines, but also all paper products, such as paper boxes, paper bags, and paper napkins, in the franchise colors with its stamped logo. The franchise agreement forbids the franchisee from purchasing paper products from a local supplier and having the colors and logo printed. This requirement is an illegal tying arrangement under Section 3, because the franchise must purchase the paper products to buy the tied product, the secret recipe mix. Paper products have nothing to do with the product sold by Fast-Food Franchise and can be purchased at lower prices from others.

Both tying arrangements and exclusive dealing contracts violate Section 2 of the Sherman Act. Under the Sherman Act, both goods and services are covered, whereas the Clayton Act covers only goods. Once, courts treated tying arrangements as *per se* illegal. Recently, however, courts have required the seller to

have economic power in the market for the tying product for such dealings to be illegal. Section 3 provisions are subject to the rule of reason today.

Section 7

The original Section 7 also was weak. In 1950, Congress passed the **Celler–Kefauver Act**, which strengthened and expanded this section. Corporations are prohibited from merging with another corporation if the merger might reduce competition or tend to create a monopoly. Section 7 was amended again by the **Hart–Scott–Rodino Antitrust Improvements Act** of 1976. The act requires businesses that intend to merge to provide both the Federal Trade Commission and the Department of Justice with a premerger notification.

Section 8

Section 8 prohibits interlocking directorates and officers. The law forbids a person from being a director or officer in two or more competing businesses if one of them has capital, surplus, and profits exceeding $10 million as of 1990. This amount is annually reviewed and is increased or decreased based on the gross domestic product (GDP) (the total value of all goods and services produced within a country). The current maximum amount is $13,813,000.

An exception to this rule, however, allows a person to be a director of a second business if the competitive sales of either corporation are less than $1,381,300, that is, 10 percent, of the larger amount. Section 8 also allows a person to be a director if the total competitive sales of both corporations is less than 4 percent of the corporation's total sales.

Actual monopolization is unnecessary under the Clayton Act, as is any attempt to monopolize. The act does not require that an injury to competition be demonstrated. Therefore, the burden of proof for violations of the Clayton Act is less than for violations of the Sherman Act. In short, the Clayton Act reaches (prohibits) practices before a monopoly actually occurs.

Federal Trade Commission Act

In 1914, Congress passed the Federal Trade Commission Act, which created the Federal Trade Commission (FTC) as a "trust-busting" agency.[8] This bipartisan, independent administrative agency is composed of five commissioners. At any given time, no more than three commissioners can be from the same political party.

The FTC Act, as originally passed in 1914, was very weak. In 1938, Congress passed the **Wheeler-Lea Act**, which provided the FTC a dual focus: the original focus of regulating anticompetitive business behavior and the additional focus of providing consumer protection (which was covered in Chapter 15). In 1975, Congress amended the FTC Act again with the **Magnuson-Moss Federal Trade Improvement Act**, which broadened the scope of the FTC Act.

The FTC's function is to ensure that the marketplace is competitive, efficient, and free from undue restraints. The FTC's antitrust division has the authority to enforce (1) the Federal Trade Commission Act, which prohibits "Unfair methods of competition in or affecting commerce, and unfair or deceptive acts or practices in or affecting commerce" as unlawful; (2) the Clayton Act, which prohibits arrangements, mergers, and acquisitions that threaten competition; (3) the Robinson-Patman Act, which forbids price discrimination; and (4) the Hart-Scott-Rodino Antitrust Improvements Act, which requires companies to file premerger notifications.

Mergers

A **merger** is the combination of two or more businesses into one. Mergers result in one business gaining greater control of the market. Accordingly, the antitrust laws apply to mergers and prevent consolidations that would substantially reduce competition or end in a monopoly.

Section 7 of the Clayton Act is the principal statute that applies to mergers. The act prohibits "one person," including corporations, partnerships, and sole proprietorships, from acquiring another if the merger would tend to reduce competition substantially or to create a monopoly. Congress feared that a concentration of power, by merger or consolidation, potentially would facilitate collusion among sellers in the market and that such collusion would be difficult to detect.

The Hart-Scott-Rodino Antitrust Improvements Act, in addition to amending Section 7 of the Clayton Act, also provided the FTC with more powers.[9] The act required businesses planning to merge to file a premerger notification with the FTC and the Department of Justice. The FTC can enforce these notification procedures. This notification allows affected agencies to review and determine if a potential merger will violate the antitrust laws. The FTC can sue to enforce the notification procedures. Violations of these procedures subject the firms to fines up to $100,000. Three types of mergers exist: *horizontal merger, vertical merger,* and *conglomerate merger.*

Horizontal Mergers

A **horizontal merger** occurs when two or more companies merge that previously competed with the same or similar products in the same geographic area. This type of merger receives rigorous scrutiny because horizontal mergers lead to a concentration of firms in a relevant market. The FTC and the Antitrust Division of the Department of Justice (DOJ) examine horizontal mergers by reviewing the degree of concentration and market shares of merging firms.

If the merged company will gain an increased market share and at the same time less competition, it can increase its product price and diminish its product quality and service. In a concentrated marketplace, innovation can be stifled. Under these circumstances, the merger will be challenged by the DOJ and the FTC. A merger is allowed, however, when the marketplace is enhanced by increasing its efficiency and the merger does not increase the horizontal concentration of power in the marketplace.

---

[8] The Federal Trade Commission's web page is located at <http://www.ftc.gov>.

[9] For more information on premerger and the Hart-Scott-Rodino Antitrust Improvements Act, go to <http://www.ftc.gov/bc/hsr/hsr.htm>. This page also includes early termination information.

LEGAL HIGHLIGHT

Herfindahl-Hirschman Index

Businesses are required under the Hart-Scott-Rodino Antitrust Improvements Act to file a premerger notification with both the Department of Justice and the Federal Trade Commission. These agencies determine whether the horizontal merger should be permitted. Mergers that create or enhance market power are not allowed to proceed.

DOJ uses the Herfindahl-Hirschman Index (HHI), which is a commonly accepted measure of market concentration. The HHI takes into account the relative size and distribution of the firms in a market. The index approaches zero when a market consists of a large number of firms of relatively equal size. The HHI increases both as the number of firms in the market decreases and the disparity in size between those firms increases. DOJ determines whether the market is concentrated through the use of the HHI.

If the index is less than 1,000 points, the merger normally will not be questioned. If the index is between 1,000 and 1,800 points, the market is considered to be moderately concentrated. The merger likewise will not be challenged if the index increases by 100 or less after the merger. If the index is above 1,800, the market is considered to be concentrated. Thus, if the merger will increase the HHI by more than 100 points in concentrated markets, antitrust concerns are raised. The DOJ will challenge the merger in most circumstances.

The index is obtained by squaring the market shares and then adding all competitors' shares to-gether. The HHI does not use decimals, so they are multiplied by 100. The following is an example.

The Herfindahl-Hirschman Index

Firm	Market Share	Market Share x 100	Market Share Squared
A	0.30	30	900
B	0.10	10	100
C	0.40	40	1,600
D	0.05	5	25
E	0.15	15	225
HHI Number			2,850

Based on guidelines, a proposed merger of any two firms among those listed would not be allowed. For example, if D and E were to merge, the new market share would be 5 + 15, or 20. This figure squared would result in a market share of 400. Because the market share of D and E before merger would be 250 (25 + 225), the difference of 400 – 250, or 150, would be greater than 100 points on an HHI that exceeds 1,800. This merger, therefore, would be challenged.

The DOJ and the FTC have jointly issued *Horizontal Merger Guidelines*.[10] An analytical process is used to determine whether a horizontal merger will be challenged. The government uses the guidelines to evaluate the concentration of the relevant market and to determine if there will be an increase in market concentration after the merger. The DOJ also consid-ers nonmarket issues, such as ease of entry into the business and competitive strength of the merged firms. The policy is to prevent anticompetitive problems in their incipiency. The government tries to avoid unnec-essary interference with mergers that are either com-petitively beneficial or neutral.

In determining whether a horizontal merger will result in an unacceptable increase in market concen-tration, the DOJ uses a statistical formula called the **Herfindahl-Hirschman Index**. After considering the other factors and implementing this index, the DOJ de-termines whether a merger is likely to be challenged.

[10] The guidelines for horizontal mergers can be found at <http://www.ftc.gov/bc/guidelin.htm> and <http://www.usdoj.gov/atr/public/guidelines/horiz_book/hmg1.html>.

The index is featured in the Legal Highlight entitled *Herfindahl-Hirschman Index*.

Vertical Mergers

Vertical mergers occur when a company at one stage of distribution acquires a company at a higher or lower stage of distribution. The acquisition of a tire plant by an automobile manufacturer is called a **backward vertical integration**. The acquisition of a car-renting agency by the same automobile manufacturer constitutes a **forward vertical integration**. The government's approach to vertical mergers depends on a number of factors, including the definition of the relevant product and geographic markets, as well as the characteristics identified as impeding competition.

The government will attack any vertical merger that keeps competitors of either party from a segment of the market that otherwise would be open to them. The law's current theory of injury to competition in vertical mergers is contained in the concept of foreclosure. For example, a manufacturer can acquire a retailer and force the new retail subsidiary to sell the manufacturer's product. This acquisition would foreclose rival manufacturers from the market. The FTC has found that "foreclosure manifests a particularly anticompetitive character when it occurs as part of a trend toward forward integration in a concentrated market."

Conglomerate Mergers

A **conglomerate merger** is the consolidation of two or more firms dealing in unrelated products and operating in markets not horizontally or vertically linked. For example, a firm that operates motion picture theaters acquires a firm that manufactures automobile parts. Sometimes the products of the merged firms are complementary and a merger permits the marketing of additional products at very little expense.

CyberLaw

Mergers and Antitrust Concerns

Competition usually spurs firms to achieve efficiencies internally. Nevertheless, mergers, even those involving e-commerce companies, have the potential to generate significant efficiencies by permitting a better utilization of existing assets, thus, enabling the combined firm to achieve lower costs in producing a given quantity and quality than either firm could have achieved without the proposed transaction. Indeed, the primary benefit of mergers to the economy is their potential to generate such efficiencies.

As more firms involved with e-commerce propose mergers, they only will be permitted when efficiencies generated through the merger can enhance the merged firm's ability and incentive to compete. Normally, these efficiencies result in lower prices, improved quality, enhanced service, and new products.

Defenses and Exemptions

Congress and the courts have created certain defenses and exemptions to the antitrust laws. More defenses and exemptions exist, but the following are commonly used.

Defenses

The courts have upheld several defenses for businesses confronted with allegations of creating an illegal monopoly or conspiring to restrain trade. The subsections that follow describe some defenses that the courts have accepted.

Defenses to Price Discrimination. Price discrimination in violation of the Robinson-Patman Act occurs when a seller that operates interstate discriminates in the prices charged to different purchasers for goods of like grade and quality, resulting in injury to a competitor. A seller may have defenses. The three defenses to price discrimination are *meeting the competition, cost justification*, and *changing market conditions*.

The Meeting the Competition Defense. The statutory provisions of the Clayton Act allow the reduction of a price made "in good faith to meet an equally low price of a competitor." The **meeting the competition defense** allows a business to sell at a lower price to some customers if it must meet a competitor's price. But the price must be lowered to meet, not to beat, a competitive price. Price lowering must not be made with the intent to drive the competitor out of business. Also, the lower price must be for goods of similar quality to those of the competitor. Finally, the lower price to these customers must be temporary so as not to result in a competitive injury to the seller's other customers. As long as the business meets these three conditions, it may sell at a lower price to certain customers to meet competition.

The Cost-Justification Defense. It is less expensive per unit to manufacture and sell a thousand units of an item than ten units. Lower prices are permitted when the savings result from a particular customer's purchase. The seller must carry the burden of proof when using a **cost-justification defense** to price discrimination. A large-volume purchase alone does not justify a seller charging a purchaser a lower price. The seller must prove with actual evidence that the buyer's large purchase saves the seller money, such as lower transportation costs. Then the seller can pass these savings on to the large purchaser. It may be difficult to determine the proper allocation of overhead and other expenses in order to demonstrate these savings.

The Changing-Market-Conditions Defense. The **changing-market-conditions defense** to price discrimination allows a business to discontinue a product or product line or to offer a fire or bankruptcy sale. In doing so, the business may sell the product at a reduced price. This defense allows a business to discount prices on seasonal goods or goods that will deteriorate.

Other Defenses. The courts have approved various defenses to charges of violations of other parts of the antitrust laws. The following are defenses to vertical restraint, monopoly, and merger cases.

The Colgate Doctrine. The ***Colgate* doctrine** comes from *United States v. Colgate & Co.* The United States Supreme Court allowed Colgate to refuse unilaterally to deal with retailers that ignored its suggested retail prices (vertical price fixing). This refusal to deal created a vertical restraint between Colgate and its retailers (purchasers of Colgate's products). The Court emphasized that a firm can choose with whom it deals.

The Thrust-Upon Defense. A business that has a monopoly can use the **thrust-upon defense** by showing that the monopoly might have been created by the production of a superior product; by better business practices; or by events, such as owning the only restaurant in an area where all the other restaurants have

closed as a result of economic conditions. For this defense, no wrongful intent to create the monopoly must exist.

The Failing-Company and Inadequate Resources Defenses. When a company confronts complete failure with no other prospective purchasers, the courts have allowed a merger, even if it violates antitrust guidelines. This defense is known as the **failing-company defense**.

Related to this doctrine is the **inadequate-resources defense**. If a company has insufficient financial resources to compete, the courts will allow a merger with another competing company, even though the result violates antitrust guidelines.

Exemptions

Congress passed the Sherman Act, the Clayton Act, and provided the Federal Trade Commission Act with antitrust provisions. Congress also passed legislation that provides exemptions from antitrust laws. The courts, when interpreting the statutes that set out the exemptions, read the statutes very narrowly, that is, the courts try to limit exemptions.

Labor. The Norris-LaGuardia Act of 1932 and the National Labor Relations Act of 1935 protect unions from antitrust legislation. Today, unions lawfully can engage in actions, normally prohibited, as long as they act in self-interest without conspiring or combining with nonlabor groups.

Agriculture. The Clayton Act exempts agricultural organizations from the Sherman Act. The law allows many farmers to join together to form an agricultural cooperative to deal with the few purchasers of farm products. A cooperative usually forms to deal with specific types of farm products and generally does not cover every farm product that could be sold. Every member of a cooperative that deals in specific products must be involved in that aspect of farm production for the cooperative to keep the exemption.

Baseball. Although most commercial sports activities are subject to the antitrust laws, baseball is an exception. The United States Supreme Court early in the 1900s held that baseball was not commerce. Baseball's exemption is anomalous, especially because no other professional sport receives such treatment.

Insurance. The **McCarran-Ferguson Act**, enacted in 1945, exempted all activities that involve the insurance business from the antitrust laws. The primary element of the insurance business is the spreading and underwriting of policyholder risk. Strict insurance activities are exempted from the antitrust laws by the McCarran-Ferguson Act. An agreement between an insurance company and pharmacies to set the profit margin in prescription drugs, however, is subject to the antitrust laws.

Exports. Congress exempted certain activities from antitrust actions in the belief that certain goals can be better achieved through cartelization, that is, a banding together of competing firms. For example, the **Webb-Pomerene Act** exempts acts or agreements made in the course of export trade by *associations of competing producers* formed solely for the purpose of engaging in export trade. Cartelization promotes an increased national investment in the covered activities, thereby aiding the nation's balance of payments.

Congress designed the Export Trading Company Act of 1982 to increase U.S. exports of goods and services. Businesses can apply for an export trade certificate of review (ETCR). If approved, the secretary of commerce, with the concurrence of the attorney general, issues the ETCR. Persons named in the ETCR obtain limited immunity from both state and federal antitrust laws for activities that the certificate specifies. The proposed export conduct, however, cannot result in a substantial reduction of competition within the United States or restrain the export trade of any competitor of the applicant.

Political Activities. The **Noerr-Pennington Doctrine** derives from two United States Supreme Court cases. Basically, the Court held that "the Sherman Act does not prohibit two or more persons from associating together in an attempt to persuade the legislature or the executive to take particular action with respect to a law that would produce a restraint or a monopoly." In other words, businesses can work with (lobby) Congress to pass appropriate favorable laws.

State Government. In general, state governments (which include city and county governments) may take actions that regulate economic activity; these actions are exempt from antitrust laws. The state govern-

ment, however, must have a state policy and must actively supervise the regulated activity.

The United States Supreme Court has held that not all state or local government actions are exempt from federal antitrust laws. For example, a city government may not grant a cable company exclusive rights to service the city.

Enforcement of Antitrust Laws

Criminal enforcement of the Sherman Act is handled exclusively by the Department of Justice (as are all criminal actions brought on behalf of the U.S. government). Civil enforcement of the Sherman Act also is the responsibility of the Department of Justice. State attorney generals and private parties may file civil lawsuits when they have been harmed.

The Clayton Act, which has primarily civil provisions,[11] is enforced by the Federal Trade Commission, Department of Justice, state attorneys general, and private parties. The Federal Trade Commission Act is enforced exclusively by the FTC.

Enforcement by the Federal Trade Commission

The FTC enforces the Federal Trade Commission Act and Sections 2, 3, 7, and 8 of the Clayton Act. The FTC will investigate a business's anticompetitive conduct. During the investigation, the FTC sends the business a copy of the complaint and a proposed form of a consent order that contains a cease-and-desist order. If the business agrees, the cease-and-desist order is entered and the proceedings end. The business agrees to cease (stop) committing the unlawful acts and to desist (restrain) from committing the acts in the future.

At any time, the business and the FTC may come to an agreement and a consent order will be entered. If the business has also been sued in a civil lawsuit, the consent order protects the accused business. The plaintiff cannot use the FTC's case against the accused in any civil lawsuit when the business enters into an agreement for a consent order.

---

[11] Section 14 of the Clayton Act includes the act's only criminal sanctions and is not discussed in this textbook.

If the business fails to reply or responds negatively to the proposed form of the consent order, the FTC issues the complaint. An administrative agency proceeding takes place to determine whether the business violated the antitrust laws.

After hearing all the evidence, the administrative law judge (ALJ) may find in favor of the business. The FTC then must decide whether to appeal the ALJ's decision. If the FTC decides against appealing, the case ends.

If the ALJ agrees with the FTC's position, the ALJ may issue an order, which the business may appeal. An appellate court reviews the order. If the order stands, the business that violates the order in the future is subject to fines up to $10,000 per day for each day of continued violation.

Enforcement by the Department of Justice

The Antitrust Division of the Department of Justice enforces the criminal aspects of the Sherman Act and the civil provisions in both the Sherman Act and Sections 2, 3, 7, and 8 of the Clayton Act. The DOJ and the FTC each have authority to enforce the Clayton Act. To use their resources more efficiently, each agency clears proposed investigations with the other.

The DOJ investigates a business that it (DOJ) believes to be committing violations of the Sherman Act or the Clayton Act. DOJ can decide to pursue criminal or civil action in federal district court. If the DOJ and the business agree, they settle the case out of court. The agreement (settlement) results in a consent judgment issued by the district court judge. The court must find that the settlement is in the national interest.

The issues in antitrust cases are extremely complex and often take years to litigate. Settlements usually can shorten the time period to reach the end of the case and can reduce the cost of enforcement. Settlements can occur at any time prior to or during the trial. Although settlements usually reduce costs, they sometimes are reached near the trial's end. Probably one of the best examples of a settlement that occurred after both a lengthy and costly investigation and a trial is the breakup of American Telephone and Telegraph. See the Legal Highlight entitled *The Breakup of AT&T* for details.

If negotiations fail, the DOJ will set the case for trial in federal district court. If the court finds in favor of the business, the DOJ must decide whether to appeal the decision. If the decision is not appealed, the case ends.

If the court finds in favor of the DOJ, it can seek a range of remedies from the court against the defendant, such as injunction, confiscation, divestiture, or dissolution. If the court grants the DOJ's request, a remedy will be ordered. With an injunction, the court orders the business to stop permanently its antitrust conduct. In other types of cases, the court can order confiscation (seizure) of goods that are in interstate commerce.

The defendant business can be ordered to divest (to sell off or withdraw from) another business that it owns. For example, the court ordered a wholesale meat packing business to sell its retail butcher shops.

In an extreme case, a dissolution (to end) order can be issued to terminate the business. The business must file articles of dissolution with the state government that created it, so that the business can be dissolved and then go out of business.

The DOJ can file a lawsuit alleging the U.S. government was harmed as a result of the antitrust activities of a business. In these cases, the statute allows the DOJ to recover up to three times the amount of the harm suffered by the government.

After an investigation, DOJ may decide that the business committed criminal acts. Any person violating either Section 1 or Section 2 of the Sherman Act is subject to criminal prosecution for a felony. In criminal cases, DOJ settles a high percentage of antitrust cases through the use of **nolo contendere** pleas. When a business enters a *nolo contendere* plea, it does not admit guilt, but will not fight the case. The court may treat the plea as if the defendant had pleaded guilty and impose the same penalty as if a guilty plea had been entered. The business may choose this plea because it cannot be used in civil cases that may be pending against it. The plea also saves money that the business would have spent in litigating a lengthy case.

If the defendant fails to use the *nolo contendere* plea, the DOJ will take the case to a criminal trial. The court will find the defendant guilty or not guilty. If the court convicts the person or business, the person can be fined up to $350,000, can be imprisoned for three years, or both. A corporation can be fined up to $10 million.

LEGAL HIGHLIGHT

The Breakup of AT&T

American Telephone and Telegraph (AT&T) was a utility regulated by the various state utility commissions. The first case brought by the Department of Justice against AT&T for antitrust activities began in 1949 and ended with a consent decree in 1956 that was a victory for AT&T. The decree merely enjoined AT&T from engaging in any business other than the furnishing of common carrier communications services, the very area in which it held a near monopoly.

Technology advances combined with AT&T's growth convinced the DOJ to renew its investigation. In 1974, following an investigation, DOJ filed a new antitrust lawsuit against AT&T, Western Electric, and Bell Telephone Laboratories, Inc. At the time the lawsuit was filed, AT&T had three million shareholders, over one million employees, an annual payroll of over $21 billion, and assets worth more than those of General Motors, Ford, Chrysler, General Electric, and IBM combined.

AT&T had a near monopoly on long-distance telephone service and controlled nearly all local telephone operating companies (twenty-two in all), which provided AT&T control of nearly 80 percent of all the country's telephones. Western Electric and AT&T had agreed in 1882 that Western Electric had the exclusive right to supply all of AT&T's telephone equipment. Between 1901 and 1913, Western Electric negotiated exclusive contracts with all the local operating companies to supply them with all telephone equipment. The state utility commissions did not regulate Western Electric's profits.

Bell Laboratories served as the research arm and was owned half by AT&T and half by Western Electric. Bell Laboratories and Western Electric developed and standardized products for use by the local operating companies.

The dispute between DOJ and AT&T was waged for six years over jurisdictional issues and involved an expensive, lengthy process. The trial opened on January 15, 1981, and recessed immediately after opening statements. Negotiations continued, but the parties could not reach a settlement. On March 4, 1981, the trial resumed. The DOJ presented more than 100 witnesses and thousands of documents. AT&T moved to have the case dismissed, but the presiding judge, Judge Green, strongly denied the motion, stating that the DOJ had presented a strong case and that AT&T would have a difficult time overcoming the weight of the evidence. AT&T presented 250 witnesses and thousands of documents. On January 8, 1982, within two weeks of when AT&T estimated its case would end, a settlement was announced.

The nineteen-page consent judgment allowed AT&T to maintain its nationwide long-distance telephone network. AT&T was ordered to divest itself of (sell) the twenty-two local telephone operating companies. They reorganized into what was then called the seven "Baby Bells."[a] Because the seven Baby Bells would not have any loyalty to Western Electric and were free to identify other suppliers, the court refrained from ordering AT&T to divest Western Electric. The court also ordered the seven Baby Bells to allow AT&T's long-distance competitors equal access to the local telephone distribution system. The order also allowed AT&T to enter into communications and computer services and to enter the computer and electronics industries without restrictions, except that AT&T could not engage in electronic publishing.

The settlement and subsequent consent judgment reached between AT&T and DOJ has been reviewed and modified through the years. The effect of the court order, however, still stands. It broke up the largest monopoly ever achieved in the United States.

[a] After the breakup of AT&T, the seven regional telephone companies were Ameritech, Bell Atlantic, Bell South, NYNEX, Pacific Telesis, Southwestern Bell, and US West. A number of these companies have been merged into other telecommunications companies.

Enforcement by State Attorneys General and Private Parties

The Hart-Scott-Rodino Antitrust Improvements Act of 1976 amended the Clayton Act. This act authorizes state attorneys general and private parties, for the first time, to file civil lawsuits under the Clayton Act and the Sherman Act. The act authorizes state attorneys general to sue on behalf of the residents of their respective states.

The states can sue for three times the amount of damage caused by a firm that has violated the Clayton Act or the Sherman Act and also to recover attorneys' fees. For example, if 3,000 residents have been harmed, but only by a $10 amount, the individual does not have the economic incentive to file a lawsuit against the an-titrust violator. The state attorney general can file an action on their behalf and recover three times the amount of the harm, plus attorneys' fees. This case usually is too small for the FTC or the DOJ to be interested in, but a state attorney general may very well be interested in pursuing this type of case.

The act allows private parties harmed by a firm's anticompetitive acts to recover up to three times their damages and their attorneys' fees. The private party often is another business harmed by a competitor engaging in illegal activity. Usually, if only one or two firms have been harmed, neither the federal nor state government is interested in suing. This act allows the victim to pursue its own case rather than relying on federal or state officials to file a lawsuit.

International Consideration

Parallel Antitrust Lawsuits

The United States has had antitrust laws for more than 100 years. Many nations, however, do not have any history of regulating anticompetitive behavior and some nations encourage and assist businesses in anticompetitive behavior.

The export and import trades account for nearly one-quarter of the U.S. gross domestic product. As the U.S. economy becomes increasingly globalized, the threat to business freedom and consumer welfare from foreign cartel activity increases. A **cartel** is a combination of producers that join together to control the production, sale, and price of goods or services and potentially to obtain a monopoly or near monopoly over a particular industry or product. The Oil Producing Exporting Countries (OPEC) is an example of a cartel. Cartels range from being very effective, such as when they achieve a monopoly, to less effective, such as when they are unable to control production, sale, or prices.

Congress passed the **International Antitrust Enforcement Assistance Act (IAEAA)** of 1994. The statute provides antitrust guidance to businesses engaged in international operations, concerning the enforcement policies of the DOJ and the FTC. The law improves the ability of law enforcement agencies to gather evidence from abroad for use in U.S. antitrust enforcement cases. The statute also authorizes the DOJ and the FTC to assist foreign antitrust authorities on a reciprocal basis.

The European Union (EU) has had antitrust laws since its inception. Articles 85 and 86 of the Treaty of Rome[12] are modeled after the U.S. antitrust laws. Article 85 prohibits concerted anticompetitive conduct, such as price fixing and limiting of markets. Article 86 aims at monopolistic practices and market domination.

EU regulations implement Article 85 and Article 86. The regulations determine whether a product concentration creates or strengthens a dominant position as the result of effective competition. The question is whether the product concentration significantly impedes the common market or whether it is incompatible with the common market. The EU law also prohibits and regulates the confidentiality requirements of an antitrust investigation. The member states have given the EU sovereign authority to administer or enforce antitrust laws.

The EU recognizes opportunities for cooperation in antitrust investigations between the EU and the United States. One example is the parallel antitrust cases brought against Microsoft Corporation by both the United States and the EU. In these cases, Microsoft was charged with a horizontal restraint.[13] Microsoft required original equipment manufacturers (OEMs), that is, computer hardware manufacturers, to sign contracts to install Microsoft's disk operating system (MS-DOS). The contract indicated two payment methods. The OEM could pay for MS-DOS per installation, but the cost was prohibitive on an individual computer basis. Using the cheaper method, the OEMs paid for MS-DOS on every computer manufactured, rather than just for the computers on which MS-DOS was installed. This type of contract was a disincentive for OEMs to install other operating systems, such as IBM's operating system OS/2, because they would have to pay another fee in addition to that already paid to Microsoft.

The parallel lawsuits were filed at Microsoft's request so that the same rules in both the United States and the EU would apply. The case was settled, and Microsoft revised its contract so that the OEMs pay a fee per computer on which MS-DOS actually is installed. Although the parallel case occurred prior to the 1994 adoption of the IAEAA, it signals unprecedented cooperation between two sovereigns to enforce antitrust laws. The IAEAA will encourage more parallel lawsuits to be filed in the future.

In 1997, the Department of Justice charged Microsoft with violating this agreement. The DOJ al-

---

[12] A brief review of the history of the EU follows. In 1957, the Treaty of Rome provided for a common market that eventually led to the European Economic Community (EEC). The Single European Act of 1987, amending the Treaty of Rome, provided for the economic union of the western European nations. During the time period from 1987 to 1994, the name evolved from the EEC to the European Community (EC). In 1993, the Treaty on European Union (commonly called the Maastricht Treaty) amended the Treaty of Rome. The Maastricht Treaty in 1994 created the European Union (EU) and provided for a political union of the western European nations. Many parts of the original Treaty of Rome remain in effect, such as the antitrust provisions.

[13] Information on the *United States v. Microsoft* case is located at <http://www.findlaw.com/01topics/01antitrust/microsoft.html>.

leged that Microsoft violated the court order by requiring OEMs to license and distribute Microsoft's Internet browser, called Internet Explorer, as a condition of licensing Microsoft's operating system. Microsoft also made it almost impossible to delete this program. The Justice Department sought, among other things, the breakup of Microsoft into two companies and a court order prohibiting Microsoft from requiring OEMs to install Internet Explorer along with Microsoft's operating system.

At the federal district court level, after a lengthy trial the court found Microsoft guilty of violations of Section 2 of the Sherman Act for the maintenance of a monopoly power by anticompetitive means. The court noted that no current products were available for users of personal computers worldwide that could substituted for the Windows operating systems without incurring substantial costs. As a result, the court inferred that Microsoft could set the price of a license substantially above that which would be charged in a competitive market and leave the price at that level without losing customers.

Microsoft was found guilty of violations of Section 1 of the Sherman Act. Microsoft was liable for illegal tying of the browser, Internet Explorer, with the Windows operating system. This tying action by Microsoft forced its customers to take Internet Explorer as a condition of obtaining Windows.

The court noted first, that Microsoft did not concede that any of its business practices violated the Sherman Act and had failed to amend its conduct. Second, Microsoft, despite credible evidence of antitrust violations, continued to do business as it had in the past and indicated that it may operate the same in future markets. Third, the court found Microsoft to be untrustworthy. In an earlier proceeding a preliminary injunction had been issued. Microsoft's purported compliance with the injunction, the court noted, was illusory and its explanation of its actions were disingenuous. The trial court ordered Microsoft to submit a proposed plan of divestiture, one that would divide Microsoft into two companies. Microsoft appealed the court's findings to the D.C. Circuit Court of Appeals. The case is expected to reach the U.S. Supreme Court.

LEGALLY SPEAKING
Avoiding Antitrust Violations

You are the marketing director of a firm that recently patented a revolutionary product similar to plastic, but with the strength of steel, the breathing ability of leather, the smoothness of silk, and the flexibility of rubber. Your business goal is to maximize profits without running afoul of the antitrust laws.

In preparing a detailed marketing plan to reach your goal, you recognize one large benefit granted by federal law. Since your product was patented, you have an automatic exemption to the antitrust laws in the event that your product occupies a monopoly position in the marketplace.

You must pay attention, however, to other antitrust aspects. The following list itemizes some areas of caution:

✔ Sell this product at the same price to competing distributors unless filling large orders creates cost savings.

✔ Refrain from requiring the distributors to sell at a given price unless you have retained title to the product.

✔ Refrain from setting the maximum price of the goods.

✔ Do not require the purchase of one product to be based on the purchase of other products.

This checklist provides you with several examples of how a business must be concerned with antitrust violations even when the law grants it the right to create a monopoly.

Chapter Summary

The three major antitrust statutes include the Sherman Act, the Clayton Act, and the Federal Trade Commission Act. The federal law attempts to prevent anticompetitive acts by businesses, to support an innovative marketplace, and to maximize consumer choice, all of which contribute to a free market economy. Anticompetitive business practices can result in a monopoly, in restraint of trade, or in substantially reducing competition.

In 1890, Congress passed the Sherman Act, which has two sections. The first section makes it illegal to enter into any contract, combination, or conspiracy in restraint of trade or commerce. The second section makes it illegal to monopolize or attempt to monopolize any trade or commerce. Violations of either section may result in a criminal felony conviction. The major defense to the Sherman Act is that business conduct is subject to the rule of reason. Certain conduct, such as price fixing, is conclusively a *per se* violation of the Sherman Act. The Department of Justice can pursue both civil and criminal lawsuits under the Sherman Act. State attorney generals and private parties can seek up to three times the amount of damage caused by violations of the Sherman Act.

The Clayton Act was adopted in 1914. This statute makes specific conducts, including price discrimination, exclusive dealing, tying arrangements, certain types of mergers, and interlocking directorships and officerships, violations of the antitrust law. Violations of the Clayton Act are subject to civil lawsuits.

Sections of the Clayton Act have been modified over the years. The Robinson-Patman Act in 1936 amended Section 2. The Celler-Kefauver Act in 1950 and the Hart-Scott-Rodino Antitrust Improvements Act in 1976 both amended Section 7. The last act also required businesses to provide both the Department of Justice and the Federal Trade Commission with premerger notification. The Department of Justice, the Federal Trade Commission, state attorneys general, and private parties can pursue various remedies for violations of the Clayton Act. The Federal Trade Commission Act also was adopted in 1914.

A number of exemptions to the antitrust laws also exist. These exemptions include labor unions, agricultural organizations, baseball, insurance, certain foreign trade groups, and certain activities conducted by individual states. The Webb-Pomerene Act allows cooperatives to file for an exemption from antitrust laws when competing overseas. The Export Trading Company Act of 1982 allows individual businesses to file for an export trade certificate of review. If approved, the business receives limited immunity from antitrust laws when operating in international markets.

In 1994, Congress passed the International Antitrust Enforcement Assistance Act. The act provides antitrust guidance to businesses that operate internationally. It improves the ability to gather evidence from overseas. The DOJ and the FTC are authorized to provide assistance to foreign antitrust authorities when pursuing antitrust violations.

Using the World Wide Web

The Federal Trade Commission has enforcement and administrative responsibilities under thirty-seven separate acts. They are grouped here in three categories: (1) statutes relating to both the competition and consumer protection missions, (2) statutes relating principally to the competition mission, and (3) statutes relating principally to the consumer protection mission. The statutes are available on the FTC's web site. Also available at the FTC's web site is a glossary of terms.

The home page of the Department of Justice's Antitrust Division is responsible for civil and criminal enforcement of the antitrust statutes, with the exception of the Federal Trade Commission Act. Antitrust cases brought by the DOJ can be found at the DOJ web site.

Finding the Law on the Web

Federal Trade Commission, statutes
    http://www.ftc.gov/ogc/stats.htm
Federal Trade Commission, glossary
    http://www.ftc.gov/ftc/glossary.htm
Department of Justice, Antitrust Division, cases
    http://www.usdoj.gov/atr/cases3/index.htm
Department of Justice, list of other antitrust sites
    worldwide
    http://www.usdoj.gov/atr/contact/otheratr.htm

Chapter Web Sites

Department of Justice
    http://www.usdoj.gov/

Department of Justice, Antitrust Division
http://www.usdoj.gov/atr/index.html

Federal Trade Commission, Antitrust Division
http://www.ftc.gov/ftc/antitrust.htm

Federal Trade Commission, Antitrust guidelines
http://www.ftc.gov/bc/guidelin.htm

Antitrust Case Summary Browser created by
Anthony D. Becker, Ph.D.
http://www.stolaf.edu/people/becker
/antitrust/antitrust.html

Yahoo!, antitrust information
http://dir.yahoo.com/government/law

American Bar Association, antitrust matters
http://www.abanet.org/

United States v. Socony-Vacuum Oil Co.
http://caselaw.findlaw.com/scripts/getcase.pl?court
=US&navby=case&vol=310&page=150#150

Exxon Mobil Corporation
http://www.exxon.mobil.com/

Standard Oil Co. of New Jersey v. United States
http://caselaw.findlaw.com/scripts/getcase.pl?navby
=case&court=US&vol=221&page=1

State Oil Company v. Khan
http://caselaw.findlaw.com/cgi=bin/getcase.pl?
court=US&vol=000&invol=96-871

Brooke Group Ltd. v. Brown & Williamson Tobacco Corporation
http://caselaw.findlaw.com/scripts/getcase.pl?navby
=case&court=US&vol=509&page=209

Federal Trade Commission
http://www.ftc.gov

Hart-Scott-Rodino Antitrust Improvements Act
http://www.ftc.gov/bc/hsr/hsr.htm

Guidelines for horizontal mergers
http://www.ftc.gov/bc/guidelin.htm
and
http://www.alston.com/resources/article.cfm?id=44

United States v. Microsoft
http://www.findlaw.com/01topics/01antitrust
/microsoft.html

Hieros Gamos, Comprehensive Law and
Government Portal
http://www.hg.org/

Microsoft cases
http://www.usdoj.gov/atr/cases3/index.htm
and
http://www.findlaw.com/01topics/01antitrust
/microsoft.html

Web Activities

21–1 You are a businessperson. How can you, as an individual or businessperson, help keep the market competitive? Go to the Federal Trade Commission's web site at <http://www.ftc.gov>, click on "Antitrust/Competition." Scroll down to "Antitrust Menu," click on "Promoting Competition, Protecting Consumers: A Plain English Guide to Antitrust Laws." Click on "Keeping Markets Competitive."

21–2 The public often thinks that little is being done concerning persons who violate antitrust laws. Go to the Hieros Gamos Comprehensive Law and Government Portal web site at <http://www.hg.org/>. Click on "200 Legal and Government Topics," then scroll down and click on "Anti-trust and Unfair Competition." Scroll down and click on "Today's HG Anti-trust and Competition News." (The link at the top of the page does not seem to work.) Pick a story about a potential merger. Does the article explain the laws that are involved? Go to the FTC or DOJ web pages. Is there any information posted about the merger that is in the news?

Key Terms

antitrust law
backward vertical
integration
beneficiary
cartel
Celler-Kefauver Act
changing-market-
conditions defense
Clayton Act
Colgate doctrine
conglomerate merger

cost-justification defense
exclusive dealing contract
failing-company defense
forward vertical
integration
group boycott
Hart-Scott-Rodino
Antitrust
Improvements Act
Herfindahl-Hirschman
Index

horizontal market division
horizontal merger
horizontal price fixing
inadequate-resources
defense
International Antitrust
Enforcement Assis-
tance Act (IAEAA)
Magnuson-Moss
Federal Trade
Improvement Act

market power
McCarran-Ferguson Act
meeting the competition
defense
merger
monopoly
Noerr-Pennington
Doctrine
nolo contendere
per se rule
price discrimination

professional association	Robinson–Patman Act	trade association	vertical restraint
relevant geographic market	rule of reason	trust	Webb-Pomerene Act
relevant product market	Sherman Act	trustee	Wheeler-Lea Act
resale price maintenance agreement	territorial and customer division	trustor	
restraints of trade	thrust-upon defense	tying arrangement	
		vertical merger	

Questions and Case Problems

21–1 Price Setting Discuss fully whether each of the following situations violates the Sherman Act.

a. Genovese Foods, Inc., is the leading seller of frozen Italian foods in the northeastern United States. Various retail outlets that sell Genovese products compete closely and customers are very price conscious. Genovese conditions its sales to retailers with the retailer's agreement to offer the products within a specific price range. Within this range, the retailer can set any price that the retailer believes to be appropriate.

b. Zimmermann, Inc., Hicks, Inc., and Micro, Inc., compete in the manufacture and sale of microwave ovens sold primarily on the West Coast. As a patriotic gesture and to assist the unemployed, the three competitors agree to lower their prices on all microwave models by 20 percent for a three-month period, which includes the Fourth of July and Labor Day.

c. Best Beer, Inc., sells beer to distributors all over the United States. Best Beer sends to each of its distributors a recommended price list, explaining that past records indicate that beer sold at these prices should ensure the distributor a reasonable rate of return. The price list clearly states that Best Beer's sale of the beer to the distributor is not conditioned on the distributor's reselling the beer at the recommended price and that the distributor may freely set the price.

21–2 Sherman Act, Section 1 Innovative Appliance Store is a new appliance retail seller in Sunwest City. Innovative's unique sales techniques and financing have caused a substantial loss of sales for the appliance department of Depressed Department Store. Depressed is a large department store that is part of a large chain with substantial buying power. Depressed told a number of appliance manufacturers that if they continued to sell to Innovative, Depressed would discontinue its large volume of purchases from these manufacturers. The manufacturers immediately stopped selling appliances to Innovative. Innovative filed suit against Depressed and the manufacturers, claiming that their actions constituted an antitrust violation. Depressed and the manufacturers can prove that Innovative is a small retailer with a small portion of the market because the relevant market was not substantially affected. They claim that they are innocent of restraint of trade. Discuss fully whether an antitrust violation occurred.

21–3 Clayton Act, Section 7 The partnership of Montoya and Marsh is engaged in the oil wellhead service industry in New Mexico and Colorado. They presently hold about 40 percent of the market for this service. The firm of West, Williams, and Wilson, Inc., competes with the Montoya-Marsh partnership in the same geographic area. The West corporation holds approximately 35 percent of the market. Montoya and Marsh acquire West's stock and assets. Discuss which antitrust law has been primarily violated.

21–4 Sherman Act Harcourt Brace Jovanovich Legal and Professional Publications (HBJ) is the nation's largest provider of bar review materials and lecture services. From 1976 to 1979, HBJ offered a Georgia bar review course in direct competition with BRG of Georgia, Inc. (BRG). In early 1980, both companies entered into an agreement that gave BRG an exclusive license to market HBJ's material in Georgia. Both agreed that HBJ would not compete with BRG in Georgia and that BRG would not compete with HBJ outside of Georgia. Under the agreement HBJ received $100 per student enrolled by BRG and 40 percent of all revenues over $350. The price of BRG's course increased from $150 to $400 following the agreement. After being sued by persons enrolled in the bar review course, both companies defended on the grounds that no *per se* violation occurred under a geographic market allocation theory, because they refrained from dividing the relevant market in which they had previously competed. Who should prevail? Explain. [*Palmer v. BRG of Georgia*, 498 U.S. 46, 111 S. Ct. 401, 112 L. Ed. 2d 349 (1990)]

21–5 Tying Agreement Febco, Inc., manufactured lawn and turf equipment. Colorado Pump and Supply Co. was a wholesale distributor of such equipment in the Colorado area. Colorado Pump distributed a control device for sprinkling systems. Although Febco manufactured one of the better sprinkler controls, a number of other manufacturers competed in the field with competitively priced and satisfactory substitutes for Febco's controllers. In an agreement between Febco and Colorado Pump, Colorado Pump received the right to distribute Febco products, provided that it stocked its complete product line. Industry data proved that in this line of goods, distributors needed to protect the "goodwill" of manufacturers by carrying a complete line of manufacturer's goods or none at all. Does the requirement by Febco that Colorado Pump stock an entire line of Febco products constitute an illegal tying arrangement? Explain. [*Colorado Pump and Supply Co. v. Febco, Inc.*, 472 F.2d 637 (10th Cir. 1973)]

21–6 Rule of Reason Sylvania sold its televisions directly to franchised retailers. Sylvania limited the number of franchises granted for any given area and required each franchise to sell Sylvania products from only the franchise locations. A franchise did not constitute an exclusive territory. Furthermore, Sylvania retained sole discretion to increase the number of retailers in an area, depending on the success or failure of existing retailers in developing their market. Continental T.V., Inc., a Sylvania franchisee, withheld payments owed for Sylvania products after a dispute over Continental's bid to add locations. John P. Maguire & Co., the finance company that handled the credit arrangements between Sylvania and its franchisees, sued Continental for payment and for return of secured merchandise (the televisions). In turn, Continental claimed that Sylvania violated Section 1 of the Sherman Act by entering into and by enforcing franchise agreements that allowed the sale of Sylvania products only in specified locations. Was this a violation of the Sherman Act? Explain. [*Continental TV, Inc. v. GTE Sylvania, Inc.*, 433 U.S. 36, 97 S. Ct. 2549, 53 L. Ed.2d 568 (1977)]

21–7 Sherman Act, Section 1 American Oil Co. produced and distributed oil, gas, and related products. Olson was engaged in bulk distribution and retail sales of oil products. Early in 1967, American decided to acquire control of Olson's bulk distribution operations by purchasing substantially all of Olson's bulk assets. Thereafter, American hired Lawrence McMullin to assume control of the Olson operation for American. Under the agreement, McMullin took charge of the Olson plant and was paid on a commission basis in lieu of salary for the bulk petroleum sales that he procured. In addition, the contract between American and McMullin imposed certain territorial limitations and price restrictions on sales resulting from McMullin's operations. Could the agreement between McMullin and American Oil that

imposed price restrictions and territorial controls on McMullin's operations violate Section 1 of the Sherman Act? Explain. [*American Oil Co. v. McMullin*, 508 F.2d 1345 (10th Cir. 1975)]

21–8 Sherman Act, Section 1 The National Collegiate Athletic Association (NCAA) plays an important role in regulating amateur collegiate sports. As a result of various surveys and reports, the NCAA concluded that telecasting games adversely affected college football game attendance and seriously threatened the athletic system in the United States. The NCAA subsequently imposed regulations that restrained member colleges from negotiating and contracting for the telecasting of college football games. Some member colleges asserted that colleges with major football programs deserved greater input in the formulation of football television policy than they presently had in the NCAA. In addition, NCAA announced that it would take disciplinary action against member colleges that proceeded to enter into a television agreement with the National Broadcasting Company (NBC) on their own. Has the Sherman Act been violated in this case? Does the rule of reason or *per se* analysis apply to the NCAA's television plan? Explain. [*National Collegiate Athletic Association v. Board of Regents of the University of Oklahoma,* 468 U.S. 85, 104 S. Ct. 2948, 82 L. Ed. 2d 70 (1984)]

21–9 Rule of Reason Thompson Everett, Inc. (Everett), the plaintiff, was an independent advertising representative. In this capacity, the plaintiff bought advertising for its clients. The defendants, however, had exclusive contracts to sell advertising for the cable companies; thus, Everett was forced to purchase cable advertisements for its clients through the defendants. Everett claimed that these exclusive contracts violated Section 1 of the Sherman Act in that they unreasonably restrained trade. The defendants contended that they had independently entered into these contracts, that these agreements should be subject to the rule of reason, and that in the interpretation of this rule the product market should include all media rather than just cable advertising. Who should prevail? Explain. [*Thompson Everett, Inc. v. National Cable Adv.*, 850 F. Supp. (E. D. Va. 1994)]

21–10 Internet The case of *United States v. Microsoft* is available at many web sites. Compare the information reported at the Department of Justice's web site with the information reported at the FindLaw web site.

The series of Microsoft cases can be accessed at the Department of Justice's web site at <http://www.usdoj.gov/atr/cases3/index.htm>. The FindLaw web site is <http://www.findlaw.com/01topics/01antitrust/microsoft.html>.

Chapter 22 Legislative Control over Labor and Labor Relations

Labor disgraces no man; unfortunately you occasionally find men disgrace labor.

Speech at Midland International Arbitration Union, Birmingham, England, 1877
Ulysses Grant, 1822–1885
Eighteenth president of the United States of America, 1869–1877

Outline

Ethical Consideration

Should a Business Have a Pension Plan?

You own a small business that manufactures commercial-grade carpeting. You pay your employees either on an hourly or a commission basis. You always have been concerned about the welfare of your employees and their families. Because of this concern, you provide a pension plan. As you review your financial statements, however, you realize that the expense of the pension plan is 5 percent of the business's gross sales. In the competitive global environment, this cost will impede your ability to remain competitive. You consider whether to increase your employees' pay and eliminate the pension benefits.

Many of your employees believe that they will retire comfortably with income from Social Security, and they are not concerned with retirement benefits. Most of your employees are under forty and do not realize that in 2000 the maximum annual benefit paid by Social Security to persons aged sixty-five who paid the maximum amount into Social Security was $13,781. The average Social Security benefit was far less and was insufficient to support a person beyond a minimum standard of living. As a result, because economic costs increase, many senior citizens are forced onto welfare programs and become an economic drain on taxpayers.

Today, as the population ages, the average number of years between retirement and death is increasing. In 1934, when Social Security was enacted, the retirement age was sixty-five. At that time less than 4 percent of the population was sixty-five or older. Today, 4 percent of the population is more than ninety years old. Predictions suggest that the Social Security system will pay a reduced retirement by the time people who currently are in their twenties or thirties reach retirement age, if Congress fails to act to ensure financial security for the Social Security trust fund.

The 1980s saw a major decrease in the benefits offered by businesses to their employees. Employers cut or eliminated pension plans. By the mid-1980s, more than half of all workers were not covered by any pension plan. When these plans were abolished, the employers normally increased the hourly rate paid to employees. Some studies have shown that employees did not take the increase in pay and place it in a retirement plan.

You consider your knowledge about the Social Security system in deciding whether to end the pension plan and increase your employees' wages. What ethical responsibilities do you have for making provisions for the retirement of your youthful employees? Use the ethical model presented in Chapter 2 and reprinted on the inside front cover to develop your answer.

Introduction

In the past, the freedom to contract, as applied to employment, gave rise to perceived inequities in the employer–employee relationship and resulted in abuses, such as, child labor, dangerous working conditions, and worker discrimination. These abuses produced two major responses in the United States. First, the federal government passed national legislation setting work standards, prohibiting discrimination, and creating safety laws. Second, workers began to unionize to gain a more powerful position in bargaining with management.

The earliest attempts by Congress to set employment standards were ruled unconstitutional on grounds that the laws infringed on an individual's right to contract. Over time, the courts began to limit employers' power in employment contracts and to recognize Congress's constitutional power to regulate employment practices under the commerce clause of Article I, Section 8, of the U.S. Constitution.

Today, unions make up less than 20 percent of the American workforce. Governmental employees, both federal and state, make up 15 percent of the workforce. Sixty-five percent of all American workers are employed at will (without a written contract covering a period of time). Regardless of the worker's contractual category, the employer must meet certain minimum standards for pay, hours, and working conditions. This chapter discusses the legislation that protects employees. Then it looks at the rights of employees to form unions and describes unions' functions.

Your online business, Artiste Login Products, Inc., employs a number of employees. Which federal and state laws apply to your business? Should you lease employees for your business or should you hire independent contractors? All businesses need to answer these questions.

Fair Labor Standards Act

The **Fair Labor Standards Act (FLSA)** of 1938 established minimum wage requirements[1] and overtime standards.[2] The act also prohibits certain types of child labor. The Department of Labor[3] (DOL) enforces the FLSA. The department has many record-keeping requirements with which businesses must comply. The DOL also determines if businesses are complying with the FLSA. Failure to file reports or maintain required government-mandated reports can result in criminal prosecution.

Who Is Covered?

The FLSA is an extensive statute based on the commerce clause of Article I of the Constitution. Commerce is the production, sale, and purchase of goods of any type. The commerce clause gives Congress the power to regulate interstate and foreign commerce.

The FLSA affects more than 70 million full-time and part-time workers. The fundamental standards set forth in the act apply to workers employed in government, unions, and private industry. For the FLSA to apply to employees in private industry, the employee must be (1) engaged in commerce, (2) engaged in production of goods to be placed in commerce, or (3) employed in an enterprise engaged in commerce.

The first two categories involve the "employee test," which considers the nature of the employee's work, not the nature of the business. In the third category, the controlling factor is the nature of the business. If the enterprise is covered, all the employees are covered, regardless of the relationship between their duties and commerce.

The FLSA explains that certain employer actions constitute a punishable violation of the statute and the rules promulgated under it. Understanding the meaning of "employer" for purposes of the act is key to determining the actions that violate the statute.

The FLSA's definition of the term *employer* is extremely broad. An employer "includes any person acting directly or indirectly in the interest of an employer in relation to an employee." An individual, such as a corporate officer who actively participates in the running of a business including the employment practices of the business, is an employer within the meaning of the statute. Such an individual will be liable personally, along with the corporation, for any violations of the act and, therefore, will be liable for the payment of any fines under the act.

An employer who violates the FLSA is liable in a civil action to the employee, who may recover from the employer unpaid wages, overtime compensation, liquidated damages, and reasonable attorneys' fees. Courts are authorized by the statute to issue injunctions restraining further violations. The employer may be prosecuted criminally by the federal government. If found guilty, the employer may be punished by a fine of up to $10,000 for the first offense and by a fine of up to $10,000, plus imprisonment for up to six months, for subsequent violations.

Exempt Employees

Congress allows exemptions to the act; otherwise, businesses could not function. The statute narrowly defines each exemption.

The employer must meet each element of the statutory exemption. Some of the industries exempted from the FLSA include agriculture, commercial fishing, some retail service businesses, and domestic services. In addition, many white-collar positions are not covered by the act because these individuals are believed to be capable of protecting themselves from the employer abuses that the FLSA prohibits.

Wage and Hour Requirements

Both state and federal statutes govern workers' minimum wage and maximum hour requirements. For the most part, state laws are consistent with the FLSA. Most businesses are subject to the federal act; thus, the FLSA is the most important guarantee of proper treatment for employees.

---

[1] For the history of the minimum wage, go to the following Department of Labor web site: <http://www.dol.gov/dol/esa/public/minwage/main.htm>.

[2] For information on minimum wage and overtime standards, go to <http://www.dol.gov/dol/asp/public/programs/handbook/flsa.htm>.

[3] The Department of Labor's home page is <http://www.dol.gov/>.

Wages. The minimum wage was initially $0.25 an hour in 1938. Periodically, Congress has increased this amount. In 1997, the minimum wage was raised to $5.15 an hour. The increases in the minimum wage over the years are shown in Exhibit 22–1.

The FLSA provides for an exception to the minimum wage in the case of tipped employees, defined as those who customarily and regularly receive more than $20 a month in tips. In such cases, the employer may consider the tips as part of the wages, but the wage credit (tips) must not exceed 50 percent of the minimum wage.

The federal government has not preempted this area. A state or local government can set a higher minimum wage than the current federal minimum wage. The state or local law applies only within that government's jurisdiction. No conflict with federal law exists since the FLSA only sets a minimum wage.

Hours. An employer must pay employees for all hours worked in a week. The definition of working time, however, is not completely clear. Generally, the hours worked—those for which an individual must be paid at least the minimum wage and must be included when computing total hours worked to determine overtime hours—encompass all the time that an employee is actually at work or is required to be on duty and that the employee is not free to use for her own purposes.

For example, police officers are regularly required to be at work twenty minutes ahead of the hour, at 7:40 A.M., to change into their uniforms and be in formation by 8 A.M. The officers must be paid for those twenty minutes in addition to their eight-hour shifts.

The calculation and payment of overtime wages can be confusing and is usually the source of many employer–employee misunderstandings. Violations of FLSA's requirement for overtime wages can occur easily because the formulas for determining overtime pay are complex and appear at times to be unfair and illogical.

The FLSA stipulates that when an employee has worked in excess of forty hours for one work week, that employee must be paid no less than one and one-half times his regular hourly rate for any hours worked in excess of forty. Overtime is not one and one-half times minimum wage, but one and one-half times the employee's regular wages.

Exhibit 22–1 Federal Minimum Wage Chart

Year	Minimum Wage
1938	$0.25
1945	$0.45
1950	$0.75
1960	$1.15
1965	$1.25
1970	$1.60
1975	$2.10
1980	$3.10
1981	$3.35
1990	$3.30
1991	$4.25 ($3.61 was a training wage that could be paid for a maximum of 180 days)
1996	$4.75
1997	$5.15 ($4.25 is a training wage paid to those under twenty years of age during the first 90 days on the job)

Investigation and Enforcement Procedures. The Wage and Hour Division (WHD)[4] of the Department of Labor has the primary responsibility for enforcing and administering the FLSA. The WHD has officers throughout the United States who conduct investigations and gather data on wages, hours, and other employment conditions.

The FLSA provides several methods for recovering unpaid wages. Methods include supervision by the WHD of the employer's payment of back wages, court action by the secretary of labor to collect unpaid wages, a lawsuit by the employee for unpaid wages and attorneys' fees, and an injunction obtained by the secretary of labor to restrain employers from further FLSA violations.

[4] For information on the Wage and Hour Division of the Department of Labor, see <http://www.dol.gov/dol/esa/public/aboutesa/whdabot.htm>.

Exemptions and Requirements under the Minimum Wage and Overtime Laws

Certain employees are exempt from both the minimum wage and overtime provisions of the FLSA. Some of the exempt employees include:

1. Executive, administrative, and professional employees, including teachers in elementary or secondary schools
2. Employees of certain enterprises, if the annual gross income of the business is under $500,000
3. Employees of seasonal amusement or recreational businesses
4. Employees of small newspapers that have a circulation of less than 4,000
5. Switchboard operators of small telephone companies with less than 750 stations
6. Sailors employed on foreign vessels
7. Employees engaged in fishing operations
8. Certain farm workers
9. Casual babysitters and people employed as companions to the elderly or infirm.

Employers are required to keep records on their nonexempt workers. The following items must be kept on file for the employees who are subject to minimum wage and overtime provisions:

1. Personal information, including name, home address, occupation, gender, and birth date
2. Hour and day when the workweek begins
3. Total hours worked each workweek and workday
4. Total daily or weekly straight-time earnings
5. Regular hourly pay rate for any week when overtime is worked
6. Total overtime pay for the workweek
7. Deductions from or additions to wages
8. Total wages paid each pay period
9. Date of payment and pay period covered.

Child Labor Laws

The FLSA provisions that govern child labor[5] are straightforward and the penalties for violating these standards are severe. The child labor laws are part of public policy. They ensure that each minor has the opportunity to attend school. They also prohibit the employment of children in hazardous jobs or under working conditions that endanger their health or well-being.

An individual who is over seventeen years old falls outside of the statute's child labor provisions. Minors between the ages of sixteen and seventeen can be employed with restrictions. Certain industries are considered to be dangerous and, therefore, off limits to sixteen- and seventeen-year-olds. In addition, children between fourteen and fifteen years old may be employed only in specially approved jobs, including at retail stores, restaurants, and service stations.

Children under the age of fourteen can only work in certain occupations, such as agricultural employment, and are subject to FLSA regulations requiring school obligations. Young actors, actresses, and performers also are exempt, when certain conditions from the FLSA prohibitions against child labor are met.

[5] Information on child labor in the United States is located at <http://www.dol.gov/dol/asp/public/programs/handbook/childlbr.htm>. For an international perspective, see the web site of the International Labour Organization for facts about international child labor at <http://www.ilo.org/> but you must type in child. Additional information is located in the statement by Mr. Michel Hansenne, director-general, International Labour Office, to the Conference on Child Labour, "Combating the Most Intolerable Forms of Child Labour: A Global Challenge" (Olso, October 29, 1997), <http://www.ilo.org/public/english/235press/speeches/ams97feb.htm>.

Retirement and Income Security

Federal and state governments have established programs and laws to cover the financial impact on employees of retirement, disability, death, hospitalization, and unemployment. The Social Security Administration[6] administers many of the laws in this area.

Social Security

The key federal law in this area is the **Social Security Act**[7] of 1935. Social Security is more formally known as **Old Age, Survivors, and Disability Insurance (OASDI)**. Both employers and employees must contribute in equal amounts under the **Federal Insurance Contributions Act (FICA)** to help fund Social Security. The contribution amount is a percentage of the employee's annual wage base. (The annual wage base is the maximum amount of an employee's wages that are subject to the tax.)

Social Security pays a monthly benefit to employees when they retire, if they have contributed to FICA. If a worker takes early retirement between ages sixty-two and sixty-four, Social Security will pay a reduced amount. The percentage increases the longer a worker waits to collect. If a retiree waits until age sixty-five, she is eligible for the full monthly benefit. The age for full retirement is increased gradually. See Exhibit 22–2 for details.

Social Security disability benefits are available to workers at any age who become disabled prior to retirement age. If a worker reaches age sixty-five, disability benefits are called retirement benefits and the monthly amount remains the same. Minors with disabilities also may collect disability benefits.

For workers who die, the nonworking spouse and minor children may collect survival benefits. Minor children receive more benefits from Social Security than any other federal program. More than 1.9 million children receive survivor's benefits in any year. Out of 100 parents who die leaving minor children, 98 percent of the children qualify for these benefits.

The nation's largest health insurance program, **Medicare**,[8] covers 37 million people. It provides health coverage for people sixty-five years old and older and for those with disabilities who are under age sixty-five. The Health Care Financing Administration (HCFA)[9] administers Medicare.

Medicare has two parts. One pertains to hospital costs and the other to nonhospital medical costs, such as doctors' office visits. People who have Medicare hospital insurance can obtain additional medical insurance for small monthly premiums that increase as medical care costs increase.

For decades, full-retirement age was sixty-five. Beginning with people born in 1938 or later, however, the full-retirement age increases gradually until it reaches sixty-seven for people born after 1959. The following chart shows the steps in which the age will increase.

Exhibit 22–2 **Full-Retirement Age Chart**

Year of Birth	Full Retirement Age
1937 or earlier	65
1938	65 and 2 months
1939	65 and 4 months
1940	65 and 6 months
1941	65 and 8 months
1942	65 and 10 months
1943–1954	66
1955	66 and 2 months
1956	66 and 4 months
1957	66 and 6 months
1958	66 and 8 months
1959	66 and 10 months
1960 and later	67

---

[6] The Social Security Administration's web site is <http://www.ssa.gov/>.

[7] For information about Social Security, go to <http://www.ssa.gov/about.htm>. For a history of the Social Security Act, see <http://www.ssa.gov/history/law.html>.

[8] For information about Medicare, see these web sites: <http://www.ssa.gov/ mediinfo.htm> and <http://www.hcfa.gov/medicare/medicare.htm>.

[9] HCFA has a web page at <http://www.hcfa.gov/>.

LEGAL HIGHLIGHT

Social Security and You

Before the government pays you any Social Security benefits, you must have earned credit for a certain amount of work, measured in "quarters of coverage." You earn a maximum of four quarters a year (three months is a quarter). If the Social Security Act covers your job, you have an individual lifetime earnings record established at the Social Security Administration (SSA) headquarters in Baltimore, Maryland. Your earnings are reported under your name and Social Security number. You should check on your Social Security statement every three years to ensure that your record is properly credited.

Use one of these methods to obtain your Personal Earnings and Benefit Estimate Statement (PEBE). First, call the SSA at 1-800-SSA-1213 (1-800-772-1213) and request your PEBE. Second, visit your local SSA office, fill out the "Request for Statement of Earnings," and send it in. Third, you can download the forms used to request your PEBE at the Social Security Administration web site: <http://www.ssa.gov/>. You then fill out the form and mail it in. Fourth, if you have security software on your computer, you can check your PEBE online. Additionally, the SSA automatically sends a PEBE to people approaching retirement age.

The PEBE provides a summary of your account, listing the last three years individually. You can correct a mistake immediately (yes, by sending in another form along with your W-2 forms). If a mistake appears in your record at retirement, your Social Security check will be reduced because your account inaccurately reflects the amount of money you have actually paid into Social Security.

The following chart indicates the distribution of each dollar that you pay into Social Security.

Distribution of a Dollar Paid into Social Security

Dollar	Distributed
70 cents	Paid into a trust fund that pays monthly benefits to retirees and their families and to surviving spouses and children of workers who have died.
19 cents	Paid into a trust fund that pays for the health care of all Medicare beneficiaries.
11 cents	Paid into a trust fund that pays benefits to people with disabilities and their families.
less than 1 cent	Administrative costs paid from the trust funds.

The Social Security trust fund invests the money not used to pay benefits and administrative expenses in U.S. government bonds, generally considered the safest of all investments. Congress has borrowed from the Social Security trust funds to pay for other services and projects provided to citizens.

Will Social Security be available when you need it? The Social Security's Board of Trustees prepares an annual report on the financial soundness of the Social Security program. As currently structured, Social Security can pay benefits for the next three decades. To correct the long-term funding problem, Congress needs to act.

The media often state that Social Security will be broke in the future. If Congress does nothing, the trust fund will be able to pay benefits for many decades at a reduced rate. To see if Congress has the time needed to make changes to protect Social Security, visit the SSA web site where you can read the SSA trustees' studies on this topic.

Private Retirement Plans

Employers may offer retirement plans to their employees. These plans supplement Social Security benefits. The **Employee Retirement Income Security Act** **(ERISA)**[10] of 1974 governs the financing, vesting, and administration of private pension plans for workers. The

[10] Information on ERISA can be found at <http://www.dol.gov/dol/asp/public/programs/handbook/erisa.htm>.

Department of Labor (through the Pension Benefit Guaranty Corporation and the Labor Management Services Administration) and the Treasury Department enforce ERISA's provisions.

Unemployment Compensation

The **Federal Unemployment Tax Act (FUTA)** of 1954 established a federal–state partnership to cover unemployed workers. FUTA operates through the state system to provide unemployment compensation to eligible individuals—those who worked a certain minimum number of weeks, earned wages in a certain amount, and are currently involuntarily out of work.

Unemployment insurance is funded by employers who pay into the fund. The proceeds are paid to qualified unemployed workers.

The cost of administering the unemployment insurance program is paid by the federal government out of the tax collected. This program is not a welfare program in that the unemployed person does not have to show a need to receive benefits. The decision to grant or deny benefits is based on whether the individual is willing and able to work and was involuntarily terminated. The following case concerns whether the employer was entitled to reimbursement on Social Security and FUTA taxes paid.

Case 22.1

Cleveland Indians Baseball Company v. United States

United States Court of Appeals, Sixth Circuit, 2000
215 F.3d 1325

BACKGROUND AND FACTS Major League Baseball Clubs (Clubs) and the Major League Baseball Players Association (MLBPA) were involved in three separate grievances in 1990. The MLBPA claimed that the Clubs breached the collective bargaining agreement (CBA) with respect to free agency rights of the baseball players in 1986, 1987, and 1988. After an arbitration panel issued a series of rulings adverse to the Clubs, the Clubs and the MLBPA settled their grievances on December 21, 1990. The settlement required the Clubs to contribute $280 million to a custodial account for distribution to affected players according to the MLBPA framework approved by the arbitration panel.

The Cleveland Indians Baseball Company's (Cleveland) share of the settlement fund was $610,000 for the 1986 season and $1,457,848 for the 1987 season. Cleveland received the funds in 1994 and distributed those funds to the following affected players: eight players employed in 1986 and fifteen players employed in 1987. Unsure as to the tax treatment of these distributions, Cleveland paid FICA and FUTA taxes on the total funds as if the payments were wages for services rendered in 1994. Cleveland paid these tax obligations in April 1994 and January 1995. None of the affected players, however, performed services for Cleveland in 1994 or 1995. Cleveland filed this action seeking reimbursement of the FICA and FUTA taxes paid to the United States.

Cleveland sought a refund of FICA and FUTA taxes claiming that (1) a portion of the funds paid to Cleveland and disbursed to its former players constituted nontaxable interest; and (2) the noninterest portion was not taxable because the funds were damages for the wrongful breach of the CBA and not wages for services rendered. Finally, even if the payments constituted wages for services rendered rather than interest and damages, Cleveland argued that it should have paid taxes at the 1986 and 1987 tax rates applicable when the services were rendered. Because the 1986 and 1987 FICA and FUTA taxes of each of the affected players had been paid up to the maximum required amount from another source, Cleveland asserted that it was entitled to a full refund if the payments were determined to be wages for services rendered in 1986 and 1987.

The government initially disputed Cleveland's claims. Both parties eventually agreed, however, that $629,000 of the payments from the settlement fund to affected players constituted interest and were not subject to FICA and FUTA taxes. Cleveland was entitled to a refund for taxes paid on the interest portion of the settlement. The parties also agreed that the remaining portion of the payments, approximately $2 million, constituted back-wage payments, earnings that would have been paid in 1986 and 1987 but for the Clubs' breach of the CBA. The court needed to determine the appropriate tax year for the back-wage payments made in 1994 for services rendered in the 1986 and 1987 baseball seasons.

PER CURIAM

. . . .

In the district court, the government and [Cleveland] agreed that our decision in *Bowman v. United States* directly addressed this precise issue. The *Bowman* court held that "a settlement for back wages should not be allocated to the period when the employer finally pays but 'should be allocated to the periods when the regular wages were not paid as usual.'" Following *Bowman*, the district court entered judgment in favor of [Cleveland] and ordered the United States to refund the FICA and FUTA taxes paid on the settlement disbursements designated as back wages, including interest from the dates on which the payments were made.
. . . .

Here, our precedent clearly indicates that the statutory provision in question requires settlements for back wages to be allocated to the period in which they were earned or should have been paid, and not to the period in which the back wages were actually disbursed. The government contends that *Bowman* was wrongly decided, arguing that the plain language, legislative history and applicable FICA and FUTA Treasury Regulations demonstrate that back wages are subject to tax in the year in which payment is made and not in which the services were rendered. In addition, the government cites cases from our sister circuits that are at odds with our *Bowman* holding. Despite these arguments, the government "agrees with taxpayer that the issue presented in this case was decided in *Bowman*."

Even if we were persuaded by the government's argument, we are bound by the *Bowman* decision.
. . . .

DECISION AND REMEDY The decision of the trial court was upheld. The baseball club was able to recover all sums it had paid for both Social Security and unemployment taxes for the players.

CRITICAL THINKING: POLITICAL CONSIDERATION In the normal course of events, if the baseball club paid the wages to the players in 1986 and 1987, it would have also paid both the Social Security and unemployment taxes. An arbitration panel found that the baseball club violated its own collective bargaining agreement with the players. The result in this case, however, was that this baseball club and other clubs did not have to pay these taxes because these taxes had been paid from another source. Is this a just result?

Other Statutes for Employee Protection

Over the years, a variety of state and federal statutes have provided protection to employees. Workers' compensation laws protect employees and their families financially from the risk of accidental injury, death, or disease resulting from their employment. Employers are required by federal laws to provide their employees with health and safety protection on the job. Employees must be informed by their employers when a plant will permanently close. Workers are entitled to leave when they or their family members are ill. Finally, workers are entitled to some privacy in the workplace. The following sections discuss these statutes.

State Workers' Compensation Acts

Workers' compensation laws provide economic protection for workers who are injured on the job. These laws provide for payment of hospital and medical costs incurred by an injured person. The worker also receives disability pay until he can return to the job. In most cases, this income is much less than the worker's regular pay. If a worker is killed on the job, his family receives death benefits. A state agency with administrative quasi-judicial powers administers workers' compensation laws. All rulings of these agencies are subject to review by the courts.

The right to recover under workers' compensation laws is provided to the injured employee without regard to the negligence or fault of the employer. The right to recover is predicated on the employment relationship and the fact that the injury arose out of the employment. Basically, employers are under a system of strict liability, which was discussed in Chapters 8 and 11. Few, if any, defenses exist for employers in workers' compensation cases.

The simple, two-pronged test for determining employee eligibility for workers' compensation consists of the following questions:

1. Was the injury accidental?
2. Did the injury arise out of and in the course of employment?

Intentionally inflicted self-injuries are not considered accidental and are not covered. In the past, heart attacks or other medical problems arising from preexisting disease or physical conditions were not covered. Recently, however, the courts have started to treat these medical problems as covered under the act. Some states have limited by legislation the recovery possible when an employee suffers a heart attack.

In most cases, an employee cannot bring legal action against an employer while receiving workers' compensation benefits, but can bring action against third persons who may have caused the injuries. The following case discusses the question of whether an employee's injuries were caused by the intentional or reckless conduct of the employer and, if so, whether the employee can obtain damages in addition to workers' compensation.

Case 22.2

Myrick v. Luhrs Corporation

District Court of Appeal of Florida, Fifth District, 1997
689 So. 2d 416

BACKGROUND AND FACTS Myrick, the plaintiff, amputated several of his fingers while operating a cut-off saw for his employer, Luhrs Corporation, the defendant. When Luhrs acquired the saw, it was equipped with various safety devices including (1) a work-presence sensor, which was designed so that the saw could function only if materials intended to be cut were on the saw's cutting table; (2) a double palm button safety interlock, which allowed the saw's activation only if both of the operator's hands were on the palm buttons, which were situated far enough from the cutting mechanism to preclude contact between the operator's hands and the cutting mechanism; (3) numerous safety warnings, prominently displayed on various surfaces of the saw, advising any operator of those aspects of operation most likely to result in serious injury or death; (4) a safety panel enclosing the saw's inner workings to prevent unintended operation of the saw; and (5) a free-swinging saw mechanism, allowing the quick removal of any object contacting with the saw blade.

Over a period of time, Luhrs removed all of these safety devices. As a result, Myrick injured himself and suffered from physical pain and suffering, mental anguish, loss of the capacity for the enjoyment of life, loss of future earning capacity, and medical expenses.

Myrick appealed a trial court's order that ruled that Myrick was limited to his remedies under the Florida Workers' Compensation Act. Myrick claimed that Luhrs had committed an intentional act.

Judge W. SHARP

The courts have long concluded that intentional acts or torts are not included in the scope of the workers' compensation statute. A potential basis for liability survives the workers' compensation exclusivity provisions, if an employer has engaged in intentional acts designed to result in, or that are substantially certain to result in the injury or death of an employee. The injury suffered must be a virtual certainty, not just a strong probability stemming from the employer's actions.

This is a close case. Myrick has alleged that his employer's removal of the various safety devices from the chop saw created a virtual certainty of injury or death to the operator.

. . . .

Reading Myrick's complaint most strongly in his favor as we must do, he alleged his employer deliberately removed or disabled five essential safety devices designed to allow an operator to run the saw without exposing himself to certain danger. Myrick also alleged that he had no knowledge or warning he was being exposed to danger by merely operating the saw. From these allegations, one can infer some cover-up on the part of the employer. Whether Myrick can sustain these allegations with sufficient proofs at a summary judgment or trial, is a different question, not ripe for our consideration.

DECISION AND REMEDY The court allowed Myrick to proceed in the trial court on his intentional tort claim unrestricted by the workers' compensation act.

CRITICAL THINKING: LEGAL ISSUE If employees can sue an employer for an intentional tort, should employees be able to sue when they are injured as a result of the employer's negligent conduct?

Health and Safety Protection

The **Occupational Safety and Health Act**[11] of 1970 was passed to ensure safe and healthful working conditions for practically every employee in the country. The act created the **Occupational Safety and Health Administration (OSHA)**,[12] the Occupational Safety and Health Review Commission, and the National Institute for Occupational Safety and Health. OSHA promulgates and enforces workers' safety and health standards. It also conducts inspections and investigations, requires employers to keep detailed records of worker injuries and illnesses, and conducts research.

OSHA's enforcement policy is twofold. First, it deals with egregious situations on a case-by-case basis,

using violation-by-violation citations. Second, it enforces settlements at the corporate, rather than at the plant, level. Both policies allow OSHA to seek large penalties. In addition to assessing civil penalties, OSHA has the power to close a plant.

OSHA first employed the egregious citation strategy against Union Carbide in 1986 after finding flagrant disregard for record-keeping requirements. Violation-by-violation citations and the corresponding penalties were issued for each of the hundreds of instances of the alleged record-keeping infractions. OSHA also sought penalties for alleged violations ranging from $4 million from John Morrell Corporation for health violations in its meat-packing plants to $7 million from USX Corporation steel plants for safety violations.

Despite OSHA's efforts, every year more than 6,000 Americans die from workplace injuries, an estimated 50,000 people die from illnesses caused by workplace chemical exposures, and 6 million people suffer nonfatal workplace injuries. Injuries alone cost

---

[11] OSHA has posted a searchable version of the Occupational Safety and Health Act at <http://www.osha-slc.gov/OshAct_toc/OshAct_toc_by_sect.html>.

[12] The home page for the Occupational Safety and Health Administration is <http://www.osha.gov/>.

the economy more than $110 billion a year. Many of these workplace injuries and illnesses are predictable and preventable.

To increase worker health and safety and to decrease paperwork, OSHA is changing its focus. To spur the spread of health and safety programs, employers will be offered a clear choice: partnership or traditional enforcement.

OSHA will work with firms that create and implement strong and effective health and safety programs as a partner. For firms with a history of endangering their employees and that indicate an unwillingness to change, OSHA will rigorously enforce the law without compromise to assure serious consequences for violators.

Most OSHA inspections are initiated as the result of an employee's written complaint. OSHA protects the identity of the complaining employee. As an added protection, the act prohibits the discharge of, or any discrimination against, an employee who, by submitting a formal complaint against an employer, exercises her rights under the statute. An employee, who believes that she has been discriminated against for bringing possible violations to OSHA's attention, may file a complaint. An investigation will be conducted and, if appropriate, a lawsuit may be filed on behalf of the employee in federal court.

In the following case, the question arose as to whether the business had actual or constructive notice of an OSHA regulation. Actual notice occurs when the person has the information or is aware that he possesses the information. Constructive notice is based on a rule of law and not on the facts of a particular situation. The law deems that a person has constructive notice if he should have known about the information.

Case 22.3

Corbesco Inc. v. Dole

United States Court of Appeals, Fifth Circuit, 1991
926 F.2d 422

BACKGROUND AND FACTS　Corbesco, Inc., is an industrial roofing and siding installation company that was hired to install flat metal roofs and siding over the skeletal structure of five aircraft hangars at the Chennault Air Base in Lake Charles, Louisiana.

Before the ironworkers could lay the aluminum sheet metal roofing, they had to install insulation. To accomplish this, they would shake the insulation rolls out onto the exposed grid of rafters, just as one might shake out a bedspread over a bed.

The ironworkers had to stand or kneel on the edge of the roof. Because the workers had to maintain their balance while leaning over the edge, high winds were very dangerous. Corbesco regularly sought wind and weather forecasts from the National Weather Service.

On April 2, 1987, Roger Mathew was on his knees shaking out insulation when a gust of wind caught the sheet of insulation that he held and pulled him forward. He lost his balance and fell sixty feet through the open structure of steel to the concrete below. Mathew was killed by the fall. The record did not reveal whether Corbesco had telephoned the National Weather Service that day.

The Occupational Safety and Health Administration regulation required safety nets "when workplaces are more than 25 feet above ground or water surface, or other surfaces where the use of ladders, scaffolds, catch platforms, temporary floors, safety lines, or safety belts is impractical."

The OSHA compliance officer inspected the hangar where Mathew had fallen. The OSHA officer cited Corbesco and assessed a $1,000 penalty for failing to install a safety net under the roof. Both the OSHA compliance officer and Corbesco agreed that only safety nets were practical. After being cited, Corbesco installed a safety net in the unfinished hangar. Corbesco filed a notice of contest with the Department of Labor to dispute the OSHA citation and penalty.

An administrative law judge (ALJ) held a hearing. Corbesco proved that the custom of the industry was that ironworkers did not use safety nets while working on flat roofs.

OSHA inspectors had made several inspections of the hangar construction project while roofing work was in progress. None had instructed Corbesco to use safety nets.

Corbesco argued that it had no knowledge of the regulation and had no way of knowing that it was in violation. Corbesco had a good safety program. The ALJ reduced the penalty to $50. Corbesco petitioned the appellate court to review the ALJ's decision.

Although the case fails to clarify the point, Corbesco may have appealed the $50 penalty for any number of reasons including higher insurance rates as a result of the OSHA citation, to have a clean record with OSHA, or to preclude liability to Mathew's estate beyond workers' compensation. The court was bound by the ALJ's finding of fact.

Circuit Judge THORNBERRY

. . . .

. . . [T]he Secretary has the burden to prove that Corbesco had actual or constructive notice [of the regulation that] required it to install a safety net. . . .

. . . .

Falling from the edge of a flat roof is not a common hazard in the roofing industry. Nevertheless, the Commission has frequently held that the regulation requires an employer to furnish either a safety net or one of the other enumerated safety devices if its employees are working near the perimeter of a flat roof more than twenty-five feet above the ground; the roof cannot serve as a temporary floor. . . . Though the wording of the regulation remains imprecise, the Commission has now elucidated its meaning. In the light of these decisions, Corbesco had a duty to at least inquire whether it had to install safety nets under the hangars. Therefore, we find that Corbesco had constructive notice of the duties imposed upon it, and its constitutional rights were not violated.

. . . .

The Secretary did not violate Corbesco's right to due process because Corbesco had constructive notice that it was required to install safety nets under its crew while they were working in the edge of a flat roof some sixty feet above a concrete floor. . . . A reasonable construction company in Corbesco's position would have known about these interpretations of this standard.

DECISION AND REMEDY The court held that because Corbesco had constructive notice of the regulation, it was required to install safety nets while the ironworkers were working on the edge of a flat roof some sixty feet above a concrete floor. Corbesco had a duty to at least inquire of OSHA as to whether it had to install a safety net.

Corbesco did not argue that it was not economically feasible to install safety nets in the aircraft hangars. If any construction company believes the cost of complying with an OSHA standard will outweigh the benefits of enhanced safety, the company can seek a variance from the standard rather than wait until it is cited. In this case, Corbesco failed to pursue this alternative.

CRITICAL THINKING: POLITICAL CONSIDERATION Why should a business be held liable for violating a regulation when the government inspectors failed to bring the regulation to its attention?

CyberLaw

Filing Complaints Online

Cyberlaw is very actively used within the employment field. Most governmental agencies have a web site for persons to research a given area of labor law. But what is recently being developed on web sites is the ability to file a complaint with the agency.

For example, a business may be operating in a dangerous condition that affects employee safety and health. An employee may anonymously report this condition to the Occupational Safety and Health Administration. They may do this over the Internet.[13] Other governmental agencies in the future will follow the example of allowing complaints to be filed online.

The problem confronting a business is how to deal with these complaints when they do not have any basis. A disgruntled employee may file a report just to get even with the boss. This report is made with the understanding that the employee's name will never be disclosed. This secrecy is not fair to the businessperson who is following the law. But a rule that allowed disclosure might discourage an employee from reporting a dangerous condition because, otherwise, he might be terminated if his identity were disclosed. Obviously, the employer would ensure that the termination is on other grounds than that of filing the report, because, the employer is liable if the termination is based solely on the filing of the report.

The employee who files the complaint, even if done from his personally owned computer at home, must be aware of a pitfall: If the employer sues the employee, the employer may request the court to seize the employee's computer in order for the employer's computer expert to examine the hard drive for any e-mails or computer files concerning the matter. Of course, the employee may raise an objection with the court and provide reasons why the court should not issue a seizure order for the computer. If the court does grant the request, however, the employer effectively has access to everything on the employee's computer.

Plant Closing Law

In 1988, Congress passed the **Worker Adjustment and Retraining Notification Act (WARN)**, more commonly called the **Plant Closing Act**, requiring businesses to notify employees sixty days in advance if a plant will close. Businesses also must give workers advance notice of a mass layoff that includes more than one-third of the company's employees. WARN applies to businesses employing more than 100 employees.

Family and Medical Leave Act

Passed in 1993, the **Family and Medical Leave Act**[14] provides that employees can take up to twelve weeks of unpaid leave for the birth or adoption of a child, for the care of an immediate family member, or for a serious health condition. The act requires that the employee must have worked for the employer for at least twelve months and must have worked 1,250 hours before being eligible for leave.

A thirty-day notice must be provided to the employer whenever possible. Accrued paid leave, such as vacation or sick time, may be used as part of the twelve weeks. The twelve weeks may be consecutive or may be taken in blocks of time or by working a reduced workweek. For the birth or adoption of a child, however, the worker must take consecutive leave unless the employer agrees to intermittent leave.

Employers with fifty employees or more are subject to the act. Thus, nearly one-half of the nation's workforce is covered. If a health plan is part of the employee's benefit package, the employer must maintain the health plan during the leave period.

Once the leave is over, the employer must reinstate the worker to the same or an equivalent job. Medical verification of the employee's or the family member's condition may be requested. Key salaried employees who are among the highest paid 10 percent in the company may be exempted by the employer, if the absence would cause the employer substantial and grievous economic harm.

The Labor Department has issued the Birth and Adoption Unemployment Compensation Rule, which

---

[13] The web address for reporting dangerous conditions is <http:www.osha.gov/as/opa/worker/complain.html>.

[14] Information on the Family and Medical Leave Act is given at the following web site: <http://www.dol.gov/dol/asp/public/programs/handbook/fmla.htm>.

provides for partial wage replacement under the unemployment compensation program. This rule is on a voluntary and experimental basis. It offers a parent unemployment compensation if leave is taken or he or she otherwise leaves employment following the birth or adoption of a child.

Medical Coverage

Two federal statutes have protected many persons from losing their medical insurance when they leave their employment. The **Consolidated Omnibus Budget Reconciliation Act (COBRA)** was passed in 1985. Prior to this act's passage, a worker's group health coverage was terminated when the worker lost her job, reduced the hours, or changed employment.

Now, when employees are terminated, change employment, or lose health coverage because of reduced work hours, they may buy group coverage for themselves and their families for a limited time period, usually no longer than eighteen months.

The act requires health plans to notify employees entitled to COBRA benefits of the right to continue benefits provided by the plan. Employees must accept coverage within sixty days or lose all rights to benefits. Once the former employee chooses COBRA coverage, he may be required to pay for the premium. The cost of the insurance is at the same rate as the former employer's contribution, plus a 2 percent surcharge.

The second statute, the **Health Insurance Portability and Accountability Act (HIPAA)**,[15] passed in 1996, protects employees when they change jobs. The word *portability* is a misnomer because the insurance plan does not move with the employee. When a person moves from one employer to another, she must be accepted and charged the same premium for the new employer's group health insurance. The second employer health care plan must cover the employee and that person's family, including any preexisting medical problems.

HIPAA prohibits insurance companies from immediately discontinuing coverage under a plan. An insurance company must follow a specific and detailed set of regulations to stop offering a health plan under COBRA.

Neither statute requires a business to offer medical coverage. If the employer stops offering a group health plan, the employee must be allowed to purchase an individual plan, regardless of his health status.

Privacy Rights of Employees

The right of privacy is not stated explicitly in the U.S. Constitution. In 1928, the United States Supreme Court established the right of privacy. Justice Louis D. Brandeis (1916–1939) wrote that it is "the right to be let alone—the most comprehensive of rights and the right most valued by civilized man." The Court based this right on the Fourth Amendment's prohibition against illegal searches and seizures by the government.

Employees use the right of privacy to oppose testing for acquired immune deficiency syndrome (AIDS) and to limit the distribution of information contained in an employee's employment record. Other areas of privacy include polygraphs, drug testing, and employee records.

Polygraphs. For many years, both the government and private businesses used polygraph tests as a condition for employment, retention, or promotion. These tests presented one major problem: They had to be subjectively interpreted by an individual, so their validity was based on the training and knowledge of the interviewer. Many innocent persons were denied employment based on inaccurate polygraph test interpretations.

To rectify this situation, Congress adopted the **Employee Polygraph Protection Act**[16] of 1988, making polygraph use unlawful except under restricted conditions. Among these exceptions are (1) national defense; (2) ongoing investigations; (3) drug security, drug theft, or drug diversion investigations; and (4) armored car and security personnel.

The major exception to the act is that of ongoing investigations. To request an employee take a polygraph test, an employer must meet three conditions. First, the test must be administered in connection with an ongoing investigation involving economic loss or injury to

[15] Also referred to informally as the Kassebaum-Kennedy Act, so named for the act's sponsors in the Senate, Senator Nancy Kassebaum, Republican, Kansas, and Senator Edward M. Kennedy, Democrat, Massachusetts. The act often is incorrectly referred to as the Kennedy-Kassebaum Act. The Republicans held the majority of the seats in the Senate when the act was passed, so the Republican name is placed before the Democrat name.

[16] Information concerning employees' rights is located at <http://www.dol.gov/dol/asp/public/programs/handbook/eppa.htm>.

the employer's business. Second, the employee must have had access to the property that is the subject of the investigation. Third, the employer must have a reasonable suspicion that the employee was involved in the incident under investigation. The polygraph questions must relate to the incident. The employee can stop the test at any time. An employee must voluntarily take the test and cannot be fired solely for refusing to take a polygraph, without additional supporting evidence establishing that the employee was involved in a theft, embezzlement, or other unlawful activity against the employer.

Drug Testing. Approximately 70 to 75 percent of substance abusers—nearly 10 million people—are employed. One of every twelve full-time employees admits to current use of illicit drugs, while one in every ten admits to abusing alcohol. Drug- and alcohol-related problems are one of the four top reasons for the rise in workplace violence. Substance abuse costs businesses $10 billion annually.

Employers face a real impact on the bottom line when employees abuse substances. Some employers try to screen out a potential problem by testing applicants for drugs prior to hiring. Drug testing prior to hiring is legal.

Employers should have a workplace substance abuse program. An employer can test an employee if the employer believes the employee to be under the influence of alcohol or drugs while at work. Employees who hold sensitive jobs, such as national security employees, are tested randomly. Persons involved with aviation, railroads, trucking, or other jobs involved with public safety also are subject to random drug testing.

The real problem with random drug testing lies in testing people who work in nonsensitive jobs. The states are split on this issue, and Congress has not set a public policy. Some courts have found that random testing violates an individual's reasonable and legitimate expectation of privacy because of the personal information obtainable from a person's body fluids.

Employee Records. Two legal theories apply to the use and distribution of information contained in an employee's personnel file: defamation and invasion of the right to privacy. A defamation case is founded on an employer's communicating harmful information about a current or former employee. Courts grant most of these communications a limited privilege. As long as an em-

ployer is communicating with a prospective new employer, no legal issue arises unless the employee proves the first employer's comments to have been made maliciously. To limit a claim that an employer released the information with the intent of harming a former employee, an employer should disclose only the basic employment history. This information would be limited to job title, dates of employment, and ending salary.

If, in contrast, an employer communicates to current employees that a terminated employee was fired on the basis of ethical or other reasons, this communication can give rise to legal problems. These statements exceed the limited privilege that the law grants. Further, this communication can be considered an invasion of the right to privacy, even if the disclosure were true.

Labor Laws

Labor relations concern the relationship between management and labor over employment conditions. A union is an organization of employees who join together to secure more favorable working conditions, pay, and benefits for the employees. Unions represent employees[17] and often are referred to as organized labor.

Employees vote for a union to represent them during collective bargaining. Collective bargaining is a process of negotiating an agreement between an employer and the authorized representative, the union, concerning working conditions, including wages, hours, safety, and other employment working conditions.

The history of labor relations stretches back to the early 1800s. Workers joined together to request from management working conditions that were better than those where criminals labored. Workers gradually formed labor unions that advocated better working conditions. Employers discouraged union activity, sometimes forcibly, by employing strike breakers who would physically assault or even kill striking employees. Employers fired union organizers and union members and replaced them with immigrants who worked for cheaper wages.

Early legislation and agencies protecting employee rights, such as the National War Labor Board, which operated during World War I, were often temporary.

[17] A history of labor activities worldwide is located at <http://www.iisg.nl/~ialhi/>.

Genetic Testing

Medical biotechnology now can determine genetic information from minute bits of blood and tissue samples. Genetic information can point out certain characteristics in an individual that may lead to a disease process, such as colon cancer, or an inherited disease, such as Huntington's chorea. Carrying a genetic characteristic is not a disability until it develops into a physical disease.

Cases exist in which individuals have been discriminated against on the basis of results of genetic testing. As testing becomes more widely available and less expensive, more problems will arise in the employment field. For a small business, the cost of insurance becomes a financial problem.

Regardless of the size of a business, the employer must be concerned with the employee's privacy. Because federal law prohibits discrimination against people, the employer must take steps to prevent harassment and discrimination within the workplace against a person who has a disease characteristic or an inherited disease.

Employers, employees, and the government are working together to reach a resolution regarding testing employees when genetic information may be found. A recent government study showed that genetic information cannot really be separated from the rest of the employee's medical information. The report recommended that the employee's entire medical file be protected.

Congress also restricted early legislation to a particular industry, such as the railroad industry. Congress passed the Railway Labor Act of 1926, which required railroads and their employees to attempt to enter into employment agreements through representatives chosen by each side.

Until the early 1930s, laws at the federal and state levels generally favored management. Beginning in 1932, however, Congress passed a number of statutes that improved the workers' rights to join unions and to engage in collective bargaining.

Today, employees in the public and private sectors have the right to organize and to bargain collectively. With the major exceptions of the military and some law enforcement employees, public employees have a statutory right to organize and bargain collectively, although generally they cannot strike.

The expanded Railway Labor Act covers rail and air carrier employees. Federal statutes fail to cover small businesses that do not affect interstate commerce. This chapter does not cover government employees, employees of small businesses, or rail and air carrier employees.

Four major statutes passed by Congress over a period of thirty years govern labor relations in the private sector. The purpose of these laws is to provide for peaceful and stable labor relations at the national level.

The four statutes are the Federal Anti-Injunction Act of 1932, the National Labor Relations Act of 1935, the Labor-Management Relations Act of 1947, and the Labor-Management Reporting and Disclosure Act of 1959. The following sections review these four statutes.

Federal Anti-Injunction Act

Congress protected peaceful strikes, picketing, and boycotts in 1932 with the passage of the **Federal Anti-Injunction Act**, more commonly known as the **Norris–LaGuardia Act**. The statute restricted the federal courts' power to issue injunctions against unions engaged in peaceful strikes. In effect, the act declared a national policy permitting employees to organize.

National Labor Relations Act

The **National Labor Relations Act (Wagner Act)** of 1935 established employees' rights to engage in collective bargaining and to strike. The Wagner Act created the **National Labor Relations Board (NLRB)**,[18] which is an independent federal agency

---

[18] The web site for the NLRB is <http://www.nlrb.gov/>. The NLRB members and general counsel can be found at <http://www.nlrb.gov/board.html>. Decisions and opinions of the NLRB can be found at <http://www.nlrb.gov/decision.html>.

that administers the act. The functions of the NLRB are discussed in more detail in a later section.

The Wagner Act defined a number of practices by employers as being unfair to labor:

1. Interference with employees' efforts to form, join, or assist labor organizations

2. An employer's domination of a labor organization or financial contribution or other types of support

3. Discrimination in the hiring of, or awarding of tenure to, employees based on union affiliation

4. Discrimination against employees for filing charges under the act or giving testimony under the act

5. Refusal to bargain collectively with the duly designated representative of the employees.

Until this act was passed, an employer could refuse to bargain with a union. Now, an employer is required to recognize the union as a bargaining power if the employees so decide by a neutral election.

The following case concerns whether the employer committed an unfair labor practice by refusing to allow the nonemployee union organizers into the employer's parking lot. Section 7 of the National Labor Relations Act guarantees employees the right of self-organization. The employer cannot place any restrictions on this right, unless it can demonstrate that a restriction is necessary to maintain production or discipline. This case questions whether Section 7 applies to nonemployee organizers.

Case 22.4

Lechmere, Inc. v. National Labor Relations Board

Supreme Court of the United States, 1992
502 U.S. 527, 112 S. Ct. 841, 117 L. Ed. 2d 79
http://caselaw.findlaw.com/scripts/getcase.pl?navby=search&linkurl=<%LINKURL%>&graphurl=<%GRAPHURL%>&court=US&case=/us/502/527.html

BACKGROUND AND FACTS Local 919 of the United Food and Commercial Workers Union, AFL-CIO, tried to organize the 200 employees at a retail store owned and operated by Lechmere, Inc. The store is located in the Lechmere Shopping Plaza in Newington, Connecticut. The strip mall includes Lechmere and thirteen smaller satellite stores not owned by Lechmere. A forty-six-foot-wide grassy strip, which is primarily public property, separates the mall property from a turnpike.

The union began its campaign to organize the store's employees, none of whom was represented by a union, in June 1987. After a full-page advertisement in a local newspaper drew little response, nonemployee union organizers entered Lechmere's parking lot, placing handbills on the windshields of cars parked in a corner of the lot used mostly by employees. Lechmere's manager immediately confronted the organizers, informed them that Lechmere prohibited solicitation or handbill distribution of any kind on its property, and asked them to leave. They did so and the handbills were removed. The scenario was repeated several times. The organizers relocated to the public grassy strip, from where they attempted to pass out handbills to automobiles entering the lot during hours (before opening and after closing) when they assumed the drivers to be primarily store employees.

For one month, the union organizers returned daily to the grassy strip and to the picket line. (A picket line is established by a union outside the employer's business where the union members often carry signs to demonstrate opposition to the employer's actions, to dissuade people from buying, to prevent strike breakers from entering, or as in this case, to organize a union.) After the first month, they picketed intermittently for another six months. They also recorded the license plate numbers of cars parked in the employee parking area. With the cooperation of the Connecticut Department of Motor Vehicles, they secured the names and addresses of some forty-one nonsupervisory employees (roughly 20 percent of the store's total). The union sent four mailings to these employees. The union made some attempts to reach employees at home or by telephone. Only one signed union authorization card was returned.

The union filed an unfair labor practice charge against Lechmere on the ground that Lechmere barred the nonemployee organizers from its property. A hearing was held. The administrative law judge (ALJ) recommended that Lechmere be ordered to cease and desist from barring the union organizers from the parking lot and to post signs in conspicuous places that Lechmere would not prohibit the union from distributing union literature.

The National Labor Relations Board (NLRB) adopted the ALJ's recommendations. Lechmere appealed. The appellate court denied Lechmere's petition for review and enforced the NLRB's order. Lechmere appealed to the United States Supreme Court.

Justice THOMAS delivered the opinion of the Court.

. . . .

. . . The ALJ below observed that "the facts herein convince me that reasonable alternative means [of communicating with Lechmere's employees] were available to the Union[.]" . . .

We cannot accept the Board's conclusion, because it "rest[s] on erroneous legal foundations." As we have explained, the exception to [the law] is a narrow one. It does not apply wherever nontrespassory access to employees may be cumbersome or less than ideally effective, but only where "the *location of a plant and the living quarters of the employees place the employees beyond the reach* of reasonable union efforts to communicate with them." Classic examples include logging camps, mining camps, and mountain resort hotels. [The] exception was crafted precisely to protect the § 7 rights of those employees who, by virtue of their employment, are isolated from the ordinary flow of information that characterizes our society. The union's burden of establishing such isolation is, as we have explained, "a heavy one," and one not satisfied by mere conjecture or the expression of doubts concerning the effectiveness of nontrespassory means of communication.

The Board's conclusion in this case that the union had no reasonable means short of trespass to make Lechmere's employees aware of its organizational efforts is based on a misunderstanding of the limited scope of this exception. Because the employees do not reside on Lechmere's property, they are presumptively not "beyond the reach" of the union's message. Although the employees live in a large metropolitan area (Greater Hartford), that fact does not in itself render them "inaccessible." . . . Their accessibility is suggested by the union's success in contacting a substantial percentage of them directly, via mailings, phone calls, and home visits. Such direct contact, of course, is not a necessary element of "reasonably effective" communication; signs or advertising also may suffice. In this case, the union tried advertising in local newspapers; the Board said that this was not reasonably effective because it was expensive and might not reach the employees. Whatever the merits of that conclusion, other alternative means of communication were readily available. Thus, signs (displayed, for example, from the public grassy strip adjoining Lechmere's parking lot) would have informed the employees about the union's organizational efforts. (Indeed, union organizers picketed the shopping center's main entrance for months as employees came and went every day.) Access to employees, not success in winning them over, is the critical issue—although success, or lack thereof, may be relevant in determining whether reasonable access exists. Because the union in this case failed to establish the existence of any "unique obstacles" that frustrated access to Lechmere's employees, the Board erred in concluding that Lechmere committed an unfair labor practice by barring the nonemployee organizers from its property.

DECISION AND REMEDY The Court decided that Section 7 of the National Labor Relations Act applies to the employer's workers who try to organize themselves and applies only derivatively to nonemployees who try to organize the employees. The exemption becomes effective when the employees are beyond the reach of reasonable union efforts to communicate with the employees, such as employees in logging camps, mining camps, and mountain resort hotels.

In this case the nonemployee organizers could communicate reasonably effectively through signs or advertising. Lechmere had not committed an unfair labor act by barring nonemployee organizers from Lechmere's parking lot.

CRITICAL THINKING: POLITICAL CONSIDERATION Why are there labor laws?

Labor-Management Relations Act

The **Labor-Management Relations Act (Taft-Hartley Act)** of 1947 amended the Wagner Act. This act contains provisions protecting employers, as well as employees. The act was opposed bitterly by organized labor groups, because it provided a detailed list of unfair labor activities. Moreover, a free speech amendment allowed employers to propagandize against unions prior to any NLRB election. The following are some unfair labor practices by unions:

1. Threatening or committing violence
2. Fining employees who cross picket lines after they have resigned from the union
3. Coercing the employer in its selection of representatives for collective bargaining
4. Discriminating against nonunion workers without legitimate union objectives being served
5. Refusing to bargain collectively with an employer.

Both the Wagner and the Taft-Hartley Acts address *closed shops* and *union shops*. A **closed shop** occurs when a business requires union membership from its workers as a condition of employment. The Taft-Hartley Act made closed shops illegal because they put the unions, rather than the employers, in charge of hiring.

A **union shop** does not require membership as an employment prerequisite but can, and usually does, require that workers join the union after a specified amount of time on the job. In an **agency shop**, union membership is not a prerequisite to hiring, and workers are not required to join the union after being hired. Workers, however, can be required to pay an amount equal to initiation fees and union dues, the theory being that these people enjoy the benefits of the union. The Taft-Hartley Act allows individual states to pass their own **right-to-work laws**. A right-to-work law makes it illegal for union membership to be required for continued employment. Thus, union shops are illegal in states with right-to-work laws.

One of the most controversial aspect of the Taft-Hartley Act was the eighty-day cooling-off period. This provision allows federal courts to issue injunctions against strikes that would create a national emergency. The president of the United States can obtain such a court injunction that will last eighty days. For example, President Dwight D. Eisenhower (1953–1961) applied the eighty-day injunction to striking steelworkers in 1959, President Richard M. Nixon (1969–1974) applied it to striking longshoremen in 1971, President Jimmy Carter (1977–1981) to striking coal miners in 1978, and President William J. Clinton (1993–2001) to striking airline employees in 1996.

Labor-Management Reporting and Disclosure Act of 1959

The **Labor-Management Reporting and Disclosure Act (Landrum-Griffin Act)** of 1959 instituted an employee bill of rights, as well as reporting requirements for union activities. This act regulates internal union business, such as union elections. Elections of officers must be regularly scheduled, using secret ballots. Ex-convicts are precluded from holding union office. Union officials are accountable for union property and for union funds. Members have the right to attend and to participate in union meetings, to nominate officers, and to vote in most union proceedings.

The National Labor Relations Board, Office of General Counsel, and Regional Offices

The National Labor Relations Board enforces all of these statutes. The NLRB handles nearly all employer

LEGAL HIGHLIGHT
Organizing Institute

Labor union membership declined sharply during the 1980s, with losses of 200,000 members annually. To stop this decline, the American Federation of Labor and Congress of Industrial Organizations (AFL-CIO) created the Organizing Institute in 1989.

The institute's mission is to promote and foster union organizing. It offers training sessions to interest people in careers as union organizers. Graduates employed with international unions affiliated with the AFL-CIO are full-time, paid union organizers. The institute offers various programs designed to assist unions in the area of external organizing.

The following unions directly participate in the training program by providing intern and apprentice campaigns and by hiring graduates: American Federation of State, County, and Municipal Employees (AFSCME), American Federation of Teachers (AFT), Communications Workers of America (CWA), Hotel

Employees and Restaurant Employees (HERE), International Brotherhood of Teamsters (IBT), International Longshoremen's and Warehousemen's Union (ILWU), Service Employees International Union (SEIU), United Auto Workers (UAW), United Brotherhood of Carpenters and Joiners (UBC), United Food and Commercial Workers (UFCW), United Mineworkers of America (UMWA), United Steelworkers of America (USWA), Laborers International Union of North America (LIUNA), Oil, Chemical, and Atomic Workers (OCAW), and Union of Needletrades, Industrial and Textile Employees (UNITE).

The institute recruits labor organizers not only from members of unions but also from college campuses. Has the Organizing Institute visited your campus? For more information, see the Organizing Institute's web page at <http://www.aflcio.org /orginst/index.htm>.

---

and employee labor issues, with the exception of airlines, railroads, agriculture, and government labor issues.

The NLRB has two principal functions: (1) to oversee union elections[19] and (2) to prevent employers or unions from engaging in unfair and illegal antiunion activities and unfair labor practices.[20] The NLRB has two major, separate components. First, the board itself consists of five members who are appointed by the president and confirmed by the Senate. The board members have staggered five-year terms and may be removed only for neglect of duty or malfeasance.

Second, the general counsel is appointed by the president and confirmed by the Senate. The general counsel is independent from the board and is responsible for the investigation and prosecution of unfair labor practice cases and for the general supervision of the NLRB field offices in the processing of cases. Of the

approximately 35,000 unfair labor charges filed each year, the general counsel finds nearly one-third to have merit. Of these meritorious cases, over 90 percent are settled.

The board has the usual administrative powers. The NLRB supervises elections with secret ballots in which the employees determine if a union will represent them in collective bargaining. The board then certifies the union selected by the majority of employees as the collective bargaining agent.

The general counsel is responsible for investigating and prosecuting unfair labor practices. All attorneys employed by the NLRB—except administrative law judges and attorneys who are members of the NLRB's staff—are supervised by the general counsel's office. The general counsel represents the NLRB in injunction proceedings in federal courts and in appeals to the circuit courts.

Regional offices of the NLRB are under the direction of a regional director and a regional attorney. The regional director reports to the NLRB on election matters and to the general counsel on unfair labor practice proceedings.

---

[19] Information on representative cases is located at <http://www .nlrb.gov/tri-rcas.html>.
[20] Information on unfair labor practices cases is located at <http://www.nlrb.gov/tri-ulp.html>.

Complaints filed by regional directors are heard initially by ALJs who have delegated authority from the NLRB. If appealed, the ALJ's decision serves as a recommendation to the board. Board decisions may be appealed to the court of appeals and, from there, to the Supreme Court of the United States.

Remedies

The NLRB has broad discretionary authority to fashion appropriate remedies. The courts have held that the board's orders will be overturned only if remedies ordered fail to fairly effectuate NLRA policies.

The board may issue cease-and-desist orders and also may require a person to take an action designed to carry out the purposes of the labor acts. For instance, the board may order reinstatement of an employee who is discharged wrongfully, along with the payment of back wages and the restoration of seniority.

When union election results are contested, the board may order new elections if unfair labor practices are deemed to have influenced the outcome. Alternatively it may, in certain instances, require an employer to bargain with the appropriate union without holding a new election.

Organizing a Collective Bargaining Unit

Section 7 of the Wagner Act guarantees that employees have the right to form, join, or assist labor organizations. The employees or a union that wants to represent the employees may start organization efforts. A collective bargaining unit is composed of the employees who have a community of interest. The union needs 30 percent of these employees to show that they want a representation election, that is, an election to determine if a union will represent the workers, and, if two or more unions seek to be elected as the workers' representative, the union that wins the election.

The most common method used by employees to show they want a representation election is through the use of authorization cards. Employees sign a card authorizing the union to act as their union. Signatures are checked against the company payroll. Once verified that 30 percent of the employees have signed, a petition for an election is sent to the NLRB. In practice, a union will usually petition for an election when it has secured authorization cards from 60 percent or more of those eligible to vote. The NLRB will set a date for the election and then will supervise the election procedure.

The employer has no duty to bargain with the union until after the union is elected and is certified by the NLRB as the employees' bargaining representative. Only one union may represent a bargaining unit of employees at one time. Although a large business may have its workforce represented by several unions, each union represents only a portion of the employees who have a community of interest. Once the union is certified, it can then begin to negotiate a collective bargaining agreement with the employer.

The Collective Bargaining Agreement

The NLRA requires both employers and the unions that represent their employees to bargain in good faith. This obligation requires the employer and union to meet at reasonable times and to confer in good faith with respect to wages, hours, and other terms and conditions of employment.

The obligation to bargain in good faith does not require the parties to come to an agreement. The purpose behind the statute is to encourage parties to negotiate enforceable contracts. Once a contract is reached it is enforceable, as the following case shows.

Case 22.5

Auciello Iron Works, Inc. v. National Labor Relations Board

Supreme Court of the United States, 1996
517 U.S. 781, 116 S. Ct. 1754, 135 L. Ed. 2d 64
http://supct.law.cornell.edu/supct/html/95-668.ZS.html

BACKGROUND AND FACTS Petitioner Auciello Iron Works had twenty-three production and maintenance employees. After a union election in 1977, the National Labor Relations Board certified as the collective bargaining representative of Auciello's employees Shopmen's Local No. 501, which was associated with the International Association of Bridge, Structural, and Ornamental Iron Workers, AFL-CIO.

During the following years, the company and the union negotiated a series of collective bargaining agreements, one of which expired on September 25, 1988. The employees went on strike. Negotiations continued, nonetheless, and, on November 17, 1988, Auciello presented the union with a complete contract proposal. On November 18, 1988, the picketing stopped, and nine days later, the union telegraphed its acceptance of the outstanding offer.

The very next day, however, Auciello told the union that it doubted that a majority of the employees supported the union and, for that reason, disavowed the collective bargaining agreement. Auciello based its doubt on the facts that nine employees had crossed the picket line, that thirteen employees had given it signed forms indicating their resignation from the union, and that sixteen had expressed dissatisfaction with the union. Auciello knew these facts nine days prior to the union's accepting the contract.

In January 1989, the NLRB's General Counsel charged Auciello with violations of the National Labor Relations Act. An administrative law judge found that a contract existed between the parties and that Auciello's withdrawal from it violated the act. The board affirmed the administrative law judge's decision.

Justice SOUTER delivered the opinion of the Court.

. . . .

The object of the National Labor Relations Act is industrial peace and stability, fostered by collective bargaining agreements providing for the orderly resolution of labor disputes between workers and employees. To such ends, the Board has adopted various presumptions about the existence of majority support for a union within a bargaining unit, the precondition for service as its exclusive representative. The first two are conclusive presumptions. A union "usually is entitled to a conclusive presumption of majority status for one year following" Board certification as such a representative. A union is likewise entitled under Board precedent to a conclusive presumption of majority status during the term of any collective bargaining agreement, up to three years. "These presumptions are based not so much on an absolute certainty that the union's majority status will not erode," as on the need to achieve "stability in collective bargaining relationships." They address our fickle nature by "enabl[ing] a union to concentrate on obtaining and fairly administering a collective bargaining agreement" without worrying about the immediate risk of decertification and by "remov[ing] any temptation on the part of the employer to avoid good faith bargaining" in an effort to undermine union support.

. . . .

We hold that the Board reasonably found an employer's precontractual, good faith doubt inadequate to support an exception to the conclusive presumption arising at the moment a collective bargaining contract offer has been accepted.

DECISION AND REMEDY The Supreme Court found that the employer committed an unfair labor practice by disavowing a collective bargaining contract to which the employer and union had agreed. Even though the employer had a good-faith belief that the union did not have the support of a majority of employees when it made the contract, the contract was still binding.

CRITICAL THINKING: LEGAL ISSUE Was it reasonable for the court to force the employer the keep the agreement that it made with a union when the union may have lost the support of the current employees?

Duty of Fair Representation

Both in negotiating and in administering a collective bargaining agreement, a union has an implied duty of fair representation for the employees it represents. A union must act fairly, impartially, and in good faith. The right to determine eligibility for its own membership remains with the union, but it is nevertheless obligated in collective bargaining to represent nonunion or minority union members without hostile discrimination, fairly, impartially, and in good faith.

The union has the power to exercise its discretion in contract negotiations with management. The union can make reasonable distinctions among types of employees in matters of pay, vacation time, and medical benefits, based on differences, such as seniority, type of work performed, competence, and skill.

Strikes

Of the several types of strikes allowed, two types are common: *economic strikes* and *unfair labor practices strikes*. **Economic strikes**, the most common type of strike, are economic in nature, that is, the employees strike for higher wages and benefits. Management may permanently replace economic strikers. The strikers, however, are entitled to priority when management rehires after the strike. Furthermore, management cannot discriminate against these strikers.

Unfair labor practices strikes occur when management violates the law. Earlier in the chapter unfair labor practices were discussed. When this type of strike ends, management must give the job back to the striking employee. Otherwise, management effectively would be rewarded for committing illegal practices prohibited by the Wagner Act.

Labor Side Agreement to NAFTA

The North American Free Trade Agreement (NAFTA) became effective in 1994, joining together the United States, Canada, and Mexico for trading purposes. Part of NAFTA is a supplemental agreement officially entitled the North American Agreement on Labor Cooperation (NAALC).[21] This part of NAFTA legislates protections for labor in the three countries. The NAALC enforces these protections through a system of cooperation, consultation, and the possibility of monetary penalties.

The NAALC established a Commission for Labor Cooperation. The commission consists of three primary parts. The first and most important is the governing council, which is composed of the labor ministers of the three member countries. The second part is the secretariat, a support organization to the council that consists of an executive director and fifteen staffers. Finally, each country has a National Administrative Office (NAO), which provides technical support within the country.

If a country fails to enforce its own labor laws to protect its workers, the council can apply greater pressure on a case-by-case basis by convening one of two committees, the Evaluation Committee of Experts (ECE) or an arbitral panel. The three-member ECE considers a country's pattern of practice in enforcing a fairly broad range of standards, including occupational

---

[21] The text of the North American Agreement on Labor Cooperation is located at <http://www.sice.oas.org/trade/nafta/Labor-C1.stm>.

safety and health labor standards. The ECE must study the particular problem at hand and issue a report with recommendations. Each party must then submit its written response to the ECE.

An arbitral panel examines alleged persistent patterns of failure by a country to enforce effectively its own labor laws and standards relating to three specific areas only: occupational safety and health, minimum wage, and child labor. The arbitral panel must make findings, determinations, and recommendations.

The panel also may establish an action plan and impose monetary penalties against a country. If a country fails to pay a monetary penalty assessed by the arbitral panel, the complaining countries may reimpose tariffs up to the penalty's limit, but for no more than the equivalent of $20 million (U.S.) for the first year, and for no more than 0.007 percent of the total trade in goods between the countries for any year thereafter. If Canada fails to pay an assessed monetary penalty, it can be forced to pay the fine through its own court system.

The ECE and arbitral panels are not authorized to examine matters relating to three important labor law principles: freedom of association (the right to organize unions), the right to bargain collectively, and the right to strike. If a country fails to enforce its laws governing these principles, no penalties can be assessed, and tariffs cannot be reimposed.

The NAOs serve as contact points through which other government agencies and NAOs may access information and assistance in NAFTA-related labor matters. The NAOs consult with one another periodically about labor laws and market conditions in the other two countries. Reviews are also conducted to determine whether the countries are enforcing their labor laws. The U.S. NAO is housed in the Department of Labor; the Canadian NAO is a division of Labor Canada; and the Mexican NAO is located within the Ministry of Labor.

The NAALC encourages each country to enforce its own labor laws. It does not require any country to pass laws that are not already on the books. Furthermore, no country has the authority to enforce labor laws in another country's territory.

International Consideration

Perspectives on Employment

Under international agreements, many industries move their production facilities from developed nations to countries that have cheap labor. Generally, workers in developing countries lack the protections and benefits that are normal for workers in developed nations. Benefits, such as health and safety protections, union contracts, Social Security, workers' compensation, and unemployment benefits, are unavailable.

Some countries even use prison labor to produce products cheaply. These products are then sent overseas to developed countries and sold at a price below domestic manufacturing costs. International agreements allow confiscation of the illegally imported items if this practice is detected.

In most of the developed world, an employee has a vested right to his job. The 1982 International Labour Organization's[22] Convention on Termination at the Initiative of the Employer recognized this practice. The United States is not a signatory to this convention, although most of the Western European countries have ratified it. The convention recognizes that an employee can be terminated only for cause.

The philosophical belief of the United States is that the employer controls all costs, including that of labor. As a result, an employer can terminate employees in cost–cutting measures aimed at maintaining competitiveness. A employee may be terminated with cause based on the employee's performance or without cause as long as the employer does not have a bad motive.

---

[22] The web site for the International Labour Organization is <http://www.ilo.org/>.

LEGALLY SPEAKING

What to Do If You Suspect That Some of Your Employees Want a Union

One of your long-term employees informs you that some of your employees are discussing unionizing. Do not panic. Just because your employees discuss union formation does not necessarily mean a union will form. Even if a union is formed, a strike or other negative actions that historically have occurred with union organization will not necessarily be taken against your firm. In fact, many companies today find that better communications with employees result from union recognition.

One major reason for which employees vote for a union is to achieve better communications between the employees and management. The business fails to keep its employees informed about problems that it confronts. These problems can involve business competition, new governmental regulations, higher taxes, or higher costs to maintain employee benefits.

When confronted with these problems, a business may forget the importance of informing its employees and involving them in making decisions. The employees feel neglected by management. The best way to stop a union's organizational effort is to open communication lines with employees and to make them feel valued. Open communications should be offered on a continual basis to foster a good relationship with employees, not only as a reaction to union-organization activity.

What actions can you take to convince your employees not to organize a union?

- ✔ Communicate with your employees. Stress the benefits they presently receive and compare them with the benefits offered by other area businesses.

- ✔ Ensure that your employees know the total cost to them for membership in the union, including initiation fees, assessments to support other unions that strike, and monthly dues.

- ✔ Outline the company's sources of funds.

- ✔ Stress that an employee strike could take months, if not years, from which to recover financially.

- ✔ Explain that employers can legally replace strikers with other workers, if the strike involves economic issues.

(continued)

✔ Send letters to your employees' residences explaining these issues. Married employees' spouses will be involved in making the union decision. Sending a personal message to your employees' residences also indicates your concern for the worker.

✔ Prohibit union organizers from distributing material in work areas if the restriction is based on safety factors.

✔ Stop nonemployees from entering your property because they can be considered trespassers.

✔ Have employees report union organizers' threats.

Organizing activities are protected by the National Labor Relations Act. The following acts are considered to be unfair labor practices:

✔ Do not question individuals about their union activities.

✔ Do not threaten to discharge an employee for union activities or threaten to close the plant if a union is elected.

✔ Do not state that benefits will decrease or that overtime will be cut if the union wins the election.

✔ Do not offer to increase benefits or income during the period of the organizing drive.

✔ Do not stop the distribution of material in work areas by your own employees during breaks and while at lunch. These periods are considered the employees' free time.

Be honest with your employees. Communicate early and often. Do not wait until the union organizers have arrived. It may be later than you think.

Chapter Summary

Federal law has a significant impact on both the relationship between employers and their employees as well as labor-management relations. The Fair Labor Standards Act (FLSA) establishes a minimum wage per hour for employees, overtime pay provisions requiring time-and-a-half of normal pay for any work over forty hours per week, certain record-keeping requirements, and child labor protection. Although some types of employees are exempt, most businesses are bound by this act. The Department of Labor enforces the FLSA.

Federal and state acts govern other labor-related issues as well. Social Security provisions include Old Age, Survivors, and Disability Insurance (OASDI) and Medicare. Unemployment compensation helps the worker financially until a new job is found. Workers' compensation laws cover employees injured or killed on the job. The Occupational Safety and Health Act (OSHA) helps to ensure safe and healthful working conditions for workers.

The Family and Medical Leave Act allows a worker to take unpaid leave to care for a family member who is ill or for a child's birth or adoption. The Consolidated Omnibus Budget Reconciliation Act (COBRA) requires that a former employee be allowed to purchase health insurance. The Health Insurance Portability and Accountability Act (HIPAA) allows a person who is covered by a group health plan to move to a second job. If the second employer also has a group health plan, the employee is covered in full, including any preexisting medical conditions. Other laws govern employees' privacy rights, including the use of polygraphs, drug testing, and employee records.

Congress passed the following four statutes that govern management-labor relations: Federal Anti-Injunction Act (Norris-LaGuardia Act), National Labor Relations Act (Wagner Act), Labor-Management Relations Act (Taft-Hartley Act), and Labor-Management Reporting and Disclosure Act (Landrum-Griffin Act). The Federal Anti-Injunction Act declared a national policy permitting workers to organize, and their right to peaceful strikes, picketing, and boycotts. The act restricted the power of federal courts to issue injunctions against striking unions.

The National Labor Relations Act established the National Labor Relations Board and defined certain acts by management as unfair labor practices. The NLRB oversees representation elections in which workers vote to determine if they want to be represented by a union. The Labor-Management Relations Act amended the Wagner Act. The act forbids closed shops, but allows union shops and agency shops. States are allowed to adopt right-to-work laws whereby only agency shops are allowed. Unfair labor practices by unions are set out in the statute. The president of the United States can determine that a strike will create a national emergency and can seek a court injunction against it.

The Labor-Management Reporting and Disclosure Act created an employee bill of rights. The act regulates internal union business, such as elections.

The NLRB enforces all four statutes. The NLRB supervises representation elections. The Office of General Counsel handles the investigations of all unfair labor practices charges brought either by management or by the union.

Both management and the union must bargain collectively in good faith. The Wagner Act allows workers to decide if they want to be represented by a union. Usually, employees fill out authorization cards, and if over 30 percent of the employees sign, a petition for an election is filed with the NLRB. Once a union has been elected and certified by the NLRB, the union represents all the employees. The union, both in negotiating and in administering a collective bargaining agreement, has an implied duty of fair representation for the employees it represents, even if an employee is not a union member.

Using the World Wide Web

Information about the government agencies and labor unions is readily available on the Internet. See the following chart for web sites for labor unions.

Finding the Law on the Web

LaborNet, Directory of Unions, Labor Organizations and Labor Resources
http://www.igc.org/igc/ln/hg/unions.html
American Federation of Labor and Congress of Industrial Organizations (AFL-CIO)
http://www.aflcio.org/
Teamsters Union
http://www.teamster.org/
Institute of Global Communications
http://www.labornet.org

Chapter Web Sites

Department of Labor, history of minimum wage
http://www.dol.gov/dol/esa/public/minwage/main.htm
Department of Labor, minimum wage and overtime standards
http://www.dol.gov/dol/asp/public/programs/handbook/flsa.htm
Department of Labor
http://www.dol.gov/
Department of Labor, Wage and Hour Division
http://www.dol.gov/dol/esa/public/aboutesa/whdabot.htm
Department of Labor, child labor in the United States
http://www.dol.gov/dol/asp/public/programs/handbook/childlbr.htm

International Labour Organization, facts about international child labor
http://www.ilo.org/; type in child
Statement by Mr. Michel Hansenne, director-general, International Labour Office, to the Conference on Child Labour, "Combating the Most Intolerable Forms of Child Labour: A Global Challenge" (Olso, October 29, 1997)
http://www.ilo.org/public/english/235press/speeches/ams97feb.htm
Social Security Administration
http://www.ssa.gov/
Social Security Administration, information about
http://www.ssa.gov/about.htm
Social Security Administration, history of the Social Security Act
http://www.ssa.gov/history/law.html
Medicare
http://www.ssa.gov/mediinfo.htm
and
http://www.hcfa.gov/medicare/medicare.htm
Health Care Financing Administration
http://www.hcfa.gov/
Employee Retirement Income Security Act (ERISA)
http://www.dol.gov/dol/asp/public/programs/handbook/erisa.htm
Occupational Safety and Health Act, searchable version
http://www.oshaslc.gov/OshAct_toc/OshAct_toc_by_sect.html
Occupational Safety and Health Administration (OSHA)
http://www.osha.gov/
Occupational Safety and Health Administration, reporting dangerous conditions
http://www.osha.gov/as/opa/worker/complain.html

Department of Labor, Family and Medical Leave Act
  http://www.dol.gov/dol/asp/public/programs
  /handbook/fmla.htm

Department of Labor, Employee Polygraph
  Protection Act
  http://www.dol.gov/dol/asp/public/programs
  /handbook/eppa.htm

History of labor activities worldwide
  http://www.iisg.nl/~ialhi/

National Labor Relations Board (NLRB)
  http://www.nlrb.gov/

National Labor Relations Board, members and
  general counsel
  http://www.nlrb.gov/board.html

National Labor Relations Board, decisions and opinions
  http://www.nlrb.gov/decision.html

Lechmere, Inc. v. National Labor Relations Board
  http://caselaw.findlaw.com/scripts/getcase.pl?navby
  =search&linkurl=<%LINKURL%>&graphurl=
  <%GRAPHURL%>&court=US&case=/us
  /502/527.html

National Labor Relations Board, representative cases
  http://www.nlrb.gov/tri-rcas.html

National Labor Relations Board, unfair labor
  practices cases
  http://www.nlrb.gov/tri-ulp.html

American Federation of Labor and Congress of
  Industrial Organizations (AFL-CIO),
  Organizing Institute
  http://www.aflcio.org/orginst/index.htm

Auciello Iron Works, Inc. v. National Labor Relations Board
  http://supct.law.cornell.edu/supct/html
  /95-668.ZS.html

North American Agreement on Labor Cooperation
  http://www.sice.oas.org/trade/nafta/Labor-C1.stm

International Labour Organization
  http://www.ilo.org/

Free Advice
  http://www.freeadvice.com

Morgan Stanley Dean Witter
  http://www.deanwitter.com

Web Activities

22–1 You are employed. Occasionally, your employer will request you work more than forty hours in a week. Your employer, however, does not want to pay you time-and-a-half for your overtime, but instead provides you compensatory time. Is this legal? Go to <http://www.freeadvice.com> and click on the title "Employment (Labor) Law"; do not click on any of the subtitles. Scroll down until you reach the question about whether your employer can insist that you, a nonexempt employee, must take paid time off rather than paying you cash for overtime. What is the answer? Near this question is a question about work-related activities after the business is closed. For example, you are required to make bank deposits and drop off the mail on the way home. Should you be paid for this extra work?

22–2 Your employer has a retirement plan. Go to <http://www.freeadvice.com> and under "Employment (Labor) Law" click on the subtitle "Pensions & Benefits." Scroll down until you reach the question "What parts of a pension plan does ERISA cover?" What parts does ERISA cover?

Key Terms

agency shop
closed shop
Consolidated
  Omnibus Budget
  Reconciliation Act
  (COBRA)
economic strike
Employee Polygraph
  Protection Act
Employee Retirement
  Income Security Act
  (ERISA)

Fair Labor Standards Act
  (FLSA)
Family and Medical
  Leave Act
Federal Anti-Injunction
  Act (Norris–
  LaGuardia Act)
Federal Insurance
  Contributions Act
  (FICA)
Federal Unemployment
  Tax Act (FUTA)

Health Insurance
  Portability and
  Accountability Act
  (HIPAA)
Labor-Management
  Relations Act
  (Taft-Hartley Act)
Labor-Management
  Reporting and
  Disclosure Act
  (Landrum-Griffin Act)
Medicare

National Labor
  Relations Act
  (Wagner Act)
National Labor
  Relations Board
  (NLRB)
Norris–LaGuardia Act
Occupational Safety and
  Health Act
Occupational Safety and
  Health Adminis-
  tration (OSHA)

Old Age, Survivors, and
   Disability Insurance
   (OASDI)
Plant Closing Act

right-to-work laws
Social Security Act
unfair labor practices
   strike

union shop
workers' compensation
   law

Worker Adjustment
   and Retraining
   Notification Act
   (WARN)

Questions and Case Problems

22–1 Workers' Compensation Workers' compensation statutes cover the injuries, disease, or death of employees while at work. Professor Able is employed by a private university in California. Prior to traveling to a professional meeting, he requests permission and travel money to attend the meeting. The university grants permission, but does not grant travel money. After the meeting, but three hours prior to his airplane trip to return home, he visits a cathedral that is noted for its beauty. When he emerges from the cathedral, he stumbles down the stairs and injures himself. An ambulance transports him to the hospital, where an emergency room physician treats and releases him in time to catch the return flight. Are his injuries covered by workers' compensation? Did the injuries occur while he was at work? Explain.

22–2 Child Labor Hamburger Joint is a nationwide fast-food outlet franchise. The management is interested in teenage unemployment; consequently, it created a program for hiring teens. The program will hire fifty people in each teenage bracket. The fourteen-year-olds will be janitors, the fifteen-year-olds will take orders at the counter, the sixteen-year-olds will cook, and the seventeen-year-olds will drive company vehicles to deliver food orders. Do you see any violations of the child labor laws in this program? Explain.

22–3 Overtime Wages Joseph owns an interstate business engaged in manufacturing and selling boats. Joseph has 500 nonunion employees. Representatives of these employees approach Joseph, seeking a four-day, ten-hours-per-day workweek. Joseph is concerned that this proposal will require him to pay his employees time-and-a-half after eight hours per day. Discuss fully which federal act concerns Joseph and whether the proposal will require Joseph to pay time-and-a-half.

22–4 Workers' Compensation Bernice Aranda was employed as a secretary and normally worked from eight to five. She was leaving her job for the evening. While she was walking to her vehicle, another automobile driven by an escaped convict and chased by the police suddenly appeared at a high speed and struck Bernice.

Because she was still on the employer's property, was she covered by workers' compensation? Explain.

22–5 Labor Organizing Yeshiva University is a private university. The faculty association, acting as a bargaining agent for the full-time faculty members, filed a petition with the National Labor Relations Board. The university opposed this action because faculty members are managerial personnel, outside the jurisdiction of the NLRB. Are the college professors managers or workers? Explain. [*NLRB v. Yeshiva University*, 444 U.S. 672, 100 S. Ct. 856, 63 L. Ed. 2d 115 (1979)]

22–6 Overtime Jiffy June Farms properly paid overtime to its employees. It entered into a collective bargaining agreement with the union that exempted Jiffy from paying time-and-a-half for overtime, but that increased basic wages considerably. The lower court found this contract to be a willful violation of the Fair Labor Standards Act. Can the workers waive their rights to overtime pay? Explain. [*Coleman v. Jiffy June Farms*, 458 F.2d 1139 (5th Cir. 1972)]

22–7 Labor Organizing The General Drivers, Warehousemen & Helpers Union attempted to organize the drivers of the Q-1 Motor Express, an interstate trucking company. Supervisors threatened drivers to stay away from the organizers. The president of Q-1, Schroering, confronted organizer Denham. Schroering told Denham that the company attorney told him that to thwart the union, he could fire all the drivers, close the company down, and then reopen seventy-two hours later with new drivers because he was not going to permit a "half-ass union [to] come in and try to tell him how to run his business." The company granted a pay increase during the height of the organizing campaign. Was the employees' right to organize violated under the labor laws? Explain. [*NLRB v. Q-1 Motor Express, Inc.*, 25 F.3d 473 (7th Cir. 1994)]

22–8 OSHA At an REA Express, Inc., shipping terminal, a conveyor belt became inoperative because of an electrical circuit short. The manager called a licensed electrical contractor. When the contractor arrived, REA's maintenance supervisor was in the circuit breaker room.

The floor was wet, and the maintenance supervisor was using sawdust to soak up the water. The licensed electrical contractor attempted to fix the short circuit while standing on the wet floor, and he was electrocuted. Simultaneously, REA's maintenance supervisor, who was standing on a wooden platform, was burned and knocked unconscious. The Occupational Safety and Health Administration wanted to fine REA Express $1,000 for failure to furnish a place of employment free from recognized hazards. What was the result? Explain. [*REA Express, Inc. v. Brennan*, 495 F.2d 822 (2d Cir.1974)]

22–9 OSHA The Occupational Safety and Health Administration issued a regulation that allowed employees to refuse to perform an assigned task if a reasonable apprehension of death or serious injury in accomplishing it existed. Whirlpool Corp. had a plant that produced appliances. Within the plant the appliances were transported by a conveyor belt that was near the ceiling. To protect employees below, Whirlpool installed a screen to stop any appliances that occasionally fell. To remove fallen parts from the screens, maintenance workers were required to climb out onto the screen. In the past, several workers had fallen through the screen to the floor below and one had been killed. Whirlpool issued an order restricting employees from walking on the screens because the old screens were being replaced by stronger screens. Several weeks after the workers had fallen through the screen, management ordered two workers onto an area that still had the old screens. When they refused the order, they were dismissed from their shift and were issued written reprimands to be placed in their employment files. They filed a complaint with OSHA. The secretary of labor filed suit and sought to have the reprimands removed and to recover the lost pay. Who prevailed in this case? Explain. [*Whirlpool Corp. v. Marshall*, 445 U.S. 1, 100 S. Ct. 883, 63 L. Ed. 2d 154 (1980)]

22–10 Internet Having enough money set aside for retirement is an issue that most people face. Some financial services have forms online to help you to determine the amount of money that you will need. For one such form, go to Morgan Stanley Dean Witter's web site at <http://www.deanwitter.com>. Fill out the form and submit the result. Find web sites that provide a similar service.

Chapter 23

Employment Law and Equal Opportunity

Outline

Laborin' men an' laborin' women
Hev one glory an' one shame;
Ev'y thin' thet's done inhuman
Injers all on 'em the same.

The Biglow Papers, Series 1, No. 1, Stanza 10,
1848
James Russell Lowell, 1819–1891
American poet, critic, essayist, editor, and
diplomat, minister to Spain, 1877–1880, and
ambassador to Great Britain, 1880–1885

Ethical Consideration

The Glass Ceiling: A Relic of the Past or a Reality of the Present?

You are Bill Nail, the general manager of Spikes Construction Company, a heavy construction firm that primarily builds freeways. You hired Sue Sure to work in the accounting department. She is a good employee and has received raises over the years. She is well liked because she has a nice disposition in spite of her outspoken position that men generally treat women poorly in the work environment.

When the director of the accounting department has a heart attack, Sure's name is proposed to take his place. Although you know that Sure is very capable, you are worried about bringing a woman into upper management, which until now has been exclusively male. You believe that your management team likes the current all-male atmosphere that allows for sexual jokes, strong language, drinks, and easy companionship—in other words, the good old boy network. The past behavior of some members of the upper management team, in terms of language and actions, may be viewed by Sure as harassing. Further, you are concerned with her ability to deal effectively with the company's suppliers and with its subcontractors on tough accounting issues, such as, denying full payment to an outraged subcontractor because it failed to fully perform its contract.

Do you promote Sure or do you conduct a search that will most likely result in the hiring of a strong male executive to fill the vacancy? Use the ethical model presented in Chapter 2 and reprinted on the inside front cover to develop your answer.

Introduction

At common law, both employment agreements between businesses and their employees and contracts between management and labor unions were considered private contractual matters. Common law provided little or no protection to employees or labor union members against arbitrary and discriminatory actions by employers or labor unions.

Not until the National Labor Relations Act (Wagner Act) of 1935 did employees gain some statutory protection. This act prohibits employers from discriminating against employees or job applicants because of their union activity. Within a decade after the Wagner Act, the U.S. Supreme Court prohibited certain forms of racial discrimination by unions. Statutes passed later broadened the regulations governing labor–management relations.

In the past, discrimination in hiring, retention, promotion, and firing was common in the workplace. Discrimination was based on many factors. Most onerous was discrimination based on race, color, religion, national origin, and gender. In 1964, Congress took legislative action to address these problems.

This chapter will examine the federal antidiscrimination laws and the agency charged with enforcing these antidiscriminatory statutes. We also will discuss affirmative action.[1]

Your online business, Artiste Login Products, Inc., has a number of employees. New businesses located on the web are not usually unionized, but this may change in the future. Even though the employees of Artiste are not unionized, as an employer, Artiste needs to be aware of the federal labor and antidiscrimination laws.

The Civil Rights Act of 1964, Title VII

The cornerstone law on antidiscrimination in the employment field is **Title VII of the Civil Rights Act of 1964**.[2] This act prohibits discrimination in all areas of employment on the basis of race; color; religion; national origin; or sex (gender), including pregnancy, childbirth, or abortion; and sexual harassment. Coverage extends to employees of private employers and to employees of local, state, and federal governments. The **Equal Employment Opportunity Commission (EEOC)** was created by the Civil Rights Act.

Title VII does not prohibit discrimination based on immigration status, physical disability, or age. Other statutes discussed in the chapter prohibit discrimination on these grounds.

Covered Employment Situations under Title VII

Title VII covers three situations: (1) employers with at least fifteen workers, (2) labor unions with at least fifteen members, and (3) employment agencies. For Title VII to apply, the activities of the employer, labor union, or employment agency must be part of, or must affect, interstate commerce, which the courts interpret very broadly.

Types of Discrimination

The EEOC uses the following two theories when determining if discrimination has occurred: **disparate treatment** (classes are treated differently by design) and **disparate impact** (a seemingly neutral requirement impacts the classes differently). Claims based on these two discrimination types can be combined in the same lawsuit when appropriate.

Disparate Treatment. The simplest form of discrimination involves disparate treatment, that is, treating members of one class differently from members of other classes. This discrimination occurs by design, because the employer intentionally discriminates. In the past, for example, newspapers carried two different help-wanted columns, one for men and one for women.

The plaintiff employee must establish a *prima facie* case of discrimination in cases involving hiring, promotion, or salary increase. A *prima facie* **case** is one in which the evidence presented by the plaintiff will prove the case until contradicted and overcome by other evidence presented by the defendant. For example, a health spa places an advertisement seeking men to work at the spa. A woman applies for the position. Her application is rejected. In a *prima facie* case, she must show that (1) she is a member of a protected class, in this case (she is a woman which is protected), (2) she applied and was qualified for the job, (3) her application was rejected, and (4) the employer continued to seek applicants for the job or that a person in an unprotected class was hired. When she shows this *prima facie* case, the defendant must respond.

The defendant may be successful in rebutting the *prima facie* case if the defendant has a valid legal reason for hiring only men. For instance, the health spa would employ only men to staff the men's locker room.

Disparate Impact. Sometimes employment practices may appear neutral on the surface, but, without any intent to do so, the practices adversely affect a protected class. This unintentional discrimination is the nature of disparate impact discrimination cases. Statistics show the adverse impact of the practice on a protected class and often provide the only way to establish a *prima facie* case.

For example, a woman applies for the position of troubleshooter with an electrical utility company. A troubleshooter determines the cause of a problem and then makes the repairs. Some repairs require digging while others require the climbing of utility poles. The job notice states a number of requirements, one of which requires the applicant to be six feet, two inches tall, and another of which requires two years of field experience. The company turns down the female applicant because she is only five feet, eight inches, although she has the work experience. She must show that (1) she is a member of a protected class, (2) she applied and was qualified for the job, (3) her application was rejected, and (4) the employer continued to seek applicants for the job or a person in an unprotected class was hired.

Once she has established the *prima facie* case, the defendant utility company has the burden of providing legitimate, nondiscriminatory reasons for the applicant's not being hired. For example, the utility company could show that it required the applicant to be six feet, two inches tall because the performance in the position requires a person to reach up to certain heights in order to make repairs without the aid of a ladder.

If the defendant can rebut the *prima facie* case, the plaintiff must prove that the reason articulated by the employer is not legitimate. The plaintiff must convince the judge or jury that the reason is a pretext (not true) to cover up a discriminatory employment practice. She can challenge the height requirement by showing that few women are six feet, two inches tall. Unless the utility company can show a legitimate reason for the height requirement, the plaintiff should prevail in this case. The requirement of a physical height of six feet, two inches appears neutral on its face, but has a disparate impact on women and some ethnic groups.

In the following case, the United States Supreme Court reviews an employment practice that appeared neutral, but in fact had a disparate impact on African-American employees. This case was the first to find a disparate impact. Prior to this case, businesses often required a high school diploma for many positions. The diploma requirement resulted in African Americans being discriminated against because in those days many lacked a high school education. In this case, the company practiced intentional discrimination against African Americans prior to the passage of the Civil Rights Act of 1964.

Case 23.1

Griggs v. Duke Power Co.

Supreme Court of the United States, 1971

401 U. S. 424 91 S. Ct. 849, 28 L. Ed. 2d 158

http://caselaw.findlaw.com /scripts/casesearch.pl? CiRestriction=401+U.S.+424 &court=US

BACKGROUND AND FACTS Thirteen African Americans brought this class action suit against their employer, Duke Power Company. Prior to July 2, 1965, the effective date of the Civil Rights Act of 1964, the company had hired African Americans in only one of its five departments, the Labor Department. The highest paying jobs in the Labor Department paid less than the lowest paying jobs in the other departments, in which only whites were employed. In 1955, the company instituted a policy of requiring a high school diploma for initial assignment to any department except labor. When the company abandoned its policy of restricting African Americans to the Labor Department in 1965, Duke Power made completion of high school a prerequisite for transfer from labor to any other department.

In 1965, in addition to the high school diploma, the company added a further requirement for new employees in all departments other than labor—satisfactory scores on two tests, one testing general intelligence and the other measuring the ability to learn to perform a particular job. Employees who lacked a high school education now could qualify for transfer to other departments by passing the two aptitude tests.

The district court found that the company had followed a policy of overt racial discrimination prior to the enactment of the Civil Rights Act of 1964, but that its discriminatory conduct had ceased. The court of appeals concluded that no discriminatory purpose in the adoption of the diploma and test requirements existed and, therefore, no violation of the Civil Rights Act occurred. The Supreme Court then reviewed the case to determine if these requirements were unlawful under Title VII if they were not shown to be job related.

Justice BURGER delivered the opinion of the Court.

The objective of Congress in the enactment of Title VII is plain from the language of the statute. It was to achieve equality of employment opportunities and to remove barriers that have operated in the past to favor an identifiable group of white employees over other employees. Under the Act, practices, procedures, or tests neutral on their face, and even neutral in terms of intent, cannot be maintained if they operate to "freeze" the status quo of prior discriminatory employment practices.

The Court of Appeals' opinion, and the pretrial dissent, agreed that, on the record in the recent case, "whites register far better on the Company's alternative requirements" than Negroes. This consequence would appear to be directly traceable to race. Basic intelligence must have the means of articulation to manifest itself fairly in a testing process. Because they are Negroes, petitioners have long received inferior education in segregated schools and this Court expressly recognized these differences in *Gaston County v. United States*. There, because of the inferior education received by Negroes in North Carolina, this Court barred the institution of a literacy test for voter registration on the ground that the test would abridge the right to vote indirectly on account of race. Congress did not intend by Title VII, however, to guarantee a job to every person regardless of qualifications. In short, the Act does not command that any person be hired simply because he was formerly the subject of discrimination, or because he is a member of a minority group. Discriminatory preference for any group, minority or majority, is precisely and only what Congress has proscribed. What is required by Congress is the removal of artificial, arbitrary, and unnecessary barriers to employment when the barriers operate invidiously to discriminate on the basis of racial or other impermissible classification.

. . . The Act proscribes not only overt discrimination but also practices that are fair in form, but discriminatory in operation. The touchstone is business necessity. If an employment practice which operates to exclude Negroes cannot be shown to be related to job performance, the practice is prohibited.

DECISION AND REMEDY The judgment of the court of appeals was reversed. The Supreme Court held that diploma and test requirements had to be job related. Duke Power had to prove that the test and degree requirements were necessary for the job.

CRITICAL THINKING: MANAGERIAL PERSPECTIVE How does a manager assure that a test is job related?

Equal Employment Opportunity Commission

The Equal Employment Opportunity Commission (EEOC)[3] is an independent administrative agency that has five members, each appointed by the president and confirmed by the Senate. No more than three members may be from the same political party. Each serves a five-year term.

The EEOC is responsible for the administration and enforcement of the Equal Pay Act of 1963, Title VII of the Civil Rights Act of 1964, the Age Discrimination in Employment Act of 1967, and the Americans with Disabilities Act of 1990.

EEOC Enforcement

The EEOC can issue interpretive guidelines and regulations, but these do not have the force of law. Rather, they provide notice of the commission's enforcement policy. The EEOC may require employers to keep statistics and records of employment and employment practices.

The EEOC, with its investigatory powers, has broad authority to require the production of documentary evidence, to hold hearings, and to subpoena and examine witnesses under oath. When a person files charges or when the commission members determine that a pattern or practice of illegal discrimination exists, a lawsuit can be filed. The EEOC has the opportunity to attempt conciliation between the parties prior to filing a suit.

EEOC Procedures

Any person claiming harm may file a charge of discrimination with the EEOC. A member of the EEOC or any person may likewise file a charge and whoever files is called the charging party.

Generally speaking, the charge must be filed within 180 days after the discriminatory action. Within 10 days of the filing of a charge with the EEOC, the agency must notify the employer. Once notified, the employer is prohibited from retaliation against the charging employee.

Once the employer has been notified, the EEOC investigates the charge. If it finds reasonable cause to believe that the federal law has been violated, it attempts to resolve the dispute by informal means. When

[3] The EEOC's web page is <http://www.eeoc.gov/>. The EEOC's National Enforcement Plan is available at <http://www.eeoc.gov/nep.html>.

informal means fail to result in a settlement, the EEOC may bring an action thirty days after the charge is filed.

Even when both the EEOC and the company are willing to accept a settlement, the charging party retains the right to sue. If, however, the EEOC does not find reasonable cause to believe a violation has occurred, it notifies the charging party and informs her of the right to pursue the matter in court. The charging party has only ninety days to file a lawsuit.

The 1991 Civil Rights Act[4] provides workers with the right to recover compensatory and punitive damages if harassment or other intentional discrimination occurred. Before the court awards money damages, the employee must demonstrate that the employer engaged in a discriminatory practice with malice or reckless indifference. The act sets limits on the combined compensatory and punitive damages based on a sliding scale: for companies with 14 to 100 employees, $50,000; 101 to 200 employees, $100,000; 201 to 500 employees, $200,000; and over 501 employees, $300,000.

The 1991 Civil Rights Act limits remedies when hiring is at issue. An applicant can obtain an injunction, attorneys' fees, and court costs. The applicant for a job cannot recover back pay.

Pattern and Practice of Discrimination

The Equal Employment Opportunity Commission will bring a lawsuit against an employer when a pattern and practice of discrimination is evident. Because the government initiates the lawsuit, it bears the burden of establishing a *prima facie* case of discrimination by proving a pattern and practice of discrimination.

The government must show that a protected class suffers from discrimination because of a company's standard operating procedure. For example, the government can make a *prima facie* case by showing large statistical disparities between the general workforce's racial composition and that of the company's employees. The government can strengthen its case by presenting evidence of specific instances of discrimination.

In 1995, the EEOC adopted the National Enforcement Plan, which identifies priority issues and creates a plan for administrative enforcement and litigation of the four laws within its jurisdiction. The EEOC does not pursue every case it receives, but focuses on the cases in which the court decision will receive the business community's attention.

Categories of Discrimination

Title VII prohibits discrimination on a nonjob criterion, such as race or color; religion; national origin; or gender, including pregnancy, childbirth, or abortion; and sexual harassment. The following sections discuss these different categories of discrimination.

Discrimination Based on Race or Color

Discrimination in employment on the basis of race or color has existed in this country for more than 300 years.[5] During the last 100 years, the government has made serious attempts to live up to the Declaration of Independence: "We hold these truths to be self-evident, that all men are created equal."

The Civil Rights Acts of 1866, 1870, 1875, 1964, and 1991, along with the Thirteenth, Fourteenth, and Fifteenth Amendments (called the Civil War Amendments) to the Constitution, make racial discrimination illegal. The Civil Rights Act of 1866 specifically made it illegal to discriminate, contractually or otherwise, based on race. The 1866 Civil Rights Act today is used primarily in nonemployment cases, while Title VII is used for employment cases.

The 1866 act prohibits government officials from discriminating against people "under the color of law." For example, a police officer cannot stop a person solely on the basis of his race. The police officer, by stopping someone, acts under the color of law, that is, as if a legitimate reason existed to stop the person. If the police officer received a report that someone fitting the detained person's description robbed a bank, the stop would be legitimate and on a nondiscriminatory basis.

Discrimination Based on Religion

Of all the categories listed in Title VII, religion is the only one protected under the First Amendment of the U.S. Constitution. It reads in part:

---

[4] The 1991 Civil Rights Act is at the same site as Title VII, <http://www.eeoc.gov/laws/vii.html>. The act is also available separately at <http://www.eeoc.gov/laws/cra91.html>.

[5] For facts about race/color discrimination, see <http://www.eeoc.gov/facts/fs-race.html>.

LEGAL HIGHLIGHT
Discrimination and Education

Like businesses, educational facilities cannot discriminate on the basis of gender, color, race, or national origin. But different federal statutes cover education organizations. Title IX of the Civil Rights Act of 1964 bans discrimination involving race, color, or national origin by any school that receives federal assistance. Practices that are prohibited are providing services, financial aid, or other benefits on a discriminatory basis.

Title IX of the Education Amendments of 1972 covers sexual discrimination. It provides that "no person in the United States shall, on the basis of sex, be excluded from participation in, be denied the benefits of, or be subjected to discrimination under any program or activity receiving federal assistance." The law applies to educational facilities. Discrimination in any area, including health, physical education, industrial arts, business, vocational, technical, home economics, music, or adult education courses, is banned.

A few exceptions allow classes to be segregated based on sex. Separate classes for discussing human sexuality, athletic segregation for sports involving bodily contact, or music classes for students whose vocal range or quality is best expressed in all-male or -female choruses are legal.

Congress shall make no law respecting an establishment of religion, or prohibiting the free exercise thereof . . . .

Employers may not discriminate against employees on the basis of religion, unless the employer itself is a religious organization. Title VII exempts religious associations and religious educational institutions from the prohibition against discrimination on the basis of religion. For example, a Christian church would not hire a Jewish rabbi to officiate at its services. Whenever these organizations hire employees for nonreligious purposes, however, they are prohibited from discriminating on the basis of race, gender, or national origin. For example, the religious association may not discriminate on the basis of race, gender, or national origin for the position of fund-raiser.

An employer must make reasonable accommodations to an employee's religious practices, beliefs, or observances, as long as the employer can do so without undue hardship in the conduct of its business.[6] Reasonable accommodation must be made for a person's religious clothing and religious observation day, such as Sunday.

The employer need only accommodate the employee's religious beliefs when the consequence to the employer is minimal. For example, an employee requests a vacation day to observe a religious holiday six months in advance. That request should be approved, especially if other employees do not observe the holiday.

On the other hand, if an employee works for an airline, it does not have to allow the employee every Sunday off. The employee knew when she was hired that people are needed to work twenty-four hours a day every day of the year because of the nature of the business. If the airline gave the employee every Sunday off, this schedule would be unfair to other employees who also may want some Sundays off. The employer, however, cannot target an employee by always scheduling the employee on her religious observation day intending that the person quit.

Discrimination Based on National Origin

Title VII prohibits discrimination based on national origin,[7] but fails to define the term. By case law, national origin refers to the country in which a person is born or from which his or her ancestors came. In 1980, the EEOC issued guidelines that defined national origin discrimination to include denial of equal employment

---

[6] For more facts about discrimination based on religion, see <http://www.eeoc.gov/facts/fs-relig.html>.

[7] For more facts about discrimination based on national origin, see <http://www.eeoc.gov/facts/fs-nator.html>.

LEGAL HIGHLIGHT

What's in a Name?

The National Organization for Women threatened, in October 1982, to file charges against a local police department in Palm Beach County, Florida. The patrol cars were emblazoned with the word "patrolman," and the local group believed that this discouraged women from applying for police jobs.

Concern with this type of language may seem at first to be misplaced. But language is an important barometer of the society that uses it. For example, if a language contains phrases like lady lawyer or woman doctor, you can be sure that women are new to these fields in that society. Language also directs and limits thoughts and ideas. When you hear the word fireman or policeman, it is hard to think of a woman in uniform. But any youngster could grow up to be a firefighter or police officer.

Under Title VII, employers generally may not use advertisements that indicate, through language or otherwise, any preference in hiring for a particular race, color, religion, gender, or national origin. Similarly, the Age Discrimination in Employment Act forbids help-wanted advertisements that imply that older workers need not apply. An advertisement for a "gal Friday" or for an "ambitious young salesperson," for example, might be unacceptable on both counts.

Are prospective applicants really deterred by these language cues and other indications, such as listing certain help-wanted advertisements under gender-segregated columns that are headed "Jobs—Male Interest"? Some studies show this to be the case. In one study, fifty-two women were asked to rate their willingness to apply for each of thirty-two jobs.[a]

When the jobs were separated and labeled by gender, less than half of the women were as likely to apply for male-interest as for female-interest jobs. When the same advertisements were listed alphabetically with no reference to gender, more than 80 percent of the women preferred the male-interest jobs. This result was not surprising in at least one respect: these jobs averaged higher pay.

[a] Testimony of Sandra L. Rem and Daryl J. Bem, then of the Department of Psychology at Carnegie Mellon University, reproduced in Hearings on Section 805 of H. R. 16098, pp. 892–894, Special Subcommittee on Education of the House Committee on Education and Labor, July 31, 1970.

---

opportunity because of an individual's, or his or her ancestors', place of origin, or because an individual has the physical, cultural, or linguistic characteristics of a national origin group.

Title VII's prohibition of national origin discrimination forbids a foreign corporation that conducts business in the United States from discriminating in favor of its own nationals. This prohibition is waived if such discrimination specifically is permitted by a treaty.

Discrimination Based on Gender

Title VII prohibits discrimination based on gender. Title VII, however, does not prohibit employment discrimination based on sexual or affectional preferences, nor does it protect transsexuals.

Protective state legislation, such as laws that prevented women from lifting more than twenty pounds of weight or from working at night, have been struck down. The protective state legislation often prevented women from obtaining higher paying jobs. Under EEOC guidelines, state statutes may not be used as a defense to a charge of illegal gender discrimination.

Gender-plus discrimination is also illegal under Title VII. This discrimination involves discrimination based on gender, plus an additional element. For example, in the past women with preschool-age children were refused employment. Title VII makes it illegal for an employer to refuse to hire these women when the employer hires men with preschool-age children. An employer may not require female employees to be single if male employees may be married. In the past, male teachers could be married, but women teachers were required to remain single to keep their jobs.

Gender Discrimination Based on Pregnancy.
Title VII was amended in 1978 by the **Pregnancy Discrimination Act**.[8] This act redefined gender discrimination to include discrimination based on pregnancy, childbirth, or related medical conditions. Based on this amendment, health and disability insurance plans must cover pregnancy, childbirth, or related medical conditions in the same way that they cover any other temporary disability.

[8] For more facts about pregnancy discrimination, see <http://www.eeoc.gov/facts/fs-preg.html>.

An employer must provide leaves of absence for pregnant women on the same terms and conditions as those provided to any other worker who has a temporary disability. A woman who is pregnant cannot be forced to take a maternity leave for any specified period of time. As long as she can perform her duties, she must be allowed to work. The 1978 amendment applies to both married and unmarried women and to any aspect of employment.

The following case involves disparate treatment, gender discrimination prohibitions, and pregnancy discrimination prohibitions under the 1964 Civil Rights Act and the Pregnancy Discrimination Act.

Case 23.2

Automobile Workers v. Johnson Controls, Inc.

Supreme Court of the United States, 1991
499 U.S. 187, 111 S. Ct. 1196, 113 L. Ed. 2d 158

BACKGROUND AND FACTS Johnson Controls, Inc., manufactures batteries. In the manufacturing process, the element lead is a primary ingredient. Occupational exposure to lead entails health risks, including the potential harm to any fetus carried by a female employee.

Before the Civil Rights Act of 1964, Johnson Controls did not employ any women in battery manufacturing. In June 1977, the company adopted a policy of warning any woman of childbearing age of the potential hazards of working in such a job and then having the woman sign a statement that she had been advised of the risks. Between 1979 and 1983, eight women became pregnant. Their blood lead levels were regarded as critical by the Occupational Safety and Health Administration (OSHA).

In 1982, Johnson Controls shifted from a policy of warning to a policy of excluding women. In 1984, the United Automobile, Aerospace, and Agricultural Implement Workers of America, United Automobile Workers, and others filed a class-action suit challenging the Johnson Controls fetal-protection policy as gender discrimination that violated Title VII of the Civil Rights Act of 1964.

Justice BLACKMUN delivered the opinion of the Court.

. . . .

The bias in Johnson Controls' policy is obvious. Fertile men, but not fertile women, are given a choice as to whether they wish to risk their reproductive health for a particular job. [T]he Civil Rights Act of 1964 prohibits sex-based classifications in terms and conditions of employment, in hiring and discharging decisions, and in other employment decisions that adversely affect an employee's status. Respondent's fetal-protection policy explicitly discriminates against women on the basis of their sex. The policy excludes women with childbearing capacity from lead-exposed jobs and so creates a facial [outward] classification based on gender.

. . . .

First, Johnson Controls' policy classifies on the basis of gender and childbearing capacity, rather than fertility alone. Respondent does not seek to protect the unconceived children of all its employees. Despite evidence in the record about the debilitating effect of lead exposure on the male reproductive system, Johnson Controls is concerned only with the harms that may befall the unborn offspring of its female employees. . . . Johnson Controls' policy is facially discriminatory because it requires only a female employee to produce proof that she is not capable of reproducing.

Our conclusion is bolstered by the Pregnancy Discrimination Act of 1978 (PDA) in which Congress explicitly provided that, for purposes of Title VII, discrimination "on the basis of sex" includes discrimination because of or on the basis of pregnancy, childbirth, or related medical conditions. The Pregnancy Discrimination Act has now made clear that, for all Title VII purposes, discrimination based on a woman's pregnancy is, on its face, discrimination because of her sex. In its use of the words "capable of bearing children" in the 1982 policy statement as the criterion for exclusion, Johnson Controls explicitly classifies on the basis of potential for pregnancy. Under the PDA, such a classification must be regarded, for Title VII purposes, in the same light as explicit sex discrimination. Respondent has chosen to treat all its female employees as potentially pregnant; that choice evinces discrimination on the basis of sex.

We concluded above that Johnson Controls' policy is not neutral because it does not apply to the reproductive capacity of the company's male employees in the same way as it applies to that of females.

. . . .

DECISION AND REMEDY The Court found that the policy was discriminatory on its face by requiring only women to prove themselves incapable of reproducing. The decision to work is that of the employed woman, not that of the employer.

CRITICAL THINKING: MANAGERIAL PERSPECTIVE How does a business protect itself from liability when employees work with hazardous materials? Can the employer have the employee waive any claims to future illness? Can the employee waive the rights to claims for illness on behalf of his or her unborn children?

Gender Discrimination in Pension Plans and Life Insurance.

On the whole, women have a longer life expectancy than men. As a result, virtually all pension and annuity plans formerly required either that women pay into the plan a higher annual amount to receive the same yearly retirement benefits or that women pay the same annual amount but retire with a lower annual income.

Today, pension plans and life insurance plans must treat retirees as individuals rather than as classes of men or women. Even though women as a class live longer than men, many women die earlier than the average man, and many men outlive the average woman. Insurance plans now consider other factors in determining rates and benefits, such as smoking habits.

Gender Discrimination Using Sexual Harassment.

By the late 1970s, federal courts began ruling that sexual harassment constituted illegal gender discrimination under Title VII.[9] Although Title VII fails to define sexual harassment, the Equal Employment Opportunity Commission adopted a regulation that defines sexual harassment as follows:

Unwelcome sexual advances, requests for sexual favors, and other verbal or physical conduct of a sexual nature constitute sexual harassment when (1) submission to such conduct is made either explicitly or implicitly a term

[9] For facts about sexual harassment, see <http://www.eeoc.gov/facts /fs-sex.html>.

or condition of an individual's employment, (2) submission to or rejection of such conduct by an individual is used as the basis for employment decisions affecting such individual, or (3) such conduct has the purpose or effect of unreasonably interfering with an individual's work performance or creating an intimidating, hostile, or offensive work environment.

The guidelines recognize two kinds of harassment: (1) *quid pro quo* (Latin for "something for something" or "one valuable thing for another") and (2) hostile environment. The *quid pro quo* harassment occurs when the employee's pay, hours, promotion, termination, or other conditions of employment depend on whether the employee submits to the unwelcome or unsolicited verbal or physical conduct of a sexual nature.

A hostile environment exists when employees are subjected to unwanted sexual innuendos, vulgarity, suggestive conduct or touching, or propositioning for sexual favors by coemployees, supervisors, or customers, even though submission to sexual demands is not a condition of continued employment. If this unwanted conduct interferes with an employee's job performance or creates an intimidating, hostile, or offensive environment, the conduct is illegal.

The courts have held that sexual harassment applies to both male–female and female–male harassment.

Unlawful harassment occurs even when the harasser is unaware that his conduct creates a hostile working environment. To prove a sexual harassment case, the employee must show that the conduct was of a sexual nature, that it was unwelcome, and that it was severe or pervasive enough in nature to alter the conditions of employment.

The employer may be held liable for illegal sexual harassment perpetrated in the company. To hold an employer liable for a hostile work environment, the employee must meet a two-part test. First, the employer must have known or should have known of the sexual harassment in the workplace. Second, on notification, the employer must have failed to take prompt and corrective action. When an employer has a valid sexual harassment policy and procedure in place and responds in a timely and meaningful manner to the claim, the employer will not be held liable. An employer is strictly liable, however, when the case is based on a *quid pro quo* harassment.

The next case involves the behavior of the male president of a business toward a female business manager. The case dealt with whether the conduct was so abusive that it amounted to work environment harassment on the basis of gender, resulting in a violation of Title VII even though she did not claim an economic or tangible injury.

Case 23.3

Harris v. Forklift Systems, Inc.

Supreme Court of the United States, 1993
510 U.S. 17, 114 S. Ct. 367, 126 L. Ed. 2d 295
http://caselaw.findlaw.com /scripts/casesearch.pl? CiRestriction=harris+v.+ Forklift+Systems%2C+Inc.& court=US

BACKGROUND AND FACTS Teresa Harris worked as a manager at Forklift Systems, Inc., from April 1985 until October 1987. Charles Hardy was Forklift's president.

Hardy often insulted Harris because of her gender and often made her the target of unwanted sexual innuendos. In the presence of other employees, Harris made statements such as "You're a woman, what do you know" and "We need a man as the rental manager." At least once, he told her that she was "a dumb ass woman." Once he suggested that the two of them "go to the Holiday Inn to negotiate a raise."

In mid-August 1987, Harris complained to Hardy, who was surprised that Harris was offended and claimed that he was only joking. He apologized and promised to stop. Based on this assurance, Harris stayed on the job.

In early September, however, while Harris arranged a deal with one of Forklift's customers, Hardy asked her in front of other employees, "What did you do, promise the guy some sex Saturday night?"

On October 1, 1987, Harris collected her paycheck and quit. She brought action on the basis that the above comments created an abusive work environment for her because of her gender.

The federal district court found that these statements did not create an abusive environment. The court determined that although these statements offended Harris, they were not so severe as to affect seriously Harris's psychological well-being and should not have interfered with her work performance. The appellate court affirmed this decision, which was appealed to the United States Supreme Court.

Justice O'CONNOR delivered the opinion of the Court.

. . . .

Title VII of the Civil Rights Act of 1964 makes it "an unlawful employment practice for an employer . . . to discriminate against any individual with respect to his compensation, terms, conditions, or privileges of employment, because of such individual's race, color, religion, sex, or national origin." As we made clear in *Meritor Savings Bank v. Vinson*, this language "is not limited to 'economic' or 'tangible' discrimination. The phrase 'terms, conditions, or privileges of employment' evinces a congressional intent 'to strike at the entire spectrum of disparate treatment of men and women' in employment," which includes requiring people to work in a discriminatory hostile or abusive environment. When the workplace is permeated with "discriminatory intimidation, ridicule, and insult," that is "sufficiently severe or pervasive to alter the conditions of the victim's employment and create an abusive working environment," Title VII is violated.

This standard, which we reaffirm today, takes a middle path between making actionable any conduct that is merely offensive and requiring the conduct to cause a tangible psychological injury. As we pointed out in *Meritor,* "mere utterance of an . . . epithet which engenders offensive feelings in a [sic] employee" does not sufficiently affect the conditions of employment to implicate Title VII. Conduct that is not severe or pervasive enough to create an objectively hostile or abusive work environment-an environment that a reasonable person would not find hostile or abusive is beyond Title VII's purview. Likewise, if the victim does not subjectively perceive the environment to be abusive, the conduct has not actually altered the conditions of the victim's employment, and there is no Title VII violation.

But Title VII comes into play before the harassing conduct leads to a nervous breakdown. A discriminatorily abusive work environment, even one that does not seriously affect employees' psychological well-being, can and often will detract from employees' job performance, discourage employees from remaining on the job, or keep them from advancing in their careers. Moreover, even without regard to these tangible effects, the very fact that the discriminatory conduct was so severe or pervasive that it created a work environment abusive to employees because of their race, gender, religion, or national origin offends Title VII's broad rule of workplace equality. . . .

. . . Certainly Title VII bars conduct that would seriously affect a reasonable person's psychological well-being, but the statute is not limited to such conduct. So long as the environment would reasonably be perceived, and is perceived, as hostile or abusive, there is no need for it also to be psychologically injurious.

DECISION AND REMEDY   The Supreme Court reversed the decisions of the two lower courts and held that if conduct adversely affected the work environment in such a manner that it would reasonably be perceived, or is perceived, as hostile or abusive, a Title VII violation has occurred.

CRITICAL THINKING: MANAGERIAL PERSPECTIVE   How should a business handle a sexual harassment complaint?

The next case involves the sexual harassment of a male by other male coworkers. The question presented to the United States Supreme Court was whether same–sex harassment behavior violated Title VII.

Case 23.4

Oncale v. Sundowner Offshore Services, Inc.

Supreme Court of the United States, 1998

523 U.S.75, 118 S. Ct. 998, 140 L. Ed. 2d 201

http://caselaw.findlaw.com /scripts/casesearch.pl? CiRestriction=510+U.S.+17 &court=US

BACKGROUND AND FACTS Oncale, the plaintiff, worked for Sundowner Offshore Services, a defendant, on a Chevron U.S.A., Inc., oil platform in the Gulf of Mexico. Oncale was married and the father of several children. He was employed as a roustabout on an eight-man crew which included the following defendants: John Lyons, Danny Pippen, and Brandon Johnson. Lyons, the crane operator, and Pippen, the driller, had supervisory authority. On several occasions, Lyons, Pippen, and Johnson forcibly subjected Oncale to sex-related, humiliating actions in the presence of the rest of the crew. Pippen and Lyons also physically assaulted Oncale in a sexual manner, and Lyons threatened him with rape.

Oncale's complaints to supervisory personnel produced no remedial action; in fact, the company's safety compliance clerk, Valent Hohen, told Oncale that Lyons and Pippen "picked [on] him all the time too" and called him a name suggesting homosexuality.

Oncale eventually quit, asking that his pink slip reflect that he "voluntarily left due to sexual harassment and verbal abuse." When asked at his deposition why he left Sundowner, Oncale stated, "I felt that if I didn't leave my job, that I would be raped or forced to have sex." Oncale filed a complaint against Sundowner and the others alleging sex discrimination in his employment. The district court held that "Mr. Oncale, a male, has no cause of action under Title VII for harassment by male co-workers." Oncale appealed. The Court of Appeals for the Fifth Circuit affirmed the district court's holding.

Justice SCALIA delivered the opinion for a unanimous Court.

. . . .

We see no justification in the statutory language or our precedents for a categorical rule excluding same–sex harassment claims from the coverage of Title VII. As some courts have observed, male-on-male sexual harassment in the workplace was assuredly not the principal evil Congress was concerned with when it enacted Title VII. But statutory prohibitions often go beyond the principal evil to cover reasonably comparable evils, and it is ultimately the provisions of our laws rather than the principal concerns of our legislators by which we are governed. Title VII prohibits "discriminat[ion] . . . because of . . . sex" in the "terms" or "conditions" of employment. Our holding that this includes sexual harassment must extend to sexual harassment of any kind that meets the statutory requirements.

DECISION AND REMEDY The judgment reversed that of the Fifth Circuit. The Supreme Court concluded that sex discrimination consisting of same-sex sexual harassment was actionable under Title VII. Oncale could pursue his lawsuit against the defendants.

CRITICAL THINKING: MANAGERIAL PERSPECTIVE Will the Supreme Court's decision transform Title VII into a general civility code for the American workplace?

Equal Pay Act

The **Equal Pay Act**[10] of 1963 is an amendment to the Fair Labor Standards Act of 1938. The act is limited in scope because it prohibits gender-based discrimination in matters of wages. Pay for women and men for equal work on jobs that require equal skills, effort, and responsibility and that are performed under similar conditions must be equal. Job content rather than job description controls in all cases.

For the equal pay requirements to apply, the act requires that male and female employees work at the same establishment. The issue is whether the jobs performed by the two employees are substantially equal rather than the equivalence of the employees' skills and training.

Small differences in job content fail to justify higher pay for one gender. The courts look to the primary duties involved in comparable jobs. For example, a "barber" and "beautician" perform essentially equal work, as do a "tailor" and a "seamstress."

Enforcement

The EEOC or private parties may bring suit under the Equal Pay Act. If, however, the government sues on behalf of a particular employee, that employee loses the right to sue, unless the employee already has brought suit.

All suits must be started within two years of the violation, or within three years if the violation is willful. Each payday amounts to a new violation. No employer may retaliate against an employee who brings suit or attempts to enforce her rights under the act.

Employers may not reduce the wages of men in order to be in compliance with the act. Rather, the wages of women must be increased. Back pay for up to two years (three years if the violation is willful) is available to the successful employee. Liquidated damages equal to the amount of back pay, plus attorneys' fees will be awarded, unless reasonable grounds exist for the employer to form a good-faith belief that it acted lawfully.

Exceptions

The Equal Pay Act provides specific exceptions. Pay differentials are allowed when based on seniority systems, merit systems, piecework, production bonus systems, or any considerations other than gender. These systems must be created in good faith and not created with the intention of specifically avoiding the act.

Bona fide training programs also may justify pay discrimination. As with the seniority or merit system, the training program must be formal and communicated to employees. If, however, a training program excludes female employees, payment of a premium to male trainees is indefensible.

Age Discrimination in Employment Act

Congress passed the **Age Discrimination in Employment Act (ADEA)**[11] in 1967 to protect older workers. Before 1967, employers often refused to hire older workers or would fire longtime workers in their fifties and sixties. Younger workers who worked for lower wages and cost the company less in terms of medical benefits because they were younger replaced these older employees. Additionally, if the employer fired an older worker before he was vested in a retirement program, the employer would benefit by not paying out retirement funds.

Amendments have changed the original act to protect persons forty or older, with no upper age limit. The ADEA applies to employers that have twenty or more nonseasonal employees, labor unions with twenty-five or more members, and any employment agency. Most federal, state, and local government employees also are covered. Government workers in policymaking positions, however, are not covered.

Age discrimination is prohibited in all aspects of employment decisions. Discrimination in hiring, firing, promotions, compensation, privileges, or any other terms or conditions of employment is unlawful. Employment advertisements classified toward younger workers are illegal, although an advertisement can

[10] The text of the Equal Pay Act is located at <http://www.eeoc.gov/laws/epa.html>.

[11] The text of the Age Discrimination in Employment Act is located at <http://www.eeoc.gov/laws/adea.html>.

LEGAL HIGHLIGHT

A Spouse Can Get Out of a Debt under Federal Law

The Equal Credit Opportunity Act (Chapter 14) forbids creditors from discriminating when granting credit based on gender, age, marital status, race, color, religion, national origin, or a person's income being derived from public assistance. The loan officer must make loan decisions based on a person's creditworthiness. The act's purpose is to prevent discrimination by a lender based on extraneous factors.

Financial institutions generally require both husband and wife to sign loan papers. Under federal regulations, "a creditor shall not require the signature of an applicant's spouse . . . on the credit instrument if the applicant qualifies under the creditor's standards of creditworthiness for the amount and terms of the credit requested" (12 C.F.R. § 9202.7).

Three state supreme courts and several federal district courts have found the statute to be violated when a financial institution requires both signatures when one spouse could obtain credit alone if he or she were single. The practical effect of these decisions is that only the spouse who takes out the loan is responsible for repaying it.

---

call for persons forty or older. Because persons under forty are unprotected, these advertisements are not discriminatory.

In 1990, Congress amended the ADEA with the **Older Workers Benefit Protection Act (OWBPA)**,[12] which prohibits discrimination in benefits packages. The exception occurs when employers can justify age-based reductions in employee benefits plans by significant cost considerations. For example, a person who accepts early retirement will receive a lower retirement income than a person who works longer and retires at an older age. The person who works longer contributes more to her retirement benefits so is entitled to more income from those retirement benefits.

The EEOC is charged with investigating and enforcing the ADEA and the OWBPA. In addition, the law allows an individual to sue in civil court. This right to sue ends if the EEOC takes action to enforce the individual's right.

Recovery includes back wages, attorneys' fees, and equitable relief, such as hiring, reinstatement to the old job, and promotion. The act requires that the employer raise the wages of the person who suffered discrimination and the employer cannot reduce the wage of any

employee to comply with the act. Criminal sanctions can be sought if an employer forcibly resists, opposes, impedes, intimidates, or interferes with EEOC representatives in the performance of their duties.

Americans with Disabilities Act

The **Americans with Disabilities Act (ADA)**[13] of 1990 provides federal civil rights protection to people with disabilities. Congress set a national mandate prohibiting discrimination in business and public settings against people with disabilities. Employers with fifteen or more employees may not discriminate against a qualified applicant with a disability.

The act defines a person with disabilities as any person who (1) has a physical or mental impairment that substantially limits one or more of the person's major life activities, (2) has a record of such an impairment, or (3) is regarded as having such an impairment. This protection extends to persons who have recovered from earlier disabilities, such as a person whose

---

[12] The text of the Older Workers Benefit Protection Act is located at the same web page as the Age Discrimination in Employment Act: <http://www.eeoc.gov/laws/adea.html>.

[13] The Americans with Disabilities Act is located at <http://www.eeoc.gov/laws/ada.html>. For facts, see <http://www.eeoc.gov/facts/fs-ada.html>. The Department of Justice's web site on the Americans with Disabilities Act is located at <http://www.usdoj.gov/crt/ada/adahom1.htm>. The Americans with Disabilities Act Document Center is located at <http://janweb.icdi.wvu.edu/kinder/>.

cancer is in remission and who currently is cancer free. In the past, this person would not have been protected. The act also extends protection to persons with acquired immune deficiency syndrome (AIDS) or who are HIV (human immunodeficiency virus) positive.

Employers also must make "reasonable accommodations" to facilitate the employment of people with disabilities. These accommodations include making facilities accessible, restructuring jobs, accommodating work schedules, and providing training policies and materials to qualified applicants.

Employers may show undue hardship and thus be excused from making reasonable accommodations. The defense of undue hardship means that significant difficulty or expense is involved in making reasonable accommodations. It includes a review of the employer's overall financial resources.

An explosion of litigation has occurred in this area. Employees' number one complaint is back problems, followed closely by mental disability. The most common mental claim is depression, with the requested accommodation being a flexible schedule or time off. Problems can be caused by other employees who do not claim a disability, but who see a fellow employee receiving a benefit, such as a flexible schedule, that they lack.

A potential liability exists for a business that reacts improperly to a disability claim. An employee must show that he was disabled within the statute's definition, that the employee was qualified to perform the essential functions of the job, and that the employee had suffered an adverse employment action under circumstances giving rise to possible discrimination.

The key issue is whether the employer knew an employee to be disabled or treated the employee as disabled. If so, then the employer must reasonably accommodate the employee.

A business may confront its largest losses in this area. For example, in *Miners v. Cargill Communications, Inc.*,[14] Miners, the employee, was observed on several occasions consuming alcoholic beverages during working hours. Cargill offered her an opportunity to attend a chemical dependency treatment program because her supervisor suspected that she might be an alcoholic. When she refused this program, Cargill immediately terminated her.

The court found that the employee had made out a *prima facie* case of discrimination under the ADA. Cargill regarded her as being an alcoholic, thus making her disabled. She was terminated because her employer believed that she was an alcoholic. The attempted accommodation was invalid because the employer had no real evidence that the employee was an alcoholic. The bottom line is that a business must be careful to avoid unjustified conclusions regarding employee disability. Ironically, Miners could have been terminated without liability if Cargill had a policy restricting employees from drinking while working.

Statutory Defenses

Prohibitions under Title VII and the other laws against discrimination are subject to the following three main statutory exceptions:

1. Bona fide occupational qualifications (BFOQs)
2. Bona fide seniority or merit systems
3. Professionally developed ability tests.

The following sections discuss these defenses.

Bona Fide Occupational Qualifications

Title VII allows discrimination in hiring based on gender, religion, or national origin if certain occupational criteria are met. An employer can never discriminate on the basis of race. A business can discriminate if it can demonstrate a **bona fide occupational qualification (BFOQ)**, which is a qualification reasonably necessary to that particular business's normal operation.

If the employer is sued for discrimination, the employer can use the defense of a BFOQ. The defendant employer has the burden to establish a BFOQ defense. To do so, the defendant must show the alleged discrimination to be a business necessity.

The courts interpret such a defense very narrowly. For example, courts may allow the BFOQ defense for situations in which gender or national origin is inherently part of the job qualification, such as for a wet nurse or for actor authenticity. Customer preference, on the other hand, is not a BFOQ. For example, if an airline surveys its customers and finds a preference for women flight attendants, the courts will refuse this customer preference as a BFOQ.

[14] 113 F.3d 820 (1997).

Bona Fide Seniority or Merit Systems

Statutes allow differences in the terms, conditions, or privileges of employment based on a **bona fide seniority or merit system**. The differences, however, cannot result from an intent to discriminate.

Most collective bargaining agreements between management and labor unions include detailed seniority systems. Indeed, such seniority systems are one of the most important aspects of collective bargaining agreements. A seniority system means that the newest employee would be the first laid off in a workplace reduction.

For a seniority system to qualify as an exception to Title VII, the system must be bona fide. A seniority system needs four factors to be bona fide:

1. The system must apply equally to all persons

2. The seniority units (that is, occupational groupings for purposes of hiring, promoting, and terminating) must follow industry practices, and the units must constitute separate collective bargaining units

3. The seniority system must not have its genesis in racial discrimination

4. The system must not be incorporated for any illegal racial purposes.

Professionally Developed Ability Tests

Employers may give and act on the results of any **professionally developed ability test**. The test measures specific abilities related to job performance. An ability test, its administration, and the actions based on the results must not be intended to discriminate illegally.

If the test eliminates a disproportionate number of protected class members, the employer must meet the burden of proving that the particular test is job related. Validation studies that meet professional standards ordinarily prove job relation. For example, if a business hires a person to research on a computer and the web, it can test a prospective employee for her computer skills. This job cannot require the applicant to take a graduate school admission test.

Prior to the 1991 Civil Rights Act, confusion existed as to whether a business could use race-norming methods to evaluate tests. To race-norm a test means to vary cutoff scores based on a person's race, color, religion, gender, or national origin. This practice became illegal under the 1991 act.

The 1991 act also prohibits quotas. In the past, quotas set a maximum number of people who could be hired or admitted, such as a quota on the number of Roman Catholics hired or admitted to a university. Quotas traditionally excluded people once the maximum amount was reached. Congress passed acts that require that goals be met (not quotas) in order to ensure that people were included.

Immigration Acts

The **Immigration Reform and Control Act** of 1986 has two purposes. First, the act provides for civil and criminal sanctions for employers. Employers suffer penalties if they (1) fail to verify their workers' employment eligibility and (2) knowingly hire any individual unauthorized to work. Second, employers cannot discriminate against workers based on their national origin or lack of citizenship if they are qualified to work in the United States.

The employer is responsible for verifying the worker's eligibility for work by using Form I-9, Employment Eligibility Verification, supplied by the Immigration and Naturalization Service (INS), which is part of the Department of Justice. The INS enforces the verification part of the act.

The form's completion involves a four-step process. First, on the first day of employment, the employer provides a Form I-9 to the new worker.

Second, the statute outlines which document a prospective employee must provide to show that he is eligible to work in this country. The employee chooses the documents to present to complete the form. The employer must honor documents that on their face reasonably appear to be genuine. The employer must accept any document designated as acceptable by law.

Third, the employer reviews and completes the form. Fourth, the employer files the form in the employer's office separately from the worker's employment file because it contains information not pertinent to employment decisions.

The usual method is to file these forms in alphabetical order by year because, first, the INS can easily inspect the files and, second, the employer must retain the form for one year after termination or three years after hiring. This filing method simplifies the determination of when forms may be destroyed.

During the hiring process, an employer may not adopt a blanket policy of preferring qualified citizens over qualified aliens, however, because this practice violates the antidiscrimination laws. The federal government determines eligibility to work and employers may not discriminate against eligible workers. If the federal government authorizes an alien who holds a government issued card, such as an Alien Registration Card ("green card"), to work in the United States, the employer must accept the card as proof of eligibility to work. The Department of Justice, Office of Special Counsel, is charged with investigating the claims of workers who believe they have been discriminated against.

The **Immigration Act** of 1990 was the first comprehensive overhaul of legal immigration in twenty-five years. The previous law favored immigration based on family ties with U.S. citizens or nationals. The new law favors immigrants based on their potential ability to contribute to the economy. Managers, professionals, and skilled laborers have preference under this law.

Affirmative Action

The current scope of **affirmative action** is primarily an outgrowth and continuation of attempts to remedy past legally authorized discriminatory practices that resulted in economic deprivation. Those traditionally discriminated against were women and minorities. Affirmative action is based on a series of presidential executive orders.

In 1961, President John F. Kennedy (1961–1963) created a Committee on Equal Employment Opportunity. His executive order, which first coined the term "affirmative action," called for the design of measures to achieve nondiscrimination.

President Lyndon B. Johnson (1963–1969) in 1965 issued an executive order requiring the federal government and federal construction contractors to implement affirmative action to ensure equality of employment opportunity regardless of race, religion, and national origin. In 1968, gender was added to the protected categories.

President Richard M. Nixon (1969–1974) signed an executive order in 1970 extending the plan to all federal contractors. As President Nixon remembered,

"A good job is as basic and important a civil right as a good education is necessary and right. We would not impose quotas, but would require federal contractors to show affirmative action to meet the goals of increasing minority employment."

Unfortunately, the term *affirmative action* does not enjoy a clear and widely shared definition. Affirmative action refers to remedial steps taken to improve work opportunities for women and for racial and ethnic minorities who suffered economic harm because as classes they were deprived of job opportunities in the past. Under the Civil Rights Act of 1964, women and racial and ethnic minorities were designated as protected classes. By the same token, the Civil Rights Acts and affirmative action executive orders do not tolerate discrimination against white males based on their color or gender.

In the past, discrimination usually was sanctioned either by laws or by the government failing to prevent these inequities. Affirmative action is a process applied through a set of programs, some of which are required by court orders, some by national and state legislation, and some by administrative regulation.

Today, affirmative action is implemented by the federal government and federal contractors adopting affirmative action plans. The purpose of these plans is to improve job opportunities for protected classes. When measurable improvement in hiring, training, and promoting minorities and females is shown, the object of affirmative action has been met.

Affirmative action plans identify and work toward the elimination of artificial barriers to equal employment. A workforce analysis determines if women and protected minorities are being discriminated against. An affirmative action plan establishes timetables and goals (not quotas) to correct any substantial disparities. If an employer makes a good-faith effort to meet timetables and goals, it meets the requirements of affirmative action.

The employer must publicize the existence of its affirmative action program, both internally and externally. Supervisors and managers must be educated concerning the company's policy and of their responsibilities in implementing it. Recruitment sources also must be advised of the company policy. The company must take active steps to expand its traditional recruitment sources to include those sources likely to result in a higher flow of protected minority and female applicants. Finally, the employer must establish a procedure for monitoring the program's success.

At times, a person with better qualifications was denied a job opportunity when employers hired or promoted a lesser qualified individual from a protected class. The person with the lesser qualifications must be minimally qualified for the job to be selected. Opponents believe that affirmative action is prohibited by Title VII, which prohibits discrimination against anyone based on protected classifications.

Although affirmative action plans are adopted to remedy discrimination, these plans may cause, at times, reverse discrimination, that is, discrimination against a white male occurs. The issue of reverse discrimination was decided by the United States Supreme Court in the following case.

Case 23.5

Johnson v. Transportation Agency

Supreme Court of the United States, 1987
480 U.S. 616, 107 S. Ct.1442,
94 L. Ed. 2d 61

BACKGROUND AND FACTS The Santa Clara County Transportation Agency voluntarily adopted an affirmative action plan for hiring and promoting minorities and women in 1978. The plan provided that in making promotions to jobs that traditionally had been segregated, the person's gender and ethnicity could be considered. The plan set short-range goals and annually adjusted these goals so that they could serve as a realistic guide for actual employment decisions. The long-term goal was to have a workforce whose composition reflected the proportion of minorities and women in the local area's general workforce.

In 1979, the agency announced a vacancy for a road dispatcher. Twelve employees applied for the promotion, including Joyce, a woman, and Johnson, a man. Both were deemed qualified for the job after their applications had been reviewed by two panels. Johnson tied for second place, while Joyce ranked next lower by two points. The case fails to explain what happened to the person who placed first or the person who tied with Johnson. At the time, the agency never had employed a woman as a road dispatcher. A panel that reviewed both records recommended Johnson for promotion.

The agency's affirmative action coordinator was responsible for informing the agency's director of opportunities for the agency to accomplish its objectives under the affirmative action plan. The coordinator recommended that Joyce be hired for the job after he reviewed both applications with their respective qualifications, test scores, expertise, and background and considered affirmative action matters.

The director accepted the coordinator's recommendation and promoted Joyce. He considered the two-point difference in her ranking to be insignificant as he looked at the whole picture.

Johnson filed a complaint with the Equal Employment Opportunity Commission based in part on reverse discrimination. In other words, he did not receive the job because he was a man, therefore, he was discriminated against. He received a right-to-sue letter from the EEOC. The district court held for Johnson. The Ninth Circuit Court of Appeals, however, overturned that decision. The U.S. Supreme Court granted *certiorari*.

Justice BRENNAN delivered the opinion of the Court.

. . . .

It is clear that the decision to hire Joyce was made pursuant to an Agency plan that directed that sex or race be taken into account for the purpose of remedying underrepresentation. The Agency Plan acknowledged the "limited opportunities that have existed in the past" for women to find employment in certain job classifications "where women have not been traditionally employed in significant numbers." As a result, observed the Plan, women were concentrated in traditionally

female jobs in the Agency, and represented a lower percentage in other job classifications than would be expected if such traditional segregation had not occurred.
. . . .

We next consider whether the Agency Plan unnecessarily trammeled the rights of male employees or created an absolute bar to their advancement. . . . The Plan expressly states that "[t]he 'goals' established for each Division should not be construed as 'quotas' that must be met." Rather, the Plan merely authorizes that consideration be given to affirmative action concerns when evaluating qualified applicants. As the Agency Director testified, the sex of Joyce was but one of numerous factors he took into account in arriving at his decision. . . . [T]he Agency Plan requires women to compete with all other qualified applicants. No persons are automatically excluded from consideration; and are able to have their qualifications weighed against those of other applicants.
. . . .

We therefore hold that the Agency appropriately took into account as one factor the sex of Diane Joyce in determining that she should be promoted to the road dispatcher position. The decision to do so was made pursuant to an affirmative action plan that represents a moderate, flexible, case-by-case approach to effecting a gradual improvement in the representation of minorities and women in the Agency's work force. Such a plan is fully consistent with Title VII, for it embodies the contribution that voluntary employer action can make in eliminating the vestiges of discrimination in the workplace.

DECISION AND REMEDY The judgment of the court of appeals was affirmed. The agency had appropriately taken into account Joyce's gender as one factor in determining her promotion. The Supreme Court found that the agency's plan was moderate and flexible and that it provided a case-by-case approach to reaching the long-term goal of improvement in the representation of minorities and females in the agency's workforce.

CRITICAL THINKING: MANAGERIAL CONSIDERATION What provisions should be included in a business's affirmative action plan?

Affirmative action covers other activities besides employment. Both federal and state levels of government have attempted to assist minority-owned businesses. The governments provide assistance by giving preference to minority-owned companies. Additional compensation is paid if a contract is entered with such a business. In the following case, the United States Supreme Court decided whether the requirement to prefer a minority-owned company in a federal construction contract was constitutional.

Case 23.6

Adarand Constructors, Inc. v. Slater

Supreme Court of the United States, 2000

528 U.S. 216, 120 S. Ct. 722, 145 L. Ed. 2d 650

http://www.supremecourtus .gov/opinions/99pdf /99-295.pdf

BACKGROUND AND FACTS This case is unique in that the U.S. Supreme Court heard and decided the case twice, once in 1996 (*Adarand I*) and again in 2000 (*Adarand II*). The basic facts of this case are as follows. Congress adopted the Intermodal Surface Transportation Efficiency Act of 1991 (ISTEA), an appropriations measure for the Department of Transportation (DOT). Congress had a long-standing policy that favored contracting with small socially and economically disadvantaged businesses when a federal contract was involved. To effectuate that policy, ISTEA directed 10 percent of the appropriated contracting funds be spent on contracting with disadvantaged businesses. ISTEA of 1991 updated the previous ISTEA legislation.

To qualify for that status, the disadvantaged business had to be certified as owned and controlled by socially and economically disadvantaged individuals. DOT did not issue certificates, but relied on certifications from two main sources. The Small Business Administration certified businesses for all types of federal procurement programs. State highway agencies certified businesses for purposes of federally assisted highway projects. The certifying entity presumed that socially disadvantaged persons were black, Hispanic, Asian Pacific, Subcontinent Asian, Native Americans, or members of other groups designated from time to time by the Small Business Administration. State highway agencies must in addition have presumed that women were socially disadvantaged. Small businesses owned and controlled by persons who are not members of the preferred groups could be certified, but only if they demonstrated social disadvantage.

In 1989, the Central Federal Lands Highway Division (CFLHD), part of the U.S. Department of Transportation (DOT), awarded a prime contract for a highway construction project in the state of Colorado to Mountain Gravel & Construction Company. The prime contract included a subcontractor compensation clause. This clause was required by the Small Business Act to be included in all prime contracts entered into by all federal agencies. Under this clause, the prime contractor was rewarded for subcontracting with disadvantaged business enterprises. This clause was required in all prime contracts under the 1991 ISTEA and the previous ISTEA.

Mountain Gravel solicited bids from subcontractors for the guardrail portion of the contract. Adarand is a Colorado-based highway construction company specializing in guardrail work. Adarand, whose principal is a white male, submitted the low bid on the guardrail portion of the project.

Gonzales Construction Company, certified by the Colorado Department of Transportation (CDOT), submitted a higher bid. The prime contract provided that Mountain Gravel would receive additional compensation if it hired a certified company. Gonzales was certified, but Adarand was not. Mountain Gravel would have contracted with Adarand except for receiving the additional compensation from the federal government for contracting with a socially and economically disadvantaged business.

Adarand brought legal action. Adarand alleged that the subcontractor compensation clause and, in particular, the race-based presumption that forms its foundation, violated its Fifth Amendment right to equal protection. The Tenth Circuit upheld the use of the clause and the presumption. Adarand appealed to the U.S. Supreme Court. Because DOT's use of race-based measures should have been subjected to strict scrutiny, the U.S. Supreme Court reversed the case and remanded it back to the district court for a rehearing based on the strict scrutiny standard.

On remand, the district court held that the clause and presumption failed the strict scrutiny test because the clause and presumption were not narrowly tailored. Specifically, the court held the presumption that members of the enumerated racial groups are socially disadvantaged to be both overinclusive and underinclusive, because it includes members of those groups who are not disadvantaged and excludes members of other groups who are. The district court enjoined DOT from using the clause and its presumption. The case was appealed to the Tenth Circuit.

Shortly thereafter, and while the appeal was still pending, Adarand filed a second suit in the district court, this time naming as defendants certain Colorado officials, and challenging (on the same grounds) the Colorado's use of the federal guidelines in certifying disadvantaged business enterprises for federally assisted projects.

Shortly after the second suit was filed, Colorado altered its certification program in response to the district court's decision in *Adarand II*. Specifically, Colorado did away with the presumption of social disadvantage for certain minorities and women, and in its place required that all applicants certify on their own statement that each of the firm's majority owners "has experienced social disadvantage based upon the effects of racial, ethnic or gender discrimination." Colorado required no further showing of social disadvantage by any applicant. The new certification program had not been approved by the U.S. Department of Transportation. Petitioner requested and received disadvantaged business certification from CDOT.

Meanwhile, on learning that CDOT had certified Adarand as a disadvantaged business, the Tenth Circuit held that the cause of action was moot and vacated the District Court's judgment favorable to Adarand. A petition for the writ of *certiorari* was filed by Adarand with the U.S. Supreme Court, which granted the writ.

PER CURIAM

. . . .

In so holding, the Tenth Circuit "confused mootness with standing," and as a result placed the burden of proof on the wrong party. If this case is moot, it is because the Federal Government has accepted CDOT's certification of petitioner as a disadvantaged business enterprise, and has thereby ceased its offending conduct. Voluntary cessation of challenged conduct moots a case, however, only if it is "absolutely clear that the allegedly wrongful behavior could not reasonably be expected to recur." And the "'heavy burden of persua[ding]' the court that the challenged conduct cannot reasonably be expected to start up again lies with the party asserting mootness."

Because respondents cannot satisfy this burden, the Tenth Circuit's error was a crucial one. As common sense would suggest, and as the Tenth Circuit itself recognized, DOT accepts only "valid certification[s]" from state agencies. As respondents concede, however, DOT has yet to approve—as it must—CDOT's procedure for certifying disadvantaged business enterprises. . . .

DOT has promulgated regulations outlining the procedure state highway agencies must follow in certifying firms as disadvantaged business enterprises. As described earlier, those regulations require the agency to presume that "women, Black Americans, Hispanic Americans, Native Americans, Asian-Pacific Americans, Subcontinent Asian Americans, or other minorities found to be disadvantaged by the Small Business Administration," are socially disadvantaged. Before individuals not members of those groups may be certified, the state agency must make individual determinations as to disadvantage. . . . CDOT's new procedure under which petitioner was certified applies no presumption in favor of minority groups, and accepts without investigation a firm's self-certification of entitlement to disadvantaged-business status. Given the material differences (not to say incompatibility) between that procedure and the requirements of the DOT regulations, it is not at all clear that CDOT's certification is a "valid certification," and hence not at all clear that the Subcontractor Compensation Clause requires its acceptance.

Before the Tenth Circuit, respondents took pains to "expres[s] no opinion regarding the correctness of Colorado"s determination that [petitioner] is entitled to [disadvantaged-business] status." Instead, they stated flatly that "in the event there is a third-party challenge to [petitioner's] certification as a [disadvantaged business enterprise] and the decision on the challenge is appealed to DOT, DOT may review the decision to determine whether the certification was proper." In addition, DOT itself has the power to require States to initiate proceedings to withdraw a firm's disadvantaged status if there is "reasonable cause to believe" that the firm "does not meet the eligibility criteria" set forth in the federal regulations. Given the patent incompatibility of the certification with the federal regulations, it is far from clear that these possibilities will not become reality. Indeed, challenges to petitioner's disadvantaged-business status seem quite probable now that the Tenth Circuit, by vacating *Adarand II*, has eliminated the sole basis for petitioner's certification in the first place.

. . . .

It is no small matter to deprive a litigant of the rewards of its efforts, particularly in a case that has been litigated up to this Court and back down again. Such action on grounds of mootness would be justified only if it were absolutely clear that the litigant no longer had any need of the judicial protection that it sought. Because that is not the case here, the petition for writ of *certiorari* is granted, the judgment of the United States Court of Appeals for the Tenth Circuit is reversed, and the case is remanded for further proceedings consistent with this opinion.

DECISION AND REMEDY The Court held in the first case that all governmental action, by either the state or federal government based on racial or other classifications, should be subjected to detailed judicial inquiry to ensure that the personal right to equal protection of the laws has not been infringed. Any such classifications must be analyzed by a reviewing court under strict scrutiny and will be upheld only if they are narrowly tailored measures that further compelling governmental interests. In the second case, the Supreme Court found that the issue as to mootness was not sustained in that the DOT may not accept the Colorado approach as to when a company can be certified as being disadvantaged.

CRITICAL THINKING: POLITICAL PERSPECTIVE Should a business owned by a minority or a woman have a preference in obtaining government contracts?

Over the years many states have adopted their own affirmative action plans through either legislation or administrative rulings. The criticism that affirmative action leads to reverse discrimination has existed since its inception.

As a reaction to this criticism, some states have moved to eliminate affirmative action. California is one of these states. The voters amended the California constitution by adopting a measure that removed any statute or regulation that granted preferential treatment to current and prospective state government employees based on race, gender, color, ethnicity, or national origin. This constitutional provision was upheld by the United States Court of Appeals, Ninth Circuit, as conforming with the equal protection clause of the U.S. Constitution. The Supreme Court of the United States refused to hear the case, thus, the California law is valid.

LEGAL HIGHLIGHT

Posting of Labor Laws

Specific employee information notices must be posted at every separate business location. The federal government requires information to be posted on the Occupational Safety and Health Act, Federal Minimum Wage Notice, Employee Polygraph Protection Act, Equal Employment Opportunity Commission/Age Discrimination, and the Family and Medical Leave Act.

State governments can require other mandatory posters, such as workers' compensation, and job safety and health protection information. Failure to do so may result in federal and state penalties. Does your employer comply with these requirements?

Protection for Members of the Military Reserve Force and National Guard

As the active-duty military force in the United States is reduced in size, more reliance is placed on the members of the military reserve force and the National Guard. Employers who saw their workers called up for duty in Operation Desert Storm and in conflicts in Somalia, Haiti, and Bosnia, to name a few, learned that the federal law protects those workers.

The Uniformed Services Employment and Reemployment Rights Act (USERRA), enacted October 1994 and significantly updated in October 1996 and 1998, provides protection and rights of reinstatement to employees who participate in the National Guard and Reserve.[15] Federal law requires these service members to do two weeks of active duty, commonly called summer camp, and to be called up for active duty during a national or international crisis.

An employer cannot discriminate against a person because he serves in the reserve force or the National Guard. An employer, therefore, cannot refuse to hire a person on this basis. An employer must reemploy returning persons without loss of seniority and must restore all benefits to them. Using an escalator as an analogy, an employer must place the returning employee back on the escalator where the employee would have been if she had remained on the job. If the

employee's position has been eliminated, the employer must place the worker in a similar position.

If the job changes in the reservist's absence, the reservist must accept the changed job. The returning person is entitled to all cost-of-living pay raises, but not to merit pay. The reservist cannot be discharged without cause for six months after returning to work.

If a business refuses to hire or to reemploy a reserve force or National Guard member, a federal court can order the business to offer the person a job. If an employer refuses to comply with the law, the U.S. attorney can bring appropriate action on behalf of the individual. All back wages and benefits can be sought by the applicant dating back to the time at which the business illegally refused the person the job.

CyberLaw

Workplace Privacy

Millions of businesses and households use the World Wide Web. Many computers are capable of using a webcam (camera), downloading and uploading streaming video, and telephony (using the computer as a telephone). Some web sites are devoted to watching people at work. Up to now, letting people watch you at work through the web sites has been voluntary.

The computer used at work can be connected to a webcam that allows the world and supervisors to see what the employees are doing. Employers have the ability to track everything done by employees on their

---

[15] The National Committee for Employer Support of the Guard and Reserve can be found at <http://www.esgr.org/>.

computers. Employers can track the number of hours spent playing computer or web games, spent shopping on the web, and time using the computer as a telephone talking with family and friends around the world, and, of course, they can read employees' e-mail. Employees wearing badges with encoded stripes can be tracked as they move through the work buildings.

Computers manufactured after 1996 come equipped with microphones. The employer can install a software program that can listen to everything said near the computer.

Technology has progressed to the point where faces can be logged into databases. Faces of people on streets can be recorded by a street camera for later comparison with faces in the database, such as criminals. Will your employer be able to track you on your private time, shopping, driving, or visiting a government office to file a complaint?

International Consideration

Progress against Discrimination

In the 1960s, the United States started to develop its antidiscrimination laws. The process has continued as further discrimination patterns have become apparent. Most countries have not developed laws as stringent as those in the United States. Few countries provide protection for alien workers, prevent discrimination based on religious beliefs, or provide help based on race or color. Still, international progress in this area slowly is being made.

The European Union (EU) has adopted nonbinding legislation prohibiting sexual harassment. The code is a guide for employers and unions in all 15 EU member countries. Until this legislation was adopted, individual countries had no laws specifically prohibiting sexual harassment. The EU, however, has laws requiring equal pay for work of equal value for men and women. In addition, EU members have laws providing mandatory paid parental leave and requiring management to hold a woman's position open until she returns from maternity leave. A combination of government, management, and union programs provides child care.

The 1991 Civil Rights Act, Title VII of the Civil Rights Act of 1964, and the Americans with Disabilities Act apply to all U.S.-based companies operating in foreign nations. These statutes apply to U.S. employees working for U.S. companies overseas. Employers must comply with these statutes unless doing so would violate the foreign country's laws.

The United States protects older workers from discrimination. The benefits of hiring and continuing to employ older workers are being discovered by management around the world. For example, a retail firm in Great Britain, annoyed at the high turnover of its younger workers, decided to hire workers over age fifty-five. Much to the firm's surprise, the benefits were immediate. Absenteeism dropped dramatically, losses from employee theft decreased, employee turnover dropped, and fewer workers' compensation claims were reported. Customer satisfaction went up and business increased. The older workers took more interest in knowing the products and explaining them to customers. The workers' politeness was very much appreciated by the customers. The experiment was such a success that the firm plans to hire more older workers in its other stores.

LEGALLY SPEAKING

Discriminatory Questions

One of the more important business procedures is the hiring of new employees. Before an individual is hired, most businesses have standard employment applications or questions. Some of the information sought may be considered discriminatory in nature. Questions that can be discriminatory sometimes take forms like these:

1. What is your maiden name?
2. How old are your children? How old is your youngest child?
3. What is your birth date?
4. Have you ever declared bankruptcy?
5. Are you married? (Single? Divorced? Separated? Widowed?)
6. (A more subtle form of the same question): Is there anyone in your life who strongly influences your decisions?
7. Who will care for your children while you are working?
8. How long have you lived at your present address?
9. What is your father's name?
10. Have you ever had your wages garnished?
11. Where do you bank? Do you have any loans outstanding?
12. Do you own or rent your home?
13. Were you ever arrested?
14. What religious group do you belong to? What is the name of your priest? (rabbi? minister?)
15. Where does your husband (wife, father, mother) work?
16. How did you learn to speak Spanish (German, Russian, and so on)?

17. List for me all the societies, clubs, and lodges you belong to.

Thinking through these questions before they come up will help an applicant to handle them in the best way. They may never come up. If they do, though, there are options. Answering militantly ("I'll see you in court for asking me that!") is a no-win choice. Answering something like "Legally I do not have to provide you with that information" is not the best option either.

Try to answer so as to (1) deflect that line of questioning courteously, (2) give the interviewer some useful, helpful information, and (3) not put him or her in the wrong. Suppose the interviewer has asked, "How will you have your children cared for while you work?" One way to answer is "If you'll show how this question is related to my ability to do a good job for you, I'll be glad to answer." Or applicants can say child care is all taken care of and then refer to their record of low absenteeism in their current job, despite family responsibilities.

Another way is to try to think why the interviewer is asking a particular question—why he or she is worried about how you will have your children cared for—and restate the question behind the question. You might say, "If by asking me that question you really mean, 'Will I be on the job every day, on time, and ready to give my full attention and energy to the job?,' the answer is most definitely 'Yes.'"

A third option is a little riskier but sometimes effective. If the rapport up until that question has been pleasant and if you are pretty sure that you are not talking to an ogre, you might be able to laugh pleasantly and say, "I'll bet you didn't really mean to ask me that question, did you?"

Most often, interviewers will back away from the "don't ask" questions if the applicants show in a low key and courteous way that they want to answer only questions directly related to their qualifications for the job. If the interviewer does not back away, the applicant might reconsider whether he or she really wants to work for this type of organization. Worse than not being hired is being hired by an organization where you would be unhappy. Before the interview, consider this checklist:

✔ Think through all the possible questions, good and bad, that you might be asked.

✔ Determine how you will respond.

✔ Update your research on the company.

The last part of the interview usually consists of the interviewer's question: "Now what questions do you have that I can answer?" If you have researched the company, you should have a number of questions you can ask to show your interest and knowledge.

Source: Business Correspondence for Today, by J. W. Gilsdorf. Copyright 1989. Reprinted by permission of John Wiley & Sons, Inc.

Chapter Summary

The major federal statutory provisions that seek to prevent discrimination in employment are the Equal Pay Act of 1963, Title VII of the Civil Rights Act of 1964, the Age Discrimination in Employment Act of 1967, Older Workers Benefit Protection Act of 1990, and the Americans with Disabilities Act of 1990. Gender discrimination; pregnancy discrimination; sexual harassment; pension plans and life insurance plans; and discrimination based on religion, national origin, or race are prohibited.

Title VII prohibits discrimination for employment based on race, color, religion, national origin, and gender. It covers employers with fifteen or more employees, labor unions with fifteen or more members, and employment agencies.

Two basic legal theories underlie actions based on Title VII. According to the disparate treatment theory, the treatment of any individual that differs from the treatment of other employees based on background or gender is discrimination. Under the disparate impact theory, although on the surface a certain practice is not discriminatory, its effect can discriminate against a protected class. Under either theory, the employer can be found liable.

The Equal Employment Opportunity Commission (EEOC) is charged with the enforcement of Title VII. A person files a charge with the EEOC, which then attempts to settle the potential dispute.

The employer has three statutory defenses to any action under Title VII: (1) bona fide occupational qualifications, (2) bona fide seniority or merit systems, and (3) professionally developed ability tests.

The Immigration Reform and Control Act of 1986 places the burden on the employer to screen applicants and prohibits discrimination on the basis of citizenship or national origin. The employer records the documents that the applicant provides to show that she or he is a citizen or a qualified alien. Members of the military reserve force and National Guard are also protected against discrimination by federal statute.

Affirmative action is the process of improving work opportunities for women and minorities who have been discriminated against in the past. The idea behind affirmative action plans is that if a member of a protected class has the necessary requirements for a job, that individual should receive preference in hiring, training, and promotion. The United States Supreme Court has approved the concept of affirmative action.

Using the World Wide Web

The legal aspects of employment and labor law are provided on many sites on the World Wide Web. Nearly everyone has worked, so employment law is of importance to many. Type into any search engine the name of a statute within the employment and labor law and a number web sites will appear.

Finding the Law on the Web

U.S. Commission on Civil Rights
http://www.usccr.gov
Free Advice, Employment (Labor) Law
http://www.freeadvice.com
Cornell University, Legal Information Institute
http://www.law.cornell.edu/topics/employment
_discrimination.html

Chapter Web Sites

Legal Information Institute, employment discrimination information
http://www.law.cornell.edu/topics/employment
_discrimination.html
Equal Employment Opportunity Commission, Title VII
http://www.eeoc.gov/laws/vii.html
Griggs v. Duke Power Co.
http://caselaw.findlaw.com/scripts/casesearch.pl?
CiRestriction=401+U.S.+424&court=US
Equal Employment Opportunity Commission (EEOC)
http://www.eeoc.gov/
Equal Employment Opportunity Commission,
National Enforcement Plan
http://www.eeoc.gov/nep.html

1991 Civil Rights Act, amending Title VII
http://www.eeoc.gov/laws/vii.html
and
http://www.eeoc.gov/laws/cra91.html
Equal Employment Opportunity Commission,
race/color discrimination facts
http://www.eeoc.gov/facts/fs-race.html
Equal Employment Opportunity Commission,
religious discrimination facts
http://www.eeoc.gov/facts/fs-relig.html
Equal Employment Opportunity Commission,
national origin discrimination facts
http://www.eeoc.gov/facts/fs-nator.html
Equal Employment Opportunity Commission,
pregnancy discrimination facts
http://www.eeoc.gov/facts/fs-preg.html
Equal Employment Opportunity Commission,
sexual harassment facts
http://www.eeoc.gov/facts/fs-sex.html
Harris v. Forklift Systems, Inc.
http://caselaw.findlaw.com/scripts/casesearch.pl?
CiRestriction=harris+v.+Forklift+Systems%2C+
Inc.&court=US
Oncale v. Sundowner Offshore Services, Inc.
http://caselaw.findlaw.com/scripts/casesearch.pl?
CiRestriction=510+U.S.+17&court=US
Equal Pay Act
http://www.eeoc.gov/laws/epa.html
Age Discrimination in Employment Act
http://www.eeoc.gov/laws/adea.html
Older Workers Benefit Protection Act
http://www.eeoc.gov/laws/adea.html

Americans with Disabilities Act
http://www.eeoc.gov/laws/ada.html
Americans with Disabilities Act, facts
http://www.eeoc.gov/facts/fs-ada.html
Department of Justice, Americans with Disabilities Act
http://www.usdoj.gov/crt/ada/adahom1.htm
Americans with Disabilities Act Document Center
http://janweb.icdi.wvu.edu/kinder
Adarand Constructors, Inc. v. Slater
http://www.supremecourtus.gov/opinions/99pdf
/99-295.pdf
National Committee for Employer Support of
the Guard and Reserve
http://www.esgr.org/
'Lectric Law Library
http://www.lectlaw.com/temp.html

Web Activities

23–1 All it takes to cause a supervisor problems is for an employee to accuse another employee of sexual harassment. What should the supervisor do? Go to 'Lectric Law Library at <http://www.lectlaw.com/temp.html>. Click on under the heading "Specifically for Employers" and then on the subheading "Avoiding Sexual Harassment for Supervisors." What advice is provided for supervisors when this issue arises?

23–2 You are an employer with a number of members of the military reserve force and National Guard. Go to the National Committee for Employer Support of the Guard and Reserve web site at <http://www.esgr.org/>. Click on "Employers Info." What tips can you use to support your employees who serve in the armed forces?

Key Terms

affirmative action
Age Discrimination in Employment Act (ADEA)
Americans with Disabilities Act (ADA)
bona fide occupational qualification (BFOQ)

bona fide seniority or merit system
disparate impact
disparate treatment
Equal Employment Opportunity Commission (EEOC)
Equal Pay Act

Immigration Act
Immigration Reform and Control Act
Older Workers Benefit Protection Act (OWBPA)
Pregnancy Discrimination Act

prima facie case
professionally developed ability test
Title VII of the Civil Rights Act of 1964

Questions and Case Problems

23–1 Civil Rights Act, Title VII Discuss fully which of the following constitute a violation of the 1964 Civil Rights Act, Title VII as amended.

a. Causeway, Inc., is a consulting firm with ten employees who travel on consulting jobs in seven states. Causeway has an employment record of hiring only white males.

b. Filmtex, Inc., is making a film about Africa. Filmtex needs to employ 100 extras for this picture. Filmtex advertises in major newspapers in southern California for the hiring of these extras. The advertisement states that only African Americans need apply.

c. Green is a major processor of cheese sold throughout the United States. Green employs 100 employees at its principal processing plant. The plant is located in Windward City, which has a population that is 50 percent white and 25 percent African American, with the balance Hispanic American, Asian American, and other minorities. Green requires a high school diploma as a condition of employment on its cleanup crew. Three-fourths of the city's white population complete high school, compared with only one-fourth of the city's minority population. Green's cleaning crew is all white.

23–2 Age Discrimination in Employment For thirty years, Christine McKennon worked for Nashville Banner Publishing Company (Banner) before being terminated. She believed she was terminated from her job because of her age. She filed suit in federal district court alleging that her discharge violated the Age Discrimination in Employment Act. In preparation for the case, Banner took McKennon's deposition in which she admitted that she had copied and taken home several confidential documents bearing on the company's financial condition. A few days after the deposition, Banner sent McKennon a letter declaring that removal and copying of the records violated her job responsibilities and advising her again that she was terminated. Banner conceded to discriminating against McKennon because of her age, but her misconduct also provided grounds for her termination. The district court granted the summary judgment, which was affirmed by the appellate court. The case was appealed to the United States Supreme Court. What was the result? Explain. [*McKennon v. Nashville Banner Publishing Co.*, 513 U.S. 352, 115 S. Ct. 879, 130 L. Ed. 2d 852 (1995)]

23–3 Civil Rights Act, Title VII The state of Connecticut required applicants to take a written examination before being considered for a supervisor position. Of those taking the test, whites had a 79 percent passing rate and African Americans had a 34 percent passing rate. The state of Connecticut showed, however, that more African American than whites were promoted from the eligibility list. The state argued that this "bottom line" was a defense to the discrimination suit. Was this a valid defense? Explain. [*Connecticut v. Teal*, 457 U.S. 440, 102 S. Ct. 2525, 72 L. Ed. 2d 130 (1982)]

23–4 Affirmative Action The city of Memphis, Tennessee, implemented an affirmative action plan. In 1981, the city confronted severe deficits and had to lay off a considerable number of employees. The city announced that it would follow the last-hired/first-fired rule. This policy was contrary to the city's affirmative action plan in that it would cause a large number of African Americans to be terminated. The district court ordered the city to modify the layoff plan to reduce the number of African Americans adversely affected. The case was appealed to the United States Supreme Court. The issue presented was whether a seniority plan that was not intentionally discriminatory would be upheld when the effect was to lay off large numbers of African Americans. What decision do you think the Court reached? Explain. [*Firefighters Local Union No. 1784 v. Stotts*, 467 U.S. 561, 104 S. Ct. 2576, 81 L. Ed. 2d 483 (1984)]

23–5 Civil Rights Act, Title VII Elizabeth Hishon was employed as an associate attorney for a large law firm in Atlanta, Georgia. The firm had more than 100 lawyers but never made a woman a firm partner. The district court held that Title VII was not applicable to the selection of partners in a law firm because partners are owners, not employees, of a firm. Do you think that the district court was correct? Explain. [*Hishon v. King & Spalding*, 467 U.S. 69, 104 S. Ct. 2229, 81 L. Ed. 2d 59 (1984)]

23–6 Age Discrimination in Employment Western Airlines required all of its pilots to retire at age sixty to conform with the Federal Aviation Administration's regulation. Criswell was physically fit and wanted to continue flying past the age of sixty. When he was required to retire, he instituted action. Was this age requirement a valid BFOQ? Explain. [*Western Airlines v. Criswell*, 472 U.S. 400, 105 S. Ct. 80, 86 L. Ed. 2d 321 (1985)]

23–7 Civil Rights Act, Title VII Five employees, white and African American, were terminated by Omni Georgia and replaced by five people of Korean origin.

The supervisor who terminated the employees was of Japanese origin. The five terminated employees brought action based on violation of Title VII. Was the law violated? Explain. [*Bullard v. Omni Georgia*, 640 F.2d 632 (5th Cir. 1981)]

23–8 Civil Rights Act, Title VII Hasselman was required to wear a "revealing and provocative" uniform while working as a lobby attendant in a large office complex. She was subjected to repeated sexual harassment by different people. Finally, she refused to wear the uniform and was terminated. Was her termination a violation of Title VII? Explain. [*EEOC v. Sage Realty Corp.*, 507 F. Supp. 599 (S.D.N.Y. 1981)]

23–9 Civil Rights Act, Title VII Velva Wise was employed by Mead Corp. She and another employee were involved in a fight. Prior to this fight, four other reported fights among employees had occurred. Only one person had been fired because of fighting, and this was a male who had been involved in two out of the four fights. Wise claimed that Mead discriminated against her when she was terminated. Was she correct?

Explain. [*Wise v. Mead Corp.*, 614 F. Supp. 1131 (M. D. Ga. 1985)]

23–10 Internet As an employer, you are concerned about an investigation being conducted by the Equal Employment Opportunity Commission (EEOC) concerning a sexual harassment complaint. Go to the EEOC's web page at <http://www.eeoc.gov/>. On the right side, under "Laws, Regulations, and Policy Guidance," click on "Enforcement Guidances and Related Documents." Scroll to the bottom until you see "Enforcement Guidance on Harris v. Forklift Sys., Inc. Date issued 9/9/93," then click on it. Scroll to the bottom until you see "Charge Processing." What are the three steps investigators should look for in their investigation?

Note: The "Policy Guidance on Current Issues of Sexual Harassment Date issued 3/19/90" referred to in the "Charge Processing" is available on the previous web page directly below "Enforcement Guidance on Harris v. Forklift Sys., Inc. Date issued 9/9/93."

Chapter 24

Environmental Law

To waste, to destroy, our natural resources, to skin and exhaust the land instead of using it so as to increase its usefulness, will result in undermining in the days of our children the very prosperity which we ought by right to hand down to them amplified and developed.

Message to Congress, December 3, 1907
President Theodore Roosevelt, 1858–1919
Twenty-sixth president of the United States of America, 1901–1909
Nobel Peace Prize, 1906

Outline

Ethical Consideration

Balancing the Needs to Protect the Environment and to Meet Current Exigencies

Your company produces a variety of pesticides, including one that eradicates virtually all insects. This particular product, called Life Protector, is banned in the United States because it is highly toxic and poses dangers to farm workers, the general environment, and consumers who ingest the toxic residue. In spite of these dangers, many developing nations use this highly efficient product because it allows crops to grow in insect-infested locations.

Although your company has placed warning labels on the product that list specific rules for its proper handling and application, environmental organizations inform your company that poor, illiterate farm workers apply Life Protect or without wearing gloves, breathing apparatuses, or other protective devices required for safety. Your company also has information that the pesticide is being overapplied in many areas and is seeping into the groundwater, creating the potential for severe and long-lasting environmental damage.

You are disturbed by the many reports of the product's misuse. You consider either stopping production or demanding proof that Life Protector is being used correctly before distributing it in a particular country. When you raise these concerns with foreign purchasers, however, they assure you that they are aware of the dangers and are doing the best they can to regulate the pesticide's use. They also contend that the potential for harm, especially in the future, is greatly outweighed by the current need to feed their vast numbers of citizens. They even say that it is better for a few people to die from Life Protector than for many to starve without sufficient crops. Do you continue to manufacture Life Protector and distribute it as you have done in the past, or do you attempt to control its use? Use the ethical model presented in Chapter 2 and reprinted on the inside front cover to develop your answer.

Introduction

Bhopal, *Exxon Valdez*, Chernobyl—each name spells an environmental disaster. Scientific research has discredited traditional beliefs that air, water, and land can absorb and cleanse waste products without being harmed. As our society and the world become more urbanized, concerns grow about the degradation of the environment.

Economic growth, greater wealth, and the proliferation of synthetic products that resist decomposition have motivated policymakers to seek strategies to clean up, reduce, and finally prevent pollution. Environmental laws focus on protecting nature and restraining the people whose activities upset the earth and its delicate life-sustaining ecosystems. These laws also regulate human pollution of air, water, and land.

Your online business, Artiste Login Products, Inc., must comply with the environmental laws. The business uses raw material, such as bronze for sculptures. Artiste also uses various types of paints for its canvas paintings and for specially manufactured dinnerware. The bronze material and paints that are left over from these processes must be disposed of in accordance with federal and state statutes. Otherwise, Artiste is subject to civil and criminal penalties. Anyone who orders improper disposal, such as dumping the material in a lake or river, may face prison time.

This chapter covers past, present, and future methods for handling pollution problems. The chapter reviews federal legislation that covers clean air, water, noise, and toxic substances. Administrative agencies implement most of these federal laws through regulations and criminal prosecutions.

Historical Background

Environmental concerns are not new. In medieval England, the English Parliament passed a number of laws that regulated the burning of soft coal. In the United States, those harmed could seek common law restitution by suing under one of several theories: private nuisance, trespass, negligence, and strict liability.

Property owners historically were granted relief by the courts under the common law doctrine of private nuisance from pollution. The individual had to be able to identify a pollution source that caused a distinct harm to himself separate from harm affecting the general public. A nuisance occurred when a person used her property in a manner that adversely affected a neighbor's property. Thus, if a factory polluted the air and killed a farmer's crops, the farmer could recover damages from the factory.

Nuisance suits that resulted in specific relief for individuals were inadequate when the harm from pollution could not be identified as affecting specific groups as opposed to the public at large. Under the common law, citizens were denied relief without showing specific harm. If a group of citizens wanted to stop a new development that would cause significant water pollution, the group would be denied any relief under the doctrine of private nuisance on the ground that the harm to the group did not differ from the harm borne by the general public. When the public is harmed, only the government can sue under the common law theory of public nuisance.

Another common law cause of action is trespass. Trespass is defined as the intentional or unintentional intrusion on another's land uninvited, regardless of whether any physical damage is done. Traditionally, to be successful in a trespass suit, the landowner had to prove a direct physical invasion of the land, such as the dumping of debris on the property. Today, trespass occurs often in subtler fashion, for example, through radiation pollution or through permeation by a harmful invisible gas. A trespass suit will provide recovery when these invasions harm plant life or destroy animals. Today, under either the trespass or nuisance theory, courts require the plaintiff to show both invasion and harm.

In addition to the torts of nuisance and trespass, injured parties may file a common law negligence action. The basis for a negligence suit is a business's failure to use reasonable care toward an individual's foreseeable injury. Failure to use pollution controls may give rise to an action for negligence, for example, when contamination of the air produces respiratory illnesses in employees and neighboring residents.

Courts have allowed injured parties to recover under the theory of strict liability in tort. Businesses that engage in ultrahazardous activities, such as blasting operations or transporting of radioactive material, are liable for injuries that these activities cause, even if the

businesses exercised the utmost care. With strict liability, the injured party does not need to prove the damages resulted from the party's fault (failure to use due care).

Inherent problems exist in pursuing any of these remedies. Historically, the common law limited relief from pollution to situations in which the harm was caused by two or more independent sources. For example, if a number of firms pollute the air, a harmed individual could sue any individual firm. Until early in the twentieth century, however, the plaintiff was unable to sue all of the factories simultaneously. Thus, specific proof of damages in individual actions often was impossible.

These difficulties in seeking relief in pollution cases, coupled with the fact that tort theory initially only allowed for money damages and thus was ineffective in preventing environmental harms, ultimately gave rise to the federal and state legislation that today regulates and controls activities affecting the environment.

Regulation by State Government

State governments have some authority in regulating the environment. The private tort actions just noted take place under state laws. Federal legislation permits direct state or local governmental control of the environment. Many states have statutes against polluting the air, the water, and the general environment.

State laws range from restricting the amount of emissions from motor vehicles to requiring state environmental impact statements for developments above a certain size or monetary amount and to restricting the disposal of toxic material. These laws vary from one state to another because each state has its own problems. State environmental laws influence business decisions. Many of these state statutes were passed under pressure from the federal government.

Several states, for example, have attempted to regulate the dumping of bottles and cans through the use of what are commonly called "bottle bills." The following case illustrates the implementation of one of the first statutes of this kind of regulation.

Case 24.1

American Can Co. v. Oregon Liquor Control Commission

Court of Appeals, Oregon, 1973

15 Or. App. 618, 517 P.2d 691

BACKGROUND AND FACTS The state of Oregon adopted a law prohibiting the use of nonreturnable containers for beer and carbonated beverages. The law also prohibited the sale of metal beverage containers that used detachable pull-top opening devices. The American Can Company filed a lawsuit against the Oregon Liquor Control Commission attacking the validity of the statute, claiming violation of equal protection and due process clauses of the Fourteenth Amendment and the commerce clause of the U.S. Constitution. The trial court upheld the law. American Can Company appealed.

Judge TANZER

. . . .

The primary legislative purpose of the bottle bill is to cause bottlers of carbonated soft drinks and brewers to package their products for distribution in Oregon in returnable, multiple-use deposit bottles toward the goals of reducing litter and solid waste in Oregon and reducing the injuries to people and animals due to discarded "pull tops."

. . . .

. . . [T]he introduction of any new circumstance affecting competition will cause economic winners and economic losers throughout the industry as it readjusts to that new circumstance. The evidence is that plaintiffs expect to be among the losers, unless, of course, they are able to make marketing adjustments.

Economic loss restricted to certain elements of the beverage industry must be viewed in relation to the broader loss to the general public of the state of Oregon which the legislature sought, by enactment of the bottle bill, to avoid. The availability of land and revenues for solid waste disposal, the cost of litter collection on our highways and in our public parks, the depletion of mineral and energy resources, the injuries to humans and animals caused by discarded pull tops, and the esthetic blight on our landscape, are all economic, safety and esthetic burdens of great consequences which must be borne by every member of the public. The legislature attached higher significance to the cost to the public than they did to the cost to the beverage industry, and we have no cause to disturb that legislative determination.

The bottle bill is not discriminatory against interstate commerce and is not intended to operate to give Oregon industry a competitive advantage against outside firms. The ban on pull tops and the deposit-and-return provisions apply equally to all distributors and manufacturers whether Oregon-based or from out of state. According to plaintiffs' testimony, the economic burden of the industry's adjustment to the change will be shared by Oregon businesses as well as non-Oregon businesses. . . .

. . . .

Plaintiffs' . . . constitutional challenges having failed, we hold the bottle bill to be a valid exercise of Oregon's police power. In doing so, we acknowledge having had the benefit of an able analysis by the trial court.

DECISION AND REMEDY The appellate court affirmed the trial court's ruling that Oregon legitimately exercised its state police power in passing laws concerning solid waste disposal. It recognized the additional cost to the beverage industry, but the court would not accept that cost as a justification for overturning a legislative enactment. Hence, the bottle bill was upheld.

CRITICAL THINKING: POLITICAL CONSIDERATION Can any business ethically justify opposition to control over bottles and cans?

Regulation by Local Government

County and municipal local governments control certain environmental aspects. Zoning laws adopted by local governments control the land use. Many communities have adopted ordinances controlling the appearance of buildings. Both usage and appearance regulations have a direct impact on the local government.

Currently, Americans generate about 160 million tons of solid waste per year. Packaging is one form of solid waste that rapidly is increasing. Compact discs, for example, are placed in larger containers in order to prevent theft. Food is packaged in individual servings to provide convenience and to reduce food waste. Both types of packaging result in increased solid wastes. Cities and counties have the primary responsibility for disposing of this and other types of garbage. Landfills take 85 percent of the solid wastes, while only 8 percent is incinerated. The rest, including glass, newspapers, and cans, is recycled.

Ordinances controlling outdoor billboards, anti-noise laws prohibiting certain levels of noise from being heard beyond the business premises, and laws banning smoking indoors are examples of local government regulations. Political decisions in these areas often are hard to make. If smoking is banned in restaurants, will the patrons go to restaurants in the next city? Less patronage means less income for businesses, which leads to fewer taxes collected by the local government and, thus, less money available for programs.

Private Litigation

Private parties can recover damages or obtain injunctions for environmental harms under a combination of statutory and common law provisions. The Clean Air Act, the Clean Water Act, and the Noise Control Act, for example, authorized private lawsuits for violations of air, water, and noise pollution standards.

Class-action lawsuits may be filed under these statutes. A **class-action lawsuit** is a suit brought by a limited number of individuals on behalf of a much larger group. These particular lawsuits are brought against companies that pollute the air or water, that make excessive noise, or that have handled or use hazardous substances. The plaintiffs can claim personal injury damages or diminution in property values as a result of exposure to environmental hazards. The remedy in class-action suits is the recovery of money, rather than pollution control.

Some federal statutes give the government the exclusive right to file lawsuits for violations of environmental protection regulations. When the government has the exclusive right to sue, state governments and private parties are limited to assisting the federal authorities in the lawsuit.

Regulation by the Federal Government

Congress has changed its attitude toward the environment over the decades. In the first stage, described in the section titled "Historical Background," little was done to prevent environmental damage or to control pollution. The second stage began in the 1960s, when Congress enacted statutes aimed at environmental cleanup. In the third stage, Congress continued its interest in cleaning up the environment while expanding its focus toward the goal of preventing pollution in the first place. Keep in mind that all the federal statutes described in the following sections represent a financial or health cost to someone: the government, the business community, or the individual.

During the 1960s and 1970s, neither federal nor state governments brought many environmental criminal prosecutions. In the 1980s, this attitude changed and the change continues today. During the early 1980s, the Environmental Protection Agency, the U.S. Department of Justice (DOJ), and the offices of state attorneys general together established special units designed exclusively for the investigation and prosecution of environmental crimes.

Since 1982, the U.S. Department of Justice has brought more than 1,100 indictments for environmental crimes. Of this total, 825 plea bargains were entered into or a trial was held and convictions were obtained. A plea bargain is a process in criminal court in which the defendant bargains with the prosecutor to plead guilty, usually on a reduced charge compared to the original charge, such as pleading guilty to manslaughter when the original charge was murder. More than 430 years of prison time were imposed, of which 227 years were actually served. More than $254 million was paid in criminal fines. For example, Rockwell International was fined $18.5 million for hazardous waste and water quality criminal violations at the Rocky Flats nuclear weapons plant near Denver, Colorado. Exxon was fined $125 million for the Valdez, Alaska, oil spill. This spill was discussed in detail in Chapter 2.

National Environmental Policy Act

The **National Environmental Policy Act (NEPA)** of 1969 created the **Environmental Protection Agency (EPA)**.[1] The EPA makes the regulatory rules for the various federal environmental acts.

NEPA also mandated the **environmental impact statement (EIS)**. The EIS is undertaken by the particular federal agency that proposes to build or fund a project. For example, the Federal Bureau of Investigation (FBI) needs to construct a new building to house its fingerprinting center. The FBI must file an EIS that analyzes the impact on the environment of the proposed building. Every proposed major *federal* project or *federally* funded project must have an EIS. The EIS has become an instrument for private citizens, businesses, and federal agencies to help shape the final outcome of federal projects.

The EIS must contain (1) the environmental impact of the proposed action; (2) any adverse effects to the environment, along with alternative actions that might be taken; and (3) the irreversible effects that the action might create.

Air Pollution

Federal involvement with air pollution goes back to the 1950s, when Congress authorized funds for air pollution research. In 1963, Congress passed the **Clean Air Act**,[2] which focused on multistate air pollution and provided assistance to states for the implementation of antipollution measures. Various amendments over the years have strengthened the government's authority to regulate air quality. In 1990, Congress passed a sweeping overhaul of the Clean Air Act. The reform measures provided stronger cleanup provisions and formulated prevention measures.

Air pollution silently damages human and animal health, vegetation, lakes, and forests. The original act distinguished between two types of air pollutants. The first type causes death or serious illness at low levels and is discussed in the subsection titled *Air Toxics*. The second type are criteria pollutants, so named because the EPA must issue criteria documents identifying the effects of each pollutant. These pollutants are discussed in the subsection titled *National Ambient Air Quality Standards*.

Although both types of pollutants were included in the original Clean Air Act, the 1990 amendments gave the EPA more authority. In 1989, Congress found determined that more than 150 million people were still living in areas that failed to meet the air quality standards. The reasons for the failure to achieve healthy air are diverse.

State Implementation Plans.
Although the 1990 Clean Air Act is a federal law affecting the entire country, the states do much of the work to carry out the act. The EPA sets limits on the amounts of different pollutants that can be in the air anywhere in the United States. These limitations ensure that all Americans have the same basic environmental protections. The law allows individual states to set stronger pollution controls, but states are prohibited from adopting weaker pollution controls than those set by the EPA.

Each state must take a complete emissions inventory of all polluters, designating them as stationary or mobile. The law recognizes that states should take the lead in carrying out the Clean Air Act because pollution control problems often require special understanding of local industries, geography, housing patterns, traffic patterns, and climate conditions.

Although taking an emissions inventory sounds like a relatively easy task, sometimes the source of an

---

[1] The web site for the Environmental Protection Agency is <http://www.epa.gov>.

[2] A copy of the Clean Air Act can be obtained at <http://www.law.cornell.edu/uscode/42/7403.shtml>.

LEGAL HIGHLIGHT

Benefits and Costs of the Clean Air Act

Recently, the EPA conducted a study to estimate and report the benefits and costs of historical air pollution control programs under the Clean Air Act by comparing the differences between two scenarios: (1) an actual scenario reflecting historical economic and environmental conditions observed with the Clean Air Act in place and (2) a hypothetical scenario projecting the economic and environmental conditions that would have prevailed without the federal, state, and local programs developed pursuant to the goals of the 1970 and 1977 Clean Air Acts.

Using a sophisticated array of computer models, the EPA found that by 1990 the differences between the scenarios were so great that, under the so-called "no-control" case, an additional 205,000 Americans would have died prematurely and millions more would have suffered illnesses ranging from mild respiratory symptoms to heart disease, chronic bronchitis, asthma attacks, and other severe respiratory problems. In addition, the lack of Clean Air Act controls on leaded

gasoline use would have resulted in IQ (Intelligence Quotient) loss in children and major increases in hypertension, heart disease, and stroke in adults. Other quantified benefits expressed in dollar terms included visibility improvements, improvements in some agricultural crop yields, improved worker attendance and productivity, and reduced household soiling damage.

When the human health, human welfare, and environmental effects were added up for the entire twenty-year period, the total benefits of Clean Air Act programs were estimated to be about $6 trillion to about $50 trillion, with a mean estimate of about $22 trillion. These benefits represented the value Americans place on avoiding the dire air quality conditions and dramatic increases in illness and premature death that would have prevailed without the 1970 and 1977 Clean Air Acts and their associated state and local programs. By comparison, the actual costs of achieving the pollution reductions observed over the twenty-year period were $523 billion, a small price for the benefits received.

---

emission is elusive, such as dust sources, particularly in arid areas of the western United States. Air pollution often travels from its source in one state to another state. In many metropolitan areas, people live in one state and work or shop in another. Air pollution generated from cars and trucks as people and goods move about daily spreads throughout the interstate area. The Clean Air Act encourages the creation of interstate commissions to develop regional strategies for cleaning up air pollution.

Air pollution also moves across national borders. The law covers pollution that originates in Mexico and Canada and drifts into the United States and vice versa.

Under the Clean Air Act, each state was required to develop its own **state implementation plan (SIP)**. A SIP is a collection of state regulations for cleaning up polluted areas. The state must involve the public, through hearings and opportunities to comment, in the development of its SIP.

EPA approves each SIP, and if a SIP is unacceptable, the EPA can take over enforcement of the Clean Air

Act in that state. The EPA assists the states by providing scientific research, expert studies, engineering designs, and money to support clean air programs.

National Ambient Air Quality Standards.
The EPA uses six criteria pollutants as indicators of air quality.[3] The EPA has set a maximum concentration above which adverse effects on human health may occur. These threshold concentrations are called the **National Ambient Air Quality Standards (NAAQS)**. These standards set uniform, nationwide ambient air quality standards.

Primary ambient standards are adopted to protect public health. These standards set the lowest level of pollution at which an effect on health is observed and include a safety margin. Primary standards are based on

---

[3] More information about ozone and particulate matter and related programs can be found on the EPA's Office of Air Quality Planning and Standards web page: <http://www.epa.gov/oar/oaqps/>.

LEGAL HIGHLIGHT

Outer Continental Shelf Activities

Air pollution comes from unlikely sources, such as the outer continental shelf (OCS) activities. Translated, this term refers to offshore drilling and to ships causing emissions in excess of 500 tons of oxides of nitrogen (NOx) annually. The emissions from constructing one drilling platform are 350 tons of NOx.

Drilling a single exploration well can exceed 100 tons of NOx. A major offshore oil project easily exceeds the air pollution caused by 100,000 automobiles that meet 1988 California emission standards, each traveling 10,000 miles. The 1990 Clean Air Act marked the beginning of regulation of OCS activities. The standards for controlling this source of pollution are the same as those for similar onshore areas.

the impact of air quality on human health without consideration of the costs in attaining the standards.

Secondary ambient standards protect public welfare. These standards protect against adverse impacts on human welfare, such as visibility, vegetation, animals, wildlife, crops, buildings, transportation, and property. Secondary ambient standards must be attained within a reasonable time period.

The six criteria pollutants for which ambient standards have been set are ozone, lead, sulfur dioxide, particulates, nitrogen dioxide, and carbon monoxide. Three potentially critical pollutants are ozone, carbon monoxide, and particulates.

Ozone is fatal at high concentrations. Of the ozone people inhale, 90 percent is never exhaled. It reacts rapidly with cells and irritates and inflames the lungs. Nearly 58 million people in the United States live in areas with high ozone concentrations.

Carbon monoxide absorbs more readily into blood than does oxygen. Carbon monoxide displaces oxygen and threatens bodily functions. High concentrations are fatal. Because it poses particular harm to fetal development, pregnant women are especially at risk. Nearly 1.4 million pregnant women live in areas with high concentrations of carbon monoxide. Motor vehicles are the single largest source of ozone and carbon monoxide pollution. As a result, an annual $2 fee is assessed on motor vehicle registration in areas where the air quality fails to meet the standards.

Particulate matter measuring less than ten microns in diameter (PM-10) can produce a range of effects from temporary lung dysfunction to death. A micron is a unit of length equal to one-millionth of a meter. Particulates come from wood stoves, power station emissions, exhausts from diesel vehicles, and common dust.

Particulates impair visibility so much that the National Park Service reports that scenic views are visually impaired 90 percent of the time. People in the United States spend $40 billion per year in health-care costs because of particulate matter. Legislators anticipate that if the new air quality standards are met by the year 2003, the amount saved in health costs will offset the plan's estimated $2.79 billion in pollution control costs.

Attainment and Nonattainment Areas.

A geographic area that meets or does better than the National Ambient Air Quality Standards is called an **attainment area**. The Clean Air Act defines a **nonattainment area** as a locality where air pollution levels persistently exceed National Ambient Air Quality Standards.[4]

Designating an area nonattainment is a formal rule-making process and EPA normally takes this action only after the area exceeds air quality standards for several consecutive years. Nonattainment areas fall into one of five classifications based on the air pollution's severity: (1) marginal area, (2) moderate area, (3) serious area, (4) severe area, or (5) extreme area.

---

[4] The Clean Air Act and Amendments of 1990 define a "nonattainment area" as a locality where air pollution levels persistently exceed National Ambient Air Quality Standards. Designating an area nonattainment requires a formal rule-making process (see Chapter 6). The EPA normally takes this action only after air quality standards have been exceeded for several consecutive years. The EPA lists all the nonattainment sites at <http://www.epa.gov/airs/nonattn.html>.

LEGAL HIGHLIGHT

Even Lawn Mowers Pollute

Gasoline-powered lawn mowers, edgers, trimmers, and leaf blowers pollute the atmosphere. One gasoline-powered lawn mower used for one hour releases into the air as much pollution as thirty automobiles will release during the same time period. And if you live in Southern California, this makes for a lot of smog.

First seen in 1903, Los Angeles suffered a severe smog attack in 1947.[a] Deciding that it was time for action, Los Angeles created the Los Angeles County Air Pollution Control District. By 1953, a task force recommended the following steps be taken within Los Angeles County:

- Reduce hydrocarbon emissions by cutting vapor leaks from refineries and fueling operations.
- Establish automobile exhaust standards.
- Burn propane instead of diesel in trucks and buses.
- Slow the growth of heavily polluting industries.
- Ban open trash burning.
- Develop a rapid transit system.

The Air Pollution Control District evolved into the South Coast Air Quality Management District (AQMD).[b] It serves as the smog control agency for all or portions of Los Angeles, Orange, Riverside, and San Bernardino Counties, California, where 14 million people breathe the dirtiest air in the United States.

[a] In London, in December 1952, a killer smog so thick that residents could see no more than three feet claimed 4,000 lives.
[b] The Southern California AQMD web site is <http://www.aqmd.gov/>.

What actions does the AQMD recommend today for you to do?

- Purchase an electric or battery-powered lawn mower.
- Use water-based paints labeled "zero-VOC" (volatile organic compound) when painting homes. The lower the VOC content, the better.
- When reroofing a home, use a lighter shade of roofing material to reduce the need for air conditioning and cut electricity bills in the summer. Plant trees for shade.
- Fire up the barbecue briquettes with an electric probe instead of starter fluid, or use a barbecue fueled by natural gas or propane.
- Purchase high-fuel efficiency and low-emissions automobiles, or even an electric vehicle.
- When filling the car's gas tank, latch the nozzle on to avoid breathing toxic gasoline fumes. Avoid topping off the gas tank to prevent spilling fuel, a significant source of air pollution.
- Keep the car tuned.
- Car pool and consolidate errands whenever possible to reduce driving.
- Report smoking vehicles, faulty gasoline nozzles, and industrial or commercial polluters suspected of violating air quality regulations to the proper authorities.

Although the Los Angeles area still suffers from smog, the air is cleaner than it has been for decades.

Market Approaches. The 1990 Clean Air Act includes many features designed to clean up air pollution as efficiently and inexpensively as possible. The act encourages businesses to choose the best ways to reach pollution cleanup goals. These new flexible programs are called market-based approaches. For instance, the acid rain cleanup program offers businesses choices of methods for reaching their pollution reduction goals and includes pollution allowances that can be traded, bought, and sold. Gasoline refiners receive credits for producing cleaner gasoline than required, which they can use when their gasoline fails to meet cleanup requirements.

The federal government allows companies that pollute, such as utilities, a limited ability to pollute. Otherwise, the electrical utilities in some major metropolitan areas would have to cease operations. But sometimes these limited allowances are insufficient to cover actual pollution so a utility is allowed a number of credits to trade for a limited ability to continue to pollute.

Comparison of two companies, Clean Utility and Dirty Utility, illustrates the trading market operation. Clean Utility has installed emission control and therefore releases only small amounts of pollution. Dirty Utility has not yet been able to afford the costly pollution controls. Under the regulations, both utilities can pollute up to 100 tons of sulfur dioxide a year. Clean Utility releases only 10 tons per year, while Dirty Utility releases 150 tons. Dirty Utility can release 100 tons legally, and can purchase credits for the other 50 tons. Clean Utility can sell credits for the 90 tons that it does not release because of the pollution controls it installed.

These credits are traded on the Chicago Board of Trade. Recently, the credits rose from $68.14 to $110.36 for each ton that is discharged into the atmosphere. Trading of these credits gives a business an additional reason to install antipollution equipment.

Air Toxics. Hazardous air pollutants are toxic and generally cancer causing. Toxic releases from major manufacturing facilities amount to approximately 2.7 billion pounds a year. Cancer incidences may be as high as 500,000 fatal cases for Americans alive in 1992.

In 1985, in Institute, West Virginia, the Union Carbide plant had an accidental toxic release one year after the Bhopal incident (discussed in detail in Chapter 2). An Occupational Safety and Health Administration (OSHA) investigation discovered 221 safety and health violations at Union Carbide's Institute plant. OSHA imposed a fine of $1.38 million for willful disregard of health and safety.

Accidental releases of extremely hazardous substances during a recent four-year period caused 309 deaths, 11,341 injuries, and the evacuation of 464,677 people from homes and jobs. Seventy percent of the events occurred at stationary facilities, and 30 percent were related to transportation.

As a result of the harm caused by air toxics, the EPA established a list of hazardous air pollutants, and the list can be amended as needed. A national air toxics clearinghouse was established to coordinate and disseminate information.

Acid Rain. Acid rain is extremely corrosive and can damage humans and materials. It can dissolve heavy metals and destroy materials such as stone, rubber, zinc, steel, leather, and paint. Congress convened a task force to investigate acid rain and to study the impact of acid rain on bodies of water, forests, and crops.

Ozone Layer and Climate Protection. The earth's main shield against the sun's harmful ultraviolet radiation is the ozone layer. Scientific evidence now shows that this layer is being destroyed. At the same time, global warming, commonly called the *greenhouse effect*, has been detected. The national goal is to correct these two problems.

First, the government has programs in place to eliminate the emissions that destroy the ozone layer (for example, chlorofluorocarbon-based automobile refrigerants will no longer be manufactured). Second, the emissions that have led to, and that perpetuate, the warming of the climate are being reduced.

The EPA has issued standards to protect the ozone. The most recent standards are based on averaging air quality over an eight-hour block of time instead of the one-hour used previously. This new standard helps protect people who spend significant time outdoors. The air quality standard is an average concentration of pollutants over an eight-hour period during a week, month, or year.

Enforcement. The EPA can issue administrative citations for which the penalties can go up to $200,000 in any given case. Criminal liability can be imposed for unlawful releases of toxic pollutants, including negligent releases.[5] The Office of Enforcement and Compliance Assurance (OECA) works in partnership with EPA regional offices, state governments, tribal governments, and other federal agencies to ensure compliance with the nation's environmental laws. Employing an integrated approach of compliance assistance, compliance incentives, and innovative civil and criminal enforcement, OECA and its partners seek to maximize compliance and reduce threats to public health and the environment.

[5] The Office of Regulatory Enforcement (ORE) is located within the EPA. The ORE's web site is located at <http://es.epa.gov/oeca/>. Some penalties that have been imposed are available for review at <http://www.epa.gov/ozone/enforce>.

LEGAL HIGHLIGHT

Enforcement by EPA

The Environmental Protection Agency regulates approximately 8 million government and business sources of potential pollution. The EPA has a number of devices to ensure compliance that are backed by a program of compliance monitoring and civil and criminal penalties. In a partnership with the state governments, the EPA has delegated enforcement to state and local government. On average, the states conduct 80 percent of the inspections and are responsible for 84 percent of the formal enforcement actions.

In 1999, the EPA conducted 21,410 inspections and started 3,935 civil judicial and administrative enforcement actions. As a result of its enforcement program, 6.8 billion pounds of pollutants were not placed in the environment. Polluters spent more than $3.6 billion to correct violations and to take the steps necessary to prevent further pollution.

Some examples are the following:

- The EPA and the Department of Justice announced a settlement with seven manufacturers of diesel engines. Although the engines were set to meet the EPA requirements and were tested at that setting, the manufacturers advised purchasers (trucking companies, bus companies, and other users) on how to readjust the engine settings. At the new settings, the engines polluted the air. The settlement will prevent 75 million tons of harmful pollutants from entering the atmosphere between the years 1999 and 2025. The manufacturers paid a $83.4 million penalty, the largest civil penalty ever for violations of environmental laws.

- The EPA and the state of Georgia reached a settlement with the city of Atlanta. The city paid a civil penalty of $700,000 and agreed to bring its sewer system into compliance with the Clean Water Act and the Georgia Water Quality Control Act. Atlanta is implementing a $27.5 million program to create a greenway corridor and to clean up various streams. Lastly, Atlanta paid a $2.5 million penalty, the largest Clean Water Act penalty ever assessed against a municipality.

- Royal Caribbean Cruises, Ltd., pled guilty to twenty-one violations and paid an $18 million for violating the Clean Water Act and the Oil Pollution Act. Video-toting passengers captured a number of violations on videotape, including the dumping of waste oil and hazardous chemicals into the ocean. Royal Caribbean also made false statements to the Coast Guard. The cruise line agreed to institute a five-year environmental compliance plan.

- The EPA has an audit policy. If a company conducts an audit and discovers violations, it can self-report those problems and can apply for penalty relief. The EPA granted relief to GTE after more than 600 Emergency Planning and Community Right-to-Know Act and Spill Prevention Control and Countermeasures violations at 314 GTE facilities in twenty-one states were reported. It was the largest EPA settlement reached through the EPA's self-disclosure policy. Seventeen telecommunications companies found, disclosed, and corrected more than 2,000 environmental violations at more than 600 facilities nationwide.

The EPA operates nine Compliance Assistance Centers designed to help small businesses and small governmental entities, such as towns and counties, to comply with their obligations under the environmental laws. The centers offer plain English summaries of the regulations and provides a number technical resources. A survey of those covered reflected positive results. More than 50 percent reported a cost savings and more than 75 percent indicated environmental improvements. More than 80 percent found the centers to be useful in understanding environmental regulations.

Water Pollution

Federal regulations governing water pollution can be traced back over a century to the **Rivers and Harbors Act** of 1886, amended in 1890 and in 1899.

These regulations required a permit for discharging or depositing refuse in navigable waterways. The courts determined that even hot water can be considered refuse because it affects fish and aquatic plant life.

Clean Water Regulation. The most important and comprehensive legislation plan to eliminate pollution in our waters took place in 1972. The 1972 **Clean Water Act** established these goals: (1) to make waters safe for swimming, (2) to protect fish and wildlife, and (3) to eliminate the discharge of pollutants into the water. Regulations for the most part specify that businesses and governments install the best available technology.

The act requires both municipal and industrial dischargers to apply for permits before they discharge wastes into the nation's navigable waters. The act also confers legal standing on citizens (or organizations) when their interests are affected by parties that violate EPA or state standards. Both injunctive relief and damages can be sought through claims under the act. Like the Clean Air Act, anyone bringing legal action under this Act may not obtain damages personally. All damages that are recovered are required to be turned over to the federal government. The following case involves private parties filing an action against a polluter of water.

Case 24.2

Friends of the Earth, Inc. v. Laidlaw Environmental Services, Inc.

Supreme Court of the United States, 2000
528 U.S. 120, 120 S. Ct. 693,
145 L. Ed. 2d 610
http://supct.law.cornell.edu
/supct/html/98-822.ZS.html

BACKGROUND AND FACTS The defendant, Laidlaw Environmental Services, Inc., purchased a hazardous waste incinerator facility in South Carolina, that included a wastewater treatment plant. Shortly after Laidlaw acquired the facility, the South Carolina Department of Health and Environmental Control (DHEC) granted Laidlaw a permit authorizing the company to discharge treated water into the North Tyger River.

The permit placed limits on Laidlaw's discharge of pollutants into the river, including mercury, an extremely toxic pollutant. Once the permit was received, Laidlaw began to discharge pollutants into the waterway; repeatedly, Laidlaw's discharges exceeded the limits set by the permit.

Friends of the Earth, Inc. (FOE), took the preliminary step necessary to filing suit. A letter was sent to Laidlaw notifying the company of FOE's intention to file a citizen suit against it under the act after the expiration of the requisite sixty-day notice period. Shortly thereafter, Laidlaw's lawyer contacted DHEC to ask whether DHEC would consider filing a lawsuit against Laidlaw.

Laidlaw's reason for requesting that DHEC file a lawsuit against it was to bar FOE's proposed citizen suit. DHEC agreed to file a lawsuit against Laidlaw; the company's lawyer drafted the complaint for DHEC and paid the filing fee. On the last day before FOE's sixty-day notice period expired, DHEC and Laidlaw reached a settlement requiring Laidlaw to pay $100,000 in civil penalties and to make "every effort" to comply with its permit obligations.

FOE filed a citizen suit against Laidlaw alleging noncompliance with the National Pollutant Discharge Elimination System (NPDES) permit and seeking an award of civil penalties. Laidlaw moved to dismiss the action on the ground that the citizen suit was barred by DHEC's prior action against the company. The district court held that DHEC's action against Laidlaw had not been "diligently prosecuted"; consequently, the court allowed FOE's citizen suit to proceed. The district court found that Laidlaw had violated the mercury limits on 489 occasions between 1987 and 1995 and further found that after FOE initiated the suit, but before the court rendered its judgment, Laidlaw violated the mercury discharge limitation in its permit 13 more times.

The district court found that Laidlaw had gained a total economic benefit of $1,092,581 as a result of its extended period of noncompliance with the mercury discharge limit in its permit. The court imposed a civil penalty of $405,800. The district court stated that the penalty was appropriate, taking into account the judgment's "total deterrent effect." In reaching this determination, the court "considered that Laidlaw will be required to reimburse plaintiffs for a significant amount of legal fees."

FOE appealed the civil penalty judgment, arguing that the penalty was inadequate. Laidlaw cross-appealed, arguing that FOE lacked standing to bring the suit and that DHEC's action qualified as a diligent prosecution precluding FOE's litigation.

The Court of Appeals for the Fourth Circuit . . . held that the case had become moot. The appellate court held that the elements of standing—injury, causation, and redressability—must persist at every stage of review or else the action becomes moot. The court of appeals reasoned that the case had become moot because the only remedy available was civil penalties payable to the government and that payment would not redress any injury FOE suffered.

After the court of appeals issued its decision but before the Supreme Court granted *certiorari,* the entire incinerator facility in Roebuck was permanently closed, dismantled, and put up for sale, and all discharges from the facility permanently ceased. Laidlaw, however, did not surrender its permit.

The U.S. Supreme Court granted *certiorari.* The Court discussed whether the case was moot and whether FOE had standing to sue.

Justice GINSBURG delivered the opinion of the Court.

. . . .

This case presents an important question concerning the operation of the citizen-suit provisions of the Clean Water Act. . . . In the Clean Water Act citizen suit now before us, the District Court . . . assess[ed] a civil penalty of $405,800. The "total deterrent effect" of the penalty would be adequate to forestall future violations, the court reasoned, taking into account that the defendant "will be required to reimburse plaintiffs for a significant amount of legal fees and has, itself, incurred significant legal expenses."

. . . .

We reverse the judgment of the Court of Appeals. The appellate court erred in concluding that a citizen suitor's claim for civil penalties must be dismissed as moot when the defendant, albeit after commencement of the litigation, has come into compliance. . . . A defendant's voluntary cessation of allegedly unlawful conduct ordinarily does not suffice to moot a case. . . .

. . . .

In *Lujan v. Defenders of Wildlife,* we held that, to satisfy Article III's standing requirements, a plaintiff must show (1) it has suffered an "injury in fact" that is (a) concrete and particularized and (b) actual or imminent, not conjectural or hypothetical; (2) the injury is fairly traceable to the challenged action of the defendant; and (3) it is likely, as opposed to merely speculative, that the injury will be redressed by a favorable decision. An association has standing to bring suit on behalf of its members when its members would otherwise have standing to sue in their own right, the interests at stake are germane to the organization's purpose, and neither the claim asserted nor the relief requested requires the participation of individual members in the lawsuit.

Laidlaw contends first that FOE lacked standing from the outset . . . because the plaintiff organizations failed to show that any of their members had sustained or faced the threat of any "injury in fact" from Laidlaw's activities. In support of this contention Laidlaw points to the District Court's finding, made in the course of setting the penalty amount, that there had been "no demonstrated proof of harm to the environment" from Laidlaw's mercury discharge violations. . . .

The relevant showing for purposes of Article III standing, however, is not injury to the environment but injury to the plaintiff. To insist upon the former rather than the latter as part of the standing inquiry is to raise the standing hurdle higher than the necessary showing for success on the merits in an action alleging noncompliance with an NPDES permit. Focusing properly on injury to the plaintiff, the District Court found that FOE had demonstrated sufficient injury to establish standing. For example, FOE member Kenneth Lee Curtis averred in affidavits that he lived a half-mile from Laidlaw's facility; that he occasionally drove over the North Tyger River, and that it looked and smelled polluted; and that he would like to fish, camp, swim, and picnic in and near the river between 3 and 15 miles downstream from the facility, as he did when he was a teenager, but would not do so because he was concerned that the water was polluted by Laidlaw's discharges. . . .

Other members presented evidence to similar effect. . . .

. . . .

. . . Here, the civil penalties sought by FOE carried with them a deterrent effect that made it likely, as opposed to merely speculative, that the penalties would redress FOE's injuries by abating current violations and preventing future ones—as the District Court reasonably found when it assessed a penalty of $405,800.

. . . .

Satisfied that FOE had standing under Article III to bring this action, we turn to the question of mootness.

The only conceivable basis for a finding of mootness in this case is Laidlaw's voluntary conduct—either its achievement by August 1992 of substantial compliance with its NPDES permit or its more recent shutdown of the Roebuck facility. It is well settled that a defendant's voluntary cessation of a challenged practice does not deprive a federal court of its power to determine the legality of the practice. "[I]f it did, the courts would be compelled to leave '[t]he defendant . . . free to return to his old ways.'" In accordance with this principle, the standard we have announced for determining whether a case has been mooted by the defendant's voluntary conduct is stringent: "A case might become moot if subsequent events made it absolutely clear that the allegedly wrongful behavior could not reasonably be expected to recur." The "heavy burden of persua[ding]" the court that the challenged conduct cannot reasonably be expected to start up again lies with the party asserting mootness.

The Court of Appeals justified its mootness disposition by reference to *Steel Co.,* which held that citizen plaintiffs lack standing to seek civil penalties for wholly past violations. In relying on *Steel Co.,* the Court of Appeals confused mootness with standing. The confusion is understandable, given this Court's repeated statements that the doctrine of mootness can be described as "the doctrine of standing set in a time frame: The requisite personal interest that must exist at the commencement of the litigation (standing) must continue throughout its existence (mootness)."

. . . .

Standing doctrine functions to ensure, among other things, that the scarce resources of the federal courts are devoted to those disputes in which the parties have a concrete stake. In contrast, by the time mootness is an issue, the case has been brought and litigated, often (as here) for years. To abandon the case at an advanced stage may prove more wasteful than frugal. This argument from sunk costs does not license courts to retain jurisdiction over cases in which one or both of the parties plainly lacks a continuing interest, as when the parties have settled or a plaintiff pursuing a nonsurviving claim has died. . . .

. . . .

Laidlaw also asserts, in a supplemental suggestion of mootness, that the closure of its Roebuck facility, which took place after the Court of Appeals issued its decision, mooted the case. The facility closure, like Laidlaw's earlier achievement of substantial compliance with its permit requirements, might moot the case, but—we once more reiterate—only if one or the other of these events made it absolutely clear that Laidlaw's permit violations could not reasonably be expected to recur. The effect of both Laidlaw's compliance and the facility closure on the prospect of future violations is a disputed factual matter. FOE points out, for example—and Laidlaw does not appear to contest—that Laidlaw retains its NPDES permit. These issues have not been aired in the lower courts; they remain open for consideration on remand.

DECISION AND REMEDY The Court found that even with Laidlaw closing the plant, the case was not moot. The Court found that the FOE satisfied the requirements to bring an action under the Clean Water Act and left it to the trial court to determine the civil penalties.

CRITICAL THINKING: POLITICAL QUESTION Why do you think that the government has not banned all pollution? After all, this would save our planet. Explain your answer.

Oil Pollution. In 1990, the **Oil Pollution Act** was signed into law. The act is a result of the *Exxon Valdez* oil spill off the Alaskan shore and other spills that occurred during the same period. Spills containing a variety of polluting elements happened to the Delaware River, the Arthur Kill, Montana's Whitefish Lake, the southern California coast, and Galveston Bay. Both the EPA and the U.S. Coast Guard have responsibilities under this act.

The strict liability limit increased eightfold. For a spill equivalent to that of the *Exxon Valdez,* the liability cap has been increased from $14.3 million to $114 million under the act. This liability is in addition to damages that may be awarded under other theories. Liability now covers cleanup costs, natural resource damages, losses to subsistence resources, and costs to local government.

The $1 billion Oil Spill Liability Trust Fund (OSLTF), established under the act, is financed by oil companies. The OSLTF is used for costs not directly paid by a responsible party and for "mystery spills" when the responsible party cannot be identified. In the future, new oil tankers must be double hulled, and single-hulled tankers are scheduled to be phased out by 2015. The statute also established the Oil Spill Recovery Institute, a research center.

Quality Standards. Every day millions of gallons of wastewater flow into effluent treatment plants, are cleaned, and are returned to navigable streams. Today, the quality standard for the water leaving the treatment plants is higher than that applied to drinking water supplied to homes. A higher cleaning standard also has been imposed for water containing toxic wastes than for water with normal pollutants.

Wetlands. Land that lies between solid land and open bodies of water, such as lakes, large rivers, or the ocean, is designated as wetlands. Often under water, wetlands are home to wildlife and birds.

In the past, wetlands were filled in by developers, and homes and businesses were built on the filled wetlands. Today, a permit issued by the Army Corps of Engineers is necessary to fill in wetlands. The following case involves an agency representing municipalities that wanted to fill in wetlands with nonhazardous solid wastes.

Case 24.3

Solid Waste Agency of Northern Cook County v. U.S. Army Corps of Engineers

Supreme Court of the United States, 2001

531 U.S. 159, 121 S. Ct. 675, 148 L. Ed. 2d 576

BACKGROUND AND FACTS   Petitioner, the Solid Waste Agency of Northern Cook County (SWANCC), was a consortium of twenty-three suburban Chicago cities and villages that united in an effort to locate and develop a disposal site for nonhazardous solid waste. SWANCC found a 533-acre parcel, which had been the site of a sand and gravel pit mining operation for three decades until 1960. Long since abandoned, a forest grew over the old mining site and its excavation trenches evolved into scattered permanent and seasonal ponds of varying size.

The municipalities decided to purchase the site for disposal of their nonhazardous solid waste. By law, SWANCC was required to file for various permits from Cook County and the state of Illinois before it could begin operation. In addition, because the operation called for the filling of some of the permanent and seasonal ponds, SWANCC contacted the U.S. Army Corps of Engineers (Corps) to determine if a federal landfill permit was required under § 404(a) of the Clean Water Act (CWA).

Section 404(a) grants the Corps authority to issue permits "for the discharge of dredged or fill material into the navigable waters at specified disposal sites." The term "navigable waters" is defined under the act as "the waters of the United States, including the territorial seas." The Corps has issued regulations defining the term "waters of the United States" to include

waters such as intrastate lakes, rivers, streams (including intermittent streams), mudflats, sandflats, wetlands, sloughs, prairie potholes, wet meadows, playa lakes, or natural ponds, the use, degradation or destruction of which could affect interstate or foreign commerce. . . . 33 CFR § 328.3(a)(3) (1999).

In an attempt to "clarify" the reach of its jurisdiction, the Corps stated in its Migratory Bird Rule that § 404(a) extends to intrastate waters:

a. Which are or would be used as habitat by birds protected by Migratory Bird Treaties; or

b. Which are or would be used as habitat by other migratory birds which cross state lines; or

c. Which are or would be used as habitat for endangered species; or

d. Used to irrigate crops sold in interstate commerce.

The Corps initially concluded that it had no jurisdiction over the site because it contained no "wetlands." After the Illinois Nature Preserves Commission informed the Corps that a number of migratory bird species had been observed at the site, the Corps reconsidered and ultimately asserted jurisdiction over the site pursuant to subpart (b) of the Migratory Bird Rule. The Corps found that approximately 121 bird species had been observed at the site, including several known to depend on aquatic environments for a significant portion of their life requirements. Thus, on November 16, 1987, the Corps formally "determined that the seasonally ponded, abandoned gravel mining depressions located on the project site, while not wetlands, did qualify as 'waters of the United States' . . . based upon the following criteria: (1) the proposed site had been abandoned as a gravel mining operation; (2) the water areas and spoil piles had developed a natural character; and (3) the water areas are used as habitat by migratory bird [sic] which cross state lines."

SWANCC filed suit in federal district court challenging both the Corps' jurisdiction over the site. The district court granted summary judgment to respondents on the jurisdictional issue. On appeal to the Court of Appeals for the Seventh Circuit, SWANCC renewed its attack on respondents' use of the Migratory Bird Rule to assert jurisdiction over the site. SWANCC argued that respondents had exceeded their statutory authority in interpreting the Clean Water Act (CWA) to cover nonnavigable, isolated, intrastate waters based on the presence of migratory birds and, in the alternative, that Congress lacked the power under the commerce clause to grant such regulatory jurisdiction.

The Court of Appeals held that under the constitution the Congress has the authority to regulate such waters based on "the cumulative impact doctrine, under which a single activity that itself has no discernible effect on interstate commerce may still be regulated if the aggregate effect of that class of activity has a substantial impact on interstate commerce." The aggregate effect of the "destruction of the natural habitat of migratory birds" on interstate commerce, the court held, was substantial because each year millions of Americans cross state lines and spend more than a billion dollars to hunt and observe migratory birds. The court of appeals then turned to the regulatory question. The court held that the CWA reaches as many waters as the commerce clause allows and, given its earlier commerce clause ruling, it therefore followed that respondents' Migratory Bird Rule was a reasonable interpretation of the act.

SWANCC filed with the U.S. Supreme Court, which granted *certiorari*.

Chief Justice REHNQUIST delivered the opinion of the Court.

. . . .

Where an administrative interpretation of a statute invokes the outer limits of Congress' power, we expect a clear indication that Congress intended that result. This requirement stems from our prudential desire not to needlessly reach constitutional issues and our assumption that Congress does not casually authorize administrative agencies to interpret a statute to push the limit of congressional authority. This concern is heightened where the administrative interpretation alters the federal–state framework by permitting federal encroachment upon a traditional state power. ("[U]nless Congress conveys its purpose clearly, it will not be deemed to have significantly changed the federal–state balance"). Thus, "where an otherwise acceptable construction of a statute would raise serious constitutional problems, the Court will construe the statute to avoid such problems unless such construction is plainly contrary to the intent of Congress."

Twice in the past six years we have reaffirmed the proposition that the grant of authority to Congress under the Commerce Clause, though broad, is not unlimited. Respondents argue that the "Migratory Bird Rule" falls within Congress' power to regulate intrastate activities that "substantially affect" interstate commerce. They note that the protection of migratory birds is a "national interest of very nearly the first magnitude," and that, as the Court of Appeals found, millions of people spend over a billion dollars annually on recreational pursuits relating to migratory birds. These arguments raise significant constitutional questions. For example, we would have to evaluate the precise object or activity that, in the aggregate, substantially affects interstate commerce. This is not clear, for although the Corps has claimed jurisdiction over petitioner's land because it contains water areas used as habitat by migratory birds, respondents now, post litem motam, focus upon the fact that the regulated activity is petitioner's municipal landfill, which is "plainly of a commercial nature." But this is a far cry, indeed, from the "navigable waters" and "waters of the United States" to which the statute by its terms extends.

These are significant constitutional questions raised by respondents' application of their regulations, and yet we find nothing approaching a clear statement from Congress that it intended § 404(a) to reach an abandoned sand and gravel pit such as we have here. Permitting respondents to claim federal jurisdiction over ponds and mudflats falling within the "Migratory Bird Rule" would result in a significant impingement of the States' traditional and primary power over land and water use. Rather than expressing a desire to readjust the federal–state balance in this manner, Congress chose to "recognize, preserve, and protect the primary responsibilities and rights of States . . . to plan the development and use . . . of land and water resources . . . ." We thus read the statute as written to avoid the significant constitutional and federalism questions raised by respondents' interpretation, and therefore reject the request for administrative deference.

. . . .

DECISION AND REMEDY The Court held that the Migratory Bird Rule exceeded the authority granted to the U.S. Army Corps of Engineers. The water involved here was not a navigable waterway in that this was solely an intrastate waterway with no ability to navigate it.

CRITICAL THINKING: POLITICAL ISSUE In the past, when deciding issues involving interstate commerce, the U.S. Supreme Court has upheld federal statutes and administrative rules by looking at the governed area in the aggregate. In this case, the U.S. Supreme Court did not follow this approach. Do you think the Court adequately explained why it did not follow this concept?

Other Regulations. In 1972, Congress passed the **Marine Protection, Research, and Sanctuaries Act.** This act established a system of permits that regulates the discharge and introduction of materials into coastal waters and continuous marine areas.

The **Safe Drinking Water Act** of 1974 authorized the EPA to establish standards for safe drinking water purity. All owners or operators of public water systems must comply with health-related standards. The law focuses on all waters actually or potentially designated for use for drinking water, whether located aboveground or underground. The rules, which are similar to those of the Clean Water Act, provide that states assume the primary responsibility for complying with national standards. The federal government assumes responsibility if states fail to institute or enforce drinking water standards. In most cases, explicit penalties are imposed on parties that pollute the water. The polluting party also can be required to clean up the pollution or to pay the cost of doing so.

Nuclear Wastes

Millions of pounds of nuclear waste, in both liquid and solid form, are generated each year. Most of this waste is radioactive and will remain dangerous for thousands

of years. In 1982, Congress passed the **Nuclear Waste Policy Act (NWPA).** This act required the building of a permanent repository for the disposal of spent nuclear fuel and high-level wastes. In the meantime, Congress provided that a monitored retrievable storage (MRS) facility could be built as a temporary measure until the permanent site was developed.

Shore Protection

In the 1980s, medical wastes, such as needles and bandages, washed ashore on New Jersey beaches crowded with bathers. Soon other reports of such garbage washing ashore caused the local governments to react quickly by closing the beaches. Federal statutes now forbid the indiscriminate disposal into the oceans of potentially infectious medical waste. Regulations provide for proper disposal.

Similarly, Congress passed a statute, entitled the **Shore Protection Act**[6] of 1988, that controls the disposal of solid wastes in oceans and lakes. The act created a permit system to track and control the solid

---

[6] A copy of this act can be obtained at <http://www.law.cornell.edu/uscode/33/2601.shtml>.

waste as it is transported to its final place of disposal. The law also provides for study and recommendations as this problem grows.[7]

Noise Pollution

In 1972, Congress prescribed standards and regulations for the control of aircraft noise, including sonic booms, and the control of sound emissions of railroad and motor vehicles involved in interstate commerce. The **Noise Control Act** of 1972 established the goal of creating an environment free from noise that injures public health and welfare. The courts ruled that local noise control is preempted when state regulations conflict with those established by federal statutes.

The Federal Aviation Administration, the Environmental Protection Agency, and the Department of Transportation administer regulations under the Noise Control Act. The EPA, for example, can establish noise emission levels for equipment, motors, and engines. It also reviews production processes, verifies reports for compliance with the law, conducts audit tests, and inspects manufacturers' records.

Toxic Substances

The **Toxic Substances Control Act**[8] was passed in 1976. This law requires the EPA to track more than 75,000 industrial chemicals produced or imported into the U.S. The EPA can investigate harmful effects from new chemical compounds. Manufacturers, processors, and other organizations planning to use chemicals are required to first determine their effect on human health and the environment. The EPA regulates those toxic substances that potentially create a hazard or an unreasonable risk of injury. This act supplements the Clean Air Act.

Pesticide and Herbicide Control

The use of chemical pesticides to kill insects and herbicides to kill weeds has significantly increased agricultural productivity. A growing body of evidence,

however, shows that the environment has failed to absorb residuals from these chemicals. In some cases, buildups of residuals have killed animals. Some potential long-term effects detrimental to the public also have been identified.

The original regulations governing pesticides were established by the **Federal Insecticide, Fungicide, and Rodenticide Act** of 1947, as amended in 1972 by the **Federal Environmental Pesticide Control Act**. The Environmental Protection Agency requires that pesticides cannot cause unreasonable harm to the environment.

Pesticides must be (1) registered before they can be sold; (2) certified, labeled, and used only for approved applications; and (3) used in amounts that meet established limits when they are applied to crops that provide food for animals or people. The EPA also inspects manufacturing establishments. In some situations, it controls the supply of pesticides to keep hazardous chemicals off the market. Substances that are identified as harmful are subject to suspension and cancellation of registration. The applicators of pesticides must take an examination before being certified to use and apply these chemicals.

Waste Disposal

Waste disposal can occur on the land, in the water, or in the air. Thus, regulations protecting these resources from pollution also apply to waste disposal. In 1965, Congress passed the **Solid Waste Disposal Act**, an act designed to reduce solid waste disposal by encouraging the recycling of waste and the reuse of materials by society. The act encourages the development and use of technology that converts garbage into useful products.

The **Resource Conservation and Recovery Act (RCRA)** of 1976, as amended in 1984, governs EPA studies and recommendations on solid waste disposal, ranging from glass and plastic waste to landfill used at airports. The RCRA provides a cradle-to-grave (from creation to disposal) tracking system of hazardous waste. Both the federal and state governments regulate companies that generate, store, transport, dispose of, or handle hazardous waste at any time. The EPA issues permits for, and conducts on-site inspections of, hazardous waste facilities.

RCRA was amended by the **Hazardous and Solid Waste Amendments (HSWA)** in 1984.

[7] The Office of Ocean and Coastal Resource Management mission is to effectively manage multiple uses of the nation's coastal and ocean resources. Its web address is <http://www.ocrm.nos.noaa.gov/welcome.html>.

[8] The full act is available at <http://www.law.cornell.edu/uscode/15/2601.shtml>.

HSWA required the phasing out of the land disposal of hazardous waste. The act provides for stringent hazardous waste management standards and a comprehensive underground storage tank program.

In 1980, Congress passed the **Comprehensive Environmental Response, Compensation, and Liability Act (CERCLA)**,[9] commonly known as the Superfund. When hazardous waste finds its way into the soil, the polluter must pay for the land to be cleaned up to drinking water standards. In other words, after the cleanup, a person should be able to drink the water that comes from the ground. If the polluter cannot be found, the Superfund monies are used to clean up the site. The trust fund is mandated to be at $8.5 billion. Residential property is exempt from this act.

In 1986, the Superfund law was amended by the **Emergency Planning and Community Right-to-Know Act (EPCRA)** to increase the information about the presence of hazardous chemicals in communities and their release into the environment. Each state appoints a State Emergency Response Commission (SERC) to plan a response to such a hazardous release.

The polluter comes from one of these categories: (1) the generator of the wastes disposed of at the site; (2) the transporter of the wastes to the site; (3) the owner or the tenant who operated the site at the time of the waste disposal; (4) the current owner and operator of the site; or (5) a lending institution, if it managed the property. Companies are liable for their past actions in waste disposal.

In the past, the Superfund mandated a strict and harsh liability standard. Multiple defendants had *joint and several liability*, which means that one or more of the responsible parties may be sued. If the court renders a money judgment on the plaintiff's behalf, the

money may be collected from one or all of the wrongdoers. Usually, the defendants jointly pay their respective share of the judgment. At other times, a company that is responsible for only a fraction of the share of the judgment may be held liable to pay all of the judgment. This happens when the other codefendants are unable to pay their share.

As a result of the harshness of strict liability, a number of reforms were adopted. Today, a polluter pays a proportional cost of the cleanup in a ratio to its degree of fault. The government rarely pursues a small-volume polluter. Any monies collected by the government for polluting a particular site is spent on cleaning up that site.

Heavy pesticide use, leaking underground storage tanks (LUST), and general waste disposal have made real property subject to cleanup. The practical effect of this law is seen in the purchase of real property. Under the act, the land's owner is liable and must clean it up. Cleanup costs may range from a few hundred dollars to millions. Today, a lending institution requires verification that the soil is free from contamination before it lends money for a buyer to purchase the property. Additionally, before the lender repossesses any property, it must verify that no environmental problems exist.

Three defenses exist: (1) act of God, (2) act of war, and (3) act of a third party (an innocent purchaser can use this defense). A property owner will not be liable if someone dumps hazardous waste on the property without permission. The innocent purchaser defense occurs when a person purchases property without knowledge of, or without reason to know of, the hazardous waste already on the property.

In the following case, a current land owner seeks damages from the prior owner under the Superfund provisions. The property was purchased in 1977 and the CERCLA statute was passed in 1980. Even though no law existed when the property was sold, the CERCLA statute applied retroactively to the land's seller.

---

[9] A copy of this act can be obtained at <http://www.law.cornell.edu/uscode/42/9601.shtml>.

Case 24.4

Amoco Oil Co. v. Borden, Inc.

United States Court of
Appeals, Fifth Circuit, 1989
889 F.2d 664

BACKGROUND AND FACTS In 1977, Amoco Oil Company wanted to purchase certain property from Borden, Inc. The parties discussed two prices: $1.8 million for the site "as is" or $2.2 million if Borden removed the phosphogypsum, a combination of phosphorus and gypsum, a by-product of the fertilizer manufacturing process. Amoco accepted the "as is" option.

The Texas Department of Water Resources informed Amoco that phosphogypsum is radioactive. Amoco hired several consultants to measure the radioactivity. The consultants' reports revealed various elevated radiation levels throughout the site. The site was secured with fences and guards to prevent access. Amoco claimed that cleanup costs would be between $11 million and $17 million.

Amoco sued Borden on a number of counts, including sharing liability under the Superfund (CERCLA). Borden's primary defenses against liability were (1) that the levels of radiation emanating from the site were not high enough to be considered a release of a hazardous substance within the meaning of CERCLA and (2) that the property was sold "as is" and that this fact and the doctrine of caveat emptor precluded a finding of liability.

Circuit Judges BROWN, REAVLEY, and HIGGINBOTHAM

. . . .

The term "release" is defined to mean: any spilling, leaking, pumping, pouring, emitting, emptying, discharging, injecting, escaping, leaching, dumping, or disposing into the environment (including the abandonment or discarding of barrels, containers, and other closed receptacles containing any hazardous substance or pollutant or contaminant).

. . . .

Borden's actions met the release requirement in two ways. First, it did so by disposing of the phosphogypsum and highly radioactive wastes on the property. . . . Second, the gas emanating from the radionuclides constitutes a release within the meaning of the statute. . . .

. . . .

It is undisputed that Amoco's property falls within the statutory definition of a "facility"; that Borden is a responsible party within the meaning of CERCLA, and that the statutory defenses to liability are inapplicable. . . .

. . . .

The hazard on the property constitutes an indivisible harm. As an owner of a facility that continues to release a hazardous substance, Amoco shares joint and several liability for remedial actions with Borden. When one liable party sues another to recover its equitable share of the response costs, the action is one for contribution, which is specifically recognized under CERCLA.

Under that provision, a court has considerable latitude in determining each party's equitable share. After deciding the appropriate remedial action, the court will have to determine each party's share of the costs. Possible relevant factors include: the amount of hazardous substances involved; the degree of toxicity or hazard of the materials involved; the degree of involvement by parties in the generation, transportation, treatment, storage, or disposal of the substances; the degree of care exercised by the parties with respect to the substances involved; and the degree of cooperation of the parties with government officials to prevent any harm to public health or the environment. Additionally, the circumstances and conditions involved in the property's conveyance, including the price paid and discounts granted, should be weighed in allocating response costs.

Borden . . . claim[s] that the equities in this case require Amoco to bear the full cost of cleanup. However, because both parties are liable under CERCLA, this is a question more properly decided by the district court, after it has determined the proper scope of the cleanup efforts.

DECISION AND REMEDY The case was sent back to the trial court to decide the equitable share that each party must pay. CERCLA imposes responsibility on every owner of real property that contains hazardous materials and creates joint and several liability in these situations.

CRITICAL THINKING: POLITICAL CONSIDERATION In the past, when a person purchased a property under the term "as is," that was interpreted as taking the property with all faults. This meant that a purchaser could not bring legal action against the seller for problems with the property. This decision changed this rule. Should this rule have been changed for a Superfund property?

Occasionally, the acts of a business or individual will violate both the RCRA and CERCLA because these statutes overlap. The next case shows companies and individuals to be in violation of the RCRA when the hazardous waste was transported, as well as in violation of CERCLA for failing to report the dumping of this same waste.

Case 24.5

United States v. MacDonald & Watson Waste Oil Co.

United States Court of Appeals, First Circuit, 1991
933 F.2d 35

BACKGROUND AND FACTS Master Chemical Company, located in Boston, Massachusetts, manufactured chemicals primarily for use in the shoe industry. Among the chemicals Master Chemical used was toluene, which it stored in a 2,000-gallon underground storage tank. When Master Chemical personnel discovered in the late fall of 1982 that water was entering the tank and contaminating the toluene, the tank was emptied and its use discontinued. Some toluene had leaked out and contaminated the soil.

Master Chemical retained an environmental consulting firm to prepare a study. The environmental consulting firm solicited a bid from MacDonald & Watson Waste Oil Company for the excavation, transportation, and disposal of the toluene-contaminated soil. Although MacDonald & Watson was in the business of transporting and disposing of waste oils and contaminated soil, it lacked a permit to dispose of solid wastes, such as soil, at all of its disposal sites. The disposal facility in Rhode Island was leased from Narragansett Improvement Company (NIC). MacDonald & Watson operated the disposal facility under NIC's Resource Conservation and Recovery Act (RCRA) permit that authorized the disposal of liquid hazardous wastes and soils contaminated with non-hazardous wastes, such as petroleum products. Neither MacDonald & Watson nor NIC had a permit authorizing the disposal of solid hazardous wastes, such as toluene-contaminated soil, at this disposal facility.

Master Chemical accepted the bid from MacDonald & Watson to remove the waste and clean up the site. The defendant Slade, an employee of MacDonald & Watson, signed the contract on behalf of MacDonald & Watson. A MacDonald & Watson employee stamped the transportation manifests "Non-hazardous in Rhode Island, Accepted for Processing."

The Environmental Protection Agency discovered that the toluene-contaminated soil was disposed of at facility that had only a permit for soil that was not contaminated with a hazardous waste. The EPA referred the matter to the Department of Justice for criminal prosecution.

In a complicated trial, the court convicted several employees of MacDonald & Watson, several employees of NIC, and both businesses, MacDonald & Watson and NIC, on various criminal charges. One employee, Ritarossi, supervised the soil's transportation. He was convicted of knowingly transporting and causing the transportation of hazardous waste, namely, toluene and soil contaminated with toluene, to a facility that lacked a permit, in violation of the RCRA. Following is a small portion of the judge's decision that discusses Ritarossi's conviction.

Circuit Judge LEVIN H. CAMPBELL

. . . .

Ritarossi contends that the evidence was insufficient to prove that he either knew that the material shipped to NIC was subject to RCRA regulation as toluene-contaminated soil or to prove he knew the substance and limitations of NlC's permit. However, Ritarossi could be found to have signed several of the "Authorization to Accept Shipment" forms which describes the "spilled material" as toluene and provides "toluene and gravel" as the "Description of petroleum product spilled and material spilled into." [A witness from Master Chemical] testified that he discussed the circumstances surrounding the leaking toluene tank with Ritarossi during excavation of the tank. Moreover, [the] environmental consultant testified that he asked Ritarossi to include options in MacDonald & Watson's bid both for disposal at MacDonald & Watson's facility and for disposal at an out-of-state RCRA secure landfill because the consultant did not know whether MacDonald & Watson had the proper permits to dispose of the material at their facility. We find sufficient evidence from which the jury could determine that Ritarossi knew the material was toluene-contaminated soil and also to infer that he either knew that NlC's permit did not permit acceptance of such material or, at very least, willfully failed to determine the material's status under NlC's permit. . . . .

We conclude that the reportable quantity for the toluene-contaminated soil was 1,000 pounds. . . . It was never a subject of dispute that the toluene-contaminated soil was delivered to the [disposal facility] in other than nine 25-yard dump trucks and one 20-yard dump truck. We see no basis on which it could be rationally concluded by any juror that less than 1,000 pounds of contaminated soil was released.

DECISION AND REMEDY The RCRA was violated when Ritarossi authorized the transportation of the contaminated soil knowing (or willfully failing to find out) that it would be dumped in an unauthorized disposal facility without the proper permits. Failure to report the solid hazardous waste's dumping was a criminal violation of CERCLA.

CRITICAL THINKING: MANAGEMENT CONSIDERATION If you were employed in a business that might have problems with hazardous materials through accidental discharge, how would you protect yourself from criminal and civil liability?

The **Pollution Prevention Act (PPA)** was passed in 1990. It focuses on reducing the amount of pollution through cost-effective changes in production, operation, and use of raw materials. The reduction of pollution is more desirable and fundamentally different than managing waste or controlling pollution. This act focuses on increasing the efficiency in the use of energy, water, or other natural resources through conservation. Some conservation practices are recycling, reduction of pollution at its source, and the use of renewable energies, such as solar energy.

CyberLaw

Record Research on the Web

The section *Legally Speaking*, found later in this chapter, discusses the three phases of an environment audit required by the Environmental Protection Agency. Within phase I surface analysis, one step is to review the public records of ownership for at least the last fifty years. These records reflect the business activities conducted on the land, such as gasoline station, photography shop, dry cleaning business, restaurant business, or farming.

All of these businesses just mentioned use hazardous materials that today are required by regulation to be disposed of in a specific manner. Realizing that these types of businesses have been previous owners of the real estate should send out a red flag that environmental problems might exist. For example, the gasoline station handles oil, gas, and underground storage tanks; in the past, the process of developing film included silver and lead; dry cleaners handle solvent chemicals; restaurants use cooking oils and cleaning supplies; and farming involves pesticides and herbicides. In addition to ownership, public records show past and existing environmental cleanup liens.

A search of the public records for the first phase currently can be achieved through the use of the World Wide Web (WWW) in a only few counties.[10] These counties have placed their public records of property ownership on the web. The placement of the recorded documents on a web site allows any person to access this information from a home or office. No longer is it necessary to travel to the local recording office to research the names of those who have owned the property. Although today not many states and counties have placed the documents recorded in the county on the web, as money becomes available, more government recording offices will place these records on the web as a routine matter.

Endangered Species Act

Congress adopted the **Endangered Species Act (ESA)** in 1973 both to conserve the species themselves and to protect the ecosystems of the endangered species. Endangered species, unlike timber, are nonrenewable resources. In a congressional hearing, the assistant secretary of the interior testified "that half of the recorded extinctions of mammals over the past 2,000 years have occurred in the most recent 50-year period."

Federal agencies are mandated to conserve endangered species. The secretary of the interior enforces the ESA. In 1993, Congress created the National Biological Survey to catalog all species within the United States. Species include mammals, birds, reptiles, fish, crustaceans, trees, flowers, and grasses. A total of 853 species were placed on the endangered species list during the 1980s and 1990s. Today, the Department of Interior lists 632 endangered species (326 are plants) and 190 threatened species (78 are plants).

In the past, the government focused on one endangered species at a time. Today, the approach is broader because it considers ecosystems. An ecosystem is a community of animals, birds, insects, trees, bushes, plants, flowers, grasses, bacteria, fungi, and soil types, just to mention a few items. If a large enough portion of land that comprises an ecosystem is preserved, such as the Florida Everglades, everything within the land is protected. It is believed that this holistic approach will prevent any one species from becoming extinct because the community is interrelated and interdependent. For example, a species of birds may depend on one type of tree, but the tree is dependent on a particular type of soil or flooding condition. To protect only the bird may be useless if its habitat is destroyed.

Private individuals can challenge a federal agency's decision involving endangered species. In the case of *Bennett v. Spear*[11] the United States Supreme Court

---

[10] An example of a progressive county is Maricopa County, Arizona, where public records are accessible through the web. See <http://recorder.maricopa.gov/recorder/imaging/>.

[11] 520 U.S.154, 117 S. Ct. 1154, 137 L. Ed. 2d 281 (1997); located on the web at <http://supct.law.cornell.edu/supct/html/95-813.ZS.html>.

Exhibit 24–1 Costs of Protecting Some Endangered Species

Species	Cost
Atlantic green turtle	$88,236,000
Loggerhead turtle	$85,947,000
Blunt-nosed leopard lizard	$70,252,000
Kemp's Ridley sea turtle	$63,600,000
Colorado squawfish	$57,770,000
Black-capped vireo	$53,538,000
Swamp pink	$29,026,000

Source: National Wilderness Institute.

allowed private persons to challenge actions of the Department of Interior involving the maintenance of minimum water levels on several lakes to protect two endangered species of fish. The private persons who would have been affected by this federal action because they depended on water for irrigation challenged the acts of the government. The Court stated that they had standing to litigate this issue.

Exhibit 24–1 shows the expensive costs of protecting a few endangered species. When a species is placed on the endangered list, the Department of Interior can restrict the free use of private property and can slow or stop economic development on it.

In the following case, the United States Supreme Court had to decide whether the secretary of the interior had the authority to define the terms "harm" and "taking" under the act. The Court's determination would result in limiting the use of public and private land.

Case 24.6

Babbitt v. Sweet Home Chapter

Supreme Court of the United States, 1995
515 U.S. 687, 115 S. Ct. 2407, 132 L. Ed. 2d 597
http://supct.law.cornell.edu /supct/html/94-859.ZS.html

BACKGROUND AND FACTS The plaintiffs are families, small landowners, and logging companies, dependent on the forest products industries in the Pacific Northwest and in the Southeast, and organizations that represent their interests. They brought this action against the petitioner, Secretary of the Interior Bruce Babbitt. They challenged the validity of the regulation adopted by the Department of Interior that defined the term "harm" under the Endangered Species Act (ESA).

This act contains a variety of protections designed to save from extinction those species that the secretary of the interior designates as endangered or threatened. The statute specifically prohibits anyone from taking any fish or wildlife that are on the endangered or threatened list. The statute defines the statutory term "take" or "taking" as to "harass, harm, pursue, hunt, shoot, wound, kill, trap, capture, or collect."

The act did not define the term "harm," but the secretary defined harm as an "act which actually kills or injures wildlife." Harm may include significant modification or degradation of the wildlife's habitat when it would actually kill or injure wildlife by significantly altering essential behavioral patterns, such as breeding, feeding, or sheltering.

Congress had developed a permit system for takings that otherwise were illegal. The plaintiffs had not obtained a permit for any takings. The plaintiffs challenged the statute and the secretary's regulation defining "harm," particularly the inclusion of habitat modification and degradation in the definition. Their complaint alleged that application of the regulation defining harm to the red-cockaded woodpecker, an endangered species, and to the northern spotted owl, a threatened species, had injured them economically.

The district court held for the plaintiffs. The appellate court reversed the trial court but restricted the regulation's implementation. The secretary of the interior appealed to the United States Supreme Court.

Justice STEVENS delivered the opinion of the Court.

. . . .

. . . [T]he broad purpose of the ESA supports the Secretary's decision to extend protection against activities that cause the precise harms Congress enacted the statute to avoid. . . . [W]e described the Act as "the most comprehensive legislation for the preservation of endangered species ever enacted by any nation." . . . [T]he 1973 Act applied to all land in the United States and to the Nation's territorial seas. As stated in . . . the Act, among its central purposes is "to provide a means whereby the ecosystems upon which endangered species and threatened species depend may be conserved."

. . . .

. . . [T]he fact that Congress in 1982 authorized the Secretary to issue permits for takings that would otherwise prohibit, "if such taking is incidental to, and not the purpose of, the carrying out of an otherwise lawful activity," strongly suggests that Congress understood [the statute] to prohibit indirect as well as deliberate takings. The permit process requires the applicant to prepare a "conservation plan" that specifies how he intends to "minimize and mitigate" the "impact" of his activity on endangered and threatened species, making clear that Congress had in mind foreseeable rather than merely accidental effects on listed species. . . . Congress' . . . permit provision supports the Secretary's conclusion that activities not intended to harm an endangered species, such as, habitat modification, may constitute unlawful takings under the ESA unless the Secretary permits them.

DECISION AND REMEDY The Court concluded that the secretary of the interior reasonably construed Congress' intent by defining harm to include habitat modification. The Court found that if a species is either endangered or threatened, the secretary may restrict economic activity on both public and private land. Congress had authorized the secretary to issue permits for takings that otherwise were prohibited. The plaintiffs had no permit, so the law applied to them.

CRITICAL THINKING: POLITICAL CONSIDERATION What action could the plaintiffs have taken instead of instituting legal action?

Judicial Limits

In the first half of the 1970s, federal and state legislators enacted many statutes that regulate environmental quality. Judicial interpretations of these statutes generally have given broad discretionary powers to the administrative agencies that carry out these statutes' directives.

Beginning in the mid 1970s, however, the courts began to place stricter limits on administrative discretion. Court decisions imposed a **cost–benefit standard** on administrative decisions.[12] Under the cost-benefit standard, courts will consider the cost of an action and compare it with the benefit that may result from the action. For example, in *Union Electric Co. v.*

Environmental Protection Agency,[13] the utility claimed that it would cost $500 million to comply with the Clean Air Act and that this sum could not be obtained through financial markets. The United States Supreme Court turned down this argument and held that the clean air regulations "are expressly designed to force regulated sources to develop pollution control devices that might at the time appear to be economically or technologically infeasible."

---

[12] See the Environmental Protection Agency's web site on cost–benefit analysis at <http://www.epa.gov/ebtpages/ecostbenefitanalysis.html>.
[13] 427 U.S. 246, 96 S. Ct. 2518, 49 L. Ed. 2d 474 (1976).

Economic and Environmental Concerns

Everyone is in favor of protecting the environment. Everyone is in favor of earning an honest living. But what happens when these two values conflict? This conflict is played out when environmentalists clash with the logging industry. In the Pacific Northwest, for example, the loggers are pitted against those who want to protect old-growth forests and spotted owls.

The logging industry either owns the land it logs or leases the land from the federal or state government and then operates under permits to log the forest. This work creates employment and thus a tax base. The monies earned by employees support other private industries, such as grocery and furniture stores, and also generate taxes paid to the local and federal governments. Since the 1920s, many logging companies have cooperated with the Save-the-Redwoods League and the Sierra Club.

If the spotted owl, along with the Harris's hawk, Henslow's sparrow, loggerhead shrike, seaside sparrow, snowy plover, and vermilion flycatcher, is placed on the endangered species list, this effectively would stop all logging. The designation would protect 1.5 million acres of old-growth forest from future logging. Keep in mind that since the pilgrims arrived in the early 1600s, more than 90 percent of the original woodland in the United States has been destroyed.

Is it ethical to protect birds and forests over the jobs of people who are generally second- and third-generation loggers—especially since these people contribute to the community's economic basis?

Most old-growth wood is shipped overseas for use in other countries. Should this be allowed? Would the decision differ if the old-growth wood were used in the United States?

Destruction of habitat poses the greatest threat to the survival of wild species. Birds, animals, and plants have evolved over centuries to survive in specific environments. Destruction of the old-growth forests would mean the destruction of some species. Each species plays a part in the ecosystem's delicate balance. Is it ethical to allow these wild species to perish?

Environmental Side Agreement to NAFTA

The United States, Mexico, and Canada, in addition to signing the North American Free Trade Agreement (NAFTA) and the North American Agreement on Labor Cooperation (NAALC was discussed along with NAFTA in Chapter 22), signed the North American Agreement on Environmental Cooperation. This side agreement establishes, maintains, and enforces each country's domestic environmental law.

The agreement encourages public participation in the lawmaking and enforcement process. Provisions include government-to-government dispute settlement procedures for patterns of failure to enforce domestic environmental statutes effectively. The side agreement also creates mechanisms for collaboration among the parties.

The environmental side agreement establishes the Commission on Environmental Cooperation (CEC), which is a council composed of each country's top environmental officials. The CEC also includes an independent secretariat under the direction of an executive director and a joint advisory committee composed of nongovernmental organizations from the three countries to advise the council.

Under the agreement, any individual or organization residing in any of the three countries may file a complaint with the secretariat alleging that a country failed to enforce its environmental laws. The secretariat determines whether the complaint warrants a response. After the offending country responds, on a two-thirds vote, the record is made public. If evidence exists that a continuing pattern has developed that violates environmental law, an action plan will be established to correct the situation. If this plan of action fails, monetary assessments can be imposed. If an assessment is not paid, trade sanctions may be imposed on the United States and Mexico. Monetary sanctions enforceable by a court order can be imposed on Canada.

International Consideration

Global Antipollution Actions

Pollution knows no international boundaries. The radioactive pollution from Chernobyl was detected over a weekend by Sweden and Norway before it was reported by the former Union of Soviet Socialist Republics. The radioactivity eventually encircled the earth and led to a ban of agricultural products from some countries because some products, such as milk, plants, and grain crops, contained radioactive elements.

The more developed nations have passed legislation similar to that of the United States. The European Union (EU), then called the European Community, passed the Single Europe Act, which requires it to issue a comprehensive regulatory scheme to protect the environment. Adopted in 1987, this program contains laws similar to those of the United States.

The less developed countries have fewer resources for protecting the environment. In 1992, a number of nations signed the Climate Change Treaty,[14] which is sponsored by the United Nations. This treaty set out a number of meetings that would establish goals and timetables. In 1997, a conference was held in Kyoto, Japan, to set legal global limits on the emissions of carbon dioxide and other "greenhouse" gases—mostly by-products of fossil fuel burning—that trap the heat that Earth emits.[15]

The conference wrapped up two years of negotiations to determine a compromise formula assigning various levels of gas reductions to the thirty-four industrialized countries. Two main proposals emerged. The European Union wanted industrialized nations to reduce greenhouse gas emissions to 15 percent below 1990 levels by 2010. The United States, on the other hand, suggested lowering emissions only to 1990 levels.

Although most parties agree that global warming is taking place, the question of how to handle the problem remains.[16] On one side, the automobile manufacturers,

coal companies, and oil producers argued that no timetables should be imposed to meet goals for the reduction of carbon dioxide and other gases. On the other side, companies selling fuel-efficient technologies, environmentalists, and insurance companies that pay damages caused by global warming, such as for flood or hurricane damage claims, supported specific reductions.

Less developed nations want and need industrial development and are willing to accept pollution to obtain that goal. Slowly, however, these countries are making ecological progress. For example, the **Association of Southeast Asian Nations (ASEAN)** is an intergovernmental agency of Indonesia, Malaysia, the Philippines, Singapore, and Thailand that was founded in 1967. This organization seeks economic and cultural cooperation among its members. In 1985, ASEAN's members entered into the Agreement on the Conservation of Nature and Natural Resources. In this agreement, each county recognized its responsibility for controlling pollution and preventing it from migrating to other countries.

Global international treaties making up the Ozone Treaties are the **Montreal Protocol on Substances that Deplete the Ozone Layer**, which has been modified five times, London (1990), Copenhagen (1992), Vienna (1995), Montreal (1997), and Beijing (1999). The protocol aims to reduce and eventually eliminate the emissions of man-made ozone-depleting substances.

The Montreal Protocol was signed by twenty-four nations in 1987. This treaty is unique in that its goal is to prevent pollution rather than simply to provide cleanup measures. The treaty requires all nations to reduce both production and consumption of chemicals that deplete the ozone layer. Production of the most damaging ozone-depleting substances was eliminated, except for a few critical uses, by 1996 in developed countries and will be eliminated by 2010 in developing countries.[17]

Under the auspices of the United Nations Environment Programme, various nations sponsored the **Vienna Convention on the Protection of the Ozone Layer** in 1985. Through this convention, governments committed themselves to protect the ozone layer and to cooperate with each other in scientific research to improve understanding of the atmospheric processes.

[14] See the Congressional Research Service, Report for Congress, 98-2: Global Climate Change Treaty: The Kyoto Protocol, at <http://www.cnie.org/nle/clim-3.html>.
[15] The Kyoto Conference has a web site at <http://www.cop3.de/>.
[16] For more information about research on the topic of climate warming, see the Hadley Center for Climate Prediction and Research located at <http://www.meto.gov.uk/sec5/CR_div/Brochure/>. The Hadley Center provides data based on temperature records dating back to the mid-nineteenth century. The data are considered among the most reliable in climate science.

[17] See the United Nations Environment Programme web page entitled *The Ozone Secretariat* at <http://www.unep.org/ozone/>.

The **United Nations Convention on the Law of the Sea**[18] imposes on signatory members the duty to avoid polluting the oceans from land or from vessels, including legislation against dumping raw wastes from ships. Many video-toting vacationers on cruise ships have taped a number of incidents of cruise ships violating the law.

The **Convention on the Law of the Non-navigational Uses of International Watercourses**[19]

---

[18] The United Nations' Oceans and Law of the Sea Home Page is located at <http://www.un.org/Depts/los/index.htm>.
[19] The United Nations' International Law Commission's web site for this convention is at <http://www.un.org/law/ilc/texts/nnavfra.htm>.

of 1997 provides for the exchange of information among countries if water-related hazards occur. Another article requires nations to take all measures to prevent harmful conditions, such as toxic chemical spills.

The United Nations Educational, Scientific, and Cultural Organization (UNESCO) also supports pollution control.[20] It has been particularly successful in compiling data and arranging for regional agreements to stop pollution. In addition, the World Bank requires pollution controls as part of each applicant's business plan before it loans for industrial purposes.

---

[20] The UNESCO home page is at <http://www.unesco.org/>.

LEGALLY SPEAKING

Considerations When Purchasing Real Property

A person must be very careful when purchasing real property. In the past, one had to consider zoning laws, financing, and engineering studies of the land and any projected buildings. Today, a purchaser must take into consideration the various federal statutes concerning the environment. If an environmental hazard exists on the property, the property owner must correct it. In reality, only one defense is available: that of the innocent purchaser. Auditing can help a purchaser establish this defense.

The Environmental Protection Agency (EPA) issued a policy statement on auditing. An environmental audit has three parts that may be implemented: (1) a surface analysis (phase 1) and (2) a technical subsurface study (phase II). If necessary, a cleanup becomes phase III. A phase II study is very expensive and normally is unnecessary if phase I does not reveal an environmental problem. Legally, neither audit is required. Without an audit, however, the EPA takes a hard stand against a purchaser claiming no knowledge. Generally, an audit is required to meet the innocent purchaser defense.

A professional known as an environmental consultant should perform a phase I analysis. The public records of ownership for at least the last fifty years must be reviewed. The names in the public record may reveal the types of business ac-

tivities in which previous owners, such as an oil company, engaged. The public record also shows existing environmental cleanup liens.

The consultant reviews aerial photographs that might show prior use of the property. He or she examines federal, state, and local records to identify building permits and reports or environmental records of previous land use. A visual inspection of the property and adjacent property also is necessary, because hazardous materials may have migrated from an adjoining property onto the property for sale.

The phase II audit includes physical sampling and testing. The soil and groundwater are sampled to identify and isolate the type and extent of the contamination. A phase II audit is accomplished only when a phase I audit indicates environmental problems. Phase III occurs when the property is cleaned up. Potential purchasers and their lending institutions always should perform a phase I audit before purchasing raw land. Otherwise, they may be held liable.

Prior to purchasing real estate, the purchaser should investigate the property by completing the following actions:

✔ Review the public records to investigate information about the prior use of the property over the prior years. Prior usage as a gasoline station or a dry cleaners should be a red flag that chemicals may exist.

✔ Review photographs of the area that were taken over past decades to see if any past property use might have caused environment problems. Photographs sometimes can be obtained from public utilities, private compa-

nies, or government offices. Compare the photographs with the public records.

✔ Check for building permits. If the building has been modified, does it meet current standards?

✔ Make a visual inspection of the property and adjacent land. A condition on a neighboring property may contaminate this property.

Chapter Summary

Private persons and state and local governments have sued polluters to protect the environment. The lawsuits focus on the tort theories of nuisance, trespass, negligence, and strict liability. Most private suits faced legal defenses that prevented a party from successfully restricting activity that has harmed or might harm the environment. Local government tried to protect the environment by regulating building design and noise and by controlling the use of property through zoning laws.

Congress in 1969 passed the Environmental Protection Act and created the Environmental Protection Agency. The law requires an environmental impact statement (EIS) for projects using federal funds or built by federal agencies. The EIS is prepared to determine the effect of the federal project on the environment.

The federal government has passed a number of statutes, including the Clean Air Act, that was last amended in 1990. The 1990 act requires states to create state implementation plans, which are intended to inventory air polluters. The Clean Water Act was passed to make the waters safe for swimming, to protect fish and wildlife, and to eliminate the discharge of pollutants into the waters. The Oil Pollution Act placed strict liability

limits on oil polluters, created the Oil Spill Liability Trust Fund, and established the Oil Spill Recovery Institute.

The Nuclear Waste Policy Act governs the disposal of spent nuclear fuel and high-level wastes. The Shore Protection Act controls the disposal of solid wastes in oceans and lakes. The Noise Control Act protects the public's health and welfare from excessive noise.

The Resource Conservation and Recovery Act provides a cradle-to-grave tracking system of hazardous waste. The Comprehensive Environmental Response, Compensation, and Liability Act requires polluters and land owners to clean up the hazardous waste sites.

In 1973, Congress passed the Endangered Species Act, administered by the Department of Interior. The act protects those species that are endangered or threatened on private or public land.

The courts attempt to balance the adverse effect of activities that affect the environment with the cost of protecting the environment. The courts use the cost–benefit standard on administrative decisions. The courts consider the cost of the EPA's action with the benefit that may result from the action.

Using the World Wide Web

EPA's Office of Air and Radiation (OAR) deals with issues that affect the quality of our air and protection from exposure to harmful radiation. OAR develops national programs, technical policies, and regulations for controlling air pollution and radiation exposure. Areas of concern to OAR include indoor and outdoor air quality, stationary and mobile sources of air pollution, radon, acid rain, stratospheric ozone depletion, radiation protection, and pollution prevention.

Finding the Law on the Web

Environmental Protection Agency, Green Book, nonattainment areas
http://www.epa.gov/oar/oaqps/greenbk/
UN Convention on Climate Change
http://www.unfccc.de/

Environmental Protection Agency, Office of Air
and Radiation
http://www.epa.gov/oar/

Chapter Web Sites

Environmental Protection Agency
http://www.epa.gov
Clean Air Act
http://www.law.cornell.edu/uscode/42/7403.shtml
Environmental Protection Agency, Office of Air Quality
Planning and Standards
http://www.epa.gov/oar/oaqps/
Environmental Protection Agency, nonattainment areas
http://www.epa.gov/airs/nonattn.html
Southern California Air Quality Management District
http://www.aqmd.gov/
Environmental Protection Agency, Office of
Regulatory Enforcement
http://es.epa.gov/oeca/
Environmental Protection Agency, penalties
http://www.epa.gov/ozone/enforce
*Friends of the Earth, Inc. v. Laidlaw Environmental Services,
Inc.*
http://supct.law.cornell.edu/supct/html
/98-822.ZS.html
Shore Protection Act
http://www.law.cornell.edu/uscode/33/2601.shtml
National Oceanic and Atmospheric Administration,
Office of Ocean and Coastal Resource
Management
http://www.ocrm.nos.noaa.gov/welcome.html
Toxic Substances Control Act
http://www.law.cornell.edu/uscode/15/2601.shtml
Comprehensive Environmental Response,
Compensation, and Liability Act (CERCLA)
http://www.law.cornell.edu/uscode/42/9601.shtml
Bennett v. Spear
http://supct.law.cornell.edu/supct/html
/95-813.ZS.html
Maricopa County, Arizona, County Recorder's Office
http://recorder.maricopa.gov/recorder/imaging/
Babbitt v. Sweet Home Chapter
http://supct.law.cornell.edu/supct/html
/94-859.ZS.html

Environmental Protection Agency, cost–benefit analysis
http://www.epa.gov/ebtpages
/ecostbenefitanalysis.html
Kyoto Protocol, Congressional Research Service,
Report for Congress, 98-2: Global Climate
Change Treaty
http://www.cnie.org/nle/clim-3.html
Kyoto Conference
http://www.cop3.de/
Hadley Center for Climate Prediction and Research
http://www.meto.gov.uk/sec5/CR_div/Brochure/
United Nations Environment Programme,
The Ozone Secretariat
http://www.unep.org/ozone/
United Nations, Oceans and Law of the Sea home page
http://www.un.org/Depts/los/index.htm
United Nations' International Law Commission,
Convention on the Law of the Non-navigational
Uses of International Watercourses
http://www.un.org/law/ilc/texts/nnavfra.htm
Environmental Defense
http://www.scorecard.org/env-releases/cap/
Environmental Protection Agency, nonattainment areas
http://www.epa.gov/oar/oaqps/greenbk/

Web Activities

24–1 Air pollution is a serious problem. What is the air
pollution quality of your community? Go to a scorecard,
which is maintained by Environmental Defense, an
independent organization that monitors air quality.
The web address is <http://www.scorecard.org
/env-releases/cap/>.

24–2 You are interested in working for the Environmental Protection Agency and wonder how many
laws the agency enforces. Go the EPA's web site at
<http://www.epa.gov/>. Click on "Laws &
Regulations" on the left side. On the next page, click on
"Introduction." Scroll toward the bottom to the list of
laws. How many laws does the agency enforce?

Key Terms

Association of Southeast
Asian Nations
(ASEAN)
attainment area
class-action lawsuit
Clean Air Act
Clean Water Act
Comprehensive
Environmental
Response,
Compensation,
and Liability Act
(CERCLA)
Convention on the
Law of the Non-
navigational Uses
of International
Watercourses
cost-benefit standard

Emergency Planning and
Community
Right-to-Know Act
(EPCRA)
Endangered Species Act
(ESA)
environmental impact
statement (EIS)
Environmental
Protection Agency
(EPA)
Federal Environmental
Pesticide Control Act
Federal Insecticide,
Fungicide, and
Rodenticide Act
Hazardous and Solid
Waste Amendments
(HSWA)

Law of the Navigational
Uses of International
Watercourses
Marine Protection,
Research, and
Sanctuaries Act
Montreal Protocol on
Substances that
Deplete the Ozone
Layer
National Ambient Air
Quality Standards
(NAAQS)
National Environmental
Policy Act (NEPA)
Noise Control Act
nonattainment area
Nuclear Waste Policy Act
(NWPA)
Oil Pollution Act

Pollution Prevention Act
(PPA)
Resource Conservation
and Recovery Act
(RCRA)
Rivers and Harbors Act
Safe Drinking Water Act
Shore Protection Act
Solid Waste Disposal Act
state implementation
plan (SIP)
Toxic Substances
Control Act
United Nations
Convention on the
Law of the Sea
Vienna Convention on
the Protection of the
Ozone Layer

Questions and Case Problems

24–1 Nuisance Oakhill is a development-home build-ing corporation that primarily develops retirement com-munities. Washington Feeds owns several feed lots in Buckeye. Oakhill purchased 20,000 acres of farmland in the same area and began building and selling homes on this acreage. In the meantime, Washington Feeds contin-ued to expand its feedlot business. Eventually only 500 feet separated the two operations. Because of the odor and flies from the feedlots, Oakhill found it difficult to sell the homes in its development. Oakhill wants to enjoin Washington Feeds from operating its feedlots in the vicinity of the retirement home development. Under what theory would Oakhill file this action? Explain.

24–2 Noise Control Act Flylight, Inc., manufactures a 250-seat passenger airplane that is fuel efficient and that travels at a cruising speed of 900 miles per hour. The plane is only cost effective for flights of 1,000 miles or more. Traveling at 900 miles per hour creates a sonic boom lasting for no more than five seconds. The sound measured during the five-second period exceeds aircraft noise levels established by the Environmental Protection Agency. Should Flylight, Inc., aircraft be banned from flying over the United States? Explain.

24–3 Clean Water Act Atlantic Richfield Co. (ARCO) had an accidental oil spill, which it reported to the Coast Guard in accordance with the law. ARCO cleaned up the oil spill to the Coast Guard's satisfaction. The Coast Guard assessed a civil penalty for this acci-dental discharge. ARCO refused to pay, claiming that it cleaned up the spill and that the spill was accidental. ARCO also argued that such penalties are criminal. The federal government sued to collect the penalty. What was the result? Explain. [*United States v. Atlantic Richfield Co.*, 429 F. Supp. 830 (E. D. Pa. 1977)]

24–4 National Environmental Policy Act The Government Services Administration (GSA) entered into an agreement with a private individual to construct a building to the GSA's specifications and to lease it to the GSA. Under the contemplated lease provision, the GSA would use the entire building for a five-year (re-newable) period. As many as 2,300 government employ-ees would be assigned to the building, and most would commute by automobile. The cost of the lease was ap-proximately $11 million. The GSA proceeded with its plans for the building without preparing an environ-mental impact statement. Was a statement necessary?

Explain. [*S. W. Neighborhood Assembly v. Eckard*, 445 F. Supp. 1195 (D.D.C. 1978)]

24–5 Standing to Sue Citizens Against Toxic Sprays, Inc., was an organization established to challenge the use of toxic sprays in places where they could be harmful to humans, animals, or vegetation. The group sought to enjoin the U.S. Forest Service from using the herbicide TCDD, because of its hazardous effect on people who breathed it. TCDD was used only in national forests, not in any residential areas. Citizens Against Toxic Sprays alleged that some of its members were affected by the use of TCDD in two of the national forests because they lived near them, worked in them, or used them for recreational activities. Does Citizens Against Toxic Sprays, Inc., have the standing to sue the U.S. Forest Service? Explain. [*Citizens Against Toxic Sprays, Inc., v. Bergland*, 428 F. Supp. 908 (1977)]

24–6 Wetlands A dispute arose over 153 acres of undeveloped land owned by Leslie Salt Company. The land abuts the San Francisco National Wildlife Refuge and lies approximately one-quarter mile from the Newark Slough, a tidal arm of the San Francisco Bay. The condition of the property in 1985 resulted from artificial changes during the last 100 years. Starting out as pastureland, it was excavated for salt until 1959. The salt pits remained and temporarily filled with water during the winter rainy season. Fish lived in the ponds and migratory birds used the pits as habitat during the winter and spring. An endangered species, the salt marsh harvest mouse, also inhabited the property.

The California Department of Transportation (Caltrans) constructed culverts adjacent to Leslie's land. Caltrans breached the levee on the wildlife refuge adjacent to Leslie's property, which allowed water to flow through the culverts onto Leslie's land. Caltrans failed to place effective floodgates on the culverts, creating wetlands conditions over time. In 1985, Leslie started to dig a ditch to drain and fill in the land. The Army Corps of Engineers (Corps) became aware of this activity and issued a cease-and-desist order pursuant to its authority under the Clean Water Act. The Corps claimed jurisdiction over the majority of the property, which Leslie then challenged. What result and why? [*Leslie Salt Co. v. United States*, 896 F.2d 354 (9th Cir. 1989)]

24–7 Nuisance Judy Godwin began construction of her home. At about the same time, Exxon began the construction of a "separation" plant 700 feet north of the home site. The residence and plant were completed at about the same time. The plant emitted noise, vibration, and sulfurous odors around the clock. These gave Godwin headaches and the odor prevented her from

inviting friends to her residence. What legal theories could she use against Exxon? What result would be obtained under them? Explain. [*Exxon Corp., U.S.A. v. Dunn*, 474 So.2d 1269 (Fla. Dist. Ct. App. 1985)]

24–8 Clean Water Act Interpretation of the language in environmental statutes is very important. The Clean Water Act authorizes private citizens to commence a civil action for an injunction and/or the imposition of civil penalties in federal district court against any person "alleged to be in violation" of the conditions of a National Pollutant Discharge Elimination System (NPDES) permit. The NPDES is a federal statute that authorizes permits to be granted to businesses that apply for permission to discharge effluent into a river or lake. The permit limits the amount and type of effluent authorized to be discharged. Between 1981 and 1984, Gwaltney of Smithfield repeatedly violated the conditions of its NPDES permit by exceeding authorized effluent limitations. Because of the installation of new equipment, Smithfield's last reported violation occurred in May 1984. Nevertheless, in June 1984, having given notice of its intent to sue to the Environmental Protection Agency and to sue state authorities, as required by the act, the Chesapeake Bay Foundation filed a suit alleging that Smithfield "has violated . . . [and] will continue to violate its NPDES permit." Smithfield filed a motion to dismiss, alleging that the federal statute required that it be in violation of the act at the time the action was filed. What was the result? Explain. [*Gwaltney of Smithfeld v. Chesapeake Bay Foundation*, 484 U.S. 49, 108 S. Ct. 376, 98 L. Ed. 2d 306 (1987)]

24–9 Endangered Species Act The secretary of the interior declared a small fish known as the snail darter to be endangered under the Endangered Species Act of 1973. The snail darter lived in a portion of the Little Tennessee River in which more than $100 million dollars had been spent on the Tellico Dam's construction. The secretary ordered all federal agencies to take action to ensure that the critical habitat of the snail darter was maintained. A group of concerned citizens brought legal action to stop any further construction of the dam on the basis that if the dam were completed, all the snail darters would be killed. Should the court grant an injunction to stop the construction? Explain. [*Tennessee Valley Authority v. Hill*, 437 U.S. 153, 98 S. Ct. 2279, 57 L. Ed. 2d 117 (1978)]

24–10 Internet The EPA web site lists all the ozone nonattainment areas by state, area, and county. Is your area listed as a nonattainment area? Go to <http://www.epa.gov/ttncaaa1/title1/bgilbert/greenbk/oncs.htm> to find out.

Appendix A Constitution of the United States of America

Note: THE FOLLOWING TEXT IS A TRANSCRIPTION OF THE CONSTITUTION. TO ASSIST THE READER, TEXT IN ITALICS REPRESENTS SECTIONS THAT HAVE BEEN AMENDED OR SUPERSEDED. TEXT IN SMALL CAPS REPRESENTS INFORMATIONAL MATERIAL.

Preamble

WE THE PEOPLE of the United States, in Order to form a more perfect Union, establish Justice, insure domestic Tranquility, provide for the common defence, promote the general Welfare, and secure the Blessings of Liberty to ourselves and our Posterity, do ordain and establish this Constitution for the United States of America.

Article I

Section 1. All legislative Powers herein granted shall be vested in a Congress of the United States, which shall consist of a Senate and House of Representatives.

Section 2. The House of Representatives shall be composed of Members chosen every second Year by the People of the several States, and the Electors in each State shall have the Qualifications requisite for Electors of the most numerous Branch of the State Legislature.

No Person shall be a Representative who shall not have attained to the Age of twenty five Years, and been seven Years a Citizen of the United States, and who shall not, when elected, be an Inhabitant of that State in which he shall be chosen.

Representatives and direct Taxes shall be apportioned among the several States which may be included within this Union, according to their respective Numbers, which shall be determined by adding to the whole Number of free Persons, including those bound to Service for a Term of Years, and excluding Indians not taxed, three fifths of all other Persons.[1] The actual Enumeration shall be made within three Years after the first Meeting of the Congress of the United States, and within every subsequent Term of ten Years, in such Manner as they shall by Law direct. The Number of Representatives shall not exceed one for every thirty Thousand, but each State shall have at Least one Representative; and until such enumeration shall be made, the State of New Hampshire shall be entitled to chuse three, Massachusetts eight, Rhode Island and Providence Plantations one, Connecticut five, New York six, New Jersey four, Pennsylvania eight, Delaware one, Maryland six, Virginia ten, North Carolina five, South Carolina five, and Georgia three.

When vacancies happen in the Representation from any State, the Executive Authority thereof shall issue Writs of Election to fill such Vacancies.

The House of Representatives shall chuse their Speaker and other Officers; and shall have the sole Power of Impeachment.

Section 3. The Senate of the United States shall be composed of two Senators from each State, *chosen by the Legislature thereof*[2] for six Years; and each Senator shall have one Vote.

---

[1] Changed by the XIV amendment.
[2] Changed by the XVII amendment.

Immediately after they shall be assembled in Consequence of the first Election, they shall be divided as equally as may be into three Classes. The Seats of the Senators of the first Class shall be vacated at the Expiration of the second Year, of the second Class at the Expiration of the fourth Year, and of the third Class at the Expiration of the sixth Year, so that one third may be chosen every second Year; *and if Vacancies happen by Resignation, or otherwise, during the Recess of the Legislature of any State, the Executive thereof may make temporary Appointments until the next Meeting of the Legislature, which shall then fill such Vacancies.*[3]

No Person shall be a Senator who shall not have attained to the Age of thirty Years, and been nine Years a Citizen of the United States, and who shall not, when elected, be an Inhabitant of that State for which he shall be chosen.

The Vice President of the United States shall be President of the Senate, but shall have no Vote, unless they be equally divided.

The Senate shall chuse their other Officers, and also a President pro tempore, in the Absence of the Vice President, or when he shall exercise the Office of President of the United States.

The Senate shall have the sole Power to try all Impeachments. When sitting for that Purpose, they shall be on Oath or Affirmation. When the President of the United States is tried, the Chief Justice shall preside: And no Person shall be convicted without the Concurrence of two thirds of the Members present.

Judgment in Cases of Impeachment shall not extend further than to removal from Office, and disqualification to hold and enjoy any Office of honor, Trust, or Profit under the United States: but the Party convicted shall nevertheless be liable and subject to Indictment, Trial, Judgment, and Punishment, according to Law.

Section 4. The Times, Places and Manner of holding Elections for Senators and Representatives, shall be prescribed in each State by the Legislature thereof; but the Congress may at any time by Law make or alter such Regulations, except as to the Places of chusing Senators.

The Congress shall assemble at least once in every Year, and such Meeting shall *be on the first Monday in December,*[4] unless they shall by Law appoint a different Day.

Section 5. Each House shall be the Judge of the Elections, Returns, and Qualifications of its own Members, and a Majority of each shall constitute a Quorum to do Business; but a smaller Number may adjourn from day to day, and may be authorized to compel the Attendance of absent Members, in such Manner, and under such Penalties as each House may provide.

Each House may determine the Rules of its Proceedings, punish its Members for disorderly Behavior, and, with the Concurrence of two thirds, expel a Member.

Each House shall keep a Journal of its Proceedings, and from time to time publish the same, excepting such Parts as may in their Judgment require Secrecy; and the Yeas and Nays of the Members of either House on any question shall, at the Desire of one fifth of those Present, be entered on the Journal.

Neither House, during the Session of Congress, shall, without the Consent of the other, adjourn for more than three days, nor to any other Place than that in which the two Houses shall be sitting.

Section 6. The Senators and Representatives shall receive a Compensation for their Services, to be ascertained by Law, and paid out of the Treasury of the United States. They shall in all Cases, except Treason, Felony and Breach of the Peace, be privileged from Arrest during their Attendance at the Session of their respective Houses, and in going to and returning from the same; and for any Speech or Debate in either House, they shall not be questioned in any other Place.

No Senator or Representative shall, during the Time for which he was elected, be appointed to any civil Office under the Authority of the United States, which shall have been created, or the Emoluments whereof shall have been increased during such time; and no Person holding any Office under the United States, shall be a Member of either House during his Continuance in Office.

Section 7. All Bills for raising Revenue shall originate in the House of Representatives; but the Senate may propose or concur with Amendments as on other Bills.

---

[3] Changed by the XVII amendment.

[4] Changed by the XX amendment.

Every Bill which shall have passed the House of Representatives and the Senate, shall, before it become a Law, be presented to the President of the United States; If he approve he shall sign it, but if not he shall return it, with his Objections to the House in which it shall have originated, who shall enter the Objections at large on their Journal, and proceed to reconsider it. If after such Reconsideration two thirds of that House shall agree to pass the Bill, it shall be sent together with the Objections, to the other House, by which it shall likewise be reconsidered, and if approved by two thirds of that House, it shall become a Law. But in all such Cases the Votes of both Houses shall be determined by Yeas and Nays, and the Names of the Persons voting for and against the Bill shall be entered on the Journal of each House respectively. If any Bill shall not be returned by the President within ten Days (Sundays excepted) after it shall have been presented to him, the Same shall be a Law, in like Manner as if he had signed it, unless the Congress by their Adjournment prevent its Return in which Case it shall not be a Law.

Every Order, Resolution, or Vote, to which the Concurrence of the Senate and House of Representatives may be necessary (except on a question of Adjournment) shall be presented to the President of the United States; and before the Same shall take Effect, shall be approved by him, or being disapproved by him, shall be repassed by two thirds of the Senate and House of Representatives, according to the Rules and Limitations prescribed in the Case of a Bill.

Section 8. The Congress shall have Power To lay and collect Taxes, Duties, Imposts and Excises, to pay the Debts and provide for the common Defence and general Welfare of the United States; but all Duties, Imposts and Excises shall be uniform throughout the United States;

To borrow Money on the credit of the United States;

To regulate Commerce with foreign Nations, and among the several States, and with the Indian Tribes;

To establish an uniform Rule of Naturalization, and uniform Laws on the subject of Bankruptcies throughout the United States;

To coin Money, regulate the Value thereof, and of foreign Coin, and fix the Standard of Weights and Measures;

To provide for the Punishment of counterfeiting the Securities and current Coin of the United States;

To establish Post Offices and post Roads;

To promote the Progress of Science and useful Arts, by securing for limited Times to Authors and Inventors the exclusive Right to their respective Writings and Discoveries;

To constitute Tribunals inferior to the supreme Court;

To define and punish Piracies and Felonies committed on the high Seas, and Offenses against the Law of Nations;

To declare War, grant Letters of Marque and Reprisal, and make Rules concerning Captures on Land and Water;

To raise and support Armies, but no Appropriation of Money to that Use shall be for a longer Term than two Years;

To provide and maintain a Navy;

To make Rules for the Government and Regulation of the land and naval Forces;

To provide for calling forth the Militia to execute the Laws of the Union, suppress Insurrections and repel Invasions;

To provide for organizing, arming, and disciplining the Militia, and for governing such Part of them as may be employed in the Service of the United States, reserving to the States respectively, the Appointment of the Officers, and the Authority of training the Militia according to the discipline prescribed by Congress;

To exercise exclusive Legislation in all Cases whatsoever, over such District (not exceeding ten Miles square) as may, by Cession of particular States, and the Acceptance of Congress, become the Seat of the Government of the United States, and to exercise like Authority over all Places purchased by the Consent of the Legislature of the State in which the Same shall be, for the Erection of Forts, Magazines, Arsenals, dock-Yards, and other needful Buildings;—And

To make all Laws which shall be necessary and proper for carrying into Execution the foregoing Powers, and all other Powers vested by this Constitution in the Government of the United States, or in any Department or Officer thereof.

Section 9. The Migration or Importation of such Persons as any of the States now existing shall think proper to admit, shall not be prohibited by the Congress prior to the Year one thousand eight hundred and eight, but a Tax or duty may be imposed on such Importation, not exceeding ten dollars for each Person.

The privilege of the Writ of Habeas Corpus shall not be suspended, unless when in Cases of Rebellion or Invasion the public Safety may require it.

No Bill of Attainder or ex post facto Law shall be passed.

No Capitation, or other direct, Tax shall be laid, *unless in Proportion to the Census or Enumeration herein before directed to be taken.*[5]

No Tax or Duty shall be laid on Articles exported from any State.

No Preference shall be given by any Regulation of Commerce or Revenue to the Ports of one State over those of another: nor shall Vessels bound to, or from, one State be obliged to enter, clear, or pay Duties in another.

No Money shall be drawn from the Treasury, but in Consequence of Appropriations made by Law; and a regular Statement and Account of the Receipts and Expenditures of all public Money shall be published from time to time.

No Title of Nobility shall be granted by the United States: And no Person holding any Office of Profit or Trust under them, shall, without the Consent of the Congress, accept of any present, Emolument, Office, or Title, of any kind whatever, from any King, Prince, or foreign State.

Section 10. No State shall enter into any Treaty, Alliance, or Confederation; grant Letters of Marque and Reprisal; coin Money; emit Bills of Credit; make any Thing but gold and silver Coin a Tender in Payment of Debts; pass any Bill of Attainder, ex post facto Law, or Law impairing the Obligation of Contracts, or grant any Title of Nobility.

No State shall, without the Consent of the Congress, lay any Imposts or Duties on Imports or Exports, except what may be absolutely necessary for executing its inspection Laws: and the net Produce of all Duties and Imposts, laid by any State on Imports or Exports, shall be for the Use of the Treasury of the United States; and all such Laws shall be subject to the Revision and Controul of the Congress.

No State shall, without the Consent of Congress, lay any Duty of Tonnage, keep Troops, or Ships of War in time of Peace, enter into any Agreement or Compact with another State, or with a foreign Power, or engage in War, unless actually invaded, or in such imminent Danger as will not admit of delay.

Article II

Section 1. The executive Power shall be vested in a President of the United States of America. He shall hold his Office during the Term of four Years, and, together with the Vice President, chosen for the same Term, be elected, as follows:

Each State shall appoint, in such Manner as the Legislature thereof may direct, a Number of Electors, equal to the whole Number of Senators and Representatives to which the State may be entitled in the Congress; but no Senator or Representative, or Person holding an Office of Trust or Profit under the United States, shall be appointed an Elector.

The Electors shall meet in their respective States, and vote by Ballot for two Persons, of whom one at least shall not be an Inhabitant of the same State with themselves. And they shall make a List of all the Persons voted for, and of the Number of Votes for each; which List they shall sign and certify, and transmit sealed to the Seat of the Government of the United States, directed to the President of the Senate. The President of the Senate shall, in the Presence of the Senate and House of Representatives, open all the Certificates, and the Votes shall then be counted. The Person having the greatest Number of Votes shall be the President, if such Number be a Majority of the whole Number of Electors appointed; and if there be more than one who have such Majority, and have an equal Number of Votes, then the House of Representatives shall immediately chuse by Ballot one of them for President; and if no Person have a Majority, then from the five highest on the List the said House shall in like Manner chuse the President. But in chusing the President, the Votes shall be taken by States, the Representation from each State having one Vote; A quorum for this Purpose shall consist of a Member or Members from two thirds of the States, and a Majority of all the States shall be necessary to a Choice. In every Case, after the Choice of the President, the Person having the greater Number of Votes of the Electors shall be the Vice President. But if there should remain two or more who have equal Votes, the Senate shall chuse from them by Ballot the Vice President.[6]

The Congress may determine the Time of chusing the Electors, and the Day on which they shall give their Votes; which Day shall be the same throughout the United States.

---

[5] Changed by the XVI amendment.

[6] Changed by the XII amendment.

No person except a natural born Citizen, or a Citizen of the United States, at the time of the Adoption of this Constitution, shall be eligible to the Office of President; neither shall any Person be eligible to that Office who shall not have attained to the Age of thirty five Years, and been fourteen Years a Resident within the United States.

In Case of the Removal of the President from Office, or of his Death, Resignation or Inability to discharge the Powers and Duties of the said Office, the same shall devolve on the Vice President, and the Congress may by Law provide for the Case of Removal, Death, Resignation or Inability, both of the President and Vice President, declaring what Officer shall then act as President, and such Officer shall act accordingly, until the Disability be removed, or a President shall be elected.[7]

The President shall, at stated Times, receive for his Services, a Compensation, which shall neither be increased nor diminished during the Period for which he shall have been elected, and he shall not receive within that Period any other Emolument from the United States, or any of them.

Before he enter on the Execution of his Office, he shall take the following Oath or Affirmation: "I do solemnly swear (or affirm) that I will faithfully execute the Office of President of the United States, and will to the best of my Ability, preserve, protect and defend the Constitution of the United States."

Section 2. The President shall be Commander in Chief of the Army and Navy of the United States, and of the Militia of the several States, when called into the actual Service of the United States; he may require the Opinion, in writing, of the principal Officer in each of the executive Departments, upon any Subject relating to the Duties of their respective Offices, and he shall have Power to grant Reprieves and Pardons for Offenses against the United States, except in Cases of Impeachment.

He shall have Power, by and with the Advice and Consent of the Senate to make Treaties, provided two thirds of the Senators present concur; and he shall nominate, and by and with the Advice and Consent of the Senate, shall appoint Ambassadors, other public Ministers and Consuls, Judges of the supreme Court, and all other Officers of the United States, whose Appointments are not herein otherwise provided for, and which shall be established by Law; but the Congress may by Law vest the Appointment of such inferior Officers, as they think proper, in the President alone, in the Courts of Law, or in the Heads of Departments.

The President shall have Power to fill up all Vacancies that may happen during the Recess of the Senate, by granting Commissions which shall expire at the End of their next Session.

Section 3. He shall from time to time give to the Congress Information of the State of the Union, and recommend to their Consideration such Measures as he shall judge necessary and expedient; he may, on extraordinary Occasions, convene both Houses, or either of them, and in Case of Disagreement between them, with Respect to the Time of Adjournment, he may adjourn them to such Time as he shall think proper; he shall receive Ambassadors and other public Ministers; he shall take Care that the Laws be faithfully executed, and shall Commission all the Officers of the United States.

Section 4. The President, Vice President and all civil Officers of the United States, shall be removed from Office on Impeachment for, and Conviction of, Treason, Bribery, or other high Crimes and Misdemeanors.

Article III

Section 1. The judicial Power of the United States, shall be vested in one supreme Court, and in such inferior Courts as the Congress may from time to time ordain and establish. The Judges, both of the supreme and inferior Courts, shall hold their Offices during good Behaviour, and shall, at stated Times, receive for their Services a Compensation, which shall not be diminished during their Continuance in Office.

Section 2. The judicial Power shall extend to all Cases, in Law and Equity, arising under this Constitution, the Laws of the United States, and Treaties made, or which shall be made, under their Authority;—to all Cases affecting Ambassadors, other public Ministers and Consuls;—to all Cases of admiralty and maritime Jurisdiction;—to Controversies to which the United States shall be a Party;—to Controversies between two or more States;—*between a State and Citizens of another State;*[8]—between Citizens of different States;—

---

[7] Changed by the XXV amendment.

[8] Changed by the XI amendment.

between Citizens of the same State claiming Lands under Grants of different States, and between a State, or the Citizens thereof, and foreign States, Citizens or Subjects.

In all Cases affecting Ambassadors, other public Ministers and Consuls, and those in which a State shall be a Party, the supreme Court shall have original Jurisdiction. In all the other Cases before mentioned, the supreme Court shall have appellate Jurisdiction, both as to Law and Fact, with such Exceptions, and under such Regulations as the Congress shall make.

The Trial of all Crimes, except in Cases of Impeachment, shall be by Jury; and such Trial shall be held in the State where the said Crimes shall have been committed; but when not committed within any State, the Trial shall be at such Place or Places as the Congress may by Law have directed.

Section 3. Treason against the United States, shall consist only in levying War against them, or, in adhering to their Enemies, giving them Aid and Comfort. No Person shall be convicted of Treason unless on the Testimony of two Witnesses to the same overt Act, or on Confession in open Court.

The Congress shall have Power to declare the Punishment of Treason, but no Attainder of Treason shall work Corruption of Blood, or Forfeiture except during the Life of the Person attainted.

Article IV

Section 1. Full Faith and Credit shall be given in each State to the public Acts, Records, and judicial Proceedings of every other State. And the Congress may by general Laws prescribe the Manner in which such Acts, Records and Proceedings shall be proved, and the Effect thereof.

Section 2. The Citizens of each State shall be entitled to all Privileges and Immunities of Citizens in the several States.

A Person charged in any State with Treason, Felony, or other Crime, who shall flee from Justice, and be found in another State, shall on Demand of the executive Authority of the State from which he fled, be delivered up, to be removed to the State having Jurisdiction of the Crime.

No Person held to Service or Labour in one State, under the Laws thereof, escaping into another, shall, in Consequence of any Law or Regulation therein, be discharged from such

Service or Labour, but shall be delivered up on Claim of the Party to whom such Service or Labour may be due.[9]

Section 3. New States may be admitted by the Congress into this Union; but no new State shall be formed or erected within the Jurisdiction of any other State; nor any State be formed by the Junction of two or more States, or Parts of States, without the Consent of the Legislatures of the States concerned as well as of the Congress.

The Congress shall have Power to dispose of and make all needful Rules and Regulations respecting the Territory or other Property belonging to the United States; and nothing in this Constitution shall be so construed as to Prejudice any Claims of the United States, or of any particular State.

Section 4. The United States shall guarantee to every State in this Union a Republican Form of Government, and shall protect each of them against Invasion; and on Application of the Legislature, or of the Executive (when the Legislature cannot be convened) against domestic Violence.

Article V

The Congress, whenever two thirds of both Houses shall deem it necessary, shall propose Amendments to this Constitution, or, on the Application of the Legislatures of two thirds of the several States, shall call a Convention for proposing Amendments, which, in either Case, shall be valid to all Intents and Purposes, as part of this Constitution, when ratified by the Legislatures of three fourths of the several States, or by Conventions in three fourths thereof, as the one or the other Mode of Ratification may be proposed by the Congress; Provided that no Amendment which may be made prior to the Year One thousand eight hundred and eight shall in any Manner affect the first and fourth Clauses in the Ninth Section of the first Article; and that no State, without its Consent, shall be deprived of its equal Suffrage in the Senate.

Article VI

All Debts contracted and Engagements entered into, before the Adoption of this Constitution shall be as

---

[9] Repealed by the XIII amendment.

valid against the United States under this Constitution, as under the Confederation.

This Constitution, and the Laws of the United States which shall be made in Pursuance thereof; and all Treaties made, or which shall be made, under the Authority of the United States, shall be the supreme Law of the Land; and the Judges in every State shall be bound thereby, any Thing in the Constitution or Laws of any State to the Contrary notwithstanding.

The Senators and Representatives before mentioned, and the Members of the several State Legislatures, and all executive and judicial Officers, both of the United States and of the several States, shall be bound by Oath or Affirmation, to support this Constitution; but no religious Test shall ever be required as a Qualification to any Office or public Trust under the United States.

Article VII

The Ratification of the Conventions of nine States shall be sufficient for the Establishment of this Constitution between the States so ratifying the Same.

Attest: William Jackson, Secretary

Done in Convention by the unanimous Consent of the Senate present the Seventeenth Day of September in the Year of our Lord one thousand seven hundred and Eighty seven and of the Independence of the United States of America the Twelfth. In witness whereof, We have hereunto subscribed our Names,

G°. Washington
   Presidt and deputy from Virginia

Delaware
   Geo: Read
   Gunning Bedford jun
   John Dickinson
   Richard Bassett
   Jaco: Broom

Maryland
   James McHenry
   Dan of St Thos. Jenifer
   Danl. Carroll

Virginia
   John Blair
   James Madison Jr.

North Carolina
   Wm. Blount
   Richd. Dobbs Spaight
   Hu Williamson

South Carolina
   J. Rutledge
   Charles Cotesworth Pinckney
   Charles Pinckney
   Pierce Butler

Georgia
   William Few
   Abr Baldwin

New Hampshire
   John Langdon
   Nicholas Gilman

Massachusetts
   Nathaniel Gorham
   Rufus King

Connecticut
   Wm. Saml. Johnson
   Roger Sherman

New York
   Alexander Hamilton

New Jersey
   Wil: Livingston
   David Brearley
   Wm. Paterson
   Jona: Dayton

Pennsylvania
   B. Franklin
   Thomas Mifflin
   Robt. Morris
   Geo. Clymer
   Thos. FitzSimmons
   Jared Ingersoll
   James Wilson
   Gouv Morris

The First 10 Amendments to the Constitution as Ratified by the States

Note: THE FOLLOWING TEXT IS OF THE FIRST 10 AMENDMENTS TO THE CONSTITUTION. THESE AMENDMENTS WERE RATIFIED DECEMBER 15, 1791, AND FORM WHAT IS KNOWN AS THE "BILL OF RIGHTS."

THE PREAMBLE TO THE BILL OF RIGHTS

CONGRESS OF THE UNITED STATES
BEGUN AND HELD AT THE CITY OF NEW-YORK, ON
WEDNESDAY THE FOURTH OF MARCH, ONE
THOUSAND SEVEN HUNDRED AND EIGHTY NINE.

THE CONVENTIONS OF A NUMBER OF THE STATES, HAVING AT THE TIME OF THEIR ADOPTING THE CONSTITUTION, EXPRESSED A DESIRE, IN ORDER TO PREVENT MISCONSTRUCTION OR ABUSE OF ITS POWERS, THAT FURTHER DECLARATORY AND RESTRICTIVE CLAUSES SHOULD BE ADDED: AND AS EXTENDING THE GROUND OF PUBLIC CONFIDENCE IN THE GOVERNMENT, WILL BEST ENSURE THE BENEFICENT ENDS OF ITS INSTITUTION.

RESOLVED BY THE SENATE AND HOUSE OF REPRESENTATIVES OF THE UNITED STATES OF AMERICA, IN CONGRESS ASSEMBLED, TWO THIRDS OF BOTH HOUSES CONCURRING, THAT THE FOLLOWING ARTICLES BE PROPOSED TO THE LEGISLATURES OF THE SEVERAL STATES AS AMENDMENTS TO THE CONSTITUTION OF THE UNITED STATES, ALL, OR ANY OF WHICH ARTICLES, WHEN RATIFIED BY THREE FOURTHS OF THE SAID LEGISLATURES, TO BE VALID TO ALL INTENTS AND PURPOSES, AS PART OF THE SAID CONSTITUTION; VIZ.

ARTICLES IN ADDITION TO, AND AMENDMENT OF THE CONSTITUTION OF THE UNITED STATES OF AMERICA, PROPOSED BY CONGRESS AND RATIFIED BY THE LEGISLATURES OF THE SEVERAL STATES, PURSUANT TO THE FIFTH ARTICLE OF THE ORIGINAL CONSTITUTION.

Amendment I [1791]

Congress shall make no law respecting an establishment of religion, or prohibiting the free exercise thereof; or abridging the freedom of speech, or of the press; or the right of the people peaceably to assembly, and to petition the Government for a redress of grievances.

Amendment II [1791]

A well regulated Militia, being necessary to the security of a free State, the right of the people to keep and bear Arms, shall not be infringed.

Amendment III [1791]

No Soldier shall, in time of peace be quartered in any house, without the consent of the Owner, nor in time of war, but in a manner to be prescribed by law.

Amendment IV [1791]

The right of the people to be secure in their persons, houses, papers, and effects, against unreasonable searches and seizures, shall not be violated, and no Warrants shall issue, but upon probable cause, supported by Oath or affirmation, and particularly describing the place to be searched, and the persons or things to be seized.

Amendment V [1791]

No person shall be held to answer for a capital, or otherwise infamous crime, unless on a presentment or indictment of a Grand Jury, except in cases arising in the land or naval forces, or in the Militia, when in actual service in time of War or public danger; nor shall any person be subject for the same offence to be twice put in jeopardy of life or limb; nor shall be compelled in any criminal case to be a witness against himself, nor be deprived of life, liberty, or property, without due process of law; nor shall private property be taken for public use, without just compensation.

Amendment VI [1791]

In all criminal prosecutions, the accused shall enjoy the right to a speedy and public trial, by an impartial jury of the State and district wherein the crime shall have been committed, which district shall have been previously ascertained by law, and to be informed of the nature and cause of the accusation; to be confronted with the witnesses against him; to have compulsory process for obtaining witnesses in his favor, and to have the Assistance of Counsel for his defence.

Amendment VII [1791]

In Suits at common law, where the value in controversy shall exceed twenty dollars, the right of trial by jury shall be preserved, and no fact tried by jury, shall be otherwise re-examined in any Court of the United States, than according to the rules of the common law.

Amendment VIII [1791]

Excessive bail shall not be required, nor excessive fines imposed, nor cruel and unusual punishments inflicted.

Amendment IX [1791]

The enumeration in the Constitution, of certain rights, shall not be construed to deny or disparage others retained by the people.

Amendment X [1791]

The powers not delegated to the United States by the Constitution, nor prohibited by it to the States, are reserved to the States respectively, or to the people.

Amendments 11–27 to the Constitution of the United States

Amendment XI [1798]

PASSED BY CONGRESS MARCH 4, 1794. RATIFIED FEBRUARY 7, 1795.
Note: ARTICLE III, SECTION 2, OF THE CONSTITUTION WAS MODIFIED BY AMENDMENT XI.

The Judicial power of the United States shall not be construed to extend to any suit in law or equity, commenced or prosecuted against one of the United States by Citizens of another State, or by Citizens or Subjects of any Foreign State.

Amendment XII [1804]

PASSED BY CONGRESS DECEMBER 9, 1803. RATIFIED JUNE 15, 1804.

The Electors shall meet in their respective states, and vote by ballot for President and Vice-President, one of whom, at least, shall not be an inhabitant of the same state with themselves; they shall name in their ballots the person voted for as President, and in distinct ballots the person voted for as Vice-President, and they shall make distinct lists of all persons voted for as President, and of all persons voted for as Vice-President, and of the number of votes for each, which lists they shall sign and certify, and transmit sealed to the seat of the government of the United States, directed to the President of the Senate;—The President of the Senate shall, in the presence of the Senate and House of Representatives, open all the certificates and the votes shall then be counted;—The person having the greatest number of votes for President, shall be the President, if such number be a majority of the whole number of Electors appointed; and if no person have such majority, then from the persons having the highest numbers not exceeding three on the list of those voted for as President, the House of Representatives shall choose immediately, by ballot, the President. But in choosing the President, the votes shall be taken by states, the representation from each state having one vote; a quorum for this purpose shall consist of a member or members from two-thirds of the states, and a majority of all states shall be necessary to a choice. *And if the House of Representatives shall not choose a President whenever the right of choice shall devolve upon them, before the fourth day of March next following, then the Vice-President shall act as President, as in the case of the death or other constitutional disability of the President.*[10] The person having the greatest number of votes as Vice-President, shall be the Vice-President, if such number be a majority of the whole number of Electors appointed, and if no person have a majority, then from the two highest numbers on the list, the Senate shall choose the Vice-President; a quorum for the purpose shall consist of two-thirds of the whole number of Senators, and a majority of the whole number shall be necessary to a choice. But no person constitutionally ineligible to the office of President shall be eligible to that of Vice-President of the United States.

Amendment XIII [1865]

PASSED BY CONGRESS JANUARY 31, 1865. RATIFIED DECEMBER 6, 1865.

Section 1. Neither slavery nor involuntary servitude, except as a punishment for crime whereof the party shall have been duly convicted, shall exist within the United States, or any place subject to their jurisdiction.

[10] Superceded by Section 3 of the XX amendment.

Section 2. Congress shall have power to enforce this article by appropriate legislation.

Amendment XIV [1868]

PASSED BY CONGRESS JUNE 13, 1866. RATIFIED JULY 9, 1868.

Section 1. All persons born or naturalized in the United States, and subject to the jurisdiction thereof, are citizens of the United States and of the State wherein they reside. No State shall make or enforce any law which shall abridge the privileges or immunities of citizens of the United States; nor shall any State deprive any person of life, liberty, or property, without due process of law; nor deny to any person within its jurisdiction the equal protection of the laws.

Section 2. Representatives shall be apportioned among the several States according to their respective numbers, counting the whole number of persons in each State, excluding Indians not taxed. But when the right to vote at any election for the choice of electors for President and Vice President of the United States, Representatives in Congress, the Executive and Judicial officers of a State, or the members of the Legislature thereof, is denied to any of the male inhabitants of such State, *being twenty-one years of age,*[11] and citizens of the United States, or in any way abridged, except for participation in rebellion, or other crime, the basis of representation therein shall be reduced in the proportion which the number of such male citizens shall bear to the whole number of male citizens twenty-one years of age in such State.

Section 3. No person shall be a Senator or Representative in Congress, or elector of President and Vice President, or hold any office, civil or military, under the United States, or under any State, who having previously taken an oath, as a member of Congress, or as an officer of the United States, or as a member of any State legislature, or as an executive or judicial officer of any State, to support the Constitution of the United States, shall have engaged in insurrection or rebellion against the same, or given aid or comfort to the enemies thereof. But Congress may by a vote of two-thirds of each House, remove such disability.

[11] Changed by Section 1 of the XXVI amendment.

Section 4. The validity of the public debt of the United States, authorized by law, including debts incurred for payment of pensions and bounties for services in suppressing insurrection or rebellion, shall not be questioned. But neither the United States nor any State shall assume or pay any debt or obligation incurred in aid of insurrection or rebellion against the United States, or any claim for the loss or emancipation of any slave; but all such debts, obligations and claims shall be held illegal and void.

Section 5. The Congress shall have power to enforce, by appropriate legislation, the provisions of this article.

Amendment XV [1870]

PASSED BY CONGRESS FEBRUARY 26, 1869. RATIFIED FEBRUARY 3, 1870.

Section 1. The right of citizens of the United States to vote shall not be denied or abridged by the United States or by any State on account of race, color, or previous condition of servitude.

Section 2. The Congress shall have power to enforce this article by appropriate legislation.

Amendment XVI [1913]

PASSED BY CONGRESS JULY 2, 1909. RATIFIED FEBRUARY 3, 1913.

The Congress shall have power to lay and collect taxes on incomes, from whatever source derived, without apportionment among the several States, and without regard to any census or enumeration.

Amendment XVII [1913]

PASSED BY CONGRESS MAY 13, 1912. RATIFIED APRIL 8, 1913.

The Senate of the United States shall be composed of two Senators from each State, elected by the people thereof, for six years; and each Senator shall have one vote. The electors in each State shall have the qualifications requisite for electors of the most numerous branch of the State legislatures.

When vacancies happen in the representation of any State in the Senate, the executive authority of such

State shall issue writs of election to fill such vacancies: Provided, That the legislature of any State may empower the executive thereof to make temporary appointments until the people fill the vacancies by election as the legislature may direct.

This amendment shall not be so construed as to affect the election or term of any Senator chosen before it becomes valid as part of the Constitution.

Amendment XVIII [1919] [Repealed]

PASSED BY CONGRESS DECEMBER 18, 1917. RATIFIED JANUARY 16, 1919. REPEALED BY XXI AMENDMENT.

Section 1. After one year from the ratification of this article the manufacture, sale, or transportation of intoxicating liquors within, the importation thereof into, or the exportation thereof from the United States and all territory subject to the jurisdiction thereof for beverage purposes is hereby prohibited.

Section 2. The Congress and the several States shall have concurrent power to enforce this article by appropriate legislation.

Section 3. This article shall be inoperative unless it shall have been ratified as an amendment to the Constitution by the legislatures of the several States, as provided in the Constitution, within seven years from the date of the submission hereof to the States by the Congress.

Amendment XIX [1920]

PASSED BY CONGRESS JUNE 4, 1919. RATIFIED AUGUST 18, 1920.

The right of citizens of the United States to vote shall not be denied or abridged by the United States or by any State on account of sex.

Congress shall have power to enforce this article by appropriate legislation.

Amendment XX [1933]

PASSED BY CONGRESS MARCH 2, 1932. RATIFIED JANUARY 23, 1933.

Section 1. The terms of the President and Vice President shall end at noon on the 20th day of January, and the terms of Senators and Representatives at noon on the 3d day of January, of the years in which such terms would have ended if this article had not been ratified; and the terms of their successors shall then begin.

Section 2. The Congress shall assemble at least once in every year, and such meeting shall begin at noon on the 3d day of January, unless they shall by law appoint a different day.

Section 3. If, at the time fixed for the beginning of the term of the President, the President elect shall have died, the Vice President elect shall become President. If the President shall not have been chosen before the time fixed for the beginning of his term, or if the President elect shall have failed to qualify, then the Vice President elect shall act as President until a President shall have qualified; and the Congress may by law provide for the case wherein neither a President elect nor a Vice President elect shall have qualified, declaring who shall then act as President, or the manner in which one who is to act shall be selected, and such person shall act accordingly until a President or Vice President shall have qualified.

Section 4. The Congress may by law provide for the case of the death of any of the persons from whom the House of Representatives may choose a President whenever the right of choice shall have devolved upon them, and for the case of the death of any of the persons from whom the Senate may choose a Vice President whenever the right of choice shall have devolved upon them.

Section 5. Sections 1 and 2 shall take effect on the 15th day of October following the ratification of this article.

Section 6. This article shall be inoperative unless it shall have been ratified as an amendment to the Constitution by the legislatures of three-fourths of the several States within seven years from the date of its submission.

Amendment XXI [1933]

PASSED BY CONGRESS FEBRUARY 20, 1933. RATIFIED DECEMBER 5, 1933.

Section 1. The eighteenth article of amendment to the Constitution of the United States is hereby repealed.

Section 2. The transportation or importation into any State, Territory, or possession of the United States for delivery or use therein of intoxicating liquors, in violation of the laws thereof, is hereby prohibited.

Section 3. This article shall be inoperative unless it shall have been ratified as an amendment to the Constitution by conventions in the several States, as provided in the Constitution, within seven years from the date of the submission hereof to the States by the Congress.

Amendment XXII [1951]

PASSED BY CONGRESS MARCH 21, 1947. RATIFIED FEBRUARY 27, 1951.

Section 1. No person shall be elected to the office of the President more than twice, and no person who has held the office of President, or acted as President, for more than two years of a term to which some other person was elected President shall be elected to the office of President more than once. But this Article shall not apply to any person holding the office of President when this Article was proposed by the Congress, and shall not prevent any person who may be holding the office of President, or acting as President, during the term within which this Article becomes operative from holding the office of President or acting as President during the remainder of such term.

Section 2. This article shall be inoperative unless it shall have been ratified as an amendment to the Constitution by the legislatures of three-fourths of the several States within seven years from the date of its submission to the States by the Congress.

Amendment XXIII [1961]

PASSED BY CONGRESS JUNE 16, 1960. RATIFIED MARCH 29, 1961.

Section 1. The District constituting the seat of Government of the United States shall appoint in such manner as the Congress may direct:

A number of electors of President and Vice President equal to the whole number of Senators and Representatives in Congress to which the District would be entitled if it were a State, but in no event more than the least populous state; they shall be in addition to those appointed by the states, but they shall be considered, for the purposes of the election of President and Vice President, to be electors appointed by a state; and they shall meet in the District and perform such duties as provided by the twelfth article of amendment.

Section 2. The Congress shall have power to enforce this article by appropriate legislation.

Amendment XXIV [1964]

PASSED BY CONGRESS AUGUST 27, 1962. RATIFIED JANUARY 23, 1964.

Section 1. The right of citizens of the United States to vote in any primary or other election for President or Vice President, for electors for President or Vice President, or for Senator or Representative in Congress, shall not be denied or abridged by the United States, or any State by reason of failure to pay any poll tax or other tax.

Section 2. The Congress shall have power to enforce this article by appropriate legislation.

Amendment XXV [1967]

PASSED BY CONGRESS JULY 6, 1965. RATIFIED FEBRUARY 10, 1967.

Section 1. In case of the removal of the President from office or of his death or resignation, the Vice President shall become President.

Section 2. Whenever there is a vacancy in the office of the Vice President, the President shall nominate a Vice President who shall take office upon confirmation by a majority vote of both Houses of Congress.

Section 3. Whenever the President transmits to the President pro tempore of the Senate and the Speaker of the House of Representatives his written declaration that he is unable to discharge the powers and duties of his office, and until he transmits to them a written declaration to the contrary, such powers and duties shall be discharged by the Vice President as Acting President.

Section 4. Whenever the Vice President and a majority of either the principal officers of the executive departments or of such other body as Congress may by law provide, transmit to the President pro tempore of the Senate and the Speaker of the House of Representatives their written declaration that the President is unable to discharge the powers and duties of his office, the Vice President shall immediately assume the powers and duties of the office as Acting President.

Thereafter, when the President transmits to the President pro tempore of the Senate and the Speaker of the House of Representatives his written declaration that no inability exists, he shall resume the powers and duties of his office unless the Vice President and a majority of either the principal officers of the executive department or of such other body as Congress may by law provide, transmit within four days to the President pro tempore of the Senate and the Speaker of the House of Representatives their written declaration that the President is unable to discharge the powers and duties of his office. Thereupon Congress shall decide the issue, assembling within forty-eight hours for that purpose if not in session. If the Congress, within twenty-one days after receipt of the latter written declaration, or, if Congress is not in session, within twenty-one days after Congress is required to assemble, determines by two-thirds vote of both Houses that the President is unable to discharge the powers and duties of his office, the Vice President shall continue to discharge the same as Acting President; otherwise, the President shall resume the powers and duties of his office.

Amendment XXVI [1971]

PASSED BY CONGRESS MARCH 23, 1971. RATIFIED JULY 1, 1971.

Section 1. The right of citizens of the United States, who are eighteen years of age or older, to vote shall not be denied or abridged by the United States or by any State on account of age.

Section 2. The Congress shall have power to enforce this article by appropriate legislation.

Amendment XXVII [1992]

ORIGINALLY PROPOSED SEPTEMBER 25, 1789. RATIFIED MAY 7, 1992.

No law, varying the compensation for the services of the Senators and Representatives, shall take effect, until an election of Representatives shall have intervened.

Appendix B · The Uniform Commercial Code (Excerpts)*

Article 1. GENERAL PROVISIONS.

Part 2. General Definitions and Principles of Interpretation.

§ 1-201. General Definitions.

Subject to additional definitions contained in the subsequent Articles of this Act which are applicable to specific Articles or Parts thereof, and unless the context otherwise requires, in this Act:

(6) "Bill of lading" means a document evidencing the receipt of goods for shipment issued by a person engaged in the business of transporting or forwarding goods, and includes an airbill. "Airbill" means a document serving for air transportation as a bill of lading does for marine or rail transportation, and includes an air consignment note or air waybill.

(15) "Document of title" includes bill of lading, dock warrant, dock receipt, warehouse receipt or order for the delivery of goods, and also any other document which in the regular course of business or financing is treated as adequately evidencing that the person in possession of it is entitled to receive, hold and dispose of the document and the goods it covers. To be a document of title a document must purport to be issued by or addressed to a bailee and purport to cover goods in the bailee's possession which are either identified or are fungible portions of an identified mass.

(19) "Good faith" means honesty in fact in the conduct or transaction concerned.

(20) "Holder" with respect to a negotiable instrument, means the person in possession if the instrument is payable to bearer or, in the case of an instrument payable to an identified person, if the identified person is in possession. "Holder" with respect to a document of title means the person in possession if the goods are deliverable to bearer or the order of the person in possession.

(32) "Purchase" includes taking by sale, discount, negotiation, mortgage, pledge, lien, issue or re-issue, gift or any other voluntary transaction creating an interest in property.

(39) "Signed includes any symbol executed or adopted by a party with present intention to authenticate a writing.

(43) "Unauthorized" signature means one made without actual, implied or apparent authority and includes a fogery.

(45) "Warehouse receipt" means a receipt issued by a person engaged in the business of storing goods for hire.

(46) "Written" or "writing" includes printing, typewriting or any other intentional reduction to tangible form.

§ 1-203. Obligation of Good Faith.

Every contract or duty within this Act imposes an obligation of good faith in its performance or enforcement.

---

*The Uniform Commercial Code. ©The American Law Institute and the National Conference of Commissioners on Uniform State Laws. Excerpts from the UCC are reprinted with permission.

§ 1–205. Course of Dealing and Usage of Trade.

(1) A course of dealing is a sequence of previous conduct between the parties to a particular transaction which is fairly to be regarded as establishing a common basis of understanding for interpreting their expressions and other conduct.

(2) A usage of trade is any practice or method of dealing having such regularity of observance in a place, vocation or trade as to justify an expectation that it will be observed with respect to the transaction in question. The existence and scope of such a usage are to be proved as facts. If it is established that such a usage is embodied in a written trade code or similar writing the interpretation of the writing is for the court.

(3) A course of dealing between parties and any usage of trade in the vocation or trade in which they are engaged or of which they are or should be aware give particular meaning to and supplement or qualify terms of an agreement.

(4) The express terms of an agreement and an applicable course of dealing or usage of trade shall be construed wherever reasonable as consistent with each other; but when such construction is unreasonable express terms control both course of dealing and usage of trade and course of dealing controls usage of trade.

(5) An applicable usage of trade in the place where any part of performance is to occur shall be used in interpreting the agreement as to that part of the performance.

(6) Evidence of a relevant usage of trade offered by one party is not admissible unless and until he has given the other party such notice as the court finds sufficient to prevent unfair surprise to the latter.

Article 2. SALES.

Part 1. Short Title, General Construction and Subject Matter.

§ 2-104. Definitions: "Merchant"; "Between Merchants"; "Financing Agency".

(1) "Merchant" means a person who deals in goods of the kind or otherwise by his occupation holds himself out as having knowledge or skill peculiar to the practices or goods involved in the transaction or to whom such knowledge or skill may be attributed by his employment of an agent or broker or other intermediary who by his occupation holds himself out as having such knowledge or skill.

(2) "Financing agency" means a bank, finance company or other person who in the ordinary course of business makes advances against goods or documents of title or who by arrangement with either the seller or the buyer intervenes in ordinary course to make or collect payment due or claimed under the contract for sale, as by purchasing or paying the seller's draft or making advances against it or by merely taking it for collection whether or not documents of title accompany the draft. "Financing agency" includes also a bank or other person who similarly intervenes between persons who are in the position of seller and buyer in respect to the goods (Section 2-707).

(3) "Between merchants" means in any transaction with respect to which both parties are chargeable with the knowledge or skill of merchants.

§ 2-105. Definitions: Transferability; "Goods"; "Future Goods"; "Lot"; "Commercial Unit".

(1) "Goods" means all things (including specially manufactured goods) which are moveable at the time of identification to the contract for sale other than the money in which the price is to be paid, investment securities (Article 8) and things in action. "Goods" also includes the unborn young of animals and growing crops and other identified things attached to realty as described in the section on goods to be severed from realty (Section 2-107).

(2) Goods must be both existing and identified before any interest in them can pass. Goods which are both existing and identified are "future" goods. A purported present sale of future goods or of any interest therein operates as a contract to sell.

(3) There may be a sale of a part interest in existing identified goods.

(4) An undivided share in an identified bulk of fungible goods is sufficiently identified to be sold although the quantity of the bulk is not determined. Any agreed proportion of such a bulk or any quantity thereof agreed upon by number, weight or other measure may to the extent of the seller's interest in the bulk be sold to the buyer who then becomes an owner in common.

(5) "Lot" means a parcel or a single article which is the subject matter of a separate sale or delivery, whether or not it is sufficient to perform the contract.

(6) "Commercial unit" means such a unit of goods as by commercial usage is a single whole for purposes of sale and division of which materially impairs its character or value on the market or in use. A commercial unit may be a single article (as a machine) or a set of articles (as a suite of furniture or an assortment of sizes) or a quantity (as a bale, gross, or carload) or any other unit treated in use or in the relevant market as a single whole.

Part 2. Form, Formation and Readjustment of Contract.

§ 2-201. Formal Requirements; Statute of Frauds.

(1) Except as otherwise provided in this section a contract for the sale of goods for the price of $500 or more is not enforceable by way of action or defense unless there is some writing sufficient to indicate that a contract for sale has been made between the parties and signed by the party against whom enforcement is sought or by his authorized agent or broker. A writing is not insufficient because it omits or incorrectly states a term agreed upon but the contract is not enforceable under this paragraph beyond the quantity of goods shown in such writing.

(2) Between merchants if within a reasonable time a writing in confirmation of the contract and sufficient against the sender is received and the party receiving it has reason to know its contents, it satisfies the requirements of subsection (1) against such party unless written notice of objection to its contents is given within ten days after it is received.

(3) A contract which does not satisfy the requirements of subsection (1) but which is valid in other respects is enforceable

(a) if the goods are to be specially manufactured for the buyer and are not suitable for sale to others in the ordinary course of the seller's business and the seller, before notice of repudiation is received and under circumstances which reasonably indicate that the goods are for the buyer, has made either a substantial beginning of their manufacture or commitments for their procurement; or

(b) if the party against whom enforcement is sought admits in his pleading, testimony or otherwise in court that a contract for sale was made, but the contract is not enforceable under this provision beyond the quantity of goods admitted; or

(c) with respect to goods for which payment has been made and accepted or which have been received and accepted (Sec. 2-606).

§ 2-204. Formation in General.

(1) A contract for sale of goods may be made in any manner sufficient to show agreement, including conduct by both parties which recognizes the existence of such a contract.

(2) An agreement sufficient to constitute a contract for sale may be found even though the moment of its making is undetermined.

(3) Even though one or more terms are left open a contract for sale does not fail for indefiniteness if the parties have intended to make a contract and there is a reasonably certain basis for giving an appropriate remedy.

§ 2-205. Firm Offers.

An offer by a merchant to buy or sell goods in a signed writing which by its terms gives assurance that it will be held open is not revocable, for lack of consideration, during the time stated or if no time is stated for a reasonable time, but in no event may such period of irrevocability exceed three months; but any such term of assurance on a form supplied by the offeree must be separately signed by the offeror.

§ 2-206. Offer and Acceptance in Formation of Contract.

(1) Unless otherwise unambiguously indicated by the language or circumstances

(a) an offer to make a contract shall be construed as inviting acceptance in any manner and by any medium reasonable in the circumstances;

(b) an order or other offer to buy goods for prompt or current shipment shall be construed as inviting acceptance either by a prompt promise to ship or by the prompt or current shipment of conforming or non-conforming goods, but such a shipment of non-conforming goods does not constitute an acceptance if the seller seasonably notifies the buyer that the shipment is offered only as an accommodation to the buyer.

(2) Where the beginning of a requested performance is a reasonable mode of acceptance an offeror who is not notified of acceptance within a reasonable time may treat the offer as having lapsed before acceptance.

§ 2-207. Additional Terms in Acceptance or Confirmation.

(1) A definite and seasonable expression of acceptance or a written confirmation which is sent within a reasonable time operates as an acceptance even though it states terms additional to or different from those offered or agreed upon, unless acceptance is expressly made conditional on assent to the additional or different terms.

(2) The additional terms are to be construed as proposals for addition to the contract. Between merchants such terms become part of the contract unless:

> (a) the offer expressly limits acceptance to the terms of the offer;

> (b) they materially alter it; or

> (c) notification of objection to them has already been given or is given within a reasonable time after notice of them is received.

(3) Conduct by both parties which recognizes the existence of a contract is sufficient to establish a contract for sale although the writings of the parties do not otherwise establish a contract. In such case the terms of the particular contract consist of those terms on which the writings of the parties agree, together with any supplementary terms incorporated under any other provisions of this Act.

§ 2-209. Modification, Rescission and Waiver.

(1) An agreement modifying a contract within this Article needs no consideration to be binding.

(2) A signed agreement which excludes modification or rescission except by a signed writing cannot be otherwise modified or rescinded, but except as between merchants such a requirement on a form supplied by the merchant must be separately signed by the other party.

(3) The requirements of the statute of frauds section of this Article (Section 2-201) must be satisfied if the contract as modified is within its provisions.

(4) Although an attempt at modification or rescission does not satisfy the requirements of subsection (2) or (3) it can operate as a waiver.

(5) A party who has made a waiver affecting an executory portion of the contract may retract the waiver by reasonable notification received by the other party that strict performance will be required of any term waived, unless the retraction would be unjust in view of a material change of position in reliance on the waiver.

Part 3. General Obligation and Construction of Contract.

§ 2-302. Unconscionable Contract or Clause.

(1) If the court as a matter of law finds the contract or any clause of the contract to have been unconscionable at the time it was made the court may refuse to enforce the contract, or it may enforce the remainder of the contract without the unconscionable clause, or it may so limit the application of any unconscionable clause as to avoid any unconscionable result.

(2) When it is claimed or appears to the court that the contract or any clause thereof may be unconscionable the parties shall be afforded a reasonable opportunity to present evidence as to its commercial setting, purpose and effect to aid the court in making the determination.

§ 2-305. Open Price Term.

(1) The parties if they so intend can conclude a contract for sale even though the price is not settled. In such a case the price is a reasonable price at the time for delivery if

> (a) nothing is said as to price; or

> (b) the price is left to be agreed by the parties and they fail to agree; or

> (c) the price is to be fixed in terms of some agreed market or other standard as set or recorded by a third person or agency and it is not so set or recorded.

(2) A price to be fixed by the seller or by the buyer means a price for him to fix in good faith.

(3) When a price left to be fixed otherwise than by agreement of the parties fails to be fixed through fault of one party the other may at his option treat the contract as cancelled or himself fix a reasonable price.

(4) Where, however, the parties intend not to be bound unless the price be fixed or agreed and it is not fixed or agreed there is no contract. In such a case the buyer must return any goods already received or if unable so to do must pay their reasonable value at the time of delivery and the seller must return any portion of the price paid on account.

§ 2–306. Output, Requirements and Exclusive Dealings.

(1) A term which measures the quantity by the output of the seller or the requirements of the buyer means such actual output or requirements as may occur in good faith, except that no quantity unreasonably disproportionate to any stated estimate or in the absence of a stated estimate to any normal or otherwise comparable prior output or requirements may be tendered or demanded.

(2) A lawful agreement by either the seller or the buyer for exclusive dealing in the kind of goods concerned imposes unless otherwise agreed an obligation by the seller to use best efforts to supply the goods and by the buyer to use best efforts to promote their sale.

§ 2–307. Delivery in Single Lot or Several Lots.

Unless otherwise agreed all goods called for by a contract for sale must be tendered in a single delivery and payment is due only on such tender but where the circumstances give either party the right to make or demand delivery in lots the price if it can be apportioned may be demanded for each lot.

§ 2–308. Absence of Specified Place for Delivery.

Unless otherwise agreed

(a) the place for delivery of goods is the seller's place of business or if he has none his residence; but

(b) in a contract for sale of identified goods which to the knowledge of the parties at the time of contracting are in some other place, that place is the place for their delivery; and

(c) documents of title may be delivered through customary banking channels.

§ 2–309. Absence of Specific Time Provisions; Notice of Termination.

(1) The time for shipment or delivery or any other action under a contract if not provided in this Article or agreed upon shall be a reasonable time.

(2) Where the contract provides for successive performances but is indefinite in duration it is valid for a reasonable time but unless otherwise agreed may be terminated at any time by either party.

(3) Termination of a contract by one party except on the happening of an agreed event requires that reasonable notification be received by the other party and an agreement dispensing with notification is invalid if its operation would be unconscionable.

§ 2–310. Open Time for Payment or Running of Credit; Authority to Ship Under Reservation.

Unless otherwise agreed

(a) payment is due at the time and place at which the buyer is to receive the goods even though the place of shipment is the place of delivery; and

(b) if the seller is authorized to send the goods he may ship them under reservation, and may tender the documents of title, but the buyer may inspect the goods after their arrival before payment is due unless such inspection is inconsistent with the terms of the contract (Section 2–513); and

(c) if delivery is authorized and made by way of documents of title otherwise than by subsection (b) then payment is due at the time and place at which the buyer is to receive the documents regardless of where the goods are to be received; and

(d) where the seller is required or authorized to ship the goods on credit the credit period runs from the time of shipment but post-dating the invoice or delaying its dispatch will correspondingly delay the starting of the credit period.

§ 2-312. Warranty of Title and Against Infringement; Buyer's Obligation Against Infringement.

(1) Subject to subsection (2) there is in a contract for sale a warranty by the seller that

(a) the title conveyed shall be good, and its transfer rightful; and

(b) the goods shall be delivered free from any security interest or other lien or encumbrance of which the buyer at the time of contracting has no knowledge.

(2) A warranty under subsection (1) will be excluded or modified only by specific language or by circumstances which give the buyer reason to know that the person selling does not claim title in himself or that he is purporting to sell only such right or title as he or a third person may have.

(3) Unless otherwise agreed a seller who is a merchant regularly dealing in goods of the kind warrants that the goods shall be delivered free of the rightful claim of any third person by way of infringement or the like but a buyer who furnishes specifications to the seller must hold the seller harmless against any such claim which arises out of compliance with the specifications.

§ 2-313. Express Warranties by Affirmation, Promise, Description, Sample.

(1) Express warranties by the seller are created as follows:

(a) Any affirmation of fact or promise made by the seller to the buyer which relates to the goods and becomes part of the basis of the bargain creates an express warranty that the goods shall conform to the affirmation or promise.

(b) Any description of the goods which is made part of the basis of the bargain creates an express warranty that the goods shall conform to the description.

(c) Any sample or model which is made part of the basis of the bargain creates an express warranty that the whole of the goods shall conform to the sample or model.

(2) It is not necessary to the creation of an express warranty that the seller use formal words such as "warrant" or "guarantee" or that he have a specific intention to make a warranty, but an affirmation merely of the value of the goods or a statement purporting to be merely the seller's opinion or commendation of the goods does not create a warranty.

§ 2-314. Implied Warranty: Merchantability; Usage of Trade.

(1) Unless excluded or modified (Section 2-316), a warranty that the goods shall be merchantable is implied in a contract for their sale if the seller is a merchant with respect to goods of that kind. Under this section the serving for value of food or drink to be consumed either on the premises or elsewhere is a sale.

(2) Goods to be merchantable must be at least such as

(a) pass without objection in the trade under the contract description; and

(b) in the case of fungible goods, are of fair average quality within the description; and

(c) are fit for the ordinary purposes for which such goods are used; and

(d) run, within the variations permitted by the agreement, of even kind, quality and quantity within each unit and among all units involved; and

(e) are adequately contained, packaged, and labeled as the agreement may require; and

(f) conform to the promises or affirmations of fact made on the container or label if any.

(3) Unless excluded or modified (Section 2-316), other implied warranties may arise from course of dealing or usage of trade.

§ 2-315. Implied Warranty: Fitness for Particular Purpose.

Where the seller at the time of contracting has reason to know any particular purpose for which the goods are required and that the buyer is relying on the seller's skill or judgment to select or furnish suitable goods, there is unless excluded or modified under the next section an implied warranty that the goods shall be fit for such purpose.

§ 2-316. Exclusion or Modification of Warranties.

(1) Words or conduct relevant to the creation of an express warranty and words or conduct tending to negate or limit warranty shall be construed wherever reasonable as consistent with each other; but subject to the provisions of this Article on parol or extrinsic evidence (Section 2-202) negation or limitation is inoperative to the extent that such construction is unreasonable.

(2) Subject to subsection (3), to exclude or modify the implied warranty of merchantability or any part of it the language must mention merchantability and in case of a writing must be conspicuous, and to exclude or modify any implied warranty of fitness the exclusion must be by a writing and conspicuous. Language to exclude all implied warranties of fitness is sufficient if it states, for example, that "There are no warranties which extend beyond the description on the face hereof."

(3) Notwithstanding subsection (2)

(a) unless the circumstances indicate otherwise, all implied warranties are excluded by expressions like "as is", "with all faults" or other language which in common understanding calls the buyer's attention to the exclusion of warranties and makes plain that there is no implied warranty; and

(b) when the buyer before entering into the contract has examined the goods or the sample or model as fully as he desired or has refused to examine the goods, there is no implied warranty with regard to defects which an examination ought in the circumstances to have revealed to him; and

(c) an implied warranty can also be excluded or modified by course of dealing or course of performance or usage of trade.

(4) Remedies for breach of warranty can be limited in accordance with the provisions of this Article on liquidation or limitation of damages and on contractual modification of remedy (Sections 2-718 and 2-719).

§ 2-317. Cumulation and Conflict of Warranties Express or Implied.

Warranties whether express or implied shall be construed as consistent with each other and as cumulative, but if such construction is unreasonable the intention of the parties shall determine which warranty is dominant. In ascertaining that intention the following rules apply:

(a) Exact or technical specifications displace an inconsistent sample or model or general language of description.

(b) A sample from an existing bulk displaces inconsistent general language of description.

(c) Express warranties displace inconsistent implied warranties other than an implied warranty of fitness for a particular purpose.

§ 2-318. Third Party Beneficiaries of Warranties Express or Implied.

Note: *If this Act is introduced in the Congress of the United States this section should be omitted. (States to select one alternative.)*

Alternative A

A seller's warranty whether express or implied extends to any natural person who is in the family or household of his buyer or who is a guest in his home if it is reasonable to expect that such person may use, consume or be affected by the goods and who is injured in person by breach of the warranty. A seller may not exclude or limit the operation of this section.

Alternative B

A seller's warranty whether express or implied extends to any natural person who may reasonably be expected to use, consume or be affected by the goods and who is injured in person by breach of the warranty. A seller may not exclude or limit the operation of this section.

Alternative C

A seller's warranty whether express or implied extends to any person who may reasonably be expected to use, consume or be affected by the goods and who is injured by breach of the warranty. A seller may not exclude or limit the operation of this section with respect to injury to the person of an individual to whom the warranty extends.

§ 2-319. F.O.B. and F.A.S. Terms.

(1) Unless otherwise agreed the term F.O.B. (which means "free on board") at a named place, even though

used only in connection with the stated price, is a delivery term under which

> (a) when the term is F.O.B. the place of shipment, the seller must at that place ship the goods in the manner provided in this Article (Section 2-504) and bear the expense and risk of putting them into the possession of the carrier; or

> (b) when the term is F.O.B. the place of destination, the seller must at his own expense and risk transport the goods to that place and there tender delivery of them in the manner provided in this Article (Section 2-503);

> (c) when under either (a) or (b) the term is also F.O.B. vessel, car or other vehicle, the seller must in addition at his own expense and risk load the goods on board. If the term is F.O.B. vessel the buyer must name the vessel and in an appropriate case the seller must comply with the provisions of this Article on the form of bill of lading (Section 2-323).

(2) Unless otherwise agreed the term F.A.S. vessel (which means "free alongside") at a named port, even though used only in connection with the stated price, is a delivery term under which the seller must

> (a) at his own expense and risk deliver the goods alongside the vessel in the manner usual in that port or on a dock designated and provided by the buyer; and

> (b) obtain and tender a receipt for the goods in exchange for which the carrier is under a duty to issue a bill of lading.

(3) Unless otherwise agreed in any case falling within subsection (1)(a) or (c) or subsection (2) the buyer must seasonably give any needed instructions for making delivery, including when the term is F.A.S. or F.O.B. the loading berth of the vessel and in an appropriate case its name and sailing date. The seller may treat the failure of needed instructions as a failure of cooperation under this Article (Section 2-311). He may also at his option move the goods in any reasonable manner preparatory to delivery or shipment.

(4) Under the term F.O.B. vessel or F.A.S. unless otherwise agreed the buyer must make payment against tender of the required documents and the seller may not tender nor the buyer demand delivery of the goods in substitution for the documents.

§ 2-320. C.I.F. and C. & F. Terms.

(1) The term C.I.F. means that the price includes in a lump sum the cost of the goods and the insurance and freight to the named destination. The term C. & F. or C.F. means that the price so includes cost and freight to the named destination.

(2) Unless otherwise agreed and even though used only in connection with the stated price and destination, the term C.I.F. destination or its equivalent requires the seller at his own expense and risk to

> (a) put the goods into the possession of a carrier at the port for shipment and obtain a negotiable bill or bills of lading covering the entire transportation to the named destination; and

> (b) load the goods and obtain a receipt from the carrier (which may be contained in the bill of lading) showing that the freight has been paid or provided for; and

> (c) obtain a policy or certificate of insurance, including any war risk insurance, of a kind and on terms then current at the port of shipment in the usual amount, in the currency of the contract, shown to cover the same goods covered by the bill of lading and providing for payment of loss to the order of the buyer or for the account of whom it may concern; but the seller may add to the price the amount of the premium for any such war risk insurance; and

> (d) prepare an invoice of the goods and procure any other documents required to effect shipment or to comply with the contract; and

> (e) forward and tender with commercial promptness all the documents in due form and with any indorsement necessary to perfect the buyer's rights.

(3) Unless otherwise agreed the term C. & F. or its equivalent has the same effect and imposes upon the seller the same obligations and risks as a C.I.F. term except the obligation as to insurance.

(4) Under the term C.I.F. or C. & F. unless otherwise agreed the buyer must make payment against tender of the required documents and the seller may not tender nor the buyer demand delivery of the goods in substitution for the documents.

§ 2–322. Delivery "Ex-Ship".

(1) Unless otherwise agreed a term for delivery of goods "ex-ship" (which means from the carrying vessel) or in equivalent language is not restricted to a particular ship and requires delivery from a ship which has reached a place at the named port of destination where goods of the kind are usually discharged.

(2) Under such a term unless otherwise agreed

(a) the seller must discharge all liens arising out of the carriage and furnish the buyer with a direction which puts the carrier under a duty to deliver the goods; and

(b) the risk of loss does not pass to the buyer until the goods leave the ship's tackle or are otherwise properly unloaded.

§ 2–324. "No Arrival, No Sale" Term.

Under a term "no arrival, no sale" or terms of like meaning, unless otherwise agreed,

(a) the seller must properly ship conforming goods and if they arrive by any means he must tender them on arrival but he assumes no obligation that the goods will arrive unless he has caused the non-arrival; and

(b) where without fault of the seller the goods are in part lost or have so deteriorated as no longer to conform to the contract or arrive after the contract time, the buyer may proceed as if there had been casualty to identified goods.

§ 2–326. Sale on Approval and Sale or Return; Consignment Sales and Rights of Creditors.

(1) Unless otherwise agreed, if delivered goods may be returned by the buyer even though they conform to the contract, the transaction is

(a) a "sale on approval" if the goods are delivered primarily for use, and

(b) a "sale or return" if the goods are delivered primarily for resale.

(2) Except as provided in subsection (3), goods held on approval are not subject to the claims of the buyer's creditors until acceptance; goods held on sale or return are subject to such claims while in the buyer's possession.

(3) Where goods are delivered to a person for sale and such person maintains a place of business at which he deals in goods of the kind involved, under a name other than the name of the person making delivery, then with respect to claims of creditors of the person conducting the business the goods are deemed to be on sale or return. The provisions of this subsection are applicable even though an agreement purports to reserve title to the person making delivery until payment or resale or uses such words as "on consignment" or "on memorandum". However, this subsection is not applicable if the person making deliver

(a) complies with an applicable law providing for a consignor's interest or the like to be evidenced by a sign, or

(b) establishes that the person conducting the business is generally known by his creditors to be substantially engaged in selling the goods of others, or

(c) complies with the filing provisions of the Article on Secured Transactions (Article 9).

(4) Any "or return" term of a contract for sale is to be treated as a separate contract for sale within the statute of frauds section of this Article (Section 2–201) and as contradicting the sale aspect of the contract within the provisions of this Article on parol or extrinsic evidence (Section 2–202).

§ 2–327. Special Incidents of Sale on Approval and Sale or Return.

(1) Under a sale on approval unless otherwise agreed

(a) although the goods are identified to the contract the risk of loss and the title do not pass to the buyer until acceptance; and

(b) use of the goods consistent with the purpose of trial is not acceptance but failure seasonably to notify the seller of election to return the goods is acceptance, and if the goods conform to the contract acceptance of any part is acceptance of the whole; and

(c) after due notification of election to return, the return is at the seller's risk and expense but a merchant buyer must follow any reasonable instructions.

(2) Under a sale or return unless otherwise agreed

(a) the option to return extends to the whole or any commercial unit of the goods while in substantially their original condition, but must be exercised seasonably; and

(b) the return is at the buyer's risk and expense.

§ 2-328. Sale by Auction.

(1) In a sale by auction if goods are put up in lots each lot is the subject of a separate sale.

(2) A sale by auction is complete when the auctioneer so announces by the fall of the hammer or in other customary manner. Where a bid is made while the hammer is falling in acceptance of a prior bid the auctioneer may in his discretion reopen the bidding or declare the goods sold under the bid on which the hammer was falling.

(3) Such a sale is with reserve unless the goods are in explicit terms put up without reserve. In an auction with reserve the auctioneer may withdraw the goods at any time until he announces completion of the sale. In an auction without reserve, after the auctioneer calls for bids on an article or lot, that article or lot cannot be withdrawn unless no bid is made within a reasonable time. In either case a bidder may retract his bid until the auctioneer's announcement of completion of the sale, but a bidder's retraction does not revive any previous bid.

(4) If the auctioneer knowingly receives a bid on the seller's behalf or the seller makes or procures such a bid, and notice has not been given that liberty for such bidding is reserved, the buyer may at his option avoid the sale or take the goods at the price of the last good faith bid prior to the completion of the sale. This subsection shall not apply to any bid at a forced sale.

Part 4. Title, Creditors and Good Faith Purchasers.

§ 2-401. Passing of Title; Reservation for Security; Limited Application of This Section.

Each provision of this Article with regard to the rights, obligations and remedies of the seller, the buyer, purchasers or other third parties applies irrespective of title to the goods except where the provision refers to such title. Insofar as situations are not covered by the other provisions of this Article and matters concerning title become material the following rules apply:

(1) Title to goods cannot pass under a contract for sale prior to their identification to the contract (Section 2-501), and unless otherwise explicitly agreed the buyer acquires by their identification a special property as limited by this Act. Any retention or reservation by the seller of the title (property) in goods shipped or delivered to the buyer is limited in effect to a reservation of a security interest. Subject to these provisions and to the provisions of the Article on Secured Transactions (Article 9), title to goods passes from the seller to the buyer in any manner and on any conditions explicitly agreed on by the parties.

(2) Unless otherwise explicitly agreed title passes to the buyer at the time and place at which the seller completes his performance with reference to the physical delivery of the goods, despite any reservation of a security interest and even though a document of title is to be delivered at a different time or place; and in particular and despite any reservation of a security interest by the bill of lading

(a) if the contract requires or authorizes the seller to send the goods to the buyer but does not require him to deliver them at destination, title passes to the buyer at the time and place of shipment; but

(b) if the contract requires delivery at destination, title passes on tender there.

(3) Unless otherwise explicitly agreed where delivery is to be made without moving the goods,

(a) If the seller is to deliver a document of title, title passes at the time when and the place where he delivers such documents; or

(b) if the goods are at the time of contracting already identified and no documents are to be delivered, title passes at the time and place of contracting.

(4) A rejection or other refusal by the buyer to receive or retain the goods, whether or not justified, or a justified revocation of acceptance revests title to the goods in the seller. Such revesting occurs by operation of law and is not a "sale."

§ 2-403. Power to Transfer; Good Faith Purchase of Goods; "Entrusting".

(1) A purchaser of goods acquires all title which his transferor had or had power to transfer except that a purchaser of a limited interest acquires rights only to the extent of the interest purchased. A person with voidable title has power to transfer a good title to a good faith purchaser for value. When goods have been delivered under a transaction of purchase the purchaser has such power even though

  (a) the transferor was deceived as to the identity of the purchaser, or

  (b) the delivery was in exchange for a check which is later dishonored; or

  (c) it was agreed that the transaction was to be a "cash sale", or

  (d) the delivery was procured through fraud punishable as larcenous under the criminal law.

(2) Any entrusting of possession of goods to a merchant who deals in goods of that kind gives him power to transfer all rights of the entruster to a buyer in ordinary course of business.

(3) "Entrusting" includes any delivery and any acquiescence in retention of possession regardless of any condition expressed between the parties to the delivery or acquiescence and regardless of whether the procurement of the entrusting or the possessor's disposition of the goods have been such as to be larcenous under the criminal law.

[Publisher's Editorial Note: If a state adopts the repealer of Article 6—Bulk Transfers (Alternative A), subsec. (4) should be read as follows:]

(4) The rights of other purchasers of goods and of lien creditors are governed by the Articles on Secured Transactions (Article 9) and Documents of Title (Article 7).

Part 5. Performance.

§2-501. Insurable Interest in Goods; Manner of Identification of Goods.

(1) The buyer obtains a special property and an insurable interest in goods by identification of existing goods as goods to which the contract refers even though the goods so identified are nonconforming and he has an option to return or reject them. Such identification can be made at any time and in any manner explicitly agreed to by the parties. In the absence of explicit agreement identification occurs

  (a) when the contract is made if it is for the sale of goods already existing and identified;

  (b) if the contract is for the sale of future goods other than those described in paragraph (c), when goods are shipped, marked or otherwise designated by the seller as goods to which the contract refers;

  (c) when the crops are planted or otherwise become growing crops or the young are conceived if the contract is for the sale of unborn young to be born within twelve months after contracting or for the sale of crops to be harvested within twelve months or the next normal harvest season after contracting whichever is longer.

(2) The seller retains an insurable interest in goods so long as title to or any security interest in the goods remains in him and where the identification is by the seller alone he may until default or insolvency or notification to the buyer that the identification is final substitute other goods for those identified.

(3) Nothing in this section impairs any insurable interest recognized under any other statute or rule of law.

§ 2-502. Buyer's Right to Goods on Seller's Insolvency.

(1) Subject to subsection (2) and even though the goods have not been shipped a buyer who has paid a part or all of the price of goods in which he has a special property under the provisions of the immediately preceding section may on making and keeping good a tender of any unpaid portion of their price recover them from the seller if the seller becomes insolvent within ten days after receipt of the first installment on their price.

(2) If the identification creating his special property has been made by the buyer he acquires the right to recover the goods only if they conform to the contract for sale.

§ 2-509. Risk of Loss in the Absence of Breach.

(1) Where the contract requires or authorizes the seller to ship the goods by carrier

(a) if it does not require him to deliver them at a particular destination, the risk of loss passes to the buyer when the goods are duly delivered to the carrier even though the shipment is under reservation (Section 2-505); but

(b) if it does require him to deliver them at a particular destination and the goods are there duly tendered while in the possession of the carrier, the risk of loss passes to the buyer when the goods are there duly so tendered as to enable the buyer to take delivery.

(2) Where the goods are held by a bailee to be delivered without being moved, the risk of loss passes to the buyer.

(a) on his receipt of a negotiable document of title covering the goods; or

(b) on acknowledgment by the bailee of the buyer's right to possession of the goods; or

(c) after his receipt of a non-negotiable document of title or other written direction to deliver, as provided in subsection (4)(b) of Section 2-503.

(3) In any case not within subsection (1) or (2), the risk of loss passes to the buyer on his receipt of the goods if the seller is a merchant; otherwise the risk passes to the buyer on tender of delivery.

(4) The provisions of this section are subject to contrary agreement of the parties and to the provisions of this Article on sale on approval (Section 2-327) and on effect of breach on risk of loss (Section 2-510).

§ 2-510. Effect of Breach on Risk of Loss.

(1) Where a tender or delivery of goods so fails to conform to the contract as to give a right of rejection the risk of their loss remains on the seller until cure or acceptance.

(2) Where the buyer rightfully revokes acceptance he may to the extent of any deficiency in his effective insurance coverage treat the risk of loss as having rested on the seller from the beginning.

(3) Where the buyer as to conforming goods already identified to the contract for sale repudiates or is otherwise in breach before risk of their loss has passed to him, the seller may to the extent of any deficiency in his effective insurance coverage treat the risk of loss as resting on the buyer for a commercially reasonable time.

§ 2-513. Buyer's Right to Inspection of Goods.

(1) Unless otherwise agreed and subject to subsection (3), where goods are tendered or delivered or identified to the contract for sale, the buyer has a right before payment or acceptance to inspect them at any reasonable place and time and in any reasonable manner. When the seller is required and authorized to send the goods to the buyer, the inspection may be after their arrival.

(2) Expenses of inspection must be borne by the buyer but may be recovered from the seller if the goods do not conform and are rejected.

(3) Unless otherwise agreed and subject to the provisions of this Article on C.I.F. contracts (subsection (3) of Section 2-321), the buyer is not entitled to inspect the goods before payment of the price when the contract provides

(a) for delivery "C.O.D." or on other like terms; or

(b) for payment against documents of title, except where such payment is due only after the goods are to become available for inspection.

(4) A place or method of inspection fixed by the parties is presumed to be exclusive but unless otherwise expressly agreed it does not postpone identification or shift the place for delivery or for passing the risk of loss. If compliance becomes impossible, inspection shall be as provided in this section unless the place or method fixed was clearly intended as an indispensable condition failure of which avoids the contract.

Part 6. Breach, Repudiation and Excuse.

§ 2-609. Right to Adequate Assurance of Performance.

(1) A contract for sale imposes an obligation on each party that the other's expectation of receiving due performance will not be impaired. When reasonable grounds for insecurity arise with respect to the

performance of either party the other may in writing demand adequate assurance of due performance and until he receives such assurance may if commercially reasonable suspend any performance for which he has not already received the agreed return.

(2) Between merchants the reasonableness of grounds for insecurity and the adequacy of any assurance offered shall be determined according to commercial standards.

(3) Acceptance of any improper delivery or payment does not prejudice the aggrieved party's right to demand adequate assurance of future performance.

(4) After receipt of a justified demand failure to provide within a reasonable time not exceeding thirty days such assurance of due performance as is adequate under the circumstances of the particular case is a repudiation of the contract.

§ 2-615. Excuse by Failure of Presupposed Conditions.

Except so far as a seller may have assumed a greater obligation and subject to the preceding section on substituted performance:

(a) Delay in delivery or non-delivery in whole or in part by a seller who complies with paragraphs (b) and (c) is not a breach of his duty under a contract for sale if performance as agreed has been made impracticable by the occurrence of a contingency the nonoccurrence of which was a basic assumption on which the contract was made or by compliance in good faith with any applicable foreign or domestic governmental regulation or order whether or not it later proves to be invalid.

(b) Where the causes mentioned in paragraph (a) affect only a part of the seller's capacity to perform, he must allocate production and deliveries among his customers but may at his option include regular customers not then under contract as well as his own requirements for further manufacture. He may so allocate in any manner which is fair and reasonable.

(c) The seller must notify the buyer seasonably that there will be delay or non-delivery and, when allocation is required under paragraph (b), of the estimated quota thus made available for the buyer.

Part 7. Remedies.

§ 2-708. Seller's Damages for Non-Acceptance or Repudiation.

(1) Subject to subsection (2) and to the provisions of this Article with respect to proof of market price (Section 2-723), the measure of damages for non-acceptance or repudiation by the buyer is the difference between the market price at the time and place for tender and the unpaid contract price together with any incidental damages provided in this Article (Section 2-710), but less expenses saved in consequence of the buyer's breach.

(2) If the measure of damages provided in subsection (1) is inadequate to put the seller in as good a position as performance would have done then the measure of damages is the profit (including reasonable overhead) which the seller would have made from full performance by the buyer, together with any incidental damages provided in this Article (Section 2-710), due allowance for costs reasonably incurred and due credit for payments or proceeds of resale.

§ 2-709. Action for the Price.

(1) When the buyer fails to pay the price as it becomes due the seller may recover, together with any incidental damages under the next section, the price

(a) of goods accepted or of conforming goods lost or damaged within a commercially reasonable time after risk of their loss has passed to the buyer; and

(b) of goods identified to the contract if the seller is unable after reasonable effort to resell them at a reasonable price or the circumstances reasonably indicate that such effort will be unavailing.

(2) Where the seller sues for the price he must hold for the buyer any goods which have been identified to the contract and are still in his control except that if resale becomes possible he may resell them at any time prior to the collection of the judgment. The net proceeds of any such resale must be credited to the buyer and payment of the judgment entitles him to any goods not resold.

(3) After the buyer has wrongfully rejected or revoked acceptance of the goods or has failed to make a payment due or has repudiated (Section 2-610), a seller who is held not entitled to the price under this section

shall nevertheless be awarded damages for non-acceptance under the preceding section.

§ 2-712. "Cover"; Buyer's Procurement of Substitute Goods.

(1) After a breach within the preceding section the buyer may "cover" by making in good faith and without unreasonable delay any reasonable purchase of or contract to purchase goods in substitution for those due from the seller.

(2) The buyer may recover from the seller as damages the difference between the cost of cover and the contract price together with any incidental or consequential damages as hereinafter defined (Section 2-715), but less expenses saved in consequence of the seller's breach.

(3) Failure of the buyer to effect cover within this section does not bar him from any other remedy.

§ 2-713. Buyer's Damages for Non-Delivery or Repudiation.

(1) Subject to the provisions of this Article with respect to proof of market price (section 2-723), the measure of damages for non-delivery or repudiation by the seller is the difference between the market price at the time when the buyer learned of the breach and the contract price together with any incidental and consequential damages provided in this Article (Section 2-715), but less expenses saved in consequence of the seller's breach.

(2) Market price is to be determined as of the place for tender or, in cases of rejection after arrival or revocation of acceptance, as of the place of arrival.

§ 2-715. Buyer's Incidental and Consequential Damages.

(1) Incidental damages resulting from the seller's breach include expenses reasonably incurred in inspection, receipt, transportation and care and custody of goods rightfully rejected, any commercially reasonable charges, expenses or commissions in connection with effecting over and any other reasonable expense incident to the delay or other breach.

(2) Consequential damages resulting from the seller's breach include

   (a) any loss resulting from general or particular requirements and needs of which the seller at the time of contracting had reason to know and which could not reasonably be prevented by cover or otherwise; and

   (b) injury to person or property proximately resulting from any breach of warranty.

§ 2-716. Buyer's Right to Specific Performance or Replevin.

(1) Specific performance may be decreed where the goods are unique or in other proper circumstances.

(2) The decree for specific performance may include such terms and conditions as to payment of the price, damages, or other relief as the court may deem just.

(3) The buyer has a right of replevin for goods identified to the contract if after reasonable effort he is unable to effect cover for such goods or the circumstances reasonably indicate that such effort will be unavailing or if the goods have been shipped under reservation and satisfaction of the security interest in them has been made or tendered.

Article 3. COMMERCIAL PAPER.

Part 1. General Provisions and Definitions.

§ 3-103. Definitions.

(a) In this Article:

   (1) "Acceptor" means a drawee who has accepted a draft.

   (2) "Drawee" means a person ordered in a draft to make payment.

   (3) "Drawer" means a person who signs or is identified in a draft as a person ordering payment.

   (4) "Good faith" means honesty in fact and the observance of reasonable commercial standards of fair dealing.

   (5) "Maker" means a person who signs or is identified in a note as a person undertaking to pay.

   (6) "Order" means a written instruction to pay money signed by the person giving the instruction. The instruction may be addressed to any person, including the person giving the instruction, or to one or more persons jointly or in the alternative

but not in succession. An authorization to pay is not an order unless the person authorized to pay is also instructed to pay.

(7) "Ordinary care" in the case of a person engaged in business means observance of reasonable commercial standards, prevailing in the area in which the person is located, with respect to the business in which the person is engaged. In the case of a bank that takes an instrument for processing for collection or payment by automated means, reasonable commercial standards do not require the bank to examine the instrument if the failure to examine does not violate the bank's prescribed procedures and the bank's procedures do not vary unreasonably from general banking usage not disapproved by this Article or Article 4.

(8) "Party" means a party to an instrument.

(9) "Promise" means a written undertaking to pay money signed by the person undertaking to pay. An acknowledgement of an obligation by the obligor is not a promise unless the obligor also undertakes to pay the obligation.

(10) "Prove" with respect to a fact means to meet the burden of establishing the fact (Section 1-201(8)).

(11) "Remitter" means a person who purchases an instrument from its issuer if the instrument is payable to an identified person other than the purchaser.

§ 3-104. Negotiable Instrument.

(a) Except as provided in subsections (c) and (d), "negotiable instrument" means an unconditional promise or order to pay a fixed amount of money, with or without interest or other charges described in the promise or order, if it:

(1) is payable to bearer or to order at the time it is issued or first comes into possession of a holder;

(2) is payable on demand or at a definite time; and

(3) does not state any other undertaking or instruction by the person promising or ordering payment to do any act in addition to the payment of money, but the promise or order may contain (i) an undertaking or power to give, maintain, or protect collateral to secure payment, (ii) an authorization or power to the holder to confess judgment or realize on or dispose of collateral, or (iii) a waiver of the

benefit of any law intended for the advantage or protection of an obligor.

(b) "Instrument" means a negotiable instrument.

(c) An order that meets all of the requirements of subjection (a), except paragraph (1), and otherwise falls within the definition of "check" in subsection (f) is a negotiable instrument and a check.

(d) A promise or order other than a check is not an instrument if, at the time it is issued or first comes into possession of a holder, it contains a conspicuous statement, however expressed, to the effect that the promise or order is not negotiable or is not an instrument governed by this Article.

(e) An instrument is a "note" if it is a promise and is a "draft" if it is an order. If an instrument falls within the definition of both "note" and "draft," a person entitled to enforce the instrument may treat it as either.

(f) "Check" means (i) a draft, other than a documentary draft, payable on demand and drawn on a bank or (ii) a cashier's check or teller's check. An instrument may be a check even though it is described on its face by another term, such as "money order."

(g) "Cashier's check" means a draft with respect to which the drawer and drawee are the same bank or branches of the same bank.

(h) "Teller's check" means a draft drawn by a bank (i) on another bank, or (ii) payable at or through a bank.

(i) "Traveler's check" means an instrument that (i) is payable on demand, (ii) is drawn on or payable at or through a bank, (iii) is designated by the term, "traveler's check" or by a substantially similar term, and (iv) requires, as a condition to payment, a countersignature by a person whose specimen signature appears on the instrument.

(j) "Certificate of deposit" means an instrument containing an acknowledgement of a bank that a sum of money has been received by the bank and a promise by the bank to repay the sum of money. A certificate of deposit is a note of the bank.

§ 3-105. Issue of Instrument.

(a) "Issue" means the first delivery of an instrument by the maker or drawer, whether to a holder or nonholder, for the purpose of giving rights on the instrument to any person.

(b) An unissued instrument, or an unissued incomplete instrument that is completed, is binding on the maker or drawer, but nonissuance is a defense. An instrument that is conditionally issued or is issued for a special purpose is binding on the maker or drawer, but failure of the condition or special purpose to be fulfilled is a defense.

(c) "Issuer" applies to issued and unissued instruments and means a maker or drawer of an instrument.

§ 3-106. Unconditional Promise or Order.

(a) Except as provided in this section, for the purposes of Section 3-104(a), a promise or order is unconditional unless it states (i) an express condition to payment, (ii) that the promise or order is subject to or governed by another writing, or (iii) that rights or obligations with respect to the promise or order are stated in another writing. A reference to another writing does not of itself make the promise or order conditional.

(b) A promise or order is not made conditional (i) by a reference to another writing for a statement of rights with respect to collateral, prepayment, or acceleration, or (ii) because payment is limited to resort to a particular fund or source.

(c) If a promise or order requires, as a condition to payment, a countersignature by a person whose specimen signature appears on the promise or order, the condition does not make the promise or order conditional for the purposes of Section 3-104(a). If the person whose specimen signature appears on an instrument fails to countersign the instrument, the failure to countersign is a defense to the obligation of the issuer, but the failure does not prevent a transferee of the instrument from becoming a holder of the instrument.

(d) If a promise or order at the time it is issued or first comes into possession of a holder contains a statement, required by applicable statutory or administrative law, to the effect that the rights of a holder or transferee are subject to claims or defenses that the issuer could assert against the original payee, the promise or order is not thereby made conditional for the purposes of Section 3-104(a); but if the promise or order is an instrument, there cannot be a holder in due course of the instrument.

§ 3-107. Instrument Payable in Foreign Money.

Unless the instrument otherwise provides, an instrument that states the amount payable in foreign money may be paid in the foreign money or in an equivalent amount in dollars calculated by using the current bank-offered spot rate at the place of payment for the purchase of dollars on the day on which the instrument is paid.

§ 3-108. Payable on Demand or at Definite Time.

(a) A promise or order is "payable on demand" if it (i) states that it is payable on demand or at sight, or otherwise indicates that it is payable at the will of the holder, or (ii) does not state any time of payment.

(b) A promise or order is "payable at a definite time" if it is payable on elapse of a definite period of time after sight or acceptance or at a fixed date or dates or at a time or times readily ascertainable at the time the promise or order is issued, subject to rights of (i) prepayment, (ii) acceleration, (iii) extension at the option of the holder, or (iv) extension to a further definite time at the option of the maker or acceptor or automatically upon or after a specified act or event.

(c) If an instrument, payable at a fixed rate, is also payable upon demand made before the fixed date, the instrument is payable on demand until the fixed date and, if demand for payment is not made before that date, becomes payable at a definite time on the fixed date.

§ 3-109. Payable to Bearer or to Order.

(a) A promise or order is payable to bearer if it:

(1) states that it is payable to bearer or to the order of bearer or otherwise indicates that the person in possession of the promise or order is entitled to payment;

(2) does not state a payee; or

(3) states that it is payable to or to the order of cash or otherwise indicates that it is not payable to an identified person.

(b) A promise or order that is not payable to bearer is payable to order if it is payable (i) to the order of an identified person or (ii) to an identified person or order. A promise or order that is payable to order is payable to the identified person.

(c) An instrument payable to bearer may become payable to an identified person if it is specially indorsed pursuant to Section 3-205(a). An instrument payable to an identified person may become payable to bearer if it is indorsed in blank pursuant to Section 3-205(b).

§ 3-110. Identification of Person to Whom Instrument Is Payable.

(a) The person to whom an instrument is initially payable is determined by the intent of the person, whether or not authorized, signing as, or in the name or behalf of, the issuer of the instrument. The instrument is payable to the person intended by the signer even if that person is identified in the instrument by a name or other identification that is not that of the intended person. If more than one person signs in the name or behalf of the issuer of an instrument and all the signers do not intend the same person as payee, the instrument is payable to any person intended by one or more of the signers.

(b) If the signature of the issuer of an instrument is made by automated means, such as a check-writing machine, the payee of the instrument is determined by the intent of the person who supplied the name or identification of the payee, whether or not authorized to do so.

(c) A person to whom an instrument is payable may be identified in any way, including by name, identifying number, office, or account number. For the purpose of determining the holder of an instrument, the following rules apply:

(1) If an instrument is payable to an account and the account is identified only by number, the instrument is payable to the person to whom the account is payable. If an instrument is payable to an account identified by number and by the name of a person, the instrument is payable to the named person, whether or not that person is the owner of the account identified by number.

(2) If an instrument is payable to:

(i) a trust, an estate, or a person described as trustee or representative of a trust or estate, the instrument is payable to the trustee, the repre-

sentative, or a successor of either, whether or not the beneficiary or estate is also named;

(ii) a person described as agent or similar representative of a named or identified person, the instrument is payable to the represented person, the representative, or a successor of the representative;

(iii) a fund or organization that is not a legal entity, the instrument is payable to a representative of the members of the fund or organization; or

(iv) an office or to a person described as holding an office, the instrument is payable to the named person, the incumbent of the office, or a successor to the incumbent.

(d) If an instrument is payable to two or more persons alternatively, it is payable to any of them and may be negotiated, discharged, or enforced by any or all of them in possession of the instrument. If an instrument is payable to two or more persons not alternatively, it is payable to all of them and may be negotiated, discharged, or enforced only by all of them. If an instrument payable to two or more persons is ambiguous as to whether it is payable to the persons alternatively, the instrument is payable to the persons alternatively.

§ 3-111. Place of Payment.

Except as otherwise provided for items in Article 4, an instrument is payable at the place of payment stated in the instrument. If no place of payment is stated, an instrument is payable at the address of the drawee or maker stated in the instrument. If no address is stated, the place of payment is the place of business of the drawee or maker. If a drawee or maker has more than one place of business, the place of payment is any place of business of the drawee or maker chosen by the person entitled to enforce the instrument. If the drawee or maker has no place of business, the place of payment is the residence of the drawee or maker.

§ 3-112. Interest.

(a) Unless otherwise provided in the instrument, (i) an instrument is not payable with interest, and (ii) interest on an interest-bearing instrument is payable from the date of the instrument.

(b) Interest may be stated in an instrument as a fixed or

variable amount of money or it may be expressed as a fixed or variable rate or rates. The amount or rate of interest may be stated or described in the instrument in any manner and may require reference to information not contained in the instrument. If an instrument provides for interest, but the amount of interest payable cannot be ascertained from the description, interest is payable at the judgment rate in effect at the place of payment of the instrument and at the time interest first accrues.

§ 3-113. Date of Instrument.

(a) An instrument may be antedated or postdated. The date stated determines the time of payment if the instrument is payable at a fixed period after date. Except as provided in Section 4-401(c), an instrument payable on demand is not payable before the date of the instrument.

(b) If an instrument is undated, its date is the date of its issue or, in the case of an unissued instrument, the date it first comes into possession of a holder.

§ 3-114. Contradictory Terms of Instrument.

If an instrument contains contradictory terms, typewritten terms prevail over printed terms, handwritten terms prevail over both, and words prevail over numbers.

§3-115. Incomplete Instrument.

(a) "Incomplete instrument" means a signed writing, whether or not issued by the signer, the contents of which show at the time of signing that it is incomplete but that the signer intended it to be completed by the addition of words or numbers.

(b) Subject to subsection (c), if an incomplete instrument is an instrument under Section 3-104, it may be enforced according to its terms if it is not completed, or according to its terms as augmented by completion. If an incomplete instrument is not an instrument under Section 3-104, but, after completion, the requirements of Section 3-104 are met, the instrument may be enforced according to its terms as augmented by completion.

(c) If words or numbers are added to an incomplete instrument without authority of the signer, there is an alteration of the incomplete instrument under Section 3-407.

(d) The burden of establishing that words or numbers were added to an incomplete instrument without authority of the signer is on the person asserting the lack of authority.

§ 3-116. Joint and Several Liability; Contribution.

(a) Except as otherwise provided in the instrument, two or more persons who have the same liability on an instrument as makers, drawers, acceptors, indorsers who indorse as joint payees, or anomalous indorsers are jointly and severally liable in the capacity in which they sign.

(b) Except as provided in Section 3-419(e) or by agreement of the affected parties, a party having joint and several liability who pays the instrument is entitled to receive from any party having the same joint and several liability contribution in accordance with applicable law.

(c) Discharge of one party having joint and several liability by a person entitled to enforce the instrument does not affect the right under subsection (b) of a party having the same joint and several liability to receive contribution from the party discharged.

§ 3-117. Other Agreements Affecting Instrument.

Subject to applicable law regarding exclusion of proof of contemporaneous or previous agreements, the obligation of a party to an instrument to pay the instrument may be modified, supplemented, or nullified by a separate agreement of the obligor and a person entitled to enforce the instrument, if the instrument is issued or the obligation is incurred in reliance on the agreement or as part of the same transaction giving rise to the agreement. To the extent an obligation is modified, supplemented, or nullified by an agreement under this section, the agreement is a defense to the obligation.

§ 3-118. Statute of Limitations.

(a) Except as provided in subsection (e), an action to enforce the obligation of a party to pay a note payable at a definite time must be commenced within six years after the due date or dates stated in the note or, if a due date is accelerated, within six years after the accelerated due date.

(b) Except as provided in subsection (d) or (e), if demand for payment is made to the maker of a note payable on demand, an action to enforce the obligation of a party to pay the note must be commenced within six years after the demand. If no demand for payment is made to the maker, an action to enforce the note is barred if neither principal nor interest on the note has been paid for a continuous period of 10 years.

(c) Except as provided in subsection (d), an action to enforce the obligation of a party to an unaccepted draft to pay the draft must be commenced within three years after dishonor of the draft or 10 years after the date of the draft, whichever period expires first.

(d) An action to enforce the obligation of the acceptor of a certified check or the issuer of a teller's check, cashier's check, or traveler's check must be commenced within three years after demand for payment is made to the acceptor or issuer, as the case may be.

(e) An action to enforce the obligation of a party to a certificate of deposit to pay the instrument must be commenced within six years after demand for payment is made to the maker, but if the instrument states a due date and the maker is not required to pay before that date, the six-year period begins when a demand for payment is in effect and the due date has passed.

(f) An action to enforce the obligation of a party to pay an accepted draft, other than a certified check, must be commenced (i) within six years after the due date or dates stated in the draft or acceptance if the obligation of the acceptor is payable at a definite time, or (ii) within six years after the date of the acceptance if the obligation of the acceptor is payable on demand.

(g) Unless governed by other law regarding claims for indemnity or contribution, an action (i) for conversion of an instrument, for money had and received, or like action based on conversion, (ii) for breach of warranty, or (iii) to enforce an obligation, duty, or right arising under this Article, and not governed by this section must be commenced within three years after the [cause of action] accrues.

Part 2. Negotiation, Transfer, and Indorsement.

§ 3-201. Negotiation.

(a) "Negotiation" means a transfer of possession, whether voluntary or involuntary, of an instrument by a person other than the issuer to a person who thereby becomes its holder.

(b) Except for negotiation by a remitter, if an instrument is payable to an identified person, negotiation requires transfer of possession of the instrument and its indorsement by the holder. If an instrument is payable to bearer, it may be negotiated by transfer of possession alone.

§ 3-202. Negotiation Subject to Rescission.

(a) Negotiation is effective even if obtained (i) from an infant, a corporation exceeding its powers, or a person without capacity, (ii) by fraud, duress, or mistake, or (iii) in breach of duty or as part of an illegal transaction.

(b) To the extent permitted by other law, negotiation may be rescinded or may be subject to other remedies, but those remedies may not be asserted against a subsequent holder in due course or a person paying the instrument in good faith and without knowledge of facts that are a basis for rescission or other remedy.

§ 3-203. Transfer of Instrument; Rights Acquired by Transfer.

(a) An instrument is transferred when it is delivered by a person other than its issuer for the purpose of giving to the person receiving delivery the right to enforce the instrument.

(b) Transfer of an instrument, whether or not the transfer is a negotiation, vests in the transferee any right of the transferor to enforce the instrument, including any right as a holder in due course, but the transferee cannot acquire rights of a holder in due course by a transfer, directly or indirectly, from a holder in due course if the transferee engaged in fraud or illegality affecting the instrument.

(c) Unless otherwise agreed, if an instrument is transferred for value and the transferee does not become a holder because of lack of indorsement by the transferor, the transferee has a specifically enforceable right to the unqualified indorsement of the transferor, but negotiation of the instrument does not occur until the indorsement is made.

(d) If a transferor purports to transfer less than the entire instrument, negotiation of the instrument does not occur. The transferee obtains no rights under this Article and has only the rights of a partial assignee.

§ 3–204. Indorsement.

(a) "Indorsement" means a signature, other than that of a signer as maker, drawer, or acceptor, that alone or accompanied by other words is made on an instrument for the purpose of (i) negotiating the instrument, (ii) restricting payment of the instrument, or (iii) incurring indorser's liability on the instrument, but regardless of the intent of the signer, a signature and its accompanying words, terms of the instrument, place of the signature, or other circumstances unambiguously indicate that the signature was made for a purpose other than indorsement. For the purpose of determining whether a signature is made on an instrument, a paper affixed to the instrument is a part of the instrument.

(b) "Indorser" means a person who makes an indorsement.

(c) For the purpose of determining whether the transferee of an instrument is a holder, an indorsement that transfers a security interest in the instrument is effective as an unqualified indorsement of the instrument.

(d) If an instrument is payable to a holder under a name that is not the name of the holder, indorsement may be made by the holder in the name stated in the instrument or in the holder's name or both, but signature in both names may be required by a person paying or taking the instrument for value or collection.

§ 3–205. Special Indorsement; Blank Indorsement; Anomalous Indorsement.

(a) If an indorsement is made by the holder of an instrument, whether payable to an identified person or payable to bearer, and the indorsement identifies a person to whom it makes the instrument payable, it is a "special indorsement." When specially indorsed, an instrument becomes payable to the identified person and may be negotiated only by the indorsement of that person. The principles stated in Section 3-110 apply to special indorsements.

(b) If an indorsement is made by the holder of an instrument and it is not a special indorsement, it is a "blank indorsement." When indorsed in blank, an instrument becomes payable to bearer and may be negotiated by transfer of possession alone until specially indorsed.

(c) The holder may convert a blank indorsement that consists only of a signature into a special indorsement by writing, above the signature of the indorser, words identifying the person to whom the instrument is made payable.

(d) "Anomalous indorsement" means an indorsement made by a person who is not the holder of the instrument. An anomalous indorsement does not affect the manner in which the instrument may be negotiated.

§ 3–206. Restrictive Indorsement.

(a) An indorsement limiting payment to a particular person or otherwise prohibiting further transfer or negotiation of the instrument is not effective to prevent further transfer or negotiation of the instrument.

(b) An indorsement stating a condition to the right of the indorsee to receive payment does not affect the right of the indorsee to enforce the instrument. A person paying the instrument or taking it for value or collection may disregard the condition, and the rights and liabilities of that person are not affected by whether the condition has been fulfilled.

(c) If an instrument bears an indorsement (i) described in Section 4-201(b), or (ii) in blank or to a particular bank using the words "for deposit," "for collection," or other words indicating a purpose of having the instrument collected by a bank for the indorser or for a particular account, the following rules apply:

(1) A person, other than a bank, who purchases the instrument when so indorsed converts the instrument unless the amount paid for the instrument is received by the indorser or applied consistently with the indorsement.

(2) A depositary bank that purchases the instrument or takes it for collection when so indorsed converts the instrument unless the amount paid by the bank with respect to the instrument is received by the indorser or applied consistently with the indorsement.

(3) A payor bank that is also the depositary bank or that takes the instrument for immediate payment over the counter from a person other than a collecting bank converts the instrument unless the proceeds of the instrument are received by the indorser or applied consistently with the indorsement.

(4) Except as otherwise provided in paragraph (3), a payor bank or intermediary bank may disregard

the indorsement and is not liable if the proceeds of the instrument are not received by the indorser or applied consistently with the indorsement.

(d) Except for an indorsement covered by subsection (c), if an instrument bears an indorsement using words to the effect that payment is to be made to the indorsee as agent, trustee, or other fiduciary for the benefit of the indorser or another person, the following rules apply:

(1) Unless there is notice of breach of fiduciary duty as provided in Section 3-307, a person who purchases the instrument from the indorsee or takes the instrument from the indorsee for collection or payment may pay the proceeds of payment or the value given for the instrument to the indorsee without regard to whether the indorsee violates a fiduciary duty to the indorser.

(2) A subsequent transferee of the instrument or person who pays the instrument is neither given notice nor otherwise affected by the restriction in the indorsement unless the transferee or payor knows that the fiduciary dealt with the instrument or its proceeds in breach of fiduciary duty.

(e) The presence on an instrument of an indorsement to which this section applies does not prevent a purchaser of the instrument from becoming a holder in due course of the instrument unless the purchaser is a converter under subsection (c) or has notice or knowledge of breach of fiduciary duty as stated in subsection (d).

(f) In an action to enforce the obligation of a party to pay the instrument, the obligor has a defense if payment would violate an indorsement to which this section applies and the payment is not permitted by this section.

§ 3-207. Reacquisition.

Reacquisition of an instrument occurs if it is transferred to a former holder, by negotiation or otherwise. A former holder who reacquires the instrument may cancel indorsements made after the reacquirer first became a holder of the instrument. If the cancellation causes the instrument to be payable to the reacquirer or to bearer, the reacquirer may negotiate the instrument. An indorser whose indorsement is canceled is discharged, and the discharge is effective against any subsequent holder.

Part 3. Enforcement of Instruments.

§ 3-301. Person Entitled to Enforce Instrument.

"Person entitled to enforce" an instrument means (i) the holder of the instrument, (ii) a nonholder in possession of the instrument who has the rights of a holder, or (iii) a person not in possession of the instrument who is entitled to enforce the instrument pursuant to Section 3-309 or 3-418(d). A person may be a person entitled to enforce the instrument even though the person is not the owner of the instrument or is in wrongful possession of the instrument.

§ 3-302. Holder in Due Course.

(a) Subject to subsection (c) and Section 3-106(d), "holder in due course" means the holder of an instrument if:

(1) the instrument when issued or negotiated to the holder does not bear such apparent evidence of forgery or alteration or is not otherwise so irregular or incomplete as to call into question its authenticity; and

(2) the holder took the instrument (i) for value, (ii) in good faith, (iii) without notice that the instrument is overdue or has been dishonored or that there is an uncured default with respect to payment of another instrument issued as part of the same series, (iv) without notice that the instrument contains an unauthorized signature or has been altered, (v) without notice of any claim to the instrument described in Section 3-306, and (vi) without notice that any party has a defense or claim in recoupment described in Section 3-305(a).

(b) Notice of discharge of a party, other than discharge in an insolvency proceeding, is not notice of a defense under subsection (a), but discharge is effective against a person who became a holder in due course with notice of the discharge. Public filing or recording of a document does not of itself constitute notice of a defense, claim in recoupment, or claim to the instrument.

(c) Except to the extent a transferor or predecessor in interest has rights as a holder in due course, a person does not acquire rights of a holder in due course of an instrument taken (i) by legal process or by purchase in an execution, bankruptcy, or creditor's sale or similar proceeding, (ii) by purchase as part of a bulk transaction not in ordinary course of business of the transferor, or (iii) as the successor in interest to an estate or other organization.

(d) If, under Section 3-303(a)(1), the promise of performance that is the consideration for an instrument has been partially performed, the holder may assert rights as a holder in due course of the instrument only to the fraction of the amount payable under the instrument equal to the value of the partial performance divided by the value of the promised performance.

(e) If (i) the person entitled to enforce an instrument has only a security interest in the instrument and (ii) the person obliged to pay the instrument has a defense, claim in recoupment, or claim to the instrument that may be asserted against the person who granted the security interest, the person entitled to enforce the instrument may assert rights as a holder in due course only to an amount payable under the instrument which, at the time of enforcement of the instrument, does not exceed the amount of the unpaid obligation secured.

(f) To be effective, notice must be received at a time and in a manner that gives a reasonable opportunity to act on it.

(g) This section is subject to any law limiting status as a holder in due course in particular classes of transactions.

§ 3-303. Value and Consideration.

(a) An instrument is issued or transferred for value if:

(1) the instrument is issued or transferred for a promise of performance, to the extent the promise has been performed;

(2) the transferee acquires a security interest or other lien in the instrument other than a lien obtained by judicial proceeding;

(3) the instrument is issued or transferred as payment of, or as security for, an antecedent claim against any person, whether or not the claim is due;

(4) the instrument is issued or transferred in exchange for a negotiable instrument; or

(5) the instrument is issued or transferred in exchange for the incurring of an irrevocable obligation to a third party by the person taking the instrument.

(b) "Consideration" means any consideration sufficient to support a simple contract. The drawer or maker of an instrument has a defense if the instrument is issued without consideration. If an instrument is issued for a promise of performance, the issuer has a defense to the extent performance of the promise is due and the promise has not been performed. If an instrument is issued for value as stated in subsection (a), the instrument is also issued for consideration.

§ 3-304. Overdue Instrument.

(a) An instrument payable on demand becomes overdue at the earliest of the following times:

(1) on the day after the day demand for payment is duly made;

(2) if the instrument is a check, 90 days after its date; or

(3) if the instrument is not a check, when the instrument has been outstanding for a period of time after its date which is unreasonably long under the circumstances of the particular case in light of the nature of the instrument and usage of the trade.

(b) With respect to an instrument payable at a definite time the following rules apply:

(1) If the principal is payable in installments and a due date has not been accelerated, the instrument becomes overdue upon default under the instrument for nonpayment of an installment, and the instrument remains overdue until the default is cured.

(2) If the principal is not payable in installments and the due date has not been accelerated, the instrument becomes overdue on the day after the due date.

(3) If a due date with respect to principal has been accelerated, the instrument becomes overdue on the day after the accelerated due date.

(c) Unless the due date of principal has been accelerated, an instrument does not become overdue if there is default in payment of interest but no default in payment of principal.

§ 3-305. Defenses and Claims in Recoupment.

(a) Except as stated in subsection (b), the right to enforce the obligation of a party to pay an instrument is subject to the following:

(1) a defense of the obligor based on (i) infancy of the obligor to the extent it is a defense to a simple contract, (ii) duress, lack of legal capacity, or illegality of the transaction which, under other law, nullifies the obligation of the obligor, (iii) fraud that induced the obligor to sign the instrument with neither knowledge nor reasonable opportunity to learn of its character or its essential terms, or (iv) discharge of the obligor in insolvency proceedings;

(2) a defense of the obligor stated in another section of this Article or a defense of the obligor that would be available if the person entitled to enforce the instrument were enforcing a right to payment under a simple contact; and

(3) a claim in recoupment of the obligor against the original payee of the instrument if the claim arose from the transaction that gave rise to the instrument; but the claim of the obligor may be asserted against a transferee of the instrument only to reduce the amount owing on the instrument at the time the action is brought.

(b) The right of the holder in due course to enforce the obligation of a party to pay the instrument is subject to defenses of the obligor stated in subsection (a)(1), but is not subject to defenses of the obligor stated in subsection (a)(2) or claims in recoupment stated in subsection (a)(3) against a person other than the holder.

(c) Except as stated in subsection (d), in an action to enforce the obligation of a party to pay the instrument, the obligor may not assert against the person entitled to enforce the instrument a defense, claim in recoupment, or claim to the instrument (Section 3-306) of another person, but the other person's claim to the instrument may be asserted by the obligor if the other person is joined in the action and personally asserts the claim against the person entitled to enforce the instrument. An obligor is not obliged to pay the instrument if the person seeking enforcement of the instrument does not have rights of a holder in due course and the obligor proves that the instrument is a lost or stolen instrument.

(d) In an action to enforce the obligation of an accommodation party to pay an instrument, the accommodation party may assert against the person entitled to enforce the instrument any defense or claim in recoupment under subsection (a) that the accommodated party could assert against the person entitled to enforce

the instrument, except the defense of discharge in insolvency proceedings, infancy, and lack of legal capacity.

§ 3-306. Claims to an Instrument.

A person taking an instrument, other than a person having rights of a holder in due course, is subject to a claim of a property or possessory right in the instrument or its proceeds, including a claim to rescind a negotiation and to recover the instrument or its proceeds. A person having rights of a holder in due course takes free of the claim to the instrument.

§ 3-307. Notice of Breach of Fiduciary Duty.

(a) In this section:

(1) "Fiduciary" means an agent, trustee, partner, corporate officer or director, or other representative owing a fiduciary duty with respect to an instrument.

(2) "Represented person" means the principal, beneficiary, partnership, corporation, or other person to whom the duty stated in paragraph (1) is owed.

(b) If (i) an instrument is taken from a fiduciary for payment or collection or for value, (ii) the taker has knowledge of the fiduciary status of the fiduciary and (iii) the represented person makes a claim to the instrument or its proceeds on the basis that the transaction of the fiduciary is a breach of fiduciary duty, the following rules apply:

(1) Notice of breach of fiduciary duty by the fiduciary is notice of the claim of the represented person.

(2) In the case of an instrument payable to the represented person or the fiduciary as such, the taker has notice of the breach of fiduciary duty if the instrument is (i) taken in payment of or as security for a debt known by the taker to be the personal debt of the fiduciary, (ii) taken in a transaction known by the taker to be for the personal benefit of the fiduciary, or (iii) deposited to an account other than an account of the fiduciary, as such, or an account of the represented person.

(3) If an instrument is issued by the represented person or the fiduciary as such, and made payable to the fiduciary personally, the taker does not have notice of the breach of fiduciary duty unless the taker knows of the breach of fiduciary duty.

(4) If an instrument is issued by the represented person or the fiduciary as such, to the taker as payee, the taker has notice of the breach of fiduciary duty if the instrument is (i) taken in payment of or as security for a debt known by the taker to be the personal debt of the fiduciary, (ii) taken in a transaction known by the taker to be for the personal benefit of the fiduciary, or (iii) deposited to an account other than an account of the fiduciary, as such, or an account of the represented person.

§ 3–308. Proof of Signatures and Status as Holder in Due Course.

(a) In an action with respect to an instrument, the authenticity of, and authority to make, each signature on the instrument is admitted unless specifically denied in the pleadings. If the validity of a signature is denied in the pleadings, the burden of establishing validity is on the person claiming validity, but the signature is presumed to be authentic and authorized unless the action is to enforce the liability of the purported signer and the signer is dead or incompetent at the time of trial of the issue of validity of the signature. If an action to enforce the instrument is brought against a person as the undisclosed principal of a person who signed the instrument as a party to the instrument, the plaintiff has the burden of establishing that the defendant is liable on the instrument as a represented person under Section 3-402(a).

(b) If the validity of signatures is admitted or proved and there is compliance with subsection (a), a plaintiff producing the instrument is entitled to payment if the plaintiff proves entitlement to enforce the instrument under Section 3-301, unless the defendant proves a defense or claim in recoupment. If a defense or claim in recoupment is proved, the right to payment of the plaintiff is subject to the defense or claim, except to the extent the plaintiff proves that the plaintiff has rights of a holder in due course which are not subject to the defense or claim.

§ 3–309. Enforcement of Lost, Destroyed, or Stolen Instrument.

(a) A person not in possession of an instrument is entitled to enforce the instrument if (i) the person was in possession of the instrument and entitled to enforce it when loss of possession occurred, (ii) the loss of possession was not the result of a transfer by the person or a lawful seizure, and (iii) the person cannot reasonably obtain possession of the instrument because the instrument was destroyed, its whereabouts cannot be determined, or it is in the wrongful possession of an unknown person or a person that cannot be found or is not amendable to service of process.

(b) A person seeking enforcement of an instrument under subsection (a) must prove the terms of the instrument and the person's right to enforce the instrument. If that proof is made, Section 3-308 applies to the case as if the person seeking enforcement had produced the instrument. The court may not enter judgment in favor of the person seeking enforcement unless it finds that the person required to pay the instrument is adequately protected against loss that might occur by reason of a claim by another person to enforce the instrument. Adequate protection may be provided by any reasonable means.

§ 3–310. Effect of Instrument on Obligation for Which Taken.

(a) Unless otherwise agreed, if a certified check, cashier's check, or teller's check is taken for an obligation, the obligation is discharged to the same extent discharge would result if an amount of money equal to the amount of the instrument were taken in payment of the obligation. Discharge of the obligation does not affect any liability that the obligor may have as an indorser of the instrument.

(b) Unless otherwise agreed and except as provided in subsection (a), if a note or an uncertified check is taken for an obligation, the obligation is suspended to the same extent the obligation would be discharged if an amount of money equal to the amount of the instrument were taken, and the following rules apply:

(1) In the case of an uncertified check, suspension of the obligation continues until dishonor of the check or until it is paid or certified. Payment or certification of the check results in discharge of the obligation to the extent of the amount of the check.

(2) In the case of a note, suspension of the obligation continues until dishonor of the note or until it is paid. Payment of the note results in discharge of the obligation to the extent of the payment.

(3) Except as provided in paragraph (4), if the check or note is dishonored and the obligee of the obligation for which the instrument was taken is the person entitled to enforce the instrument, the obligee may enforce either the instrument or the obligation. In the case of an instrument of a third person which is negotiated to the obligee by the obligor, discharge of the obligor on the instrument also discharges the obligation.

(4) If the person entitled to enforce the instrument taken for an obligation is a person other than the obligee, the obligee may not enforce the obligation to the extent the obligation is suspended. If the obligee is the person entitled to enforce the instrument but no longer has possession of it because it was lost, stolen, or destroyed, the obligation may not be enforced to the extent of the amount payable on the instrument, and to that extent the obligee's rights against the obligor are limited to enforcement of the instrument.

(c) If an instrument other than one described in subsection (a) or (b) is taken for an obligation, the effect is (i) that stated in subsection (a) if the instrument is one on which a bank is liable as maker or acceptor, or (ii) that stated in subsection (b) in any other case.

§ 3–311. Accord and Satisfaction by Use of Instrument.

(a) If a person against whom a claim is asserted proves (i) that person in good faith tendered an instrument to the claimant as full satisfaction of the claim, (ii) the amount of the claim was unliquidated or subject to a bona fide dispute, and (iii) the claimant obtained payment of the instrument, the following subsections apply.

(b) Unless subsection (c) applies, the claim is discharged if the person against whom the claim is asserted proves that the instrument or an accompanying written communication contained a conspicuous statement to the effect that the instrument was tendered as full satisfaction of the claim.

(c) Subject to subsection (d), a claim is not discharged under subsection (b) if either of the following applies:

(1) The claimant, if an organization, proves that (i) within a reasonable time before the tender, the claimant sent a conspicuous statement to the person against whom the claim is asserted that com-

munications concerning disputed debts, including an instrument tendered as full satisfaction of a debt, are to be sent to a designated person, office, or place, and (ii) the instrument or accompanying communication was not received by that designated person, office, or place.

(2) The claimant, whether or not an organization, proves that within 90 days after payment of the instrument, the claimant tendered repayment of the amount of the instrument to the person against whom the claim is asserted. This paragraph does not apply if the claimant is an organization that sent a statement complying with paragraph (1)(i).

(d) A claim is discharged if the person against whom the claim is asserted proves that within a reasonable time before collection of the instrument was initiated, the claimant, or an agent of the claimant having direct responsibility with respect to the disputed obligation, knew that the instrument was tendered in full satisfaction of the claim.

§ 3–312. Lost, Destroyed, or Stolen Cashier's Checks, Teller's Check, or Certified Check.

(a) In this section:

(1) "Check" means a cashier's check, teller's check, or certified check.

(2) "Claimant" means a person who claims the right to receive the amount of a cashier's check, teller's check, or certified check that was lost, destroyed, or stolen.

(3) "Declaration of loss" means a written statement, made under penalty of perjury, to the effect that (i) the declarer lost possession of a check, (ii) the declarer is the drawer or payee of the check, in the case of a certified check, or the remitter or payee of the check, in the case of a cashier's check or teller's check, (iii) the loss of possession was not the result of a transfer by the declarer or a lawful seizure, and (iv) the declarer cannot reasonably obtain possession of the check because the check was destroyed, its whereabouts cannot be determined, or it is in the wrongful possession of an unknown person or a person that cannot be found or is not amenable to service of process.

(4) "Obligated bank" means the issuer of a cashier's check or teller's check or the accepter of a certified check.

(b) A claimant may assert a claim to the amount of a check by a communication to the obligated bank describing the check with reasonable certainty and requesting payment of the amount of the check, if (i) the claimant is the drawer or payee of a certified check or the remitter or payee of a cashier's check or teller's check, (ii) the communication contains or is accompanied by a declaration of loss of the claimant with respect to the check, (iii) the communication is received at a time and in a manner affording the bank a reasonable time to act on it before the check is paid, and (iv) the claimant provides reasonable identification if requested by the obligated bank. Delivery of a declaration of loss is a warranty of the truth of the statements made in the declaration. If a claim is asserted in compliance with this subsection, the following rules apply:

(1) The claim becomes enforceable at the later of (i) the time the claim is asserted, or (ii) the 90th day following the date of the check, in the case of a cashier's check or teller's check, or the 90th day following the date of the acceptance, in the case of a certified check.

(2) Until the claim becomes enforceable, it has no legal effect and the obligated bank may pay the check or, in the case of a teller's check, may permit the drawee to pay the check. Payment to a person entitled to enforce the check discharges all liability of the obligated bank with respect to the check.

(3) If the claim becomes enforceable before the check is presented for payment, the obligated bank is not obliged to pay the check.

(4) When the claim becomes enforceable, the obligated bank becomes obliged to pay the amount of the check to the claimant if payment of the check has not been made to a person entitled to enforce the check. Subject to Section 4-302(a)(1), payment to the claimant discharges all liability of the obligated bank with respect to the check.

(c) If the obligated bank pays the amount of a check to a claimant under subsection (b)(4) and the check is presented for payment by a person having rights of a holder in due course, the claimant is obliged to (i) refund the payment to the obligated bank if the check is paid, or (ii) pay the amount of the check to the person having rights of a holder in due course if the check is dishonored.

(d) If a claimant has the right to assert a claim under subsection (b) and is also a person entitled to enforce a cashier's check, teller's check, or certified check which is lost, destroyed, or stolen, the claimant may assert rights with respect to the check either under this section or Section 3-309.

Part 4. Liability of Parties.

§ 3-401. Signature.

(a) A person is not liable on an instrument unless (i) the person signed the instrument, or (ii) the person is represented by an agent or representative who signed the instrument and the signature is binding on the represented person under Section 3-402.

(b) A signature may be made (i) manually or by means of a device or machine, and (ii) by the use of any name, including a trade or assumed name, or by a word, mark, or symbol executed or adopted by a person with present intention to authenticate a writing.

§ 3-402. Signature by Representative.

(a) If a person acting, or purporting to act, as a representative signs an instrument by signing either the name of the represented person or the name of the signer, the represented person is bound by the signature to the same extent the represented person would be bound if the signature was on a simple contract. If the represented person is bound, the signature of the representative is the "authorized signature of the represented person" and the represented person is liable on the instrument, whether or not identified in the instrument.

(b) If a representative signs the name of the representative to an instrument and the signature is an authorized signature of the represented person, the following rules apply:

(1) If the form of the signature shows unambiguously that the signature is made on behalf of the represented person who is identified in the instrument, the representative is not liable on the instrument.

(2) Subject to subsection (c), if (i) the form of the signature does not show ambiguously that the signature is made in representative capacity or (ii) the

represented person is not identified in the instrument, the representative is liable on the instrument to a holder in due course that took the instrument without notice that the representative was not intended to be liable on the instrument. With respect to any other person, the representative is liable on the instrument unless the representative proves that the original parties did not intend the representative to be liable on the instrument.

(c) If a representative signs the name of the representative as drawer of a check without indication of the representative status and the check is payable from an account of the represented person who is identified on the check, the signer is not liable on the check if the signature is an authorized signature of the represented person.

§ 3-403. Unauthorized Signature.

(a) Unless otherwise provided in this Article or Article 4, an unauthorized signature is ineffective except as the signature of the unauthorized signer in favor of a person who in good faith pays the instrument or takes it for value. An unauthorized signature may be ratified for all purposes of this Article.

(b) If the signature of more than one person is required to constitute the authorized signature of an organization, the signature of the organization is unauthorized if one of the required signatures is lacking.

(c) The civil or criminal liability of a person who makes an unauthorized signature is not affected by any provision of this Article which makes the unauthorized signature effective for the purposes of this Article.

§ 3-404. Imposters; Fictitious Payees.

(a) If an imposter, by use of the mails or otherwise, induces the issuer of an instrument to issue the instrument to the imposter, or to a person acting in concert with the imposter, by impersonating the payee of the instrument or a person authorized to act for the payee, an indorsement of the instrument by any person in the name of a person who, in good faith, pays the instrument or takes it for value or for collection.

(b) If (i) a person whose intent determines to whom an instrument is payable (Section 3-110(a) or (b)) does not intend the person identified as payee to have any interest in the instrument, or (ii) the person identified

as payee of an instrument is a fictitious person, the following rules apply until the instrument is negotiated by special indorsement:

(1) Any person in possession of the instrument is its holder.

(2) An indorsement by any person in the name of the payee stated in the instrument is effective as the indorsement of the payee in favor of a person who, in good faith, pays the instrument or takes it for value or for collection.

(c) Under subsection (a) or (b), an indorsement is made in the name of a payee if (i) it is made in a name substantially similar to that of the payee or (ii) the instrument, whether or not indorsed, is deposited in a depositary bank to an account in a name substantially similar to that of the payee.

(d) With respect to an instrument to which subsection (a) or (b) applies, if a person paying the instrument or taking it for value or for collection fails to exercise ordinary care in paying or taking the instrument and that failure substantially contributes to loss resulting from payment of the instrument, the person bearing the loss may recover from the person failing to exercise ordinary care to the extent the failure to exercise ordinary care contributed to the loss.

§ 3-405. Employer's Responsibility for Fraudulent Indorsement by Employee.

(a) In this section:

(1) "Employee" includes an independent contractor and employee of an independent contractor retained by the employer.

(2) "Fraudulent indorsement" means (i) in the case of an instrument payable to the employer, a forged indorsement purporting to be that of the employer, or (ii) in the case of an instrument with respect to which the employer is the issuer, a forged indorsement purporting to be that of the person identified as payee.

(3) "Responsibility" with respect to instruments means authority (i) to sign or indorse instruments on behalf of the employer, (ii) to process instruments received by the employer for bookkeeping purposes, for deposit to an account, or for other disposition, (iii) to prepare or process instruments for

issue in the name of the employer, (iv) to supply information determining the names or addresses of payees of instruments to be issued in the name of the employer, (v) to control the disposition of instruments to be issued in the name of the employer, or (vi) to act otherwise with respect to instruments in a responsible capacity. "Responsibility" does not include authority that merely allows an employee to have access to instruments or bank or incomplete instrument forms that are being stored or transported or are part of incoming or outgoing mail, or similar access.

(b) For the purpose of determining the rights and liabilities of a person who, in good faith, pays an instrument or takes it for value or for collection, if an employer entrusted an employee with responsibility with respect to the instrument and the employee or a person acting in concert with the employee makes a fraudulent indorsement of the instrument, the indorsement is payable if it is made in the name of that person. If the person paying the instrument or taking it for value or for collection fails to exercise ordinary care in paying or taking the instrument and that failure substantially contributes to loss resulting from the fraud, the person bearing the loss may recover from the person failing to exercise ordinary care to the extent the failure to exercise ordinary care contributed to the loss.

(c) Under subsection (b), an indorsement is made in the name of the person to whom an instrument is payable if (i) it is made in a name substantially similar to the name of that person or (ii) the instrument, whether or not indorsed, is deposited in a depositary bank to an account in a name substantially similar to the name of that person.

§ 3–406. Negligence Contributing to a Forged Signature or Alteration of Instrument.

(a) A person whose failure to exercise ordinary care substantially contributes to an alteration of an instrument or to the making of a forged signature on an instrument is precluded from asserting the alteration or the forgery against a person who, in good faith, pays the instrument or takes it for value or for collection.

(b) Under subsection (a), if the person asserting the preclusion fails to exercise ordinary care in paying or taking the instrument and that failure substantially

contributes to loss, the loss is allocated between the person precluded and the person asserting the preclusion according to the extent to which the failure of each to exercise ordinary care contributed to the loss.

(c) Under subsection (a), the burden of proving failure to exercise ordinary care is on the person asserting the preclusion. Under subsection (b), the burden of proving failure to exercise ordinary care is on the person precluded.

§ 3–407. Alteration.

(a) "Alteration" means (i) an unauthorized change in an instrument that purports to modify in any respect the obligation of a party, or (ii) an unauthorized addition of words or numbers or other change to an incomplete instrument relating to the obligation of a party.

(b) Except as provided in subsection (c), an alteration fraudulently made discharges a party whose obligation is affected by the alteration unless that party assents or is precluded from asserting the alteration. No other alteration discharges a party, and the instrument may be enforced according to its original terms.

(c) A payor bank or drawee paying a fraudulently altered instrument or a person taking it for value, in good faith and without notice of the alteration, may enforce rights with respect to the instrument (i) according to its original terms, or (ii) in the case of an incomplete instrument altered by unauthorized completion, according to its terms as completed.

§ 3–408. Drawee Not Liable on Unaccepted Draft.

A check or other draft does not of itself operate as an assignment of funds in the hands of the drawee available for its payment, and the drawee is not liable on the instrument until the drawee accepts it.

§ 3–409. Acceptance of Draft; Certified Check.

(a) "Acceptance" means the drawee's signed agreement to pay a draft as presented. It must be written on the draft and may consist of the drawee's signature alone. Acceptance may be made at any time and becomes effective when notification pursuant to instructions is given or the accepted draft is delivered for the purpose of giving rights on the acceptance to any person.

(b) A draft may be accepted although it has not been signed by the drawer, is otherwise incomplete, is overdue, or has been dishonored.

(c) If a draft is payable at a fixed period after sight and the acceptor fails to date the acceptance, the holder may complete the acceptance by supplying a date in good faith.

(d) "Certified check" means a check accepted by the bank on which it is drawn. Acceptance may be made as stated in subsection (a) or by a writing on the check which indicates that the check is certified. The drawee of a check has no obligation to certify the check, and refusal to certify is not dishonor of the check.

§ 3-410. Acceptance Varying Draft.

(a) If the terms of a drawee's acceptance vary from the terms of the draft as presented, the holder may refuse the acceptance and treat the draft as dishonored. In that case, the drawee may cancel the acceptance.

(b) The terms of a draft are not varied by an acceptance to pay at a particular bank or place in the United States, unless the acceptance states that the draft is to be paid only at that bank or place.

(c) If the holder assents to an acceptance varying the terms of a draft, the obligation of each drawer and indorser that does not expressly assent to the acceptance is discharged.

§ 3-411. Refusal to Pay Cashier's Checks, Teller's Checks, and Certified Checks.

(a) In this section, "obligated bank" means the acceptor of a certified check or the issuer of a cashier's check or teller's check brought from the issuer.

(b) If the obligated bank wrongfully (i) refuses to pay a cashier's check or certified check, (ii) stops payment of a teller's check, or (iii) refuses to pay a dishonored teller's check, the person asserting the right to enforce the check is entitled to compensation for expenses and loss of interest resulting from the nonpayment and may recover consequential damages if the obligated bank refuses to pay after receiving notice of particular circumstances giving rise to the damages.

(c) Expenses or consequential damages under subsection (b) are not recoverable if the refusal of the obligated bank to pay occurs because (i) the bank suspends payments, (ii) the obligated bank asserts a claim or defense of the bank that it has reasonable grounds to believe is available against the person entitled to enforce the instrument, (iii) the obligated bank has a reasonable doubt whether the person demanding payment is the person entitled to enforce the instrument, or (iv) payment is prohibited by law.

§ 3-412. Obligation of Issuer of Note or Cashier's Check.

The issuer of a note or cashier's check or other draft drawn on the drawer is obliged to pay the instrument (i) according to its terms at the time it was issued or, if not issued, at the time it first came into possession of a holder, or (ii) if the issuer signed an incomplete instrument, according to its terms when completed, to the extent stated in Sections 3-115 and 3-407. The obligation is owed to a person entitled to enforce the instrument or to an indorser who paid the instrument under Section 3-415.

§ 3-413. Obligation of Acceptor.

(a) The acceptor of a draft is obliged to pay the draft (i) according to its terms at the time it was accepted, even though the acceptance states that the draft is payable "as originally drawn" or equivalent terms, (ii) if the acceptance varies the terms of the draft, according to the terms of the draft as varied, or (iii) if the acceptance is of a draft that is an incomplete instrument, according to its terms when completed, to the extent stated in Sections 3-115 and 3-407. The obligation is owed to a person entitled to enforce the draft or to the drawer or an indorser who paid the draft under Section 3-414 or 3-415.

(b) If the certification of a check or other acceptance of a draft states the amount certified or accepted, the obligation of the acceptor is that amount. If (i) the certification or acceptance does not state an amount, (ii) the amount of the instrument is subsequently raised, and (iii) the instrument is then negotiated to a holder in due course, the obligation of the acceptor is the amount of the instrument at the time it was taken by the holder in due course.

§ 3-414. Obligation of Drawer.

(a) This section does not apply to cashier's checks or other drafts drawn on the drawer.

(b) If an unaccepted draft is dishonored, the drawer is obliged to pay the draft (i) according to its terms at the time it was issued or, if not issued, at the time it first came into possession of a holder, or (ii) if the drawer signed an incomplete instrument, according to its terms when completed, to the extent stated in Sections 3-115 and 3-407. The obligation is owed to a person entitled to enforce the draft or to an indorser who paid the draft under Section 3-415.

(c) If a draft is accepted by a bank, the drawer is discharged, regardless of when or by whom acceptance was obtained.

(d) If a draft is accepted and the acceptor is not a bank, the obligation of the drawer to pay the draft if the draft is dishonored by the acceptor is the same as the obligation of an indorser under Section 3-415(a) and (c).

(e) If a draft states that it is drawn "without recourse" or otherwise disclaims liability of the drawer to pay the draft, the drawer is not liable under subsection (b) to pay the draft if the draft is not a check. A disclaimer of the liability stated in subsection (b) is not effective if the draft is a check.

(f) If (i) a check is not presented for payment or given to a depositary bank for collection within 30 days after its date, (ii) the drawee suspends payments after expiration of the 30-day period without paying the check, and (iii) because of the suspension of payments, the drawer is deprived of funds maintained with the drawee to cover payment of the check, the drawer to the extent deprived of funds may discharge its obligation to pay the check by assigning to the person entitled to enforce the check the rights of the drawer against the drawee with respect to the funds.

§ 3-415. Obligation of Indorser.

(a) Subject to subsections (b), (c), and (d) and to Section 3-419(d), if an instrument is dishonored, an indorser is obliged to pay the amount due on the instrument (i) according to the terms of the instrument at the time it was indorsed, or (ii) if the indorser indorsed an incomplete instrument, according to its terms when completed, to the extent stated in Sections 3-115 and 3-407. The obligation of the indorser is owed to a person entitled to enforce the instrument or to a subsequent indorser who paid the instrument under this section.

(b) If an indorsement states that it is made "without recourse" or otherwise disclaims liability of the indorser, the indorser is not liable under subsection (a) to pay the instrument.

(c) If notice of dishonor of an instrument is required by Section 3-503 and notice of dishonor complying with that section is not given to an indorser, the liability of the indorser under subsection (a) is discharged.

(d) If a draft is accepted by a bank after an indorsement is made, the liability of the indorser under subsection (a) is discharged.

(e) If an indorser of a check is liable under subsection (a) and the check is not presented for payment, or given to a depositary bank for collection, within 30 days after the day the indorsement was made, the liability of the indorser under subsection (a) is discharged.

§ 3-416. Transfer Warranties.

(a) A person who transfers an instrument for consideration warrants to the transferee and, if the transfer is by indorsement, to any subsequent transferee that:

(1) the warrantor is a person entitled to enforce the instrument;

(2) all signatures on the instrument are authentic and authorized;

(3) the instrument has not been altered;

(4) the instrument is not subject to a defense or claim in recoupment of any party which can be asserted against the warrantor; and

(5) the warrantor has no knowledge of any insolvency proceeding commenced with respect to the maker or acceptor or, in the case of an unaccepted draft, the drawer.

(b) A person to whom the warranties under subsection (a) are made and who took the instrument in good faith may recover from the warrantor as damages for breach of warranty an amount equal to the loss suffered as a result of the breach, but not more than the amount of the instrument plus expenses and loss of interest incurred as a result of the breach.

(c) The warranties stated in subsection (a) cannot be disclaimed with respect to checks. Unless notice of a claim for breach of warranty is given to the warrantor within 30 days after the claimant has reason to know of the breach and the identity of the warrantor, the liability of the warrantor under subsection (b) is discharged to the extent of any loss caused by the delay in giving notice of the claim.

(d) A [cause of action] for breach of warranty under this section accrues when the claimant has reason to know of the breach.

§ 3-417. Presentment Warranties.

(a) If an unaccepted draft is presented to the drawee for payment or acceptance and the drawee pays or accepts the draft, (i) the person obtaining payment or acceptance, at the time of presentment, and (ii) a previous transferor of the draft, at the time of transfer, warrant to the drawee making payment or accepting the draft in good faith that:

(1) the warrantor is, or was, at the time the warrantor transferred the draft, a person entitled to enforce the draft or authorized to obtain payment or acceptance of the draft on behalf of a person entitled to enforce the draft;

(2) the draft has not been altered; and

(3) the warrantor has no knowledge that the signature of the drawer of the draft is unauthorized.

(b) A drawee making payment may recover from any warrantor damages for breach of warranty equal to the amount paid by the drawee less the amount the drawee received or is entitled to receive from the drawer because of the payment. In addition, the drawee is entitled to compensation for expenses and loss of interest resulting from the breach. The right of the drawee to recover damages under this subsection is not affected by any failure of the drawee to exercise ordinary care in making payment. If the drawee accepts the draft, breach of warranty is a defense to the obligation of the acceptor. If the acceptor makes payment with respect to the draft, the acceptor is entitled to recover from any warrantor for breach of warranty the amounts stated in this subsection.

(c) If a drawee asserts a claim for breach of warranty under subsection (a) based on an unauthorized indorsement of the draft or an alteration of the draft, the warrantor may defend by proving that the indorsement is effective under Section 3-404 or 3-405 or the drawee is precluded under Section 3-406 or 4-406 from asserting against the drawee the unauthorized indorsement or alteration.

(d) If (i) a dishonored draft is presented for payment to the drawer or an indorser or (ii) any other instrument is presented for payment to a party obliged to pay the instrument, and (iii) payment is received, the following rules apply:

(1) The person obtaining payment and a prior transferor of the instrument warrant to the person making payment in good faith that the warrantor is, or was, at the time the warrantor transferred the instrument, a person entitled to enforce the instrument or authorized to obtain payment on behalf of a person entitled to enforce the instrument.

(2) The person making payment may recover from any warrantor for breach of warranty an amount equal to the amount paid plus expenses and loss of interest resulting from the breach.

(e) The warranties stated in subsections (a) and (d) cannot be disclaimed with respect to checks. Unless notice of a claim for breach of warranty is given to the warrantor within 30 days after the claimant has reason to know of the breach and the identity of the warrantor, the liability of the warrantor under subsection (b) or (d) is discharged to the extent of any loss caused by the delay in giving notice of the claim.

(f) A [cause of action] for breach of warranty under this section accrues when the claimant has reason to know of the breach.

§ 3-418. Payment or Acceptance by Mistake.

(a) Except as provided in subsection (c), if the drawee of a draft pays or accepts the draft and the drawee acted on the mistaken belief that (i) payment of the draft had not been stopped pursuant to Section 4-403 or (ii) the signature of the drawer of the draft was authorized, the drawee may recover the amount of the draft from the person to whom or for whose benefit payment was made or, in the case of acceptance, may revoke the acceptance. Rights of the drawee under this subsection are not affected by failure of the drawee to exercise ordinary care in paying or accepting the draft.

(b) Except as provided in subsection (c), if an instrument has been paid or accepted by mistake and the case is not covered by subsection (a), the person paying or accepting may, to the extent permitted by the law governing mistake and restitution, (i) recover the payment from the person to whom or for whose benefit payment was made or (ii) in the case of acceptance, may revoke the acceptance.

(c) The remedies provided by subsection (a) or (b) may not be asserted against a person who took the instrument in good faith and for value or who in good faith changed position in reliance on the payment or acceptance. This subsection does not limit remedies provided by Section 3-417 or 4-407.

(d) Notwithstanding Section 4-215, if an instrument is paid or accepted by mistake and the payor or acceptor recovers payment or revokes acceptance under subsection (a) or (b), the instrument is deemed not to have been paid or accepted and is treated as dishonored, and the person from whom payment is recovered has rights as a person entitled to enforce the dishonored instrument.

§ 3-420. Conversion of Instrument.

(a) The law applicable to conversion of personal property applies to instruments. An instrument is also converted if it is taken by transfer, other than a negotiation, from a person not entitled to enforce the instrument or a bank makes or obtains payment with respect to the instrument for a person not entitled to enforce the instrument or receive payment. An action for conversion of an instrument may not be brought by (i) the issuer or acceptor of the instrument or (ii) a payee or indorsee who did not receive delivery of the instrument either directly or through delivery to an agent or a co-payee.

(b) In an action under subsection (a), the measure of liability is presumed to be the amount payable on the instrument, but recovery may not exceed the amount of the plaintiff's interest in the instrument.

(c) A representative, other than a depositary bank, who has in good faith dealt with an instrument or its proceeds on behalf of one who was not the person entitled to enforce the instrument is not liable in conversion to that person beyond the amount of any proceeds that it has not paid out.

Part 5. Dishonor.

§ 3-501. Presentment.

(a) "Presentment" means a demand made by or on behalf of a person entitled to enforce an instrument (i) to pay the instrument made to the drawee or a party obliged to pay the instrument or, in the case of a note or accepted draft payable at a bank, to the bank, or (ii) to accept a draft made to the drawee.

(b) The following rules are subject to Article 4, agreement of the parties, and clearing-house rules and the like:

(1) Presentment may be made at the place of payment of the instrument and must be made at the place of payment if the instrument is payable at a bank in the United States; may be made by any commercially reasonable means, including an oral, written, or electronic communication; is effective when the demand for payment or acceptance is received by the person to whom presentment is made; and is effective if made to any one of two or more makers, acceptors, drawees, or other payors.

(2) Upon demand of the person to whom presentment is made, the person making presentment must (i) exhibit the instrument, (ii) give reasonable identification and, if presentment is made on behalf of another person, reasonable evidence of authority to do so, and (. . .) sign a receipt on the instrument for any payment made or surrender the instrument if full payment is made.

(3) Without dishonoring the instrument, the party to whom presentment is made may (i) return the instrument for lack of a necessary indorsement, or (ii) refuse payment or acceptance for failure of the presentment to comply with the terms of the instrument, an agreement of the parties, or other applicable law or rule.

(4) The party to whom presentment is made may treat presentment as occurring on the next business day after the day of presentment if the party to whom presentment is made has established a cut-off hour not earlier than 2 p.m. for the receipt and processing of instruments presented for payment or acceptance and presentment is made after the cut-off hour.

§ 3-502. Dishonor.

(a) Dishonor of a note is governed by the following rules:

(1) If the note is payable on demand, the note is dishonored if presentment is duly made to the maker and the note is not paid on the date of presentment.

(2) If the note is not payable on demand and is payable at or through a bank or the terms of the note require presentment, the note is dishonored if presentment is duly made and the note is not paid on the day it becomes payable or the day of presentment, whichever is later.

(3) If the note is not payable on demand and paragraph (2) does not apply, the note is dishonored if it is not paid on the day it becomes payable.

(b) Dishonor of an unaccepted draft other than a documentary draft is governed by the following rules:

(1) If a check is duly presented for payment to the payor bank otherwise than for immediate payment over the counter, the check is dishonored if the payor bank makes timely return of the check or sends timely notice of dishonor or nonpayment under Section 4–301 or 4–302, or becomes accountable for the amount of the check under Section 4-302.

(2) If a draft is payable on demand and paragraph (1) does not apply, the draft is dishonored if presentment for payment is duly made to the drawee and the draft is not paid on the day of presentment.

(3) If a draft is payable on a date stated in the draft, the draft is dishonored if (i) presentment for payment is duly made to the drawee and payment is not made on the day the draft becomes payable or the day of presentment, whichever is later, or (ii) presentment for acceptance is duly made before the day the draft becomes payable and the draft is not accepted on the day of presentment.

(4) If a draft is payable on elapse of a period of time after sight or acceptance, the draft is dishonored if presentment for acceptance is duly made and the draft is not accepted on the day of presentment.

(c) Dishonor of an unaccepted documentary draft occurs according to the rules stated in subsection (b)(2), (3), and (4), except that payment or acceptance may be delayed without dishonor until no later than the close of the third business day of the drawee following the day on which payment or acceptance is required by those paragraphs.

(d) Dishonor of an accepted draft is governed by the following rules:

(1) If the draft is payable on demand, the draft is dishonored if presentment for payment is duly made to the acceptor and the draft is not paid on the day of presentment.

(2) If the draft is not payable on demand, the draft is dishonored if presentment for payment is duly made to the acceptor and payment is not made on the day it becomes payable or the day of presentment, whichever is later.

(e) In any case in which presentment is otherwise required for dishonor under this section and presentment is excused under Section 3-504, dishonor occurs without presentment if the instrument is not duly accepted or paid.

(f) If a draft is dishonored because timely acceptance of the draft was not made and the person entitled to demand acceptance consents to a late acceptance, from the time of acceptance the draft is treated as never having been dishonored.

§ 3-503. Notice of Dishonor.

(a) The obligation of an indorser stated in Section 3-415(a) and the obligation of a drawer stated in Section 3-414(d) may not be enforced unless (i) the indorser or drawer is given notice of dishonor of the instrument complying with this section or (ii) notice of dishonor is excused under Section 3-504(b).

(b) Notice of dishonor may be given by any person; may be given by any commercially reasonable means, including an oral, written, or electronic communication; and is sufficient if it reasonably identifies the instrument and indicates that the instrument has been dishonored or has not been paid or accepted. Return of an instrument given to bank for collection is sufficient notice of dishonor.

(c) Subject to Section 3-504(c), with respect to an instrument taken for collection by a collecting bank, notice of dishonor must be given (i) by the bank before midnight of the next banking day following the banking day on which the bank receives notice of dishonor of the instrument, or (ii) by any other person within 30 days following the day on which the person receives notice of dishonor. With respect to any other instrument, notice of dishonor must be given within 30 days following the day on which dishonor occurs.

§ 3–504. Excused Presentment and Notice of Dishonor.

(a) Presentment for payment or acceptance of an instrument is excused if (i) the person entitled to present the instrument cannot with reasonable diligence make presentment, (ii) the maker or acceptor has repudiated an obligation to pay the instrument or is dead or in insolvency proceedings, (iii) by the terms of the instrument presentment is not necessary to enforce the obligation of indorsers or the drawer, (iv) the drawer or indorser whose obligation is being enforced has waived presentment or otherwise has no reason to expect or right to require that the instrument be paid or accepted, or (v) the drawer instructed the drawee not to pay or accept the draft or the drawee was not obligated to the drawer to pay the draft.

(b) Notice of dishonor is excused if (i) by the terms of the instrument notice of dishonor is not necessary to enforce the obligation of a party to pay the instrument, or (ii) the party whose obligation is being enforced waived notice of dishonor. A waiver of presentment is also a waiver of notice of dishonor.

(c) Delay in giving notice of dishonor is excused if the delay was caused by circumstances beyond the control of the person giving the notice and the person giving the notice exercised reasonable diligence after the cause of the delay ceased to operate.

§ 3–505. Evidence of Dishonor.

(a) The following are admissible as evidence and create a presumption of dishonor and of any notice of dishonor stated:

(1) a document regular in form as provided in subsection (b) which purports to be a protest;

(2) a purported stamp or writing of the drawee, payor bank, or presenting bank on or accompanying the instrument stating that acceptance or payment has been refused unless reasons for the refusal

are stated and the reasons are not consistent with dishonor.

(3) a book or record of the drawee, payor bank, or collecting bank, kept in the usual course of business which shows dishonor, even if there is no evidence of who made the entry.

(b) A protest is a certificate of dishonor made by a United States consul or vice consul, or a notary public or other person authorized to administer oaths by the law of the place where dishonor occurs. It may be made upon information satisfactory to that person. The protest must identify the instrument and certify either that presentment has been made or, if not made, the reason why it was not made, and that the instrument has been dishonored by nonacceptance or nonpayment. The protest may also certify that notice of dishonor has been given to some or all parties.

Part 6. Discharge and Payment.

§ 3–601. Discharge and Effect of Discharge.

(a) The obligation of a party to pay the instrument is discharged as stated in this Article or by an act or agreement with the party which would discharge an obligation to pay money under a simple contract.

(b) Discharge of the obligation of a party is not effective against a person acquiring rights of a holder in due course of the instrument without notice of the discharge.

§ 3–602. Payment.

(a) Subject to subsection (b), an instrument is paid to the extent payment is made (i) by or on behalf of a party obliged to pay the instrument, and (ii) to a person entitled to enforce the instrument. To the extent of the payment, the obligation of the party obliged to pay the instrument is discharged even though payment is made with knowledge of a claim to the instrument under Section 3-306 by another person.

(b) The obligation of a party to pay the instrument is not discharged under subsection (a) if:

(1) a claim to the instrument under Section 3-306 is enforceable against the party receiving payment and (i) payment is made with knowledge by the payor that payment is prohibited by injunction or similar process of a court of competent jurisdiction,

or (ii) in the case of an instrument other than a cashier's check, teller's check, or certified check, the party making payment accepted, from the person having a claim to the instrument, indemnity against loss resulting from refusal to pay the person entitled to enforce the instrument; or

(2) the person making payment knows that the instrument is a stolen instrument and pays a person it knows is in wrongful possession of the instrument.

§ 3-603. Tender of Payment.

(a) If tender of payment of an obligation to pay an instrument is made to a person entitled to enforce the instrument, the effect of tender is governed by principles of law applicable to tender of payment under a simple contract.

(b) If tender of payment of an obligation to pay an instrument is made to a person entitled to enforce the instrument and the tender is refused, there is discharge, to the extent of the amount of the tender, of the obligation of an indorser or accommodation party having a right of recourse with respect to the obligation to which the tender relates.

(c) If tender of payment of an amount due on an instrument is made to a person entitled to enforce the instrument, the obligation of the obligor to pay interest after the due date on the amount tendered is discharged. If presentment is required with respect to an instrument and the obligor is able and ready to pay on the due date at every place of payment stated in the instrument, the obligor is deemed to have made tender of payment on the due date to the person entitled to enforce the instrument.

§ 3-605. Discharge of Indorsers and Accommodation Parties.

(a) In this section, the term "indorser" includes a drawer having the obligation described in Section 3-414(d).

(b) Discharge, under Section 3-604, of the obligation of a party to pay an instrument does not discharge the obligation of an indorser or accommodation party having a right of recourse against the discharged party.

(c) If a person entitled to enforce the instrument agrees, with or without consideration, to an extension of the due date of the obligation of a party to pay the instrument, the extension discharges an indorser or accommodation party having a right of recourse against the party whose obligation is extended to the extent the indorser or accommodation party proves that the extension caused loss to the indorser or accommodation party with respect to the right of recourse.

(d) If a person entitled to enforce an instrument agrees, with or without consideration, to a material modification of the obligation of a party other than an extension of the due date, the modification discharges the obligation of an indorser or accommodation party having a right of recourse against the person whose obligation is modified to the extent the modification causes loss to the indorser or accommodation party with respect to the right of recourse. The loss suffered by the indorser or accommodation party as a result of the modification is equal to the amount of the right of recourse unless the person enforcing the instrument proves that no loss was caused by the modification or that the loss caused by the modification was an amount less than the amount of the right of recourse.

(e) If the obligation of a party to pay an instrument is secured by an interest in collateral and a person entitled to enforce the instrument impairs the value of the interest in collateral, the obligation of an indorser or accommodation party having a right of recourse against the obligor is discharged to the extent of the impairment. The value of an interest in collateral is impaired to the extent (i) the value of the interest is reduced to an amount less than the amount of the right of recourse of the party asserting discharge, or (ii) the reduction in value of the interest causes an increase in the amount by which the amount of the right of recourse exceeds the value of the interest. The burden on proving impairment is on the party asserting discharge.

(f) If the obligation of a party is secured by an interest in collateral not provided by an accommodation party and a person entitled to enforce the instrument impairs the value of the interest in collateral, the obligation of any party who is jointly and severally liable with respect to the secured obligation is discharged to the extent the impairment causes the party asserting discharge to pay more than that party would have been obliged to pay, taking into account rights of contribution, if impairment had not occurred. If the party asserting discharge is an accommodation party not entitled to discharge under subsection (e), the party is deemed to have a right to contribution based on joint and several liability rather than a right to reimbursement. The burden of proving impairment is on the party asserting discharge.

(g) Under subsection (e) or (f), impairing value of an interest in collateral includes (i) failure to obtain or maintain perfection or recordation of the interest in collateral, (ii) release of collateral without substitution of collateral of equal value, (iii) failure to perform a duty to preserve the value of collateral owed, under Article 9 or other law, to a debtor or surety or other person secondarily liable, or (iv) failure to comply with applicable law in disposing of collateral.

(h) An accommodation party is not discharged under subsection (c), (d), or (e) unless the person entitled to enforce the instrument knows of the accommodation or has notice under Section 3-419(c) that the instrument was signed for accommodation.

(i) A party is not discharged under this section if (i) the party asserting discharge consents to the event or conduct that is the basis of the discharge, or (ii) the instrument or a separate agreement of the party provides for waiver of discharge under this section either specifically or by general language indicating that parties waive defenses based on suretyship or impairment of collateral.

Article 4. BANK DEPOSITS AND COLLECTIONS.

Part 1. General Provisions and Definitions.

§4-102. Applicability.

(a) To the extent that items within this Article are also within Articles 3 and 8, they are subject to those Articles. If there is conflict, this Article governs Article 3, but Article 8 governs this Article.

(b) The liability of a bank for action or non-action with respect to an item handled by it for purposes of presentment, payment, or collection is governed by the law of the place where the bank is located. In the case of action or non-action by or at a branch or separate office of a bank, its liability is governed by the law of the place where the branch or separate office is located.

§ 4-103. Variation by Agreement; Measure of Damages; Action Constituting Ordinary Care.

(a) The effect of the provisions of this Article may be varied by agreement, but the parties to the agreement cannot disclaim a bank's responsibility for its lack of good faith or failure to exercise ordinary care or limit the measure of damages for the lack or failure. However, the parties may determine by agreement the standards by which the bank''s responsibility is to be measured if those standards are not manifestly unreasonable.

(b) Federal Reserve regulations and operating circulars, clearing-house rules, and the like have the effect of agreements under subsection (a), whether or not specifically assented to by all parties interested in items handled.

(c) Action or non-action approved by this Article or pursuant to Federal Reserve regulations or operating circulars is the exercise of ordinary care and, in the absence of special instructions, action or non-action consistent with clearing-house rules and the like or with a general banking usage not disapproved by this Article, is prima facie the exercise of ordinary care.

(d) The specification or approval of certain procedures by this Article is not disapproval of other procedures that may be reasonable under the circumstances.

(e) The measure of damages for failure to exercise ordinary care in handling an item is the amount of the item reduced by an amount that could not have been realized by the exercise of ordinary care. If there is also bad faith it includes any other damages the party suffered as a proximate consequence.

§ 4-104. Definitions and Index of Definitions.

(a) In this Article, unless the context otherwise requires:

(1) "Account" means any deposit or credit account with a bank, including a demand, time, savings, passbook, share draft, or like account, other than an account evidenced by a certificate of deposit;

(2) "Afternoon" means the period of a day between noon and midnight;

(3) "Banking day" means the part of a day on which a bank is open to the public for carrying on substantially all of its banking functions;

(4) "Clearing house" means an association of banks or other payors regularly clearing items;

(5) "Customer" means a person having an account with a bank or for whom a bank has agreed to collect items, including a bank that maintains an account at another bank;

(6) "Documentary draft" means a draft to be presented for acceptance or payment if specified documents, certificated securities (Section 8-102) or instructions for uncertificated securities (Section 8-308), or other certificates, statements or the like are to be received by the drawee or other payor before acceptance or payment of the draft;

(7) "Draft" means a draft as defined in Section 3-104 or an item, other than an instrument, that is an order;

(8) "Drawee" means a person ordered in a draft to make payment;

(9) "Item" means an instrument or a promise or order to pay money handled by a bank for collection or payment. The term does not include a payment order governed by Article 4A or a credit or debit card slip;

(10) "Midnight deadline" with respect to a bank is midnight on its next banking day following the banking day on which it receives the relevant item or notice or from which the time for taking action commences to run, whichever is later;

(11) "Settle" means to pay in cash, by clearing-house settlement, in a charge or credit or by remittance, or otherwise as agreed. A settlement may be either provisional or final;

(12) "Suspends payments" with respect to a bank means that it has been closed by order of the supervisory authorities, that a public officer has been appointed to take it over, or that it ceases or refuses to make payments in the ordinary course of business.

§ 4-105. "Bank"; "Depository Bank"; "Payor Bank"; "Intermediary Bank"; "Collecting Bank"; "Presenting Bank".

In this Article:

(1) "Bank" means a person engaged in the business of banking, including a savings bank, savings and loan association, credit union, or trust company.

(2) "Depository bank" means the first bank to take an item even though it is also the payor bank, unless the item is presented for immediate payment over the counter;

(3) "Payor bank" means a bank that is the drawee of a draft;

(4) "Intermediary bank" means a bank to which an item is transferred in course of collection except the depository or payor bank;

(5) "Collecting bank" means a bank handling an item for collection except the payor bank;

(6) "Presenting bank" means a bank presenting an item except a payor bank.

§ 4-108. Time of Receipt of Items.

(a) For the purpose of allowing time to process items, prove balances, and make the necessary entries on its books to determine its position for the day, a bank may fix an afternoon hour of 2 P.M. or later as a cutoff hour for the handling of money and items and the making of entries on its books.

(b) An item or deposit of money received on any day after a cutoff hour so fixed or after the close of the banking day may be treated as being received at the opening of the next banking day.

§ 4-109. Delays.

(a) Unless otherwise instructed, a collecting bank in a good faith effort to secure payment of a specific item drawn on a payor other than a bank, and with or without the approval of any person involved, may waive, modify, or extend time limits imposed or permitted by this [Act] for a period not exceeding two additional banking days without discharge of drawers or indorsers or liability to its transferor or a prior party.

(b) Delay by a collecting bank or payor bank beyond time limits prescribed or permitted by this [Act] or by instructions is excused if (i) the delay is caused by interruptions of communication or computer facilities, suspension of payments by another bank, war, emergency conditions, failure of equipment, or other circumstances beyond the control of the bank, and (ii) the bank exercises such diligence as the circumstances require.

§ 4-110. Electronic Presentment.

(a) "Agreement for electronic presentment" means an agreement, clearing-house rule, or Federal Reserve regulation or operating circular, providing that presentment of an item may be made by transmission of an image of an item or information describing the item ("presentment notice") rather than delivery of the item itself. The agreement may provide for procedures governing retention, presentment, payment, dishonor, and other matters concerning items subject to the agreement.

(b) Presentment of an item pursuant to an agreement for presentment is made when the presentment notice is received.

(c) If presentment is made by presentment notice, a reference to "item" or "check" in this Article means the presentment notice unless the context otherwise indicates.

§ 4-111. Statute of Limitations.

An action to enforce an obligation, duty, or right arising under this Article must be commenced within three years after the [cause of action] accrues.

Part 2. Collection of Items; Depositary and Collecting Banks.

§ 4-202. Responsibility for Collection or Return; When Action Timely.

(a) A collecting bank must exercise ordinary care in:

(1) presenting an item or sending it for presentment;

(2) sending notice of dishonor or nonpayment or returning an item other than a documentary draft to the bank's transferor after learning that the item has not been paid or accepted, as the case may be;

(3) settling for an item when the bank receives final settlement; and

(4) notifying its transferor of any loss or delay in transit within a reasonable time after discovery thereof.

(b) A collecting bank exercises ordinary care under subsection (a) by taking proper action before its midnight deadline following receipt of any item, notice, or settlement. Taking proper action within a reasonably longer time may constitute the exercise of ordinary care, but the bank has the burden of establishing timeliness.

(c) Subject to subsection (a)(1), a bank is not liable for the insolvency, neglect, misconduct, mistake, or default of another bank or person or for loss or destruction of an item in the possession of others or in transit.

§ 4-203. Effect of Instructions.

Subject to Article 3 concerning conversion of instruments (Section 3-420) and restrictive indorsements (Section 3-206), only a collecting bank's transferor can give instructions that affect the bank or constitute notice to it, and a collecting bank is not liable to prior parties for any action taken pursuant to the instructions or in accordance with any agreement with its transferor.

§ 4-204. Methods of Sending and Presenting; Sending Directly to Payor Bank.

(a) A collecting bank shall send items by a reasonably prompt method, taking into consideration relevant instructions, the nature of the item, the number of those items on hand, the cost of collection involved, and the method generally used by it or others to present those items.

(b) A collecting bank may send:

(1) an item directly to the payor bank;

(2) an item to a nonbank payor if authorized by its transferor; and

(3) an item other than documentary drafts to a nonbank payor, if authorized by Federal Reserve regulation or operating circular, clearing-house rule, or the like.

(c) Presentment may be made by a presenting bank at a place where the payor bank or other payor has requested that presentment be made.

§ 4-205. Depositary Bank Holder of Unindorsed Item.

If a customer delivers an item to a depositary bank for collection:

(1) the depositary bank becomes a holder of the item at the time it receives the item for collection if the customer at the time of delivery was a holder of the item, whether or not the customer indorses the item, and, if the bank satisfies the other requirements of Section 3-302, it is a holder in due course; and

(2) the depositary bank warrants to collecting banks, the payor bank or other payor, and the drawer that the amount of the item was paid to the customer or deposited to the customer's account.

§ 4-209. Encoding and Retention Warranties.

(a) A person who encodes information on or with respect to an item after issue warrants to any subsequent collecting bank and to the payor bank or other payor that the information is correctly encoded. If the customer of a depositary bank encodes, that bank also makes the warranty.

(b) A person who undertakes to retain an item pursuant to an agreement for electronic presentment warrants to any subsequent collecting bank and to the payor bank or other payor that retention and presentment of the item comply with the agreement. If a customer of a depositary bank undertakes to retain an item, that bank also makes this warranty.

(c) A person to whom warranties are made under this section and who took the item in good faith may recover from the warrantor as damages for breach of warranty an amount equal to the loss suffered as a result of the breach, plus expenses and loss of interest incurred as a result of the breach.

§ 4-211. When Bank Gives Value for Purposes of Holder in Due Course.

For purposes of determining its status as a holder in due course, a bank has given value to the extent it has a security interest in an item, if the bank otherwise complies with the requirements of Section 3-302 on what constitutes a holder in due course.

Part 3. Collection of Items: Payor Banks.

§ 4-302. Payor Bank's Responsibility for Late Return of Item.

(a) If an item is presented to and received by a payor bank, the bank is accountable for the amount of:

(1) a demand item, other than a documentary draft, whether properly payable or not, if the bank, in any case in which it is not also the depositary bank, retains the item beyond midnight of the banking day of receipt without settling for it or, whether or not it is also the depositary bank, does not pay or return

the item or send notice of dishonor until after its midnight deadline; or

(2) any other properly payable item unless, within the time allowed for acceptance or payment of that item, the bank either accepts or pays the item or returns it and accompanying documents.

(b) The liability of a payor bank to pay an item pursuant to subsection (a) is subject to defenses based on breach of a presentment warranty (Section 4-208) or proof that the person seeking enforcement of the liability presented or transferred the item for the purpose of defrauding the payor bank.

§ 4-303. When Items Subject to Notice, Stop-Payment Order, Legal Process, or Setoff; Order in Which Items May Be Charged or Certified.

(a) Any knowledge, notice, or stop-payment order received by, legal process served upon, or setoff exercised by a payor bank comes too late to terminate, suspend, or modify the bank's right or duty to pay an item or to charge its customer's account for the item if the knowledge, notice, stop-payment order, or legal process is received or served and a reasonable time for the bank to act thereon expires or the setoff is exercised after the earliest of the following:

(1) the bank accepts or certifies the item;

(2) the bank pays the item in cash;

(3) the bank settles for the item without having a right to revoke the settlement under statute, clearing-house rule, or agreement;

(4) the bank becomes accountable for the amount of the item under Section 4-302 dealing with the payor bank's responsibility for late return of items; or

(5) with respect to checks, a cutoff hour no earlier than one hour after the opening of the next banking day after the banking day on which the bank received the check and no later than the close of that next banking day or, if no cutoff hour is fixed, the close of the next banking day after the banking day on which the bank received the check.

(b) Subject to subsection (a), items may be accepted, paid, certified, or charged to the indicated account of its customer in any order.

Part 4. Relationship Between Payor Bank and Its Customer.

§ 4-401. When Bank May Charge Customer's Account.

(a) A bank may charge against the account of a customer an item that is properly payable from the account even though the charge creates an overdraft. An item is properly payable if it is authorized by the customer and is in accordance with any agreement between the customer and bank.

(b) A customer is not liable for the amount of an overdraft if the customer neither signed the item nor benefited [*sic*] from the proceeds of the item.

(c) A bank may charge against the account of a customer a check that is otherwise properly payable from the account, even though payment was made before the date of the check, unless the customer has given notice to the bank of the postdating describing the check with reasonable certainty. The notice is effective for the period stated in Section 4-403(b) for stop-payment orders, and must be received at such time and in such manner as to afford the bank a reasonable opportunity to act on it before the bank takes any action with respect to the check described in Section 4-303. If a bank charges against the account of a customer by a check before the date stated in the notice of postdating, the bank is liable for damages for the loss resulting from its act. The loss may include damages for dishonor of subsequent items under Section 4-402.

(d) The bank that in good faith makes payment to a holder may charge the indicated account of its customer according to:

(1) the original terms of the altered item; or

(2) the terms of the completed item, even though the bank knows the item has been completed unless the bank has notice that the completion was improper.

§ 4-402. Bank's Liability to Customer for Wrongful Dishonor; Time of Determining Insufficiency of Account.

(a) Except as otherwise provided in this Article, a payor bank wrongfully dishonors an item if it dishonors an item that is properly payable, but a bank may dishonor an item that would create an overdraft unless it has agreed to pay the overdraft.

(b) A payor bank is liable to its customers for damages proximately caused by the wrongful dishonor of an item. Liability is limited to actual damages proved and may include damages for an arrest or prosecution of the customer or other consequential damages. Whether any consequential damages are proximately caused by the wrongful dishonor is a question of fact to be determined in each case.

(c) A payor bank's determination of the customer's account balance on which a decision to dishonor for insufficiency of available funds is based may be made at any time between the time the item is received by the payor bank and the time that the payor bank returns the item or gives notice in lieu of return, and no more than one determination need be made. If, at the election of the payor bank, a subsequent balance determination is made for the purpose of reevaluating the bank's decision to dishonor the item, the account balance at that time is determinative of whether a dishonor for insufficiency of available funds is wrongful.

§ 4-403. Customer's Right to Stop Payment; Burden of Proof of Loss.

(a) A customer or any person authorized to draw on the account if there is more than one person may stop payment of any item drawn on the customer's account or close the account by an order to the bank describing the item or account with reasonable certainty received at a time and in a manner that affords the bank a reasonable opportunity to act on it before any action by the bank with respect to the item described in Section 4-303. If the signature of more than one person is required to draw on an account, any of these persons may stop payment or close the account.

(b) A stop-payment order is effective for six months, but it lapses after 14 calendar days if the original order was oral and was not confirmed in writing within that period. A stop-payment order may be renewed for additional six-month periods by a writing given to the bank within a period during which the stop-payment order is effective.

(c) The burden of establishing the fact and amount of loss resulting from the payment of an item contrary to a stop-payment order or order to close an account is on the customer. The loss from payment of an item contrary to a stop-payment order may include damages for dishonor of subsequent items under Section 4-402.

§ 4-404. Bank Not Obliged to Pay Check More Than Six Months Old.

A bank is under no obligation to a customer having a checking account to pay a check, other than a certified check, which is presented more than six months after its date, but it may charge its customer's account for a payment made thereafter in good faith.

§ 4-405. Death or Incompetence of Customer.

(a) A payor or collecting bank's authority to accept, pay, or collect an item or to account for proceeds of its collection, if otherwise effective, is not rendered ineffective by incompetence of a customer of either bank existing at the time the item is issued or its collection is undertaken if the bank does not know of an adjudication of incompetence. Neither death nor incompetence of a customer revokes the authority to accept, pay, collect, or account until the bank knows of the fact of death or of an adjudication of incompetence and has reasonable opportunity to act on it.

(b) Even with knowledge, a bank may for 10 days after the date of death pay and certify checks drawn on or before that date unless ordered to stop payment by a person claiming an interest in the account.

§ 4-406. Customer's Duty to Discover and Report Unauthorized Signature or Alteration.

(a) A bank that sends or makes available to a customer a statement of account showing payment of items for the account shall either return or make available to the customer the items paid or provide information in the statement of account sufficient to allow the customer reasonably to identify the items paid. The statement of account provides sufficient information if the item is described by item number, amount, and date of payment.

(b) If the items are not returned to the customer, the person retaining the items shall either retain the items or, if the items are destroyed, maintain the capacity to furnish legible copies of the items until the expiration of seven years after receipt of the items. A customer may request an item from the bank that paid the item, and that bank must provide in a reasonable time either the item, or, if the item has been destroyed or is not otherwise obtainable, a legible copy of the item.

(c) If a bank sends or makes available a statement of account or items pursuant to subsection (a), the customer must exercise reasonable promptness in examining the statement or the items to determine whether any payment was not authorized because of an alteration of an item or because a purported signature by or on behalf of the customer was not authorized. If, based on the statement or items provided, the customer should reasonably have discovered the unauthorized payment, the customer must promptly notify the bank of the relevant facts.

(d) If the bank proves that the customer failed, with respect to an item, to comply with the duties imposed on the customer by subsection (c), the customer is precluded from asserting against the bank:

(1) the customer's unauthorized signature or any alteration on the item, if the bank also proves that it suffered a loss by reason of the failure; and

(2) the customer's unauthorized signature or alteration by the same wrongdoer on any other item paid in good faith by the bank if the payment was made before the bank received notice from the customer of the unauthorized signature or alteration and after the customer had been afforded a reasonable period of time, not exceeding 30 days, in which to examine the item or statement of account and notify the bank.

(e) If subsection (d) applies and the customer proves that the bank failed to exercise ordinary care in paying the item and that the failure substantially contributed to loss, the loss is allocated between the customer precluded and the bank asserting the preclusion according to the extent to which the failure of the customer to comply with subsection (c) and the failure of the bank to exercise ordinary care contributed to the loss. If the customer proves that the bank did not pay the item in good faith, the preclusion under subsection (d) does not apply.

(f) Without regard to care or lack of care of either the customer or the bank, a customer who does not within one year after the statement or items are made available to the customer (subsection (a)) discover and report the customer's unauthorized signature on or any alteration on the item is precluded from asserting against the bank the unauthorized signature or alteration. If there is a preclusion under this subsection, the payor bank may not recover for breach or warranty under Section 4-208 with respect to the unauthorized signature or alteration to which the preclusion applies.

§ 4-407. Payor Bank's Right to Subrogation on Improper Payment.

If a payor bank has paid an item over the order of the drawer or maker to stop payment, or after an account has been closed, or otherwise under circumstances giving a basis for objection by the drawer or maker, to prevent unjust enrichment and only to the extent necessary to prevent loss to the bank by reason of its payment of the item, the payor bank is subrogated to the rights

(1) of any holder in due course on the item against the drawer or maker;

(2) of the payee or any other holder of the item against the drawer or maker either on the item or under the transaction out of which the item arose; and

(3) of the drawer or maker against the payee or any other holder of the item with respect to the transaction out of which the item arose.

Article 9. SECURED TRANSACTIONS; SALES OF ACCOUNTS AND CHATTEL PAPER.

Part 1. General Provisions.

§ 9-102. Definitions and Index of Definitions.

(a) In this article:

(1) "Accession" means goods that are physically united with other goods in such a manner that the identity of the original goods is not lost.

(2) Except as used in "account for," "account" means a right to payment of a monetary obligation, whether or not earned by performance, (i) for property that has been or is to be sold, leased, licensed, assigned, or otherwise disposed of, (ii) for services rendered or to be rendered, (iii) for a pol-

icy of insurance issued or to be issued, (iv) for a secondary obligation incurred or to be incurred, (v) for energy provided or to be provided, (vi) for the use or hire of a vessel under a charter or other contract, (vii) arising out of the use of a credit or charge card or information contained on or for use with the card, or (viii) as winnings in a lottery or other game of chance operated or sponsored by a State, governmental unit of a State, or person licensed or authorized to operate the game by a State or governmental unit of a State. The term includes a health-care-insurance receivable. The term does not include (i) a right to payment evidenced by chattel paper or an instrument, (ii) a commercial tort claim, (iii) a deposit account, (iv) investment property, (v) a letter-of-credit right, or (vi) a right to payment for money or funds advanced or sold, other than a right arising out of the use of a credit or charge card or information contained on or for use with the card.

(3) "Account debtor" means a person obligated on an account, chattel paper, or general intangible. The term does not include a person obligated to pay a negotiable instrument, even if the instrument constitutes part of chattel paper.

(4) Except as used in "accounting for," "accounting" means a record:

(A) authenticated by a secured party;

(B) indicating the aggregate unpaid secured obligations as of a date not more than 35 days earlier or 35 days later than the date of the record; and

(C) identifying the components of the obligations in reasonable detail.

(5) "Agricultural lien" means an interest, other than a security interest, in farm products:

(A) which secures payment or performance of an obligation for:

(i) goods or services furnished in connection with a debtor's farming operation; or

(ii) rent on real property leased by a debtor in connection with its farming operation;

(B) which is created by statute in favor of a person that:

(i) in the ordinary course of its business furnished goods or services to a debtor in connection with a debtor's farming operation; or

(ii) leased real property to a debtor in connection with the debtor's farming operation; and

(C) whose effectiveness does not depend on the person's possession of the personal property.

(6) "As-extracted collateral" means:

(A) oil, gas, or other minerals that are subject to a security interest that:

(i) is created by a debtor having an interest in the minerals before extraction; and

(ii) attaches to the minerals as extracted; or

(B) accounts arising out of the sale at the wellhead or minehead of oil, gas, or other minerals in which the debtor had an interest before extraction.

(7) "Authenticate" means to:

(A) sign; or

(B) execute or adopt a symbol, or encrypt a record in whole or in part, with present intent to:

(i) identify the authenticating party; and

(ii) adopt, accept, or establish the authenticity of a record or term.

§ 9-108. Sufficiency of Description.

(a) Except as otherwise provided in subsections (c), (d), and (e), a description of personal or real property is sufficient, whether or not it is specific, if it reasonably identifies what is described.

(b) Except as otherwise provided in subsection (d), a description of collateral reasonably identifies the collateral if it identifies the collateral by: (1) specific listing; (2) category; (3) except as otherwise provided in subsection (e), a type of collateral defined in [the Uniform Commercial Code]; (4) quantity; (5) computational or allocational formula or procedure; or (6) except as otherwise provided in subsection (c), any other method, if the identity of the collateral is objectively determinable.

(c) A description of collateral as "all the debtor's assets" or "all the debtor's personal property" or using words of similar import does not reasonably identify the collateral.

(d) Except as otherwise provided in subsection (e), a description of a security entitlement, securities account, or commodity account is sufficient if it describes: (1) the collateral by those terms or as investment property; or (2) the underlying financial asset or commodity contract.

(e) A description only by type of collateral defined in the [Uniform Commercial Code] is an insufficient description of: (1) a commercial tort claim; or (2) in a consumer transaction, consumer goods, a security entitlement, a securities account, or a commodity account.

§ 9-109. Scope.

(a) Except as otherwise provided in subsections (c) and (d), this article applies to:

(1) any transaction, regardless of its form, that creates a security interest in personal property or fixtures by contract;

(2) an agricultural lien;

(3) a sale of an account, chattel paper, payment intangible, or promissory note;

(4) a consignment;

(5) a security interest arising under Section 2-401, 2-505, 2-711(3), or 2A-508(5), to the extent provided in Section 9-110; and

(6) a security interest arising under Section 4-210 or 5-118.

(b) The application of this article to a security interest in a secured obligation is not affected by the fact that the obligation is itself secured by a transaction or interest to which this article does not apply.

(c) This article does not apply to the extent that:

(1) a statute, regulation, or treaty of the United States preempts this article;

(2) another statute of this State expressly governs the creation, perfection, priority, or enforcement of a security interest created by this State or a governmental unit of this State;

(3) a statute of another State, a foreign country, or a governmental unit of another State or a foreign country, other than a statute generally applicable to security interests, expressly governs creation, perfection, priority, or enforcement of a security interest created by the State, country, or governmental unit; or

(4) the rights of a transferee beneficiary or nominated person under a letter of credit are independent and superior under Section 5-114.

(d) This article does not apply to:

(1) a landlord's lien, other than an agricultural lien;

(2) a lien, other than an agricultural lien, given by statute or other rule of law for services or materials, but Section 9-333 applies with respect to priority of the lien;

(3) an assignment of a claim for wages, salary, or other compensation of an employee;

(4) a sale of accounts, chattel paper, payment intangibles, or promissory notes as part of a sale of the business out of which they arose;

(5) an assignment of accounts, chattel paper, payment intangibles, or promissory notes which is for the purpose of collection only;

(6) an assignment of a right to payment under a contract to an assignee that is also obliged to perform under the contract;

(7) an assignment of a single account, payment intangible, or promissory note to an assignee in full or partial satisfaction of a preexisting indebtedness;

(8) a transfer of an interest in or an assignment of a claim under a policy of insurance, other than an assignment by or to a health-care provider of a health-care-insurance receivable and any subsequent assignment of the right to payment, but Sections 9-315 and 9-322 apply with respect to proceeds and priorities in proceeds;

(9) an assignment of a right represented by a judgment, other than a judgment taken on a right to payment that was collateral;

(10) a right of recoupment or set-off, but:

(A) Section 9-337 applies with respect to the effectiveness of rights of recoupment or set-off against deposit accounts; and

(B) Section 9-404 applies with respect to defenses or claims of an account debtor;

(11) the creation or transfer of an interest in or lien on real property, including a lease or rents thereunder, except to the extent that provision is made for:

(A) liens on real property in Sections 9-203 and 9-308,

(B) fixtures in Section 9-334;

(C) fixture filings in Sections 9-501, 9-502, 9-512, 9-516, and 9-519; and

(D) security agreements covering personal and real property in Section 9-604;

(12) an assignment of a claim arising in tort, other than a commercial tort claim, but Sections 9-315 and 9-322 apply with respect to proceeds and priorities in proceeds; or

(13) an assignment of a deposit account in a consumer transaction, except that Sections 9-315 and 9-322 apply with respect to proceeds and priorities in proceeds.

Part 2. Effectiveness of Security Agreement; Attachment of Security Interest; Rights of Parties to Security Agreement.

§ 9-203. Attachment and Enforceability of Security Interest: Proceeds; Supporting Obligations; Formal Requisites.

(a) A security interest attaches to collateral when it becomes enforceable against the debtor with respect to the collateral, unless an agreement expressly postpones the time of attachment.

(b) Except as otherwise provided in subsections (c) through (i), a security interest is enforceable against the debtor and third parties with respect to the collateral only if:

(1) value has been given;

(2) the debtor has rights in the collateral or the power to transfer rights in the collateral to a secured party; and

(3) one of the following conditions is met:

(A) the debtor has authenticated a security agreement that provides a description of the collateral and, if the security interest covers timber to be cut, a description of the land concerned;

(B) the collateral is not a certificated security and is in the possession of the secured party under Section 9-313 pursuant to the debtor's security agreement;

(C) the collateral is a certificated security in registered form and the security certificate has been delivered to the secured party under Section 8-301 pursuant to the debtor's security agreement; or

(D) the collateral is a deposit account, electronic chattel paper, investment property, or a letter-of-credit right, and the secured party has control under Section 9-104, 9-105, 9-106, or 9-107 pursuant to the debtor's security agreement.

(c) Subsection (b) is subject to Section 4-210 on the security interest of a collecting bank, Section 5-118 on the security interest of a letter-of-credit issuer or nominated person, Section 9-110 on a security interest arising under Article 2 or 2A, and Section 9-206 on security interests in investment property.

(d) A person becomes bound as debtor by a security agreement entered into by another person if, by operation of law other than this article or by contract: (1) the security agreement becomes effective to create a security interest in the person's property; or (2) the person becomes generally obligated for the obligations of the other person, including the obligation secured under the security agreement, and acquires or succeeds to all or substantially all of the assets of the other person.

(e) If a new debtor becomes bound as debtor by a security agreement entered into by another person:

(1) the agreement satisfies the requirements of subsection (b)(3) with respect to existing or after-acquired property of the new debtor to the extent the property is described in the agreement; and

(2) another agreement is not necessary to make a security interest in the property enforceable.

(f) The attachment of a security interest in collateral gives the secured party the rights to proceeds provided by Section 9-315 and is also attachment of a security interest in a supporting obligation for the collateral.

(g) The attachment of a security interest in a right to payment or performance secured by a security interest or other lien on personal or real property is also attachment of a security interest in the security interest, mortgage, or other lien.

(h) The attachment of a security interest in a securities account is also attachment of a security interest in the security entitlements carried in the securities account.

(i) The attachment of a security interest in a commodity account is also attachment of a security interest in the commodity contracts carried in the commodity account.

Part 3. Perfection and Priority.

§ 9-310. When Filing Required to Perfect Security Interest or Agricultural Lien; Security Interests and Agricultural Liens to Which Filing Provisions Do Not Apply.

(a) Except as otherwise provided in subsection (b) or Section 9-312(b), a financing statement must be filed to perfect all security interests and agricultural liens.

(b) The filing of a financing statement is not necessary to perfect a security interest:

(1) that is perfected under Section 9-308(d), (e), (f), or (g);

(2) that is perfected under Section 9-309 when it attaches;

(3) in property subject to a statute, regulation, or treaty described in Section 9-311(a);

(4) in goods in possession of a bailee which is perfected under Section 9-312(d)(1) or (2);

(5) in certificated securities, documents, goods, or instruments which is perfected without filing or possession under Section 9-312(e), (f), or (g);

(6) in collateral in the secured party's possession under Section 9-313;

(7) in a certificated security which is perfected by delivery of the security certificate to the secured party under Section 9-313;

(8) in a deposit account, electronic chattel paper, investment property, or a letter-of-credit right which is perfected by control under Section 9-314;

(9) in proceeds which is perfected under Section 9-315; or

(10) that is perfected under Section 9-316.

(c) If a secured party assigns a perfected security interest or agricultural lien, a filing under this article is not required to continue the perfected status of the security interest against creditors of and transferees from the original debtor.

§ 9-312. Perfection of Security Interests in Chattel Paper, Deposit Accounts, Documents, Goods Covered by Documents, Instruments, Investments, Investment Property, Money, Letter-of-Credit Rights, and Money; Perfection by Permissive Filing; Temporary Perfection without Filing or Transfer of Possession.

(a) [**Perfection by filing permitted.**] A security interest in chattel paper, negotiable documents, instruments, or investment property may be perfected by filing.

(b) [**Control or possession of certain collateral.**] Except as otherwise provided in Section 9- 315(c) and (d) for proceeds:

(1) a security interest in a deposit account may be perfected only by control under Section 9-314;

(2) a security interest in a letter-of-credit right may be perfected only by control under Section 9-314, except as otherwise provided in Section 9-308(d); and

(3) a security interest in money may be perfected only by the secured party's taking possession under Section 9-313.

(c) [**Goods covered by nonnegotiable document.**] While goods are in the possession of a bailee that has issued a negotiable document covering the goods:

(1) a security interest in the goods may be perfected by perfecting a security interest in the document; and

(2) a security interest perfected in the document has priority over any security interest that becomes perfected in the goods by another method during that time.

(d) [**Goods covered by nonnegotiable document.**] While goods are in the possession of a bailee that has issued a nonnegotiable document covering the goods, a security interest in the goods may be perfected by:

(1) issuance of a document in the name of the secured party;

(2) the bailee's receipt of notification of the secured party's interest; or

(3) filing as to the goods.

(e) [**Temporary perfection: new value.**] A security interest in certificated securities, negotiable documents, or instruments is perfected without filing or the taking of possession for a period of 20 days from the time it attaches to the extent that it arises for new value given under an authenticated security agreement.

(f) [**Temporary perfection: goods or documents made available to debtor.**] A perfected security interest in a negotiable document or goods in possession of a bailee, other than one that has issued a negotiable document for the goods, remains perfected for 20 days without filing if the secured party makes available to the debtor the goods or documents representing the goods for the purpose of:

(1) ultimate sale or exchange; or

(2) loading, unloading, storing, shipping, transshipping, manufacturing, processing, or otherwise dealing with them in a manner preliminary to their sale or exchange.

(g) [**Temporary perfection: delivery of security certificate or instrument to debtor.**] A perfected security interest in a certificated security or instrument remains perfected for 20 days without filing if the secured party delivers the security certificate or instrument to the debtor for the purpose of:

(1) ultimate sale or exchange; or

(2) presentation, collection, enforcement, renewal, or registration of transfer.

(h) [**Expiration of temporary perfection.**] After the 20-day period specified in subsection (e), (f), or (g) expires, perfection depends upon compliance with this article.

§ 9–320. Buyer of Goods.

(a) Except as otherwise provided in subsection (e), a buyer in ordinary course of business, other than a person buying farm products from a person engaged in farming operations, takes free of a security interest created by the buyer's seller, even if the security interest is perfected and the buyer knows of its existence.

(b) Except as otherwise provided in subsection (e), a buyer of goods from a person who used or bought the goods for use primarily for personal, family, or household purposes takes free of a security interest, even if perfected, if the buyer buys:

(1) without knowledge of the security interest;

(2) for value;

(3) primarily for the buyer's personal, family, or household purposes; and (4) before the filing of a financing statement covering the goods.

(c) To the extent that it affects the priority of a security interest over a buyer of goods under subsection (b), the period of effectiveness of a filing made in the jurisdiction in which the seller is located is governed by Section 9-316(a) and (b).

(d) A buyer in ordinary course of business buying oil, gas, or other minerals at the wellhead or minehead or after extraction takes free of an interest arising out of an encumbrance.

(e) Subsections (a) and (b) do not affect a security interest in goods in the possession of the secured party under Section 9-313.

Part 5. Filing.

§ 9–504. Indication of Collateral.

A financing statement sufficiently indicates the collateral that it covers if the financing statement provides:

(1) a description of the collateral pursuant to Section 9-108; or

(2) an indication that the financing statement covers all assets or all personal property.

Part 6. Default.

§ 9–609. Secured Party's Right to Take Possession after Default.

(a) A secured party has the right on default to take possession of the collateral.

(b) A secured party may take possession of collateral:

(1) pursuant to judicial process; or

(2) if it takes possession without breach of the peace, without judicial process.

(c) If a debtor so agrees, a secured party may require a debtor to assemble the collateral and make it available to the secured party at a place to be designated by the secured party which is reasonably convenient to both parties.

(d) Without removal, a secured party:

(1) may render equipment unusable; and

(2) may dispose of collateral on a debtor's premises under Section 9-610.

§9–610. Disposition of Collateral after Default.

(a) A secured party after default may sell, lease, license, or otherwise dispose of any or all of the collateral in its present condition or following any commercially reasonable preparation or processing.

(b) Every aspect of a disposition of collateral, including the method, manner, time, place, and other terms, must be commercially reasonable. If commercially reasonable, a secured party may dispose of collateral by public or private proceedings, by one or more contracts, as a unit or in parcels, and at any time and place and on any terms.

(c) A secured party may purchase collateral:

(1) at a public sale; or

(2) at a private sale only if the collateral is of a kind that is customarily sold on a recognized market or the subject of widely distributed standard price quotations.

(d) A contract for sale, lease, license, or other disposition includes the warranties relating to title, possession, quiet enjoyment, and the like which by operation of law accompany a voluntary disposition of property of the kind subject to the contract.

(e) A secured party may disclaim or modify warranties under subsection (d): (1) in a manner that would be effective to disclaim or modify the warranties in a voluntary disposition of property of the kind subject to the contract of disposition; or (2) by communicating to the purchaser a record evidencing the contract for disposition and including an express disclaimer or modification of the warranties.

(f) A record is sufficient to disclaim warranties under subsection (e) if it indicates "There is no warranty relating to title, possession, quiet enjoyment, or the like in this disposition" or uses words of similar import.

§ 9-615. Application of Proceeds of Disposition; Liability for Deficiency and Right to Surplus.

(a) A secured party shall apply or pay over for application the cash proceeds of disposition in the following order to:

(1) the reasonable expenses of retaking, holding, preparing for disposition, processing, and disposing, and, to the extent provided for by agreement and not prohibited by law, reasonable attorney's fees and legal expenses incurred by the secured party;

(2) the satisfaction of obligations secured by the security interest or agricultural lien under which the disposition is made;

(3) the satisfaction of obligations secured by any subordinate security interest in or other lien on the collateral if:

(A) the secured party receives from the holder of the subordinate security interest an authenticated demand for proceeds before distribution of the proceeds is completed; and

(B) if a consignor has an interest in the collateral, the subordinate security interest or lien is senior to the interest of the consignor; and

(4) a secured party that is a consignor of the collateral if the secured party receives from the consignor

an authenticated demand for proceeds before distribution of the proceeds is completed.

(b) If requested by a secured party, a holder of a subordinate security interest or other lien shall furnish reasonable proof of the interest or lien within a reasonable time. Unless the holder does so, the secured party need not comply with the holder's demand under subsection (a)(3).

(c) A secured party need not apply or pay over for application noncash proceeds of disposition under this section unless the failure to do so would be commercially unreasonable. A secured party that applies or pays over for application noncash proceeds shall do so in a commercially reasonable manner.

(d) If the security interest under which a disposition is made secures payment or performance of an obligation, after making the payments and applications required by subsection (a) and permitted by subsection (c):

(1) unless subsection (a)(4) requires the secured party to apply or pay over cash proceeds to a consignor, the secured party shall account to and pay a debtor for any surplus; and

(2) the obligor is liable for any deficiency.

(e) If the underlying transaction is a sale of accounts, chattel paper, payment intangibles, or promissory notes:

(1) the debtor is not entitled to any surplus; and

(2) the obligor is not liable for any deficiency.

(f) The surplus or deficiency following a disposition is calculated based on the amount of proceeds that would have been realized in a disposition complying with the requirements of this part to a transferee other than the secured party, a person related to the secured party, or a secondary obligor if:

(1) the transferee in the disposition is the secured party, a person related to the secured party, or a secondary obligor; and

(2) the amount of proceeds of the disposition is significantly below the range of proceeds that a complying disposition to a person other than the secured party, a person related to the secured party, or a secondary obligor would have brought.

(g) A secured party that receives cash proceeds of a disposition in good faith and without knowledge that the receipt violates the rights of the holder of a security interest or other lien that is not subordinate to the security interest or agricultural lien under which the disposition is made:

(1) takes the cash proceeds free of the security interest or other lien;

(2) is not obligated to apply the proceeds of the disposition to the satisfaction of obligations secured by the security interest or other lien; and

(3) is not obligated to account to or pay the holder of the security interest or other lien for any surplus.

§ 9-620. Acceptance of Collateral in Full or Partial Satisfaction of Obligation; Compulsory Disposition of Collateral.

(a) Except as otherwise provided in subsection (g), a secured party may accept collateral in full or partial satisfaction of the obligation it secures only if:

(1) the debtor consents to the acceptance under subsection (c);

(2) the secured party does not receive, within the time set forth in subsection (e), a notification of objection to the proposal authenticated by:

(A) a person to which the secured party was required to send a proposal under Section 9-621; or

(B) any other person, other than the debtor, holding an interest in the collateral subordinate to the security interest that is the subject of the proposal;

(3) if the collateral is consumer goods, the collateral is not in the possession of the debtor when the debtor consents to the acceptance; and (4) subsection (e) does not require the secured party to dispose of the collateral.

(b) A purported or apparent acceptance of collateral under this section is ineffective unless:

(1) the secured party consents to the acceptance in an authenticated record or sends a proposal to the debtor; and

(2) the conditions of subsection (a) are met.

(c) For purposes of this section:

(1) a debtor consents to an acceptance of collateral in partial satisfaction of the obligation it secures only if the debtor agrees to the terms of the acceptance in a record authenticated after default; and

(2) a debtor consents to an acceptance of collateral in full satisfaction of the obligation it secures only if the debtor agrees to the terms of the acceptance in a record authenticated after default or the secured party:

(A) sends to the debtor after default a proposal that is unconditional or subject only to a condition that collateral not in the possession of the secured party be preserved or maintained;

(B) in the proposal, proposes to accept collateral in full satisfaction of the obligation it secures; and

(C) does not receive a notification of objection authenticated by the debtor within 20 days after the proposal is sent.

(d) To be effective under subsection (a)(2), a notification of objection must be received by the secured party:

(1) in the case of a person to which the proposal was sent pursuant to Section 9-621, within 20 days after notification was sent to that person; and

(2) in other cases:

(A) within 20 days after the last notification was sent pursuant to Section 9-621; or

(B) if a notification was not sent, before the debtor consents to the acceptance under subsection (c).

(e) A secured party that has taken possession of collateral shall dispose of the collateral pursuant to Section 9-610 within the time specified in subsection (g) if:

(1) 60 percent of the cash price has been paid in the case of a purchase-money security interest in consumer goods; or

(2) 60 percent of the principal amount of the obligation secured has been paid in the case of a non-purchase-money security interest in consumer goods.

(f) To comply with subsection (e), the secured party shall dispose of the collateral:

(1) within 90 days after taking possession; or

(2) within any longer period to which the debtor and all secondary obligors have agreed by authenticating a record including a statement to that effect after default.

(g) In a consumer transaction, a secured party may not accept collateral in partial satisfaction of the obligation it secures.

§ 9-625. Remedies for Secured Party's Failure to Comply with Article.

(a) If it is established that a secured party is not proceeding in accordance with this article, a court may order or restrain collection, enforcement, or disposition of collateral on appropriate terms and conditions.

(b) Subject to subsections (c) and (f), a secured party is liable for damages in the amount of any loss caused by a failure to comply with this article. Loss caused by a failure to comply with a request under Section 9-210 may include loss resulting from the debtor's inability to obtain, or increased costs of, alternative financing.

(c) Except as otherwise provided in Section 9-628:

(1) a person that, at the time of the failure, was a debtor, was an obligor, or held a security interest in or other lien on the collateral may recover damages under subsection (b) for its loss; and

(2) if the collateral is consumer goods, a person that was a debtor or a secondary obligor at the time a secured party failed to comply with this part may recover for that failure in any event an amount not less than the credit service charge plus 10 percent of the principal amount of the obligation or the time-price differential plus 10 percent of the cash price.

(d) A debtor whose deficiency is eliminated under Section 9-626 may recover damages for the loss of any surplus. However, a debtor or secondary obligor whose deficiency is eliminated or reduced under Section 9-626 may not otherwise recover under subsection (b) for noncompliance with the provisions of this part relating to collection, enforcement, disposition, or acceptance.

(e) In addition to any damages recoverable under subsection (b), the debtor, consumer obligor, or person named as a debtor in a filed record, as applicable, may recover $500 in each case from:

(1) a secured party that fails to comply with Section 9-208;

(2) a secured party that fails to comply with Section 9-209;

(3) a person that files a record that the person is not entitled to file under Section 9-509(a);

(4) a secured party that fails to cause the secured party of record to file or send a termination statement as required by Section 9-513(a) or (c);

(5) a secured party that fails to comply with Section 9-616(b)(1) and whose failure is part of a pattern, or consistent with a practice, of noncompliance; or

(6) a secured party that fails to comply with Section 9-616(b)(2).

(f) A debtor or consumer obligor may recover damages under subsection (b) and, in addition, $500 in each case from a person that, without reasonable cause, fails to comply with a request under Section 9-210. A recipient of a request under Section 9-210 which never claimed an interest in the collateral or obligations that are the subject of a request under that section has a reasonable excuse for failure to comply with the request within the meaning of this subsection.

(g) If a secured party fails to comply with a request regarding a list of collateral or a statement of account under Section 9-210, the secured party may claim a security interest only as shown in the statement included in the request as against a person that is reasonably misled by the failure.

The Sherman Act (Excerpts) 15 U.S.C.A. §§ 1 and 2

Section 1. Trusts, etc., in restraint of trade illegal; penalty.

Every contract, combination in the form of trust or otherwise, or conspiracy, in restraint of trade or commerce among the several States, or with foreign nations, is declared to be illegal. Every person who shall make any contract or engage in any combination or conspiracy hereby declared to be illegal shall be deemed guilty of a felony, and, on conviction thereof, shall be punished by fine not exceeding $10,000,000 if a corporation, or, if any other person, $350,000, or by imprisonment not exceeding three years, or by both said punishments, in the discretion of the court.

Section 2. Monopolizing trade a felony; penalty.

Every person who shall monopolize, or attempt to monopolize, or combine or conspire with any other person or persons, to monopolize any part of the trade or commerce among the several States, or with foreign nations, shall be deemed guilty of a felony, and, on conviction thereof, shall be punished by fine not exceeding $10,000,000 if a corporation, or, if any other person, $350,000, or by imprisonment not exceeding three years, or by both said punishments, in the discretion of the court.

The Clayton Act (Excerpts) 15 U.S.C.A. §§ 13 *et seq.*

Section 2. Discrimination in price, services, or facilities. [15 U.S.C.A. § 13]
(SECTION 2 WAS AMENDED BY THE ROBINSON–PATMAN ACT.)

(a) Price; selection of customers.

It shall be unlawful for any person engaged in commerce, in the course of such commerce, either directly or indirectly, to discriminate in price between purchasers of commodities of like grade and quality, . . . where such commodities are sold for use, consumption, or resale within the United States or any Territory thereof . . . and where the effect of such discrimination may be substantially to lessen competition or tend to create a monopoly in any line of commerce, or to injure, destroy, or prevent competition with any person who either grants or knowingly receives the benefit of such discrimination, or with customers of either of them: Provided, That nothing herein contained shall prevent differentials which make only due allowance for differences in the cost of manufacture, sale, or delivery resulting from the differing methods or quantities in which such commodities are to such purchasers sold or delivered: Provided, however, That the Federal Trade Commission may, after due investigation and hearing . . . fix and establish quantity limits, . . . as to particular commodities or classes of commodities, where it finds that available purchasers in greater quantities are so few as to render differentials on account thereof unjustly discriminatory or promotive of monopoly in any line of commerce; and the foregoing shall then not be construed to permit differentials based on differences in quantities greater than those so fixed and established: And provided further, That nothing herein contained shall prevent persons engaged in selling goods, wares, or merchandise in commerce from selecting their own customers in bona fide transactions and not in restraint of trade: And provided further, That nothing herein contained shall prevent price changes from time to time where in response to changing conditions affecting the market for or the marketability of the goods concerned, such as but not limited to actual or imminent deterioration of perishable goods, obsolescence of seasonal goods, distress sales under court process, or sales in good faith in discontinuance of business in the goods concerned.

(b) Burden of rebutting prima facie case of discrimination.

Upon proof being made, at any hearing on a complaint under this section, that there has been discrimination in price or services or facilities furnished, the burden of rebutting the prima facie case thus made by showing justification shall be upon the person charged with a violation of this section, and unless justification shall be affirmatively shown, the Commission is authorized to issue an order terminating the discrimination: Provided, however, That nothing herein contained shall prevent a seller rebutting the prima facie case thus made by showing that his lower price or the furnishing of services or facilities to any purchaser or purchasers was made in good faith to meet an equally low price of a competitor, or the services or facilities furnished by a competitor.

(c) Payment or acceptance of commission, brokerage, or other compensation.

That it shall be unlawful for any person engaged in commerce, in the course of such commerce, to pay or grant, or to receive or accept, anything of value as a commission, brokerage, or other compensation, or any allowance or discount in lieu thereof, except for services rendered in connection with the sale or purchase of goods, wares, or merchandise, either to the other party to such transactions or to an agent, representative, or other intermediary therein where such intermediary is acting in fact for or in behalf, or is subject to the direct or indirect control, of any party to such transaction other than the person by whom such compensation is granted or paid.

(d) Payment for services or facilities for processing or sale.

That it shall be unlawful for any person engaged in commerce to pay or contract for the payment of anything of value to or for the benefit of a customer of such person in the course of such commerce as compensation or in consideration for any services or facilities furnished by or through such customer in connection with the processing, handling, sale, or offering for sale of any products or commodities manufactured, sold, or offered for sale by such person, unless such payment or consideration is available on proportionally equal terms to all other customers competing in the distribution of such products or commodities.

(e) Furnishing services or facilities for processing, handling, etc.

That it shall be unlawful for any person to discriminate in favor of one purchaser against another purchaser or purchasers of a commodity bought for resale, with or without processing, by contracting to furnish or furnishing, or by contributing to the furnishing of, any services or facilities connected with the processing, handling, sale, or offering for sale of such commodity so purchased upon terms not accorded to all purchasers on proportionally equal terms.

(f) Knowingly inducing or receiving discriminatory price.

That it shall be unlawful for any person engaged in commerce, in the course of such commerce, knowingly to induce or receive a discrimination in price which is prohibited by this section.

Section 3. Sale, etc., on agreement not to use goods of competitor. [15 U.S.C.A. §14]

It shall be unlawful for any person engaged in commerce, in the course of such commerce, to lease or make a sale or contract for sale of goods, wares, merchandise, machinery, supplies, or other commodities, whether patented or unpatented, for use, consumption, or resale within the United States or . . . other place under the jurisdiction of the United States, or fix a price charged therefor, or discount from, or rebate upon, such price, on the condition, agreement, or understanding that the lessee or purchaser thereof shall not use or deal in the goods, wares, merchandise, machinery, supplies, or other commodities of a competitor or competitors of the lessor or seller, where the effect of such lease, sale, or contract for sale or such condition, agreement, or understanding may be to substantially lessen competition or tend to create a monopoly in any line of commerce.

Section 4. Amount of recovery; prejudgment interest. [15 U.S.C.A. § 15]

[A]ny person who shall be injured in his business or property by reason of anything forbidden in the antitrust laws may sue therefor in any district court of the United States in the district in which the defendant resides or is found, or has an agent, without respect to the amount in controversy, and shall recover threefold the damages by him sustained, and the cost of suit, including a reasonable attorney's fee. . . .

Section 4A. Suits by United States; amount of recovery; prejudgment interest. [15 U.S.C.A. § 15a]

Whenever the United States is hereafter injured in its business or property by reason of anything forbidden in the antitrust laws it may sue therefor in the United States district court for the district in which the defendant resides or is found or has an agent, without respect to the amount in controversy, and shall recover threefold the damages by it sustained and the cost of suit.

Section 4B. Limitation of actions. [15 U.S.C.A. § 15b]

Any action to enforce any cause of action under sections 4 or 4A shall be forever barred unless commenced within four years after the cause of action accrued. No cause of action barred under existing law on the effective date of this act shall be revived by this Act.

Section 4C. Actions by State attorneys general. [15 U.S.C.A. § 15c]

(a) Parens patriae; monetary relief; damages; prejudgment interest

(1) Any attorney general of a state may bring a civil action in the name of such State, as parens patriae on behalf of natural persons residing in such State, in any district court of the United States having jurisdiction of the defendant, to secure monetary relief as provided in this section for injury sustained by such natural persons to their property by reason of any violation of the Sherman Act. The court shall exclude from the amount of monetary relief awarded in such action any amount of monetary relief (A) which duplicates amounts which have been awarded for the same injury, or (B) which is properly allocable to (i) natural persons who have excluded their claims pursuant to subsection (b)(2) of this section, and (ii) any business entity.

(2) The court shall award the State as monetary relief threefold the total damage sustained as described in paragraph (1) of this subsection, and the cost of suit, including a reasonable attorney's fee.

. . . .

(b) Notice; exclusion election; final judgment.

(1) In any action brought under subsection (a)(1) of this section, the State attorney general shall, at such times, in such manner, and with such content as the court may direct, cause notice thereof to be given by publication. If the court finds that notice given solely by publication would deny due process of law to any person or persons, the court may direct further notice to such person or persons according to the circumstances of the case.

(2) Any person on whose behalf an action is brought under subsection (a)(1) may elect to exclude from adjudication the portion of the State claim for monetary relief attributable to him by filing notice of such election with the court within such time as specified in the notice given pursuant to paragraph (1) of this subsection.

(3) The final judgment in an action under subsection (a)(1) shall be res judicata as to any claim under section 4 of this Act by any person on behalf of whom such action was brought and who fails to give such notice within the period specified in the notice given pursuant to paragraph (1) of this subsection.

(c) Dismissal or compromise of action.

An action under subsection (a)(1) shall not be dismissed or compromised without the approval of the court, and notice of any proposed dismissal or compromise shall be given in such manner as the court directs.

(d) Attorneys' fees

In any action under subsection (a) of this section—

(1) the amount of the plaintiffs' attorney's fee, if any, shall be determined by the court; and

(2) the court may, in its discretion, award a reasonable attorney's fee to a prevailing defendant upon a finding that the State attorney general has acted in bad faith, vexatiously, wantonly, or for oppressive reasons.

Section 6. Antitrust laws not applicable to labor organizations. [15 U.S.C.A. § 17]

The labor of a human being is not a commodity or article of commerce. Nothing contained in the antitrust laws shall be construed to forbid the existence and operation of labor, agricultural or horticultural organizations, instituted for the purposes of mutual help, and not having capital stock or conducted for profit, or to forbid or restrain individual members of such organizations from lawfully carrying out the legitimate objects thereof; nor shall such organizations or the members thereof, be held or construed to be illegal combinations or conspiracies in restraint of trade, under the antitrust laws.

Section 7. Acquisition by one corporation of stock of another. [15 U.S.C.A. § 18] (SECTION 7 WAS AMENDED BY THE CELLER-KEFAUVER ACT AND THE HART-SCOTT-RODINO ANTITRUST IMPROVEMENT ACT.)

No person engaged in commerce . . . shall acquire, directly or indirectly, the whole or any part of the stock or other share capital and no person subject to the jurisdiction of the Federal Trade Commission shall acquire the whole or any part of the assets of another person engaged also in commerce . . . or in any activity affecting commerce in any section of the country, the effect of such acquisition may be substantially to lessen competition, or to tend to create a monopoly.

No person shall acquire, directly or indirectly, the whole or any part of the stock or other share capital and no person subject to the jurisdiction of the Federal Trade Commission shall acquire the whole or any part of the assets of one or more persons engaged in commerce, where in any line of commerce in any section of the country, the effect of such acquisition, of such stocks or assets, or of the use of such stock by the voting or granting of proxies or otherwise, may be substantially to lessen competition, or to tend to create a monopoly.

This section shall not apply to persons purchasing such stock solely for investment and not using the same by voting or otherwise to bring about, or in attempting to bring about, the substantial lessening of competition . . .

. . . .

Section 8. Interlocking directorates and officers. [15 U.S.C.A. § 19]

(a)(1) No person shall, at the same time, serve as a director or officer in any two corporations (other than banks, banking associations, and trust companies) that are—

(A) engaged in whole or in part in commerce; and

(B) by virtue of their business and location of operation, competitors, so that the elimination of competition by agreement between them would constitute a violation of any of the antitrust laws;

if each of the corporations has capital, surplus, and undivided profits aggregating more than $10,000,000 as adjusted pursuant to paragraph (5) of this subsection.

(2) Notwithstanding the provisions of paragraph (1), simultaneous service as a director or officer in any two corporations shall not be prohibited by this section if—

(A) the competitive sales of either corporation are less than $1,000,000, as adjusted pursuant to paragraph (5) of this subsection;

(B) the competitive sales of either corporation are less than 2 per centum of that corporation's total sales; or

(C) the competitive sales of each corporation are less than 4 per centum of that corporation's total sales.

For purposes of this paragraph, "competitive sales" means the gross revenues for all products and services sold by one corporation in competition with the other, determined on the basis of annual gross revenues for such products and services in that corporation's last completed fiscal year. For the purposes of this paragraph, "total sales" means the gross revenues for all products and services sold by one corporation over that corporation's last completed fiscal year.

(3) The eligibility of a director or officer under the provisions of paragraph (1) shall be determined by the capital, surplus and undivided profits, exclusive of dividends declared but not paid to stockholders, of each corporation at the end of that corporation's last completed fiscal year.

(4) For purposes of this section, the term "officer" means an officer elected or chosen by the Board of Directors.

(5) For each fiscal year commencing after September 30, 1990, the $10,000,000 and $1,000,000 thresholds in this subsection shall be increased (or decreased) as of October 1 each year by an amount equal to the percentage increase (or decrease) in the gross national product, as determined by the Department of Commerce or its successor, for the year then ended over the level so established for the year ending September 30, 1989. As soon as practicable, but not later than October 30 of each year, the Federal Trade Commission shall publish the adjusted amounts required by this paragraph.

(b) When any person elected or chosen as a director or officer of any corporation subject to the provisions hereof is eligible at the time of his election or selection to act for such corporation in such capacity, his eligibility to act in such capacity shall not be affected by any of the provisions hereof by reason of any change in the capital, surplus and undivided profits, or affairs of such corporation from whatever cause, until, the expiration of one year from the date on which the event causing ineligibility occurred.

The Federal Trade Commission Act (Excerpts) 15 U.S.C.A. §§ 41 *et seq.*

Section 5. Unfair methods of competition unlawful; prevention by Commission. [15 U.S.C.A. §§ 45a and 45l]

(a) Declaration of unlawfulness; power to prohibit unfair practices; inapplicability to foreign trade.

(1) Unfair methods of competition in or affecting commerce, and unfair or deceptive acts or practices in or affecting commerce, are hereby declared unlawful.

(2) The Commission is empowered and directed to prevent persons, partnerships, or corporations . . . from using unfair methods of competition in or affecting commerce and unfair or deceptive acts or practices in or affecting commerce.

. . . .

(l) Penalty for violation of order; injunctions and other appropriate equitable relief.

Any person, partnership, or corporation who violates an order of the Commission after it has become final, and while such order is in effect, shall forfeit and pay to the United States a civil penalty of not more than $10,000 for each violation, which shall accrue to the United States and may be recovered in a civil action brought by the Attorney General of the United States. Each separate violation of such an order shall be a separate offense, except that in the case of a violation through continuing failure to obey or neglect to obey a final order of the Commission, each day of continuance of such failure or neglect shall be deemed a separate offense. In such actions, the United States district courts are empowered to grant mandatory injunctions and such other and further equitable relief as they deem appropriate in the enforcement of such final orders of the Commission.

National Labor Relations Act (Excerpts) 29 U.S.C.A. §§ 151 *et seq.*

Section 3. National Labor Relations Board. [15 U.S.C.A. §§ 153(a) and 153(d)]

(a) Creation, composition, appointment, and tenure; Chairman; removal of members.

The National Labor Relations Board (hereinafter called the "Board") . . . is . . . an agency of the United States, shall consist of five . . . members, appointed by the President by and with the advice and consent of the Senate . . . for terms of five years each. . . . The President shall designate one member to serve as Chairman of the Board. Any member of the Board may be removed by the President, upon notice and hearing, for neglect of duty or malfeasance in office, but for no other cause.

. . . .

(d) General Counsel; appointment and tenure; powers and duties; vacancy.

There shall be a General Counsel of the Board who shall be appointed by the President, by and with the advice and consent of the Senate, for a term of four years. The General Counsel of the Board shall exercise general supervision over all attorneys employed by the Board (other than administrative law judges and legal assistants to Board members) and over the officers and employees in the regional offices. He shall have final authority, on behalf of the Board, in respect of the in-vestigation of charges (of unfair labor charges), and in respect of the prosecution of such complaints before the Board, and shall have such other duties as the Board may prescribe or as may be provided by law. In case of a vacancy in the office of the General Counsel the President is authorized to designate the officer or employee who shall act as General Counsel during such vacancy, but no person or persons so designated shall so act (1) for more than forty days when the Congress is in session unless a nomination to fill such vacancy shall have been submitted to the Senate, or (2) after the adjournment sine die of the session of the Senate in which such nomination was submitted.

Section 7. Rights of employees as to organization, collective bargaining, etc. [29 U.S.C.A. § 157]

Employees shall have the right to self-organization, to form, join, or assist labor organizations, to bargain collectively through representatives of their own choosing, and to engage in other concerted activities for the purpose of collective bargaining or other mutual aid or protection, and shall also have the right to refrain from any or all of such activities except to the extent that such right may be affected by an agreement requiring membership in a labor organization as a condition of employment as authorized in section 8(a) (3) of this title.

Federal Civil Rights Acts (Excerpts) including the Americans with Disabilities Act (Excerpts) 42 U.S.C.A. §§ 1981 *et seq.*

CHAPTER 21. CIVIL RIGHTS.

SUBCHAPTER I. GENERALLY.

Section 1981. Equal rights under the law. [42 U.S.C.A. § 1981 (1866)]

(a) Statement of equal rights.

All persons within the jurisdiction of the United States shall have the same right in every State and Territory to make and enforce contracts, to sue, be parties, give evidence, and to the full and equal benefit of all laws and proceedings for the security of persons and property as is enjoyed by white citizens, and shall be subject to like punishment, pains, penalties, taxes, licenses and exactions of every kind, and no other.

(b) "Make and enforce contracts" defined.

For purposes of this section, the term "make and enforce contracts" includes the making, performance, modification, and termination of contracts, and the enjoyment of all benefits, privileges, terms, and conditions of the contractual relationship.

(c) Protection against impairment.

The rights protected by this section are protected against impairment by nongovernmental discrimination and impairment under color of State law.

Section 1981a. Damages in cases of intentional discrimination in employment. [42 U.S.C.A. § 1981a (1991)]

(a) Right of recovery

(1) Civil rights. In an action brought by a complaining party under section 706 or 717 of the Civil Rights Act of 1964 against a respondent who engaged in unlawful intentional discrimination (not an employment practice that is unlawful because of its disparate impact) prohibited under section 703, 704, or 717 of the Act, and provided that the complaining party cannot recover under section 1981 of this title, the complaining party may recover compensatory and punitive damages as allowed in subsection (b) of this section, in addition to any relief authorized by section 706(g) of the Civil Rights Act of 1964, from the respondent.

(2) Disability. In an action brought by a complaining party under the powers, remedies, and procedures set forth in section 706 or 717 of the Civil Rights Act of 1964 (as provided in section 107(a) of the Americans with Disabilities Act of 1990) against a respondent who engaged in unlawful intentional discrimination (not an employment practice that is unlawful because of its disparate impact) under section 791 of Title 29 and the regulations implementing section 791 of Title 29, or who violated the requirements of section 791 of Title 29 or the regulations implementing section 791 of Title 29 concerning the provision of a reasonable accommodation, or section 102 of the Americans with Disabilities Act of 1990, committed a violation of section 102(b)(5) of the Act, against an individual, the complaining party may recover compensatory and punitive damages as allowed in subsection (b) of this section, in addition to any relief authorized by section 706(g) of the Civil Rights Act of 1964, from the respondent.

(3) Reasonable accommodation and good faith effort. In cases where a discriminatory practice involves the provision of a reasonable accommodation pursuant to section 102(b)(5) of the Americans with Disabilities Act of 1990 or regulations implementing section 791 of Title 29, damages may not be awarded under this section where the covered entity demonstrates good faith efforts, in consultation with the person with the disability who has informed the covered entity that accommodation is needed, to identify and make a reasonable accommodation that would provide such individual with an equally effective opportunity and would not cause an undue hardship on the operation of the business.

(b) Compensatory and punitive damages.

(1) Determination of punitive damages. A complaining party may recover punitive damages under this section against a respondent (other than a government, government agency or political subdivision) if the complaining party demonstrates that the respondent engaged in a discriminatory practice or discriminatory practices with malice or with reckless indifference to the federally protected rights of an aggrieved individual.

(2) Exclusions from compensatory damages. Compensatory damages awarded under this section shall not include backpay, interest on backpay, or any other type of relief authorized under section 706(g) of the Civil Rights Act of 1964.

(3) Limitations. The sum of the amount of compensatory damages awarded under this section for future pecuniary losses, emotional pain, suffering, inconvenience, mental anguish, loss of enjoyment of life, and other nonpecuniary losses, and the amount of punitive damages awarded under this section, shall not exceed, for each complaining party—

(A) in the case of a respondent who has more than 14 and fewer than 101 employees in each of 20 or more calendar weeks in the current or preceding calendar year, $50,000;

(B) in the case of a respondent who has more than 100 and fewer than 201 employees in each of 20 or more calendar weeks in the current or preceding calendar year, $100,000; and

(C) in the case of a respondent who has more than 200 and fewer than 501 employees in each of 20 or more calendar weeks in the current or preceding calendar year, $200,000; and

(D) in the case of a respondent who has more than 500 employees in each of 20 or more calendar weeks in the current or preceding calendar year, $300,000.

(4) Construction. Nothing in this section shall be construed to limit the scope of, or the relief available under, section 1981 of this title.

(c) Jury trial.

If a complaining party seeks compensatory or punitive damages under this section—

(1) any party may demand a trial by jury; and

(2) the court shall not inform the jury of the limitations described in subsection (b)(3) of this section.

(d) Definitions.

As used in this section:

(1) Complaining party. The term "complaining party" means—

(A) in the case of a person seeking to bring an action under subsection (a)(1) of this section, the Equal Employment Opportunity Commission, the Attorney General, or a person who may bring an action or proceeding under title VII of the Civil Rights Act of 1964; or

(B) in the case of a person seeking to bring an action under subsection (a)(2) of this section, the Equal Employment Opportunity Commission, the Attorney General, a person who may bring an action or proceeding under section 749a(a)(1) of Title 29, or a person who may bring an action or proceeding under title I of the Americans with Disabilities Act of 1990.

(2) Discriminatory practice. The term "discriminatory practice" means the discrimination described in paragraph (1), or the discrimination or the violation described in paragraph (2), of subsection (a) of this section.

Section 1982. Property rights of citizens. [42 U.S.C.A. §1982 (1866)]

All citizens of the United States shall have the same right, in every State and Territory, as is enjoyed by white citizens thereof to inherit, purchase, lease, sell, hold and convey real and personal property.

Section 1983. Civil action for deprivation of rights. [42 U.S.C.A. § 1983 (1871)]

Every person who, under color of any statute, ordinance, regulation, custom, or usage, of any State or Territory or the District of Columbia, subjects, or causes to be subjected, any citizen of the United States or other person within the jurisdiction thereof to the deprivation of any rights, privileges, or immunities secured by the Constitution and laws, shall be liable to the party injured in an action at law, suit in equity, or other proper proceeding for redress.

SUBCHAPTER II. PUBLIC ACCOMMODATIONS. [Title II of the Civil Rights Act of 1964]

Section 201. Prohibition against discrimination or segregation in places of public accommodation. [42 U.S.C.A. § 2000a]

(a) Equal access.

All persons shall be entitled to the full and equal enjoyment of the goods, services, facilities, privileges, advantages, and accommodations of any place of public accommodation, as defined in this section, without discrimination on the ground of race, color, religion, or national origin.

(b) Establishments affecting interstate commerce or supported in their activities by State action as places of public accommodation; lodgings; facilities principally engaged in selling food for consumption on the premises; gasoline stations; places of exhibition or entertainment; other covered establishments.

Each of the following establishments which serves the public is a place of public accommodation within the meaning of this title if its operations affect commerce, or if discrimination or segregation by it is supported by State action:

(1) any inn, hotel, motel, or other establishment which provides lodging to transient guests, other than an establishment located within a building which contains not more than five rooms for rent or hire and which is actually occupied by the proprietor of such establishment as his residence;

(2) any restaurant, cafeteria, lunchroom, lunch counter, soda fountain. . . .

(3) any motion picture house, theater, concert hall, sports arena, stadium. . . .

. . . .

(d) Support by State action.

Discrimination or segregation by an establishment is supported by State action within the meaning of this subchapter if such discrimination or segregation (1) is carried on under color of any law, statute, ordinance, or regulation; or (2) is carried on under color of any custom or usage required or enforced by officials of the State or political subdivision thereof; or (3) is required by action of the State or political subdivision thereof.

(e) Private establishments.

The provisions of this subchapter shall not apply to a private club or other establishment not in fact open to the public, except to the extent that the facilities of such establishment are made available to the customers or patrons of an establishment within the scope of subsection (b) of this section.

Section 202. Prohibition against discrimination or segregation required by any law, statute, ordinance, regulation, rule or order of a State or State agency. [42 U.S.C.A. § 2000a-1]

All persons shall be entitled to be free, at any establishment or place, from discrimination or segregation of any kind on the ground of race, color, religion, or national origin, if such discrimination or segregation is or purports to be required by any law, statute, ordinance, regulation, rule, or order of a State or any agency or political subdivision thereof.

Section 203. Prohibition against deprivation of, interference with, and punishment for exercising rights and privileges secured by section 2000a or 2000a-1 of this title. [42 U.S.C.A. § 2000a-2]

No person shall (a) withhold, deny, or attempt to withhold or deny, or deprive or attempt to deprive, any person of any right or privilege secured by section 201 or 202, or (b) intimidate, threaten, or coerce, or attempt to intimidate, threaten, or coerce any person with the purpose of interfering with any right or privilege secured by section 201 or 202, or (c) punish or attempt to punish any person for exercising or attempting to exercise any right or privilege secured by section 201 or 202.

SUBCHAPTER VI. EQUAL EMPLOYMENT OPPORTUNITIES. [Title VI of the Civil Rights Act of 1964 and 1991]

Section 703. Unlawful Employment Practices. [42 U.S.C.A. § 2000e-2]

(a) Employer practices.

It shall be an unlawful employment practice for an employer—

(1) to fail or refuse to hire or to discharge any individual, or otherwise to discriminate against any individual with respect to his compensation, terms, conditions, or privileges of employment, because of such individual's race, color, religion, sex, or national origin; or

(2) to limit, segregate, or classify his employees or applicants for employment in any way which would deprive or tend to deprive any individual of employment opportunities or otherwise adversely affect his status as an employee, because of such individual's race, color, religion, sex, or national origin.

(b) Employment agency practices.

It shall be an unlawful employment practice for an employment agency to fail or refuse to refer for employment, or otherwise to discriminate against, any individual because of his race, color, religion, sex, or national origin, or to classify or refer for employment any individual on the basis of his race, color, religion, sex, or national origin.

(c) Labor organization practices.

It shall be an unlawful employment practice for a labor organization—

(1) to exclude or to expel from its membership, or otherwise to discriminate against, any individual because of his race, color, religion, sex, or national origin;

(2) to limit, segregate, or classify its membership or applicants for membership, or to classify or fail or refuse to refer for employment any individual, in any way which would deprive or tend to deprive any individual of employment opportunities, or would limit such employment opportunities or otherwise adversely affect

his status as an employee or as an applicant for employment, because of such individual's race, color, religion, sex, or national origin; or

(3) to cause or attempt to cause an employer to discriminate against an individual in violation of this section.

(d) Training programs.

It shall be an unlawful employment practice for any employer, labor organization, or joint labor-management committee controlling apprenticeship or other training or retraining, including on-the-job training programs to discriminate against any individual because of his race, color, religion, sex, or national origin in admission to, or employment in, any program established to provide apprenticeship or other training.

(e) Businesses or enterprises with personnel qualified on basis of religion, sex, or national origin; educational institutions with personnel or particular religion.

Notwithstanding any other provision of this sub-chapter, (1) it shall not be an unlawful employment practice for an employer to hire and employ employees, for an employment agency to classify, or refer for employment any individual, for a labor organization to classify its membership or to classify or refer for employment any individual, or for an employer, labor organization, or joint labor-management committee controlling apprenticeship or other training or retraining programs to admit or employ any individual in any such program, on the basis of his religion, sex, or national origin in those certain instances where religion, sex, or national origin is a bona fide occupational qualification reasonably necessary to the normal operation of that particular business or enterprise, and (2) it shall not be an unlawful employment practice for a school, college, university, or other educational institution or institution of learning to hire and employ employees of a particular religion if such school, college, university, or other educational institution or institution of learning is, in whole or in substantial part, owned, supported, controlled, or managed by a particular religion or by a particular religious corporation, association, or society, or if the curriculum of such school, college, university, or other educational institution or institution of learning is directed toward the propagation of a particular religion.

(f) Members of Communist Party or Communist–action or Communist-front organizations.

As used in this subchapter, the phrase "unlawful employment practice" shall not be deemed to include any action or measure taken by an employer, labor organization, joint labor-management committee, or employment agency with respect to an individual who is a member of the Communist Party of the United States or of any other organization required to register as a Communist-action or Communist-front organization. . .

(g) National security.

Notwithstanding any other provision of this subchapter, it shall not be an unlawful employment practice for an employer to fail or refuse to hire and employ any individual for any position, for an employer to discharge any individual from any position, or for an employment agency to fail or refuse to refer any individual for employment in any position, or for a labor organization to fail or refuse to refer any individual for employment in any position, if—

(1) the occupancy of such position, or access to the premises in or upon which any part of the duties of such position is performed or is to be performed, is subject to any requirement imposed in the interest of the national security of the United States . . . and

(2) such individual has not fulfilled or has ceased to fulfill that requirement.

(h) Seniority or merit system; quantity or quality of production; ability tests; compensation based on sex and authorized by minimum wage provisions.

Notwithstanding any other provision of this subchapter, it shall not be an unlawful employment practice for an employer to apply different standards of compensation, or different terms, conditions, or privileges of employment pursuant to a bona fide seniority or merit system, or a system which measures earnings by quantity or quality of production or to employees who work in different locations, provided that such differences are not the result of an intention to discriminate because of race, color, religion, sex, or national origin, nor shall it be an unlawful employment practice for an employer to give and act upon the results of any professionally developed ability test provided that such test, its administration or action upon the results is not designed, intended or used to discriminate because of race, color, religion, sex, or national origin. . . .

. . . .

(j) Preferential treatment not be granted on account of existing number or percentage imbalance.

Nothing contained in this subchapter shall be interpreted to require any employer, employment agency, labor organization, or joint labor-management committee subject to this subchapter to grant preferential treatment to any individual or to any group because of the race, color, religion, sex, or national origin of such individual or group on account of an imbalance which may exist with respect to the total number or percentage of persons of any race, color, religion, sex, or national origin employed by any employer, referred or classified for employment by any employment agency or labor organization, or admitted to, or employed in, any apprenticeship or other training program, in comparison with the total number or percentage of persons of such race, color, religion, sex, or national origin in any community, State, section, or other area, or in the available work force in any community, State, section, or other area.

(k) Burden of proof in disparate impact cases.

(1)(A) An unlawful employment practice based on disparate impact is established under this subchapter only if—

(i) a complaining party demonstrates that a respondent uses a particular employment practice that causes a disparate impact on the basis of race, color, religion, sex, or national origin and the respondent fails to demonstrate that the challenged practice is job related for the position in question and consistent with business necessity; or

(ii) the complaining party makes the demonstration described in subparagraph (C) with respect to an alternative employment practice and the respondent refuses to adopt such alternative employment practice.

(B)(i) With respect to demonstrating that a particular employment practice causes a disparate impact as described in subparagraph (A)(i), the complaining party shall demonstrate that each particular challenged employment practice causes a disparate impact, except that if the complaining party can demonstrate to the court that the elements of a respondent's decisionmaking process are not capable of separation for analysis, the decisionmaking process may be analyzed as one employment practice.

(ii) If the respondent demonstrates that a specific employment practice does not cause the disparate impact, the respondent shall not be required to demonstrate that such practice is required by business necessity.

(C) The demonstration referred to by subparagraph (A)(ii) shall be in accordance with the law as it existed on June 4, 1989, with respect to the concept of "alternative employment practice."

(2) A demonstration that an employment practice is required by business necessity may not be used as a defense against a claim of intentional discrimination under this subchapter.

(3) Notwithstanding any other provision of this subchapter, a rule barring the employment of an individual who currently and knowingly uses or possesses a controlled substance, as defined in schedules I and II of section 102(6) of the Controlled Substances Act other than the use or possession of a drug taken under the supervision of a licensed health care professional, or any other use or possession authorized by the Controlled Substances Act or any other provision of Federal law, shall be considered an unlawful employment practice under this subchapter only if such rule is adopted or applied with an intent to discriminate because of race, color, religion, sex, or national origin.

(l) Prohibition of discriminatory use of test scores.

Alteration of test results. It shall be an unlawful employment practice for a respondent, in connection with the selection or referral of applicants or candidates for employment or promotion, to adjust the scores of, use different cutoff scores for, or otherwise alter the results of, employment related tests on the basis of race, color, religion, sex, or national origin.

(m) Impermissible consideration of race, color, religion, sex, or national origin in employment practices.

Except as otherwise provided in this subchapter, an unlawful employment practice is established when the complaining party demonstrates that race, color, religion, sex, or national origin was a motivating factor for any employment practice, even though other factors also motivated the practice.

(n) Resolution of challenges to employment practices implementing litigate or consent judgments or orders.

(1)(A) Notwithstanding any other provision of law, and except as provided in paragraph (2), an employment practice that implements and is within the scope of a litigated or consent judgment or order that resolves a claim of employment discrimination under the Constitution or Federal civil rights laws may not be challenged under the circumstances described in paragraph (B).

(B) A practice described in subparagraph (A) may not be challenged in a claim under the Constitution or Federal civil rights laws—

(i) by a person who, prior to the entry of the judgment or order described in subparagraph (A), had—

(I) actual notice of the proposed judgment or order sufficient to apprise such person that such judgment or order might adversely affect the interests and legal rights of such person and that an opportunity was available to present objections to such judgment or order by a future date certain; and

(II) a reasonable opportunity to present objections to such judgment or order; or

(ii) by a person whose interests were adequately represented by another person who had previously challenged the judgment or order on the same legal grounds and with a similar factual situation, unless there has been an intervening change in law or fact.

(2) Nothing in this subsection shall be construed to—

(A) alter the standards for intervention under rule 24 of the Federal Rules of Civil Procedure or apply to the rights of parties who have successfully intervened pursuant to such rule in the proceeding in which the parties intervened;

(B) apply to the rights of parties to the action in which a litigated or consent judgment or order was entered, or of members of a class represented or sought to be represented in such action, or of members of a group on whose behalf relief was sought in such action by the Federal Government;

(C) prevent challenges to a litigated or consent judgment or order on the ground that such judgment or order was obtained through collusion or fraud, or is transparently invalid or was entered by a court lacking subject matter jurisdiction; or

(D) authorize or permit the denial to any person of the due process of law required by the Constitution.

(3) Any action not precluded under the subsection that challenges an employment consent judgment or order described in paragraph (1) shall be brought in the court, and if possible before the judge, that entered such judgment or order. Nothing in this subsection shall preclude a transfer of such action pursuant to section 1404 of Title 28.

Section 704. Other Unlawful Employment Practices. [42 U.S.C.A. § 2000e-3]

(a) Discrimination for making charges, testifying, assisting, or participating in enforcement proceedings.

It shall be an unlawful employment practice for an employer to discriminate against any of his employees or applicants for employment, for an employment agency, or joint labor-management committee controlling apprenticeship or other training or retraining, including on-the-job training programs, to discriminate against any individual, or for a labor organization to discriminate against any member thereof or applicant for membership, because he has opposed any practice made an unlawful employment practice by this subchapter, or because he has made a charge, testified, assisted, or participated in any manner in an investigation, proceeding, or hearing under this subchapter.

(b) Printing or publication of notices or advertisements indicating prohibited preference, limitation, specification, or discrimination; occupational qualification exception.

It shall be an unlawful employment practice for an employer, labor organization, employment agency, or joint labor-management committee controlling apprenticeship or other training or retraining, including on-the-job training programs, to print or publish or cause to be printed or published any notice or advertisement relating to employment by such an employer or membership or any classification or referral for employment by such a labor organization, or relating to any classification or referral for employment by such an employment agency, or relating to admission to, or employment in, any program established to provide apprenticeship or other training by such a joint-labor-management committee, indicating any preference, limitation, specification, or discrimination, based on race, color, religion, sex, or national origin, except that such a notice or advertisement may indicate a preference, limitation, specification, or discrimination based on religion, sex or national origin when religion, sex, or national origin is a bona fide occupational qualification for employment.

CHAPTER 45. FAIR HOUSING.

SUBCHAPTER I. GENERALLY.

Section 803. Discrimination in the sale or rental of housing and other prohibited practices. [42 U.S.C.A. § 3604]

. . . [I]t shall be unlawful—

(a) To refuse to sell or rent after the making of a bona fide offer, or to refuse to negotiate for the sale or rental of, or otherwise make unavailable or deny, a dwelling to any person because of race, color, religion, sex, familial status, or national origin.

(b) To discriminate against any person in the terms, conditions, or privileges of sale or rental of a dwelling, or in the provision of services or facilities in connection therewith, because of race, color, religion, sex, familial status, or national origin.

(c) To make, print, or publish, or cause to be made, printed, or published any notice, statement, or advertisement, with respect to the sale or rental of a dwelling that indicates any preference, limitation, or discrimination based on race, color, religion, sex, handicap, familial status, or national origin, or an intention to make any such preference, limitation, or discrimination.

(d) To represent to any person because of race, color, religion, sex, handicap, familial status, or national origin that any dwelling is not available for inspection, sale, or rental when such dwelling is in fact so available.

(e) For profit, to induce or attempt to induce any person to sell or rent any dwelling by representations regarding the entry or prospective entry into the neighborhood of a person or persons of a particular race, color, religion, sex, handicap, familial status, or national origin.

(f)(1) To discriminate in the sale or rental, or to otherwise make unavailable or deny, a dwelling to any buyer or renter because of a handicap of—

(A) that buyer or renter;

(B) a person residing in or intending to reside in that dwelling after it is so sold, rented, or made available; or

(C) any person associated with that buyer or renter.

(2) To discriminate against any person in the terms, conditions, or privileges of sale or rental of a dwelling, or in the provision of services or facilities in connection with such dwelling, because of a handicap of—

(A) that person; or

(B) a person residing in or intending to reside in that dwelling after it is so sold, rented, or made available; or

(C) any person associated with that person.

(3) For purposes of this subsection, discrimination includes—

(A) a refusal to permit, at the expense of the handicapped person, reasonable modifications of existing premises occupied or to be occupied by such person if such modifications may be necessary to afford such person full enjoyment of the premises except that, in the case of a rental, the landlord may where it is reasonable to do so condition permission for a modification on the renter agreeing to restore the interior of the premises to the condition that existed before the modification, reasonable wear and tear excepted;

(B) a refusal to make reasonable accommodations in rules, policies, practices, or services, when such accommodations may be necessary to afford such person equal opportunity to use and enjoy a dwelling; or

(C) in connection with the design and construction of covered multifamily dwellings for first occupancy after the date that is 30 months after September 13, 1988, a failure to design and construct those dwellings in such a manner that—

(i) the public use and common use portions of such dwellings are readily accessible to and usable by handicapped persons;

(ii) all the doors designed to allow passage into and within all premises within such dwellings are sufficiently wide to allow passage by handicapped persons in wheelchairs; and

(iii) all premises within such dwellings contain the following features of adaptive design:

(I) an accessible route into and through the dwelling;

(II) light switches, electrical outlets, thermostats, and other environmental controls in accessible locations;

(III) reinforcements in bathroom walls to allow later installation of grab bars; and

(IV) usable kitchens and bathrooms such that an individual in a wheelchair can maneuver about the space.

CHAPTER 26. EQUAL OPPORTUNITY FOR INDIVIDUALS WITH DISABILITIES.

42 U.S.C.A. § 12101.
Findings and purpose.

(a) Findings

The Congress finds that—

(1) some 43,000,000 Americans have one or more physical or mental disabilities, and this number is increasing as the population as a whole is growing older;

(2) historically, society has tended to isolate and segregate individuals with disabilities, and, despite some im-

provements, such forms of discrimination against individuals with disabilities continue to be a serious and pervasive social problem;

(3) discrimination against individuals with disabilities persists in such critical areas as employment, housing, public accommodations, education, transportation, communication, recreation, institutionalization, health services, voting, and access to public services;

(4) unlike individuals who have experienced discrimination on the basis of race, color, sex, national origin, religion, or age, individuals who have experienced discrimination on the basis of disability have often had no legal recourse to redress such discrimination;

(5) individuals with disabilities continually encounter various forms of discrimination, including outright intentional exclusion, the discriminatory effects of architectural, transportation, and communication barriers, overprotective rules and policies, failure to make modifications to existing facilities and practices, exclusionary qualification standards and criteria, segregation, and relegation to lesser services, programs, activities, benefits, jobs, or other opportunities;

(6) census data, national polls, and other studies have documented that people with disabilities, as a group, occupy an inferior status in our society, and are severely disadvantaged socially, vocationally, economically, and educationally;

(7) individuals with disabilities are a discrete and insular minority who have been faced with restrictions and limitations, subjected to a history of purposeful unequal treatment, and relegated to a position of political powerlessness in our society, based on characteristics that are beyond the control of such individuals and resulting from stereotypic assumptions not truly indicative of the individual ability of such individuals to participate in, and contribute to, society;

(8) the Nation's proper goals regarding individuals with disabilities are to assure equality of opportunity, full participation, independent living, and economic self-sufficiency for such individuals; and

(9) the continuing existence of unfair and unnecessary discrimination and prejudice denies people with disabilities the opportunity to compete on an equal basis and to pursue those opportunities for which our free

society is justifiably famous, and costs the United States billions of dollars in unnecessary expenses resulting from dependency and nonproductivity.

(b) Purpose

It is the purpose of this chapter—

(1) to provide a clear and comprehensive national mandate for the elimination of discrimination against individuals with disabilities;

(2) to provide clear, strong, consistent, enforceable standards addressing discrimination against individuals with disabilities;

(3) to ensure that the Federal Government plays a central role in enforcing the standards established in this chapter on behalf of individuals with disabilities; and

(4) to invoke the sweep of congressional authority; including the power to enforce the fourteenth amendment and to regulate commerce, in order to address the major areas of discrimination faced day-to-day by people with disabilities.

Appendix H The Uniform Partnership Act (Excerpts)

Section 6. Partnership Defined.

(1) A partnership is an association of two or more persons to carry on as co-owners a business for profit.

(2) But any association formed under any other statute of this state, or any statute adopted by authority, other than the authority of this state, is not a partnership under this act, unless such association would have been a partnership in this state prior to the adoption of this act; but this act shall apply to limited partnerships except in so far as the statutes relating to such partnerships are inconsistent herewith.

Section 8. Partnership Property.

(1) All property originally brought into the partnership stock or subsequently acquired by purchase or otherwise, on account of the partnership, is partnership property.

(2) Unless the contrary intention appears, property acquired with partnership funds is partnership property.

(3) Any estate in real property may be acquired in the partnership name. Title so acquired can be conveyed only in the partnership name.

(4) A conveyance to a partnership in the partnership name, though without words of inheritance, passes the entire estate of the grantor unless a contrary intent appears.

Section 9. Partner Agent of Partnership as to Partnership Business.

(1) Every partner is an agent of the partnership for the purpose of its business, and the act of every partner, including the execution in the partnership name of any instrument, for apparently carrying on in the usual way the business of the partnership of which he is a member binds the partnership, unless the partner so acting has in fact no authority to act for the partnership in the particular matter, and the person with whom he is dealing has knowledge of the fact that he has no such authority.

(2) An act of a partner which is not apparently for the carrying on of the business of the partnership in the usual way does not bind the partnership unless authorized by the other partners.

(3) Unless authorized by the other partners or unless they have abandoned the business, one or more but less than all the partners have no authority to:

(a) Assign the partnership property in trust for creditors or on the assignee's promise to pay the debts of the partnership,

(b) Dispose of the good-will of the business,

(c) Do any other act which would make it impossible to carry on the ordinary business of a partnership,

(d) Confess a judgment,

(e) Submit a partnership claim or liability to arbitration or reference.

(4) No act of a partner in contravention of a restriction on authority shall bind the partnership to persons having knowledge of the restriction.

Section 10. Conveyance of Real Property of the Partnership.

(1) Where title to real property is in the partnership name, any partner may convey title to such property by a conveyance executed in the partnership name; but the partnership may recover such property unless the partner's act binds the partnership under the provisions of paragraph (1) of section 9, or unless such property has been conveyed by the grantee or a person claiming through such grantee to a holder for value without knowledge that the partner, in making the conveyance, has exceeded his authority.

(2) Where title to real property is in the name of the partnership, a conveyance executed by a partner, in his own name, passes the equitable interest of the partnership, provided the act is one within the authority of the partner under the provisions of paragraph (1) of section 9.

(3) Where title to real property is in the name of one or more but not all the partners, and the record does not disclose the right of the partnership, the partners in whose name the title stands may convey title to such property, but the partnership may recover such property if the partners' act does not bind the partnership under the provisions of paragraph (1) of section 9, unless the purchaser or his assignee, is a holder for value, without knowledge.

(4) Where the title to real property is in the name of one or more or all the partners, or in a third person in trust for the partnership, a conveyance executed by a partner in the partnership name, or in his own name, passes the equitable interest of the partnership, provided the act is one within the authority of the partner under the provisions of paragraph (1) of section 9.

(5) Where the title to real property is in the names of all the partners a conveyance executed by all the partners passes all their rights in such property.

Section 13. Partnership Bound by Partner's Wrongful Act.

Where, by any wrongful act or omission of any partner acting in the ordinary course of the business of the partnership or with the authority of his co-partners, loss or injury is caused to any person, not being a partner in the partnership, or any penalty is incurred, the partnership is liable therefor to the same extent as the partner so acting or omitting to act.

Section 15. Nature of Partner's Liability.

All partners are liable

(a) Jointly and severally for everything chargeable to the partnership under sections 13 and 14.

(b) Jointly for all other debts and obligations of the partnership; but any partner may enter into a separate obligation to perform a partnership contract.

Section 16. Partner by Estoppel.

(1) When a person, by words spoken or written or by conduct, represents himself, or consents to another representing him to any one, as a partner in an existing partnership or with one or more persons not actual partners, he is liable to any such person to whom such representation has been made, who has, on the faith of such representation, given credit to the actual or apparent partnership, and if he has made such representation or consented to its being made in a public manner he is liable to such person, whether the representation has or has not been made or communicated to such person so giving credit by or with the knowledge of the apparent partner making the representation or consenting to its being made.

  (a) When a partnership liability results, he is liable as though he were an actual member of the partnership.

  (b) When no partnership liability results, he is liable jointly with the other persons, if any, so consenting to the contract or representation as to incur liability, otherwise separately.

(2) When a person has been thus represented to be a partner in an existing partnership, or with one or more persons not actual partners, he is an agent of the persons consenting to such representation to bind them to the same extent and in the same manner as though he were a partner in fact, with respect to persons who rely upon the representation. Where all the members of the existing partnership consent to the representation, a partnership act or obligation results; but in all other

cases it is the joint act or obligation of the person acting and the persons consenting to the representation.

Section 17. Liability of Incoming Partner.

A person admitted as a partner into an existing partnership is liable for all the obligations of the partnership arising before his admission as though he had been a partner when such obligations were incurred, except that this liability shall be satisfied only out of partnership property.

Section 18. Rules Determining Rights and Duties of Partners.

The rights and duties of the partners in relation to the partnership shall be determined, subject to any agreement between them, by the following rules:

(a) Each partner shall be repaid his contributions, whether by way of capital or advances to the partnership property and share equally in the profits and surplus remaining after all liabilities, including those to partners, are satisfied; and must contribute towards the losses, whether of capital or otherwise, sustained by the partnership according to his share in the profits.

(b) The partnership must indemnify every partner in respect of payments made and personal liabilities reasonably incurred by him in the ordinary and proper conduct of its business, or for the preservation of its business or property.

(c) A partner, who in aid of the partnership makes any payment or advance beyond the amount of capital which he agreed to contribute, shall be paid interest from the date of the payment or advance.

(d) A partner shall receive interest on the capital contributed by him only from the date when repayment should be made.

(e) All partners have equal rights in the management and conduct of the partnership business.

(f) No partner is entitled to remuneration for acting in the partnership business, except that a surviving partner is entitled to reasonable compensation for his services in winding up the partnership affairs.

(g) No person can become a member of a partnership without the consent of all the partners.

(h) Any difference arising as to ordinary matters connected with the partnership business may be decided by a majority of the partners; but no act in contravention of any agreement between the partners may be done rightfully without the consent of all the partners.

Section 25. Nature of a Partner's Right in Specific Partnership Property.

(1) A partner is co-owner with his partners of specific partnership property holding as a tenant in partnership.

(2) The incidents of this tenancy are such that:

(a) A partner, subject to the provisions of this act and to any agreement between the partners, has an equal right with his partners to possess specific partnership property for partnership purposes; but he has no right to possess such property for any other purpose without the consent of his partners.

(b) A partner's right in specific partnership property is not assignable except in connection with the assignment of rights of all the partners in the same property.

(c) A partner's right in specific partnership property is not subject to attachment or execution, except on a claim against the partnership. When partnership property is attached for a partnership debt the partners, or any of them, or the representatives of a deceased partner, cannot claim any right under the homestead or exemption laws.

(d) On the death of a partner his right in specific partnership property vests in the surviving partner or partners, except where the deceased was the last surviving partner, when his right in such property vests in his legal representative. Such surviving partner or partners, or the legal representative of the last surviving partner, has no right to possess the partnership property for any but a partnership purpose.

(e) A partner's right in specific partnership property is not subject to dower, curtesy, or allowances to widows, heirs, or next of kin.

Section 30. Partnership Not Terminated by Dissolution.

On dissolution the partnership is not terminated, but continues until the winding up of partnership affairs is completed.

Section 31. Causes of Dissolution.

Dissolution is caused:

(1) Without violation of the agreement between the partners,

(a) By the termination of the definite term or particular undertaking specified in the agreement,

(b) By the express will of any partner when no definite term or particular undertaking is specified,

(c) By the express will of all the partners who have not assigned their interests or suffered them to be charged for their separate debts, either before or after the termination of any specified term or particular undertaking,

(d) By the expulsion of any partner from the business bona fide in accordance with such a power conferred by the agreement between the partners;

(2) In contravention of the agreement between the partners, where the circumstances do not permit a dissolution under any other provision of this section, by the express will of any partner at any time;

(3) By any event which makes it unlawful for the business of the partnership to be carried on or for the members to carry it on in partnership;

(4) By the death of any partner;

(5) By the bankruptcy of any partner or the partnership;

(6) By decree of court under section 32.

Section 32. Dissolution by Decree of Court.

(1) On application by or for a partner the court shall decree a dissolution whenever:

(a) A partner has been declared a lunatic in any judicial proceeding or is shown to be of unsound mind,

(b) A partner becomes in any other way incapable of performing his part of the partnership contract,

(c) A partner has been guilty of such conduct as tends to affect prejudicially the carrying on of the business,

(d) A partner willfully or persistently commits a breach of the partnership agreement, or otherwise so conducts himself in matters relating to the partnership business that it is not reasonably practicable to carry on the business in partnership with him,

(e) The business of the partnership can only be carried on at a loss,

(f) Other circumstances render a dissolution equitable.

(2) On the application of the purchaser of a partner's interest under sections 28 or 29 [should read 27 or 28];

(a) After the termination of the specified term or particular undertaking,

(b) At any time if the partnership was a partnership at will when the interest was assigned or when the charging order was issued.

Section 35. Power of Partner to Bind Partnership to Third Persons after Dissolution.

(1) After dissolution a partner can bind the partnership except as provided in paragraph (3).

(a) By any act appropriate for winding up partnership affairs or completing transactions unfinished at dissolution;

(b) By any transaction which would bind the partnership if dissolution had not taken place, provided the other party to the transaction

(I) Had extended credit to the partnership prior to dissolution and had no knowledge or notice of the dissolution; or

(II) Though he had not so extended credit, had nevertheless known of the partnership prior to dissolution, and, having no knowledge or notice of dissolution, the fact of dissolution had not been advertised in a newspaper of general circulation in the place (or in each place if more than one) at which the partnership business was regularly carried on.

(2) The liability of a partner under paragraph (1b) shall be satisfied out of partnership assets alone when such partner had been prior to dissolution

(a) Unknown as a partner to the person with whom the contract is made; and

(b) So far unknown and inactive in partnership affairs that the business reputation of the partnership could not be said to have been in any degree due to his connection with it.

(3) The partnership is in no case bound by any act of a partner after dissolution

(a) Where the partnership is dissolved because it is unlawful to carry on the business, unless the act is appropriate for winding up partnership affairs; or

(b) Where the partner has become bankrupt; or

(c) Where the partner has no authority to wind up partnership affairs; except by a transaction with one who

(I) Had extended credit to the partnership prior to dissolution and had no knowledge or notice of his want of authority; or

(II) Had not extended credit to the partnership prior to dissolution, and, having no knowledge or notice of his want of authority, the fact of his want of authority has not been advertised in the manner provided for advertising the fact of dissolution in paragraph (1bII).

(4) Nothing in this section shall affect the liability under Section 16 of any person who after dissolution represents himself or consents to another representing him as a partner in a partnership engaged in carrying on business.

Section 40. Rules for Distribution.

In settling accounts between the partners after dissolution, the following rules shall be observed, subject to any agreement to the contrary:

(a) The assets of the partnership are:

(I) The partnership property,

(II) The contributions of the partners necessary for the payment of all the liabilities specified in clause (b) of this paragraph.

(b) The liabilities of the partnership shall rank in order of payment, as follows:

(I) Those owing to creditors other than partners,

(II) Those owing to partners other than for capital and profits,

(III) Those owing to partners in respect of capital,

(IV) Those owing to partners in respect of profits.

(c) The assets shall be applied in the order of their declaration in clause (a) of this paragraph to the satisfaction of the liabilities.

(d) The partners shall contribute, as provided by section 18(a) the amount necessary to satisfy the liabilities; but if any, but not all, of the partners are insolvent, or, not being subject to process, refuse to contribute, the other partners shall contribute their share of the liabilities, and, in the relative proportions in which they share the profits, the additional amount necessary to pay the liabilities.

(e) An assignee for the benefit of creditors or any person appointed by the court shall have the right to enforce the contributions specified in clause (d) of this paragraph.

(f) Any partner or his legal representative shall have the right to enforce the contributions specified in clause (d) of this paragraph, to the extent of the amount which he has paid in excess of his share of the liability.

(g) The individual property of a deceased partner shall be liable for the contributions specified in clause (d) of this paragraph.

(h) When partnership property and the individual properties of the partners are in possession of a court for distribution, partnership creditors shall have priority on partnership property and separate creditors on individual property, saving the rights of lien or secured creditors as heretofore.

(i) Where a partner has become bankrupt or his estate is insolvent the claims against his separate property shall rank in the following order:

(I) Those owing to separate creditors,

(II) Those owing to partnership creditors,

(III) Those owing to partners by way of contribution.

International Top-Level Domain (ITLD)

Entity (Short Name in English)	Code	Entity (Short Name in English)	Code	Entity (Short Name in English)	Code	Entity (Short Name in English)	Code
Afghanistan	AF	Bosnia and Herzegowina	BA	Cook Islands	CK	France, Metropolitan	FX
Albania	AL	Botswana	BW	Costa Rica	CR	French Guiana	GF
Algeria	DZ	Bouvet Island	BV	Cote D'Ivoire (Ivory Coast)	CI	French Polynesia	PF
American Samoa	AS	Brazil	BR	Croatia	HR	French Southern Territories	TF
Andorra	AD	British Indian Ocean Territory	IO	Cuba	CU	Gabon	GA
Angola	AO	Brunei Darussalam	BN	Cyprus	CY	Gambia	GM
Anguilla	AI	Bulgaria	BG	Czech Republic	CZ	Georgia	GE
Antarctica	AQ	Burkina Faso	BF	Denmark	DK	Germany	DE
Antigua and Barbuda	AG	Burundi	BI	Djibouti	DJ	Ghana	GH
Argentina	AR	Cambodia	KH	Dominica	DM	Gibraltar	GI
Armenia	AM	Cameroon	CM	Dominican Republic	DO	Greece	GR
Aruba	AW	Canada	CA	East Timor	TP	Greenland	GL
Australia	AU	Cape Verde	CV	Ecuador	EC	Grenada	GD
Austria	AT	Cayman Islands	KY	Egypt	EG	Guadaloupe	GP
Azerbaijan	AZ	Central Africa Republic	CF	El Salvador	SV	Guam	GU
Bahamas	BS	Chad	TD	Equatorial Guinea	GQ	Guatemala	GT
Bahrain	BH	Chile	CL	Eritrea	ER	Guinea	GN
Bangladesh	BD	China	CN	Estonia	EE	Guinea–Bissau	GW
Barbados	BB	Christmas Island	CX	Ethiopia	ET	Guyana	GY
Belarus	BY	Cocos (Keeling) Islands	CC	Falklands Islands or Malvinas	FK	Haiti	HT
Belgium	BE	Colombia	CO	Faroe Islands	FO	Heard and McDonald Islands	HM
Belize	BZ	Comoros	KM	Fiji	FJ	Honduras	HN
Benin	BJ	Congo	CG	Finland	FI	Hong Kong	HK
Bermuda	BM			France	FR	Hungary	HU
Bhutan	BT						
Bolivia	BO						

Entity (Short Name in English)	Code	Entity (Short Name in English)	Code	Entity (Short Name in English)	Code	Entity (Short Name in English)	Code
Iceland	IS	Marshall Islands	MH	Poland	PL	Syrian Arab Republic	SY
India	IN	Martinique	MQ	Portugal	PT	Taiwan, Province	
Indonesia	ID	Mauritania	MR	Puerto Rico	PR	of China	TW
Iran (Islamic Republic of)	IR	Mauritius	MU	Qatar	QA	Tajikistan	TJ
		Mayotte	YT	Reunion	RE	Tanzania, United	
Iraq	IQ	Mexico	MX	Romania	RO	Republic of	TZ
Ireland	IE	Micronesia		Russian Federation	RU	Thailand	TH
Israel	IL	(Federated		Rwanda	RW	Togo	TG
Italy	IT	States of)	FM	St. Helena	SH	Tokelau	TK
Jamaic	JM	Moldova,		Saint Kitts and		Tonga	TO
Japan	JP	Republic of	MD	Nevis	KN	Trinidad and Tobago	TT
Jordan	JO	Monaco	MC	Saint Lucia	LC	Tunisia	TN
Kazakhstan	KZ	Mongolia	MN	St. Pierre and		Turkey	TR
Kenya	KE	Montserrat	MS	Miquelon	PM	Turkmenistan	TM
Kiribati	KI	Morocco	MA	Saint Vincent and		Turks and Caicos	
Korea, Democratic People's Republic of	KP	Mozambique	MZ	the Grenadines	VC	Islands	TC
		Myanmar	MM	Samoa	WS	Tuvalu	TV
Korea, Republic of	KR	Namibia	NA	San Marino	SM	Uganda	UG
Kuwait	KW	Nauru	NR	Sao Torme and		Ukraine	UA
Kyrgyzstan	KG	Nepal	NP	Principe	ST	United Arab Emirates	AE
Lao People's Democratic Republic	LA	Netherlands	NL	Saudi Arabia	SA	United Kingdom	UK
		Netherlands Antilles	AN	Senegal	SN	United States	US
Latvia	LV	New Caledonia	NC	Seychelles	SC	United States	
Lebanon	LB	New Zealand	NZ	Sierra Leone	SL	Minor Outlying	
Lesotho	LS	Nicaragua	NI	Singapore	SG	Islands	UM
Liberia	LR	Niger	NE	Slovakia	SK	Uruguay	UY
Libyan Arab Jamahiriya	LY	Nigeria	NG	Slovenia	SI	Uzbekistan	UZ
		Niue	NU	Solomon Islands	SB	Vanuatu	VU
Liechtenstein	LI	Norfolk Island	NF	Somalia	SO	Vatican City State	
Lithuania	LT	Northern Mariana Islands	MP	South Africa	ZA	(Holy See)	VA
Luxembourg	LU	Norway	NO	South Georgia and the South Sandwich Islands	GS	Venezuela	VE
Macau	MO	Oman	OM			Viet Nam	VN
Macedonia, former Yugoslav Republic	MK	Pakistan	PK	Spain	ES	Virgin Islands (British)	VG
		Palau	PW	Sri Lanka	LK	Virgin Islands (U.S.)	VI
Madagascar	MG	Panama	PA	Sudan	SD	Wallis and Futuna	
Malawi	MW	Papua New Guinea	PG	Suriname	SR	Islands	WF
Malaysia	MY	Paraguay	PY	Svalbard and Jan Mayen Islands	SJ	Western Sahara	EH
Maldives	MV	Peru	PE			Yemen	YE
Mali	ML	Philippines	PH	Swaziland	SZ	Yugoslavia	YU
Malta	MT	Pitcairn	PN	Sweden	SE	Zaire	ZR
				Switzerland	CH	Zambia	ZM
						Zimbabwe	ZW

Critical Thinking

Whether examining a court case, making an ethical decision, or making a business decision, critical thinking skills are essential. Critical thinking requires a reasoning process and the evaluation of that process.

But how does one develop critical thinking skills? One process that applies these skills includes gathering the evidence, determining the issue, using a reasoning process, and reaching a conclusion.

Evidence

Evidence supports the reasons that lead to the conclusion. The issue is the focal point of the debate in the law. You need to gather all the **relevant evidence**—that is, evidence that is important and connected to the issue. The gathering of evidence is an ongoing process. Evidence consists of *facts, statistics,* and *documents.*

A **fact** is information that actually exists—that is, the reality or the truth. A fact can be a piece of empirical data on which all parties agree. For example, the U.S. government needed to standardize the calendar across the nation, so at the beginning of the twentieth century, it adopted a standardized calendar. Thus, in lawsuit, the judge can accept that July 4, 2001, was a Wednesday.

A fact may also be an observed event, past or present. **Testimony** consists of statements, commonly given in a court proceeding, by a witness to establish facts. A word of caution is necessary, however. The observer may filter or interpret facts. As a result, facts are subject to misinterpretation because they can be clouded by opinion or perspective.

Opinions are distinguishable from facts. An **opinion** is a personal judgment, sometimes based on in-complete evidence. For example, unless the statement "Drivers of red Porsches always speed" can be supported by empirical data or statistics, it is an opinion that should be ignored.

A **professional opinion**, when based on objective evidence, can lead to a valid conclusion. For example, a real estate appraiser may render an opinion as to the value of a particular piece of real estate.

The second type of evidence is **statistics**, which is the science that deals with the collection, analysis, and interpretation of numerical data. Advertisements, books on business trends, and cost-of-living indexes apply statistics.

Statistics is one way to gather evidence to prove a point. For example, you are severely injured in an automobile accident. You can use statistics to calculate your projected lifetime earnings before and after the accident. Employment discrimination cases often apply statistics to determine if the number of minorities and women working for a company reflects the ratio in the general population.

Documents are the third type of evidence. A document is any written or printed evidence that is used to establish a fact. A document may be a copy of official records, such as, birth or death certificates, minutes of a meeting, or accounting records, or letters.

All of these documents are evidence to establish certain facts. For example, a person is charged with filing accounting papers meant to mislead the lender as to the true worth of the borrower. The papers reflected that the borrower's house is worth $500,000, but two months previously the owner sold the house for $300,000. The documents detailing the house sale at

$300,000 established its value as well as the fact that the borrower no longer owned the house when he claimed it as part of his assets. These documents can help to establish the borrower's intent to defraud the lender by overstating the house's value by a significant amount.

The omission of evidence affects the reasoning process, often resulting in an incorrect conclusion. The omitted evidence, however, must be relevant. The inclusion of immaterial evidence also can lead to an error in the reasoning process. Reasoning errors, thus, can occur through inclusion of irrelevant facts or exclusion (omission) of relevant facts.

Issue

Following the gathering of evidence, the issue is stated. The issue briefly states the dispute or controversy. In court cases, the sentence stating the issue often starts with the words "whether" or "the issue in this case." The following are examples of how a court may state an issue:

● "This appeal turns on whether the trial court's interpretation of the contract is reasonable."

● "This court must determine whether a new trial is required by reason of juror coercion."

● "We address, in this case, the proper interpretation of the Education Code."

Reasoning Process

Reasoning is used to justify a position in an argument. An **argument** is concerned with discovering and conveying the best judgment about a truth through an appeal to reason. The person who makes the argument must clarify and support the reasons to arrive at rational conclusions.

The two basic reasoning processes are *inductive reasoning* and *deductive reasoning*. **Inductive reasoning** uses specific pieces of evidence to draw a conclusion which is probably true, while **deductive reasoning** uses a generalization, which, when applied to a specific instance, will result in a true or certain conclusion. More simply, inductive reasoning starts from the specific to derive the general, while deductive reasoning is the opposite; it starts from the general to derive the specific.

An example of inductive reasoning is a test for quality using a Japanese method of sampling output from a production process. The sample consists of the first item and the last item. If these two items are perfect, it is induced that all items in between are perfect. With inductive reasoning, the conclusion is a probability when based on valid evidence, while with deductive reasoning, when the premise is true, the conclusion must be true.

Because thinking processes rarely fit into neat, separate boxes, the separation of these two reasoning processes in many situations is almost impossible. The following sections discuss the two processes and potential reasoning fallacies in more detail.

Inductive Reasoning. Inductive reasoning is the process of looking at specific instances to arrive at a conclusion. A person starts with a particular experience and proceeds to a generalization. For example, you are bitten by two dogs. You conclude that all dogs bite. In reality, there is no logical movement from the evidence to the conclusion. Inductive reasoning, thus, leads to probabilities, not certainties. A **probability** can reasonably be expected to happen or to be true on the basis of the evidence, but cannot be proven to a certainty.

Inductive reasoning is the basis of common sense. Most people use their past experience (or evidence they have found) to predict the future by forming a conclusion. The results of the inductive reasoning process always are subject to some doubt. The conclusion, however, generally will be true, if the evidence is unflawed and carefully applied. Your conclusion, all dogs bite, is flawed because your evidence, the two previous dog bites, is flawed based on your small sample size.

Inductive reasoning uses four reasoning processes. These four are *generalizing, hypothesizing, analogies,* and *tracing cause and effect*. These four processes often overlap. In fact, often two or three of these processes are used simultaneously. To clarify reasoning, people should distinguish among these processes.

The most common form of inductive reasoning is **generalizing**. Generalization uses a properly sized database, then finds a sample that is typical for the class that is being generalized. The database must be sufficiently large, for the generalization to be valid, and the database should demonstrate a clearly identifiable trend.

The following problem involves generalization: during the past four years, you have purchased four used cars. Each car gave you lots of problems. At the end of the fourth year, your particular experience leads you to generalize that all used cars are clunkers. The conclusion has a probability, but not a certainty, of being true. This example will be revisited later under the category "Hasty Generalization."

Similar to generalizing is **hypothesizing**. An hypothesis is a provisional theory that attempts to explain the problem. The hypothesis helps to limit the investigation. Once the hypothesis is stated, enough data must be gathered to prove or disprove it. A hypothesis should be revised until it has been followed through to its conclusion; the evidence either supports or disproves the hypothesis.

Crimes often are solved by hypothesizing. For example, from the evidence gathered, you theorize that the butler committed the crime. That hypothesis limits the investigation to the butler. Now more evidence must be gathered to prove or disprove the hypothesis.

Analogies establish similarities between characteristics of two things on which a comparison may be based. In reasoning, one thing is identified as similar to another thing in a certain respect, allowing a conclusion to be inferred. For example, an analogy can be drawn between a human heart and a pump. A court can draw an analogy in its reasoning process. For example, a group gathers the signatures needed to put an initiative on the ballot for voter approval at the next election. The initiative becomes a state statute when the voters approve. People who opposed the statute sue in court to have the statute blocked as unconstitutional. The attorney general must defend the statute's constitutionality because it is state law. The initiative's original proposers also defend the statute. The court had to decide whether only the attorney general can defend the lawsuit or the original proposers could also defend the statute. The court drew an analogy between the state attorney general and the group. The court reasoned that if the state attorney general was qualified to defend the statute's constitutionality, which was created by the ballot initiative, the initiative's principal sponsor was also qualified to defend the statute's constitutionality.

The process of **tracing cause and effect** attempts to relate a situation, the cause, to a series of events, the effects. Often effects are more visible and more easily identified; finding the cause is harder. Once the cause is determined, dealing with the cause should change the effect at the same time.

For example, you try to start your car by turning the key. The engine groans, but fails to ignite. You think that the battery is at fault because it might have one or more dead cells. You observe that the radio does not play, the headlights are dim, and the electric windshield wipers and windows do not work. All of these effects result from a dead battery. The dead battery causes the effect of the engine failing to ignite. The items that reinforce your belief are discovered by tracing cause and effect. In this case, it is a probability that the battery is dead, not a certainty, until you test the battery. In a murder case, investigators look for a cause knowing that the effect was death. The cause can determine the type of criminal charges, such as, first degree, second degree, or manslaughter. Did the accused plan to kill the person? Or did the accused's speeding cause him to hit and kill a pedestrian?

Deductive Reasoning. Deductive reasoning starts with a conclusion (a generalization, such as "All persons are mortal."). This conclusion is applied to a specific instance. (Aristotle is a person.) Those truths result in another conclusion. (Therefore, Aristotle is a mortal.) Deductive reasoning is a form of argument that consists of a major premise and a minor premise that connect to the conclusion, which helps to visualize the argument.

A major premise deals with an entire class or category and with a single characteristic of that class or category. The minor premise applies the category to a specific instance. For example:

Major Premise: All dogs (category) are four-legged animals (characteristic).

Minor Premise: I own a dog (category),

Connection: therefore,

Conclusion: my dog (category) is four legged (characteristic).

The principal rule in constructing the minor premise is that it applies a specific instance to the major class or category, never to the characteristic. For example:

Major Premise: All dogs (category) are four-legged animals (characteristic).

Minor Premise: I own a four-legged animal (characteristic),

Connection: therefore,

Conclusion: I own a dog (category)?

In this case, no conclusion is possible. You used the characteristic in the minor premise instead of the category.

Breaking down the argument into parts allows for easier testing for fallacies, or errors. For the conclusion to be true, the premise must be true. Remember, however, that the argument is true within its own terms, but not necessarily true when applied to the world at large.

Both the inductive reasoning and the deductive reasoning processes are prone to errors. The following sections deal with some problems with the reasoning process.

Fallacies in Reasoning

The reasoning process is based on various types of evidence. As a result, the reasoning process is prone to fallacies. To evaluate the evidence, its source must be reliable. Evidence is compromised when an argument diverts attention or manipulates emotions.

Consider the following exclamations. All used cars are clunkers! Heavy metal music incites drug use! All politicians are liars! These statements reflect a lack of critical thinking. Any conclusion reached by a person who listened to the first statement (an example of a fallacy in the evidence by classifying all used cars into one category), the second statement (an example of diverting attention from other causes of drug use), or the third statement (an example of an emotional appeal by using the unpopularity of politicians) will inevitably be faulty. Often people try to win over others either through reasoning or through emotional appeals to a conclusion that may or may not be true.

Errors in the reasoning process, thus, fall into these categories: (1) *errors gathering or using the evidence*, (2) *fallacies using diversion tactics*, or (3) *fallacies using emotional appeals*. Remember, however, that reasoning errors may fall into more than one category.

Errors in the Evidence. Failure of the evidence falls into five general categories: (1) hasty generalization, (2) forming too few hypotheses, (3) asserted conclusion or circular reasoning, (4) faulty dilemma, or (5) faulty analogy. These different categories are not mutually exclusive.

Hasty Generalization. A hasty generalization results from using too few or atypical samples. In the previous case concerning your bad experience with used cars, the generalization, all used cars are clunkers, is not a true statement, even though you based your conclusion on your true experience. Generalizations can be based on limited personal experience, a sample size that is too small, or an atypical sample.

For example, you read in the newspaper over a period of six months that six different pit bull dogs bit people. You conclude that all pit bull dogs are mean and vicious. This example demonstrates a hasty generalization. To make an accurate generalization, you should find out the number of dog bites reported in the six months, the breeds of dog that bit people, and the circumstances surrounding the bites. As a potential dog buyer, your hasty generalization may be useful to determine the breed of dog to purchase. As a city council member deciding whether to pass a city ordinance concerning pit bull dogs, your hasty generalization is insufficient for making public policy decisions.

Forming Too Few Hypotheses. Similar to a hasty generalization is the error of forming too few hypotheses (theories), sometimes called a "rush to judgment." This error occurs when a person forms only one or two hypotheses, for which enough evidence must be gathered to prove or disprove a theory. Failure to keep an open mind to alternative theories may cause a person to overlook important ideas.

There is a difference between a hasty generalization and having too few hypotheses. A hasty generalization uses a database that is too small or atypical samples. Forming a hypothesis equates to developing a theory. From some given facts a number of theories develop to explain those facts. As more evidence is gathered, theories that fail to explain the facts are eliminated.

This error frequently occurs during the course of research. In an attempt to prove a particular hypothesis, very relevant evidence is overlooked or, worse, deliberately omitted. When the evidence fails to support the first hypothesis, it must be modified or discarded entirely and a new one must be formed.

An example follows: A woman, who is separated from her husband, is found murdered in her apartment. The husband lives two miles away. If you, as an investigator, suspect only the husband to the exclusion of others, you have formed too few hypotheses. (The husband killed her.) By initially forming too few hypotheses, you may ignore evidence that may lead to another possible suspect. (A serial killer or a current boyfriend killed her.)

Asserted Conclusion or Circular Reasoning. An asserted conclusion or circular reasoning denies a person an opportunity to examine evidence that forms the basis of the conclusion. The conclusion becomes the evidence. For example, you watch an hour-long television show that plays police videotapes. Each tape graphically shows criminals' violence against police officers. You conclude that all television shows are violent. Your evidence is the one-hour police television documentary, which, of course, demonstrates your conclusion that all television shows are violent.

Faulty Dilemma. This fallacy in reasoning employs the device of offering two apparent alternatives: The speaker or writer argues for the first, and the second is unacceptable. Politicians often employ this device, such as "You either vote for me and help preserve the Constitution or vote for my opponent and join the forces trying to destroy it."

Faulty Analogy. The speaker or writer who uses a faulty analogy uses a false comparison. For example, a panel discusses the proposed regulations on air quality standards from the Environmental Protection Agency (EPA). One member states that if these proposed regulations had been sent to the Food and Drug Administration (FDA), the proposed regulations would be rejected because they fail to meet the FDA's high standards. While this statement sounds true, it is a false analogy because Congress has set different standards for each agency. The research and development of the EPA regulations must meet requirements set by Congress for the EPA, not those set for another agency, the FDA.

The following sections discuss diversion tactics.

Diversion Tactics.
Diversion tactics distract a person's concentration from the evidence. Three favorite techniques are (1) stacking the evidence, (2) the loaded question, and (3) ignoring the question.

Stacking the Evidence. In stacking evidence, the facts are arranged before or after the event to demonstrate the chosen action to be correct. For example, you are on a search committee to fill a vacancy for a corporate office. One prominent committee member states that "Cartier is the person who should be appointed to the board. A Harvard graduate, she has been on the congressional staff for years, is personable, and is in favor of lower taxes." You would want to know more about Cartier, but with such a stacked endorsement, you may believe it inappropriate to question the person making the statements.

Loaded Question. A loaded question provides the listener with two ostensible choices. An example is the question "When did you stop beating your spouse or are the beatings continuing?" Or, the supervisor who asks an employee, "Well, Able, how did you screw up today?" incorporates the assumption that Able has already failed in his job. The statement is posed in the form of a question, but is loaded with negative information.

Ignoring the Question. In ignoring the question, the listener hears and evades the question. The answer contains information that sounds as if the question were being answered, but in reality the reply is unresponsive to the question. This technique is used often by people who are interviewed, particularly on television or radio shows. Politicians are particularly skilled in ignoring the question and giving a short speech on a topic they want to emphasize.

For example, Pol Politician is asked "How do you think the new laws on welfare reform will affect children?" Pol answers "Finally welfare recipients, who have been bilking the taxpayers for years, will have to get off the dole and get jobs like the rest of us. Welfare reform will save millions, force people to be moral by working for their food, and this benefits the country." The answer sounds great, but Pol failed to reveal how children will fare under the new law.

The following sections address reasoning errors based on emotional appeals.

Emotional Appeals.
All emotional appeals depend on the blind transfer of feelings from one issue to another without recourse to reason. Emotional appeals invoke feelings and passions while diverting attention from the argument. Six types of emotional appeal are: (1) name calling, (2) glittering generality, (3) snob appeal, (4) plain folks appeal, (5) bandwagon appeal, and (6) appeal to authority.

Name Calling. Name calling is characterized by such statements as "computer geeks" or "brainy nerds." These titles are designed to sway the listener into lumping people into one mold. Another example follows. When the EPA sent out proposed regulations for air quality standards, an opponent called the proposed regulations unworkable because they were based on "junk science." This type of name calling often stops further inquiry, which, if pursued in this case, would show that the EPA based its proposed regulations on the results of 256 research projects. Name calling has a negative connotation, stirs the emotions, and diverts attention from the reasoning process.

Glittering Generality. A glittering generality involves the name of a product or service or obtaining an endorsement that appeals to others without noting the product's characteristics. When the royal family of Great Britain patronizes a shop enough times, the shop, with permission from the royal family, can display an emblem that denotes that the royal family shops there. People shop in these stores merely because the royal family has in the past. These stores may or may not have a higher quality of goods than other similarly situated stores. A glittering generality creates a positive appeal but also stirs the emotions and diverts attention from the reasoning process.

Snob Appeal. The snob appeal caters to human ambition, connecting a higher social status with a product or idea. An advertisement, for example, may read "All the better people are moving to Estrella Estates." The advertisement evades the definition of "better people" and, more importantly, their reasons for moving to Estrella Estates.

Plain Folks Appeal. The reverse of the snob appeal and glittering generalities, the plain folks appeal creates contempt for status items. For example, an advertisement might read "Buy a log cabin in beautiful Lakeside Estates. Return to nature and the simple life and leave the hustle and bustle of the city." Returning to nature and the simple life may turn out to be hauling water, using a cellular telephone, chopping wood for heat, and reading by propane lamp. Did the advertisement cover these facts?

Bandwagon Appeal. The bandwagon appeal applies peer pressure to convince people to accept or reject an item or idea because "it is the thing to do." The bandwagon appeal is based on the principle that if an idea is accepted by a group, an individual would be presumptuous to reexamine it. For example, some teenagers smoke because their friends smoke. Of course, the real issue, that smoking affects the smoker's health, is not examined.

Appeal to Authority. Often talk shows use the emotional appeal technique. Talk show hosts will have lawyers on the show to discuss prominent court cases. The authority is clear; the guests are lawyers. The question is whether these guests really are knowledgeable about this type of case. Is the case under discussion a criminal one, while the guest has limited criminal trial experience. What are the qualifications of this expert?

Conclusion or Holding

A conclusion is the assessment or decision of the one making the argument. In court cases, a conclusion is called a *holding*. In this textbook, the holding of the court establishes the party that prevailed in the lawsuit. In inductive reasoning, the conclusion comes last. In deductive reasoning, a conclusion is used to reach another conclusion.

Fallacies or errors in reasoning distract attention from the problem. The person engaged in faulty reasoning is not held to answer because the diversion focuses attention elsewhere. Understanding diversion tactics allows individuals to defend against them. Failure to ask the right questions can be expensive.

The processes of critical thinking are difficult to apply. Reorganizing logical fallacies requires practice and discipline. The mark of a good thinker is the ability to form logical, coherent arguments, to ask thoughtful and probing questions, and to see fallacies in the reasoning process.

RULES TO REMEMBER

The following list for briefing a case appears simple. In many appellate cases, however, the application of that list is more difficult than it appears. The following rules will help you.

1. *What are the facts?* Facts rarely come in neat packages. Facts in a real situation or in a hypothetical situation remain constant. Just give the facts. As a saying goes, "Don't argue with the facts." because people often like to add to, subtract from, or otherwise alter or embellish the facts.

   a. *Relevant facts.* Determine relevant facts. Not all facts included in a problem relate to the problem (the issue). Choose the facts that are germane to the problem and discard the facts that are insignificant.

b. *Missing facts.* Determine missing information. Rarely are all the facts known that surround a particular situation. It is important to recognize the problem (the issue) and the missing information.

2. *What is the issue?* Determine the important issue (or issues). In the court's view, what is the problem that the parties want resolved?

3. *What is the rule of law or holding?* Determine the rule of law to be applied. The court looks first to statutes, then to regulations by administrative agencies, previously decided cases, or sometimes a mixture of these sources. Choose the rule or rules appropriate to the issue (the holding in the case).

4. *What is the reasoning?* Determine the court's reasons for applying the rule of law to the given facts. Ask if the reasoning is clear or ambiguous.

5. *What are the ethical considerations in the court's reasoning?* Determine the ethical issues involved. Ethical issues are discussed in Chapter 2. Look at the ethical conduct of each party. Determine the ethical norm used by the court in its reasoning.

6. *Don't confuse the facts with the law.* The facts of the case are not the legal reason. Keep the facts separate from the law. Following is an example from everyday life.

You are in your automobile traveling down the highway at thirty miles per hour. The speed limit is twenty miles per hour. A police officer stops you and issues you a ticket for speeding ten miles per hour over the speed limit. Why were you ticketed? You might say, "I received a ticket because I was speeding." This statement gives the facts as the law.

After you are ticketed, you continue driving your automobile on the highway at thirty miles per hour. In this section of the highway, the minimum speed is forty miles per hour and the maximum is fifty-five miles per hour. A police officer stops you and issues you a ticket for driving too slowly. Why were you ticketed by the police officer? If you use the same reason, "I received a ticket because I was speeding," the reason does not fit the facts. The facts are the same; you were traveling at thirty miles per hour.

The rule of law is used to state the answer. In the first case, you received a ticket because the statute (rule of law) set the speed limit for this particular section of road at twenty miles per hour, and you exceeded the limit. In the second case, you received a ticket because the statute (rule of law) set the minimum speed limit for this particular section of highway at forty miles per hour.

The statute determines the proper speed for different types of driving conditions. The statute reveals the rule of law indicating the particular speed for a specific section of roadway.

Selected World Wide Web Addresses

United States Government General Information

FirstGov, your first click to the U.S. government;
a complete web site to all government web sites.
http://www.firstgov.gov

Consumer Information Center
http://www.pueblo.gsa.gov

Declaration of Independence
http://lcweb2.loc.gov/const/declar.html
or
http://www.nara.gov/exhall/charters/charters.html

Federal Business Opportunities
http://www.fedbizopps.gov/

Federal Consumer Information Center,
National Contact Center (operates like a federal
Yellow Pages)
http://www.info.gov

Federal Consumer Information
http://www.pueblo.gsa.gov/money.htm

Federal Statistics
http://www.whitehouse.gov/WH/html
/govstats.html

Federalist Papers
http://lcweb2.loc.gov/const/fedquery.html

Government Information Locator Service
http://www.access.gpo.gov/su_docs/gils
/index.html

GovNews Project
http://govnews.org

Government Printing Office Online Databases
http://www.access.gpo.gov/su_docs/db2.html

National Archives and Records Administration (NARA)
http://www.nara.gov/

NARA, Exhibit Hall
http://www.nara.gov/exhall/exhibits.html

NARA, Office of the Federal Register
http://www.access.gpo.gov/nara/index.html

U.S. Constitution
http://lcweb2.loc.gov/const/constquery.html
or
http://www.nara.gov/exhall/charters/charters.html

U. S. Government Manual
http://www.access.gpo.gov/nara/nara001.html

U.S. Government Printing Office
http://www.access.gpo.gov

World Wide Web Virtual Library
http://www.law.indiana.edu/v-lib

United States Government Libraries

Library of Congress (LOC)
http://lcweb.loc.gov

LOC, online services
http://lcweb.loc.gov/homepage/online.html

LOC, searchable electronic global library
http://lcweb.loc.gov/homepage/lchp.html

LOC, U.S. Copyright Office
http://www.loc.gov/copyright/

Department of Energy Library
http://www.energy.gov/library/index.html

National Agricultural Library
http://www.nalusda.gov

National Library of Education
http://www.ed.gov/NLE

National Library for the Environmental
Protection Agency
http://www.epa.gov/natlibra/

National Library of Medicine
http://www.nlm.nih.gov
National Library Service for the Blind and Physically
Handicapped
http://lcweb.loc.gov/nls/nls.html
National Resources Library, Department of Interior
http://www.doi.gov/nrl/
National Transportation Library
http://www.bts.gov/NTL/
Newspaper and Current Periodical Reading Room
http://lcweb.loc.gov/global/ncp/ncp.html

Article I, Legislative Branch

General Accounting Office (GAO)
http://www.gao.gov
Library of Congress, THOMAS site, provides
legislative information on current and past bills.
http://thomas.loc.gov
United States Capitol
http://www.aoc.gov
U.S. Code of Federal Regulations
http://www.access.gpo.gov/nara/cfr
/cfr-table-search.html
U.S. Code
http://law2.house.gov/uscode.htm
or
http://www.law.cornell.edu/uscode/
U.S. Code, Table of Popular Names
http://www.law.cornell.edu/uscode/topn/
U.S. Electoral College
http://www.nara.gov/fedreg/elctcoll/index.html
U.S. House of Representatives
http://www.house.gov
U.S. House of Representatives, Office of the Clerk
http://clerkweb.house.gov/mbrcmtee
/mbrcmtee.htm
U.S. Senate
http://www.senate.gov
U.S. Senators
http://www.senate.gov/senators/index.cfm

Article II, Executive Branch and Executive Departments

Executive Office of the President
http://www.whitehouse.gov/eop_agencies.html
Department of Agriculture
http://www.usda.gov
Department of Commerce
http://www.doc.gov

Department of Defense
http://www.defenselink.mil
Department of Education
http://www.ed.gov
Department of Energy
http://www.doe.gov
Department of Health and Human Services
http://www.dhhs.gov
Department of Housing and Urban Development
http://www.hud.gov/
Department of the Interior
http://www.doi.gov
Department of Justice
http://www.usdoj.gov
Department of Labor
http://www.dol.gov
Department of State
http://www.state.gov
Department of Transportation
http://www.dot.gov
Department of Treasury
http://www.ustreas.gov
Department of Veterans Affairs
http://www.va.gov

Executive Office of the President

Council of Economic Advisers
http://www.whitehouse.gov/cea/index.html
Council on Environmental Quality
http://www.whitehouse.gov/ceq/index.html
Domestic Policy Council
http://www.whitehouse.gov/dpc/index.html
National Economic Council
http://www.whitehouse.gov/nec/index.html
National Security Council
http://www.whitehouse.gov/nsc/index.html
Office of Administration
http://www.whitehouse.gov/oa/index.html
Office of Management and Budget (OMB)
http://www.whitehouse.gov/omb/index.html
Office of National AIDS Policy
http://www.whitehouse.gov/onap/index.html
Office of National Drug Control Policy
http://www.whitehousedrugpolicy.gov/index.html
Office of Science and Technology Policy
http://www.ostp.gov/index.html
Office for Women's Initiative and Outreach
http://www.whitehouse.gov/women/index.html
President's Foreign Intelligence Advisory Board
http://www.whitehouse.gov/pfiab/index.html

United States Trade Representative
http://www.ustr.gov/
Vice President of the United States
http://www.whitehouse.gov/president/vpbio.html
White House
http://www.whitehouse.gov

Department of Agriculture

Welcome to the U.S. Department of Agriculture
http://www.usda.gov/welcome.html
Agricultural Marketing Services
http://www.ams.usda.gov/
Center for Nutrition Policy Promotion
http://www.usda.gov/cnpp/
Food and Nutrition Sources
http://www.fns.usda.gov/fns/
Food Safety and Inspection
http://www.fsis.usda.gov/index.htm
Foreign Agriculture Service
http://www.fas.usda.gov/
Forest Service
http://www.fs.fed.us
Natural Resources Conservation Service
http://www.ams.usda.gov/
Research, Education, and Economics Mission
http://www.reeusda.gov/ree/
Rural Development
http://www.rurdev.usda.gov/

Department of Commerce

Office of the Secretary of Commerce
http://osecnt13.osec.doc.gov/public.nsf/docs/os
Census Bureau
http://www.census.gov
Bureau of Economic Analysis
http://www.bea.doc.gov
Bureau of Export Administration
http://www.bxa.doc.gov/
Economic Development Administration
http://www.doc.gov/eda/
Economic Statistics Administration
http://www.esa.doc.gov/
International Trade Administration
http://www.ita.doc.gov
Minority Business Development Agency
http://www.mbda.gov/
National Environment Satellite, Data,
and Information Service
http://www.nesdis.noaa.gov/
National Oceanic and Atmospheric Administration
http://www.noaa.gov

National Telecommunications and Information
Administration
http://www.ntia.doc.gov/
National Weather Service
http://www.nws.noaa.gov
National Technical Information Service
http://www.fedworld.gov/ntis/ntishome.html
National Institute of Standards and Technology
http://www.nist.gov
Patent and Trademark Office
http://www.uspto.gov
Statistical Abstract
http://www.census.gov/stat_abstract
STAT–USA database
http://www.stat-usa.gov
Topographically Integrated Geographic Encoding and
Referencing System (TIGER)
http://tiger.census.gov
Technology Administration
http://www.ta.doc.gov/

Department of Defense

Office of the Secretary of Defense
http://www.defenselink.mil/pubs/almanac/osd.html
Armed Services Board of Contract Appeals
http:// www.law.gwu.edu/ASBCA/
Department of the Army (U.S. Army)
http://www.army.mil
U.S. Army, Judge Advocate General
http://www.goarmy.com/job/jag/jag.htm
Department of the Air Force (USAF)
http://www.af.mil/
USAF, Alternative Dispute Resolutions
http://www.adr.af.mil/
USAF, Judge Advocate General
http://hqja.jag.af.mil/
Department of the Navy (USN)
http://www.navy.mil
USN, Judge Advocate General Corps
http://www.jag.navy.mil/
U.S. Marine Corps
http://www.usmc.mil
Joint Service Schools
http://fedgate.org/fg_jss.htm
National Guard Bureau
http://www.ngb.dtic.mil/
Naval Observatory Master Clock
http://tycho.usno.navy.mil
Unified Combatant Commands
http://www.defenselink.mil/pubs/almanac
/unified.html

Department of Education

Office of the Secretary of Education
http://www.ed.gov/offices/gen_ed_org/mgmt.html
National Center for Education Statistics
http://nces.ed.gov/edstats/
Free Application for Federal Student Aid
http://www.ed.gov/offices/OPE/express.html
Office of Educational Technology
http://www.ed.gov/Technology/
Student Financial Assistance Programs
http://www.ed.gov/offices/OSFAP/Students/

Department of Energy

Secretary of Energy
http://www.energy.gov/aboutus/history/abraham.html
Alternative Fuels Data Center
http://www.afdc.doe.gov
Data and prices
http://www.energy.gov/dataandprices/index.html
Energy efficiency
http://www.energy.gov/efficiency/index.html
Energy Efficiency and Renewable Energy Network
http://www.eren.doe.gov
Energy Information Administration
http://www.eia.doe.gov
Energy sources and production
http://www.energy.gov/sources/index.html
Environmental quality
http://www.energy.gov/environ/index.html
Federal Energy Regulatory Commission
http://www.ferc.fed.us/
National security
http://www.energy.gov/security/index.html
Science and technology
http://www.energy.gov/scitech/index.html
U.S. Department of Energy Business Page
http://www.pr.doe.gov/prbus.html

Department of Health and Human Services

Office of the Secretary of the Department of Health and Human Services
http://www.hhs.gov/agencies/os.html
Centers for Disease Control
http://www.cdc.gov
Food and Drug Administration
http://www.fda.gov
Health Care Financing Administration
http://www.hcfa.gov/

Medicare
http://www.hcfa.gov/medicare/medicare.htm
Medicaid
http://www.hcfa.gov/medicaid/medicaid.htm
National Institutes of Health
http://www.nih.gov/
Office of Public Health and Science
http://phs.os.dhhs.gov/
Surgeon General
http://www.surgeongeneral.gov/sgoffice.htm

Department of Housing and Urban Development

Secretary of Housing and Urban Development
http://www.hud.gov/about/secretary
Buying a first home
http://www.hud.gov/buying/index.cfm
Office of Fair Housing and Equal Opportunity
http://www.hud.gov/fhe/fheo.html
Government National Mortgage Association (Ginniemae)
http://www.ginniemae.gov/
Marketplace
http://www.hud.gov/business.html

Department of Interior

Secretary of Interior
http://www.doi.gov/secretary/
Bureau of Indian Affairs
http://www.doi.gov/bureau-indian-affairs.html
Bureau of Land Management
http://www.blm.gov
Bureau of Reclamation
http://www.usbr.gov/main/index.html
Coastal Ecosystems
http://www.fws.gov/~cep/cepcode.html
Endangered Species Program
http://endangered.fws.gov/index.html
Fish and Wildlife Service
http://www.fws.gov/
Minerals Management Service
http://www.mms.gov/
National Wetlands Inventory
http://www.nwi.fws.gov
National Park Service
http://www.nps.gov
National Register of Historic Places
http://www.cr.nps.gov/nr/
National Wildlife Refuge System
http://bluegoose.arw.r9.fws.gov/

Office of Surface Mining
http://www.osmre.gov/
U.S. Geological Survey
http://www.usgs.gov
Water Resources of the United States
http://water.usgs.gov/

Department of Justice
Attorney General
http://www.usdoj.gov/ag/index.html
Antitrust Division
http://www.usdoj.gov/atr/index.html
Civil Division
http://www.usdoj.gov/civil/home.html
Civil Rights Division
http://www.usdoj.gov/crt/crt-home.html
Criminal Division
http://www.usdoj.gov/criminal
/criminal-home.html
Drug Enforcement Administration
http://www.usdoj.gov/dea/
Environment and Natural Resources Division
http://www.usdoj.gov/enrd/enrd-home.html
Federal Bureau of Investigation
http://www.fbi.gov
Federal Bureau of Prisons
http://www.bop.gov/
Foreign Claims Settlement Commission
http://www.usdoj.gov/fcsc/
Immigration and Naturalization Service
http://www.ins.usdoj.gov/graphics/index.htm
National Central Bureau of INTERPOL
http://www.usdoj.gov/usncb/
Tax Division
http://www.usdoj.gov/tax/
U.S. Attorneys
http://www.usdoj.gov/usao/eousa/usaos.html
U.S. Marshals Service
http://www.usdoj.gov/marshals/

Department of Labor
Secretary of Labor
http://www.dol.gov/dol/_sec/welcome.html
Bureau of Labor Statistics
http://stats.bls.gov
Employment Standards Administration
http://www.dol.gov/dol/esa/
Occupational Safety and Health Administration
http://www.osha.gov

Pension and Welfare Benefits Administration
http://www.dol.gov/dol/pwba
Veterans' Employment and Training Service
http://www.dol.gov/dol/vets/

Department of State
Secretary of State
http://www.state.gov/secretary
Bureau of Consular Affairs
http://travel.state.gov
Embassies and consulates worldwide
http://travel.state.gov/links.html
International Information Programs
http://usinfo.state.gov/
Passport Services and Information
http://www.travel.state.gov/passport_services.html
Travel warnings
http://www.travel.state.gov/travel_warnings.html

Department of Transportation
Secretary of Transportation
http://www.dot.gov/ost/
Bureau of Transportation Statistics
http://www.bts.gov
Federal Aviation Administration
http://www.faa.gov
Federal Highway Administration
http://www.fhwa.dot.gov/
Federal Motor Carrier Safety Administration
http://www.fmcsa.dot.gov/
Federal Railroad Administration
http://www.fra.dot.gov/site/index.htm
Federal Transit Administration
http://www.fta.dot.gov
Maritime Administration
http://www.marad.dot.gov/
National Highway Traffic Safety Administration
http://www.nhtsa.dot.gov
Saint Lawrence Seaway Development Corporation
http://www.dot.gov/slsdc/
Surface Transportation Board
http://www.stb.dot.gov/
U.S. Coast Guard http://www.uscg.mil/

Department of Treasury
Secretary of the Treasury
http://www.ustreas.gov/press/officers/
Bureau of Alcohol, Tobacco, and Firearms
http://www.atf.treas.gov/

Bureau of Engraving and Printing
http://www.bep.treas.gov/
Bureau of Public Debt
http://www.publicdebt.treas.gov/
Electronic Services
http://www.irs.ustreas.gov/prod/elec_svs
/index.html
Federal Law Enforcement Training Center
http://www.ustreas.gov/fletc/
Financial Management Service
http://www.fms.treas.gov/
Internal Revenue Service (IRS)
http://www.irs.ustreas.gov
IRS, tax questions
http://www.irs.ustreas.gov/prod/ind_info
/tax_trails/index.html
Office of the Comptroller of the Currency
http://www.occ.treas.gov/
Office of Thrift Supervision
http://www.ots.treas.gov/
U.S. Mint
http://www.usmint.gov
U.S. Customs Service
http://www.customs.ustreas.gov/
U.S. Secret Service
http://www.ustreas.gov/usss/

Department of Veterans Administration

Secretary of the Veterans Administration
http://www.va.gov/opa/bios/index.htm
Education Benefits (G.I. Bill)
http://www.gibill.va.gov/
Home Loan Guaranty Services
http://www.homeloans.va.gov/
National Cemetery Administration
http://www.cem.va.gov/
Veteran Data and Information
http://www.va.gov/vetdata/
Veterans Benefits Administration
http://www.vba.va.gov/
Veterans Health Administration
http://www.va.gov/About_VA/Orgs/vha/
Vocational Rehabilitation and Employment Services
http://www.vba.va.gov/bln/vre/vbsvre.htm

Article III, Judicial Branch

Federal Judicial Center
http://www.fjc.gov

Federal Judiciary home page
http://www.uscourts.gov/
Judiciary Now: The Latest News and Features
http://www.uscourts.gov/judnow/index.html
Federal Judiciary home page links
http://www.uscourts.gov/links.html
Supreme Court of the United States
http://www.supremecourtus.gov/
First Circuit Court of Appeals
http://www.uscourts.gov/allinks.html#all
Second Circuit Court of Appeals
http://www.uscourts.gov/allinks.html#all
Third Circuit Court of Appeals
http://www.uscourts.gov/allinks.html#all
Fourth Circuit Court of Appeals
http://www.uscourts.gov/allinks.html#all
Fifth Circuit Court of Appeals
http://www.uscourts.gov/allinks.html#all
Sixth Circuit Court of Appeals
http://www.uscourts.gov/allinks.html#all
Seventh Circuit Court of Appeals
http://www.uscourts.gov/allinks.html#all
Eighth Circuit Court of Appeals
http://www.uscourts.gov/allinks.html#all
Ninth Circuit Court of Appeals
http://www.uscourts.gov/allinks.html#all
Tenth Circuit Court of Appeals
http://www.uscourts.gov/allinks.html#all
Eleventh Circuit Court of Appeals
http://www.uscourts.gov/allinks.html#all
D.C. Circuit Court of Appeals
http://www.uscourts.gov/allinks.html#all
U.S. Court of Appeals for the Federal Circuit
http://www.uscourts.gov/allinks.html#all
U.S. Court of International Trade
http://www.uscit.gov/
U.S. Court of Appeals for the Armed Forces
http://www.armfor.uscourts.gov/
U.S. Court of Federal Claims
http://www.law.gwu.edu/fedcl/
United States Sentencing Commission
http://www.ussc.gov/
U.S. Tax Court
http://www.ustaxcourt.gov/
American Judicature Society
http://www.ajs.org/

United States Government Independent Establishments, Government Corporations, and Quasi-Official Agencies

Advisory Council on Historic Preservation
http://www.achp.gov/

African Development Foundation
http://www.adf.gov/

Broadcasting Board of Governors
http://www.ibb.gov/bbg/

Central Intelligence Agency
http://www.odci.gov/

United States Commission on Civil Rights
http://www.usccr.gov/index.html

Commodity Futures Trading Commission
http://www.cftc.gov/

Consumer Product Safety Commission
http://www.cpsc.gov/

Corporation for National Service
http://www.cns.gov/

Corporation for Public Broadcasting
http://www.cpb.org

Defense Nuclear Facilities Safety Board
http://www.dnfsb.gov/

Environmental Protection Agency (EPA)
http://www.epa.gov/

EPA, air
http://www.epa.gov/ebtpages/air.html

EPA, air and radiation
http://www.epa.gov/oar/oarhome.html

EPA, cleanup
http://www.epa.gov/ebtpages/cleanup.html

EPA, compliance and enforcement
http://www.epa.gov/ebtpages
/complianceenforcement.html

EPA, economics
http://www.epa.gov/ebtpages/economics.html

EPA, ecosystems
http://www.epa.gov/ebtpages/ecosystems.html

EPA, emergencies
http://www.epa.gov/ebtpages/emergencies.html

EPA, environmental management
http://www.epa.gov/ebtpages
/environmentalmanagement.html

EPA, human health
http://www.epa.gov/ebtpages/humanhealth.html

EPA, industry
http://www.epa.gov/ebtpages/industry.html

EPA, information sources
http://www.epa.gov/epahome/resource.htm

EPA, pesticides
http://www.epa.gov/ebtpages/pesticides.html

EPA, pollutants and toxics
http://www.epa.gov/ebtpages/pollutants.html

EPA, pollution prevention
http://www.epa.gov/ebtpages
/pollutionprevention.html

EPA, research
http://www.epa.gov/ebtpages/research.html

EPA, treatment and control
http://www.epa.gov/ebtpages/treatmentcontrol.html

EPA, wastes
http://www.epa.gov/ebtpages/wastes.html

EPA, water
http://www.epa.gov/ebtpages/water.html

Equal Employment Opportunity Commission
http://www.eeoc.gov/

Export-Import Bank
http://www.exim.gov/

Federal National Mortgage Association (Fannie Mae)
http://www.fanniemae.com/

Farm Credit Administration
http://www.fca.gov/

Federal Communications Commission
http://www.fcc.gov/

Federal Deposit Insurance Corporation
http://www.fdic.gov/

Federal Election Commission
http://www.fec.gov/

Federal Emergency Management Agency (FEMA)
http://www.fema.gov/

FEMA, National Flood Insurance Program
http://www.fema.gov/nfip/

FEMA, Project Impact
http://www.fema.gov/impact/

FEMA, U.S. Fire Administration
http://www.usfa.fema.gov/

Federal Housing Finance Board
http://www.fhfb.gov/

Federal Labor Relations Authority
http://www.flra.gov/index.html

Federal Maritime Commission
http://www.fmc.gov/

Federal Mediation and Conciliation Service
http://www.fmcs.gov/

Federal Mine Safety and Health Administration
http://www.msha.gov/

Federal Retirement Thrift Investment Board
http://www.frtib.gov/

Federal Trade Commission
http://www.ftc.gov/

Freddie Mac
http://www.freddiemac.com/
General Services Administration
http://www.gsa.gov/
Government asset sales
http://www.financenet.gov/financenet/sales
/salefed.htm
Inter-American Foundation
http://www.iaf.gov/
International Broadcasting Bureau
http://www.ibb.gov/
Legal Services Corporation
http://www.lsc.gov/
Merit Systems Protection Board
http://www.mspb.gov/
National Aeronautics and Space Administration
http://www.nasa.gov/
National Capital Planning Commission
http://www.ncpc.gov/
National Credit Union Administration
http://www.ncua.gov/
National Endowment for the Arts
http://arts.endow.gov/
National Endowment for the Humanities
http://www.neh.fed.us/
National Labor Relations Board
http://www.nlrb.gov/
National Mediation Board
http://www.nmb.gov/
National Railroad Passenger Corporation (AMTRAK)
http://www.nmb.gov/
National Security Agency
http://www.nsa.gov/
National Science Foundation
http://www.nsf.gov/
National Transportation Safety Board
http://www.ntsb.gov/
Nuclear Regulatory Commission
http://www.nrc.gov/
Occupational Safety and Health Review Commission
http://www.oshrc.gov/index.html
Office of Federal Housing Enterprise Oversight
http://www.ofheo.gov/
Office of Government Ethics
http://www.usoge.gov/
Office of Personnel Management
http://www.opm.gov/
Office of Special Counsel
http://www.osc.gov/
Overseas Private Investment Corporation
http://www.opic.gov/

Peace Corps
http://www.peacecorps.gov/
Pension Benefit Guaranty Corporation
http://www.pbgc.gov/
Postal Rate Commission
http://www.prc.gov/main.asp
Railroad Retirement Board
http://www.rrb.gov/
Security and Exchange Commission (SEC)
http://www.sec.gov/
SEC, EDGAR database
http://www.sec.gov/edgarhp.htm
Selective Service System
http://www.sss.gov/
Small Business Administration (SBA)
http://www.sba.gov
SBA, financing your business
http://www.sba.gov/financing/
SBA, expanding your business
http://www.sba.gov/expanding/
SBA, regional offices
http://www.sbaonline.sba.gov/regions
/regionmap.html
SBA hot links
http://www.sba.gov/hotlist
Smithsonian Institution
http://www.si.edu/
Social Security Administration (SSA)
http://www.ssa.gov/
SSA, online site map
http://www.ssa.gov/sitemap.htm
Social Security Handbook
http://www.ssa.gov/OP_Home/handbook
/ssa-hbk.htm
State Justice Institute
http://www.statejustice.org/
Tennessee Valley Authority
http://www.tva.gov/
Trade and Development Agency
http://www.tda.gov/
United States Chemical Safety and Hazard
Investigation Board
http://www.chemsafety.gov/
United States Commission on Civil Rights
http://www.usccr.gov/
United States Agency for International Development
http://www.usaid.gov/
United States Institute of Peace
http://www.usip.org/
United States International Information Program
http://usinfo.state.gov/

United States International Trade Commission
http://www.usitc.gov/
United States Postal Service
http://www.usps.gov/

Federal Reserve System

Federal Reserve Board
http://www.federalreserve.gov/
Twelve federal reserve districts
http://www.clev.frb.org/fedlinks.htm
Federal Reserve Bank of Atlanta
http://www.frbatlanta.org
Federal Reserve Bank of Boston
http://www.bos.frb.org
Federal Reserve Bank of Chicago
http://www.frbchi.org
Federal Reserve Bank of Cleveland
http://www.clev.frb.org
Federal Reserve Bank of Dallas
http://www.dallsfed.org
Federal Reserve Bank of Kansas City
http://www.kc.frb.org/
Federal Reserve Bank of Minneapolis
http://woodrow.mpls.frb.fed.us
Federal Reserve Bank of New York
http://www.ny.frb.org
Federal Reserve Bank of Philadelphia
http://www.libertynet.com/rol/default.asp
Federal Reserve Bank of Richmond
http://www.rich.frb.org/
Federal Reserve Bank of St. Louis
http://www.stls.frb.org
Federal Reserve Bank of San Francisco
http://www.frbsf.org

Presidential Libraries

National Archives and Records, presidential gifts
http://www.nara.gov/exhall/treasures/giftmain.html
Overall presidential web site
http://www.ibiblio.org/lia/president/
Overall presidential libraries web site
http://www.ibiblio.org/lia/president/pres-home.html
Overall all presidential web sites
http://www.ibiblio.org/lia/president/pressites/
Overall first ladies web sites
http://www.ibiblio.org/lia/president/FirstLadies/
George Bush (1989-1993)
http://bushlibrary.tamu.edu/

Jimmy Carter (1977-1981)
http://carterlibrary.galileo.peachnet.edu/
Dwight D. Eisenhower (1953-1961)
http://www.eisenhower.utexas.edu/ddehp.htm
Gerald R. Ford (1974-1977)
http://www.lbjlib.utexas.edu/ford/
Rutherford B. Hayes (1877-1881)
http://www.rbhayes.org/
Herbert Hoover (1929-1933)
http://www.hoover.nara.gov/
Lyndon Baines Johnson (1963-1969)
http://www.lbjlib.utexas.edu/
John Fitzgerald Kennedy (1961-1963)
http://www.cs.umb.edu/jfklibrary/index.htm
William McKinley (1897-1901)
http://www.mckinley.lib.oh.us/
Richard Nixon (1969-1974)
http://www.nixonfoundation.org/
Ronald W. Reagan (1981-1989)
http://www.reaganlibrary.net/
Franklin D. Roosevelt (1933-1945)
http://www.fdrlibrary.marist.edu/
Harry S Truman (1945-1953)
http://www.trumanlibrary.org/

Media Web Sites

ABC Network, an over-the-air general television network
http://abc.go.com/
Business Week
http://www.businessweek.com/
CBS Network, an over-the-air general television network
http://www.cbs.com/
CNBC (Cable NBC), a cable network that focuses on business news
http://www.cnbc.com/
CNN, a cable 24/7 news network
http://www.cnn.com/
C-Span (Cable Satellite Public Affairs Network); broadcasts live sessions of the U.S. House of Representatives, U.S. Senate, and other meetings of public interest; often mistaken for a government-owned network, it is in fact a private network owned and operated by a consortium of the cable networks
http://www.c-span.org
The Economist
http://www.economist.com
Financial Times
http://news.ft.com/ft/

Fortune
http://www.fortune.com/fortune/
Forbes
http://www.forbes.com/
International Herald Tribune
http://www.iht.com/frontpage.html
MSNBC, a subsidiary of General Electric Company and Microsoft
http://www.msnbc.com/
NBC Internet (NBCi), a subsidiary of General Electric Company
http://home.nbci.com
Newseum
http://www.newseum.org
Wall Street Journal
http://public.wsj.com/home.html

Legal, Business, Political, and Other Web Sites

A law.com Company
http://www.law.com/
AllBusiness.com
http://www.allbusiness.com
American Bankruptcy Institute
http://www.abiworld.org
American Bar Association
http://www.abanet.org
American Civil Liberties Union, workers' rights
http://www.aclu.org/issues/worker/hmwr.html
Association of Trial Lawyers of America
http://www.ATLA.org
Atlas of U.S. presidential elections
http://www.uselectionatlas.org
Better Business Bureau
http://www.bbb.org
businessCreditUSA
http://businesscreditusa.com/
Copyright & Fair Use, Stanford University Library
http://fairuse.stanford.edu/
Electric Frontier Foundation, privacy issues
http://www.eff.org
Electronic Privacy Information
http://www.epic.org
Environmental Defense
http://www.edf.org
Equal Employment Advisory Council
http://www.eeac.org

Executive Planet.com
http://www.executiveplanet.com/
Government Guide
http://www.governmentguide.com
Government Online
http://www.govspot.com/
Hoovers Online, The Business Network
http://www.hoovers.com/
Internet Legal Resources Guide
http://www.ilrg.com
Investment Company Institute
http://www.ici.org
Justice on Campus
http://joc.mit.edu
Jurist, The Legal Education Network
http://www.jurist.law.pitt.edu/
LawOffice.com
http://www.lawoffice.com
'Lectric Law Library, irreverent look at the law with serious law pages
http://www.lectlaw.com
Market Guide, Inc.
http://www.marketguide.com
National Academy of Elder Law Attorneys, Inc.
http://www.naela.com/
National Academy of Sciences
http://www.nas.edu
National Technology Transfer Center
http://www.nttc.edu
Natural Resources Defense Council
http://www.nrdc.org
9to5 National Association of Working Women
http://www.9to5.org
Nolo
http://www.nolo.com
Politics.com
http://www.politics.com
Red Herring
http://www.redherring.com
Rhodes College, Political Science Resources, The Burrow Library
http://www.rhodes.edu/pshtmls/psnet.html
Sierra Club
http://www.sierraclub.org
Society for Human Resource Management
http://www.shrm.org
Stanford University
http://www.stanford.edu/
Transparency International
http://www.transparency.org/

U.S. Army Corps of Engineers
http://www.usace.army.mil/
U.S. Business Advisor, Small Business Administration
http://www.business.gov/
West Group
http://www.westgroup.com/
West Group, law schools
http://lawschool.westlaw.com/
Work & Woman
http://www.worknwoman.com
Yahoo, government and law web site
http://dir.yahoo.com/government/law/

Legal Search Engines, Directories, and Indexes

AALLNET, Association of Law Libraries
http://www.aallnet.org/index.asp
American Law Sources On-line (ALSO)
http://www.lawsource.com/also/
CataLaw, meta-index of law and government
http://www.catalaw.com
Center for Information Law and Policy
http://www.cilp.org
Chicago Kent Law Links, index of law-related
meta-indexes
http://www.kentlaw.edu/clc/lrs/lawlinks
/meta.shtml
CNN Law Section
http://www.cnn.com/law
Cornell Legal Information Institute
http://www.law.cornell.edu/
Court TV Law Center
http://www.courttv.com
FindLaw
http://www.findlaw.com
Georgetown University Law Center
http://www.ll.georgetown.edu/
Great American Web Site
http://www.uncle-sam.com
Indiana University College of Law Library,
new law-related sites
http://www.law.indiana.edu/v-lib/

Law.com
http://www.law.com
Martindale Lawyer Locator
http://www.martindale.com/

International Law Web Sites

Australasian Legal Information Institute, Australian law
http://austlii.law.uts.edu.au
BUBL Information Service, British law sources
http://www.bubl.ac.uk
Council of Europe, European treaties
http://conventions.coe.int
Directorate on Competition of the Commission
of the European Union
http://www.europa.eu.int/comm/competition/
European Union
http://www.europa.eu.int
European Union, European Union treaties
http://www.europa.eu.int/abc/obj/treaties/en
/entoc.htm
ForInt-Law, Washburn University School of Law Library,
international and multilateral treaties
http://www.washlaw.edu/forint/alpha/t/treaties.htm
Legal research on international law issues
http://www.lib.uchicago.edu/~llou/forintlaw.html
National Law Center for Inter-American Free Trade
http://www.natlaw.com/index.htm
Organization of American States
http://www.oas.org
Organization of American States, Foreign Trade
Information System
http://www.sice.oas.org
United Nations
http://www.un.org
United Nations, web site locator
http://www.unsystem.org
U.S. treaties
http://www.senate.gov/activities/treaties.html
World Intellectual Property Organization
http://www.wipo.org
World Trade Organization
http://www.wto.org

Spanish Equivalents for Important Legal Terms in English

Abandoned property: bienes abandonados

Acceptance: aceptación; consentimiento; acuerdo

Acceptor: aceptante

Accession: toma de posesión; aumento; accesión

Accommodation indorser: avalista de favor

Accommodation party: firmante de favor

Accord: acuerdo; convenio; arregio

Accord and satisfaction: transacción ejecutada

Act of state doctrine: doctrina de acto de gobierno

Administrative law: derecho administrativo

Administrative process: procedimiento o metódo administrativo

Administrator (-trix): administrador (-a)

Adverse possession: posesión de hecho susceptible de proscripción adquisitiva

Affirmative action: acción afirmativa

Affirmative defense: defensa afirmativa

After-acquired property: bienes adquiridos con posterioridad a un hecho dado

Agency: mandato; agencia

Agent: mandatorio; agente; representante

Agreement: convenio; acuerdo; contrato

Alien corporation: empresa extranjera

Allonge: hojas adicionales de endosos

Answer: contestación de la demande; alegato

Anticipatory breach, or anticipatory repudiation: anuncio previo de las partes de su imposibilidad de cumplir con el contrato

Appeal: apelación; recurso de apelación

Appellate jurisdiction: jurisdicción de apelaciones

Appraisal right: derecho de valuación

Arbitration: arbitraje

Arson: incendio intencional

Articles of partnership: contrato social

Artisan's lien: derecho de retención que ejerce al artesano

Assault: asalto; ataque; agresión

Assignment of rights: transmisión; transferencia; cesión

Assumption of risk: no resarcimiento por exposición voluntaria al peligro

Attachment: auto judicial que autoriza el embargo; embargo

Bailee: depositario

Bailment: depósito; constitución en depósito

Bailor: depositante

Bankruptcy trustee: síndico de la quiebra

Battery: agresión; física

Bearer: portador; tenedor

Bearer instrument: documento al portador

Bequest or legacy: legado (de bienes muebles)

Bilateral contract: contrato bilateral

Bill of lading: conocimiento de embarque; carta de porte

Bill of Rights: declaración de derechos

Binder: póliza de seguro provisoria; recibo de pago a cuenta del precio

Blank indorsement: endoso en blanco

Blue sky laws: leyes reguladoras del comercio bursátil

Bond: título de crédito; garantía; caución

Bond indenture: contrato de emisión de bonos; contrato del empréstito

Breach of contract: incumplimiento de contrato

Brief: escrito; resumen; informe

Burglary: violación de domicilio
Business judgment rule: regla de juicio comercial
Business tort: agravio comercial

Case law: ley de casos; derecho casuístico
Cashier's check: cheque de caja
Causation in fact: causalidad en realidad
Cease-and-desist order: orden para cesar y desistir
Certificate of deposit: certificado de depósito
Certified check: cheque certificado
Charitable trust: fideicomiso para fines benéficos
Chattel: bien mueble
Check: cheque
Civil law: derecho civil
Close corporation: sociedad de un solo accionista o de un grupo restringido de accionistas
Closed shop: taller agremiado (emplea solamente a miembros de un gremio)
Closing argument: argumento al final
Codicil: codicilo
Collateral: garantía; bien objeto de la garantía real
Comity: cortesía; cortesía entre naciones
Commercial paper: instrumentos negociables; documentos a valores commerciales
Common law: derecho consuetudinario; derecho común; ley común
Common stock: acción ordinaria
Comparative negligence: negligencia comparada
Compensatory damages: daños y perjuicios reales o compensatorios
Concurrent conditions: condiciones concurrentes
Concurrent estates: condominio
Concurrent jurisdiction: competencia concurrente de varios tribunales para entender en una misma causa
Concurring opinion: opinión concurrente
Condition: condición
Condition precedent: condición suspensiva
Condition subsequent: condición resolutoria
Confiscation: confiscación
Confusion: confusión; fusión
Conglomerate merger: fusión de firmas que operan en distintos mercados
Consent decree: acuerdo entre las partes aprobado por un tribunal
Consequential damages: daños y perjuicios indirectos
Consideration: consideración; motivo; contraprestación
Consolidation: consolidación

Constructive delivery: entrega simbólica
Constructive trust: fideicomiso creado por aplicación de la ley
Consumer protection law: ley para proteger el consumidor
Contract: contrato
Contracts under seal: contrato formal o sellado
Contributory negligence: negligencia de la parte actora
Conversion: usurpación; conversión de valores
Copyright: derecho de autor
Corporation: sociedad anómina; corporación; persona juridica
Co-sureties: cogarantes
Counterclaim, or cross-complaint: reconvención; contrademanda
Counteroffer: contraoferta
Course of dealing: curso de transacciones
Course of performance: curso de cumplimiento
Covenant: pacto; garantía; contrato
Covenant not to sue: pacto or contrato a no demandar
Covenant of quiet enjoyment: garantía del uso y goce pacífico del inmueble
Creditors' composition agreement: concordato preventivo
Crime: crimen; delito; contravención
Criminal law: derecho penal
Cross-examination: contrainterrogatorio
Cure: cura; cuidado; derecho de remediar un vicio contractual
Customs receipts: recibos de derechos aduaneros

Damages: daños; indemnización por daños y perjuicios
Debit card: tarjeta de débito
Debtor: deudor
Debt securities: seguridades de deuda
Deceptive advertising: publicidad engañosa
Deed: escritura; título; acta translativa de domino
Defamation: difamación
Delegation of duties: delegación de obligaciones
Demand deposit: depósito a la vista
Depositions: declaración de un testigo fuera del tribunal
Derivative suit: acción judicial entablada por un accionista en nombre de la sociedad
Devise: legado; deposición testamentaria (bienes inmuebles)

Directed verdict: veredicto según orden del juez y sin participación activa del jurado

Direct examination: interrogatorio directo; primer interrogatorio

Disaffirmance: repudiación; renuncia; anulación

Discharge: descargo; liberación; cumplimiento

Disclosed principal: mandante revelado

Discovery: descubrimiento; producción de la prueba

Dissenting opinion: opinión disidente

Dissolution: disolución; terminación

Diversity of citizenship: competencia de los tribunales federales para entender en causas cuyas partes intervinientes son cuidadanos de distintos estados

Divestiture: extinción premature de derechos reales

Dividend: dividendo

Docket: orden del día; lista de causas pendientes

Domestic corporation: sociedad local

Draft: orden de pago; letra de cambio

Drawee: girado; beneficiario

Drawer: librador

Duress: coacción; violencia

Easement: servidumbre

Embezzlement: desfalco; malversación

Eminent domain: poder de expropiación

Employment discrimination: discriminación en el empleo

Entrepreneur: empresario

Environmental law: ley ambiental

Equal dignity rule: regla de dignidad egual

Equity security: tipo de participación en una sociedad

Estate: propiedad; patrimonio; derecho

Estop: impedir; prevenir

Ethical issue: cuestión ética

Exclusive jurisdiction: competencia exclusiva

Exculpatory clause: cláusula eximente

Executed contract: contrato ejecutado

Execution: ejecución; cumplimiento

Executor (-trix): albacea

Executory contract: contrato aún no completamente consumado

Executory interest: derecho futuro

Express contract: contrato expreso

Expropriation: expropriación

Federal question: caso federal

Fee simple: pleno dominio; dominio absoluto

Fee simple absolute: dominio absoluto

Fee simple defeasible: dominio sujeta a una condición resolutoria

Felony: crimen; delito grave

Fictitious payee: beneficiario ficticio

Fiduciary: fiduciaro

Firm offer: oferta en firme

Fixture: inmueble por destino, incorporación a anexación

Floating lien: gravamen continuado

Foreign corporation: sociedad extranjera; U.S. sociedad constituída en otro estado

Forgery: falso; falsificación

Formal contract: contrato formal

Franchise: privilegio; franquicia; concesión

Franchisee: persona que recibe una concesión

Franchisor: persona que vende una concesión

Fraud: fraude; dolo; engaño

Future estate: bien futuro

Garnishment: embargo de derechos

General partner: socio comanditario

General warranty deed: escritura translativa de domino con garantía de título

Gift: donación

Gift *causa mortis*: donación por causa de muerte

Gift *inter vivos*: donación entre vivos

Good faith: buena fe

Good-faith purchaser: comprador de buena fe

Holder: tenedor por contraprestación

Holder-in-due course: tenedor legítimo

Holographic will: testamento ológrafico

Homestead exemption laws: leyes que exceptúan las casas de familia de ejecución por duedas generales

Horizontal merger: fusión horizontal

Identification: identificación

Implied-in-fact contract: contrato implícito en realidad

Implied warranty: garantía implícita

Implied warranty of merchantability: garantía implícita de vendibilidad

Impossibility of performance: imposibilidad de cumplir un contrato

Impostor: imposter

Incidental beneficiary: beneficiario incidental; beneficiario secundario

Incidental damages: daños incidentales

Indictment: auto de acusación; acusación

Indorsee: endorsatario
Indorsement: endoso
Indorser: endosante
Informal contract: contrato no formal; contrato verbal
Information: acusación hecha por el ministerio público
Injunction: mandamiento; orden de no innovar
Innkeeper's lien: derecho de retención que ejerce el posadero
Installment contract: contrato de pago en cuotas
Insurable interest: interés asegurable
Intended beneficiary: beneficiario destinado
Intentional tort: agravio; cuasi-delito intencional
International law: derecho internacional
Interrogatories: preguntas escritas sometidas por una parte a la otra o a un testigo
Inter vivos **trust:** fideicomiso entre vivos
Intestacy laws: leyes de la condición de morir intestado
Intestate: intestado
Investment company: compañia de inversiones
Issue: emisión

Joint tenancy: derechos conjuntos en un bien inmueble
Joint tenancy with right of survivorship: derechos conjuntos en un bien inmueble en favor del beneficiario sobreviviente
Judgment n.o.v.: juicio no obstante veredicto
Judgment rate of interest: interés de juicio
Judicial process: acto de procedimiento; proceso jurídico
Judicial review: revisión judicial
Jurisdiction: jurisdicción

Larceny: robo; hurto
Law: derecho; ley; jurisprudencia
Lease: contrato de locación; contrato de alquiler
Leasehold estate: bienes forales
Legal rate of interest: interés legal
Legatee: legatario
Less-than-freehold estate: menos de derecho de dominio absoluto
Letter of credit: carta de crédito
Levy: embargo; comiso
Libel: libelo; difamación escrita
Life estate: usufructo
Limited partner: comanditario

Limited partnership: sociedad en comandita
Liquidation: liquidación; realización
Lost property: objetos perdidos

Majority opinion: opinión de la mayoría
Maker: persona que realiza u ordena; librador
Mechanic's lien: gravamen de constructor
Mediation: mediación; intervención
Merger: fusión
Mirror-image rule: fallo de reflejo
Misdemeanor: infracción; contravención
Mislaid property: bienes extraviados
Mitigation of damages: reducción de daños
Moral hazard: riesgo moral
Mortgage: hypoteca
Motion to dismiss, or demurrer: excepción parentoria
Municipal law: derecho municipal
Mutual fund: fondo mutual

Negotiable instrument: instrumento negociable
Negotiation: negociación
Nominal damages: daños y perjuicios nominales
Novation: novación
Nuncupative will: testamento nuncupativo

Objective theory of contracts: teoria objetiva de contratos
Offer: oferta
Offeree: persona que recibe una oferta
Offeror: oferente
Order paper: instrumento o documento a la orden
Original jurisdiction: jurisdicción de primera instancia
Output contract: contrato de producción

Parol evidence rule: regla relativa a la prueba oral
Partially disclosed principal: mandante revelado en parte
Partnership: sociedad colectiva; asociación; asociación de participación
Past consideration: causa o contraprestación anterior
Patent: patente; privilegio
Pattern or practice: muestra o práctica
Payee: beneficiario de un pago
Penalty: pena; penalidad
Per capita: por cabeza
Perfection: perfeción
Performance: cumplimiento; ejecución

Personal defenses: excepciones personales

Personal property: bienes muebles

Per stirpes: por estirpe

Plea bargaining: regateo por un alegato

Pleadings: alegatos

Pledge: prenda

Police powers: poders de policia y de prevención del crimen

Policy: póliza

Positive law: derecho positivo; ley positiva

Possibility of reverter: posibilidad de reversión

Precedent: precedente

Preemptive right: derecho de prelación

Preferred stock: acciones preferidas

Premium: recompensa; prima

Presentment warranty: garantía de presentación

Price discrimination: discriminación en los precios

Principal: mandante; principal

Privity: nexo jurídico

Privity of contract: relación contractual

Probable cause: causa probable

Probate: verificación; verificación del testamento

Probate court: tribunal de sucesiones y tutelas

Proceeds: resultados; ingresos

Profit: beneficio; utilidad; lucro

Promise: promesa

Promisee: beneficiario de una promesa

Promisor: promtente

Promissory estoppel: impedimento promisorio

Promissory note: pagaré; nota de pago

Promoter: promotor; fundador

Proximate cause: causa immediata o próxima

Proxy: apoderado; poder

Punitive, or exemplary, damages: daños y perjuicios punitivos o ejemplares

Qualified indorsement: endoso con reservas

Quasi-contract: contrato tácito o implícito

Quit-claim deed: acto de transferencia de una propiedad por finiquito, pero sin ninguna garantía sobre la validez del título transferido

Ratification: ratificación

Real defenses: defensas legitimas o legales

Real property: bienes immuebles

Reasonable doubt: duda razonable

Rebuttal: refutación

Recognizance: promesa; compromiso; reconocimiento

Recording statutes: leyes estatales sobre registros oficiales

Redress: reparación

Reformation: rectificación; reforma; corrección

Rejoinder: dúplica; contrarréplica

Release: liberación; renuncia a un derecho

Remainder: substitución; reversión

Remedy: recurso; remedio; reparación

Replevin: acción reivindicatoria; reivindicación

Reply: réplica

Requirements contract: contrato de suministro

Rescission: rescisión

Res judicata: cosa juzgada; res judicata

Respondeat superior: responsabilidad del mandante o del maestro

Restitution: restitución

Restrictive indorsement: endoso restrictivo

Resulting trust: fideicomiso implícito

Reversion: reversión; sustitución

Revocation: revocación; derogación

Right of contribution: derecho de contribución

Right of reimbursement: derecho de reembolso

Right of subrogation: derecho de subrogación

Right-to-work law: ley de libertad de trabajo

Robbery: robo

Rule 10b-5: Regla 10b-5

Sale: venta; contrato de compreventa

Sale on approval: venta a ensayo; enta sujeta a la aprobación del comprador

Sale or return: venta con derecho de devolución

Sales contract: contrato de compraventa; boleto de compraventa

Satisfaction: satisfacción; pago

Scienter: a sabiendas

S corporation: S corporación

Secured party: acreedor garantizado

Secured transaction: transacción garantizada

Securities: volares; titulos; seguridades

Security agreement: convenio de seguridad

Security interest: interés en un bien dado en garantía que permite a quien lo detenta venderlo en caso de incumplimiento

Service mark: marca de identificación de servicios

Signature: firma; rúbrica

Slander: difamación oral; calumnia

Sovereign immunity: immunidad soberana

Special indorsement: endoso especial; endoso a la orden de una person en particular

Specific performance: ejecución precisa, según los términos del contrato

Spendthrift trust: fideicomiso para pródigos

Stale check: cheque vencido

Stare decisis: acatar las decisiones, observar los precedentes

State exemption laws: leyes que exceptúan los estados

Statutory law: derecho estatutario; derecho legislado; derecho escrito

Stock: acciones

Stock split: fraccionamiento de acciones

Stock warrant: certificado para la compra de acciones

Stop-payment order: orden de suspensión del pago de un cheque dada por el librador del mismo

Strict liability: responsabilidad uncondicional

Summary judgment: fallo sumario

Tangible property: bienes corpóreos

Tenancy at will: inguilino por tiempo indeterminado (según la voluntad del propietario)

Tenancy by sufferance: posesión por tolerancia

Tenancy by the entirety: locación conyugal conjunta

Tenancy for years: inguilino por un término fijo

Tenancy in common: specie de copropiedad indivisa

Tender: oferta de pago; oferta de ejecución

Testamentary trust: fideicomiso testamentario

Testator (-trix): testador (-a)

Third-party-beneficiary contract: contrato para el beneficio del tercero-beneficiario

Tort: agravio; cuasi-delito

Totten trust: fideicomiso creado por un depósito bancario

Trade acceptance: letra de cambio aceptada

Trademark: marca registrada

Trade name: nombre comercial; razón social

Traveler's check: cheque del viajero

Trespass to land: ingreso no authorizado a las tierras de otro

Trespass to personalty: violación de los derechos posesorios de un tercero con respecto a bienes muebles

Trust: fideicomiso; trust

Ultra vires: ultra vires; fuera de la facultad (de una sociedad anónima)

Unanimous opinion: opinión unámine

Unconscionable contract or clause: contrato leonino; cláusula leonino

Underwriter: subscriptor; asegurador

Unenforceable contract: contrato que no se puede hacer cumplir

Unilateral contract: contrato unilateral

Union shop: taller agremiado; empresa en la que todos los empleados son miembros del gremio o sindicato

Usage of trade: uso comercial

Usury: usura

Valid contract: contrato válido

Venue: lugar; sede del proceso

Vertical merger: fusión vertical de empresas

Voidable contract: contrato anulable

Void contract: contato nulo; contrato inválido, sin fuerza legal

Voir dire: examen preliminar de un testigo a jurado por el tribunal para determinar su competencia

Voting trust: fideicomiso para ejercer el derecho de voto

Waiver: renuncia; abandono

Warranty of habitability: garantía de habitabilidad

Warranty of possession: garantía de posesión

Watered stock: acciones diluídos; capital inflado

White-collar crime: crimen administrativo

Writ of attachment: mandamiento de ejecución; mandamiento de embargo

Writ of *certiorari*: auto de avocación; auto de certiorari

Writ of execution: auto ejecutivo; mandamiento de ejecutión

Writ of mandamus: auto de mandamus; mandamiento; orden judicial

Glossary

A

abandoned property Property discarded by the true owner who has no intention of reclaiming it.

absolute privilege Applies to judicial and legislative proceedings where defamatory statements are made, but the maker cannot be held liable under conditions protected by law.

acceptance Voluntary act by word or by conduct of the offeree that shows assent or agreement to the terms of the offer.

acceptor Drawee who, by signature, agrees to pay a drawer's instrument.

accession Something added on, as in value added to a piece of personal property by labor or materials.

accord and satisfaction An agreement to settle a disputed debt. The accord is the offer and the satisfaction is normally the payment of the amount.

accounting A remedy in equity whereby the court requires a finding as to the amount of money due and owing.

accredited investor Investor who is not likely to need government protection when making investment decisions; includes institutional investors, seller's directors and officers, individual investors with large annual incomes or net worths, and any corporation or charitable organization with total assets of more than $5 million.

act of state doctrine Doctrine created by the judiciary that provides that the judicial branch of one country will not examine the validity of public acts committed by a recognized foreign government within its own territory.

actual authority Authority held by an agent of a principal; consists of expressed and applied authority.

actual knowledge Knowledge in fact.

actual malice Refers to a statement made with the knowledge that it is false or with reckless disregard of whether or not it is false.

actus reus Criminal conduct.

administrative agency Agency of the federal government created by the executive or legislative branch for a specific purpose; endowed with legislative, executive, and judicial powers, agency interprets and enforces congressional statutes and rules.

administrative law Body of law that governs the powers, procedures, and practices of administrative agencies.

Administrative Procedure Act of 1946 (APA) Federal statute that acts as a constitution for administrative agencies; provides standardized administrative agency practices and governs how an administrative agency conducts its business.

administrative regulation Rules adopted by administrative agencies to implement and administer statutes. They have the force of law, absent successful challenge in the courts.

adversary system System in which the judge or jury acts as the decision maker between two opposing sides, the plaintiff and defendant, at trial.

adverse possession Means of obtaining title to land without a deed being delivered. To establish title, the adverse possessor must prove nonpermissive use that is actual, open, notorious, exclusive,

and adverse for the period prescribed by statute.

affidavit Short written statement of facts given under oath and sometimes used as evidence in court.

affirm Act of appellate court when deciding to uphold a lower court's decision.

affirmative action Based on an executive order issued by the U.S. president requiring the federal government and businesses that contract with the federal government to affirmatively seek out people in protected classes based on race, religion, national origin, or sex, in order for the workforce to reflect the makeup of the community.

affirmative defense A defense raised in answer to an attempt to defeat the allegations in a complaint.

affirmative disclosure order An order from a FTC administrative law judge requiring a seller to place affirmative disclaimers in its advertising disclosing that the product will not benefit all members of the public and specifying which members will not be aided; a remedy for past deceptive advertisements.

Age Discrimination in Employment Act (ADEA) A federal statute that protects older workers from discrimination in matters of hiring, promotions, and layoffs.

age of majority Age when a person is no longer a minor, which is set by state statute.

agency by estoppel Occurs when a principal leads a third person to believe that another person is the principal's agent.

agency shop Under federal law, states may pass a statute whereby workers cannot be required to be members of a union, but it might require workers to pay an amount equal to initiation fees and union dues under the theory that these workers enjoy the benefits of the union.

agent Person or business who agrees to represent another person or business.

agreement The act of two or more persons who express a mutual and common purpose.

alien corporation Corporation that originated outside the United States, but does business within the United States.

alternative dispute resolution Speedy and just means of resolving a dispute at a reasonable cost to both the parties and to the taxpayers; for example, arbitration, conciliation.

American Arbitration Association Private nonprofit organization established in 1926, whose purpose is to foster study of arbitration, to perfect the techniques of arbitration law, and to advance the science of arbitration for the prompt and economic settlement of disputes.

Americans with Disabilities Act (ADA) A federal statute amending the Civil Rights Act prohibiting discrimination against people with disabilities.

analytical school of law Approach to the study of law that uses logical analysis to extract the principles underlying a legal code.

annual percentage rate (APR) True rate of interest being charged on a yearly basis.

answer Document filed by defendant that answers a complaint and admits or denies the allegations stated in the complaint.

antitrust laws Laws that regulate economic competition in order to prevent monopolists from controlling the economy.

apparent authority See *agency by estoppel.*

appellant The party appealing a case to a higher court.

appellate courts Courts of appeal or courts of review; courts whose subject-matter jurisdiction is limited to hearing appeals.

appellate jurisdiction Power of appeals courts to hear appeals only on issues of law, not on issues of fact.

appellee The party defending an appeal of a case to a higher court.

arbitration Procedure in which the parties to a dispute submit their case to an impartial third person (arbitrator).

arbitrator Person selected by the parties to a dispute to make a decision based on evidence submitted by both parties.

arson Intentional, willful, and malicious burning of another's or one's own property.

articles of dissolution Resolution adopted by a corporation's board of directors and majority shareholders when the decision has been made to cease operation of the corporation.

articles of incorporation Initial incorporation process that provides basic information about the corporation and is the primary source of authority for future operation of the business.

articles of organization These articles are prepared for a limited liability company. They normally have a brief statement of who are the owners and/or managers of the business. This document is normally filed in a public office.

assault Intentional act (not excused or allowed on grounds of self-defense or defense of others) that creates in another person a reasonable, imminent apprehension of fear of harm.

assignee Third party to whom rights of a party to a contract have been transferred.

assignment A transfer of all or part of one's property, interest, or rights.

assignor Original party to a contract who assigns rights to a third party.

Association of Southeast Asian Nations (ASEAN) Organization among some southeast Asian nations that seeks economic and cultural cooperation among its member nations: Indonesia, Malaysia, the Philippines, Singapore, and Thailand.

assumption of risk Doctrine that says a plaintiff is barred from legal recovery if plaintiff entered into a known and appreciated danger that caused the plaintiff injury or damage.

attainment area Geographic area defined by the Clean Air Act where air pollution levels meet or exceed the minimum requirements mandated by the National Ambient Air Quality Standards.

attempt Intent along with some overt action to commit a criminal act that falls short of committing the act itself.

automatic stay In bankruptcy law, an order that stops or suspends all civil litigation against a debtor.

avoidance In bankruptcy law, power invested in a trustee to rescind a debtor's obligations.

award Arbitrator's decision.

B

backward vertical integration When a business goes back up the supply chain and merges with a supplier; for instance, when an automobile manufacturer purchases an automobile parts manufacturing company.

bailee Person who is entrusted with personal property and who holds the property for a limited time.

bailor Person who owns personal property and who entrusts that property to another for a limited time period.

bankruptcy A federal right guaranteed under Article I, Section 8, of the U.S. Constitution allowing the bankrupt to reorganize or discharge debts.

bankruptcy fraud Dishonesty with the bankruptcy court on the part of the person who has declared bankruptcy.

Bankruptcy Reform Acts of 1978, 1994, and 2001 Federal statutes that govern bankruptcy law.

bargain and sale deed Deed that conveys title to real property to a purchaser, but it does not warrant or guarantee title.

battery An intentional act that results in harm to another person as a result of physical contact.

bearer Person who has physical possession of a negotiable instrument.

bearer paper Instrument that is payable to any person holding the paper. May start as order paper that is converted to bearer paper through use of a blank indorsement. Contrast with *order paper.*

beneficiary Person who benefits from the income of property placed in a trust.

Berne Convention for the Protection of Literary and Artistic Works Agreement signed in 1988 that provides citizens of other countries that are signatories with the same copyright protections that it provides its own citizens.

beyond a reasonable doubt A high level of proof that requires a jury to be convinced the defendant committed the crime.

bilateral contract Contract in which one person makes an offer and receives an acceptance from the offeree; most contracts are of this nature.

bill of exchange Draft drawn upon the buyer of the goods; used as one type of method of making payments when dealing internationally.

bill of information Varies from state to state. Normally, the prosecutor submits an affidavit to a judge who then issues the bill of information charging a person with a crime. Used instead of a grand jury indictment.

bill of lading Document used in the transportation industry that indicates who holds title to goods or who has a right to possession of the goods.

bill of sale A sworn document use to transfer ownership of personal property.

binding arbitration Arbitration that is binding once parties have agreed in writing to submit a controversy to arbitration. A legal action cannot be brought if the parties have agreed to submit a controversy to arbitration.

blue sky laws Statutes that regulate the sales of securities within a state.

board of directors Board consisting of directors elected by shareholders to set and oversee a corporation's overall policies and management. The board hires officers to implement policy set by the board and to oversee the daily operations of the corporation.

bona fide occupational qualification (BFOQ) Job requirement that is unique and specific to a job but that could be discriminatory; for example, the requirement that a wet nurse be female is a BFOQ, and this fact would be a possible defense to an employment discrimination charge.

bona fide seniority or merit system A system allowing differences in the terms, conditions, or privileges of employment based on a seniority or merit system, but the differences cannot result from an intent to discriminate. Commonly, a system that is the result of a union contract.

bond Method of financing (as for a business) that is a long-term commitment in which the loan earns interest at a fixed rate, and repayment to the creditor is commonly secured by property.

breach of contract Failure to perform what a party is under an absolute duty to perform based on an express or an implied-in-fact contract.

bribery Crime of offering, giving, receiving, or soliciting something of value for the purpose of influencing an official in the discharge of his or her public or legal duties. In some states,

covers private persons, such as business executives.

browser Computer software program that provides a graphical user interface with the World Wide Web.

burglary Act of entering into the building of another with the intent to commit a felony.

bylaws Statutes of a corporation setting forth the internal rules of management for the corporation.

business format franchise Franchise for which the franchisor provides the franchisee with the right to use a franchisor's trademark. The franchisee is responsible for the manufacture and sale of the end product.

business judgment rule Law stating that directors and officers will not be held liable for honest errors in business decisions if they made the decisions as reasonable and prudent businesspersons and in good faith.

C

cartel A combination of producers that join to control the production, sale, and price of goods or services and potentially to obtain a monopoly or near monopoly over a particular industry or product.

case law See *common law.*

cashier's check Draft in which the bank is both the drawer and drawee.

causation Action that causes something to be produced or to happen. One of the elements necessary to prove negligence.

cease-and-desist order This order is an administrative remedy that directs a person to refrain from engaging in further violative conduct. Several major federal agencies have the authority to issue these orders. If they are violated the business can be fined damages and eventually be held in contempt of court.

Celler-Kefauver Act Section 7 of the Clayton Act, established in 1950; controls corporate mergers.

certificate of deposit (CD) Acknowledgment by a bank of the receipt of money; carries an agreement to repay the money with interest.

certified check Check that is recognized and accepted by a bank office as a valid appropriation of the specified amount drawn against the funds held by the bank.

challenge for cause During *voir dire*, an attorney's request to dismiss a prospective juror because of apparent bias.

chancellor In early England, the principal minister who handled petitions for redress. In American law, this is the name given in some states to the judge of a court of chancery.

changing-market-conditions defense In an antitrust price discrimination case, this defense is used by a business to show that a business is selling a product at a lower price because it was discontinuing a product or product line or was offering the items at fire or bankruptcy sale prices.

chattel real Chattel that concerns real property, such as a lease.

check Paper drawn on a bank, ordering it to pay a sum of money on demand.

choice-of-forum clause A clause used in international contracts that designates the forum, or location, in which the case will be heard in the event of any dispute.

choice-of-law clause Clause in an international business contract that designates the forum in which adjudication will take place and the substantive law that will be applied in the event of any dispute.

civil law The legal rights and duties that exist among persons or between citizens and their government. Not criminal law.

civil law system Based on the continental European legal system, which deals strictly with statutory provisions and does not take into consideration decisions by courts.

class-action lawsuit Suit brought by a limited number of individuals on behalf of a much larger group.

Clayton Act Federal statute enacted in 1941 to strengthen federal antitrust laws; aimed at restraining specific monopolistic practices.

Clean Air Act A federal statute that mandates antipollution controls by air polluters, such as utilities; provides assistance to states for the implementation of antipollution measures.

Clean Water Act A federal statute that established the goals of (1) making water safe for swimming, (2) protecting fish and wildlife, and (3) controlling or eliminating the discharge of pollutants into the water.

clear and convincing evidence The level of proof that requires a plaintiff to present evidence that goes beyond a well-founded doubt. This level of proof falls between that of a preponderance of the evidence and the level of proof needed in a criminal case, which is evidence beyond a reasonable doubt.

close corporation Corporation with a small number of shareholders, often family members. Its stock is not traded publicly.

closed shop Firm that recognizes union membership by its workers as a condition for employment.

Colgate doctrine Rule that resulted from United States v. Colgate decision in which the U.S. Supreme Court allowed Colgate to refuse unilaterally to deal with retailers who did not follow suggested retail prices; that is, Colgate can deal with whomever it desires.

collateral contract Express written contract made by a third person who guarantees to pay a debt or perform a duty to one party (the creditor) of an original contract if the original debtor is unable to do so.

collateral installment note Negotiable instrument that is payable in installments, during which time the owner of the negotiable instrument has a lien against the maker's personal property.

collateral note Written promise to pay secured by the payee-creditor in which the maker-debtor creates a lien against his or her personal property.

collect on delivery (C.O.D.) Delivery method in which the delivery company collects from the buyer the money owed for goods when it delivers them.

comity Deference that one nation gives to the laws and judicial decrees of another nation, based on respect.

commerce clause Clause in the U.S. Constitution that gives Congress the power "to regulate commerce with foreign nations, and among the several states, and with the individual tribes."

common law Body of judge-made law comprised of principles and the rules of how these principles relate to the government and to the security of persons and property.

common stock Method of financing a business in which stock is held by a shareholder and carries voting rights and the right to a share of the profits of the business if a dividend is declared; has indefinite duration unless redeemed by the corporation.

community property Property of married couples in which each spouse owns an undivided half interest in any property acquired during the marriage.

compact See *treaty.*

comparative negligence Doctrine that enables computation of both the plaintiff's and the defendant's negligent acts when determining recovery amounts.

compensatory damages Award to the injured party as a result of a lawsuit to make up for the monetary loss suffered because the other party breached the contract.

complaint Type of pleading issued by the plaintiff to the defendant that states the purpose of the lawsuit.

Comprehensive Environmental Response, Compensation, and Liability Act (CERCLA) A federal statute requiring polluting hazardous waste to be cleaned up by the polluter; if the polluter cannot be found, monies appropriated to the act are used. Commonly known as Superfund.

computer crime Crime committed by use of a computer; for example, electronic thefts of money through issuing an extra paycheck, shaving funds, or depositing funds in personal accounts.

Computer Software Rental Amendments Act A federal statute that allows a computer program's copyright holder to control the rental, leasing, or lending of the computer program after the first sale.

concurrent jurisdiction Power to hear a case held by both federal and state courts.

concurrent powers Power of either Congress or state legislatures to make laws on the same subject matter.

confiscation Taking property without proper public purpose or just compensation being awarded.

confusion Mixing one person's personal property that is fungible with another's fungible goods, such as grains. Once mixed, no way exists to reseparate the goods.

conglomerate merger Consolidation of two or more firms dealing in unrelated products and operating in markets not horizontally or vertically linked.

consent decree Agreement signed by an administrative law judge after the government and business have reached a voluntary agreement. This type of decree can be enforced in court.

consequential damages Foreseeable damages that result when a party breaches a contract.

consideration Something of legal value given in exchange for a promise; essential element of a contract.

consignment Situation in which an owner of goods turns the goods over to a person who sells this type of goods and who agrees to sell them in the ordinary course of business.

Consolidated Omnibus Budget Reconciliation Act (COBRA) A federal statute providing that when an employee leaves an employer, the employee may buy group health coverage for themselves and their families for a limited time period, usually no longer than eighteen months.

conspiracy Occurs when two or more persons plan, along with some overt action, to commit a criminal act.

constitutional law Public law that involves questions of whether the government has the power to act.

constructive knowledge Knowledge that is imputed, such as what the agent knows, the principal knows; or, for example, what is publicly recorded is presumed to be known by all persons.

constructive notice All documents that are recorded in a public office, such as a county recorder's office. A public recording provides every person the ability to find the recorded document. This public recording means that every person either has actual notice or has imputed knowledge of the information actually recorded. If the information is imputed to a person, it is said that he or she has constructive notice of the publicly recorded document.

Consumer Credit Cost Disclosure Act See *Truth-in-Lending Act.*

Consumer Credit Protection Act (CCPA) Federal statute that is the primary source of federal law covering credit transactions; enforced by several federal agencies.

consumer credit transaction Transaction that occurs when a consumer enters into a contract to purchase an item and at the same time receives credit from the seller or a financial institution to purchase the item specified in the contract.

Consumer Leasing Act A federal statute act requiring full disclosure of all financial terms in consumer leasing contracts.

Consumer Product Safety Act A federal statute that created the Consumer Product Safety Commission, which is designed to protect consumers from unreasonable risk of injury from hazardous consumer products.

Consumer Reporting Reform Act A federal statute requiring all credit bureaus to provide toll-free numbers and to make an employee, not a recording, available when a consumer calls a credit bureau. Amended the Consumer Reporting Act.

contract Promise or set of promises for the breach of which the law gives a remedy, and the performance of which the law in some way recognizes as a duty.

contract for future goods Contract for the sale of goods that do not yet exist.

contractual agreement to arbitrate Arbitration established by contractual agreement entered into either before or after a dispute occurs.

contributory negligence Negligence on the part of both parties; each party contributes to the negligence.

convention Law adopted by an international organization that was created by a treaty.

Convention on the Law of the Non-navigational Uses of International Watercourses Convention providing for the exchange of information among countries if water-related hazards occur; includes an article requiring nations to take all measures to prevent harmful conditions, such as toxic chemical spills.

Convention on the Limitation Period in the International Sale of Goods Convention that established unified rules for determining the statute of limitations in a lawsuit.

conversion Taking personal property from its rightful owner or possessor and placing it in the service of another; civil law side of stealing.

copyright Right granted by statute to the author or originator of certain literary or artistic productions.

corporation A legal entity created by the state or federal government and owned by shareholders.

corrective advertising order An order from a FTC administrative law judge requiring a seller to alert consumers to false statements in past advertising.

cost and freight (C.&F.) Delivery term that indicates that the purchase price of goods includes freight charges of those goods during transportation.

cost, insurance, and freight (C.I.F.) Delivery term that indicates that the purchase price of goods includes insurance and freight charges of those goods during transportation.

cost–benefit standard Standard created by statute and applied by courts; involves considering the cost of an action and comparing it with the benefit that may result from the action.

cost-justification defense In an antitrust price discrimination case, this defense is used by a business to show that the cost was lower per unit to manufacture or transport; therefore, the sale of the unit at lower cost is justified.

counterclaim Claim in which the defendant sets forth allegations against the claims made by the plaintiff in a lawsuit.

Counterfeit Access Device and Computer Fraud and Abuse Act Act that makes it a federal crime to knowingly access a computer to obtain restricted federal government information, to obtain financial records from financial institutions, or to obtain consumer reports from consumer reporting agencies. It also made it a crime to counterfeit or use unauthorized access devices to obtain items of value or to traffic in such devices.

counteroffer Rejection of original offer and the simultaneous making of a new offer.

countervailing duty Import tax equal to the grant extended to an exporter by its home country to encourage exportation or to assist the exporters in meeting competition.

course of dealing Principle encouraged by the Uniform Commercial Code that defers to previous conduct between parties of a contract to establish a basis for understanding and interpreting their expressions in a current contract.

court of equity Court that grants a legal means to enforce personal rights or to correct a wrong.

Court of International Trade (CIT) Court that has the power of a federal district court involving trade matters, such as dumping and countervailing duty.

court of law Court that grants a monetary damage award.

court's opinion Decision by the court.

courts of appeal Courts of review.

covenant not to compete This clause can be included in one of two types of agreements, either the purchase of a business or an employment contract. The seller of the business or the employee agrees not to compete against the other party to the contract. These clauses are valid if they are reasonable both as to time and area.

covenant not to sue Contract between two parties in which one party waives the right to sue the other party, usually in return for a settlement.

cover Ability to obtain goods similar to those required by the contract, after it has been breached, from other available sources.

creditor beneficiary Person who purchases the right to receive proceeds owed under a contract. Has the right to institute legal action to enforce rights under the original contract.

criminal law Body of law that deals with violations of wrongs committed against society as a whole.

cross-claim Claim brought by a defendant against a codefendant.

cumulative preferred stock Stock in a corporation that carries the right to accumulate unpaid dividends and has preference at dissolution of the corporation.

Currency Transaction Report (CTR) Report required by federal law that must be submitted by financial institutions (1) if they suspect criminal activity by a customer who is involved in a financial transaction of $1,000 or more or (2) when a single transaction of a series of related transactions of currency amounts to more than $10,000.

customs brokers Licensed people who conduct customs business on behalf of others.

D

damages for pain and suffering Damages awarded to compensate the plaintiff who has endured pain and suffering as a result of the defendant's actions.

debenture Form of bond that is unsecured.

debt securities Bonds of debentures that represent a loan to the corporation.

deceit See *fraud*.

decree Decision that determines a party's equitable rights in a case before a court.

deed Writing signed by an owner of property by which title to the property is transferred to another.

defamation Act of making any untrue statement or statements that harm the reputation of another person or corporation.

defamation by computer Production by a computer of erroneous information about a person's credit standing or business reputation that may impair the person's ability to obtain further credit.

default judgment Court order awarding one party everything it requested because opposing party failed to respond in time.

defendant Person being sued and accused of causing harm by a plaintiff.

deficiency judgment Award that represents the deficient amount (difference between the mortgage debt and the amount received from the proceeds of the foreclosure sale).

delegation Transfer of a contract's duties to another person.

demand draft See *sight draft*.

demurrer Defendant's motion to dismiss the complaint, stating that, even if the facts are true, their legal consequences are such that there is no reason to go further with the lawsuit and no need for the defendant to present an answer.

deontology Philosophical practice of defining and adhering to an absolute set of standards by which ethical behavior can be measured.

deposition Sworn oral testimony by opposing party or by witness(es) taken by interrogatories, not in open court.

derivative authority Authority accorded the agent by the principal to carry out the principal's business.

Digital Millennium Copyright Act (DMCA) A federal statute that limits the liability of online service providers for copyright infringement and covers other issues, such as distance education, libraries, and webcasting of sound recordings.

director (of a corporation) Person elected by shareholders to oversee the corporation's overall policies and management. The board of directors hires officers to implement the policy and to oversee the daily operations of the corporation.

disaffirm Person who has a legal right to rescind a contract and therefore does not have a duty to perform.

discharge To perform a contract fully.

disclosed principal Principal whose identity is known by the third party at the time the contract is made by the agent.

discovery Process of obtaining information from opposing party or from witnesses in a lawsuit.

disgorgement This order is issued by the SEC to require a wrongdoer to return any profits that have been made in violation of the security laws.

dishonest employee rule A theft using checks by an employee who endorses legitimate checks made out to the employer and cashes the check or deposits these checks into a banking account not controlled by the employer.

disparagement of goods False statement made about a person's product.

disparate impact Employment discrimination practice that appears neutral on the surface but that actually affects a protected class adversely.

disparate treatment Employment discrimination practice in which treatment of a certain class differs from the treatment of other employees or applicants.

dissociation The end of a relationship with a partnership.

dissolution Through court action, an order terminating a business entity so that it no longer exists.

dissolve The act of a corporation liquidating itself in preparation for going out of business.

distributorship franchise Type of franchise where a manufacturing concern (franchisor) licenses a dealer (franchisee) to sell its products; for example, an automobile dealership.

diversity of citizenship cases Cases involving: (1) citizens of different states, (2) a foreign country as plaintiff and citizens of a state or different states, or (3) citizens of a state and citizens or subjects of a foreign country where the amount in controversy is greater than $50,000 and does not involve a federal question.

divestiture Through court action, an order taking away from a defendant something of value, such as illegally gained profits or property used in the commission of a crime.

doctrine of exhaustion of remedies A business or person must use all procedures for appeal of an administrative agency before filing an action in court.

doctrine of laches Rule that states that individuals who fail to look out for their rights until after a reasonable time has passed will not be helped.

doctrine of *respondeat superior* Rule that makes the principal liable for the agent's torts if the torts are committed within the scope of the agency or the scope of employment.

doctrine of selective incorporation Under the Fourteenth Amendment, the U.S. Supreme Court has applied many, but not all, clauses of the first ten amendments to the states.

document of title Paper representing ownership of goods.

domestic corporation Corporation doing business in the state in which it was incorporated.

donee beneficiary Person who receives the proceeds of a contract as a gift even though not a party to the contract. Often has the right to institute legal action to enforce rights under the original contract.

double jeopardy Protection provided in the Fifth Amendment that says a person cannot be tried by the same level of government more than once for the same crime.

draft Unconditional written order; debt owed by the drawee to the drawer.

drawee Debtor of the drawer.

drawer One who creates or executes the order-to-pay instrument.

due diligence defense Under the Securities Act of 1933, a defense available to a defendant who signed a false statement about a security, but did so after a good faith attempt to verify the truth of the statement

due process clause Part of the Fifth and Fourteenth Amendments.

dumping Practice of selling goods in the buyer's country below the price costs to manufacture in, and transport from, the seller's country.

duress Compulsion by threat; forcing someone to do something out of fear.

E

easement Right of a person to make limited use of another person's property without taking anything from the property.

easement by prescription A right to a nonpossessory interest in real property by establishing the right contrary to, and without the permission of, the owner.

economic school of law Approach to the study of law that holds that most laws may be evaluated in accordance with economic theory; developed by Richard A. Posner in the 1970s.

economic strike Strike in which employees seek economic benefits, such as higher wages and benefits; management may permanently replace the striking employees, although these employees have priority when management rehires after the strike.

Electronic Communications Privacy Act A federal crime to intercept an electronic communication at the point of or during transmission, when transmitted through a router or server, or after receipt by the intended recipient; includes any electronic transfer of signals.

Electronic Data Gathering, Analysis, and Retrieval (EDGAR) System that performs automated collection, validation, indexing, acceptance, and forwarding of submissions by companies that are required by law to file forms with the SEC.

Electronic Freedom of Information Act A federal statute that makes it possible for the public to have free electronic access to government documents on the Internet without having to make a formal request under the Freedom of Information Act.

electronic funds transfer (EFT) Automatic payment or direct deposit using teller machines, point-of-sale systems, and automated clearinghouses.

embezzlement Fraudulent conversion of another's property or money by a person in lawful possession of that property.

Emergency Planning and Community Right-to-Know Act (EPCRA) A federal statute requiring the release of information to affected communities about the presence of hazardous chemicals and their release into the environment.

eminent domain Power of government to condemn land in order to take it for public use.

Employee Polygraph Protection Act A federal statute making polygraph use unlawful except under restricted conditions, including (1) national defense; (2) ongoing investigations; (3) drug security, drug theft, or drug diversion investigations; and (4) armored car and security personnel.

employment law State and federal statutes that define the relationship between an employer and its employees.

Employee Retirement Income Security Act (ERISA) Federal statute that established a supplement to social security to be set up by employers for their employees.

employment at will This form of employment exists when there is no contractual arrangement for the employee to work for a given time period such as one year. The employer may terminate the employee with or without cause.

enabling act Congressional legislation that creates an administrative agency, determines its structure, and defines its powers.

Endangered Species Act (ESA) A federal statute designed to conserve endangered species and protect their ecosystems.

entitlement program Government program that administers benefits to those who qualify for them. Economic regulation to control the public welfare.

enumerated powers Provisions in the U.S. Constitution that delegate certain powers to the three branches of the federal government.

environmental impact statement (EIS) Any federal agency that will build or fund the building of a project must conduct an EIS under the National Environmental Policy Act. The EIS must contain information on the (1) environmental impact of project, (2) any adverse effects that might result, and (3) the irreversible effects that the action might create.

Environmental Protection Agency (EPA) Federal agency created in 1970 that assembles various organizations responsible for environmental protection.

Equal Access to Justice Act A federal statute that allows an individual or small business to recover legal fees, expert witness fees, and other expenses involving an action by the U.S. government, if the government action was not substantially justified.

Equal Credit Opportunity Act Federal statute that forbids discrimination based on race, sex, religion, national origin, marital status, age, or person's income from public assistance in determinations of creditworthiness.

Equal Employment Opportunity Commission (EEOC) Five-member commission created in 1964 to administer Title VII; members are appointed by the president of the United States with consent of the Senate; issues interpretive guidelines and regulations but does not have force of law; investigates, holds hearings, keeps statistics.

Equal Pay Act Amendment to the Fair Labor Standards Act of 1938, administered by the EEOC; prohibits discrimination based on sex in wages paid for equal work on jobs which performance requires equal skills, effort, and responsibility and that are performed under similar conditions (job content rather than job description).

equal protection clause Legal right in the Fourteenth Amendment that holds that government must treat similarly situated individuals in a similar manner.

equity remedy Remedy granted by court; an appropriate remedy, based on fairness, justice, and honesty is awarded to the harmed party in order to correct the situation.

equity securities Shares of stock representing an ownership interest in a corporation.

estoppel To bar, to impede, to stop.

ethics Principles used to differentiate right from wrong and govern a person's conduct.

exclusive dealing contract Legal vertical restraint of trade in which the manufacturer or distributor may require the retailer not to sell products of competing firms, provided there is no boycott but each decision is made on an individual basis.

exclusive jurisdiction Power to hear a case held by only a federal court (as in federal crimes, bankruptcy, patents, copyrights, and suits against the United States) or by only a state court (as in divorce, probate, and adoption cases).

executed contract Contract that is fully performed.

executive agency See *line agency.*

executive agreement Agreement made by the president of the United States without need for the consent of the Senate; used in making agreements with foreign countries.

executive branch Branch of the U.S. government that includes the president and is charged with enforcing the law; the powers of the president, as established in Article II of the Constitution.

executory contract Contract that has not been performed.

exempt property Debtor's property protected by state or federal statute from seizure by a creditor of a debtor or trustee in bankruptcy; such property cannot be sold. Contrast with *nonexempt property.*

exempt security Security issued by governments, nonprofit organizations, and certain businesses that is exempt from registration under the Securities Act of 1933.

exempt transaction Transaction that is exempt from the registration requirements of the Securities Act of 1933. See *small offering exemption, private offering exemption,* and *intrastate offering exemption.*

Exon–Florio provision Allows the U.S. president to prevent the purchase by a foreign business of any U.S. firms, such as airline companies or defense companies, if such purchase would threaten national security.

Export Administration Act A federal statute that governs the export of goods and restricts the export of goods and technology in the military field when release of these would be detrimental to the United States.

Export-Import Bank (Eximbank) Created by Congress, a bank that provides financial assistance, primarily in the form of credit guarantees, to exporting and importing firms.

Export Trading Company Act A federal statute designed to increase U.S. exports of goods and services; allows competing producers to apply for an exemption from antitrust laws for business conducted overseas if the U.S. government grants the export trade certificate of review.

exporting Selling of goods manufactured in, and sent from, the domestic country to a foreign country.

express authority Authority that provides an agent with specific instructions on behalf of the principal.

express contract Contract in which the terms are stated exactly whether written or spoken.

express warranty Explicit statements made by the seller to the buyer regarding the condition or quality of the goods purchased.

expropriation Government seizure of a privately owned business or goods for a proper public purpose and with just compensation.

extortion The obtaining of property from another, with his or her consent, but the consent is induced by wrongful use of actual or threatened force, violence, fear, or under color of official right.

F

fact finding Investigative process by which a third party will investigate the issues and make findings of fact to present to the court or other body charged with ruling on the issues.

factor A factor is one who provides short-term financing, from 30 to 180 days, to businesses exporting to developed countries. The exporter sells the export receivable to the factor who in turn is paid by the importer or its import factor. The factor works in developed countries in order to use the banking, legal, and accounting systems when necessary. The difference between a factor and using a letter of credit is that a factor provides nonbank financing while a letter of credit is issued by a bank.

failing-company defense Defense used by a business to justify a merger with a company confronting with complete failure and no known prospective purchasers. In such a case, the courts may allow a merger that could create a monopoly.

Fair Packaging and Labeling Act (FPLA) A federal statute that requires certain disclosures by any firm that packages or labels consumer products.

False Claims Act A federal statute authorizing government to sue any party filing a fraudulent payment claim for products or services.

Fair Credit Billing Act Amendment to Truth-in-Lending Act (TILA) that requires creditors to correct errors promptly and without damage to a person's credit rating.

Fair Credit Reporting Act Title VI of the Consumer Credit Protection Act, which requires that consumers be informed of the nature and scope of a credit investigation, the kind of information that is being compiled, and the names of persons who will be receiving the report.

Fair Debt Collection Practices Act Part of the Consumer Credit Protection Act; adopted in 1977, it prohibits certain practices in the collection of consumer debt by debt collection agencies.

Fair Labor Standards Act (FLSA) Federal statute that established minimum wage, overtime standards, record-keeping, and child labor prohibitions; provides for administrative procedures for the enforcement of and compliance with these standards as they apply to employees engaged in commerce, production of goods to be placed in commerce, or employees of an enterprise engaged in commerce.

false imprisonment Intentional confinement or restraint of another person without justification.

False Statement Act A federal statute that makes criminal making a false statement to the U.S. government to obtain a monetary return. The making of a false statement is a crime.

Family and Medical Leave Act A federal statute providing that employees can take up to twelve weeks of unpaid leave for the birth or adoption of a child, for the care of an immediate family member, or for a serious health condition.

Federal Anti-Injunction Act A federal statute restricting the federal courts' power to issue injunctions against unions engaged in peaceful strikes. Also known as the Norris-LaGuardia Act.

Federal Arbitration Act Federal statute favoring arbitration that withdraws from the states the power to require a judicial forum for the resolution of disagreements if the parties by contract have agreed to solve the problem by arbitration.

Federal Environmental Pesticide Control Act A federal statute that amends the Federal Insecticide, Fungicide, and Rodenticide Act.

Federal Insecticide, Fungicide, and Rodenticide Act A federal statute that requires licensing of those handling and applying insecticides, fungicides, and rodenticides; requires EPA to inspect manufacturing sites; EPA controls supply of pesticides to keep hazardous chemicals off the market. Pesticides must be (1) registered before they can be sold; (2) certified, labeled, and used only for approved applications; and (3) used in amounts that meet established limits when they are applied to crops that provide food for animals or people.

Federal Insurance Contribution Act Federal statute that provides funding for the social security program.

federal question case Case with a legal question that involves the federal Constitution, treaty, or statute. Federal courts have jurisdiction over federal question cases.

Federal Trade Commission Act of 1914 Federal statute that created the Federal Trade Commission.

Federal Unemployment Tax Act (FUTA) Federal statute that established a state system of providing unemployment compensation to eligible individuals.

federalism System of government organization in which state governments and the federal government share powers.

fee simple defeasible Type of estate of real property for which the title can be taken away automatically from the current owner under certain conditions created by the original seller.

fee simple absolute Estate in property in which the owner has the greatest aggregation of rights, privileges, and power possible; is indefinite in duration.

fee simple subject to a condition subsequent Type of estate of real property for which the title can be taken away from the current owner if a specified event occurs as set out by the original seller.

felony Crime punishable by imprisonment in a federal or state penitentiary for more than one year, by fine, or by death.

fictitious name filing Filing with a public office and prepared by the owner of a business to alert the public to the fact that he or she is doing business under a fictitious name.

fictitious payee rule A theft using checks by an employee who writes checks drawn on the employer's bank that are payable to a fictitious payee.

fiduciary duty Duty of an agent to act on behalf of the principal with the utmost good faith.

finance charge Total amount of interest paid on a loan.

financing statement Document required by the UCC and signed by a debtor that describes the goods used as collateral in a security agreement and must be filed in a public office in order to be effective against all persons.

firm offer Under the UCC, Section 2-205, a firm offer is created when a merchant makes a written, signed offer to buy or sell goods and indicates in the offer that the offer is irrevocable. The purchaser does not need to pay the merchant to hold the offer open if the time period is less than three months.

fixture Object affixed to realty by roots, embedded in it, or permanently attached by cement, nails, bolts, plaster, or screws.

Food, Drug, and Cosmetic Act A federal statute that created the Food and Drug Administration and also prohibits adulteration or misbranding of food, drugs, and cosmetics.

foreclosure A judicial document filed by a mortgagee-creditor against a mortgagor-debtor that exercises the mortgagee's lien right under the mortgage to have the real property sold for nonpayment of a note for real property. With a deed of trust, a foreclosure can be a nonjudicial action by a trustee.

foreign corporation Corporation doing business in a state other than the one in which it was incorporated.

Foreign Corrupt Practices Act of 1977 (FCPA) Federal statute that prohibits bribes given to foreign government officials by representatives of American companies and their directors, officers, shareholders, employees, or agents for the purpose of obtaining or retaining business for the American company.

foreseeability Test for proximate cause that asks whether the defendant's unreasonable conduct could have been foreseen to cause the plaintiff's injury or damage.

forfaiter A forfaiter is one who provides medium- to long-term financing from 180 days to ten years to businesses exporting or working in developing countries. A forfaiter will purchase an export receivable from the exporter. The export receivable is guaranteed by the country's bank or the country itself where the work or item was delivered.

forgery Crime of obtaining goods by false pretenses.

formal contract Written contract between parties.

formal rule making Rule making that requires an agency to conduct a hearing before it can adopt a rule. Contrast with *informal rule making*.

forward-looking statement A statement issued by a business that projects earnings and losses.

forward vertical integration When a business goes forward in the supply chain and merges with a purchaser; for instance, when an automobile manufacturer purchases a car rental company.

franchise Arrangement in which the owner of a trademark, a trade name, or copyright licenses another person under specified conditions or limitations to use the trademark, trade name, or copyright in marketing goods or services.

franchisee The holder of a franchise.

franchisor A franchisor licenses a franchisee to use the franchisor's trademark, trade name, or copyright in the marketing of specific goods and services.

fraud Involving (1) a misrepresentation of material facts, (2) the intent to deceive or the reckless disregard of the facts' truthfulness, (3) the knowledge that the facts are false, (4) the victim's justifiable reliance on these facts, and (5) damages.

free on board, destination (F.O.B. destination) Transportation term denoting that risk and title of goods transfer to the buyer on notification that goods have arrived at the destination.

free on board, point of shipment (F.O.B.) Transportation term denoting that risk and title of goods transfer to the buyer on delivery of the goods to the transportation company.

Freedom of Information Act of 1966 (FOIA) Amendment to the Administrative Procedure Act that makes all nonexempt information held by federal agencies available to the public.

freehold estate Estate in real property of uncertain duration.

freight forwarders Licensed businesses that arrange the transportation of goods.

full faith and credit clause Clause in the U.S. Constitution that mandates the enforcement of a state's valid judgment, decree, or order in other states.

full warranty A promise that ensures some type of buyer satisfaction in case a product is defective; provides for free repair or replacement of any defective part.

fungible goods Identical goods by nature or usage of trade, such as grains.

G

garnishment Statutory procedure in which a person's property in possession of another is applied to payment of that person's debts.

General Agreement on Tariffs and Trade (GATT) The GATT was created in 1948 as only an agreement. Since then it has grown to be both an agreement and an organization. Several rounds of GATT have been negotiated over the decades in order to continually update the tariff and trade rules. The GATT organization was replaced by the World Trade Organization (WTO) in 1995.

general jurisdiction Power to hear almost any subject matter in a lawsuit; authority of the court of original jurisdiction.

general license General authority to ship and export goods; not a license in the usual sense.

general partner In a business, a partner who has unlimited liability.

general policy statement Statement that sets out in broad terms the particular philosophy, mission, and objectives of a government agency.

general warranty deed Deed that provides the buyer protection against defects in the title to land.

gift Voluntary transfer of ownership of property.

government agency Administrative agency created by Congress to administer a quasi-business venture generating its own revenue; for example, U.S. Postal Service.

goods All things that are movable and tangible.

gratuitous agency Occurs when an agent performs services without compensation.

gray-market goods Foreign-manufactured goods for which a valid U.S. trademark has been registered; also known as a *parallel import*.

group boycott Per se violation of the Sherman Act in which a group refuses to deal with some third party or parties.

H

hardware Computer equipment itself.

Hart-Scott-Rodino Antitrust Improvement Act A federal statute requiring businesses that intend to merge to provide the Federal Trade Commission and the Department of Justice with a premerger notification.

Hazardous and Solid Waste Amendments (HSWA) A federal statute requiring the phasing out of land disposal of hazardous waste; provides for stringent hazardous waste management standards and a comprehensive underground storage tank program.

Health Insurance Portability and Accountability Act (HIPAA) A federal statute mandating that when a person moves from one employer with group health insurance to another employer with group health insurance, the new group health insurance company must accept that person and charge the same premium and may not exclude or charge a higher premium for a preexisting medical condition.

hearsay evidence Out-of-court information given by someone other than a witness to prove the truth of a contested fact. Not allowed at trial.

Herfindahl-Hirschman Index Statistical formula used by the Department of Justice to determine nonmarket considerations of a proposed merger, such as the ease of entry into the business and the resulting competitive strength of the merged firms.

historical school of law Approach to the study of law based on the origin and history of the legal system; looks to the past to discover what the principles of contemporary law should be.

holder Person who possesses negotiable instruments drawn, issued, or indorsed to his or her order or to the bearer or in blank.

holder in due course (HDC) Special-status transferee of a negotiable instrument.

homestead exemption Exemption of certain types of real and personal property from levy of execution or attachment in the event of mortgage default and deficiency judgment.

horizontal market division Per se violation of the Sherman Act that involves dividing a market for the sale of a specific product among competitors.

horizontal price fixing Occurs when two or more potential competitors on the same level set a fixed price for their goods or services.

horizontal merger Merger of comparable companies.

I

identified goods Existing goods that have been identified to a particular contract.

illusory promise A statement that appears to be a promise but in reality does not create any contractual obligation.

Immigration Act A federal statute that overhauled previous immigration acts, changing the emphasis from immigration based on family ties with U.S. citizens or nationals to immigration based on the potential ability of the immigrant to contribute to the economy.

Immigration Reform and Control Act A federal statute providing for civil and criminal sanctions for employers if they fail to verify their workers' employment eligibility and knowingly hire any individual unauthorized to work. Also, employers cannot discriminate against workers based on their national origin or lack of citizenship.

implied authority Authority that is ordinary in that type of business.

implied-in-fact contract Contract formed in whole or in part from the conduct of the parties.

implied-in-law contract This contract exists when one person is unjustly enriched at the expense of another. No actual contract actually exists, but the law implies a promise to pay by the person who has been enriched.

implied warranty of authority When a person acts for another, he or she guarantees that he or she has the right to so act.

implied warranty of fitness for a particular purpose Warranty that arises when any seller knows the particular purpose for which a buyer will use the goods and knows the buyer is relying on the seller's skill and judgment to select suitable goods.

implied warranty of merchantability Warranty that goods are reasonably fit for the purpose for which they are sold, are properly packaged and labeled, and are of proper quality; arises in the sale of goods by a merchant who deals in goods of that kind.

importing Buying of goods manufactured in a foreign country that are brought into the domestic country.

impostor rule A theft using a check by a person posing as the person entitled to the check.

inadequate-resources defense Defense used by a company to justify a merger with a business that has inadequate financial resources to compete. In such a case, the courts may allow a merger that could create a monopoly.

incidental beneficiary Person who receives a benefit from a contract in an indirect way, even though the person is not a party to the contract and has no right to enforce the contract.

incorporator Person who starts a corporation.

independent agency Administrative agency that is not under the control of the president or Congress but is freestanding; has a commission created by Congress and is headed by a commissioner.

independent contractor Person who contracts with another to do something for him or her but who is not controlled by the other or subject to the other's right to control with respect to his or her physical conduct in the performance of the undertaking.

indictment Formal charge of wrongdoing issued by a grand jury prior to trial.

indorsee Person who receives a signed negotiable instrument from an indorser.

indorsement Signature of the person known as the indorser written on the back of the instrument itself.

indorser Anyone, other than the maker or acceptor, who signs a negotiable instrument.

insider trading Under Section 16, the act by any director, officer, or shareholder holding 10 percent or more of any one class of stock who buys and sells or sells and buys within six months. Under Section 10(b), the act by any director, officer, majority shareholder, or anyone having access to or receiving information of a nonpublic nature from an insider who uses the nonpublic information to trade.

Insider Trading and Securities Fraud Enforcement Act A federal statute that amended the Insider Trading Sanctions Act by enlarging the types of people subject to civil liability and provided the SEC with the power to reward informants, required securities firms to prevent insider trading, and increased criminal penalties.

Insider Trading Sanctions Act (ITSA) A federal statute that gave the SEC additional powers to institute legal action against any person who trades on nonpublic information through a national securities exchange or a registered broker-dealer.

infliction of mental distress Intentional act that involves extreme and outrageous conduct and that results in severe emotional distress to another.

informal contract Written or oral contract.

informal rule making Rule making that consists of notice and comment; most commonly used by administrative agencies to promulgate rules.

injunction Equitable remedy in which an order is issued to a person or a business to refrain from doing wrongful act(s).

in personam jurisdiction Jurisdiction over the person.

in rem jurisdiction Jurisdiction over property.

installment note Negotiable instrument that is payable in installments.

intangible property Property that possesses an invisible value, such as an annuity, checks, or bonds, and is reported by a piece of paper with rights recognized by law.

intended beneficiary Person who intended to benefit from the contract as either a creditor beneficiary or a donee beneficiary.

intentional interference with a contractual or business relationship Tort in which the plaintiff must prove the defendant intentionally induced the breach of a valid contractual or business relationship.

intentional tort Intentional acts that cause injuries either against the person or against property.

InterAmerican Convention on International Commercial Arbitration (Panama Convention) Convention that created the agreement among the United States, Mexico, and Latin American countries to submit disputes surrounding commercial transactions to arbitration.

intermediate scrutiny test Discrimination test for which two requirements must be met: (1) an important governmental objective and (2) a substantial relationship between the means and the end.

international agent A specialized type of agent that can help a business find buyers in another country.

International Antitrust Enforcement Assistance Act (IAEAA) A federal statute providing antitrust guidance to businesses engaged in international operations, concerning the enforcement policies of the Department of Justice and the Federal Trade Commission.

International Court of Justice (ICJ) Principal judicial organ of the United Nations.

international custom General practice among nations that is accepted as law.

international law Law considered legally binding among otherwise independent nations.

International Organization of Securities Commission Organization created by the International Securities Enforcement Cooperation Act to cooperate with other countries in regulating the securities markets and transactions.

International Securities Enforcement Cooperation Act Act that allows the SEC to cooperate with other countries to regulate security markets and transactions.

International Trade Administration (ITA) Promotes world trade and strengthens the international trade and investment position of the United States; part of the Department of Commerce.

International Trade Commission (ITC) Independent agency that imposes tariff adjustments and import quotas for goods.

international trade.

interpretive rule Statement by an administrative agency as to how it interprets the statute it is charged with administering; published in the Federal Register.

interrogatories Written questions sent to the opposing party that must be answered under oath.

Interstate Land Sales Full Disclosure Act A federal statute designed to decrease the opportunities for fraud and deception when consumers purchase property they have not seen. Developers are required to (1) make full disclose their financial position; (2) register with the Office of Interstate Land Sales Registration within the Department of Housing and Urban Development before commencing sales; and (3) provide purchasers with a copy of a property report before a contract is signed.

intrastate offering exemption Offerings made within the boundaries of one state by a seller who resides in that state. Federal regulations do not apply to these types of offerings.

invasion of privacy An intentional act that invades a person's intangible right to be left alone.

issue To deliver a negotiable instrument for the first time.

issuer Party, such as a corporation or limited partnership, that issues securities.

J

joint tenancy with right of survivorship Situation in which two or more persons own an undivided interest in either personal or real property, and, on the death of one of the joint tenants, his or her interest transfers to the remaining joint tenant, not to his or her heirs.

judgment Verdict that has been signed by a judge and that states who won the case and the conditions of the award.

judgment rate Interest rate set by statute and used when the parties to a negotiable instrument or other contracts have failed to specify an interest rate.

judicial arbitration Compulsory, court-mandated arbitration.

judicial branch Branch of the U.S. government that consists of the federal judicial system and its powers as established by Article III of the U.S. Constitution.

judicial deference Term meaning that a court does not reverse an agency action unless the court finds that agency in violation of a condition set out by the Administrative Procedure Act.

judicial review Process for deciding whether a law is in conflict with the mandates of the Constitution.

judicial sale Sale conducted by a sheriff, as directed by a court order, to sell off property seized from a nonpaying debtor.

jurisdiction Power of a court to hear a particular dispute, civil or criminal, and to make a binding decision.

jurisprudence Science or philosophy of law.

K

know-how license License granted to a foreign licensee by a U.S. business to use a trade secret or the know-how to use certain technology.

L

Labor Management Relations Act Also known as the Taft-Hartley Act; amendment to the Wagner Act that provides protection for employers as well as employees in labor-related issues.

Labor Management Reporting and Disclosure Act Also known as the Landrum-Griffith Act; statute that established an employee bill of rights and reporting requirements for union activities; regulates internal union business.

landlord Owner of a piece of property that is rented to a tenant.

Lanham Act A federal statute prohibiting false descriptions about products or services in advertisements; forbids deceptive advertising that is likely to mislead.

larceny Wrongful or fraudulent taking and carrying away by any person of the personal property of another.

law System that gives order to society; a system of moral conduct by which society achieves justice; a body of rules.

law merchant Rules resulting from the resolution of disputes and from transactions of merchants and other commercial traders; consists primarily of general customs of the trades that remain law unless displaced by specific statutes.

lease Transfer of real or personal property by landlord or lessor to the tenant or lessee for a period of time in exchange for a consideration (usually payment of rent); on termination, the property reverts to the lessor.

legal benefit Occurs when a person obtains something that he had no prior legal right to obtain.

legal detriment Occurs when a person does, or promises to do, something that he had no prior legal duty to perform or when the person gives up the legal right.

legal entity Individuals and various forms of business that can sue and be sued in a court, pay taxes, and hold title to property.

legal ethics Moral and professional duties that lawyers owe other lawyers, their clients, the courts, and the public.

legal fiction A construction by the law to reach a just result.

legal realists school of law School that stresses the pragmatic and empirical sides of law; looking at how well the law meets the needs of society.

legal remedy Remedy awarded by the court; the harmed party could be awarded land, money, items of value, or a combination of all three.

legislative branch Branch of the U.S. government that consists of Congress and its powers as established by Article I of the U.S. Constitution.

letter of credit Contract used in international business that assures the seller of payment while assuring the buyer that payment will not be made until all terms and conditions of the instrument are complied with.

letter ruling Document stating the official position of a federal administrative agency with respect to a particular issue.

libel Act of false and malicious statements in writing to others about another person or business.

life estate Type of ownership of real property for the life of an individual.

limited jurisdiction Jurisdiction limited to certain subject matters.

limited liability company (LLC) This is a new form of organization that allows the owners to have limited liability like a corporation, but treats the organization as a partnership (which does not pay taxes) for tax purposes. The owners may lose their investment in the business if it fails, but otherwise are not liable for other debts of the business.

limited liability partnership This form of organization is of recent origin. It allows partners to have limited liability from the debts of the business. All of the rules of a general partnership apply to this business organization except for limited liability. In a regular general partnership all of the partners are liable for the debts of the business.

limited partner In a limited partnership, a partner who has limited liability up to the amount of his or her contribution to capital.

limited partnership A business that is created by statute where there must be at least one general partner and one limited partner.

limited warranty A promise that is limited in its scope of coverage. Less than a full warranty.

line agency Administrative agency under the direct control of the president of the United States; for example, the Department of Labor.

liquidated damages Amount stipulated in a contract to serve as the measure of damages in case of a breach.

liquidated debt A debt that is not disputed between the contracting parties.

liquidation The selling of assets so they can be converted into cash.

long-arm statute A state statute that allows a court to obtain jurisdiction over a defendant who lives outside that state.

lost property Property that is not voluntarily left and forgotten.

M

Magnuson-Moss Federal Trade Improvement Act A federal statute that broadened the scope of the Wheeler-Lea Act; eliminated holder-in-due course rights when consumer goods are financed; provided FTC with more enforcement powers.

Magnuson-Moss Warranty Act Federal statute designed to prevent deception in warranties by making them easier to understand; enforced by the Federal Trade Commission.

mailbox rule Under common law, an acceptance is effective when dispatched when it uses the same means of communication as the offer.

maker Person who signs and issues a promissory note agreeing to pay a certain sum of money.

manager The person(s) who manage(s) a limited liability company, as determined by the operating agreement for the company.

manufacturing or processing plant franchise Type of franchise in which the franchisor transfers to the franchisee essential ingredients or the formula to make a particular product.

Marine Protection, Research, and Sanctuaries Act A federal statute that established a system of permits that regulates the discharge and introduction of materials into coastal waters and continuous marine areas.

market power The business becomes so dominate in the marketplace that it no long competes but instead can force its decisions on other competitors.

Market Reform Act A federal statute that addresses the stability of U.S. securities markets when extraordinarily volatile situations occur.

maskwork A series of related images, fixed or encoded, in a three-dimensional pattern on a silicon chip. The pattern is layered in a series, so that each image has a pattern. Similar to a film negative that is black on clear plastic. As it is processed into a picture, various layers of plastic with images are placed on top of one another. Eventually the final product, a colored photograph, is produced. May be copyrighted.

McCarran–Ferguson Act A federal statute exempting all activities that involve insurance businesses from the antitrust laws.

med/arb Hybrid system that first uses mediation and then arbitration to reach a resolution.

mediation Process of promoting voluntary compromise or resolution of a dispute usually initiated before arbitration.

Medicare Health insurance program administered by the Social Security Administration to people sixty-five years of age and older and for those under sixty-five years of age who are disabled.

meeting the competition defense In an antitrust price discrimination case, this defense is used by a business to justify its selling of a product at a lower price to some customers to meet a competitor's price.

member As used in this textbook, the owner(s) of a limited liability company.

mens rea Criminal intent.

merchant Under the UCC, a person who regularly deals in a particular type of goods.

merchant protection legislation A state statute that allows a merchant to detain a suspected shoplifter, provided that reasonable cause for suspicion exists and that the detention is executed in a reasonable way.

merger Combination of two or more firms into one firm.

merit registration State security registration that is reviewed for its merits rather than just for its disclosures.

minitrial A form of alternative dispute resolution in which the parties present their arguments or part of a case to a judge or advisory jury that renders a decision in order to encourage settlement.

mirror–image rule A common law rule that requires an offeree's acceptance to match the offeror's offer exactly.

misapplication of trust funds A special form of embezzlement in which funds entrusted to a person or business are not used for their original intention.

misdemeanor Crime punishable by a fine or by confinement for up to a year; for example, trespass or disorderly conduct.

mislaid property Property that has been placed somewhere by the owner voluntarily and then inadvertently forgotten.

misrepresentation A factually incorrect statement or conduct made during contract negotiations on which the other party relies.

Model Business Corporation Act (MBCA) A model statute that has had its major provisions adopted by most states.

Money Laundering Control Act A federal statute that requires the tracking of large sums of currency to prevent the free flow of currency gained from criminal acts.

monopoly Situation in which a business has exclusive control or nearly total control of the market share of a particular business or even of a whole industry.

Montreal Protocol on Substances that Deplete the Ozone Layer Protocol aimed at reducing and eventually eliminating the emissions of man-made ozone-depleting substances.

mortgage Special type of lien against real property to secure repayment of a debt.

mortgage note Type of collateral note used to buy a house.

mortgagee Creditor or lender; the beneficiary of the mortgage.

mortgagor Debtor or borrower who creates a mortgage on real estate.

motion Application made to a judge by a party to a lawsuit seeking relief for a wrong committed or asserting a procedural right.

motion to dismiss See *demurrer.*

multiple product order An order from an FTC administrative law judge requiring a seller's future advertisements for specific products to be accurate. Order covers more products than the product involved in a past false advertisement.

mutual assent Meeting of the minds of the offeror and the offeree; offer must be made by one person and accepted by another for the same item or service.

mutual mistake Mistake made by both of the contracting parties as to either the identity or existence of the subject matter of the contract.

N

National Ambient Air Quality Standards (NAAQS) Standards set by the Environmental Protection Agency that regulate uniform nationwide ambient air quality standards.

National Environmental Policy Act (NEPA) Federal statute established in 1970 that created the Council of Environmental Quality and mandated that an environmental impact statement be prepared for every recommendation or report on legislation or major federal action significantly affecting the quality of the environment.

National Export Strategy Expanded and streamlined program to promote U.S. exports by the federal government.

National Labor Relations Act Also known as the Wagner Act; federal statute enacted in 1935 that established rights of employees to engage in collective bargaining and to strike.

National Labor Relations Board (NLRB) Agency created by the Wagner Act to oversee union elections and to prevent employers from engaging in unfair and illegal union-labor activities and practices.

national law Body of law that pertains to a particular nation.

National Securities Markets Improvement Act A federal statute that ended dual regulation (by the state and federal governments) of investment advisers by providing the SEC authority over any adviser who manages $25 million or more of assets.

national treatment Required under World Trade Organization (WTO) rules, a nondiscrimination principle that calls for an importing country to treat goods from other WTO member countries as if they were domestic goods.

natural law school Approach to the study of law that holds ethics to be the source of legal authority; ethical values are used to make legal decisions.

negative option rule Federal Trade Commission rule that requires book, video, and other similar clubs to provide members enough time to respond if they choose to decline a monthly selection.

negligence Conduct that falls below the duty of care and that results in another's personal injury or property damage.

negotiable To make an instrument negotiable, it must be in writing and signed, be an unconditional promise or order to pay a fixed amount of money, payable to bearer or order, and payable on demand or at a definite time.

negotiable instrument A specialized written document signed by the debtor acknowledging a debt to be paid on demand or at a specified time in the future. The document is an unconditional promise or order to pay a fixed sum of money.

negotiation Process in which two or more people meet to discuss their differences and attempt to arrive at a settlement that is acceptable to both.

Noerr-Pennington Doctrine Derives from two U.S. Supreme Court cases that allows businesses to work together to lobby Congress to pass appropriate favorable laws.

Noise Control Act A federal statute establishing the goal of creating an environment free from noise that injures public health and welfare.

nolo contendere Plea by the defendant that does not admit guilt but that allows the court to impose the same penalty as for a guilty plea.

nonattainment area Geographic area defined by the Clean Air Act where air pollution levels persistently exceed national ambient air quality standards.

nonexempt property Debtor's property that is not protected by state or federal statute from seizure and sale by a creditor or trustee in bankruptcy with proceeds from sale used to pay off the outstanding debts. Contrast with *exempt property*.

nonfreehold estate Chattel real; estate consisting of possession of land without possessing a freehold estate in it.

normal trade relations Required under the World Trade Organization (WTO) rules, a nondiscrimination principle that calls for equal treatment of goods exported and imported among countries that are members of WTO. Formerly called most-favored-nation principle.

Norris-LaGuardia Act Federal statute established in 1932 that permits employees to organize and restricts federal courts from issuing injunctions against unions engaged in peaceful strikes.

novation Written agreement entered into by all the parties in which one party is substituted for another party; that is, one party is completely dismissed, and another party is substituted.

nuisance Improper activity that interferes with another's enjoyment or use of his or her property.

Nuclear Waste Policy Act (NWPA) A federal statute requiring the building of a permanent repository for the disposal of spent nuclear fuel and high-level wastes.

O

objective standard of care All persons must act as a reasonable and prudent person would act under the same facts or circumstances. One of the elements necessary to prove negligence.

obtaining goods or money by false pretenses Crime of obtaining title to another's property using an intentionally false statement of a past or existing fact with the intent to defraud another.

Occupational Safety and Health Act Federal statute that requires health and safety protections for employees at their place of employment.

Occupational Safety and Health Administration (OSHA) Organization that promulgates and enforces workers' safety and health standards, conducts inspections and investigations, keeps records, and performs research.

offer In contract law, conduct or statement by a person with the objective intent to be bound that proposes definite terms and is communicated to the other party, permitting that person receiving the offer to accept or reject it.

offeree Person receiving the offer.

offeror Person making the offer.

officer (of a corporation) Person hired by a corporation's board of directors to implement policy set by the board and to oversee the daily operations of the corporation.

Oil Pollution Act A federal statute that increased the strict liability limit eightfold for spills containing polluting elements. Liability fines cover cleanup costs, natural resource damages, losses to subsistence resources, and costs to local government.

Old Age, Survivors, and Disability Insurance (OASDI) Another name for Social Security, which provides retirement and disability payments and acts as a life insurance annuity by providing funds to minor children whose parent(s) is(are) deceased.

Older Workers Benefit Protection Act (OWBPA) A federal statute prohibiting employers from discrimination in benefits packages for older workers.

Omnibus Trade and Competitiveness Act (OTCA) A federal statute having four purposes: (1) to authorize the negotiation of reciprocal trade agreements; (2) to strengthen U.S. trade laws; (3) to improve the development and management of U.S. trade strategy; and (4) through these actions, to improve living standards in the world.

operating agreement Agreement in a limited liability company that determines who will have the responsibility of management, control, and division of profits.

operation of law Broad concept used by a court or statute to impose rights or liabilities on a party without any action taken by the party.

option contract Contract separate from the main contract that removes the offeror's right to revoke an offer for the time period specified in the option; money for time.

order Decision of the administrative law judge; final disposition of a case between the government and a party in a lawsuit.

order paper Instrument that is payable to a specific person. May start as bearer paper that is converted to order paper by designating the next holder. Contrast with *bearer paper*.

ordinance Law enacted by a city or county legislative body.

original jurisdiction Jurisdiction held by the original court, the trial court.

overt act An act committed in anticipation of committing a criminal act.

P

parallel import See *gray-market imports*.

Paris Convention for the Protection of Industrial Property Convention that attempts to achieve uniformity in the patent area by having countries adopt a universal system of granting and recognizing patents.

parol evidence rule Rule that allows courts to prevent being placed into evidence any oral statements made prior to or at the time of a written contract's signing; also known as the *best evidence rule*.

partially disclosed principal Principal whose identity is not known by the third party but the third party knows that the agent is acting for a principal at the time the contract is made.

partially protected speech Speech that cannot be regulated by the government, but can be restricted as to time and place, but must be fully truthful.

partnering This term is used in large construction contracts to assist in building a framework to handle any disputes that may arise among the contractors. Normally a neutral facilitator arranges a procedure to handle these disputes in an expeditious manner. The purpose is to take care of small disputes when they arise in order to prevent larger disputes.

partnership A business that is run for profit in which two or more people have an undivided, and sometimes unequal, ownership interest.

partnership by estoppel When a person allows his name to be used in a partnership and does not deny it when others imply that he is a partner. The person becomes liable as if he really were a partner.

pass-through tax treatment The passing of profits and losses through a partnership, limited liability company, or S corporation to the individual owners for federal taxation purposes.

patent Grant from the government that conveys and secures to an inventor the exclusive right to make, use, and sell an invention for a period of seventeen years.

patent license License granted to a foreign licensee by a U.S. business that allows access to and use of a patent.

payee Bearer of an instrument.

payment order Under the UCC, Article 4A, order for an electronic transfer of funds that deletes money from the originator's account and places it in the payee's account.

per se **rule** Illegality that requires for proof only the fact that an agreement existed; for example, horizontal price fixing.

peremptory challenge During *voir dire*, an attorney's request that a prospective juror be dismissed for an unstated reason.

perfection A series of steps a secured party must take to protect its rights in the collateral against all persons.

personal defense A defense against paying a negotiable instrument to an ordinary holder; it is not a defense against a holder in due course.

personal property All property that is basically movable and is not real property.

petition Written request made to a court.

petty offense Civil offense not classified as a crime, which is punishable by a fine, imprisonment, or both; for example, a traffic violation.

pierce the corporate veil Action taken by a court to ignore the corporate structure and look to the shareholders' personal assets to satisfy corporate obligations.

plaintiff Person filing a lawsuit to seek relief from harm.

Plant Closing Act See *Worker Adjustment and Retraining Notification Act.*

plead To present a case before a court.

pleading Document written by one of the parties to a lawsuit and sent to the other parties and to the court to be included in the judge's case file; provides information to the other parties.

police power Authority possessed by states to regulate private activities in order to protect or promote the health, safety, morals, or general welfare of their citizens.

Pollution Prevention Act (PPA) A federal statute that focuses on the reduction of the amount of pollution through cost-effective changes in production, operation, and use of raw materials.

power of attorney Notarized written document that grants a person the authority to perform acts on another person's behalf, such as signing papers, opening accounts, or making purchases.

precedent Decision made in a previous, similar case that is used to decide the outcome of a current case.

preemption doctrine Doctrine that allows Congress to act exclusively in areas that affect primarily national, as opposed to local, matters. If Congress chooses to preempt a particular area, the states no longer have any authority to enact legislation in that area.

preferential lien As defined by federal statute, a lien voluntarily made by a debtor, prior to a bankruptcy, to enable a favored creditor to receive payments prior to payments owed to other creditors.

preferential payment As defined by federal statute, payments made within a specific time period by a debtor to favored creditors, but not to all creditors, prior to the filing of a bankruptcy.

preferred stock Equity security in a corporation that carries certain preferences, such as dividends at a fixed rate; may or may not carry voting rights and is entitled to preference over common

stock in payment of assets in the event the corporation is liquidated.

Pregnancy Discrimination Act A federal statute that redefined gender discrimination to include discrimination based on pregnancy, childbirth, or related medical conditions.

preponderance of the evidence To prevail in a lawsuit, the level or proof that requires a plaintiff to present evidence that is just slightly more persuasive than the defendant's evidence.

pretrial hearing Hearing that serves to identify and narrow the subject matter that is in dispute and to plan the course of the trial.

price discrimination Occurs when the same goods or services are sold to competing purchasers at different prices.

prima facie **case** Evidence presented by the plaintiff that will prove the case unless contradicted and overcome by other evidence presented by the defendant.

principal Person or business who hires an agent to represent them.

Privacy Act 1974 amendment to the Administrative Procedures Act that protects individuals who are citizens or legal aliens from uncontrolled transfer of certain personal information to federal agencies for nonroutine uses.

private judge A judge, usually retired, who is hired by parties to resolve a dispute because of his or her subject matter expertise in the area of the dispute. Also called a *referee*.

private law Subdivision of substantive law; addresses direct dealings between persons.

private nuisance Tort that interferes with the property interest of a limited number of individuals.

private offering exemption Securities offered to only a few people and exempt from registration with the SEC.

Private Securities Litigation Reform Act A federal statute that curtails lawsuits against businesses based on securities law violations.

privilege and immunities clause Clause that prevents one state from discriminating against the citizens of another state based solely on their residency.

privilege of immunity Person cannot be held liable for defamatory statements when made under conditions that are protected by law.

privileged information Information obtained through a confidential communication in a protected relationship, such as an attorney–client, husband–wife (in some states), or priest–penitent relationship. Not allowed at trial.

privity of contract Requirement that an injured party suing for product liability must have been a party to the original contract.

probable cause Reasonable ground for supposing that an individual has committed a crime.

probate Legal process of settling a person's estate by collecting property owned by the deceased, paying his debts, and transferring ownership of the deceased's property to his heirs.

procedural due process Guarantee granted to individuals that requires any government decision to take a person's life, liberty, or property to be made fairly.

procedural law Established methods or processes of enforcing the rights created by substantive law.

procedural rule Type of administrative agency rule that governs the internal practices of an agency.

process Document that is an order coming from the court, signed by the judge or representative; three stages of process exist: issued, served, filed.

product liability Potential responsibility that a manufacturer or seller has for injuries or damages caused by defective goods.

production Means of acquiring ownership of personal property by creating that property.

professional agent One who handles contracts in a particular field; for example, real estate broker.

professional association Organized group of professionals with common interests; subject to antitrust laws.

professionally developed ability test Tests that can be given by employers to potential employees to measure specific abilities related to job performance. An ability test, its administration, and the actions based on the results must not be intended to discriminate illegally.

promisee Person receiving the promise.

promisor Person making the promise.

promissory estoppel Doctrine that prevents the promisor from revoking the offer.

promissory note Written promise to pay made between two parties; payable at a definite time or on demand.

promoter Person who takes the preliminary steps to organize a corporation.

prospectus Document the supplies information to prospective buyers of a security.

protected speech Speech that cannot be restricted or regulated in any manner by the government, thus allowing a full exchange of ideas to take place.

Protection of Semiconductor Chip Products Act A federal statute that allows the maskwork of a semiconductor chip to be copyrighted.

protocol Official agreement between different countries' diplomats that does not have the force of a treaty.

proximate cause Reasonable, causal relationship between a defendant's unreasonable conduct and the plaintiff's injury or damage. Limits the defendant's liability as a result of the misconduct. One of the elements necessary to prove negligence.

proxy Written authorization empowering another person to act for the signer at, for instance, a shareholders' meeting.

public welfare Government protection and entitlement programs that benefit the public at large.

public law Subdivision of substantive law; addresses the relationship between individuals and their government.

public nuisance Crime that disturbs or interferes with the public.

punitive damages Damages awarded to punish a party for intentional and willful conduct that he or she knew at the time would harm someone.

purchase money security loan Security interest created as part of a purchase agreement.

Q

qualified indorsement Instrument of indorsement used by the indorser to disclaim or limit liability on the instrument.

qualified privilege The law gives a limited right of protection to a person who makes defamatory statements, as long as they are made under conditions protected by law.

quasi in rem **jurisdiction** Jurisdiction over the interests of particular persons in particular property.

quasi-contract Implied-in-law contract in which the parties did not make any promise by word or conduct but the law imposed a promise on the party who benefited.

quasi-executive function Administrative agency power to ensure compliance with the rules and to conduct investigations.

quasi-judicial function Administrative agency power to prosecute cases, render judgments, and impose penalties if violations occur.

quasi-legislative function Administrative agency power to promulgate rules that have the effect of law.

quasi-official agency Created by Congress, but the agency does not have the same authority as line, independent, or government agencies.

quiet title action Action filed in court whereby the court determines who has title to real property.

quitclaim deed Deed conveying to the buyer whatever interest the grantor had in the property, if any.

quota Limit, as on the number of goods that can be imported to a country.

R

Racketeer Influenced and Corrupt Organizations Act of 1970 (RICO) Amendment to the Organized Crime Control Act of 1970; designed to control the investment by organized crime into legitimate businesses and to force forfeiture of any profits made as a result of such criminal activity.

ratification Occurs when a principal approves a contract, by word or by action, that has been negotiated by a purported agent. Ratification binds the principal to the agent's acts and treats the acts or contracts as if the principal had authorized them.

rational basis test Discrimination test that does not involve a protected class. Two requirements must be met: (1) a legitimate governmental interest and (2) a rational relationship between the governmental interest and the means used to accomplish that interest.

reaffirm As defined by federal statute, an agreement by a debtor with a creditor to repay debts that could have been forgiven by bankruptcy court.

real defense A complete defense against paying a negotiable instrument to any owner.

Real Estate Settlement Procedures Act (RESPA) Federal statute that governs the purchase of a house and the borrowing of money to pay for it.

real property Land and the objects permanently attached to it.

receiving stolen goods Crime in which the recipient of the stolen goods knows or should have known that the goods were stolen.

recording statute State statute that allows certain documents, such as deeds and liens, to be recorded in a specified public office so prospective buyers or lenders are provided with a way to check a property's history and to determine any outstanding claims against the property's title.

red herring prospectus Preliminary prospectus; so named because the legend printed across it is in red ink and states that the SEC registration has been filed but is not yet effective.

reformation of the contract Rewriting of the contract because of errors in the written document.

registration statement Document filed with the SEC by a business that desires to issue a security; provides information about the business, such as the names of directors and officers and financial and economic information.

regular trustee Court-appointed trustee who is elected or appointed to represent the creditors in a specific bankruptcy case. Contrast *U.S. trustee.*

Regulation A An SEC rule that provides a simplified registration statement for issues of $1.5 million or less in one year.

Regulation D An SEC rule that has three provisions that exempt different situations from registration.

Regulatory Flexibility Act 1980 amendment to the Administrative Procedures Act that requires an agency to publish in the Federal Register twice each year a special regulatory flexibility agenda.

rejection In contract law, act of refusing to accept an offer.

relevant geographic market Part of the structural analysis used by the courts to determine whether a monopoly exists; considers the area where the product is sold, transportation costs, and how far consumers must travel to purchase the product.

relevant product market Part of the structural analysis used by the courts to determine whether a monopoly exists; considers the characteristics of the product, its substitutes.

remand Act of sending a case back to a lower court to carry out the appellate court's decision.

remedy Relief provided for an innocent party when the other party has breached a contract.

remedy at law Legal remedy awarded by the court; the harmed party could be awarded land, money, or items of value, or a combination of all three.

reorganization Also known as Chapter 11 in a business bankruptcy filing; situation in which the creditors and debtors formulate a plan under which the debtor pays a portion of the debts and is discharged of the remainder, and the debtor is allowed to continue in business.

reply Pleading filed by a plaintiff in response to a defendant's counterclaim.

repossession Situation in which the secured party takes possession of the collateral covered by the security agreement in the event of default.

request for physical or mental examination Court order requiring a party to a lawsuit to submit to an examination by a doctor.

request to produce Court order requiring a party to a lawsuit to make available physical evidence it has in its possession.

res ipsa loquitur Latin for "the thing speaks for itself." Doctrine that says the event causing the damage must not occur in the absence of negligence, the conduct of the plaintiff or any other third party could have caused the event, and the defendant owes the plaintiff a duty of reasonable care.

res judicata Rule that states once a case has been fully litigated, neither party can institute another action based on the same facts or circumstances.

resale price maintenance Vertical restraint of trade in which the buyer and the seller agree to the price at which the buyer will resell the product.

rescission Remedy that cancels the agreement and returns the parties to the contract to the status quo; may be by mutual consent, by conduct, or by decree of a court of equity.

Resource Conservation and Recovery Act (RCRA) A federal statute governing Environmental Protection Agency studies and recommendations on solid waste disposal; provides a creation-to-disposal tracking system for hazardous waste.

response See *answer.*

Restatement, Second Body of law created by the judiciary and revised in 1979; covers the areas of law regarding contracts, property, trusts, and torts.

restitution Equitable remedy in which a person is restored to his or her original position prior to loss or injury, or is

placed in the same position as if a breach had not occurred.

restraint of trade Agreement among competitors that has a wrongful intent to increase prices on products or services by minimizing competition.

restricted securities Securities acquired in unregistered, private sales from an issuer.

restrictive indorsement Indorsement on an instrument that requires the indorser to comply with certain instructions regarding the funds involved.

retention Under the merit system, judges who were originally appointed must stand for election to retain their judicial office.

reverse Act of appellate court when deciding to disagree with a lower court's decision.

Revised Model Business Corporation Act (RMBCA) A model statute that revised the then-existing law by simplifying its procedures.

Revised Uniform Limited Partnership Act (RULPA) A uniform statute that has been adopted by several states that revised the then-existing limited partnership rules.

Revised Uniform Partnership Act (RUPA) A uniform statute that has been adopted by many states that revised the then-existing partnership laws. Under this act, a partnership is treated as an entity rather than as a collection of individuals

revocation Withdrawing of the offer by the offeror.

right-to-work laws Statutes making it illegal for union membership to be required for employment.

robbery Wrongful or fraudulent taking and carrying away by any person of the personal property of another, involving the use of fear or force.

Robinson-Patman Act Section 2 of the Clayton Act; promotes economic equality in the purchasing and selling of goods; prohibits price discrimination.

Rivers and Harbors Act A federal statute regulating the discharge into or depositing of refuse in navigable waterways.

Rule 10b–5 Rule issued by the SEC implementing Section 10(b) of the Securities Exchange Act of 1934 that makes it unlawful for any person, directly or indirectly, to defraud or mislead anyone in the purchase or sale of a security.

Rule 144 An SEC rule that allows an owner of a securities to sell them if they have been held for more than one year and adequate public information is available.

Rule 144A An SEC rule that allows a safe harbor for the owner when reselling securities to qualified institutional buyers or registered broker-dealers.

Rule 415 An SEC rule, known as shelf registration, that allows an issuer to register stock without needing to sell it. The stock is placed on a shelf to be sold at a later time.

Rule 504 An SEC rule stating that a noninvestment company can sell up to $1 million in securities that it issues in any one year without registration if the company does not advertise or make any general solicitations.

Rule 505 An SEC rule stating that a private, noninvestment company may sell up to $5 million in securities in any one year to any number of accredited investors and no more than 35 unaccredited investors if the company does not advertise or make any general solicitations.

Rule 506 An SEC rule stating that a private, noninvestment company may offer an unlimited number of securities if they generally do not solicit or advertise them.

rule of reason Doctrine by which the court reviews all the circumstances of a case to decide whether the defendant's practice was an unreasonable restraint on trade.

S

S corporation A corporation that is treated as a partnership for federal tax purposes.

Safe Drinking Water Act A federal statute authorizing the Environmental Protection Agency to establish standards for safe drinking water purity.

safe harbor exemption An SEC rule that exempts parties from having to register certain securities.

sale on approval Contract clause that states that no sale occurs until the ultimate consumer is satisfied.

sale or return Contract clause that states that the business purchaser can return the goods if not sold. Buyer has risk of loss and title unless the goods are returned.

scam bankruptcy A plan to swindle creditors by purchasing goods in ad-

vance, while at the same time planning a bankruptcy proceeding.

scienter Guilty knowledge that is greater than simple negligence.

scope of employment Within the time and space of a work assignment.

Section 10(b) Section of the Securities Exchange Act of 1934 that makes it unlawful to use or employ, in connection with the purchase or sale of a security, any deceptive device.

Section 16 Section of the Securities Exchange Act of 1934 that requires directors, officers, and owners of more than 10 percent of the shares of any one class of stock of a company registered with the SEC to file reports of their holdings and transactions with the SEC; such persons are known as "insiders."

Section 18 Section of the Securities Exchange Act of 1934 that requires publicly held corporations registered with the SEC to file periodic and intermittent reports that include audited financial statements, current financial status, and securities holdings.

secured transaction Type of transaction secured by collateral.

Securities Act of 1933 First securities regulation statute enacted by Congress; often referred to as the "truth in securities" law because it requires full and truthful disclosure by companies issuing securities.

Securities and Exchange Commission (SEC) Federal body that regulates securities, financial markets, business practices, and specific industries, such as stockbrokers.

Securities Enforcement Remedies and Penny Stock Reform Act A federal statute that strengthens the enforcement powers of the SEC and regulates the penny stock market.

Securities Exchange Act of 1934 A federal statute that (1) ensures the integrity of stock and securities sold through national stock exchanges and over-the-counter markets; (2) informs the investing public of the financial condition of a business; (3) protects the public from fraudulent activity; and (4) created the Securities and Exchange Commission.

Securities Investor Protection Corporation (SIPC) A corporation created by Congress that manages a fund that protects investors from the financial harm caused when stockbrokerage houses fail.

security An investment of money or other consideration in a common enterprise, with the investor expecting a profit and with the profit derived primarily through the efforts of a promoter or a third party other than the investor.

self-defense Doctrine that gives a person the right to defend his or her person.

self-incrimination Protection provided in the Fifth and Fourteenth Amendments that says a person cannot be forced to testify against himself or herself.

server Computer software program that allows mainframe and personal computers to host World Wide Web sites.

service mark Mark used to distinguish the services of one person from those of another; the title, character names, or other distinctive features of radio and television programs may be registered as service marks.

shelf registration See *Rule 415*.

Sherman Act A federal statute that attempts to end monopolies and restraints of trade.

Shore Protection Act A federal statute controlling the disposal of solid wastes in oceans and lakes.

sight (demand) draft Instrument payable on sight when the holder presents it for payment.

slander Act of verbally making false and malicious statements to others about another person or business.

slander of title Defaming the title a person has to his or her property and possibly preventing the sale of the property.

small offering exemption Offerings from an issuer that are not large enough for the federal government to regulate; includes certain types of bank loans, privately negotiated sales of securities to large institutional investors, and business-venture promotions by a few closely related persons.

Social Security Act Federal statute that established a federal insurance program covering the financial impact of retirement, death, disability, hospitalization, and unemployment of a worker through contributions by a worker and his or her employer.

software Programming involved with a computer system.

sole proprietorship A business owned by one person.

Solid Waste Disposal Act A federal statute designed to reduce solid waste disposal by encouraging the recycling of waste and the reuse of materials by society.

sovereign immunity Doctrine that states a person cannot sue the government without its permission.

special indorsement Indorsement on an instrument that indicates a specific person to whom the indorser intends to make the instrument payable.

special warranty deed Deed in which the seller warrants that he or she has not previously done anything to lessen the value of the real estate for sale.

specific performance Equitable remedy in which the defendant is ordered to perform the act(s) promised in the contract.

spending power Authority possessed by the federal and state governments to spend public monies.

spot rate Market rate for goods or exchange rate for currencies.

stakeholder Persons or entities affected by the activities of a business, such as shareholders, employees, customers, suppliers, government, and the community or public at large.

standing to sue Doctrine that requires a litigant to demonstrate a direct harm as a result of the other party's action.

stare decisis "Let the decision stand"; the practice of deciding a case with reference to former decisions.

state implementation plan (SIP) Plan required by the 1991 Clean Air Amendments that requires states to collect information about mobile and stationary sources of pollution and to issue regulations for cleaning up polluted areas.

statute Law passed by Congress or a state legislature.

statute of frauds Statute providing that certain contracts are not enforceable in court unless they are in writing and signed by the party to be charged.

statute of limitations Statutes that set limitations on the amount of time that can elapse during which a lawsuit must be filed.

statutory duty Obligation imposed by a legislative act.

statutory law Body of law enacted by state and federal legislatures.

statutory liens Liens granted by statute, such as a landlord's lien against the tenant's property for nonpayment of rent.

stay Court order to stop a proceedings.

stop-payment order Request made by a customer that his or her bank stop payment on an issued check.

straight bankruptcy Bankruptcy in which the debtor lists debts and turns his or her assets over to a trustee for settlement of the bankruptcy action.

strict scrutiny test Discrimination test for which two requirements must be met: (1) a compelling government interest and (2) use of the least restrictive means available to satisfy that interest.

strict liability Situation in which no defenses exist; applies to dangerous activities where all risk and responsibility for injury is assumed by the party involved or doing the hazardous activity.

subject matter jurisdiction Jurisdiction that limits the type of cases a court can hear as a result of the subject of the case or the amount of money disputed.

subpoena Process document that secures the attendance of a witness at a trial.

subpoena *duces tecum* Process document that requires evidence to be brought to court.

substantial evidence Evidence that a reasonable person might accept as adequate to support a conclusion.

substantive due process Doctrine that holds that the content or substance of a piece of legislation must be in compliance with the Constitution.

substantive law Law that defines, describes, regulates, and creates legal rights and obligations of individuals with respect to each other.

substantive rule Administrative agency rule that is not procedural or interpretive in nature.

summary judgment Written request by either party to a lawsuit to the court to grant judgment on grounds that there is no genuine issue of material fact and the requesting party is entitled to judgment as a matter of law.

summons Process document that requires the defendant to defend against the claim of the plaintiff in a lawsuit.

sunset law Law that establishes the automatic expiration date for an administrative agency.

Sunshine Act Amendment to the Administrative Procedures Act that prohibits administrative agencies from holding secret meetings.

supremacy clause Clause in Article VI of the Constitution that governs the

relationship between the states and the federal government; the federal Constitution, statutes, and treaties take priority over state laws if a conflict arises between the two.

T

tangible property Visible property that has physical existence; for example, land, cattle, buildings, computers.

tariff Tax placed on imported goods based on either an ad valorem or a flat-rate basis.

tenancy by the entirety Ownership where the husband and wife own property without separate transfer rights.

taxing power Authority possessed by the federal government and state governments to levy and collect taxes.

temporary restraining order (TRO) A person is ordered for a temporary time to refrain from an activity.

tenancy at will Rental agreement in which either the tenant or the landlord can terminate the tenancy without notice.

tenancy by sufferance Possession of land without right; not a true tenancy.

tenancy for years Nonfreehold estate created by express contract by leasing property for a specific period of time.

tenancy from period to period Nonfreehold estate created by a lease that does not specify length of time but states that rent is to be paid at certain intervals.

tenancy in common Co-ownership in which two or more persons can own an undivided fractional interest in the property, but, on one tenant's death, that interest passes to his or her heirs.

tenant Person who rents a piece of property from the landlord (owner).

tender Offer of money or goods.

termination The final act of a partnership when it goes out of business.

termination statement Statement showing that a debt has been paid.

territorial and customer division Where competitors engage in an agreement to divide sales among certain customers or territory and agree not to compete for those customers or territory.

theft of trade secrets Tort of stealing confidential information.

third-party complaint Complaint filed against a party who was not an original party to the lawsuit.

thrust-upon defense Defense used by a business to justify its monopoly that it is selling a superior product or follows better business practices and, hence, the monopoly was created through no wrongful act or intent on the business's part.

time draft Draft that is payable at a definite future time.

tippee People to whom material information about a security is given that could be used for insider trading.

tipper People who give out material information about a security that could be used for insider trading.

Title VII of the Civil Rights Act of 1964 Federal statute that prohibits discrimination in all areas of employment on the basis of race, color, religion, national origin, sex, including pregnancy, childbirth, and abortion, by state, local, and federal agencies and employers of at least fifteen employees and involved in or a part of interstate commerce; administered by the Equal Employment Opportunity Commission.

tombstone advertisement Written advertising for a security that simply tells the investor where and how to obtain a particular security's prospectus; so named because it is outlined in black and resembles a tombstone.

tort French word meaning "wrong"; wrongdoing for which a civil action in court is possible.

Toxic Substances Control Act A federal statute requiring the Environmental Protection Agency to track more than 75,000 industrial chemicals produced or imported into the United States in order to regulate those toxic substances that potentially create a hazard or an unreasonable risk of injury to people. This act supplements the Clean Air Act.

trade acceptance Draft frequently used with the sale of goods in which the purchaser becomes liable to pay the draft. Equivalent to note receivable of the seller and note payable of the buyer, a trade acceptance permits the seller to raise money on it before it is due.

Trade Act A federal statute that governs trade; first time Congress granted the U.S. president fact-track authority, now called trade promotion authority.

Trade Agreement Act A federal statute that regulates the practice of dumping in the United States.

trade association Group of organized competitors pursuing a common interest, such as dissemination of information, advertising campaigns, codes of conduct; subject to antitrust laws.

trade promotion authority Procedure passed by Congress requiring it, once the U.S. president has signed a trade agreement with another country or countries, either to approve or disapprove of the agreement as signed; amendments are not allowed. Formerly called fast-track authority.

trade regulation rule Administrative rule issued by the FTC that applies to an industry's policies and practices; this rule has the force of law.

trademark Distinctive mark, motto, device, or implement that a manufacturer stamps, prints, or otherwise affixes to the goods it produces.

Trademark Counterfeiting Act A federal statute that makes dealing in goods or services under a counterfeit trademark a federal crime.

traveler's check Draft from a financial institution.

treaty Agreement or contract between two or more nations that must be authorized and ratified by the supreme power of each nation.

tribunal administrator Person who manages the administrative matters and all communication between the parties and the arbitrator in an arbitration.

trust Legal entity in which a trustee holds title to property for the benefit of another.

trustee Person who holds title to the property placed in a trust and manages the property for the benefit of the beneficiaries.

trustor Person who creates a trust and names the trustee and beneficiary.

Truth-in-Lending Act (TILA) Title I of the Consumer Credit Protection Act; deals with deceptive credit practices and requires notice and disclosure to prevent sellers and creditors from taking unfair advantage of consumers.

tying arrangement Arrangement in which the buyer must purchase one item in order to purchase the tied product.

U

unaccredited investor An investor who is likely to need protection when making investments. Compare with *accredited investor.*

unconscionable contract or clause Clause in a contract, or the entire contract, that is so one-sided as to be unjust after considering the needs of the particular case.

undercapitalization Situation of a corporation when it has insufficient capital (money and property).

undisclosed principal Principal whose identity is totally unknown by the third party and the third party has no knowledge that the agent is acting in an agency capacity at the time the contract is made.

undue influence Arises from special relationships that allow one party to greatly influence another, thus overcoming the weaker party's free will.

unenforceable contract Contract that began as a valid contract, but for some legal reason cannot now be enforced against the other party.

unfair labor practices strike Strike whereby workers strike because management is alleged to be in violation of the law. If workers are correct, management must rehire these workers.

unfair or deceptive acts or practices Language contained in the Wheeler-Lee Act to enable the FTC to provide consumers with protections from these types of acts or practices. Not defined by statue, but interpreted by the courts on a case-by-case basis.

Uniform Arbitration Act Act designed to make legislation on arbitration more uniform throughout the country; has been adopted by 34 states and the District of Columbia.

Uniform Commercial Code (UCC) Uniform act consisting of eleven articles that applies to both interstate and intrastate business transactions governing the conduct of business among individuals and businesses.

Uniform Consumer Credit Code (UCCC) Comprehensive body of rules governing the most important aspects of consumer credit; has been adopted by only a few states.

Uniform Limited Partnership Act (ULPA) A uniform statute that has been adopted by many states that established the rules for limited partnerships.

Uniform Partnership Act (UPA) A uniform statute adopted by most states that establishes the law on general partnerships.

unilateral contract Contract in which a person makes a promise that requires in return an act (not a promise) by the other party; for example, a reward situation.

unilateral mistake Mistake made by one of the contracting parties.

union shop Business that does not require union membership of applicants in order to be hired but can and usually does require workers to join the union after a specific period of time on the job.

United Nations Commission on International Trade Law (UNCITRAL) Commission that develops model laws that cover international commercial transactions.

United Nations Convention on International Bills of Exchange and Promissory Notes Agreement among nations concerning the rules governing documents that are orders to pay (bills of exchange) and promises to pay (promissory notes).

United Nations Convention on the Law of the Sea Convention imposing on signatory members the duty to avoid polluting the oceans from land or from vessels; includes legislation against dumping raw wastes from ships.

United Nations Convention on the Recognition and Enforcement of Foreign Arbitral Awards (New York Convention) Convention that created the agreement that allows the enforcement of arbitrated awards in any of the signature.

Universal Copyright Convention Agreement signed in 1952 that grants an author copyright protection in other countries that are signatories when the work is first published and notification given to the other country's copyright office.

unliquidated debt A disputed debt is called an unliquidated debt. This dispute occurs when one person claims more is owed than what the other party believes is owed.

unprotected speech Any speech not protected by the First Amendment. Includes dangerous speech, fighting words, speech that incites violence or revolution, defamatory speech, obscenity, and child pornography.

U.S. Customs Service Service housed within the Department of Treasury that assesses and collects customs duties, excise taxes, fees, and penalties owed on imported merchandise.

U.S. trade representative Chief representative of the United States in the formulation of trade policy and in activities involving bilateral and multilateral trade negotiations; cabinet-level official with the rank of ambassador.

U.S. trustee Government employee in an administrative position within the bankruptcy court who monitors the administration of bankruptcy cases. Contrast *regular trustee*.

usage of trade Principle encouraged by the Uniform Commercial Code that calls for the application of the rules of a particular trade to fill in missing terms in a contract or to guide a court when interpreting a contract clause.

use of the mails to defraud Crime of (1) mailing a writing for the purpose of executing a scheme to defraud or (2) an organized scheme to defraud by false pretenses.

use permit Permit issued by a governmental body that grants permission to operate a given type of business in a certain area.

usury Rate of interest that is above the amount allowed by statute; applies to cash loans only.

utilitarianism Approach to establishing ethical standards based on the consequences of an action.

V

valid contract Contract that meets all requirements of a contract to be enforced in a court.

validated license Limited authority to ship and export certain types of high-technology goods; limits or prohibits certain types of high-technology goods from being shipped to countries of concern that may pose a military threat to the United States.

variance Exception to a zoning ordinance.

venue Particular geographic area within a judicial district where a suit should be brought.

verdict Decision of the jury.

vertical merger Merger of a company at one stage of production with another company at a higher or lower stage of production.

vertical restraint Trade practice that involves firms at different levels of the production and distribution process and that violates antitrust laws.

Vienna Convention on the Law of Treaties Convention that codified the entire body of law on treaties; covers issues such as the legal difference between treaties and other types agreements, constitutional limitations on treaty-making powers, terminology, legal designation of parties, and general rules that apply to interpreting treaties.

Vienna Convention on the Protection of the Ozone Layer Convention through which governments committed themselves to protecting the ozone layer and to cooperating with each other in scientific research to improve understanding of the atmospheric processes.

void agreement Agreement in which the purpose is illegal and hence cannot be enforced by law.

voidable contract Situation in which one party to a contract is bound but the other party may disaffirm it; for example, a contract by a minor.

voir dire The process of selecting a jury, during which attorneys can question prospective jurors to determine bias.

W

warehouse receipt Document that indicates who holds title to goods or who has a right to possession of the goods stored by a distributor.

warrant To promise a fact or facts shall be as represented in a contract or negotiable instrument.

warranty of title Guarantee to the buyer that the goods are not stolen, have no lien against them, and do not infringe a patent or copyright.

Webb-Pomerene Act A federal statute exempting acts or agreements made in the course of export trade by associations of competing producers formed solely for the purpose of engaging in export trade.

Wheeler-Lea Act A federal statute strengthening the power of the Federal Trade Commission to regulate anticompetitive business behavior and to provide consumer protection.

whistleblower Person who discloses wrongful behavior on the part of a company or person.

white-collar crime Monetary offense usually against a business; nonviolent crimes committed by corporations or by individuals against corporations.

winding up The process whereby the assets of a partnership are sold and proceeds distributed.

Worker Adjustment and Retraining Notification Act (WARN) A federal statute requiring businesses to notify employees sixty days in advance if a plant will close. Businesses must also give workers advance notice if more then one-third of a company's employees will be laid off. Also known as the Plant Closing Act.

workers' compensation laws Laws that provide economic protection for workers who are injured or killed on the job.

World Trade Organization (WTO) Created by the Uruguay Round of GATT in 1994, the WTO has two purposes: to administer the GATT and the dispute-resolution system. The WTO replaced the 47-year-old GATT organization on January 1, 1995, although the GATT organization and the WTO will both be in place while the administrative duties are transferred.

writ of attachment Process document issued after judgment has been made by the court; may take the form of an order to take or seize property or persons to bring them under control of the court.

writ of *certiorari* Formal notice from the U.S. Supreme Court or other appellate courts that it will accept a case for review.

writ of execution Process document issued after judgment has been made by the court; puts in force the court's decree or judgment.

writ of garnishment Process document issued after judgment has been made by the court; garnishes the wages or property of the party at fault.

Table of Cases

Index

I-10 ● *Index*

Generalizing/generalizations, A-91–A-92
  glittering, A-95
  hasty, A-93
Genetic testing, 708
Geographic market, 673–674
Gifts, 508
Ginsburg, Ruth Bader, 82
Glantz, Stanton A., 53
Global economy
  environmental law, 781–782
  ethics, 44, 47
Good faith
  collective bargaining and, 713
    case involving, 714–715
  negotiable instruments and, 362
Goods, 317, 318–319. *See also* Bill of lading;
    Exporting; Title
  disparagement of, 232
  fungible, 508
  gray-market, 408
    case involving, 408–410
  importing, 394, 419, 421
    case involving, 419–421
  international conventions on, 286, 312, 344
  obtaining by false pretenses, 205
  specially manufactured, 328–330
    case involving, 330–332
  stolen, 205
  tariffs, 394
Government, 47–48. *See also* Federal
    government; State governments
Government agencies, 167, 168. *See also*
    Administrative agencies
"Governmentese," 173, 181
Grand jury, 200
Gratuitous agency, 540
Gray-market goods, 408
  case involving, 408–410
Greek philosophers, 36
Gross, Allen J., 621
Group boycotts, 666–667
Group of Eight (G-8), 425
Guarantee debt of another, contracts to, 300
Guardians, 312
Guidelines for Multinational Enterprises, 60
"Guidelines on Multinational Corporations,"
    489
"Guides against Bait Advertising," 478
Guilty *versus* nonguilty decision, 200–201
Gulf Cooperation Council, 395

H

Habeas corpus, writ of, 7
Hall, Kermit, 5, 8
Hamilton, Alexander, 136
Hammurabi, 350–351
Handshakes, 293
Hardware (computer), 511
Harmonized Tariff Schedule of the United
    States (HTSUS), 419–421
Hart-Scott-Rodino Antitrust Improvements
    Act, 677, 685
Hazardous and Solid Waste Amendments
    (HSWA), 772–773
Hazelwood, Joseph J., 51
Health and Human Services, U.S.
    Department of, A-100

Health Care Financing Administration, 697
Health Insurance Portability and
    Accountability Act (HIPAA), 706
Hearings
  administrative adjudication, 174
  arbitration, 114–115
  pretrial, 88
Hearsay evidence, 89, 174
Hendrickson, Sue, 500
Herfindahl-Hirschman Index (HHI),
    679–680
Higher Education Amendments, 666
Hinkley, John, 218
Historical school of law, 23, 26
Holders, 352, 361
Holders in due course, 353, 361–362
  case involving, 362–364
  ethical dilemma of, 350
  federal limitation on rights of, 367
Holdings, in court cases, 27, A-95
Holmes, Oliver Wendell, Jr., 5
Home equity loans, 562
Homestead exemption, 449
Hooters Rules, 122–123
Hope diamond, 16
Horizontal market division, 660, 662
  case involving, 662–665
Horizontal mergers, 678–680
  Guidelines, 679
Horizontal price fixing, 660–661
  case involving, 661–662
Hotel Employees and Restaurant Employees
    (HERE), 712
Hours (workers), 695
Housing and Urban Development, U.S.
    Department of, 487, A-100
HTML (Hypertext Markup Language), 27
HTTP (Hypertext Transfer Protocol), 27
Hurricane Andrew, 104
Hurricane insurance, 254
Hyatt Regency Hotel skywalks collapse,
    Kansas City, 244
Hypertext Markup Language (HTML), 27
Hypertext Transfer Protocol (HTTP), 27
Hypothesizing/hypotheses, A-91, A-92
  error of forming too few, A-93

I

IAEAA (International Antitrust Enforcement
    Assistance Act), 686
Identified goods, 318
Identity theft, 481–482
Iguchi, Toshihide, 646–647
Illegality, offer termination and, 273
Illusory promises, 282
  case involving, 282–284
Immigration Act, 740
Immigration Reform and Control Act,
    739–740
Immunity
  privilege of, 232, 234
  sovereign, 158
Implied authority, 532, 533
  case involving, 534–536
Implied contracts, 264, 267
Implied warranties
  of authority, 542

disclaimers/defenses against, 340–341
of fitness for a particular purpose, 340
of merchantability, 339–340
Implied-in-fact contracts, 264, 267
Implied-in-law contracts, 264
Import factor, 414–415
Importing, 394, 419, 421
  case involving, 419–421
Impostor rule, 374–376
Impracticability, 328
In personam jurisdiction, 66–67, 78
In rem jurisdiction, 70
Inadequate-resources defense, 681
Incapacity, 217–218
Incidental beneficiaries, 306
Incidental damages, 329
Incorporators, 589
Incoterms, 345
Independent agencies, 167–168
Independent contractors, 547–549
Indictments, 200
Individual bankruptcy, 454–455
Indorsees, 358
Indorsements, 358–359, 361
  illustrated, 360
Indorsers, 358
Inductive reasoning, A-91–A-92
Infliction of mental distress, 232
Informal contracts, 264, 267
Informal rule making, administrative
    agencies', 172
Information. *See also* Freedom of
    Information Act; Personal information
  administrative agencies and, 175
  labor laws posting of, 746
  privileged, 89
Infringement, 245, 407
  case involving, 246–248
Inherent authority. *See* Implied authority
Inheritance, 502, 508
Injunctions, 16–17
  against strikes, 708, 711
Injury, 238
  personal, 229, 232–234
    case involving, 230–231
  strict liability, 243
Insider trading, 634, 642–643, 645, 646–647.
    See also Section 10(b)
  case involving, 643–644
Insider Trading and Securities Fraud
    Enforcement Act, 620, 645, 647
Insider Trading Sanctions Act, 620, 645
Inspection, right of, 329
Installment note, 354
Institute for Civil Justice, RAND
    Corporation, 105–107, 128, 252
Insurance, 254–255
  antitrust exemption for, 682
  consumer complaints and, 287
  employer-provided medical, 528
  gender discrimination in, 732
  product liability, 345
Insurance agents, 533
Insurance certificate, 419
Intangible property, 496
Intellectual property rights, 511–512, 516
  case involving, 513–514
  Web resources, 522–523

Official-language clause, 414
Oil, Chemical, and Atomic Workers
    (OCAW), 712
Oil Pollution Act, 768
Oil Spill Liability Trust Fund (OSLTF), 768
Oil Spill Recovery Institute, 768
Old Age, Survivors, and Disability Insurance
    (OASDI), 697
Older Workers Benefit Protection Act
    (OWBPA), 737
Oligopolistic market, 677
Omnibus Trade and Competitiveness Act
    (OTCA), 405
    Exon-Florio provision, 520
Online ADR, 120
Ono, Masatoshi, 334
Open account exporting, 414
Opening statements (trials), 88
Operating agreements, 561
Operation of law, 273
    agency relationship termination by, 547
    discharge by, 309
    negotiable instrument defenses and, 366
Opinions
    court's, 26
    as evidence, A-90
Option contracts, 269
Oral contracts, 299–300
    case involving, 301–302
    parol evidence rule and, 302
Order paper, 353
    converting to bearer paper, 365
    negotiating, 365
Orders, 16, 174
Ordinances, 6
Organization for Economic Cooperation and
    Development (OECD), 60, 394
    consumer credit recommendations, 456
    "Guidelines on Multinational Corporations,"
    489
Organization of American States (OAS), 425
Organized Crime Control Act, 208–209
Organizing Institute, 712
Original jurisdiction, 73
Overdrafts, 370
Overt (criminal) acts, 203
Overtime laws, 696
OWBPA (Older Workers Benefit Protection
    Act), 737
Ownership
    corporate transfer factors, 561
    personal information, during bankruptcies,
    515
    of personal property, 506–508
    real property interest, 499–502
    slander of title and, 232
    transfer of real property, 502–506
Ozone layer and climate protection, 763

P

Paid information programs, 204
Pain and suffering, damages for, 251
Panama Convention, 126
Parallel imports, 408–410
Paris Convention for the Protection of
    Industrial Property, 520
Parol evidence rule, 302

Partially disclosed principals, 541–542
Partially executed contracts, 267
Partially protected speech, 145–148
Partnering, 125
Partnership by estoppel, 565
Partnerships, 559, 564–571
    agreements, 583–584
    capital and funding, 565
    duration and termination, 568–571
    liability, 566–567
        case involving, 567–568
    limited, 559, 571–574
    limited liability, 559, 581–582
    versus limited liability companies, 575–576
    management and control, 565–566
Pass-through tax treatment, 574
Patent and Trademark Office (PTO),
    511–512
Patents, 511–512
    infringement of, 245
    licenses for, 612
    websites, 256
Payee, 353. *See also* Indorsements
    fictitious, 374–376
    material alteration by, 366
Payment orders, 377
Payments, automatic, 377
Penny stock reform, 647
Pension Benefit Guaranty Corporation, 168
Pension plans, 693. *See also* Retirement
    gender discrimination in, 732
People's Republic of China, 395
PEOs (professional employer organizations),
    549–550
Per se rule, 660–667
    group boycotts, 660, 666–667
    horizontal market division, 660, 662
        case involving, 662–665
    horizontal price fixing, 660–661
        case involving, 661–662
Peremptory challenges (of jurors), 88
Perfection, 380–381
    case involving, 381–383
Performance
    agent's duty of, 538
    discharge by, 308
    sales and, 328–332
Person(s)
    jurisdiction over, 66–67
        case involving, 67–69
    wrongs against, 229, 232–234
        case involving, 230–231
Personal defenses, 366–367
Personal Earnings and Benefit Statement
    (PEBE), 698
Personal information
    Federal Trade Commission on, 481–482
    ownership during bankruptcy, 515
    privacy issues, 153, 154
    on warranties, 463
Personal injury, 229, 232–234
    case involving, 230–231
Personal jurisdiction, 66–67
    case involving, 67–69
Personal property, 495–496
    ownership of, 506–508
    trespass to, 234
Petitions, 81

Petroleum Marketing Practices Act, 611
Petty offenses, 195, 197
Pfizer, defective heart valves, 244
Philosophies of law, 23, 26, 32
Physical examination, requests for, 85
Piercing the corporate veil, 595, 596–599
Pinto, Ford, 201
Plain English contracts, 30
*Plain English Handbook, A: How to Create
    Clear SEC Disclosure Documents,* 624
Plain folks appeals, A-95
Plaintiffs, 19
Plaintiff's case, 89–90
Plant Closing Act, 705
Plato, 36
Plea bargains, 759
Plead, 81
Pleadings, 81
Point-of-sale systems, 377
Point-of-shipment contracts, 321, 322
Police powers, 137
Political activities, antitrust exemption for, 682
Political crime, 188
Political Web sites, A-106–A-107
Pollution credits, 763
Pollution Prevention Act (PPA), 777
Polygraphs, 706–707
Ponzi schemes, 196, 208, 475
Possession, 506–507
    perfection upon, 381
    risk of loss and, 325
Postal fraud, 205–206
Postdating checks, 387
Power of attorney, 529
Precedents, 7
Predatory losses, 677
Preemption doctrine, 139, 341
    case involving, 341–343
Preferential liens, 451
    case involving, 451–452
Preferential payments, 451
Preferred stock, 593–594
Pregnancy Discrimination Act, 731
    case involving, 731–732
Preponderance of evidence, 90, 228
President, Executive Office of
    affirmative action and, 740
    labor strikes and, 711
    Web resources, A-98–A-99
Presidential libraries, Web resources for, A-105
Pretrial hearings, 88
Pretrial motions, 85, 88
Preventive law, 30
Price discrimination, 674
    case involving, 675–677
    defenses, 680–681
Price fixing. *See* Horizontal price fixing
Prima facie case, 725, 728
Primary ambient air quality standards,
    760–761
Principals, 528
    agent relationship with, 531–537
    disclosed, 541
    duties to agents, 540–541
    partially disclosed, 541–542
    undisclosed, 541–542
Print advertisements, 482
Prior existing debt rule, 285